sociology

Third Edition

James Fulcher and John Scott

OXFORD
UNIVERSITY PRESS

OXFORD
UNIVERSITY PRESS

Great Clarendon Street, Oxford OX2 6DP

Oxford University Press is a department of the University of Oxford.
It furthers the University's objective of excellence in research, scholarship,
and education by publishing worldwide in

Oxford   New York

Auckland   Bangkok   Buenos Aires   Cape Town   Chennai
Dar es Salaam   Delhi   Hong Kong   Istanbul   Karachi   Kolkata
Kuala Lumpur   Madrid   Melbourne   Mexico City   Mumbai   Nairobi
Sao Paulo   Shanghai   Singapore   Taipei   Tokyo   Toronto

and an associated company in Berlin

Oxford is a registered trade mark of Oxford University Press
in the UK and in certain other countries

Published in the United States
by Oxford University Press Inc., New York

British Library Cataloguing in Publication Data
Data available

Library of Congress Cataloging in Publication Data

Typeset by Graphicraft Limited, Hong Kong
Printed in Spain
on acid-free paper by Graficas Estella S.A.

ISBN 978-0-19-928500-6

10 9 8 7 6 5 4 3 2 1

To all students of sociology, whoever they are

and wherever they may be

brief contents

detailed contents

about the authors

James Fulcher teaches sociology at the University of Leicester and has long experience as the course leader of an introductory sociology course. His main interests have been in the comparative study of the historical development of different societies. He has carried out research into the distinctive features of the social democratic model of society and has written a comparative study of the development of employment relations in Britain and Sweden, *Labour Movements, Employers, and the State: Conflict and Cooperation in Britain and Sweden* (1991). He has also been particularly interested in the distinctive features of Japanese society and the intriguing question of how the Japanese were able to beat the West at its own game by escaping colonial domination and becoming first a military and then an economic superpower. Interest in these societies led him to explore the issue of whether globalization was leading to the convergence of all societies towards a common model of capitalism or whether they were maintaining their historic distinctiveness. He discusses this and takes up many related issues, such as the origins of capitalism, its stages of development, its global spread, and its crisis tendencies in *Capitalism: A Very Short Introduction* (2003). He believes that sociology provides not only the best way to approach these very important questions but also the only way in which we can make sense of the world we live in, grasp our place within it, and ultimately understand ourselves.

John Scott teaches sociology at the University of Essex and was formerly Professor of Sociology at the University of Leicester. His interests in introductory sociology derive from his long involvement as editor of the student magazine *Sociology Review*. His main research interests cover the areas of economic and political sociology, social stratification, and social theory. He has undertaken comparative studies of business organization and capitalist class formation, most especially concentrating on Britain, the United States, and Japan. His principal publications in this area include *Capitalist Property and Financial Power* (1986) and *Corporate Business and Capitalist Classes* (1997). He has also undertaken detailed studies of the formation and current structure of the British upper class and the relationship between wealth and poverty. The major publications in this area include *Who Rules Britain?* (1991) and *Poverty and Wealth* (1994). His larger theoretical ideas on theories of power and class have been discussed in *Stratification and Power* (1996) and *Power* (2001). He has developed a view of social theory as a continuing area of intellectual debate that lies at the heart of the sociological enterprise, emphasizing the continuing importance of the formative ideas of the 'classical' writers as well as contemporary contributions. These arguments have been set out in *Sociological Theory* (1995) and *Social Theory* (2006). These empirical and theoretical interests have led to a long engagement with issues of research methodology, with major contributions to discussions of documentary research (*A Matter of Record*, 1990) and social network analysis (*Social Network Analysis: A Handbook*, 1992 and 2000).

about the book

We enjoyed writing and revising this book, and we hope that you will enjoy reading it. Our aim has been to write a book that is comprehensive and interesting, but also easy to read. We have included many special textbook features to help you find your way through what is a complex subject, and these are listed in the 'How to use this book' section.

In this third edition we have maintained the same broad approach to sociology that has worked well in previous editions but, in addition to generally updating and revising the text, we have made important changes to reflect areas of growing interest, to extend and improve the book's special features, and to provide a clearer structure.

New to this edition

- New or greater coverage of the sociological imagination; consumer cities; crime and deviance; disability; social capital; the collective office; emotional labour; job satisfaction; the life course; the workfare state; global terror; the impact of new information technologies on social life.

- Creation of 'Workshops' that consolidate the end-of-chapter material and include brand new 'Media Watch' stories that examine articles from the media and relate them back to the core chapter issues.

- Addition of new part headings, in order to clarify the book's structure and group the chapters more appropriately.

Focus of the book

This book is mainly focused on contemporary British society but it is important to set this in historical perspective. Many of the most strongly held ideas found in Britain today, such as beliefs about 'sex' and 'race', which we explore in Chapters 5 and 6, originated in the nineteenth century or earlier. Recent and far-reaching changes in the relationship between the state and society, which we examine in Chapter 15, attempted to reverse a century of expansion in the role of the state and return to an earlier age when market forces ruled. You will find that in all of our substantive chapters we set recent changes in the context of the longer-term development of society.

It is important also to take account of the experience of other societies and you will find that we often discuss particular questions from a comparative point of view. For example, we make comparisons with many other countries when we discuss recent changes in the British welfare state in Chapter 15. We refer to the Japanese case when we examine changes in education in Chapter 9 and changes in work organization and work relationships in Chapters 14 and 17. We look at changes in patterns of political power in Russia, when we explore elite theories in Chapter 20.

With globalization, it is, anyway, no longer sensible to separate one society sharply from another. What happens in one society is often very closely related to what happens in another. Indeed, some would say that we now live in a 'global society' where the boundaries between countries no longer matter, an issue that we discuss in Chapter 16, which is devoted to globalization. We consider it so important to take account of globalization that we have also included either a section or a box on globalization in every chapter.

The structure of the book

Part One is concerned with the broad areas of *Theories and Methods*. Its chapters provide a general discussion of sociology and many of the theories and methods that you will come across in other chapters. You may indeed find it useful to treat these Part One chapters as reference sources to turn to when you wish to explore a theoretical question further or consider the issues raised by use of a particular method. You do not have to read the Part One chapters first and you should certainly not feel that you have to understand everything in Part One before you go further into the book.

Part Two examines the construction of *Social Identities*. We begin in Chapter 4 by considering the process of socialization, the formation of social identities, and the way people present themselves to others. We highlight issues of role learning and changes occurring across the life course. Then, in Chapters 5 and 6, we explore two fundamental aspects of identity: gender and ethnicity. In Chapter 7 we consider how people acquire deviant identities. In Chapter 8 we examine the bodily aspects of identity, discussing here the medicalization of mental illness, and the significance of conceptions of the body for views of disability, cosmetic surgery, and eating disorders.

Part Three deals with *Culture, Knowledge, and Belief*. In Chapter 9 we examine the acquisition of culture and knowledge through education, and its significance for inequality and economic success. In Chapter 10 we consider the communication of ideas and images through the media, and their influence on the way that people feel, think, and behave. In Chapter 11 we examine religious belief, its decline through processes of secularization and its revival in recent times, with the rise of new religions and the growth of fundamentalist movements in religion.

Part Four covers *Social Organization and Control*. We examine here the main levels of social organization, beginning with the family in Chapter 12 before moving to larger structures with city and community in Chapter 13 and organizations in Chapter 14. In Chapter 15 we examine the development of the nation state and its transformation since the 1970s. Then in Chapter 16 we consider the impact of globalization on the nation state, and examine global movements of capital and people, before discussing whether we now live in a global society.

Part Five deals with *Production, Inequalities, and Social Divisions*. We begin by examining production, through the topics of work, employment and leisure, in Chapter 17. Many social inequalities are grounded in work and employment relationships, and we move on to analyse inequality, poverty, and wealth in Chapter 18. In the Chapter 19 discussion of stratification we examine the organization of inequalities into hierarchies of class and status. Finally, in Chapter 20, we consider the relationship between class and power, before discussing whether class divisions have now been displaced by new social divisions and social movements.

There are many connections between these parts, and between various chapters. For example, while gender, ethnicity, and class are most fully discussed in Chapters 5, 6, and 19 respectively, every chapter in this book refers to them. Thus, the relationship between all three and educational achievement is discussed in Chapter 9, while their media representation is examined in Chapter 10. We draw attention to the more important of these links through our 'Connections' boxes but we also cross-reference many others in the text.

The chapters of Parts Two, Three, Four, and Five have a common organization. Each begins with an '*Understanding . . .*' section, in which we review the principal theoretical debates and the main concepts that are relevant to the subject of the chapter. The sections that follow look in detail at the studies and research carried out in the area and consider how they relate to the theoretical debates. After examining longer-term tendencies, often going back into the nineteenth century or earlier, we concentrate in the later sections of each chapter on recent changes and contemporary issues.

We are keen to hear your ideas about this new edition. Visit our website at www. oxfordtextbooks.co.uk/orc/fulcher3e/ or send us your feedback at fulcherandscott.uk@oup.com and let us know what you think of it!

James Fulcher and John Scott
August 2006

how to use this book

Chapter-opening vignettes

Each chapter begins with a short story drawn from the mass media, to illustrate a key issue covered in the chapter you are about to read and show its relevance to everyday life.

How to lie with statistics

'The secret language of statistics, so appealing in a fac[t] sensationalize, inflate, confuse, and oversimplify. Stat[istics] terms are necessary in reporting the mass data of soci[al] conditions, "opinion" polls, the census. But without w[riters] honesty and understanding and readers who know wha[t] only be semantic nonsense.'

Source: Huff (1954: 8).

Global focus   Inequality across the globe

The richest 1 per cent in the world (about 50 million people) have as much income as the poorest 57 per cent (about 2.7 billion people). This inequality reflects a global distribution of poverty: 80 per cent of the world's population have incomes below the US and European poverty lines. Two-thirds of the world's population is worse off than the poorest 10 per cent of Americans. This poverty is concentrated in Africa, India, and Bangladesh. While average age at death is 75 or older in North America, Australia, and Western Europe, it falls to 60 or so across continental Europe

Africa and $26[...]
show a growing [...]
the growth of p[...]
  These inequ[...]
putes that hav[...]
Organization. [...]
Union, the Uni[...]
to take accoun[...]
tariffs on the a[...]

'Global focus' boxes

No society can be understood in isolation. 'Global focus' boxes have been included throughout the chapter text to place the topics under discussion into an international context, and to compare social identities and structures across a number of different cultures.

'Controversy and debate' boxes

It is important that you are aware of the lively debates that are going on within sociology and their relevance to controversial issues in wider society. 'Controversy and debate' boxes aim to make you think about the contested nature of sociological ideas and become critical thinkers.

Controversy and debate   Islam and women

The relationship between Islam and patriarchy has become an issue of contemporary debate. Extreme examples of the subordination and exclusion of women can certainly be found in Islamic countries and communities. In Afghanistan under the Taliban regime, women were excluded from employment, education, hospital care, and political life. In Saudi Arabia, they are not allowed to vote or even drive cars. In some Islamic communities women are forbidden to show their faces in public and have to cover themselves head-to-toe in the *burka*. In

- to inherit fro[m
- to participat[e
- to be regarde[d

Jawad argues t[hat
improved great[ly
deteriorated af[ter
were taken awa[y
public life. The [

'Frontiers' boxes

'Frontiers' boxes take you to the edge of the subject and give you a taste of the more innovative and ground-breaking research that is taking place within the discipline, to keep you abreast of important developments and complement the core ideas in the textbook.

Frontiers   Internet democracy

Can the Internet solve the problems faced by democracy? It has been claimed that the Internet provides a 'technology of democracy' by making information freely available, facilitating communication, and enabling organization by opposition or campaign groups. It has also been argued that it can counteract declining popular participation and involvement in the political process, as shown by low turnout figures at elections.

The Internet does provide a way of accessing information, and one that is independent of selection and manipulation by

The Internet groups. It is a tions, such as t an absolutely c for loosely orga anti-capitalist, campaigns, suc the organizatio exiled oppositi however, that t

New technology   E-Universities?

It is claimed that information and communication technology (ICT) is transforming education. What matters, however, is how it is used. E-moderators (teachers and trainers who work with learners online) can adopt different roles. Gilly Salmon (2004: chapter 6) has sketched out four scenarios, which are not predictions but a way of helping us to think about the range of possibilities and the choices that we face. She takes us on a voyage to a new planetary system.

Planet Contenteous

Planet Nomad

This planet pro wireless techn carried, then w Learning is ind through projec least negotiate They may work globe. They are boundaries. Th

'New technology' boxes

We live in a world of rapid and transforming technological change! These boxes focus on the impact of such changes on the way we live and the character of our society, and provide examples of the effect of the Internet and new forms of communication on societal groups.

'Theory and methods' boxes

Questions of theory and method are absolutely central to sociology and so these boxes have been included throughout the chapter text to highlight particular research tools, techniques or problems and draw your attention to particular theoretical issues.

THEORY AND METHODS

Karl Marx

Voted the greatest ever philosopher.
© Getty Images/Hulton Archive

Karl Marx (1818–83) was born in Trier, Germany. He studied law at Bonn and

in 1844 (Engels 1845), and he collaborated with Marx on a number of works, including *The Communist Manifesto* (Marx and Engels 1848).

Marx found it difficult to complete books. A number of his most important studies were published long after his death, thanks to the editorial work of Engels and others. The most important of his early works, where he set out a theory of 'alienation', was the *Economic and Philosophical Manuscripts* (Marx 1844), published only in 1932. After *The Communist Manifesto*, he went on to produce a series of massive drafts for *Capital*, a critical study of economic theory and the economic basis of society. Only volume one (Marx 1867) was published in his lifetime.

There is some controversy about the relationship between the works of the older, mature Marx of the 1860s and those of the youthful Marx of the 1840s.

'Briefings'

'Briefing' boxes have been included throughout the chapter text to showcase a miscellany of interesting and relevant examples, questions, and issues, to help expand your general knowledge of sociology and the arguments presented in each chapter.

Briefing: wild children

Kamala (about 8 years old) and Amala (about 1½) were discovered in India in 1920, living as part of a pack of wolves. After their rescue they were seen to walk on all fours, to eat and drink with their mouths, directly from the plate, and at night they howled. No one knows how they came to live with wolves rather than in a human group. Amala did not survive the discovery for long. She died within a year. Kamala, however, lived to be 18. By the time that he died, he had learned to walk upright and to wear clothes, but he had learned to speak only a few words.

A boy called Ramu, also discovered living with wolves, was taken to an orphanage run by Mother Theresa. He continued to hunt chickens at night but, although he learned to dress, he never learned to speak before he died, aged 10, in 1985.

The truth of these accounts of 'wild children' has been questioned, but evidence from the case of Genie, an American child, supports the general position. Genie was systematically abused by her parents and was kept away

type of person, attributed to h ticular label th type of person person may ta terms of that i they *are* that ki

Social ident sonality chara reliability), th identity. They istics and attrib categories, or social identiti labels as woma clerk, mechani of these identit tional roles, so and others cor roles. Neverth real or imagi characteristics whom people by others.

Someone id

---

which they have no real choice. Ultimately they may remain free, but in practice they are constrained.

> **Connections**
> You will understand more about Weber's views on rational economic action when you have read our discussion of *The Protestant Ethic and the Spirit of Capitalism* in Chapter 11, pp. 411–12. You may like to read that discussion now.

'Connections' feature

There are many important links between chapters and so our 'Connections' feature suggests ways in which you can follow up on a point and link it to related discussions elsewhere in the book.

'Stop and reflect' summaries

At the end of each main section of a chapter you will find 'Stop and reflect' summaries that remind you of the points that have been made and suggest things that you should think about before you move on to the next main section, to aid your revision.

 Stop and reflect

In this section we have looked at a number of aspects of research design and methodology.

- Research design is the whole process of planning a project that relates to theoretical concerns and is easily researchable. It involves issues relating to purposes, methods, styles, and strategies of research.

- Is it usefu a fundame qualitativ

- Triangula involves o of one cor

End-of-chapter workshop

At the end of every chapter you will find a 'Workshop' that comprises a series of case studies and exercises for revision and debate, to help you develop skills in critical analysis and apply your learning to new situations.

Case studies

Each case study focuses on an important piece of sociological research to keep you up to date with the latest thinking and help you to understand the implications of these research findings for the world around you.

Workshop 6

 Study 6 The art of being black

In *The Art of Being Black* (1996), Claire Alexander explored the ways in which young black Britons construct their cultural identities. She recognized that common cultural representations of black youths saw them in stereotypical terms drawn from cultural imagery of the black mugger, the Rastafarian drug dealer, and the rioter. Such labelling of them as 'problems' led to their high levels of alienation from mainstream white society.

through the particular and di
Ethnic identities, therefore, are
ing to the particular situations
The method that Alexander
participant observation among
in east, north-west, and west L
at work, and during their leis

'Media watch' stories

'Media watch' stories examine contemporary articles from the local media and relate them back to the key issues raised in the chapter, to help you think about the relevance of sociological ideas in modern society.

 Media watch 7 Mobile crime

The problem of crime is often depicted as a problem of youth crime, so you will find it useful to consider some aspects of this. Look back at our discussion of mobile phone theft at the beginning of this chapter, p. 235.

The British government's youth crime adviser, Lord Warner, the Chairman of the Youth Justice Board, has seen these trends in crime as showing the growing importance of gang crime committed by young people against other young people. He claims

- The Con. Where one gang m lures him, or her, to where t waiting.
- The Trap. A robbery that tak a gang's territory and is sur

Consult the official statistic website listed in the 'Online r

Discussion points

Discussion points have been included to allow you to focus on important sociological issues raised in the chapter in greater detail, and develop strong skills in sociological argument.

 Discussion points

Educational capital

- How useful are the concepts of 'cultural capital' and 'social capital' in enabling us to understand patterns of educational advantage and disadvantage?

Read the sections on these concepts in 'Education and inequality' and make sure that you understand the meaning of these concepts.

- Why did greater choice of s education policy?
- What are the implications o inequality? Does everyone
- What are the disadvantages
- Do you think that there sho
- Should parents be offered

'Explore Further' section

To take your learning further, further reading lists and web links have been provided to help you locate supplementary sources of information that will aid your revision and coursework.

 Explore further

The following cover most of the issues dealt with in this chapter:

Ball, S. (2004) (ed.), *The Routledge Falmer Reader in the Sociology of Education* (London: Routledge Falmer). *A personal collection of classic and contemporary texts.*

Coffey, A. (2001), *Education and Social Change* (Buckingham: Open University Press). *A careful, reflective and theoretically informed examination of current issues in the sociology of education and*

complex interaction of gender a the views of Muslim boys.

Ball, S. (2003), *Class Strategies a Middle Classes and Social Advan A theoretically informed discussi interviews with parents and chil*

Brown, P., and Hesketh, A. (with *Mismanagement of Talent: Emp Economy* (Oxford: Oxford Unive

online resource centre

 www.oxfordtextbooks.co.uk/orc/fulcher3e/

The Online Resource Centre that accompanies this book provides students and instructors with ready-to-use teaching and learning materials. These resources are free of charge and designed to maximise the learning experience.

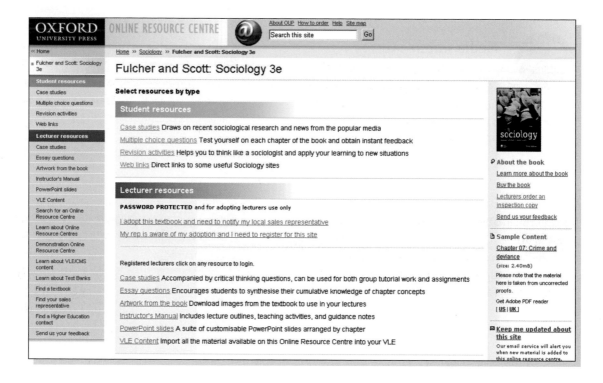

FOR STUDENTS

Multiple-choice questions

The best way to reinforce your understanding of sociology is through frequent and cumulative revision. As such, a bank of self-marking multiple-choice questions has been provided for each chapter of the text, and includes instant feedback on your answers and cross-references back to the textbook to assist with independent self-study.

Web links

A series of annotated web links organised by chapter has been provided to point you in the direction of important associations, articles, reports, research papers and other sources of relevant sociological information. These links will help keep you informed of the latest developments in the field.

Revision activities

A suite of interactive revision activities have been prepared to help you to think like a sociologist and apply your learning to new situations. Activities include questions about key sociology concepts: simply click a button to access detailed feedback on your answers.

Case studies

Sometimes the best way to understand sociological ideas is through story: as such, each chapter is supplemented by a fresh case study that draws on recent sociological research and news from the popular media, to help you grasp core concepts and strengthen your skills in case analysis.

FOR LECTURERS

Case studies

A further collection of relevant and engaging case studies has been provided for use in group tutorial work and assignments. These cases have high student relevance and appeal, focus on new and emerging themes in sociology, and are accompanied by critical thinking questions for students.

Essay questions

A bank of diverse and challenging essay questions has been provided to enrich the assessment program. Each question is designed to encourage students to synthesise their cumulative knowledge of chapter concepts and demonstrate the linkages between them.

Instructor's Manual

A practically-focused and comprehensive Instructor's Manual has been provided for new and experienced lecturers, and includes lecture outlines, guidance notes on how the textbook features may be used in class, and teaching activities for tutorials and seminars.

PowerPoint Slides

A suite of customisable PowerPoint slides has been included for use in lecture presentations. Arranged by chapter theme, the slides may also be used as hand-outs in class.

acknowledgements

We have many people to thank for their contribution to the long and complex process of producing this third and extensively revised edition and its accompanying website.

We are most grateful to the Oxford editorial team, to Angela Adams and Amie Barker (Commissioning Editors), Nicola Bateman (Production Editor), Sarah Bury (Copy Editor), Tim Branch (Designer), David Carles (Proofreader), and, especially, Jane Clayton (Development Editor), for her pain-staking work and steady encouragement in developing the special features of this new edition, bringing the project to fruition, and overcoming the various hurdles along the way. The book builds heavily on the two previous editions and we would like to acknowledge the important contributions made to these by Angela Griffin and Tim Barton. Many thanks to Julie O'Shea for her picture research and to Alice Chadwick, Lucy Dawkins, Alan Felstead and Hymers College (Hull) for their imaginative photography.

We would like to thank the many reviewers for the detailed and very helpful comments they have given us at various stages in the process of writing and rewriting this edition, who include but are not limited to:

- Patrick Baert, University of Cambridge
- Matthew Bond, University of Kent
- Emma Casey, Kingston University
- Helen Corr, University of Strathclyde
- Justin Cruickshank, University of Birmingham
- Nick Ellison, Durham University
- Jack Fawbert, De Montfort University
- David Inglis, University of Aberdeen
- Christopher Jackman, Roehampton University
- William Keenan, Nottingham Trent University
- Mike McBeth, Bath Spa University
- Janice McLaughlin, University of Newcastle
- Samantha Punch, University of Stirling.

Last but not least, we wish to thank those involved in producing the material for the extensive, informative, and innovative website that accompanies the book: Will Keenan, Nottingham Trent University, for providing the bank of essay and short-answer questions; Susie Scott, University of Sussex, for writing the case studies; and Shaminder Takhar, London South Bank University, for constructing the comprehensive Instructor's Manual.

thinking sociologically: theories and methods

PART ONE

what is sociology?

Contents

01

We introduce you to sociology in this chapter. We begin by explaining why we think that you should study sociology, and by telling you what you can get out of it and what you can use it for. We go on to tackle two fundamental questions. Sociologists study society but what do we mean by this term? How do sociologists study society—is sociology a science?

Why study sociology?

Sociology enables us to understand the world we live in but also to understand ourselves, for we are the products of that world. This understanding can help us to gain more control over our lives but it can also be put to more practical uses as well.

Understanding our world

We live in a world of extraordinary choice. Our choice of food to eat, holiday destinations to visit, and television channels to watch seems almost limitless. We can to some extent choose our own identity, by constructing a lifestyle that suits us or creating a new persona in a virtual community on the Net. We can select the body shape that we want and through a combination of diet, exercise, and cosmetic surgery at least try to change our body accordingly. The provision of greater choice, whether in education or health care, has become one of the main priorities of government policy.

Although we have a strong sense of choice, we are also subject to social pressures that seem often to make these choices for us. We are under pressure to conform to other people's ideas of how we should look and how we should live. While we may think that we choose certain products or decide to hold certain views, we are manipulated by advertisers, media moguls, and spin doctors. Many people anyway feel that work pressures and shortage of time leave them with very little opportunity to do anything but get up in the morning, work all day, and do the housework or look after the children when they get home at night.

We also live in a world where the ability to choose varies enormously between people. In Britain the poor, the unemployed, the single parent, the refugee, all have less choice than others. In many African, Asian, or Latin American countries, many people just struggle to survive from day to day. Choice is, therefore, unequally distributed and has become steadily more so, as inequality has increased—not only within our own society but also in the world as a whole, for the gap between rich and poor countries has been widening as well.

How are we to understand and explain this strange world we live in, a world that gives us choice but also takes it away, that provides some with enormous choice but others with very little, that makes people think that they have choice when they often have hardly any? It is, above all, sociology that has tackled these issues and you will find that they come up again and again in this book, when we examine the way that beliefs, values, and identities are shaped and created; or analyse inequalities of class, gender, and ethnicity; or discuss the influence of the mass media on the way that we think and behave; or consider the conflicting pressures of work demands and household obligations.

Understanding our place in the world

Sociology enables us not only to understand the world around us, but also our place within it. This is not just a matter of where we live, important as this is, but of where we are located within social structures and the changes taking place in these structures.

Sociologists use the term **social structure** to refer to any relatively stable pattern of relationships between people. In our panel of four sociologists (see pp. 6–7), C. Wright Mills refers to the structure of 'society as a whole' but any social group, however big or small, from a family to a political party, has a social structure. So does any organization, such as a university, a business corporation, or a hospital. There are also the wider structures of class, gender, and ethnicity that stretch across a whole society and, indeed, beyond it. Some organizations, such as transnational corporations, cross national boundaries, and national societies themselves exist within a global structure of international relationships.

By describing such structures, sociology provides us with a map of society within which we can locate ourselves, so that we can begin to understand the social forces that act upon us. These structures are, however, constantly changing and one of the main tasks of sociology is to understand

and explain social change and the impact that it has on people. You will find that most of our chapters are centrally concerned with processes of social change.

Some recent changes that have in one way or another impacted on all of us are:

- Advances in communications that have made it possible to transfer huge quantities of information and money instantly across the world, and enabled the emergence of an electronic world of cyberculture, virtual communities, and anonymous identities.

- The decentralization of cities, as superstores, hospitals, hotels, and leisure complexes have moved from the centre to the edge of the city, and the transformation of city centres by a rapidly expanding night-time world of pubs and clubs where bouncers rule.

- Changes in family life, as more people have decided to live on their own, more couples have cohabited without marriage, women have increasingly found employment in paid work, divorce rates have risen, and the number of single-parent families has increased.

- The transformation of work, with the decline of old industries and the expansion of service occupations requiring emotional labour, while more flexible and less secure forms of part-time and temporary work have spread, and more employees now telework from home.

- Increasing inequality, as more people have experienced poverty and exclusion, and the gap has widened not only between the rich and the poor within societies but also between rich and poor countries.

You will find that we discuss all these changes and many others in this book. Each may seem to be quite distinctive in character, but they have many processes in common and are interconnected in various ways. Globalization, for example, is involved in all of them and connects one process of change with another. It is sociology that has the concepts that enable us to comprehend these processes of change and grasp the connections between them.

Understanding ourselves

Above all, sociology enables us to understand ourselves. The way that we think, behave, and feel, indeed our identity, is socially produced. It is only through a knowledge and understanding of the social processes that

How has city life been changed by the growth of superstores?
© Lucy Dawkins

turn us into the people we are that we can truly understand ourselves.

Socialization is the general term that sociologists use for this process. We use this term because it is a process that makes us into social and cultural beings, that turns an individual into a member of society. It begins with upbringing and continues through education but does not stop there, for it goes on throughout our lives. Every time that we join a new group, perhaps of first years at university or colleagues at work, a process of socialization starts. Whenever we enter a new stage in life, we learn to play certain roles, for example the role of a parent, later of a grandparent. Socialization is so fundamental to understanding how a society works that we discuss it at length in Chapter 4.

Socialization also provides us with an identity. Our sense of **personal identity** seems so strong and so individual that we tend to think it results from some process going on mysteriously inside us that makes us who we *really* are. Sociology shows, however, that identities are socially constructed. Even such basic personal characteristics as sex, race, and age are socially not biologically constructed.

Thus, although the categories we place ourselves in, as 'men' or 'women', 'blacks' or 'whites', 'young' or 'old',

---

THEORY AND METHODS

Sociologists reflect on their subject

C. Wright Mills

'The sociological imagination enables its possessor to understand the larger historical scene in terms of its meaning for the inner life and the external career of a variety of individuals. . . . The sociological imagination enables us to grasp history and biography and the relations between the two within society. That is its task and its promise. . . . those who have been imaginatively aware of the promise of their work have consistently asked three sorts of questions:

1 What is the structure of this particular society as a whole? What are its essential components, and how are they related to one another? How does it differ from other varieties of social order? Within it, what is the meaning of any particular feature for its continuance and for its change?

2 Where does this society stand in human history? What are the mechanics by which it is changing? What is its place within and its meaning for the development of humanity as a whole? How does any particular feature we are examining affect, and how is it affected by, the historical period in which it moves?. . .

3 What varieties of men and women now prevail in this society and in this period? And what varieties are coming to prevail? In what ways are they selected and formed, liberated and repressed, made sensitive and blunted?'

Source: Mills, C. W. (1959), *The Sociological Imagination* (New York: Oxford University Press), 5–7.

C. Wright Mills (1916–62) was an American sociologist well-known for his criticism of abstract approaches in sociology, and his belief that sociology should relate the 'personal troubles' of the individual to the 'public issues' of social structure. Apart from *The Sociological Imagination*, he is most well known for *White Collar: The American Middle Classes* (New York: Oxford University Press), 1951; and *The Power Elite* (New York: Oxford University Press), 1956.

Peter Berger

'A more adequate representation of social reality now would be the puppet theatre, with the curtain rising on the little puppets jumping about on the ends of their invisible strings, cheerfully acting out the little parts that have been assigned to them in the tragi-comedy to be enacted. . . . We see the puppets dancing on their miniature stage, moving up and down as the strings pull them around, following the prescribed course of their various little parts. We learn to understand the logic of this theatre and we find ourselves in its motions. We locate ourselves in society and thus recognize our own position as we hang from its subtle strings. For a moment we see ourselves as puppets indeed. But then we grasp a decisive difference between the puppet theatre and our own drama. Unlike the puppets, we have the possibility of stopping in our movements, looking up and perceiving the machinery by which we have been moved. In this act lies the first step towards freedom.'

Source: Berger, P. (1963), *Invitation to Sociology: A Humanistic Perspective* (Harmondsworth: Penguin), 140, 199.

Peter Berger (1929–) is an American sociologist, who (with Thomas Luckmann) wrote *The Social Construction of Reality: A Treatise in the Sociology of Knowledge* (Harmondsworth: Penguin), 1966. Two other well-known books by him are: *The Sacred Canopy: Elements of a Sociological Theory of Religion* (New York: Doubleday), 1969; *The Capitalist Revolution: Fifty Propositions about Prosperity, Equality, and Liberty* (Aldershot: Wildwood House), 1987.

'healthy' or 'sick', refer to physical characteristics, they are, none the less, social categories that reflect certain culturally specific ways of thinking about people. For example, the notion that there are two sexes may appear self-evident but it emerged quite recently in European history (see Chapter 5, pp. 157–9). What happens is that we learn these categories through socialization and then see ourselves as having the characteristics that these categories specify.

Freeing ourselves

A knowledge of the social structures that constrain us, and the social processes that give us identities, does not, however, condemn us to passivity. Indeed, the reverse is the case, for by making us aware of the forces acting upon us, sociology also enables us to see them for what they are, resist them if we wish to, and, to some (but only some) extent, free ourselves from them.

This point is made well by two of the sociologists in our panel of four (see pp. 6–7). Berger uses the metaphor of the puppet theatre to represent 'social reality'. He suggests that, as in a puppet theatre, people act out certain parts that are prescribed for them, and are pulled this way and that by the 'invisible strings' of society. Through sociology, they can, however, see the strings that pull them and the social machinery that operates the strings. Once they do this they are no longer puppets and have taken 'the first step towards freedom'.

THEORY AND METHODS

Sociologists reflect on their subject

Zygmunt Bauman

'One could say that the main service the art of thinking sociologically may render to each and every one of us is to make us more *sensitive*; it may sharpen up our senses, open our eyes wider so that we can explore human conditions which thus far had remained all but invisible. Once we understand better how the apparently natural, inevitable, immutable, eternal aspects of our lives have been brought into being through the exercise of human power and human resources, we will find it hard to accept once more that they are immune and impenetrable to human action—our own action included. Sociological thinking is, one might say, a power in its own right, an *anti-fixating* power. It renders flexible again the world hitherto oppressive in its apparent fixity; it shows it as a world which could be different from what it is now. It can be argued that the art of sociological thinking tends to widen the scope, the daring and the practical effectiveness of your and my *freedom*. Once the art has been learned and mastered, the individual may well become just a bit less manipulable, more resilient to oppression and regulation from outside, more likely to resist being fixed by forces that claim to be irresistible.'

Source: Bauman, Z. (1990), *Thinking Sociologically* (Oxford: Basil Blackwell), 16.

Zygmunt Bauman (1925–) has been Professor of Sociology at the Universities of Leeds and Warsaw. Among his many reflections on sociological theory and contemporary society are *Modernity and the Holocaust* (Cambridge: Polity Press), 1989; *Globalization: The Human Consequences* (Cambridge: Polity Press), 1998; *Liquid Modernity* (Cambridge: Polity Press), 2000. A second edition of *Thinking Sociologically* (written with Tim May) was published in 2001.

Steve Bruce

'To summarize, whatever reservations we may have about how closely actual scientists conform to the high standards set in their programmatic statements about what they do and why it works, we need not doubt that the natural sciences offer the best available template for acquiring knowledge about the material world. Critical reasoning, honest and diligent accumulation of evidence, subjecting ideas to test for internal consistency and for fit with the best available evidence, seeking evidence that refutes rather than supports an argument, engaging in open exchanges of ideas and data unconstrained by ideological commitments: all of those can be profitably adopted by the social sciences. However, we need to appreciate the differences between the subject matter of the natural and the human sciences. People think. They act as they do, not because they are bound to follow unvarying rules but because they have beliefs, values, interests, and intentions. That simple fact means that, while some forms of sociological research look rather like the work of chemists or physicists, for the sociologist there is always a further step to take. Our notion of explanation does not stop at identifying regular patterns in social action. It requires that we understand.'

Source: Bruce, S. (1999*b*), *Sociology: A Very Short Introduction* (Oxford: Oxford University Press), 18–19.

Steve Bruce (1954–) has been Professor of Sociology at the University of Aberdeen since 1991. He is the author of *The Edge of the Union: The Ulster Loyalist Political Vision* (Oxford: Oxford University Press), 1994; *Religion in Modern Britain* (Oxford: Oxford University Press), 1995; *Choice and Religion: A Critique of Rational Choice Theory* (Oxford: Oxford University Press), 1999*a*; and many other publications in the sociology of religion.

Bauman similarly points out that through sociology we can become aware of, and can then explore, the previously invisible social context of our lives. This means that we become aware of the social forces that shape our lives. It also means that we discover that what seemed natural or inevitable, is actually the result of human actions. To return to Berger's metaphor, we find out that it is in fact people who are pulling the puppets' strings. Once we realize this, we understand that things do not have to be the way they are. If human actions make the world the way it is, then the world can be changed. If the way we live is not the fixed result of human nature, then we can live differently.

People have, for example, often thought that patterns of behaviour are biologically determined when they are not. It has been widely believed that the different roles performed by men and women are biologically prescribed. This can lead to the false idea that for biological reasons men are not fitted to be, say, nurses and women to be, say, pilots. In Britain, beliefs of this sort became established in the nineteenth century as men sought to exclude women from many occupations and confine them to domestic and caring roles. Knowledge of the way this idea became established and the socializing processes that maintain it help us to understand that gender role differences are socially constructed (we discuss this in Chapter 5). This awareness makes it possible to challenge them and change them, as has clearly happened, for there are now many male nurses and female pilots.

Applying sociology

You may reasonably say that this is all very well but what is sociology useful for? Sociology may provide plenty of knowledge and understanding but what else can it do?

Sociological knowledge has important applications in many areas of work. It has made major contributions to the study of social problems and the work of those

A female RAF pilot—gender role expectations can be challenged and changed.

© Crown/RAF

who seek to deal with them. Thus, sociologists have carried out research into drug use, crime, violence, industrial disputes, family problems, and mental illness, to name some of the more well-known problems of society. Indeed, no investigation of the causes and consequences of these social problems would be complete without an input from sociology.

Sociologists have not only, however, been concerned with explaining why some people behave in problematic ways. They are also interested in the deeper sources of such behaviour in, say, the patterns of family relationships, the structure of organizations, or the distribution of resources. They are concerned, too, with the processes that lead to the treatment of certain actions as problematic, as deviant or criminal behaviour. Why, for example, are poor people prosecuted for failing to pay the community charge, when the rich are allowed to avoid paying taxes by shifting their money into tax havens?

Sociology has made a central contribution to the study of management and the training of managers. Sociologists have researched the structures that enable organizations to function productively and efficiently. They have asked what kinds of structure and what styles of management facilitate creativity and innovation. One of the most important contributions of sociology here has been to penetrate beneath the surface of things. They have shown how apparently well-designed organizations are disrupted by internal conflicts. They have revealed the unintended consequences of rules and regulations (see Chapter 14, p. 539).

Those sociologists working in this area have not, however, just focused on issues of organizational efficiency. They are also concerned with the perspectives of those who work for organizations. How meaningful do employees find the work that they do? How do they meet the requirements of the employer but continue carrying out their work in a professional way and protect themselves against exploitation. One of the current frontiers here (see Chapter 14, p. 559 and Chapter 17, p. 670) is the struggle between managers and employees in call centres and, more generally, in the 'emotional labour' of customer service work.

In the application of sociology, there is a constant tension between those who seek to use it to deal with organizational and social problems by making social control more effective and those who use it to reveal exploitation, domination, and manipulation.

Careers in sociology

What can *you* do with sociology? How can sociology help you in finding a career?

One possible career is to become a professional sociologist, carrying out sociological research and communicating its results. This might be in an educational institution but not necessarily, as there are many other organizations, such as specialized research institutes and think tanks, that employ professional sociologists. Sociology is an exceptionally rewarding area in which to do research. It is an enormously diverse and dynamic field, with frontiers opening up in all directions, as our Frontiers boxes and end-of-chapter Studies will show. The range of methods involved, which stretch from large-scale quantitative surveys to intensive observational studies of the social life of small groups, provides scope for many different skills and inclinations. Research is, furthermore, not just a matter of acquiring knowledge, but also of developing the ideas, concepts, and methods of sociology itself.

As a subject to teach, it has much to offer, as it deals all the time with topics and issues that are central to the lives of those being taught. As you teach sociology you can draw on the experiences of those you are teaching, using their daily lives to illustrate sociological theories and concepts, while using sociology to provide them with a greater understanding of their situation in the world, the forces acting upon them, and the sources of their own beliefs and identities. Those who teach in schools and colleges can play their part in developing the subject by contributing articles to such publications as the *Sociology Review* or writing pieces for sociology websites.

Most sociology graduates will probably not, however, go into teaching or research careers. What other things can sociologists do? Sociology is not a vocational subject, in the sense of providing a training for a specific occupation. It is, however, relevant to a very wide range of occupations, and this broad range of occupational destinations makes sociology a good choice for those who have not decided what career they wish to pursue or simply want to keep their options open. You *can* be sure that a subject that gives you a greater understanding of social situations, social interaction, and human behaviour in general, will provide you with insights that will come in useful whoever employs you and whatever you do.

The skills and knowledge of the sociologist also become increasingly relevant as information about people becomes more and more central to the functioning of the society we live in. Most expanding occupations, in such areas as marketing, public relations, opinion formation, the media, human resource management, education, research, and social policy, depend on the collection, analysis, and communication of information about people, and this is, after all, what sociologists do.

What is society?

Most would agree that sociologists study **society** but what do we mean by this term? It is used in many different ways in sociology but most commonly to refer to a national unit, as in British society, though some would argue that we now live not in distinct national societies but a global one. It is not really possible to give a short definition of something as complex as a society and the easiest way to get a sense of what it means is to examine its main aspects in turn. These are also the main lines of enquiry along which sociology has developed.

A complex of institutions

Institutions are the established practices that regulate the various activities that make up social life. Some examples of institutions are marriages, markets, educational curricula, religious rituals, and laws, which in their different ways all give order to different aspects of the way that we live. In contemporary societies, these institutions, and also the organizations associated with them, are highly specialized. Thus, the educational, economic, political, military, and religious activities of society each have specialized institutions and organizations.

We speak of a complex of institutions because these specialized institutions are closely interrelated with each other. Consider, for example, educational institutions and their organizations. In Britain, public-sector schools, colleges, and universities are dependent on political institutions for their funding. It is ultimately the government that decides how much money to distribute to them. Governments are themselves dependent on the economy. The amount of money that the government has to spend on education depends on how much it can raise in taxes. While this is partly a political question, it also depends on the state of the economy. This itself depends, however, on education, for it is education that supplies the economy with skilled labour. This has been an important issue in Britain since the 1970s, for it has been claimed that education has not been giving people the skills that the economy needs (see Chapter 9, pp. 345–8).

These interrelationships mean that institutions should not be studied in isolation from each other. Sociologists cannot, of course, study everything simultaneously and they tend to specialize in the study of particular areas, such as the family or religion or the media. Most of this book is divided into chapters that specialize in distinct areas of this sort. To achieve a complete understanding of what is going on in any one of these areas, you must always, however, bear in mind its links with others. In this book we have indicated what we see as the more important links through cross-references and Connections boxes.

It is one of the distinctive features of sociology that it is concerned with whole societies. As C. Wright Mills put it (see p. 6), sociologists should ask: 'What is the structure of this particular society as a whole?' Sociology is the only subject that sees societies as 'wholes' in this way. This distinctive perspective means that it overlaps with many other fields of specialized enquiry. Economics and politics, for example, are subjects in their own right, which explore in detail the workings of the areas concerned and the issues specific to them. Economic and political institutions are, however, crucial to the functioning of any society and there is also, therefore, a sociology of economic life and a sociology of politics, which address the relationships between these areas and the wider society.

Sociology's concern with whole societies and all activities that occur within them means that any aspect of social life can become a field within sociology. Indeed, one of the exciting and dynamic things about sociology is the way that new specialities are constantly opening up within it as sociologists begin to explore new areas of activity that have not been studied before or have newly emerged through social change. Examples of new fields are the sociology of tourism, and the sociology of the body.

A multi-level structure

In discussing society as a complex of institutions we have been operating at one particular level, the national level, of society. People do commonly see themselves as members of national societies. If someone asks you which society you belong to, you will probably reply that you live in, say, British or American or Indian society. If you live in Britain, you might of course prefer to say that you live in Scottish or Welsh society, for nationality is a contentious matter, which we discuss in Chapter 16, pp. 619–21. The point that

Figure 1.1 Institutional interdependence

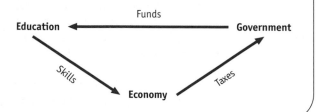

Education and politics—why are politicians so interested in education?

© EMPICS

we are making, here, however, is that the national level is one level of social organization but only one level.

Another level is that of interpersonal, face-to-face interactions in small group situations. During their daily lives people interact with each other in patterned ways. They will usually be members of small groups, such as a **family** or **household** unit (see Chapter 12), but also of work-groups and friendship circles, perhaps of gangs or sports teams, and you can no doubt think of other small groups that are important in your life. People also interact with others on a more transitory basis. Indeed, urban sociologists have argued that city life is a 'world of strangers', where people interact with others that they know very little about (see Chapter 13, p. 494). Some sociologists have been primarily interested in these small groups and interpersonal interactions (see Chapter 2, pp. 51–6), and the study of such interactions is indeed an essential part of sociology. These interactions are, however, structured by larger social units and interpersonal behaviour cannot be explained solely in terms of face-to-face interaction patterns.

One such larger social unit is the **organization** (see pp. 537–8). Business corporations, churches, hospitals, and schools are all examples of such organizations. Organizations are designed to carry out a particular social activity and will usually have a clearly stated and specific goal. They will also have a defined membership and will generally require their members to follow certain rules of behaviour. Whether their members actually do so is another matter and one that has preoccupied the sociology of organizations. All such organizations do, however, have a definite

authority structure which controls the membership but also generates opposition and creates internal conflict.

Another larger and less formal social unit is the **community**. Two centuries or so ago most people lived in small, relatively self-sufficient and self-contained communities in villages or small towns, where everyone knew everyone else. Industrialization and urbanization disrupted communities of this sort and brought large numbers of people who did not know each other together. As we show in Chapter 13, pp. 495–6, new kinds of community have, however, established themselves within cities. Furthermore, the Internet has made possible the emergence of virtual communities, which we discuss on pp. 518–19. Many people still see themselves as members of communities of one kind or another.

Whether or not people feel that they are members of a community, they are inevitably members of a larger social unit, the **nation state**, which during the nineteenth and twentieth centuries became steadily more important in people's lives. With the development of the nation state, national institutions emerged. At its centre is the state apparatus itself, but there are also national educational systems, national health services, national armies, and national churches, to name some of the more obvious examples. As members of a nation state, people have the rights and responsibilities of citizens of that state, and a sense of national identity. We examine the development of nations and nation states in Chapter 16, pp. 628–9.

Nation states are not, however, self-sufficient, for they are interlinked with each other and interdependent in complex ways. These links developed particularly strongly

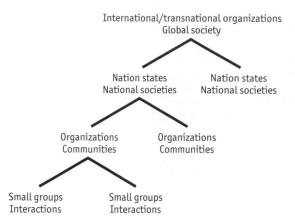

Figure 1.2 Society as a multi-level structure

International/transnational organizations
Global society

Nation states
National societies

Nation states
National societies

Organizations
Communities

Organizations
Communities

Small groups
Interactions

Small groups
Interactions

with industrialization, which made national economies highly dependent on one another through an international division of labour. The industrial societies specialized in producing manufactured goods for the world as a whole, while other parts of the world specialized in producing food for the workers, and raw materials for the factories, of the industrial societies.

National societies have become more closely interlinked through a process known as **globalization**, which we discuss at length in Chapter 16. The world—the globe—has become a 'smaller' place, as a result of improvements in communication which make possible travel to most places within a day or so, while information can be transmitted instantly to any part of it. Nowadays, some companies are global corporations operating in large numbers of countries on every continent. There are also global political organizations, such as the United Nations, and global movements such as Greenpeace. As well as being citizens of national societies, people are also arguably members of a global society.

As society has developed, social units have become steadily larger in their scale. Thus, communities became parts of national societies and national societies have become parts of a global society. This raises the issue of how smaller-scale units relate to larger ones. Do larger-scale units supersede smaller ones? There are literatures on the decline of the family, the decline of community, and, more recently, the decline of the nation state as a global society has emerged. We examine the debates on these issues in the chapters concerned with these units. Arguably, smaller-scale units have, however, not so much disappeared as changed, as society has become multi-level in character. There are many important questions here for sociologists as they examine the relationships between the overlapping units that make up human society.

A structure of inequality and domination

In our discussion of society as a complex of institutions, we emphasized the way in which each organized a particular activity for the society as a whole. Some groups benefit more, however, from these activities than others and seek to maintain or increase their advantages. Societies are characterized by inequality between dominant and dominated groups. Structures of inequality may stretch right across a society, indeed across the whole world, as a dominant group tries to gain control of all areas of activity and secure benefits in all aspects of life. We particularly address the issues raised by inequality in Chapters 18 and 19, but you will find them cropping up throughout the book.

There are various dimensions of inequality within national societies. There are class inequalities between, say, aristocracies and commoners or employers and workers. There are ethnic inequalities between, say, whites, Asians, and African Caribbeans. There are gender inequalities between men and women. In some societies, religion or nationality have become major lines of division. There are also inequalities between national societies, for increasing global integration has not resulted in greater international equality, as we show in Chapter 16.

The study of inequality and its consequences brings up a number of important issues that have been much discussed in sociology. These can be grouped under three headings:

- social stratification;
- social control;
- social conflict.

Social stratification. **Social stratification** is concerned with the way in which a structure of layers, or strata, emerge within society. Typically there is a top layer of the rich and powerful, a bottom layer of the poor and powerless, and various other layers in between. Important questions that are raised are the number of layers that exist in a society, where the boundaries between them should be drawn, the ease with which people can move between them (social

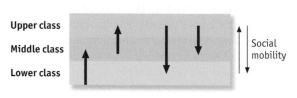

Figure 1.3 Social stratification by class

Upper class

Middle class

Lower class

Social mobility

Are communities alive and well in the contemporary city?
© Lucy Dawkins

mobility), and the way in which the layers persist and change from one generation to the next.

Social control. This raises the question of how inequality is maintained. How do the upper layers dominate and exploit those below them and maintain their various advantages? One way is through control of the use of force—typically through control of the military and police forces of a society. Sociologists generally emphasize, however, that there are more subtle means of control that operate by influencing beliefs and attitudes. Thus, it has been variously argued that people are controlled through education, religion, the mass media, or social policy, and we discuss these arguments in the chapters on these areas.

Social conflict. Here the issue is whether and under what conditions inequality generates conflict. Do the

mechanisms of social control break down? Do those in the lower layers organize themselves to improve their situation and challenge the domination of society by those with wealth and power? Under what conditions, for example, can workers organize themselves collectively to demand higher wages and challenge the power of the employer? Under what conditions do women organize themselves through feminist movements to challenge male domination?

The study of inequality is linked to the study of institutions and their interrelationships, for the rich and powerful maintain their wealth and power by controlling the institutions of society. Similarly, those who challenge their position have to contest their control of these institutions. Thus, the study of this aspect of society is closely related to the issues we raised in our discussion of institutions.

Structure and culture

We have been making much reference to structures but there are aspects of a society that sociologists treat as its cultural rather than structural features. A society not only has an institutional structure and a structure of inequality, it also has ideas and beliefs. It is these ideas and beliefs that are described as its **culture**, together with their symbolic representation through communicative and creative activities. A symbol is simply a representation, such as a word or an image or a gesture, which embodies and communicates an idea. Indeed, beliefs and ideas cannot exist without symbolic representation. It is hard to see how a belief in a god can exist without the word 'god' and without representations of a god. Symbols also convey feelings, as when a representation of a god, say a painting or a sculpture, expresses feelings of religious devotion.

Beliefs are concerned with both ideas about the way things *are* and ideas about how they *ought* to be. Ideas about how things are include beliefs about the nature of things—the physical world, human nature, and the character of society. Ideas about how things ought to be are embodied in values and norms:

- **Values** specify what people ought to do. Thus, the belief that people should accumulate wealth or the belief that they should live in harmony with the natural environment both express values, though rather different ones.
- **Norms** are rules of behaviour that regulate how people behave. A typical norm, for example, is the rule that people should not accumulate wealth by stealing from each other. Such norms are often embodied in laws.

Beliefs about the way that the world *is* and the way that it *ought to be* are commonly linked together by religion and politics. Thus, Christianity contains ideas about God's creation of the world and the belief that human beings are naturally sinful. Christianity also emphasizes certain values, such as love and charity, and provides a set of norms, such as the prohibition of sexual behaviour outside marriage. Political beliefs, such as socialism or liberalism, similarly link together ideas about the nature of society and distinctive visions of what a society should be like.

The term culture also refers to the communicative and creative activities that express ideas and feelings. It is often used to refer to the *high* culture of a society, its collections of paintings, its opera houses, and great works of literature. But there is also its *popular* culture, and this has become an area of growing interest in sociology, which we discuss in Chapter 10. Cinema, popular music, magazines, and soap operas are part of our culture in this sense. Activities as various as gardening, craftwork, dressing, cooking, and talking are all creative activities that can be considered part of culture.

Indeed, the term culture is often used in a very broad way to refer to the general customs and way of life of a society or a group within it, as in references to, say, American culture or working-class culture. Culture in this sense includes the way that people meet and greet each other, the way they behave towards each other at work and at leisure, their sporting and religious activities, and so on. Indeed, all social activity has a cultural aspect, for all social actions have meaning and therefore express the ideas of a culture.

The question then arises of the relationship between social structure and culture, an issue that has been much debated in sociology. Some sociologists, such as C. Wright Mills, see sociology's task as the explanation of a person's situation by reference to the wider social structure that constrains and shapes the circumstances of that person's life. Others, notably some post-modern theorists (see pp. 64–5), claim that cultural representations are the only social reality. There are no external structures and the only reality is what people believe about the world. This leads them to a cultural relativism where all beliefs are equally valid and scientific investigation is impossible.

Most sociologists would argue that neither structural determinism nor cultural relativism enable us to properly explain and understand social life. To do this we do need to refer to the relationships, organizations, and institutions which can best be thought of as structures external to the individual. We need also to refer to the cultural beliefs and ideas that people hold about the world, which give their actions meaning.

Structure and culture are not, however, independent of each other. The beliefs that people hold are, for example, shaped through the institutional and organizational structures of education, the media, and religion. These institutions may in turn be created or reformed because of the ideas and beliefs of those who control them. Statements of this kind can only be made if we distinguish between structure and culture, give both some explanatory weight, and examine the relationship between them.

Is sociology a science?

In the previous section we discussed what sociologists mean by society. Here we take up issues raised by the way in which they study it. The question of whether sociology should be considered a science has been hotly debated both inside and outside the subject. It is an interesting and important question that enables us to explore the nature of the subject, its distinctiveness, and its relationships with other subjects. Before discussing it, we must, however, first consider what is meant by science.

What is science?

It is commonly thought that scientists are simply engaged in the discovery and collection of facts. Scientists do not, however, just look around to see what they can discover, for scientific enquiry is directed by the theoretical concerns of scientists. Scientific *ideas* lie behind the design of experiments or the search for data. The discovery of 'dark matter' by astronomers provides a good example. The 'dark matter' of the universe was not exactly visible, by its very nature, and astronomers discovered it not because they came across it but because the currently dominant theory of the origins of the universe suggested that there had to be far more matter in the universe than could be accounted for by its visible material.

The conventional idea of a fact is of something that is observed existing 'out there'. Scientific observations have, however, to be interpreted and made sense of *before* they can become facts. Interpretation always involves explanatory ideas and this returns us again to the importance of theories. Another example from astronomy can be used to demonstrate this. The existence of 'black holes' is now an accepted fact in astronomy. The discovery of this fact did result from observations of the behaviour of stars but the concept of a 'black hole' depends also upon a theory of what happens when matter becomes so highly concentrated that nothing can escape its gravitational pull.

Science is both an *empirical* and a *theoretical* enterprise. In saying that it is empirical we mean that it is based on observations. The word *empirical* is derived from the Greek word for experience and refers to the observational work that provides us with experience of the world. In saying that science is theoretical we mean that it also involves systematic thought about the world. A *theory* is a logically connected set of ideas. Theories guide empirical work and are used to interpret and explain its observations, which may or may not fit existing theories. If they do not fit it, the theory needs at least to be revised and may have to be

abandoned. Science advances through the constant interplay of theoretical and empirical work.

While it is important to be clear about the logic of scientific activity, it is also important to bear in mind the scientific spirit. By this we mean the set of ideals which motivate and guide scientific work. Science is both *rational* and *critical*. It is rational in that it rejects explanations of the world that are based on religious beliefs or mysterious forces, rather than reasoned thought. It is critical, as it questions received ideas and accepted beliefs. It is concerned with establishing the truth about how the world is and how things actually work, rather than how they ought to be or how they are supposed to be.

This does not mean that scientists lack values and beliefs. Like anyone else, they hold values and beliefs, which may well influence what they do. For example, scientists concerned about the state of the natural environment might well carry out research into global warming. Values and beliefs should not, however, influence the scientist's investigation or interpretation of observations. Thus, however concerned such a scientist might be about this issue, if the observations did not support the theory of global warming, the scientist would be expected to say so.

We have in some ways presented an idealized picture of science. Most scientific enquiry is driven by the requirements of industry or government rather than the pursuit of knowledge. Scientists sometimes suppress results that do not fit their theories or might damage their careers, because they conflict with their employer's interest in a particular policy or product. Research results are faked by some researchers who are more concerned to achieve publications and advance their careers than advance knowledge. At the heart of science there is, none the less, an ideal of disinterested enquiry into the nature of things and it is against this ideal that the work of scientists is judged.

Is sociology a natural science?

The first sciences to develop were the natural sciences and they therefore became the model for scientific activity. Some sociologists adopted this model and tried to develop a natural science of human behaviour. Most contemporary sociologists would, however, argue that society cannot be studied in this way. Social behaviour is in important respects quite different from natural behaviour.

Human actions are meaningful, for whatever human beings do means something to them. They act in the context of beliefs and purposes that give their actions meaning and shape the way that they behave. If sociologists are to understand and explain human behaviour, they have to take account of the meanings that people give to their actions.

Thus, no universal statements can be made about human behaviour, for the same behaviour means different things in different societies. Let us take eating practices as a simple example. The eating of roast beef has been traditional in England and regarded as one of the distinctive features of English life. In India, however, cows are considered sacred by Hindus and may not be killed, let alone eaten. On the other hand, while the eating of dogs in the Far East is commonplace, it is quite abhorrent to most British people. Behaviour considered quite normal in one society is unacceptable in another. No general statements can therefore be made about human eating behaviour in the way that they can about the eating behaviour of animals.

Human behaviour is also different because people think about what they are doing. They are at least partly aware of the forces acting upon them and can resist these forces and act differently. Thus, while the eating of snails and frogs' legs is not a normal feature of the British diet and is generally viewed in Britain with some disgust, some British people may consider that there is no good reason for rejecting these foods. They may decide that it must be possible to enjoy them, if the French eat them with such relish, and may then try them out. Similarly vegetarians may reject traditional British beef-eating practices. Behaviour is not entirely culture bound because people can break out of their culture and, indeed, change it. However, whether they do so is not simply a matter of choice, for those who break away from established patterns will themselves be distinctive in certain ways. They may, for example, be more educated.

> ↻ *Connections*
> Weber particularly emphasized the importance to sociological explanation of understanding the meaning of human action. See Chapter 2, pp. 39–42.

Given this cultural content of social behaviour, we cannot explain it just by making observations of it. To be explained, human actions have to be understood. This special requirement of sociology comes out clearly in the reflections of the sociologists in our panel (see pp. 6–7). Thus, after arguing that many of the features of natural science should be adopted by the sociologist, Steve Bruce insists that the sociologist must go further. As he puts it: 'Our notion of explanation does not stop at identifying regular patterns in social action. It requires that we understand.'

Is sociology a science at all?

Some have, however, questioned whether there can be a science of society at all. If sociology has to understand what people do, is there any real difference between sociology and common sense?

The answer to this question is a resounding yes.

In their everyday lives people are too involved in what is going on around them to have any detachment from it. They are immersed in their own situations, their own families, their own work relationships, their own friendship and leisure patterns. These colour their view of the world. Their knowledge of the world is limited to the situations that they have experienced. They generally interpret their own and other people's behaviour in terms of preconceived ideas and beliefs. In doing so they make little distinction between the way the world is and the way they think it ought to be. Their experience is fitted into these ideas and beliefs, which are important to their sense of identity, and they are therefore usually very reluctant to alter them.

The sociologist's knowledge of the world is very different. Sociology builds up a knowledge of society that is not based upon the experience of one individual but accumulated from the research of large numbers of sociologists. This is knowledge of many different aspects of many different societies at many different times. It is a cumulative knowledge that is constantly increasing through further research. This bank of knowledge means that the experience of large numbers of people in many very different situations and from very different cultures is available to the sociologist.

Sociologists are trained to develop their ideas in a logical, disciplined, and explicit way by constructing theories, which are quite unlike the everyday beliefs of common sense. These ideas are made explicit, because their assumptions have been brought into the open, thought about, and justified. Logical connections are made between the various ideas that make up a theory so that its train of thought can be followed. Theories are also subject to the scrutiny of other sociologists, who will critically examine their assumptions and check the logic of their arguments.

Sociologists then test out their theories in an objective and systematic way. They do not assume that they know the answers or that their theory is right. They demonstrate the truth or falsity of their ideas by collecting appropriate information, using a wide variety of methods to do this. These range from large-scale surveys to the small-scale, in-depth, participant observation of particular situations. Sociologists draw on many different sources of material, from documents to census data or interview responses. As we show in Chapter 3, pp. 73–6, different methods are appropriate to different issues and different situations but can also be used to complement and check upon each other. As with their theories, their methods and the way that they interpret their data are open to the scrutiny of other sociologists.

Sociology is then a science. It has explicit theories and collects data in an objective and systematic way, in order to check those theories and revise them if they are found wanting. As we showed above, it is not a natural science because there are important differences between the social and natural worlds as objects of study, differences that actually require sociologists to go beyond the methods of the natural sciences. It is a social science, not a natural science, but a science none the less.

The sociological imagination

Sociologists have, however, argued strongly that a scientific approach is insufficient on its own. C. Wright Mills famously insisted that the mechanical application of the rules of scientific method was not enough, that the understanding of social structures required a special quality of mind, the **sociological imagination** (Mills 1959 and 2000). In the panel on p. 6 we have quoted some of his words on this.

Anthony Giddens has taken up this idea in his 'brief but critical introduction' to sociology. As Giddens puts it: 'The practice of sociology . . . demands invoking what C. Wright Mills has aptly called the "sociological imagination".' Giddens takes this to mean that there are 'several related forms of sensibility indispensable to sociological analysis' (Giddens 1986: 13). These are:

- historical sensibility;
- anthropological insight;
- critical sensitivity.

Historical sensibility enables us to understand the distinctiveness of the society we live in. This is a society which has been transformed by industrialization and the rise of the nation state. It is a society where there is a very high rate of technological change. Yet all this has happened quite recently and during most of human history people lived very differently in small, self-sufficient, and traditionally minded communities. To appreciate what is distinctive about our world, we have to compare it with past worlds, and you will find that we do this in most of our chapters.

Anthropological insight is necessary to enable us to appreciate the diversity of human society. Giddens here refers to the work of social anthropologists who provided us with a knowledge and understanding of the functioning, the beliefs, and way of life of non-industrial societies that are very different from our own. Apart from enabling us to comprehend human diversity, this knowledge helps us to combat an ethnocentrism that judges other societies from the standpoint of ours. This ethnocentrism has considered our own society to be superior and therefore justified in 'the greedy engulfing of other modes of life by industrial capitalism' (Giddens 1986: 20).

The exercise of these two sensibilities makes possible the third, *critical* sensitivity. Through the *historical* and *anthropological* sensibilities we can escape the 'strait-jacket' of the society that we live in and discover that very different societies with other ways of organizing life, other institutions, and other beliefs, have existed and continue to exist. This enables us to examine critically our own society and consider alternative ways of living and thinking, alternative organizations and institutions.

Why, one may ask, does all this require *imagination*? An effort of imagination is required because, to acquire these sensibilities, sociologists have to go beyond their immediate day-to-day experience of the world. They have to grasp quite abstract concepts of structure and process that enable them to make sense of the workings of the wider society and its historical development. They have to make an imaginative leap to understand ways of living and organizing that are very different from the ones that they know. They have to get 'inside the heads' of other people so that they can understand their actions and the meanings they attach to them. As you read this book you will find that you have to develop and exercise your sociological imagination in all these ways.

◆ *Chapter summary*

In this chapter we discussed a number of general issues raised by the subject of sociology. We began by exploring why one should study sociology:

- We argued that it enables us to understand the world that we live in and our place within that world.
- In doing so, it enables us to understand ourselves, and self-understanding can help us to free ourselves.

- It also has many practical applications to the understanding of social problems, though it is also concerned with how certain kinds of behaviour come to be defined as 'a problem'.

We then moved on to consider what sociologists mean by society:

- Societies consist of a complex of interdependent institutions.

- Societies are, however, organized at different levels, from the small group, through the community and the organization, to the nation state, and the global level.

- Societies also consist of structures of inequality and domination.

- There is a cultural dimension to society, consisting of people's beliefs and their symbolic representation in actions and objects.

  Lastly, we discussed whether sociology should be considered a science:

- Science involves systematic observation and the development of theories to explain observations.

- Sociology is not a natural science because social behaviour is different from natural behaviour.

- The explanation of social behaviour requires an understanding of the meaning of actions.

- Sociology is, none the less, a social science that is based on systematic observational methods and the construction of explicit theories.

- Sociology also requires the exercise of a 'sociological imagination', to grasp concepts, conceive alternatives, and understand the meaning of human action.

 ## *Key concepts*

- community
- culture
- family
- globalization
- household
- institutions

- nation state
- norms
- organization
- personal identity
- science
- socialization

- social stratification
- social structure
- society
- sociological imagination
- values

Workshop 1

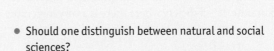

Discussion points

Sociology and science

- What do you consider to be the key features of a science?

- Do scientists simply carry out observations that discover facts?

- What do you think facts are?

- How well does sociology fit your definition of science?

- Is there any reason to suppose that sociology is not a science?

- Should one distinguish between natural and social sciences?

- What do we mean by 'common sense'?

- Is sociology different from common sense?

- Should sociology be considered superior to common sense?

Explore further

The following references, some of which we have quoted in our panel on pp. 6–7, all provide interesting and perceptive discussions of the nature of sociology:

Bauman, Z., and May, T. (2001), *Thinking Sociologically* (2nd edn., Oxford: Basil Blackwell).

Berger, P. (1963), *Invitation to Sociology: A Humanistic Perspective* (Harmondsworth: Penguin).

Bruce, S. (1999), *Sociology: A Very Short Introduction* (Oxford: Oxford University Press).

Jenkins, R. (2002), *Foundations of Sociology* (Basingstoke: Palgrave Macmillan).

Mills, C. W. (1959), *The Sociological Imagination* (2nd edn., New York: Oxford University Press, 2000).

Online resources

Visit the Online Resource Centre that accompanies this book to access more learning resources and other interesting material on what sociology is about at:

www.oxfordtextbooks.co.uk/orc/fulcher3e/

The website of the British Sociological Association, where you can find general information about the subject, including another answer to the question 'What is sociology?',

and advice about career opportunities for sociologists, is at:

www.britsoc.co.uk/

For a comprehensive but carefully selected list of sociology web links, with very helpful descriptions of what can be found at each one, visit:

www.intute.ac.uk/socialsciences/

theories and theorizing

Contents

'That's all very well in theory'

How often have you heard someone say 'That's all very well in theory' or 'Well, I know how it ought to work in theory'? The implication of these statements is that 'theory', no matter how logical or clear-cut, can never grasp the realities of a situation and so is a poor guide to action. Theory is seen as abstract and irrelevant, perhaps as produced by those who live in 'ivory towers' and do not understand what the 'real world' is like. Sometimes, theory is seen as an evaluative, ideological position that contrasts with a sombre reliance on 'the facts'. This view is particularly strong in popular discussions of the social world. Sociologists are criticized for theorizing, rather than getting on with more important things, much as Nero was supposed to have fiddled while Rome burned. This view often goes hand in hand with the assertion that sociological theory is, in any case, mere jargon: commonplace ideas are dressed up in scientific mumbo-jumbo language. From this point of view, theory consists simply of spinning out long but essentially meaningless words: the jargon is a smokescreen for ignorance or platitudes. The implication is clear: sociological theorizing is not the kind of thing that any self-respecting person need be concerned with.

The popular criticisms of theory misunderstand what theory is all about. Theory is—or should be—an attempt to describe and explain the real world. In a very important sense, it is impossible to know anything about the real world without drawing on some kind of theoretical ideas. Sociological theories are attempts to highlight aspects of social situations that are of interest by drawing out their general features. They abstract from the particular and unique features of events and situations in order to isolate those things that they have in common and that can, therefore, guide us in understanding events and situations that we have not yet encountered.

It is undoubtedly true that sociologists can be as susceptible to prejudice and jargon as anybody else. Perhaps they have sometimes adopted cumbersome terminology in a misguided attempt to justify their claims to a scientific status in the face of exactly these kinds of objections. However, any scientific activity must employ specialized technical terms in its theories, and these terms will not always be comprehensible to the person in the street. It is also the case that many sociological concepts originate in everyday terms, and these must be given a more precise and technical meaning if they are not to be misunderstood.

Theory lies at the heart of sociology. It enables us to understand and explain the nature of the social world. Many sociological theories are concerned with specific social phenomena or with explaining particular social

> **⤵ Connections**
>
> Theory can be difficult and demanding. You will not necessarily understand all that we say in this chapter the first time that you read it. However, you should not worry about this. It is not your fault. The problem lies with the complexity of the theories and—it has to be said—with the failure of certain theorists to present their ideas clearly. You will find it best to skim through the chapter as a whole, not worrying too much about the detail. You can spend more time on the parts that you find easiest to handle. Treat the whole chapter as a reference source, as something to come back to as and when you read the 'Understanding' sections of the book. Theory is best handled in the context of particular empirical issues.

processes. They concern such things as crime, health, education, or politics, or they concern deviance, socialization, or stratification. You will encounter many such theories in the various chapters of this book. These theories are, however, connected into larger theoretical frameworks that try to grasp the most general features of social life as a whole. It is these theories that we will look at in this chapter. We will outline the key ideas of the main theorists, and we will show how their ideas are related to the issues that we raise in the other chapters of the book.

There is no single theory to which all sociologists subscribe. There are, instead, a number of different theories, each of which has its advocates and its detractors. These theories are sometimes presented as mutually opposed to each other and as defining rival positions from which sociologists must choose. It is sometimes assumed that adherents of one theory have nothing to learn from considering any others. Some textbooks, for example, present their readers with a range of different theoretical positions on each topic and imply that all are equally valid. It is as if you enter the sociological supermarket and see, laid out on the shelves in front of you, 'Marxism', 'functionalism', 'feminism', 'interactionism', and so on. You walk down the aisles, picking up those theories that appeal to you or that have the best packaging. Having made your choice, you return home to use your new theories.

Theoretical choice is not like this. The choice between theories is not made on the basis of individual preference ('I just don't like functionalism') or political standpoint ('I'm working class, so I'm a Marxist'). Preferences and politics do, of course, enter into sociology, but they do not determine the merits of particular theories. The choices that we must make among theoretical positions are shaped, above all, by empirical considerations. When judging a theory, what really matters is its capacity to explain what is happening in the real world. Theories must always be tested through empirical research. As we show in this and the next chapter, the 'facts' are not quite as straightforward as this statement suggests. However, the point still remains. Theories are attempts to describe and explain the social world. Their merits and limitations depend, ultimately, on their ability to cope with what we know about that world.

We will show that the leading theorists of the sociological tradition have attempted, in their different ways, to understand the modern world. They have each, however, concentrated on particular aspects of that world. None has given a full and complete picture. The least satisfactory theorists are, in fact, those who have tried to move, prematurely, towards that comprehensive picture. The most powerful theories are those that have emphasized a particular aspect of the social world and have concentrated their attention on understanding that aspect. In doing so, they neglect or put to one side the very processes that other theories take as their particular concern.

If it is possible to produce a comprehensive understanding of the social world, this is likely to result from the slow synthesis of these partial viewpoints. In so far as the social world is constantly changing, it is undoubtedly true that any such synthesis would not last long before it, too, needed to be revised. Theoretical change and the development of new theories are constant features of scientific activity. Even in such a well-developed field as physics, there are numerous partial theories that have not yet been synthesized into a larger and more comprehensive theory.

For the present, then, different theories must be seen, in principle, as complementary to one another. We must emphasize that we are not proposing that all theories are of equal value, or that they can simply be hashed together in some unwieldy mixture. Some theories are bad theories that have received no support from empirical research. Even the useful theories have their particular strengths and, of course, their particular weaknesses. Each theory must be assessed against the facts that are relevant to its particular concerns, not against those that are more relevant to some other theory. By the end of this chapter you should have some appreciation of how the various sociological theories do, indeed, complement one another. You should begin to see how, collectively, they provide a picture of the social world that is far better than any of them can provide alone.

In this chapter we place great emphasis on the historical development of sociological theory. Theories constructed over 100 years ago are, of course, likely to have been superseded, in many respects, by more recent theories. Many of them, however, still have a great deal of relevance for us today, and most contemporary theories have developed out of the ideas of the nineteenth-century theorists. It is possible to gain a better understanding of them if these lines of development are traced.

We begin with an overview of the earliest attempts to establish a science of sociology, and we go on to show how these attempts were the basis of the classical statements of sociology produced around the turn of the twentieth century. The section on 'Academic sociology established' looks at the three main theoretical traditions of the twentieth century: structural-functionalist theories, interaction theories, and conflict theories. We conclude the chapter with a sketch of the feminist and post-modernist theorists whose arguments have moved sociological debates on to a broader set of issues, and we indicate some of the implications of globalization for social theorizing. We consider these arguments at greater length in the various chapters of Part Two. In this chapter and throughout the book you will find that we consider both classic and contemporary theorists, treating them as participants in the same great intellectual enterprise that is sociology.

Pioneers of social theory

For as long as people have lived in societies, they have tried to understand them and to construct theories about them. So far as we know, people have always lived in societies, and so social theory has a long history. For much of this history, however, these attempts at understanding have looked very different from what we currently mean by the word sociology. Early attempts at social understanding had a greater similarity to myths or to poetry than they did to science, and many of these attempts were religious or highly speculative in character. The creation of a distinctively scientific approach to social understanding is, in fact, a very recent thing. While the philosophers of ancient Greece developed many ideas about social and political life, it is only since the seventeenth century, and then mainly in Europe, that there has been anything that could truly be called a science of society.

The origins of a *scientific* perspective on social life can be traced to the European Enlightenment of the seventeenth and eighteenth centuries. The Enlightenment marked a sea change in the whole cultural outlook of European intellectuals. In one field after another, rational and critical methods were adopted and religious viewpoints were replaced by scientific ones. It was in this period that the very idea of science first emerged.

The greatest of the early achievements of the Enlightenment were the philosophy of Descartes and the physics of Newton. Writing in the middle decades of the sixteenth century, Descartes set out a view of intellectual enquiry as the attempt to achieve absolutely certain knowledge of the world, using only the rational and critical faculties of the mind. From this point of view, science is the attempt to construct theories that can be assessed against the evidence of the human senses. Observation and direct experience of the world provide the raw materials for scientific work. The rational and critical faculties of the scientist guide the way that these are accounted for. In Newton's physics, this method led to the construction of elegant mathematical theories that saw the behaviour of physical objects in relation to their mass, volume, and density, and to the forces of gravity and magnetism. The German philosopher Kant drew out the wider implications of this approach to knowledge and his arguments were central to attempts to extend Enlightenment ideas to the analysis of the social world.

During the eighteenth century, the scope of scientific knowledge in physics was enlarged, and the same scientific method led to advances in chemistry, biology, and many other specialist fields. Progress in the construction of a scientific sociology was much slower. At first, social life was understood in almost exclusively individual terms. Those who explored social life tried to explain it as resulting from the behaviour of rational, calculating individuals who sought only to increase their own happiness and satisfaction. They were aware that individuals lived in societies, but they saw societies only as collections of individuals. They had not grasped what most people now take for granted: that individuals cannot be understood in isolation from the social relations into which they are born and without which their lives have no meaning.

In Britain and France, and later in Germany, a more properly *social* perspective was gradually developed. British theorists were particularly concerned with economic activities and economic relations and have often been described as taking a **materialist** view of social life. For them, the central features of social life were the struggle over economic resources and the inequalities and social divisions to which this gave rise. Many French and German writers, on the other hand, highlighted the part played by moral values and ideas, and they have been described as **idealist** theorists. These theorists saw societies as possessing a cultural spirit that formed the foundation of their customs and practices.

Social development and evolution

The first systematic theories of social life to achieve a major influence were those of Georg Hegel and Auguste Comte. Hegel built on the work of his German predecessors to construct a comprehensive idealist theory of society and history. Similar concerns are apparent in the work of Comte, though he was a more self-consciously scientific writer who owed a great deal to the economic analyses of the earlier materialists. Where Hegel remained satisfied with a very general account of the nature of the distinctive social element in human life, Comte tried to analyse this into its constituent elements. These were, he said, aspects of the structure of social systems. Both writers identified long-term processes of social change that they described as processes of social development. Herbert Spencer, writing later in the nineteenth century, carried all these themes forward. He saw society as a social organism that developed over time through a process of social evolution.

Hegel: society as spirit

The inspiration behind Hegel's ideas was the philosophy of Immanuel Kant, the next great landmark in philosophical thought after Descartes. Kant's central argument was that scientific knowledge had to be seen as an active and creative production of the human mind. All observations, Kant argued, depend upon the particular ways in which experiences are interpreted in relation to current cultural concerns. According to Hegel, the interpretation of experience reflects the 'spirit' of the culture. This term, taken from Montesquieu (1748), referred to the general principles and underlying ideas that lay behind the particular customs and practices of a society. The spirit of a culture shapes the subjective ideas and meanings on which individuals act, and so Hegel saw individuals as the mere embodiments of a cultural spirit. There is, then, a one-to-one relationship between cultural spirit, social institutions, and social actions. Hegel saw actions and institutions as simply the means through which cultural ideas and values are formed into a social reality.

> **⊃ Connections**
> Hegel's ideas are complex and his works are difficult to read. At this stage, you should not try to track down his books. If you ever do feel able to tackle him, you should start with his *Philosophy of Right* (Hegel 1821). Do not expect an easy ride!

Hegel saw history as involving a gradual shift from local to more global social institutions. In the earliest stages, family and kinship defined the basic social pattern. People's lives were contained within localized communities that were tied tightly together through bonds of kinship and family obligations. The family spirit prevailed. These communal forms of social life were followed in Europe and in certain of the great civilizations of the world, by societies in which the division of labour and market relations tied local communities into larger societies. Hegel saw these societies as marked by deep divisions into unequal social classes and as driven by the commercial spirit of property-owners and merchants.

In his own time, Hegel identified the beginnings of a new stage of social development. The nation state was becoming the key social institution. In contemporary societies, he held, the state embodied the spirit of the people as a whole and not just the spirit of a particular class or kinship group. This was what he called the *world spirit*, a universal and all-embracing cultural spirit that marked the end point of historical development.

Hegel's work, while pioneering, was not yet sociology. He saw history as the automatic and inevitable expression of an abstract spirit into the world. Spirit itself was seen as the active, moving force in social life. Yet spirit was an unsatisfactory idea and was not analysed in a scientific way. Hegel personified spirit, seeing it as some kind of active and creative force. Furthermore, when Hegel looked to what it is that drives the human spirit itself, he discovered God. The holy spirit lies behind the human spirit, and social development is seen as the progressive realization of God's will.

Hegel's work drew together many of the insights of the French idealists and put them into a comprehensive general framework. Its religious character, however, meant that he had few direct followers. Some aspects of his thought were taken ahead, in a very different direction, by Karl Marx, as we will shortly show. Idealism had its greatest impact on the development of sociology in France. The key writer here was Comte, who was the first to set out a comprehensive, if flawed, account of a theoretical science of society.

Comte and Saint-Simon

It is thanks to Comte that the science of society is called 'sociology', as it was he who invented the word in 1839 to describe the system of ideas that he had developed. Comte, however, was carrying forward and enlarging some of the ideas that he had learned from his teacher and first employer, Saint-Simon. Comte's intellectual and personal relationship to Saint-Simon was very close, but a disagreement between the two men led Comte to deny the importance of Saint-Simon and to exaggerate the originality of his own work. Despite this, it is undoubtedly Comte's efforts at systematizing and unifying the science of society that made possible its later professionalization as an academic discipline.

Saint-Simon was a radical, but eccentric aristocrat who popularized the idea of what he called *positive science*. The term positive means definite and unquestionable, and Saint-Simon used it to describe the precise or exact sciences based on observation and mathematics that he saw emerging in one intellectual field after another. This led him to advocate the building of a positive 'science of man', a psychological and social science of the human mind. Once this science had been achieved, he held, we would be well on the way to possessing a complete knowledge of everything that exists. At this point, the various positive sciences could be unified into a single 'positive philosophy'.

The work of Saint-Simon was confused and unsystematic, and he recognized that he needed a collaborator. Comte, who had been convinced by the work of Montesquieu and Condorcet that there was a pressing need for a social science, took on this task and worked closely with Saint-Simon from 1817 to 1824. It was this period of intellectual apprenticeship that gave Comte the confidence to begin to construct the outlines of the positive philosophy and its positive science of society.

A positive science of society

Comte's importance in the history of sociology is due to the particular method that he proposed and his general view of

THEORY AND METHODS

Auguste Comte

Inventor of the word 'sociology'.

© Bibliotheque Nationale, Paris/The Bridgeman Art Library

Isidore Auguste Marie François Xavier Comte (1798–1857) was born in Montpellier. After an unspectacular education, during which his political interests led him into conflict with the authorities, he settled in Paris.

He was a dogmatic and self-important individual, whose arrogance made it difficult for him to establish secure relationships. His intellectual relationship to Saint-Simon was stormy, and ended a year before the death of Saint-Simon in 1825. His personal life was equally unstable. Comte's early life was marked by periods of depression and paranoia, and his marriage broke down because of his extreme jealousy.

Comte decided on the plan for his life work while still working for Saint-Simon. He planned a *Course in Positive Philosophy*, which he delivered in public lectures and published in serial form between 1830 and 1842. The *Course* eventually ran to six volumes, covering the whole of what he took to be established knowledge in mathematics, astronomy, physics, chemistry, biology, and sociology. The part on sociology (which he originally called 'social physics') was its

centrepiece and took up three of the six volumes.

Having completed this task, Comte went on to write what he considered to be even more important, the *System of Positive Polity*. This, too, was a multi-volume work and was completed in 1854, just three years before his death. The *System* set out a summary of his position and his programme for the social reconstruction of European society. This reconstruction involved the establishment of a 'Religion of Humanity', a religion that abandoned dogma and faith and was itself constructed on a scientific basis. Sociology was to be the core of this religion, with sociologists replacing priests as the expert teachers and policy-makers.

Comte's works are difficult to get hold of in English editions, but you might like to scan some of the extracts reprinted in K. Thompson (1976).

the subject matter of sociology. The method that Comte proposed for sociology was that of positive science. He held that sociology could advance human understanding only if it emulated the other positive sciences in its approach. Comte was not saying that sociology had slavishly to follow the natural sciences. On the contrary, he was very concerned to emphasize that each of the major disciplines had its own distinctive subject matter, which had to be studied in its own right and could not be reduced to the subject matter of any other science. His point was simply that there was only one way of being scientific, whatever the subject matter of the science.

Comte's **positivism** presented science as the study of observable phenomena. The scientist must make direct observations of those things that are of interest, examining their similarities and differences, and investigating the order in which they occurred. These observations had then to be explained by theoretical laws, or logical connections. These laws stated causal relationships between observed events, so allowing the scientist to predict the occurrence of events. If, for example, we have a law stating that intellectual unrest is a cause of political instability, then the observation of intellectual unrest would lead us to predict

a period of political instability. The task of the scientist is to produce theories that are able to arrive at just these kinds of laws.

While many of the details of Comte's sociology are no longer accepted by sociologists, his main principles have largely been accepted and they now form a part of the mainstream of the subject. His key insight was that societies had to be understood as complex *systems*. They are organic wholes with a unity similar to that of biological organisms. The human body, for example, is a biological system of parts that are connected together into a living whole. Similarly, a society may be seen as a cohesive and integrated whole. The parts of a society are not simply individuals, but social institutions. A society consists of family and kinship institutions, political institutions, economic institutions, religious institutions, and so on. These do not exist in isolation but are interdependent parts of the whole social system. Change in any one institution is likely to have consequences for the other institutions to which it is connected.

Comte identified two broad branches of sociology, corresponding to two ways in which social systems could be studied:

- *social statics*: the study of the coexistence of institutions in a system, their structures and their functions;
- *social dynamics*: the study of change in institutions and systems over time, their development and progress.

The study of social statics is similar to the study of organization or anatomy in biology. It looks at the **social structure** of a social system, at the way in which the institutions that make up the system are actually connected to each other. Comte argues that the aim of social statics is to produce *laws of coexistence*, principles concerning the interdependence of social institutions.

The main elements of a society, according to Comte, are its division of labour, its language, and its religion. It is through a division of labour—a socially organized distribution of productive tasks—that people are able to satisfy their material needs. Through their language they communicate with each other and pass on the knowledge and values that they have learned. Through their religion, they can achieve a sense of common purpose and of working towards a common goal. These elements are all cemented together into the overall social structure.

The connections between the parts of a social system are studied by identifying their **functions**. We will come back to this idea later in this chapter. In general terms, however, Comte used the term function to refer to the contribution that particular institutions or practices make to the rest of the society, the part that they play in reproducing or maintaining it in existence by contributing to its solidarity or coherence. Comte saw a coherent society as a 'healthy' society. Those systems that show a high level of solidarity, consensus, or coherence work more smoothly and are more likely to persist than those with only a low level of coherence. Coherent societies are in a healthy state of balance or equilibrium, with all their parts working well together. In some situations, however, societies, like other organisms, may be in a 'pathological' condition of imminent breakdown or collapse. If their parts are not functioning correctly, they will not have the kind of coherence that they need to survive.

The study of social dynamics is concerned with the flow of energy and information around a social system and, therefore, with the ways in which societies change their structures in certain ways. Structural change is what Comte calls development or progress. The aim of social dynamics is to produce *laws of succession* that specify the various stages of development through which a particular social system is expected to move.

Comte saw the emergence of positive science itself as something that could be explained by the most important law of succession that sociologists possess. This was what he called the law of the three stages. According to this law, the religious ideas produced by the human mind pass through three successive stages, and particular types of social institution correspond to each of them. These three stages are the theological, the metaphysical, and the positive. In the theological stage, people think in exclusively supernatural terms, seeing human affairs as resulting from the actions of gods and other supernatural beings. In the metaphysical stage, theological ideas are abandoned and people begin to think in terms of more abstract spiritual forces such as 'Nature'. Finally, the positive stage is one in which these abstractions give way to scientific observation and the construction of empirical laws.

Comte saw the theological stage as having lasted in Europe until the fourteenth century. This period involved a vast range of human societies from the simplest tribal societies to more complex kingdoms. The metaphysical stage lasted from the fourteenth century until about 1800, and Comte saw its development as having been closely linked with the rise of Protestantism. Societies in the metaphysical stage were militaristic and feudal societies that depended on a vast agricultural base. The positive stage began early in the nineteenth century and corresponds to what Comte called **industrial society**. This term, now so taken for granted, was first used by Saint-Simon and was taken up by Comte to describe the type of society that was gradually maturing in the Europe of his day. The term industrial was initially contrasted with earlier 'militaristic' types of society, and was intended to suggest that social life had become organized around the peaceful pursuit of economic welfare rather than the preparation for war. More specifically, an industrial society is one organized around the achievement of material well-being through an expanding division of labour and a new technology of production. This kind of society is headed by the entrepreneurs, directors, and managers, who are the technical experts of the new industrial technology.

THEORY AND METHODS

Positivism

For Comte, the positivist approach in science simply involves an emphasis on rational, critical thought and the use of evidence. In many contemporary discussions, however, it is presented as a much narrower and more restricted idea. 'Positivist' is often used almost as a term of abuse, and is applied to those who use mathematics or social surveys. This kind of distortion is not helpful. You will find it much easier to handle sociological debates if you avoid trying to label people as positivists and non-positivists. If you must use the word, try to use it as Comte intended. Bear in mind, however, that Comte tied positive science to positive politics and his religion of humanity.

As it developed, however, industrial society created great inequalities of income. The resentment that the poor felt towards the wealthy was responsible for a pathological state of unrest and social crisis. The only long-term solution to this, Comte argued, was for a renewed moral regulation of society through the establishment of a new, rational system of religion and education. This would establish the moral consensus that would encourage people to accept the inevitable inequalities of industrialism.

Comte's political aspirations were unfulfilled, and his religion of humanity inspired only small and eccentric groups of thinkers. His view of the need for a critical and empirical science of society, however, was massively influential and secured the claims of his sociology to a central place in intellectual discussions. His particular view of the development of modern industrial society rested on a rather inadequate historical understanding of pre-modern societies, but he accurately identified many of its most important characteristics. His concept of the industrial society has continued to inform debates about the future development of modern societies.

Spencer and social evolution

The materialist tradition in Britain had its major impact on the growth of economic theory (usually termed political economy), where a long line of theorists attempted to uncover the way in which the production of goods is shaped by the forces of supply and demand. In the work of Herbert Spencer this was combined with ideas drawn from the work of Comte to form a broader sociological theory.

THEORY AND METHODS
....

Herbert Spencer

Herbert Spencer (1820–1903) was born in Derby and was privately educated in mathematics and physics. He started work in the new railway industry, and became a successful railway engineer. His intellectual interests in geology and biology, and his interest in political issues, led him to publish a number of articles, and in 1848 he decided to move into journalism. His first book was *Social Statics*. This and a series of papers on population and evolution were followed by a major work that was to take the whole of the rest of his life to complete. Like Comte, he aimed at an encyclopaedic summary of human knowledge; a 'synthetic philosophy'. He published this work in his *Principles of Biology*, *Principles of Psychology*, *Principles of Sociology*, and *Principles of Ethics*.

Spencer's sociological works are difficult to get hold of and it is probably better to approach him through the extracts reprinted in Andreski (1976).

Spencer was seen by many people as the direct heir to Comte, although this was certainly not how he saw himself. Although he gave far less attention to religious and intellectual factors than did Comte, there is, nevertheless, a great similarity in their views. It is also true to say, however, that Spencer remained very close to the British tradition in giving a great emphasis to individual action. Spencer took forward Comte's idea that societies were organic systems, but he also emphasized that they must be seen in terms of individuals and their actions.

Spencer adopted Comte's distinction between social statics and social dynamics as the two main branches of his sociology. His social statics stressed the idea of society as an organism. Each part in a society is specialized around a particular function and so makes its own distinctive contribution to the whole. A society is an integrated and regulated system of interdependent parts. Much of Spencer's work in sociology consisted of the attempt to describe these interdependencies in general terms and as they are found in actual societies.

His most distinctive contribution to sociology, however, was his emphasis on the principle of **evolution** in his social dynamics. Evolutionary ideas achieved a great popularity in Victorian Britain following the publication of Darwin's *On the Origin of Species* in 1859. The debate over Darwin's work made widely known the idea that biological species evolve through a constant struggle for existence in which only the fittest can survive. Those species that are best adapted to the biological conditions under which they live are more likely to survive than those that are only weakly adapted or not adapted at all. In fact, the phrase 'survival of the fittest' had been introduced by Spencer some years before Darwin published his work, and both Darwin and Spencer acknowledged that the idea of a struggle for existence came from Malthus's (1798) work on population.

Spencer's great contribution to the debate over evolution, however, was his advocacy of the principle of *social* evolution. This consisted of two processes:

- structural differentiation;
- functional adaptation.

Structural differentiation is a process through which simple societies develop into more complex ones. This idea was modelled on the biological process through which, as Spencer saw it, advanced organisms had more differentiated and specialized parts than less advanced ones. In all spheres of existence, he held, there is an evolution from the simple to the complex. In the social world, structural differentiation involves the proliferation of specialized social institutions.

Spencer saw simple societies as organized around family and kinship relations, and as achieving their material needs through hunting and gathering. Few aspects of social life are specialized, and everything is, ultimately, organized through kinship. Gradually, however, separate governmental and economic institutions are formed and systems of communication are established. Many activities previously organized through the family come to be organized through these specialized institutions. As a result, the family loses some of its functions, which have been 'differentiated' into the specialized institutions. Over time, the specialized institutions are themselves subject to structural differentiation. Governmental institutions, for example, become differentiated into separate political and military institutions.

The reason why structural differentiation occurs, Spencer held, is that it allows societies to cope with the problems and difficulties that they face in their material environment (physical conditions, climate, natural resources) and from other societies. This process of coping with the environment is what Spencer called *functional adaptation*. Structural differentiation allows societies to become better adapted, and so a changing environment is associated with an increasing level of structural differentiation.

The nineteenth century, according to Spencer, was a period in which industrial societies were beginning to evolve. These societies were well adapted to the conditions under which people then lived. They were highly differentiated social systems with only a very loose degree of overall regulation. Individuals had a great degree of autonomy in an industrial society, and further evolution depended on the maintenance of their intellectual, economic, and political freedoms. Spencer tried to explore what he saw as the balance between individual freedom and collective welfare in industrial societies. Adam Smith had argued that the economic market operates as a 'hidden hand' to ensure that the greatest level of economic happiness results from individually selfish behaviour. Spencer extended this argument and held that all the structurally differentiated institutions of contemporary societies could be seen as working, generally in unintended ways, to produce the greatest collective advantages. There is a natural harmony or coherence that results only from the rational, self-interested actions of free individuals. Spencer was, therefore, opposed to state intervention of any kind, whether in the sphere of education, health, or the economy. Individuals had to be left to struggle for existence with each other. The fittest would survive, and this was, he argued, in the best interest of society as a whole.

Karl Marx

We have looked at two writers who were engaged in a common intellectual exercise. Despite the differences in their views, Comte and Spencer both produced pioneering

versions of a science of sociology. Karl Marx too aspired to build a science of society, but he was very much on the margins of the intellectual world and he did not describe himself as a sociologist. To the extent that he took any account of the work of the sociologists, he was critical of it. This failure of Marx to identify himself as a sociologist reflects the fact that the word was still very new and, for many people, it still described only the specific doctrines of Comte and Spencer. As we will see in 'The formative period of sociology', pp. 32–43, it was only in the next generation of social theorists that Marx's ideas began to receive any proper recognition as a part of the same *sociological* enterprise as the works of Comte and Spencer.

The inspiration for Marx's work was the growth of the European labour movement and of socialist ideas. He tried to tie his philosophical and scientific interests to the needs of this labour movement. Marx was trained in the tradition of Hegel's philosophy, studying at Berlin just a few years after Hegel's death, but he was also influenced by the British materialist tradition. He saw the work of writers such as Ferguson and Millar as providing the basis for an understanding of the power and significance of the labour movement, but only if combined with the historical perspective of Hegel.

Marx's model of society

The central idea in Marx's early work was **alienation**. This described the way in which the economic relations under which people work can change their labour from a creative act into a distorted and dehumanized activity. As a result, people do not enjoy their work or find satisfaction in it. They treat it as a mere means to ensuring their survival (by providing themselves with a wage) and therefore their ability to turn up the next week to work once more. In this way, work and its products become separate or 'alien' things that dominate and oppress people.

Marx accounted for alienation in terms of property relations and the division of labour. The economy, he held, is central to the understanding of human life. He argued that the existence of private property divides people into **social classes**. These are categories of people with a specific position in the division of labour, a particular standard of living, and a distinct way of life. The basic class division is that between property-owners and propertyless workers. The existence of classes and of social inequality was first highlighted by the British materialists, and Marx saw his own contribution as showing how and why these classes are inevitably drawn into conflict with each other. This he did in his later work for *Capital* (1867). Classes, he argued, are involved in relations of exploitation. The property-owning class benefits at the expense of the propertyless, and this leads the classes to struggle over the distribution of economic resources.

THEORY AND METHODS

Karl Marx

Voted the greatest ever philosopher.

© Getty Images/Hulton Archive

Karl Marx (1818–83) was born in Trier, Germany. He studied law at Bonn and Berlin. His radical political views led him into a journalistic career, but this was cut short by the suppression of the various journals for which he wrote. He fled to Paris in 1843, to Brussels in 1845, and, finally, to London in 1848. It was in London that he spent the rest of his life. His massive tomb can still be seen in Highgate cemetery.

Marx began to work on a series of philosophical and economic books while in Paris, and he spent the rest of his life studying, engaging in radical politics, and writing articles for newspapers and periodicals. He was able to use his time in this way only because of the financial support from his friend and collaborator Friedrich Engels.

Engels (1820–95) was the son of a wealthy cotton manufacturer. Like Marx, he was involved in radical politics and intellectual work, but he was sent to Manchester by his father to manage the English branch of the family firm. This gave him the financial independence to support both himself and Marx. Engels wrote an important study of poverty, *The Condition of the Working Class in England*

in 1844 (Engels 1845), and he collaborated with Marx on a number of works, including *The Communist Manifesto* (Marx and Engels 1848).

Marx found it difficult to complete books. A number of his most important studies were published long after his death, thanks to the editorial work of Engels and others. The most important of his early works, where he set out a theory of 'alienation', was the *Economic and Philosophical Manuscripts* (Marx 1844), published only in 1932. After *The Communist Manifesto*, he went on to produce a series of massive drafts for *Capital*, a critical study of economic theory and the economic basis of society. Only volume one (Marx 1867) was published in his lifetime.

There is some controversy about the relationship between the works of the older, mature Marx of the 1860s and those of the youthful Marx of the 1840s. For some commentators, the early works on alienation were immature exercises that he later abandoned. For others, however, exploitation and alienation are closely related ideas. A close reading of Marx's texts shows that there is a great deal of continuity and that the so-called *Grundrisse* (Marx 1858) is a key link between the two phases of his work.

Marx's central idea of the organization of a society into a base and a superstructure (discussed in the text) drew a comparison with architecture. If the superstructure of a building (its walls and roof and the internal layout of the rooms) is to remain solid and not fall down, then it must stand on solid foundations that run deep into the ground. Marx saw kinship, politics, and ideology as the various levels of the social superstructure, and he saw these standing on the firm foundations of an economic base comprising the forces and relations of production. The superstructure is the most obvious and visible aspect of the social structure, but the base is the essential—if hidden—support for it.

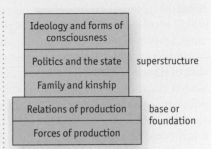

Ideology and forms of consciousness	
Politics and the state	superstructure
Family and kinship	
Relations of production	base or foundation
Forces of production	

Marx remains an influential theorist. In a poll carried out for a BBC radio programme in 2005, Marx was voted the greatest ever philosopher—he received 28 per cent of the 30,000 votes cast.

Useful discussions of Marx's ideas can be found in Giddens (1971) and Craib (1997). There is more detail in McLellan (1971), which contains some extracts from Marx's own work. A good biography is McLellan's *Karl Marx: His Life and Thought* (McLellan 1973). If you want to try to understand Marx's economic theory, you should try Mandel's (1967) *The Formation of the Economic Thought of Karl Marx*. A good collection of electronic texts by Marx can be found at

http://eserver.org:16080/marx/

Links to the ideas of Marx and other Marxists can be found at

www.marxists.org/

A useful biographical overview is at www.historyguide.org/intellect/marx.html

➔ The details of Marx's work are discussed in various parts of this book. You will find them in the following chapters:

- alienation and the nature of work *Chapter 17*
- poverty *Chapter 18*
- class relations and class polarization *Chapter 19*
- labour organization, ruling class, politics, and the state *Chapters 14, 20*
- religion and ideology *Chapter 11*

Marx saw societies as social systems that could be divided into two quite distinct parts: the **base** and the **superstructure**. The economy and class relations comprise what he called the material base or substructure of society. The base always involves a particular **mode of production**. By this term, Marx referred to the technical and human resources of production and the specific property relations and division of labour under which they are used. This economic base is the foundation upon which a superstructure of political, legal, and customary social institutions is built. It is also the basis of various forms of consciousness and knowledge. The ideas that people form, Marx said, are shaped by the material conditions under which they live. They must be regarded as what he called **ideologies**.

There has been much controversy as to how Marx's division of the social system into a base and a superstructure is to be interpreted. In its most general sense, it is simply a claim that only those societies that are able to ensure their material survival, through an efficiently organized system of production, will be able to sustain any other social activities. People must eat and have adequate clothing and shelter before they can stand for parliament, write poetry, or engage in sociology. The economic system acquires a compulsive power that shapes all other social activities because of the priority that has to be given to meeting basic economic needs.

Some of Marx's followers, along with his critics, have claimed, however, that he was setting out a form of economic determinism that allowed no autonomy at all for politics and culture. According to this view, political institutions and cultural ideas simply reflect economic divisions and struggles. While Marx did sometimes seem to suggest that the economy should be seen in this way, he was too sophisticated to accept such a deterministic position. Indeed, the claims for his work made by some of his followers led him to make the famous remark 'I am not a Marxist'.

Comte and Spencer saw social systems, in their normal states, as characterized by harmony and cohesion. Marx's view, on the other hand, recognized conflict and division as normal features of all societies. There are divisions not only within the economic base (between classes), but also between base and superstructure. While a superstructure normally reinforces and supports the economic base, it can frequently come into contradiction with it. By this, Marx meant that the form taken by the superstructure obstructs the further development of the mode of production. If production is to expand any further, the superstructure must be transformed to re-establish a closer correspondence with the economic base.

Historical materialism

Social systems develop over time as a result of the contradictions that develop within their economies. Marx's materialism, then, was a specifically **historical materialism**, the name by which Marxism is often known. Historical materialism is a theory of the transition from one mode of production to another.

Marx distinguished a number of modes of production that he used to chart the sequences of historical development that resulted from increases in the level and scale of production. The simplest, least-developed forms of society were those in which the mode of production could be described as *primitive communism*. In this type of society, property is owned by the community as a whole, and the community itself is organized around bonds of kinship.

Marx argued that, as technology develops and production expands, so the property relations must change. If they do not, societies will not be able to continue to expand their powers of production. Out of the simple form of primitive communism, then, systems with private property and more complex divisions of labour evolve. In these societies, there are distinct political institutions and, in many cases, centralized states.

Marx often suggests that the evolutionary line in western Europe led from the primitive communism of the Germanic and Celtic tribes, through the slave-owning systems of ancient Greece and Rome, and on to the feudal states of the medieval period. Feudal societies centred on the division between landowners and unfree labourers, who must work for the landlord as well as for themselves. Eastern Europe and the Near East followed a similar progression, but passed through an 'Asiatic' stage instead of a feudal one. It is to feudalism that Marx traced the emergence of the capitalist societies to which he gave his greatest attention.

The form of society that was emerging in western Europe at the time that Marx was writing was not simply an industrial society (as Comte had argued) but a specifically **capitalist society**. Beginning in the towns and commercial centres of the feudal world, a class of private property-owners had become the most important economic force. Since at least the sixteenth century, these capitalists had built plants, workshops, and factories in which they employed large numbers of workers. Capitalist entrepreneurs generated profits for themselves through a system of market exchange and the employment of wage labour. Marx held that these capitalists eventually became the **ruling classes** of their societies. They displaced the old feudal landowners, often through violent revolutions such as that in France from 1789 to 1799. They were responsible for the alienation, exploitation, and oppression of the workers who actually produced the goods that provided them with their profits.

As capitalist societies developed, Marx argued, exploitation grew and their superstructures no longer encouraged economic growth. If production was to continue to

THEORY AND METHODS

Modes of production

Marx recognized six main modes of production, each defined by a particular type of property ownership and labour:

- primitive communism—relatively egalitarian, communal property;
- ancient—slave-owning systems;
- Asiatic—despotic and bureaucratic control;
- feudalism—serfdom, combined with urban commercial centres;
- capitalism—wage labour and private property;
- advanced communism—re-establishes communal property.

In each of these modes of production, the productive forces are developed to a different level. Before the stage of advanced communism they are also marked by growing levels of exploitation and alienation.

Do not worry about the details of this scheme. We will introduce some of these, where relevant, in other chapters. You might like to compare Marx's scheme with the stages of development identified by Hegel, Comte, and Spencer.

expand, property relations and the whole superstructure had to be swept away in a revolution. This time, however, it would be a revolution of the workers, who would displace the capitalist ruling class. Workers, Marx held, would become conscious of their alienation and of the need to change the conditions that produced it. They would join together in radical political parties and, in due course, would overthrow the capitalist system. A workers' revolution, Marx rather optimistically thought, would abolish alienation, exploitation, and oppression, and it would establish a new and more advanced form of communist production.

A theory of knowledge

Marx derived a distinct philosophical position from his social theory. He accepted that the natural sciences might produce absolute and certain knowledge about the physical world, as Descartes and Kant had argued, but he held that this was not possible for the social sciences. The social world could not be known objectively, but only ever from particular standpoints. These standpoints were those provided by the class backgrounds of the observers. Members of a dominant class do, quite literally, see the social world differently from those who stand below them in the class hierarchy.

All social knowledge, then, is relative or ideological. It is historically determined by the class position of the knower. There is no standpoint outside the class structure, and so there can be no impartial or completely objective knowledge of the social world. For Marx, commitment is unavoidable. Social knowledge—and therefore social science—reflects a political commitment to one side or another in the struggle of classes.

Marx accepted the logical conclusion that his own theories were relative. They were relative, not to the standpoint of his own class, but to that of his adopted class. This was the **proletariat**, the subordinate class of the capitalist system. He believed that theorists who adopted the standpoint of this subordinate class, the oppressed and exploited class, were able to achieve a deeper and more adequate understanding of their society than those who were tied to the standpoint of the ruling class. It was for this reason that he did not hesitate to present his core ideas in a political manifesto for the communist movement (Marx and Engels 1848).

By contrast, he saw the ideas of almost all other social theorists as adopting the standpoint of the ruling, capitalist class. Classical economics and the sociologies of Comte and Spencer were, for Marx, uncritical expressions of the capitalist or **bourgeois** world-view. Their ideas could serve the labour movement only if they were subjected to rigorous criticism. Hence, he subtitled his major work on economics (1867) 'A Critique of Political Economy'. Unless bourgeois thought was subjected to criticism from the standpoint of the proletariat, it would remain simply an intellectual defence of the existing social order.

Marx's work provides a powerful challenge to the ideas of Comte. Where Comte emphasized that modern societies were *industrial societies* ruled by benign industrialists, Marx saw them as *capitalist societies* ruled by an oppressive capitalist class. Marx also differed from Comte in his stress on the importance of conflict and struggle in human history and in his emphasis on the economic basis of social life. Marx's claim to have produced a complete and comprehensive social theory cannot be upheld, but it is undoubtedly true that he highlighted many factors that had been minimized or ignored by Comte and Spencer.

> **Connections**
> Marx saw all social knowledge as relative to the class standpoint of the observer. What social divisions, other than class, could he have seen as providing distinctive standpoints on the social world? Do you agree with his rejection of the possibility of 'objectivity'? Come back and consider this question again when you have read our discussions of Max Weber and of feminist theories.

◈ *Stop and reflect*

This section has traced the early stages of scientific sociology from the Enlightenment thinkers through to the pioneering statements of Comte, Spencer, and Marx. Although you are not expected to understand or recall everything that we have written about them, you should try to make sure that you have some familiarity with their key ideas.

- The idea of a *science* of society was a product of the European Enlightenment of the seventeenth and eighteenth centuries.

- Only gradually was an understanding of the distinctively *social* features of human life separated from an understanding of *individuals*.

- Why do you think that these early social theories differed so much in their main themes and ideas?

The pioneering statements of a specifically sociological approach are found in the works of Comte and Spencer. An alternative approach, that of Marx, broadened out this emerging form of social thought.

Comte established the idea of sociology as a *positive science* that explained empirical observations through causal laws.

- Both Comte and Spencer used a distinction between social statics and social dynamics. Social statics is concerned with the structure and functioning of social systems. Social dynamics is concerned with their development over time.

- Spencer saw social development as a process of structural differentiation, shaped by functional adaptation.

- How useful do you think it is to make a distinction between 'industrial' societies and the 'militant' societies of the past?

While Marx also saw societies as systems that could be studied in terms of their structures and development over time, he placed more emphasis on the part played by conflict and struggle in social development.

- Marx saw economic activity as fundamental to social life. Work, property, and the division of labour form the economic *base* of society, its mode of production. They are the basis of class divisions that result in the alienation and exploitation of labour.

- Social development has followed a sequence of modes of production from primitive communism through feudalism to contemporary capitalist societies.

- Political and legal institutions, together with cultural values and ideologies form the superstructure of society and are shaped by the economic base.

- Was Marx correct to see class conflict as the means through which the base and the superstructure of a capitalist society can be transformed and a new society created?

The formative period of sociology

The period from the 1880s to the 1920s was one in which sociology began to be established as a scientific discipline in the universities of Europe and North America. Increasing numbers of professors began to call themselves sociologists or to take sociological ideas seriously. Their work is often referred to as 'classical sociology'. Both Spencer and Marx had their heirs and followers. In Britain, Spencer's ideas were developed in a more flexible way by Leonard Hobhouse, the first person to hold a sociology professorship in a British university. In the United States, William Sumner developed versions of Spencer's ideas that had a considerable influence, and Lester Ward developed a sociology that owed rather more to Comte.

Marx's ideas were taken up in the leading Communist parties of Europe and, even before his death, they began to be codified into 'Marxism'. Those who regarded themselves as Marxists shared his identification with the proletariat. Marxism was seen not simply as a theoretical framework but as the basis for the political programme of the labour movement. The country in which Marxism had the greatest impact was Russia, where the revolution of 1917 led to the dominance of the Communist Party and the enshrinement of Marxism as the official ideology of the Soviet Union. The political content of Marxism limited its influence in academic sociology. While there was some attempt to grapple with his ideas—especially in Germany—Marxism was a neglected tradition of thought until the 1960s.

Sociology thrived most strongly in France and Germany, where a number of important theorists began to construct more disciplined and focused theoretical frameworks that could be used in detailed empirical investigations. In France, there was the work of Le Play, Tarde, and, above all, Durkheim. In Germany, the leading theorists were Tönnies, Simmel, and Weber. In terms of their impact on the later development of sociology, it is Durkheim and Weber who must be seen as the key figures.

Émile Durkheim

Émile Durkheim saw one of his principal academic tasks as the construction of a philosophical basis for a *science* of sociology. He wanted to show that sociology could be a rigorous scientific discipline that was worthy of a place in the university system. An understanding of Durkheim's thought, then, must begin with this philosophy of science and his attempt to produce a distinctive view of the nature of sociology.

The nature of social facts

According to Durkheim, the subject matter of sociology is a distinctive set of **social facts**. These are not just any facts that happen to concern people's lives in societies. They are quite specific phenomena that can be sharply distinguished from the facts studied by other scientists. They are, in particular, distinct from the facts of individual consciousness studied by psychology and the organic facts of individual bodies studied by biology. They are the things that define the specific intellectual concerns of sociology.

Durkheim characterizes social facts as ways of acting, thinking, or feeling that are collective, rather than individual, in origin. Social facts have a reality *sui generis*. This is a Latin phrase that Durkheim uses to mean 'of its own type' or 'distinctive to itself'. Because this was a difficult idea for others to understand—and it is still not completely understood by many critics of sociology—he set out his views at some length.

Durkheim gives as an example of a social fact what later writers would call a role. There are, he says, certain established ways of acting, thinking, or feeling as a brother, a husband, a citizen, and so on. They are, in the most general sense, expected, required, or imposed ways of acting, thinking, or feeling for those who occupy these positions. They are conventional ways of behaving that are expected by others and that are established in custom and law.

Social facts are collective ways of acting, thinking, or feeling. They are not unique to particular individuals, but originate outside the consciousness of the individuals who act, think, or feel in this way. They most often involve a sense of obligation. Even when people feel that they are

---

THEORY AND METHODS

Émile Durkheim

The study of social facts.

© Bibliothèque Nationale de France

Émile Durkheim (1858–1917) was born in Épinal, France. He studied social and political philosophy at the École Normale Supérieure in Paris, reading deeply into the works of Montesquieu and Rousseau. He studied for a year in Germany. He taught educational theory at Bordeaux from 1887 to 1902, after which he moved to a professorship at the Sorbonne in Paris. He made a close, but critical study of the work of Comte, and he produced a number of exemplary sociological studies. In 1913, only four years before his death, he was allowed to call himself Professor of Sociology.

Durkheim's key works appeared regularly and became the basis of a distinctive school of sociology. His major writings were *The Division of Labour in Society* (1893), *The Rules of the Sociological Method* (1895), *Suicide: A Study in Sociology* (1897), and *The Elementary Forms of the Religious Life* (1912). He founded a journal (the *Année Sociologique*) that became a focus for his work. One of his principal followers was his nephew, Marcel Mauss, who produced some important work himself (Durkheim and Mauss 1903; Mauss 1925).

The texts by Giddens (1971) and Craib (1997) give useful discussions of Durkheim. More detail and a biographical account can be found in Lukes (1973). A good brief introduction is K. Thompson (1982). Useful attempts to set up Durkheim home pages are **www.relst.uiuc.edu/durkheim/**

and

www.emile-durkheim.com/

You will find useful links to many Durkheim sites at **http://elvers.stjoe.udayton.edu/history/people/Durkheim.html**

➲ **You will find more detailed discussions of Durkheim's principal ideas in various parts of this book:**

- religion *Chapter 11*
- education *Chapter 9*
- anomie and the division of labour *Chapter 17*

acting through choice or free will, they are likely to be following a pattern that is more general in their society and that they have acquired through learning and training. We learn what is expected of us quite early in life, and these expectations become part of our own personality.

Social facts, then, are *external* to the individual. They do not, of course, actually exist outside individual minds, but they do originate outside the mind of any particular individual. They are not created anew as each individual chooses what to do. They are passed from generation to generation and are received by particular individuals in a more or less complete form. Individuals are, of course, able to influence them and contribute to their development, but they do so only in association with other individuals. It is in this sense that social facts are the collective products of a society as a whole or of particular social groups.

Because they are matters of expectation, obligation, or deep commitment, social facts also have a 'compelling and coercive power', which Durkheim summarizes by the term *constraint*. This constraint may be expressed in punishment, disapproval, rejection, or simply the failure of an action to achieve its goal. Thus, someone who breaks the law by killing another person is likely to face arrest, trial, and imprisonment or execution. On the other hand, someone who misuses language is simply likely to be misunderstood. Durkheim remarks, for example, that he is not forced to speak French, nor is he punished if he does not, but he will be understood by his compatriots only if he does in fact use the rules and conventions of French vocabulary and grammar.

Durkheim emphasizes that social facts are very difficult to observe. Indeed, they are often observable only through their effects. We cannot, for example, observe the role of husband, but only particular individuals acting as husbands. Similarly, we cannot observe the grammar of a language, but only the speech of particular individuals. Social facts are, in general, invisible and intangible and their properties have to be discovered indirectly. By observing the actions of large numbers of people who act in similar ways, for example, we may be able to infer the existence of the role of husband. By observing a large number of conversations, we may be able to infer the existence of particular rules of grammar.

In some cases, however, social facts may appear to be more visible. They may, for example, be codified in laws, summarized in proverbs, set down in religious texts, or laid down in books of grammar. Durkheim makes clear, however, that these laws, proverbs, texts, and books are not themselves the social facts. Social facts are mental, not physical, and what we have are simply the attempts that individuals have made to bring these social facts to consciousness and to make them explicit. These explicit formulations can, nevertheless, be useful sources of evidence about social facts and can be employed alongside the direct observation of actions in any investigation into social facts.

Studying social facts

Durkheim's approach to the study of social facts owes a great deal to Comte's positivism. It was set out as a set of rules or principles that Durkheim thought should guide the scientific sociologist. The first of these directly reflected Comte's contrast between metaphysical thought and positive science, though Durkheim cast it in a more convincing form. The first rule simply says 'consider social facts as things'.

What Durkheim meant by this was that it was necessary to abandon all preconceived ideas and to study things as they really are. He held that all sciences must do this if they are to be objective and of any practical value. The transformation of alchemy into chemistry and of astrology into astronomy occurred because the practitioners of the new sciences abandoned the common-sense preconceptions that they relied on in their everyday lives. Instead, they made direct observations of natural phenomena and constructed theories that could explain them. Sociology, Durkheim argued, must move in the same direction. It must treat its objects—social facts—as 'things'.

Our natural, everyday attitudes towards social facts tend to be shaped by religious and political preconceptions and by personal prejudices. We use a whole range of everyday concepts such as the state, the family, work, crime, and so on, and we tend to assume (with little or no evidence) that these are universal features of human life. We assume, for example, that all families in all societies are more or less the same as the families that we are familiar with in our own social circle. Such ideas, as Marx recognized, are ideological. They reflect our particular social position. While Marx simply accepted that all thought was ideological,

---

THEORY AND METHODS

Social facts

Social facts 'consist of manners of acting, thinking and feeling external to the individual, which are vested with a coercive power by virtue of which they exercise control over him' (Durkheim 1895: 52). Social facts are characterized by:

- externality;
- constraint.

Some social facts are collective representations: shared ways of thinking about a group and its relations to the things that affect it. Examples of collective representations are myths, legends, and religious ideas. Others are institutions. These are modes of behaviour that are long established in a society or social group.

Durkheim saw a fundamental distinction between ideology and science. Those who adopt the scientific attitude, he said, must abandon all the accepted ideas of their social group and attempt to construct new concepts that directly grasp the real nature of things. Preconceived ideas come from outside science; scientific concepts are generated from within scientific practice itself.

Durkheim's claim that we need to study things, rather than rely on preconceptions, is, perhaps, too simple. While he correctly identified the need to avoid the prejudice and distortion that often results from preconceived ideas, he was mistaken in his belief that it was possible to observe things independently of *all* concepts. Marx's philosophy, for all its problems, recognized that the things that exist in the world can be known only through concepts. As we will see, Max Weber, too, recognized this and produced a rather better account of scientific knowledge than did Durkheim.

Nevertheless, the core of what Durkheim was trying to establish remains as a valuable insight. He stressed that, if sociology is to be a science, it must engage in research that collects evidence through the direct observation of social facts. This must be done through the adoption of an attitude of mind that is as open as possible to the evidence of the senses. We cannot substitute prejudice and ideology for scientific knowledge.

Durkheim's approach to the study of social facts makes a distinction between two complementary aspects of sociological explanation. These are **causal explanation** and **functional analysis**. Of the two, causal explanation is the more fundamental. In a causal explanation, the origins of a social fact are accounted for in relation to the other social facts that brought it into being. The punishment attached to a crime, for example, may express an intense collective sentiment of disapproval. The collective sentiment, then, is the cause of the punishment. If the sentiment did not exist, the punishment would not occur.

> ### ➲ *Connections*
> Showing causal relationships is not quite as straightforward as Durkheim implies. The fact that variations in *A* are followed by variations in *B* may not indicate that *B* is caused by *A*. The variations could indicate that both *A* and *B* are caused by some other, as yet unknown, third factor. We look at this problem in Chapter 18, pp. 743–4, where we consider it in relation to occupational achievement.

Functional analysis is concerned with the *effects* of a social fact, not with its causes. It involves looking at the part that a social fact plays in relation to the *needs* of a society or social group. The term 'need' refers simply to those things that must be done if a society is to survive. More generally, the function of something is the part that it plays in relation to the adaptation of a society to changing circumstances.

The nature of functional analysis is shown in Figure 2.1. This model simplifies Durkheim's account of the function of religion in a society. Durkheim argued that religion helps to meet a society's need for social solidarity. High levels of religious observance tie people together and so increase the level of social solidarity; low levels of religious observance, on the other hand, reduce the level of social solidarity. This is matched by the effects of social solidarity on religion. If the level of social solidarity is too low, then individualistic impulses may threaten the survival of

---

Figure 2.1 Functional analysis

This model is based on Durkheim's account of suicide, which we discuss on pp. 37–9 below, and the view of social solidarity that we set out on pp. 36–7. You might find it useful to come back to this diagram after you have read our account of social differentiation and social solidarity.

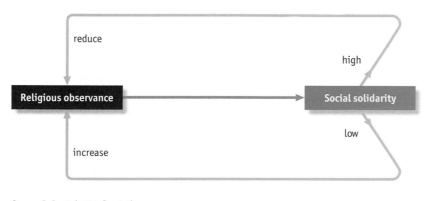

Source: J. Scott (1995: fig. 6.2).

THEORY AND METHODS
....

Rules of the sociological method

Durkheim (1895) set out a number of rules or principles. We have considered only the most important of these. A simplified and slightly shortened version of his list is:

- consider social facts as things;
- cause and function must be investigated separately;
- a particular effect always follows from the same cause;
- a full explanation of a social fact involves looking at its development through all the stages of its history;
- social facts must be classified according to their degree of organization;
- a social fact is normal for a given type of society when it is found in the average example of the type;
- a social fact is normal when it is related to the general conditions of collective life in a type of society.

Reread the discussion of Durkheim's philosophy and identify the paragraphs in which we discuss each of these rules.

In the title of his book, *Rules of the Sociological Method*, Durkheim uses the word 'method' in the sense of a philosophy of science or 'methodology' of science. He is not talking about the specific research methods that we discuss in Chapter 3.

the society. Stability can be maintained only if religious observance increases and a higher level of social solidarity is re-established. If, on the other hand, the level of social solidarity becomes too high, individual creativity may be stifled, and a reduction in the level of religious observance may be required. Religion and social solidarity are, then, interdependent.

There is much in this view of functional analysis that remains unclear. In particular, it does not show what mechanisms actually ensure that increases or reductions in religious observance take place. Durkheim minimizes this problem by equating need with 'goal' or 'purpose'. That is, he assumes that people consciously and deliberately act to meet social needs. Most later writers have rejected this view and have tried to show that the meeting of needs is often an unintended and unrecognized consequence of social action.

Social differentiation and social solidarity

Durkheim applied his scientific method in his great book on the development of modern society (Durkheim 1893). This book, the first that he wrote, was an attempt to examine **social differentiation**, the specialization of activities into a complex structure of occupations. Durkheim label-

led this the **division of labour**, using this term to refer not only to the differentiation of economic activities, but also to the specialization of political, administrative, legal, scientific, and other tasks. The division of labour was a principal topic of investigation for economists, but Durkheim wanted to show that their understanding of it was limited. The division of labour, which had achieved an unprecedented scale in modern society, was not simply an economic matter. It was central to the very cohesion and integration of modern societies.

Durkheim's book is divided into two parts: the first is concerned with the causal explanation of the division of labour and the second with its functional analysis. Durkheim's discussion of the causes of the division of labour is the shorter part of the book and can be dealt with briefly. He argued that the division of labour can occur only when communal societies give way to more organized societies. Communal societies are divided into 'segments' (families, clans, local villages) and have little or no division of labour. Each segment is self-sufficient. As segments break down, however, individuals are brought into greater and more intimate contact with those in other parts of their society. This expansion in the scale of social interaction depends on increasing population density and on the emergence of cities and commercial centres. These all bring about an increase in what Durkheim called **dynamic density**. This refers to an increase in the number of social relationships and therefore in the amount of communication and interaction between the members of a society.

A growing population density leads to more and more people carrying out the same activities. This results in growing competition and an ever increasing struggle to survive. The only way that this competition can be reduced is by people becoming more specialized in their activities. Self-sufficient households may, for example, become specialized in farming, milling, brewing, weaving, and other tasks. They begin to form a division of labour. The division of labour, Durkheim argues, develops in direct proportion to the dynamic density. As the dynamic density of a society increases, so the division of labour becomes more marked. Hence, growth in the scale of societies over time produces ever more complex and differentiated societies.

Far more attention has been given to Durkheim's functional analysis of the division of labour. In this part of the book, he looks at the consequences that the division of labour has for the wider society. In a division of labour, he argues, people's actions are complementary and interdependent. The division of labour creates not simply exchange relationships in a market system, but a feeling of **solidarity** that becomes an essential factor in the integration of the society as a whole.

Social solidarity consists of the *integration* of individuals into social groups and their *regulation* by shared norms. As a social fact, solidarity cannot be observed directly, but only through its external indicators. Durkheim argued that the most important external indicator of social solidarity is the system of law. In societies with an extensive division of labour, he argued, the law tends to be restitutive rather than repressive. Legal procedures attempt to restore things to the way that they were before a crime occurred. Punishment for its own sake is less important. This, Durkheim says, indicates a sense of solidarity that is tied to cooperation and reciprocity. Durkheim calls this **organic solidarity**. People are tied together through relations of trust and reciprocity that correspond to their economic interdependence, and each sphere of activity is regulated through specific types of norms.

The organized, organic solidarity that is produced by the division of labour is contrasted with the **mechanical solidarity** of traditional, communal societies. In these undifferentiated societies that are characteristic of the pre-modern, pre-industrial world, social solidarity revolves around a sense of similarity and a consciousness of unity and community. Conformity in such a society is maintained through the repressive force of a strong system of shared beliefs.

Organic solidarity is a normal or integral feature of modern society, but it may fail to develop in some. In the early stages of the transition from pre-industrial to industrial society, Durkheim argued, there is a particular danger that abnormal forms of the division of labour will develop. The normal condition of organic solidarity encourages a high level of individual freedom, controlling this through the normative systems that Durkheim called moral individualism. The abnormal forms of the division of labour, however, lack this moral framework, and individual actions are left uncontrolled. The two abnormal situations that he describes are egoism and anomie.

Egoism is that situation where individuals are not properly integrated into the social groups of which they are members. **Anomie** is the situation where individual actions are not properly regulated by shared norms. Durkheim saw anomie and egoism as responsible for the economic crises, extremes of social inequality, and class conflict of his day. As we show below, he also saw them as responsible for high rates of suicide. All of these problems, he held, would be reduced when the division of labour was properly established and organic solidarity instituted in its normal form.

Suicide and social solidarity

Durkheim's best-known book is his study of suicide (Durkheim 1897). His aim in this book was not only to provide an account of suicide but also to illustrate how his methodology could be applied to even the most individual of acts. The book was intended to serve as a model of sociological explanation.

Durkheim demonstrated that the taking of one's life, apparently the most individual and personal of acts, was socially patterned. He showed that social forces existing outside the individual shaped the likelihood that a person would commit suicide. Suicide rates are therefore social facts. He demonstrated this by showing how suicide rates varied from one group to another and from one social situation to another. Some of the main variations that he identified were as follows:

- *Religion*. Protestants are more likely to commit suicide than Catholics. The suicide rate is much higher in Protestant than Catholic countries. Similar differences could also be found between Protestant and Catholic areas within the same country.

- *Family relationships*. Those who were married are less likely to commit suicide than those who are single, widowed, or divorced. Whether people had children or not is also very important. Indeed, the suicide rate for married women is lower than that for single women only if they had children.

- *War and peace*. The suicide rate drops in time of war, not only in victorious but also in defeated countries. Thus, Germany defeated France in the war of 1870 but the suicide rate fell in both countries.

- *Economic crisis*. Suicide rates rise at times of economic crisis. It might be expected that a recession that causes bankruptcies, unemployment, and increasing poverty would send up the suicide rate. Suicide rates also rise, however, when economies boom. It is not worsening economic conditions but sudden *changes* in them that causes suicide rates to rise.

This demonstration of systematic variations in the suicide rate showed that suicide cannot be explained solely in terms of the psychology of the individual. Even the taking of one's own life is socially organized behaviour and therefore requires sociological explanation.

In order to provide an explanation, Durkheim put forward a sociological theory of suicide that would account for these variations. Durkheim's theory of suicide was based on the idea that it was the degree of social solidarity that explained variations in suicide rates. If a person is only loosely connected into a society or social group, then he or she is more likely to commit suicide. If their level of solidarity is too strong, then this, too, could lead to a higher suicide rate.

His theory went further than this, however, for he distinguished between two aspects of social connection, which he called *integration* and *regulation*. Integration refers to the strength of the individual's attachment to social groups. Regulation refers to the control of individual desires and aspirations by group norms or rules of behaviour. This distinction led him to identify four types of suicide, which correspond to low and high states of integration and regulation (see Figure 2.2):

Figure 2.2 Durkheim's typology of suicide

There has been much discussion in the media about the motives of suicide bombers. How do you think that Durkheim would classify these suicides?

Type	Degree of solidarity	Social situation	Psychological state	Examples
Egoistic	Low	Lack of integration	Apathy, depression	Suicides of protestants and single people
Anomic	Low	Lack of regulation	Irritation, frustration	Suicides during economic crisis
Altruistic	High	Excessive integration	Energy and passion	Suicides in primitive societies; military suicides
Fatalistic	High	Excessive regulation	Acceptance and resignation	The suicide of slaves

- egoistic suicide;
- anomic suicide;
- altruistic suicide;
- fatalistic suicide.

Egoistic suicide results from the weak integration of the individual that we have shown he described as 'egoism'. The higher suicide rate of Protestants is one example of it. Protestantism is a less integrative religion than Catholicism, for it places less emphasis on collective rituals and emphasizes the individual's direct relationship with god. Those who are single or widowed or childless are also weakly integrated and therefore more prone to suicide. War, on the other hand, tends to integrate people into society and therefore reduces the suicide rate. This form of suicide was called egoistic because low integration leads to the isolation of the individual, who becomes excessively focused on the self or ego.

Anomic suicide results from the lack of regulation that Durkheim described as anomie. Durkheim believed that people would only be content if their needs and passions were regulated and controlled, for this would keep their desires and their circumstances in balance with each other. Changes in their situation, such as those brought about by economic change or divorce, could upset this balance. In these circumstances, the normal regulation of a person's life breaks down and they find themselves in a state of anomie. This word means normlessness, lacking any regulation by shared norms.

Altruistic suicide is the opposite of egoistic suicide. In this case, it is not that social bonds are too weak but, rather, that they are too strong. People set little value on themselves as individuals, or they obediently sacrifice themselves to the requirements of the group. Durkheim saw this form of suicide as characteristic of primitive societies, though it was also found among the military, where there is a strong emphasis on the importance of loyalty to the group. He used the term altruistic to convey the idea that the individual self is totally subordinated to others.

Fatalistic suicide is the opposite of anomic suicide and results from an excessively high regulation that oppresses the individual. Durkheim gives as an example the suicide of slaves, but he considered this type to be of little contemporary significance and he limited his discussion of it to a footnote.

Durkheim recognized that egoism and anomie are often found together, as, for example, when a divorce occurs. This both isolates people and leaves their lives in an unregulated state. He was, however, careful to distinguish between the social processes involved in egoism and anomie, on the one hand, and the states of mind that each produced, on the other hand. One of the most notable features of Durkheim's theory of suicide, and one that is often overlooked by commentators, is that he shows the consequences of social conditions for an individual's psychological state. He demonstrated not only that the behaviour of the individual was social but also that the individual's internal world of feelings and mental states was socially produced.

Thus, Durkheim argued that the social isolation characteristic of egoistic suicide results in apathy or depression. Anomic suicide is associated with a much more restless condition of irritation, disappointment, or frustration. When lack of regulation leads desires and ambitions to get out of control, people become upset and frustrated by their inability to achieve them. Altruistic suicide is generally accompanied by an energy and passion quite opposite to the apathy of egoism. Durkheim did not discuss the psychological state characteristic of fatalistic suicide but it would seem to involve a mood of acceptance and resignation.

Since Durkheim, the study of suicide has moved on and later sociologists have pointed to problems with the methods that he used. The main problem was that the suicide rates on which he based his study were calculated from official statistics. These depended on coroners' decisions on the classification of deaths as suicides and it has been shown that their practices vary (Douglas 1967;

J. M. Atkinson 1978). For a death to be suicide, it must be intentional, and the assessment of intention is difficult, particularly if no suicide note is left. This leaves a lot of room for interpretation and considerable scope for others, such as friends and relatives of the dead person, to influence coroners' decisions. The existence of social variations in suicide rates cannot, however, be denied, and Durkheim's fundamental point, that the apparently most individual of acts requires sociological explanation, stands.

> **➲ Connections**
> We discuss many of the general problems that arise with the use of official statistics in Chapter 3, pp. 103–6.

Max Weber

Max Weber worked as an economic historian and a lawyer, but he also worked along with other social scientists in Germany to develop a distinctively sociological perspective on these issues. His approach to sociology, however, was very different from that of Durkheim. Weber argued that sociology had to start out not from *structures* but from people's *actions*. This contrast between a sociology of structure and a sociology of action, two complementary perspectives on social life, was to mark the whole of the subsequent development of sociology.

We will begin by discussing Weber's general approach to social science, and we will then look at his application of this approach in his investigations into the development of European societies.

Concepts, values, and science

Durkheim said that the sociologist must consider social facts as things, disregarding all preconceptions. Weber set out a more complex position, arguing that observation was impossible without concepts of some kind. In his principal essay on this subject (Max Weber 1904), he set out to show that this was perfectly compatible with the production of objective scientific knowledge.

Taking his lead from Kant, Weber argued that there can be no knowledge of things as they actually exist, independently of thought. To have knowledge is to give meaning to the world and to interpret it in some way. The world does not simply present itself to our senses already interpreted. It must be interpreted in the light of what is significant to the observer. An area of land, for example, may be of interest as a place for physical exercise, an environment for flora and fauna, a beautiful landscape, the site of a historical ruin, and so on. The particular interest that we bring to our observation leads us to focus on different aspects of the world and to use different concepts to interpret it. All observers, scientists included, carve out particular aspects of reality to give them meaning and significance.

The concepts that are used to give this meaning to the world, Weber argued, derive from cultural **values**. It is our values that tell us which aspects of reality are significant and which are insignificant. All concepts are 'value relevant'. They are relative to particular cultural values. Those who hold on to feminist values, for example, are likely to focus on the relationships between men and women and to develop such concepts as patriarchy to describe the domination of women by men. Those who hold on to communist values, on the other hand, are likely to focus on the relationships between workers and property-owners and to develop such concepts as exploitation to describe these relationships. Values differ considerably from one social group to another, and they change over time. There are no universally valid values, and so there can be no universally valid scientific concepts. There are a large number of possible value standpoints, and reality can only ever be known from particular value-relevant points of view.

This does not mean, however, that all knowledge is simply arbitrary or merely subjective. Scientific knowledge can be objective, despite being value-relevant. This is possible if sociologists adopt strict and disciplined methods of investigation. They must be critical in their use of concepts and evidence, and they must follow strict logical principles in their reasoning. It must be possible for any other sociologist to replicate the research and test the results. On this basis, a feminist and a communist may disagree over which concepts are most useful for studying the modern world, but they should each be able to see whether the other has been honest, rational, and critical in carrying out his or her research.

In this way, Weber also distinguished quite clearly between *factual judgements* and *value judgements*. Sociologists, like all scientists, come to objective factual judgements about what is happening in the world. They may also make subjective value judgements about those things in the world of which they approve or disapprove. These value judgements, however, are no part of science. That someone disapproves of inequality has no bearing upon the question of how great the level of inequality might be in any particular society. The latter is a purely empirical matter, a matter of fact. When a scientist makes a value judgement, he or she is making an ethical or political statement, not a scientific statement. Weber went to great lengths to show that those who allowed their value judgements to interfere with scientific activities were abandoning the principles of science and the pursuit of objective knowledge.

THEORY AND METHODS

Max Weber

The study of social action.

© Bildarchiv Preussischer Kulturbesitz

Max Weber (1864–1920) was born in Erfurt, Germany, but spent most of his early life in Berlin. He studied law at the University of Heidelberg—his father was a lawyer—and did further academic work at Berlin and Göttingen. He was particularly interested in Roman law and agrarian relations, and he undertook a number of studies in economic history. He became Professor of Economics at Freiburg in 1893, and in 1896 he moved to Heidelberg. Following a dispute with his father, he suffered a mental breakdown and gave up his teaching post the following year. Although he was later able to continue with research and writing, he did not fully return to university teaching until 1917, when he was appointed to a professorship at Munich. Weber was actively involved in liberal politics, and he was a member of the German delegation to the Versailles peace conference after the First World War.

Much of Weber's work appeared as essays in journals, appearing in book form only later in his life or after his death. His most influential work was his study of Protestantism and the rise of capitalism (Max Weber 1904–5), and he produced related studies of religion in China (1915) and India (1916). His key works on economic and political sociology were not completed in his lifetime and were brought together for publication after his death (Max Weber 1914, 1920).

Giddens (1971) and Craib (1997) both provide very useful accounts of Weber's work. The standard biography is that written by his wife (Marianne Weber 1926). Parkin (1982) gives a good, brief introduction. You can find attempts to set up home pages for Weber at

www.faculty.rsu.edu/~felwell/Theorists/Weber/Whome.htm

and

www2.fmg.uva.nl/sociosite/topics/weber.html

the latter containing a lot of his texts online.

⮕ You will find detailed discussions of Weber's main ideas in the following chapters:

- **religion and rationality**
  Chapter 11
- **social stratification** *Chapter 19*
- **bureaucracy** *Chapter 14*
- **authority and the state**
  Chapter 15

> ⮕ *Connections*
>
> Weber's argument is very difficult to follow at many points, so do not worry if you have problems with it at first. It is probably one of the most difficult things that you will come across in sociology. The important point is that Weber rejected the idea that we all experience the world in exactly the same way. He concluded that there can be a number of equally legitimate ways of doing sociology. Come back to Weber's argument after you have completed the rest of this chapter.

The final element in Weber's scientific method is the **ideal type**. The principal concepts used by social scientists are constructions for specific scientific purposes. They are logical, ideal constructions from one-sided, value-relevant standpoints. From our particular perspective, we pull together those aspects of reality that are of interest to us and forge them into an idealized model. They can, therefore, be seen as idealizations in the sense that they do not actually exist in reality. These are 'ideal' because they are analytical or conceptual, not because they are desirable or perfect. Ideal types are conceptual models that help us to understand the real world. Such ideal types as capitalism, the nation state, and bureaucracy are not themselves realities. They are analytical devices that are constructed by social scientists in order to understand the more complex reality that actually exists.

This is also true, in many respects, for the natural sciences. The concept of H_2O, for example, is an idealization that does not exist in reality. Actual samples of water contain impurities and additives of all kinds, and it is only under highly artificial, laboratory conditions that it is possible to isolate pure H_2O. In the social sciences, laboratory experimentation is not usually possible and so sociologists are never likely to observe things that correspond precisely to their ideal types. Class and gender relations, for example, only ever exist in combination and alongside many other factors.

Understanding social actions

The most important ideal types for sociology are, according to Weber, types of social action. The more complex ideal types are nothing more than intricate patterns of action, so a typology of action can provide the building blocks for sociological investigations. Weber's emphasis on action marks another area where he differs from Durkheim. Social structures are not seen as external to or independent of individuals. All social structures must be seen as complex, interweaving patterns of action. They have a reality as social facts only when individuals define them as things with a separate existence. Sociologists can describe political activity in terms of the concept of the state only if particular forms of administration and decision-making have already been reified—defined as things—by the people involved in them.

Weber identified four ideal types of action as the fundamental building blocks for sociology:

- instrumentally rational action;
- value-rational action;
- traditional action;
- affectual action.

Action is *instrumentally rational* when people adopt purely technical means for the attainment of their goals. The action involves a clear goal or purpose, and means are chosen as the best or most efficient ways of achieving it. The capitalist entrepreneur calculates the most efficient and economic means for attaining the maximum profit from a particular line of business. The party leader calculates the particular combination of policy proposals that will maximize the party's vote in forthcoming elections. Weber argues that much of the economic, political, and scientific action that involves rational choice and decision-making approximates to this type of action.

Value-rational action, on the other hand, is action that is rational in relation to some irrational or arbitrarily chosen value. The religious believer who prays and gives alms to the poor may be acting in a value-rational way. He or she is acting this way for its own sake and as an absolute duty, and no account at all is taken of instrumental considerations. In this type of action, there is no discrete or easily observable goal, even if a believer hopes that his or her actions might lead to salvation. In the case of value-rational action, there is no suggestion that actions are technically appropriate in cause–effect terms. They are, however, rational in the methods that they adopt for expressing particular values.

Traditional action is that kind of action that is unreflective and habitual. It barely involves any degree of rationality at all. Traditional action is carried out as a matter of routine, with little or no conscious deliberation. People simply act in the way that they always have done in that kind of situation in the past. Many everyday actions have this traditional, habitual character. Finally, *affectual* action is that which directly expresses an emotion, taking no account of its connection to any specific goals or values. Angry outbursts of violence, for example, would be seen as affectual in nature.

Because these four types of action are ideal types, they do not exist in reality. All concrete patterns of action are likely to be interpretable in terms of more than one type. For example, the actions of a manager in a large business enterprise faced with the need to set a wage level for its employees may involve aspects of all four types of action. The manager may instrumentally calculate the financial consequences of different rates of pay, but may also rule out extremely low pay and certain forms of coercion as contrary to his or her values. The manager may also respond unreflectively to the wage negotiations, seeing them in the way that he or she has done in the past, and making knee-jerk reactions to trade-union proposals. Finally, a breakdown of negotiations may involve angry recriminations as one side or the other walks away from the bargaining table and storms out into the street.

In order to decide how closely a particular course of action corresponds to these and other ideal types, it is necessary to use a technique that Weber sees as central to sociology. This is the technique of **understanding** (*Verstehen* in German). The aim of a social science, says Weber, is to use ideal types as a way of understanding the meanings that people give to their actions. These meanings include their intentions and motives, their expectations about the behaviour of others, and their perceptions of the situations in which they find themselves. Sociologists must infer these meanings from their observations of people's actions, thereby aiming at an interpretative understanding of them. This involves *empathizing* with those that they study, though it does not mean *sympathizing* with them.

We may not approve of serial murder, for example, but we can hope to explain it only if we get close enough to serial murderers to begin to see the world as they see it. We must exercise empathy by trying to identify with them up to the point at which we can comprehend *why* they acted as they did. We do not, however, sympathize with them or condone their actions. To go beyond empathy to sympathy is to make the same mistake as those who go beyond factual judgements to value judgments.

Traditionalism and rationality

Weber's philosophy of science led him to reject deterministic systems of explanation. The causal explanations that sociologists produce must always be rooted in an interpretative understanding of the subjective meanings that individuals give to their actions. Any study of social development must recognize the part played by individual action, and Weber stressed that individuals have free will. Individuals have the power to act freely and not simply as the occupants of class positions or social roles. The future is open and undetermined, it cannot be predicted. The explanations of modern industrial capitalism and the predictions of its future given by Marx and Durkheim would be unacceptable to Weber.

The transition from feudal, pre-industrial societies to modern industrial capitalism is seen by Weber in terms of a shift in the typical meanings that individuals give to their actions. Europe, he argued, had undergone a process of **rationalization**. This involves a shift from value-rational actions to instrumentally rational actions. In medieval societies, people's actions were oriented to absolute religious and political values, while in modern societies they engage in a rational calculation of the likely effects of different courses of action. Political authority in modern society, for example, is based on formal, legal procedures, rather than ultimate religious values such as the divine right of kings.

In medieval societies, furthermore, a great deal of everyday action was not rational at all. It was traditional in character. Indeed, tradition itself was treated as an absolute value in many situations. In modern societies, on the other hand, more and more areas of social life have been opened up to rational, reflective considerations. Thus, economic actions have come to be based on market calculations and contractual relations, rather than on fixed ways of living rooted in traditional styles of life.

Much everyday action in modern societies, of course, remains traditional in character. It continues unreflectively and in routine ways with little direct concern for immediate ends or ultimate values. Traditional forms of action may even acquire a new importance in modern societies. This is clear from Weber's consideration of contemporary economic actions. He holds that religious values motivated the actions of those who became the first generations of calculating capitalist entrepreneurs, but later generations of individuals were more likely to continue with their business activities simply because they had become a matter of routine. As they become mere cogs in huge bureaucratic machines, their work becomes a 'dull compulsion' about which they have no real choice. Ultimately they may remain free, but in practice they are constrained.

> **⟳ Connections**
>
> You will understand more about Weber's views on rational economic action when you have read our discussion of *The Protestant Ethic and the Spirit of Capitalism* in Chapter 11, pp. 411–12. You may like to read that discussion now.

 # *Stop and reflect*

In this section we have looked at the two leading figures of the classical period of sociology, Durkheim and Weber. Durkheim was the principal French sociologist and founder of an approach that emphasized social structures as the fundamental social facts. He set this out in an account of the basic principles of sociology.

- Social facts are ways of acting, thinking, or feeling that are both external and constraining. They are collective products, and individuals experience them as coercive or obligatory.

- Social facts are to be studied as things, through observation rather than on the basis of prejudice and preconception. Although they cannot always be observed directly, social facts can be observed indirectly through their effects on individual actions.

- Do you agree with Durkheim's view that even such an individual act as taking one's own life is socially patterned and can be explained sociologically?

- Durkheim said that in causal explanation social facts are accounted for in terms of the other social facts that brought them into being; in functional analysis social facts are examined in relation to the part that they play in relation to the survival or adaptation of other social facts. How useful is it to make this distinction?

Durkheim applied this sociological approach in a number of substantive studies of the division of labour, suicide, education, and religion. We discuss a number of these studies in other chapters. These were seen as aspects of a general account of social development.

- Social solidarity comprises the integration of individuals into social groups and their regulation by shared norms. Durkheim contrasted the mechanical solidarity of traditional societies with the organic solidarity of modern societies.

- One of the central problems of contemporary society was the pathological state of individualism that Durkheim described as involving egoism and anomie. Egoism and anomie are associated with particular psychological conditions and rates of suicide.

- How did Durkheim understand the relationship between social differentiation and social solidarity?

Weber, as one of a number of important German sociologists, tried to build a sociology of social action that was sensitive to the meanings and motives that shaped people's behaviour.

- Social reality can only ever be studied through the use of concepts that reflect cultural values. Knowledge of social reality is objective only if it results from the rational and critical use of these concepts in a scientifically disciplined way.

- While all concepts are value relevant, Weber emphasizes the need to distinguish clearly factual judgements from value judgements.

- Sociological concepts are ideal types and do not correspond to things that actually exist in reality. They are the basic building blocks of sociological analysis and grasp particular aspects of reality.

- Is Weber's typology of action—instrumentally rational action, value-rational action, traditional action, and affectual action—a useful way of approaching the study of social interaction?

- How easy is it to understand social actions by empathizing with those who are studied?

Weber rejected all forms of structural determinism, emphasizing the open-ended character of social life. He did, however, undertake a number of studies of social development, including the important study of religion that we look at in Chapter 11.

- Western societies had experienced a process of rationalization. This was a growth in the significance of rational motivations and a shift from value-rational to instrumentally rational considerations.

- In modern, capitalist societies, market calculation and contractual relations have achieved a central significance.

- Although capitalist economic actions originated in religiously motivated actions, they had come to be a mere matter of routine and dull compulsion.

- Can the growth of standardized production and distribution—a process often referred to as 'McDonaldization'—be seen as an example of the rationalization that Weber described?

Academic sociology established

In the hands of Durkheim, Weber, and their contemporaries, sociology finally became established, by the first decade of the twentieth century, as a legitimate science with a place in the system of university teaching and research. Although there were still few professors of sociology—and sociology was barely taught in schools—a sociological perspective had been established in the study of history, law, politics, education, religion, and many other areas of specialization. Figure 2.3 summarizes the origins of their ideas and the main lines of development in sociology into the first half of the twentieth century.

There were, of course, great differences in the theoretical positions that were put forward by those who called themselves 'sociologists'. Durkheim and his followers stressed the importance of structure in social life, seeing societies as systems of structured relationships. The German sociologists, such as Weber, tended to emphasize action as the central concept, showing that all social structures were, ultimately, to be explained as the outcome of human actions.

These positions must not be seen as stark alternatives to one another. In the early days of academic sociology it was easy for Durkheim and Weber each to believe that his particular theory was uniquely appropriate for the study of social life. Indeed, some writers today still suggest that there is a great gulf between structure and action perspectives

and that only one of them can be correct. As soon as one tries to do any sociological work, however, it becomes clear that the two approaches are complementary.

Durkheim and Weber were emphasizing different aspects of a highly complex reality. Social life involves *both* structure and action. Some sociologists have tried to combine both aspects in the same theory, but these attempts have not been particularly successful. There may one day be a single, all-encompassing theory, but it is probably a long way from completion (but see Giddens 1976). The point is that sociologists need to develop a theoretical understanding of both the structural aspects of social life and their shaping by social actions. Distinct theoretical traditions may continue to exist, but they must cooperate in studies of particular phenomena.

In the generation that followed Durkheim and Weber, their leading ideas were consolidated and further developed, though there were no major advances for some time. The mainstream of academic sociology in Europe and America owed most to the ideas of Durkheim. Sociology and intellectual life generally were suppressed in Germany during the 1930s and 1940s, and this limited the wider impact of the ideas of Weber and his contemporaries.

In Britain and the United States, Durkheim's ideas were welded into a theoretical framework that came to be described as 'structural functionalism', or simply as

Figure 2.3 The development of sociology up to the 1940s

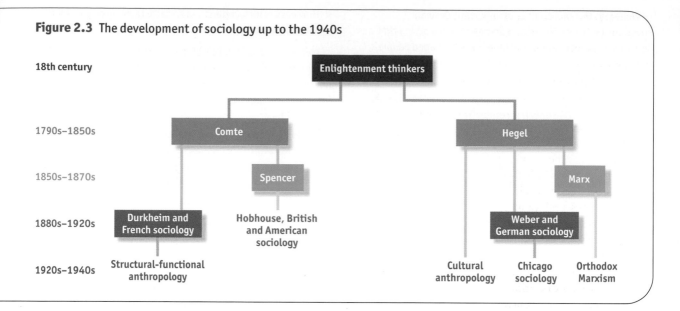

'functionalism'. Much of this theoretical work was undertaken in the study of small-scale, tribal societies of the kind that Durkheim had studied for his own investigations into religion (1912), and many functionalists called themselves anthropologists rather than sociologists.

Much of the sociological research that was undertaken in the first thirty years or so of the twentieth century ignored theoretical issues. Work by Booth, Rowntree, and others in localities and communities across Britain, for example, investigated poverty and inequality with little concern for how these could be explained in terms of the overall structure of British society. The principal exception to this neglect of theory was to be found in the United States, where the new Department of Sociology at Chicago —the first full department in the world—was associated with a large number of local studies that drew explicitly on European traditions of theory.

Like the anthropologists, the Chicago sociologists made a major contribution to fieldwork methods, but they did so from very different theoretical traditions. In

---

THEORY AND METHODS

Social anthropology

Social anthropology is the term often used to describe the work of those sociologists who specialize in the study of small-scale, pre-industrial societies.

Most influential among the early followers of Durkheim was Alfred Radcliffe-Brown, a Cambridge-trained anthropologist who carried out fieldwork in Australia and in the Andaman Islands of the Indian Ocean. His work (Radcliffe-Brown 1922, 1930) reported on religious ritual and kinship in tribal societies, and he drew out some general conclusions in a series of essays (Radcliffe-Brown 1952). Radcliffe-Brown inspired the work of Lloyd Warner, an American who undertook investigations in Australian tribal societies and small American towns during the 1930s and 1940s (Warner and Lunt 1941). Radcliffe-Brown added little to Durkheim's own ideas, but he popularized the idea that theories had to be applied in detailed fieldwork studies.

Bronislaw Malinowski developed this fieldwork tradition in Britain. He carried out some early research on native Australian kinship, but his most important work was undertaken in the Trobriand Islands of the Pacific. His main books (Malinowski 1922, 1929, 1935) emphasized the need to study all social phenomena in terms of their functions in relation to other social phenomena and in relation to the structure of the society as a whole. He further emphasized that this kind of research could most easily be undertaken by living in a society and trying to grasp its whole way of life.

Franz Boas carried forward a similar fieldwork method in the United States, though his work owed a great deal to Hegel as well as to Durkheim. Boas (1911) emphasized the importance of culture and the need to grasp the inner spirit of the culture as a whole. He and his many students carried out a series of studies of native American tribes and small communities in the Pacific. While Malinowski saw functional analysis in relation to material and environmental factors, Boas set out a more cultural or idealist theory.

their work, they paid little attention to Durkheim, finding their main inspiration in German sociology. The main influence was not Weber but his friend Georg Simmel. The Chicago sociologists took up, in particular, the German writers' emphasis on action and interaction, combining this with an awareness of the part played by group conflict in social life. Their main studies were concerned with the city of Chicago itself (Park and Burgess 1925), and they began to develop theoretical ideas that would achieve their fullest recognition only after the Second World War.

Figure 2.3 shows how these various strands of thought relate to the wider development of sociological theory. From the 1940s, and for at least a generation, sociological theorists continued to build on these foundations. By the 1950s, when sociology had begun to break through its old national boundaries, the theoretical landscape had been transformed. Theoretical debates crystallized into a smaller number of separate positions, each of which had a far more international character than before. Three principal traditions of thought dominated sociological debate: structural functionalism, symbolic interactionism, and a number of conflict theories.

Structural-functionalist theories

Post-war structural functionalism had its roots in the sociology of Durkheim and the social anthropology of the inter-war years. However, its leading figure came from a very different background. Talcott Parsons, who was to dominate sociology for more than two decades, was trained in economics, spending periods of time in Britain and Germany. He began, in the 1930s, to explore the relationship between economics and sociology and to build a novel philosophical basis for sociology. After this, and influenced by some early work by Robert Merton (1936, 1949), Parsons began to set out his own version of structural-functionalist theory. This theory exercised a great influence on the development of sociology and it is currently being developed as systems theory.

The action frame of reference

In *The Structure of Social Action* (Parsons 1937), Parsons set out to synthesize the insights of Durkheim and Weber. Durkheim, it will be recalled, had stressed the need to consider social facts as things and to abandon all theoretical preconceptions. Weber, on the other hand, said that observation was impossible without concepts and that all concepts were value-relevant. Parsons would not go along with either of these positions, though he recognized that each writer had glimpsed a part of the truth.

Parsons called his synthesis of the two positions **analytical realism**. It was analytical in that, like Weber, he recognized that all observations were dependent on concepts. But it was also realist in that, like Durkheim, he saw these observations telling us something about what the world was actually like (Scott 1995). He argued that we must use concepts to make observations, but we must check our observations against evidence.

The particular concepts needed in sociology, Parsons said, comprise an **action frame of reference**. This is a set

---

THEORY AND METHODS

Talcott Parsons

Talcott Parsons (1902–79) was the son of a clergyman. He studied economics at Amherst, and then undertook postgraduate research at the London School of Economics and at Heidelberg. He taught economics from 1926 to 1931, when he switched to sociology at Harvard University. His early works were concerned with the relationship between economics and sociology, as this had been seen by Weber, Pareto, and the British economist Alfred Marshall. Under the influence of the biologist L. J. Henderson, Parsons began to take Durkheim's work more seriously and in 1937 he produced his first book, *The Structure of Social Action*. Parsons remained at Harvard throughout his academic career.

Parsons has a reputation for his impenetrable prose style and the large number of new, long words that he invented. His work is certainly difficult. Do try to read Parsons's work, but do not expect to understand it all at a first reading.

After his first book, his most important works were the massive *Social System* (1951), a book on the family (Parsons and Bales 1956), one on the economy (Parsons and Smelser 1956), and two shorter volumes on social development (Parsons 1966*b*, 1971). Some of his more accessible work has been reprinted in a collection of essays (Parsons 1954). A valuable and brief introduction to his work is Hamilton (1983).

➲ You will find more detailed discussions of Parsons's work in the following chapters:

- socialization and social roles *Chapter 4*
- family and kinship *Chapter 12*
- health and illness *Chapter 8*
- social stratification *Chapter 19*

> ⮞ *Connections*
>
> If you are interested in philosophical issues, you should look back at our discussion of Durkheim on social facts and Weber on value relevance before continuing. We do not intend to go very far into these issues. You may prefer to look further at them when you have studied more sociology. Once you have tackled a few substantive topics, you may find it easier to struggle with some philosophy! For those who do want to read further, some good discussions are Keat and Urry (1975) and Williams and May (1996).

of concepts that allow sociologists to talk about social action rather than about physical events or biological behaviour. This frame of reference had begun to emerge in the work of the classical sociologists. Each started from his own distinctive theoretical position, but they had gradually and unconsciously begun to move towards a similar theoretical approach to social life. This approach was the action frame of reference.

According to the action frame of reference, any action involves five basic elements:

- *actors*: the people who actually carry out the actions;
- *ends*: the goals that these people pursue;
- *means*: the resources that are available to achieve these ends;
- *conditions*: the particular circumstances in which actions are carried out;
- *norms*: the standards in relation to which people choose their ends and means.

Parsons holds that sociologists must construct models of action using these elements. To do this, they must try to understand things and events as they appear to the actors involved. The various ideal types and general concepts that are used in sociological explanations, according to Parsons, must be compatible with these basic principles of the action frame of reference. You will probably recognize how much Parsons owed to Weber here.

This action frame of reference became the basis of the structural functionalism built by Parsons, Merton, and others from the 1940s. In undertaking this task, they drew heavily on the ideas of Durkheim. They built a set of concepts that could describe the *structural* features of social life, but that were grounded in the *action* frame of reference. Societies, and social groups of all kinds, were seen as *social systems* that consisted of mutually dependent parts, such as roles, institutions, and organizations. These parts together formed the social structure. The task of sociological analysis was to identify these parts and to show the functions that they fulfil in the system as a whole.

Social structure

Structural functionalists see the structure of a society as a normative framework. It consists of the norms that define the expectations and obligations that govern people's actions and so shape their social relations. At the heart of this normative framework are definitions of the various social positions that are linked together into a complex social division of labour. There may be, for example, family positions such as husband, wife, and child, economic and professional positions such as teacher, miller, doctor, and banker, and such other positions as student, priest, politician, and so on.

Those who occupy social positions are expected to behave in certain ways. These expectations define the social **roles** that are attached to the positions. A role is a cluster of normative expectations that set out a script for social actors in particular social positions. It defines standards of appropriate and inappropriate behaviour, telling people what is 'normal' or expected behaviour in particular situations. A teacher, for example, knows how he or she ought to behave in relation to pupils, parents, head teachers, governors, and others who play their parts in the same school and in the wider educational system (Merton 1957; Gross *et al.* 1958).

Many norms are quite specific and concern just one role. Others, however, may be very general in their scope. These generalized norms, rooted in widely shared cultural values, are termed social institutions by structural functionalists. Institutions, then, are established and solidified sets of norms that cross-cut social roles and help to tie them together. The institutions of property, contract, and the market, for example, help to define a large number of economic and occupational roles. Similarly, the institutions of kinship and marriage regulate a range of family roles, and the institutions of bureaucratic administration and democratic leadership regulate political roles. Structural functionalists recognize a tendency for positions, roles, and institutions to cluster together into more or less distinct subsystems. A society may, for example, consist of an economic system, a political system, an educational system, a system of social stratification, and so on. At its most general, then, the structure of a social system might be described in terms of the connections between such subsystems. A simplified structural-functionalist model is shown in Figure 2.4.

The key to the stability and cohesion of a social structure, argue structural functionalists, is **socialization**. In their infancy and childhood, as well as in their later life, individuals learn the norms of their society. They come to learn what is expected of them and of those with whom they are likely to come into contact. They learn, in short, how to be an acceptable member of their society. The cultural values

Figure 2.4 A model of social structure

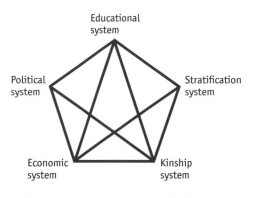

and social norms that people learn are, according to many structural functionalists, widely shared in the society. That is to say, they assume the existence of a social consensus, an agreement over the basic principles that will regulate social life. All members of a society, for example, are seen as sharing a broad commitment to the same values, beliefs, and ideas. Merton (1938b), however, has recognized that this consensus may be far from perfect. Individuals may be committed to some aspects of their culture, while rejecting or remaining neutral about others. He used this insight to develop a very important theory of anomie.

> ➲ *Connections*
> Merton's concept of anomie is not exactly the same as Durkheim's, although they are closely related. Whenever you come across the word 'anomie', make sure that you know how it is being used.
>   In Chapter 4, pp. 125–7, you will find a full discussion of the structural-functionalist view of socialization on which Merton relies.

The starting point for this theory is Merton's discussion of culture. The culture of a society, he holds, specifies the *ends* or goals that people should pursue and the *means* that they are expected to follow in achieving them. People's goals include such things as promotion at work, pleasing a husband or wife, learning to drive a car, writing a book, passing an examination, and so on. Means are those things that help to achieve these goals: working hard, money, physical skills, power, etc. Where people are fully socialized into their culture, they will be committed to the ends and the means that are held out to them. They will be conformists who follow only culturally approved goals and use only culturally approved means. Someone may, for example, desire a pleasant and well-decorated home and will work hard to earn the money required. The

conformist would not even consider stealing the money from others. If, however, a culture emphasizes the ends much more than the means, leaving the means only loosely regulated, people's commitment to the approved means —and therefore their conformity to social norms—may be eroded. This is especially likely where the material structure of opportunities available to people makes it difficult for them to achieve the approved ends. The conditions under which they must act may mean, for example, that they lack the resources that are needed for the means to which they are supposed to be committed. It is the rift between culturally approved ends and means that Merton calls anomie. In a situation of anomie, conformity is far from automatic.

Merton suggests that his model is particularly applicable to a modern society such as the United States, where financial success in an occupation is a central social value. Contemporary culture, he says, places great emphasis on the need to maximize income. It also requires that individuals should pursue this end through occupational achievement: they should work diligently and efficiently in order to be promoted to a higher salary. The distribution of resources, however, makes it difficult for people to compete on an equal basis in this race for financial success. Not all people have the same opportunities to enter well-paid employment, for example. Divisions of class, gender, and ethnicity set limits on the chances that they are able to enjoy. In this situation, their commitment to the prescribed means may be weakened, especially if they are given less cultural emphasis than the overriding goal of success.

Merton argues that there are four possible responses to this anomie, as shown in Figure 2.5. The first possible response is what he calls *innovation*. The innovator is someone who responds to these cultural strains by rejecting the legitimate means and employing illegitimate ones. Criminal activities aimed at financial gain are typical innovative acts. This is particularly likely to occur, Merton argues, among the poorest members of society who have fewest opportunities. Merton recognizes this also as the response of those who are relatively successful, but who are willing to 'bend the rules' and engage in fraud and embezzlement to increase their income.

Ritualism is the second possible response to anomie. Here, people decide that they have little chance of attaining any significant success and so reject this as a goal. They remain, however, loosely committed to the conventional means. They simply go through the motions in a ritualistic way, with little or no commitment to the approved goal. The time-serving bureaucrat who rigidly follows rules and procedures, regardless of the consequences, is a typical ritualist. Such a person, if challenged about the consequences of his or her actions, is likely to respond that 'I'm only

Figure 2.5 Conformity and responses to anomie

Robert Merton was born in 1910 and died in 2003. He studied under Talcott Parsons and published important papers on roles, anomie, and functional analysis. You will find applications of his model of anomie to the rise of new religions in Chapter 11, pp. 430–3, and to drug use in Chapter 7, pp. 257–60. A useful introduction to his thought is Crothers (1987). Check the Merton home page at www.faculty.rsu.edu/~felwell/Theorists/Merton/

	Ends	Means
Conformity	+	+
Innovation	+	−
Ritualism	−	+
Retreatism	−	−
Rebellion	±	±

+ acceptance;
− rejection;
± rejection of dominant values and acceptance of alternative values.

doing my job'. Ritualistic bureaucrats are likely to be fatalistic, resigned to their lot. They feel that they have no control over their lives.

The third response to anomie is *retreatism*. The retreatist decides to reject both the means and the ends prescribed by the culture. This is the response of the drop-out, of whom Merton sees the hobo or vagrant as the typical example. Others have suggested that persistent deviant drug use may also be the action of a retreatist. Merton's analysis of retreatism, however, fails to recognize that many of those who drop out of conventional society establish new conventions for themselves in deviant subcultures. This is the case for many drug users and vagrants.

The retreatist response, therefore, is difficult to distinguish from *rebellion*, where the legitimate ends and means are rejected but are replaced by alternative ends and means that may challenge conventional values. Radical political action, aimed at altering the distribution of resources or the political system, is, for Merton, the typical response of the rebel. This claim can be seen as Merton's reformulation of Durkheim's idea that organized class conflict can be seen as a consequence of anomie.

Functional analysis

Structural functionalists have developed and clarified the method of functional analysis outlined by Durkheim, making it the centrepiece of their work. Both Spencer and Durkheim, like many of their contemporaries, had seen parallels between societies and biological organisms. For Spencer, societies were to be seen as 'social organisms'

that could be studied by the same scientific methods as biological organisms. The most important part of any scientific investigation, he held, is to uncover the functions carried out by the various structures of the organism. The function of the heart in the human body, for example, is to maintain the circulation of the blood. In sociology, Spencer suggested, we must investigate such things as the functions of government and ritual. In Durkheim's work, functional analysis was drawn out more clearly and set alongside causal explanation at the heart of sociological explanation.

The functional method has been much misunderstood. Some critics of structural functionalism have claimed that it involves the idea that societies literally are the same as biological organisms, or that social facts can be reduced to biological facts. These misunderstandings are, in part, the result of the misleading language used by many functionalists. Nevertheless, functional analysis is an important aspect of any sociological investigation into how societies work, and its core ideas are quite straightforward. The functionalist method sees any system as having *needs* or requirements. If a system is to survive and to continue in more or less its current form, then these needs must be met in some way. The function of a structure is the contribution that it makes to meeting a need, and a functional analysis consists in identifying the processes through which these needs are met.

The idea of a need is quite simple. A human body needs food if it is to survive; it will die without this food. However, it is important to recognize that there is nothing automatic about the meeting of needs. The need for food does not, in itself, cause food to become available. Many people across the world do, in fact, starve to death. It is for this reason that Durkheim tried to separate cause from function.

How, then, can functional analysis be used in the study of societies? The first step is to identify the needs of the society. A society is assumed to be a relatively self-contained unit that can be treated as a well-bounded system. As such, it has many internal needs. These include the biological and psychological needs of its members (for example, their needs for food and company) and the need to maintain its boundaries and identity. Some of these needs can be met, in whole or in part, from its own internal resources. The need to socialize infants, for example, can be met through the educational efforts of its already socialized members, such as the infant's parents.

However, many needs can be met only if the society draws on resources from its external environment. This external environment comprises the natural world that surrounds the society, together with the other societies and social groups with which it has contacts. A society must adapt itself to its external environment, and the environment must be adapted to its needs. For example, if a large society is to feed its members, then crops must be planted and harvested, soil must be improved and irrigated, commodities must be imported, minerals must be mined and converted into ploughs and tractors, and so on. To achieve this kind of environmental adaptation, a society needs to restructure itself by establishing ways of handling its external relations and, perhaps, altering its own boundaries.

The initial internal needs, then, lead to external needs. As a result of its restructuring, the society may face new internal needs. If, for example, a system of food production is established, a society will then need to ensure that the pace and level of production are, in some degree, coordinated with its actual food requirements and that the resources given over to this production do not prevent it from meeting any of its other needs. Social systems, then, are dynamic systems, constantly altering their structures as the ways in which they meet, or fail to meet, their needs change.

It is important to emphasize again that needs will not be inevitably or automatically met, though some functionalists have tended to assume that they will. The needs of a social system are simply the conditions that are necessary for its survival in its current form. These conditions will actually be met only if, for whatever reason, people carry out the actions that meet them. The need does not itself cause the action that meets it.

A number of theorists have attempted to compile lists of the needs or functional requirements of a social system (Aberle *et al.* 1950; Levy 1966). The most influential was that of Parsons himself, though this was not without its critics. Parsons arrived at a classification of functional needs by looking at two aspects or dimensions of them:

- whether they are *internal* or *external* to the system;
- whether they involve the *ends* or the *means* of action.

As we have already shown, some needs are internal to the system itself, while others are external to it. Parsons defines internal needs as those that concern the integrity and cohesion of a social system. External needs, on the other hand, concern the facilities and resources that must be generated from its environment. Whether they are internal or external, needs may be relevant to either the means or the ends of action. In the former case, they are concerned with the production and accumulation of human and physical resources for use in the future, while in the latter they involve the immediate use and consumption of resources in current actions.

According to Parsons—who followed Spencer on this— the gradual differentiation of social activities into structurally distinct roles, institutions, and subsystems is a response to attempts to meet functional needs. He held that a model of a social system can be constructed by cross-classifying the two dimensions that he identified, as shown in Figure 2.6. According to this model, any social system has four functional needs, and its structures can be classified according to which of the four functions they are mainly concerned with. This model lies at the heart of Parsons's work, and versions of it can be found throughout his books. It has come to be known as the Parsonian boxes.

The four functions shown in Figure 2.6 are adaptation, goal attainment, integration, and latency. **Adaptation** is the need to accumulate and control resources from the environment so that they are available for future actions. Parsons said that this need is met through the economic structures of production, distribution, and exchange. **Goal attainment** is the need to mobilize existing resources in relation to individual and collective goals. This, he said, can be met through the political structures of decision-making and executive control.

Integration is the need to ensure the cohesion and solidarity of the social system itself. Parsons introduced the term societal community to designate the structures concerned with this function. The term refers not only to localized community structures of kinship and neighbourhood, but also to the larger bonds of national and ethnic community and of social stratification. Finally, **latency** (or 'pattern maintenance') is the need to build up a store of motivation and commitment that can be used, when required, for all the various activities of the society. Institutions such as the family and education, where

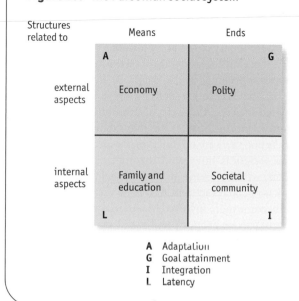

Figure 2.6 The Parsonian social system

Structures related to	Means	Ends
external aspects	**A** Economy	Polity **G**
internal aspects	Family and education	Societal community
	L	**I**

A   Adaptation
G   Goal attainment
I   Integration
L   Latency

people are socialized into the values and norms of their society, are the main structures concerned with this need. These structures are much less likely to become differentiated than are other structures, and they remain closely tied to the structures of the societal community.

Parsons's language sometimes gives the impression that needs are automatically met. Perhaps Parsons did, on occasion, believe this. He maintained, however, that structural functionalism was rooted in the action frame of reference, which showed that functions would be met only if people acted in ways that actually did meet these needs. This point has been clarified by Merton (1949), who shows that functions are generally met, if at all, as the unintended consequences of human action. One of the strongest criticisms of Parsons has been that he failed to analyse action as thoroughly as structure and function. Although he claimed to base his arguments on the action frame of reference, action played a minor part in his work. A structural-functionalist model that focuses on the structural level of analysis must be complemented by an analysis of action.

The evolution of modern society

One of the main concerns of structural-functionalist theorists was to use their ideas to build an account of the development of modern society. They tried to show that the need to adapt to changing functional needs drove societies in a definite direction. Though no one intended it to occur, traditional agricultural societies underwent a process of *modernization* that brought into being the new social institutions that comprise modernity. Modern societies, then, are the results of long processes of structural differentiation that were shaped by the need to adapt to changing environments and the unintended consequences of the responses made to this need. This argument has been most clearly stated by Parsons, who placed it in the context of a larger theory of social evolution.

The baseline for studying social evolution, according to Parsons, is provided by the 'primitive' hunting and gathering societies (Parsons 1966b). In these relatively undifferentiated societies, the societal community is formed from a network of kinship relations that extend across the whole society and there are no functionally specialized structures. Each society is integrated through its shared religious beliefs, which provide an all-embracing cultural framework for people's actions. As these societies increase in size and become more involved in settled agriculture, so structures of private property and social stratification begin to develop to organize the new systems of production. When societies achieve this level of complexity, they may require systems of chiefhood or kingship to coordinate them.

Across the world, tribes and chiefdoms prevailed for thousands of years. In certain circumstances, however,

development to even more complex forms of social organization occurred. In Egypt and Mesopotamia, more complex forms of agriculture were associated with the building of large systems of irrigation. Social stratification became sharper, religion came under the control of a specialized priesthood, and political control became stronger. By the third millennium BC, these societies had evolved into *advanced intermediate* societies that had both a historic religion and an imperial political system. Similar developments occurred somewhat later in China, India, and the Roman world. Following Comte, Parsons sees their religions becoming more philosophical and metaphysical in character.

The breakthrough to modern forms of society, Parsons said, occurred in medieval Europe in the centuries following the collapse of the Roman Empire and the gradual rebuilding of royal structures. Political and scientific spheres of action were differentiated from the previously all-encompassing religious structures, and a separate sphere of economic action also appeared. Private property, the market, and the division of labour expanded, forming specialized elements in the economies of the European societies. From the eighteenth century, industrialism and democracy transformed the ways in which the adaptation and goal-attainment functions were met, and more fully modern societies were formed. Nation states and industrial technologies were the characteristic institutions of these modern societies, which were characterized by the spread of bureaucracy and market relations. Modern social institutions developed especially rapidly in the United States, where pre-modern survivals were very much weaker, and it became the characteristically modern society of the twentieth century.

Systems theory

The structural functionalism of Parsons came under heavy criticism from those who stressed interaction and conflict, and whose views we consider below. These critics argued, in particular, that structural functionalism overemphasized the importance of value consensus and of socialization into these values. A number of writers associated with structural functionalism have attempted to come to terms with these criticisms and have developed a form of structural functionalism that takes the conflict of values and social groups more seriously, but retains the structural focus of the original structural functionalism. These theorists have generally defined their position as neofunctionalism or simply systems theory. Jeffrey Alexander (1985, 1988) and Neil Smelser in the United States and Niklas Luhmann (1982, 1984) in Germany have been the key figures in this theoretical work.

Neofunctionalism and systems theory hold that social systems need not be perfectly integrated and coherent, as

Parsons tended to imply. There can be contradictions, strains, and tensions among the various parts of a social system, and these are quite likely to generate conflict and change in the structure of a society. According to Luhmann, these are the driving forces in a process of structural differentiation. Early forms of society, he argues, are organized around core institutions of kinship and religion but, over time, distinct spheres of action and structure split off from these core social institutions. Specialized economic, political, legal, scientific, educational, and other social systems are, therefore, differentiated from each other and may come to operate according to different values and norms. This process, which Parsons saw as one of modernization, is, according to Luhmann, an integral feature of change in all social systems. It is the outcome of often incompatible system processes, and it creates further incompatibilities.

The arguments of the neofunctionalists and systems theorists do not mark a fundamental change from the earlier structural functionalism. What they show, rather, is how to use structural-functionalist ideas in a more flexible way and how to build theoretical explanations that are more sensitive to the conflict and change that is such an obvious feature of social life.

Interaction theories

Structural functionalism provided the mainstream of sociological thought from the 1940s until at least the 1970s, and it remains an important part of contemporary sociology. With its roots in Comte, Spencer, and Durkheim, it is at the heart of the sociological tradition. However, it was never unchallenged. Many critics pointed out that, despite its advocacy of an action frame of reference, it did not really take sufficient account of action. In providing a comprehensive theory of social structures and their functions, it minimized the active and creative part played by social action. This concern for social action has a long history, and we have shown how it was central to the work of Weber and his contemporaries in Germany. However, it was a subordinate trend within sociology, and it has achieved a wider impact only since the 1960s. Writers critical of structural functionalism returned to the founding statements of Weber and, above all, the early Chicago sociologists in an attempt to construct a full-blown sociology of action. In this section, we will look at two related theories of interaction: the symbolic interactionism of the Chicago school and the phenomenological theories developed from a reconsideration of Weber's typology of action.

Symbolic interactionism

Symbolic interactionism was nurtured in the Department of Sociology at Chicago from the 1920s to the 1950s.

However, it originated outside Chicago and it has, since the 1950s, spread far beyond it. The core of the sociological work carried out at Chicago was a series of empirical studies in the city of Chicago itself. The theoretical framework used to organize these studies and to explain some of their results stressed the struggle of social groups for resources and their competition over the use of space in the city. When they wished to explain what was going on within each of these groups and how individuals responded to their situations, they drew on the ideas that later came to be called symbolic interactionism.

This was a theory of action that originated in the philosophical and psychological studies of William James, carried out at Harvard towards the end of the nineteenth century. William James, brother of the novelist Henry James, was not a particularly sophisticated philosopher. He had a number of insightful ideas, but he expressed these in a rather homespun and over-simple way. He did, however, nurture the brilliant work of the eccentric Charles Peirce. The works of James and Peirce together laid the foundations of the philosophical position of pragmatism, and it was this approach to knowledge and meaning that was transformed into symbolic interactionism.

Pragmatism holds that ideas are produced and used in practical situations. The knowledge that people acquire is not like a photograph. It is not a mental copy of things that actually exist in reality. It is, rather, an attempt to understand the world well enough to make practical sense of it and to act effectively. James summarized this point of view in the claim that truth consists simply of those ideas that happen to work. Knowledge is true if it helps us to get by in our practical actions. It is this practical or *pragmatic* test that gave the philosophical position its name. Peirce's work added much subtlety to this basic argument. In particular, he presented pragmatism as a theory of *meaning*, rather than simply a theory of truth. What Peirce argued was that the meaning of a concept is given by the way in which that concept is used. What we mean by a chair is something to sit on when we wish to relax, and many different physical objects can meet this need. Similarly, one of the things that we mean by a mother is someone who looks after children. There can be no abstract definitions of these concepts that identify essential characteristics of what chairs or mothers 'really' are. They simply mean whatever they are used to refer to in practical everyday situations.

These arguments were developed—and made much clearer—in the works of John Dewey, Charles Cooley, William Thomas, and George Mead. It was Thomas and Mead, after they joined the staff at Chicago, who began to convert pragmatist ideas into a sociological theory of action. Mead was by far the more sophisticated writer of the two. He had undertaken his postgraduate studies in Germany, and he found many congenial ideas in the

German philosophical and sociological tradition. Weber was, of course, an influence on him, but the most important of the German theorists in the shaping of Mead's position was Georg Simmel. Work by Simmel was translated and published in the *American Journal of Sociology*, the journal of the Chicago Department, and through these translations Simmel had a major impact on the new theory.

Mead argued that individuals give meaning to the world by defining and interpreting it in certain ways. The world is never experienced directly, but always through the ideas that we hold about it. The meaning of reality is, in a fundamental sense, the meaning that we *choose* to give to it. Thomas summarized this point of view in the statement that 'When men define situations as real, they are real in their consequences'. What he meant by this is that the actions of men (and women) depend far more on how they define a situation than on the situation itself. People define situations and act upon those definitions. As a pragmatist, however, Thomas stressed that these definitions were not simply arbitrary and artificial constructions. Only those definitions that are useful in practical actions are likely to persist in use for any time.

This becomes clearer if we consider the example of a bus. A bus exists as a purely physical object, an assemblage of metal, plastic, rubber, fabric, and so on. Its meaning for us, however, depends on how we choose to define it. In calling it a bus, we define it as something that will follow a particular route, stop at particular places, and pick up people who pay to take a journey. Redundant buses, however, have been defined and used as social centres, caravans, chicken coops, and works of art. Each of these definitions —and many others—is compatible with the particular physical object that, in other circumstances, we define as a bus. What makes its definition as a bus appropriate is our practical success in being able to use it to travel to our destination. What is true of the bus is true of all social objects. It is possible to define things in any of a number of different ways, and the effective definition is simply the one that works when people come to act on their definitions.

These definitions cannot be unique to particular individuals, or they will not work. The concept of a bus, for example, is one that is useful only because it is widely shared. It is a concept shared by all those interested in its operations: passengers, drivers, conductors, inspectors, traffic police, ministers of transport, and so on. Many of these people acquire their identities from the idea of the bus. It is, for example, impossible to have bus drivers unless we have the concept of a bus. It is usually possible to rely on a bus service because there are widely shared definitions and conventions concerning timetabling, queuing, and fare-paying. A widely shared meaning, communicated to us by others, has a greater reality than does an idiosyncratic one, and it is more likely to be useful in practical situations.

The definitions that people use are constructed from the *symbols* (the names and labels for objects) that are available to them in their culture. Spoken and written words, together with pictures, images, and other conventional signs, convey information and are used by people to give meaning to the situations in which they find themselves. These symbols are learned and communicated through interaction with others. This is why the theoretical position has come to be called **symbolic interactionism**.

This name was coined by Herbert Blumer (1966), who also did much to popularize it and to mark out its distinctiveness from mainstream structural-functionalist sociology. According to Blumer, societies were not fixed and objective structures. What we call 'society' is the fluid and flexible networks of interaction within which we act. To describe these overlapping networks of interaction as structures, Blumer held, is to reify them and to distort the part that individuals play in creating and altering them through action. This led Blumer to reject all talk of structures, systems, and functional needs. There are simply actions, interactions, and their consequences for individuals.

Others in the symbolic interactionist tradition have been less extreme in their opposition to mainstream sociology. They have seen symbolic interactionism as concerned merely with those aspects of action and interaction

---

THEORY AND METHODS

Georg Simmel

Georg Simmel (1858–1917) was born in Berlin, Germany. He spent most of his academic career at the University of Berlin. He studied philosophy, but he taught and wrote on both philosophy and sociology. During his lifetime he was probably better known than Weber among other sociologists.

Simmel stressed the need to study the *forms* of social relationships, rather than their content. He explored such things as the relations of insiders to outsiders, relations of domination and subordination, relations of conflict, and the significance of the size of groups. His ideas were developed in a book called *Sociology* (Simmel 1908), most of which has been translated in K. H. Wolff (1950). Simmel was particularly concerned with uncovering the distinctive features of contemporary urban life, and he set out these ideas in an essay on the metropolis and a book called *The Philosophy of Money* (Simmel 1900). A good home page for Simmel is **http://socio.ch/sim/index_sim.htm**, though some parts of this are in German.

Controversy and debate Social construction

The idea of social construction has been derided by many opponents of sociology, who see the things we encounter in our everyday lives as 'obvious' and unproblematic. All social phenomena, however, involve a degree of social construction. The case of a bus—discussed in the text—is typical of all social definitions, which is why we have discussed it at such length. Whenever we employ words to refer to objects in our social world, we are, quite literally, *constructing* them as meaningful social objects that we can take account of in our actions.

Try to think about the implications of attempting to redefine some common social objects. What would happen if you defined a table as a chair? What consequences would follow if you defined newly washed curtains as paint covers? (Don't try this one at home!) When you have considered these relatively simple cases, you might think about the consequences of defining an unmarried man as a homosexual rather than a bachelor.

that have not been given their due attention in structural functionalism. This is, for example, the case with Erving Goffman, whose work owes as much to Durkheim as it does to Mead (Collins 1994: 218).

Connections

The arguments of Mead, Goffman, and other symbolic interactionists figure prominently in this book. You will find substantial discussions of their core ideas in the following chapters:

- **self, roles, identity** *Chapter 4*
- **deviance and social reaction** *Chapter 7*
- **social construction of health** *Chapter 8*
- **organizations** *Chapter 14*

Goffman's work, undertaken between the 1950s and the 1970s, gave particular attention to face-to-face interaction and small-scale social contexts. He called his approach *dramaturgical* (Goffman 1959). By this he meant that it was a theory of action that uses the metaphor of drama in a theatre to examine people's abilities to present particular images of themselves in their interactions with others. Goffman used such terms as actor, audience, and, of course, role in his theory. Actors play their parts in interaction, and they attempt to give their audiences convincing performances.

In their interactions, Goffman said, people aim to create a particular impression or image of themselves in the eyes of others. Goffman calls this image the **self**. People present this image to others through using techniques of impression management that help them to control the performances that they give. The image that they present will vary according to the expectations of the audience. The self that is presented to friends at a club on a Friday night is likely to be very different from that presented to a bank manager in an interview about an overdrawn account. The self that is presented to parents at home is likely to be different again. Whenever we wish others to think of us as a particular kind of person, we try to present exactly that image to them.

Goffman has emphasized the ability that people have to manipulate the images that they present to others. However, symbolic interactionism also shows that images and conceptions of self can be imposed on people by their audiences. The social process is an interplay of action and reaction, an interplay in which each actor interprets and responds to all others. Interaction involves a reciprocal and continuous negotiation over how situations are to be defined. A definition of the situation is the joint construction of the participants in interaction. Consensus exists only when this definition has been established and agreed by all involved. Though often implicit, this negotiation is necessary because any definition can be contested by others. What we call reality is constructed through social interaction; it is a socially constructed reality. Where there is disagreement, and dissension, the individual or group that is most powerful may be able to impose a definition of the situation on all others. They have the power to ensure that their views prevail.

This point of view became the cornerstone of the trends in the sociology of deviance that powerfully enlarged symbolic interactionism during the 1960s and 1970s (Becker 1963). This work stressed the way in which the *labels* used to define behaviour by those with the power to enforce them could influence the actions of those who were labelled. The use of such labels as 'criminal', 'junkie', 'queer', and so on defines behaviour as deviant by identifying it as a departure from social norms and attributing certain characteristics to the person labelled. Through their reactions to a person's behaviour, then, an audience of labellers may cause her or him to take on the image that is held out.

Phenomenological approaches to interaction

While symbolic interactionism mounted an increasingly successful challenge to the excessive claims made by some structural functionalists, it, too, was challenged in the 1960s by what claimed to be a more radical perspective on interaction. This was the approach of **phenomenology** that originated in the philosophy of Edmund Husserl. During the 1920s and 1930s, Husserl began to produce what he saw as the fundamental basis for all knowledge. The aim of his philosophy was to describe the contents of people's experiences of their world. Husserl's work inspired a number of diverse approaches to sociology. The most influential has, perhaps, been that of Alfred Schütz, who saw his task as that of uncovering the content and form of everyday interpersonal experiences of the social world. Schütz took as his fundamental question, how is Weber's typology of action possible? That is, he asked how the types of action could be justified, on philosophical grounds, as the necessary basis for sociological research.

The work of Husserl and Schütz appeared rather idiosyncratic, and it was not until the 1960s that it really began to inspire specific approaches to sociology. In the works of Berger and Luckman (1966) and Douglas (1967), phenomenological ideas were used in order to investigate the taken-for-granted reality that people construct in the face of the reactions of others. These writers have stressed the way in which the everyday world comes to be seen as natural, inevitable, and taken for granted. People are born into a prestructured meaningful world, and they rarely question it in later life. This taken-for-granted reality has the character of a Durkheimian social fact. As well as being objective, however, it is also subjective.

The everyday world is seen as the product of human subjectivity. It is a product of human action that is *reified*— made into a thing—whenever people forget that it is a human product and begin to take it for granted. The language that we use is the principal means through which we reify social reality. An example might be the very use of the terms symbolic interactionism and phenomenological sociology as names for loose and diverse collections of writers. Use of these particular labels gives the impression that these approaches have more unity and reality than is, in fact, the case. Repetition of the words in textbooks, essays, and examination questions reinforces the taken-for-granted assumption that they exist as sharply defined schools of thought. When we give a name to something, we make it appear as something that is separate from us, external to us, and that is solid and substantial. Berger and Luckman show how this creates the apparent solidity of

'the family', while Douglas argues that suicide is a similarly reified term.

These phenomenological approaches began to rediscover some of the themes raised in classical German sociology and to translate them into contemporary concerns. They stressed, as Weber had done, that all social realities have to be studied from the standpoint of the subjective meanings given to them by individual actors. As they were being developed, however, yet another phenomenological approach was being developed from Schütz's work. This was the ethnomethodology of Harold Garfinkel and Aaron Cicourel. Ethnomethodology originated in papers written by Garfinkel in the 1950s (see the essays collected in Garfinkel 1967), and it was taken up by others in the 1960s and 1970s.

Garfinkel criticizes Parsons and other structural functionalists for treating people as what he calls *cultural dopes*. Structural functionalists assumed that people were simply socialized into a cultural consensus and so had no real freedom of action. They acted in their roles as if they were puppets, controlled by the social system. In place of this point of view, Garfinkel stresses individual autonomy. He holds that the objective reality of everyday life is something that people struggle to achieve in their practical actions: it is, he says, a 'practical accomplishment'.

In accounting for their actions and for the actions of others, people continually create and recreate their social world. Their accounts, however, are never complete but always leave something implicit or taken for granted. People rely on their audiences sharing a background of assumptions that allow them to fill in the gaps for themselves and so to understand what is being said. Organizational accounts, such as police records, medical records, and personnel files, for example, contain gaps and incomplete information that can be filled in by their readers. They are descriptions of actions and interactions that are seen as meaningful by those involved and that provide a satisfactory basis for action. They are not, however, so easily readable by non-participants, who are less likely to share the background knowledge and assumptions employed by those in the organization.

An important part of this taken-for-granted background is a sense of social structure that people use to interpret and account for the actions of others. People explain actions by showing that they are exactly the kinds of things that people in that situation would do. They see it as a part of their role, for example. These interpretative processes are not normally visible, and ethnomethodology assigns itself the special task of uncovering them in order to demonstrate what is really going on in the routine activities of everyday life. They believe that this can be achieved through experimental interventions in social life. Taken-for-granted realities have to be disrupted or challenged so

THEORY AND METHODS
. . . .

Ethnomethodology

Sociology is often criticized for using too many big words and phrases. Our use of phenomenology and ethnomethodology might have convinced you that these critics are right. Don't panic! Many professional sociologists still find it difficult to pronounce the words, let alone spell them. Concentrate on the ideas and do not get caught up on the words themselves. To help you along, however, the word 'ethnomethodology' has two elements in it: *ethno*, meaning 'people', and *methodology*, meaning 'how things are done'. So ethnomethodology simply means 'how people do things'.

If you find that you struggle to keep clear the meanings of sociology's specialized words, you should try regularly consulting a good sociological dictionary or encyclopaedia, such as *The Oxford Dictionary of Sociology* (3rd edn., 2005).

that people are forced to reflect on what they are doing. Only in this way can the ethnomethodologist obtain any proper knowledge about these processes. Garfinkel suggested, for example, that his students should react to their parents as they would if they were merely a lodger. This forced parents to bring out into the open the normally taken-for-granted assumptions about how children ought to behave in relation to their parents.

Rational choice theory

A final approach to action and interaction focuses not on interpretative processes and the construction of meaning, but on rational choices and calculative decision-making. This theory of action draws heavily on the models of action used by economists to explain producer and consumer choices in markets, but its advocates argue that such models can be applied to actions in the political, religious, familial, ethnic, and other spheres, as well as to the economic sphere. One of the most important formulations of rational choice theory was given by George Homans (1961), but it has also been developed by Peter Blau (1964), James Coleman (1990), and Jon Elster (1989).

What these theories have in common is the view that all actions are oriented towards goals and that people choose those means that are likely to be most effective in attaining them. They choose from a range of alternative courses of action by calculating the chances they have of achieving their goals. In doing so, they consider the rewards and costs that are attached to each alternative. Some of these rewards and costs will, of course, be monetary, but many are not. Choosing whether to earn money from employment or to obtain it through theft, for example, involves the obvious

monetary rewards but also involves considering the time costs involved, the amount of effort, the hardship that will be caused, the social approval or disapproval that will be experienced, and so on. Similarly, the choice between voting or staying at home on an election day involves considering the time and effort required and the strength of commitment to the democratic process. While some of these rewards and costs are tangible material factors and others are less tangible symbolic and emotional factors, all are seen as equally subject to rational calculation. People must find a way of comparing very different rewards and costs and deciding what course of action is, overall, most rewarding or least costly to them.

This kind of theory is often described as game theory, as the emphasis on rational and strategic calculation is comparable with that required by the rules of games such as poker and chess. People are seen as acting exclusively on the basis of simple strategic principles in pursuit of a series of 'moves' that will ensure they 'win' their various social encounters.

Homans and Blau described their approach as 'exchange theory' in order to emphasize that they were dealing especially with interaction rather than with isolated rational actions. When people encounter one another, each tries to maximize their profit—or minimize their loss—by gaining rewards and avoiding costs. Any interaction, therefore, involves an exchange of some kind: there may be an exchange of goods for money, as in an economic transaction, an exchange of love for financial support, an exchange of loyalty for political support, and so on. In successful, ongoing interactions, each participant will tend to have ensured that the overall reward that they earn is greater than could be earned for any other interaction: if this were not the case, they would have abandoned the interaction in favour of that other alternative.

Blau argues, however, that many interactions may, in fact, involve unbalanced exchange: one person will be gaining more than the other. People may, for example, undertake a course of action that is costly to them if they think that, in the long term, they will benefit in some way. On the other hand, people may continue with an unprofitable relationship simply because other possibilities have been shut off from them. A married woman, for example, may remain with a violent husband because she has no realistic possibility of finding employment or housing on her own.

Larger claims have been made for rational choice theory (Downs 1957; G. Becker 1976, 1981), and it has proved to give valuable insights into many aspects of social life. Its fundamental limitation, however, is that it cannot properly take account of precisely those features that are central to symbolic interactionism. In order to apply a rational choice model of action, it is necessary to draw on other action theories to show how people are able to construct a definition

Controversy and Debate Action and system

The opposition between structural-functionalist theories and interactionist theories can be usefully seen in terms of their central concepts of system and action. Where the concept of action points to issues of *agency* and will, the concept of system points to issues of *structure* and determinism. The contrast should not be taken too far, but it highlights a real difference in focus.

Action

- The actions of individuals are the basic elements in social life. They are the building blocks of sociology.
- Individuals define situations and construct social reality.
- Sociologists must understand actions in terms of their subjective meanings.
- Individuals improvise and create their own roles on the basis of what they learn during their socialization.

System

- Social structures are the basic elements in social life. They have a reality over and above individuals.
- Social reality is external to individuals and constrains their actions.
- Sociologists must look at the functional connections among the structural parts of social systems.
- Individuals conform to the role expectations that they learn during their socialization.

of the situation and how their norms and values influence the decisions that they make.

Theories of action prospered because of the failure of structural functionalists to pay serious attention to action and interaction. They promised a sociology that properly considered the creative element that human beings bring to their social relations. Symbolic interactionists, phenomenologists, and ethnomethodologists, in their various ways, aimed to uncover the processes of communication and interaction that allowed people to make sense of their social worlds and to construct the structures that structural functionalists treated simply as social facts. Many advocates of these theories, however, claimed that the matters that concerned structural functionalists could safely be forgotten. In saying this, they overstated their case. Action and structure are not alternative explanatory principles but complementary ones.

Conflict theories

The analysis of conflict has a long history, yet structural functionalism developed as an approach that placed far more emphasis on consensus and cohesion. This was one of the reasons why Marx—who saw conflict as playing a central part in social life—refused to identify himself as a sociologist. While some sociologists recognized the importance of conflict, they had little impact on the mainstream of academic sociology. Marxism was, of course, a major influence on the work of Weber and other German sociologists, but this tradition itself was of secondary

importance until after the Second World War. The growing dissatisfaction with structural functionalism as a complete and all-embracing theory of social life was associated not only with a growing interest in theories of interaction but also with attempts to recover an awareness of conflict.

Those who saw structural functionalism as paying too much attention to consensus looked to conflict theories for an expansion of the intellectual tools available to them. They highlighted, instead, the part played by divisions, power, force, and struggle. They looked at the ways in which groups came to be organized for collective action, entered into conflict with one another, and established relations of domination and control. No single theory of conflict has dominated the field, but a great many views of conflict have been put forward. We will look at four of the most influential arguments—those of Ralf Dahrendorf, John Rex, C. Wright Mills, and Jürgen Habermas.

Authority, resources, and conflict

In the section on 'Interaction theories' we showed that Weber had an important influence on some of the American symbolic interactionists. His major impact, however, has been on conflict theorists. Weber's discussion of social action has been a particularly fruitful source of ideas, and the most important writers to develop this into conflict theories were Dahrendorf (1957), Rex (1961), and Mills (1959). Dahrendorf argues that structural functionalists presented, in effect, a consensus theory. They looked at only one side of reality, ignoring the existence of conflict and division. The theory of consensus, then, needed to be complemented by a theory of conflict. Dahrendorf wanted to use ideas from Weber and Marx to build a theory of conflict. He did not, however, see any need to bring consensus and conflict theories together into a new synthesis. Each theory had something separate to offer. Consensus theory illuminated some aspects of reality, while a conflict theory would be better able to illuminate others.

At the heart of Dahrendorf's theory of conflict is **authority**. In all organizations, he argues, there is an unequal distribution of authority that creates a division between the dominant and the subordinate, between those who rule and those who are ruled. In a business organization, for example, there is a division between managers and workers, in a state there is a division between the elite and the mass of citizens, and in a church there is a division between clergy and laity.

Where consensus theorists focus on the normative expectations attached to social positions, Dahrendorf looks at their **interests**. A person's interests are those things that are advantageous or disadvantageous, given his or her position in society. Those in ruling positions have an interest in the structure of authority as it is and so will act to maintain it. Those they rule, on the other hand, have an interest in altering the distribution of authority and will try to change it in order to improve their positions. Individuals may not always be aware of their own interests, as they rarely have a complete and perfect knowledge of the circumstances that they face. This lack of knowledge may often lead people to act in ways that disadvantage them. Because of these differences in interest and outlook, rulers and ruled will tend to be formed into what Dahrendorf calls social classes. These are the bases from which trade unions, political parties, and other associations are recruited. These **interest groups** come into conflict with one another and are the actual driving forces in social change.

Rex focuses on social divisions that originate in the distribution of economic, political, and cultural resources, rather than the distribution of authority. He sees economic resources as fundamental, and he draws on a number of ideas from Marx to explore the conflicts that result from the unequal distribution of economic resources. He shows that classes are formed around differences of property and market situation and that they struggle with each other over this distribution. Agricultural land, company shares, factories, and houses, for example, are sources of power for their owners, who tend to come into conflict with those who lack these resources and seek to alter their distribution. Similar divisions are produced around political and cultural resources, and there is a close correspondence between the various distributions. Whole societies tend to

be divided into sharply defined classes and these become organized for conflict through the kinds of interest groups described by Dahrendorf.

Collective action by conflict groups establishes what Rex calls a *balance of power*. In some situations, a powerful group may be able to impose its ideas and values on others, establishing a dominant ideology. In other situations, however, the conflicting groups may be more equally balanced and so the institutions of the society will reflect a compromise between the values of the two groups. Occasionally, the members of a subordinate group may be able to carry through revolutionary actions aimed at transforming their society.

Mills drew heavily on symbolic interactionist ideas to provide a social psychological basis for his arguments, but his core ideas focused on the class divisions of societies and the ways that these organized political power and cultural processes. His particular concern was to explore the ways in which personal experiences and problems were linked to possible issues of structural change. Individual biographies, he said, must be related to the historical development of social structures.

> **⊃ Connections**
> Dahrendorf, Rex, and Mills talk about the division of societies into conflicting classes. However, they mean different things by this. For Dahrendorf, classes are defined by authority relations, while Rex and Mills see them as defined by economic and other resources, but Mills gives particular attention to their participation in political and military power. You will find a discussion of these issues in 'Class and status', Chapter 19, pp. 773–7, and 'Elitist theories', Chapter 20, pp. 822–4.

Social structures, according to Mills, must be explored through uncovering the processes through which they are integrated. Social systems may be integrated through consensus and the 'correspondence' among their social institutions, but also through processes of 'coordination' that reflect the society's conflicts and tensions. In a situation of coordination, one or more institutional orders predominates over others and regulates their relations with each other (Gerth and Mills 1953: chapter 12). The clearest examples of this are provided by totalitarian societies in which there is a dominance of the political institutions, which are organized into single-party states. Even in the United States and similar capitalist societies, however, Mills saw a close association between the political, economic, and military institutions, and an overlapping of power relations among them (Mills 1956). Ordinary people, as a result, have become increasingly powerless and feel that they can do little to influence the decisions that shape their lives. The United States has become, then, a 'mass society', divided between the powerful elite and the powerless masses. The task for sociology is to uncover and explore this link between historical trends and individual experiences (Mills 1959: chapter 1).

> ⤳ *Connections*
>
> This might be a useful point at which to review Marx's main ideas, as you will find they help you to understand the following section on 'Critical theory'. Look back at our whole discussion of Marx on pp. 28–31.

Critical theory

Rex, Dahrendorf, and Mills made use of ideas from Marx and Weber. Marx's recognition of conflict, however, was kept alive even more strongly in Marxist political parties and in the works of a number of Marxist theorists. Of most importance in developing Marx's ideas were the so-called critical theorists. They have suggested that a renewed understanding of Marx's ideas will allow sociologists to advance beyond its conventional concerns and, indeed, beyond Marxism itself.

The idea of critique was, in many ways, a part of the Marxist tradition from its beginnings. This was certainly the way that Marx saw his own work. In the Marxism of the Russian, German, and other European Communist parties, however, Marx's thought was transformed into an uncritical and dogmatic system of theory. This began to change in the 1920s, when a number of independent thinkers started to develop a critique of established Marxism. Antonio Gramsci in Italy and Karl Korsch and Gyorgy Lukács in Germany were the pioneers in developing a form of Marxism that broke with dogmatic styles of thought and also took the political and cultural spheres more seriously than earlier Marxists (see Lukács 1923). Many of these ideas were taken up by Marxists such as Theodor Adorno and Max Horkheimer in Frankfurt and the United States during the 1930s and 1940s. Although these ideas had little impact outside Marxist circles, they helped to change the direction of Marxist thought, and their ideas were taken up by radical writers in the 1960s and 1970s. Prominent among these has been Jürgen Habermas.

Some of Habermas's most important work has concerned issues of scientific method, where he has tried to clarify the nature of a truly critical theory. All knowledge, he argues, develops in relation to what he calls the **cognitive interests** of social groups. These are the particular social interests that shape people's needs for knowledge.

THEORY AND METHODS

Jürgen Habermas

A critical theory of society.
© Getty Images/Darren McCollester

Jürgen Habermas (1929–) studied under Theodor Adorno, a leading figure in critical theory, at Frankfurt. It is here that he has spent most of his academic career. He produced a number of essays on philosophy and scientific method in the 1960s (Habermas 1967, 1968), and he began to engage with the radical student movement. His initial attempt to construct a sociological account of this new movement (Habermas 1968–9) owed as much to Weber as it did to Marx.

Habermas set out the basis of a critical theory of modern society, along with a research programme to study it, in *Legitimation Crisis* (1973). Through the 1970s he worked on the more general theoretical principles underlying this, publishing the results in his *Theory of Communicative Action* (1981*a*, 1981*b*). Since completing this, he has concentrated rather more on philosophical issues and on engaging with his political and philosophical critics.

Critical theorists' views on the mass media are discussed in Chapter 10.

A good account of Habermas's early work can be found in McCarthy (1978), and a brief overview of his whole output can be found in Pusey (1987). The best accounts of the wider context of critical theory are Jay (1973) and Held (1980). General websites on critical theorists can be found at

www.uta.edu/huma/illuminations/

and

http://home.cwru.edu/~ngb2/Pages/Intro.html

⤳ You can find more on the applications of Habermas's theory in other parts of this book:

● state and crisis *Chapter 15*

● social movements *Chapter 20*

There are three of these cognitive interests, each of which is associated with a particular kind of knowledge:

- an interest in technical control;
- an interest in practical understanding;
- an interest in emancipation.

An interest in *technical control*, argues Habermas, is inherent in the whole way in which human labour is organized for productive purposes. Labour involves an attempt to use and to transform the resources provided by the natural environment, and it stimulates people to acquire the kind of knowledge that will help them to control the natural world. The natural sciences and industrial technology are based on what he calls empirical–analytical knowledge of the kind produced in the positive sciences. This knowledge, he says, provides the kind of objective information that can be used to make explanations and predictions that will help to ensure the technical success of our actions.

An interest in *practical understanding*, on the other hand, is fundamental to human communication and interaction in everyday settings. In their interactions, people need to attain some kind of understanding of one another. They must build up a degree of consensus and shared understanding if their actions are not to collapse into mutual incomprehension and conflict. The cultural disciplines, concerned with understanding texts, are based on what he calls historical–hermeneutic knowledge. (You need not worry about the precise meaning of all the long words that Habermas uses.) This knowledge provides the interpretations and meanings that make practical understanding possible.

Habermas sees approaches to the social world as having tended towards one or the other of these two types of knowledge. The positivism of Comte, Durkheim, and structural functionalism more generally has followed the natural-science model and has aimed at producing empirical–analytical knowledge for a positive science of society. The interpretative work of Weber and the interactionist theorists, on the other hand, has been closer to the cultural studies and has aimed at producing historical–hermeneutic knowledge.

Both forms of knowledge have their uses, but Habermas sees neither of them as giving a satisfactory base for social theory. Both the main traditions of sociological thought are partial and one-sided. They are limited and distorted by the underlying cognitive interests around which they are organized. Only an emancipatory interest, he holds, can produce the kind of knowledge that can synthesize these two partial perspectives.

An interest in *emancipation* is what is required if distorted forms of knowledge and action are to be overcome. Habermas holds that people can be liberated from ideology and error only through what he calls critical–dialectical thought. Once liberated, they can go on to achieve the kind of autonomy and self-determination that Marx saw as the ultimate goal of human history. An interest in emancipation develops along with the evolution of human society, and Marx was the first to construct a properly critical theory appropriate to this interest.

This is how Habermas locates his own work, along with that of the earlier critical theorists. An interest in human emancipation, he argues, requires that all knowledge is subjected to criticism. To be true to the interest that motivated Marx's work, it is necessary to go beyond it and to reconstruct it continually in the light of changing circumstances. Societies have changed since Marx's death, and a critical theory must reflect these changes. In contemporary societies there are new sources of division, unforeseen by Marx. It is no longer possible to see the working class as the sole agents of revolutionary change. A challenge to the system may come from any of its many oppressed social groups. For some time, critical theorists saw the radical student movement as the group most likely to initiate social change, but they now recognize a great variety of groups from the women's movement to environmental and anti-militarist movements.

Habermas's critical theory, then, is critical of contemporary social theories for their distorted views of social reality, but it is also self-critical. Critical theory must continually reassess its own foundations and the specific theories that it builds on them. Habermas's own major work (1981*a*, 1981*b*) was cast in exactly this spirit. It is an attempt at a comprehensive reconstruction of Marx's social theory, but it makes this reconstruction by critically reconsidering also the work of structural functionalists and interaction theorists. All of these strands are synthesized by Habermas.

With structural functionalism and systems theory, Habermas emphasizes the importance of systems and structures, seeing these concepts as especially applicable to the economic and political systems of modern societies. However, he builds an awareness of conflict and social division into his account of these social systems. With interaction theories, on the other hand, he recognizes the importance of communication and meaning, which he sees as essential for understanding face-to-face encounters in everyday life. These face-to-face situations comprise what he calls the *lifeworld* through which people's experiences are formed into human communities.

These two traditions of theory, Habermas says, highlight different aspects of social reality. Modern societies, for example, are organized around the separation of systems of economic and political relations from a communal lifeworld of interpersonal interactions. The systems are concerned with the integration of actions and relations into more or less coherent and coordinated wholes. They are

Controversy and debate Consensus and conflict

While the opposition between consensus and conflict perspectives can be exaggerated, there are real differences that it is important to recognize. The approaches can be contrasted in terms of their main concepts and themes.

Consensus

- Norms and values are the basic elements of social life. There is a consensus over them.
- People conform because they are committed to their societies and their rules.
- Social life depends on cohesion and solidarity.
- People tend to cooperate with one another.

Conflict

- Interests are the basic elements of social life. They are the sources of conflict.
- People react to one another on the basis of inducement and coercion.
- Social life involves division and exclusion.
- People tend to struggle with one another.

Source: Adapted from Craib (1984: 60).

➔ You might like to consider whether Habermas adequately combines consensus and conflict themes in his work.

studied by tracing the functional connections among the structures and the parts that they play in the maintenance of the system as a whole. Habermas, like Marx, stresses that it is important to look at contradictions within these systems as well as at their coherence. The lifeworld is concerned with the harmonization of the meanings given to actions in the communal life of social groups. It is studied by examining the shared ideas and values that form the taken-for-granted cultural framework for interaction.

Stop and reflect

In this section we have identified three broad approaches to sociological theory, and have argued that they have to be seen as grasping different aspects of a complex reality. They are, therefore, complementary rather than alternative approaches. These three approaches are structural-functionalist theories, interaction theories, and conflict theories.

The main source of inspiration for structural-functionalist theories was the work of Durkheim, who laid its foundations in the classical period. You might like to remind yourself about his key ideas.

- The key figure in the construction of structural-functionalist ideas was Talcott Parsons, who saw his task as that of synthesizing the ideas inherited from the classical writers. He set out the basis for this in his action frame of reference, according to which the basic elements in any course of action are actors, ends, means, conditions, and norms.
- The structure of a society is the normative framework that defines its social positions and their social relations in a division of labour. The normative expectations attached to social positions define the roles to be played by their occupants.
- Dislocations between culturally approved ends and structurally available means establish conditions of anomie. Individuals respond to anomie through innovation, ritualism, retreatism, or rebellion.
- The function of any structure is its contribution to meeting the needs of the system of which it is a part. At the most general level, needs include the internal needs of the system and its adaptation to its external environment. Parsons recognized four fundamental needs: adaptation, goal attainment, integration, and latency.
- Neofunctionalism and systems theory try to retain an emphasis on structure and system, but they combine this with a sensitivity to conflict and change.
- Is it accurate to describe Parsons as a 'consensus' theorist?
- Does Parsons's account of social life involve a conservative bias?

A diverse range of interaction theories have attempted to provide the analysis of action that tends to get lost in the work of the structural functionalists. We considered symbolic interactionism, phenomenological approaches, ethnomethodology, and rational choice theory.

- Symbolic interactionism originated in pragmatist philosophy, which held that the truth of theories and concepts depends on their value in practical actions.
- Central to symbolic interactionism is the idea of the definition of the situation. By acting in terms of their definition of the situation, people construct and make meaningful the objects of their social world. Definitions are built in interaction through processes of self-presentation, labelling, and negotiation.
- Are symbolic interactionists correct to claim that their approach provides a more subtle and flexible approach to that of Parsons?
- Phenomenological approaches focus their attention on the taken-for-granted contents of everyday consciousness. Ethnomethodology, originating in the work of Garfinkel, takes this one step further and examines the processes through which people sustain a taken-for-granted sense of reality in their everyday encounters.
- Rational choice theory, using an economic model of action, sees people as making rational calculations about the rewards and costs involved in their interactions with others.

- Why do these various interaction theories make such different assumptions about the nature of social action?

The works of Weber and Marx inspired a number of theories that put conflict at the centre of their attention. These theorists criticized the structural-functionalist mainstream for its overemphasis on consensus.

- Dahrendorf saw conflict as originating in the distribution of authority, while Rex saw it as originating in the distribution of resources. Both writers saw interest groups as recruited from classes and as engaged in struggles that lead to social change.
- Mills emphasized the emergence of a power elite as the central element in contemporary class structure.
- Why have these conflict theories been seen as posing such a challenge to the sociology of theorists such as Parsons?
- Critical theory aimed at a reconstruction of Marxism so as to combine its recognition of social divisions and social conflict with an awareness of how societies had changed since the death of Marx.
- Habermas placed his analysis of conflict and collective action in the context of a theory of the relationship between economic and political systems, on the one hand, and a communal lifeworld, on the other.
- Is Habermas correct to see a strong relationship between knowledge and interests in science?

New directions in sociology

Structural-functionalist, interactionist, and conflict theories continue to provide the theoretical core of contemporary sociology, but they have not gone unchallenged. The rise of a strong and powerful women's movement in the 1970s led many women to challenge not only the male domination of senior positions in sociology but also the intellectual content of sociology itself. A number of influential *feminist theories* challenged what they saw as the male bias in all the leading traditions of social theory. These have, they argued, ignored women and the part played by gender divisions. While feminists found much of value in existing social theory, they suggested that nothing less than its whole-scale reconstruction was needed if this bias was to be overcome.

A different challenge to the mainstream has come from the *theorists of the post-modern*. They have argued that contemporary societies have undergone a transformation that cannot be grasped by our existing intellectual tools. All existing forms of theory, including most feminist theories, are seen as too closely tied to the structures of modern societies. They must be replaced by new forms of theorizing that are better fitted to the *post-modern* condition that we have entered.

We will look at these theoretical approaches in turn. You will find that our discussions of particular topics in Part Two of this book draw on these theories as well as the mainstream theories. Indeed, the suggested shift from modern forms of regulated, centralized, and organized social life to post-modern flexible and pluralistic forms is one of the principal ideas that we explore. While we are critical of the idea of post-modern society, you will find that the chapters in this book look at contemporary changes in relation to the issues raised by theorists of the post-modern condition.

Feminist theories

Feminist writers have posed a fundamental and comprehensive challenge to all existing social theories and to their attempts to inform and interpret empirical research. They have attempted nothing less than a long-overdue reformulation of the way in which sociologists—and other social scientists—have tried to understand modern societies. This transformation of theories and research is still under way, and it has not gone unchallenged by those who cling to existing styles of work. We look at the impact of these arguments in the various chapters that follow, and particularly in Chapter 5, where we look at the central issue of gender divisions and gender identities. In this chapter we will concentrate on the philosophical questions that they have raised about the status of knowledge in sociology.

We showed on p. 31 that Marx saw all social knowledge as related to the class position of the observer or theorist. This view was echoed by Lukács, an early influence on critical theory. Lukács held that the standpoint of the proletariat—the working class—was the only one that allowed its occupants to grasp the real nature of their society as a whole. In Habermas's formulation of critical theory, knowledge was related to deeper and more general cognitive interests. For Habermas, it was the standpoint corresponding to the emancipatory interest that allowed people a broader and deeper perspective on social reality than knowledge built from the standpoint of technical and practical interests.

One of the most significant and far-reaching features of contemporary sociology has been the way in which these kinds of argument have been taken up and extended by feminist writers. The main thrust of feminist thought has been the claim that knowledge is related to divisions of sex and gender. Put simply, men and women have different experiences and so have different standpoints from which they construct their knowledge. All social knowledge is related to the gender of the observer or theorist.

At one level there is an agreement among Marxists, critical theorists, and feminists, all of whom see aspects of social position and social action as determining what people can know about their world. Conventional, mainstream theories are seen, variously, as based on bourgeois, technical and practical, or male standpoints. Those who occupy these dominant and privileged positions in society are tied closely to the system from which they benefit; their ideas can do little but legitimate and reinforce existing social relations. Conventional science is neither objective nor neutral. Liberating and critical theories, on the other hand, are built from proletarian, emancipatory, or female standpoints. Those who occupy subordinate or oppressed social positions are uniquely able to challenge the social order and to produce knowledge that is critical of it.

Feminists, then, suggest that mainstream theory must be seen as *malestream* theory. It is rooted in patriarchal relations that embody male power over women and that establish the male standpoint on knowledge. The technical character of scientific knowledge and its emphasis on objectivity reflects a male way of seeing the world. This **gendering** of knowledge is denied, ignored, or

unacknowledged by mainstream theorists, virtually all of whom have been male. Women, it is claimed, are invisible in social theory and in social research. Studies of people are, in reality, studies of men. This gendered knowledge, feminists argue, must be challenged by theorizing and research conducted from a female or feminist standpoint.

> **Connections**
>
> Gender differences are those differences of masculine and feminine identity that are linked to biological differences of sex. We discuss these issues at length in Chapter 5, pp. 159–64, where various strands in feminist thought are identified.
>
> Knowledge is said to be gendered when its content and its structure express specifically masculine or feminine characteristics. Look back over this chapter and see how few female theorists have been mentioned: can you find any? Is this simply bias on the part of two male authors, or is something deeper involved? When you have read more widely into sociological theory, you might like to see if you can find any female theorists who could have been mentioned in our sections on 'Pioneers of social theory' and 'The formative period of sociology'.

A feminist standpoint is held to yield knowledge that is radically different from malestream knowledge (Hartsock 1983; Harding 1986). The human mind, feminists argue, does not acquire knowledge in abstraction and detachment from the world. It is only through the senses and through bodily involvement in real situations that knowledge is possible. Differences of sex and gender, it is held, lead men and women to have quite different patterns of bodily involvement and experience, and so knowledge is necessarily *embodied*. Women have primary responsibility for childbirth, mothering, and domestic labour, and they learn to behave in distinctly female ways. They have quite different ways of being and acting in the world, and their lives are characterized by a much greater intensity of feeling and emotion than is typical for men. Through 'patriarchal' structures and processes they are excluded from or marginalized in their participation in many areas of public political and economic life. The public world of patriarchal, malestream ideas and institutions comprises the 'relations of ruling' through which men dominate women (D. Smith 1987).

Knowledge acquired from a feminist standpoint, then, is deeply marked by this subjectivity. Feminists do not, of course, see this as a failing, though this is how subjectivity has often been seen in mainstream theory. According to feminists, their standpoint gives women distinct advantages in the pursuit of knowledge. They have access to whole areas of social life that are inaccessible or unavailable to men.

Controversy and debate   Knowledge and standpoints

There are many different feminist approaches, and not all accept this particularly strong version of the argument for the feminist standpoint. There is, however, a broad agreement about the features that are supposed to characterize malestream and feminist knowledge. These are set out below. While malestream writers place a positive value on the things listed on the left-hand list, feminists see these in a negative light and stress the importance of things on the right-hand list.

Malestream	Feminist	Malestream	Feminist
● rationality	● emotion	● detachment	● embodied
● facts	● experiences	● public	● private
● objectivity	● subjectivity	● culture	● nature
● neutral	● personal		

You might have noticed an interesting ambiguity in these arguments. It is the distinctive standpoint of women that has been identified, yet the theory describes itself as a 'feminist-standpoint' theory rather than a female-standpoint or feminine-standpoint theory. Is it valid to equate a female standpoint with a specifically feminist consciousness?

Feminist writers have raised crucial issues about the gendered character of scientific methodology and empirical research. They have also suggested that sociological theory itself is gendered. Their argument suggests that such concepts as structure, system, and action may themselves be part of the malestream world-view. This is a difficult position to uphold, as feminists have developed their criticisms by drawing on precisely these concepts. There are, for example, structural feminists, interactionist feminists, and feminists who draw on Marxist ideas about conflict. It seems that these most general concepts of sociological theory are not intrinsically gendered, although they have often been *used* in gendered ways. That is, arguments about structure, action, and conflict are not, in themselves, malestream discussions. They become part of the malestream when they are discussed exclusively in terms of the world of male experience and involvement. For example, theories of class structure have tended to focus on men's class position and have either ignored women or derived their class positions from those of their husbands, partners, and fathers.

Feminist critics of the malestream have correctly identified, in particular, the gaps and the absences that have characterized substantive sociological work. This substantive work has, for example, tended to emphasize class as the overriding social division. Until feminist critics raised the problem, little or no attention was given to the significance of gender divisions or to the theorization of the body and the emotions (Shilling 1993; B. Turner 1996).

However, in showing that knowledge is gendered and in promoting the claims of the feminist standpoint over malestream knowledge, feminist writers tend to accept many of the characteristics and consequences of contemporary gender differences. They argue that women have a distinctive standpoint because of their oppression, and they go on to advocate the cultivation of this standpoint. A truly critical and radical position would challenge this very differentiation of male and female and would try to overcome the oppression that it produces.

Feminist standpoint theorists have, of course, realized this problem, and they have made some attempts to overcome it. Harding (1986), for example, has tried to explore the ways in which feminist knowledge can be enlarged into knowledge that is not gendered at all. Current feminist standpoints are seen as transitional and as destined to be transformed in the future into a broader form of knowledge that is neither male nor female in character. Butler (1993) has argued for the need to reject all taken-for-granted ideas about fixed gender divisions. Gendered identities are constructed through interaction and are inherently flexible and malleable. It is for this reason that Butler advocates 'gender bending' actions that challenge established identities and open up new possibilities.

The original formulations of feminist standpoint theories were based on the idea that the specific experiences of women were common to *all* women. A number of writers have reminded us, however, that women's experiences are shaped, also, by ethnicity and sexual orientation, as well as by such factors as class, age, and disability. Black feminist writers, for example, have challenged mainstream white feminists, on the grounds that they ignore the distinct experiences of women of colour (Hill Collins 1990).

A recognition of such diversity poses a number of challenges for sociological theory. Because they are factors that also divide men, the simple dichotomy of male and female must be abandoned. Middle-class women and middle-class men, for example, may have more in common with each other than do middle-class women and working-class women. More importantly, these divisions cross-cut each other and prevent the construction of any single female standpoint. There is no single category of 'woman': there are black middle-class women, Asian working-class women, white gay women, and so on.

The feminist criticism of sociological thought has opened up possibilities for other critiques of the mainstream: black and anti-racist perspectives, 'queer theories', post-colonial theories, and many others have all been proposed. The end result of the critique of the mainstream seems to be a proliferation of competing perspectives. This proliferation has been encouraged and welcomed by the contemporary theoretical approach that we consider in the next section.

Post-modernism and theory

Throughout the 1960s there was a growing recognition that conventional science did not live up to the image of positive science presented in the philosophy textbooks. The focus of these discussions was not the social sciences but the natural sciences.

The leading figure in reconstructing the image of natural science was Thomas Kuhn, who stressed that science did not deal with *given* facts but *created* its facts. Scientists, he argued, worked within communities of theorists and researchers who shared certain basic concepts and methods. Without these shared preconceptions, no factual knowledge was possible. Scientists employ what Kuhn called *paradigms* of knowledge that tell them what to look for in their experiments and that help them to explain away observations that did not fit their preconceived theories (Kuhn 1962).

Eventually, Kuhn said, the sheer bulk of the observations that had been ignored would become so great that support for a paradigm might begin to crumble. Younger scientists might begin to use a new one that was better able to handle these observations. The history of science, then, is a sequence of theoretical revolutions in which paradigms replace one another periodically. It is impossible, said Kuhn, to describe this in terms of scientific *progress* or the *advance* of knowledge, as there is no way of comparing the results produced by scientists using different paradigms. Each paradigm creates its own facts, and there are no theory-neutral facts that we can use to decide among them. The paradigm that survives is one that is able to attract the largest number of new recruits and the highest levels of research funding. As so often in the political world, might makes right. Theoretical approaches are, therefore, *different* from each other, but it is much more difficult to say whether any one is *better* or more truthful than another.

Kuhn's ideas were enthusiastically taken up in sociology, as his argument suggested that the differences between the natural sciences and the social sciences were not so great as many people assumed. Sociologists did not need to feel inferior about the theoretical disputes that ran through the discipline. As in physics, chemistry, biology, and astronomy, the clash of fundamental and irreconcilable theoretical positions was a sign of a healthy pluralism (Friedrichs 1970).

Kuhn was not as radical as many of his more enthusiastic supporters. His belief that a paradigm would collapse when a large number of problematic observations had accumulated implied that observations were not simply creations of the paradigm itself. If facts really were nothing other than the products of preconceived ideas, then no problematic observations would ever be made. Many of his followers conveniently ignored this point and saw Kuhn as justifying the proliferation of irreconcilable theoretical positions. Sociologists merely had to *choose* a theoretical position that appealed to them. In the world of science, they held, anything goes. There can be as many alternative positions as our imaginations can produce.

These arguments were echoed and elaborated in the works of two French writers, Foucault (1971) and Lyotard (1979). Both highlighted the plurality and diversity of scientific knowledge, and Lyotard argued that this reflected the *post-modern condition* that contemporary societies were

---

THEORY AND METHODS

Post-structuralism and post-modernism

Foucault's work is often described as 'post-structuralist', as he developed it in response to certain structuralist writers in the Marxist tradition (see Althusser 1965). We discuss his extremely important ideas at many places in this book, but particularly in Chapter 8. Foucault's work is often linked with that of Lyotard, though they differ in many ways. What they have in common is their rejection of the idea that there are overarching structures in social life, and their recognition of fragmentation and diversity in cultural and social life. Lyotard saw himself as setting out a theory of the post-modern condition, and he is generally seen as a 'post-modernist'. This position has been most forcibly developed by Baudrillard (1977).

You will find that some writers use a hyphen in post-modernism, but others prefer it without. In fact, the dictionary definition of 'postmodernism' (without a hyphen) refers to a movement of thought in art and architecture. This idea inspired contemporary writings, but the term has now acquired a different meaning. It is used in its hyphenated form to show this difference in meaning: a post-modern condition is one that goes beyond the modern condition.

- He saw individual patterns of action as shaped by the social structures in which people live. These structures have properties of their own that can be treated as distinct 'social facts'.

- Weber, who owed a great deal to Marx, developed an awareness of the importance of conflict, but he did so through a focus on the individual social actions from which social structures are built.

- He stressed the importance of understanding the subjective meaning of situations to the individuals involved and developed a distinctive methodology for studying social action.

We went on to consider the ways in which theorists of the twentieth century have elaborated on these foundations by developing structural-functionalist, symbolic interactionist, conflict, and rational choice theories.

- Talcott Parsons was the principal architect of structural-functionalist theories of *social systems*. He saw social structures as a normative order through which actions are formed into 'institutionalized' social patterns.

- Symbolic interactionists took a similar view to Weber, emphasizing the importance of the *definitions* of situations that people employ in their relations with each other. They explored the *social construction* of reality.

- Rational choice theories focused on one particular type of action from Weber's scheme—instrumentally rational action—and saw this as the basis of a general theory of action. They saw individuals as motivated by rewards and costs, calculating the most advantageous courses of action to take.

- Conflict theories combined elements from both Weber and Marx, aiming to highlight those aspects of social structure that were down-played in the 'normative' theories of structural functionalism. They highlighted resources, divisions, interests, and coercion.

In our final section, we considered some recent developments in theory that have introduced some novel and fundamentally important challenges to prior forms of theorizing.

- Feminist writers have criticized the male standpoint on rationality and objectivity that they see at the heart of conventional sociology.

- Black feminists stressed that female experiences, too, are diverse and women are divided by issues of ethnicity and class. This has encouraged a greater awareness of diversity and plurality in sociological understanding.

- Post-modern theorists have contributed to this debate by emphasizing the complete relativism of knowledge. They deny that there can be any objective or impartial viewpoint from which 'scientific' knowledge can be built.

Key concepts

- action frame of reference
- adaptation
- alienation
- analytical realism
- anomie
- authority
- base
- bourgeois
- capitalist society
- causal explanation
- cognitive interests
- division of labour
- dynamic density
- evolution
- function
- functional analysis
- gendering
- goal attainment
- historical materialism
- idealist
- ideal type
- ideologies
- industrial society
- integration
- interest group
- interests
- latency
- materialist
- mechanical solidarity
- mode of production
- organic solidarity
- phenomenology
- positivism
- post-modernism
- proletariat
- rationalization
- roles
- ruling classes
- self
- social classes
- social differentiation
- social facts
- socialization
- social structure
- solidarity
- superstructure
- symbolic interactionism
- understanding
- values

Workshop 2

Study 2 How to theorize

Very few sociologists write about how to actually go about theorizing. Sociological theory is usually presented as an abstract body of ideas and it is often difficult to see how it can be applied or used in practice. Howard Becker is one of the exceptional theorists who pays attention to the *processes* through which theories are developed and applied. In his book *Tricks of the Trade* (Becker 1998), Becker takes a number of central ideas and shows how students and professional sociologists can actually use these concepts in their research. He does this through a number of 'tricks' that people can use to develop their own theoretical skills.

He notes a fundamental problem in teaching students to use theoretical concepts. Students sent out to observe delinquency and deviant behaviour in the town or city will come back to their class and say, for example, that they couldn't see the relevance of Durkheim's ideas (or Parsons', or Merton's) because they could not see any anomie. Becker notes that this involves a failure to appreciate that anomie—like all sociological concepts—is something that is inferred from observations, it is not something that is directly observed itself. This is the question of *generalization*. Observations are specific, but concepts are general. Sociological theorizing involves making a leap from the specific to the general.

How, then, do sociologists generalize? How do they move, say, from observations of drinking behaviour to statements about identities and self-conceptions? To students and outsiders it appears to be a magical leap of imagination. Becker argues, however, that it involves a trick that, once learnt, becomes second nature as a professional skill: it might appear to be magical to outsiders, but it is actually a form of learned behaviour. The key trick he identifies in developing the skill of generalization is the progressive redescription of observations.

This trick involves describing findings without using any of the identifying characteristics of the actual case. Becker illustrates this from his own work on the careers of Chicago school teachers, among whom he had carried out a series of interviews and observations. When first attempting to describe his findings he would disregard all the personal details of the individuals (names, addresses, ages, etc.) and would come up with a summary such as:

> 'These teachers make their careers by moving from school to school within the Chicago school system, rather than trying to rise to higher, better paid positions, or moving to other systems in other cities, and their moves between positions in the school system can be understood as trying to find a school in which the people they interacted with—students, parents, principals, other teachers—would act more or less the way the teachers expected them to.' (Becker 1998: 126)

This redescription is a basic summary that remains fairly close to the observations, but contains no personal or idiosyncratic detail. Most people can manage to produce such an account from their observations fairly easily. The second step in theorizing is to redescribe the research without using any of the remaining identifiers and specifically avoiding words such as 'teacher', 'school', 'pupil', 'Chicago', and so on. This might seem odd, but most people would be able to take this second step. Becker presents the following redescription:

> 'people in bureaucratic systems choose between potential positions by assessing the way all the other participants will treat them and choosing places where the balance will be best, given whatever they are trying to maximize.' (Becker 1998: 127)

This is immediately much more theoretical than the initial descriptions of observations. It is now very easy to see links between the observations and such fully theoretical concepts as rational choice and career commitment. The jump has been made by making progressively more general redescriptions of the observations. Practice makes perfect, and Becker holds that continued use of such a technique results in the researcher being able to move back and forth between concepts and data, almost without thought—it has become second nature.

Many of you will be undertaking small-scale projects. Try to apply this trick in your research and see if it helps you to discover the relevance of the sociological theories that we have discussed in this chapter. Becker's book is full of similar tricks, many of which are aimed at the integration of theory with research methods, and you will find it useful to read the whole book.

Media watch 2 Values and family breakdown

Writing in the *Daily Mail*, journalist Melanie Phillips presented the case of Julie Atkins, a divorced mother of three girls who are themselves mothers. The girls are aged 14, 15, and 18, and two of the fathers of their children are in their teens. Melanie Phillips's diagnosis of this 'baby factory' is that Julie is 'guilty of the most reckless neglect' and has failed to take responsibility for her own family. She relies on the support provided by the welfare system. This is a symptom of the 'collapse of civilized values' in contemporary Britain that has resulted in a 'culture of disrespect'. She argues that fatherless children are being reared by feckless mothers, producing a '"yob" culture and the breakdown of civility and order'. We live in a 'fractured and brutish society' that contrasts markedly with the cohesive and well-integrated society of the past in which people took individual responsibility for their own actions and subscribe to a common set of values:

> There was a time when standards of behaviour were upheld to which all would aspire and by which they would be judged. Sobriety, sexual restraint, hard work and abiding by the law were all held to be vital for civilising the masses. These virtues were policed by a combination of laws and informal sanctions such as shame or stigma.

The collapse in social values, Phillips argues, has produced a divided society. There is a division between those who subscribe to 'basic civilised codes which everyone acknowledges' and those who are 'disconnected from mainstream life and its values'. The remedy for this, she concludes, is the rebuilding of respect for established values through education and through encouraging the better parenting skills that will ensure the socialization of the next generation into these values. She seeks to 'provide children for whom all the codes of civilised life are absent with the security of absolutely rigid discipline and educational structure'.

Melanie Phillips is implicitly drawing on the kinds of consensus ideas set out by Talcott Parsons. For Parsons, societies were held together by shared cultural values, and social problems were a result of what Durkheim called anomie—the breakdown of all commitment to social values. Try to collect some articles

from other newspapers that show this same point of view. How many discussions of 'anti-social behaviour' and social problems ascribe this to a breakdown in values and social cohesion?

When you have considered this question you should try to evaluate the argument. What evidence is produced in support of the claims? More importantly, what evidence can you find that raises problems for the theory?

Some counter-evidence was presented in an article by Anastasia de Waal in the *Guardian*. She, too, looks at the decline of personal responsibility in families and the position of single-parent, female-headed households. She, however, looks at the increasing pressures on these women to hold down a job and manage their family without the material and financial support of a partner. The link between lone motherhood and welfare dependency, decried by Phillips, is more often a result of a failure of the fathers to pay their child maintenance in full. Both men and women are locked into a structure of limited employment opportunities, low pay, and poor working conditions that make it economically difficult for them to meet their responsibilities.

De Waal makes little reference to values. Instead, she emphasizes economic resources, interests, and opportunities. Read back over our discussion of Marxist theory and see if you think that arguments from Marx might be brought to bear on this. Try to construct a Marxist explanation of the causes and consequences of family breakdown.

We have encouraged you to consider two different ways of explaining a social issue from the mass media: a Parsonian explanation and a Marxist explanation. Summarize each of these theories in a table. How would you go about choosing between them? Indeed, how far should we regard them as competing theories and how far as complementary ones?

Source: Melanie Phillips, 'The Two Faces of Britain', *Daily Mail*, 25 May 2005; Anastasia de Waal, 'Paternity Rights and Parental Responsibilities', *Guardian*, 23 August 2005.

Discussion points

Look back over the 'Stop and reflect' points at the end of each section of this chapter and make sure that you understand the issues that have been highlighted. The most general issues running through the chapter can be covered by considering four questions:

- What do you understand by materialist, idealist, and positivist views of knowledge?

- What is meant by gendered knowledge, and in what sense can it be said that sociological theory is malestream theory?
- What intellectual problems, if any, can you identify in the post-modern theorists' defence of relativism and feminist views of knowledge standpoints?
- Should we abandon the idea of a social *science* and its search for objectivity? If we do abandon objectivity and

impartiality, what distinguishes sociological argument from an argument in the pub?

Theories of structure

- Consider how you would use such concepts as structure, structural differentiation, and social role in the analysis of a work situation.

- How would you characterize the social solidarity of a society, and how useful are Durkheim's concepts of mechanical solidarity and organic solidarity?

- How did Merton's concept of anomie differ from that of Durkheim? Try to think of some examples of the responses to anomie that Merton identified.

- Contemporary societies are often referred to as 'industrial societies'. What is meant by this, and what is meant by the claim that they have entered a post-industrial or post-modern condition?

Theories of interaction

- How did Weber construct his ideal types of action? What did he mean by describing them as 'ideal' types?

- What is meant by the ideas of social construction and the definition of the situation? How might these be used in a study of a school, college, or university?

- What does it mean to describe a theory of action as phenomenological? How does this relate to Weber's idea of 'understanding'?

- Why do you think we have argued that it is appropriate to consider Weber under the headings of both 'interaction theories' and 'conflict theories'?

Theories of conflict

- What does it mean to describe Marx's historical materialism, and his concepts of base and superstructure, as involving an economic determinism? Is this a valid criticism of Marx?

- How might a Marxist look for evidence of alienation, class relations, and ideology in contemporary societies?

- Has the break-up of the Soviet Union and the other Communist states of eastern and central Europe finally undermined the intellectual claims of Marxism?

- To what extent can the theories of Dahrendorf and Rex be seen as improving on Marx's ideas on class and conflict?

- Can Habermas appropriately be called a Marxist? To what extent does his introduction of the concept of the lifeworld involve a significant departure from Marxist ideas?

 Explore further

Useful overviews of the main trends in sociological theory can be found in:

Craib, I. (1997), *Classical Social Theory* (Oxford: Oxford University Press). *An excellent and very readable introduction to the ideas of Marx, Weber, Durkheim, and Simmel.*

Giddens, A. (1971), *Capitalism and Modern Social Theory* (Cambridge: Cambridge University Press). *Gives an excellent account of Marx, Weber, and Durkheim, but also puts them into the historical context of the development of European society.*

Scott, J. (1995), *Sociological Theory: Contemporary Debates* (Cheltenham: Edward Elgar). *Looks in detail at Parsons and at the various strands of theory that developed in relation to his work, including interaction theories and conflict theories.*

Scott, J. (2006), *Social Theory* (London: Sage). *Takes a thematic approach to the development of theoretical ideas and includes discussions of a large number of theorists in relation to these themes.*

More detailed discussions can be found in:

Berger, P. L., and Luckmann, T. (1966), *The Social Construction of Reality* (Harmondsworth: Allen Lane, 1971). *An important and influential statement of the phenomenological point of view.*

Dahrendorf, R. (1957), *Class and Class Conflict in an Industrial Society* (London: Routledge & Kegan Paul, 1959). *A readable statement of the need for a conflict perspective that goes beyond the ideas of Marx.*

Goffman, E. (1959), *The Presentation of Self in Everyday Life* (Harmondsworth: Penguin). *Gives a powerful extension of the symbolic interactionist position. We look at his work in more detail in Chapter 4, pp. 128–9 and Chapter 8, pp. 301–3.*

You should try to read at least one of the works of each of the leading classical theorists. The best starting points might be:

Durkheim, E. (1897), *Suicide: A Study in Sociology* (London: Routledge & Kegan Paul, 1952).

Marx, K., and Engels, F. (1848), *The Communist Manifesto* (Harmondsworth: Penguin, 1967).

Weber, Max (1904–5), *The Protestant Ethic and the Spirit of Capitalism* (Oxford: Basil Blackwell, 2002).

Online resources

Visit the Online Resource Centre that accompanies this book to access more learning resources and other interesting material on theories and theorizing at:

www.oxfordtextbooks.co.uk/orc/fulcher3e/

The views of all the principal sociologists can be assessed through the comprehensive pages set up at the 'Dead Sociologists' Society:

www.pfeiffer.edu/~lridener/DSS/DEADSOC.HTML

Important sites for studying Marx, Durkheim, and Weber can be found in the boxes dedicated to these writers earlier in this chapter.

Symbolic interactionism can be pursued through the Society for the Study of Symbolic Interactionism's own page:

http://sun.soci.niu.edu/~sssi/

Feminist thought is well represented by the Feminist Majority Foundation at:

www.feminist.org/

Many of Baudrillard's works on post-modernism are covered at:

www.uta.edu/english/apt/collab/baudweb.html

Methods and research

Contents

03

How to lie with statistics

'The secret language of statistics, so appealing in a fact-minded culture, is employed to sensationalize, inflate, confuse, and oversimplify. Statistical methods and statistical terms are necessary in reporting the mass data of social and economic trends, business conditions, "opinion" polls, the census. But without writers who use the words with honesty and understanding and readers who know what they mean, the results can only be semantic nonsense.'

Source: Huff (1954: 8).

Sociologists are often told that 'you can prove anything with statistics'. The famous quotation about there being 'lies, damned lies, and statistics' is often produced as further evidence of the unfounded scientific pretensions of sociologists. How valid is this judgement? Is the sociologist simply a scientific charlatan whose methods leave much to be desired?

We have already shown in Chapter 1, pp. 15–17 that a scientific method is essential in scientific research. Any scientist must be careful and critical of the evidence that is used to build and to test theories. Handled properly, statistical sources are an essential part of the sociological enterprise. It is their *misuse*, not their *use*, that can mislead people. In this chapter we will look at the ways in which this kind of evidence can be collected and used in sociological research and how it can help to inform public debates.

Not all sociological evidence is statistical, however. The image of the sociologist as a survey researcher processing large numbers of statistics with a computer is only a part of the truth. In fact, sociologists use a variety of methods to collect their evidence. They carry out observations and interviews, and they examine historical and contemporary documents. Our aim in this chapter is to give you an overview of the range of sociological methods and the kinds of evidence that can be used in sociological work. In the section on 'Research design and methodology' we look at the principal forms of sociological research and the ways in which they complement one another in the sociological toolbox. In 'Surveys, ethnography, and documents' we look at the main varieties of data sources and their analysis. The section on 'Displaying and using data' helps you to read the tables and charts produced by other researchers and gives you some guidance on how to produce your own. Finally, 'The ethics of social research' looks at the effects of research on the people studied and on the sociologist him or herself. It asks 'what are the ethical responsibilities of the sociologist?'

Research design and methodology

The studies that you will come across in this book and in your wider reading have used a great variety of research methods to collect their information. If you are to approach these studies critically, you need to know something about the advantages and disadvantages of the various methods that have been used. Our aim in this section is to give you some of the basic ideas about research methods that will enable you to do this.

Some of you may be carrying out a small project of your own as a part of your studies and we hope that this section will give enough information for you to make an informed choice about the kinds of research methods that you want to use. When you begin your research, you will find that you need to go beyond what we tell you and consult some of the many specialist books that give detailed guidance on the techniques and skills of sociological research (see O'Connell Davidson and Layder 1994; May 2001; Bryman 2004). Our discussion will, we hope, convey the flavour of social research, but it cannot provide you with the full recipe!

Research design

Research does not simply happen. It has to be planned in advance. This planning is called **research design**. Designing a research project involves translating general ideas and concerns into specific and researchable topics. You may start out with a general interest in, say, deviance, work, or health, but this must be made more specific before you can start to design a project. In this way, the focus of interest is narrowed down to something that can actually be investigated in an empirical study. Instead of a general wish to investigate deviance, a researcher might finally decide to look at violent street crime in urban areas, especially as this affects women. This topic is specific enough to suggest particular theoretical questions and practical issues to examine and therefore will point to the kinds of research methods that might be used.

Varieties of research

Research design involves decisions about many different aspects of the research process. We will highlight four of these. The researcher must be clear about the *purposes* of the research, the *methods* that will be used, the ways in which these methods are combined into a particular *style* of research, and the *strategy* through which these will be tied together into a coherent project.

There are many *purposes* for which research might be carried out. A researcher may be trying to please an employer, complete a Ph.D., advance the sum of human knowledge, and so on. We are focusing here, however, on the scientific purposes of a project. Robson (1993: 42) has usefully suggested that three broad scientific purposes can be identified:

- exploration;
- description;
- explanation.

A project concerned with *exploration* is one in which the researcher seeks to find out something in a new or under-researched area. The project seeks to map out the area in order to generate ideas and further questions to examine. An exploratory study asks 'What is going on here?' A researcher may, for example, try to find out how many families are living in poverty in a particular city, or where the main areas of urban deprivation are to be found.

A project with a *descriptive* purpose, on the other hand, is one where the researcher tries to construct a clearer and more comprehensive picture of something in relation to the theoretical questions from which the research began. The research will build on existing bodies of knowledge and fill in further details in order to arrive at a rounded picture of the extent or significance of something. A descriptive project might try to show how poverty, health, and diet are related together as aspects of working-class life in a particular city. Both exploration and description are concerned with reporting the facts, and they are distinguished from one another only in terms of how well defined an area is already.

When a project has an *explanatory* purpose, it seeks to go beyond reporting the facts to seek out the causes and influences that are at work. It asks 'Why is this happening?' or 'What is the most important factor in producing this?'. The theory that the researcher uses will suggest certain factors to study, or these may be drawn from previous exploratory and descriptive research. An explanatory study might try to see whether low pay, unemployment, or bad housekeeping is the most important cause of poverty.

When the most important causal factors have been identified, they may be combined into a **model** of the causal influences. A model is a simplified picture of a situation or process that tries to show how its various elements are connected to each other. A model may often be suggested by the particular theory that informs the research. Projects informed by structural-functionalist theories, for example, are likely to construct models of the functional connections among the things studied. A model may suggest one or more hypotheses that can be examined in further research. A **hypothesis** is a suggested relationship between two or more factors that can be tested against evidence. A model that links poverty to low pay, for example, may suggest the hypothesis that increasing the legal minimum rate of pay will reduce the level of poverty. A researcher whose model links poverty to unemployment, however, may draw the hypothesis that a higher rate of pay, by increasing business costs, would increase the level of unemployment and, therefore, the level of poverty.

Once the purpose of the research has been clarified, it is possible for a researcher to choose the particular *methods* to use. A research method is a particular technique for collecting or analysing evidence, and the kinds of research methods that sociologists use include questionnaires, participant observation, interviewing, the interpretation of documents, content analysis, and many others. We will look at a number of these methods in this chapter and in other parts of this book. It is important that the methods chosen relate closely to the purposes of the research and the topics that are being examined. An attempt to explain the causes of poverty in contemporary Britain, for example, might seem to require a standardized method, such as a questionnaire that can easily be administered to a large number of people. An exploratory study of the consequences of poverty for lone-parent households, on the other hand, might seem to require more informal interview techniques.

The particular methods that are chosen and combined by a researcher will often be associated with a distinctive *style* of research. A style of research comprises methods that fit well together and that tend to be associated with particular theoretical approaches and philosophical assumptions. In this chapter, we will discuss three principal styles of research:

research could be undertaken by sociologists if improved levels of funding were available.

The common element in all social surveys is the asking of questions in a more or less formal and standardized way. Information is sought on a number of matters through asking the same questions to large numbers of people and then collating the answers in order to produce a general picture. The printed list of questions used in a survey is called a **questionnaire**; the person who responds to the questions is called the **respondent**. Surveys differ in terms of the kind of questionnaire used and the way that respondents are approached. Three types of social survey are in common use:

- The *interview survey*. This is a door-to-door or street-based survey where a trained interviewer asks questions and records the answers. A questionnaire used by an interviewer is often called a schedule.

- The *postal survey*. This involves sending a questionnaire through the post to chosen addresses. This is said to be a self-administered or self-completion questionnaire, as respondents write in the answers themselves.

- The *telephone survey*. This is a more recent variation on the interview survey, the interview being carried out over the telephone, rather than face to face.

In the following sections, we will look at the two main ways in which social surveys, of whatever type, differ. We will first look at the design and construction of questionnaires, and we will then look at the principles of sampling used in surveys.

Asking questions and getting answers

The design of a questionnaire is not easy, though people often think that it is. Deciding on the topics and themes to be covered can be quite straightforward, but converting these into precise and unambiguous questions that can be used to produce sociological data involves a number of steps. Unless a question is carefully worded, there will be scope for ambiguity and misunderstanding on the part of the respondents. As a result, the answers that they give may be difficult to interpret. To deal with this problem, professional questionnaires go through a long and complicated process of drafting and evaluation before they are used in an actual survey. Even the small-scale questionnaires used in student project work need to be carefully worked out. A model of the whole process of questionnaire design is shown in Figure 3.2.

The initial stage, of course, is to decide on the specific topics that are to be investigated in the survey. This will often have been decided, in general terms, in the initial phases of research design, but it is important that they are

clarified before any attempt is made to draw up specific questions. This is usually done by building a checklist of topics that can be broken down and combined until they form a reasonably coherent and manageable list. This list is usually kept as short as possible. A questionnaire takes time to complete, and if unnecessary topics are covered, there will be less time for the respondents to provide the more important information. This means, in practice, that information that is easily available elsewhere (for example, from other surveys or from published sources) should not usually be sought.

Once a brief and workable checklist of topics has been completed, it is possible to begin to turn these topics into specific questions. When all topics have been converted into questions, a questionnaire has been produced. The most important considerations are to make the wording of the various questions as clear as possible and to decide on the order in which they should be asked. We will look at

Figure 3.2 Questionnaire design

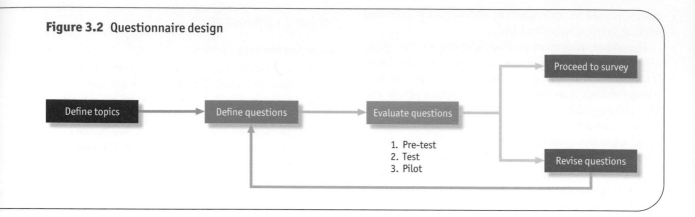

these matters in some detail later in the section. In the initial phase of questionnaire design, the aim is to produce fairly good, workable questions, but not the final, polished questions that will actually be used in the survey. Many alterations will later need to be made to the questions, and detailed polishing of grammar and vocabulary would be a waste of time in the early phases.

The draft questions must go through a process of evaluation. In the first phase of questionnaire design this is often called a *pre-test*. This involves an initial assessment of the questions by asking friends and colleagues to have a look at them and see if they can identify any obvious problems. Even experienced groups of professional survey researchers find it useful to get the opinions of professional colleagues. It is all too easy to miss problems in your own questions. Written comments on the questions, including suggestions for improvement, are usually obtained in the pre-test.

The draft questionnaire must be revised at the end of the pre-test to take account of the suggestions received. This involves reconsidering many of the same issues that arose in the first phase of question definition. In some cases, where the subject matter is complex or sensitive, this reconstruction may be quite substantial. Even if the outcome of the pre-test is positive and the draft questions all seem acceptable, it will be necessary to begin producing instructions for the interviewers or written instructions for the respondents. A questionnaire will, for example, need to have instructions added to it that tell the respondent 'Please tick the appropriate box', or 'Please go to question 8'.

Similarly, an interviewer needs written instructions about exactly how much more information to give the respondent when asking a question. An interviewer may, for example, need to probe further in relation to a respondent's answer by saying 'What exactly do you mean by . . . ?', 'Could you say a little more about . . . ?', or even just remaining silent until the respondent offers more information. If the questionnaire is to be standardized, it

is essential that all interviewers respond in similar ways to each respondent. The written instructions are an attempt to ensure that this happens. Some questions may require that a number of *prompts* be given to the respondent. A list of possible answers may need to be read out to them in a particular order, or they may have to be shown to the respondent on prompt cards. All these matters need to be set down as a part of the questionnaire in order to ensure that each response is as standardized as possible.

Once the questionnaire has been reviewed, it must again be evaluated. In the second phase of questionnaire design this is often called a *test*. In a test there will be a trial of the full questionnaire under near-normal survey conditions. This may involve a small number of respondents who are similar to those who will eventually be approached in the full survey, but far less attention is usually given to the details of who is and who is not selected for interview. The test will seek comments on the questionnaire from interviewers and, very often, from respondents. These comments will, again, feed into the next revision of the questionnaire. In some small surveys, a pre-test and test will be sufficient to resolve most problems and to allow the survey to proceed. With very large surveys, however, a third evaluation may be carried out in a *pilot* survey. This is, in effect, a full dress rehearsal for the actual survey, but using a much smaller sample. Following the test or pilot survey, the final version of the questionnaire will be produced, and if interviewers are to be used, they can be trained to carry it out.

In practice, of course, questionnaire design is rarely as clear-cut as this discussion implies. The distinction between a test and a pilot survey, as we have noted, is not always drawn, and some poorly thought-out surveys may dispense with formal testing altogether. In good surveys, however, proper testing of the questionnaire will be of great importance, and full attention will be given to all the issues that we have discussed, even if some of the stages are compressed into one another. Similarly, it must not be assumed that there will be a neat arrangement of the various phases over time. Training of interviewers, for example, begins at an early stage in the planning of the survey. In some surveys that use people who have not previously worked as interviewers on sociological projects, the test and pilot surveys may be used as means of training. Similarly, the writing of instructions for interviewers and respondents will be undertaken in parallel with the defining of the questions.

We have, so far, talked about the drafting and redrafting of questions in very general terms. It is now necessary to look at this in a little more detail. The most important consideration is to make the individual questions as short, clear, and unambiguous as possible. It is important, for example, that the terms that are used in questions should be meaningful to the respondents. Questions that ask 'Have you ever experienced anomie?' or 'Do you occupy a contradictory class location?' are unlikely to get meaningful answers from respondents, unless they happen to be sociology graduates. Similarly, questions that ask about eligibility rules for social-security entitlements will be misunderstood by all except the most knowledgeable respondents.

Even if obscure and technical terms are avoided, the actual wording of the questions may be ambiguous. A question that asks 'How often have you been to the cinema?' is not likely to produce useful information as it does not make it clear what is meant by 'often' and what time period is to be considered. It is far more useful to ask 'How often have you visited the cinema to see a film in the last year?' and then to offer a choice of, say, 'once a month', 'once every two months', 'once every three months', 'less than once every three months', and 'not at all'.

This example also illustrates the difference between 'open-ended' and 'fixed-choice' questions. In a fixed-choice question, the respondent must choose one of the alternative answers provided on the questionnaire. This has the advantage that the results of the survey can easily be totalled up. Where the respondents are allowed to reply in their own words, they have more flexibility about how they answer. In these circumstances, however, the researcher may find it more difficult to quantify the results.

One of the most important considerations in wording a question is to avoid what have been called leading questions. These are questions that lead the respondent to a particular kind of response because of the way in which they have been worded. An example of a leading question is 'Why do you think Tony Blair makes a good prime minister?' This question makes it difficult for people to reply that they do not think that he is a good prime minister. They may simply follow the lead of the interviewer and give a reason, particularly if they are offered a fixed number of choices.

The things to consider when drawing up topics and forming them into questions are numerous, and many complex issues arise. The most useful discussions of these can be found in Moser and Kalton (1979), A. N. Oppenheim (1966), and de Vaus (1991). From these and other sources we have constructed a checklist of major issues. There are ten key points to remember when constructing a questionnaire.

The first key point involves making the whole task as easy as possible for the respondent. The questions on a questionnaire must always be kept as easy and as straightforward as possible, but it is sometimes necessary to include complex questions or even questions that may appear threatening or upsetting. Many people, for example, do not like to tell strangers details about their income, and most people would feel uneasy answering questions about their involvement in criminal activities. For this reason, it is generally a good idea to begin the questionnaire with the relatively easy and non-threatening questions that respondents will be happiest to answer. If a questionnaire begins with difficult and threatening questions, respondents are less likely to cooperate or to complete it.

For the same reason, it is always a good idea to have lengthy questions that require a lot of writing towards the end of the questionnaire. If a respondent must, from the beginning, write long responses on the questionnaire, she or he is far less likely to complete the task. Where an interviewer is asking the questions, the amount of writing should, in any case, be kept to an absolute minimum. If the interviewer has to write down a great deal, mistakes may occur and the respondent is left to sit idly while the interviewer writes.

Funnelling is a useful principle in questionnaire design. It involves starting out with the more general questions on a topic and gradually making them more specific. If the amount of detail required at the beginning of a questionnaire is too great, the cooperation of the respondents is put under great strain. Respondents are more likely to give the details required if they have been led on to them by more general questions.

Using the respondent's biography to organize questions is something that, where it can be done, gives a logic and coherence to a questionnaire. If the purpose of a questionnaire is to explore work careers, then it will usually be sensible to begin with questions about the first job and then to follow through any job changes in sequence. Similarly, it is sensible to put any questions about education before those on work. Using this kind of chronological or biographical framework makes it far easier for people to organize their responses and makes it less likely that they will forget important events and information.

The first four of our key points suggest that, in general, a questionnaire should begin with easy, brief, and general

THEORY AND METHODS

A checklist for questionnaire construction: ten key points

1 *Easy*: start with straightforward and non-threatening questions.

2 *Writing*: put questions that require a lot of writing towards the end.

3 *Funnel*: questions should move from the more general to the more specific.

4 *Biography*: use the respondent's own biography to organize the questions.

5 *Transition*: when switching topics, make this as smooth as possible.

6 *Variety*: try to include a wide range of question types.

7 *Short*: keep the questionnaire as brief as possible.

8 *Attractive*: make the questionnaire as neat and well designed as possible.

9 *Code*: classify responses in advance, wherever possible.

10 *Confidentiality*: offer and maintain promises of confidentiality and anonymity wherever appropriate.

questions and move gradually towards more difficult, lengthy, and specific questions. If appropriate, it should also have a biographical structure. For short questionnaires, these principles can usually be applied quite consistently. In larger questionnaires, however, a number of separate topics may be covered and a more modular approach will be needed. If a questionnaire covers, for example, both work career and political activities, then these would usually be treated as separate sections or modules of the questionnaire. Each module might be structured in terms of the principles that we have discussed, but the overall structure of the questionnaire will be more complex.

Our next key point concerns the transition from one part of a questionnaire to another. Where there are two or more sections, the transition from one to another must be as smooth as possible. It is important to avoid a sudden switch of topic that leaves the respondent confused. When changing topic, the interviewer might say something like 'I would now like to ask you a few questions about . . .'. In a postal questionnaire, such phrases can be printed before each batch of questions begins.

The next three key points in questionnaire construction relate rather more to the appearance and feel of the questionnaire than to its content. While the subject matter or purpose of a survey may often help to ensure that respondents cooperate, this is not always the case. A subject that is of great interest to the researcher may appear unimport-

ant or baffling to the respondent. In these circumstances, the actual appearance of the questionnaire or the manner of its implementation may be critical.

Having a variety of question formats will help to retain the interest of respondents and prevent them from getting too bored. A mixture of open-ended and fixed-choice questions, for example, prevents the responses from becoming too mechanical. If the questionnaire is kept as short as possible, this will also help to retain the cooperation of the respondent. Survey researchers need to remember that respondents are giving up their time, and it is important that this is kept to a minimum. In postal surveys an attractively presented questionnaire can help to ensure that people complete it, especially if it is quite long. A questionnaire that is simply a dense list of single-spaced questions is unlikely to show a good response. Major surveys employ professional designers and specialist software packages to produce neat and attractive questions.

The coding of a questionnaire—the ninth key point on the checklist—is something that is of particular relevance to the person analysing the results. Coding is the process

THEORY AND METHODS

Attitude scaling

Many surveys ask people for their attitudes and opinions. You will find that these kinds of questions tend to have a particular format. Surveys sometimes ask attitude questions in a normal question format: 'Do you agree with the view that the monarchy is out of touch with ordinary people?' More typically, however, they involve an attempt to measure—or *scale*—the strength of an attitude.

The most common way of doing this uses a so-called *Likert scale*, named after its originator. People are given a phrase and are asked to circle a number from 1 to 5, labelled to show the strength and direction of their attitude. For example:

Some people say that the unemployed should help themselves and not be dependent on welfare benefits. Do you

1	2	3	4	5
strongly agree	agree	neither agree nor disagree	disagree	strongly disagree

If items are labelled consistently across questions, it is possible to add up scores and get an assessment of the overall strength of a person's attitudes on a particular set of issues.

This method is similar to the way that magazine quizzes claim to measure such things as 'How sexy are you?' from scored responses to questions. This was not exactly what Likert intended the method to be used for.

Controversy and debate Advantages and disadvantages of using questionnaires

Advantages

- Information is standardized and can be easily processed. This is especially useful for quantitative data.
- It is possible to collect information on a large number of people and so allow more valid generalizations to be made.
- Reliability is high: all respondents answer exactly the same questions in near identical situations. Differences in response can be assumed to reflect real differences among the respondents.
- Postal questionnaires are often the easiest and most efficient way of reaching large numbers of people.
- Postal questionnaires give great anonymity to respondents, encouraging honesty and openness.

Disadvantages

- Respondents may misrepresent or distort their views.
- Respondents may not remember relevant information.
- Large surveys can be very costly.
- Interviewers may antagonize respondents or cause biased responses if they are not properly trained.
- People may refuse to be interviewed or to complete a postal questionnaire, creating a non-response problem.
- Postal questionnaires may not be completed by the person they are addressed to, and they may not be taken seriously.

through which individual responses are converted into categories and classifications for use in the research. Sex, for example, may be coded as 'female' or 'male', and occupations may be coded into one of a set of class categories. In order to process the data more effectively, by computer, these categories are given numbers. This may be 1 for female and 2 for male, or classes numbered from 1 to 7. These numbers are generally quite arbitrary and are used simply as labels that a computer can handle more easily.

Where fixed-choice questions are used, it is very easy to *pre-code* the responses by printing the numbers beneath them or down the side of the questionnaire. Similarly, the scale points used in attitude scaling can be used as codes. Wherever pre-coding is possible, it can save a great deal of time. If pre-coding is not possible, as in the case of open-ended questions, the researcher has to look at a selection of responses after the survey has been completed and try to distinguish different types of answer. Only then is it possible to use these as codes to be applied to all completed questionnaires.

The final key point on our checklist relates to matters that we will discuss more fully in 'The ethics of social research', pp. 106–8. In order to gain the cooperation of respondents, it will often be necessary to guarantee the privacy of their responses. They must feel that no one except those on the research team will read the questionnaires. This guarantee is usually given in a covering letter sent with the postal questionnaire or verbally by the interviewer, right at the beginning of the interview. It should go without saying, of course, that a researcher should give only those guarantees that can actually be kept.

If the questionnaires are to be stored in an archive or made available to other researchers, full confidentiality may not be possible. A related issue concerns the privacy of the interview itself. If a person is interviewed in the presence of other people who can overhear what is said, this may affect her or his willingness to be completely open in answering the questions.

Ethnographic research

Ethnography simply means 'writing about people', but it has come to be used in a more specific sense to describe forms of research that try to get close to how people actually feel and experience social life. Ethnographic methods, then, are oriented towards understanding the meanings that people give to their actions. Ethnography is a form of research in which the researcher actually participates in some way in the situation being studied. This kind of research may involve observation of what people are doing, engaging them in conversations and informal interviews, or some mixture of the two. It is easiest in small-scale, face-to-face settings, though ethnographies of large organizations and communities have been carried out.

Ethnographic participation may be overt or covert. In **overt research**, researchers are open about the fact that research is being undertaken and that they are trying to obtain relevant information. In **covert research**, on the other hand, researchers keep the research a secret and try to appear to others as just ordinary participants.

Some see ethnography as including only participant observation and informal conversations, but this is rather

Ethnographic researchers can sometimes find it difficult to be unobtrusive. Edward Evans-Pritchard and the Azande.
© Pitt Rivers Museum

restrictive. Long, informal interviews, for example, have played an important part in ethnographic studies. While these have some similarities with the questionnaire-based interviews of the survey method, they have far more in common with participant observation. This kind of interviewing has often been combined with observation and the use of personal documents. The advantage of taking this rather broader view of ethnography is that it highlights its most distinctive feature, which is to explore the *qualitative* and more intimate aspects of social life. While survey research is not exclusively *quantitative*, it is far more suited to the production of quantitative data.

Ethnographic methods were developed in the fieldwork techniques of the structural-functionalist anthropologists that we discuss in Chapter 2. Anthropologists such as Malinowski went and lived among the peoples that they studied, learning their language and trying to understand their cultures. This research was, out of necessity, overt research, as there was no way in which a white anthropologist could simply pass as a member of the black societies being studied. The purposes of the research were not, of course, fully disclosed to the subjects, who had little or no conception of what research was and probably identified the anthropologist with the colonial authorities.

Similar techniques were developed in the work of the Chicago sociologists, though these involved far more covert research. This is easier when the subjects of the research are ethnically similar to the researcher. The research carried out in Chicago combined observation and conversation with more systematic interviewing and the collection of personal data. In such classic studies as those of the hobo (N. Anderson 1923), the gang (Thrasher 1927), and the jack roller (Shaw 1930), powerful techniques of ethnographic investigation were developed.

> **⊅ Connections**
>
> We briefly discuss the background to the Chicago school of sociology in Chapter 2, pp. 51–4, and you might find it useful to look at that now. Goffman's work is an important example of ethnographic research that draws on this tradition. You will find a discussion of the use of life-history interviews by the Chicago sociologists in Chapter 7, p. 246, where we look at Sutherland's work on the professional thief.

Making observations

Observation is, of course, one of the principal ways in which sociologists can collect their data. In any of the situations that we enter, we can watch people to see what they do, and we can listen to what they say and who they speak to. However, sociological observation involves more than this. It is necessary to decide when and where to observe, how to ensure observation of exactly those things

Unobtrusive observation.
© Alice Chadwick

that are of interest, and how to make sociological use of the observations. The ways in which these issues are handled depend upon the particular research role that is taken. Sociological observers have typically chosen one of three research roles:

- the complete participant;
- the participant-as-observer;
- the complete observer (Schwartz and Schwartz 1955; Gold 1958).

In the case of the *complete participant*, observers take a highly active and involved stance towards those being observed. They aim to become a member of a group or to enter an organization in order to appear to others as an ordinary participant. The researcher may, for example, take employment in a factory or hospital in order to observe fellow workers. Researchers have increasingly taken advantage of the Internet to engage in 'cyber ethnography', for example by joining chat rooms or discussion groups in order to study the other participants. Research as a complete participant is covert, as those being studied do not know that they are being observed for research purposes. This role has often been adopted in social research. In his study of a secretive religious group, Wallis (1976) joined in its activities as if he were an ordinary recruit. Another example is a study of homosexual activities in toilets, where Humphreys (1970) got to know the men and acted as a voyeur and look-out. Through participation, a researcher can observe people in many off-guard situations that would not really be open to an outsider. So long as entry to the group or organization is possible, this kind of research can be highly effective and allows the sociologist to understand activities from the standpoint of the actors concerned.

A major practical difficulty in complete participant observation is that it is difficult to ask questions or raise issues that would make it obvious that the researcher is not merely a participant. The researcher must always act in role and cannot step outside it. This may lead to such involvement in the life of the group or organization that it is impossible to maintain the distance that the research requires. A particular problem is the difficulty of recording observations. A complete participant may observe a great deal, but may not have the opportunity to write this down without arousing suspicion. In their study of a religious group, Festinger and his colleagues (1956) found that they had to make frequent trips to the lavatory in order to write up their field notes in secret. If this kind of subterfuge is not possible, observations will have to be written down many hours, and perhaps days, later, making errors and omissions very likely.

The role of the *participant-as-observer* resolves some of these problems. In this role, the researcher's purposes are overt and the actors know that research is being undertaken. This gives a researcher access to the situation to be studied, but it also allows questions to be asked and notes to be made. Research by Hargreaves (1967) and Lacey (1970) on schools used this method, as does much anthropological fieldwork. The main disadvantage of this research role is that it may be more difficult to gain entry to a group when its members know that they are going to be observed. Even if access is gained, people may be more guarded in what they say and do in the presence of the researcher.

The third observation role is that of the *complete observer* who engages in no interaction with those who are being studied. The thinking behind this is that any involvement through participation will affect the very situation that is being studied. The participant observer cannot help but affect what is happening. By avoiding any interaction, the complete observer hopes to avoid any influence on what is being observed. R. King (1978), in his study of classroom behaviour, adopted this role. He sat at the back of a classroom and refused to be involved in any way, even if spoken to.

It can be argued, of course, that the very presence of an observer—particularly an impassive and mute observer—will have just as much influence on people's actions as a participant-as-observer. In a famous set of experiments carried out at the Hawthorne electrical works in Chicago, researchers observed the behaviour of workers who were wiring electrical components (Roethlisberger and Dickson 1939). It was found that the mere presence of an observer affected the productivity of the workers. This effect of the observer on the observed has, since then, been called the *Hawthorne effect*.

> ⮩ *Connections*
> You will find a discussion of the Hawthorne researches in Chapter 14, pp. 559–60.

The only way in which the complete observer can truly avoid having any influence is by staying out of sight and becoming a covert observer. This is very difficult to arrange in real-life situations. The nearest approximations are the observations made by Bales (1950) of small-group behaviour. By using a one-way mirror, Bales was able to observe without being observed, albeit in a rather artificial laboratory setting.

The question of the influence that the observer has on the observed is a critical matter in ethnographic research. It is, of course, true that survey interviewers can influence the responses of their respondents if they do not behave in a standardized way. There is also some evidence that female interviewers generally achieve a better rapport, and therefore better results, than do male interviewers. The

Documenting women's lives?

© Lucy Dawkins

written by them. In many cases the authorship of a document may not be clear. Official documents, even when issued in the name of a particular minister, are produced by a complex administrative apparatus. In the same way, books and newspapers are the products of a division of labour in which the work of named writers is processed and reprocessed by copy editors, sub-editors, and editors. In these cases, it might be quite inappropriate to see a particular named individual as the author of a document.

Assessing the *credibility* of a document involves looking at its sincerity and accuracy. All documents are, to a greater or lesser extent, selective or distorted, as it is impossible to construct accounts that are independent of particular points of view. Nevertheless, they can be more or less credible as accounts, depending on whether an observer is sincere in the choice of a point of view from which to write and whether the account gives an accurate report from that starting point.

The sincerity of authors is related to their motives. Some people may be motivated to report on events with as much objectivity as possible. Others, however, may write to justify their own actions, to make propaganda, to deceive others, or for financial gain. The motivation is not always clear. Official documents may present themselves as factual information, but they may actually be attempts to persuade people towards a particular position or course of action. More obviously, newspapers are produced by journalists who are paid to write marketable material and who may be subject to political pressure from a proprietor.

> ### ⊃ *Connections*
> At this point you might like to consider some of the issues that we look at in Chapter 10, 'Communication and the media'. Look, in particular, at 'Ownership and control', pp. 388–90, and 'The commercialization of the media', pp. 391–2.

Even when an author has acted sincerely, the credibility of a document is affected by its accuracy. The accuracy of a report depends on the conditions under which it was compiled and how close the author was to the events reported. Historians have generally preferred to use what they call primary sources. These are first-hand accounts of events, and it is felt that they minimize any loss of accuracy due to lapses of memory and inadequate records. However, even first-hand observers may have difficulties in recording their observations in such a way that they can be used to construct accurate reports. As we noted in connection with interviews and observations, it is generally very difficult to record what is seen and heard with complete accuracy. Shorthand was invented only in the seventeenth century, and tape recorders were not available until well into the twentieth century. Accuracy of recall is, therefore, a problem even with primary sources.

The *representativeness* of a document is determined by its survival and availability. We discuss the issue of sampling in the following section. A representative sample of relevant documents will not always be needed, but it is

THEORY AND METHODS
. . . .

Primary and secondary sources

A distinction is often made between primary and secondary sources, though there is some confusion over this. For most historians, a primary source is a first-hand account produced by a participant. It involves little or no intervention by the historian. Diaries, autobiographies, letters, and many administrative documents are primary sources. Secondary sources, on the other hand, are those that have been produced by historians or others, using primary sources, and which are therefore second-hand accounts. When a historian relies on the work of other historians or commentators, instead of going to new primary sources, he or she is said to be using secondary sources.

Some sociologists have defined primary sources as consisting of data collected by researchers themselves, and secondary sources as comprising data that already exist. This means that the fieldwork data of a participant observer is correctly recognized as a primary source, but it is rather misleading to see letters and diaries as 'secondary' sources. This confusion seems to result from different concerns: historians are generally concerned with whether accounts are first-hand (participant) or second-hand; sociologists are more concerned with whether accounts are produced by a professional sociologist or by people in their everyday lives. Both points of view are important, but you may conclude that the attempt to see them in terms of a simple distinction between primary and secondary sources should be abandoned.

THEORY AND METHODS
. . . .

Official statistics

The statistics produced by governments are one of the most important sources of data available to sociologists. They cover population, crime, health, employment, and a whole range of other issues. You will find a full discussion of them in 'Using official statistics', pp. 102–6. You might want to look at that discussion when you have finished this section. Try to apply the criteria of authenticity, credibility, representativeness, and meaning while you read what we say about crime and other statistics.

To get some idea of the kinds of statistics produced in Britain, look at a recent issue of *Social Trends*.

important to know whether the chosen documents are, in fact, representative. Most documents are produced some time before they are used in research, and their users will need to know what proportion of the relevant documents have actually survived and whether they are all available for research purposes.

If documents are to survive, they must be stored in some way. This may simply involve dumping them in a cardboard box, as happens with many personal documents, or it may involve storage in a proper archive. Many public and private documents are destroyed soon after their production, while others are stored for a period and destroyed at a later date. Household receipts and many letters, for example, are often not retained at all. Because of the massive number of documents produced by modern bureaucratic organizations, it is impossible for them to retain more than a small portion. These official documents are stored while in current use and may then be 'weeded' for destruction before the remainder are transferred to an

archive. In many private organizations, however, there is no archive and all non-current documents are destroyed.

Even when documents are stored, the number that survive may decrease over time through deterioration and decay or through periodic clear-outs. The introduction of computer technology has resolved some of the problems of paper storage, as large amounts of data can be stored on a single computer disk. However, computerized records are continually updated by over-writing existing files, which means that historical records may be lost. The survival of computerized records is further threatened by the rapid pace of change in software and hardware, which can make files unreadable.

Not all documents that survive will be available for research purposes. Considerations of confidentiality and official secrecy limit access to state documents, and access to private documents may be even more difficult. State documents often enter the public sphere after a particular period of time has lapsed, this period ranging from thirty years to 150 years, but some documents may be permanently closed. Problems can be even greater in the private sphere. Researchers will often be refused access to household documents such as diaries and letters, for obvious reasons. Unless they are stored in family archives—which is unusual, except among very wealthy families—personal documents tend to be neither available nor catalogued.

The final consideration is the *meaning* of the documents that the researcher wishes to use. This involves both the literal meaning of the document and its interpretation. The literal meaning of a document is its surface or word-for-word meaning. To produce this, the researcher must be able to read the language in which it is written, know the accepted definitions of the words that are used, and be able to understand any dating systems or shorthand conventions. In the case of hand-written documents, of course, the handwriting must be legible if it is to be read at all.

Once a literal reading has been produced, the researcher can go on to the far more complex task of interpretation. This is achieved by grasping the underlying selective point of view from which the individual concepts in a text acquire their meaning. Methods of interpretation are considered more fully in other parts of this book (see especially 'Methods of media research', Chapter 10, pp. 369–70). The two principal methods are quantitative **content analysis** and qualitative **textual analysis**. Content analysis involves counting the number of times that particular words or images appear, while textual analysis concentrates on grasping the qualitative significance of these words and images.

Selection and sampling

It is rarely possible to study all of the people or documents that you are interested in. This means that you will have to rely on a small selection or 'sample' from all of those that might be available. Sampling issues are usually considered only in relation to survey methods, but they are, in fact, applicable to all forms of research. Even where a small number of cases are investigated for qualitative purposes, the researcher must still give some consideration to whether these cases are typical or untypical. Some of the implications of this for documentary research have already been discussed.

Unless a very small social group is being surveyed, it is not usually possible to include a whole population in the study. There are practical limits to the number of people who can be observed, interviewed, telephoned, or sent postal questionnaires. It may be possible to interview a few thousand people, but it is simply not possible to interview all the hundreds of thousands who live in even a small city. The only large-scale studies that do aim to cover a whole population today are the national censuses. These are carried out in Britain just once every ten years and use a very short postal questionnaire. Even this limited task is possible only because the government employs large numbers of full-time and temporary staff to collect and process the data.

> ⬧ *Connections*
>
> We discuss the development of the census and government surveys in Chapter 8, pp. 280–1. You may find it useful to return to this discussion of sampling after you have read that chapter.

In almost all research, then, it is necessary to use a **sample**. A sample is a selection drawn from the population that is being studied. The intention behind sampling is to draw a sample that will allow the researcher to generalize about the population as a whole. Sampling is a relatively recent innovation that resulted from mathematical advances made early in the twentieth century. You do not need to understand very much of the mathematics in order to understand the general principles of sampling.

Sampling rests on a particular branch of statistics called the theory of probability. Mathematical theories of probability concern the calculation of such things as the probability that a tossed coin will come up 'heads' and the probability that you will win the national lottery. Sampling is possible if we can calculate the probability that any sample will be *representative* of the population as a whole. If the probability of drawing a representative sample is the same as the probability of winning the lottery (about one in 14 million), then sampling would not be a very good idea. Fortunately, there are ways of ensuring that the probability of a representative sample is quite high. There will always be a slight chance that the particular sample drawn will give inaccurate results, but it is possible to calculate the likelihood of this and to try to keep it as low as possible.

That is almost all that you need to know about the mathematics of probability theory. All the basic principles of sampling follow from these points. The basic principle is that getting a representative sample depends on whether it is possible to calculate the probabilities involved. When this is possible, the method of sampling is called **probability sampling**. When these kinds of calculation are not possible, other methods of sampling can be used, but these cannot be relied on to the same extent as a

Sampling

There are two types of sampling: probability sampling (where the mathematical properties of the population are known) and non-probability sampling (where these mathematical properties are unknown). The 'population' referred to is a technical term that refers to all the units that are of interest, not just the population of a country. The population may be a collection of organizations or countries, or any subgroup within a country. Statisticians sometimes refer to the population as the *universe*. The main types of sampling that you will encounter are listed below. They are discussed briefly in the text.

Probability samples	Non-probability samples
• simple random	• convenience
• systematic random	• purposive
• stratified random	• snowball
• cluster	• quota
• multi-stage	

probability sample. They may produce perfectly valid results, but it is always difficult to know how confident we can be in them. We will try to explain these ideas a little further.

The basic form of probability sample is the *simple random* sample. In this, respondents or subjects are drawn at random from a complete list of all those in the population. Technically, the list is called a *sampling frame*, and it might be an electoral register, a telephone book, an attendance register, and so on. The basic requirement is that it must be a complete list, though few are perfectly complete. A telephone directory would be an acceptable sampling frame for a survey of telephone subscribers, but it would be little use for a survey of the poor (who tend not to have telephones). In many surveys today, the official postcode address file is used to generate samples of addresses.

The word random does not mean haphazard, though many non-statisticians use it this way. A sample is drawn at random when every member of the population has an equal chance of being selected. This is the same principle that is involved in drawing a playing card from a well-shuffled deck: if the deck is complete (containing fifty-two cards) and has been properly shuffled, then every card has a one in 52 chance of being selected. Similarly, the selection of winning numbers in the lottery is a random process, as every numbered ball has the same chance of being drawn. Simple random samples are often drawn for sociological surveys by using printed tables of random numbers. These

are generated by computer and are printed in books of statistical tables. If each person in the population is assigned a number, then the lists of random numbers allow the researcher to draw a simple random sample of people. Similar considerations apply in documentary research wherever there is a comprehensive list of the relevant documents to be studied. In research on women's magazines, for example, a simple random sample can be drawn by selecting random dates and using the copies of the magazines published on those dates.

A variation on simple random sampling occurs where it is not possible or is impractical to number people or to use random numbers. The so-called *systematic random* sample involves making *one* random choice of starting point in the list and then selecting occurrences on a systematic basis: say, every 10th, 50th, or 100th person. If the population contains 10,000 people, a sample of 100 could be drawn by choosing every 100th person on the list. It is crucial that the list itself should not be organized in any way that is relevant to the topic of the research. An alphabetical list, for example, would be useful for most purposes.

A more complex form of probability sample is the *stratified random* sample. This term is a little confusing, as it has nothing at all to do with the social stratification that we discuss in Chapter 19. In sampling theory, a stratum is simply a group or category that has particular characteristics in common. A population may be stratified into its male and female members, into age groups, or, of course, into social classes. Whatever criterion is used, a stratified random sample involves drawing separate random samples from each of the categories into which the population has been divided. The sampling method is usually devised so that the numbers in each category are reflected in the sample. For example, if there are equal numbers of men and women in the population, there should also be equal numbers in the sample. In some cases, however, extra numbers may be drawn from very small categories. This is most likely if the number that would otherwise appear in the sample is too small to allow any reliable conclusions to be drawn. In general, however, stratified random samples are used to ensure that the sample matches the population in all crucial respects.

In some studies, practical needs lead researchers to adapt these strict procedures. A sample of engineering workers, for example, might be drawn by making a random sample of engineering factories and then choosing all the workers in those factories. This would ensure that the sample is not too geographically dispersed, but it does involve a departure from strict probability principles. The technical term for such a method is *cluster* sampling. This form of sampling is particularly appropriate for ethnographic observation, where a researcher may, for example, make a random selection of organizations or departments and then undertake systematic participant observation of workers in each of the places selected. When this method of cluster sampling is further adapted (for example, by taking a random sample of workers in each factory), the sampling is said to be *multi-stage* sampling.

In many research situations, there is no obvious sampling frame that can be used or compiled. This means that it is not possible to draw random samples. In these circumstances, sociologists must resort to non-probability sampling. In these types of survey, the researcher tries to produce a representative sample but cannot be certain how representative it really is.

One of the most commonly used and, unfortunately, least useful non-probability sampling methods in smaller studies is to build a *convenience* sample. This involves building a sample almost by accident from those who are most conveniently to hand. Interviewing friends and neighbours or standing on a street corner and stopping passers-by are examples. Much ethnographic observation that relies on participant observation is, of necessity, of this type. The participant observer may have to take whatever opportunities there are to carry out the study and may have little chance of making an ideal selection. This method leaves the researcher open to all sorts of bias in the selection of respondents. It is, for example, all too easy to study only those people who look as if they might be helpful or cooperative, and there is no likelihood that they will be at all representative of the target population. This is, in general, a method to avoid, unless there is some way in which the representativeness of a sample can be assessed after the data have been collected. It may, for example, be possible to compare data collected with already known data about the population.

A great improvement is the adoption of *purposive* sampling. Here the researcher deliberately seeks out those who meet the needs of the project. An investigation into student attitudes may involve seeking out students in areas where they are known to live in large numbers. This kind of sampling is often associated with so-called *snowballing* techniques, in which those in an initial sample are asked to name others who might be willing to be approached. The full sample grows with each round of interviews or observations. This type of sampling has been used in studies of deviant or closed groups, where the names of members can be discovered only from those who might help in making contact.

Neither purposive nor snowball samples are useful in most large-scale surveys, and a method that tries to approximate to random sampling is most often used. This is the method of the *quota* sample. This is superficially similar to stratified random sampling, but it does not involve any statistically random procedures. In quota sampling the population is divided into categories that are known to be

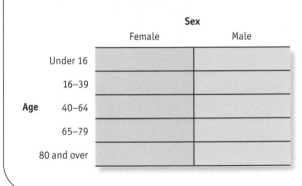

Figure 3.4 A grid for a quota sample

important and for which it is possible to get some basic information. A population might be divided by age and sex, for example, making it possible to construct a grid, as shown in Figure 3.4.

Using data from a census or a similar source, it is possible to work out how the whole population is distributed across the cells in the grid. In 2000, for example, males aged 16–29 comprised 9.2 per cent of the population of the United Kingdom, while females aged 16–29 comprised 8.7 per cent. A researcher seeking a representative sample would try to ensure that 9.2 per cent of the sample were young men and 8.7 per cent were young women. If a sample of 5,000 was to be drawn, it would need to contain 460 young men and 435 young women. These target numbers are the quotas that need to be filled, and the total quota is divided up into separate quotas for each interviewer. In such a survey, interviewers are given strict instructions that they must stop people in the street or call at houses until they achieve their particular quota.

The method of quota sampling is very widely used in large-scale surveys, as it is an economical and efficient way of achieving a sample that matches the broad and known features of a population. The actual individuals chosen, however, are not randomly selected and so it is not strictly legitimate to apply certain statistical measures to the results.

The aim of any method of sampling is to achieve a representative sample. It may fail to achieve this for two reasons. First, the sample itself may not be drawn at random. This is termed *sampling bias*. Secondly, a random sample may differ, by chance, from a truly representative sample. This is termed *sampling error*. This distinction is very important. Sampling error falls as the size of a sample increases, but this is not true of sampling bias. No matter how large a sample may be, if it has not been drawn at random it may be biased. The advantage of using a probability sample is that, if properly random methods are used, bias can be ignored and its representativeness can accurately be measured by the sampling error alone. These calculations are quite complex, and are purely technical. As a general rule, it has been found that increases in sample size above about 2,500 have little effect on the sampling error, regardless of the size of the population. For this reason, even national population samples rarely need to go above this level.

Statistics defines the ideal qualities that a sample should possess. In practice, it is difficult to meet these criteria. In actual research projects, corners have to be cut and *ad hoc* adjustments need to be made if any research at all is to be possible. Statistical purism would make research impossible. For this reason, it is important to be suspicious whenever a great battery of statistical tests and measures is reported. In some cases these may be precise reports on surveys using probability sampling, but in many other cases they are, at best, a rough-and-ready guide to how much reliance can be placed on the data. Many large-scale quota surveys, for example, cite measures of sampling error that should not, strictly, be taken seriously.

The basic problem with any sampling procedure is the problem of non-response. As we have shown, a sample has a **bias** if it is not truly representative of the population. The aim of probability sampling, and of quota sampling, is to minimize the bias in the sample. This assumes, however, that all those who are drawn in the sample will actually cooperate. In fact, a great many of those who are selected refuse to cooperate with the survey. The proportion of the sample who respond is called the **response rate**. Non-response can result from direct refusals and because people are away from home or cannot be contacted.

A certain level of non-response is acceptable and need not mean that the remaining sample will be biased. In practice, it is very difficult to achieve more than a 75 per cent response rate, meaning that virtually all surveys will involve a degree of bias. If the response rate falls below 60 per cent (i.e. more than 40 per cent of the sample are non-responders), the results cannot usually be relied on with any certainty.

It is important to note that a representative sample may often not be possible to secure. In the case of much documentary research, for example, the researcher must study those documents that happen to have survived and are available for study. This does not necessarily reduce the value of the research. What is important is that the unrepresentative character of the documents be realized and taken into account in the analysis of the results. Knowing how unrepresentative or untypical is your sample becomes the first step towards a realistic assessment of its value for your research purposes.

‹› *Stop and reflect*

In this section we have looked at the issues that arise in survey research, ethnographic research, and documentary research. We have also considered the issues of sampling that are common to all of these forms of research.

Survey research involves the use of a questionnaire to study the behaviour, attitudes, or opinions of a sample of respondents. Distinctions can be made between interview surveys, postal surveys, and telephone surveys.

- Questionnaire design involves a complex process of evaluation in which questions are drafted and modified in the light of practical tests.
- How many of the ten key points for good questionnaire design can you recall? (Check your answers on p. 82.)

Ethnographic research involves observations and conversations aimed at understanding the meanings of social actions and social situations.

- Ethnographic observation may be overt or covert and observers can take one of three research roles: complete participant, participant-as-observer, and complete observer.

- Ethnographic interviewing is semi-structured, rather than questionnaire-based. Effective interviewing relies on good interpersonal skills.
- Are ethnography and survey research completely opposed approaches to sociological investigation?

Documentary research is based on the use of written texts of all kinds.

- Documents may be personal or public documents, and the researcher may be granted varying degrees of access.
- Documents must be assessed in relation to the criteria of authenticity, credibility, representativeness, and meaning.
- Why do sociologists make so much use of documents in their research?

Whichever of these three forms of research is pursued, a number of issues in sampling must be considered.

- It is rarely possible to study all the individuals, locations, or documents that interest you. It will always be necessary to select, or to sample, in some way.

- A sample is drawn from a larger population, of which it is supposed to be representative. The most important distinction is that between probability and non-probability sampling methods.

- Within each of the methods of sampling there are a number of different types of sample: the simple random

sample, the systematic random sample, the stratified random sample, the cluster and multi-stage sample, the convenience sample, the purposive sample, and the quota sample.

- Is it ever possible to disregard issues of sampling in social research?

Displaying and using data

We have shown that research design involves constructing a researchable project from theoretical ideas. Theories are systems of concepts that are connected together through logical reasoning and that may be translatable into models and hypotheses. If models and hypotheses are to guide empirical research, the concepts must be converted into *variables*. That is, a concept must be turned into something that is measurable. This is generally seen as a process of **operationalization**, of specifying the operations needed to produce evidence relevant to the concept. A concept that is successfully operationalized, then, is specified in terms of a number of quite specific empirical indicators and measures.

Anomie, for example, was a central concept for both Durkheim and Merton. But how do we know when we have observed a situation of anomie? Unless specific indicators of anomie are set out, we cannot do so. It was for this reason that Durkheim defined anomie as an absence of normative regulation, but took such things as a lack of religious affiliation and being unmarried as indicators of this.

When a concept has been defined in terms of a set of indicators that can be used in empirical research, it is said to have been transformed into a variable. A variable consists of a concept and its indicator(s). The concept is the idea, and the indicator is the item or items on which relevant empirical data can be collected. An example of this, which we look at more fully in 'Technology and the meaning of work', Chapter 17, pp. 679–80, is the Marxist concept of alienation. Seeman (1959) took Marx's ideas about alienation and developed them into a set of measurable indicators that Blauner (1964) went on to explore in his study of work relations (see the criticism of this in Lukes 1967).

The two fundamental issues that arise in the operationalization of concepts are validity and reliability. When an indicator has been devised that gives a theoretically acceptable measure of a concept, the indicator is said to be *valid*. When the indicator can be used to generate reproducible results, it is said to be *reliable*. Blauner (1964) claimed to have produced a reliable indicator of alienation, but his Marxist critics claimed that he had failed to produce a valid one. No matter how reliable an indicator may be, if it does not relate properly to the concept that it is supposed

to measure it will be of little use. Blauner produced some valuable information about work satisfaction and work attitudes, but he did not really address the theoretical issues that Marx referred to in his discussion of alienation.

Operationalization has led to the construction of relatively uncontentious indicators of such things as urban and rural contexts, employment and self-employment, church membership, voting intention, and many other concrete concepts. It is far more difficult, however, to operationalize the more basic sociological concepts. Lukes (1974) has suggested that it is difficult to arrive at an operationalization of a concept such as power, because there are so many different views of what power is. Similar problems arise with such concepts as class, patriarchy, and ethnicity. As we show in Chapter 8, even such concepts as health, illness, and mental health are difficult to define in uncontentious ways.

The difficulty in producing valid and reliable indicators of sociological concepts has been taken by some philosophers as a sign that sociology is not scientific. If Marx's concepts, for example, cannot be given operational definitions, then Marxism cannot be a scientific theory (Popper 1959). Countering this view, Marxists and others have decried what they have called the positivist view of science. By this, they mean an approach that seeks to reduce all theoretical and conceptual issues to measurable and, perhaps, quantifiable indicators (Adorno *et al.* 1969).

However, a positive science—in the sense in which this term was used by Comte and Durkheim—need not be as narrowly quantitative as this implies. It is important to recognize that conceptual differences are an essential feature of social life. This is true for all the concepts and variables that we use. Much research, for example, makes use of the concept of sex, and we show in Chapter 5 that there are important theoretical issues surrounding the study of sex. The use of categories of ethnic origin, even if they are not presented as 'racial' categories, involve many similar issues (Burgess 1986). Even the category of age—used almost as widely in official statistics as sex—is far from straightforward, as chronologically defined categories rarely correspond to socially constructed concepts of age (Pilcher 1995).

One of the most problematic, and most widely discussed, concepts is social class. This has been used in official statistics as a routine way of summarizing occupational and employment data so that their effects on fertility, mortality, and health can be assessed. It has also been used as a fundamental concept in sociological studies on education, religion, family relations, crime, media viewing, language, and so on. The official categories of social class, though frequently used in sociological work, do not correspond in any straightforward way to any of the theoretically sophisticated concepts of social class that are current in sociology. This raises important questions about their validity and about the operationalization of sociological concepts in general. In Chapter 19, pp. 780–5, we will illustrate this through a detailed consideration of the operationalization of class and its use as a key variable in the analysis of sociological data. In the remainder of this chapter we will look at some of the practicalities of using sociological classifications and presenting sociological data. Finally, we will consider how, in the light of all this, it is possible to make use of official statistics.

Presenting data

Through the conversion of concepts into variables, sociologists are able to collect the data that they need for their research. Once these data have been collected, however, they must be organized and presented in ways that highlight their relevance for the theoretical interests that inform the research design. We are not able to look at the many specialist techniques that are available to sociologists for doing this. We can, however, look at some of the procedures that will be most relevant to you when you try to understand the results of sociological research. We will look, in particular, at the ways in which data can be presented in tables and in charts, two different ways of trying to summarize sociological data. We will also, but very briefly, consider some of the statistical measures that you may come across.

Reading a table

The best way to approach the question of how to construct a table is to consider how to read one. Tables can be quite daunting, as many people are—quite unnecessarily—frightened by numbers. There is no need for this. A table can be read in exactly the same way as a piece of prose. You simply need to know where to start.

Look at Figure 3.5 for a few moments. Where did you look first? The chances are that you glanced down the left-hand side and then across some of the numbers. This is the wrong thing to do. The first thing that you should do when reading any table is to *read the title*. This is obvious when you think about it, but people tend to ignore the obvious when it comes to tables.

The title of this table is 'A table to read', but below this you will see the original title as it appeared in *Social Trends*. This tells you that it concerns 'AIDS cases' and 'HIV-1 infected persons' and that it looks at these in relation to 'probable exposure' and 'gender'. It also tells you that the data refer to 1995. We already know quite a lot about the table, just from its title. If you are not familiar with any of the terms used in a title, you should check back through the text or consult other sources to check them out. For example, in this case you would need to know, in general terms, what AIDS is, what HIV is, and how exposure and gender are likely to be relevant. In most cases, this will be obvious to you from the content of the book or article that you are reading. In the case of this example table, of course, this may not be the case, as we have introduced it out of its original context.

The next thing that you should do is look for any notes about the table. These are usually underneath it. In this case, you will see that one of the notes relates specifically to the title. This note clarifies something about the date to which the information relates. A second note merely clarifies one of the headings in the table, so we do not need to worry about this for the moment. The final note is one that gives the original source of the data (ignore our own 'Source' reference to *Social Trends* 1996). This is often a very useful piece of information. The original source information in this table tells you that the data were produced by a centre that monitors 'communicable diseases', another term that you will need to understand. (PHLS is the Public Health Laboratory Service, though the table does not actually tell you this.) In many cases, these notes will give you some useful definitions or may give you details of any sampling method.

You can now turn to the main body of the table: but do not look at any numbers yet. Look at the headings along the top and down the left-hand side of the table. Immediately under the title you are told that the data relate to the 'United Kingdom' (not England, not Scotland, not even Great Britain, but the United Kingdom as a whole). You are also told that they are 'numbers'. It might seem obvious that the data are numbers, but this is stated in order to make it clear that you are being given the actual numbers and not percentage figures.

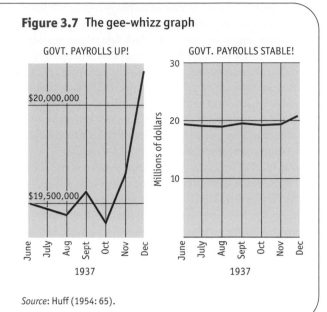

Figure 3.7 The gee-whizz graph

GOVT. PAYROLLS UP!

GOVT. PAYROLLS STABLE!

Source: Huff (1954: 65).

with which sociologists deal and they are essential to the overall picture that sociologists try to construct. Official statistics are a relatively cheap and plentiful source of data. They are constructed in ways that, in general, make it possible to assess their reliability and validity, and they are often available on a regular basis over long periods of time. For all of these reasons, sociologists have made a great deal of use of them.

There has, however, been much discussion of the very serious problems that they involve. Criminal statistics, for example, are held to underestimate the real level of crime, unemployment statistics to underestimate the actual number of people who are out of work, and so on. For some, these problems are so great that the whole idea of using statistics to study real social processes has been rejected. Indeed, some interactionists and ethnomethodologists claim that there is no such thing as a real rate of crime, unemployment, or suicide. They argue that all rates depend on definitions that are socially constructed. If this is so, the idea of using official statistics to measure them cannot make sense (Cicourel 1964; Douglas 1967; from a different theoretical perspective, see the similar point made in Hindess 1973).

These critics undoubtedly have some important arguments on their side. Suicide statistics, for example, depend on the ways in which coroners, police, and others classify deaths. This does not, however, mean that rates cannot be constructed or used. What it does mean is that whenever we use such a rate it is vital to be clear about the definitions that have been used in its construction.

Differences in rates still require explanation, and the different definitions that have been used may provide a part of that explanation. It is also possible to control, at least in part, for differences of definition. This is how Durkheim examined not only differences between countries but also differences between areas within countries. Important questions still arise, however, about how these rates might be explained. We might ask, for example, whether Durkheim's (1897) particular conclusions were valid, but the reality of suicide cannot seriously be questioned (J. M. Atkinson 1978).

Despite the problems involved in the use of official statistics, we will try to show that they remain an essential part of the sociological toolbox. So long as we are *aware* of their limitations, we can try to overcome them or, at least, be honest about the limits on the conclusions that we draw from the statistics. The problems of official statistics are, in fact, no greater than the problems of using participant observation or historical documents. One of the most valuable things that a sociologist can do is to *combine* various types of data in a single piece of research. The limitations of any one source would, wherever possible, be compensated by the advantages of another.

> ⊃ *Connections*
> If the word 'triangulation' did not spring to your mind at this point, read our discussion of combining research methods on p. 76.

Official statistics of crime

The limitations of official statistics have been most comprehensively explored in relation to statistics on crime. It does make sense to talk about rates of crime—the numbers of rapes, murders, or burglaries—and it is important to try to measure these rates. However, the available criminal statistics provide wholly inadequate measures of these rates. The criminal statistics include only those offences that are 'known to the police'. Many offences are simply not reported to the police and so do not appear in the statistics.

The rate of reporting varies quite considerably from one type of crime to another. Offences that are seen as relatively minor, such as dropping litter in a public place, may be regarded as annoying, but they are not seen as worth reporting to the police. Most murders, on the other hand, are likely to be reported, as it is an offence that is generally regarded as serious, and, in any case, it is difficult to conceal a dead body for any period of time. Rape is far less likely to be reported. While it is undoubtedly regarded as a serious crime, many women victims of rape prefer not to face police questioning. The prospect of an interrogation in court, particularly when the likelihood of a successful prosecution is seen as fairly low, discourages many from reporting their rapes.

These remarks bring out the fact that victims and others make assessments of the likely consequences of reporting crimes. They try to judge whether the police will take the report seriously, or will simply file it away and get on with other business. Similarly, they try to assess the chances that the police will solve the crime and bring the offender to book. Detection rates for many crimes are very low, and victims may simply not think it worth reporting them. Burglaries, for example, have a low detection rate, and it is largely due to pressure from insurance companies that householders report burglaries. Insurance companies will not consider a claim for any burglary that has not been reported, and so those who wish to claim on their policy must report it, no matter how unlikely they think it is that the offender will be apprehended. Where householders have not insured their property, reporting rates for burglary are low.

Victims and others also take account of whether detected offenders are likely to be charged, rather than given a warning, and, if charged, whether they are likely to be convicted in court. Where these probabilities are seen to be low, as they are for many kinds of crime, reporting is also likely to be low.

Considerations such as these lead many people to talk about the 'hidden figure' or **dark figure** of crime. Crimes known to the police are merely the tip of an iceberg (see Figure 3.8), and there is an unknown amount of unreported crime that remains invisible in official statistics. The size of the dark figure varies from one kind of crime to another. In the case of murder, for example, it is likely to be very small, while in the case of traffic speeding it is likely to be very high. One of the major problems in research on crime is the unknown size of the dark figure. It is also very difficult to assess whether those crimes that are reported to the police are a representative sample of all crimes. If they are, then it is possible to discover some important characteristics of crime and criminals from the criminal statistics. If we do not know whether they are a representative sample, then any conclusions drawn from the criminal statistics may be unfounded.

One of the ways in which this problem has been addressed in the sociology of crime is through self-report and victim studies. In self-report studies, people are asked whether they have ever committed particular offences. In victim studies, they are asked whether they have ever been the victims of particular kinds of crime. Such studies have helped to quantify the dark figure and to show how crime statistics can be used. Recent research has suggested that, overall, only 47 per cent of all offences are reported to the police, and only 27 per cent are recorded by them. Just 2 per cent of all offences result in the conviction of an offender. However, the broad *trends* in crime rates are, for the most part, accurately reflected in the statistics.

On this basis, Lea and Young have concluded that criminal statistics 'have to be interpreted with extreme caution. It is not that they are meaningless; they do reflect public, police and court definitions of crime, the disposal of limited resources and the extent of infractions thus defined; but what they do not do is tell about an independent entity called "crime"' (Lea and Young 1984: 15). If the limitations of the criminal statistics are fully recognized, this helps us to make a proper and sensitive use of them (Maguire 1994).

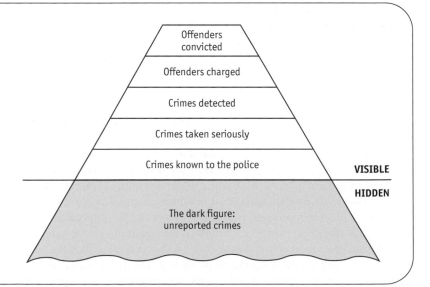

Figure 3.8 Reported and unreported crimes

social identities

PART TWO

socialization, identity, and interaction

Contents

04

Attachment disorder

When he was 5 years old, Mike was adopted by a couple who already had children of their own. His adoptive parents loved him and looked after him along with their other children, and he seemed to settle in well to family life and to school. However, his parents and teachers began to notice worrying things about his behaviour, though they tried to see these as 'normal' and as just part of growing up: he talked constantly about TV programmes, he told lies, he hurt the family pet, he did not like family members showing affection to one another but not to him, he found it difficult to make friends, he stole from his mothers' purse, and he acquired the belongings of other children. By the time that he was 12 his parents were so concerned that they took him to a child psychiatrist, but no problems were discovered. Then, when he was 14, he was found to have been sexually abusing his younger sister and was referred for social work assessment. His social workers discovered that he, too, had been sexually abused in a children's home before he was adopted, and they classed him as a low risk of re-offending. Problems continued and eventually Mike was diagnosed as having an attachment disorder. His psychiatrist said that Mike's relationship to his birth mother had been weak and inadequate. As a result, Mike engaged in behaviour that he thought would bring him some attention from those around him. His adoptive parents could find no treatment for him that they could afford, and they feared that he would end up in prison.

Source: *Guardian*, 17 April 2002.

How important are early family attachments in ensuring that children grow up to become acceptable and well-integrated members of their society, and how typical is Mike of those who are deprived of these close relationships? These questions depend on an understanding of the processes of socialization through which people learn what those in their society expect of them and how to act in autonomous ways. In this chapter, we will look at this through considering socialization, identity formation, and interaction. We show how these processes are central not only to understanding problems of 'attachment disorder' but also to *all* the actions and experiences through which people's lives are organized. Family life, education, and work all depend upon particular patterns of socialization through which people build a picture of their social world and of their own place within it.

Understanding socialization, identity, and interaction

One of the most striking things about human behaviour is that most of the things that we do are learned. While much that an animal does is determined by its biology, very little human behaviour is instinctive or fixed in this way. Children come into the world as helpless infants, and they develop into slightly less helpless adults only because they learn from their parents and from other adults how to speak, study, work, marry, vote, pray, steal, and do all the many other things with which people fill their time. All of these activities must be learned.

Animals do, of course, learn as well. Birds, for example, must learn how to fly. Many animals can even be trained by human beings to do things that are not 'natural' to them—dogs can be house trained and they can also be taught to sit up and beg for food. The dependence of human beings on learned behaviour, however, is fundamentally different from anything else that is found in the animal kingdom. While some aspects of human behaviour do have similarities with animal behaviour—particularly with that of monkeys and the higher primates—the greater part of human behaviour is qualitatively distinct from all other animal behaviour. Human beings learn to be conscious agents, capable of reflecting upon their own behaviour and of modifying it in the light of their experiences. It is this conscious, subjective element in human conduct that makes it more appropriate to describe it as 'action' than as mere 'behaviour'. Action is behaviour to which a subjective meaning has been attached and which can, therefore, be reflexively monitored by a human actor. To be a person is to *act*, not simply to behave.

This point is not always fully appreciated, and many non-sociologists have held that human behaviour can be explained in purely biological terms. As a result, the relative merits of biology and sociology have been hotly debated, though often with considerable misunderstanding on each side of the argument.

The precise relationship between biology and culture has been a matter of contention, with advocates of the most extreme positions tending to dominate the debates. For much of the nineteenth century and well into the twentieth century, the advocates of **biological determinism** held sway. Biological determinists hold that all aspects of human behaviour can be explained in terms of the universal and innate characteristics that people have as human beings. These claims have been further developed in recent years by advances in the understanding of genetics. Biological determinism has once more been forcefully promoted, most notably in the new scientific specialisms of sociobiology and evolutionary psychology.

The fundamental limitation to biological explanations of human behaviour is that, as action, it is meaningful, and not simply instinctive or reactive. Social life involves interactions through which people take account of each other's behaviour in determining their own behaviour. There is a conscious reflection on the meaning of the other's behaviour and on its significance for our own future actions. Georg Simmel called this interaction a process of 'sociation' so as to emphasize that it was the means through which all social phenomena are produced. In sociation we try to understand the actions of others, and they try to understand ours. Interaction, then, involves the establishment of mutual knowledge that allows us to predict with a greater or lesser degree of accuracy what is likely to happen in any particular situation.

This mutual knowledge consists of expectations about the kinds of things that others will or ought to do: it consists of *norms* of behaviour. A norm is a more or less conscious expectation that someone will 'normally' act in one way or another. It is a rule of behaviour, and it may be a formal prescription such as a law or moral principle or it may be a more informal expectation about what is typically likely to occur.

Norms and the larger systems of ideas and symbols that people use to understand their own and other people's behaviour comprise the **culture** of a society. Culture is learned and is quite variable from one society to another. To know how to behave in any particular society, people must be socialized into its culture. They must learn how to understand the other people that they will encounter and, in particular, they must learn the norms that prevail and that will shape their interactions.

The importance of culture in human life led some sociologists and anthropologists to formulate a position of **cultural determinism** as a counter-doctrine to biological determinism. A central figure in the promotion of cultural determinism was Margaret Mead, an anthropologist whose views we will look at later in this chapter. She undertook a series of studies that seemed to show the infinite variability of human behaviour from one culture to another and that were therefore taken as firmly establishing the claims of cultural determinism. Recently, however, some of the key elements in her account have been questioned. The way has been opened for a more sophisticated understanding of the interdependence of culture and biology, an understanding that avoids the extreme deterministic theories that have been advocated on both sides of the debate.

Identity and socialization

Human beings are social animals, and the process through which someone learns how to be a member of a particular society is termed **socialization**. It is through socialization that people acquire their culture, their specific skills and abilities, and a knowledge of what kinds of people they are. People continue to learn throughout their lives, but the first few years of life are critical. Through their interactions with others, infants gradually become aware of themselves as 'individuals'. They come to see themselves as conscious and reflective entities—agents or subjects—capable of independent and autonomous action. Central to this growing awareness is a child's conception of him or herself as a person. Without close social relationships with other people during these early years, children will fail to learn how to interact and to communicate. For ethical reasons, it is impossible to produce direct evidence for this claim by depriving human infants of social experience in an experiment. Nevertheless, evidence from observations of those children who have, for one reason or another, been brought up in isolation from normal human contact shows this to be the case. Such children may, in later life, learn basic table manners and toilet behaviour, but they have no real ability to use or to understand normal language, and they have only a very limited ability to engage in normal social interaction.

A distinction can be made between primary socialization and secondary socialization. **Primary socialization** is that which takes place in infancy and childhood, typically within a family or a small household of carers. This early socialization provides the foundation for all later learning. Through their interaction with parents or carers, children are able to learn a great deal about what it is to be a member of their particular society. They also learn such specific skills as the ability to speak their own language and to interact and communicate with others.

Secondary socialization begins in later childhood, when children begin to interact more frequently outside the household and with people other than their parents. Interacting with other children and with teachers at school,

they begin to learn a broader range of social skills and to acquire a more detailed knowledge of roles outside the family. As they get older, much of this interaction takes place beyond the direct control of their parents. During adolescence, the peer group of other adolescents becomes a particularly important agency of socialization. Secondary socialization runs parallel with formal education in contemporary societies, but much socialization takes place outside the school—for example, in clubs and on the street corner—and it continues into adult life. In a very real sense, human beings are still being socialized into their society, learning new things about it, until the very moment of their death.

Self and society

It is through socialization that a person acquires a sense of social identity and an image of his or herself as a person. People attribute personality characteristics of all sorts to themselves, and the others with whom they come into contact also define their characters and their actions in various ways. When someone is defined, or labelled, as a specific *type* of person, it can be said that a **social identity** has been attributed to him or her. A social identity, then, is a particular label that has been applied in order to indicate the type of person that someone is. As a result of the label, that person may take on the label and interact with others in terms of that identity. They may even come to feel that they *are* that kind of person.

Social identities do not refer to specific, discrete personality characteristics (such as cleverness, honesty, or reliability), though any of these may be involved in an identity. They are, rather, clusters of personality characteristics and attributes that are linked to particular social roles, categories, or groups. Examples of commonly employed social identities in contemporary societies include such labels as woman, child, father, Asian, Jew, doctor, teacher, clerk, mechanic, homosexual, drug-taker, and so on. Some of these identities are based around clearly defined occupational roles, some relate to more general social positions, and others correspond more to stereotypes than to actual roles. Nevertheless, each designates a particular type of real or imagined person, to whom particular moral characteristics and social abilities are imputed, and with whom people may identify themselves or be identified by others.

Someone identifies with a particular social type—or is identified in this way by others—when there is a feeling that the type adequately describes certain enduring features of his or her life. A social identity is regarded as being somehow fundamental to a person's whole way of being: it is what the person *is*, above all else. It should not be assumed, however, that people can identify themselves in

 Briefing: wild children

Kamala (about 8 years old) and Amala (about 1½) were discovered in India in 1920, living as part of a pack of wolves. After their rescue they were seen to walk on all fours, to eat and drink with their mouths, directly from the plate, and at night they howled. No one knows how they came to live with wolves rather than in a human group. Amala did not survive the discovery for long. She died within a year. Kamala, however, lived to be 18. By the time that he died, he had learned to walk upright and to wear clothes, but he had learned to speak only a few words.

A boy called Ramu, also discovered living with wolves, was taken to an orphanage run by Mother Theresa. He continued to hunt chickens at night but, although he learned to dress, he never learned to speak before he died, aged 10, in 1985.

The truth of these accounts of 'wild children' has been questioned, but evidence from the case of Genie, an American child, supports the general position. Genie was systematically abused by her parents and was kept away from any social contact until the age of 13. Despite being taken into care and given physical attention and social support, Genie has never learned to speak and lives in a residential home.

Source: Gleiman (1995: 73–80).

only one way. In contemporary societies, in particular, people are likely to identify themselves in a number of ways. They can be said to have multiple identities. Because of the various roles or positions that she has, for example, a woman may see herself as a woman, an Asian, *and* a doctor. Multiple identification has become more common. Instead of identifying exclusively with one particular type of person—a worker, for example—people are now more likely to identify with a variety of social types. They may shift from one identity to another according to the situation or context in which they are acting and the roles that they take on. A man may, for example, regard himself as being a teacher when he is at work, a father when he is at home, and a Labour activist when he is involved in local politics.

We will often refer to social identity simply as identity, but this is a little ambiguous. The word 'identity' is widely used to refer both to what we call social identity and to the related idea of personal identity. A social identity marks people out as, in certain respects, *the same as* others. A **personal identity** marks someone out as a *unique* and quite distinct individual. Central to a personal identity is a personal name. Personal names are attempts to individualize and so distinguish from all other people with whom a person may share one or more social identities. It is, for most people, the most immediate and important marker of personal identity.

Having a personal name marks out our individuality as a unique person. In fact, of course, few names are actually unique, as even a cursory examination of any telephone directory will show. Nevertheless, even those with quite common names regard them as being their personal property, and they can be quite disconcerted to come across other people with the same name. People feel, in the words of the football chant, that 'there's only one . . .'. A name is closely tied to other markers of individuality: signature, fingerprints, photograph, address, birth certificate, and various official identification numbers (R. Jenkins 1996: chapter 7). Where names are shared within a family or group, pet names or nicknames are often used to differentiate people and to emphasize their individuality.

Personal identity is the link between the concepts of social identity and self. Social identities are, in principle, *shared* with others. There are, for example, large numbers of people who might identify themselves as men, as English, or as engineers. The word **self**, on the other hand, is used to distinguish a person's sense of her or his own uniqueness or individuality. A sense of self is built up when people reflect on their personal history and construct a biography of how they came to be the people that they are. They grasp their various social identities and characteristics and unify them into a conception of what is particular or peculiar about them as an individual (Strauss 1959:

 ## Briefing: what is an individual?

Social identity is a person's sense of the type of person that he or she is: man, woman, black, white, tinker, tailor, soldier, sailor. Personal identity, on the other hand, is a person's sense of his or her own individuality and uniqueness and is marked by a name, personal appearance, identification numbers, and so on. A sense of self is the particular image that is associated with a personal identity, the defining characteristic of individuality. It is how people see themselves and how others see them.

The British government has announced its intention to introduce identity cards with unique identification numbers. Such cards were used during the Second World War, and have often been advocated since then. The government has proposed credit card-style identity cards that would ensure entitlements to welfare benefits and hospital treatment. Supporters of civil liberties have seen this as a fundamental threat to freedom and individuality, and a sociological study has highlighted its costs (**http://is.lse.ac.uk/idcard/identityreport.pdf**).

This kind of threat has often been explored in popular television programmes. The cult 1960s television series, *The Prisoner*, depicted the attempt by an all-pervasive power to subject the prisoner, 'Number Six' (played by Patrick McGoohan), to its control. The Prisoner was confined to a self-contained village from which escape seemed impossible. Control was exercised by a constantly changing 'Number Two', subject to an unseen 'Number One'. The prisoner's constant response to attempts to control him is 'I am not a number, I am an individual'.

The more recent television series *Star Trek: Voyager* explored this theme through the character 'Seven of Nine' (played by Jeri Ryan). Originally a member of the Borg collective, where individuality does not exist, this 'drone' was designated simply as the seventh of nine members in a particular work group—her full Borg designation was 'Seven of Nine, Tertiary Adjunct of Unimatrix Zero One'. Liberated from the collective by the Voyager crew, Seven of Nine was given a crash course of secondary socialization into the nature of individuality and her Borg designation was transformed into a personal name: her familiar name among the crew became simply 'Seven'.

❓ *Why are numbers seen as more anonymous and less individual than names?*

➦ *You will find a cultural analysis of the* Star Trek *series in Barrett and Barrett (2001).*

144–7). Only in very extreme situations where a person has a single, all-encompassing identity might a social identity and a sense of self coincide.

The sense of individuality that is central to the idea of the self is obvious from the importance that is attached to markers of personal identity in modern societies. This highlights a very significant social change. In many pre-modern societies, identities were collective and corporate. People had little sense of their own individuality. They had *public* social identities—as citizens, peasants, and lords, for example—but they had no real sense of a *private self* that was separate from these social identities. Their whole existence was tied up in the collective life that they shared with others around them. This identification with the group is fundamental to what Durkheim called mechanical solidarity.

As societies have become more complex and diversified, so a greater sense of individuality has emerged. Durkheim (1893) saw this growth of individualism as a central feature of the spread of modernity. In societies with a growing sense of individuality, there is a greater tendency to use the idea of the self. Personal names become more important as ways of distinguishing among different individuals. The development of individual names, then, is a comparatively recent feature of human history. In England, for example, it was not until the twelfth or thirteenth centuries that sur-names came into use for the majority of the population.

Gender and ethnicity interact in social identity.
© Alice Chadwick

Primary and secondary identities

The moment of birth is, in contemporary societies, the point at which social identities are first ascribed to individuals. The period of preparation for birth may, of course, involve some anticipation of the child's identity: bedrooms may be decorated, clothes bought, and so on. Not until birth, however, can a true identity be given to the child. A newborn infant is immediately identified as being a boy or a girl and, soon afterwards, is given a name. The baby's sex and name, together with the names of his or her parents, are officially recorded by a government official, and they are often announced and affirmed in a religious service. Infants are not, of course, in a position to respond to these

imputed social and personal identities—certainly not in any conscious or reflexive way—and will have little choice about them. Both the given identity and the official record are likely to remain with them throughout their life. A married woman who adopts her husband's name does so only by convention and custom, and only her 'maiden name' is shown on the marriage certificate.

Through the period of primary socialization, in infancy and childhood, the core social identities are added to. Children gradually take a more active part in the construction of their social identities. It is through these processes of primary socialization that **primary identities** of personhood, gender, and, perhaps, ethnicity are built up (R. Jenkins 1996: 62).

Personhood is a sense of selfhood and human-ness. It is something that develops quite early in infancy, but it does so only very gradually. The newborn child's first active role in determining its own identity comes as it develops a conception of its own personhood. An infant only gradually learns that it exists as something separate from its surroundings. Similarly, it slowly learns that it is capable of making things happen, that it is capable of being an agent. This involves learning a sense of difference.

> **⊃ Connections**
>
> The sexual identification of a newborn infant is not always straightforward, as we show in the opening section of Chapter 5, p. 155, where a case of intersexual identity is considered. Running through Chapter 5 you will find a discussion of the relationship between sex and gender identity.

The child learns that it is different from its cot and its toys, and that it is different from its parents. It also learns, however, that it shares certain characteristics with its parents. These shared characteristics separate the child not only from inanimate objects but also from the family pet and from other animals. In these ways, the infant begins to learn an initial sense of self and of its own human status: it learns that it is a person. This begins to develop prior to the acquisition of any language, and it seems to be a crucial precondition for developing a linguistic competence. It is, however, massively extended once a language is acquired. The sense of personhood develops rapidly as a child's language abilities expand during the second year of its life.

When a child becomes aware that it is a person, its parents or carers can begin to solidify those other social identities that they have made and recorded for it. These identities are those which the parents regard as being important defining characteristics of their own identities and circumstances. Most important among these is a gender identity—being masculine or feminine. This gender identity shapes the ways in which the parents act towards their child. Clothes, toys, and the use of language, for example, are all differentiated by gender from the very earliest hours of a child's life. In due course, gender also shapes the way that the child will act him or herself.

Closely linked to gender identity is a child's identity within its family or household. When learning that it is a boy or a girl, it typically learns that it is a child and, moreover, that it is the child of a particular mother and father. Through its parents, it may learn that it is a brother or sister, that it is a grandchild, a nephew, and so on. All of these aspects of its gendered kinship identity define it genealogically within a particular family.

An ethnic identity—membership in a particular cultural group that is defined by 'race', religion, or language—is likely to be ascribed to a child in its early years whenever ethnicity is salient to its parents and those with whom they interact. In contemporary Britain, for example, being black is highly salient for most people of African or African-Caribbean background. It is something that their children learn very early on. Being white, on the other hand, is not so salient to members of the majority ethnic group. It is not widely employed by them as a personal marker, and many white children do not learn to see themselves as being white. Where ethnicity is salient, an ethnic identity is learned as an integral part of a gendered family identity. In these circumstances, it might be said, ethnicity is an aspect of genealogy.

Primary identities are far more stable than those that are acquired later in life. As Richard Jenkins argues:

> Identities entered into early in life are encountered as more authoritative than those acquired subsequently. At most, a child can only muster a weak response of internal definition to modify or customise them. Taken on during the most foundational learning period, they become part of the individual's axiomatic cognitive furniture, 'the way things are'. Very young children lack the competence to counter successfully their external identification by others. They have limited reserves of experience and culture with which to question or resist, even were they disposed to. And they may not: during and before the process of language acquisition the human learning predisposition leaves the individual open to forceful and consequential definition by others. (R. Jenkins 1996: 62)

As the child grows up, it usually comes to think of its primary, ascribed identities as being fixed and all but unalterable. Some aspects of personal identity can be altered: given names may be shortened or modified into nicknames, and people have a certain degree of freedom to modify their name in relation to what they perceive to be its image or connotation. A man may, for example, prefer to be known as James rather than Jim, or Mick rather than Michael. This freedom rarely stretches to a complete change of name, though the law generally permits this. Parenthood and sex, however, are much more likely to be treated as permanent and unchangeable. They are seen as natural and normal features of the way the world is. Changes in these matters are likely to be seen as unthinkable or as extremely difficult, if not impossible. Despite some widely publicized court cases, it is difficult for a child to 'divorce' his or her parents, though disowning parents is slightly more common. Only a very few individuals ever reconsider their gender identity, and few of these go so far as to seek medical treatment to change or correct their sexual characteristics. Those who do, will often experience great difficulties in convincing others of their new social identity, and they may face very great difficulties in altering some aspects of their personal identity. It may be very difficult—often impossible—for example, to change the details that are recorded on a birth certificate. John Smith, who has sex-correction surgery and becomes Joan Smith, is likely to encounter resistance from others who refuse to accept that she is really female. Legislation is beginning to alter this situation. In Britain, the Gender Recognition Act of 2004 allows transsexuals, under certain circumstances, to acquire a birth certificate issued in their new name and gender.

Secondary identities, acquired during secondary socialization, are built on to a foundation provided by the

---

⊃ Connections

We discuss gender identity in greater detail in Chapter 5. Racial and ethnic identity is covered in Chapter 6, pp. 200–1. You will find our discussion of these topics very relevant to the general argument of this chapter.

primary identities. The most important secondary identity that most people acquire in modern societies is an occupational identity. Through entering the labour market and a particular type of work, they come to see themselves as the type of person who fills that occupational role. They describe themselves and are described by others as an engineer, a baker, a doctor, or a sociologist. Other secondary identities are also important, and some of these have gradually become more important than occupational identity. Leisure- and consumption-related identities, for example, have become particularly important. People may define themselves as antiques collectors, football fans, opera buffs, horse enthusiasts, and so on.

A sense of national identity has also been sharpened for many people. In Britain and the United States, for example, nationality is an important secondary identity for many members of the white majority populations. For members of their ethnic minorities, on the other hand, their primary identities as black or Asian remain highly salient and these identities are reinforced by the actions of those who exclude and oppress them. The persistence of these ethnic identities may often run counter to governmental attempts to foster a common sense of national citizenship. We will return to secondary identities later in the chapter. We discuss them more fully in various parts of this book.

Self-presentation depends on the use of appropriate props and scenery.

© John Scott

Narratives of identity

It is important not to treat identities as completely fixed or essential attributes of individuals. The identities that people see as salient vary according to the particular situations in which they find themselves. People can present themselves to one another in varying ways as they pass from one situation to another. They have a stock of identities on which they can draw as seems appropriate, much as they have a stock of clothes from which they can select according to the occasion. Identities are multiple, diverse, and constantly shifting. Of course, not all aspects of identity are completely unanchored. Primary identities are relatively stable and underpin the more shifting and transient secondary identities, and some secondary identities may be particularly salient and will shape the ways in which individuals present themselves in a range of situations. Nevertheless, the fundamental flexibility of identities must be recognized.

For many commentators, this flexibility is something that has increased in contemporary societies. The plurality and diversity of the social situations in which people find themselves in these highly differentiated societies gives a far greater scope for the deployment of multiple, but transient, self-presentations. People are no longer bound so deeply into the tight and enclosed communities that formerly sustained their unified and relatively fixed identities. These days, people have a far greater choice as to how they identify themselves to each other.

A recognition of this growing flexibility of identities has been particularly closely associated with post-modern theory (see our discussion in Chapter 2, pp. 64–5) and with those theorists who see the plurality and diversity of identities as a central feature of a post-modern condition. Identities, they argue, are not essences that lie behind forms of self-expression and self-presentation: they *are* these presentations. It is acts of self-presentation, then, that produce or 'perform' identity (Butler 1990). Identities become stabilized and relatively enduring only when continued and repeated performance fixes them in the minds of the performers and their audiences.

Zygmunt Bauman (1995), for example, has argued that the problem of identity in the past has been the problem of how to build an identity and to keep it solid and stable. In the contemporary world, on the other hand, the problem is that of avoiding complete fixity and maintaining a range of choices as to what kind of person to be. People today, Bauman argues, seek to keep their options open and pursue flexibility in the way that they are seen by others and, therefore, in their own life experiences. They no longer want to be tied down to the communal and organizational contexts that, for much of the modern period, have defined shared and fixed identities.

A particularly important strand in recent work is the argument that the production of identities must be seen in relation to the **narratives** that people construct to account for their actions. People account for their actions and offer explanations of them and, as they do so, they construct and reconstruct their own biographies, drawing selectively on their memories (Gergen and Gergen 1983; Gergen 1994). In producing these accounts, they also draw on a cultural stock of acceptable explanations, and these tend to have a standardized form. The more acceptable motivational narratives that there are, the more likely are identities to be plural and transitory.

In any society, then, there are typical, recurrent accounts that can be used to explain actions. The culture of a society comprises a number of available character types and patterns of motivation that allow people to construct stories with characteristic plots that the others with whom they interact are likely to see as acceptable accounts of their behaviour. These narratives shape their future actions and the likely reactions of others, and the available cultural stock of narratives is an outcome of the interaction, dialogue, and negotiation that makes up the social process. Narratives are, in part, self-conscious attempts to create continuity and coherence in personal experiences, but they also shift in response to the varying situations in which people find themselves. This underlines the fact that there is no 'real' identity. When people do succeed in producing a coherent account of their 'true' identity, this is a consequence of their narrative success and their ability to persuade themselves and others of this 'truth'.

The possibilities for people to present themselves in varying ways through the appropriate use of narratives has escalated with the growth of the Internet. Any form of communication at a distance—by letter, by telephone, and by e-mail—allows people to escape some of the constraints of face-to-face encounters and to present themselves in alternative ways: it is possible, for example, to say things in writing that would be very difficult to say in person. With Internet-based communication, however, this has

increased greatly. Virtual communities can be built through discussion groups, bulletin boards, and chatrooms. And contacts may be followed up through individual e-mail. This opens up new possibilities of self-presentation:

> Since participants cannot see each other, and are not obliged to reveal their names or physical location, there is considerable scope for people to reveal secrets, discuss problems, or even enact whole 'identities' which they would never do in the real world. . . . These secrets or identities may, of course, be 'real', or might be completely made up. In cyberspace, as the saying goes, no one can tell if you're talking complete garbage. (Gauntlett 2000)

People on the Net engage in 'identity play', and this may often allow them to try out an identity before presenting it in face-to-face situations. They can try out their biographical narratives in a situation from which they can easily withdraw, testing its acceptability to other people (Turkle 1995). In some cases, of course, identities may be cynically presented in order to make sexual contacts with those who may not be aware of the identity 'play' that is going on: there has been evidence, for example, of paedophiles using chat rooms to make apparently innocent contact with young children.

In the rest of this chapter, we will review the main theoretical perspectives on socialization and the formation of social identity. We will show how identities are related to the shared construction of social realities, and we will look at how emotions are socially shaped in different societies.

Theories of socialization, identity, and interaction

Three major theoretical approaches to socialization and social identity can be considered. These are role-learning theory, symbolic interactionism, and psychoanalytic theory. Although they are often seen as rival theories, they actually contribute different components to an understanding of socialization. There are, of course, many

New technology Home pages

One way in which people present themselves on the Internet is through the construction of home pages, where narrative accounts of lives and careers are presented for all who care to consult the page.

Log on to the Internet and visit some personal home pages: just type a personal name into a search engine (such as www.google.co.uk) and you will discover a number of home pages. What identities are presented on these pages, and how

would you try to judge their truthfulness? Consult the web pages of the authors and see what you can find out about *our* self-presentation:

● www.le.ac.uk/sociology/staff/djf6.html

● http://privatewww.essex.ac.uk/~scottj/index.htm

Cheung (2000) contains a useful discussion of these issues.

points on which they disagree, but their central insights are complementary viewpoints on a highly complex phenomenon.

The first approach that we will consider is role-learning theory. This stresses the importance of role behaviour in social life and, therefore, of the need to learn the norms that make up role expectations. This theory sees people as learning about various social roles and then reproducing what they have learned in their own behaviour. Symbolic interactionism, on the other hand, gives more attention to the formation of the self through social interaction. It sees role-playing as a *creative* process, not simply as the replaying of things learned during socialization. Psychoanalytic theory, the third theory that we will look at, gives particular attention to the unconscious aspects of the mind and to the ways in which emotional forces drive people towards particular patterns of action throughout their lives. The sense of self that is built up during socialization is seen as reflecting the ways in which people come to terms with these unconscious emotional forces.

Role-learning theory

Role-learning theory has been developed mainly by writers associated with the structural-functionalist approach to sociology. However, it is not only functionalists who have used it. It is a much broader approach towards the learning of social behaviour. The theory starts out from the rejection of biological reductionism that we have already looked at. The biological attributes with which infants are born give only the *potential* for social action, and these have to be developed through socialization into the normative expectations that define their social roles. People become social by learning social roles.

Social roles are treated as *social facts*: they are seen as institutionalized social relationships that are—to all intents and purposes—matters of constraint rather than of choice. People are not free to renegotiate what it is to be a doctor, a teacher, or a mother. They must largely accept the ways in which these have come to be defined within their culture. Someone employed as a teacher, for example, is seen as having very little freedom of choice about how to act when carrying out that role. He or she must follow the specific requirements and obligations that define the role. Social roles are blueprints or templates for action. They provide people with examples or illustrations of how to behave in particular roles, and these can be directly copied in their own behaviour (H. M. Johnson 1961: 135–6). Socialization is, above all, the process through which individuals learn how to perform social roles.

Conformity to learned role expectations is seen, in part, as something that results from external social pressure. This occurs because of the rewards and punishments that people apply to each other's behaviour. Role partners reward conformity and punish deviation, so bringing role performance into line with their expectations. A child seen as naughty, for example, may be smacked or offered an inducement—perhaps sweets or an extra hour of television viewing—if he or she will behave as the parents expect. In the same way, a teacher thought of as poor may suffer the rejection or disapproval of children, parents, and other teachers, and may be denied promotion opportunities by his or her head teacher. A teacher who is felt to be good, on the other hand, may be awarded a higher salary, popularity from pupils, and high status from colleagues. In these ways, role performance and role expectations are kept in line.

Role-learning theory holds, however, that this kind of external coercion and constraint is insufficient on its own. If conformity to role expectations is to continue, there must be a process of **internalization**. People must internalize their roles, making them a part of their self, and so become committed to them (Parsons 1951; Parson and Bales 1956). They must not only learn the expectations that define particular roles; they must also come to see these as requirements, as obligations. They must become integral elements in their own personality and motivation. People must *want* to act in the way that they are expected to act. These ways of acting must come to seem natural or normal to them because they are morally committed to them.

According to this point of view, a good mother does not remain good because of public approval or financial inducement—although these are, of course, seen as important. Rather, the good mother is committed to doing the best for her children simply because she loves them and knows no other way of being a mother. Ideas about what makes a good mother may vary quite widely from one culture to another, and the good mother is someone who has internalized the particular expectations of her own culture. Socially approved patterns of behaviour are so deeply ingrained in her personality that she no longer recognizes that they have their origin outside her in cultural expectations. She has truly internalized them.

Role-learning theory sees primary socialization within the family as laying the foundation for all later social learning. It is from their parents that children learn their culture and the basic roles of their society. Children internalize a large number of common social roles during their primary socialization. As well as learning the roles that become part of their own social identity, they build up an image of the basic roles of their society. They construct a mental map of its many social positions.

At the same time, people build up emotional attitudes towards these internalized representations. They can be recalled to memory and so become the objects of thought and of sentiments of approval or disapproval, desire, or aversion. Children can, for example, imagine particular social positions and the roles associated with them, and they can think and feel what it would be like to be that kind of person.

The first roles that children are likely to learn are the immediate family roles of mother, father, brother, and sister, and their own role as a child. They may also learn wider family and friendship roles (aunt, uncle, cousin, friend) and, through their play, some basic occupational roles (train driver, postman, teacher, and so on). Secondary socialization begins when children enter schools and other groups and organizations to learn specific skills. Schools, for example, are more formal means of training and instruction into specific skills and bodies of knowledge, but they also deepen and enlarge a knowledge of social roles. Indeed, socialization is a lifelong process, as individuals continue to acquire role-specific knowledge through their interactions with others in the local community, at work, and in the political sphere. In all these ways, socialization gives people a knowledge of the particular cluster of roles that define them as an individual and that give them their identities.

While stressing the process of socialization, role-learning theory itself offers no specific theory of the actual mechanisms of learning that are involved. Its major contribution has been to emphasize the link between roles and socialization. The accounts offered of how socialization actually takes place tend to draw on one or other of the two theories that we will consider later in this chapter—symbolic interactionism and psychoanalysis.

Role-learning theory emphasizes a process of **role-taking**. It sees people as taking on culturally given roles and acting them out in a rather mechanical way. People's actions are seen as almost completely determined by the cultural definitions and expectations that they have learned during their socialization. This deterministic view of social behaviour has been criticized for its 'over-socialized' view of action (Wrong 1961). From this point of view, individuals are rather misleadingly seen as the mere puppets of their culture, as having no real freedom of action in the face of the institutionalized social facts. Role-learning theory, then, over-emphasizes the degree of internalization and commitment that is normally achieved through socialization.

R. Turner (1962) has shown that individuals do, in fact, have considerable freedom in almost all situations to decide how they will act out their roles. Social roles are not tightly specified and compulsory blueprints for action, but are loose frameworks within which people must *improvise* their actions. Roles invariably allow people a degree of latitude in deciding how to conform and whether to disregard or to bend certain of the expectations that are placed upon them. Indeed, it can be said that role-learning theory overstates the degree of consensus that exists over role expectations. There may often be quite contrary views of how the occupants of particular roles should behave, and role-learning theory has taken over the strong consensus model that is found in much structural-functionalist theory.

Briefing: is a family necessary for socialization?

Some proponents of role-learning theory write as if everybody is born into the same kind of family—the conventional nuclear family that we discuss in Chapter 12. The theory is, however, quite compatible with a recognition of a much wider range of family and household patterns. The key point is that primary socialization is seen as occurring in small social groups that are organized around face-to-face interaction, and that variations in the type and composition of this social group will result in variant patterns of socialization. Role-learning theory sees the potential for 'failures' of socialization to occur wherever this kind of small-group interaction does not exist or is weakened.

For most people today, this social group remains the two-parent or lone-parent family household. If you want to pursue this further, look at our discussion of family and household in Chapter 12.

> ### ⊃ *Connections*
> You might find it useful to return quickly to our discussion of structural-functionalist theory in Chapter 2, pp. 45–50. There you will find a discussion and criticism of the idea that all societies rest upon a consensus of opinion and values.

The freedom available to people in their roles is especially apparent where—as is typically the case—people have to play two or more conflicting roles at the same time. A woman who is in paid employment as a teacher, but who also has childcare responsibilities as a mother, will often have to juggle the expectations that are attached to the two roles of teacher and mother. She must construct a course of action that will, she hopes, meet at least the more pressing demands of both work and home. This is likely to involve her disregarding many other expectations and acting in ways that have not been explicitly scripted in the cultural definition of the role.

It is important to recognize, then, that people create and modify the roles that they play. Socialization does not programme people in the same way that a computer can be programmed to behave in certain ways (Giddens 1976: 160–1). People are active, not passive: they *make* roles, rather than simply *take* them. In order to develop this point of view, it is necessary to draw on the work of George Mead and the symbolic interactionists.

Symbolic interactionism

We showed in Chapter 2 that the key figures in the development of symbolic interactionism were George Mead and Erving Goffman. It was Mead's ideas on the social construction of the self that were later developed by Goffman (1959) and extended into a theory of the social *presentation* of the self.

Mead held that sociological analysis must always start out from the meanings that objects have for individuals. These meanings are not 'given' in the nature of the objects themselves. A meaning is a social construction. It is a definition that is decided through communication and negotiation and in relation to shared interests and concerns. The social construction of meaning is a process that depends upon the communication of meanings within and between social groups.

The social process is a complex pattern of socially constructed meanings, both other people and social objects depending on the social context for their meanings. A man identifies the particular other people with whom he interacts as, for example, his wife, his boss, his friend, his bus driver, and so on. These people, in turn, define him as a husband, subordinate, friend, or passenger. A central tenet of symbolic interactionism is that the way in which a person is labelled is highly fateful. A child who is called a thief when taking something that belongs to someone else may eventually come to see him or herself as having the character of thief if the accusation is repeated often enough.

The games children play help them to learn about social identities.
© Alice Chadwick

Similarly, the various objects that we use in our interactions—houses, offices, buses, pubs, beds, desks, coins, and glasses—are also socially constructed. They have no intrinsic meaning as physical objects. A limestone cave in Somerset, for example, may be a dwelling place, a storage area for cheese, or a tourist attraction, depending on whether it is being used by a Neolithic hunter-gatherer, a nineteenth-century dairy farmer, or a twenty-first-century entrepreneur in the leisure industry. A particular knife can be defined as a cooking implement, a letter opener, or a means of suicide. Indeed, objects are, of course, produced with their social meanings in mind. Social interaction is a process in which these constructions and definitions are used and built up.

Mead argued that the creation and use of meanings depends upon individuals consciously monitoring their own actions. It is only when they have developed a sense of their own self that this is possible. A self is constructed through a process of socialization in which children, and adults, must continually come to terms with the reactions of others to their actions. Mead saw play activities as the means through which young children initially develop into social beings. In their games, children imitate what they have seen their mothers, fathers, and other adults doing. By playing 'house' or 'mothers and fathers', for example, they gradually begin to learn how it might feel to *be* a mother or father. Mere imitation is unreflective copying. Mead saw this as characteristic only of very young infants who had not developed a symbolic capacity. Once they have learned to understand and manipulate symbols and have, in particular, acquired an image of their self and of others, they will always interpret and reflect upon what they see others do. They imagine alternatives and assess these alternatives in relation to the likely reactions of others.

Mead called this process taking the role of the other. The role of the mother, for example, is taken on and explored by a young girl in her games, as the mother is typically the most salient person in her life. She is a **significant other**, an interaction partner who is especially important in an emotional sense. In her play, however, the child does not simply copy her own particular mother, but improvises motherly behaviour from her rudimentary understanding of the role expectations that are attached to motherhood. As the child's play becomes more complex, particularly through play with siblings and other children, so her understanding of these role expectations becomes gradually more refined.

By acting out the role of a parent towards a child, Mead argued, the child also comes to acquire a conception of self, an idea of 'me' as someone who can be the object of other people's attention. In Mead's terminology, there are two aspects to the self: the 'I' and the 'me'. The I is the source of action, but other people observe and react towards the me. The me is the social self, constructed through interactions with others and reflecting the attitudes that they adopt. The me has been termed the 'reflected' or 'looking-glass self' (Cooley 1902) because it is a reflection of the attitudes of others.

The social self is seen as having developed by about the age of 4 or 5. At about 8 or 9, children's play activities become more detached from the roles of particular others (their mother or their father) and they begin to take on the attitude of what Mead calls the **generalized other**. They begin to infer the common or widely held values of their society by generalizing from particular adults to society in general. They begin to consider how other people in general within their society might react to particular kinds of actions, and they may also begin to objectify these attitudes as norms and standards of conduct that have a *moral* authority. The attitudes of the generalized other become the voice of their moral conscience. Through constructing a sense of self and moral conscience, children become

properly socialized members of their society, and they can begin to broaden their experience of the world through their secondary socialization.

Play involves pretending to be something other than what one really is: the child pretends to be a mummy or a teacher. Goffman (1959) has argued that, in important respects, people continue to play with one another when they interact in adult life. When they take on a particular role, they must interpret it creatively in their actions. As we have seen, roles are not fixed blueprints, but loose guides to action. People must play their social roles in the same way that professional actors play theatrical roles. Goffman holds that people are like actors on the stage, and they employ props and scenery in their interactions in order to try to convince others that they really are what they claim to be. Their aim is to give a convincing dramatic performance in front of their audience.

A man who is employed as a hospital doctor, for example, might typically wear a white coat or hang a stethoscope around his neck in order to symbolize his medical competence. In addition to their construction as technical objects for medical investigations, they are constructed as objects that symbolize the professional status of the doctor and the special social position that he or she occupies. The scenery against which the doctor acts will typically include a couch, screen, sink, table, cabinets, and the particular coloured paintwork that define the room as a surgery rather than a kitchen, bedroom, or office. Many of the props and much of the scenery, of course, have a technical purpose, but Goffman argues that they also have a symbolic purpose that allows the doctor to persuade his or her patients that it really is all right to take their clothes off, swallow a pill, or allow them to insert a scalpel into their bodies. Without these props, patients may find it difficult to accept that person as a doctor. To sustain this acceptance, doctors must also give a convincing performance through their actions: they must try to convey an air of competence, even if they must secretly resort to a textbook or ask the advice of nurses.

Goffman's argument, then, is that social interaction is a process of **self-presentation**. We are always presenting ourselves for others to observe, and we have a considerable amount of discretion as to exactly *how* we present ourselves. People cannot usually check out all the claims that are made by those with whom they interact, and much must be taken on trust. This is why it is so easy for the confidence trickster and the fraudster to gain at the expense of others. More generally, however, we are all engaged in a more or less cynical manipulation of the others with whom we interact. We constantly try to present ourselves in the best possible light by 'bending' the truth, obscuring conflicting evidence, and employing the appropriate props.

THEORY AND METHODS

Erving Goffman

Erving Goffman (1922–82) was born in Alberta, Canada. After graduating from the University of Toronto in 1945 he began his graduate work in sociology and social anthropology at the University of Chicago. Although he cannot be unambiguously regarded as a symbolic interactionist—he owed at least as much to the structural functionalism of Durkheim—he was firmly grounded in the traditions of Chicago ethnography. His theory is sometimes described as a 'dramaturgical' theory, because it sees social life as being like a drama or theatre play. He undertook fieldwork in the Shetland Islands for his Ph.D., producing the data on social interactions that became the basis of his famous book on *The Presentation of Self in Everyday Life* (1959). In the middle of the 1950s he carried out participant observation in mental hospitals that he later published in *Asylums* (1961*b*). His first teaching post, in 1957, was at the University of California, Berkeley, where Herbert Blumer—the systematizer of symbolic interactionism—also taught. During the 1960s and 1970s Goffman undertook a long series of studies in such areas as disability, advertising, and gambling. His best-known books include *Relations in Public* (1963*a*), *Stigma* (1963*b*), and *Gender Advertisements* (1979).

Theatre actors can retreat backstage and avoid the gaze of their audience, and Goffman argues that social actors also rely on **back regions**. Much social interaction occurs in front regions, where people are on stage and acting out their roles in public. Offices, hospitals, factories, and schools are all, for most of their participants, public front regions. The back regions are those places to which people can withdraw and relax, abandoning some of the pressures of public performance. In the back regions, people can say and do things that are incompatible with the self-image that they are trying to present in public. The front region of the hospital ward, for example, may have its back-region kitchen, where nurses can get away from their patients. Similarly, the school has its staff room and common rooms, the office block has its private office areas, and so on.

For many people, their home is the ultimate back region, a private haven for relaxation away from the public world. The distinction between back region and front region is maintained within the home, however. The hall and lounge, for example, may be treated as front regions where visitors can be entertained, while the kitchen and back sitting room may be a back region that only the family can enter. Even in private, family settings, however, people must still present a self to other family members. Members of the family may, therefore, defend their own bedrooms as back regions to which they can escape from the rest of the family and 'really be themselves'.

This highlights the important ways in which Goffman has developed the concept of the self. This is no longer seen as an internal cause of action, but as an external product of action. Personal and social identities, then, need not be seen as completely fixed by an automatic process of socialization. They are presentations or performances through which people actively seek to identify themselves, in varying ways, in the eyes of others. The self that is presented in interaction is something that an individual works to produce and that depends, in large part, on the ability or willingness of others to cooperate in this:

> A correctly shaped and performed scene leads the audience to impute a self to a performed character, but this imputation—this self—is a *product* of a scene that comes off, and is not a *cause* of it. The self, then, as a performed character, is not an organic thing that has a specific location, whose fundamental fate is to be born, to mature, and to die; it is a dramatic effect arising diffusely from a scene that is presented, and the characteristic issue, the crucial concern, is whether it will be credited or discredited. (Goffman 1959: 223)

Our ability to act out multiple identities—and therefore to present different selves—is made possible by the segregation of different types of activity. We can behave as one kind of person at work, another at home, and yet another at a party because we interact with different people in each of these settings. In each setting, we present a self that conforms to the expectations of the particular audience and of which we think the audience will approve. By segregating activities in this way, we can try to ensure that those who see us in one situation will not see us in any other. Problems of self-presentation arise, however, if there is any seepage between different settings. When parents turn up at university at the beginning or end of term, for example, a student may not only find the parents' behaviour excruciatingly embarrassing, but will also experience a conflict between acting in the way that they usually act with friends at university and acting in the way that they usually act at home.

Psychoanalytic theory

Where interactionism has focused on cognitive meanings, psychoanalysis focuses more directly on *emotional* meanings. At the heart of this theory is the idea that human behaviour can be explained in terms of the relationship between the conscious and **unconscious** elements of the mind. People are seen as being motivated by unconscious drives. These are emotions of which they are unaware or that they experience only in a distorted form. Their conscious lives are dominated by the attempt to control the expression of these drives. Psychoanalysis, then, looks at the relationship between the surface structure of consciousness and the deeper structure of the unconscious.

Much early psychoanalytical theory has emphasized the biological basis of the emotions and, therefore, the ways in which people learn to try to control their 'natural' tendencies and drives. A failure to control successfully the unconscious is seen as the source of mental disorder and of mental illness. Later psychoanalysts have broadened this out and have recognized the cultural formation of these unconscious drives.

The main theorist of unconscious mental processes was Freud, who saw them as rooted in people's biological drives. Freud (1900, 1901, 1915–17) held that the biology of the human body generated unconscious drives and desires, in particular the drive for pleasurable experiences that satisfy bodily needs. The conscious mind—which Freud called the 'ego'—had to come to terms with these forces. Human action is shaped by the continuing struggle between unconscious, instinctive drives and the conscious, rational control exercised by the ego.

Freud recognized many sources of bodily pleasure that could motivate people in diverse ways—the pleasures of eating, drinking, urination, and defecation, for example, all play an important part in human motivation. It is, for example, pleasurable to eat food that satisfies a feeling of hunger. These pleasures are experienced through the senses, and Freud saw sensual pleasure as culminating in the pleasures of genital sex. For this reason, Freud virtually equated the sensual with the sexual, and he described all pleasure-seeking as having a sexual character (Freud 1905). It is undoubtedly true that he seriously overstated the significance of sexuality, and also that he tended to see this in deterministic, biological terms (Webster 1995). Nevertheless, the broader implications of his thought, as explored by later writers, concern the need to explore human bodily pleasures in the broadest sense.

In his later work, Freud added an account of a drive towards aggression that operated alongside the drive towards pleasure, although he never properly spelled out the biological basis of this aggressive drive. Later psychoanalysts, as we will show, have explained this drive in cultural terms, just as they have also given greater attention to the cultural shaping of the drive towards pleasure.

The conscious ego is seen by Freud as responding to these emotional drives on a practical, rational basis. It learns to control the ways in which they are expressed, forming them into habitual, recurrent patterns of behaviour that can be undertaken with little or no conscious deliberation. This control may involve deferring desires until they can be safely and properly expressed, but they may often be denied expression altogether. Those

> ### THEORY AND METHODS
> ....
> ### *Freud and psychoanalysis*
>
> Sigmund Freud (1856–1939) was born in Vienna and trained in medicine, specializing in nervous disorders and the use of hypnosis. From his clinical conversations with his patients, he developed his method of interpreting dreams and conscious processes in terms of deeper unconscious forces. Freud is, perhaps, best known for his emphasis on the centrality of sex in human life. As a Jew, he was forced to leave Austria when the Nazis seized power, and he spent the rest of his life in London. His key ideas were developed by his daughter, Anna Freud (1895–1982), and, above all, by Melanie Klein (1882–1960).
>
> Later psychoanalysts, who built a firm awareness of cultural diversity into Freudian theory and who departed from some of the ideas of the Freudian orthodoxy, were Alfred Adler (1870–1937), Karen Horney (1885–1962), and Harry Stack Sullivan (1892–1949).
>
> A number of writers attempted to synthesize aspects of psychoanalysis with Marxism, most notably Erich Fromm (1900–80) and Herbert Marcuse (1898–1979). More radical and controversial forms of psychoanalysis were produced by Carl Jung (1875–1961), who formulated theories of inherited unconscious symbolism, and Wilhelm Reich (1897–1957), who developed theories of the orgasm and authoritarianism.

emotions that are denied are pushed back to form the unconscious part of the mind that Freud called the 'id'.

The id was seen as a seething mass of forces formed from biological drives and their repression by the conscious mind. Through repression, these drives can be converted ('sublimated') into socially acceptable forms of behaviour. This denial of the drives, however, can mean that they return to consciousness in distorted forms. Repressed sexual desires, for example, can make themselves felt as slips of the tongue—so-called Freudian slips. They may also appear in a disguised form while dreaming, or as anxiety, hysteria, and more serious forms of mental disorder. It was this dynamic relationship between the conscious and the unconscious that Freud saw as being both a creative force and a destructive or pathological force in human action. Repression produces not only the energy that makes social life possible, it also produces forms of mental illness.

Freud argued that the core elements of the personality are formed during childhood. It is through interaction with their parents and other members of their immediate family household that infants' drives are satisfied or frustrated. A baby attempts to discover how to achieve satisfaction rather than frustration. It learns, for example, that a particular behaviour, such as a sound (a cry or, later, a word), is likely to be an effective way of influencing the carer. It is through their experiences of satisfaction and frustration that infants gradually become aware of themselves as individuals with a capacity for self-reflection and conscious thought. The conscious ego, like the unconscious id, is a product of the social interactions through which children learn how to respond to satisfaction and frustration. This is the source of the key emotions identified by psychoanalysis. Adult responses are uncertain, and infants develop a sense of *anxiety* about the reactions of their carers. Later on, they develop a sense of *guilt* about those behaviours that meet with disapproval. It is the handling of anxiety and guilt, and their consequences, that psychoanalysts have seen as the critical element in personality development.

It is in the first few years of life that this sense of self and of conscious orientation to the world develops. At this same time, a sense of morality develops. Parents place prohibitions upon a child's behaviour by punishing it and saying such things as 'don't do that, it's not right'. These parental prohibitions are gradually internalized by the child as its own sense of right and wrong, as a conscience. They become that part of the child's conscious mind that Freud called the **superego**. It is the superego that provides the standards in relation to which the demands of the id are assessed by the ego (Freud 1923). Particular kinds of sexual experience, for example, come to be judged as bad, and therefore as things that cannot be expressed in action. Mental illness results from states of anxiety or guilt that are caused by the conflict between the moral demands of the superego and the unconscious urges of the id.

Freud stressed the biological basis of people's unconscious desires, but he gradually came to give more attention to the cultural desires that they derived from their social experiences. This broadened understanding of the relationship between the biological and the cultural was taken further by a number of later psychoanalytical writers, who also moved away from Freud's overemphasis on childhood sexuality. Alfred Adler (1928), for example, held that people are motivated by a striving for power and for recognition or a sense of belonging or acceptance. They seek to be superior to others in these respects and to avoid any experience of inferiority. Feelings of inferiority are, however, inescapable, as superiority and inferiority are necessary consequences of social inequality. Adler, therefore, saw people as developing a sense of their self in relation to their perceived successes and failures. It was when people consistently felt inferior that they showed symptoms of the mental disorder that he called an **inferiority complex**.

Karen Horney (1937, 1946) opened up psychoanalysis even more. She argued that what is regarded as 'normal'

THEORY AND METHODS
....

Freud and Mead

The relationships between the psychoanalytic categories of id, ego, and superego, on the one hand, and the interactionist categories of I, me, and generalized other, on the other hand, are interesting, but far from straightforward. Mead had no real understanding of the unconscious, while Freud gave little attention to the situational presentation of self. The two approaches are, however, complementary.

The ego is the term that Freud used for the conscious mind in its broadest sense. It is similar to Mead's self, of which the I and the me are aspects. It is the interplay of the id and the ego that produces the impulsive, but reflexive, driving force that Mead termed the I. The me, on the other hand, is the 'looking-glass self', the image of how I appear to others. Where Freud gave greatest attention to the interplay of the id and the ego, Mead gave greatest attention to the 'internal conversation'—within the conscious ego—between the I and the me.

The generalized other and the superego have, perhaps, the most direct relationship to each other. They are terms for the internalized responses of others that are constructed into a supervising and controlling conscience.

varies from one culture to another, and that what is normal in one society may be regarded as neurotic in another (see also Fromm 1942; Riessman 1961). Nevertheless, Horney did still recognize that particular forms of socialization were essential for the formation of a coherent sense of self. Children who do not receive warmth or affection from their parents, Horney argued, will grow up with a deep-seated and generalized sense of anxiety. They will be unable to achieve a mental balance. Horney saw neurotic behaviours as the results of attempts to escape this 'basic anxiety'.

This move towards a proper recognition of cultural variability in socialization, and so towards a fully sociological form of psychoanalysis, culminated in the work of Harry Stack Sullivan (1939), according to whom anxiety results from a failure to realize biological and socialized needs in culturally appropriate ways. His understanding of this process has striking parallels with the arguments of the symbolic interactionists. While accepting that a drive for recognition and a sense of acceptance or of belonging was of fundamental importance in human life, Sullivan held that people are motivated to seek this from others by sustaining a particular image or *self conception* that they believe will be valued by others. In Sullivan, then, the

Freudian analysis of the unconscious—the hallmark of psychoanalysis—is united with an interactionist view of the self and self-presentation.

The three theories that we have considered in this section have been used, separately and together, to build understandings of the development of social identities. Whatever insights have been generated by each theory, a more powerful understanding can be achieved if they are used as complementary approaches to socialization.

◆ *Stop and reflect*

In this section we have discussed the relationship between cultural and biological factors in socialization and identity. We have shown that:

- Human behaviour, unlike most animal behaviour, is learned. However, neither biological determinism nor cultural determinism gives an adequate picture of social behaviour.

- Human learning involves processes of primary socialization and secondary socialization.

- People acquire social identities through their socialization. People today have multiple identities.

- Primary identities develop during primary socialization. These primary identities are those of personhood, gender, and ethnicity.

- How useful is it to distinguish between primary and secondary socialization?

We reviewed the three major theories of socialization and identity, and we have argued that they must be seen as complementary rather than competing theories. We first of all looked at role-learning theory.

- Role-learning theory stresses the importance of learning role expectations. Roles are social facts that constrain people.

- Conformity to role expectations depends upon commitment as well as rewards and punishments.

- Do you agree that role-learning theory tends to have a rather over-socialized view of action?

Next we examined the symbolic interactionist theory.

- Symbolic interactionism stresses the construction of the self in social interaction. The self is a looking-glass self that reflects the attitudes of others.

- Social actors, like theatrical actors, play roles and act out their parts in public performances. This is how people 'present' their self to others.

- How realistic is it to make parallels between social interaction and acting in a theatre?

The last theoretical framework that we looked at was that of psychoanalysis.

- Psychoanalytic theory places great emphasis on the role of unconscious emotional factors in primary socialization.

- Freud stressed the role of sexuality and, more generally, sensual factors in socialization. Later psychoanalysts have placed more emphasis on cultural factors in the formation of personality.

- Was Freud correct to see sexuality as such an important factor in human life?

Socialization and family relations

We have shown that socialization can be considered as having primary and secondary phases. Primary socialization occurs in infancy and childhood, largely within the family, while secondary socialization involves the later learning that takes place outside the family household. We discuss some aspects of this more fully in Chapter 9 and in 'Building social worlds', pp. 140–9 below. In this section, we look a little more closely at the processes of primary socialization through which a basic sense of personal and gender identity is developed. We focus on early childhood and adolescence, which highlight the significance of parental roles in socialization and the relationship between culture and biology.

It is conventional to distinguish between infancy, childhood, adolescence, youth, adulthood, maturity, and old age, all understood as stages of life between the ultimate stages of birth and death. The number and length of these stages is culturally and historically variable, and it is clear that we are dealing with socially constructed categories and not biological stages. The idea of childhood, for example, is a relatively recent construction in Western culture (Ariès 1962). The idea of the **life course** brings these stages together, pointing to similarities of experience for all those growing up in a particular society. Fundamental aspects of social identity are those that people share with others as an **age cohort**. An age cohort is a category of people who are born at the same or similar time and who, therefore, undergo life-course transitions at the same time. As a 'generation', they also have definite historical experiences in common that may have a major impact on their outlook on life (Mannheim 1927).

Childhood, ageing, and the life course

The implications of ageing for a sense of identity have been explored in works on personality development. Piaget (1924, 1932, 1936; see also Kohlberg 1981) looked at the way in which the biological maturity of children is a precondition for them to be able to engage with, and learn from, the world around them. Their sense of space, time, and number, of the nature of the physical world, and of the moral implications of their behaviour develop and are transformed through the specific kinds of 'operations' that they perform on the world as they explore it and in their infancy and in formal education. The ways in which they physically operate on the world—handling objects and manipulating them—is itself a social process, made possible by the kinds of social situation in which children are placed. It is this combination of biological maturation and social interaction that results in their move from one stage of personality development to the next. Jerome Bruner (1966) has shown how teachers can draw on this understanding of child development to devise more effective systems of learning in the school.

Noam Chomsky (1965) took a similar approach to the development of language, arguing that the acquisition of language depends upon the innate 'linguistic competence' of human beings, stressing that this can give rise to an understanding and development of language only if children are exposed to language users at an appropriate age. If they do not interact linguistically with their parents and others in the critical early years of life—around the age of 2—they will never be able to develop any sense of language or any linguistic facility. It has also been suggested that the ability to learn additional languages is greatly diminished after the age of 13, when the biological capacity for language acquisition is 'switched off' with bodily maturation.

The work of Lev Vygotsky (1934) has been especially important in stressing that the learning process identified by Piaget depends not only on physical engagement with the world but also on social interaction. For Piaget this was largely taken for granted, but Vygotsky highlights the varying ways in which social conditions can establish opportunities and constraints for children. Their ability to learn from their actions depends upon their social location. This argument is relevant also to that of Chomsky, as it highlights the social shaping of language learning. These ideas were also explored in some of the work on schooling and language acquisition undertaken by Basil Bernstein (1962).

One of the most important contributions to an understanding of personality development has come from the psychoanalytical work of Erik Erikson (1950), who is firmly rooted in the more cultural approach of writers such as Horney. Erikson argues that people go through eight stages of personality development in the course of their lives. The first four of these are those identified by Freud, but Erikson adds an important account of later adult personality development through social encounters.

The first four stages identified by Erikson are those of infancy (up to age 1), the toddler (from age 1 to 2), early childhood (from 2 to 6), and the early school years (from 6 to 12). These are closely related to Freud's ideas of the oral, anal, phallic, and latency stages, but Erikson emphasizes the specific identity problems that arise at each stage. The first stage is one in which the child can achieve a 'basic trust' in others if its needs are met by the adults (its parents) on whom it depends completely. In the second stage, children begin to do things for themselves and acquire greater autonomy in their behaviour. The third stage is one in which children are able to engage in social interaction with other children and, through play activities, learn to deal with feelings of shame and guilt and begin to take responsibility for their own actions. Finally, through their early schooling they begin to interact with more others outside their own family and can acquire a sense of intellectual competence in their own skills. Development from each stage to the next is not inevitable, but depends upon the cultural context and the social opportunities created by the adults on whom the child depends.

Between the ages of 12 and 18, children are in the stage of adolescence or youth when their lives are dominated by their developing sexuality. It is in this stage, Erikson argued, that young people are concerned with issues of identity. They are concerned with knowing who they are and how they fit in; they build a meaningful self-image. People who fail to resolve this 'identity crisis' will enter adulthood with a sense of uncertainty about their role in life and their sexuality. From the age of 18 to the late twenties, is the young adult stage in which people are concerned with establishing intimacy with others through secure emotional relationships. This is possible, he argues, only if they have successfully resolved the prior identity crisis. By the time a person enters the adulthood of their late twenties or early thirties they will, if they have resolved the 'crisis of intimacy' become concerned with 'generativity', with having and rearing children and, at the same time, building their careers. They seek to establish a home and family as a secure basis for those close to them. Finally, around the age of 50, people enter 'maturity' or the beginnings of 'old age' in which they turn from family building to their own gradual withdrawal from social life. Their children leave home and begin their own young adulthood and the person has to plan for the approach of retirement from work. Ultimately, they must face the approach of their own death, and the whole period is marked by a concern for the constant 'despair' about 'time running out'. Successful handling of this problem, Erikson claimed, involves the achievement of 'wisdom' and fulfilment.

Erikson certainly does not see any inevitability in the passage through these life-course stages. Each is marked by problems and anxieties that result from the failure to resolve the characteristic crises thrown up by changing social circumstances and bodily abilities. The resolution of each successive crisis is made easy, difficult, or impossible by the resolutions achieved in earlier crises and the mature personality is a complex sedimentation of all these stages. It is the changing social circumstances of individuals that comprise the driving force in the crises they face and the resolutions they achieve, and societies differ in the demands that they place on individuals and the opportunities that they offer for them to cope with them. The movement from one stage to the next is often marked by rituals and ceremonies that make the transition easier: a marriage ceremony, for example, is a public marker of the transition to adulthood. The socially structured ceremonials, then, are cultural markers on the life course.

Mothers, fathers, and children

All three of the theories that we have looked at in the previous section saw family relations as central to primary socialization. A helpless newborn child requires the care and support of its parents for its physical survival and security. Through this relationship to its parents, the infant also acquires its social skills, social knowledge, and sense of self. All three theories see effective socialization as involving this continuing family support. An important question, therefore, is whether primary socialization is most effective when it takes place in a conventional two-parent household with a close and intimate relationship between, in particular, the mother and child. Not all families are of this conventional form, and not all family households can provide the kind of care that the theories see as being important for normal development. The growing

importance of employment outside the household, and the increasing number of single-parent households has raised the question of whether primary socialization is adversely affected by changing family relations.

Childhood and parental deprivation

It is psychoanalysis, in particular, that sees early socialization within the family as holding the key to adult emotional development. The relationship between a baby and its adult carer is the critical factor in the development of its personality. For the satisfaction of most of their needs, young children are dependent on an adult to care for them. The baby comes to perceive the carer as the source of its pleasure, as it is only through the carer's actions that its needs can be satisfied. Bonds of attachment are made with a carer who can satisfy the baby's needs and bring it pleasure. Psychoanalysts hold that the mother is central to this. Her pregnancy—so it is argued—will normally have led her to develop strong feelings of affection towards her baby and a willingness to provide continuing care for it.

This emphasis on the role of the mother in psychoanalysis is one of the most contentious areas in psychoanalytic theory. Children who are deprived of the close and sustained attention of their mother, runs the theory, will be inadequately socialized and they will experience serious psychological problems in later life. The chief advocate of this view of maternal deprivation was John Bowlby, who held that what is 'essential for mental health is that an infant and young child should experience a warm, intimate and continuous relationship with his mother' (Bowlby 1965: 13; see also Winnicott 1965). Because of its stress on the importance of attachment to the mother, and on the negative consequences of absence, Bowlby's argument has been described as 'attachment theory'.

A close relationship between mother and child, Bowlby argued, is very weak when the child is looked after by a childminder. It is completely absent when the mother has died or has rejected the baby, and where the child, therefore, has to be brought up in residential care, an orphanage, or a hospital. Part way between these two situations, Bowlby suggested, is the experience of those children who come from so-called broken homes, where contact with their mother is limited or irregular. Most controversially, Bowlby's conclusions have sometimes been extended to the cases of children whose mothers are involved in full-time paid employment outside the household. In all of these situations, it is held, the child is deprived of the kind of close and continuing maternal attachment that is required for proper socialization.

Bowlby produced evidence to show that maternal deprivation in early life can lead to anxiety in a child, expressed in a growing depression and withdrawal from social contact. This can result in serious physical, intellectual, and social problems in a child's later life, Bowlby said, and in extreme cases it can result in physical or mental illness. The effects of protracted early separation continue into adult life, when they are difficult to reverse or to overcome. Parallels with the experiences of 'wild children' and children such as Genie have often been drawn.

The most crucial period for child development, Bowlby held, is when an infant is aged between 6 months and 1 year. Separation before this time has little psychological effect, so long as maternal care is re-established by 6 months of age. After the end of the first year, the effects of separation are, again, less stark, though Bowlby argued that serious long-term problems can occur as a result of any prolonged separation during the first three years of life. After age 3, problems of separation become less marked, and after 5 there are few significant problems for children.

A great deal of empirical evidence was produced by Bowlby to support his case—though he had no direct evidence on either lone parents or on mothers in paid employment. Nevertheless, his research has been criticized for appearing to place all the responsibility for children's psychological problems on to their mothers. In fact, Bowlby was careful not to do this. Although he held that, in contemporary Britain, the nuclear family provides the most usual context for primary socialization and that in most families mothers take the main responsibility for the care of their children, he felt that 'mothering' was an activity that could be provided by what he called a 'permanent mother-substitute'. It is the activity of mothering that is important, not the social position of the person who performs it. A 'mother-substitute' could be an aunt or grandmother providing informal help, or it could be a paid nanny. As a Kleinian psychoanalyst, however, Bowlby did see the gender of the carer as being important. He held that the mother–child relationship was a gendered relationship. Others, however, have suggested that a male carer, such as the father, could provide all the mothering that a child needs. There is nothing in the broader thesis of maternal

deprivation that requires that the principal carer should be a woman (Rutter 1972). The crucial finding highlighted by Bowlby's research was that the establishment of a close, intimate, and enduring relationship with the mother or a mother-substitute in the critical period of infancy and early childhood was necessary for effective socialization.

> **⊃ Connections**
>
> We look at the issue of gender identities in Chapter 5, pp. 159–60, where we also consider the psychoanalytic explanation offered by Chodorow. You might find it useful to review some of that argument now. What are the implications of the view that fathers can 'mother' a child?

Narratives of motherhood

Mothering, therefore, is not a 'natural' or biologically fixed activity. It is not simply an instinctive nurturing provided to a child by its biological mother. Mothering is a social activity in which both the needs of the dependent child and the responses of the person who mothers are socially constructed. They are shaped by the prevailing cultural ideas, and so the forms of mothering can be quite variable from one society to another.

While we have shown that the evidence from attachment theory does not require that this mothering be provided by the biological mother, or even by a woman, mothering is, in contemporary Western societies, a gendered task. It is a task whose social construction is inextricably tied to the social construction of the woman and of femininity and to such related social constructions as wife. These 'feminine' roles and norms form part of a larger system of cultural meanings. They are involved in such constructions as family and kinship, and through these mothering is also linked to ideas of fathering. Fatherhood and fathering are socially constructed as male tasks, linked to the ideas of manhood, masculinity, and the husband. This cluster of social meanings around parenting is the crucial element in the cognitive mappings through which people organize the upbringing of children.

The gendered character of the activity of mothering has been explored by Lawler (2000) in an empirical study of mothers and daughters. She looks, in particular, at the narratives produced by mothers to account for the ways in which they carry out their role and, in particular, to explain how they depart from the cultural idea of the 'good' mother. The mothers that she interviewed held to the idea that a child's character, its fundamental sense of identity, is inborn. They believed that children are destined by nature to be a particular kind of person and that the task of the mother is to allow this essential character to express itself. The nurturing activities of mothers are geared to providing the conditions under which the child can 'be herself'. Their daughters' adult characteristics were seen as the products of their childhood selves, so that they, too, were largely products of nature. Mothers did not, therefore, claim any responsibility for the positive achievements of their daughters: children are destined from birth to develop in certain ways, and it is felt that there is little that mothers can do to change their character or temperament. They did, however, take some responsibility for what they saw as their daughters' failings. These they saw as the results of their own failure to provide proper nurturing. In particular, they felt that they had passed on negative traits of their own to their daughters.

Lawler also examined the accounts of their upbringing produced by the grown-up daughters themselves, and she found echoes of this same narrative. There was a common feeling that their mothers had been too restrictive and had not allowed them enough independence for them to 'be themselves'. Adolescence was seen as the key period in life when conflicts with their mothers had become apparent. Their own desire for autonomy had begun to express itself at this time, and there was considerable conflict between mothers and daughters over how their independence was to be exercised. The daughters, then, felt that they had had to overcome some of the failings that they identified in their mothers, and they claimed that they would not make the same mistakes with their own daughters.

Growing up

It seems that motherhood and growing up, in contemporary Western societies, draw on cultural ideas that deny or ignore their own character as social constructions. Like all social definitions, however, they are real in their consequences for the behaviour of those who act upon them and those who are affected by this behaviour. Adolescence, in particular, becomes a battleground between parents and their children. There has been much work on this generational conflict (Pilcher 1995), and we look at some of the consequences of this for the formation of oppositional youth subcultures in Chapter 7, pp. 257–8. In this section, we turn to some of the consequences of generational conflict for the self-formation of adolescents and the impact of this on their adult lives. We look, in particular, at the work of R. D. Laing and his associates, who have provided vivid examples of the most extreme forms of breakdown in socialization. The generational conflict over autonomy that lies at the heart of the Western family, they argue, can produce serious problems of mental health. These problems, however, are to be seen as problems of the family as a whole, and not just problems for the particular member who comes to be labelled as mentally ill.

It is also important to consider the extent to which this intergenerational conflict is built into Western culture rather than being, as Lawler's mothers believed, rooted in biological universals. If adolescent conflict is not an inevitable feature of family relations, then alternative, and equally effective, patterns of socialization might be possible. A belief that adolescent conflict was not universal lay behind a classic comparative study by Margaret Mead, which tied this to a larger account of cultural determinism. This important work, though flawed, provides important insights into the cultural variability of parent–child relations.

Sanity, madness, and the family

Laing and Esterson (1964) were medically trained psychiatrists who became very critical of the biomedical assumptions behind much psychiatry. They recognized the crucial importance of social factors in the production of mental illness, but they also rejected those views that saw this mental illness as simply an individual pathology, whether psychological, genetic, or constitutional. Echoing the arguments of Szasz (1962), they held that the diagnosed patient has to be seen simply as someone who has strange experiences and behaves in strange ways, as judged by the others with whom they interact. What psychiatrists describe as mental illness is generated within families, and it is the family as a whole that should be seen as having the problem. In particular, they argue that the apparently bizarre behaviour of psychiatric patients makes perfect sense as a rational and comprehensible form of behaviour if seen in the context of the behaviour of the other members of their families.

This opposition to psychiatric approaches to mental illness earned Laing and Esterson the label 'antipsychiatrists', a label that they took on with pride to mark the distinctiveness of their social approach to mental health. The theoretical basis of their work (Laing 1960, 1961) is that of existential phenomenology, a position that shares much with cultural approaches in psychoanalysis and with symbolic interactionism. We look at the phenomenological approach in greater detail in Chapter 2. They applied this theoretical approach to the formation of the particular mental and behavioural patterns that are commonly diagnosed as schizophrenia. The exercise of autonomy and independence on the part of a child as it grows up is often experienced as threatening and worrying by its parents, who are used to controlling its behaviour closely. When parents expect that their child will continue to conform in all respects as it grows up, they may interpret its individuality and difference as worrying signs that something is 'wrong' with the child. Normal childhood and teen behaviour comes to be seen as a sign of disturbance or of illness. Laing and Esterson explored how the dynamics of family relations produced a concern for the mental health of one of its members and how medical interventions led to formal psychiatric diagnosis.

Schizophrenia is a diagnosis that gets applied to women far more often than it does to men, and it is a diagnosis that often has its roots in adolescent behaviour. In order to explore the family dynamics that lie behind this, Laing and Esterson studied a number of families of hospitalized females diagnosed as schizophrenic. Through interviews and observations, they attempted to uncover the patient's own perspective on the situation and the views and behaviour of the other family members. Their argument is built up through a number of biographical accounts of patients and their families, of which the case of Maya Abbott is typical.

➲ Connections
You will find a longer discussion of the debate over mental illness, and how sociologists have tried to understand mental disorders in Chapter 8, pp. 300–5. You might find it useful to read that discussion now.

Interviews with her parents and observations of the family together showed that Maya had consistently been seen as an isolated, apathetic, and withdrawn child. Maya's parents had found it difficult to allow their daughter to do anything of her own choice, unless it was under their supervision. The more independently that Maya acted, the more disturbed she was felt to be. Maya herself denied this interpretation of her behaviour. She felt that she was not treated as a 'person' in her own right and that her ideas and comments were not taken seriously. She claimed that her parents had never shown her any real emotion or ever allowed her to express her own emotions spontaneously. However, Maya's only point of reference judging her own behaviour was the attitude of her parents. As she grew up, she, in turn, became increasingly anxious about her own thoughts and came to feel that they might, indeed, be unusual or unnatural.

Maya's parents felt that she told them nothing about herself and was not interested in them, but they interpreted this as a sign that she possessed exceptional powers of mind reading: she did not need to communicate verbally because she could read their minds directly. They began to experiment in their relations with her, trying to catch her out in her mind reading. The things that she said or did were interpreted as signs that confirmed their belief in her strange mental powers. However, the various signals that the parents exchanged with each other as they carried out these experiments (nods, winks, smiles, etc.) were interpreted by Maya as signs that *they* were trying to influence *her* through the power of their minds. Not wanting to admit to experimenting on their daughter, her parents denied that they were signalling to each other, and Maya found it increasingly difficult to know if she was perceiving or imagining the signals. Parent and child, then, became locked into a cycle of misinterpretation and misunderstanding in which the distinction between what was 'real' and what was 'imagined' became more and more difficult to make.

Maya's confusions, as the youngest and weakest member of the family were the 'symptoms' that resulted in her diagnosis as a schizophrenic. She was taken to her doctor and referred to psychiatrists, who diagnosed her as suffering from 'ideas of influence'. The symptom of her schizophrenia was that she felt that she 'influenced' other people and that they 'influenced' her. Laing and Esterson argue, however, that these apparent delusions of influence made complete sense if they were seen in the context of the interpersonal relations of her family: 'Much of what could be taken to be paranoid about Maya arose because she mistrusted her own mistrust. She could not really believe that what she thought was going on was going on' (Laing and Esterson 1964: 40).

Thus, Maya's confusion, anxiety, and withdrawal were a rational and comprehensible response to her experiences in her interaction with her parents. They appeared to be irrational and bizarre to her parents because they were unaware of their own anxieties and confusions and the effects that these had on their daughter. Maya's behaviour appeared as symptomatic of schizophrenia to her doctors because they were unaware of the family interactions that gave them their meaning. What psychiatrists and others treated as individual 'illness' became perfectly understandable behaviour when seen in its interpersonal context.

Laing and Esterson concluded that the problems of living that Maya and others like her experience are wrongly and unhelpfully seen as organic, psychiatric illnesses. Treatment based on such diagnoses, they argue, cannot alleviate the problems. Such women could be helped only by bringing the whole family to an understanding of their situation and of the interpersonal spiral of misunderstanding into which they have locked themselves. The interpersonal knots must be unravelled through therapeutic work with the whole family. While the validity of their argument as a complete explanation of schizophrenia has been disputed, they provide a compelling account of how behaviour that appears bizarre or irrational can be understood in terms of the family dynamics involved in socialization.

Adolescence in its cultural context

Franz Boas was the leading American anthropologist of the 1920s and was a firm advocate of cultural determinism. He expected to find that non-Western societies such as the Pacific territory of Samoa would show a completely different approach to adolescence from that found in the United States and in Europe. Differences of culture, he argued, would result in different experiences of growing up. If people of the same physiological age could behave in radically different ways, then the problems faced by adolescents in the United States had to be explained in cultural terms. They could not be explained simply in terms of the biological aspects of puberty and adolescence. To explore and, he hoped, establish this idea, he sent a young graduate student, Margaret Mead, to undertake some fieldwork.

Mead's study (1928) was undertaken in the small island of Ta'u, part of the Samoan group of islands. Samoa was an American colony and naval base, and Ta'u itself was heavily dependent on its trading relations with the United States navy. Although still a tribal society, its chiefs were highly Westernized. Mead concentrated her attention on a sample of twenty-five local girls, who ranged in age from 14 to 20. She lived in a house belonging to the only white family on the island and, working from the house—and using the school building during the holidays—she talked with the girls and began to collect much information about their lives. She claimed that, by contrast with adolescent girls in the United States, those in Samoa had a very easy and stress-free life. This, she thought, reflected the overall balance and moderation of Samoan culture.

Life in Samoa, Mead held, was easy and relaxed, with little or no conflict. Its inhabitants lacked any deep feelings, and they had no strong passions. As they did not get worked up about day-to-day matters, they were rarely drawn into stressful or hostile relationships. Children grew up in large extended families and had no strong attachment to their individual parents. They were, instead, embedded in diffuse, warm relationships with large numbers of adults. They learned, early on, not to act impulsively. Samoa, then, was a very harmonious society. Its people, Mead claimed, were happy and well adjusted.

In this idyllic society, adolescence was the age of maximum ease and freedom. When they entered adolescence, Samoans were free to engage in sexual activity promiscuously. Mead claimed that this reflected the adult view of sex in Samoa: it was an enjoyable and playful activity that should not be taken too seriously.

The girls that Mead studied grew up with a great deal of sexual knowledge. This was unavoidable when large extended families lived in single-room houses with little or no privacy. They began to masturbate in early childhood, generally at 6 or 7, and homosexual relationships were not uncommon during puberty. Adolescence was a time for erotic dancing and singing, and playful heterosexual relations emerged naturally out of this sexual experimentation.

As a result of this, Mead argues,

> adolescence represented no period of crisis or stress, it was instead an orderly developing of a set of slowly maturing interests and activities. The girls' minds were perplexed by no conflicts, troubled by no philosophical queries, beset by no remote ambitions. To live as a girl with many lovers as long as possible and then to marry in one's own village, near one's own relatives, and to have many children, these were uniform and satisfying ambitions. (M. Mead 1928: 129)

Mead contrasted this with the typical adolescent experience in the United States. Adolescence there was widely seen as a period of great emotional turmoil. Conflict between parents and their children was rife. Because the ease and balance of Samoan adolescence could be related to the central features of Samoan culture, Mead argued that adolescence in the United States must be seen as reflecting the peculiarities of its culture. The biological universals of puberty and biological maturation, she claimed, have little or no direct impact on people's actions and relationships. Behaviour is shaped, above all else, by the culture into which people are born and socialized.

Mead's study became widely accepted as an exemplary proof of cultural determinism and as a final repudiation of biological determinism. By the 1960s it had become the most widely read of any anthropology book and it was a popular best-seller. Mead's reputation was confirmed by her studies in New Guinea (1930, 1935), where she explored the extent of cultural variation in gender relations. The three societies that she studied—those of the Arapesh, the Mundugumor, and the Tchambuli—appeared to show all possible permutations of masculinity and femininity.

THEORY AND METHODS

Margaret Mead

Margaret Mead (1901–78) was no relation to George Mead. She studied anthropology at Columbia University, and it was her Samoan fieldwork that made her name and that became the most influential anthropological work of all time. This was published as *Coming of Age in Samoa* (1928). A few years later, she carried out some related work into adolescence in the Admiralty Islands, producing *Growing Up in New Guinea* (1930). Pursuing her interest in cultural variation, she later carried out work, also in the Pacific, on sex and gender roles for her books *Sex and Temperament in Three Primitive Societies* (1935) and *Male and Female* (1950). She felt very marginal to the male academic world and followed a career as Curator of the American Museum of Natural History in New York. Her work on culture closely paralleled the influential ideas of Ruth Benedict on native Americans (1934) and on Japan (1946).

Taken together, they further reinforced the claims of cultural determinism.

In Arapesh society, both men and women were gentle, caring, and passive, while in Mundugumor society both were assertive and sexually aggressive. By contrast with the United States and other Western societies, then, neither of these societies showed any significant gender differentiation. They varied considerably, however, in the type of personality that they valued most highly. Arapesh personality was similar to Western femininity, while Mundugumor personality was similar to Western masculinity. In the third society that she studied, the Tchambuli, Mead identified a sharp differentiation of gender roles, and she claimed that these varied in the opposite direction to the United States. Tchambuli men decorated themselves and gossiped with each other, while Tchambuli women were assertive and competent in practical affairs.

Mead's study, then, showed that the situations described by Laing and Esterson (1964) were culturally specific. Laing and Esterson were correct to look at the social factors and to reject biological explanations of schizophrenia, as the adolescent conflicts they described simply did not occur in Samoa. However, while the general thrust of Laing and Esterson's argument is now accepted, some of Mead's conclusions have been challenged. Culture, as we have shown, is an important determinant of human behaviour, but it is not the only determinant and it is not so all-pervasive as Mead had argued. Mead believed that she had conclusively refuted the thesis of biological determinism. The single study of Samoa seemed sufficient to show that there were no universal biologically determined stages of social development. The New Guinea studies simply added more weight to her argument for cultural determinism. These conclusions have been questioned.

The limits to culture

This challenge to cultural determinism was clarified in a systematic criticism of Margaret Mead's research. Her work had been so influential that only a demonstration of its flaws could show that the importance of culture should not be overstated.

The critique of Mead was set out in a book by Freeman (1984), which showed that she had been seriously misled in her Samoan studies. She had undertaken only very limited fieldwork, and she had a rather poor understanding of the language. In fact, she had got it all wrong. Drawing on a wide range of less well-known anthropological studies and on his own period of more than five years of detailed fieldwork, Freeman conveys a very different picture of Samoa and of its adolescents. Samoan society, he says, is highly competitive and beset by conflict. Far from being the stable, peaceful, and cohesive society that Mead had claimed, it has much aggression, violence, and rape. Child-

rearing is far from being the open and flexible system that Mead had described. It centres on firm parental authority and harsh discipline.

Above all, however, Freeman rejects Mead's account of adolescent sexual behaviour. He shows that virginity at marriage is held in extremely high esteem. A central aspect of marriage ceremonies throughout Western Polynesia is the ritual deflowering of the young bride in public by her husband to-be. Through this violent and humiliating ritual assault, the girl's virginity is publicly demonstrated by a flow of blood. Mead had reported such occasions, but she had claimed them to be mere empty rituals that could easily be avoided and were of no significance. In fact, they have been central to Samoan culture. Given the great importance that is attached to virginity, it is unlikely that adolescent promiscuity would be at all widespread. Young girls have always, in fact, been tightly controlled by their parents and by other members of their kinship group. They would themselves ensure that they maintained their purity—whether out of moral commitment or fear of public shame—until their marriages.

Why, then, does Freeman think that Mead could have got things so wrong? When she began to speak to the girls about their sexual behaviour, her lack of fluency in their language meant that she was unaware of the subtle nuances of speech and of the emotional state of her interviewees. Freeman met one of the girls in 1987, by which time she was a rather elderly lady. She told him that she and the

---

THEORY AND METHODS

Problems of participant observation

Mead's difficulties highlight important methodological problems in participant observation. The usual method in anthropological fieldwork is for the researcher to live as a participant in the society that is being studied for a period of one or more years. The fieldworker must learn the language and talk to the locals in order to try to understand their culture from within. Margaret Mead spent only two months studying the Samoan language, and she completed her fieldwork in just five months. In this time, she lived with a white, American family, not with a Samoan family, and she relied on rather formal and uncomfortable interviews. She reports very few of her own observations in the book. Instead of a close ethnographic encounter, Mead relied upon hearsay and on observation at a distance. In these circumstances, she had little or no way of checking the narratives produced by the girls with whom she spoke.

- Look at 'Ethnographic research', Chapter 3, pp. 83–9. What lessons do you think that other ethnographers can learn from Mead's study?

other girls had been so embarrassed by the questions that Mead had asked them that they had playfully lied to her. They created a picture of promiscuity and sexual freedom that accorded so well with what Mead had hoped to discover that she had not questioned its truth.

Mead's views have, however, been supported by other studies, and her wider conclusions are still accepted as valid (Orans 1996). The criticisms of her Samoan study, however, suggest that there are greater similarities with patterns of growing up in the United States than she had wanted to find. To this extent, biological maturation and its consequences for adolescent behaviour cannot be ignored. Cultural variation may not be quite as extreme as she thought. Nevertheless, it is clear from her work that patterns of socialization and their outcomes are shaped by the cultural context of the societies in which they take place.

‹› *Stop and reflect*

This section has looked at primary socialization within families. We first looked at a number of issues concerning personality development.

- A child's intellectual, linguistic, and moral development depends upon both biological maturation and interaction with the world. Social interaction is a crucial aspect of the latter.

- The human life course involves the complex negotiation of a series of 'stages' of development, each marked by characteristic social constraints and involving specific subjective responses.

- Should the sociologist accept that biology sets the conditions under which human behaviour and personality can be shaped by culture and social relations?

We then looked at issues related to mothering and motherhood:

- The attachment of a child to its carer is important for the development of its sense of self and its later psychological health. This attachment is built up through the carer's 'mothering' of a child.

- The task of mothering a child can be undertaken by a carer who need not be the biological mother and who may be a mother-substitute.

- Is mothering an instinctive, biological response or a socially constructed activity?

When we turned to look at adolescence and its shaping by family relations we showed that:

- Adolescence in contemporary Western societies is a period of conflict between parents and children over a child's exercise of its growing independence.

- In certain situations this conflict over independence and autonomy can result in the child being labelled as 'troubled' or, in extreme cases, mentally ill.

- What limits might there be to the cultural determination of adolescent behaviour?

Building social worlds

Secondary socialization builds on the foundations of primary socialization, and it allows people to build the social worlds in which they live and into which the next generation will be born. Central to this world-building activity is the playing of social roles. People learn the social roles that comprise their society and they play these roles out in their interactions with others. They do not, however, mechanically act out tightly defined roles. We showed in our discussion of role-learning theory that people do not simply 'take' roles: they 'make' them. That is, they learn merely the outlines or general patterns that define roles, acquiring this knowledge from their observations of large numbers of individuals as well as from formal learning.

When they come to act in a role themselves, they must improvise their actions on the basis of these learned patterns. In doing so, they contribute to the reproduction and, perhaps, the transformation of these roles.

As we showed in Chapter 2, Berger and Luckman drew on phenomenological ideas to show that the social structures that surround and constrain us must be seen as socially constructed realities. Individuals encounter one another with their varying, and perhaps conflicting, views about the character of the situation in which they find themselves. They negotiate an agreed meaning—a definition of the situation—which then becomes the reality to which they orient themselves. It becomes, over time, taken for granted, and those involved may forget that they built it. When they pass on their knowledge to their children and to younger members of their society, it may be acquired by these others as a fixed and completely given reality that is beyond question and unchangeable. Most social realities are perceived as somewhere between these two extremes, neither unchangeable nor easily renegotiable but capable of change, through individual or collective action, given the appropriate time, effort, and inclination.

Role-playing and the building of social worlds is not a purely calculative activity. People have emotional commitments to the norms and ideas that they have learned. This emotional aspect to socializaton has been particularly emphasized by psychoanalysts, though Freudian theory has tended to see the emotions as fixed biological drives. An implication of all that we have looked at so far, however, is that emotions must be seen as socially constructed and, therefore, as culturally variable. There is a biological basis to emotions, but the ways in which these are shaped and expressed reflects cultural factors. Work based on this important idea has shown that many roles involve the performance of 'emotional labour' and that contemporary societies have generated high levels of emotional anxiety that are difficult to handle.

Constructing realities

The argument that secondary socialization is central to the building of social worlds can be illustrated from a number of areas. We look first of all at the marital roles of husband and wife in order to consider how these roles are creatively performed, on the basis of outline cultural 'scripts', by all of those who marry. Marital partners build a family world into which their own children are born and in which these children will, in turn, learn how they, in due course, may produce themselves as husbands and wives. We look at this same process of world building in occupational roles, taking hospital nursing as our example. Any occupational role is performed by those who have learned the basics of the role before they enter it, but who must learn—and create—its details at the same time that they play it.

Once they are constructed, social realities must be maintained. Because social roles are only partially defined in the culture and so are creatively performed by their occupants, there is a constant risk that they might be disrupted by those whose definitions of the situation differ or who have been less well socialized. Taking the example of medical investigations, we show how the various participants must cooperate to minimize the effects of these disruptions.

Constructing a marriage

The roles played by men and women in their marital relationships—the roles of husband and wife—are learned as very general cultural typifications or templates. These pre-defined typifications of what it is to be a husband or wife give only a very general guidance on how to act in these domestic roles. They are outline scripts whose details are produced and reproduced in the negotiated interactions of the marital partners.

Berger and Kellner (1970) have explored the construction of these roles within the private sphere of the household. It is within the household that all family relations have their focus, and each family is felt by its members to be a sub-world, an area of interaction that is segregated from more public spheres of interaction and within which people generally feel that they are free to express themselves as individuals and to produce the kind of world in which they can feel comfortable and relaxed. It is in such a context that the most basic meanings and identities that people live by can be produced.

The starting point for constructing a family and its small-scale sub-world is the construction of the marital roles of husband and wife. Berger and Kellner see this as a new stage of socialization, following on from socialization in childhood and adolescence. The wedding ceremony itself is the crucial rite of passage that marks the entry of the marital partners into a new household and a new stage of life.

In forming a marital partnership, those who are still relative strangers to one another gradually come to know each other better and, at the same time, they construct, through their actions, their own particular performances as husband and wife. They bring to their marital interactions the highly generalized cultural typifications that they have learned through observing their own parents and others in marital relationships, and through reading and watching television. They also draw on those wider cultural themes that run through these typifications: such themes as romantic love, sexual fulfilment, self-realization through love, family relationships, and so on. It is in these general and very abstract scripts that people acquire the means through which they can extend and enlarge on what is expected of them and can invent new forms of husbandly and wifely behaviour:

> Their society has provided them with a taken-for-granted image of marriage and has socialized them into an anticipation of stepping into the taken-for-granted roles of marriage. All the same, these relatively empty projections now have to be actualised, lived through, and filled with experiential content by the protagonists. This will require a dramatic change in their definitions of reality and of themselves. (Berger and Kellner 1970: 58)

The first step in this is coming to be seen as a unit—a 'couple' or an 'item'—rather than as two completely separate individuals. They must convince themselves, as well as others, that this is the way in which they should be seen.

Each partner's identity must be reconstructed as the partners come to be seen—by those outside the relationship and by the partners themselves—as conjoined: they are seen, and they see themselves, as a unit. Each partner must align his or her definitions of situations with those of their partner. Only in this way can their actions within the marital relationship be coordinated.

Each husband is the most significant other to the wife, and vice versa. People enter this process, however, with only a partial awareness of what they are doing. They generally believe that they remain largely unchanged within their new relationship. They believe that they have a fixed social identity, rooted in their experiences of developing as a child and a youth. For this reason, they typically believe that their fundamental identity remains as something that is not culturally variable. They experience their change of identity on marriage as a series of encounters with particular others who now define them, in important respects, differently. In responding to these definitions, however, they construct themselves as a husband or a wife and their identity is slowly and inexorably transformed: old friends are dropped and old relationships transformed, new joint friendships are formed, and new, shared experiences are built up.

A new shared definition of reality is constructed and is constantly redefined through conversation and interaction and through encounters with those outside the marital relationship. When children are born, their existence strengthens the identity of the marital relationship. The children refer to the partners as 'Mummy' and 'Daddy', reinforcing their identity as parents as well as husband and wife.

> ⮏ *Connections*
>
> The Berger and Kellner argument focuses on the conventional marriage relationship and the conventional family. They tend to give a rather idealized view of the family. How well do you think the argument applies to non-marital partnerships and the cohabitation of men and women? How much of their argument do you think applies to same-sex partnerships and 'marriages'?

Being a nurse

The improvised construction of roles also occurs in the world of employment, where much secondary socialization takes place. The nature of this role behaviour is particularly well illustrated in a study of nursing that was carried out by Davina Allen (2001). Allen focused on the character of nursing as a gendered occupational role, as a specific occupational position in the division of labour that is disproportionately filled by women. Like many 'caring' occupations, nursing originated in the voluntary work that

was undertaken by many women as an extension of their domestic role, as wife and mother, within the family. Although now organized in hospitals and medical practices and undertaken as paid employment, nursing is still influenced by its origins.

Allen shows that contemporary nursing has come to be shaped by two competing ideas of work organization: 'professionalism' and 'managerialism'. The idea of professionalism sees nursing as organized around a moral obligation to provide care as autonomous and trained experts. The idea of managerialism, on the other hand, depicts the nurse as an employee at a particular career grade in a bureaucratic organization and as subject to the authority of supervisors (Dingwall *et al.* 1988; Witz 1992). The larger context for these rival ideas was a complex of changes in health policy and nurse education during the 1990s. The introduction of the internal market, accountability, and managerialism to the health service had an impact on many occupations, including nursing. At the same time, however, nurse education came to emphasize greater professionalism through degree-level training. In particular, Project 2000 emphasized the autonomy of clinical nursing and the need for a 'holistic' approach to patient care.

> ⮏ *Connections*
>
> You will find a discussion of wider changes in working practices in Chapter 17, pp. 704–7 and Chapter 14, pp. 559–63. Policy changes are considered in Chapter 15, pp. 601–3.

These changes led to much debate over the nature of the nurse role, leading to much greater uncertainty for nurses as to how their role should actually be performed on the wards and in surgeries. Nurses come to their training with only a general idea of what it is to be a nurse, and their training and the reorganization of nursing and health care has meant that their concrete formal knowledge about the role—as against their purely technical, medical knowledge—was ambiguous and uncertain. The reforms reshaped the cultural templates of the nurse role, making them even less certain than before. The meaning of the role had to be reconstructed and renegotiated in the day-to-day interactions of those who were actually undertaking the task of nursing in hospitals and medical units.

Allen focuses on the issues of role conflict that arise within the role-set of the nurse. Merton's (1957) contribution to structural functionalism and role-learning theory had been to introduce this idea of the role-set to describe all those pairs of roles that are regularly involved in structured relationships with each other. Thus, Allen identifies role relations among nurses of various grades as well as role relations between nurses and support workers, management, doctors, and patients. Each of the relations in this role-set is an area of negotiation and has the potential for conflict. The boundaries and the links that make up the role-set are contested and subject to constant negotiation.

Allen's study involved observations and interviews in two hospitals in the Midlands. Her focus was on the ward nurses and the ways in which they organized their work. In particular, she was concerned with how they organized the teamwork that was required by the new nursing practices.

In wards dominated by managerialist ideas, conflict between junior and senior nurses was especially marked. The junior nurses claimed that senior staff did not devolve responsible jobs to them but retained control over them in order to boost their own status in the ward hierarchy. The junior nurses saw the senior nurses as too bureaucratic and regulatory, and they opposed this in the name of what they saw as their own—professional—'patient centredness'.

In units that were dominated by ideas of professionalism, on the other hand, senior nurses saw themselves as coordinating rather than controlling. As a result, there was less conflict over work allocation. However, the senior staff in these units were less happy with the situation. The senior nurses felt that their job had little real content to it: much primary nursing care was devolved to the junior nurses, and the senior nurses were left with more paperwork and administration.

Thus, staff experienced role strains, expressed as boundary disputes over participation in patient care. These strains reflected the role realignment that had been required by Project 2000, though the ways in which they were worked out depended upon the particular negotiated interactions of nurses in the various kinds of ward and medical unit: 'Nurses are subject to conflict and ambiguous ideologies. The professional rhetoric of "new nursing" emphasizes their status as autonomous practitioners but as employees in a managed organization they are expected to render obedience to superiors and conform to formal rules and regulations' (Allen 2001: 75).

These strains deeply affected their sense of professional identity: What did it now mean to identify oneself as a 'nurse'? The general public may have an image of nursing drawn from the differing views in accounts of Florence Nightingale and from television programmes such as *Casualty*, *No Angels*, or *ER*, but nurses themselves had a far less clear idea of what nursing means in practice and

Doctor's, nurses, and other medical staff spend more time in managerial work.

© Getty Images/Nicholas Russell

how their work relates to the larger division of labour in health care.

These ambiguities were also apparent in concerns over the demarcation between nursing work and the work undertaken by unqualified support staff. Project 2000 reforms had introduced the new occupation of health-care assistant, and there was much ambiguity over the boundaries between this and professional nursing. Where the organization of ward-level care put great emphasis on the work of the ward team as a whole, the boundary was very blurred, especially in the non-technical areas of work. Allen notes that there were also implications for the nurse–patient boundary, as patients themselves had become more actively involved in routine care tasks such as the keeping of records, maintaining fluid balances, and making some technical measurements and adjustments to equipment.

It was in relation to management, however, that conflict was especially marked. Nurses recognized the gendered character of both nursing and management, routinely referring to managers as 'the men in suits'. The relation between managers and nurses was a gendered power relationship: men holding authority over the women who were undertaking the caring work. Many nurses felt that the increased paperwork that they were expected to do undermined their ability to participate fully in professional patient care and involved them in tasks that were properly the sphere of management. Those who were employed in the grade of 'nurse manager' were pulled in both directions and tended to see themselves playing an intermediary role, as translating central requirements into more professional and collegial forms whenever possible. However, they tended to be seen as outsiders by both the managers and other nurses.

Nurses followed flexible working practices that led them into areas that were often regarded as the province of junior doctors—it was often easier to make a decision on the spot than it was to consult a doctor. This gave the nurses greater autonomy, but was a source of conflict with doctors.

The boundaries of nursing work are produced in particular practical situations where nurses come into contact with patients, other professionals, and managers. The ways in which these boundaries are produced, however, are constrained by the general institutional context and the combination of competing managerial and professional ideas. They are further constrained by consumerist ideas that try to give patients rights as 'customers' of the health-care system. This led to conflicts with the more traditional 'service' orientation that nurses had long held to.

Changes in the organization of health care make it more than ever impossible for nurses to immediately undertake their work on the basis of their generic training and its induction of them into the nursing role. They cannot simply 'take' a pre-existing nurse role and play it out. They must 'make' this role for themselves through their conflict and negotiation with others involved in the provision and receipt of health care.

Sustaining medical definitions

In interaction, people build and sustain shared definitions of reality that define the various situations that they enter. It is rarely the case that there is a single, consensual definition of reality—as some forms of structural functionalism have argued. There are usually 'counter-realities' or, at the very least, counter-themes that oppose or qualify any dominant definition. Any dominant definition is likely to be the outcome of complex negotiations among a group of actors. For this reason, the participants must work hard to maintain the dominance of their preferred reality, and their ability to sustain it depends on their power, on the resources that they can bring to bear on the situation.

Emerson illustrates these processes through her investigation in a gynaecological clinic. Like any medical examination, a gynaecological examination involves the sustaining of a medical definition of reality that justifies forms of intrusion that are not normally permissible in interpersonal encounters: doctors must be able to ask highly personal questions and to interfere with another person's body, and this is possible only if the participants agree to maintain a medical definition of reality. In a gynaecological examination, however, these problems are especially acute because the personal intrusions concern the genitals: 'Since a woman's genitals are commonly accessible only in a sexual context, sexual connotations come readily to mind. Although most people realize that sexual responses are inappropriate, they may be unable to dismiss the sexual reaction' (Emerson 1970: 76).

Thus, the medical definition is countered by a sexual definition of reality that continually threatens to undermine the medical definition and so make medical intervention impossible. Doctors and medical staff must work hard to prevent the patients from seeing the examination in sexual terms. The medical definition gives staff the right to carry out their work, and it minimizes any threat to the dignity of the patient.

They do this by adopting a matter-of-fact stance, implying that 'this happens all the time' and 'nothing unusual is going on'. They make it clear that they are not interested in the aesthetics of the patient's body and that 'their gaze takes in only medically pertinent facts' (Emerson 1970: 78). The aim is to convey the idea that the patient is regarded as a technical object—they are concerned with the biological body and not with the self that inhabits it. At the same time, however, a doctor must acknowledge the patient as a person, as without this there will not be the necessary cooperation. Some of the counter-themes, then, must be recognized and brought into play alongside the medical definition of reality.

The complexity of the medical encounter results from the need to balance these contradictory elements. Various routine ways of doing this are established:

- Props and scenery are utilized to emphasize the clinic as a 'medical space': decoration, equipment, titles, nameplates, uniforms, and announcements all work to this end.

- Rituals of respect are employed. For example, the patient's body is covered so that only the part to be examined is uncovered, and a female nurse may act as 'chaperone' to a male doctor.

- The use of technical language and impersonal forms to refer to the patient's genitals helps to depersonalize and desexualize the conversation: medical staff refer to 'the vagina', not 'your vagina'. Similarly, they may use oblique terms when addressing the patient, such as referring to problems 'down below'.

- A nonchalant demeanour.

A crucial problem, however, is that patients are less well socialized into these norms and routines, and so there is the ever present possibility that they may do or say things that disrupt the medical definition of reality. They may show signs of embarrassment, such as blushing, which emphasize the sexual aspects of the situation and make it more difficult for medical staff to adopt an impersonal and technical orientation. Similarly, displays of modesty or of concern over the aesthetics of the body show that the patient has not fully accepted the requirements of the medical definition of reality.

 Briefing: medical assaults

Newspapers regularly report cases of doctors who sexually assault their female patients. The power inherent in the doctor–patient relationship makes it difficult for women, in vulnerable situations and seeking medical help, to resist such assaults. It can be very difficult for them to prove their cases against the doctor.

❓ *What does Emerson's argument suggest about the causes of such behaviour by doctors? Are they, too, less well socialized into the norms of medical investigations, or is their commitment to these norms overridden by stronger motivations?*

➲ *You might like to look at newspaper archives, surfing the Internet, to collect reports from recent cases and see if you can come up with any evidence on this.*

Where such things occur, doctors and nurses adopt strategies to neutralize the disruptions. One strategy is to continue to maintain a nonchalant demeanour, not acknowledging the patient's disruptive actions and hoping that a medical definition will re-establish itself. Often it may be necessary to redefine behaviour: signs of embarrassment, for example, may be defined as signs of 'pain', so reasserting a medical interpretation of the behaviour. Humour may also be used to acknowledge but defuse disruptions by channelling them away from the doctor–patient encounter. Conversations with nurses, for example, are safe ways in which patients' fears and concerns can be addressed before they meet the doctor.

Emotions and reflexivity

We have looked at the construction of social realities through interaction, exploring the cognitive images of social life and the normative expectations that people build up to shape their actions towards each other. In this section we look at the idea that human emotions can also be seen as socially constructed. The part played by emotions in social life was particularly stressed by psychoanalytical writers, but many of them—and most notably Freud himself—saw these emotions as natural, biological factors that were a fixed and universal element in human motivation. Those who incorporated a cultural dimension into psychoanalysis were particularly concerned to emphasize the interdependence of culture and biology: culture shapes, or constructs, not only the ways in which emotions are expressed, but also the very emotions themselves. This is not to deny the biological, bodily aspects of emotion—this cannot be ignored. However, the meaning and experience of anxiety, love, fear, and so on are culturally variable.

In this section we will look at the social construction of emotions through an important study by Arlie Hochschild, which examines this through an investigation into the organization of particular kinds of work and their implications for self and identity. Hochschild draws on the work of symbolic interactionists—and on Goffman, in particular—to complement the insights of psychoanalysis. We also look at the argument of those writers who have seen contemporary societies as particularly likely to develop high levels of anxiety because they are structured around a growing awareness of the risks inherent in modern social life.

Emotional presentations

Hochschild sees an emotion as a socially constructed mode of response that links bodily feelings to specific objects and circumstances. Bodily feelings sensitize us to certain objects or aspects of our environment, and it is our cultural definition of the situation that picks out or identifies these objects and aspects and so makes them meaningful in relation to our feelings. We can call up particular emotions by imagining situations that would evoke them, or we can suppress an emotion by suppressing the images that would evoke it. The whole social setting in which someone lives and works (as Emerson showed for the medical context) may be constructed in order to ensure that a particular emotional feeling occurs among the participants.

These ideas are applied to work contexts through the concept of **emotional labour**. Any concrete form of labour, Hochschild argues, has physical, mental, and emotional aspects to it. It involves the physical coordination of the body, the mental planning of actions, and the emotional inducement or suppression of feelings. Hochschild defines emotional labour as the use of techniques of emotion management, or 'emotion work', to control the emotions that must be expressed as an integral part of a particular process of labour. Emotional labour, she holds, is undertaken whenever a job 'requires one to induce or suppress feeling in order to sustain the outward countenance that produces the proper state of mind in others' (Hochschild 1983: 7).

Emotion work involves the application of norms that Hochschild calls 'feeling rules' (Hochschild 1983: 18). These are the cultural norms that shape emotions and determine how they are presented or performed in interaction. The ways in which actors perform their particular emotions may be more or less consciously managed. The cultural control of emotions may typically be a matter of routine, giving the appearance of spontaneous or uncontrolled emotion, but it may also be subject to conscious control in the same way as any other aspect of self-presentation.

All occupations involve emotional labour, to a greater or lesser extent. In some, however, the presentation of positive emotions is more obvious. This is the case, for example, of the nurses discussed in an earlier section, where 'caring' involves an emotional element as well as a purely technical element. Similar considerations apply to many occupations in the service sector, where the ways in which a worker relates to others is central to the work itself. In these cases, specific feeling rules may be imposed by employing organizations in order to ensure the public display of feeling. This results in a 'transmutation' of private acts of feeling: people try to feel what they ought to feel and what they are obliged to display in their public acts.

Hochschild looks at situations where the norms that shape emotions are set by the managers of an organization, who thereby require their employees to exercise emotion management in ways that they might not otherwise have chosen. Particular forms of emotional expression are required as an integral feature of the performance of particular kinds of labour. In this situation, specific kinds of display are required—smiling, being polite, saying 'have a nice day', and so on—so that customers or clients of the organization will believe that the worker actually feels concern for their pleasure or well-being.

She looks at this through the case of airline cabin crew in the American company Delta Airlines. Flight attendants —stewards, stewardesses, pursers, etc.—are the most visible part of an airline, and the growth of commercial competition from the 1930s led airline companies to focus on the flight attendant in their advertising. The high point of this was the 1950s and 1960s. Delta Airlines chose an image of the ideal flight attendant to represent the company as a whole, and as a southern company they chose a southern image: 'The image they chose . . . was that of a beautiful and smartly dressed Southern white woman, the supposed epitome of gracious manners and warm personal service' (Hochschild 1983: 93).

The company developed systems of staff selection and training aimed at producing flight attendants who conformed to this ideal. They also used advertising slogans and images that sexualized the attendant. All this meant that the attendant's work had to express emotions that were appropriate to this imagery. The successful candidates in the selection process were those who were aware of the feeling rules that had to be applied and who were willing to take them seriously. Interview manuals stressed sincerity, a friendly smile, enthusiasm, vivaciousness, and similar qualities, and they emphasized the importance of using the right body language (such as maintaining eye contact). Applicants were screened for an 'outgoing middle-class sociability' (Hochschild 1983: 97).

During training it was made clear that cabin crew members would keep their jobs only so long as they lived and worked as a particular type of person. They had to maintain the correct physical appearance (make-up, clothing, weight), personal behaviour (smoking, drinking, hours of sleep), and, above all, emotion management. Flight attendants were expected to show particular kinds of feelings and were trained in the techniques that would achieve this. Attendants were told to regard the plane as their home and to treat passengers as if they were guests. Imagining the plane in this way helped to evoke the emotions of care and hospitality that the airline required.

In the case of angry or troublesome passengers, attendants were taught to treat them in the same way as they would treat naughty children. They must maintain a good-humoured but firm approach and not react with anger themselves. Again, conjuring up the image of dealing with children allowed the attendant to evoke the appropriate emotional response towards the unruly passenger.

It was emphasized by the trainers that the emotional presentation had to be 'sincere': attendants had to act from the heart rather than acting in an obviously unnatural way.

That is, they were required, through their displays, actually to produce the emotion in themselves. Everything that the attendants do in their job, then, involves them in emotion work.

The airline industry changed rapidly from the 1970s. Larger and faster planes were introduced, and journey times became shorter. Discount fares, family travel, and greater competition meant that passengers were no longer simply the affluent business travellers. These changes make it more difficult for cabin crew to perform their emotional labour effectively. Attendants must give greater priority to safety and to other technical skills, leaving less time and energy for emotion work. As a result, Hochschild argues, attendants have reasserted a claim to their own emotions and to a greater autonomy in deciding their appearance. They display positive emotions by acting superficially rather than from the heart. This brings them into greater conflict with the airline company managers. The managers, in response, have attempted to recruit lower paid and more submissive ethnic minority employees in an attempt to build a workforce that can be drilled into the 'proper' performance of emotional labour.

> **⊃** *Connections*
> Try to think of other examples of work that involves high levels of emotional labour. How do selection and training processes bring this about?

Anxiety and risk

Psychoanalytical writers, and Adler in particular, stressed the part played by anxiety in human life. Anxiety was seen as resulting from the cultural demands placed upon the impulses of the id, and Adler saw it as the root of the inferiority complex. The question of anxiety has recently been taken up by a number of writers who see it as having an increased importance in contemporary Western societies because of the fundamental social changes that they have experienced (Wilkinson 2001). In particular, it is argued that the increasing risks faced by people in their everyday lives generates high levels of anxiety.

Among the earliest writers to point in this direction were David Riesman (1961) and C. Wright Mills (1959). Riesman recognized what he called a 'diffuse anxiety' as a characteristic personality feature in America, while Mills identified economic dislocations, military conflicts, urban disorganization, and family breakdown as the structural conditions responsible for this growing anxiety. According to some, this anxiety is a fundamental social malaise that produces a deep cultural pessimism (Bailey 1988).

At the heart of the contemporary discussions of anxiety is the idea of the **risk society**, postulated by Beck (1992).

Beck argues that the increase in technologically and socially generated dangers—as against purely natural disasters—in modern societies has encouraged the growth of a 'risk consciousness'. This is a predisposition to express anxieties about these dangers in the language of risk.

The risks that concern people are what Giddens (1990) has called 'manufactured risks'. These are risks that result from the effects of human actions on the world, through technologies of production and all of the other social practices that people are involved in. The whole of nature has been transformed by human activity, and there are few parts of the global human environment that have not been affected by this. Ostensibly 'natural' disasters, such as famines and floods, are increasingly the results of environmental changes brought about by industrial and urban life. Strikingly, these risks are overwhelmingly produced in the advanced societies of the West, but they are overwhelmingly experienced in the poor countries of the world. There is a global distribution of risk. Within the advanced societies themselves, there is not only a perception of this globalization of risk, but also an awareness of the internal risks that the advanced societies face. There is less certainty concerning both the personal relations of intimacy, marriage, and family and the public relations of work, employment, and politics.

In the contemporary world, Beck argues, there is an increasing awareness of the dangers that face whole populations and that, indeed, operate on a global scale. This awareness is overwhelmingly derived from the output of the mass media. The hazards that can result from genetically modified foodstuffs, reproductive technologies,

 ## Briefing: to vaccinate or not to vaccinate?

There has been much anxiety among parents in Britain over the possible risks to children of the MMR triple vaccine for measles, mumps, and rubella. Reports of differences of opinion among medical experts, and uncertainty within the government meant that many parents preferred to face the risk that their children would catch one of the diseases rather than the risk of damage from a side-effect of the vaccine. The government commissioned a full investigation, which came up with a clear statement that there was no significant risk attached to the vaccination, but many parents saw this as simply another opinion and remained very confused and anxious about what course of action to take.

For background on this see
www.mmrthefacts.nhs.uk/

ecological change, and so on, are reported and discussed in the newspapers and on television, and the ways in which these reports are constructed shapes people's perceptions of the risks that are involved in them. A shared sense of crisis or catastrophe may be generated among readers and viewers, and people tend to become very anxious about their own fate and their particular circumstances. They perceive the world as a dangerous world, a runaway world (Giddens 1999) over which they have little or no control. Such a consciousness evokes feelings of anxiety that are attached to the world in general, rather than to specific dangers or problems. This is Riesman's diffuse anxiety.

Scientific knowledge and scientific experts are of little help in reducing this anxiety. They may be seen as responsible for the technologically induced risks, and a growth in knowledge that people have about the risks that they

face may simply serve to increase their level of anxiety. Scientific experts will often disagree among themselves over the likely consequences of particular actions, and people become critical of science and scientists and feel that they must come to their own conclusions.

Giddens has seen this growth in anxiety in terms of the implications of modernity for the formation of identities. He holds that people seek to cope with everyday life by 'bracketing-off', or disregarding, the uncertainties and dangers of the world. They try to build everyday social realities that cocoon them from these dangers and allow them to get on with the routines of daily life.

In pre-modern societies, this framework of routine was provided by tradition and custom: people had to make few decisions or choices and could simply rely on the ways that things had always been done. Their fates and destinies in

Global focus Tourism and identity

Most secondary identities—identities of occupation, class, politics, and religion—have been tied to the boundaries of nation states. This is at its clearest in a person's 'national' identity as British, French, German, American, and so on. But does this still apply in an era of globalization? John Urry (2002) has explored this through an investigation into the ideas of travel and tourism. What does it mean when a person identifies themselves as a 'tourist': are they a 'national' citizen in a 'foreign' country, or is the tourist a distinctively transnational or global identity?

Tourism is a specifically modern phenomenon that arose with the creation of a distinction between 'work' and 'leisure' in modern societies. In pre-modern societies there was no distinction between paid work and unpaid leisure, and so there was no possibility of travelling for leisure. The journey and the stay that make up a tour or holiday are to places other than the normal places of residence and work, for purposes not directly connected with work, and for a specified period of time. The person who travels in this way adopts a specific identity: that of the tourist. According to Urry, the tourist identity involves the adoption of what he calls the tourist gaze. That is, the tourist is someone who looks on things and places in a particular and distinct way that is not that of the local resident or worker. The tourist gazes on 'sights', recording them in photographs and postcards in order to be able to recreate them in memory at a later date. What the tourist sees, however, is not the 'real' place (whatever that may be), but the image of that place that has been constructed through the various tourist professionals that have arisen around the holiday and travel industries of the modern world.

Tourism initially involved travel within one's own country, except for the very rich. The typical holiday into the first half of

the twentieth century was a short break at a seaside resort. As air travel became cheaper in the second half of the twentieth century, foreign holidays became more usual, and foreign travel has increasingly involved travelling great distances and to a greater variety of places.

More than ever before, tourist venues are specifically constructed for the tourist gaze: the clearest examples of this are, perhaps, the various Disneyland resorts. A tourist is separated from his or her normal routines and places of work and residence, and is, at the same time, not a part of the place that he or she visits. The tourist, then, is a detached figure, a cultural nomad in a simulated reality.

The global growth of tourism has meant that the immense international flows of people are, for the most part, flows of tourists. Global realities are constructed through the images present in the tourist gazes. Constructions of nationhood are, increasingly, constructions by and for tourists from outside the nation. People's own sense of national identity reflects the constructions of the global tourist industry, and nations must compete to present themselves in images and as spectacles that will appeal to a large number of visitors. National identity is no longer so closely linked to a sense of territory, but is more closely related to a sense of the image of a particular place. Britain, for example, projects an international image of its history and national heritage. At the same time, the very idea of travel and mobility becomes central to people's identities. They no longer define themselves simply by the places where they live and work; they also define themselves by the places to which they can travel and, therefore, by the very idea of travel and movement.

life were fixed, and they had to play a largely passive part in the world. In modern societies, with their high degree of individualism and the disappearance of traditional ideas in the face of critical, rational reflection, this is no longer the case, as people must make individual decisions for themselves.

Modern societies, Giddens argues, rest upon a culture of 'reflexivity', a cultural requirement to constantly monitor, assess, and modify one's own actions in the light of their likely consequences. The self is a 'reflexive project' (Giddens 1991: 32), a constantly reconstructed identity that is legitimated through the production of appropriate narratives. People are compelled to take responsibility for deciding and building their own identities and for constructing a constantly changing 'narrative of the self'. They become what Bauman (1995) has called 'pilgrims': they travel through their lives towards a chosen destination

forming and reforming their identities as they travel (see also Bauman 1993). Even successfully socialized individuals, Giddens argues, can face anxieties that swamp these efforts and impel individuals into a state of constant diffuse anxiety over their own identity and their place in the world.

The growth of risk society and its risk consciousness, then, generates the kinds of concerns that make it impossible for individuals to ignore the dangers that they face. The emergence of the reflexive project of building the self and the expansion of risk consciousness means that these modern societies have seen a growth in expert systems that are aimed at helping individuals to live with their anxieties. The growth of academic sociology and psychology are examples of this, but it is manifested, in particular, in the massive growth of therapy and counselling in all areas of life.

 *Stop and reflect*

We have looked at a number of aspects of the construction of social reality and the operation of secondary socialization.

- Social realities are actively constructed by the participants and must be maintained and sustained in their interactions.

- A person's identity is reconstructed as his or her social relationships develop and are transformed.

- Does an emphasis on social construction imply that all human behaviour is culturally determined? How adequate would such a view be?

These processes occur in many work situations where secondary socialization takes place:

- Occupational roles often involve conflicting demands that have to be met. Staff respond to these strains by reconstructing and redefining their roles.

- The emergence of counter-realities has to be prevented in order to sustain dominant definitions of reality.

- Can you think of examples of the ways in which the maintenance of definitions of reality involves the use of specific routines and practices?

Finally, we looked at a number of aspects of the emotional dimension to social interaction:

- Many work tasks involve people in the performance of much emotional labour, and work organizations may require particular forms of emotional display.

- The growth of a risk consciousness has resulted in high levels of anxiety over the nature of these risks and their consequences.

- What is meant by the claim that the reflexive reconsideration of identity has become a central feature of contemporary social life?

Chapter summary

In the section on 'Understanding socialization, identity, and interaction' we discussed a number of issues concerning the relationship between culture and biology and the ways in which these have been considered in theories of socialization and identity. We showed that:

- Human behaviour is learned and there is no fixed human nature determined by biology.

- Biological factors condition or constrain cultural formation but do not determine social behaviour.

- A sense of identities and self develops through primary and secondary socialization.

Three major theories of socialization and identity were considered, and we suggested that they are complementary ways of understanding these issues.

- Role-learning theory focuses on the ways in which conformity to role expectations results from socialized commitments and practical constraints. People are, however, active creators and interpreters of their roles.

- Symbolic interactionist theory focuses on the social construction of a sense of self. This self takes over and reflects the attitudes of others.

- Psychoanalytic theory focuses on unconscious emotions and drives, particularly those of sexuality and sensual desire. Later psychoanalysts recognized the shaping power of cultural factors.

In 'Socialization and family relations' we considered issues of personality development in relation to practices of mothering and stages in the family life cycle. We showed that:

- Social interaction is a crucial condition for the intellectual, linguistic, and moral development of a child. Development is not simply a matter of biological maturation.

- The life course must be seen as a series of 'stages' characterized by specific social constraints and opportunities and to which individuals respond subjectively in constructing their sense of self.

- 'Mothering' is a crucial aspect of socialization, though this mothering may be undertaken by a carer who is not the biological mother. It is the quality and intimacy of the relationship that is important, not the sex or gender of the carer.

- Conflicts between parents and children are particularly marked in adolescence in contemporary Western societies, and this can lead to a child being labelled as 'troubled' or, in extreme cases, mentally ill.

In 'Building social worlds', we concentrated on aspects of secondary socialization, showing that social realities are actively constructed by the participants and need to be actively maintained and sustained through their interactions.

- Social identities are constantly reconstructed and reshaped as people's social relationships change.

- In the sphere of work, people frequently have to juggle with conflicting expectations from both within the world of work and from outside. This is handled by reconstructing and redefining roles. This involves building and relying on specific routines and practices that help to manage day-to-day encounters.

- Emotional labour is an integral aspect of most work situations and many jobs require an active display of emotions by their occupants.

- Contemporary work patterns are associated with levels of uncertainty and insecurity that generate a risk consciousness and high levels of anxiety. People no longer have fixed and secure work identities but must constantly and reflexively rebuild their identities.

Key concepts

- age cohort
- back regions
- biological determinism
- cultural determinism
- culture
- emotional labour
- generalized other
- inferiority complex
- internalization

- life course
- narratives
- personal identity
- primary identities
- primary socialization
- risk society
- role-taking
- secondary identities

- secondary socialization
- self
- self-presentation
- significant other
- social identity
- socialization
- superego
- unconscious

Workshop 4

Study 4 Negotiating shyness

A recent study has explored the presentation of self among those who regard themselves, and are regarded by others as 'shy'. Susie Scott (2005, 2007) examines shyness in terms of concepts drawn from the work of George Mead and Erving Goffman. She sees shyness as a social role that has to be negotiated in everyday life through presentational strategies in which those who regard themselves as shy attempt to conceal this discrediting identity from others and to create an illusion of competence.

Shyness is often seen in individualistic terms as a psychological 'problem', but Scott interprets the subjectivity of shy persons rather differently. Anxiety about interactional encounters with others is normal and widespread, but some individuals may experience extreme and uncontrollable attacks of anxiety about social encounters that inhibit them from full participation and lead them to withdraw from or avoid front-stage situations. Such individuals, when they have to enter social situations, tend to blush, stammer, or exhibit other behavioural responses that betray their anxiety to the others with whom they interact. These others act towards them on the basis of cultural stereotypes of shyness and, through their stigmatizing and discrediting responses, they lead the socially anxious to come to perceive themselves as shy. Their image of self derives from the reactions of others, and they perceive a 'shy me'—the shy self perceived by others. In taking on the social expectations about shyness, they come to play the shy role.

Those who take on the shy role as an aspect of their social identity come to see themselves as relatively incompetent: they regard themselves as lacking in the social skills that others possess, and their perceived lack of social skills leads to further avoidance of interaction or to discrediting performances. They act in terms of an image of the generalized other as a 'competent other': other people are able to handle public, front-stage encounters with ease because they have none of the anxieties or inadequacies possessed by the shy person. Others are socially competent extroverts, whereas the shy person feels a socially incompetent introvert. The adoption of the shy role has led to an internalization of shyness that makes it appear as an individual psychological problem rather than a socially generated condition.

Scott suggests that anxiety is far more widespread than commonly assumed. Those whom the shy person regards as socially competent may also experience anxiety about personal encounters but may be better able to handle them without succumbing to the shy role. The shy can, on occasion, pass as normal or competent. If they are able to learn the techniques that they observe in others, they may be able to give a convincing display of competence in social interaction and so may be less likely to be treated as shy. The fact that others do not define them in terms of their shyness allows them to begin to break with the shy role, despite their continuing anxiety. One such technique is to deflect attention from oneself. Asking a question that encourages others to talk, for example, means that one's own quietness becomes less apparent.

You might like to consider how best to undertake sociological studies of shyness. How can a sociologist go about interviewing or observing people who avoid social encounters? Look at Scott's study and see how she resolved this methodological problem.

If you were to observe social encounters in a public place, how would you know whether you are observing the actions of competent persons or the actions of shy persons who are passing as competent?

Media watch 4 What is a mother?

When Bob Geldof said that there was no significant difference in what a mother or a father can give a child, many disagreed. The *Guardian*'s 'parents' page' decided to explore the range of views on this and invited six people—three men and three women—to set out their thoughts (*Guardian*, 10 May 2002).

Dina Rabinovitch, a writer, based her views on the biology of motherhood. The fact that it is women who get pregnant and give birth, she argues, creates an intense bond—the child grows inside its mother's body, each adapting to the bodily rhythms of the other, and this physical tie creates a unique emotional tie.

She concludes that fathers cannot provide the kind of immediate and intense emotional support that comes 'naturally' to the mother. Although mothers and fathers are complementary in socialization, the mother relationship is primary. The author Kate Figes also sees fathers and mothers as complementary, but she rejects any idea that pregnancy and childbirth create an 'instinctive' bond between mother and child. Parenting is learned, she says, through trial and error, and what matters is not the sex of the parent but whether they quickly learn to be a 'good' parent.

Peter Howarth, a magazine editor, took a very different view, recognizing that mothers and fathers are complementary and that there is a 'powerful maternal bond', he stresses the particular importance of fathering. He grew up without a father, and it was while bringing up his own child that he began to realize what he had lost when he was a child. Richard Reeves, a business consultant for organizations wanting to set up 'father-friendly' workplaces, supported this view and believed that work must be reorganized to allow both parents to participate equally in a child's upbringing. Rather than stressing the complementarity of mothers and fathers, Richard holds that they are virtually interchangeable. The one thing that men cannot do, he argues, is breast feed, but they can do everything else just as well as women. The only reason that women tend to be better at parenting is that they have had more opportunity to develop the skills. If work was organized differently, men could also develop those skills.

Jack O'Sullivan, founder of a father's pressure group, points to medical studies that show that fathers can do just as well in feeding and nurturing their children, and he argues that there is a long history to the part played by men in bringing up their children. Maureen Freely, however, contrasts today with the 1950s when, she argues, the assumption was that 'real men didn't waste time on their children'. She points out that her own father, though involved in full-time employment, was very involved in her upbringing. The contribution of fathers, she argues, is invisible because it does not square with the image of the real man, because their contribution is invisible, it is seen as dispensable. The task for parents in families, she argues, is to negotiate ways in which they can each put their children before their jobs.

- Look back at our discussion of maternal deprivation and attachment theory and see how these various views relate to the theoretical debates that we considered. Do any of the contributors question the gendered character of mothering? How many of them recognize that not all children are born into conventional nuclear families.

- Carry out some brief interviews with members of your own family—male and female—and see if their views are similar to those reported in the *Guardian*. Do you expect to come up with any different views?

Discussion points

Look back over the 'Stop and reflect' points at the end of each section of this chapter and make sure that you understand the points that have been highlighted.

Socialization, personhood, and identity

In 'Understanding socialization' and 'Theories of socialization and identity' we considered a number of conceptual and theoretical ideas in learning a sense of self and social identity, and we compared and contrasted the main concepts used by symbolic interactionists and psychoanalysts:

- What is meant by primary and secondary identities?
- How would you distinguish between primary socialization and secondary socialization?
- How do psychoanalysts understand personality in terms of the superego, sexuality, and guilt?

Childhood, parenthood, and life course

In the section on 'Socialization and family relations' we looked at a number of issues related to motherhood, fatherhood, and childhood, and we saw these as socially constructed roles that correspond to particular stages in the life course.

- Consider the arguments from attachment theory about the significance of mothering. What are the problems with the idea of 'maternal deprivation'?
- How useful is it to see individual personalities as developing according to a particular sequence of developmental stages?

The social construction of reality

'Building social worlds' looked at the construction of social realities and at their cognitive, normative, and emotional dimensions.

- What do you understand by the term 'social construction'? How is this related to the ideas of self-presentation and role-playing?
- What does it mean to talk about role-making rather than role-taking?

Explore further

Good general reading on the issues discussed in this chapter can be found in:

Goffman, E. (1959), *Presentation of Self in Everyday Life* (Harmondsworth: Penguin). *A highly readable and illuminating account of everyday interaction. A sociological classic.*

Jenkins, R. (1996), *Social Identities* (London: Routledge). *A useful overview of debates in the area.*

Strauss, A. L. (1959), *Mirrors and Masks: The Search for Identity* (London: Martin Robertson, 1977). *A useful and well-written statement of the social-constructionist position.*

Becker, H. *et al.* (1961), *Boys in White* (New York: John Wiley; New Brunswick, NJ: Transaction, 1977). *An important study of the secondary socialization of trainee doctors in a medical school.*

Parsons, T., and Bales, R. (1956), *Family, Socialization and Interaction Process* (London: Routledge & Kegan Paul). *A useful but badly written statement of role-learning theory that tries to integrate it with psychoanalytic ideas.*

Hochschild, A. (1983), *The Managed Heart: Commercialization of Human Feeling* (Berkeley and Los Angeles: University of California Press). *An important and influential study of the social construction of emotions.*

Giddens, A. (1991), *Modernity and Self-Identity* (Cambridge: Polity Press). *Looks at the relationship between large-scale processes of modernization and the formation of a sense of self and individuality.*

Online resources

Visit the Online Resource Centre that accompanies this book to access more learning resources and other interesting material on socialization, identity, and interaction at:

www.oxfordtextbooks.co.uk/orc/fulcher3e/

On social interactionism, see the Society for the Study of Symbolic Interactionism at:

http://sun.soci.niu.edu/~sssi/

More specifically on G. H. Mead is the Mead Project at:

http://spartan.ac.brocku.ca/~lward/

although be aware that not all the links from this page work.

Psychoanalytic theory can be approached through Freud at:

http://users.rcn.com/brill/freudarc.html

(where many sources, including excerpts from his major works, are to be found).

The anti-psychiatry of R. D. Laing is well-covered at:

http://laingsociety.org/

The so-called attachment disorder is discussed at:

www.attachmentdisorder.net

Susie Scott's Shyness and society website can be found at:

www.sussex.ac.uk/Users/ss216/

sex, gender, and sexuality

Contents

05

Intersex

'Anna was never told the truth about her condition, or the real reason she underwent surgery at the age of 20. After seeking advice from her doctor about her failure to menstruate, Anna was sent to a London hospital for examination, where she was told she had lumps in her abdomen that needed to be removed. After surgery, she was prescribed a high dosage of the female hormone oestrogen and discharged with little follow-up. "I felt confused, like something was very wrong. But didn't understand what was happening", says Anna, now 44 . . .

What Anna slowly discovered in medical journals was that she had a rare genetic disorder called androgen insensitivity syndrome (AIS), also classed as an intersex condition. This meant that although externally she looked like a girl, she had no womb or ovaries, her vagina was undeveloped, and her body produced high levels of testosterone. The lumps that doctors removed when she was 20 were undescended testes . . .

Anna has a feminine voice. She keeps her greying, curly hair cropped short and swept back from her face in a hair band. She never wears a skirt or dress. On the day we meet she is dressed casually in jeans and sweatshirt. She does not look masculine. She says she does not look on herself as either male or female but, rather, "mixed gender" and has tended to avoid close relationships. "Society likes to categorise you, and I do not fit neatly with people's expectations. I just deal with it myself. I rarely talk about it." She then adds quietly, as if talking to herself: "It is like being continually punished for a crime I never committed."'

Source: Christine Toomey, 'The Worst of both Worlds', *The Sunday Times Magazine*, 28 October 2001.
© Times Newspapers Limited, 2001

People take it for granted that we are born male or female and that our biology determines which sex we are. Some are, however, born with a mixture of male and female characteristics that is labelled 'intersex'. In some cultures intersex children have been treated as special and unique creations that are highly valued, but in contemporary Western societies they are forced into one sex or the other. They are categorized as either male or female and their bodies are then required to fit these categories.

This is a particular example of the more general process through which people are made to fit the requirements of their sex, requirements which are specified by the society in which they live. This process generally starts at birth when they are given male or female names, which identify their sex. They are then brought up to be male or female. Throughout their lives they will be expected to behave in the ways considered appropriate to either men or women.

In this chapter we explore the social processes that make us men or women. We investigate the origins of contemporary beliefs about sex and gender and their significance for the way that people think, feel, and behave. We also examine the relationships of power and inequality between men and women, and discuss whether these relationships have changed.

Understanding sex, gender, and sexuality

In this section we examine the basic concepts used in studying the differences between men and women, theories of the inequalities between them, and the relationship between sex and sexuality.

Sex, gender, and sexuality

In understanding the differences between men and women, we must first make a basic distinction between sex and gender. The term **sex** refers to the physical and anatomical characteristics considered to distinguish *male* and *female* bodies from each other. These include differences in their chromosomes, reproductive organs, hormones, and physical appearance. **Gender** refers to differences in the way that men and women in a particular society are expected to feel, think, and behave. Thus, males are typically expected to feel, think, and behave in a *masculine* way, and females in a *feminine* way.

It was thought at one time that sex determined gender, that differences in the way that men and women behave are biologically rooted in their sex. Thus, differences in their occupations were seen as resulting from differences in their biological make-up that fitted them for very different kinds of work. Nurses were women because women were naturally more caring than men, while soldiers were men because they were naturally more aggressive.

While some people still hold these views, they cannot explain the different occupations of men and women. Many occupations that were once regarded as a male or female preserve have been opened up to the other sex. If women can become competent members of the armed forces and men can become competent nurses, the fact that nurses are predominantly women and soldiers are mainly men cannot have a biological explanation. Gender must therefore be distinguished from sex.

Sexuality too must be separated from sex. The word 'sex' is commonly used to describe sexual behaviour, as in the phrase 'having sex'. We must, however, clearly distinguish between sex, as referring to the physical and anatomical characteristics of men and women, and sexual behaviour, which refers to the activities that they find physically arousing. These activities are extremely diverse and are clearly not simply the result of their sex.

A person's sexuality is not just a description of his or her sexual practices. A person's sexuality refers also to those aspects of his or her identity, lifestyle, and community associated with these activities. Furthermore, these aspects of sexuality are not just the result of particular kinds of sexual behaviour but also shape that behaviour, for the adoption of a lifestyle or identity itself influences sexual behaviour. Sociologists argue that sexuality is not biologically given but is socially constructed.

Sex

A person's sex might seem to be a simple biological matter. Are we not born male or female? Does not our biology give us either a male or a female body? This section will show that the distinction between male and female bodies is a much more complex matter that involves social processes and requires sociological as well as biological explanation.

Determining sex

The basic biological difference between men and women is that a man has one X and one Y chromosome, while a woman has two X chromosomes. These chromosomal differences are responsible for primary sexual characteristics, that is for the internal reproductive organs (testes or ovaries) that develop in a particular individual, the hormones that circulate around their bodies, and the outward form taken by their reproductive organs (a penis or a vagina).

Our genes do not, however, simply produce two sexes. As our opening piece shows, some people cannot be classified at birth as male or female and are described as **intersex**. This may be because they have extra chromosomes or lack one chromosome. In other cases, the chromosomes do not produce clearly male or female bodies for genetic or hormonal reasons. Indeed, Fausto-Sterling (2000) has claimed that five different sexes can be biologically distinguished. Medical interventions have commonly occurred to turn intersex babies into males or females, though recently there has been a greater willingness to leave intersex people to decide their own destinies. The United Kingdom Intersex Association campaigns against the idea that intersexed people should be forced to conform to the two-sex social norm.

There are also some people who fit perfectly well the biological requirements of one sex but consider that they belong elsewhere. This occurs when a person who appears biologically male or female identifies with the other sex.

Such people typically feel that they are 'trapped in the wrong body' or 'born with the wrong sex'. They may well seek hormonal treatment or reconstructive surgery to give them the biological characteristics of the sex they believe they should be. These *transsexuals* should not be confused with *transvestites*, who do not believe that their sex should be different but adopt the dress of the other sex because they find it pleasurable to do so.

There is considerable variation in secondary sexual characteristics, such as body size. On average men are taller than women but this does not mean that all women are shorter than all men. The two distributions overlap. Many men are shorter than many women, and many women are taller than many men. There is, however, a cultural expectation that men will be taller. If a tall woman marries a short man and the difference cannot be remedied by heel sizes, the man may well have to stand on a box for wedding photographs! Other characteristics can be more easily changed. Weight and body shape can be altered by exercise and dieting, cosmetic surgery and hormonal treatments. The physical differences between male and female bodies are not just an outcome of their biology.

While sex and gender must be conceptually distinguished, sex characteristics should not be seen as independent of gender identities, for these identities specify the characteristics that the bodies of men and women should have (see box on 'Gendering sex'). Gendered conceptions of maleness and femaleness that require men and women to have different bodies have led to the widespread adoption of dieting and exercise regimes, cosmetic surgery and, in intersex cases, more dramatic medical and surgical interventions, that exaggerate the biological differences between men and women.

Sexes

The physical differences between the sexes should not then be seen as biologically determined. This is not just, however, a matter of how the body is shaped to fit gendered conceptions of the two sexes. The whole idea that there are two sexes is itself a particular way of thinking about the differences between men and women.

According to Thomas Laqueur (1990), this is, historically speaking, a quite recent way of thinking. For two millennia, from the time of the ancient Greeks to the eighteenth century, a 'one-sex model' dominated ways of thinking about men and women. People were, of course, aware of differences between men and women but did not think of them as two different sexes. Women were regarded as a less developed version of men. The 'two-sex model' that is now dominant only came into existence during the eighteenth and nineteenth centuries (we examine its emergence and consequences later in this chapter, on pp. 170–1).

The importance of this change in the way that the differences between men and women were seen can hardly be exaggerated. The whole idea that men and women have contrasting bodily characters, that 'men are from Mars and women are from Venus' stems from the two-sex model. This model has had enormous implications for sexual categories and sexual identities, as the section on 'Sexuality'

THEORY AND METHODS

Gendering sex

Judith Butler has reversed the notion that sex determines gender by arguing in her influential book, *Gender Trouble* (1990), that gender shapes sex. She rejected essentialist ideas of men and women that treat them as having a fixed and opposite character, ideas that were bound up with a 'stable and oppositional heterosexuality' (1990: 30). She is here very critical of those feminists who think that all women have the same underlying character and share a common identity. Indeed, Butler was opposed to the whole notion that there is some inner male or female self that makes us think and behave in male and female ways.

Butler argued that sex is shaped by gender discourses, which prescribe male and female ways of behaving by providing 'scripts' that people then perform. It is the repeated *performance* of actions according to these scripts that makes bodies male and female. She developed the concept of **performativity** to describe the formation of the character of men and women through these repeated performances.

For example, dominant conceptions of masculinity provide a male script, emphasizing physical toughness, which men are expected to display. This leads men to develop their muscles and engage in physical aggression, by, say, using their fists to resolve conflicts. These 'performances' result in men appearing more muscular and physically aggressive than women and this is then seen as an external manifestation of their nature. Physical toughness comes to be regarded as a biological characteristic of the male sex but it is, in fact, the result of a repeated acting out of beliefs about how men should be.

Butler considered that gendered ideas about the nature of men and women could be subverted by transgressive acts that cross the boundaries set up by gender scripts. Drag and cross-dressing show that men and women can challenge gender scripts by adopting the appearance of the other sex. But are these acts really subversive, since they perpetuate the association of maleness and femaleness with opposite ways of dressing and behaving? Do they not reinforce gender scripts? Can you think of changes in dress that are more subversive?

A drag queen prepares for a night out—is this a subversive act?

© Alice Chadwick

will show. It also assisted the emergence of a feminist movement by freeing women from the notion that they were merely an inferior version of men.

We have now moved a long way from the idea that the physical differences between male and female bodies are the result of biological differences alone. Our actual bodies are to a considerable extent shaped by gendered beliefs about these differences and the practices associated with these beliefs. The whole notion that men and women are two different sexes that are opposite in character is itself cultural not biological. Sex cannot just be left to biologists and is part of the subject-matter of sociology as well.

Gender

The rejection of biological explanations of gender differences resulted in their explanation by reference to **gender-roles** that specify the ways in which men and women are expected to feel, think, and behave. These prescribe not only the kinds of work that men and women are expected to do but the feelings they can express and everyday aspects of their behaviour, such as the way that they speak and dress. The term **sex-roles** has been widely used to express the same idea but we refer to gender-roles because the behaviour of men and women is shaped by beliefs about gender.

Gender socialization

These gender-roles are learned through the process of socialization, which begins in the family and continues through education and indeed throughout life, for agencies of socialization, such as the media, continue to shape people's behaviour long after they have become adults.

> **⊃ Connections**
> You may find it helpful to refer here to our detailed discussion of role-learning and socialization theories in Chapter 4, pp. 124–32.

There is plenty of evidence to support this account of gender differences. It has been shown that boys and girls are brought up differently from the moment they are born. In Britain they are, for example, commonly dressed in different colours, blue for a boy and pink for a girl. This may seem a trivial observation but these differences in clothing elicit powerful differentiating responses from

adults. In one experiment, reported in Brewer (2001), the same baby was first dressed in pink and then in blue. Adults immediately assumed that pink meant female and blue meant male. The child was then handled and spoken to quite differently. When in pink the baby was described as beautiful, when in blue as strong. Different futures were imagined and projected on to the child, according to the presumed sex.

It is through such processes that boys and girls learn that they are different and acquire gendered identities. Children know whether they are boys or girls as soon as they can talk. By the time that they are three or four years old they see these differences as biological and permanent. They then begin to inhabit different worlds in which each plays only with children of its own sex and avoids contact with the other, thereby reinforcing gender divergence (Brewer 2001).

Behaviourist approaches argue that all this occurs simply through reward and punishment. When boys and

Like mother, like daughter—learning gender-roles.

© Alice Chadwick

girls act in the ways that are prescribed by gender-roles, they are rewarded. When they act in other ways, they are punished. Rewards and punishments involve subtle forms of social approval and disapproval, as well as material rewards or physical punishment. Children themselves reinforce the process by ridiculing behaviour that violates gender norms. The playground and the street are important sites of socialization. Socialization into gender-roles does clearly involve mechanisms of reward and punishment but are these sufficient to explain the differentiation of male and female identities?

Those working within the Freudian tradition (see Chapter 4, pp. 129–32) provide a very different account that emphasizes the dynamics of personality formation, the significance of emotion, and the intimate relationships of parents and children. Nancy Chodorow (1978) argued that all infants have a close attachment to their mothers. Because mothers have the main responsibility for child-rearing, children tend to identify with them. Soon, however, they come to conform to gendered expectations of their behaviour. Boys and girls are dressed differently, spoken to in different ways, given different kinds of toys and different amounts of attention and encouragement.

Boys are encouraged to achieve their distinct 'masculine' identity by breaking their close attachment to their mothers and stopping 'feminine' behaviour. They acquire values of independence and achievement, and find it more difficult to express their emotions in close relationships. Girls are encouraged to retain a strong identification with their mothers and copy their behaviour. Through this identification they grow up with a more emotional and sensitive outlook. Distinct masculine and feminine personalities are reinforced in school, by the mass media, and at work.

In her focus on early years, personality formation, and emotional relationships between parents and children, Chodorow provides an understanding of the gendering of personality and an explanation of the contrast between female sensitivity and male assertiveness. Her approach has, however, been criticized for perpetuating male and female stereotypes at a time when male and female identities are changing, when some men are becoming more sensitive and some women more assertive. It has also been seen as a rather culture-bound theory based on the experience of a small number of middle-class, white, and two-parent families.

A knowledge of socialization processes is indispensable to an account of the mechanisms that produce gender differences but socialization theory faces two major problems:

- social change;
- individual choice.

First, there is its inability to accommodate social change. Changes in male and female behaviour and identity suggest that early socialization is less than permanent in its effects. Arguably, this is because socialization is a lifelong process that involves periodic resocializations, so that changes in society feed through to the way that men and women feel and behave through such agencies as the mass media. Furthermore, different agencies of socialization may come into conflict by promoting alternative ways of living. For example, commercially driven changes in media representations and styles may conflict with those instilled by families and schools. These more complex views of the socialization process do, at the very least, call into question both the emphasis in much of the socialization literature on early experiences and the idea of fixed gender-roles and identities.

Secondly, socialization theory leaves little room for choice, or for people's activity and creativity in shaping their own lives. A more post-modern approach to the formation of identity would see it as constructed through choice of lifestyle and emphasize the part played by consumption in this. People can create (and recreate) their identities through the objects and experiences they buy. They can experiment with the wide range of lifestyles made available through the media and the market-place. If taken too far, the individualism of this approach can, however, neglect the power of stereotypes in shaping lifestyles and the commercial forces that drive their creation.

The concepts of socialization and gender-role rescued the study of the differences between men and women from biological determinism. They provided a convincing account of the ways in which gender differences in role and personality are acquired, reinforced, and perpetuated. The problem is that they became somewhat determinist themselves and left little room for human agency, for change or choice. Post-modern approaches have then gone to the other extreme and made it appear as though identities could be adopted and created more or less at will. To understand gender we need to take a balanced view, which accepts human agency but recognizes that this operates within the constraints of powerful socializing institutions, from the family to the mass media.

Patriarchy

Although socialization could explain the persistence of gender differences, once they had come into existence, it could not account for the inequalities between men and women. The concept of patriarchy emerged in the feminist literature to describe and explain these inequalities. In this section we consider the meaning of patriarchy, different approaches to it, and the criticisms that have been made of it.

Patriarchy originally meant domination by the father and was used by social anthropologists to describe family structures where the father rather than the mother ruled. In the feminist literature it came to mean male domination in general and this is now the main way that it is used in sociology. Within the feminist literature there are a number of different approaches to patriarchy.

Marxist feminists have emphasized the interconnections between capitalism and patriarchy. They have argued that the subordination of women in the household benefits the capitalist employer by providing free domestic labour. There is a domestic division of labour between the male 'breadwinner', who takes paid employment, and the housewife, who looks after the household and brings up the children. The wife's domestic labour is essential to the capitalist economy, both because it meets the home needs of the male wage-earner, enabling him to work long hours, and brings up the next generation of workers. This essential work is, however, unpaid labour that costs the employer nothing at all.

> **⊃ Connections**
>
> The domestic division of labour is discussed in detail in Chapter 12, pp. 476–8.

According to radical feminists, such as Kate Millett (1970) and Shulamith Firestone (1971), patriarchy is not, however, specifically associated with capitalism but is found in all known societies. Some indeed argue that men and women comprise 'sex classes'. Men, as the dominant class, oppress women and exploit them economically, politically, and sexually. This domination has its clearest expression in the intimate personal relationships of love, sex, and marriage, which are claimed to be subject to the constant threat of male violence. Millett famously argued that the 'personal is political', for men use their personal relationships with women, especially their sexual relations, to dominate and control them. These two perspectives were combined by some feminists, such as Heidi Hartmann (1981) and Sylvia Walby (1986) in a 'dual systems' approach which saw women as exploited both by men and by capital.

Some feminists have seen family relationships as the main site of patriarchy. Christine Delphy (1977) argued that these were central to the oppression of women, since they enabled men to exploit the unpaid labour of their wives or partners. She referred to the household as 'the domestic mode of production', in order to emphasize that productive work went on in the home as well as the workplace. Housework was, in her view, as productive and important as any other kind of work. Within the domestic mode of production men held a superior position and controlled the distribution of money and goods within the family. The family was, therefore, the main institution for the exploitation of women by men.

According to Walby (1990), however, there are multiple patriarchal structures that cumulatively produce male domination. She identified six such structures:

Controversy and debate Feminisms

There have always been different positions within the feminist movement. Three broad positions of **feminism** can be identified and are briefly outlined here.

Liberal feminism has been concerned primarily with equal rights for women. Key issues have been the right to vote, the ending of discrimination against women, and equal opportunities for women. Liberal feminism has not tried to transform society but to establish equality with men within the existing social order. Legislation was the main means of achieving this. Because of its emphasis on equality, liberal feminism saw men and women as essentially the same in character.

Socialist feminism combined feminism with the Marxist critique of capitalism and its liberal politics, seeing patriarchal relations as being inextricably tied to capitalist relations of production. Key issues were domestic labour and female wage labour, the role of the family in the reproduction of male labour, and the role of the state in the reproduction of the family.

Radical feminism rejected the liberal programme of legislative reform and instead engaged in direct action and political opposition, aimed at challenging the basis of the social and political order. Patriarchy was not specific to capitalism but a universal feature of human society. Particular attention was given to love, sex, and reproduction, which were seen as closely linked to male domination, and violence towards women. This was often a 'difference' feminism that considered women to be different from men and superior to them.

⊃ Note that we discuss feminist theory in more detail in Chapter 2, pp. 61–4.

- household production;
- employment relations;
- the state;
- male violence;
- sexual relations;
- cultural institutions.

She argued that there are two main forms of patriarchy, *private* and *public* (see Figure 5.1). Patriarchy in the nineteenth century took a mainly *private* form with individual males exploiting women's labour in the household and excluding women from public life. Household production was its dominant structure. The private form continued to exist in the twentieth century but by then, as a result of feminist organization, women had forced their way into the public sphere. This was only a limited success, for women were now subject to the *public* form of patriarchy, in which the state and employment relations were the

Figure 5.1 Private and public patriarchy

Form of patriarchy	Private	Public
Dominant structure	Household production	Employment/State
Wider patriarchal structures	Employment/State	Household production
	Sexuality	Sexuality
	Violence	Violence
	Culture	Culture
Period	Nineteenth century	Twentieth century
Mode of expropriation	Individual	Collective
Patriarchal strategy	Exclusionary	Segregationist

Source: Walby (1990: table 1.1, p. 24).

Controversy and debate Islam and women

The relationship between Islam and patriarchy has become an issue of contemporary debate. Extreme examples of the subordination and exclusion of women can certainly be found in Islamic countries and communities. In Afghanistan under the Taliban regime, women were excluded from employment, education, hospital care, and political life. In Saudi Arabia, they are not allowed to vote or even drive cars. In some Islamic communities women are forbidden to show their faces in public and have to cover themselves head-to-toe in the *burka*. In others, women have their clitorises surgically mutilated to prevent them experiencing sexual pleasure. Under some applications of sharia law women may find themselves punished, even stoned to death, if they become pregnant out of wedlock, even if this has resulted from rape. These practices have been justified by reference to the Qu'ran and other teachings of the founder of Islam, the prophet Muhammad.

Haifaa Jawad (1998) has claimed, however, that these interpretations of the holy writings of Islam are quite wrong. According to the Qu'ran and other holy texts, a woman has the following rights:

- to own and manage money and property;
- to marry whom she pleases and initiate divorce;
- to become educated;
- to keep her family name;
- to have sexual pleasure within marriage;

- to inherit from her parents and family;
- to participate actively in politics and decision-making;
- to be regarded as equal to men.

Jawad argues that the position of women in Arabia actually improved greatly with the advent of Islam, but then deteriorated after the death of Muhammad, as their rights were taken away and they were increasingly excluded from public life. The contemporary position of women in Islamic communities is the result of cultural and social practices that are nothing to do with Islam itself. Fundamentalists who oppress women have not returned to the original texts, as they claim, but only offer 'a distorted image of Islam'.

Jawad does not, however, believe that the best way forward for Muslim women is to adopt Western values, as some elite women in Islamic countries and some Islamic women in Western countries have done. She argues that this approach alienates the broad mass of Muslims from the women's movement. Muslim women should instead seek to achieve equality in an 'authentic Islamic way' by basing their demands on the original teachings of Islam.

In 2005, at a meeting in Spain, Islamic feminists launched what they hoped would be a global movement to liberate muslim women, under the banner of a 'gender jihad'. This was described by one of the organizers as 'a struggle against male chauvinist, homophobic or sexist readings of the Islamic sacred texts' (*Guardian*, 31 October 2005).

dominant structures and patriarchy operated in a more collective way. Women were no longer excluded from work but they were still segregated in lower-grade and lower-paid work.

This debate over patriarchy has focused on the development of patriarchal institutions in industrial societies but religions too are a major source of patriarchal beliefs. There has been much recent concern with the assertive patriarchy of Islamic fundamentalism (see box on 'Islam and women'), though all the other major religions—Christianity, Confucianism, Hinduism, and Judaism—contain patriarchal beliefs and practices. In Christianity, for example, god is generally represented as a male authority figure, while all the apostles were male, and priests have until recently been exclusively male and in its Roman Catholic branch still are. In her book *Gyn/Ecology*, Mary Daly (1978) provides many examples from all the major religions of the religious practices that subordinate women.

The concept of patriarchy enabled sociology to move beyond sex-roles and examine the power differences between men and women, but in recent years it has been strongly criticized (see Acker 1989; Bradley 1989; Pollert 1996).

First, there is the problem of its explanatory value. If patriarchy is a universal feature of human society, it cannot help us understand the evident differences between societies in the relationships between men and women. Similarly, it cannot account for changes in these relationships. To explain variations or changes we have to go outside the concept of patriarchy.

Secondly, there is the problem of how patriarchy itself is to be explained. If it is universal, it is hard to avoid ending up with some kind of biological determinism. Some feminists have explained its universality by reference to the relations of dependence at the heart of human reproduction. Women are dependent on men for their material needs while they are involved in the long human process of child-rearing. Patriarchy is, therefore, ultimately explained by the biology of reproduction, which produces human infants dependent on parental care for a long time. Biological determinism has been rejected on principle by Walby and many other feminists, but without it patriarchy appears to hang in the air without any explanation of why it should exist.

There is, thirdly, the problem of structural determinism. Patriarchy often appears to be a simple monolithic structure of domination that somehow exists 'behind the scenes'. The analysis is of institutions rather than social practices. There is little sense of the way that institutions have to be maintained through people's actions or of the ways that they can resist, subvert, and change them.

There is, fourthly, the problem of treating men and women as if each were a homogeneous category. The early radical feminists minimized differences between women by emphasizing their common reproductive experiences and, therefore, their common fate and destiny. This emphasis has been one of the cornerstones of feminist politics, involving as it does the idea that there is a specifically female way of seeing and feeling, a distinctive 'standpoint' from which women view the world (see Chapter 2, p. 63). This standpoint has been seen as the basis of a feminist consciousness expressed and nurtured in the organizations and practices of the women's movement.

Many recent feminist writers have criticized the idea that there is some essential female experience that divides *all* women from *all* men. These critics point to the diversity of female experience and, by implication, of male experience too. Black feminists, for example, have argued that feminism is simply the outlook of white, middle-class women and that it fails to recognize the distinctiveness of black women's experiences. Sarah Delamont has argued that 'class differences between women are more powerful than any gender-based similarities' (2001: 111).

The work of those who have used the concept of patriarchy should not, however, be dismissed because of these criticisms. To start with, there are many differences in the way that it is used by different theorists and particular criticisms are more relevant to some than others. The analysis of patriarchy has anyway generated an immense amount of knowledge and understanding of how institutions constrain the relationships between men and women. What should be abandoned, however, is any notion that the concept of patriarchy can provide some simple and all-embracing explanation of these relationships.

The gender order

An alternative and influential way of analysing the relationship between gender and power has been presented by Robert Connell. While Connell was concerned with the same central issue as feminist writers—the description, analysis, and explanation of male domination—his work reflected the growing interest in masculinity and what is happening to men. His first book, *Gender and Power* (1987), developed a framework for the analysis of gender and this was followed by *Masculinities* (1995).

Social practices are at the heart of his conception of gender. He defined gender as 'practice organized in terms of, or in relation to, the reproductive division of people into male and female' (Connell 1987: 140). Gender is not ultimately a matter of institutions but of practices, of what people actually do. They can resist and subvert structures and, within an overall pattern of male domination, there are areas where women dominate. Structures can only be maintained through the policing of practices, and this, importantly, means the practices of men as well as those of women.

A society has what he called an overall **gender order**, which consists of a hierarchy of masculinities and femininities. At the top of this hierarchy is **hegemonic masculinity**, a dominant set of ideas that establish the superiority of the male. Heterosexuality is at the core of hegemonic masculinity but this also involves the valuation of toughness, physical strength, authority, and aggression. Film characters and sporting heroes provide models of masculinity. Most men cannot live up to this masculine ideal but engage in a 'complicit masculinity', as they benefit from the male domination provided by the hegemonic version. Other forms of 'subordinated masculinity' exist, notably 'homosexual masculinity', which is stigmatized and subordinated by practices of exclusion, abuse, violence, and discrimination. Heterosexual men who do not live up to the masculine model are also subjected to some of these practices.

> **⊃** *Connections*
>
> Hegemony is a widely used concept in sociology, which we discuss in Chapter 10, p. 364 and Chapter 20, pp. 821–2.

There is also a hierarchy of femininities, though this is less pronounced. There is no hegemonic femininity, because femininity is subordinate to masculinity, and cannot therefore be hegemonic. **Emphasized femininity** is at the top of the hierarchy of femininities. Connell described this as involving:

> the display of sociability rather than technical competence, fragility in mating scenes, compliance with men's desire for titillation and ego-stroking in office relationships, acceptance of marriage and childcare as a response to labour-market discrimination against women. (Connell 1987: 187)

Arguably, just as most men have difficulty living up to images of the 'real man', most women have difficulty living up to the idealized images of 'emphasized femininity'. There are also other femininities that resist or reject emphasized femininity but these are not so vigorously subordinated as the masculinities that challenge hegemonic masculinity. Instead they are marginalized, through a cultural exclusion that hides them from view.

Connell's awareness of gender diversity and concern with actual practices leads him to highlight crisis tendencies in the gender order, the conflicts of sexual politics, and alternative futures. The family, sexuality, and work are the key arenas in which these crisis tendencies and conflicts are played out. Connell considered whether the actual abolition of gender would be a feasible project but thought that this would lead to cultural impoverishment, as gender has been so central to art and, indeed, everyday life, to both eroticism and imagination. He proposed instead a

The gender order in a shooting gallery?
© Alice Chadwick

restructuring of gender that would permit greater gender diversity and remove inequalities between men and women.

Although Connell criticized earlier conceptions of patriarchy, he had, none the less, his own theory of it. He certainly viewed existing societies as patriarchal in character but presented a theory of patriarchy that focused on the role of hegemonic masculinity in maintaining male domination. The key contributions he has made to the study of patriarchy are:

- an analysis of gender as *practice*;
- a much more differentiated view of gender.

The diversity of both masculinities and femininities is central to his view of gender, as is the relationships between different masculinities and between different femininities. Patriarchy is not just a matter of the domination of women by men but also of the domination of some men by other men and some women by other women.

Sexuality

We argued earlier that sexuality is socially constructed, not biologically determined. This is, however, a much debated question and some still hold an 'essentialist' view of sexuality. According to this view, a person's sexual preferences are fixed by their nature at birth. Whether a person is, for example, homosexual or heterosexual is to do with their inborn nature and cannot be changed. This notion has received a recent revival with the idea that homosexuality is genetically determined. We begin this section with a discussion of this issue before going on to examine the main categories of sexuality and their significance.

Becoming homosexual

Scientific studies have reportedly identified genetic differences between heterosexual and homosexual men, and there has been much recent media interest in the discovery of a 'gay gene'. These studies do not, however, show that homosexuality is genetically determined, for the most that they claim is that there is an inherited disposition or tendency towards homosexual behaviour, not a biological determination of it. The scientific credentials of the studies have, anyway, been heavily criticized by other scientists and there is currently no general acceptance among biologists of the existence of a genetic disposition of this kind.

Whatever the status of these studies, whether a person is 'gay' or not cannot result simply from their biology. Being 'gay' refers not just to sexual practices but to the assumption of a sexual identity that is social in character. It is certainly possible that some genetic disposition to sexual preferences may be discovered but the meanings that are attributed to these preferences and the ways in which they are expressed in behaviour are not themselves matters of biology.

Homosexual activities conventionally labelled as deviant have been seen as perfectly normal in many societies, including ancient Greece and traditional Japan. Whether an activity is treated as deviant or normal is a matter of social definition, and social definitions vary from one society to another. These social definitions are transmitted and adopted through socialization.

The work of Ken Plummer (1975) has shown very clearly that sexual deviance—specifically, male homosexuality—can best be understood if it is seen as a process of social learning. Plummer argues that sexual socialization involves learning to define oneself as a sexual being and then managing that definition and its consequences for other aspects of one's life. People gradually become committed to a particular sexual identity and the sexual practices associated with it.

The period of adolescence is critical for adult sexual identity. At a time when the biological changes of puberty are occurring, sexual identity becomes crystallized. It is in the peer group, rather than the family, that this adolescent sexual socialization takes place. This is a time when boys tend to enter into casual and irregular exploratory sexual encounters with other boys. Mutual masturbation, for example, has been especially common at single-sex boys' schools.

In most cases, these are transient encounters but in some circumstances boys may come to see them as signs of homosexual inclinations. This is likely if they have other reasons for feeling different from other boys. A boy may, for example, be more interested in art, literature, or hairstyles than in football or aggressive sports, and may be seen as a 'sissy'. Feelings of cultural and sexual difference may be reinforced by parents, teachers, or other boys making remarks about a boy's 'effeminacy'.

A self-identification as 'homosexual' may then be reinforced by social isolation. Feelings of guilt or shame aroused by the negative image of homosexuality in the wider culture may contribute to this isolation. A boy may keep his feelings about his identity secret and become increasingly solitary. Solitude will in turn strengthen his sexual identity because it cuts him off from the possibility of heterosexual experiences.

Some may remain solitary and keep their identity secret for the whole of their lives, passing as heterosexual. Others, however, 'come out' as homosexuals. Coming out is an open avowal of homosexuality that allows greater, and more open, contact with others perceived to be similar. By meeting those who share their identity and with whom they can feel at ease, they come into contact with alternative, more positive views of homosexuality, and are able to reconstruct their sense of self in more positive terms. They fully enter the homosexual role and become committed to a 'gay' identity. Through contacts with other homosexuals in clubs, pubs, and elsewhere, they are drawn into a subculture of homosexuality that provides both opportunities for meeting sexual partners and meanings that legitimate their new sexual identity.

Sexualities

The above discussion presumes the existence of distinct sexual identities. It is indeed commonly taken for granted that people are heterosexual, homosexual, or possibly bisexual, that everyone (except the disabled—see box on 'Disability and sexuality' on p. 167) can be placed in one of these categories. The categories themselves are, however, social in origin and reflect a particular way of thinking about sex and sexuality.

They came into use as a means of classifying people in the nineteenth century, when a new language of sexuality

THEORY AND METHODS

Telling sexual stories

We live in a world in which 'it's good to talk' and people are encouraged to verbalize their feelings. Plummer (1995) has explored the ways in which sexual identities of all kinds are explored and reconstructed through the production of narrative accounts of personal biography.

Plummer saw the collection of these sexual narratives as an important way of understanding the changing meanings of sexuality. Some narratives are published in books, magazines, or broadcasts, but he also wanted to collect the private ones recounted only among small circles of friends or, perhaps, only to oneself. Although using the word 'story' to describe these accounts, Plummer is not implying that they are fictional. A sexual story is a reconstruction of a person's sexual biography from the standpoint of his or her current situation. It is a genuine attempt to make sense of the person's experiences and moral career.

Plummer shows that the sexual narratives of those who came out as gay during the 1960s and 1970s have a common pattern in which sexual suffering is survived and then overcome. The most significant act in the development of homosexuality is coming out and announcing one's gayness to others. Those who have come out tell their stories to friends, colleagues, and others. The telling of sexual stories in a gay club, for example, helps to reinforce the storytellers' identities through shared experiences and creates a sense of solidarity that can sustain them in the future.

Gay and lesbian accounts of coming out tend to follow a common storyline. This begins with a frustrated or stigmatized erotic desire for someone of one's own sex. It moves on to explorations of childhood and youth in an attempt to uncover 'motives' and 'memories', feelings of unhappiness and difference, that would 'explain' this desire. The accounts then proceed to a crisis or turning point—perhaps a 'discovery'—that leads to a complete reconsideration of the past and the building of a new identity, often with the help of others in the same situation. A sense of identity and community is established. Subcultures of homosexuality—gay social worlds— are crucial conditions for the production of these accounts.

Plummer suggests that a similar pattern is found in other sexual stories—of sexual abuse, sex addiction, pornography, fetishism, and rape experiences. In the case of rape, for example, he suggests that from the 1960s and 1970s there was a recasting of women's narratives of rape in the same 'suffering, surviving, and surpassing' structure that has just been described.

These sexual stories, as they become public, enter into a new politics of what Plummer calls 'intimate citizenship'. They contribute to a broadening of cultural self-understanding. The dominance of the expert or the authority figure—the doctor, the psychologist, and even the sociologist —is broken, and participants are able to make their own views known and can begin to shape a more autonomous cultural and political agenda.

➲ In addition to published sources, Plummer used a range of personal contacts to encourage people to write down their sexual stories or to provide them in interviews.

➲ Look at our discussion of documentary research in Chapter 3, pp. 90–3, and see what problems you can identify in this research design. You might like to look at Plummer's own methodological discussion in his book *Documents of Life* (Plummer 2001).

---

derived from the two-sex model (see the section on 'sexes' above) spread. It was this model that made possible such categories as **heterosexuality**, **homosexuality**, and **bisexuality**, which all depend on the notion of two sexes and are inconceivable without it.

The important point to grasp here is that terms like 'heterosexual' and 'homosexual' (and 'lesbian') are not simply words that describe particular kinds of sexual behaviour. They carry with them all sorts of assumptions about it that derive from nineteenth-century ways of thinking. The classification of people into these categories implies that only certain kinds of people engage in particular sexual practices. The term 'homosexual', for example, implies that sexual acts between men (and between women) occur only within a distinct group called homosexuals. Both men and women had engaged in sexual acts with people of the same sex before the nineteenth century but had not been treated as a distinct kind of person.

According to the dominant discourse of the nineteenth century, heterosexuality was the only normal sexuality and this belief has been so strong that the term 'compulsory heterosexuality' has been used to convey its force (Rich 1980a). In more recent years, those engaging in same-sex relationships have rejected the negative valuation of homosexuality by adopting the new, and more positive sounding 'gay' label. In doing this, they have also, however, perpetuated the distinction between different sexualities. Indeed, some gays have seized hold of the notion of

Out and about—what is the sociological significance of 'coming out'?

© Alice Chadwick

a 'gay gene' in order to argue that being gay is as natural as being heterosexual. Bisexuals challenged nineteenth-century categories more fundamentally by crossing the boundary between heterosexuality and homosexuality, though the very term 'bisexual' showed that a two-sex model still underlay their thinking.

It was **queer theory**, which emerged in the United States during the 1980s, that mounted a thoroughgoing intellectual challenge to nineteenth-century categories. Queer theory not only opposed the idea that heterosexuality was the only normal and natural sexuality, but also rejected the notion of homosexuality as a distinct category of people and behaviour. It rejected all 'binary divides' that separated sexes and sexualities. The theoretical basis for rejecting existing categories was the argument that these did not reflect real differences, biological or otherwise, but a particular *discourse* (see Chapter 6, p. 203 for a discussion of this concept). These categories were part of the language of heterosexual dominance (Stein and Plummer 1994).

Queer theory threw out the notion of distinct sexual identities. It shared with post-modern theorizing a much looser and more decentred conception of identity, recognizing that there are many strands to any one person's identity. Furthermore, individuals could construct and reconstruct themselves through their choice of lifestyles, moving across categories and boundaries as they pleased (Epstein 1994).

The message of queer theory is that the sexual categories that people customarily use are socially produced and not biological in origin. These categories have powerfully constrained people's beliefs, identities, and behaviour but

Controversy and debate Disability and sexuality

This head waiter that I knew well . . . came up to me and said, 'You can't can you . . . ?' I said, 'Can't what?' . . . I knew what he meant. I thought, I'll drag this out a bit, and he said, 'Well, you can't have sex, can you?' And I said, 'Why ever not?' And he said, 'Well, you can't walk . . .' And I said, 'You walk while you're having sex? I haven't seen that in the Kama Sutra!' (Paula, quoted by Shakespeare 2003: 144)

Disabled people commonly report that they are treated by the non-disabled as though lacking both sex and sexuality. They are, however, disabled not by their bodies, which have desires and are capable of sexual activity, but by society. Shakespeare rejects the medicalization of the disabled and claims that 'in general, the problems of disabled sexuality are not caused by the impairment itself, but by the way people with that particular impairment are viewed and treated in society' (2003: 148). He also argues that while some disabled people,

particularly those in residential institutions, find that their sexuality is denied and others have experienced sexual abuse, they should not be treated as victims. Some of the disabled people that he studied had found their disability sexually liberating, because it freed them from both sexual norms and the pressure to perform, and encouraged them to experiment and explore their sexual potential. Shakespeare concludes that the social barriers to disabled sexuality should be removed by educating those who work with them to recognize their sexual rights and needs, but notions of 'normal sex' should not be imposed on them.

❓ What social processes lead to the treatment of the disabled as non-sexual beings?

❓ What problems might be raised by facilitating normal sexual behaviour by the disabled?

when people understand that the categories are social in origin, they can challenge them, liberate themselves from them, and then freely choose how they live.

Queer theory is not only a sociological analysis of the origins and significance of social categories but also a political project (we examine the queer movement on p. 187).

Some have found this perspective personally liberating but its whole argument that sexual categories have no real existence outside a particular discourse is open to sociological criticism. It neglects the power of the socialization process, the strength of gender-roles, the creation of distinct identities, and the solidarity of communities based upon them.

◆ *Stop and reflect*

We began this section by distinguishing between the concepts of sex, gender, and sexuality. Make sure that you are clear about the distinctive meanings of these terms and the relationships between them.

- Some people believe that differences in the behaviour of men and women are biologically determined. Why do sociologists reject this idea?

We then examined 'sex'.

- The term 'sex' refers to the biological and physical differences between men and women.
- Is the notion that there are two sexes simply a reflection of human biology?

We moved on to consider 'gender' and 'patriarchy'.

- We argued that socialization can account for the persistence of gender differences but cannot explain them.

- Theories of patriarchy try to provide possible explanations of gender differences but the concept of patriarchy is problematic.
- Consider whether Connell's approach is an advance on earlier theories of patriarchy?

Finally in this section we discussed 'sexuality'.

- A person's sexuality refers not only to the practices they find sexually stimulating but also to related aspects of identity, lifestyle, and community.
- Why should sociologists be sceptical of the notion of a 'gay gene'?
- Our conventional categories of sexuality are derived from the 'two-sex model' established in the nineteenth century.
- Consider whether the terms 'heterosexual' and 'homosexual' are simply a description of sexual practices.

Separating identities

In this section we examine the processes through which the identities of men and women were created in nineteenth-century Britain. The idea that men and women were different did not originate then but it was at this time that what are now thought of as their 'traditional' identities became firmly established. These identities are closely linked to the power relations between men and women, and we examine the interconnections between gender identities, patriarchy, and feminism. We then go on to consider the interaction between identity formation and the emergence of distinct sexualities, for it was also at this time that heterosexuality and homosexuality were first sharply differentiated from each other.

Separating spheres

The separation of male and female spheres was central to the separation of identities. The world of public affairs, of politics and work, became increasingly a male sphere, while the home became a female sphere. This separation of spheres was closely connected with the growing separation of home and work but it was also a patriarchal process, for the exclusion of women from the public world and their confinement in the home was one of the main ways in which men dominated them. Separation and exclusion also generated, however, the first organized feminist movement, which began to challenge patriarchy in the second half of the nineteenth century.

Patriarchal exclusion

The development of industrial capitalism concentrated paid work in factories and offices away from the home. Workplace and home also became spatially separated, particularly for the middle class. Residential areas, such as Edgbaston in Birmingham, or Islington in London, were built well away from the business and industrial parts of these cities. Home and work were separated further by the growth of suburbs, from which people commuted by rail to work.

The separation of home from work provided the conditions in which a clear separation of male and female spheres could take place. In the middle class, the world of business outside the home became seen as a male sphere and the private world of home and children a female one. Thus, Catherine Hall (1982*b*) has pointed out that informal business partnerships between husbands and wives gave way to formal business partnerships between men. The woman's business was now to look after home and children, with the assistance of servants. Women were excluded from male professions, as is well shown by changes in medicine at this time (see box on 'Gender and medicine').

An ideology of female domesticity legitimated this separation of spheres. The notion that women's primary responsibility lay in the home was not new but it was given much greater moral force in the early nineteenth century. Hall has noted that in government reports during the 1830s and 1840s 'working wives and mothers are presented as something unusual and immoral' (Hall 1998: 195). Religion contributed significantly to this ideology through the evangelical movement in the Anglican Church, which spread a 'religion of the household' that sharply separated the moral life of the home from the evils of public life, treating the home as a female sphere and public life as a male sphere.

The separation of spheres was linked to the construction of contrasting gender identities. Women were expected to be passive, dependent, and caring, while men were required to be strong, protective, and active. Women were seen as sensitive, emotional creatures, men as rational and calculating. These conceptions of masculine and feminine character strengthened patriarchal ideology and practice by making it appear as though the different roles of men and women expressed differences in their nature (Davidoff 1990).

In the working class, the situation was initially different. Industrialization resulted in a growing separation of the home from production but this did not automatically result in the exclusion of women from paid work. It was not only men that were employed in the new factories but women and children too, for they provided employers with cheaper labour. There was, however, a reaction against the employment of women, in part because of the growing strength of the ideology of domesticity but also because it threatened the interests of men. Male-dominated trade unions kept women out of the more skilled and better-paid trades, while they were also excluded from some occupations by legislation (Walby 1986).

Women were certainly not wholly excluded from paid work. Large numbers of them were employed as servants, though this was an extension of their domestic roles. Many also still worked in factories, particularly in the textiles industry, or carried out 'homework' for employers in their own houses. Later, in the twentieth century, the expansion of white-collar work led to the recruitment of women to white-collar jobs. Women's paid work was, however, generally considered secondary to their domestic work and men were seen as the breadwinners who earned a 'family wage' to provide for the needs of the whole family.

 ## Briefing: gender and medicine

In the early nineteenth century, women were excluded from medical practice. Previously health care had been provided by travelling and community-based healers, many of whom had been women.

> By the mid-nineteenth century . . . medical diagnosis and treatment had become the exclusive prerogative of medical men, and women had become restricted to the care of the sick, as nurses, and to the attendance of women during natural labour, as midwives. (Witz 1992: 75)

Exclusion occurred when the market provision of medical care was expanding and new forms of organizational control were being established. These involved the state registration of medical practitioners after 1858 and the regulation of entry to the medical professions by teaching hospitals and Royal Colleges, which were controlled by men

Women responded by seeking to gain entry to medical education in order to gain the qualifications required for medical practice. When their first attempts to do this through existing institutions were frustrated, another and more successful strategy was pursued through the opening in 1874 of a new medical school, the London School of Medicine for Women.

❷ *Can the nineteenth-century exclusion of women from medicine be explained by reference to patriarchy? In thinking about this, read our discussion of patriarchy on pp. 161–3.*

Figure 5.2 Spheres and identities

	Male	Female
Spheres	Work/politics	Home
	Public	Private
Identities	Active	Passive
	Rational	Emotional
	Independent	Dependent

> **Connections**
> We discuss the employment of women in Chapter 17,
> pp. 705–7.

A separation of spheres had then occurred in both the middle and the working classes, though they were less sharply defined in the working class. Both ideological, economic, and residential changes brought this separation about. It was a process of patriarchal exclusion, though patriarchy alone cannot explain why it occurred. With the separation of spheres the identities of men and women became more sharply differentiated.

Challenging patriarchy

The separation of spheres excluded women but also stimulated and enabled the growth of organized feminism.

What came, much later, to be called first-wave feminism emerged in the nineteenth century. Feminist ideas were not new—they had first appeared during the eighteenth-century Enlightenment—but it was in 1856 that the first British feminist organization, the 'Ladies of Langham Place', was founded. In 1859 the Langham Place group launched a *Society for Promoting the Employment of Women*, which set up an employment exchange to find work for women. They also sought to gain property rights for women and in the 1860s began the campaign for women's right to vote.

It was the separation of spheres that actually enabled women to organize. Their confinement in the home provided middle-class women, who could afford servants to do the domestic work, with the time to meet and organize. As the name of this first organization suggests, it was indeed middle-class women who led and dominated the early feminist movement (Banks 1981).

The separatism that excluded women became the basis of the feminist counter-attack. Access to medical education was a key battleground and a separate medical school was set up for women in London (see box on 'Gender and medicine' on p. 169). A separatist strategy was pursued more widely within education, with the establishment of schools for girls in which they would be taught by women (see Chapter 9, p. 338). As Anne Witz has put it, there was a 'widespread adoption of separatist methods by middle-class women as they forged spaces within which they could participate in the public sphere' (1992: 195). Charities, the care of the sick and the poor were other areas that women came to dominate, indeed to monopolize.

In the working class, the situation was, as we have seen, rather different, for although processes of exclusion had operated there too, many women were, none the less, employed in paid work. Most trade unions excluded women, however, and in the last quarter of the nineteenth century a number of women's union organizations, such as the Women's Trade Union League and the National Federation of Women Workers were created (Walby 1986). A separatist strategy was pursued here too.

There were, however, limits to such a strategy. While it enabled women to at least partially escape domesticity and establish a certain independence, it did not directly challenge male control of the central organizations and institutions of British society. Women had made some significant inroads into public affairs but, as Walby has argued (see p. 162), a private patriarchy that sought to confine them in the home had been replaced by a public patriarchy. Men used their control of public organizations and institutions to keep women in a subordinate position.

Separating sexes

The separation of spheres distinguished the roles and activities of men and women, who were now seen as fundamentally different in character. We now look at the grounding of these character differences in the quite new belief that men and women were biologically different sexes.

The two-sex model

We argued earlier that the idea that men and women are different sexes is a comparatively recent idea (see p. 157). Indeed, according to Thomas Laqueur (1990), men and women were not thought of as separate sexes before the eighteenth century. In a striking turn of phrase he claimed that 'sometime in the eighteenth century, sex as we know it was invented' (1990: 149).

Before this time, when anatomists examined male and female bodies they did not see them as having different organs. The vagina was considered an interior penis, another tube through which sperm passed. Ovaries were internal testicles. Women's organs were simply less developed versions of men's. It was thought that they were less developed because women were 'cooler and moister beings', which also meant that they were less active than men and their mental capacities less developed.

According to Laqueur (1990), this 'one-sex' model was replaced by a 'two-sex' model during the eighteenth century. This did not, however, happen due to greater knowledge or the advance of science but resulted from new ways of thinking. A new view of men and women as separate sexes can be found in the ideas of both French and Scottish thinkers during the period of the Enlightenment. Old ways of thinking were then demolished by the revolutionary changes and political struggles that followed during the later eighteenth and the nineteenth centuries.

THEORY AND METHODS

Foucault on homosexuality

'There is no question that the appearance in nineteenth-century psychiatry, jurisprudence, and literature of a whole series of discourses on the species and subspecies of homosexuality, inversion, pederasty, and "psychic hermaphrodism" made possible a strong advance of social controls into this area of "perversity"; but it also made possible the formation of a "reverse" discourse: homosexuality began to speak on its own behalf, to demand that its legitimacy or "naturality" be acknowledged, often in the same vocabulary, using the same categories by which it was radically disqualified.' (Foucault 1976: 101)

➔ We discuss Foucault's concept of discourse on p. 203.

responsible for their sexuality or judged as immoral in their behaviour. The notion of a 'gay gene' (see p. 165) has recently been used in this way to defend 'gay' sexual practices.

Thus, in the nineteenth century sexuality became central to the identities of men and women. Heterosexuality had become a defining feature of the hegemonic masculinity of nineteenth-century Britain. Those who engaged in same-sex practices were now treated as a quite distinct group of 'homosexuals'. Changes in discourse were quite fundamental to these new distinctions, which can be traced back to the emergence of the two-sex model, for this made it linguistically possible to distinguish between hetero-sexuality and homosexuality.

Deviant identities

While the category 'homosexual' emerged from the dominant discourse of the time, a distinct homosexual identity resulted from the formation of sexual subcultures. These raised the distinctiveness of deviant groups and enabled their members to provide mutual support. They also made it possible for them to resist and challenge negative images and develop their own more positive view of themselves.

In England signs of a 'homosexual' subculture first emerged in London during the late seventeenth and eighteenth centuries. This had 'its own network of meeting houses and distinctive gestures, language, dress, and pick-up signals' (Shoemaker 1998: 83). It was also characterized by the growth of effeminacy, with its 'mollies' adopting the dress, appearance, and behaviour of women. But the only regular members of the subculture were, it seems, the 'professionals', who sold their sexual services and behaved effeminately, while many others from varied social backgrounds participated occasionally (Weeks 1989: 110).

According to Weeks, it was not until the later nineteenth century that a separate homosexual community and identity became established.

Between the 1850s and the 1930s a complex sexual community had developed in many American as well as European cities, which crossed class, racial, gender and age boundaries, and which offered a focus for identity development. (Weeks 1985: 192)

It was also during this period that organized movements of male homosexuals appeared. These organizations assisted those in trouble with the law and sought reform of the various laws that criminalized homosexual acts.

A female homosexual subculture was much slower to emerge. By the end of the nineteenth century there were certainly lesbian meeting-places but there is little evidence of a subculture as such. The roles assigned to women, beliefs about female sexuality, and women's lack of independence made it difficult for a distinctive lesbian identity to emerge. It was in the 1920s that such an identity first became clearly visible and also at that time that **lesbianism** became a social issue and attempts were made to criminalize it (Weeks 1989).

It is important to be clear that the idea that all men or women who engage in same-sex sexual activities are 'homosexuals' involves very particular beliefs about sexuality. They were treated as such by the dominant ideology, while the formation of a distinctive subculture and identity has meant that some people have come to see themselves in this way. It is well known, however, that much same-sex activity, for example in schools, the armed forces, and prisons, is situational in character and does not involve the assumption of a homosexual identity. Furthermore, many people outside these situations who have same-sex sexual experiences do not participate in homosexual subcultures or do so only occasionally. Some who have same-sex experiences see themselves as bisexual or indeed heterosexual rather than homosexual and do not identify with homosexual groups at all.

◆ *Stop and reflect*

In this section we have analysed the separating out of distinct male and female identities in the nineteenth century.

We began by examining the emergence of distinct male and female spheres.

- Domestic life became a female sphere and public life a male sphere.
- Distinct gender identities became associated with these spheres.
- Consider the implications of this separation for gender power relationships.
- What was the significance of separation for the rise of feminism?

By the nineteenth century men and women were seen as different sexes.

- Make sure that you understand what is meant by the idea that sex was 'invented' in the eighteenth century.
- What is meant by the 'biologization' of the 'two-sex' model?
- What were the implications of this model for the power relationships between men and women?

The separation of sexes also led to the separation of sexualities.

- The two-sex model made possible the distinction between 'heterosexuality' and 'homosexuality'.
- Male homosexuality has been treated with less tolerance than female homosexuality. Why do you think this happened?
- If people engage in sexual activity with people of the same sex, does this mean that they are 'homosexuals'?

Blurring identities

The separation of people into categories is one of the most important ways in which one group asserts and maintains its dominance over another. It provides a basis for systematic discrimination and exclusion, and enables those who are dominant to treat those they dominate as different and inferior by nature.

Separation and exclusion can also, however, create situations that assist those who are dominated to organize themselves, establish their own identity, and challenge the dominant group. We showed in the previous section how separation provided the basis for the growth of feminism and deviant sexual subcultures. Another well-known example of this process is the growth of a black power movement out of the segregation of black people. This is probably a necessary stage in the successful contesting of domination by a dominated group but organization on the basis of separateness also confines and limits the challenge. If a dominant group is to be displaced, the separation of identities must itself be challenged.

In this section we examine more recent processes that have blurred at least partially the sharply differentiated identities established in the nineteenth century. We again examine spheres, sexes, and sexualities but this time looking at recent changes to see whether the separateness of the nineteenth century has broken down. Are men and women becoming more like each other in their attitudes, the way they behave, and the way they think of themselves?

> **⊙ Connections**
>
> You can follow up on many of the issues raised in this section by going to other chapters:
>
> - On women in employment see Chapter 17, pp. 705–7.
> - On girls' increasing success in education see Chapter 9, pp. 339–41.
> - On changes in the domestic division of labour see Chapter 12, pp. 476–8.
> - On divorce see Chapter 12, pp. 467–9.

Spheres?

The confinement of women in the home was the central feature of the separation of male and female spheres in the nineteenth century but in recent times far more women have entered paid work and participated in politics. New waves of feminism have challenged male domination. Has the separation of the spheres broken down?

Women in employment

Between 1851 and 1951 there was little change in the proportion of women entering paid work and their participation rate was roughly half that of men. Since then there has been a big increase in women's participation and the gender gap in employment rates has now almost

As housework and childcare still fall disproportionately on women, they still affect women's access to paid work and women's earnings. About 90 per cent of part-time work is done by women, largely because of their domestic responsibilities, and part-time work is paid at lower rates. The gap between male and female earnings is much greater among couples with children than couples without (*Social Trends* 2006: table 5.4). Furthermore, some women can only do poorly paid homework because of their childcare responsibilities.

Occupations remain highly gendered. Indeed, one of the main reasons for the narrowing of the gap between male and female rates of employment is the decline of men's occupations, such as mining and other forms of heavy manual work, and the growth of women's service occupations, such as cleaning and catering. Women's occupations are still largely extensions of their 'traditional' domestic roles. They are also disproportionately drawn into occupations that involve emotional labour, which again is linked to their caring role in the household. Unfortunately for them, it is these occupations that are the lowest paid. In 2002 the ten lowest-paid occupations were in catering, caring, and cleaning, and 80 per cent of the workers who did these jobs were women (Toynbee 2002).

It is not only that particular occupations tend to recruit either men or women. There are also barriers to those who seek to enter occupations considered inappropriate to their sex. In Britain, equal opportunities legislation bans open discrimination but occupational cultures can isolate or ridicule those who seek to cross gender boundaries. One form that ridicule can take is a questioning of the sexuality of someone of the 'wrong' sex. Men who work in caring occupations may be labelled 'gay', while women employed in manual work in garages or building sites may be called 'dykes' (Charles 2002).

In some occupations women have broken through gender barriers. This is particularly the case in the professions. There were few women in financial services, law, and medicine fifty years ago but now there are many. Women have also made some inroads into the armed forces (see box on 'Fighting women' on p. 176) and the police (see Study 5 at the end of this chapter). This is not, however, to say that women have achieved equality with men. There is still a tendency to sideline women into particular jobs that women are considered best suited for, and there are still glass ceilings, while professional bodies are still largely controlled by men. The control of business is still largely a male preserve with women comprising only 11 per cent of the directors of the top 100 British companies (Equal Opportunities Commission 2006, www.eoc.org.uk/pdf/sexandpower_GB_2006.pdf).

The growing employment of women has at least reduced the separation of spheres, particularly in the middle class.

Is the public sphere still a man's world?
© Alice Chadwick

disappeared. While this is mainly due to the growing employment of women, it is also substantially due to the declining employment of men. As women's participation in the labour market has increased, so has their participation in trade unions. These previously highly patriarchal organizations have been significantly feminized (Rees 1992).

If women are doing more paid work, does this mean that men are doing more work in the domestic sphere? Although mechanization of housework may have reduced the time that has to be spent on it, someone has to do this. One solution has been the employment of other people to do it and there is evidence that this has been increasing. In many households this is not, however, financially possible. As we show in Chapter 12, pp. 476–8, there is some evidence of greater male participation in housework, particularly when men are unemployed, but it is still disproportionately done by women.

Controversy and debate Fighting women?

According to the tests carried out by the Combat Effectiveness Gender Study, which was presented to the chiefs of staff of the British armed forces in 2001, most women are not physically suitable for front-line service.

These tests were queried by Alice Mahon, MP, who said: 'I suspect that many of these tests were flawed. If women compete physically with men, then obviously most will fail. The truth is that most fighting these days is done from 20,000 feet.'

Claire Ward, another MP, took a different view, after spending a year with the Royal Marines as part of a scheme to provide MPs with experience of military life. 'I arrived with the view that women should have the right to do this and told them so. But after a year my mind changed. I don't think women are physically built for it, and I also think that while the lads I knew were mature and calm, they are trained to be very aggressive and, let's be frank, to kill, often with bare hands. I believe firmly in equality, but men and women are different.'

Women's access to military occupations has varied between the services. In the navy, 73 per cent of jobs were reportedly available to them but they were excluded from the Marines, the Special Boat Squadron, and submarines. In the army, the figure was 70 per cent but they were excluded from the infantry, armoured units, and the SAS. The situation was different in the Royal Air Force, where women could enter 96 per cent of jobs and become fighter pilots (Clark 2002).

Access is one thing and entry is another, and in the RAF only 36 of 2,120 pilots were reported to be women, though at Cranwell College, where pilots are trained, women in pilots' uniform have apparently been a common sight. With Nicky Smith becoming the commander of the 84 helicopter squadron, a woman had just become a squadron leader for the first time (Craig 2002).

❷ Do you think this means that women are overcoming barriers to occupational entry or does it show that little has really changed?

❷ What information would you need to assess whether there is greater gender equality in the armed forces?

There has been less change in the working class, partly because there always was less separation there. Delamont has indeed claimed that 'the mass of women are working as they did in 1893' (2001: 93).

Women in politics

After a long campaign all adult women finally received the vote in 1928. In 1979 Margaret Thatcher became Britain's first woman prime minister, though there were still only 19 women MPs. Have women truly entered the public sphere of politics?

The representation of women did increase considerably in the 1987 election (41 MPs), the 1992 election (60), and above all the 1997 election (120). It was claimed that in 1997, with 18 per cent of MPs, women had become a 'critical mass', with the potential to 'initiate changes in organizational structures, gender relations and political agendas' (Puwar 1997: 3). It was also crucial that women occupied ministerial positions and in 1997 five obtained Cabinet office. After the 2001 election, the representation of women dropped back slightly to 115 MPs before rising again to 128 in 2005.

Puwar (1997) reports that, even so, women have faced many problems in parliament. As transgressing interlopers, women MPs had to prove themselves before they were taken seriously. Many found that media interest was

Controversy and debate Women's political dilemma

'If they overcome their many political differences to act as women in the interests of women, they exclude themselves from the main political arena and are unlikely to secure ministerial positions. If they operate primarily as members of a political party and rise up the political hierarchy, they become successful politicians but lose their capacity to act as women in the interests of women. Simply being a woman in a position of power may make little difference to the position of women in general, as was shown by the career of Margaret Thatcher, who "repeatedly denied the gender significance of her achievements".' (Pilcher 1999: 151)

❷ Which ministerial positions in the government are currently filled by women?

❷ Do you think that these ministers are doing anything to improve the position of women in British society?

A 'businessman's lunch'—is this phrase now out-of-date?
© Alice Chadwick

primarily in them as women, in their appearance, their families, or their sex-life, and they were not taken seriously as political figures. Male colleagues often treated them in the same way and opponents used sexist language when attacking them, while the House of Commons was historically very much a 'male space', with organizations and procedures designed for men. The women MPs have certainly challenged male practices but they are still a minority facing an uphill struggle.

Even though women were heavily underrepresented at the time, there have been important legislative changes in their favour. These were the Equal Pay Act of 1970, the Sex Discrimination Act of 1975, and the Equal Value Amendment of 1984, which widened pay comparisons under the Equal Pay Act to include men and women doing work of equal value. Then the 1994 extension of many of the rights of full-time workers to part-time workers particularly benefited women because so many of them do part-time work. This legislation has not made women equal but

it has had a considerable impact on women's pay, helped women to challenge and remove open discriminatory practices, and put equal opportunities firmly on the agenda of employers in particular and organizations in general (Walby 1997).

The presence of women in parliament actually had little to do with this legislation. As Walby (1997) has shown, it was the European Union that played the key role in forcing a reluctant British state to make these changes. They were also a response to feminist demands backed by the labour movement. Arguably, women have had a greater political impact through feminism than through participation in formal political institutions.

New/old feminisms

It is no coincidence that the key legislation in the 1970s followed a period of renewed growth and radicalism in the feminist movement. After the 1920s victory of the campaign for the vote, the feminist movement had entered a period of relative weakness and division until the emergence of the second-wave feminism of the Women's Liberation Movement in the 1960s (Banks 1981; Pilcher 1999).

Second-wave feminism was itself far from unified but its various parts combined to produce the major impact that it had on Western societies in the 1970s. In line with our distinctions between different strands of feminism in the box on p. 161, three main branches of second-wave feminism can be identified.

The liberal 'equal rights' strand can be traced back to the eighteenth-century Enlightenment and had earlier culminated in the campaign for the vote. The revival of equal rights demands led directly to the call for equal pay and the ending of discrimination.

Radical feminists did not believe that legislation would achieve anything and emphasized liberation for women rather than equality with men. There were many threads within this anarchic and loosely organized strand of feminism. Some pursued a separatist strategy of 'life without men' and set up women's communes or advocated a militant lesbianism. Radical feminism did frontally attack patriarchy and therefore posed a more direct and general challenge to male domination than liberal feminism had done.

The socialist strand allied feminism with the labour movement. The labour movement had been historically a patriarchal organization that excluded women but in the 1960s radicals became more influential and the unions supported equal rights demands. The labour movement was at the peak of its strength in the 1960s and 1970s and its adoption of the demand for equal pay and an end to discrimination added industrial muscle to the feminist movement. The labour movement could supply the organizational resources that other strands rather lacked.

Global focus International differences in gender inequality

The World Economic Forum (WEF) has published a league table of countries according to the size of their gender gap. Countries are ranked by the extent to which they have reduced the inequality between men and women.

1	Sweden	30	Colombia
2	Norway	31	Russian Federation
3	Iceland	32	Uruguay
4	Denmark	33	China
5	Finland	34	Switzerland
6	New Zealand	35	Argentina
7	Canada	36	South Africa
8	United Kingdom	37	Israel
9	Germany	38	Japan
10	Australia	39	Bangladesh
11	Latvia	40	Malaysia
12	Lithuania	41	Romania
13	France	42	Zimbabwe
14	Netherlands	43	Malta
15	Estonia	44	Thailand
16	Ireland	45	Italy
17	United States	46	Indonesia
18	Costa Rica	47	Peru
19	Poland	48	Chile
20	Belgium	49	Venezuela
21	Slovak Republic	50	Greece
22	Slovenia	51	Brazil
23	Portugal	52	Mexico
24	Hungary	53	India
25	Czech Republic	54	Korea
26	Luxembourg	55	Jordan
27	Spain	56	Pakistan
28	Austria	57	Turkey
29	Bulgaria	58	Egypt

The gender gap combines five equally weighted measures:

1 *Economic participation*—women's presence in the workforce;

2 *Economic opportunity*—the quality of women's involvement, e.g. occupational distribution of women, number of women in managerial positions, duration of maternity leave, wage inequalities;

3 *Political empowerment*—the representation of women in decision-making structures and their voice in formulating policies;

4 *Educational attainment*—literacy rates, enrolment rates, years of education;

5 *Health and well-being*—access to nutrition, healthcare, reproductive facilities, together with safety.

While the overall position of countries is of interest, the combination of different measures presents problems. A high position on some dimensions combined with a low position on others may result in a middle position that does not mean very much. Differences in the position of a given country on the various measures are themselves of considerable interest. Thus, the United Kingdom scored high on educational attainment (4) and political empowerment (5) but much lower on economic participation (21), health and well-being (28), and economic opportunity (41).

The data used are partly statistics from publicly available sources and partly based on a 2004 survey of 9,000 business leaders by the WEF, which is an international organization based in Geneva. Many countries were excluded because of the non-availability of data.

Sources: UN Millennium Project Task Force on Education and Gender Equality (2005); World Economic Forum (2005).

Think about the following questions:

❓ What groupings of countries emerge from their positions in the league table? What is it that these countries have in common. Are there countries that seem out of place and why do you think they are?

❓ Why do you think that the United Kingdom scores so differently on the various dimensions?

❓ How useful is a league table of this kind? Consider the problems posed by the methods used, the availability of data, and the meaning of rank position.

Frontiers Where is feminism now?

Do we live in a 'post-feminist' world where feminism has largely achieved its goals or does it still have a mission? Two recent books on feminism suggest that it is still needed, though they disagree over the direction it should take.

In *The New Feminism* (1998), Natasha Walter argues that there is still plenty of discrimination against women and that women still need to pursue financial, educational, and legal equality with men. To be successful in achieving equality, feminists must, however, abandon the slogan that 'the personal is political'. While this has performed an important function in drawing attention to the way in which the power differences between men and women penetrated, often violently, into women's personal and domestic lives, it has now become a handicap. It distracts attention from the campaign for equal rights and alienates women because its focus on the conflicts of personal life is associated with a 'man-hating' feminism.

In *The Whole Woman* (1999), Germaine Greer rejects equal rights feminism to argue that women do not so much need

equality with men as liberation from them. Equal rights legislation has not removed male domination and women still seek to mould themselves into bodies and lives shaped by male conceptions of what women should be like. She claims that the campaign for equality with men accepts male definitions of how the world should be and seeks to turn women into men. Women should instead assert their distinctive qualities and make their own world. Greer's feminism belongs to the 'difference strand' of feminism that emerged in the 1960s, though it can be traced back to the nineteenth-century feminist belief that women were different and superior (see our discussion of this on p. 171).

Post-feminism is discussed in Pilcher (1999: 3). Recent feminist work is examined in Jowett (2001).

❷ Do you think that feminism has achieved so many of its goals that women no longer need it?

❷ Are women still dominated by male conceptions of how they should look and behave?

The feminist movement undoubtedly played a crucial part in bringing about changes that improved the position of women, but these were not, however, just the result of feminist organization and activity. Broad changes in the economy and in education were also crucial. We saw above that occupational changes led to the growing employment of women. The post-Fordist shift to more flexible patterns of employment was also very important, as it resulted in the expansion of part-time employment, which made it much easier for women to take up paid work. Employment then gave them greater independence at home and made it easier to leave or end marriages that they found unsatisfactory. Education too played a key part, for it was the growing educational success of girls that enabled them to acquire the qualifications that they needed to enter the professions.

Legislation, occupational changes, and access to education provided opportunities but women had to seize them. That women did so was because women themselves were changing. We will next examine changes in the character of men and women, and the relationship between them.

Sexes?

We argued earlier (see p. 170) that the concept of two distinct sexes emerged in the eighteenth century and was hardened in the nineteenth by the belief that the differences between them were essentially biological. The growth

of feminism, the increasing employment of women, and the rise of sociology have chipped away at this biological essentialism. Have we now returned to a 'one-sex' view of men and women? It has certainly been argued that the behaviour of men and women has been converging in recent years. In this section (and in Media Watch 5 at the end of the chapter) we consider whether women have become more like men and whether men have become more like women.

Changing women

Women in Western societies have become less focused on domestic life and more on paid work, which is nowadays a normal and continuing feature of most women's lives. In Britain most women used to give up work when they married but by the 1960s they were working until they had their first child and then returning to work once childcare responsibilities had diminished. The amount of time spent out of work due to childcare responsibilities has steadily declined, in part because women have had fewer children but also because they have resumed work sooner. Indeed, women with dependent children have increasingly combined childcare with not only part-time but also full-time work (Pilcher 1999).

There is evidence too that the aspirations of girls have changed. Sue Sharpe (1994) compared the expectations of a group of girls in the 1970s and 1990s. She found that

Controversy and debate A global revolution?

Is globalization revolutionizing the position of women? In his BBC Radio 4 Reith Lectures of 1999, Anthony Giddens suggested that it is:

> Traditional family systems are becoming transformed, or are under strain, in many parts of the world, particularly as women stake claim to greater equality. There has never before been a society, so far as we know from the historical record, in which women have been even approximately equal to men. This is a truly global revolution in everyday life, whose consequences are being felt around the world in spheres from work to politics.

There is no doubt that globalization has in various ways resulted in a world-wide increase in the employment of women. Transnational corporations, such as Gap and Nike, employ young women as cheap factory labour in countries such as Cambodia and Indonesia. Global communications make it possible for European and American companies to employ teleworking women in secretarial and clerical work in the West Indies or the Philippines. The growth of global tourism has provided work for women in hotels, catering, tour organization, and the sex industry all over the world. There has been an extensive international migration of women from poor countries to meet the increasing demand for their labour in rich countries.

But does this growing employment give women greater equality? Employment can provide the basis for greater independence but whether it does so depends on the context in which it occurs. If women are simply cheap or, in the sex industry, degraded labour, controlled and exploited by men both at work and at home, it is hard to see how this improves their position. This is not just a matter of how patriarchal a particular society may be but of a woman's class (and ethnic) position in that society. Educated middle-class women with jobs in the professions or media careers are, and this applies

to any society, in a very different position from women working in the fields or in sweatshops or in bars.

Globalization is not just, however, an economic process and its political aspects have made possible the growth of global women's movements and organizations. Feminist movements now have a global reach. The United Nations has sponsored a series of World Conferences on Women and has provided the framework for many regional women's conferences and meetings. The International Labour Organization has worked to establish world-wide standards for the employment of homeworkers, who are mainly female.

Global communications have also enabled women suffering oppression in highly patriarchal societies to make their situation known to the outside world and seek its support. This was, for example, the case in Afghanistan where the Taliban regime systematically excluded and confined women. The Revolutionary Association of the Women of Afghanistan (RAWA) used the Internet to generate international awareness and build a network of support. Its website is listed at the end of this chapter.

In some societies globalization has stimulated a patriarchal reaction. This has particularly occurred where traditional values and relationships have been threatened by Western ideas and patterns of consumption. Some fundamentalist religious movements are trying to force women back into traditional roles, modes of dress, and behaviour. In considering the significance of globalization, one must take into account not only the globalizing processes themselves but also responses to them.

Sources: Giddens (1999); Cohen and Kennedy (2000*b*); Ehrenreich and Hochschild (2003).

❷ **Do you think that we can speak of a 'global revolution' taking place in the position of women?**

---

the 1970s group looked for love, marriage, and children. The 1990s group were primarily concerned with jobs and careers. Jane Pilcher (1999) has claimed that it is these changed expectations that probably account for the growing success of girls in school. Educational success then facilitates career success and successful women act as role-models, which raise girls' expectations further.

There can also be little doubt that in the last forty years women in western societies have become more independent. Their growing employment was crucial to this, as it reduced their economic dependence on the breadwinning

male. There were two other key changes, both of which occurred in 1960s Britain:

- divorce law reform;
- oral contraception.

Marriage was one of the central institutions of patriarchy and greater ease of divorce helped women to escape marital constraints, though it also helped men avoid family responsibilities. The availability of the contraceptive pill meant that women could reliably control when and whether they had children. These changes made possible

Frontiers From netball to football

'Football, once considered so unfeminine that the authorities banned women from playing, is overtaking netball as the sport most widely played by women in England.

The Football Association . . . says that there has been such an increase in interest in football that the number of registered female players has nearly doubled in the past two years.

Part of the reason for this is the higher media profile of the game, with England ladies' matches being shown live on satellite television, and a BBC drama series, *Playing the Field*, about a women's football team. . . . The higher profile of women's football has been matched at grassroots level in England, with thousands of projects set up in the past decade to coach girls and provide clubs and leagues for them to play in.

Between the 1998/99 season and the 2000/01 seasons, the number of girl football players (under 16 years old) increased by 87 per cent from 19,200 to 36,000, according to the FA's 2001 audit. The number of women players has increased by 15 per cent from 16,900 to 19,366.'

Source: Jenny Booth, 'Netball Kicked into Touch by Women's soccer', *Sunday Telegraph*, 27 January 2002. © Telegraph Group Limited, 2002.

❷ Why do you think that the number of female players has been increasing so rapidly?

❷ What does this increase tell us about changes in women?

the higher divorce rates, single-parent families, and childless career women that are characteristic of contemporary British society and sharply distinguish it from the society of the first half of the twentieth century.

Increased employment, higher educational qualifications, greater interest in careers, and more independence have all resulted in women behaving more like men. Another arena in which this has occurred is sport, with women engaging increasingly in what was previously considered to be a male preserve (see box on 'From netball to football'). The convergence of behaviour is associated with a unisex convergence of dress and appearance.

The lives of women have changed but does this mean that ideas of what it means to be a woman have changed as well?

There is certainly evidence of change in femininities, particularly in media representations of them. Angela McRobbie's research showed that in magazines for girls and young women, older, more romantic, notions of what it means to be a woman have been increasingly mocked, while their content has focused on sexuality rather than love. McRobbie suggested that this has 'extended the possibilities of what it is to be a woman' (1996: 178).

A different indication of how women view themselves is the way that they see their bodies. This is particularly significant because of the rapidly expanding possibilities of body modification, which enable women (and men) to reconstruct themselves in an attempt to match reality to image. Dieting, exercise regimes, cosmetic surgery, and hormonal therapy have all become commonplace and highly commercialized activities. While all these ways of changing the body are to some extent a matter of indi-

vidual choice, they are, like any other form of consumption, subject to commercial pressures and constrained by gendered beliefs about how the female body should look and be presented.

> ➔ *Connections*
>
> Femininities are discussed on p. 164 of this chapter.
>
> Media representations of women are discussed in more detail in Chapter 10, pp. 377–8.
>
> You can follow the issue of body modification by referring to our discussion of anorexia in Chapter 8, pp. 309–11.

Overwhelmingly, body modification is used to make women slimmer, younger in appearance, and sexually attractive to men. Unisex has its limits! Styles may change but there seems little recent change in the kind of body that most women seek to have and keep. The availability of new technologies has, it appears, put pressure on women to conform all the more to male conceptions of women. As Pilcher has put it:

> Therefore whilst for individual women these techniques have advantages, for women as a whole they can be argued to represent a cumulative narrowing of the range of valuable femininities within a masculine-dominated culture. (Pilcher 1999: 106)

Changes in women's behaviour, expectations, and appearance show them becoming in some ways more like men. Conceptions of the female body, and the time and money expended on body modification, tell, however, a different story. This is the age-old story of women emphasizing their difference and making themselves attractive to

Has femininity changed?
© Alice Chadwick

men by conforming to male conceptions of how their bodies should look.

Changing men

Women have been changing. What about men? In this section we examine first the challenge posed to male identity and then the male response.

Notions of a general male superiority have come under attack as individual women have demonstrated that they can be as successful as men in business, the media, and politics. It is important to be clear here that to argue this is not to claim that women have become equal with men in any of these fields. Individual women have, however, broken through exclusive barriers and this is of great symbolic importance. If a woman can be prime minister or head of the British intelligence service or a chief constable or a barrister or a newscaster or a chief executive, this refutes the idea that only men are able to do these things.

Do women change their bodies just to please men?
© Alice Chadwick

Changes in employment patterns have undermined traditional notions of the male role. The idea of the male as breadwinner has been weakened by the equalizing of economic activity rates, which has resulted from the decline of male, as well as the rise of female, employment. Job expectations have changed too and men have found themselves called upon to show more feminine skills, to be more flexible, more accommodating, and more responsive to clients and customers (see our discussion of customer service work in Chapter 17, pp. 683–4).

As male employment has declined and women have gone out to work, men have come under pressure to do domestic and childcare work. If in a particular household men are unemployed and women are earning money, there are good reasons for maintaining a domestic division of labour but reversing the sex-roles. There is some evidence of this taking place, as we show in Chapter 12, p. 477. There is also considerable evidence of the persistence of traditional roles in the household but it is significant that these roles have lost some of their previous legitimacy. Whether or not they actually do this, men are increasingly expected to do housework and care for children.

Masculinity itself has been assailed. Frank Mort (1996) claimed that there had been a radical change in male identity with the emergence of the 'new man'. A new image of man that feminized male identity was projected in the media during the 1980s. This presented men as caring and cooperative, abandoning masculine aggressiveness and competitiveness. The 'new man' was more sensitive and more emotional, more concerned with appearance, more interested in cosmetics and style. In the media the male body became sexualized in much the same way as the female body had long been.

While Mort saw this as a broad change in culture, Tim Edwards (1997) has argued that it is a more limited phenomenon associated with marketing and advertising. It is a result not so much of some male identity crisis caused by changing employment patterns and feminism as of the expanding market for male fashion. This was generated by the individualist consumerism of the 1980s and the high purchasing power of young men in growing occupations, such as financial services, advertising, and marketing. Demographic changes meant that there were more single men and childless couples, with money to spend on fashion products. The 'new man' was, according to Edwards, largely restricted to these particular social groups. Furthermore, Edwards argues that many traditional images of masculinity can still be found in the men's magazines that appealed to these groups.

Indeed, evidence can be found of the reassertion of traditional masculinities. Connell (1995) showed this occurring within 'masculinity therapy'. This grew up in the 1960s in response to the feminist challenge to traditional

The 'new man'—myth or reality?
© Alice Chadwick

gender-roles and was initially concerned with 'curing' men of the 'disease' of masculinity. In the 1980s, however, masculinity therapy completely changed its character and became concerned with the restoration of a traditional masculinity. Men went off to 'bush camps', where they engaged in drumming, hunting, and warrior activities in search of the 'deep masculine' within them.

Masculinity was asserted in other ways, such as the emergence, particularly in the United States, of movements celebrating the gun and defending the right to carry it. Another example was 'gay-bashing', for the coming-out of gays threatened the heterosexual component of traditional masculine identity. Yet another was the reassertion of patriarchal authority by religious movements.

Connell also argued that the questioning of male identity should not lead us to suppose that men are losing their grip, for they have continued to dominate industry, the military, politics, and the media. As he put it, the defence of hegemonic masculinity has 'formidable resources' and has been 'impressively successful' (Connell 1995: 216).

Changes in employment patterns and gender relationships have clearly not destroyed masculinity. The notion of a 'new man' did certainly emerge in the 1980s but there has subsequently been a reassertion and commercial exploitation of masculinity that feeds off much of its traditional content.

We may conclude that in some ways the two sexes have converged, for the work and home lives of men and women have become more similar. Unisex in fashion and the idea of the 'new man' are symptomatic of this. The 'two-sex' model has not, however, disappeared and the belief that there are fundamental biological differences between the two sexes may well be as strong as ever, while contrasting notions of femininity and masculinity continue to keep the sexes apart. Indeed, the challenge to men has arguably stimulated them to reassert their masculinity, while many women still identify with, in Connell's words (see p. 164), a 'subordinated femininity'.

Sexualities?

In this section we consider the impact of changes in relationships between the sexes on sexuality. If the lives of men and women have become more similar, does this mean that women's sexual behaviour has become more like men's? Have the boundaries between different sexualities become blurred?

Sexual revolution

Premarital sex seems to have increased throughout the twentieth century. Nineteen per cent of married women born before 1904 reported that they had sex before their marriage. The proportion rose to 36 per cent among those born between 1904 and 1914, and by 1934 it had reached 43 per cent. There is some evidence that these rates varied by class. Virginity at marriage seems to have been most likely in poorer families and least likely among wealthier families. This must, in part, reflect the relative lack of opportunities for premarital sex for those who lived in small, cramped houses. A study of sexual behaviour in the working-class districts of Bolton in 1939 reported that for most young, unmarried couples the streets, parks, and back alleys were all that were available for their 'courting'. For this reason, large numbers of those interviewed in a survey in 1946 said that they would have had sex before marriage if they had had the opportunity to do so (J. Burke 1994).

The first half of the twentieth century was a period of considerable sexual ignorance for most people. They knew little about human anatomy, the causes of pregnancy, and contraception. This ignorance meant that rates of illegitimacy, abortion, and sexual disease were high. Nevertheless, rates of illegitimacy fell from the 1870s until the 1940s. This suggests that, when premarital sex resulted in pregnancy, a marriage rapidly followed (L. Hall 1991; see also T. Harrison 1949).

In the 1960s, however, what has often been called the 'sexual revolution' began to separate sexuality from marriage. The availability of the contraceptive pill played a major part in this, though it also reflected important changes in attitudes and the growth of a women's liberation movement. For many women, sex was now no longer something that happened only in marriage in order to produce children but an activity in its own right. Sexual satisfaction became a need and an expectation.

This was, arguably, particularly liberating for women, who had been more constrained than men by the sex-within-marriage norm that had earlier prevailed. The 'double standard' had turned a blind eye to the sexual escapades of men but not those of women. Furthermore, survey evidence from the 1940s suggests that women were more likely than men to be dissatisfied with marital sex (Charles 2002).

Women's sexual needs were now recognized and, indeed, commercialized. Women were no longer expected to be sexually inactive. In the age of *Cosmopolitan*, their magazines no longer just provided information about cooking, home-care, and family problems but also gave sexual information and advice. Pornography specifically for women became more available, while male strip shows for women appeared long before *The Full Monty*.

But was this a liberation? Some have argued that it was the very reverse of this. Sexual liberation made women more available to men and less able to resist their demands. Women also became more vulnerable to male exploitation in the sex industry with the growth of pornography, which

exploits women to meet, mainly, the sexual needs of men. Some feminists here converged with 'new right' moralists in their condemnation of the sexual revolution. A similar debate is now taking place over the interpretation of 'raunch' culture, with some feminist writers arguing that this is not sexual liberation so much as a commercialized pandering to male desires.

The double standard of sexual inequality has not disappeared. Social surveys have reported that men continue to have more partners than women. If men sleep around, they are still considered to be demonstrating their virility, but if women do the same, they are still called 'slags'. Men still discard women when they become older and seek younger female partners but women who seek younger male partners meet with social disapproval (Pilcher 1999).

National survey material suggests that the sexual behaviour of British women has been converging with that of men, though major differences persist (see Figure 5.3). Thus, according to the 2000 survey, women in Britain as a whole reported nearly twice as many 'lifetime' heterosexual partners as those interviewed in 1990 but still only about half the number of partners reported by the men. Similarly, a substantially higher proportion of women were having two or more relationships at the same time but this was still more common among men. In at least one respect, however, women had caught up with men. In the 2000 survey the same proportions of men and women reported having same-sex partnerships during the past five years.

There is evidence in the 2000 survey for a convergence of the ages at which boys and girls have their first sexual intercourse (Wellings *et al.* 2001). This is shown by a

Women's sexual needs recognized and commercialized.
© Alice Chadwick

Figure 5.3 Changes in sexual behaviour in Britain 1990–2000[a]

	Men		Women	
	1990	2000	1990	2000
Average number of heterosexual partners during lifetime	8.6	12.7	3.7	6.5
Average number of heterosexual partners during past five years	3.0	3.8	1.7	2.4
Ever had homosexual partners	3.6%	5.4%	1.8%	4.9%
Percentage with homosexual partners during past five years	1.5%	2.6%	0.8%	2.6%
Percentage with concurrent partners during past year[b]	11.4%	14.6%	5.4%	9.0%

[a] The data come from randomly selected respondents at stratified samples of addresses in Britain. The same questions were used in 1990 and 2000.
[b] Partnerships are defined as concurrent if the first sexual act with the more recent partner preceded the last act with the previous partner.

Source: A. Johnson *et al.* (2001).

comparison of older and younger age groups. There was a big difference in the proportions of men and women aged 40–44 who had had their first sexual intercourse before the age of 16 (27 per cent of males and 17 per cent of females). But for those aged 20–24, women were actually more likely than men to have had their first intercourse before 16 (26 per cent of males and 28 per cent of females). In the youngest age group, those aged 16–19, boys were again ahead but not by much (30 per cent of males and 26 per cent of females). Not too much should be made of small variations but the contrast between those over 40 and those under 25 is clear. There are, however, dangers in generalizing about men and women, for a later article has shown considerable variation by ethnicity in the proportions of both men and women having their first intercourse before the age of 16 (Fenton *et al.* 2005).

Heterosexuality and homosexuality

Although women have behaved sexually increasingly like men, it has been argued that this convergence has not diminished the force of compulsory heterosexuality or, therefore, the male domination intimately associated with it. According to Nickie Charles:

> Although attitudes towards sexual behaviour may have become more liberal, there is evidence that the linkage of sex with male-dominated heterosexuality is as strong at the beginning of the 21st century as it was in the immediate post-war years and that changes in sexual behaviour have resulted in women being able to behave more like men but in male-dominated ways. Thus they can engage in sexual activity and demand more and better orgasms, but the sexuality they engage in is overwhelmingly on men's terms. (2002: 149)

The survey results shown in Figure 5.3 indicate that heterosexuality is still overwhelmingly dominant. Two

qualifications must be made to this, however. First, these figures indicate that during the 1990s same-sex relationships increased rapidly, even if from a low base. Secondly, the figures produced by the same survey for Greater London show that a much higher percentage of people have at some time had same-sex partnerships than in the rest of Britain. According to the 2000 survey, one in ten Greater London men and one in fifteen Greater London women had had same-sex partnerships at some time in their lives.

The most significant change in homosexuality is the emergence of strong and open 'gay' identities since the 1960s. The very term gay was created to value positively a same-sex culture and to distance same-sex relationships from the negative associations that the term homosexuality had carried since the nineteenth century. An important feature of this new culture has been its rejection of the notion that same-sex activity violates male and female identities. As Weeks has put it:

> *Sexual* identity, at least in the lesbian or gay subcultures of the west, has broken free from *gender* identity. You can now be gay and a 'real man', lesbian and a true (or even better) woman. (1985: 191, original italics)

It is important, however, to emphasize again that only some of those who engage in same-sex activity participate in or identify with these cultures. It is also the case that some of those who participate in these cultures are not sexually active. This point has been made particularly with reference to lesbianism, where solidarity between members of a sisterhood rather than a common sexuality has been considered by some to be the true basis of a lesbian subculture (Rich 1980).

The emergence of openly gay cultures has been interconnected with the decriminalization of homosexuality

Is there more toleration now of openly gay couples?

© Alice Chadwick

and the acceptance of gay lifestyles. Homosexuality was substantially, if not completely, decriminalized in Britain by the 1967 Sexual Offences Act. Toleration of gay lifestyles has increased, notably with the emergence of gay villages in some cities (see Chapter 13, p. 517). Significantly, gay couples have increasingly laid claim to the same legal status as married couples and in December 2005 they were allowed to register civil partnerships (see Chapter 12, p. 468).

Liberalization has not been unopposed, for the new permissiveness of the 1960s provoked a 'new moralism'. The rise of the New Right, in combination with the spread of AIDS, which was seen by some as clear proof of the dangers of sexual liberation, led to a growing political conflict between liberationists and moralists during the 1980s and after. This conflict has intensified with the rise of fundamentalist groups claiming that religious texts prohibit homosexuality.

The assertion of gay cultures has been something of a two-edged sword. It has given homosexuals a voice, an identity, a positive image, and a collective organization that could provide mutual support and campaign on their behalf to demand an end to discrimination against them. It also, as Weeks (1985) has pointed out, can lead to 'ghettoization', providing a target for gay-bashing and stimulating a backlash against homosexuality. Furthermore, the claim that gays are naturally different maintains the nineteenth-century distinction between the heterosexuality of the majority and the homosexuality of a minority. Nineteenth-century categories are in this way not so much challenged or subverted as perpetuated. A hegemonic masculinity centred on heterosexuality may be defied but the consequence may be that it is also reinforced.

Bisexuality and queerness

As we suggested earlier (see p. 167), it is bisexuality and, above all, the queer movement that have really challenged the categories of the nineteenth century and the cultures and identities derived from them.

The very term 'bisexuality' preserves the notion of two different sexes but it also transgresses sexual boundaries and provokes not only heterosexual but homosexual condemnation. Some defenders of heterosexuality have considered bisexuality more depraved than homosexuality, while gays and lesbians have attacked it as compromising gay identities and undermining the gay movement. Bisexuals have counter-attacked by arguing that it is bisexuality that is natural and that everyone is naturally bisexual. Although homosexuality and heterosexuality might have seemed the most obvious opponents in battles over sexual identity, they could coexist as separate worlds, while bisexuality crossed their boundaries and threatened both (Weeks 1985).

There is a bisexual subculture but, given its lack of clear boundaries, it has been less militant and less organized than gay and lesbian groups. There are, none the less, many local bisexual groups, national and international bisexual organizations, and websites that enable bisexuals to meet, maintain contact, support each other, exchange information, and promote their cause. The World Wide Web is a valuable resource for a loose network of this kind, which is not centred in communities with a bounded sexual identity.

The queer movement is broader still and includes a wide range of 'deviant' sexual groups. It originated with the emergence of a group of activists calling themselves the Queer Nation in a number of cities in the United States during the 1980s. 'Queer' was originally a term of abuse directed at 'abnormal' homosexuals but it became a rallying cry for radical lesbians and gays who proclaimed their queerness and revelled in it. As Steven Epstein has put it: 'the invocation of the "Q-word" is an act of linguistic reclamation, in which a pejorative term is appropriated by the stigmatized group so as to negate the term's power to wound' (1994: 195). The movement was intellectually

New technology Identity play on the Internet

The Internet has provided new opportunities for experimentation with sexual identities. Participants in chat rooms and bulletin boards cannot see each other and do not have to disclose their real names or their location. They can assume identities that social constraints would normally prevent them adopting. They can allow their imaginations to run riot in experimental acts of cybersex. Webcams do, of course, mean that they can see each other if they wish to but the freedom of anonymous interaction has become more available than ever before. As Gauntlett has put it:

> Because the internet breaks the connection between outward expressions of identity and the physical body which (in the real world) makes those expressions, it can be seen as a space where queer theory's approach to identity can really come to life. (2000: 15)

For a more detailed discussion of Internet identities, see Chapter 4, p. 124.

---

highly self-conscious and was associated with the development of 'queer theory', which we discussed on pp. 167–8.

The queer movement did not seek toleration or acceptance by heterosexuals or their recognition of the minority rights of gays. It directly challenged the whole idea that heterosexuality was normal and natural. It was associated with a confrontational politics and its members engaged in many provocative actions, such as same-sex 'kiss-ins' in 'straight' bars.

It also rejected the internal divisions of sexual deviance. In its new meaning, the term 'queer' was stretched to include not only gays and lesbians but also bisexuals and all those, such as transvestites and transsexuals, who crossed sex and gender boundaries and in any way subverted heterosexual normality. In its rejection of categories and identities it meshed with contemporary tendencies to see sexual behaviour as, like any other aspect of life, a matter of lifestyle choice.

In spite of this challenge, the heterosexuality/homosexuality discourse has remained dominant in most people's ways of thinking and talking. As we argued earlier in our discussion of queer theory, the capacity of the dominant ideology and the socialization process to perpetuate the 'h' categories should not be underestimated. Furthermore, as we noted above, by proclaiming their difference, 'orthodox' gay cultures and communities have themselves reinforced the 'h' discourse.

‹› *Stop and reflect*

In this section we have been considering whether the identities separated in the nineteenth century have in recent times become blurred.

We first looked at male and female spheres.

- There is some evidence of the decline of separate spheres in the area of employment but occupations are still in many ways gendered.
- Consider how important feminism has been in breaking down this separation. What other social changes have been involved?

We then discussed whether the differences between the sexes had diminished.

- List ways in which men and women have become more similar.
- List ways in which their attitudes, behaviours, and identities still appear to be distinctive.
- List ways in which male and female bodies are becoming more alike or more different.

In the last section we returned to sexualities. We considered whether sexualities have been losing their distinctiveness.

- There is evidence of the convergence of male and female sexual behaviour, though significant differences remain and there is still a 'double standard'.
- Has sexuality become simply a matter of lifestyle choice?

Chapter summary

In 'Understanding sex, gender, and sexuality' we examined the concepts of sex, gender, and sexuality, and the theoretical issues they raised.

Sex refers to the biological and physical differences between men and women:

- The notion that there are two sexes is not just a reflection of the biological differences between men and women but a historically specific way of thinking about these differences.
- The sex differences between men and women are at least partly the result of gendered conceptions of maleness and femaleness.

Gender refers to differences in the way that men and women in a particular society are expected to feel, think, and behave:

- Socialization can explain the persistence of gender differences but cannot explain social change, leaves little room for agency and choice, and cannot account for gender inequalities.
- Theories of patriarchy have provided important explanations of gender inequalities but many of their assumptions have been criticized.
- Connell's conception of a 'gender order' has provided a more differentiated analysis of masculinities and femininities.

Sexuality refers to activities found physically arousing but also to linked aspects of identity, lifestyle, and community:

- A person's sexuality is constructed through a process of social learning.
- The conventional categories of sexuality do not just describe sexual practices but carry with them assumptions about sexual behaviour.

In 'Separating identities' we examined the mainly nineteenth-century processes that separated out spheres, sexes, and sexualities.

The separation of male and female spheres distinguished male and female roles and activities:

- Domestic life became a female sphere and the public life of employment and politics a predominantly male sphere.
- The separation of spheres excluded women from many activities but also enabled the growth of the first feminist organizations.

The nineteenth century also saw the separation of men and women as different sexes:

- According to Laqueur (1990), a two-sex model emerged during the eighteenth century.

- Sex differences were biologised during the nineteenth century.
- The separation of the sexes enabled the growth of feminism.

The separation of the sexes was closely associated with the separation of sexualities:

- Men were thought to be sexually active in nature and women passive.
- The notion of two sexes made possible the categories of heterosexuality and homosexuality.
- Distinct homosexual identities and subcultures began to emerge.

In 'Blurring identities' we considered whether the identities separated in the nineteenth century have converged in recent years.

We first examined what had happened to the male and female spheres:

- Women have entered further into the male sphere by increasingly taking paid employment, though occupations are still gendered.
- Women have achieved greater representation in parliament and government but have experienced marginalization in male-dominated political institutions.
- Important equal opportunities legislation has been passed, in part because of the renewed vigour of 1960s feminism.

We went on to discuss whether women have become more like men and men more like women.

- Women have become more independent and more focused on work and career, and in these respects more like men.
- Conceptions of the female body still emphasize the differences between men and women, and the male view of the female body remains dominant.
- The 'new man' feminization of male identity has arguably been outweighed by the reassertion of traditional masculinity.

We then considered whether sexual life is still shaped by nineteenth-century ideas and categories:

- There has been some convergence of male and female behaviour, though significant differences remain.
- The queer movement has rejected sexual categories and, for some, sexuality has become a matter of lifestyle choice and experimentation.
- There is still a sharp distinction between a dominant heterosexuality and a subordinate homosexuality.

Key concepts

- bisexuality
- emphasized femininity
- feminism
- gender
- gender order
- gender-role

- hegemonic masculinity
- heterosexuality
- homosexuality
- intersex
- lesbianism
- patriarchy

- performativity
- queer theory
- sex
- sex-role
- sexuality

Workshop 5

Study 5 Gender and policing

In *Gender and Policing: Sex, Power and Police Culture*, Louise Westmarland (2001) reports on an ethnographic study of police work. This was a three-year study of two police forces, one in a rural and one in an urban area. The main method used was observation of the police on patrol, though Westmarland tried to make herself an 'informed stranger' by carrying out interviews and focus group discussions before making her observations.

The police force has become an important area of research in the study of gender because it is a traditionally male area of work that has increasingly recruited women and has been forced by legislation to integrate them by abolishing their segregation in a separate force. By 2000 women comprised 17 per cent of police officers in England and Wales. Although women are disproportionately in the lower ranks, they were promoted at a higher rate in the 1990s and by 2000 there were twelve women assistant chief constables (8 per cent of the total) and three women chief constables (6 per cent). It is, none the less, one of the few remaining occupations where the masculine virtues of toughness and physical strength are still valued, where 'men can still act as men'.

Does the recruitment and promotion of women mean that police work is no longer gendered? It has been claimed that women are segregated in low-status work dealing with women and children. Segregation results from assumptions made about 'embodied expertise'. Women are considered better at caring for children, because of childbirth, and men better at tasks that may involve fighting, because of their physical strength. Westmarland

did find evidence for this kind of segregation. In one child and family protection unit, there were fourteen women officers and only three men, though in the other there were seventeen women and fifteen men. The senior positions in both units were filled by men.

She cautions us, however, against the assumption that all the women involved were forced into this work by men. In focus group discussions many women said that they preferred it, had chosen it, and did not consider it of low status. Some simply regarded it as a step on the way to a higher rank or to other duties, which they could move on to when opportunities arose. It was also not always assumed that women were best at dealing with children. After one male officer stated in a focus group that 'a woman is naturally less intimidating to a child', another disagreed and declared that 'I could speak to a child a hell of a lot better than a policewoman who hasn't had children. I've got three children of my own' (Westmarland 2001: 74).

The allocation of work was, anyway, different out on patrol and this is where Westmarland's observational approach has enabled her to correct misconceptions of the *actual* work done by women officers. When women officers were on patrol, they were not deployed according to the character of the incident. Bureaucratic procedures meant that they were called to deal with incidents according to priorities and dispatch systems, not according to whether they involved women or children.

Where this did not apply was in incidents involving child sexual abuse. This is partly explained by the legal requirement that women officers must be present. There was also a belief among both men and women that women were better at handling the emotional side of these cases. This reflects the much wider and well-established practice of women being responsible for 'emotional labour' (see our discussion on this in Chapter 4, pp. 146–7).

When out on patrol women officers achieved the same percentage of arrests as men. Indeed, this study actually found the women making more arrests than the men did for crimes, such as aggravated house burglary and car crime, that involved physical force. Westmarland declares that 'the traditional image of the high adrenalin, "macho cop" arrest being made only by men now seems unsupportable' (2001: 185).

There was, none the less, still a strong culture of masculinity in the police force. Women officers might make as many arrests as men but the men did not consider that it was right to expose them to violence in this way. There was a 'van culture' of sexual bragging and sexist comments about passing women. An exaggerated masculinity was particularly manifest in some departments, notably those concerned with 'cars, guns, and horses'—that is the elite traffic department with its fast cars, the firearms departments, and the mounted branch. These were something of a refuge for men who did not like working with women or carrying out 'female' tasks that might involve caring.

This study supports earlier work in showing that, although far more women have been recruited to the police force, police work is still highly gendered. Its ethnographic methods have, how-ever, demonstrated the complexity and limits of the gendering process. It shows that women police officers are not just pushed around by men but are actively involved in choosing work and pursuing their careers. It also shows that out on patrol women can act as men, that, to quote Westmarland, there is an 'equality of opportunity on the streets' (2001: 188).

This case study illustrates many of the concepts and processes examined in this chapter. Try answering the following questions:

- ❓ What evidence does this study provide of the gendering of occupations?
- ❓ Does it suggest that this gendering is diminishing?
- ❓ Does this study show that the police force is a patriarchal organization?
- ❓ What evidence can you find here of hegemonic masculinity? Is this a more useful concept for the analysis of the police force than patriarchy?

Compare this ethnographic account with the portrayal of the police in a television police drama (record a police drama so that you can analyse it more carefully).

- ❓ What points of similarity and what points of difference can you identify?
- ❓ How do you think the requirements of a drama affect the representation of men and women in the police force?

 ## Media watch 5 Ladettes

'Ladette' came into use in the media during the later 1990s but has now made it into the *Oxford English Dictionary* (2001). This defines a ladette as:

> A young woman characterized by her enjoyment of social drinking, sport, or other activities typically considered to be male-oriented, and often by attitudes or behaviour regarded as irresponsible or brash; (usually) one of a close-knit social group.

Too much drinking is central to characterizations of the ladette and there is certainly evidence that young women have been drinking more in recent years and behaving more like men in this respect. According to the Office for National Statistics (ONS 2004), the proportion of men exceeding weekly recommended benchmarks rose only from 26 per cent to 27 per cent between the years 1988 and 2003, but the proportion of women doing this rose from 10 per cent to 17 per cent. The increase was much more pronounced among women aged 16–24, as Figure 5.4 shows. Note that weekly recommended benchmarks were 21 units of alcohol for men and 14 for women. A unit is roughly equivalent to half a pint of beer or cider, a small glass of wine, or a 25 ml measure of spirits.

Some of the media explanations of young women's increased alcohol consumption are: the rising number of women in higher education; the rising employment and income of women; the changing character of clubs and pubs; the marketing strategies of the drinks industry; TV programmes like *Friends* and *Sex in the City*.

Figure 5.4 Young adults exceeding weekly benchmarks of alcohol consumption, Great Britain (%)

	1988	2002
Males aged 16–24	31	37
Females aged 16–24	15	33

Source: ONS (2004).

Figure 5.5 Those born in 1987 binge drinking three times or more in the last thirty days, in selected European countries, 2003 (%)

	Males	Females
France	13	7
Germany	31	24
Ireland	31	33
Italy	19	8
Sweden	18	14
United Kingdom	26	29

Source: ESPAD (2003).

International survey data suggest that this is a particularly British (and Irish) phenomenon. The ESPAD (European School Survey Project on Alcohol and other Drugs) survey of 35 European countries showed that it was only in these two countries that binge drinking among 15 and 16 year-old girls exceeded that among 15 and 16 year-old boys. Binge drinking is defined as 'having five or more drinks in a row' (ESPAD 2003).

How is the distinctive British drinking pattern to be explained? There has been frequent comment in Britain on differences in eating and drinking cultures between North European and Mediterranean countries. Arguably, the distinctiveness of drinking patterns in Britain may, however, have more to do with British economic policy, changes in British cities (see Chapter 13, pp. 532–3), and the neo-liberal capitalism that has flourished in Britain since the 1980s (see Chapter 15, pp. 601–2).

This would all suggest that the 'ladette' is a new phenomenon. Carolyn Jackson and Penny Tinkler (2007, forthcoming) have, however, argued that there is nothing new about fears that girls are behaving badly. They give examples from the years at the end of the First World War, when 'flappers' or 'modern girls' were described in very similar ways. They point out that excessive drinking was central to their characterization too.

Why have the drinking habits of girls attracted so much negative comment? Concerns were raised then as now about the health problems and various dangers to social order posed by the misbehaviour of young women. More fundamentally, Jackson

and Tinkler suggest that these negative representations are a reaction to the threat they pose to the gender order. When girls behave like boys, they transgress gender boundaries and challenge the dominant conceptions of masculinity and femininity that project contrasting images of men and women. In particular, they violate the conception of women as domestic carers.

Jackson and Tinkler argue that (both then and now) the media interest in, and negative characterization of, the behaviour of girls is not just a reflection of changes in behaviour and the social problems these may cause. It is also a response to:

- the social advances made by women;
- anxiety about the behaviour of the young;
- the growing consumer power of young women;
- the mass media's thirst for stories.

As they put it: 'Ladettes and modern girls are products of a backlash against the perceived power of "unsettled" and power-hungry female youth in a society where media spectacle and/or moral panics are the lifeblood of the newspaper industry' (Jackson and Tinkler 2007, forthcoming).

Sources: ESPAD (2003), *European School Survey Project on Alcohol and Other Drugs*, at **www.espad.org/**; *Guardian*, 19 March 2004; *Independent*, 15 December 2004; ONS (2004), *Living in Britain 2002* (London: Office for National Statistics), p. 170; *The Oxford English Dictionary*, at **http:// dictionary.oed.com/**; Jackson, C. and Tinkler, P. (2007, forthcoming), '"Ladettes" and "Modern Girls": "Troublesome" Young Femininities', *Sociological Review*.

This material raises many questions about gendered behaviour, changes in the behaviour of men and women, and perceptions of these changes. Consider the following questions:

❷ What other changes in gendered behaviour patterns might be associated with changes in drinking patterns?

❷ How can these changes in drinking patterns be explained?

❷ What does use of the term 'ladette' tell us about social perceptions of changes in the behaviour of women?

❷ What are the implications of this material for Connell's characterization of the 'gender order' (see pp. 163–4)?

❷ Does the material in this example show that there are no longer significant differences between male and female identities?

Discussion points

Patriarchy

How useful is the concept of patriarchy in helping us to under-stand and explain gender inequalities? Read the sections on 'Patriarchy' and 'The gender order'. Make sure you are clear about the meaning of this term and the different ways in which it has been used.

- What has this concept contributed to the study of gender?
- What problems does its use raise?
- Has Robert Connell provided a better approach to the study of gender.

Identities

How different are male and female identities? Read the part of the chapter called 'Separating identities'.

- What were the main features of the male and female identities established in the nineteenth century?

- What processes led to the formation of these identities?
- Why have people thought that male and female identities are biological in character?
- Are there any good reasons for supposing that they are?

Gender convergence

Are men and women becoming more alike? Read the part of the chapter called 'Blurring identities'.

List the ways in which men and women are becoming more alike. Consider how men and women appear, what they do, the attitudes they hold, and the way they see themselves.

- List the ways in which you think they are still different in character.
- Do you think that men and women will eventually behave in the same way?
- Could gender differences become a thing of the past?

Explore further

The following provide introductory surveys of the position of women in British society:

Charles, N. (2002), *Gender in Modern Britain* (Oxford: Oxford University Press). *Covers all areas of society in a theoretically informed but very clear way and deals with men as well as women.*

Delamont, S. (2001), *Changing Women, Unchanged Men? Sociological Perspectives on Gender in a Post-industrial Society* (Buckingham: Open University Press). *This strongly argued book addresses exactly this question—Have women changed but not men?—and concludes that women have not really changed either.*

Pilcher, J. (1999), *Women in Contemporary Britain* (London: Routledge). *A very clear and comprehensive examination of the position of women in all areas of society.*

For clear definitions of the concepts used in gender studies, followed by brief but detailed discussions of their usage and the issues this raises see:

Pilcher, J., and Whelehan, I. (2004), *50 Key Concepts in Gender Studies* (London: Sage).

Latest reflections from one of the main theorists of gender:

Connell, R. W. (2002), *Gender and Power: Society, the Person, and Sexual Politics* (Cambridge: Polity Press).

A knowledge of the history of gender is indispensable to an understanding of the concepts and categories that still dominate the way people think about it:

Shoemaker, R. (1998), *Gender in English Society, 1650–1850: The Emergence of Separate Spheres* (London: Longman). *This book provides a detailed and comprehensive account of their origins.*

Weeks, J. (1985), *Sexuality and its Discontents: Meanings, Myths, and Modern Sexualities* (London: Routledge). *A frequently reprinted book that provides a highly perceptive, sociologically informed account of the historical development of contemporary concerns with sexuality.*

There are many interesting and diverse readers that cover the issues dealt with in this chapter:

Backett-Milburn, K., and McKie, L. (2001) (eds.), *Constructing Gendered Bodies* (Basingstoke: Palgrave). *Brings together many theoretical and research pieces on a fashionable and important theme that is crucial to the discussion of the relationship between sex and gender.*

Ehrenreich, B., and Hochschild, A. R. (2003), *Global Women: Nannies, Maids and Sex Workers in the New Economy* (London: Granta). *A wide-ranging collection of studies examining female migration and the globalization of women's work.*

Weeks, J., Holland, J., and Waites, M. (2003) (eds.), *Sexualities and Society* (Cambridge: Polity Press). *A diverse and interdisciplinary collection of pieces that includes the writings of many of the big-name theorists and researchers in this field.*

Williams, C. L., and Stein, A. (2002) (eds.), *Sexuality and Gender* (Oxford: Blackwell). *Another wide-ranging and up-to-date reader on the interrelationships between sex, gender, and sexuality.*

Online resources

Visit the Online Resource Centre that accompanies this book to access more learning resources and other interesting material on sex, gender, and sexuality at:

www.oxfordtextbooks.co.uk/orc/fulcher3e/

For further material on queer theory and Judith Butler's approach, including a helpful interview with Judith Butler, browse:

www.theory.org.uk/resources.htm

To find out more about the Revolutionary Association of the Women of Afghanistan visit:

www.rawa.org/

The Social Science Information Gateway web page on Sex and Gender lists lots of useful sites:

www.intute.ac.uk/socialsciences/sociology/

The Equal Opportunities Commission Sex and Power report looks at the representation of women in senior positions in private and public organizations and can be found at

www.eoc.org.uk/

A series of articles in *The Guardian* on 'gender issues' is available at

www.guardian.co.uk/gender/

racial and
ethnic identities

Contents

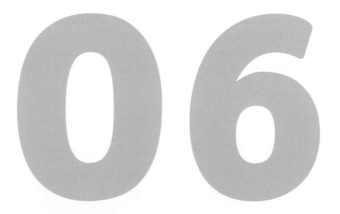

06

Race and racism

'On current demographic trends, we, the native British people, will be an ethnic minority in our own country within sixty years. To ensure that this does not happen, and that the British people retain their homeland and identity, we call for an immediate halt to all further immigration, the immediate deportation of criminal and illegal immigrants, and the introduction of a system of voluntary resettlement whereby those immigrants who are legally here will be afforded the opportunity to return to their lands of ethnic origin assisted by a generous financial incentives both for individuals and for the countries in question. We will abolish the "positive discrimination" schemes that have made white Britons second-class citizens. We will also clamp down on the flood of "asylum seekers", all of whom are either bogus or can find refuge much nearer their home countries.'[1]

The British National Party split from its predecessor, the National Front, in 1982 and built its current programme under the leadership of John Tyndall. In 1983 it became the first explicitly racist party to win a seat in a British local council election. Under its current, and younger, leader Nick Griffin, it achieved some success in the local elections of 2002 and 2003. In the 2005 general election it secured 0.7 per cent of the national vote. Its racist programme claims to defend the British people against the dangers of racial interbreeding. Nick Griffin has said that only the BNP is aware that 'our ancient cultural and ethnic identities are being submerged in a sea of colour'.[2]

Griffin made his point in the context of an argument that black and white people are genetically distinct from each other. The Human Genome Project, he argues, establishes this, but most scientists are too frightened to state it openly. Scientists fear speaking against the liberal orthodoxy and political correctness that denies the reality of race.

Source 1: British National Party policy statement on www.bnp.org.uk/policies.html

Source 2: www.bnp.org.uk/articles/article11.html

What is the real basis to these claims? Are there human 'races', and do biological and cultural problems follow from the 'mixing' of races? These are the crucially important questions that we look at in this chapter. In the past, racial ideas were very widely accepted and were seen as unproblematic. Large numbers of people advocated or tolerated programmes of genetic population control. The demise of those programmes and the weakening of the racial ideas on which they rested is not a mere matter of the rise of political correctness. We will show that there is no biological basis to race and that racial categories have to be seen as social constructions through which people exercise power and control over each other. We will look at the effects of racial classification on cultural differences, and we will trace the ways in which racial and ethnic identities have shaped people's relations with each other.

Understanding race and ethnicity

The claim that genetic differences divide human beings into distinct racial categories has a long history. Such races are seen as marked by differences in skin colour, hair type, body form, blood group, and other physical characteristics. Those who accept the reality of racial differences have often taken the further step of attributing the existence of cultural diversity to them. Just as the personality differences between men and women have been seen as consequences of their biological sexual differences, so the cultural differences between black and white people, for example, have been seen as expressions of biological racial differences. Whatever reality, or lack of reality, can be given to the idea of biological race, racial thinking has had significant social consequences for the groups identified as 'races'. If we are to understand race and its relation to cultural difference, we must understand how the idea of racial difference came about.

Racial thinking

The word 'race' came to be used in English during the sixteenth century to refer to types, kinds, or groupings of people or things. In relation to people, it originally described the various human populations that were believed to have been dispersed from the biblical homeland after the Flood and the fall of the Tower of Babel. The diversity of physical and cultural types found in Europe and the lands that were being encountered in the European exploration of the world were seen as descending from this initial dispersion. The word could, therefore, be applied to differentiate Germans, Celts, Normans, Jews, Africans, and others. It was only much later that 'race' came to have the specific meaning of types of people who were distinguished from each other by their inherited biological characteristics. This happened during the period of European colonization when European expansion into the Pacific, the Americas, and Africa led to a far greater awareness of human diversity in respect of skin colour and other visible physical characteristics, on the one hand, and cultural practices, on the other. Biologists and the early social theorists sought a way of describing and accounting for the differences between the European colonialists and the native Americans and Africans that they colonized and enslaved. Eighteenth-century biologists dispensed with much of the biblical framework and used the word 'race' to refer simply to the various physical types into which they thought the human species could be divided.

Race and science

One of the earliest attempts to produce a systematic classification of human races was that of the medical scientist Johann Blumenbach towards the end of the eighteenth century. Blumenbach distinguished the Caucasian, Mongolian, Ethiopian, American, and Malayan races. A little later, the anatomist Léopold Cuvier made a simpler distinction between the white, yellow, and black races. More and more physical studies of the anatomy of individuals from different populations were carried out, leading to more refined and elaborate classifications. The Caucasian or European population, for example, was sometimes divided into Gothic (Teutonic or German), Slavic, Celtic (Gallic), and other races. These racial categories were used by nineteenth-century writers to explain political and economic conflicts between nations and the divisions within such multinational empires as Austria-Hungary.

> ⊃ *Connections*
>
> Many of the writers on race based their arguments on anatomical measurements, taking skull size, for example, as an indicator of brain size. You will find a discussion of this argument in relation to intelligence in Chapter 18, pp. 731–2. You might also like to refer to our discussion of the work of Lombroso in criminology, as he used similar measures and some racial ideas to classify criminal types (Chapter 7, pp. 236–7). Theories of racial stratification and conflict are briefly discussed in Chapter 19, pp. 772–3.

These anatomical classifications were often associated with beliefs about the moral qualities of the various races. The white or Caucasian race was invariably seen as morally superior to the yellow and black races. The impoverished and enslaved position of Africans and those of African descent, for example, was seen as a direct consequence of their smaller brain size and as being responsible for their 'childlike' characteristics and their 'inferior' or 'backward' cultural development.

This scientifically grounded idea of race became possible because of the emergence of new ways of understanding the origins and formation of the world of human beings. Biblical accounts of creation were challenged in the nineteenth century by new thinking in geology and biology, where ideas of 'development' and 'evolution' were stressed. Human biological differences, it now appeared, had to be seen as the result of long processes of development in which, over the course of many generations, the populations living under different climatic and environmental conditions across the globe became gradually more distinct in their biological traits.

Central to the success of these ideas was the publication, in 1859, of Charles Darwin's *Origin of Species*, which, after much intellectual opposition from the religious orthodoxy, firmly established the idea that all human characteristics were the result of a 'natural selection' through which those characteristics that best helped individuals to adapt to their specific environment (for example, by allowing them to benefit from particular kinds of food or to avoid particular kinds of disease) would tend to be perpetuated over generations through breeding. Darwinism and the idea of evolution are not necessarily racialist in character, but the popularization of Darwin's ideas in the nineteenth century undoubtedly favoured the growth of racial thinking. It encouraged the view that races could be seen in an evolutionary framework, with the Caucasian as the highest, most evolved, and most civilized race and the Negro or African as the least advanced race.

Central to the spread of racial thinking was the discovery of the genetic mechanism that made possible evolution by natural selection. Gregor Mendel, studying variation in plants, suggested that offspring inherited minute particles of 'germ matter'—now termed 'genes'—that determined their biological characteristics. He showed that offspring inherited genes from each parent and that their own biological characteristics depended on the particular ways in which this genetic material was combined at the moment of conception. In particular, he showed that offspring inherited genetic characteristics and possibilities that may not be apparent in their own features but may be passed on to their offspring and find their expression in them.

The child of brown-eyed and blue-eyed parents, for example, will have brown eyes. However, the child will also inherit the gene for blue eyes, though this remains inactive. If, however, they reproduce with a brown-eyed person who also had a blue-eyed parent, then their children may be born with blue eyes. Mendel and later genetic researchers have shown how such patterns of inheritance can be explained and predicted for many observable biological traits.

The idea that racial traits are fixed and inherited led many people to consider policies of selective breeding. If one race is culturally superior to another, it was held, then governments should prevent any breeding between the two races, which could result only in a decline in the cultural standard of the superior race. Whites, for example, should not marry or have children with blacks if they want to maintain the intelligence and cultural superiority of their race. This advocacy of the complete biological segregation of the races was given its strongest expression in the racial thought of the Nazis in Germany during the 1930s and 1940s. Nazi thought contrasted the superior characteristics of the white 'Aryan' race with the 'inferior' characteristics of the Jews and, under the leadership of Adolf Hitler, Nazis attempted to bring about the complete physical elimination of the Jews from Europe.

In reaction to the political racism of the Second World War, the United Nations sponsored a scientific dialogue on race between biologists and social scientists. This resulted in a joint statement—called the Moscow Declaration—in 1964. This statement concluded that there was no scientific basis for conventionally identified race categories, and it effectively discouraged scientists from using the term to describe human biological variations. Those variations in biological traits that do exist within and between human populations can be explained by the inheritance of genes, but they do not constitute discrete 'racial' categories. All human populations can interbreed without problem, and so there is a single human species with no obvious way of delineating any 'subspecies' or races. 'Race', the Moscow Declaration concluded, is simply an outdated term, a hangover from unscientific ways of thinking. This view has been reinforced by later scientific work.

 ## Briefing: who is black and who is white?

It is difficult to relate skin colour directly to genetic inheritance. Dennis Barber, a white bank manager from Staffordshire, discovered that he is the direct descendant of a black African slave who was brought to England in the eighteenth century. Despite his white appearance, Dennis carries genes that could result in his own descendants being born with dark features. It has been estimated that the number of slaves and other black people that lived in Britain in the eighteenth century means that one in five white British people has a direct black ancestor.

Recent research has suggested that 30 per cent of 'white' Americans have some black parentage in their family history, and roughly 18 per cent of 'black' Americans have white ancestry. About 10 per cent of African Americans are 50 per cent white by ancestry.

Source: Sunday Telegraph, 3 October 1999; **www.isteve.com/2002_How_White_Are_Blacks.htm**

Briefing: Adolf Hitler

Adolf Hitler (1889–1945) was born in Austria. He dropped out of school, intending to follow an artistic career, but he failed to gain entry to the Vienna Academy. He dodged military service and moved to Germany, where he volunteered for army service during the First World War. After the war he spied on political parties as a paid informer of the authorities, but he gradually became drawn into open political action. He joined a small party, transforming it into the National Socialist German Workers' Party and forming a paramilitary 'brown-shirt' movement.

The Nazis—as they became known—took an extreme right-wing and anti-Jewish position. Hitler was imprisoned after an attempt to overthrow the Bavarian government in 1923. After his release, he cultivated the support of big business and the established political parties, and became German Chancellor (prime minister) in 1933. He immediately set up a framework of terror and abandoned constitutional restraints. Hitler built up the German army, invaded Austria and Czechoslovakia, and following his invasion of Poland he found himself embroiled in war against Britain and France in 1939.

One of the principal elements in Hitler's outlook was his anti-Semitism—anti-Jewish sentiment—which he built into an ideology that justified the exclusion of Jews from most forms of employment, the confiscation of their property, and their wholesale persecution. His ideas were set out in the book that he wrote while in prison, *Mein Kampf* (1925), and they were implemented in the 'final solution'. This was a policy to remove Jews and other 'degenerates' (such as gypsies and homosexuals) from German territory to concentration and extermination camps such as Belsen, Dachau, and Auschwitz. More than six million people were murdered by the Nazis in the gas chambers at these camps.

Is it all in the genes?

Genetic accounts of human differentiation have shown clearly that variations and differences in genetic structure from one individual to another are not obviously expressed in simple differences in, say, skin colour. Skin colour is not determined by any major genetic difference, but by a combination of relatively minor ones. These genetic differences are, in any case, the results of differences in climate and other environmental factors operating over the generations. Differences in skin colour are also not directly associated with any of the vastly more extensive genetic differences that produce other physical differences.

One such genetic trait is the blood group. But even this does not support the idea of racial difference. People can be classified as type A, B, AB, or O and according to the rhesus factor, and the pattern of distribution of blood types has been shown to be quite distinct from one human population to another. Nevertheless, attempts to produce discrete racial categories based on externally observable characteristics have proved unsuccessful, as the overlap in these types between populations is too great.

Although advances in genetics have led scientists to recognize the important causal effect that genes can have on human behaviour, biology has also shown that separate human populations do not have the degree of genetic uniformity that would warrant a scientific description of them as races. The observable characteristics that have been linked to the use of the term race (skin colour, hair type, facial form, and so on) are the outcome of a whole cluster of genetic and other biological factors that operate under particular environmental conditions. While certain natural clusterings of genetic differences can be found in different human populations, these are the results of normal reproduction within those populations as they have developed over time. These patterns of biological difference change as the boundaries of the populations change. They do not correspond to any lines of racial division.

Genes are stored in chromosomes, 23 pairs of them in each cell. One chromosome—the so-called Y chromosome—is specific to human beings and is the determinant of male sex characteristics. As it appears only in males, it can be used to trace genetic inheritance through the male line. Biologists have found that variations in the genetic patterns on the Y chromosome are related to the degree of biological separation: the longer that two populations have been separate and distinct from each other, the more different are the Y chromosomes carried by their men. This research showed the common African origin of all human populations, but it brought out some striking patterns of similarity and difference. The genetic similarities between Chinese and native Australians, for example, are greater than those between either group and Europeans. The Europeans, however, have close genetic similarities with South Asians. The sharpest genetic differences distinguish African populations from *all* other human populations, although the variation within each group is vast.

Individual differences in detailed genetic characteristics (so-called within-group differences) are much greater than population differences (between-group differences) and they vastly outweigh any differences among conventionally defined skin-colour categories. Two randomly chosen English men, for example, may differ far more from one another in genetic terms than do a typical English and Nigerian man. Similarly, the 'Black' and the 'White' populations in the United States are both internally quite diverse in their genes. Compared with other animal species, human beings are, overall, extremely homogeneous in genetic terms. There are no identifiable sub-species. There is no scientific basis for any conception of biological races in human populations.

The social construction of race

If human populations are not to be called 'races', is there any role for the word in sociological analysis? This is a very contentious question, as the word carries strong moral and political connotations. For many sociologists, as we will show, there is, indeed, a useful role for a properly theorized concept of race. According to this point of view, a human grouping is a 'race' not because of their biological characteristics but because they are socially constructed as a race. If they and others construct their personal and cultural characteristics in terms of a presumed biological or genetic descent, then they can be called a race. In using the word 'race' to describe such a group, the sociologist is simply recognizing the ways in which people themselves use the term to describe one another. The sociologist is not describing the group as a biological race—we have shown that such an idea cannot be sustained—but is recognizing an important element in social consciousness. When people identify themselves as a race, or are identified in this way by others, their actions are shaped by the specifically racial discourse that has been built up since the eighteenth century, and sociological analysis has to be sensitive to this and to its consequences.

Biological race cannot be regarded as a serious scientific concept. Nevertheless, it remains an important term in political debate. It is a central term in those political beliefs that draw on now discredited biological ideas to define social differences and so to justify the oppression and exclusion of those from particular social groups, who are deemed to be naturally inferior. Much prejudice and discrimination against cultural minorities continues to be justified in racial terms.

The use of the term 'race', then, rests on beliefs in the significance of supposed biological differences that are seen as determining social differences. **Race** is a purely social construct, based on the observed physical and cultural characteristics of individuals and on discredited racial theories (Banton 1987). To understand how this is possible, it is necessary to examine the relationship between race and ethnicity.

Ethnic identities and racialization

Ethnicity is a general category for describing collective identities. Ethnic groups are defined by their sense of sharing a distinct culture that can be traced back to the historical or territorial origins of the group. Ethnic groups build an 'imagined community' (B. Anderson 1991), an image of themselves as a collectivity. The solidarity and group consciousness of an ethnic group are organized around this idea of origin and cultural history (A. Smith 1986). Hall (1989) has stressed that ethnicity can also be rooted in a history of common experiences such as those of the exclusion and discrimination experienced by minority groups at the hands of a majority.

Ethnicity, then, involves defining groups by a shared history or culture, a common geographical origin, a common language or religion, or a common set of experiences. Ethnic identifiers based on common history, language, or religion include Asian, Black, Muslim, Scottish, Jewish, Basque, Kurd, Slav, and British. Ethnicity is often expressed in a common language, though merely having a common language does not necessarily confer ethnicity. Hebrew and Arabic are the basis of distinct ethnic identities, while the English language is now a global language spoken by people of many ethnicities, and those who identify themselves as 'Asian' may speak Punjabi, Gujarati, Urdu, Bengali, or Pashto. The same is true of religion: Judaism is strongly associated with Jewish ethnicity, Christianity is a religious system common to those of many ethnicities, and Asians may be Hindu, Sikh, Jain, Buddhist, or Muslim. Nationalism, such as that of the Scots and the Palestinians, is a form of ethnic identity based on attachment to a particular territory and to claims for a political sovereign state to promote and defend national interests (A. Smith 1991). The colonial and post-colonial experience, for example, has shaped and transformed ethnic and racial identities in both the former imperial powers and their ex-colonies. The racial exclusion that has shaped the experience of many migrant groups in Britain is the basis of their identification of themselves as 'Black' British, though this is a precarious sense of identity and the cultural differences that distinguish the various minorities lead them to fragment into their constituent ethnicities: into Asian and African-Caribbean ethnicities, for example. Most recently in Britain, the sharing of an Islamic heritage and the experience of oppression and exclusion has led many otherwise diverse groups to identify themselves as 'Muslims'. Many ethnic groups have constructed an identity and sense of community for themselves, despite the fact that they have been widely dispersed across the world. Transnational

Jewish and Chinese identities, for example, have been built in the face of long histories of **diaspora**—of global dispersion from their original homelands.

While having a specifically cultural identity, ethnic groups are not purely cultural phenomena. In any concrete situation these cultural representations are entwined with class and political divisions that determine the power and resources that are available to the ethnic groups (Anthias 1992: 28–9). This means that ethnic groups can be identified in objective terms and not simply on the basis of their more transient and variable subjective identities.

Ethnic origin and ethnic identity

This involves a distinction between *ethnic origin* and *ethnic identity*. While subjective identification with a particular ethnic category is an important element in ethnicity, ethnicity cannot be reduced to this sense of identity. Ethnic origins can be traced in commonalities of religion, language, history, etc., even if those who originate in these groups do not make their origins a central element in their social identity (Berthoud 1998; Platt 2005*b*). Ethnic group membership is both normative and relational. Groups with common origins must have some collective awareness of their origins and some shared ideas and norms if they are to count as an ethnic group; however, this does not require a complete consensus of individual members over any particular label of identity. Similarly, an ethnic group is not simply a collection of self-identifying members. It rests on the recognition and acceptance by other members of the group and involvement in social relations and everyday interactions. Identities contribute to a common ethnic origin when they are sustained and reproduced over many generations within a particular population, but origin and identity may differ in the short run.

Such objective categories of ethnic group membership are what government censuses have tried to measure when asking questions about ethnic origin, and sociological surveys have found that people themselves recognize and use similar categories to those of the census (Modood *et al.* 1997). In Britain, such categories as Pakistani, Indian, Bangladeshi, and African Caribbean are the principal ethnic groups classified by ethnic origin. In the United States, the census recognizes many distinct 'European' ethnicities (German, Italian, Irish, Polish, Dutch, etc.), various 'native American' and 'Hispanic' (Mexican, Puerto Rican, Cuban), 'African', and numerous 'Asian' (Chinese, Japanese, Filipino, Korean, etc.) categories. In both societies, the specific labels that individuals adopt to identify themselves ethnically are diverse and vary over time, and the crucial issue for sociological investigation is to examine the changing relationship between ethnic origin and ethnic identity.

Figure 6.1 Ethnic composition of the population in England and Wales, 1991 and 2001

Ethnic identity	%	
	1991	2001
White	94.5	92.1
Black Caribbean	0.9	1.0
Black African	0.4	0.8
Black other	0.3	0.2
Indian	1.5	1.8
Pakistani	0.9	1.3
Bangladeshi	0.3	0.5
Chinese	0.3	0.4
Other	0.9	2.0

Source: Mason (2000: table 4.1) and **www.statistics.gov.uk/cci/nugget.asp?id=273**. See also Joshi (1989: 183) and Skellington (1992).

While it is notoriously difficult to formulate survey questions that will accurately uncover people's felt sense of ethnic identity, some indications of this ethnic diversity can be found in the recent censuses and some surveys. Since 1991, people have been asked about their ethnic identity. People were asked an open question about how they would define their own ethnicity, with the results shown in Figure 6.1.

Just over three million people in England and Wales (7.2 per cent of the population) identified themselves as members of a non-white ethnic group. Almost a half of these people claimed a broadly Asian identity, identifying themselves as Indian, Pakistani, or Bangladeshi, and about a third defined themselves as black.

Racialization and racial discourse

A race relations situation exists wherever ethnic relations have been racialized. This **racialization** occurs whenever ethnic identities and group boundaries are defined in specifically racial terms, that is in terms of colour and biological difference (Miles 1989; Anthias and Yuval-Davis 1993). Racialization often involves the imposition of racial identity on a minority by a powerful majority, but this is not always the case.

The use of the language of race divides populations from each other on the basis of assumed and essential biological differences, supposedly reflected in their 'stock' or their collective inheritance of biological traits. As such, racial language transforms ethnic differences that are, in reality, in constant flux into absolute and fixed categorizations.

➔ **Connections**

Issues of nationhood and nationalism are discussed at greater length in 'Nation states, nations, and nationalism', in Chapter 16, pp. 619–21. You will find it useful to think about that discussion in the light of what we say here about ethnicity and the language of race.

It builds separate and distinct social groups out of permeable and overlapping human differences (Gilroy 1987).

Race, then, must not be seen as a scientific concept. It is a social construct used by people in their everyday discussions and encounters, and that figures in political debates. When sociologists use the word, they use it to reflect the ways that people have racialized their relations with each other. While the term has often been used by dominant groups to reinforce their dominance over subordinate ethnic groups, it has also been taken over by subordinate groups themselves as the basis of an identity that would enhance their resistance to their social exclusion and subordination. The emergence of a Black Power movement in the United States during the 1960s and its promotion of the slogan 'Black is Beautiful', for example, involved a positive assertion of collective racial identity by African-Americans.

The idea of race is popularized through **racist discourse**. A racist discourse is a set of ideas, meanings, and representations that structures people's communication and encounters with each other and that serves to advantage some 'races' and to disadvantage others. A racist discourse has its greatest social impact when it informs significant social actions and practices and becomes embodied in social institutions. These social institutions therefore come to discriminate against certain racially defined ethnic groups. The term **racism** has been used to describe those structures and processes of disadvantage and inequality that are built around a racist discourse.

Despite this close relationship between racism and racist discourse, racism can exist even where there is no explicit use of racial concepts by those involved. The term **institutional racism** has been used to describe those situations where a racialized ethnic group is systematically disadvantaged by the ways in which social institutions that may not be built around explicit racist ideas nevertheless operate. People may not employ racist ideas—they may even disavow them—but they may, nevertheless, be involved in structures and processes that systematically disadvantage certain ethnic groups. This is a racism that rests upon a diffuse racialization of ethnic difference, but is inscribed within social institutions and their effects and not only, if at all, in the attitudes and beliefs of those who participate in them. It is a particular and extreme form of institutionalized ethnic disadvantage.

➔ **Connections**

The idea of institutional racism achieved notoriety through the Macpherson Report on the murder of Stephen Lawrence, but the concept originated in the Black Power arguments of the 1960s (Carmichael and Hamilton 1968). We discuss this idea and the Lawrence case on pp. 228–9 below.

'Black is Beautiful': expressing ethnic identity.

© Alice Chadwick

THEORY AND METHODS
....

Discourse

In its most general sense, the word 'discourse' refers to a more or less systematic argument, whether spoken or written. It has come to be used in literature and social science to refer to any system of statements, arguments, and theories that is organized around particular underlying themes, concepts, and assumptions. So, a racist discourse consists of a whole set of shared ideas about 'race' and racial difference. Foucault has emphasized that any discourse embodies and reinforces the power relations among the groups that it defines. A racist discourse advantages some ethnic groups and disadvantages others. It is in this sense that Foucault has said that 'knowledge' always implies 'power'.

Discourse analysis is particularly associated with the method of 'deconstruction' advocated by post-structuralist writers. They argue that discourses tend to be confusing and lacking in coherence: statements and accounts reflect the inconsistencies and contradictions that exist among the underlying concepts. The deconstruction of a discourse involves digging down below its surface content to these underlying inconsistencies and contradictions. You do not need to worry too much about the details of this position, but you might like to look at our discussion of Foucault in Chapter 8, pp. 276–9, and Chapter 14, pp. 541–3.

You will find a further discussion of this idea on pp. 206–7 below.

Theories of race and ethnicity

Racial thinking and racial discourse have been explored in a number of sociological theories. In this section, we will look at three particularly influential theoretical approaches that have explored the impact of these ideas on social life. The first of these concerns the relationship between race and citizenship. It explores the ways in which racial categorization can contradict and undermine the ability of racialized ethnic groups to participate fully in their societies. This theoretical approach was developed in the 1930s and 1940s in the United States as a way of understanding the continued exclusion of African-Americans from the rights and advantages secured by other ethnic minorities. The second theoretical approach stresses the relationship between race and colonialism. Developed, in particular, by British sociologists during the 1960s, it looks at the ways in which migrants to an imperial society are defined by racial categories that are rooted in the colonial encounter. This

colonial racialization structures their experience of disadvantage in the 'host' society. The final theoretical approach that we consider looks at racial discourse itself. Developed during the 1980s, it examines the ways in which racial categories are constructed and their role in the formation of collective identities.

Theories of race and citizenship

This theoretical approach is particularly associated with Lloyd Warner (1936), who argued that the expansion of black African-Americans had to be seen in relation to the more common experience of migrants to a new society. Migrant ethnic groups tend to enter low and disadvantaged social positions when they first arrive in a society: they arrive with few resources, they generally speak a different language, and they have few connections with other members of the society. In a relatively open society such as the United States, however, it is normal for the members of these ethnic groups to improve their situation gradually. They build up their resources, secure better education and jobs, and, perhaps over two or three generations, they rise up the social hierarchy. The positions held by members of the ethnic minorities in the distribution of resources, opportunities, and power, therefore, become indistinguishable from those of the rest of the population. They are distributed according to their individual abilities and resources, not according to their ethnic origin. This view is summarized in the idea of the ethnic **melting pot** of the big city: the city mixes people together, regardless of their origins, and the various ethnic minorities become 'assimilated' and 'acculturated'. This happened, Warner argued, with East European Jews, Poles, Italians, Germans, Irish, and many other migrants to Chicago, New York, and other North American cities in the nineteenth and early twentieth century.

Warner held that the ethnic melting pot did not work for the former slave population of black African-Americans. Their exclusion during the slave period is, of course, obvious. They were taken to North America specifically in order to carry out menial and subordinate tasks, and they were held in this position through force and coercion. With the ending of slavery and the migration of large numbers of African-Americans to the northern states, however, this might have been expected to change: the ethnic melting pot of the open society should have ensured their gradual acceptance and incorporation into mainstream society. Warner argued, however, that the racial attitudes of the slave period persisted and were responsible for continued prejudice and discrimination by whites against blacks.

Warner saw this as a clash between two value systems. One set of values was rooted in the slavery of the southern states and defined African-Americans as a distinct and inferior category of people. These values were expressed in institutions, attitudes, and practices that were at their strongest in the southern states, where they divided blacks and whites into separate communities and prevented them from encountering each other in anything other than purely instrumental and routine interactions. The other set of values comprised the liberal values that underpinned the American creed of democracy and equality. These values were stronger in the northern, metropolitan cities than they were in the south, but even here there was a conflict. Dollard (1937) took a similar view, describing a conflict between the 'dominant American mores' and the 'regional mores' of the south. If the normal pattern for ethnic minorities was incorporation into the mainstream society by virtue of the dominant values, opportunities for assimilation by African-Americans were limited by the persistence of the southern values. Their exclusion was sharpest wherever the southern values were at their strongest.

Black–white relations, then, show a complex pattern of social stratification. Southern values create a status division that cross-cuts class divisions. Black Americans form a distinct 'caste', which is fixed in its social position and with its members unable to move up the social hierarchy. In using the term 'caste', Warner did not mean that race relations in the United States are identical to patterns of stratification in India. Rather, he was trying to emphasize that both situations involve sharp and immutable divisions based around ideas of colour and the 'polluting' effects of racial contacts.

> ⮩ **Connections**
> We discuss the ideas of class and status in Chapter 19, pp. 773–7, and you may want to look at that discussion now. We look at caste as it exists in India, and you should consider how Warner's use of the term differs from this.
>
> Warner was a structural-functionalist theorist, stressing the function of values in creating and sustaining group solidarity. You might find it useful to look at our discussion of this kind of theorizing in Chapter 2, pp. 45–51.

This idea that there is a cultural conflict at the heart of American race relations was taken further in an important study by the Swedish sociologist Gunnar Myrdal (1944). Myrdal described the dominant or core social values as the 'American creed'. This is central to American nationalism and gives Americans their ideas on America's historical mission or destiny as a society. The creed is taught in schools and churches, enunciated in courts, and espoused in the mass media. It is embodied in the ideas of equality, liberty, and citizenship, and it defines the principles that most Americans claim ought to apply in their dealings with each other.

Myrdal argued that American society is marked, nevertheless, by major discrepancies between the ideals of the creed and the actual practices that people engage in. The gap between ideal and practice is particularly great in the case of black Americans. The exclusion faced by black Americans is rooted in the fact that, unlike other ethnic minorities, they are 'coloured' and are accorded an inferior social status. As Warner argued, they form a subordinate caste whose attitudes and outlook (including, in particular, their relative lack of self-respect and self-confidence) are the result of their social exclusion. African-Americans have not had the opportunities to exercise in full the civil, political, and economic rights of citizenship formally accorded to them in the American creed. They are second-class citizens.

The cultural contradiction between the American creed and the assumption of caste inferiority generates disadvantages for black Americans that reinforce their purely economic disadvantages. There is a double confounding of economic disadvantage and caste exclusion:

> When we say that Negroes form a lower caste in America, we mean that they are subject to certain disabilities solely because they are 'Negroes' in the rigid American definition and not because they are poor and ill-educated. It is true, of course, that their caste position keeps them poor and ill-educated on the average, and that there is a complex circle of causation, but in any concrete instance at any given time there is little difficulty in deciding whether a certain disability or discrimination is due to a Negro's poverty or lack of education, on the one hand, or his caste position, on the other hand. (Myrdal 1944: 669)

Initially developed as an account of black–white relations in the United States in the 1930s and 1940s, this theoretical approach has been very influential and it has also been taken up in Britain. In a landmark study of the emerging pattern of race relations during the 1960s, Rose *et al.* (1969) followed Myrdal's argument and held that Britain, too, showed a clash between citizenship rights, on the one hand, and discrimination on the grounds of colour, on the other. This discrimination rests on prejudiced and stereotyped views that originate in the imperial dominance of Britain over the colonies from which the migrants arrived. Black migrants to Britain from the West Indies and Africa were prevented from enjoying the full rights of citizenship. They were excluded from full membership in British society.

> ⮩ **Connections**
> In Chapter 18, pp. 722–4 and 726 we review the legislation that has shaped the ability of ethnic minorities in Britain to exercise their citizenship rights. You will also find a fuller discussion of the idea of citizenship, and we relate this idea to wider patterns of inequality.

Optimistic versions of this theory, in both Britain and the United States, have seen the denial of full citizenship as something that is bound to be rectified. Social exclusion persists because of the incomplete modernization of cultural values and social institutions. With the enlargement of modern social institutions, the values of the old south and the imperial state would become unsustainable, and full citizenship would eventually be achieved (Parsons 1966a). The failure to achieve full citizenship is a symptom of a 'cultural lag' in the process of modernization.

Theories of race and colonialism

The second strand of theory that we will consider places imperialism and the colonial encounter of black and white at the centre of attention. Writers in this tradition agree with Warner that race attributions are a matter of culture and status, but they argue that these arise only under certain very specific structural conditions. For this reason, a race relations situation cannot be analysed in terms of culture and values alone. It has also to be seen in terms of the structure of group relations that is brought into being. These theorists ask why it is that some group differences are translated into the language of colour and biology—expressed as 'race' relations—while others are not. Warner wrote as a structural functionalist and emphasized the role of values, but we are here concerned with theorists who stress power and conflict.

> **⊃ Connections**
> You might like to review our discussion of conflict theories in Chapter 2, pp. 56–8, looking particularly at the discussion of John Rex's work.

One of the earliest writers to adopt this approach was Oliver Cromwell Cox, a black American sociologist at the University of Chicago. Cox took a Marxist approach and argued that racial thinking was tied to group relations that arise with the expansion of capitalism and colonialism. Racial thinking is an ideology that promotes the transformation of labour into a commodity and justifies, where necessary, the use of coercion to control this labour (Cox 1948). By creating a division between black and white workers, racial thinking can prevent the development of a strong and oppositional working-class consciousness. Race, therefore, contributes to the 'false consciousness' through which a dominant class justifies its power and control over a subordinate class.

Racial categorization, however, is not a feature of every class-divided society, and those who have followed Cox's lead have tried to specify the conditions under which white workers might be distinguished from black workers, with only the latter being subjected to racial stigmatization.

Particularly important in the development of this theory has been John Rex.

Rex (1970) argues that racial ideas have become popular when groups have come together through conquest into a 'colonial' structure of coercive power in which there is an unequal distribution of political rights and economic resources, and where it is possible to distinguish among the dominant and subordinate groups on the basis of their physical appearance and their culture. Conquest can take a number of different forms. It might, for example, involve settlement of a territory by economically superior groups or it might involve militaristic domination by an imperial state. Conquest brings different cultures into contact and, when the members of these cultures are physically different from one another, it is possible to take the physical differences as markers of cultural differences. It is the value system of the colonizers—the dominant social group—that shapes the whole of the colonial society. The racial ideas that developed in European science in the eighteenth and nineteenth centuries were especially important contributions to colonial racism.

Conquest and colonization have a long history and occur in a number of societies. Rex gives particular attention to those forms of conquest that have been involved in the building of the modern world. The growth of the modern world system (see Chapter 16, p. 629) occurred through the building of large political and economic empires by the European nations—initially Spain and Portugal, then Britain, France, the Netherlands, and Germany. Imperial expansion required the establishment of coercive forms of control over the labour of subordinate populations in the colonized territories. The most notable of these coercive forms, of course, was the slave system of the Americas, but Rex highlights also the use of indentured, legally tied labour and the physical confinement of workers to closed compounds.

The racial divisions of the colonies have an impact on the home society of the colonial power itself. The racial thinking that informs official and popular attitudes towards those who live in the colonies also influences attitudes within the metropolitan centres. This is most apparent where members of the colonized society migrate to the imperial society in a search for work and economic improvement.

Rights of entry for colonial subjects vary from one imperial society to another, but the second half of the twentieth century—a period of decolonization—involved large numbers of migrant workers and long-term immigrants making the journey from the former colonies to the European metropolises. The entry of economic migrants into the labour market and the wider institutions of the imperial societies were shaped by the values and attitudes towards them that prevailed in the colonial context itself.

In the early stages of migration in particular, public and official attitudes towards 'immigrants' are shaped not so much by direct knowledge—people in the metropolitan centres had little of this—but by second-hand evidence from friends, relatives, and colleagues with experience of the colonial situation. The racial ideas and stereotypes of the colony, therefore, are translated into the new metropolitan situation:

> What seems to happen is that colour is taken as an indication that a man [or woman] is only entitled to colonial status, and this means that he has to be placed outside the normal stratification system. The stratification system thus becomes extended to take account of additional social positions marked by a degree of rightlessness not to be found amongst the incorporated workers. (Rex 1970: 108)

'Coloured' immigrants, then, are confined to low-paid jobs and face limited opportunities for improvement. They do not find the opportunities for which they migrated. They are likely to experience persistent poverty and disadvantage, and they become the objects of prejudice and discrimination. Miles (1984, 1989) has argued that migration from former colonies results in the formation of 'racialized fractions' within the metropolitan classes.

Rex argues that his theoretical approach throws additional light on the racism experienced by African-American migrants from the deep south of the United States to the metropolitan cities of the north. The denial of full citizenship that was highlighted by Warner and Myrdal is not simply the result of a cultural conflict. It also reflects a structural conflict between groups in a quasi-colonial encounter. Cultural differences rest on power differences.

Representations of race in the mass media.

© Alice Chadwick

Theories of racialized discourse

The third type of theory to be considered here focuses neither on values nor on group structure. It focuses on the content and character of racial discourse itself. It looks at the ways in which the idea of race is constructed in the various ideologies produced by different groups. The approach has much in common with the Marxist-inspired arguments of Cox and Rex, but it shifts attention from the power relations to the cultural construction of identities.

The key arguments in the development of this point of view come from Stuart Hall and Paul Gilroy, though echoes of it can be found in earlier writers such as Du Bois. For these writers, race is a social construct that enters into the formation of collective identities. It is a product of specific forms of discourse and of the struggles that are involved in establishing the dominance of one form of discourse over another. The kinds of accounts and narratives that people produce define themselves and others as specific types of people with particular characteristics, and it is through such discourse that diverse and heterogeneous individuals can be forged into a collectivity. What people have in common does not pre-exist their identity, as some kind of primitive or primordial ethnicity, but results from the very processes through which an identity is constructed (Centre For Contemporary Cultural Studies 1982; see also Gilroy 1987). There is no objective basis to race; there are simply historically diverse racialized identities, which are constantly being formed and re-formed.

Initially stressing the racial construction of political and party identities, these writers have increasingly moved in a more cultural direction to explore the language through which race is constructed. They examine the racial constructions that have been built in literature and the mass media in order to examine the particular representations of race and racial identity that they embody and perpetuate. Their argument is that we live in a pluralistic world of competing constructions and that any individual or group identity will be syncretic, combining elements from all the culturally available constructions. Identities, they argue, are 'hybrid' (Bhaba 1994).

THEORY AND METHODS

Du Bois

William Edward Burghardt Du Bois was born in 1868 in Massachusetts. He was descended from slaves on both his father's and his mother's side. He graduated from Fisk University and then studied philosophy with William James at Harvard. He was awarded a postgraduate fellowship in history to study the African slave trade. While studying for this in Germany, he attended Weber's lectures. In 1894, Du Bois was appointed as a professor at a university run by the African Methodist Church and he argued for the introduction of sociology to the syllabus.

Pursuing his interests in sociology, he carried out a sociological survey of a black district in Philadelphia (Du Bois 1899). His model for this work was the London investigation undertaken by Charles Booth (see Chapter 19, pp. 737–9), and Du Bois produced a detailed study of occupational and family structure, drawing on interviews, personal observations, and official documents. He showed that the social problems of the black population were not a consequence of their biological characteristics but of the economic conditions under which they lived and their experience of segregation, prejudice, and exclusion. The real social problem was racism. Later work in this tradition,

though developing both the theory and the methods, is that of Frazier (1932) and Wilson (1987).

Du Bois was clear that the idea of race had to be seen as a social construction that was imposed on individuals and determined their identity in the eyes of others. Those designated as being of the same race share a sense of identity as part of a community, but their shared cultural traits are a product of their shared history—in the case of African-Americans this was a history of slavery, prejudice, and disadvantage. Du Bois developed the concept of 'double consciousness': African-Americans had a consciousness of themselves as both 'coloured' and 'American'.

Du Bois became heavily involved in black politics and the civil rights struggle, publishing an important series of essays (Du Bois 1903). He was critical of Booker T. Washington's conservative position, standing firmly on the left in the black struggles. He became a Director of the National Association for the Advancement of Colored People in 1910, advocating the separate development and self-reliance of black communities. He was very influential in international debates over civil rights and in 1961 he moved to Ghana and renounced his US citizenship. He died in 1963.

> **⊃ Connections**
>
> We consider some studies of mass media representations of racial groups in Chapter 10, pp. 379–80. Look at that discussion and then return to consider the specific arguments discussed here.

Hybridity has become an important way of understanding the construction of identities from the diverse and contradictory cultural sources available in any society. It is an idea that is particularly compatible with the postmodern theories that we discuss in Chapter 2 (pp. 64–5). Post-modern theory stresses the diversity and plurality of

cultural ideas and representations and the need to be aware of this diversity. There is a constant translation, negotiation, and reconstruction of identities, and collective identities often try to combine things that are logically incompatible. A social identity must be seen as an unstable synthesis of diverse ideas that can be sustained only through rhetorical and textual devices aimed at the accounts and practices through which discourses are reproduced.

There are, then, a multiplicity of racisms and racial identities, and there are diverse connections to the cultural construction of the related ideas of 'nation' and 'country'. It is this cultural complexity that leads to the opposing of 'blackness' to 'Englishness' or of 'black' to 'Asian'.

◈ *Stop and reflect*

In this section we have looked at the relationship between cultural and biological factors in the formation of racial and ethnic identities. Our discussion of race and ethnicity showed that:

- There is no scientific basis to the biological concept of race.

- The use of the term 'race' in political debates involves a racialization of ethnic differences that hardens and sharpens them.

- Do you think that a sociologist should ever use the word 'race'?

Our consideration of the major theories in this area showed that:

- Theories of race and citizenship emphasize a cultural contradiction between a dominant, liberal creed and conservative racial ideas.

- Theories of race and colonialism look at the interdependence of power and cultural construction, relating these to the colonial and post-colonial experience.

- Theories of racialized discourse look at the representations of race that figure in cultural discourses and they examine their role in the formation of identities. Such discursively formed identities are syncretic or hybrid.

Towards assimilation and incorporation?

The expansion of the modern world system involved European colonization of the 'new world' of the Americas and of Africa and of other distant parts of the globe. Central to this expansion was a slave trade through which people were taken from Africa by the colonial powers and sold in the Caribbean and North America to work on plantations set up by the European settlers. Slavery was, by the sixteenth century, already well established in Africa, where slaves were taken in warfare and sold by Arab and African slave traders. As Europeans began to settle and subject Africa, they also began to trade with the slave traders and they transported the people that they bought across the Atlantic to the Americas. Slaves and captives were sold in open markets and kept in their slavery through force and coercion. It was through the system of slavery that the tobacco, sugar, and cotton industries of North America were built (Paterson 1967, 1982).

Rigid slave systems were established across the Americas and they persisted until the abolition of the slave trade and slavery—this was abolished within the British Empire in 1833 and in the United States in 1865. The end of slavery marked the beginning of a migration of ex-slaves from the rural areas of the southern United States to the northern industrializing centres. Somewhat later, ex-slaves from the British colonies of the Caribbean began to migrate from their poor rural homes to the cities and towns of Britain. Similar migrations occurred from the colonial territories of the other European powers to their imperial centres.

This migration of ex-slave populations brought black and white groups together in the expanding cities of Europe and North America. The resulting pattern of 'race relations' was seen by policy-makers in the imperial centres as foreshadowing a process of acculturation or **assimilation**. It was assumed that the dominant and primordial culture of the metropolitan societies was carried and sustained by their white populations. The black ex-slaves, of a different ethnic background, were seen as destined to be assimilated into this dominant cultural tradition. The ethnic minorities, as 'strangers', would familiarize themselves with the new metropolitan culture and would willingly embrace it, abandoning their own 'archaic' culture. Ethnic differences would disappear and the migrants would become culturally indistinguishable from members of the majority society.

This assumption shaped perceptions of the race relations situations in the metropolitan cities. The persistence of racial conflict and inequality was seen to be a result of a racial prejudice on the part of the ethnic majority that would eventually disappear through legislative changes and a growing familiarity with members of the ethnic minorities.

Where the black experience in the United States was rooted in slavery, that in Britain was rooted in colonialism. These two histories were not, of course, separate. The slave trade with the Americas had been operated by British merchants, and the territory that became the United States was a British colony until 1776. Slavery was also established in the British colonies of the Caribbean and persisted well into the eighteenth century. Britain, however, also expanded its power into Africa itself, into the Indian subcontinent, and into many other parts of the world. The building of the British Empire was an integral feature of the emergence of the modern world system that we discuss in Chapter 16, p. 629.

British settlement and conquest led to the establishment of a variety of forms of labour in the different colonies, and in areas such as Canada and Australia the number of white settlers vastly outnumbered the indigenous populations. This shaped the timing and character of migration into Britain. Migration has generally had only a relatively small effect on overall population trends in Britain, as the numbers involved have been so small in relation to the total numbers of births and deaths. Migrants arrived in Britain from its colonies in relatively small numbers until the second half of the twentieth century. Chinese seamen with the East India Company had moved into the dockland districts of London and some other port cities by the end of the eighteenth century, and a few Indians and African Caribbeans, mainly the servants of returning colonists, had also begun to settle in Britain.

The largest group of early migrants was the Irish. As a result of migration from Ireland to the British mainland, especially after the Great Famine of the 1840s, the Irish accounted for 2.9 per cent of the population of England and Wales and almost 5 per cent of the population of London by 1851. Their descendants, together with more recent Irish migrants, are estimated to account for up to 10 per cent of the mainland British population today. A second major wave of migration, however, had little directly to do with British colonialism. Ashkenazi Jewish migrants from Germany and eastern Europe, driven out by anti-Semitic pogroms, began to arrive in Britain in the 1880s and they continued to arrive into the early part of the twentieth century. They settled in large numbers in the East End of London and in other major urban centres.

For the first thirty years of the twentieth century, Britain experienced a net loss of population through migration (emigration was greater than immigration). The reason for this was that large numbers of Britons were migrating to Canada, Australia, South Africa, and other parts of the Empire. Despite this movement of population, migration had little effect on the overall composition of the British population. Certain ethnic enclaves were formed, but they were a marginal feature of British society, which remained an ethnically homogeneous society through the first half of the twentieth century. For this reason, 'race relations' were not a significant feature of British society, and racial divisions were largely confined to the colonies themselves.

From the delta to the melting pot

In the United States, the situation was very different, as slavery had established a race relations situation in the heart of the country. Slavery in the United States was concentrated in the southern states, and stable patterns of race relations were built across the whole of the 'Deep South'. Even after the abolition of slavery, black–white relations were sharply segregated and African-Americans were systematically excluded from many areas of life. In the towns and cities of the south, the race relations pattern was similar to that described by Warner in his model of 'caste'. The growing urbanization of American society and the consequent migration of many rural blacks to the cities of the north led many observers in the 1930s and 1940s to endorse the assimilationist expectations of the race and citizenship theorists. The expanding cities, they argued, were 'melting pots' in which race relations would be forged into a new and more equal pattern.

Slave society

Slavery is a system of social stratification in which differences of status define some people as free and others as unfree. Slaves lack freedom because they are owned by others. As the objects of property relations, slaves have none of the rights of full membership in their society: they can be bought and sold and have no say in their own fate. Slaves occupy a subordinate social position and must carry out their assigned role of serving the free citizens of their society. Slavery is an ascribed status that is enforced through compulsion. The children of slaves, for example, have no choice about their status: they are born into slavery and can do nothing to alter the situation.

American slavery was closely linked with the rise of racial thinking in Western culture. Differences of colour between European colonists and African slaves became markers of ethnic differences that took a racialized form. Slaves were at the bottom of a system of social stratification that was headed by the white settlers and their descendants. At the top of the system was an upper stratum of plantation-owners who held economic and political power as well as having the highest status. The middle levels of the system consisted of small independent farmers, officials, and other white groups.

Slavery was legally abolished within the United States in 1865, following a civil war between the southern Confederate states and the northern Unionist states. Despite abolition, the racialized status of African-Americans continued to disadvantage them. Although they were formally free, ex-slaves had few real options in life. Many of them continued to work on the plantations, and their masters simply became their employers. Others became sharecroppers—tenant farmers who paid a part of their crop as rent—and they were as exploited as they had been under slavery. Nevertheless, African-Americans did acquire a legal freedom of movement and of access to public places during the era of 'Reconstruction' at the end of the nineteenth century, and this raised hopes for their full participation in US society.

Large numbers of ex-slaves moved to the cities of the north in search of work and a better way of life. An urban way of life, however, did not resolve their problems. The migrants to Chicago, Detroit, Philadelphia, New York, and other urban centres found themselves facing poor housing and job opportunities. They lived in ghetto conditions and endured long periods of unemployment.

The greater freedom experienced by African-Americans was felt as a threat by many white Americans, who had previously been able to keep a social distance between

Migrants from the West Indies arrived in Britain in large numbers from the 1940s to the 1960s.
© Getty Images/Haywood Magee

themselves and African-Americans. This fear caused many states to pass laws that restricted the rights of African-Americans, the high point of this legislation being between 1890 and the First World War. These laws limited African-American voting rights, prevented them from using the same railway carriages, bus seats, toilets, hotels, and eating places as whites, and limited them to certain schools. Social segregation was re-asserted, especially in the southern states where the system came to be known as 'Jim Crow'. This segregation was justified on the grounds that it provided 'separate-but-equal' facilities for blacks and whites, and a structure of racial segregation remained intact in many parts of the south until the 1960s, despite a growth of political radicalism among African-Americans.

The Deep South

Warner used race and citizenship theory to organize and interpret the results of his fieldwork study of black–white relations in the southern states of the United States. The states of the Deep South—most especially Georgia, the Carolinas, Mississippi, Louisiana, Alabama, and Arkansas—lay at the heart of southern slave society, and it was here that the old racial divide persisted in its sharpest form. Warner sought out a typical southern city to study, hoping to compare it with a typical northern city that he was studying. The northern, New England city of Newburyport—to which Warner had given the pseudonym 'Yankee City' (Warner and Lunt 1941)—had a relatively open and flexible pattern of ethnic relations that Warner felt contrasted sharply with the situation found in the Deep South.

For the southern study, he settled on the city of Natchez, given the pseudonym 'Old City' in his research team's publication (Davis 1941). This was a small city of about 10,000 people and was the principal cotton trading centre for the plantations of the surrounding Mississippi Delta region, a role it had established for itself in the days of slavery. At the time of the study, Natchez showed a sharp split between a white caste and a black caste. The authors argued that the social system of caste and class had evolved from the destruction of the slave system. It started as a sharp horizontal caste divide between an internally differentiated white group and the predominantly black labourers. The white caste was the dominant group and the black caste was the subordinate group. Gradually, the 'colour line' had tilted upwards slightly as black society had become more differentiated and those at its top had improved their economic position.

This system was sustained by ideas of the status superiority of whites and the inferiority of blacks, and these ideas were underpinned by the beliefs and sentiments concerning race that united each caste. These racialized attitudes were at the heart of their prejudices towards each other and were rooted in economic differences and in differentials of power. Patterns of circulation and association within each caste crystallized into relatively well-defined internal social-class boundaries, but there was no circulation or association across the colour line. There was a sharp spatial separation of the two castes: schools, cinemas, churches, jails, and public transport were all segregated, and blacks always had the least desirable facilities.

⤴ Connections

The idea of social stratification and the role of circulation and association in defining social-class boundaries is discussed in Chapter 19, pp. 771–2. If you feel unsure about the claims that are being made here, you might like to look at that now. You will find a model of a caste-like structural division in Figure 19.1, p. 771. Caste is discussed more fully on pp. 779–80.

The white caste was internally divided into three major social classes, and each of these classes showed a differentiation into more or less distinct upper and lower segments. At the top of this hierarchy was the aristocracy of 'Society' families, the old established families whose wealth originated in the cotton plantations. In the middle were the managers, professionals, and small business families, and at the bottom were the ordinary working families. Those at the bottom had a relatively low standard of living and were referred to as the 'poor whites' by their fellow caste

members. The middle and lower classes deferred to aristocratic families who dominated all the major social institutions of the city.

While there were also upper, middle, and lower levels within the black caste, these were not the same as the white social classes and there were, of course, no significant connections between them and the white classes. The upper levels of black society comprised a very small class of professionals, such as doctors and lawyers, mainly dependent on black clients, and the middle levels comprised skilled and clerical workers. The great bulk of the black population, however, formed a lower social class of porters, drivers, barbers, labourers, and tenant farmers. This class had the lowest standard of living in the city.

African-American and white societies, therefore, coexisted. Each had its own culture and social institutions. Their internal social divisions were overridden and obscured by the fundamental social gulf that was created by the colour line. While the relatively wealthy black professionals who stood at the top of the black caste were much better off than the poor whites, they were still regarded as social inferiors and were denied the full rights that were enjoyed by all whites.

According to Warner's researchers, the belief system that underpinned the idea of racial superiority in the southern states could be summarized in terms of four core ideas:

- The inherent inferiority of blacks was seen as sanctioned by God. Racial differences were seen as rooted in 'immutable, inevitable and everlasting' biological differences that made 'Negroes' primitive and animal-like. These racial differences were seen as willed by God, who had put the races in their separate places in the first place and so was happy with their continued segregation.

- It was believed that contact between races was to be avoided because of its contaminating consequences for whites. Whites believed that they would suffer through any direct contact with black people, and they saw any physical contact as bringing them into dangerous relations with those who were 'unclean', both physically and morally. Eating or drinking from the same tableware, for example, was to be avoided, as was the use of the same chairs, tables, and rooms.

- 'Negroes' were held to be unsocialized and childlike beings who lacked all of the normal social restraints and obligations. They were seen as lazy and as lacking in ambition, as having to be compelled to work, and as lacking proper respect for property and conventional sexual morality. They were naturally childlike, and could never be expected to become fully socialized members of society.

- White people claimed that they had a responsibility to protect blacks from their own failings and weaknesses. They should not put temptations in their way, and they needed to force them to do what was right or in their own best interest. These matters could not be left to their own choice, as such primitive people were incapable of properly exercising their choice (Davis 1941: 15–20).

These beliefs were the basis of exclusionary practices and symbols of subordination that established and justified white superiority. In addition to the spatial segregation of blacks and whites into distinct neighbourhoods, blacks were expected to behave in specific ways in all their inter-personal relationships with whites. They were, for example, expected to show 'respect' by touching their hat and using titles such as 'Boss' and 'Sir' when talking to a white man. Whites, for their part, would call a black man 'boy'. This was, however, modified by social class: lower-class whites showed the same kind of deference towards upper-class

---

Hooded Klansmen salute a burning cross.

© Getty Images/William F. Campbell

whites, and they were sometimes on relatively friendly terms with the blacks who lived close to them. Sexual relations were rigidly controlled. No black American could marry a white person, as this was prohibited by law in the southern states. Non-marital sex across the colour line was also disapproved of, though white men often regarded black women as legitimate objects of coercive sexual relations or of prostitution.

The colour line that divided white from black society was reflected in the explicit use of colour as a criterion of social differentiation among African-Americans themselves: light-skinned African-Americans had taken over some of the negative views that whites held about the black population. The light-skinned professionals distinguished themselves from the dark-skinned lower class, and they often used the language of colour when they disparaged their fellow blacks as 'boisterous' or 'stupid'. 'Blackness', then, was a master symbol that marked someone out as an object of disgust and contempt. The black lower class, in

---

THEORY AND METHODS

Sociology for the South

Two of the earliest books to use the word 'sociology' in their titles were produced in the southern states of the United States as justifications for its system of slavery. The racist ideas documented by Warner's fieldworkers in the 1930s and 1940s showed that many of the arguments made in these books almost one hundred years before were still an important element in southern thinking.

In 1854, George Fitzhugh published *Sociology for the South* (Fitzhugh 1854) and Henry Hughes published his *Treatise on Sociology* (Hughes 1854). These writers saw sociology as informing their criticisms of liberalism and the 'free society'. While much social thought had been socialist in character, Hughes and Fitzhugh aimed to construct a conservative and paternalistic social theory that would justify the anti-liberal principles and practices of slavery. Blacks and whites, they argued, differ in their personal, moral, and intellectual characteristics, and the childlike character of blacks makes it inappropriate to give them the same rights and freedoms as whites. Their ignorance and improvidence would simply result in social conditions worse than those in Africa. On this basis, they saw the white 'master' as the only person able to act in what is the best interest of blacks. The slave system of the Deep South, they argued, is the perfect form of social life, producing the essential conditions of life for all.

❓ How does this argument relate to the often-voiced claim that sociology shows a left-wing bias?

 Briefing: the Ku Klux Klan

The Ku Klux Klan was originally formed in 1866 by opponents of Reconstruction who wanted to retain a system of white supremacy. Its members posed as the spirits of the Confederate dead who had returned to protect Confederate principles. They covered themselves and their horses in white robes, and they covered their faces with white masks to emphasize this. They intimidated the black population of their localities through public torchlight displays and bonfires, and through the routine use of whippings and lynchings.

The organization was revived in 1915 with wider aims, and it drew on anti-Semitic ideas as well as white supremacist ones. It was a powerful political force during the 1920s, when it had between four and five million members. Legal action against the Klan and the economic problems of the 1930s, however, led to a decline in its membership. Although support for the Klan grew again during the civil rights struggles of the 1960s, it never regained its former strength. Many Klan organizations, nevertheless, still exist in the southern states.

turn, saw the black professionals as 'uppity' or pushy, and as denying their roots.

The American creed was weak in the south and clashed with strongly entrenched assumptions of white racial supremacy. There was no popular drive to implement the recognition of equal rights for all that was emphasized in the American creed. The subordination of African-Americans was maintained by local laws and by custom and habit, and these legal exclusions and sanctions were supplemented by the unofficial but publicly tolerated use of direct physical punishment. The social control exercised over African-Americans involved individual violence, collectively sanctioned beatings and whippings, and the lynch mob.

The ethnic melting pot and the ghetto

Alongside the study of Natchez, Warner's research group undertook a study of Chicago (Drake and Cayton 1945). Their aim was to explore what was happening in one of the major northern cities to which African-Americans had migrated from the Deep South.

Chicago had been a city of migrants from its earliest days. From the second half of the nineteenth century through to the First World War, successive waves of Germans, Irish, Scandinavians, Poles, East European Jews, Italians, and Greeks had arrived in the city. Black migration from the south became a significant factor after the ending of slavery, but rates of black migration were particularly high during the 'Great Migration' of 1916–19, when the growing demand for labour attracted many more rural blacks to work in the city. Migration continued at high levels through the 1920s and 1930s, and by 1944 almost one in five of the population was European born and one in ten was an African-American.

Chicago was a new, expanding city, full of opportunities, and its openness meant that its successive waves of migrants felt sure that, in time, they would secure the kinds of advantages and opportunities that were enjoyed by those who had already established themselves there. A person's ethnic origin posed few long-term problems in what rapidly came to be seen as an ethnic melting pot: a city whose vibrancy and interpersonal familiarity dissolved ethnic boundaries and forged all together into a distinctively 'American' identity.

Initially, each migrant group would settle in a particular neighbourhood, but groups would soon spread out across the city into ethnically mixed neighbourhoods. Where areas of ethnic concentration did persist, they changed their character. Areas of high German and Italian settlement, for example, might persist, but these did not remain areas of concentrated disadvantage. To a considerable degree, people *chose* to continue living there.

Warner's researchers showed that, however idealized the image of the ethnic melting pot might be, there was a con-

THEORY AND METHODS

Assimilation

The idea of the ethnic melting pot rests on a model of assimilation. This is the process through which an ethnic minority takes on the values, norms, and ways of behaving of the dominant, mainstream group and is accepted by the latter as a full member of their society.

The problem with the idea of assimilation is that it assumes that there is a social and cultural mainstream and so rests on the idea that the 'host' society is characterized by a value consensus. This may not be the case. It also assumes that there is only one way in which majority and minority groups can coexist—through the disappearance of the minority culture. In the following section we will look at an alternative idea that stresses multiculturalism.

siderable amount of truth in it. For one group, however, it just did not apply. African-American neighbourhoods had solidified and formed a significant part of Chicago's social structure. The 'Black Metropolis', or 'Black Belt', at the heart of the city was a ghetto settlement, similar to the Harlem district in New York. Over 90 per cent of blacks in Chicago were living in the ghetto during the 1940s.

> **⊃ Connections**
>
> The City of Chicago was an important sociological base for the studies undertaken by the so-called Chicago school of sociology. Their theoretical ideas are discussed in Chapter 2, pp. 51–4, and their model of the city is discussed in Chapter 13, pp. 504–5. Look at the plan in Figure 13.8 and find the Black Belt on it.

Despite the relative strength in Chicago of the American creed of citizenship equality, the persistence of racial values meant that black Americans were excluded from the full citizenship that had been gained by other ethnic minorities. Although the colour line was not as sharp as it was in the Deep South, it still existed and it divided the two societies from each other. The relative freedom and impersonality of the city allowed a certain degree of movement across the line to occur, but the colour line remained an important aspect of the African-American experience in Chicago.

The colour line defined the subordination of blacks to whites in employment and their segregation in housing. African-Americans had limited opportunities for occupational mobility and did not compete on equal terms with white Americans. They were largely restricted to low-paid and menial work and were always the first to lose their jobs in times of depression. After the Second World War, they began to enter more skilled and clerical jobs, producing an expansion in the black middle class, but a clear job ceiling remained to limit African-American opportunities. They were also limited to poor-quality housing, concentrated in the ghetto. This housing segregation determined the educational and recreational facilities that were available to black Americans. The ghetto had the highest proportion of welfare recipients and low-income earners in the city, as well as the highest rates of illegitimate births, juvenile delinquency, tuberculosis, and mental illness.

The researchers characterized this as a 'social disorganization', symptomatic of its 'slum' character and the low level of cohesion that existed among its residents. The regulatory norms that would normally commit people to the conformist behaviour of the mainstream of American society were absent, and ghetto residents lived in a state of anomie. Those norms and values that did exist simply reflected and sustained the deviant character of ghetto life.

There were, however, some relatively affluent areas within the ghetto, especially around the Washington Park district. This was the area where the homes could be found of the emerging black middle class of doctors, teachers, lawyers, shopkeepers, and insurance sellers, all of whom depended on their fellow ghetto residents. These and other 'respectable' members of ghetto society were organized around the clubs and churches and were able to generate a degree of collective solidarity and mutual support that sustained their sense of community and a distinctiveness from other ghetto residents. Excluded from many areas of white society, they nevertheless followed many of its values and aspired to join it. Their search for respectability and assimilation led them to distinguish themselves particularly sharply from the 'shadies' of the underworld, who were concentrated in the lower class and were the core of the 'disorganized' element of the community.

‹› *Stop and reflect*

In this section we have looked at the impact of colonialism and slavery on race relations in the advanced capitalist societies.

- Britain was, until the middle of the twentieth century, an ethnically homogeneous society and had few significant problems of race relations.

- The United States had a clear racialization of group relations because of the persistence of ideas and practices from the slave period.

We gave particular attention to the American situation, exploring race relations in both the Deep South and Chicago.

- A sharp racial divide existed in the Deep South, with black and white groups forming distinct 'castes' or sub-societies. These social differences were rooted in differences of economic resources and power.

- Migration to the big cities was associated with a process of assimilation for European migrants, but persistent exclusion for African-American migrants.

- How important is it to know the history of slavery if we are to understand contemporary ethnic relations in the United States?

Migration, racism, and multiculturalism

The failure of the melting pot to work in favour of African-Americans meant that divisions around the colour line grew sharper during the second half of the twentieth century. The ghettos of the large American cities continued to attract migrants from southern rural districts, but there were few opportunities for the existing residents of the ghettos to leave them. Struggles over civil rights and the social exclusion of African-Americans grew through the 1960s and conflict became a central feature of racialized ethnic relations in the United States. At the same time, new waves of migrants from Puerto Rico found that they, too, were unable to take advantage of the melting pot mechanism. The ethnic division between a white mainstream society and the black and Hispanic ghettos became a central feature of American life.

Rates of colonial immigration into Britain increased through the late 1940s, and from the middle of the 1950s into the early 1960s there was a net gain in UK population from migration. Large numbers of people from the Commonwealth (as the Empire had become) were being recruited into the expanding industries and public services to meet post-war labour shortages. These migrants were

Why do immigrants often end up in poorly paid work?
© Alice Chadwick

had been far less of a 'British' element in their education, and their religious differences set them apart.

Britain became less of an ethnically homogeneous society. Migrants and their descendants settled in large numbers in London, in Birmingham, and in many other parts of the midlands and the north. This growing ethnic diversity was associated with a growth in racialized attitudes in many sections of the white population, and 'race' became an important element in British politics and policy from the 1960s.

The numbers of both Asian and Caribbean immigrants to Britain declined from the mid-1960s, partly because of legal restrictions on immigration, and the immigrants that have arrived since then have mainly been the dependants of those who had already settled. During the 1960s there were about a quarter of a million immigrants to Britain each year, but in every year until the middle of the 1980s they were more than balanced by an even larger number of emigrants. Almost a half of all immigrants in this period came from Australia, New Zealand, and Canada (the 'Old Commonwealth' in the official terminology), the United States, or the European Community. These numbers were counterbalanced by the return of short-term migrants to the same areas and by the emigration of Britons to join relatives in the 'Old Commonwealth' or to work in other parts of Europe. Immigrants to Britain from India, Pakistan, and the Caribbean were generally long-term or permanent migrants, but they were very few in number: in the middle of the 1980s there were 21,000 migrants from the Indian subcontinent, 11,000 from African Commonwealth countries, and 3,000 from the Caribbean. Only since the middle of the 1980s has there again been a net balance of immigrants over emigrants.

Migrants and their descendants now form a significant element in the British population, and they are increasing at a much faster rate than the majority population. Where the white population has increased by 1 per cent over the last five years, the ethnic minority population has increased by 15 per cent over the same period. Ethnic minorities now account for over 7 per cent of the British population. It has been estimated that a half of the British ethnic minority population were born in the United Kingdom, showing the inadequacy of the common popular designation of them as 'immigrants'. Recent patterns of migration, however, have produced a situation where there are now more German and American migrants living in Britain than there are Bangladeshi migrants. The fastest growing groups of migrants have been those born in Albania and former Yugoslavia. Almost a half of the total ethnic minority population lives in Greater London, the second biggest concentration being in Birmingham. Other concentrations of the non-white population can be found in West Yorkshire (Bradford and Leeds), Greater Manchester, and Leicester.

overwhelmingly drawn into low-paid work. People from the former British colonies of the Caribbean, India, and Pakistan increased the ethnic diversity of the British population. Most of the early migrants were from Jamaica and the islands in the east of the Caribbean. Their cultures combined their British, French, and Spanish colonial inheritance with some African elements that had survived through the slave period. The predominant feature of their culture, however, was its 'British' character. Their schools had used English textbooks and taught British history, as if it was their own, and they were brought up to define themselves as British. Increasing numbers came from India and Pakistan, mainly from Pakistan itself, from the Gujarat and Punjab districts of India that bordered Pakistan, and from the eastern part of Pakistan that later became Bangladesh. These Asian migrants were very diverse in their culture: Sikhs came from the Punjab, Muslims from Pakistan and Bangladesh, and Hindus from Gujarat. The character of British colonialism in India meant that there

Global focus   Ethnicity, Refugees, and Asylum Seekers

National disasters, military action, and political repression have always produced large-scale movements of population as displaced groups seek new homes. Those displaced for military or political reasons have often sought a right to asylum under a state that will protect them or guarantee their freedom. In the first half of the twentieth century, large numbers of refugees fled or were expelled from Nazi Germany, Palestine, and the Soviet bloc, and in 1951 a legal definition of refugee was created under the Geneva Convention. It is from the second half of the twentieth century, however, that international conflict and tension created ever greater numbers of refugees seeking asylum in a more secure home. This has been driven, in large part, by the ethnic basis of much military and political conflict, which has meant that whole populations have been forced to seek refuge.

The collapse of the Soviet bloc and the dismantling of repressive border controls freed many in central and eastern Europe to move westwards in search of work and better living conditions. Ethnic conflict in former Soviet areas, such as Yugoslavia and the Balkans, has displaced large numbers of Bosnians, Albanians, and Kosovans. Famine and war in Africa and Asia have led to large-scale population movements in Sudan, Angola, Afghanistan, and elsewhere.

Refugees seeking asylum and work in the more affluent countries have often encountered difficulties. Countries that have previously accepted refugees, who arrived in relatively small numbers, have increasingly claimed that the large numbers of people involved make this policy more difficult to sustain.

Opposition to the entry of large numbers of 'asylum seekers' and economic migrants, like opposition to large-scale immigration, is often driven by racialized ethnic differences.

Large numbers of asylum seekers in Europe are kept in camps and detention centres—now renamed removal centres—while their fates are determined by the European immigration authorities. It can take many months to come to a decision on individual cases, and many refugees see this as no different from imprisonment. In Britain, before 1997 the average wait for a decision was twenty months, this fell to just over a year in 2000, and is now about seven months.

The largest immigration removal centre in Britain is Yarl's Wood, near Bedford, run by GSL UK Ltd. Those who are felt to be likely to evade controls may be held in jails. At its peak, the Kosovo crisis produced 71,000 asylum applications in the United Kingdom. The United Nations High Commission for Refugees estimated that in 2001 there were 169,354 refugees living in Britain. These numbers are increased by illegal entrants who arrive hidden in freight lorries. A national asylum support service undertakes the 'dispersal' of refugees while their claims are decided, offering them accommodation in specific towns and cities to prevent any concentration of large numbers of refugees in any one place.

Hostility to 'asylum seekers', like opposition to 'immigrants', has been strong in the Conservative Party and has been fuelled by the racism of groups such as the British National Party and its counterparts in other European countries.

Migration and racism

The pattern of race relations in Britain in its first phase has been clearly documented in classic studies by Sheila Patterson (1963) in London and by John Rex and Robert Moore (1967) in Birmingham. Patterson's study of Brixton was shaped by her expectation that assimilation would be the eventual outcome of the emerging pattern of race relations, but she shows clearly the obstacles to this that existed. The study that Rex and Moore undertook in Sparkbrook drew on the race and colonialism theory and the arguments of the Chicago school of sociology, and they gave much more attention to the deep sources of conflict that characterized British race relations.

Separation, exclusion, and conflict are also apparent in work on the United States. Earlier work had been documented by the assumption of assimilation and the metaphor of the melting pot. Later work showed that

assimilation was by no means automatic, especially for African-Americans, and that the structural separation of a black 'underclass' from the mainstream of white society was as sharp, if not sharper, than ever before.

Settlement and housing

Brixton is in central Lambeth, bordering on to Battersea, Wandsworth, and Camberwell. It has been a predominantly working-class district from the middle of the nineteenth century. At the time of the survey it was largely a dormitory area, with few local industries, and was attractive to migrants because of the relatively large numbers of boarding houses and bed-sit housing. Significant levels of immigration from the West Indies began in 1948. As people arrived and settled in the area, news and information was passed back to friends and relatives who were also likely to aim for Brixton when they, too, migrated.

Britain's ethnic minority groups are concentrated in certain inner city areas, such as Brick Lane in the East End of London.

© Lucy Dawkins

Patterson (1963) saw the situation in Brixton as typical of that found in many other British towns and cities, and she interpreted it as an 'immigration' situation that is complicated by the fact of racial difference. Conflict and lack of understanding result from unfamiliarity, and the settlement of colonial migrants in relatively large numbers in Brixton has brought together groups of 'strangers' who must learn to live with each other. This unfamiliarity is sharpened, however, by the sense of racial difference that marks both groups. Patterson minimized the extent of any racism in the indigenous 'host' community, and gave far more importance to the colour-consciousness of the migrants themselves. The African-Caribbean residents of Brixton at the time of her study were first generation and they were still oriented towards their original home society, to which most of them hoped to return.

The West Indian population amounted to about 5,000 by 1955 and approximately 10,000 by the early 1960s. These migrants had been attracted by job opportunities, but a national decline in employment opportunities between 1956 and 1959 made itself felt in Brixton, and levels of unemployment among recent migrants increased substantially. Poor economic opportunities among the black and white populations led those who felt themselves to be 'different' from one another to come into conflict over economic resources.

The main area of competition and conflict between black and white residents was housing. Because of the wartime destruction of much local housing and later slum clearance programmes, there was a general shortage of housing in the area. Sellers and landlords charged West Indian purchasers and tenants more than they did white families, but few West Indians made official complaints about their treatment. They recognized that going to a rent tribunal, for example, was likely to be a difficult experience for them and would only create longer-term problems with their landlord.

As a result, African-Caribbean migrants were concentrated in the worst—and relatively expensive—housing. Many were crowded into boarding and lodging houses. This housing situation did not improve as African Caribbeans began to buy property. Those who were able to build up some resources bought run-down properties on short leases and sub-let rooms to other West Indian families. Most of these families lived in overcrowded conditions, often one family to a single room. Although their own rooms were kept very clean, shared areas—toilets, kitchens, and hallways—were dirty, damp, and badly maintained. Overcrowding in houses owned by African-Caribbean landlords persisted because the landlords needed to let out as much of their property as possible in order to meet their own mortgage payments on the house.

These characteristics are similar to those described by Rex and Moore for the Sparkbrook district of Birmingham. About one-third of Sparkbrook's residents were migrants. Although the largest group was Irish (including Dubliners, country people, and travellers), there were significant numbers of recent West Indian and Pakistani arrivals. Using ideas from the Chicago writers, they looked at competitive relations among these groups in the local housing market. Sparkbrook, like Brixton, they saw as a zone of transition (Zorbaugh 1929), an area where housing quality and housing values have fallen to the point at which it is possible for poorer and migrant families to settle. The local population was formed into a number of housing classes, based on their varying ownership of and access to domestic property: owners, council tenants, private tenants, lodging-house owners, and lodging-house tenants.

> **⊃ Connections**
> You will find a further discussion of the idea of housing classes in Chapter 13, pp. 506–7.

As in Brixton, the West Indian and Pakistani immigrants were drawn into multi-occupied houses, either as tenants or, eventually, as owners who let out rooms to their fellow immigrants. Those who purchased houses had to borrow at high rates of interest and needed the help of friends to raise the deposit. The only way in which the resulting debts could be met was by letting out all spare rooms at the highest rents possible. Where Pakistani landlords, for example, tried to help fellow Pakistanis by letting them a room at favourable rents, this forced them to charge even higher rents to their other tenants.

Conflict and community

Housing segregation and the differing experiences of those in the black and white communities was a basis for serious cultural misunderstanding and provided fertile ground for the growth of hostility and conflict. Most West Indian house purchasers in Brixton had bought their houses in areas where house prices were low or where, because of the condition of the neighbourhood, they were declining. This created an impression among white families in the locality that it was the arrival of the black families that had driven down the property values, and many of them became concerned about the effects that having a West Indian neighbour might have on the value of their own home.

They were, therefore, likely to be hostile towards any movement of African-Caribbean migrants into 'white' areas. In fact, Patterson argues, any direct effect of migration on property values was confined to the more prosperous areas on the margins of the main area of settlement, and was a consequence of prejudice rather than of migration. However, the belief that property values were affected by migrant settlement fuelled local hostility. This antagonism was exacerbated by a hostility towards what were perceived as strange and unacceptable ways of behaviour in the African-Caribbean community. The white working-class residents of Brixton, predominantly of the 'respectable' working class, expected the new arrivals to conform to their—white and working-class—standards of privacy, quietness, and cleanliness. They were very critical of the poverty, overcrowding, and noise seen in West Indian households, which they saw as reflecting high levels of deviance and social disorganization. In most cases, however, this did not reflect any real difference in deviant or conformist behaviour between white and black families. Rather, it marked a difference in culture that was combined with the visible consequences of having to live in poor-quality housing and with limited resources.

The migrants shared not only a language and a religion, but also a colonial experience. They came from semi-rural backgrounds that were associated with slavery and poverty. This made for distinctive work habits, family forms, and attitudes to authority (Patterson 1963: 7). This colonial experience gave them a strong sense of their own racial identity.

The culture of the migrants to Brixton derived from the distinctively lower-class West Indian culture into which they had been born and which, until recently, had organized their lives in Jamaica, Barbados, and the other islands from which they came (Henriques 1953). This culture arrived with the migrants and formed the basis for the new way of life that they built to adapt to living in Britain.

Family life was based around informal but fairly permanent relationships between men and women, and family size tended to be large. In many cases, however, the link between men and their children was fairly weak, and fathers did not always live with their children. Family life, therefore, tended to be organized around the mother. In the early years of this migration, however, many men arrived alone, or in advance of their families, and there were many single-person households. In the West Indies,

Many West Indian migrants to Britain have been active in Pentecostal churches.
© Alice Chadwick

women had relied on the help and support of their own mothers, but as most of the mothers were still in the West Indies this was not possible in Brixton. Women tended, therefore, to feel isolated unless they had brothers or sisters who also lived locally.

West Indians in Brixton tended to be active churchgoers, a number of them attending Pentecostal churches (see Chapter 11, pp. 428–9). The churches, however, were not an active means of integration for West Indians, and few migrants were regular churchgoers. In Sparkbrook, the Asian migrants were Hindu, Muslim, and Sikh, though only the latter two had central places of worship in Birmingham. Their religious involvement, however, helped to maintain their sense of ethnic identity and their links with their country of origin.

Despite this segregation, there was little community formation among the migrants. A shared culture and shared disadvantages did not, in themselves, allow the building of a distinctive and autonomous West Indian community in Brixton. The formation of such a culture was limited by the isolation experienced by many households. Their different attitudes and behaviour brought them into conflict with members of white society, who found it difficult to understand or appreciate these cultural differences.

The white population in Brixton were deeply suspicious of foreigners and strangers, and especially of the visibly different West Indian migrants. Their thinking linked blackness with dirt and danger, and these were reinforced by—and in part derived from—the images depicted in American popular films:

> a coloured skin, especially when combined with Negroid features, is associated with alienness and with the lowest status. Primitiveness, savagery, violence, sexuality, general lack of control, sloth, irresponsibility—all these are part of the image. On the more favourable side, Negroid people are often credited with athletic, artistic, and musical gifts, and with an appealing and childlike simplicity. (Patterson 1963: 234)

Contacts between black and white in Brixton were frequent and relatively unproblematic on the buses and in shops, where they were associated with clearly defined role differences. In more informal contacts in the street and in places of leisure, there were greater attempts at mutual avoidance. While there were no official 'colour bars', as there were in parts of the United States, there was a degree of segregation. West Indian men, for example, would go to dances at the Locarno ballroom on Streatham Hill, but the white girls at the ballroom generally refused to dance with them. Disputes between white and black men at the ballroom led its owners to formulate a national policy that West Indian men could not be admitted to rock-and-roll nights unless accompanied by a partner. (This was at a time

before such policies were made illegal.) When going out for a drink, both blacks and whites tended to establish their own local pubs or sections of pubs.

Patterson argued that this resulted in an 'accommodation' between immigrant and host societies, a limited acceptance and tolerance rather than full assimilation. Their perception as 'strangers' by members of white society limits the degree to which they are offered acceptance. Patterson saw no inevitability in the move from accommodation to assimilation: whether blacks are assimilated as British citizens, she argued, depended on the attitudes of second-generation migrants and later generations of the host society.

The Rex and Moore (1967) study drew out the implications that this had for politics. Politically, Sparkbrook had shifted from being a safe Conservative area to being a safe Labour one, represented at the time by Roy (now Lord) Hattersley. The mainstay activists of the Labour Party were Irish, but few other immigrants were involved in its political or social activities. A significant number of the white working class supported the Conservative Party, which espoused the need for immigration controls, and there was some anti-black feeling among Labour supporters. However, there was little support for overtly racist parties in either national or local elections. Few West Indian or Asian migrants were involved in politics, but those few who voted in elections tended to vote Labour.

Beyond the melting pot

In the United States, such divisions were well established —and generally stronger—than in Britain. African-Americans seemed to have become fixed to the bottom of the melting pot, and many began to reject the very idea of assimilation and the idea of the melting pot. This was explored in an important study of New York by Glazer and Moynihan (1963, 1970), who showed that ethnicity remained a crucial element in social difference and social division, even in a city as large and cosmopolitan as New York.

Glazer and Moynihan argue that the end of mass migration did not lead to the merging of the black Americans into a uniform American national identity—indeed, American ethnic identities are generally very diverse. The Irish, Italians, and Poles share a common Catholic outlook that combines with their American outlook and, in the case of Irish Americans, shapes their view of the political conflicts in Northern Ireland. American Jews, on the other hand, have been significantly influenced by the Nazi persecutions of the 1930s and 1940s, and the founding of the state of Israel has remained an important part of their political outlook. These 'assimilated' groups have not abandoned their sense of national identity in favour of a simple 'American' one. They have forged a distinctive sense of collective identity that reflects both their national heritage and their distinctive experiences within the United States.

African-Americans are also likely to retain such hybrid identities, but their experience of American society is that of disadvantage and social exclusion. They remain concentrated in low-paid jobs and poor housing, and have an identity that is shaped by their continuing structural exclusion from the mainstream of American society. Despite a relative improvement in the economic circumstances of the black population, their sense of deprivation and exclusion remains. The ethnic division between them and the whites is the overriding division in American life.

Assimilation is unlikely for black Americans, who they argue are likely to develop an increasingly strong sense of their separate identity, even if their economic conditions continue to improve. They share their depressed situation with the more recent Puerto Rican migrants, but there is a sharp ethnic divide between the two groups. Some black Americans, however, have come to see themselves as part of a larger deprived group of people of colour (black, yellow, and red, combining African-American, Hispanic, Asian, and native American).

Moynihan's earlier work (1965) had highlighted what he saw as a breakdown in the fabric of black urban society in America. The accumulated disadvantages and social exclusion of African-Americans had produced a growing divide between a relatively stable middle-class group and a disorganized and demoralized lower-class group. The black middle class had not been assimilated into mainstream American society, but they had become separated from the inner-city ghetto poor who came to form what Myrdal (1962) called an 'underclass'.

> **⊃ Connections**
> We critically discuss the idea of an underclass in Chapter 18, pp. 729–31. You will find that discussion a particularly useful background to what we say here.

Moynihan traced many of the disadvantages of African-Americans to the breakdown of the lower-class family through an increase in divorce and illegitimacy. This made the large number of female, single parents dependent on welfare benefits and produced a whole generation of children who were unable to take advantage of what few opportunities were available to them. Moynihan, it is important to point out, was not seeing family breakdown as the crucial causal factor in producing disadvantage. Rather, he saw exclusion and deprivation in employment and housing, and the continued undermining of black civil rights, as having produced fertile conditions for family breakdown and, therefore, for the perpetuation of disadvantage.

THEORY AND METHODS

Black nationalist thought

Black nationalism has developed from ideas stressing the importance of autonomy and self-sufficiency in black communities. Their disadvantaged social situations give them a particular standpoint on politics and social life, and establishing a degree of self-organization and autonomy is seen as a way of developing this in a radical direction.

An early contributor to this idea was Booker T. Washington, who, around the end of the nineteenth century, advocated economic self-help through his National Negro Business League. This supported entrepreneurialism and black capitalism as a means of black empowerment. Marcus Garvey broadened this view with his idea of Pan-African solidarity. William Du Bois (whom we discuss on p. 207) was initially a follower of Washington, but he became very critical of him during the 1920s. Du Bois was a left-wing advocate of separate development and self-reliance through 'voluntary segregation'.

Black nationalism was strongly developed within the Nation of Islam (see Chapter 11, p. 434). Elijah Mohammad—originally a close associate of Marcus Garvey—converted to the Nation of Islam in the 1930s and advocated that its members should positively support black businesses. Malcolm X, a leading figure in the Nation of Islam during the 1950s and 1960s, broadened the message away from Islam to a more inclusive 'black' strategy. He was assassinated in the racial violence of 1965.

One of the most important of recent contributors to black nationalist thought was Stokely Carmichael (see Carmichael and Hamilton 1968), whose important concept of institutional racism we discuss below.

This argument was taken further by Wilson (1987), who established very clearly the structural basis of racial disadvantage in US cities. He argues that the black ghettos of New York, Chicago, and other major cities in the 1930s had been organized around a strong sense of community and collective solidarity that tied all their residents together, whatever their economic position. Middle-class, working-class, and poor African-Americans lived together and supported one another in the face of their shared exclusion from white society. By the 1960s, the black middle and working classes had moved out to the suburbs, leaving the poor blacks (and the Hispanics) in the ghettos. This broke down the relations of mutual support that had previously integrated them into a larger community. These 'truly disadvantaged' formed an economic underclass that found it ever more difficult to escape its disadvantaged conditions. Unlike Conservative commentators, however, Wilson saw the black underclass as a product of racialized social exclusion and not as a product of any lack of morality. They are victims of a vicious circle of exclusion and disadvantage.

Hybrid identities and multiculturalism

We have shown that through most of the twentieth century ethnic minority relations, in both Britain and the United States, have been shaped by a clash between the liberal idea of equal citizenship and conservative racial thinking. Official policies in both countries have stressed the need to assimilate ethnic minorities into an all-embracing mainstream culture. The ways in which these policies have been implemented has shown that these liberal assumptions have not gone unchallenged. Many members of the ethnic majority, including many of those in the legislative, executive, and administrative branches of the state, hold to racial ideas and values that undermine the liberal ideal and have prevented its implementation. Indeed, from the 1960s, state policies in Britain and other parts of Europe became more restrictive in relation to immigration, as racial thinking became a more marked feature of official thinking.

At the same time, members of the ethnic minorities have become less willing to accept the goal of assimilation. They have felt more strongly that their particular experiences and values should be remembered and should be important elements in their identities. Their identities draw on shared memories of their ethnic background and of their experiences in the society to which they have migrated. Such identities are not simple expressions of a single cultural origin, but are hybrid, composed of diverse cultural elements.

A study of black and ethnic minority people in 2005 reported that the majority considered themselves to be fully or mainly British, though still considering their ethnic origin quite or very important to them. Twenty-two per cent of black people said that they did not feel at all British. High levels of prejudice were reported. Sixty per cent of black and 54 per cent of Asian respondents had experienced name calling or verbal abuse, and 24 per cent of black and 18 per cent of Asian respondents had experienced physical attack or harassment. Over a quarter of those in all categories felt that Britain had become more racist in the previous ten years, and many had considered leaving Britain as a result: 24 per cent of black and 18 per cent of Asian respondents said that they had considered leaving the country because of their experiences of racial intolerance (ICM Research reported in *Guardian*, 21 March 2005, http://image.guardian.co.uk/sys-files/Politics/documents/2005/03/21/ICMrace.pdf).

This has encouraged new political practices aimed at sustaining collective identities that are rooted in a shared sense of difference from the white, mainstream culture. Ideas of difference have sometimes been more formally articulated as **multiculturalism**, the demand that the diversity of ethnic cultures within a society should be respected and equally valued in official policy and in everyday life. This has recently been described as 'cultural citizenship' (Pakulski 1997). Where the civil, political, and social rights of citizenship stress equality and ignore or minimize differences, the idea of cultural citizenship involves an explicit recognition of the legitimacy of cultural differences and stresses the need to establish equal rights to express these differences. This includes the right to express one's own identity. Unlike the idea of assimilation, the idea of cultural citizenship does not aim at merging differences into a single cultural framework. It seeks to establish cultural values that recognize and legitimate difference.

A sense of ethnic difference, however, is not expressed only in multiculturalism. Differences within and among ethnic minorities can undermine any common orientation, and a growth of conflict between the various minority groups is also apparent. These differing forms of consciousness are rooted in the structural differences between an advantaged majority and various disadvantaged minority groups, and their development has been tied to political conflicts over inequalities of power and resources. The growth of multiculturalist ideas and of autonomous and assertive ethnic minority communities has reinforced the tendency towards racial thinking that has been apparent in majority communities, especially in those that have been most affected by social and economic change. For many white people facing poverty, unemployment, and poor housing, 'immigrants' and racial minorities have been an easy target to blame for these problems: 'they' are taking 'our' jobs and 'our' houses. Social conditions that were actually a consequence of large-scale social changes in work and community relations that were operating at a global level were seen simply as the effects of immigration.

> **↪ Connections**
> We discuss some aspects of these larger changes in Chapter 13, pp. 515–17, Chapter 17, pp. 691–3, and Chapter 19, pp. 790–3 and 803–7.

The migrants and their descendants become the scapegoats for social problems and, therefore, the targets of hostility and, increasingly, of violence. The first significant signs of racial conflict in Britain were the Notting Hill riots of 1958, when white residents took to the streets in protest against black settlers who had moved into the area. This marked and reinforced the change in attitudes that was taking place among both black and white groups. Maverick politicians gave voice to these shifts in public opinion during the 1960s, as it became more acceptable to openly express racist ideas and opposition to black immigration. The Conservative candidate in a by-election in the Smethwick district of Birmingham achieved much notoriety when his supporters circulated leaflets proclaiming 'If you want a nigger neighbour, vote Labour'. This climate of hostility culminated in a speech by a former Conservative government minister, Enoch Powell, in 1968. In this speech, Powell spoke of British culture and society being 'swamped' by the growing number of immigrants and their families. He predicted—and, some said, encouraged—a growth in racial conflict, claiming that the rivers of Britain would soon be 'flowing with blood' as levels of racial violence increased.

By the 1970s, the character of official discourse itself was deeply marked by racial ideas and racial hostility, and this lay behind a series of restrictions on the rights of legal entry to Britain that had formerly been open to Commonwealth residents (see our discussion of 'Acts against discrimination', p. 726). In a landmark report on race relations in Britain, Rose *et al.* (1969) showed that policies concerned with the welfare of migrants, which had prevailed from 1948 until the mid-1950s, had progressively given way to policies that were aimed at the control and regulation of the entry of migrants into British society. Both main political parties were more concerned with control than with welfare. This has continued into the new millennium, with ongoing debates over the rights of Muslims and other ethnic minorities to pursue separate and segregated educational practices in 'faith schools' and over the entry of 'asylum seekers'. Such opposition has occurred across Europe and was also found in the United States. Riots in the Watts district of Los Angeles in the 1960s ignited a long series of urban riots and conflict between black and white. Such riots became a recurrent feature of race relations in Britain and the United States.

> ➲ *Connections*
>
> In Chapter 13, pp. 522–5, we look at more recent urban riots involving conflict between ethnic groups. You might find it useful to review that discussion before returning to this chapter.

Racialized politics and the new racism

Martin Barker (1981) has argued that the 1970s saw the emergence of a 'new racism'. The old racism of biological superiority and inferiority, he argues, has given way to a cultural racism that appears, on the surface, to be more benign. Feelings of difference and hostility between ethnic groups are seen as natural responses to the presence

The Anti-Nazi League challenges racism.
© Alice Chadwick

of other populations. These feelings are not typically formulated in full-blown theories and so do not appear to be racist. They are, however, based on an underlying **xenophobia**, a fear of those who are culturally different. This is, Barker argues, a more subtle form of racism in which perceived biological differences predispose people to hostility.

The new racism of the British majority population links 'British character' and 'British culture' as central elements in defining a whole way of life. This rests on an image of a cohesive, homogeneous, and solidaristic national society whose shared and 'traditional' way of life is threatened by outsiders and by those who have refused to accept and to be assimilated into this way of life. A national home is felt to be a natural place to be, and the desire to preserve a national identity is seen as equally natural. People's feelings and their culture, traditions, and way of life are the bases of their fear of outsiders; they fear that a cherished way of life, however fictional, will be lost. Those members of the majority culture who feel this way do not see themselves as

Briefing: an oath of allegiance?

Riots by Asian residents on depressed estates in Bradford and Oldham during the summer of 2001 and the terrorist attacks in New York later that year led to much adverse comment about the loyalty of Muslims to the British state. The then Home Secretary responded to such criticisms with the suggestion that those seeking British citizenship should undergo citizenship education and should swear allegiance to Britain. After some discussion an oath and pledge were introduced. The words of these are:

> I . . . do solemnly and sincerely affirm that on becoming a British citizen, I will be faithful and bear true allegiance to Her Majesty Queen Elizabeth the Second, her Heirs and Successors, according to law.

> I will give my loyalty to the United Kingdom and respect its rights and freedoms. I will uphold its democratic values. I will observe its laws faithfully and fulfil my duties and obligations as a British citizen.

For many radicals and liberals, the adoption of an oath of allegiance was an expression of the new racism described by Barker: those who refused to swear allegiance would be seen by the authorities as rejecting the British way of life and as threatening national solidarity. For many conservatives, it is a desirable affirmation of loyalty. Indeed, one Conservative Party politician argued that the loyalty of Caribbean and Asian residents in Britain could be tested by which side they cheered for in cricket test matches.

racist. In fact, they see the outsiders as the racists: it is they who have rejected the way of life of the 'host' society on racial grounds. Members of the majority, then, can claim the moral high ground: they are not racist but are simply striving to maintain a way of life that has existed for many generations. They are not rejecting or decrying the migrants' way of life, but are simply saying that they should pursue this in their home country or accept the way of life of the country to which they or their parents have migrated.

A growth of racial antagonism is apparent in the emergence of new racist political movements of a neo-fascist character from the 1970s. Examples are the *Fronte Nationale* in France, the National Front and British National Party in Britain, various Neo-Nazi groups in Germany, and the KKK in the United States (Solomos and Back 1996). The growth of such groups has been

THEORY AND METHODS

Hate crimes

Violent crimes by white men against black and Asian men are widespread, and they have increasingly come to be defined as hate crimes. They may be expressions of racialized hatred, even where an instrumental crime such as theft is involved. Street attacks, often described as 'Paki bashing', involve the targeting of individuals simply because of their ethnic background. Many racial hate crimes involve repeated harassment of individuals or families. Typical is the case of Sanjay, who was confronted by a group of white teenagers on the front lawn of his Greenwich home. The youths were throwing stones and shouting such chants as 'Go back to your own country'. Many victims of such attacks are, of course, already in their 'own country'. They were born in Britain and regard it as their home. All that marks them off as outsiders is the colour of their skin. In 1993, Stephen Lawrence was murdered in Greenwich by a group of white youths. In 2005, Anthony Walker was murdered with an axe on the streets of a prosperous Liverpool suburb following taunts and racial abuse (see **http://news.bbc.co.uk/1hi/english/special_report/1999/02/99/stephen_lawrence/281141.stm**).

Not all racial hate crimes take place between black and white, and there appears to be a hostility between different ethnic minorities. The killings of black Dexter Coleman by Asians in Bradford and of Abdul Bhatti by African-Caribbean men in Notting Hill during 2000 highlighted this issue (*Independent*, 13 September 2000), which was raised again in media discussions of the murder of Damilola Taylor, a 10 year-old Nigerian, who was reported in some newspapers as having been killed by West Indian youths as part of a campaign of harassment. The particular youths accused were cleared of the attack, and it is unclear whether the media accusations reflected a real knowledge of the interracial hatred or were, themselves, a form of racial stereotyping and harassment (*Observer*, 28 April 2002).

The theoretical and policy implications of hate crimes have been well explored in Paul Iganski's *The Hate Debate: Should Hate Be Punished as a Crime?* (2002).

➔ You can follow up on hate crimes at www.hatecrime.org

partly countered by the British Anti-Nazi League, Anti-Racist Alliance, and similar groups. The level of political violence is apparent in such events as the assassination of the Dutch racist politician (and ex-sociologist) Pim Fortuyn in 2002.

Violence against ethnic minorities by racists is a form of hate crime—crime carried out by those whose motivation is hatred of those in a particular social group. Racist organizations and parties that foster racial hatred encourage such hate crimes. Hostility towards Asian Muslims, in particular, has increased since the terrorist attacks on the World Trade Center in New York in 2001 and the London underground bombings of July 2005. 'Muslim' and 'terrorist' have become almost interchangeable terms, so far as many people are concerned. Racist organizations are able to use this suspicion of Muslims to justify hate crimes against Asians. The response of the British government to this has been to propose new legislation that would extend existing legislation and make incitement to religious hatred into a crime. At the same time, however, new official policies have targeted Muslim communities and individuals as 'problems' requiring discriminatory practices such as the stopping and searching of Asians on the street and at railway stations.

Antagonism and violence reflect the persistence of segregation in housing and employment, and political mobilization within ethnic minority communities has been associated with a growth in both residential and educational segregation.

Members of ethnic minorities are heavily represented in marginal, insecure, and low-paid jobs, and their rates of unemployment are especially high. This is especially marked for those of African, Pakistani, and Bangladeshi origin, though much less so for the Chinese, and especially Chinese women (Mason 2000: table 5.4). Their difficulties in entering the mainstream of the labour market have led them to take up forms of self-employment in great numbers. The most significant area of self-employment has been the involvement of large numbers of South Asian families in retailing, catering, and hotels. Research has shown, however, that these businesses find it more difficult to raise capital and are less profitable than comparable white businesses.

> ⊃ **Connections**
>
> We review the wider issues of ethnic inequality and division in Chapter 9 on education, Chapter 17 on work, and Chapter 18 on inequality. A very useful summary can be found in Mason (2000: chapters 5 and 6).

These economic disadvantages are reflected in the relatively great educational disadvantages of ethnic minorities. It is true that ethnic minorities have a higher participation rate in education after the age of 16, and that young Chinese, East African Asians, and Indians have particularly high levels of qualification, but this is not the case for all ethnic minorities. There is much evidence that these findings do not hold for the parental generation, while research on the schooling of those below the age of 16 has shown the considerable underachievement of most ethnic minorities. This underachievement reflects, in part, their social-class background (Troyna and Carrington 1990). However, it is also due to stereotyping by their (white) teachers, whose expectations about the relative performance of white and ethnic minority pupils tend to produce the very results that they anticipate. Even where, as is generally the case, teachers are liberal in their attitudes and show no intention to discriminate, the judgements that they make about the likely performance of different groups of students have a major impact on their actual performance.

This is one of the reasons for the growing tendency towards educational segregation. Dissatisfaction with the schooling of their children has led many ethnic minority parents to support the establishment of evening and Saturday schools and of separate 'faith' day schools. Some Muslim groups, for example, have exercised their right to 'opt out' of local authority schools and to set up grant-maintained schools along the lines of the long-established Catholic schools. As a result, many neighbourhood schools are dominated by particular ethnic minorities. As well as a segregation of white and ethnic minority housing, both Britain and the United States show a degree of segregation among the ethnic minorities themselves. For example, Bangladeshis predominate in Spitalfields, East London, while Mirpuris from Kashmir predominate in Bradford. Segregation by school is also shaped by the housing patterns found among ethnic minorities. As we have shown, ethnic minority settlement has been concentrated in particular localities. In Bradford, where many schools are almost 100 per cent Asian and others are exclusively white, the first voluntary-aided Muslim school for girls has been established.

Racial antagonism and segregation does not mean that there is no communication or sharing of concerns. The essence of hybridity is that identities are constructed from a variety of often contradictory sources. In a study of Deptford, South London, Les Back (1996) has shown this in the construction of white identity. Deptford is a riverside district where residents have long relied on the dock trades and metal working for employment. It sustained the class consciousness of a cohesive working-class community into the 1950s, after which this was undermined by economic decline. Like Brixton, it was an area of migrant settlement for people from the West Indies, who were attracted by the relatively cheap housing. The white residents of the predominantly white estate studied by Back were very hostile towards the black tenants, whom they saw as being responsible for the decline and loss of community that the area had experienced. This hostility was

Global focus Racism

We have concentrated on describing patterns of ethnic dis-advantage and racialization in the United States and the United Kingdom, but these patterns actually vary from society to society. White discrimination on the grounds of ethnicity is almost universal, but its extent and its consequences differ.

In France, colonialism has had a major influence. The French state sought to integrate its colonial territories into a single political system, giving colonial populations full citizenship status in France itself. Nevertheless, the common framework of European racism had an influence, and French writers, such as Gobineau, were central to the construction of racial theories. Today, skin colour and national origin still divide people, despite their formal equality of citizenship. High levels of immigration have led to a situation where around a quarter of the French population have origins overseas. Many of these migrants came from North Africa and the Middle East, making Islam the country's second biggest religion, and there is a high level of racist feeling among the white population, as there had been against the Jews in the past. The French government has sought to minimize the visibility of ethnic minorities by banning the wearing of religious symbols, such as the Muslim headscarf, in schools, but this has fuelled fears that the state itself is pursuing racist policies.

It might be expected that this would be different in the former colonies themselves. Brazil—formerly a colony of Portugal—has a highly diverse population and appears to be highly egalitarian. There is, nevertheless, prejudice and discrimination against those of African origin, whose ancestors arrived in the country as slaves. The inheritance from the slave period remains strong, despite the myth of racial equality. In many situations there is a fine shading of distinction according to the shading of skin colour. South Africa—colonized by the Dutch and the British—had an entrenched system of apartheid (we discuss this in Chapter 19, p. 780). Under the new multi-racial state established under the presidency of Nelson Mandela, the political and economic rights of blacks have improved and there has been little racism of blacks against the white former rulers. A Peace and Reconciliation Commission was established in South Africa as a way of bringing the violence and aggression of apartheid into the open, but in a non-confrontational and non-punitive context.

➔ For further information see Fagin and Batur (2004).

expressed in a growth in right-wing racism and electoral support for the National Front.

Among the young white people studied by Back, however, there was a great enthusiasm for many aspects of black culture. Features of black music, masculinity, and 'hardness' were all taken up by the white lads. Reggae, hip hop, and rap music, for example, became important elements in their musical culture. At the same time, however, white lads were involved in a national discourse in which racialized images of black criminals and problem families figured prominently, creating an ambiguity and ambivalence over their own cultural borrowings. Everyday language and culture, Back argues, is necessarily syncretic, as people always forge new symbolic systems out of old and inconsistent elements:

> a syncretic working-class youth culture develops that is neither black nor white but somehow a celebration of shared experience. This constitutes a volatile working-class ethnicity that draws on a rich mixture of South London, African-American and Caribbean symbols. (Back 1996: 98)

This hybrid sense of identity allows great flexibility about who can be included and who excluded. The boundaries of racial inclusion are constantly shifting, depending on the particular situation and the perceived salience of particular cultural elements. In some situations, collective identities will include both black and white together, while in other situations black youths will be excluded.

The hybridity of ethnic identities emphasizes the need to avoid any *essentialist* concept of ethnic identity. It is not only such all-embracing categories as 'black' and 'white' that imply a fixed and essential identity: all descriptions of identity, if taken as anything other than situationally specific descriptions, invoke an unchanging and inflexible essence. People will describe themselves as 'Asian', 'Muslim', or 'Bangladeshi', depending on the situation that they are in and the purposes for which they are producing the description. No person is 'really' and only 'Bangladeshi', for example. Apparently fixed identities are products of specific narratives of identity and are often tied to particular political projects and patterns of alliance. In the contemporary world, such narratives are difficult to maintain. The differences that separate groups must be constantly addressed if a common identity is to be sustained, and the cultural elements that they must combine and recombine may be incompatible. Thus, a collective identity is always in process of formation and is never finally formed (Hall 1992).

The challenge to institutional racism

We have looked a great deal at how racist attitudes have grown and have generated many of the patterns of disadvantage and exclusion that we have described. However, it is not simply a question of attitudes and ideas. Systematic disadvantage can occur as a result of the ways in which institutions operate. Institutions may operate through routines and practices that are quite different from the attitudes and preferences of those who occupy positions within them. Discriminating practices may result from prejudiced attitudes, but they may also result from institutional processes overseen by people who espouse tolerant and unbiased ideas. This is the central insight behind the concept of institutional racism that we discussed earlier (p. 202).

Institutional racism has come to the fore as a result of the Macpherson Report on the handling of a controversial murder case by the Metropolitan Police. In his report, Sir William Macpherson argues that institutional racism is:

> The collective failure of an organization to provide an appropriate and professional service to people because of their colour, culture, or ethnic origin. It can be seen or detected through unwitting prejudice, ignorance, thoughtlessness and racist stereotyping which disadvantage minority ethnic people. (Macpherson 1999: 6.34)

Macpherson's inquiry was set up by the government in response to criticisms of the ways in which the criminal justice system responded to the murder of Stephen Lawrence, a young black man, in April 1993. Stephen was assaulted and then murdered by a gang of white youths at a South London bus stop. The police were on the scene within five minutes and they received a number of tip-offs about who was responsible. There was little momentum to the police enquiries, however, and charges against two youths were dropped for lack of sufficient evidence. Stephen's parents launched a private prosecution a year later, frustrated at the response of the police. After two years, however, the private prosecution had to be withdrawn when identification evidence was ruled inadmissible. It seemed as if the investigation had got nowhere, though many people believed that they knew who was responsible. In February 1997, therefore, the *Daily Mail* carried front-page photographs of five young men that it labelled as 'murderers'.

Public outcry at the handling of the case—even the Head of the Metropolitan Police Murder Squad eventually admitted that he did not know the law relating to his own powers of arrest—led the Police Complaints Authority to set up an internal investigation, while the government asked Sir William Macpherson to carry out an independent, external inquiry. The Police Complaints Authority report was published first in December 1997, and it concluded that the police operation had been well organized and that there was no evidence of any racist conduct on the part of police officers. The Macpherson inquiry, however, took almost two years collecting evidence and points of view, publishing its final report in 1999. Prior to the publication of the report, senior police officers were aware of what was going to be recommended and they followed a public relations strategy aimed at countering its central tenets. The Assistant Police Commissioner for London apologized to the Lawrence family in mid-1998, while the Commissioner himself also acknowledged 'our failure' to respond properly.

Central to Macpherson's report was the claim to have discovered evidence for the existence of institutional racism. Not all of those outside the police accepted the idea, however. John Tyndall, then active in the British National

Is everyone in Britain racist?
© Alice Chadwick

Party, claimed it was empty rhetoric that obscured what was really happening:

> The very phrase 'institutional racism' of course conceals the hidden liberal agenda, implying that anything which protects or advances the interests of the white majority in our own country is somehow wrong, and therefore needs to be rectified. In fact, an objective examination of what is actually happening quickly reveals that the only people to be victims of serious and sustained 'institutional racism' are—you've guessed it—native British Whites! (www.spearhead-uk.com/9908-rc.html)

There has, clearly, been much dispute over the politics of institutional racism, but the sociological importance of the concept is undeniable. Sociological analysis shows that social institutions are major determinants of people's actions and that these actions cannot be explained in terms of individual attributes alone—no matter how widely shared. The importance of the concept of institutional racism, like any other process of institutional constraint, is that it shows that social exclusion and disadvantage cannot be changed by policies that are concerned with prejudice alone: direct institutional reforms are needed as well.

Macpherson's specific point was that the normal operating procedures of the police force systematically worked against the interests of non-whites and that this sustained and reinforced the overt racism that was also present in the police. The force must, therefore, reform its practices as well as attack racism and prejudice. A particular practice highlighted in the report was stop-and-search, where black people are far more likely to be singled out for investigation, but other areas included the recruitment and promotion policies that result in small numbers of black and Asian police officers, especially at senior levels.

As a result of the report, the Race Relations Act was extended to the whole of the public sector, which had previously been exempt from parts of the Act. This highlighted the fact that institutional racism is not confined to the police but is a feature of many of the central institutions, public and private, in contemporary societies. It has been argued, for example, that Home Office immigration procedures and the arrangements for dealing with asylum seekers have racist consequences. It has been shown that ethnic minority doctors are less likely to get promoted to consultant grade in hospitals, and they are likely to work in less popular specialisms and badly funded hospitals. Similar issues arise over the appointment and promotion of teachers in schools and universities. Institutional racism in schools, it has been claimed, is responsible for the poor performance of many ethnic minority children. Policies aimed at racial awareness training and equal opportunities training have been introduced in many public-sector, and some private-sector, organizations in an attempt to counter this institutional racism.

‹› *Stop and reflect*

In this section we have looked at the patterns of community relations that followed from colonial migration to Britain.

- Colonial migrants have been forced to live in poor, overcrowded housing in declining areas.
- Housing segregation produces misunderstanding and is the basis for hostility and conflict.

We also reviewed trends in ethnic relations in the United States:

- White migrants have not abandoned their sense of national identity when adopting an American one.
- African-Americans have continued to be excluded from full participation in American society, and the racialized division between black and white has sharpened.

- The movement of relatively affluent African-Americans to the suburbs has left a poor and heavily disadvantaged section in the ghettos.

- Do you think it is useful to talk about heavily disadvantaged African-Americans as an 'underclass'?

In the sphere of race policy we have identified the importance of a clash between the liberal idea of equal citizenship and conservative racism:

- Official policy in Britain and the United States has emphasized the ideal of the assimilation of ethnic minorities into mainstream culture.
- There has been a growth of racism since the 1960s, undermining the model of the ethnic melting pot.
- Is it correct to see racialized disadvantage as reflecting institutional racism as well as overt prejudice?

Chapter summary

In the section on 'Understanding race and ethnicity' we examined the ways in which cultural and biological factors entered into the formation of ethnic identities. We showed that:

- The concept of race should be abandoned as it has no scientific meaning. Its use in political discourse gives ethnic difference a false fixity.

- The use of the term 'race' in political debates involves a racialization of ethnic differences that hardens and sharpens them.

We then showed that three distinctive theoretical approaches were useful in studying ethnic difference:

- One approach centres on the concept of citizenship and the existence of cultural contradictions between dominant and other systems of ideas.

- A second approach takes the material structures of colonialism as its starting point and sees contemporary relations as reflecting the history of the colonial and post-colonial periods.

- The third theory sees the representations of race in cultural discourses as central to the construction of ethnic identities. This approach stresses hybridity.

'Towards assimilation and incorporation?' looked at the immediate consequences of colonialism and slavery and examined the degree to which ethnically diverse societies had become more integrated.

- Slavery had a strong impact on the position of African-Americans in the first half of the twentieth century, especially in the Deep South.

- Migration to cities such as Chicago led to the assimilation of many European migrants, but blacks migrating from the south experienced continued exclusion.

The section on 'Migration, racism, and multiculturalism' looked at the consequences of black and Asian migration from former British colonies in the period since the 1950s and it examined their continuing impact on contemporary ethnic relations. We also investigated recent trends in the United States. It was shown that:

- Colonial migrants experienced poor housing, employment, education, and health. White society tended to see this as reflecting cultural differences rather than social inequality and social exclusion.

- White migrants in the United States have combined their sense of national identity with a sense of American identity.

- Exclusion from full participation in American society still characterizes the position of African-Americans. Their social position is racialized.

- A structural 'underclass' has been isolated in the urban ghettos by the migration of relatively affluent African-Americans to the suburbs.

We showed, finally, that official policy in Britain and the United States is marked by a cultural contradiction between the liberal idea of equal citizenship and a conservative racism. In particular, we showed that:

- The persistence of racialized disadvantage reflects institutional racism as much as it does overt prejudice.

Key concepts

- assimilation
- diaspora
- ethnicity
- hybridity
- institutional racism
- melting pot
- multiculturalism
- race
- racialization
- racism
- racist discourse
- xenophobia

Workshop 6

Study 6 The art of being black

In *The Art of Being Black* (1996), Claire Alexander explored the ways in which young black Britons construct their cultural identities. She recognized that common cultural representations of black youths saw them in stereotypical terms drawn from cultural imagery of the black mugger, the Rastafarian drug dealer, and the rioter. Such labelling of them as 'problems' led to their high levels of alienation from mainstream white society. Her particular concern was to highlight the strengths and the ambiguities that are generated in black youth as they interpret their lived experiences in terms of specific representations of community, class, masculinity, and leisure. Black youths are affected by the labels imposed on them, they draw on their own cultural inheritance, and they interpret all of these through their own lived experience of disadvantage and oppression to produce their characteristic outlook on life and sense of identity. Her particular concern was how terms of identity articulated with conceptions of masculinity that were sustained through peer groups and involved distinctive attitudes towards women.

Alexander sees ethnic identity not simply as a label, but as a mode of being. People perform or present their identities through the particular and distinctive ways in which they act. Ethnic identities, therefore, are fluid and shifting, varying according to the particular situations in which people find themselves.

The method that Alexander employed was twelve months of participant observation among groups of young black Londoners in east, north-west, and west London. She studied them at home, at work, and during their leisure-time activities. Her aim was to act, as far as possible, as 'one of the boys'. You might spot some immediate problems in this research strategy: Alexander is a young woman of British Asian descent studying African-Caribbean young men through participant observation. Look back at our discussion of participant observation in Chapter 3, pp. 85–7 and see if you can identify the particular problems that she might have faced. Look at Alexander's own account and see how she addresses these issues.

Alexander's account provides a useful way of approaching the issues that we ask you to consider in Media watch 6. In particular she asks questions about being both 'black' and 'British'. What does her approach tell us about the imposition of official categories in censuses and surveys?

Media watch 6 Black and white answers

In the summer of 2005, some Asian community leaders asked the government to introduce US-style hyphenated terms of ethnic identity, such as Asian-British or Indian-British, for official purposes. This, it was held, would help to recognize the complexity of ethnic identity. The political commentator Yasmin Alibhai-Brown supported this idea, saying that it would allow people to show pride in their ethnic roots and in their status as a Briton. The Conservative home affairs spokesman countered that Asian British people in his constituency regarded themselves as British and that 'They don't need a government minister to tell them how to describe themselves' (http://news.bbc.co.uk/1/hi/uk/4130594.stm). This debate followed hard on the London tube and bus bombings of July 2005, which fed a growing climate of concern over 'Muslim' or 'Islamic' terrorists and their supposed links with the British Asian communities. The then-leader of the Conservative Party, Michael Howard, held that the bombings had

fundamentally changed the context in which issues of identity and multiculturalism had to be discussed. He argued, however, that 'most people in this country want to share a strong sense of British identity while recognising that this is not incompatible with a continuing attachment to other traditions' (*Guardian*, 17 August 2005).

Any term of ethnic identity is likely to be open to dispute. This problem is especially marked when observers and participants try to use an inclusive label referring to all or a large number of separate ethnic minorities. This is most obvious with the derogatory terms used by members of a majority to describe a minority, and many terms eventually acquire derogatory overtones. This is the case, for example, with 'Negro', which was once used as a neutral, descriptive term. The London bombings gave the term 'Muslim' new, and negative, meanings among many members of the white majority. Deciding on an appropriate category is particularly problematic when labels are politically contested. Many African, Caribbean, and Asian people in Britain, for example, have used the word 'black' to describe themselves as a single, racialized category. Other members of the ethnic minorities, however, challenge this usage on the grounds of the political and cultural differences that are felt to distinguish them from each other. In the United States, the term 'black' was perceived as having many negative connotations, and the term 'of colour' was preferred as a generic label for non-white minorities, though this, too, has been challenged from within the minority communities.

This same problem applies to majority groups as well. The term 'white', for example, is not routinely employed by all members of the ethnic majority in Britain and the United States, and it is a term that may be embraced by some ethnic minorities who seek to align themselves with the majority rather than a minority.

● In this book, we have tried to use the most appropriate term for the contexts and situations that we are dealing with, though it is unlikely that we have ever been able to use completely neutral terms. Turn to our discussion of Weber's ideas on value-relevance and value freedom (Chapter 2, pp. 39–40) and see what this suggests about the possibility of objective and neutral descriptions.

● You might find it informative to discuss this issue of ethnic identity with friends to see if their preferred labels of identity correspond to those that you would have predicted.

Discussion points

Discourse, science, and ideology

We have looked at a number of issues around the construction of racial ideas and their legitimation through science. While there is no basis to conventional ideas of race, racial thought has often sought a scientific grounding.

● Make sure that you understand the differences between the ideas of ethnic identity and ethnic origin. Which is the most useful in sociological analysis?

● Search the Web for information about the following and their race policies: British National Party, National Socialism, Nation of Islam, Ku Klux Klan, Conservative Party, Anti-Nazi League, Anti-Racist Alliance.

● Is there any acceptable biological meaning that can be given to the concept of race?

Racism, citizenship, and exclusion

Policy and political practices have been shaped by liberal ideas of citizenship and contradictory racist ideas. Patterns of inclusion and exclusion reflect the clash between these two sets of ideas.

● Make sure that you are clear about the meaning of prejudice, discrimination, and disadvantage as they apply in the field of ethnic relations. How would you distinguish between racism and institutional racism?

● Ethnic relations used to be seen in terms of a model of the 'assimilation' of minorities into a majority society. How do contemporary ideas of 'multiculturalism' differ from this?

Colonialism, migration, and conflict

The global context of race and ethnic relations is critically important. We looked at the impact of colonial structures on slavery and on migration from colonial to imperial centres. The historical inheritance is a major influence on contemporary patterns of power and conflict.

● How useful is it to see contemporary patterns of migration in terms of the claims of 'asylum seekers'? Is this an advance over earlier views of them as 'immigrants'?

● To what extent do contemporary ethnic relations issues result from the experience of colonialism and empire?

Explore further

Banton, M., and Harwood, J. (1975), *The Race Concept* (Newton Abbott: David and Charles). *A very useful overview of the history of racial ideas. Now partly superseded by the second edition of Banton's* Racial Theories *(Cambridge University Press, 2000).*

Mason, D. (2000), *Race and Ethnicity in Modern Britain* (2nd edn., Oxford: Oxford University Press).

Modood, T., Berthoud, R., Lakey, J., Nazroo, J., Smith, P., Virdee, S., and Beishan, S. (1997), *Ethnic Minorities in Britain: Diversity and Disadvantage* (London: Policy Studies Institute).

Online resources

Visit the Online Resource Centre that accompanies this book to access more learning resources and other interesting material on racial and ethnic identities at:

www.oxfordtextbooks.co.uk/orc/fulcher3e/

Useful overview sites for these issues are the government's Commission for Racial Equality at:

www.cre.gov.uk

and the privately financed Runnymede Trust at:

www.runnymedetrust.org

The major academic point of reference for race and ethnic relations research is the website of the Centre for Research in Ethnic Relations at Warwick University:

www.warwick.ac.uk/fac/soc/CRER_RC

The global flow of refugees can be tracked through the United States' State Department site:

www.state.gov/g/prm/

However, you should also consult Human Rights Watch for impartial reporting on repression and rights problems at

www.hrw.org/refugees

crime and deviance

Contents

07

Mobile crime

Mobile phone theft is high and is on the increase. Phones are small and easily portable, they are much in demand, and so they are easily sold on at a considerable profit. Up to three-quarters of a million mobile phones were stolen during 2001, and the figure has increased since then. Mobile phone theft now accounts for 45 per cent of all crime on the London Underground. At the end of 2003 the Home Office launched a new National Mobile Phone Crime Unit specifically to counter the growth in this crime. Two-thirds of the stolen phones are taken from young people aged between 11 and 15. The chances of being a victim of mobile phone theft are now five times greater for young people than they are for adults. Almost 12 per cent of young people, mainly young men, in Britain's inner cities are likely to fall victim to this kind of crime. Most of these crimes are committed by young people. Police statistics suggest that the typical offender is aged 14–17 and is male, black, and works as part of a gang.

This growth in mobile phone theft has been fuelled by the massive growth in mobile phone use and the increasing demand for the latest in fashionable technology. There has been no significant flagging in the innovations in design and technology that fuel demand and, therefore, crime. People continue to upgrade to new models with more advanced facilities.

Source: *Guardian*, 8 January 2002 (drawing on Home Office Research). http://news.bbc.co.uk/1/hi/uk/1748258.stm

Many people are likely to be the victim of a crime at some time in their life: phone theft, car theft, domestic burglary, or, in extreme cases, a rape or murder. Many of those who do not become victims—and some who do—will be the perpetrators of crime. Some crime seems to be the result of a long-term profession of crime. Much crime seems to have been motivated by drug use and the need to purchase illegal drugs. At the same time, growing numbers of people, including many young people, are likely to be involved in fairly regular drug use, even if they do not become involved in committing other types of offence.

How are we to understand this growth of criminality and deviance, and how are we to explain how some people come to identify with their deviant acts and come to see themselves and to be seen by others as criminals, drug users, and so on? These are the questions that we examine in this chapter. We look at various forms of deviant behaviour and the ways in which they are shaped by the criminal law and informal social relations. We ask how reliable the evidence on deviance can be when it is produced by these very forces of social control: to what extent, for example, can we put our trust in the apparent facts about mobile phone theft that we have reported above?

Understanding deviance and control

Deviance is nonconformity to social norms or expectations. For many people, the word 'deviance' is used only in relation to moral, religious, or political norms. The 'deviant' is seen as someone whose behaviour departs from normal moral standards (for example, those con-cerned with sexual behaviour), or who deviates from a political or religious orthodoxy. The sociological concept of deviance, however, takes a broader point of view and recognizes that there can be deviation from social norms of all kinds.

Along with sexual deviants, political deviants, and religious deviants must be counted those whose behaviour runs counter to legal or customary norms more generally —criminals, the mentally ill, alcoholics, and many others. What makes these people deviant is the fact that their behaviour seems to run counter to the norms of a social group. It is this that the homosexual, the prostitute, the child molester, the schizophrenic, the suicide, the radical, the heretic, the Ecstasy user, and the burglar all have in common. All of them seem to engage in behaviour that is not seen as normal in their society.

No form of behaviour is deviant in and of itself. To judge behaviour as deviant is to judge it from the standpoint of the norms of a particular social group. The defining statement for the sociological study of deviance is Becker's justly famous claim that:

> Social groups create deviance by making the rules whose infraction constitutes deviance, and by applying these rules to particular people and labelling them as outsiders. From this point of view, deviance is *not* a quality of the act the person commits, but rather a consequence of the application by others of rules and sanctions to an 'offender'. The deviant is one to whom that label has successfully been applied; deviant behaviour is behaviour that people so label. (Becker 1953: 9)

Even where there is a consensus over standards of behaviour within a society, these standards may change over time. What was formerly considered as normal, conformist behaviour may come to be seen as deviant. High levels of consensus are uncommon, and it is more typical for there to be rival definitions of normality and deviance within a society. In these circumstances, conformity to the expectations of one group may mean deviating from the expectations of another. Revolutionary terrorists, for example, may be regarded as deviants from the standpoint of established social groups, but they are seen very differently by members of their own political movement.

In all these contested situations, it is the views of the powerful that prevail, as they have the ability to make their views count. This insight is particularly associated with a so-called **labelling theory** of deviance that is closely linked to symbolic interactionism. According to this point of view, it is the fact of being labelled as a deviant by the members of a powerful or dominant social group that makes an action deviant. This is why ethnic minorities are in many societies treated as deviant groups if they are seen as violating the normal customs and practices of the majority ethnic group. Similarly, those women who depart from what is seen as normal female behaviour by, say, entering what are regarded as male occupations, might be regarded as deviant by many men and by some other women. Whether the behaviour of a person is deviant depends upon whose values are taken as being the basis for determining what is to count as normal or conformist behaviour.

In this section we will look at a number of forms of deviance. We will look at the formation of deviant identities through interaction between deviants and the agents of social control. We will show that what is deviant in one context may be conformist in another, and that the critical element is the social reaction that labels behaviour one way or another. Having discussed some of the features that are common to all forms of deviance, we will look in more detail at criminality, drug use and abuse, and sexual difference.

Biology and deviance

In the past, but also in some more recent discussions, the social dimension of deviance has often been ignored. Deviant behaviour has been seen in purely individual terms and as something to be explained by biology. From this point of view, all 'normal' individuals conform to social expectations, and so those who differ must have something wrong with them. A deviant body is seen as explaining a deviant mind and deviant behaviour. Such a claim ignores the fact that no behaviour—except, perhaps, purely automatic reflexes such as blinking in bright sunlight—can be seen independently of the meanings that it carries and the social contexts in which it occurs.

Evolution, race, and deviance

For many writers on difference and deviance in the nineteenth century, and still for some today, biology provides the key to explaining human behaviour. Nineteenth-century evolutionary theory led to the widespread acceptance of the idea that there was a 'great chain of being', an evolutionary hierarchy of species that connected humans to apes and to the lower animals. The supposed racial divisions of the human species that we discuss in Chapter 6, pp. 197–8, were all accorded their place in this evolutionary hierarchy.

It was widely believed that individuals 'recapitulate' the evolution of their species in their own biological development. They go through various animal-like stages in their foetal development and during their later development outside the womb. Particular races, it was held, had developed only to the particular level that was allowed by their biology: the white races had developed the furthest, while the black races showed an inferior development. White children, for example, were seen as having reached the same stage of evolution as black adults, who had not developed beyond these more 'childlike' characteristics and forms of behaviour.

These assumptions underpinned contemporary views of deviance. The nineteenth-century English doctor John

Down, for example, classified various forms of mental disability in terms of the 'lower' races to which their characteristics corresponded. He argued that some 'idiots' were of the 'Ethiopian' variety, some of the 'Malay' or 'American' type, and others of the 'Mongolian' type. His special study of the genetics of the latter group meant that those with Down's syndrome were, for many years, known as 'Mongols'—a derogatory label that continued to be very widely used until the 1970s. Each society tends to see its own members as being the highest, most-evolved exemplar of the human species. The Japanese, for example, saw themselves as being at the pinnacle of evolution and civilization, and their term for Down's syndrome was 'Englishism'.

The most notorious of these evolutionary approaches to deviant behaviour was the theory of crime set out by Cesare Lombroso, who held that many criminals had been born with 'atavistic' features. Criminals had definite biological failings that prevented them from developing to a fully human level. They showed, perhaps, certain ape-like characteristics, or sometimes merely 'savage' features that gave them the distinct anatomical characteristics from which they could easily be identified: large jaws, long arms, thick skulls, and so on. These atavistic features, Lombroso argued, also led them to prefer forms of behaviour that are normal among apes and savages, but are criminal in human societies. These criminal tendencies were apparent, Lombroso claimed, in their other 'degenerate' personal characteristics: the criminal, he believed, is idle, has a love of tattooing, and engages in orgies. Lombroso claimed that about 40 per cent of all criminals were 'born criminals' of this kind. They were driven into criminality by their biology. Other law-breakers were simply occasional, circumstantial offenders and did not have the 'atavistic' characteristics of the born criminal.

THEORY AND METHODS

Cesare Lombroso

Cesare Lombroso (1836–1909) was born in Verona, Italy. He worked as an army surgeon and later became a Professor of Forensic Medicine and Psychiatry at Turin. He carried out extensive investigations into the appearance and biological characteristics of convicted criminals, publishing his results in his book *L'uomo delinquente* in 1875. This book was never translated into English, but had a great influence through the presentation of its ideas in a summary form in 1911 and in the work of his disciples Ferri and Garafalo. Lombroso's ideas lived on among many psychiatrists interested in criminal behaviour.

The excesses of Lombroso's theory and the racial assumptions that underpinned it have long been discarded. However, many people still see criminality as resulting from innate characteristics. Violence and aggression, for example, are often seen not only as specifically male characteristics, but in their extreme forms as being due to genetic peculiarities. It has been proposed, for example, that many violent criminals have an extra Y chromosome in their cells. Some have suggested that rape can be explained as a consequence of normal, genetically determined male behaviour (Thornhill and Palmer 2000). In the 1990s, the success of the Human Genome Project led to many strong claims about the genetic basis of crime. The idea of the born criminal was supported in a report that 'Pimping and petty theft appear to be genetically conditioned but a person's genes have little influence on their propensity for committing crimes of violence' (*Independent*, 15 February 1994). Violence was reported to be due to a 'mild brain dysfunction in early life', and it was claimed that improved standards of health care for pregnant women could reduce violent crime by over 20 per cent (*Independent*, 8 March 1994). The link between biology and social behaviour is not this straightforward. While there may, indeed, be a biological basis to violent behaviour—and the matter is still hotly debated—the ways in which this is expressed and the consequences that flow from it depend upon the meanings that are attached to it and the particular social situations in which it occurs.

The behaviour of a soldier in time of war involves violence that is channelled into disciplined action against a national enemy. This violence is condoned and encouraged, and it may even be rewarded as heroism or bravery. The behaviour of someone at a football match who attacks a member of the opposing team's supporters involves far less violence, but it is likely to be condemned and denounced as hooliganism that must be stamped out. No biological explanation of violence can explain why one act is that of a hero and the other is that of a villain. Of course, this is not to make the absurd claim that it is only the social reaction that differs between the two cases. The point is that, while some people may have a disposition towards violent behaviour, a biological explanation can, at best, explain the disposition. It cannot explain when and how that disposition is expressed in social action, or is inhibited from expression. Nor can it explain the reactions of others to violence.

An explanation of deviance must refer to the processes of socialization through which people *learn* to give meaning to their behaviour and to the processes of discipline and regulation through which some people come to be identified as deviants and to be processed in particular ways by a system of social control.

Social reaction and deviance

There are three levels of explanation in the study of deviant behaviour. A first level of explanation is concerned with the existence of the many different forms of human behaviour that occur in any society. Biology may contribute towards an explanation of this diversity, but it can never provide the whole explanation. It is always necessary to take account of processes of socialization. A second level of explanation is concerned with the variation in norms between social groups, as manifested particularly in cultural and subcultural differences. Socialization takes place within particular social groups, and it is the norms of these groups that provide the standards for the identification of particular kinds of behaviour as deviant. The third, and final, level of explanation is concerned with the ways in which particular individuals are identified as deviants by others and so come to develop a deviant identity. This is a matter of social reaction and control.

In the rest of this section we will outline some of the general processes that are involved in deviance and control and the processes that are common to a range of deviant and conformist identities. You may like to read this through fairly quickly, not worrying about all the details, and then go on to the discussion of specific forms of deviance in the following sections. When you have read one or two of these sections, return to this general discussion of deviance and control and try to work through its details.

Primary and secondary deviation

Two key concepts in the study of deviance are primary deviation and secondary deviation, which were first systematized by Lemert (1967). **Primary deviation** is the object of the first two levels of explanation that we identified above. It is behaviour that runs counter to the normative expectations of a group, and is recognized as deviant behaviour by its members, but which is 'normalized' by them. That is to say, it is tolerated or indulged as an allowable or permissible departure from what is normally expected. It is ignored or treated in a low-key way that defines it as an exceptional, atypical, or insignificant aberration on the part of an otherwise normal person.

The **normalization** of the deviant behaviour defines it as something that is marginal to the identity of the deviator. Many justifications for the normalization of deviant behaviour are employed: a man is seen as aggressive because he is 'under stress' at work, a woman behaves oddly because it is 'that time of the month', a child is being naughty because he or she is 'overtired', an elderly woman steals from a supermarket because she is 'confused', a middle-aged man exposes himself in public because he has a 'blackout' and 'did not know what came over him', and so on.

What Lemert calls **secondary deviation**, or deviance proper, is the object of our third level of explanation. It

THEORY AND METHODS

Stigmatization

Stigmatization is a social reaction that picks out a particular characteristic and uses this to devalue a person's whole social identity. The term was introduced by Goffman (1963b) to describe the reaction of many people to those with physical disabilities. Such reactions define people as 'disabled' and others respond to them in terms of that label. The term 'stigma' has been applied more widely to any characteristic that is regarded as abnormal or unusual and that is seen as a reason for denigration or exclusion.

arises when the perceived deviation is no longer normalized and is, instead, stigmatized or punished in some way. The social reaction and its consequences become central elements in the deviator's day-to-day experiences and it shapes future actions. When public opinion, law-enforcement agencies (police, courts, and tribunals), or administrative controls exercised by the welfare and other official agencies react in an overt and punitive way, their reaction labels the person as a deviant of some kind (a thief, a welfare fraudster, a junkie, and so on). This labelling stigmatizes the behaviour and the person, who must now try to cope with the consequences of the stigma.

Stigmatization may involve the rejection, degradation, exclusion, incarceration, or coercion of the deviant, who becomes the object of treatment, punishment, or conversion (Schur 1971). Those who are stigmatized find that their lives and identities come to be organized around their deviance. They may even come to see themselves *as a* deviant—as a 'thief', as 'mentally ill', and so on—taking on many of the stigmatizing attributes of the popular and official images. Even if the deviator rejects this identity, the fact that he or she is identified in this way by others becomes an important factor in determining future behaviour.

The development of secondary deviation may, initially, involve an acceptance of the negative, stigmatizing stereotypes that others hold of the deviant. Deviants may often, however, be able to construct a more positive image of their deviance and build an identity around a rejection of the stigma. They accept the label, but, instead of merely reflecting back the public stereotype, they construct an alternative view that reflects their own experiences and those of people like them. They construct accounts—narratives—of their coming to be the kind of people that they are, and these narratives become central features of the construction and reconstruction of their identity (Plummer 1995: chapter 2). In much the same way that the Black Power movement constructed more positive images of black identity, so such movements as Gay Pride have led to the construction of positive images of homosexuality.

Not all deviance results from the conversion of primary deviation into secondary deviation through an external social reaction. Deviators may, for example, escape the attention of those who would label them, remaining 'secret deviants'. Such people may, nevertheless, move into secondary deviation precisely because of their attempts to keep their deviant behaviour secret. By *anticipating* the reactions of others, they begin to act towards themselves in terms of the stigmatized deviant identity, even if they do not embrace this identity themselves. The man who engages in homosexual acts in private, for example, may become drawn into association with other gay people because the risks of his inadvertent exposure as gay in other social situations are too great.

There is also the possibility of false accusation. Someone who has not violated expectations may, nevertheless, be labelled as a deviant and processed accordingly. Such people will experience many of the same consequences as those who have been correctly labelled. Although they may feel a sense of injustice about their wrongful accusation, they may, as a result of their experience of stigmatization, come to act in ways that are quite indistinguishable from other deviants. Such highly publicized cases of wrongful imprisonment for terrorist bombings as those of the Birmingham Six and the Guildford Four highlight the more general situation of false accusation that is apparent in, for example, the child who is wrongly punished by a teacher for cheating or the political dissidents in the Soviet Union who were officially designated as mentally ill.

Primary deviation that is not normalized does not always result in secondary deviation or commitment to a deviant identity. Many people **drift** in and out of deviant behaviour without being committed to it at all (Matza 1964). Because they are not committed to their deviant acts—they do not see them as a fundamental expression of their identity—they are able to abandon them whenever they choose, or when the circumstances are not right. Conversely, of course, they may feel able—though not required—to deviate whenever the opportunity and the inclination are present. Drift, then, is an important aspect of the structuring of deviant behaviour. Matza suggests, for example, that juvenile delinquency rarely becomes a matter of secondary deviation, precisely because juveniles drift back and forth between deviant and conformist behaviour without ever becoming committed to delinquency as a way of life.

Many of those who become involved in crime do not embrace a deviant identity—they do not see themselves as criminals, burglars, or housebreakers. Rather, they see their involvement in criminal activities as an aspect of the larger social situation in which they find themselves. They may, for example, be long-term unemployed, in serious financial hardship, and faced with the opportunity of illegal gain. Such people drift into crime for situational

reasons, and become secondary deviants only if they are unable to drift out again. Certain opportunities may be denied to them, while other courses of action become easier. They become secondary deviants if the whole structure of interests within which they act—the advantages and disadvantages, rewards and punishments—tend to force them into continued deviance. Those who have been imprisoned for theft or burglary, for example, may experience restricted employment and promotion opportunities in the outside world that make it difficult for them to abandon their criminal life and to enter or re-enter conventional occupations.

Where people do take on a deviant identity, however, their behaviour will be shaped by commitment as well as constraint. Those who have become committed to a deviant identity will be committed to a whole range of behaviours that are associated with that identity. These ways of behaving will seem more 'natural' to them than any others, and they will identify with the behaviours as much as with the label itself. Commitment and constraint generally operate together: a firmly committed deviant is more likely to face disadvantaged opportunities, and a tightly constrained deviant is more likely to feel a sense of difference from others. If their circumstances change, and these constraints alter, they may find it possible to drift out of crime once more.

Deviant roles and careers

Where deviance has become a central feature of a person's identity and way of life, it can take the form of role deviance. In this situation, a person's activities become organized into a distinct and recognizable social role to which particular normative expectations are attached. The deviant is expected to act in deviant ways: conformity to these particular role expectations confirms the person's deviant identity! Until recently, male homosexuals, for example, were widely expected to exhibit their deviance by behaving in 'effeminate' ways, and one who conformed to these expectations had adopted the public, stereotyped homosexual role.

Deviant roles, like conformist roles, often have a career structure. This is particularly likely where the role is defined within a group of deviants, rather than by public stereotypes alone. Where the deviant role involves a particular sequence of events and experiences that are common for all its occupants, role deviance becomes what has been called **career deviance**. This may be highly formalized, paralleling the kinds of career structures that are found in conventional occupations. Full-time thieves, for example, may be members of teams who make their living from their deviance and that have their own internal structures of leadership, reward, and 'promotion' (Sutherland 1937).

When organized as career deviance, the deviant role is likely also to involve what Goffman (1961*b*) has called a **moral career**. This term describes the internal or personal aspects of a career, the specific sequence of learning experiences and changes in conceptions of self and identity that occur as people follow their deviant career. It is a process through which people come to terms with their stigma and their commitment to a deviant identity. With each phase of the public career associated with the role, its occupants must reconsider their past in an attempt to make sense of their new experiences. They single out and elaborate, with the benefit of hindsight, those experiences that they believe can account for and legitimate their present situation. This is a continuous process in which their personal biography—their life story—is constantly constructed and reconstructed in the light of their changing circumstances.

Deviant groups and communities

Career deviants are especially likely to become involved with groups that support and sustain their identities and that help them to come to terms with the constrained opportunities that they face. Gangs and cliques are formed, clubs and pubs are colonized as meeting places, and organizations and agencies are set up to promote shared interests or political goals. With advances in technology, new forms of support and communication become possible. The spread of the telephone allowed people to maintain distant communication far more effectively than was possible through writing letters, and computer technology now allows global communication through the Internet and e-mail. Those who are involved in two or more of these groups will tie them into larger social networks that bond the groups into cohesive and solidaristic communities with a shared sense of identity.

Criminal gangs, for example, may be involved in localized networks of recruitment and mutual support, to which individual criminals and juvenile gangs may also be attached. These networks form those subcultures of crime that comprise an underworld. The subcultures are means through which skills and techniques can be learned and in which criminals can obtain a degree of acceptance and recognition that is denied to them by conventional groups.

Goffman (1963b) has argued that the groups of 'sympathetic others' that form the supportive subcultures of deviance comprise two distinct types of people: the own and the wise. The **own** are those who share the deviant identity. They have a common understanding of stigmatization from their personal experiences, and they may be able to help in acquiring the tricks of the trade that allow a deviant to operate more effectively, as well as by providing emotional support and company in which a deviant can feel at home. The own help people to organize a life around their deviance and to cope with many of the disadvantages that they experience.

The **wise**, on the other hand, are 'normals' who have a particular reason for being in the know about the secret life of the deviants and for being sympathetic towards it. They are accepted by the deviants and are allowed a kind of associate membership in their activities. They are those for whom the deviants do not feel the need to put on a show of normality or deviance disavowal: they can safely engage in back-region activities with them. The wise can include family members and friends, employees, and even some control agents (such as nurses or police) who have day-to-day contact with them. The own and the wise together form a network of contacts and connections that support deviants in the construction of their narratives of identity.

Some of the wise may actively support deviants in sustaining their deviance, though there are limits to the

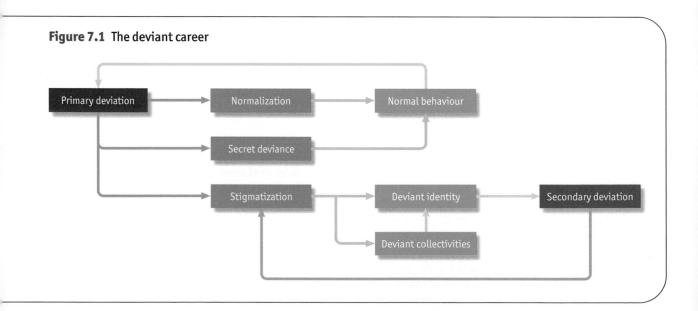

Figure 7.1 The deviant career

Embracing alternative identities at Gay Pride.

© Getty Images/Joe Raedle

> ⊙ *Connections*
>
> Look back at our discussion of Goffman's work on self-presentation in 'Symbolic interactionism', Chapter 4, pp. 128–9. You might check, in particular, our discussion of what he called 'front regions' and 'back regions'.

willingness of people to become too closely involved in activities where the stigma of deviance is likely to 'rub off' on to them. Active support, then, is most likely to come from the own, and this is particularly true where there is a need for representatives to speak or act for their interests and concerns in public. Such representatives may sometimes become very active and make a living—and a new identity—out of their role as spokespersons for particular deviant groups. They make a 'profession' of their deviance in quite a novel way, perhaps appearing in the press and on radio and television whenever issues of concern are

discussed. There are, of course, limits to this. Only certain forms of deviance are allowed to have the legitimacy of their stigmatization debated in public. Gays and the mentally ill, for example, have active and important organizations that can lobby for their interests, while thieves and burglars do not. Pressure groups on behalf of those involved in serious crime are, for the most part, limited to campaigns for prison reform and are led by the wise and by reformed offenders.

The general account of deviance and control that we have presented (summarized in Figure 7.1) must be treated with caution, as all of its elements will not apply equally to every case of deviance and stigmatized identity. It is a general framework that provides the concepts that can sensitize researchers to the specific issues that occur in particular cases. We will illustrate this by considering a number of forms of criminal behaviour. In the following chapter we will show that certain aspects of illness can also be understood as forms of deviance.

◈ *Stop and reflect*

In this section we have looked at the relationship between biological and social factors in the explanation of deviance and the formation of deviant identities. In reviewing our discussion of biology and deviance, you may like to look back to our discussion of the biology of race in Chapter 6, pp. 199–200. The main points we made in this section were:

- Early approaches to deviance drew on now-discredited evolutionary ideas. Lombroso, for example, saw 'born criminals' as 'atavistic' evolutionary forms.

- Deviance is never a purely biological fact. It depends on an act of social definition, of labelling.

- Does the labelling argument imply that biological conditions—such as genetic inheritance—are never relevant to criminality?

In considering the nature of the social reaction to deviance and its consequences, we showed that:

- It is important to distinguish between primary and secondary deviation.

- Many people drift in and out of deviance without becoming committed to it.

- Much deviation is normalized, but some is stigmatized. Stigmatized secondary deviation may involve role deviance and a deviant career.

- How useful is it to think of deviance as a 'career'?

- Deviant groups and communities are important in supporting and sustaining role deviance.

Crime and legal control

Crime is that form of deviance that involves an infraction of the criminal law. Not all laws are 'criminal'. Lawyers recognize civil law, constitutional law, and various other categories of legal norm.

Civil law, for example, concerns relations among private individuals, such as the contractual relations involved in such areas as employment relations and consumer purchasing. A person who breaks a contract by, say, unfairly dismissing someone from her or his job or failing to supply goods that are 'fit for their purpose' has infringed the civil law, and action can be taken only by the particular individual affected (the dismissed person or the unhappy consumer). The police have no right to become involved, and a completely separate system of courts is involved in hearing any civil case. The outcome of a successful civil case is some kind of 'restitution', such as financial compensation or 'damages'.

The criminal law, by contrast, consists of those legal norms that have been established by the state as a *public* responsibility, and which the police and the criminal courts have been designated to enforce. Someone who infringes the criminal law can be arrested, charged, and tried at public expense and, if found guilty, will be subject to repressive or punitive penalties such as a fine or imprisonment.

The criminal law of a society can cover a wide range of actions. In Britain, for example, it covers such acts as driving above the legal speed limit, stealing a car, breaking into a house, possessing certain drugs, forging a signature on a cheque, murdering someone, and arson. Penalties attached to these offences range from small fines for speeding to life imprisonment for murder, and, until 1998, execution for treason. The crimes that are most visible or that are perceived to be the most threatening are not necessarily those that have the greatest impact in real terms. In practice, many minor crimes are normalized: few people report cases of speeding or dropping litter, and the police may often choose to disregard such offences. Figure 7.2 shows the main types of serious offence (officially termed 'notifiable offences') recorded in the criminal statistics for England and Wales.

The statistics in Figure 7.2 show a large increase in the level of crime. A different picture emerges, however, from the British Crime Survey, which draws its evidence from a sample survey of the general public. This survey of victims and potential victims showed a fall in the amount of crime between 1995 and 2005. The figures reached a peak in 1995, but crime had fallen by 44 per cent by 2005. Both vehicle crime and burglary fell by over a half, while violent crime fell by 43 per cent. The chances of being a victim of crime fell from 40 per cent in 1995 to 24 per cent in 2005. This is the lowest level since 1981. Young men, however, are far more likely to be a victim of crime, while relatively few of those aged over 65 have been victims. People's attitudes, however, reflected the official statistics and their reporting in the media, with 61 per cent of people believing that crime had risen in the country as a whole.

Gangsters participate in a subculture of crime.

© Getty Images/Ron Gerelli

of people, project crime involves a much smaller number of large thefts. Growing affluence and, in particular, the increasing scale of business activity have meant that the potential targets of theft have become much bigger. As a result, criminals have had to organize themselves more effectively and on a larger scale if they are to be successful against these targets. Improved safes, alarm systems, and security vans can be handled only by organized teams of specialists: safe-breakers, drivers, gunmen, and so on. Such crimes, organized as one-off projects, require advanced planning and a much higher level of cooperation than is typical for craft crime.

Teams for particular projects are recruited through the cliques and connections that comprise the underworld, and these may sometimes be organized on a semi-permanent basis. The criminal underworld that existed in the East End of London from the Second World War until the 1960s, for example, contained numerous competing gangs that were held together largely by the violent hegemony of the Kray twins and their associates. The east London gangs engaged in violent feuds with their counterparts (the

Richardsons) from the south London underworld, and the leading members of the East End and south London gangs occasionally met on the neutral ground of the West End (Morton 1992; Hobbs 1994).

It is through the subculture of crime that people can be socialized into criminal identities, whether as a craft thief or a project thief. The professional thief, like the professional doctor, lawyer, or bricklayer, must develop many technical abilities and skills. He (the thief is generally male) must know how to plan and execute crimes, how to dispose of stolen goods, how to 'fix' the police and the courts, and so on. These skills must be acquired through long education and training, and it is through his involvement in the underworld that the thief can acquire them most effectively.

Based on his detailed study of a professional thief, Sutherland (1937) has shown how the person who successfully learns and applies these techniques earns high status within the underworld. The beginning thief, if successful, is gradually admitted into closer and closer contact with other thieves. It is they who can offer him 'better' work and from whom he can learn more advanced skills. Once successful, the thief dresses and behaves in distinct ways and proudly adopts the label 'thief' in order to distinguish himself from a mere 'amateur', small-time criminal. As well as gaining respect within the underworld, he may also gain a degree of recognition and respect from police, lawyers, and newspaper crime writers. These people are aware of his activities and have often accommodated themselves to professional crime: apart from the corruption that sometimes occurs, there may also be shared interests in not reacting immediately and punitively towards all crime.

Burglary as a way of life

One of the few contemporary investigations of career theft in Britain is an investigation of domestic burglaries (Maguire and Bennett 1982). Burglary is illegal entry into a building with the intent to steal. Domestic burglary was, for a long time, subject to the death penalty, and from 1861 to 1968 it carried a maximum sentence of life imprisonment. Following the Theft Act of 1968, the maximum penalty has been fourteen years' imprisonment. In practice, only just under a half of convicted burglars have been given custodial sentences.

Recognizing the problems involved in assessing rates of crime, Maguire and Bennett concluded that about 60 per cent of all burglaries were committed by a relatively small number of persistent, career criminals. The remaining 40 per cent were committed by juveniles who had drifted into delinquency and would, for the most part, drift out of it again.

Maguire and Bennett interviewed a number of persistent burglars, most of whom were committed to their criminal careers. They had, typically, carried out between 100 and 500 break-ins during their careers. They combined this with involvement in car theft, burglary from commercial premises, and cheque forgery. They were mainly young, single, and with no dependants. The men described themselves as 'thieves', or simply as 'villains', and they described their crimes as 'work' from which they could earn a living and from which they would eventually retire. Maguire and Bennett are, however, more critical of this self-image than Sutherland had been. In particular, they highlight a number of ways in which the thieves sought to neutralize the moral implications of their actions through self-serving rationalizations.

Thieves claimed, for example, that any distress suffered by the victims was no concern of theirs. They were simply doing a job, carrying on their trade, and this distress was an unavoidable consequence of their routine, professional activities. This claim was further bolstered by the claim that, in any case, they stole only from the well-to-do, who could easily afford it and who were well insured (Maguire and Bennett 1982: 61). In fact, many of their victims were

Briefing: the professional thief

In 1930 Edwin Sutherland, a sociologist at the University of Chicago, carried out lengthy research with Chic Conwell, a man involved full-time in theft between 1905 and 1925. Using the life-history method pioneered at the university, Sutherland obtained a biographical account of Conwell's life, which he used as the basis for his interpretation of thieving (Sutherland 1937).

Conwell was born in the 1880s and, after a short period of theatre work, got involved in the use of drugs and became a pimp. Through his pimping, he acquired a knowledge of other forms of crime and he worked in Chicago as a pickpocket, a shoplifter, and a confidence trickster. He spent a number of periods in prison, though only one of his sentences was for theft. He gave up both thieving and drug use after release from prison in 1925 and worked regularly until his death in 1933.

Sutherland specialized in the study of crime. He developed a view that stressed differential association: people learn criminal behaviour by coming into contact with others who define criminality in positive ways. In addition to his study of professional theft, he pioneered the study of white-collar crime (Sutherland 1949).

Sutherland's position on the professional thief was that:

> a person can be a professional thief only if he is recognized and received as such by other professional thieves. Professional theft is a group-way of life. One can get into the group and remain in it only by the consent of those previously in the group. Recognition as a professional thief by other professional thieves is the absolutely necessary, universal, and definitive characteristic of the professional thief. . . . A professional thief is a person who has the status of a professional thief in the differential association of professional thieves. (Sutherland 1937: 211)

relatively poor council house residents who could ill afford to be burgled.

Similarly, the thieves sought to boost their own status by disparaging the amateurism of the majority of 'losers', 'wankers', 'idiots', and 'cowboys' who carried out unsuccessful thefts. However, Maguire and Bennett argue, it is more accurate to see the persistent career thieves as divided into low-level, middle-level, and high-level categories on the basis of the scale of their crimes. Thieves move up and down this hierarchy a great deal over the course of their careers.

High-level burglaries are undertaken by thieves who are members of small networks of committed criminals who keep themselves separate from other, small-time criminals. Sometimes they work alone, and sometimes in pairs, but always they keep their principal criminal contacts within their network. Middle-level burglaries are carried out by those who are involved in larger and less exclusive networks of thieves with varying abilities and degrees of commitment. There is less consistent adherence to the code of mutual support, and less effective contacts with receivers of stolen goods and with other specialist criminals. Finally, low-level burglaries are undertaken by individual thieves with only loose connections to one another and who are indiscriminate in both their criminal connections and their choice of crimes.

It is at the lower level that people first enter burglary, as the loose social networks are closely embedded in the surrounding structure of the local community. In most cases, this is a process of drift by some of those who have previously been involved in juvenile delinquencies. When describing their careers, however, the thieves minimized the element of drift and presented a self-image of themselves as people who had chosen to enter careers of crime. Those who drift into lower-level burglary and become at all successful may graduate, in due course, to middle-level or high-level burglary through the contacts and connections that they make.

Those in the networks carrying out the high-level burglaries were, in a sense, at the pinnacle of the career hierarchy, though Maguire and Bennett show that they are unlikely to be at all involved in large-scale project crimes undertaken by the London gangs. Their activities are confined to housebreaking, shop-breaking, car theft, shoplifting, and cheque forgery. They have little or no involvement in such specialist crimes as hijacking lorries, bank raids, or embezzlement.

Very few burglars—even those at the high level—make a major financial success of their chosen careers, and most spent at least one period in prison. Imprisonment is not, however, a purely negative experience, as it gives the burglar an opportunity to 'widen his circle of criminal acquaintances, learn new techniques and be encouraged to try his hand at more lucrative offences' (Maguire and Bennett 1982: 67). Nevertheless, few burglars continued with burglary beyond their thirties or forties. Most drifted into what they hoped would be safer forms of work. Entry into legal employment is difficult for someone with a criminal record, and few make the transition successfully. Walsh (1986: 58–9) has shown that some burglars are able to combine career crime with a continuing involvement in legitimate employment—typically short-term jobs in the building and construction industry or in other casual work such as catering and cleaning. It seems likely that some who retire from burglary may be able to continue or to re-enter such casual and temporary work.

Career crime has probably never been a completely self-contained, full-time activity. Even in the heyday of the Victorian underworld of the East End, criminal activities were combined with casual labour and street trading, one type of work supplementing the earnings from the other (Mayhew 1861b). Hobbs (1988) has shown how the East End has long been organized around an entrepreneurial culture of wheeling and dealing, trading and fixing, that makes no sharp distinction between legal and illegal activities.

Theft may, indeed, be career crime, a way of life, but it does not take up all of a thief's time and cannot usually provide him with a regular or substantial income. Those involved in thieving, then, must combine it with other ways of gaining an income. Casual labour is combined with their own thieving and the performance of the occasional criminal task for other, more successful thieves. Those who are themselves more successful may be involved as much in trading and dealing as in thieving, and their entrepreneurial activities are likely to range from the legitimate, through various 'shady' deals, to the criminal. The full-time criminal is not a full-time thief, even if he stresses this aspect of his life in constructing his own identity. Much thieving is undertaken by those who are in low-paid or semi-legitimate work or who are unemployed (see Figure 7.3).

There is considerable evidence that the growth of the drugs market in the 1980s has sharpened a distinction between the full-time criminal and the mass of ordinary thieves. The establishment of a large and extensive market in drugs has connected together the criminal networks of London, Manchester, Birmingham, Glasgow, and other large cities. This has allowed a greater degree of organization to be achieved in the project crimes that sustain drug-trafficking. Those who are involved in this organized crime, however, have highly specialized skills—for example, in relation to VAT fraud—and are very different from those who steal hi-fis and videos from domestic premises. The significance of the drug market for ordinary thieves, as we show later in this chapter, is that it offers possibilities for casual and occasional trading in small quantities of drugs that supplement their more established sources of income (Hobbs 1994: 449, 453–4).

Gender, ethnicity, class, and crime

The public perception of crime concentrates on robbery, burglary, theft, mugging, rape, and other crimes of theft and violence. The popular view sees this crime as male, working-class activity. Professional crime is seen as the work of certain adult males and as expressing conventional notions of masculinity.

Figure 7.3 Unemployment and crime

In a period of growing unemployment during the 1990s, there was much discussion about the link between unemployment and crime. What conclusions would you draw about crime from the two graphs below? Take a few minutes to think about this. Look at our discussion of unemployment measures and the crime statistics in Chapter 3, pp. 103–5, and see if you would want to change any of your conclusions. You might like to try to find figures for unemployment and recorded crime over the period 1994–2006 to see what trend is shown for that period.

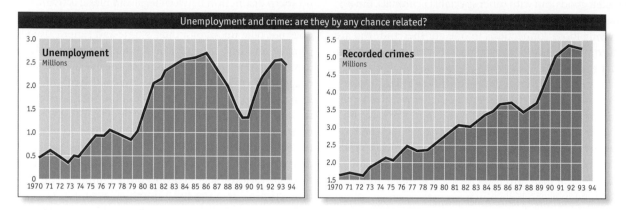

Source: *Independent on Sunday*, 4 June 1995.

This point of view does get some support from the criminal statistics, which seem to show the very small number of women who are convicted of criminal offences (see Figure 7.4); 5.9 per cent of all men in 2000 were found guilty or were cautioned for a notifiable offence, compared with 1.2 per cent of women. It also appears that the kinds of crimes committed by women are less 'serious' than those committed by men. Figures for all parts of Britain show that women have very little involvement as offenders in domestic or commercial theft, vehicle theft, or street violence, though they are often, of course, involved in these as victims. They are, however, more heavily involved in shoplifting than are men, prostitution is an almost exclusively female crime, and only women can be convicted of infanticide. There is some evidence, however, that the number and types of crime committed by women may have altered since the 1960s (Heidensohn 1985).

In a similar way to the crimes of women, many middle-class crimes are not generally regarded as 'real' crimes. While there is a great public fear of street violence and domestic burglary, there is relatively little concern about fraudulent business practices, violations of safety legislation, or tax evasion. While such offences, arguably, have much greater impact on people's lives than does the relatively small risk of theft or violence, they are either invisible to public opinion or are not seen as proper 'crimes'.

In this section we will assess the adequacy of these views of crime, exploring aspects of the crimes of women, ethnic minorities, and the affluent.

Distribution by gender, ethnicity, and class

The kinds of crimes that are committed by women, like those committed by men, reflect the gender-defined social roles that are available to them. Both men and women are

Figure 7.4 Indictable offences by gender, England and Wales, 2003 (thousands)

Offence	Males	Females
Theft and handling stolen goods	124.3	49.3
Drug offences	86.2	10.6
Burglary	29.3	2.0
Violence against the person	55.7	11.1
Criminal damage	13.2	1.8
Sexual offences	5.6	0.1
Robbery	6.8	0.9
Other indictable offences	72.1	15.4
Total	393.2	91.2

Source: *Social Trends* (2005: fig. 9.12).

involved in shoplifting, for example, but women are more likely to steal clothes, food, or low-value items. Men are more likely to steal books, electrical goods, or high-value items. This reflects the conventional domestic expectations that tie women to shopping for basic household goods in supermarkets, while men are able to shop for luxuries and extras. Put simply, both men and women tend to steal the same kinds of items that they buy (Smart 1977: 9–10). Similarly, men (especially young men) are heavily involved in vehicle crimes, including car theft, while women are heavily involved in prostitution. This involvement in prostitution can be seen as an extension of a normal feminine role that allows implicit or explicit bargaining over sex.

This connection between crime and conventional gender-roles is particularly clear in the patterns of involvement that women have in offences related to children. Those who are most responsible for childcare are, other things being equal, more likely to be involved in cruelty to children, abandoning children, kidnapping, procuring illegal abortions, and social-security frauds. Theft by women generally involves theft from an employer by those involved in domestic work or shop work. Even when involved in large-scale theft, women are likely to be acting in association with male family members and to be involved as receivers of stolen goods rather than as thieves.

There are, of course, problems in estimating the actual number of offences from the official statistics (as we show in Chapter 3, pp. 102–4), but the overall pattern is clear. Because women are less likely to be arrested and convicted for certain offences—something that we look at below—the difference between male and female involvement in crime is exaggerated by the official figures. The differing patterns of offence do, however, exist. Only in the case of sexual offences is the pattern for male and female involvement more equal, the apparent predominance of women resulting from the fact that their sexual behaviour is more likely to be treated in ways that result in conviction. The sexual double standard means that the authorities normalize much male sexual delinquency, but express moral outrage at female sexual delinquency. As Smart argues:

> None of these types of offences requires particularly 'masculine' attributes. Strength and force are unnecessary and there is only a low level of skill or expertise required. The women involved have not required training in violence, weapons or tools, or in specialised tasks like safe breaking. On the contrary the skills required can be learnt in everyday experience, and socialization into a delinquent subculture or a sophisticated criminal organisation is entirely unnecessary. (Smart 1977: 15–16)

There is growing evidence that members of ethnic minorities in Britain have become more heavily involved with the legal system since the 1960s. They are now especially likely to appear as offenders and, more particularly, as victims of crime and as police suspects. Housebreakings and other household offences show little variation among the various ethnic groups, about one-third of all households being victims of such crime.

African Caribbeans, however, are almost twice as likely as whites to be the victims of personal attacks. This is, in part, a consequence of the fact that African Caribbeans live, disproportionately, in inner-city areas where such crimes are particularly likely to take place. However, their experiences also have a racially motivated character. The growing victimization of black and Asian people reflects a real growth in racial violence and racist attacks by members of the white population. While criminal acts carried out during the urban riots of the 1980s (see Chapter 13, pp. 522–5) often had a racial aspect to them, blacks and Asians are far more likely to be the targets of racial crimes than they are to commit them. There has, nevertheless,

Suspicion: Young, black, working class boys are often stopped on 'suspicion', yet young black African Carribeans are actually the most likely to be victims of crime.

© Alice Chadwick

been a growing involvement of young African Caribbeans in many kinds of street crime.

The police hold to a widely shared prejudice that African Caribbeans, in particular, are heavily involved in crime and that special efforts need to be taken to control them. Many studies have shown the racism inherent in police actions that stop black people in the street and subject them to closer scrutiny than other members of the population (Hall *et al.* 1978; Gelsthorpe 1993). African Caribbeans are more likely than whites, and members of other ethnic minorities, to be approached by the police on suspicion, to be prosecuted, and to be sentenced. This is reflected in a growing hostility of ethnic minorities towards the police, who are often seen as racists rather than as neutral defenders of law and order.

Offences carried out by men (and women) from the middle classes are generally described as **white-collar crime** (Sutherland 1949; Croal 1992). This term originally referred to crimes and civil-law infractions committed by those in non-manual employment as part of their work. It is now used a little more broadly to refer to three categories of offence:

- *Occupational crimes* of the affluent: offences committed by the relatively affluent and prosperous in the course of their legitimate business or profession. Examples are theft from an employer, financial frauds, and insider dealing in investment companies.

- *Organizational crimes*: offences committed by organizations and businesses themselves—that is, by employees acting in their official capacities on behalf of the organization. Examples are non-payment or under-payment of VAT or Corporation Tax, and infringements of health and safety legislation leading to accidents or pollution.

- Any other crimes committed by the relatively affluent that tend to be treated differently from those of the less affluent. An example is tax evasion, which is treated differently from social-security fraud (Nelken 1994: 362–3).

The concept of white-collar crime, then, is far from clear-cut. It does, however, help to highlight the class basis of much crime. The number of people involved in white-collar crimes is barely apparent from the official statistics, as many go unrecorded. Its status as hidden crime, however, is paradoxical in view of its financial significance. It was estimated that the total cost of reported fraud alone in 1985 was £2,113 million, twice the amount accounted for by reported theft, burglary, and robbery (Levi 1987; see also M. Clarke 1990). Official estimates suggest that the actual cost of all fraud in Britain in 2003 was £13,800 million.

The relatively low representation of women in recorded crime is the main reason why female criminality has been so little researched. Lombroso and Ferrero (1895) set out a deterministic theory, based on the claimed peculiarities of female biology, which still has some influence in the late 1990s. They held that women were less highly evolved than men and so were relatively 'primitive' in character. They were less involved in crime, however, because their biology predisposed them to a passive and more conservative way of life. They were, however, weak willed, and Lombroso and Ferrero saw the involvement of many women in crime as resulting from their having been led on by others. The female drift into crime was a consequence of their weak and fickle character.

The extreme position set out by Lombroso and Ferrero has long been abandoned, but many criminologists do still resort to biological assumptions when trying to explain female criminality. Pollak (1950), for example, held that women are naturally manipulative and deceitful, instigating crimes that men undertake. What such theories fail to consider is that, if women do indeed have lower rates of criminality, this may more usefully and accurately be explained in terms of the cultural influences that shape sex–gender roles and the differing opportunities available to men and to women.

Like the crimes of women, the crimes of the affluent have been little researched. Early discussions of white-collar crime were intended as criticisms of the orthodox assumption that criminality was caused by poverty or deprivation. Those who carried out thefts as part of a successful business career, Sutherland (1949) argued, could not be seen as acting out of economic necessity. Sutherland's own account stressed that white-collar crime was *learned* behaviour and that, in this respect, it was no different from other forms of criminality. All crime, he held, resulted from the effects of 'differential association' on learning: those who interact more frequently with others whose attitudes are favourable to criminal actions are themselves more likely to engage in criminal acts.

This implies that patterns of conformity among the affluent and the deprived, among men and among women, are to be understood in the context of their wider role commitments and the interactions in which they are involved with their role partners. Those who are predisposed to see criminal actions as appropriate will, if the structure of opportunities allows it, drift into crime. There is no need to assume that women are fundamentally different from men, or that the working classes are fundamentally different from the middle classes.

Women and crime

It appears, then, that women, like men, drift into criminal actions whenever the structure of opportunities is such that it seems a reasonable response to their situation. The particular situations in which they find themselves are determined by the ways in which sex–gender identities are institutionalized in their society, and so their patterns of criminality are gendered. Cultural stereotypes about men and women, as we will show, are also a major influence on the nature of the social reaction to female criminality. The absence of strong punitive responses to most forms of female crime means that the progression from primary to secondary deviation is less likely to occur. Women may drift into crime, but they only rarely pursue criminal careers.

A form of female crime that seems to be the principal exception to this rule is prostitution. In law, a prostitute is someone who sells sex, and this is almost invariably seen as a female offence. Men involved in prostitution, other than as clients, tend to be seen as engaged in acts of 'indecency' rather than of 'soliciting' for prostitution. Under British law, a woman who has been arrested and convicted for soliciting is officially termed a 'common prostitute' and is liable to re-arrest simply for loitering in a public place. As most prostitution is arranged in public, on the streets, it is difficult for women so labelled to avoid the occasional spell in custody. They may also find it difficult to live a normal life off the streets:

> It is virtually impossible for them to live with a man or even another woman as it is immediately assumed that such people are living off immoral earnings, thereby making themselves vulnerable to a criminal charge. Also, the legal definition of a brothel, as a dwelling containing two or more prostitutes, has made it difficult for two women to live together even where only one is a prostitute. (Smart 1977: 114)

In 2006 the government in Britain announced its intention to change the law to allow up to three prostitutes to work together without their place of work being defined as a brothel.

> ⮌ *Connections*
> You might like to consider street prostitution in relation to our discussion of the gendering of space in Chapter 13, pp. 506 and 514–15. A good discussion can be found in McKeganey and Barnard (1996). While you are looking at the gendering of space in the city, you might also think about the way in which urban space is used by various ethnic groups (see p. 517 in the same chapter).

The reaction of the police is critical in determining whether a woman who breaks the law is defined as a criminal. Police work is structured around the cop culture (Reiner 1992), a culture that strongly emphasizes masculinity and that underpins the harassment and abuse of female police officers and the derogation of many female offenders.

Prostitutes, for example, are seen as flouting the domesticity of the conventional female role and have been subject to harassment and entrapment. Nevertheless, prostitutes are often able to establish a mutual accommodation with the police, an arrangement in which each can get on with their job with the minimum of interference from the other. When there is pressure on the police to take action, however, such arrangements break down. In these circumstances, prostitutes are highly vulnerable and can be quite susceptible to police persuasion and suggestion. On the other hand, women who conform to conventional role expectations are seen as in need of protection, and cautioning is more widely used for female offenders than it is for males (S. Edwards 1984: 16–19).

There is some evidence that this differential treatment of male and female offenders also occurs in the courts. Sexist assumptions in court practices have led some to suggest that women experience greater leniency than men (Mannheim 1940: 343). Others, however, have suggested that greater harshness is more likely (A. Campbell 1981). Heidensohn (1985) correctly points out that this may simply reflect the well-known lack of consistency in sentencing, though she reports evidence that supports the view that women are treated more harshly (Farrington and Morris 1983).

Indeed, Edwards (1984) has suggested that women are subjected to much closer scrutiny in courts precisely because the female offender is seen as unusual or unnatural. Women are on trial not only for their offence but for their deviation from conventional femininity. Their punishment or treatment is intended to ensure that they adjust themselves back to what is seen as a natural feminine role.

Very few convicted women are given custodial sentences. Men are two or three times more likely to be imprisoned for an offence than are women, and their sentences tend to be longer. The women who are imprisoned are mainly those who have been convicted of such things as theft, fraud, forgery, or violence. Prisons do make some attempt to recognize that women's domestic commitments are different from those of men, and a number of mother-and-baby units have been set up. Some well-publicized cases have been reported, however, of pregnant prison inmates who have been forced to give birth while manacled to a prison officer. Studies of female prisons in the United States have shown how these prisons are important sources of emotional and practical support for their inmates (Giallombardo 1966), often involving the establishment of lesbian family relationships. This appears to be less marked in Britain.

Crimes of the affluent

The crimes of the affluent, the prosperous, and the powerful can be explained in terms of the same motives as any other criminal act. They differ from 'ordinary' theft and burglary only in terms of their social organization and the social reaction to them. The character and motivation of those involved are no more, and no less, pathological than those of any others who drift into crime. White-collar crimes, however, are much less likely to result in full-time criminal careers. The nature of the social reaction makes the development into secondary deviation much less likely.

Much corporate and occupational crime takes place in the financial services industry, where changing patterns of regulation have created greater opportunities for illicit activities. The British financial system was, for much of the nineteenth and twentieth centuries, regulated in a highly informal way. Recruitment to banks, insurance companies, and other financial enterprises took place through an old-boy network centred on the public schools and the Oxford and Cambridge colleges. The Stock Exchange, as the central institution in the financial system, was at the heart of this system of informal regulation. The system rested on trust and loyalty: those who had been to school together and shared a similar social background felt that they could trust one another in their business dealings. The motto of the Stock Exchange was 'My word is my bond', and many deals were sealed on the shake of hands rather than with a written contract (Lisle-Williams 1984; M. Clarke 1986).

> **⊃ Connections**
> Recruitment to the boards of the financial enterprises that make up the City of London financial system is one aspect of the recruitment to elites and top positions in British society. You might like to look at our discussion of elites and the ruling class in Chapter 20, pp. 832–4, where we look in more detail at the part played by schooling and informal social networks.

During the 1970s the government introduced a number of changes to this system of regulation in response to the growing internationalization of the money markets. This culminated in the so-called Big Bang of October 1986, when the Stock Exchange was finally opened up to foreign competition. New codes of practice were introduced to reflect the more diverse social backgrounds of those involved in the buying and selling of currency, shares, and commodities. The old system of trust could no longer be

Is white-collar crime really victimless crime?
© Alice Chadwick

Briefing: banking crimes

The financial centres of the world economy offer great opportunities for people to make money from illegal financial activity.

During the 1990s, Baring's Bank experienced massive losses and was forced into bankruptcy when one of its employees, Nick Leeson, defrauded the Singapore branch of the bank to the sum of £830 million. Leeson was sentenced to six years in prison, but his story attracted so much attention that he was able to negotiate a book and film deal (for *Rogue Trader*) valued at more than £3 million. Early in 2002, Allied Irish Bank suspended one of its New York traders, John Rusnack, following the discovery of losses of £485 million. It was suspected that a number of currency traders had cooperated in a long-term fraud.

The big growth area for financial fraud in recent years has been online fraud, involving fraudulent access to bank accounts and credit cards, and often involving 'identity fraud'. E-mail scams and illegal card readers have enabled people to make withdrawals from bank accounts and purchase goods without the permission or knowledge of the account holder. It is estimated that bank and credit card fraud now amounts to £505 million a year. In an attempt to reduce the amount of credit card fraud, banks have introduced new 'chip and pin' cards that are claimed to be more secure. It has been suggested, however, that this has helped to increase the amount of Internet-based credit card fraud. While card fraud losses fell by 13 per cent in the first half of 2005, online card fraud has increased by 29 per cent over the same period.

Sources: Guardian, 21 February 2002; *Guardian*, 8 March 2005 and 8 November 2005; **http://news.bbc.co.uk/1/hi/business/3707290.stm**

 Carry out some searches in local and national newspapers to discover evidence on the penalties attached to different kinds of crime. (Don't forget to check the business pages as well as the general news pages.) Can you find any association between the size of any financial loss and the severity of the penalty? Which kinds of serious offence receive the lowest penalties, and which receive the highest?

relied on, and more formal mechanisms were required. The Bank of England was given greater powers of control and supervision, and in 1997 the Labour government created a new Securities and Investment Board to regulate the whole system.

The offences with which the new system of regulation has had to deal are those that have been made possible by the changing structure of the financial system. The investment management firm of Barlow Clowes, for example, set up new offshore investment funds to provide high returns to its wealthy clients who wanted to minimize their tax bills. The head of the company was found to have financed an extravagant lifestyle at the expense of the investors in the funds (M. Clarke 1990: 167–70). The growth of domestic takeover business made possible massive fraud by some directors and managers associated with Guinness and its financial advisers in 1986. These directors and managers manipulated share dealings to keep up the price of Guinness shares on the stock market and to help its takeover of another company. Their actions were the subject of an official inquiry and, later, a criminal trial that resulted in some of them being imprisoned.

Much white-collar crime is low in visibility. It tends to occur in the context of normal business routines, and it is less likely to be noticed, even by its victims. Fiddling business expenses, for example, is almost undetectable, and many employers treat it as a source of tax-free perks for their employees (Mars 1982). Large-scale fraud, when discovered, is more likely to result in an official reaction, though it will often be hushed up if it might suggest a failure of supervision or control by senior managers.

Crimes of the affluent are far more likely to be regulated by specialized enforcement agencies than by the police, and this has important consequences for the nature of the social reaction. These agencies—the Health and Safety Executive, the Factory Inspectorate, the Inland Revenue, and so on—generally have a remit to maintain and promote high standards of business and trading, and the enforcement of the criminal law is only one part of this remit (Croal 1992: chapter 5). Their officials, therefore, develop 'compliance strategies' that stress persuasion and administrative sanctions aimed at crime prevention, rather than the detection and punishment of offences. The level of prosecutions is, therefore, very low. Few cases go to court, and very few result in imprisonment. In these ways, the transition to secondary deviation is avoided.

◇ *Stop and reflect*

In this section we have looked at professional and career crimes and at the relationships between gender, class, and crime. We started out by showing that not all deviation from legal norms is criminal activity. Criminal actions involve deviation from the criminal law. In considering theft and career crime, we showed that:

- Theft has undergone a series of transformations as the wider society has changed.
- Much theft has been organized in relation to an extensive underworld, a subculture of crime that supports and sustains criminal activities.
- Is there still a criminal underworld in the major cities today?
- Career thieves adopt an identity as professional thieves, though their involvement in theft is quite variable.
- Much burglary is combined with low-paid, semi-legal, and casual work, or is carried out by those who are unemployed.

We explored the popular viewpoint that crime is a male, working-class phenomenon. Looking at gender, ethnicity, class, and crime, we showed that:

- Patterns of male and female crime differ, and they reflect differences in conventional sex–gender roles. Female criminality, for example, reflects cultural conceptions of femininity and the structure of opportunities open to women.
- There are significant variations in the attitudes of police and the courts to men and to women.
- Why does so much popular discussion explain female criminality in terms of female biology?
- African Caribbeans are twice as likely as whites to experience personal attacks. Many of these crimes are racially motivated.
- Members of ethnic minorities are more likely than whites to be stopped by the police and prosecuted in court.
- White-collar crime includes a diverse range of crimes of the affluent. Its economic impact is far more extensive than is often assumed.
- Trends in white-collar crime are related to changes in the structure of the financial system and the wider economy.
- Why are crimes of the affluent more likely to be normalized or to be regulated by bodies other than the police and the criminal courts?

Drugs and drug abuse

The use of drugs is now one of the most widely discussed forms of deviance. In its most general meaning, a drug is any chemical that can have an effect on the human body and, perhaps, a physical effect on the mind. Some drugs occur quite naturally in many widely used drinks and foods. Caffeine, for example, is found in both coffee and tea, alcohol is the basis of beer, wine, and spirits, and vitamins are found in fresh fruit and vegetables. Many drugs are used as medicines, usually under the control of doctors. Morphine, penicillin, and steroids, for example, are used very widely and under a variety of commercial trade names in hospitals, clinics, and surgeries. Many other medical drugs are freely available for purchase without prescription: aspirin, codeine, ibuprofen, and numerous other analgesic (pain-killing) drugs can be bought in any high-street pharmacy and in many supermarkets.

This broad, dictionary definition of 'drugs', however, is not what newspaper columnists, politicians, and social commentators mean when they use the word. These people generally use the word in a much narrower sense to refer to the non-medical use of drugs. This is the deliberate use of chemical substances to achieve particular physiological changes, simply for the pleasure or the other non-medical effects that they produce. It is in this sense, for example, that many parents and teachers rail against the use of drugs by children and young people. The non-medical use of drugs in the twentieth century has, indeed, been largely an activity of the young. Drug use, then, is seen as a deviant activity, as non-medical drug *abuse*. It becomes, therefore, a matter for social control. For this reason, the non-medical use or possession of many drugs has been made illegal.

There is a great deal of ambiguity over how widely this meaning of the word 'drug' is to be taken, and whether all non-medical drug use is to be regarded as a deviant activity. Many freely available products have the same characteristics as illicit drugs. Tobacco, for example, can be freely bought in shops and it is a major source of tax revenue for the government. At the same time, however, it contains nicotine, an addictive stimulant to the nervous

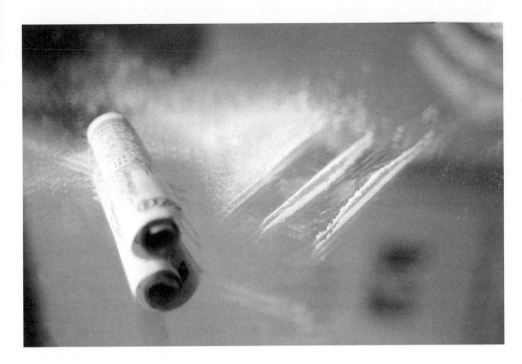

Cocaine is a widely
used illegal
substance.
© Alice Chadwick

system that is a major health hazard both to those who smoke and to those around them. Similarly, alcoholic drinks, which can have serious physiological and psychological effects if taken in large quantities, are an accepted and even encouraged part of a normal social life for most people. Like tobacco, alcohol is available in shops and supermarkets, it is a multi-million pound industry, in which many people find legitimate employment, and—unlike cigarettes—it can be advertised freely on television.

Some chemicals with domestic or industrial uses, but which can also be used to produce 'high' feelings, can be purchased quite legitimately and with even fewer restrictions. Recent research has suggested that chocolate may operate in the same way as heroin, nicotine, and cannabis, by its effect on the limbic system in the brain. Eating chocolate can produce a 'rush' or high feeling because it affects the brain in the same way as the active ingredient in cannabis. Glues and solvents, which are used as stimulants and hallucinogenics (mood-changers) by many young people, can be purchased in hardware and do-it-yourself shops. The use of heroin (a morphine derivative), cocaine, or Ecstasy (MDMA), on the other hand, is widely disapproved of and their use is surrounded by numerous legal restrictions over their acquisition and sale. Many such drugs are the objects of advertising campaigns that are aimed at discouraging their use by encouraging people to 'say no' if offered them. They can usually be obtained only from illegal sources. Medical trials have been set up in Britain, however, to investigate the part that might be played by cannabis, on prescription, in the treatment of multiple sclerosis and as a pain-killer. Morphine has long been available in pharmacies in Codeine and similar analgesic tablets, and both cocaine and morphine could be bought over the counter in British high streets until 1916. In 2002 it was announced that heroin would be made available to addicts on prescription.

The different social reaction to alcohol, chocolate, glue, and heroin cannot be explained simply in terms of the medical dangers involved in using any specific stimulant. If the potential danger was the principal determinant of the social reaction, alcohol and tobacco would have been criminalized many years ago.

Learning drug use

The idea of **addiction** to drugs is central to discussions of their non-medical uses. Addiction is seen as occurring where people have become physiologically dependent on the use of a particular drug and suffer serious and persistent withdrawal symptoms when its use is stopped. However, dependence is as much a psychological as a physiological fact and, as such, it is shaped by social factors. People must learn how to use particular drugs, and they become committed to their use only through complex social processes from which physiological dependence cannot be isolated. 'Addiction' is a medically constructed label and a social role that combines elements of the sick role and, in some cases, the criminal role.

➔ *Connections*
We look at the idea of the sick role in Chapter 8, pp. 295–7.
You may want to read our discussion now.

Drugs do, of course, have specific physiological effects: alcohol and barbiturates depress mental activity, cocaine and caffeine stimulate it, and LSD distorts experiences and perception. Their full effects, however, depend upon the social context in which they are used. Individuals who use drugs learn from one another not only the techniques that are necessary for their use, but also how to shape and to experience the kinds of effects that they produce. The non-medical use of drugs, then, is a deviant activity that, like all forms of deviance, is surrounded by normative frameworks that structure the lives of users and lead them to experience particular deviant careers and associated moral careers. 'Drug addiction' is a deviant identity that reflects a specific deviant career.

Becoming a cannabis user

In an influential study of deviant activity, Becker (1953) documented the career stages that are involved in becoming a marijuana (cannabis) user. He showed that people drift into cannabis use for a variety of reasons. Once they begin its use, however, they will—if they persist—follow a particular sequence of stages. Becker called these stages the 'beginner', the 'occasional user', and the 'regular user'. As users follow this career sequence, cannabis-smoking becomes an ever more important part of their identity. Becker shows, however, that cannabis use rarely involves full-blown secondary deviation, despite the fact that its use is illegal. Cannabis use is a low-visibility activity that rarely comes to the attention of those who might publicly stigmatize users, and so these users are less likely to progress to secondary deviation.

Becker's research was undertaken in the early 1950s, and public attitudes have altered somewhat since then. There was an increase in cannabis use in both the United States and in Britain during the 1960s. It has, since then, become accepted or tolerated in many situations. In California in 1996, for example, legal restrictions were relaxed in order to allow for its medical use in the treatment of certain cancer patients. Indeed, it has been suggested that cannabis use has become normalized for many people. Research shows that about a quarter of 16–24 year olds in Britain in 2000 had tried cannabis during the previous year. Most of these users regard their use in the same way that most adults regard alcohol and tobacco use.

In 2004, legislation came into effect in Britain that partly decriminalizes the possession of cannabis by altering its classification to that of a 'Class C' drug (the same legal status as anabolic steroids and growth hormone). This meant that possession of cannabis will no longer result in automatic prosecution but could be dealt with through an official warning. It was anticipated that the police would, in most situations, pay little attention to those who merely possess cannabis for their own use (www.urban75.com/Drugs/cannabis.html).

When Becker undertook his research, cannabis use was both illegal and surrounded by social meanings that associated it with irresponsibility, immorality, and addiction. Becker showed that, while the drug is not physically addictive, its image and its illegality led to specific patterns in its use. Unlike cigarettes, cannabis cannot be bought at the local newsagent or the supermarket—though it can be obtained in this way in the Netherlands. Most people, therefore, had neither the opportunity nor the inclination to smoke it. Those who were most likely to begin to use the drug, Becker argued, were those who were involved in social groups where there was already a degree of cannabis use. It was here that there were likely to be opportunities for new users.

Becker saw the typical locales for exploratory drug use as organized around values and activities that oppose or run counter to the mainstream values of the larger society. When he undertook his research, these had their focus in social groups around jazz and popular music, students, and 'bohemians'. These groups tended to have a more critical and oppositional stance towards conventional social standards. Participants were likely to see many other people using the drug, and their own first use was likely to become a real possibility if an opportunity presented itself. Today, when marijuana use has become more generalized among young people, exposure to its use in peer groups is likely to be the initial introduction for many young people. Someone enters the *beginner* stage in the use of cannabis when he or she is offered the opportunity to smoke it in a social situation where others are smoking, where there is a degree of social pressure to conform to group norms, and where the group itself provides a relatively safe and secluded locale away from the immediate possibility of public censure.

Becker shows that people who move from the stage of the beginner to that of the *occasional user* must learn a number of skills and abilities associated with the use of the drug. Someone willing to use the drug may know that it causes a 'high' feeling, but they are unlikely to know exactly how to produce this. The principal skill that must be learned, then, is the actual technique for smoking cannabis. This is different from that used in tobacco smoking. Only if the smoke is inhaled in the correct way, with an appropriate amount of air, can cannabis have any significant effect on a person's body and mind. Group membership is essential for the easy learning of this skill, as the new user is surrounded by those who can demonstrate it in their

THEORY AND METHODS

. . . .

Howard Becker

Howard Becker was born in 1928 and was trained at the University of Chicago. His work draws heavily on symbolic interactionism, but he places this in the larger context of the power struggles among social groups. His early work on drug use was followed by work on student doctors (Becker *et al.* 1961), education (Becker *et al.* 1968), and artistic production (Becker 1982). He has also published a number of important methodological essays (Becker 1970). His work on drug use was republished in the early 1960s (Becker 1963), when it made a major contribution to the labelling theory of deviance.

own smoking. Those who fail to learn the proper technique will never experience the physical effects of cannabis and so are unlikely to persist in using the drug.

A user must also acquire the ability to perceive the effects of the drug and, therefore, must learn what it is to be high or stoned. This is not as strange as it may seem. Users may have experiences that they fail to recognize as effects of the drug, but that others recognize as central features of their high state. Through interaction with others, new users begin to learn what signs and symptoms to look out for and what, therefore, can be taken as indicating that they have successfully learned the smoking technique. Last, but not least, they must learn to enjoy the effects of cannabis. They must learn to treat dizziness, tingling, and distortions of time and space as pleasurable experiences, rather than as unpleasant and undesirable disturbances to their normal physical and mental state. Only those who successfully acquire these skills and abilities—the smoking technique, the ability to perceive the effects, and enjoyment of the effects—will persist as cannabis users.

As occasional users, cannabis smokers acquire further justifications and rationalizations for its use, and these reinforce their continued use of the drug. The subculture of the group provides ready-made answers to many of the conventional objections to cannabis use that may be raised in their minds. Users may claim, for example, that cannabis is less dangerous than the alcohol that is tolerated and encouraged by conventional opinion. They are also likely to hold that cannabis smokers are in complete control of when and where they choose to use the drug; that the drug is not in control of them.

The regular user of cannabis can neutralize any conventional or official labels that may be applied to them by non-users. People who lack the support of other users are less likely to become regular users if they accept the stereotype of addiction or the idea that they are likely to escalate towards the use of hard drugs. If ideas of addiction, escalation, and mental weakness cannot be neutralized, smokers may revert to occasional use, rather than becoming committed, regular users.

To protect themselves from stigmatization, regular users try to learn how to control the effects of the drug, inhibiting its effects at will, so that they are able to pass as normal in front of non-users or the police. They must, nevertheless, run certain risks of detection, as regular use requires access to illegal dealers whose criminal activities may bring the user to the attention of the police. In order to minimize their chances of discovery as users, they are likely to spend more and more of their time in the company of their own, the other regular users who can provide a supportive and relatively safe environment in which to smoke.

Patterns of drug use

People learn how to use drugs in particular social contexts. Becker's work explored cannabis use in the specific context of post-war America, though his conclusions have a much wider application. In this section we will look at the changing context of drug use in Britain. We look first at an account of deviant drug use in the 1970s, and then we turn to the contemporary, normalized use of drugs by young people.

Deviant drug use

Although it was developed in the 1950s, Becker's argument retains much of its relevance for contemporary patterns of cannabis use, and it has much to say about the use of other drugs. This was first confirmed in a study undertaken by Jock Young (1971) in London. Young's primary concern, however, is the origins of the negative social reaction to cannabis use. Why is it, he asks, that there is no similar social reaction to the use of tobacco? He holds that the reason is to be found not in the drug, but in the motivation that people are seen as having for using it. Drugs that are seen as being used to aid productivity are likely to be tolerated, while those that have a purely hedonistic (pleasure-seeking) purpose are seen as 'drug abuse'.

European and North American societies tolerate or even encourage the drinking of coffee and tea, and the smoking of tobacco when working under pressure or as a 'release' from the pressure of a heavy work schedule. The worker 'earns' the right to 'relax with a smoke and a drink' after work, and people may be allowed to smoke at work if it 'helps them to concentrate'. Alcohol is widely used, and it is tolerated as a way in which people may, periodically, ease the transition from work to leisure. It is culturally normalized. It is only when alcohol is used to excess and interferes with normal, everyday activities that its use is defined as deviant. No such tolerance is allowed for the user of cannabis, which is not seen as linked in any way to work productivity. Young also points out that there can be cultural variations in response to the same drug. Andean peasants use cocaine (in the form of coca leaves) as an aid to work, and it is a normalized feature of their society. In Britain and the United States, however, cocaine is regarded very differently.

Young has shown that these variations in response to drugs can be explained in terms of the relationship between a dominant set of social values and a secondary *subterranean* set of values (Matza 1964). The dominant values of contemporary societies stress work and everyday routines, but they coexist with other values that stress the need for excitement, leisure, and pleasure. These hedonistic, or pleasure-oriented, values are subterranean because they concern experiences that can be pursued only when the demands of employment and family life have been met. It is through their work—paid employment and unpaid work in the household—that people acquire the 'right' to freely enjoy their leisure activities and to pursue the subterranean values. Young sees this as involving a socialized conflict between the desire for pleasure and the repression of this desire as people engage in their everyday activities (Marcuse 1956). Through their socialization, he argues, adults acquire a feeling of guilt about any expression of these hedonistic values that has not been earned through hard work. Subterranean values can be exercised only with restraint and only so long as they do not undermine the normal everyday realities of work and family life.

The drugs that have come to be seen as problematic in contemporary societies are those that are used to induce an escape from everyday realities into an alternative world where hedonistic values alone prevail. They are seen to be associated with subcultures that disdain the work ethic and enjoy pleasures that have not been earned through work: 'It is drug use of this kind that is most actively repressed by the forces of social order. For it is not drugtaking *per se* but the culture of drugtakers which is reacted against: not the notion of changing consciousness but the type of consciousness that is socially generated' (J. Young 1971: 137). In contemporary societies, Young argues, this kind of drug use is to be found in the inner-city subcultures and many youth subcultures.

Young found an overwhelming emphasis on drug use in the 'Bohemian youth culture' of the hippies of the 1960s. The use of mind-altering drugs was raised to a paramount position as one of the fundamental organizing principles for the identities of its members. This subculture—primarily a subculture of middle-class, student youth—was organized around spontaneity and expressivity and a rejection of work. It was in hippie culture that the main structural supports for cannabis use were found, and in the late 1960s Young documented its increasing emphasis also on the strong hallucinogenic drug LSD. What he called the delinquent youth culture, on the other hand, was more characteristic of some working-class areas. Young saw this as generating an ambivalent attitude towards drug use. While the delinquent subculture was organized around its strong emphasis on subterranean values, drug use was merely tolerated or allowed—it was not required.

Normalized drug use

Young's work was undertaken in a period of full employment and relative affluence. The period since he wrote has seen the emergence of mass unemployment and economic insecurity, exacerbated by a global recession. Despite some improvement, employment remains insecure or uncertain for many young people. Illegal drug use today is not so much focused on hippie youth who reject the work ethic. It is now more strongly emphasized by the inner-city unemployed who have little experience of or prospect for secure and regular paid employment. Some glimpses of this were apparent in Young's references to the subculture of inner-city black Americans, as it had developed from the 1920s. He saw this as strongly supportive of cannabis use and as a principal source of heroin use. Their poverty and inferior status forced them into a rejection of conventional values and an embrace of subterranean values (Finestone 1964). Indeed, this was one of the principal contexts of drug use studied by Becker. This group has recently been identified as the core of a so-called underclass—an idea that we examine in Chapters 18 and 19.

In the 1970s, 'conformist youth culture' could still be seen as fully embracing conventional culture and its conditional commitment to hedonistic values. Its members were committed to work and to family, and their leisure-time activities posed no challenge to the dominance of the conventional values. Young saw this culture as having little significance for deviant drug-taking, holding that conformist youth simply made illicit use of alcohol (which they were not supposed to buy until aged 18) for the same purposes as their parents. It is clear today, however, that cannabis use has become common within this culture since the 1980s and that there was a growth in the use of Ecstasy in the 1990s. Declining employment opportunities in a period of recession broke the link between conventional work values and hedonistic values for many young people. Where there was little or no employment, the question of 'earning' pleasure simply did not arise.

As a result, drug use has increased among all sections of youth. Almost half (47 per cent) of 16 year olds in Manchester in 1992 were reported to have used an illegal drug, generally cannabis, and just under three-quarters (71 per cent) had been in situations where drugs were available and on offer. In a national survey of 15–16 year olds in 1996, 42 per cent had used an illegal drug (Parker and Measham 1994). The British Crime Survey for 2000 found that a quarter of those aged 16–19 and over a quarter of those aged 20–24 had used cannabis during the previous twelve months. A survey in 2004 of 16–24 year olds found that 39 per cent reported that they had used illegal drugs. Cannabis was the most commonly used drug, with 30 per cent of the young adults having used it. Use of Ecstasy, cocaine, or amphetamines was much lower, at about 4–7 per cent of 16–24 year olds (*Social Trends* 2005: table 7.11). Heroin use, however, has been increasing in Britain, and the average age at which heroin users had first begun to experiment with the drug is 15. Three-quarters of the young people in inner-city areas are reported to have tried crack cocaine (a mixture of cocaine and baking soda). Class and gender show little association with drug availability and take-up, but ethnicity does. Black youths are rather more likely to come into contact with drugs than are white youths, as suggested in an earlier study by Pryce (1986), and Asians are far less likely to do so: only 32 per cent of young Asians in Manchester in 1992 reported having been offered drugs.

The ease of access to drugs such as cannabis—44 per cent of boys and 38 per cent of girls in 1996 had used it—shows that Becker's view of the importance of subcultures to occasional users must now be qualified. Changes in the urban and class conditions that sustained 'delinquent' subcultures in the past, combined with a more commercialized structure of illegal drug-trading, have resulted in a wider availability of drugs.

Drug use is now an integral, normalized part of a generalized youth culture, and not of specific class-based or deviant subcultures. Even the police are tolerant towards its use and generally caution those cannabis users who come their way. Along with music, clothes, magazines, and a love of fast cars, drugs and alcohol are a part of the everyday, pleasure-seeking experience of virtually all young people. The counter-cultural Bohemian and hippie orientations that Young identified in the 1960s are no longer an important part of this youth subculture, which is now a consumerist and leisure-oriented subculture organized around the pursuit of pleasure that is disconnected from the requirement to 'earn' it through productive work.

Despite its high profile in the news media, Ecstasy (MDMA) is far less widely used than cannabis. In a national survey in 1996, 9 per cent of boys and 7 per cent of girls reported having taken Ecstasy. Amphetamines (such as speed and whizz), LSD ('acid'), and solvents are all more widely used than Ecstasy: 20 per cent of boys and 21 per cent of girls had used solvents. Ecstasy, amphetamines, and LSD were all associated with regular involvement in dance clubs and raves, but in these venues, cannabis remains the most widely used illegal drug. Indeed, alcohol —consumed under age—was even more widespread: 94 per cent of 15–16 year olds in a national survey reported that they had consumed alcohol, generally on a regular basis. Over one-third were tobacco smokers, the rate of use and the rate of growth in use being higher among girls than among boys (Ettorre 1992; Oakley *et al*. 1992). These findings support the claim that there is now a 'poly-drug' culture in which users are not confined to the use of any one drug. Cannabis remains the drug of preference, but it is taken alongside other drugs (see Figure 7.5).

Figure 7.5 Drug use, England and Wales 2003–4

	Class	Estimated no. of users	Users (% of population)	Average price	Deaths (2003)
Cocaine	A	755,000	2.4	£40 per gram	113
Crack	A	55,000*	0.2	£15–25 per rock	Not distinguishable from cocaine
Ecstasy	A	614,000	2.0	£2–7 per pill	33
Heroin	A	43,000*	0.1	£40–90 per gram	591
LSD	A	76,000	0.2	£1–5 per tab	–
Magic mushrooms	A	260,000	0.8	–	–
Amphetamines	A/B	483,000	1.5	£8–15 per gram	33
Cannabis	C	3,364,000	10.8	£40–140 per ounce, depending on type and quality	11
All Class A		1,091,000	3.5		
Any drug		3,854,000	12.3		2,445

Sources: http://news.bbc.co.uk/1/shared/spl/hi/in_depth/drugs_uk/drugs_grid/html/default.stm, drawing on British Crime Survey 2003–4; Drugscope survey 2005. Death figures show the total number of deaths in which the specified drug was noted on a death certificate. The figures for any drug include anti-depressants and painkillers. Comparable Scottish figures can be found in Scottish Crime Survey 2003.

Not all drugs used by young people are normalized features of the conformist youth culture. Heroin use, for example, is found among less than 2 per cent of young people, and these generally have little involvement in consumerism and conventional family life. Indeed, 'conformist' drug users tend to regard heroin as a drug that would undermine their lifestyle. It is something to be avoided in favour of the more 'pleasure-oriented' drugs (M. Collison 1994). Auld *et al.* (1986) show that there is a characteristic *episodic user* of heroin: neither the occasional nor the regular user, but someone who has periods of sustained heroin use, followed by periods 'coming off' (see also Dorn and South 1987).

Retreatism and withdrawal from what is perceived as a hostile world are principal motives for those who

have experienced a lifetime of emotional and physical abuse in broken families and poor districts (Ruggiero and South 1995: 116 ff). Such users find it difficult to band together for mutual support in the deprived city areas where the homeless congregate, and their lifestyle forces them into close association with a vast criminal underworld of dealers and organized crime (Dorn *et al.* 1992). In these circumstances, heroin users are very likely to make the transition from primary to secondary deviation.

In the inner-city areas, the growth of an informal economy has been associated with the expansion of an extensive fringe of irregular activities—street-level thieving, dealing and exchange of stolen and illicit goods of all kinds (Auld *et al.* 1986). The unemployed residents of these areas seek to make more than the bare public assistance

Global focus Drug-trading

There has been a huge growth in the production and distribution of illegal drugs, and these activities have become entangled in other forms of crime, as well as in conforming and law-abiding behaviour such as money dealing, commodity trading, and political activity. The raw materials required for producing many drugs come from countries that are geographically distinct from their main users, and there has been a growing globalization of the drug trade.

Drug crops are fundamental to the agriculture of many of the world's poorest countries. Coca leaves for the production of cocaine are produced in Bolivia and Columbia, opium poppies for the production of heroin are grown in Nepal and Afghanistan, and marijuana is a cash crop in Jamaica. The consumption of these drugs, however, is concentrated in the advanced economies of Europe and the United States, and these crops are attractive to Third World farmers because of the secure and growing market available in those countries.

Local drug dealers, who buy the crops from the producers, are often involved in other, legitimate, businesses and have strong financial and political connections to the local leaders. These countries allow the dealers to sell the drugs onwards and to launder the proceeds through their other business activities. A case in London in 2002 showed that proceeds from cocaine sales were processed through corrupt *bureaux de change* and through electronic money transfers involving banks in Britain, the Isle of Man, the United States, and Colombia (*Guardian*, 18 June 2002). There are sometimes global networks of gangs and dealers, as is reported to be the case with the Chinese triads that dominated the nineteenth-century opium trade, but these networks are generally very loose. Despite the claims of the US Food and Drug Administration Agency, there is no international cartel behind

the Colombian cocaine trade, but there is an extensive and well-connected network of entrepreneurs, brokers, and minor dealers.

Large sums can be made by those in the major European and American centres who buy Third World drugs in bulk. The British Customs and Excise ran its largest ever drugs investigation, Operation Stealer, in 1997, arresting forty-four people and seizing £65 million worth of drugs from an operation that involved dealers in three continents. Those who run the biggest risks, however, are the small-scale smugglers and street dealers who handle relatively small quantities of drugs. In the same month as Operation Stealer, a young woman in Colchester was found guilty for having nineteen small packets of heroin, some heroin stuffed in a teddy bear, and some cannabis inside her bra. She was sent to jail for three years (*Guardian*, 1 July 1997; *Essex County Standard*, 18 July 1997).

Opium production was a major element in the Afghanistan conflicts. When the Taliban leadership came to power they allowed the farming and sale of opium, but they outlawed it in 2000. As the Taliban had earned a considerable amount of money from heroin, it was suspected that this was a ploy to reduce supply and increase the price for the opium stockpiled in previous years. The ending of the Taliban regime in the Afghan war meant that many farmers began to plant poppies again, and output of heroin increased. The new government offered Afghan farmers $500 per acre to destroy their fields, but drug traffickers made a counter offer of $6,400 per acre to grow opium poppies. A United Nations investigation estimated that by 2005, half a million people in Afghanistan were involved in the trafficking chain, and that the crop had an estimated annual value of $25 billion (**www.washtimes.com/national/20030811-100220-8928r.htm**).

level of income through involvement in these activities. Cannabis has, since the 1960s, become more closely tied to professional drug-dealing and, along with hard drugs such as heroin and cocaine, is traded on the streets. It has been estimated that, by 1997, the number of drug deals in London alone had reached an annual total of 30 million, with a total value of £600 million. Only around one in 4,000 street deals results in an arrest.

Through their involvement in this irregular economy, the unemployed can easily become involved in drug-dealing, and the opportunities for use are great. Small-scale users and others become drawn into large networks of organized drug crime. There is a hierarchical division of labour in the supply of drugs, and the largest rewards tend to go to those who are furthest removed from street-level dealing.

◈ *Stop and reflect*

In this section we have looked at how people learn to obtain and to use drugs for pleasure, and we traced the growing normalization of certain types of drug use.

- Is it possible to distinguish between the medical and the non-medical uses of drugs?

- People drift into drug use for a whole variety of reasons, and not all enter a career of persistent drug use. Persistent drug users pass through a series of stages in which their experiences and identities alter.

- How useful is it to see drug use as the result of a learning process of the kind described by Becker?

- The use of drugs is closely involved with ideas of work, leisure, and pleasure. The use of certain drugs has been normalized in youth culture and rates of use are now very high.

- The use of drugs and trading in them on the streets and in clubs is closely tied into large international networks of drug-trafficking and organized crime.

Organized crime, international crime, and terrorism

Crime is often seen in highly individual and informal terms, though we have tried to emphasize the ways in which it is generated in and through cultural and subcultural forms of social organization related to class, gender, and ethnic differences. It is important, however, to recognize that much criminality is professionally organized, and we have, again, tried to indicate some of the ways in which this is socially organized. In the next section, we turn to an examination of these issues of the formal social organization of crime in much greater detail. We look, in particular, at crime as a business, organized nationally and internationally in ways that challenge conventional businesses in the scale of their activities. We trace how processes of globalization have produced extensive transnational criminal organizations. We look also at the growing significance of international terrorism—the use of criminal acts for political purposes—and trace some of the parallels and connections between terrorism and organized crime.

Organized crime

We have looked at certain forms of professional, career crime in earlier parts of this chapter, but we have not discussed what is commonly referred to as 'organized crime'. This can be defined as that form of criminal activity that is organized as a business enterprise through the systematic use of administrative mechanisms, formal coordination, alliances, and joint ventures, and does so in relation to a range of markets for goods and services. Organized crime is criminal activity that goes beyond the relatively small-scale professional and gang activity considered so far. Like these, it has its roots in the specific subcultures of criminality that comprise the underworld, but it also has quite distinctive causes and conditions. Where organized crime exists, it affects the whole pattern of crime within a society. In this section we will look at the common characteristics of organized crime in the United States, Russia, Japan, and Hong Kong, commonly seen as the foci of 'Mafia' style criminality in the world today.

Mafia and *Cosa Nostra*

Public recognition of something called the Mafia or *Cosa Nostra* in the United States dates largely from the 1950s and 1960s, when a series of Senate hearings brought the activities of a number of leading Italian-American criminals to public attention. The most influential model of 'Mafia' organization is that depicted by Donald Cressey (1969), originally produced in association with a Presidential Task Force on organized crime (see also Albini 1971; Ianni and Reuss-Ianni 1972). Cressey presented a picture of a huge national confederation involved in fraud, drugs, prostitution, corruption, gambling, and violence, but also using its funds in conventional business operations such as property, finance, clubs, and restaurants. Its methods had come to parallel those of other business enterprises and it was impossible to disentangle illegal from legal activities and profits. This type of organized crime may never have been quite as tight and centralized as it seemed to the public and as it was portrayed in such films as *The Godfather*, but it was, in many ways, a distinctive form of criminal activity.

Such organized crime became a prominent feature of major American cities in the 1920s and 1930s. It is often seen as a direct outgrowth of the rural networks of support and control that proliferated in Sicily and other isolated parts of Italian society in the nineteenth century and that were transplanted to the United States by migrants from these areas. These were loose networks of friends and relations, rather than secret societies, and were organized around the 'honour' of family and locality and were involved in a wide range of neighbourhood and regional activities (Blok 1974; Boissevain 1974; Gambetta 1993). The true origins of organized crime are more recent and more complex. It arose in its contemporary form after the great waves of European migration to New York, Chicago, and other American cities and was an outgrowth of the very specific conditions of the 1920s and 1930s. The urban slums gave rise to many loosely organized groups that were rooted in their distinctive subcultures. We have already shown how similar gangs also emerged in districts of London. The emergence of such gangs can be explained by the distinctive subcultures found in lower-class areas of large cities and the corresponding differential association in which this results (Sutherland 1939). It depends also, however, on the attractiveness of an 'innovative' response to the anomie found in such areas (Merton 1938*b*).

> ⮑ *Connections*
> At this point you might like to review our discussion of Merton's account of anomie in Chapter 2, pp. 47–8.

The gangs of the major US cities became especially involved in the production and sale of 'bootleg' alcohol, made profitable by the 'Prohibition' legislation of the American state. The central participants in the bootlegging of whiskey were European immigrants and the descendents of immigrants, and both Italians and Sicilians were prominent. They were actively involved in a range of criminal activities within their neighbourhoods and became drawn into intensive conflict for customers. An alliance of Sicilian and Italian gangs was forged in 1930–1 and came to be known by outsiders as the Mafia. Far from being a direct descendent of the rural neighbourhoods, then, the gang grouping of the 1930s was a new phenomenon and a distinctive product of American society. It is true, nevertheless, that many of the leading figures in the emerging criminal gangs were recent migrants who had fled the clampdown on the Italian mafia by Mussolini's Fascist regime in the late 1920s. For all these reasons, Cressey rejected the 'mafia' label, holding that it is inaccurate and was not used by the participants themselves. Participants themselves preferred such impersonal terms as the 'organization', 'business', or 'firm', and sometimes *Cosa Nostra* ('our thing').

The organization existed, Cressey argued, as a federation of separate and autonomous family-based gangs, each of which defended its particular territory and held that it had a legitimate claim on the support of its local population. In acting 'honourably' towards 'their' people, providing them with the political influence and personal welfare they were denied by the city and national authorities, they earned the respect of people living in their neighbourhoods. This was reinforced by a structure of coercion that ensured that no one in the locality would challenge the right of the gang to monopolize its profitable ventures. Typical of such territorial groups was the Capone Mob of 1930s Chicago.

By the 1960s, Cressey argued, there were over thirty such family mobs. Each family boss—or 'Don'—had absolute authority in his territory. Through a series of cross-cutting alliances designed to protect the territorial claims of each of the gangs, a vast national organization had been built. The Organization itself had no single leader, but was run by a committee of major mobsters known as the 'Commission'. Cressey held that, by the late 1960s, the Organization was dominated by nine powerful families: three from New York, three in the surrounding cities of Buffalo, Newark, and Boston, and one each in Philadelphia, Detroit, and Chicago. The various families recognized the role of the Commission in resolving disputes and coordinating activities at a national level.

The criminal activities of a family were typically organized through a hierarchy of executive positions, running from the Don through his deputy and advisers to the

'Buffer', who acts as the interface or intermediary between the senior family members and the lower-level operatives. The Buffer had various 'Lieutenants' responsible for particular operating units, each of which had its Section Chief to liaise with the 'Soldiers' who actually operate particular activities—money lending, lotteries, vending machine rackets, protection, and so on. Beyond the level of the Soldiers, numerous non-Italians were employed or contracted for specific purposes at street level to take bets, answer telephones, sell narcotics, collect protection money, and so on.

Cressey further claimed that the Organization and its families operated according to a strict code of behaviour that governs all their activities. This code comprises five principles:

1 **Loyalty**. This is the basic injunction to respect the interests of other families and to keep silent about family activities.

2 **Rationality**. This is the requirement to act coolly and calmly in pursuit of the family's business: not to take drugs, not to get into fights, and to follow orders as a good team player.

3 **Honour**. This is tied to ideas of masculinity and patriarchalism, involving respect for women and for the senior members of the family.

4 **Courage**. Family members are to withstand pressure and punishment without complaint. This is, again, tied to a strong ethos of masculinity.

5 **Commitment**. Family members are to uphold their way of life without being drawn into the conventions of regular employment or social conformism.

Joseph Albini has warned that the Organization must be regarded not as a bureaucratic enterprise but as a loose-knit system of patron–client or network relationships (Albini 1988). As such, its structure is constantly in flux and no rigid model can describe its shape at any particular time. It is clear, nevertheless, that Cressey highlighted the ways in which such a loose-knit structure can coordinate and control the actions of its constituent gangs through both formal and informal mechanisms.

Other organized crime

Much discussion of organized crime in the United States has been concerned with that of Italian Americans, but a number of sociologists have pointed to the existence of many other forms of organized crime. Robert Davidson (1992) has documented the rise of Asian-American gangs in Chicago and other cities. Those from China, the Philippines, India, Korea, and other parts of Asia now form a significant section of the US population. In a number of areas of Asian settlement, there has been a growth of

---

THEORY AND METHODS

Official sources on crime

Much of Cressey's evidence comes from official investigations and the testimony of informers. Albini questioned the validity of this evidence, suggesting that Cressey may have been led to overstate his case.

❓ What other sources of evidence might there be on organized crime? How could a satisfactory research project be set up?

---

criminal involvement in drug trafficking, especially the trade in heroin from South East Asia. Organized gangs in American cities use their connections with Chinese triads operating from Hong Kong to obtain heroin for re-sale in the United States. Actual sales to users are handled by street gangs, but the bulk trade itself is a highly organized business.

Outside the United States, evidence for strong organized criminal gangs has been found in Japan, Russia, and other parts of Eastern Europe. Organized crime had begun to develop in the final twenty years of Communism in Russia, when corrupt and self-serving politicians used illegal means to further their own interests, but it was the collapse of Communism that really stimulated its growth. The disappearance of the strong, totalitarian state in Russia and the consequent privatization of state economic assets allowed many private individuals to amass considerable wealth through dealing in state assets. Many former Communist politicians were able to use their knowledge and connections to build up personal fortunes themselves and to join this emerging Russian 'mafia'. Organized crime has proliferated because of the economic dislocations that followed the ending of Communism, as this allowed the criminal syndicates to obtain and monopolize scarce resources from which they could benefit.

Russian organized crime, like its American counterpart, is organized through loose 'syndicates' that operate on the basis of patron–client relationships. In these relationships, a person of power or wealth helps or protects specific others (the clients), who, in return, perform services for their patron. The relationship is not a contractual, employment relationship but rests on informal patterns of trust and obligation. Hierarchies of patron–client relationships form networks of reciprocity and obligation centred on the most powerful individuals. Those involved in these networks are engaged in a range of illegal activities. Although Russia has virtually no bank robberies, bank fraud is rife and banks pay high levels of protection money to avoid becoming the targets of robberies. Forging of documents is widespread, as is illegal arms trading, including dealing in nuclear materials, prostitution, drug smuggling, money laundering, and illegal imports. Crime is so closely integrated with conventional business that it has been argued that there is a 'shadow economy' of marginal and unregulated business with its 'black market' for distributing goods. There are high levels of political corruption, giving the criminal syndicates considerable influence over the state (Albini *et al.* 1997; Varese 2001).

Organized crime in Hong Kong and mainland China originated in the 'triad' secret societies, though it now reaches beyond them. Triads are a long-standing feature of traditional Chinese society and prospered in Hong Kong during its separation from the rest of China. A triad is a family- and neighbourhood-based grouping that provides support and services for its members and organizes its activities on the basis of secrecy and elaborate rituals of membership. Acting outside, and often against, the central state, triads became involved in a range of legal and illegal activities. Triad activity in Hong Kong grew after the Communist revolution in China, when many prominent leaders were expelled from the mainland. The economic success of Hong Kong since the 1960s provided many opportunities for triads to expand their involvement in prostitution, gambling, and drugs.

Thus, while there is continuity between the traditional triads and those of today, systematic involvement in organized crime is a recent and more specific phenomenon. Triads tend to be organized as loose networks of independent gangs that regard themselves as part of a larger 'family' or clan in which there is a decentralized structure of command. The various gangs are loosely ranked as 'Red Pole', 'Blue Lantern', and ordinary. Although they cooperate for common purposes, they are also involved in recurrent and intense conflict over the pursuit of their interests.

Organized crime in Japan originated in gambling groups and itinerant dealers who banded together for mutual protection and were given official encouragement to organize markets at shrines and temples and to regulate the supply of labour for public works construction. By the early twentieth century, they were a strongly entrenched feature of Japanese society and had come to be known as *Yakuza* (Hill 2003). They were used as government tools for strike-breaking and for fighting left-wing political groups and they had strong links with right-wing political leaders. The *Yakuza* took their present form, however, after the Second World War. Industrial reconstruction and slow political liberalization created opportunities for profitable enterprise in the black markets and in the supply of labour for construction and dock work. They moved into the growing entertainment industry of bars, prostitution, and *pachinko* (pin ball), and they extended their protection

and extortion activities. Intense conflict among *Yakuza* led to the emergence of a small number of major syndicates, paralleling the structure of business groups that had developed in the conventional economy. Despite a police clamp down in the 1960s, organized crime in Japan remains highly concentrated.

Hill (2003) has established that there are currently about 90,000 men involved in organized crime in Japan and that about 40 per cent are involved in gangs affiliated to one of the three big syndicates: *Yamaguchi-gumi*, *Iwagawa-kai*, and *Sumiyoshi-kai*. The syndicates have great similarities to Cressey's model of the *Cosa Nostra* and are organized in ways that draw on the idea of the traditional family household, with its paternalistic and authoritarian patterns of control by the 'father' over junior members. Formal administrative mechanisms are also used, however, and the syndicates are organized into series of ranks such as 'boss', executive, soldier, and trainee. A *Yakuza* syndicate and its affiliated groupings are organized in relation to a tight discipline and obedience, embodied in a strict code of behaviour that is enforced, when necessary, through violence. *Yakuza* are currently involved in protection rackets, the supply of drugs, gambling, the sale of festival trinkets, prostitution, debt collection, loan sharking, rent collection, and the supply of labour through sub-contractors. In many of these areas they act under commission from conventional businesses and public authorities, which rely on the ability of the *Yakuza* to manage and manipulate their employees, shareholders, and voters through blackmail and coercion.

International crime

Organized crime, we have suggested, has certain similarities with conventional business activity. Like many businesses, those involved in organized crime have expanded their activities to an international level. Organized criminal gangs in the United States, China, Russia, and elsewhere have been involved in extensive international transactions and have increasingly begun to organize their activities on a global scale.

> **↪ Connections**
> Try to think about organized crime in relation to the general issue of globalization that we discuss in Chapter 16. You may like to have a quick look at pp. 645–9 now.

State borders have always provided opportunities for, as well as barriers to, criminal activity. Within the United States, organized crime has been able to operate under different state jurisdictions, as laws vary from one part of the country to another, and it has been only a small step further to operate across international state borders. Providing goods and services that are legal in one state but illegal in another provides great opportunities for such operations. The smuggling of alcohol and tobacco, because of variations in tax levels, is one example of such international crime that has existed for a very long time. The growing complexity of legal regulations and of the economic and political interdependence of nation states has created the immense opportunities that organized crime groups have been able to exploit. It has been argued that the globalization of the political economy has resulted in a globalization of crime (Ruggiero *et al.* 1998; Findlay 1999).

Causes and consequences

The most obvious and important criminal activity is smuggling, and this has always existed alongside and interdependently of legal international trade. The liberalization of international trade, creating global markets and encouraging business enterprises to operate freely and without regard for national borders has created a situation in which smuggling operations come to be seen, almost, as forms of 'free trade' activity. International smugglers can present themselves as providing commodities that market restrictions prevent from flowing freely across the world. Although smuggling is often thought of in terms of a tourist carrying a few hundred cigarettes or a bottle of whiskey, the scale of smuggling is immense and it is highly organized. It has been estimated that smuggling is a major global business, valued at more than $600 billion a year, especially through money-laundering operations that are closely tied to established banking and financial activities.

The transformation of the transport industry with the rise of large container ships and juggernaut lorries, has transformed the methods of smuggling. Previously, drugs such as marijuana and cocaine were smuggled into the United States in small planes and speedboats, but organized criminal groups are now transporting larger consignments in sealed containers alongside conventional cargos. Containers and sealed lorries are also used to smuggle migrants across national borders. These mechanisms are anonymous and impersonal, making it more difficult for states to trace those responsible. The flow of goods from Mexico to the United States, for example, combines both legal and illegal commodities. Drug traffickers have established factories and distribution centres in northern Mexico and have taken advantage of the deregulated trucking industry to transport their drugs into the United States alongside legitimate trade in fruit and vegetables. Within the European Union, the opening-up of national borders has made it easier for lorries to transport economic migrants, asylum seekers, and drugs into Germany, France, and Britain (Andreas 2002).

The liberalization of financial markets was intended to promote the transnational flow of capital, but it has also promoted a huge growth in money laundering. This is the process through which the proceeds from illegal activities can be converted into legal—and untraceable—financial assets through the use of multiple international bank accounts and investments in tax havens and other financial centres (Sikka 2003). This has been particularly important for organized criminal groups from Russia and Colombia.

The transformation of the international financial system has also created opportunities for new forms of crime. The almost exclusive reliance on credit cards for consumer purchases has made the copying of credit cards and the 'skimming' of credit details from them into a major criminal activity. Information from cards skimmed in a London restaurant can be used to produce cards that can, within hours, be used to make purchases in New York, Athens, or Rome. The technology required makes this an obvious area for the involvement of organized criminal groups, which have increased their level of investment in technologies for fraud in the face of the growth in international credit card trading.

 New technology Internet crime

The Internet makes it very easy for organized criminal groups to steal credit details—and even whole identities—through intercepting insecure credit card transactions. Major Internet providers and dealers, such as Microsoft and e-bay, have sought to increase the security of their systems in the face of technologies of both crime and control.

E-mail has also made new forms of crime possible. Criminal groups create e-mails and websites that appear to be those of legitimate businesses, such as banks. In a 'spamming' operation, they send e-mails to millions of Internet users in the hope that just a handful will believe the message to be genuine and will hand over their password and other account details.

Another financial scam on the Internet is the sending of 'spam' messages claiming to be from a deposed politician—generally in Nigeria—who is looking for a bank account in which to lodge millions of pounds. In return for allowing the use of an account, the Internet user is told that they will receive many thousands of pounds in commission. This is, of course, merely another way of persuading people to pass on details about their bank account, which can rapidly be emptied or used for illegal purposes.

Criminal organizations

The actors involved in international crime are many and diverse. Organized crime groups vary from one country to another, and even within countries. They are not organized in precisely the same way as large-scale business enterprises engaged in conventional activities, but they do have certain common characteristics as international actors and they use many of the same mechanisms as those conventional businesses.

Criminal groups from numerous countries extend their international scope and combine with other criminal groups in a number of ways. At its loosest, there may be a recognition of the respective spheres of influence and territories of each group, but these easily give way to mutual supplier relationships that may persist over time (P. Williams 2002). Colombian drug producers, for example, have established stable supply linkages with Italian organized criminal groups, and the latter are given exclusive rights to redistribute the drugs across western Europe. The Russian organized crime groups have established links with organized criminal groups in the Netherlands and Japan for supplying women from Eastern Europe for prostitution. Such supply relations may involve barter rather than money transactions: guns may be exchanged for drugs, for example.

Stronger forms of transnational organization occur when groups form what Williams (2002) has called tactical and strategic alliances. Short-term tactical cooperation may lead to longer-term strategic alliances that allow systematic and extensive cooperation. Drug trafficking into the United States, for example, has involved the establishment of strong strategic linkages between Colombian producers and dealers in the Dominican Republic, these links being built as their earlier reliance on Mexican intermediaries became less profitable. Most recently, the Colombian dealers have built strategic alliances with Russian groups to handle distribution through eastern and central Europe.

If there are no transnational bureaucratic criminal organizations, the loose networks do, nevertheless, have certain formal mechanisms of cooperation. It has been reported that summit meetings of major criminal groups have been used to regulate spheres of influence and to plan joint ventures. Although the participants are not, in any sense, representatives or leaders of whole national criminal gangs, the meetings do bring together many of the important criminal groups and bring some stability to international criminal activity. These meetings are complemented by bilateral meetings and by continued contacts through intermediaries. Some criminal groups, it has been suggested, have made such mediation and courier business their main activity.

Much discussion has focused on the idea that the Chinese triads of Hong Kong have expanded through the overseas Chinese communities to establish transnational triad organizations. Hong Kong has been seen as the directing centre for such global criminal activities, and the drive to globalization has been strengthened since the 1997 return of Hong Kong to rule—and strong political control—from Beijing. While Chinese organized criminal groups have certainly established strong links across national borders, there is no global triad structure. Chinese communities are diverse in their ethnicity and there is little basis for dominance by Hong Kong migrants. Chinese criminal gangs have become very active in drug smuggling and people smuggling, but they do so as parts of the larger growth in global criminal activity that has been described.

Terrorism

Terrorism is political action against a state and its citizens that pursues its goals through extreme violence, often on a spectacular or mass scale, and that is generally criminalized through legislation, proscription, and exclusion. It has become, since the 1960s, one of the most important targets for police and security service operations and it has entered the public consciousness as a major—and perhaps permanent—source of concern at work, in travel, and during leisure. X-ray and security checks at airports and other public places have become an accepted, if unwelcome, weapon in what many politicians describe as 'the war against terrorism'.

Violent political conflict has a history as long as the human species. Its organized form as the internal opposition of political groups to state authorities has a history almost as long. Eric Hobsbawm (1969) has termed this 'social banditry' when it takes the form of redistributive political action pursued through violent acts that are criminalized by the state. Social bandits engage in a range of criminal activities in support of their political aims, and their overall political strategy and tactics are labelled as criminal by the state that they attack. In rural societies, social banditry is generated by a sense of grievance and wrong-doing and a desire to secure vengeance and justice. Examples of such social banditry include the idealistic robber of the Robin Hood myth, the guerrilla or resistance fighter, and the violent avengers who terrorize their opponents.

Pacification of their societies by industrializing states, especially those that established liberal and democratic structures, greatly reduced the level of social banditry and institutionalized the legitimate and non-violent opposition of political parties. Even in these societies, however, criminalized forms of political violence could still erupt. Many European governments of the nineteenth century were concerned about the activities of 'anarchists', who were widely seen as motivated by the French revolution. Anarchists were seen as forming secret societies and organizations through which they could plot acts of violence, and a number of bombings and assassinations did take place in this period.

The most protracted forms of political violence, however, have been linked with separatist and nationalist claims, as in the Irish Republican Army (IRA) in the United Kingdom from the late nineteenth century until the establishment of the Republic of Ireland in 1922. The IRA attacked political or military targets and saw itself as engaged in a war against an imposed state.

From the 1960s, these forms of political violence were renewed, but they also began to be transformed as dispossessed groups generated by international conflicts began to take their struggles to the metropolitan and colonial states that they saw as responsible for their oppression. This was the beginning of that form of violent political conflict described as terrorism.

The violent political organizations of the late 1960s and 1970s—groups such as the IRA, the Red Army Faction, the Red Brigade, and ETA—were formed, like the IRA of fifty years earlier, as highly centralized and tightly coordinated organizations with a structure of command modelled on that of conventional armies. Indeed, many used militaristic terminology in their names and in their tactics. They emerged in the political upheavals of the 1960s and saw themselves pursuing radical, leftist policies through violent means because they were unable to pursue their goals through conventional political means. They often saw themselves as part of an international struggle, though their international links were limited and each group tended to operate on a national basis. Their targets were politicians and businessmen, embassies and banks, and national airlines.

The rise of Islamist terrorism

The first signs of a change in the nature of terrorism occurred in the wake of the Arab–Israeli War of 1967, which resulted in the dispossession of large numbers of Palestinians in the Israeli-occupied territories. The involvement of Western states in this conflict, where support generally went to Israel, led many Palestinians to see Israel and Western governments as legitimate targets for acts of violence. Many came to see their conflict in religious terms, drawing on Islam to construct an ideology of political opposition. Groups such as Al-Fatah and Hezbollah organized themselves to pursue the goal of Palestinian liberation and autonomy through all means necessary and many of their supporters came to see this as a first step in a holy war (*jihad*) through which the boundaries of the Islamic world could be extended across the

 Briefing: Islam and Islamist ideologies

It is important to recognize a distinction between Islamist ideologies and the beliefs of Islam. Islamist ideologies are those that may be based on particular interpretations of Islam but that ally this with ideas that are opposed to secularism and that support the establishment of political systems in which their interpretation of Islam is promoted against all other forms of belief. Many Muslims, whether liberal or more traditional in their beliefs, reject such views and advocate a tolerance towards other religions and systems of political belief. Many commentators incorrectly and insultingly describe some violent political groups as 'Islamic terrorists', when they should be referring to Islamist terrorism. Islamist ideology should not be seen simply as 'Islamic fundamentalism' and it should certainly not be equated with Islam *per se*.

globe. This Islamist ideology—often misunderstood as 'Islamic fundamentalism'—was strengthened by the Iranian revolution in which the regime of the Western-oriented Shah was replaced by a radical Islamic caliphate under the Ayatollah Khomeini. Iran became a major centre for fomenting and supporting Islamist terrorism, and hijack and kidnapping became the principal means through which struggles against particular states were globalized.

A continuing failure to resolve the Palestinian situation radicalized other states in the Middle East, and numerous state-sponsored terrorist organizations arose. A crucial step was taken, however, in the heart of Asia, where Russian intervention in Afghanistan led to the formation of *mujahideen* guerilla groups who went on to build training camps across the country and to build links with radicals and terrorist groups in Pakistan and the Middle East. A variety of groups began to take their struggles to an international level and to broaden their targets from the political and the military to civilians. Bombs were set off at Western embassies in Kenya and Tanzania and at US embassies in the Middle East; hotels, restaurants, and buses became targets in Israel; and the World Trade Center in New York was bombed in 1993. This shift also involved a change in tactics, as car bombs and suicide bombs became the main weapons of attack.

The most visible sign of this shift in targets was the destruction of the twin towers of the World Trade Center on 11 September 2001. In this attack, hijacked airliners were flown directly into the towers and, simultaneously, into the Pentagon in Washington. This led directly to a

US-led invasion of Afghanistan, which was seen as the coordinating and training centre of international terrorism. Osama bin-Laden, a Saudi Arabian millionaire, was identified as the leading figure in an organized terrorist group called Al-Qaeda, and the war in Afghanistan was supposed to destroy his power base. Continuing American involvement in Afghanistan fuelled Islamist radicalism and wider public opinion across the Middle East, and terror attacks continued. In the search for states supporting this spread of terrorism, the United States led an invasion of Iraq, incorrectly seen as the source of international terrorism. While this invasion successfully removed the oppressive regime of Saddam Hussein, it created yet a further pretext for Islamist violence. American and British soldiers became targets of attack by Islamist groups from Iraq and the surrounding countries, and opposition to Western governments reached a higher level than before. The direct consequences may have included further increases in political terror, most notably in night clubs in Indonesia in 2002, in the Madrid train bombs of 2004, and the London transport bombings of 2005.

> **⟳ Connections**
> You will find a full listing of recent attacks on p. 656 in Chapter 16. Pages 655–7 of that chapter also give a fuller discussion of the political context of and political responses to international terrorism.

This growth in Islamist terrorism is often interpreted on the model of the violent political conflict of the past. Thus, it is seen as the product of a centralized and coordinated organization, headed by Osama bin-Laden, that plans its numerous coordinated attacks in immense detail. Actions such as the events of 9/11 certainly require meticulous planning, but it would be wrong to see these and similar attacks as part of the master-plan of an army-like organization. We have shown that organized crime borrows certain elements from conventional business practice but applies these in a far looser and decentralized way. Islamist terrorism, too, has learned much from conventional military and security practices, but these are employed in novel ways through decentralized networks in which chains of command are complex and fragmentary.

Al-Qaeda does not exist as a monolithic organizational entity. The word means 'base' or 'model', and it was precisely to promote a model of how the Islamist cause could be promoted and to establish an intellectual base from which activists could draw inspiration (Jason Burke 2004). It was probably formed in 1988 in Pakistan as a way of helping to maintain the political unity of those who had fought against the Russians in Afghanistan. It had, however, a purely nominal existence until 1996, when bin-Laden and a number of other politico-religious factions began to build

training camps in Afghanistan and it became an important coordinating element in a larger network of militant groups. Its influence within this network came from bin-Laden's ability to provide finance, resources, and a safe basis for terrorist operations.

Actual operations are planned by the many local groups linked to this network and there is little or no overall coordination. The 9/11 bombings did involve a greater degree of planning and coordination than many other attacks before or since, and the bin-Laden group does seem to have retained overall control. The initial idea came from a group from Egypt, the United Arab Republic, and Lebanon living in Hamburg, and it was through Osama bin-Laden that a number of Saudi Arabian activists in Afghanistan were drawn in to support the operation without having any part in its planning. The finance for the operation—estimated at $500,000—came from bin-Laden and was laundered through the international banking system to make it untraceable. The American-led invasion of Afghanistan in 2001 disrupted this network and made it impossible for the country to be used as a safe base. Bin-laden set up a more mobile base in Pakistan and continued his attempts to inspire Islamist terrorism: he and his associates issued videos in support of terrorist attacks and encouraged others to follow suit. However, Al-Qaeda has even less of a directive role in this terrorism than before.

Islamist terrorism is now planned and executed by very small groups with multifarious, but loose, links to each other. Actual terrorist operations are generally planned by small groups or clusters of individuals, linked by ethnicity and family background and, perhaps, worshipping at the same mosque. The London underground attacks of 7 July 2005 were largely planned and carried out by a small group of British Asians from Leeds, while the failed attempts of later that month were undertaken by a small group of Somalis from South London. A willingness to participate in acts of terrorism is something that individuals drift into and to which they gradually become more committed as a result of their ideological radicalization through religious events and groupings allied to, but not parts of, particular mosques in their own country and in Pakistan. Loose and informal connections with people met informally, if at all, are the means through which they acquire the necessary knowledge and materials for their attacks. Those who become involved in terrorist activities know very few other participants, making it especially difficult for security services to build up intelligence through the usual mechanisms of tracing known contacts. Their acts are not an expression of widely held subcultural beliefs in their locality—indeed, public opinion in their communities is generally strongly opposed to such acts. Nevertheless, their radical views can often be interpreted by outsiders as mere religious fervour and, embedded in their localities, they may be all but invisible to these outsiders.

Stop and reflect

In this section, we have explored a number of issues relating to organized crime and violence and its increasingly transnational character. We showed that:

- Contemporary organized crime in the United States cannot simply be traced back to rural roots in the Sicilian mafia. It is a specific adaptation to contemporary economic and political conditions.

- Organized crime takes the form of loose networks, often with a family or neighbourhood base, but connected through formal mechanisms of communication and control.

- Patterns of organized crime in the United States, Russia, Japan, and Hong Kong all show a similarity and overlap with conventional business activity.

- Is organized crime a bigger social problem than informal street crime?

Drawing on parallels between organized crime and international terrorism, we showed that:

- New forms of terrorism arose from the 1960s and have had their focus in Islamist ideologies produced in the Middle East.

- International terrorism has a loosely structured organization, with acts of terrorism largely initiated and planned by small, local groups rather than by a vast international conspiracy.

- People may drift into terrorism, their radical views sustained by their subculture, but terrorist acts are not expressions of subcultural values and are not supported by Islamic communities.

- Why has Islamist terrorism led to so much hostility towards Islamic communities?

 Chapter summary

We began the chapter by considering a number of general issues in the study of crime and deviance, looking particularly at the relationship between biological and social factors and the social construction of deviant identities.

- Deviance cannot be seen as a purely biological fact or as a consequence of evolution. The crucial factor is the element of labelling through which particular acts are socially defined as deviant in one way or another.

- Drift into deviance is typical and is the means through which some primary deviation may become secondary deviation, to which people become committed and with which they identify themselves and are identified by others.

- Stigmatization is a crucial element in labelling, but much primary deviation is normalized and does not become the basis of role deviance or a deviant career.

We looked at a variety of forms of criminality, tracing their relationship to gender, ethnicity, and class, and we showed some of the distinctive features of professional or career crime:

- Conventional sex–gender roles shape male and female participation in crime. It is important to look at cultural conceptions of femininity and masculinity and at patriarchal structures of varying employment opportunities.

- Ethnic variations are also associated with criminality and with the likelihood of being the victim of a crime. Members of ethnic minorities are especially likely to experience police action against them.

- Subcultures of crime and criminal underworlds have been important in sustaining career crime.

- Within these subcultures, criminality may be combined with low-paid or casual work, and it is often carried out by those who are denied employment opportunities.

- White-collar crime is very extensive and is related to changes in the wider economy.

These issues were explored in greater depth for the particular case of drug use and abuse. We showed that:

- Many people drift into drug use, but few follow a career of persistent drug use. The use of some drugs has been normalized in youth culture and rates of use are high.

- Street and club trading in drugs is closely linked into international networks of drug trafficking and organized crime.

Turning to organized crime itself, we showed that:

- Many societies have strongly established patterns of organized crime. This is generally organized as loose networks with only minimal formal and administrative mechanisms of control.

- Organized crime is, nevertheless, increasingly organized at a transnational level and shows many similarities and overlaps with contemporary global business.

- International terrorism has many organizational similarities with organized crime.

- Involvement in terrorism must be seen in relation to the subcultures that unintentionally sustain it, but without overtly supporting it.

Key concepts

- addiction
- career deviance
- craft crime
- crime
- deviance
- drift

- labelling theory
- moral career
- normalization
- own
- primary deviation
- project crime

- secondary deviation
- underworld
- white-collar crime
- wise

Workshop 7

Study 7 Bank robbers

Martin Gill (2000) has carried out one of the few ethnographic studies of commercial robbery—that is robbery aimed at business and commercial premises and property. He interviewed a sample of 341 people imprisoned for robberies of commercial properties such as banks and building societies, or cash-in-transit vans, aiming to uncover the motives behind their robberies and to study the ways in which they identified targets and planned their crimes. Gill reports that most of the robbers had been convicted for the first time in their teens, generally for assaults, car crimes, or burglaries. Most were in their twenties before they first committed a robbery, but few regarded themselves as exclusively robbers. The overriding motive was, unsurprisingly, financial gain, but many robbers reported that their desire for money was associated with unemployment or a desire for excitement. The money gained from robberies was most typically spent on drugs, alcohol, and gambling, and on living the 'high life'. It was generally spent in a relatively short period rather than being invested to meet long-term living expenses.

Much of Gill's research concerns the organizational structure of robbery, and particularly the actual planning and carrying out of robberies. The planning of a robbery varied considerably. In the case of banks and cash-in-transit, planning took more than a week, while building society, post office, and off-licence robberies were generally planned only over a day or two. This reflected robbers' perceptions of whether a particular target was a 'soft' or 'hard' one. Supermarkets and off-licences, but also building societies, were generally regarded as soft targets that required little or no planning. Robbers might, on the spur of the moment, drive into town and look for a likely place to rob with only a very minimal reconnaissance. Large-scale cash robberies directed at banks, on the other hand, required more meticulous preparation in advance and may involve periods of surveillance. It was not uncommon in such cases to rely on information received from friends or acquaintances, and this might sometimes involve the cooperation of someone on the inside of the organization targeted. Hard targets also tended to involve more robbers: a bank or bank van may typically involve a team of three or more robbers. Physical security measures such as closed-circuit television cameras were rarely deterrents to robbery, as robbers simply hid their faces or wore disguises.

Gill draws on his results and a series of case studies to reflect on attempts to construct a typology of robbers. The clearest division that he found was that between the amateurs and the professionals, who could be distinguished by the amount of planning and organization that they did and by the sizes of their targets. There was, however, much overlap between these categories. Gill sees far more uniformity among robbers of all types, with their willingness to engage in robberies depending on their rational calculation of the particular rewards and costs involved in the specific situations in which they find themselves: their assessment of the risk and the opportunities, the presence of cameras, screens, and other security measures, and so on.

⊃ Gill stresses the rationality of robbers. Refer back to our discussion of rational action theory in Chapter 2, pp. 55–6 and see how useful you think this approach might be in explaining Gill's findings.

❷ How valid are Gill's conclusions likely to be, considering that his sample consisted of those who had been caught and convicted for their robberies?

❷ Read the case studies presented by Gill (2000 chapter 4). What evidence do they provide for the various theories of crime that we have considered in this chapter? What evidence is there for labelling processes, differential association, and drift, for example?

Media watch 7 Mobile crime

The problem of crime is often depicted as a problem of youth crime, so you will find it useful to consider some aspects of this. Look back at our discussion of mobile phone theft at the beginning of this chapter, p. 235.

The British government's youth crime adviser, Lord Warner, the Chairman of the Youth Justice Board, has seen these trends in crime as showing the growing importance of gang crime committed by young people against other young people. He claims that there are 400 'problem estates' in Britain where gangs of up to sixty members operate. These gangs are said to recruit their members from those excluded from school. Gang activity on these estates, he said, encouraged a 'culture of bullying and intimidation' that undermined authority and order at school and on the streets. They steal mobile phones, trainers, and designer clothing, they are involved in drug use, and they coerce girls into sex. This crime is missed in the British Crime Survey, Lord Warner argued, because it interviewed only those aged over 16.

Reporting on Lord Warner's views, the *Independent* newspaper identified what it held to be the five types of tactic used by these juvenile gangs:

- The Blitz. A brief attack by a group of youngsters, generally on an older person.

- The Snatch. A crime where one gang member targets the victim.

- The Confrontation. The victim is surrounded by gang members who threaten and intimidate until the targeted goods are surrendered.

- The Con. Where one gang member distracts the victim and lures him, or her, to where the other gang members are waiting.

- The Trap. A robbery that takes place when an outsider enters a gang's territory and is surrounded by its members.

Consult the official statistics on crime (see the Home Office website listed in the 'Online resources' section below) and see what information you can discover about the extent of this kind of juvenile crime. Do the statistics tell you anything about whether the perpetrators of the crime are acting as members of a gang? What are the problems of drawing any firm conclusions from these data?

Lord Warner pointed out that these kinds of crime tend to lead to custodial sentences, and he advocated a greater use of community service as a penalty. Do you think such a shift in sentencing would be successful in reducing the amount of crime and the likelihood of juvenile offenders drifting into long-term criminality?

Use the Index and the Contents page of this book to find the sections in Chapter 9 'Education' and Chapter 13 'City and community' that might be relevant to explaining youth crime. Can you find any material that would help to assess the accuracy of Lord Warner's depiction of schools and communities?

Go to your library and find some books on juvenile crime and delinquency. The classic sources are Cohen (1955) and Yablonsky (1967).

Discussion points

Review the various 'Stop and reflect' points in this chapter. You may find it useful to consider these in relation to our discussion of socialization and identity in Chapter 4. The topics that we considered can usefully be revised in three groups: the most general issues raised about deviance; general issues related to crime and criminality; and issues related to organized crime and terrorism.

Deviance, reaction, and identity

In 'Understanding deviance and control' we set out a number of general ideas that were applied to deviance in later parts of the chapter:

● How important do you think it is to distinguish between 'difference' and 'deviance'?

● Make sure that you understand the meaning of primary deviation and secondary deviation, and that you understand the role of labelling and stigmatization in establishing role deviance.

● Try to think of examples of processes of 'drift' in and out of deviance.

Many writers and commentators on deviance still look to biology for the causes of crime. Look back at our discussion of biological and cultural determinism in Chapter 4, pp. 137–40, and then consider the following questions:

● Lombroso and other biological theorists used terms such as 'atavism', 'degenerate', 'lower races', and 'born criminal'. Can these be considered to have any scientific meaning, or are they mere value judgements?

● How much attention should sociologists give to recent developments in genetics that have claimed to identify the genes responsible for particular kinds of behaviour?

Crime and criminal careers

We began our discussion of crime with an account of the distinctive features of the criminal law, distinguishing it from civil law, constitutional law, and other specialist forms of law. We then looked at criminal behaviour as a specific form of deviance. A number of the issues that we looked at concern the formal and informal social organization of crime:

● Make sure that you understand the terms craft crime, project crime, underworld, and white-collar crime.

● How plausible is it to describe career crime as a job? Why are women less likely than men to engage in a career of theft?

● What problems do you think might be involved in calculating the economic significance of corporate crime?

● Compare the data in Figures 7.2 and 7.4. Why are the numbers in each category of offence so different in the two tables? Which type of crime reported to the police is most likely to result in a conviction or caution? And which is the least likely?

Drugs and pleasure

Our sections on drugs and sexuality looked at diverse ways in which people pursue pleasure, and we paid particular attention to the ways that their actions come to be seen as conformist or deviant:

● Why is there such great diversity in the social reaction to different drugs and other mood-changing substances?

● How would you define the following terms: occasional user, regular user, addiction, hedonism, retreatism.

● Make sure that you understand the main ideas of Becker and Young.

You should give some attention to the particular methodological problems involved in trying to find accurate information about these matters. You will find some useful background in Chapter 3:

● Using the data in Figure 7.5, draw a pie chart showing the users of different types of drug. Are the data in the figure likely to be reliable? Why is this?

● What are the main problems involved in obtaining accurate information about drug use?

Organized crime and terrorism

We discussed the relationship between formal and informal mechanisms of control in the organization of criminal and terrorist actions.

● Why does the conventional view of organized crime tend to see it as tightly structured and bureaucratic?

● To what extent do you think that ideas of anomie might be useful in explaining involvement in political terrorism?

● Consider some of the issues concerning ethnicity and religion discussed in Chapters 6 and 11. How important is the existence of religious subcultures in ethnic communities for the emergence and perpetuation of terrorism?

Explore further

Good overviews of the subjects in this chapter are:

Becker, H. S. (1963), *Outsiders: Studies in the Sociology of Deviance* (New York: Free Press). *This is a landmark study that still repays a close reading.*

Heidensohn, F. (1985), *Women and Crime* (London: Macmillan). *A very useful and comprehensive overview of the gendering of criminal activity.*

Croal, H. (1992), *White Collar Crime* (Buckingham: Open University Press). *An up-to-date account of the nature and significance of white-collar crime.*

Plummer, K. (1975), *Sexual Stigma: An Interactionist Account* (London: Routledge). *A classic study of homosexuality that makes powerful use of symbolic interactionist theory.*

Further and more detailed information can be found in:

Matza, D. (1964), *Delinquency and Drift* (New York: John Wiley & Sons). *An important work that emphasizes the fact that much criminal behaviour results from 'drift' and circumstances, rather than from commitment to a criminal career.*

Goffman, E. (1963), *Stigma* (Englewood Cliffs, NJ: Prentice-Hall). *Like all of Goffman's work, this is very readable and has been massively influential. He sets out a general model of the stigmatization of deviance and difference.*

Dorn, N., Murji, K., and South, N. (1992), *Traffickers* (London: Routledge). *An important book by some of the leading figures in the study of the organized criminal drug trade.*

Young, J. (1971), *The Drugtakers* (London: McGibbon & Kee). *Young's emphasis on the hippies now seems a little outdated, but the book has much to say about the relationship between work, pleasure, and social control.*

Online resources

Visit the Online Resource Centre that accompanies this book to access more learning resources and other interesting material on crime and deviance at:

www.oxfordtextbooks.co.uk/orc/fulcher3e/

The site of the Institute of Criminology at Cambridge has many useful links:

www.crim.cam.ac.uk/library/links/crime_prevention.html

A huge site that contains almost everything you could possibly want to know (and a lot that you don't want to know) about crime and criminology:

http://faculty.ncwc.edu/toconnor/criminology.htm

The Criminology Information Service page at the University of Toronto has many links to 'grey' and alternative sources:

http://link.library.utoronto.ca/criminology/crimdoc/index.cfm

The official website on crime and law enforcement in Britain is that of the Home Office. This contains links to research reports and much statistical information:

www.homeoffice.gov.uk

International material can be found through the United Nations site on crime and criminal justice:

www.uncjin.org

On drugs, the website of the Institute for the Study of Drug Dependency is the most comprehensive available:

www.drugscope.org.uk

The leading international investigator on terrorism is Paul Wilkinson and you will find useful information on the site of his research centre at St Andrew's University:

www.st-andrews.ac.uk/academic/intrel/research/cstpv/

You can find the official viewpoint on the website of MI5, the British security service, at

www.mi5.gov.uk/

The website of MI6, the British Secret Service, can be found at

www.mi6.gov.uk/output/Page79.html

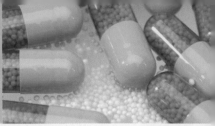

body, health, and medicine

Contents

08

Psychiatric careers

Andrew Solomon, a New Yorker, published his first novel in 1994, aged 30, but felt no enthusiasm about its critical success. He had begun to feel constantly tired, and contact with other people just seemed too much of an effort. He barely ate anything at all. He feared going to a birthday party organized for him by his family, and on his only trip outside the house on the day of the party he lost control of his bowels.

Andrew consulted his doctor, who diagnosed him as suffering from depression, and he was prescribed a course of Xanax to control his anxiety. While taking the medication he spent most of his time in bed, having to force himself to do such basic things as wash. He had to be fed, like a baby, by his father.

Over the next six months he slowly began to feel better, and he began to live a more normal life again. Though others saw him as having recovered, Andrew felt that it was simply the symptoms that had gone away and that the underlying depression remained. Feeling that death would end this, and that a serious and 'visible' illness would legitimate his death, he sought out homosexual encounters in public parks in the hope that he would get AIDS. He failed to contract the disease, but to his own surprise, he felt relieved about this and began to feel that his recovery was now really under way and that he knew how he could control his own depression.

Deborah Tallis's depression led her to overdose on her medication, and she was taken into hospital. She was classified as a risk to herself and was 'sectioned' under the Mental Health Act. She stayed in hospital for eight months. When she was released she felt herself to be back in exactly the same situation, and after another six months she was back in hospital.

As her spells of hospitalization increased, she found it more and more difficult to cope alone in the outside world. She moved continually from the community to hospital and back again over a period of more than six years. When she is in hospital, she wants only to be outside again. When she is released, her difficulties in coping and getting welfare benefits make her long for the relative security of hospital.

Sources: *Guardian*, 5 February 1997; *Observer*, 6 May 2001.

What is depression, and why is it so difficult to treat? If it is an illness, why does it seem less responsive to treatment than other diseases? In this chapter we will look at the ways in which both psychiatric and physical illnesses are subject to a process of social construction. They are the products of a long-term transformation in medical understanding that began in the eighteenth century, and they have become the objects of the political and economic activities of the state. Control over the minds and bodies of a population has become a major feature of state policy, and the nature of contemporary medicine cannot be understood in isolation from this. Deborah Tallis would be the first to recognize that her personal troubles are inextricably linked to the public issues of financing medical and welfare provision.

In the section on 'Understanding bodies' we look at the ways in which individual bodies and populations have been controlled, examining the arguments of

Foucault. Aspects of individual health and population demography are considered in 'Health, reproduction, and disability', where we present an account of the consequences of the development of industrial societies. In the final section on 'Medicine, minds, and bodies' we look at the medical control and regulation of bodies, in life and in death, and at the shaping of mental problems by medical interventions. We also consider how these interventions are related to cultural conceptions of femininity and beauty.

Understanding bodies

The role of the state in controlling the bodies of its members has been described in some detail by Michel Foucault. His work provides an essential context for understanding the development of the medical profession and of modern forms of medical practice. He relates these to the transformation of states and their capacities to exercise powers of surveillance over their populations.

Sex, bodies, and populations

Foucault sees the late eighteenth century as the crucial point in the rise of what he calls a **disciplinary society**. This is a form of society in which there was a growing concern to secure the human base of national wealth by introducing new forms of social power over human biology. These forms of power are the demographic control (or *regulation*) of whole populations, and the anatomical control (or *discipline*) of individual human bodies.

Regulating populations

The idea of a national 'population' came to be used as an economic and political category as the leading nation states strived to expand their national wealth and productive powers at the end of the eighteenth century. A population was seen not as an aggregate of individuals but as an entity in its own right, having specific properties of its own. These properties were what Durkheim (1895) was to call 'social facts'. They concerned characteristics of the nation as a whole: its level of productivity, rate of employment, rate of growth, level of national wealth, and so on. Nation states recognized that these variables depended, to a crucial degree, on the size and well-being of their population and the productive powers of its members. These, in turn, depended on the sexual behaviour of its members. As Foucault put it:

> At the heart of this economic and political problem of population was sex: it was necessary to analyse the birth rate, the age of marriage, the legitimate and illegitimate births, the precocity and frequency of sexual relations, the ways of making them fertile or sterile, the effects of unmarried life or of the prohibitions, the impact of contraceptive practices. (Foucault 1976: 25–6)

Thus, a whole new range of social facts were identified for study: rates of birth and death, trends in life expectancy, rates of suicide, levels of health and disease, patterns of diet, and so on. At a national level, there was a growing concern to suppress all forms of sexuality that were not directly linked to procreation and, therefore, to the reproduction of the population. The sexual conduct of the population became the object of analysis and a target for intervention by nation states.

The fertility, health, and welfare of a population, the crucial conditions for its reproduction, are all linked to sexual activity. Sex became a public issue to be regulated through techniques of surveillance and intervention. Observation

---

THEORY AND METHODS

Michel Foucault

Michel Foucault (1926–84) was born in Poitiers, France. He was the son of a doctor and studied philosophy at the École Normale Supérieure in Paris. While there he joined the Communists, though he left the party in the early 1950s. Disillusioned by the failure of philosophy to provide him with answers to the great questions of human existence, he turned to the study of psychology and psychopathology. He spent the period from 1952 to 1955 carrying out research into psychiatric practices in mental hospitals, and he wrote a short book on mental illness.

During academic visits to Sweden and Poland he switched his attention to the history of philosophy and science, and particularly to the history of medical science. He soon completed his first major book in this area, *Madness and Civilization* (1961), and this was rapidly followed by *The Birth of the Clinic* (1963).

More general works in history and theory and a diverse array of specialized investigations led to his masterly *Discipline and Punish* (1975). By this time he had already begun the research for what he intended to be a six-volume history of sexuality, though only parts of this (1976, 1984*a*, 1984*b*) were to appear before his death.

of birth, death, and marriage rates in censuses and surveys, the compilation of official statistics by government agencies, the undertaking of public health and housing schemes, and control over migration were all developed as ways of regulating the 'social body'.

Foucault saw the introduction of these demographic controls as the establishment of a **biopolitics** of the population. This involved new forms of discourse that shaped and gave direction to the demographic controls. Statistics and later demography, for example, defined ways of mapping a population in numerical terms and measuring its key characteristics. These new forms of knowledge became central to state policy. Indeed, the word 'statistics' has its origins in the idea of collecting facts relevant to the state. In a related way, political economy provided ways of mapping the resources that were available to a population and the division of labour through which these resources were used. The emergence and growth of sociology itself, with its concept of 'society', involved recognizing that human populations had then come to be defined by nation-state boundaries and could not be seen as mere aggregates of individuals.

Medical experts played a key part in this reorientation of social thought. According to the medical point of view, populations were complex organic wholes—social bodies—that could exhibit 'pathological' social problems that required effective treatment. This treatment could be achieved through an informed social policy that was aimed at restoring normal 'health'. The health of the social body was seen as dependent, in large part, on the health of the individual bodies from which it was composed. Public-health measures, such as sanitation and housing improvements, were seen as ways of improving the general health of the population. Fear of the effects of such diseases as cholera and typhus were eventually met by the introduction of sewerage and freshwater schemes, urban paving and rebuilding, by regulations over the burial of dead bodies, and through the expansion of hospital medicine. These public-health measures were linked to other techniques of regulation that were massively expanded during the nineteenth century. The police and the prisons, the workhouses, and poor-law welfare administration all contributed to the regulation and control of human populations.

Disciplining the body

The second form of power, anatomical control, involved new disciplines of the body. Foucault describes these as comprising the **anatomo-politics** of the body. This form of power rested on a view of the body as a mechanism with capabilities and skills that had to be optimized in order to increase its usefulness and to integrate it into efficient economic systems.

Until the eighteenth century, physical controls over the body had as their main aims the reaffirmation of the power of the state and the deterrence of others. In many cases this took the form of public spectacles of torture and execution, such as hanging, burning, disfigurement, or dismemberment. Foucault illustrated this by the kind of public execution that was set out for anyone who attempted to murder the French king:

> The flesh will be torn from his breasts, arms, thighs and calves with red-hot pincers, his right hand, holding the knife with which he committed the said parricide, burnt with sulphur, and, on those places where the flesh will be torn away, poured molten lead, boiling oil, burning resin, wax and sulphur melted together and then his body drawn and quartered by four horses and his limbs and body consumed by fire. (Foucault 1975: 3)

Anatomical controls were not, however, purely physical in nature, and Foucault traces a shift in social control from attempts to shape the *flesh* of the body to attempts to shape its *mind*. From the late eighteenth century, new techniques of social control were developed that affected the body only as a way of influencing the mind. Surveillance and the shaping of motives, operating through consciousness and language, were seen as more effective methods of control than force and coercion. This kind of control involved harnessing and intensifying the energies of the human body through the processes of treatment and training.

Disciplines of training into new habits of behaviour were the tasks of the prisons, clinics, schools, workshops, and barracks that brought people together for their various purposes. These kinds of organization began to be established from the sixteenth century, but they were massively expanded with the consolidation of the capitalist market in the nineteenth century. The emergence of scientific medicine was central to the establishment of new disciplines of the body in these organizations. Medicine and reform—the clinic and the prison—were particularly closely associated, as many forms of criminal behaviour were seen as the results of medical conditions that could be treated. The growth of psychiatric medicine, in particular, involved a close association between the criminalization and the medicalization of behaviour (Scull 1979).

Criminals were controlled through private and enclosed disciplines aimed at their reform. Prison discipline has only incidentally been concerned with physical intervention on the body. Methods of punishment were principally concerned with altering the mind in order to shape a person's motivations and desires. Inmates of the prisons were trained in new ways of behaviour so as to produce conforming, obedient individuals who could, in due course, be returned to a 'normal' and productive life. Moral training and industrial training in work habits were at the heart of this new discipline of the body.

The structure of Pentonville prison epitomizes the disciplinary gaze.

© Getty Images/Ian Waldie

> ⮕ *Connections*
>
> In Chapter 14, pp. 545–8, we discuss more fully the nature of the 'carceral' organizations in which this discipline takes place. You will find this a useful background for both the present discussion and our discussion of Goffman's work on the hospital treatment of mental patients later in this chapter.

Conceptions of health and illness in traditional societies had made little distinction between disorders of the body and disorders of the mind. They saw illness in religious terms and linked 'sickness' with 'sin'. Physicians and surgeons did not exist in most societies, and there was little or no medical treatment. Where it did occur, it was barbaric and used unfounded techniques. Even this kind of intervention was largely confined to the aristocratic and professional strata. The illnesses and emotional problems of labourers and peasants were of little concern to anyone else. For the most part, those in the rural villages remained dependent on herbal and folk remedies that were passed down by word of mouth from one generation to the next and were sometimes meted out by the local wise man ('wizard') or wise woman.

The expansion of scientific medicine in the eighteenth and nineteenth centuries changed all this and introduced characteristically modern ways of handling physical and psychological disorders. A new bio-medical model of illness was established, and doctors—as the possessors of this knowledge—established themselves as the 'experts' in the treatment of bodily ills. Centralized hospital medicine allowed doctors to use their control over knowledge to build a power base for themselves. The shift from aristocratic **client control** over medicine to autonomous **professional control** by doctors themselves meant that doctors were able to define the nature of health and to determine forms of treatment (Jewson 1976; see also T. Johnson 1972; I. Waddington 1973). Initially in the private clinics and the workhouses, and later in large public hospitals, forms of hospital medicine and general practice were slowly established through an increasingly complex division of labour that involved doctors, nurses, and other professionals, along with administrators and ancillary workers.

Central to the rise of scientific medicine was a new orientation towards the sick. The medical professions were organized around what Foucault called the **medical gaze**. This is a specific way of seeing and defining the sick that entailed specific forms of investigation, teaching, and clinical intervention. Through the medical gaze was built an image of the 'sick body' as something that could be technically manipulated. The sick were no longer seen as persons, but simply as 'pathological' or dysfunctional bodies. They were systems of organs, cells, and tissues that required treatment whenever they were subject to 'disease'. This new viewpoint culminated in the germ theory of disease that was systematized during the 1870s and 1880s. As scientific technicians, doctors could adopt a detached, neutral, and disinterested orientation towards a particular 'case' and its 'symptoms'. Each case could, furthermore, be given a clinical description that could be bureaucratically organized and filed as a 'case record'.

In all countries, medical experts have become the core members of an administrative apparatus that comprises the various levels of staff that run the wards, consulting rooms, and dispensaries. Bureaucratically organized staff have expanded continuously since the nineteenth century, and include many different categories of 'specialist' doctor (physician, surgeon, psychiatrist, dentist, geriatrician, gynaecologist, paediatrician, etc.), nurses (midwives, psychiatric nurses, district nurses, health visitors), technicians (radiographers, audiologists, haematologists), social workers, and managers. Medicine has expanded into specialized organizations (asylums, sanatoriums, isolation hospitals) and into associated and subsidiary positions and organizations: Medical Officers of Health, general-practice surgeries, health centres, pharmacies, school and occupational nursing, family-planning clinics, and residential homes for the elderly. Administrative apparatuses vary considerably in their levels of organization into health regimes. Even where state centralization has resulted in the establishment of such organizations as the National Health Service, the degree of coordination has generally been quite loose (Freidson 1970).

This looseness and lack of coherence in health regimes led Foucault to reject the concept of a health 'system'. The 'disciplinary society' is one in which organizations and agencies are interconnected in complex and extensive networks of power. However, they are rarely formed into tight and centralized systems. Foucault describes such a network as an 'archipelago'—literally, a group of islands—so as to emphasize that there is only a loose interconnection among the constituent organizations.

Controlling sexuality

Central to the new techniques of anatomical control, according to Foucault, was the attempt to discipline sexuality, which came to be seen as a central and potentially dangerous force that had to be channelled in appropriate and productive directions. In all areas of social life there was an attempt to define and to consolidate images of normality: the good worker, the well-educated child, the law-observing citizen, and so on. The 'pathologies' of the feckless, unemployed poor, the ill-educated truants, and criminals had to be controlled so that they did not 'infect' the 'healthy' members of society. The norm of sexuality was defined in relation to an image of the heterosexual couple. This was the 'Malthusian couple', whose sexual activity was limited to the procreation of children and, thereby, to increasing the size of the population. On this basis, norms of sexual development were defined that described the behaviours that were felt to be appropriate.

Public attention was directed towards the maintenance and protection of the marital, heterosexual sexuality of the 'normal' family. There was a corresponding 'medicalization of the sexually peculiar' and a 'psychiatrization of perverse pleasure' (Foucault 1976: 44). 'Unusual' and 'unnatural' forms of sexuality were identified as 'lesions', 'dysfunctions', or 'symptoms' that reflected deep organic disturbances of the body. Those who were sexually dif-

ferent were fixed in the medical gaze and isolated as objects of investigation and treatment. They were seen as suffering from 'nervous disorders' and sexual 'perversions'. Medical power drew out, isolated, and solidified these sexual disorders and made them objects of public concern, transforming many types of sexual conduct into behaviours that could be pathologized or even criminalized.

Childhood masturbation, for example, became a major target of medical attention. Described as 'onanism' and as a wasteful and dangerous activity, it was seen as something for which parents, teachers, and others needed to be constantly observant. Similarly, the male medical establishment saw female sexuality as dangerous and in need of control. Many female disorders were seen as sexual in origin. 'Idle' or 'nervous' women, for example, were seen as suffering from 'hysteria'—literally, a disorder of the uterus. Such women were in need of medical treatment that could restore them to a healthy state and, therefore, to their domestic, child-bearing, and family roles.

A whole range of sexual practices came to be identified as distinct types of 'perversion'. Psychiatric opinion recognized not only the 'homosexual', but also the 'zoophile' and the 'zooerast', the 'auto-monosexualist', the 'mixoscopophile', the 'gynecomast', the 'presbyophile', and so on (Foucault 1976: 43). Many of these categories had only a short medical life, before being superseded by newer ones. Today, for example, the 'homosexual', the 'sado-masochist', and various types of 'fetishist' form the core elements in the psychiatric imagery of contemporary sexuality.

Several perversions were also seen as carrying the threat of other forms of illness. Diseases linked to sex, such as the venereal diseases of syphilis and gonorrhoea, were seen as ever-present consequences of unnatural sexual pleasures, much as AIDS has been seen. Concern about the spread of these diseases in the nineteenth century led to great public concern over prostitution, which itself reflected male attitudes towards female sexuality.

Foucault has provided a very powerful account of the disciplines of the body and the regulation of populations in modern societies. His argument, however, tends to present a highly flexible picture of the body that recognizes few significant physical limits to the ways in which the human body can be shaped by social forces. The body is known only in and through discourse and, as a result, Foucault tends to play down the importance of the physical, material aspects of bodies that exist independently of medical and other forms of discourse. Later in this chapter we will look at some of these material features of populations and bodies before going on to consider the social construction of health and illness through medical discourse. First, however, we must give some further consideration to the idea of surveillance.

Surveillance of populations

Regulation and discipline depend on practices of **surveillance**. Those who are to be controlled through the new techniques of biopolitics and anatomo-politics must be observed and monitored by the various agencies whose job it is to supervise and superintend their behaviour. The power of surveillance has been central to the growth of nation states, which have developed complex apparatuses for collecting and processing information on those who live within their boundaries. In this section we will look at the establishment of censuses and surveys along with mechanisms for the analysis and reporting of official statistics.

The birth of the census

Central to systems of surveillance were new mechanisms for counting the population and keeping track of its growth. In Britain and in many other countries, the churches had been responsible for the regulation of births, marriages, and burials, together with occasional local censuses, since the sixteenth century. The new systems of the eighteenth and nineteenth centuries, however, established national systems backed by the full force of the law. In 1800 an Act of Parliament established a regular census, a full count of the whole English population. The first national census took place the following year and, with the sole exception of 1941, a census has been taken every ten years since then. The cost of the Statistical Service, however, led the government to set up a review of the Census in 2002. The task of the review was to see whether the kind of information collected in the census could more cheaply be collected from computerized tax and benefit records, supplemented by a sample survey. The internal review proposed that the census continue but that its results and procedures be more closely integrated with other official data sources.

In 1837 a national system of 'civil registration' was set up for England. Under this system, all births, marriages, and deaths were registered at a local office that returned these to a national office. A few years later, similar systems were set up for Scotland and Ireland (Scott 1990: chapter 4; see also Nissel 1987; Higgs 1996). This system of civil registration is still in operation and provides many of the basic demographic statistics that are published by the government.

Similar moves occurred in other countries. By the middle of the nineteenth century, registration and statistical services had been established in virtually all of the major European countries, in the United States, in Australia and New Zealand, and in Japan. Alongside the collection of data on their populations, states also began to compile statistics on crime, health, and a whole array of economic matters. Publication of statistics on court trials, for example, began in Britain in 1805, and this was followed by prison statistics in 1836 and police statistics in 1857. By the time that Durkheim carried out his investigations into suicide (Durkheim 1897), official statistics on this subject were available for a large number of countries.

The censuses in Britain are carried out by local enumerators, who issue standard forms to each household in their area. These forms require information on the names, ages, sexes, places of birth, and occupations of all members of the household, together with an indication of their marital status and their relationship to each other. To this core of information is added a varying set of questions concerning travel to work, education, housing conditions, car ownership, and ethnicity. The household forms, when completed, are used for the compilation of registers and, in recent years, computer records, and they are stored by the Office for National Statistics (ONS), formerly the Office of Population, Censuses and Surveys (OPCS).

Civil registration records are also stored by the General Register Offices for England and Wales, Scotland, and Northern Ireland, and it is from these registers that birth, marriage, and death certificates are produced. The birth registers record the name, sex, place of birth, and date of birth of each child, together with the names of its parents, the occupation of its father, and the name and address of the person (usually a parent) registering the birth. A marriage register records the date of the marriage, the names, ages, and occupations of both partners, the names and occupations of their fathers (but not of their mothers), and whether the partners were bachelor, spinster, or widowed at the time of the marriage. The death registers are much shorter, giving simply the name, age, sex, and occupations of the deceased, the cause and place of death, and the name and address of the informant.

The original records and registers from the census and civil registration are stored under conditions of official secrecy, though the census records are opened for public examination after 100 years. Staff in ONS, however, have full access to all the original records and they use them to produce periodic statistical reports. Civil registration data are summarized quarterly in a publication now called *Population Trends*, while census data are summarized in national and county reports and in the so-called small area statistics. Taken together, the census and civil registration data provide regular benchmark counts of the whole population and a record of trends between these benchmark years. In addition to aggregate totals, the statistical summaries give breakdowns and comparisons by age, sex, class (as computed from occupational data), and a whole variety of other factors.

The ONS brought together various government statistical agencies around the Government Social Survey (GSS), which had begun in 1939 as a part of the Ministry of Information. It had the task of monitoring public morale during the Second World War. Drawing on the successes achieved by many private and academic surveys, the GSS used sampling methods to obtain national data that would complement the more comprehensive data that came from the census and civil registration. The GSS produced detailed information on a whole range of topics much more cheaply than could a complete census. Some of the early wartime surveys looked at the availability of steel for corset production and shortages in domestic brushes and brooms, though more long-lasting results came from surveys on food consumption and attitudes towards sexual disease.

In the post-war period, a number of regular national surveys were established, including the Family Expenditure Survey, the General Household Survey, and the Labour Force Survey. Reports are produced from each of these annual surveys, and their statistical results are combined with census and civil registration data in such compilations as *Social Trends* (from 1970). Together with health service and other data, they have been used for periodic reports on drinking, smoking, dental health, disease and illness, employment, and numerous other issues.

The Office for National Statistics oversees various statistical publications and coordinates them with those from other government departments. Criminal statistics are collected in the Home Office, which publishes *Criminal Statistics* and various reports from the regular *British Crime Survey*; health statistics are collected by the Department of Health; employment and unemployment statistics as well as educational statistics are collected by the Department for Education and Skills, which publishes the *Employment Gazette*; and financial and trade statistics are collected in the Treasury. A cost-cutting review in 1980 made substantial cutbacks in the statistical service in order to reduce its public-service role and limit its work on social statistics, but there is still a massive output of statistical data. In 2000 'National Statistics' was formed as a central organizing agency for all government statistics.

THEORY AND METHODS

Government social surveys

In addition to occasional surveys and alongside the census and civil registration, ONS is responsible for three major social surveys that provide essential information for planners and academics.

The **Family Expenditure Survey** began in 1957 and carries out interviews with people in 11,000 households. These people keep detailed records of their expenditure over a period, and they provide details on their incomes. In addition to providing information on tax changes and on income distribution, typical patterns of expenditure can be identified. These data are used in the preparation of the Retail Price Index.

The **General Household Survey** began in 1970. It undertakes annual interviews with those aged over 16 in 12,500 households. Topics covered include household composition, housing, employment, education, health, and income. Additional topics are added from year to year. It was reduced in scope in the 1980 cost-cutting review, and it was a suspended in 1997–8 and 1999–2000 in order to save money and carry out a review. It was reinstated in 2001 and continues in operation.

The **Labour Force Survey** began in 1973. It was carried out every two years until 1983, annually from 1984 to 1991, and is now a quarterly survey. It draws its information from a regular 'panel' of individuals in 60,000 households. Questions covered in the interviews cover employment, hours worked, vocational training, education, job-search methods, nationality, and ethnicity.

➔ You can find the official government statistics home page at: www.statistics.gov.uk/. From this page you can download many statistical tables and publications. Survey work can be found at www.statistics.gov.uk/ssd/

◆ *Stop and reflect*

In this section we have examined the growth of regulation and discipline in the control of populations and human bodies. We used the ideas of Foucault to bring together a number of concerns.

- The development of nation states and the idea of a national population was an important feature of the growth of surveillance and control. Medicine and statistics were central to this.

- Medicine introduced new techniques of social control aimed at the shaping of the body and the influencing of the mind. The medical gaze introduced conceptions of the sick body and of professional expertise.

- Look at our discussion of sexuality in Chapter 5, pp. 171–3 and consider what this tells us about how control over sexuality became central to control over populations.

We also looked at the ways in which new techniques of measurement through censuses, surveys, and registration became central to social surveillance. This resulted in the collection and compilation of official statistics.

- Nation states have established regular population censuses and a number of regular surveys aimed at collecting data about their people.

- Criminal statistics, unemployment statistics, demographic statistics, and a variety of other statistics are shaped by the bureaucratic procedures through which they are produced. They reflect administrative concerns rather than sociological concepts.

- Can official statistics have any useful role in explorations of health and illness?

Health, reproduction, and disability

Foucault's work highlighted the importance of examining the ways in which populations are regulated and individual bodies are disciplined. In this section we will look at the material aspects of each of these. We will look at the material structure of populations—what Durkheim called 'social morphology'—and at the material health, disease, and diet of individual bodies. We will show that both social morphology and individual health have undergone a distinctive pattern of change since 1800.

Fertility and mortality

Total world population seems to have fluctuated at a level of about half a billion until the modern period, when it began to climb steadily. By 1950 it had risen to 2.5 billion, and in 2001 it stood at 6.1 billion. The United Kingdom, with a population of just over 59 million, has about 1 per cent of the total world population. Within the European Union, it has about the same size of population as France and Italy, but it is significantly smaller than Germany. Britain, however, is quite small and so has a very high population density (Coleman and Salt 1992; *Social Trends* 2005).

The British population figure of 59 million is a substantial increase over the figure of 38 million recorded in 1901, and the population is estimated to rise to almost 64 million by the year 2021. Despite this substantial increase, the *rate* of growth in the twentieth century was

Global focus Population

Total world population is currently around 6.2 billion people. Europe's total population (see Figure 8.1) is about half as big again as the total population of the United States. This, in turn, is half as big again as the population of Japan. Europe, the Americas, and Africa are roughly equivalent to each other in terms of population size, but by far the most populous area of the world is Asia. Almost two-thirds of the world's population lives in Asia, and almost a quarter of the world's population lives in China. The significance of this is clear when population is compared with economic development, an issue that we discuss more fully in Chapter 16. Just 20 per cent of the world's population lives in the most developed areas: in North America, Europe, Australia, New Zealand, and Japan. The remaining 80 per cent of people live in the world's poorest countries, where population growth is also most rapid. The population of India, for example, has increased by over 20 per cent each decade, and its growth in population between 1991 and 2001 was greater than the total population of Brazil, the fifth most populous country in the world. In 2001 India became the second country in the world, after China, to achieve a population of more than one billion. (See **www.censusindia.net**/)

Figure 8.1 World population, 1800–2001

Region	Population (m.)		
	1800	1900	2001
Europe	203	408	726
North America	7	82	317
Latin America, Caribbean	24	74	527
Asia	635	947	3,721
Africa	107	133	813
Oceania	2	6	31
Total	978	1,650	6,134

Note: Figures do not total exactly because of rounding in the original source.

Source: *Social Trends* (1996: table 1.21; 2002: table 1.17).

Figure 8.2 UK population, 1851–2021 (000s)

Year	England	Wales	Scotland	Northern Ireland	UK
1851	16,764	1,163	2,889	1,443	22,259
1901	30,515	2,013	4,472	1,237	38,237
1931	37,359	2,593	4,843	1,243	46,038
1961	43,561	2,635	5,184	1,427	52,807
1971	46,412	2,740	5,236	1,540	55,928
1981	46,821	2,813	5,180	1,538	56,352
1991	48,204	2,899	5,107	1,601	57,807
2001	49,450	2,910	5,064	1,689	59,113
2021 (projected)	*53,954*	*3,106*	*4,963*	*1,811*	*63,835*

Sources: Coleman and Salt (1992: table 3.1); Central Office of Information (1995: table 1); *Social Trends* (2002: table 1.1); *Population Trends 121* (2005: table 1.2).

much lower than it was in the nineteenth century. The first Census, in 1801, recorded a population of just over ten million, a figure that had doubled by 1851 and had almost doubled again by 1901. By contrast, the estimated population size for 2025 is less than double the 1901 figure. The fastest period of population growth in the twentieth century was during its first decade, and the growth rate has declined since then. Despite a small boom in the 1960s, this decline in the rate of growth was especially rapid in the last thirty years of the twentieth century and it is expected to continue. These trends are summarized in Figure 8.2.

Marriage and fertility

The size of a population and its rate of growth or decline are largely determined by the balance between fertility (births) and mortality (deaths). Whenever the birth rate is higher than the death rate, there is an increase in the so-called natural growth rate of the population. This terminology is a little unhelpful, as it implies that changes in population that are due to other factors are somehow 'unnatural'. Nevertheless, it remains the case that the balance between births and deaths is fundamental to the development of any particular population.

The basic measure of the **fertility** of a population is its so-called crude birth rate. This is the annual number of live births per 1,000 population. This widely used figure gives a result that is very similar in form to a percentage figure, but it is calculated on a base of 1,000 rather than 100. The crude birth rate in Britain stood at 35.2 per 1,000 between 1860 and 1870. It declined very rapidly from the 1870s to the 1920s, reaching 27.2 in the period 1901–10. The drop in the rate was particularly sharp while men were

away at the front during the First World War. The rate increased in the years immediately after the war, but the decline set in again fairly rapidly and continued through the 1930s.

Despite the onset of the Second World War in 1939, the birth rate increased through most of the wartime years, and there was a substantial baby boom in the years 1945–8. From a low point in the middle of the 1950s, the birth rate increased through the 1960s. This was a period of relative prosperity and affluence, and there was a second baby boom between 1957 and 1966. Following this boom, the rate declined once more, and it has continued to decline. The decline since the 1960s has been especially rapid. The crude birth rate fell from a level of 18.8 in 1964 to one of 10.8 in 2005.

As its name implies, this 'crude rate' is a very rough-and-ready figure, which does not directly reflect changes in the age and sex composition of the population. What is called the 'general fertility rate' does a rather more precise job of measurement. This is the number of births per 1,000 women in the usual child-bearing age range of 15 to 44. Figures show that this rate fell from 94 to 55 between 1964 and 2001. The general fertility rate, however, is also a little misleading, as it obscures the variations that exist from one age group to another. Age-specific fertility rates show, for example, that there were 73.3 births per 1,000 women aged 20–24 in 2004, compared with 99.4 births per 1,000 women aged 30–34.

Changes in the age-specific rates—and, therefore, in the overall birth rate—are consequences of changes in the age of marriage and the age at which child-bearing begins. If people marry late, then there will be fewer years of marriage in which they can have children. Similarly, if married women delay having their first child, they will also reduce the total number of years that are available for child-bearing. The age at marriage for women was between 25 and 26 throughout the period from 1900 to 1940. The age at marriage for men in the same period was between 27 and 28. After 1940, people began to marry much earlier, and the average marriage age had fallen to 22 for women and 24 for men by 1970. During the 1980s and 1990s, however, age at marriage began to increase once more. At the turn of the century it stood at about 24 for women and 26 for men.

Late marriage is especially marked among professional and managerial workers. Late marriage, however, does not necessarily mean that people begin their families later. As we show in Chapter 12, the rate of marriage itself has fallen as more and more people choose to cohabit. Many 'late' marriages take place between people who have already been cohabiting for some time. Nevertheless, the so-called age of maternity—the age at which a woman has her first child—has increased. In 1951 the average age at maternity

When is the right time to have a baby?
© Alice Chadwick

was 28.4 years. This fell to 27.3 in 1964, and 26.5 in 1977. During the 1980s and 1990s the age of maternity increased, and by 2005 it had risen to above 27.

Mortality

The basic measure of **mortality** is the crude death rate, the annual number of deaths per 1,000 population. Death rates were very high in the eighteenth century, but began to fall during the nineteenth century. By 1870 the rate stood at 23.0 per 1,000, and this had dropped to 13.5 by 1910. Death rates altered very little during the rest of the century, though high rates were recorded—for obvious reasons—in the wartime years. The death rate is currently between 10 and 11 persons per 1,000.

The aggregate figures, of course, mask significant differences among the age groups. There are fewer than one per 1,000 deaths among those aged between 1 and 15 years, while there are 44.7 per 1,000 among those aged 65–79 and 141.4 per 1,000 among those aged 80 or more. If crude death rates are compared across the country, the highest death rates—for obvious reasons—appear in those areas where there are relatively large numbers of retired persons. Many of these deaths are among people who have retired to the seaside. About a third of the population in East Sussex and the south of the Isle of Wight are over pension age, and these areas have the highest death rates in the country.

A more useful comparison of death rates uses the so-called standardized mortality rate, which takes account of the age structure of the population. A figure of 100 indicates that an area or group has exactly the death rate that would be expected among people of its age composition; a figure above 100 indicates higher-than-average death rates, and a figure below 100 indicates lower-than-average death rates. Using age-specific measures for Great Britain as a whole, death rates are lowest in East Anglia and the south-west, and they are highest in Scotland and the north of England.

Mortality rates reflect the increase in life expectancy that has taken place over the century. People are now living longer than ever before, and women live longer than men. Life expectancy for a male born in 2003 was about 76 years, compared with 80 for a female. The corresponding life expectancies for 1901 were 45 for men and 49 for women, an increase in average life span of 50 per cent. A hundred years earlier, in 1801, life expectancy was about 37 years (Coleman and Salt 1992: 38).

This does not mean, however, that large numbers of people died at age 37 in 1801 and at about 50 in 1901. Life expectancy at birth is very low when rates of infant mortality are high, but those who survive their childhood can expect to live rather longer than these minimal figures suggest. Although life expectancy at birth in 1901 was just under 50, those who actually managed to survive until age 45 could certainly have expected about another twenty-five years of life. Changes in life expectancy, then, reflect two quite separate changes: the rate of infant mortality and the rate of post-infant mortality.

One of the major changes in mortality during the twentieth century was the reduction in levels of infant mortality. This is officially measured by the number of deaths of infants aged under 1 year old per 1,000 live births. At the end of the nineteenth century, infant mortality accounted for one in five of all deaths. Most of these were due to diarrhoea, dysentery, and other forms of gastric infection. These were diseases of poverty, poor sanitation, and bad hygiene (Coleman and Salt 1992: 54). The rate of infant mortality fell constantly over the course of the twentieth century. It fell from 147 in 1901 to 70 in 1931, 32 in 1951, 23 in 1961, 10 in 1981, and 6.9 in 1994. The greatest improvements in infant health have been those that have increased survival chances during the critical first four weeks of life. This so-called neonatal mortality rate stood at 24.48 per 1,000 in 1951. By 2004, total infant mortality stood at 5.1 per 1,000.

Infant mortality is not constant across the country, but varies quite considerably from one region to another. Rural areas of Oxfordshire, Cambridgeshire, and Warwickshire, like the affluent districts of London, Surrey, and Hampshire, have infant mortality rates of between five and six per 1,000. The poorer urban areas of Birmingham, Wolverhampton, and Bradford have rates that are more than double these levels. Rates of infant mortality also vary by ethnicity: rates for infants born to mothers from the Caribbean and Africa are one and a half times those for mothers born in Britain.

Rates for mothers born in Pakistan were double the British-born rate.

Age, sex, and ethnicity

Any population is diverse in terms of its sex and age structure. Very slightly more than a half of all births are male, and males outnumber females in the population throughout childhood and the early years of adulthood. Death rates for males, however, are higher than they are for females at all ages, and women tend to live longer than men. As a result, women outnumber men from about the age of 50. Among those who are 80 years old or more, there are twice as many women as men.

The age composition of the population can vary quite considerably from one period to another. From the middle of the nineteenth century until the 1920s, there were relatively large numbers of infants and young children. About one-third of the population was aged 15 or less in 1901. At the same time, there were very small numbers of people aged over 70. As a result, the British population was, overall, quite young. A decline in the birth rate, however, has meant that the total number of children in the population has declined from its earlier level. About one-fifth of the population is now aged under 16, while one-sixth of the population is aged 65 or more. Baby booms in the 1940s and the 1960s (peaking in 1964) have produced bulges in the age distribution of the population in successive years as the members of these cohorts have aged. At the same time, there has been a growth in the number of elderly people. In 1993, 18.3 per cent of the population were of retirement age or above (60 for women, 65 for men), the corresponding figure having been 6.2 per cent in 1901 (see Pilcher 1995: figure 1.2). In 2000, 13 per cent of men and 18 per cent of women were aged 65 or over.

It is estimated that 23 per cent of the population will be aged 65 or over in 2031, and about a third of these people will be aged 80 or more. Those over 80 will be the survivors of the post-war baby boom, while those in their sixties will be the survivors of the 1960s baby boom. Looking at these trends in the numbers of the young and the old from a different angle, those of working age (16 to 65), whether actually working or not, made up about two-thirds of the population in 2001 and they will have fallen to below 60 per cent by 2025 (see Figure 8.3).

Britain is not unusual among advanced industrial societies in this respect, although its population is now somewhat older than the European average. The problems of an ageing population are especially marked in Japan. There are major differences, of course, from the non-industrial societies, which tend to have much younger populations. About one-third of the Chinese population is under 15 years old, and only 6 per cent are aged 65 or more. Where Britain is unusual among industrial societies is in

Briefing: an ageing population

The problems of an ageing population are increasingly debated in our newspapers and frequently make front page news. Greater life expectancy has meant that a larger number of retired people must be supported by the younger working population. This puts great pressure on the pension system, as the contributions made by those in employment are used to pay pensions for those who have retired, leaving less money available for the pensions of younger workers when it comes to their turn to retire. Low stock market values, on which many pensions depend, during the early years of the century have made this problem even worse. There have been suggestions that the age of retirement be raised to 70 from its present level of 65, as improved health has meant that people are now capable of working for longer. It has been estimated, however, that the increase in average life span may continue to grow, and the very elderly will make heavier demands on the health care system and on the need for residential care. (See *Guardian*, 10 May 2002, 25 July 2005.)

Figure 8.3 Age and gender, United Kingdom, 1961–2001

Year	% of population			
	Under 16	16–39	40–64	65 or over
1961	25	33	32	12
1971	25	33	30	13
1981	22	35	28	15
1991	20	35	29	16
	Under 16	16–34	35–64	65 or over
2001				
Male	21	26	39	14
Female	19	25	39	18

Source: *Social Trends* (2002: table 1.5 and 2005: table 1.2). See also Pilcher (1995) and Vincent (1995).

the ethnic composition of its ageing population. Members of ethnic minorities (predominantly black and Asian) are significantly younger than the rest of the population. Almost one-third of the ethnic minority population is under 16 and only less than one in ten is aged over 60. In thirty years time, if present trends continue, the population of working age will be disproportionately black and Asian, while the retired population will be disproportionately white.

We showed earlier that the so-called natural growth of a population depends upon the balance between its birth rate and its death rate. A further variable that has an effect on population, which should by no means be regarded as 'unnatural', is migration. **Immigration** (the movement of people into a country) tends to increase the population, while **emigration** (the movement of people out of a country) tends to reduce it. The net effect of migration on a population is the balance between its levels of immigration and emigration from year to year. As we show in Chapter 6, pp. 215–7, migration into Britain had little impact on the overall size of the population until relatively recently. Emigration more or less balanced immigration until the growth of immigration during the 1950s and 1960s. Migration has, however, altered the ethnic composition of the population. Just over 5 per cent of the

population now assign themselves to a non-white ethnic category, about a half of them describing themselves as Asians and about a half as 'black' Africans or African-Caribbean. The majority of these people, however, are not 'immigrants' but were born in the United Kingdom.

The demographic transition

Industrialized societies have been described as showing a particular pattern called the **demographic transition** (W. S. Thompson 1929; Kingsley Davis 1945). According to this point of view, population change shows a succession of three stages (see Figure 8.4). Stage 1, which in Britain preceded the Industrial Revolution of the eighteenth century, is a period of high death rates combined with high birth rates. As a result, population growth is fairly slow. Industrialization initiates the transition to Stage 2, where death rates begin to fall as the improved food supply increases longevity and reduces infant mortality. Birth rates, however, remain high, and so population begins to increase rapidly. This period of rapid population growth ended in Britain at the close of the nineteenth century, when birth rates began to fall. Stage 3, then, is a period of low death rates combined with low birth rates, resulting in only slow population growth.

The late and more rapid industrialization of other European countries meant that they underwent the demographic transition somewhat later than Britain. It is now the common experience of all the industrialized societies. It has been suggested that the non-industrialized countries of the world today will eventually undergo a similar transition as they industralize. Many think that this will resolve

of disease by making people less susceptible. Medical treatment, on the other hand, has mainly had an effect since the early years of the twentieth century, when techniques of vaccination and immunization improved the survival chances of infants. We look further into this in the following section.

Health and disease

One of the concerns of writers such as Malthus was the fear that population growth would outstrip food production and that this would result in famine, disease, and death on a large scale. The most pessimistic expectations have not materialized, but patterns of death and disease have changed quite markedly since the end of the nineteenth century.

The health transition

In parallel with the demographic transition that we have described, there has been a change in patterns of disease. This can be described as a **health transition**. This transition, shown in Figure 8.5, involves a change in the nature and scale of the principal diseases that have been responsible for ill health and death as societies have industrialized.

Stage 1 of the health transition is that of pre-modern, agrarian societies. The principal causes of illness and death are acute infectious diseases. These are spread from one person to another through direct contact, through polluted water, or through parasitic carriers such as fleas and mosquitoes. Diseases such as tuberculosis, malaria, and plague are endemic in these societies, along with cholera, typhus, leprosy, and sleeping sickness. Young children are particularly susceptible to measles, smallpox, and diphtheria. Whole populations are at risk from these diseases, and only the very wealthy have a degree of immunity. The incidence of these diseases is greatly affected by poor harvests and by warfare, which reduce or disrupt food supply and result in deteriorating living and working conditions. In these circumstances, epidemics are regular occurrences.

Stage 2 of the health transition, corresponding to the period of industralization, involves some improvement in the standard of living for many people, though the problem of urban poverty increases. Acute infectious diseases (particularly tuberculosis, cholera, and typhus) remain at a high level. They are, however, particularly concentrated among the new urban poor, whose living conditions make them the most vulnerable. Tuberculosis accounted for 13.2 per cent of all deaths in Britain in 1880, typhus, dysentery, and cholera accounted for 7.3 per cent, measles, scarlet fever, and whooping cough each accounted for just less than 1 per cent. Alongside these infectious diseases, respiratory diseases such as pneumonia accounted for 17.6 per cent of all deaths. Improved public health through sanitation, housing, and nutrition had some effect on the diseases of the poor, but it served mainly to confine the diseases to the poor districts and to insulate the majority of the population from their worst effects.

In Stage 3 of the health transition there is an enhanced control over infectious diseases, which fall to low levels. It is not always realized how little direct effect medical treatment had until comparatively recently. The decline in tuberculosis, for example, began in about 1850, but the tubercle bacillus was not discovered until 1882, and drug treatment was not available until 1947. Nevertheless, vaccination and the use of antibiotics from the 1930s and 1940s did have a significant effect on health, particularly on that of children. This was possible once the underlying improvements in living conditions had been made (McKeown 1979). There has been a rapid growth in medical and surgical techniques since the 1940s. As a result of these medical advances, there have been the significant falls in infant mortality and the general increase in life expectancy that we have already discussed.

In Stage 3, rates of the degenerative diseases, such as cancer, heart disease, and strokes, are high. They become the principal causes of chronic illness and death. These diseases result largely from bodily deterioration with age, or from environmental conditions (such as dietary changes

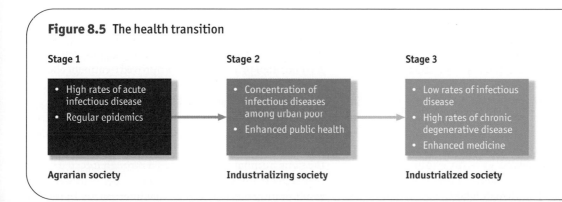

Figure 8.5 The health transition

Stage 1	Stage 2	Stage 3
• High rates of acute infectious disease • Regular epidemics	• Concentration of infectious diseases among urban poor • Enhanced public health	• Low rates of infectious disease • High rates of chronic degenerative disease • Enhanced medicine
Agrarian society	**Industrializing society**	**Industrialized society**

and the use of alcohol and tobacco) that have their greatest effects as bodies age. People now live long enough to suffer from different kinds of disease. Respiratory diseases continue to account for about one in ten of all deaths in Britain, but tuberculosis now accounts for only a fraction of 1 per cent. Circulatory diseases (those of the heart and blood vessels) now account for 46 per cent of all deaths, compared with just 7 per cent in 1880. Another major cause of death is cancer, which now accounts for 25 per cent of deaths (2.5 per cent in 1880). The incidence of lung cancer among men has declined since 1951, but among women both lung cancer and breast cancer have increased sharply since the 1960s.

Britain is now above the European Union average for both circulatory disease and cancer. The highest rates of death from cancer among European women are found in Denmark, Ireland, and Britain; the lowest rates are in Greece, Spain, and France. Among men, the highest rates of death from circulatory disease are found in Austria and Germany, and the lowest rates are those of France and Spain.

Changes in patterns of death in the twentieth century reflect, in part, a real increase in the level of such diseases as cancer as a result of changes in living conditions. An increase in smoking in the first half of the century, for example, was responsible for the increase in the prevalence of both lung cancer and heart disease. However, these trends also reflect increased life expectancy. Putting matters crudely, a greater control over infectious diseases means that people are now living long enough to face the circulatory and cancer problems of old age that their parents and grandparents avoided because they died much younger. These diseases are, therefore, commonest among the oldest age groups. By contrast, over a half of deaths among men aged 15 to 39 result from injury or poison (associated with drugs or alcohol), and not from disease at all. Many of these injuries result from road-traffic accidents, which account for nearly 40 per cent of all accidental deaths.

Health and well-being

Of course, not all people suffer from serious illnesses. A national survey in 1993 found that over three-quarters of adults rated their own health as 'good' or 'very good'. Nevertheless, about 40 per cent reported that they had a long-standing illness or disability.

On average, people see their doctor about four times each year, and it is he or she who provides most of the medical treatment that people receive. More serious illnesses are often referred on for more specialist treatment at hospitals, though this may involve a long wait until a clinic appointment or hospital bed is available. In 2005, 800,000 people in England were on waiting lists for in-patient treatment, and 39,000 had been waiting for more than five months. The British health-care system is not typical. In the United States, for example, the bulk of the

health system operates on a private basis rather than as a public service, and it is normal for paying patients to make direct approaches to specialist practitioners.

For all age groups—and among both men and women—problems of the musculoskeletal system (arthritis and rheumatism) were among the most common long-standing disorders. Among those aged 45–64, almost a quarter report these kinds of problems. For those aged 65 or over, the proportion rises, especially among women: almost two-thirds of women report such problems. Among older men, however, heart and circulatory problems outweighed arthritis and rheumatism. The most common heart and circulation problems faced by older people were high blood pressure and angina, though large numbers of people experienced diabetes or abnormal heart rhythms. Most older people, of course, experienced both musculoskeletal problems and circulatory difficulties, along with other long-term disorders.

Among the medical conditions that affect large numbers of people and that are chronic rather than physically dangerous are fatigue and sleep problems, irritability and worry, anxiety, depression, and 'stress'. People aged 35–54 are particularly likely to report that they have experienced stress or pressure in their life; men and those in non-manual jobs are more likely to report this than women and those in manual jobs. A growing amount of evidence, however, shows that medically diagnosed stress is more common among manual workers than non-manual workers. On the other hand, rates of depression are much higher among women than among men, and they are especially great among women in manual-working households.

Asthma has shown an increased incidence during the 1980s. This is an illness that is particularly likely to affect children and that has been linked to growing levels of air pollution. Many other childhood diseases, however, have shown a long-term decline. Measles and whooping cough, despite occasional epidemics, are at a lower level than they were even fifty years ago, and diseases such as diphtheria (which killed about 10,000 children each year in the second half of the nineteenth century) and polio are kept under control through immunization programmes.

A major health issue of the 1980s was AIDS (acquired immune deficiency syndrome). This is sexually transmitted, but can also be contracted through infected blood. It could often prove fatal until improved treatment allowed its effects to be kept under control. The number of new cases reported in the United Kingdom increased from 298 in 1986 to 1,785 in 1994, and 3,400 people were diagnosed in 2000. Of these known cases, about 6 per cent resulted from infection as a result of the injection of drugs. About the same number were contracted through infected blood (generally from a transfusion), and 73 per cent were as a result of unprotected homosexual intercourse. In the late 1990s, however, the number of cases resulting from sex

Global focus Health

The World Health Organization has investigated the major causes of death on a global scale. The largest single cause is heart disease, which accounts for 13.7 per cent of all deaths. In second place is cerebrovascular disease (stroke), accounting for 9.5 per cent of deaths, and in third place are deaths from acute respiratory infections. HIV/AIDS is the fourth largest killer, accounting for 4.2 per cent of deaths world-wide.

Rates of HIV infection vary considerably across the world. Although it came to prominence in the United States and Europe, the prevalence there is among the lowest in the world. Rates are higher in the countries of the former USSR and in South East Asia, but they reach their highest levels in Africa. In sixteen African countries more than 10 per cent of the population is infected with AIDS. In Zimbabwe, one-third of the population is estimated to be affected by the disease. The causes of infection vary. In the United States and Europe the disease was initially spread through unprotected gay male sex. In Eastern Europe infected intravenous drug use is the main agent, though this is responsible for a significant minority of cases in the United States and some European countries. In Africa, on the other hand, AIDS has spread predominantly through heterosexual relations. Nelson Mandela spoke out about the experience of AIDS in his own family in order to increase awareness of the issue within Africa.

When account is taken of the burden of disease—the number of years that someone lives with a debilitating disease—psychological conditions appear as an important factor. Depression is the fifth most significant cause of disease burden. In Europe and the United States, it is estimated that depression is actually the second largest cause of death if account is taken of its impact on alcohol, tobacco, and drug use and of the health consequences of these. The European country with the highest life expectancy is Sweden, where average expectancy is almost two years longer than in Britain. France and Germany have higher

Figure 8.6 Prevalence of HIV/AIDS in various countries (2002)

	% of total population
Japan	>0.01
USA	0.61
Russia	0.90
UK	0.11
Australia	0.15
Thailand	1.80
Haiti	6.10
Malawi	15.96
South Africa	20.10
Zimbabwe	33.70

rates of death from cancer (among men and women) than does Britain, though Britain has higher rates of death from heart disease.

Health problems are especially acute in the poorer countries, yet these are precisely the countries with the lowest spending on health care. Cameroon, Indonesia, Nigeria, Sri Lanka, and Sudan each spent less than 2 per cent of their GDP on health care. In Germany, 10 per cent of the national income is spent on health care, compared with 9.3 per cent in France and 6.8 per cent in Britain.

Sources: *World Health Report* (WHO, 1999); *Guardian*, 7 December 2001; **www.avert.org/aroundworld.htm**; Lichtenstein (2002: table 19.1).

between men fell and was overtaken by the rapid rise in cases due to sex between men and women. To put these numbers in context, the incidence of many less serious sexually contracted diseases is much higher, and also increasing. The number of cases of gonorrhoea and syphilis had decreased substantially, but increased sharply in the second half of the 1990s. Chlamydia, another sexually transmitted disease, shows a rising trend.

Diet and fitness

The health and fitness of a population reflect a whole complex of environmental factors. Among the most critical have been patterns of eating and exercise. Under-nourishment

was chronic throughout the eighteenth and nineteenth centuries, when large numbers of people died in the Irish famines. A lack of food left many people unhealthy and prone to infectious diseases. At the time of the Boer War (1899–1902), 38 per cent of potential army recruits were rejected as being undersized or unfit for military service.

During the twentieth century, the quality of the national diet generally improved. Levels of poverty have declined, though lack of food remains a problem for many people. Many of the poor are forced into eating cheap but unhealthy diets. Although the quantity of food eaten by the majority of the population increased over the century, its nutritional quality has not always increased at the same pace. Compared with the typical nineteenth-century diet, there has been a reduction in fibre intake and an increase in fat, sugar, and salt intake, as well as a greater consumption of alcohol and tobacco.

There have been major changes in diet since the 1960s. Most significant has been a shift from red meats (beef and lamb) and dairy products to poultry and vegetables. The increased consumption of vegetables reflects a growing level of vegetarianism and concern for healthy eating, especially among the young (P. Atkinson 1983; Twigg 1983). There has also, however, been a decline in the consumption of fresh vegetables and an increase in the consumption of processed vegetables. This is associated with a growth in the consumption of 'convenience foods' of all kinds, including sweets and snacks. A national survey for the mid-1990s found that young people in the 16–24 age group were especially likely to eat confectionery and to do so on five or six days of each week. These trends are, perhaps, reinforced by the decline in the idea of the 'family meal' as the focus of family life. Households of all kinds rely more and more on convenience foods, rather than the traditional 'hot meal' with a 'pudding', and household members eat at different times of the day (Blaxter and Paterson 1982; Murcott 1982; Charles and Kerr 1988).

Smoking has declined considerably since the early 1970s. In 1972, 52 per cent of men and 41 per cent of women were smokers. By 1994 these figures had fallen to 28 per cent and 26 per cent respectively. The fall levelled off, however, and there appears to be a growth in smoking among those in the 20–24 age group: 42 per cent of men and 39 per cent of women in this age group are now regular smokers. Similarly, the incidence of excessive drinking—consumption of alcohol above medically approved limits—is highest among both men and women in the 18–24 age group.

Disability and disadvantage

'Disability' might seem to be a straightforward idea. Many who regard themselves as fully fit in body and mind label themselves as 'able-bodied' and those who differ from them as 'disabled', as lacking in certain 'normal' physical abilities. Thus, the visually impaired, the deaf, wheelchair users, and others may all be defined as having disabilities that prevent them from leading a normal life. They are regarded as incapacitated or handicapped, as unable to take on normal social responsibilities. This leads people to operate with an individualized model of disability, treating it as an individual 'problem', as a personal tragedy, with psychological or biological causes. Many disabled people, seen as unable to live like the rest of us, are often seen as requiring incarceration in a 'home', segregated from the rest of society, where they could be looked after by professional carers (Goffman 1961b; P. Morris 1969).

This view has been questioned by those who advocate a social model of disability, first set out by pressure groups acting on behalf of the disabled. An influential statement was that of the Union of the Physically Impaired Against Segregation: 'In our view it is society which disables physically impaired people. Disability is something imposed on top of our impairments by the way we are unnecessarily isolated and excluded from full participation in society' (UPIAS 1976: 14). According to the social model of disability, disability has to be seen as a failure on the part of a society to provide appropriate services and facilities that meet the needs of those with particular impairments. Those with particular bodily impairments *become* disabled when the social conditions under which they live exclude them from participation in things that other members of their society take for granted.

Oliver (1983, 1996) has shown that this tends to medicalize a social condition and so to hand over control of a serious problem to the medical profession. Although some of the disabled may suffer from chronic illnesses, doctors cannot use their knowledge of illness to treat the disability, which has to be seen as a social condition.

Impairment and disability

This view of disability rests on a distinction being made between impairment and disability. An **impairment** exists when someone has a defective bodily part (a limb or an organ), and it includes such things as blindness and visual impairment, deafness, vocal difficulties, paralysis, amputation, arthritis, epilepsy, and problems of brain disorder and function. Impairment can result from congenital and perinatal conditions, from disease and illness, and from injury. A **disability**, on the other hand, is a disadvantage that is caused for the physically impaired by particular forms of social organization. Examples of disability include the inability to negotiate stairs, use keyboards, use telephones, read documents, get dressed, communicate, or drive a car (see Albrecht *et al.* 2001).

Thus, impairment is not, in itself, a cause of disability. A disability exists when social conditions impose restrictions on impaired people. As such, it may result from prejudice or simply from the way that accepted institutions happen to operate. What might be called institutional discrimination, like institutional racism, may disable the impaired even where none of the participants intend to do so.

It has recently been argued that 'disablism'—prejudice and institutionalized discrimination against the impaired —should be seen in the same way as sexism and racism. Disablism is a form of oppression, social exclusion, and disadvantage exercised over the impaired by other members of their society (Barnes and Mercer 2003: chapters 2 and 3).

Typically, disability results from the stigmatization of impairments (Goffman 1963*b*). Stigmatization occurs when an impairment becomes a mark of social difference that is responded to in prejudiced and socially stereotyped ways. It is treated as something that undermines the identity of the impaired person as a 'normal' member of society. A stigmatized impairment signifies a 'spoiled identity', something that is disfiguring physically or metaphorically. Goffman gives particular attention to the ways in which individuals seek to manage their spoiled identities. He looks, for example, at the ways in which they seek to avoid embarrassment and prejudice by 'passing' as normal, hiding their impairment. Davis (1961) has documented the mechanisms of 'deviance disavowal' through which impaired individuals may gradually encourage those with whom they interact to accept their impairment as unimportant or unnoticeable. In many situations, however, such disavowal is not possible and people must handle the negative reactions to their spoiled identities. In striving for 'normality', impaired people adopt coping mechanisms that enable them to present and sustain an impression of a 'capable self', rather than the 'disabled self' that others might impute on the basis of their spoiled identity (Corbin and Strauss 1985).

It is certainly important to recognize that impairment must not be seen as the cause of disability. It is also important, however, to recognize that impairment is a bodily condition or circumstance that allows the disabling processes of a society to have their effects. Some advocates of the social model of disability have deliberately emphasized a strong formulation of the model, minimizing the reality of physical impairment, in order to further a political programme of eliminating the social conditions responsible for disability. In fact, the social model has to be combined with a proper awareness of impairment as a condition that makes disability possible and that must, therefore, be analysed in its own right. Carol Thomas (1999) has argued that disability and impairment must be recognized as separate and quite distinct conditions affecting social activity:

> Disability is about restrictions of activity which are socially caused. That is, disability is entirely socially caused. But some restrictions of activity are caused by illness and impairment. Thus, some aspects of illness and impairment are disabling. But disability has nothing to do with impairment. (Thomas 1999: 39)

While the social conditions for disability must be removed, the potential for medical intervention on impairments should not be ignored. The provision of contact lenses or glasses for the short-sighted, for example, may be a far more effective solution to their impairment than treating it as a disability requiring a restructuring of the social conditions that necessitate good eyesight (the ways in which books and newspapers are produced,

the rules governing car driving, and so on). Similarly, the provision of hearing aids may be a more appropriate solution for hearing impairment than attempts to redesign televisions and radios for use by the hearing impaired. Such medical intervention on impairment may not be possible or appropriate in all cases, but it is important to recognize the interdependence of medical intervention and social change in reducing the potential for disability.

> ➔ *Connections*
> Consult some published official statistics on disability. Do these statistics recognize the distinction between impairment and disability? How useful are they likely to be in devising policies for reducing levels of disability? In considering these questions, you may like to think about the kinds of questions that need to be asked in social surveys if they are to produce better information. For example, could questions on difficulties in holding or grasping objects be rephrased as questions about the design of objects?

Learning spoiled identities

Some of these issues have been explored in relation to blindness and deafness. Robert Scott (1969) has looked at the ways in which the medical and care services that are available to blind people reinforce the kind of behaviour that is expected by the experts who provide the services. Those taken into 'special' schools and training organizations are rewarded when they conform to staff expectations—they are praised for their 'insight' into their own condition and they are punished when they deviate from them—and they are criticized for 'resisting' the views of staff. In these ways, their behaviour and their own sense of identity is shaped into a dependent role—the blind role—that is seen as a normal and natural consequence of the impairment.

In their study of deafness, Evans and Falk (1986) looked at the effects on deaf children of attending a residential school. They show how children who are born deaf are socialized into the expectations of the official culture of the school. In learning the sign language that allows them to communicate with staff and with each other, they also learn the attitudes and identity expected of them. They are schooled for the world of the deaf rather than being schooled for living in a hearing world. This is not a completely deterministic process. Some visually impaired people, Scott shows, resist these definitions, despite the punishing sanctions applied by the service providers. They may calculatedly and manipulatively adapt the blind role when it suits their purposes, maintaining an independent sense of identity, or they may actively oppose the institutionalization of the blind role.

In many cases, however, the social reaction to impairment and the construction of a disability role is based around a discourse of 'rehabilitation'. Wendy Seymour (1998) has shown how those with spinal-chord injuries are encouraged by health professionals to recognize and address the 'damage' to their bodies and to reassess the ways in which they might live in the future. This discourse revolves around an ideal of how the body should be and a model of the ways in which a disabled person can be brought back towards this ideal image. In some cases this may be allied with the medical interventions aimed at reconstructing the body and transforming it into a more 'normal' form. Such attempts have sometimes encountered resistance from the disabled themselves, especially where they have the support of groups of similar others. Some deaf parents of deaf children, for example, oppose the use of cochlear implant operations, which restore an approximation to normal hearing in the completely deaf, on the grounds that such interventions deny the identity that a child already has within a deaf community with its own way of life and way of communicating.

◆ *Stop and reflect*

This section has presented a large number of statistics about population and health, and these cannot be summarized here. You will find it useful to glance back over the various tables and diagrams that we have given.

- Population change is the result of the balance between fertility, mortality, and migration.
- In modern societies, changes in population can be described in terms of a demographic transition. The demographic transition is associated with a parallel health transition.
- Causes of illness and death have altered considerably with the development of industrial societies.
- Is it useful to see impairment as a condition distinct from disability, and to see the latter as the result of stigmatization and social exclusion?

Medicine, minds, and bodies

Illness is now generally seen as having an objective, physical reality. It is a result of the influence of germs, viruses, and other specific biological agents. Our discussion in 'Health, reproduction, and disability' may have seemed to accept, rather uncritically, the idea that there can be an objective and straightforward definition of health. It should be clear from our discussion of Foucault, however, that this is not the case. It is now necessary to return to this theme and look more critically at the ideas of health and illness.

The conditions that are recognized as illnesses vary quite considerably from one society to another, as do the particular ways in which they are defined and treated. For the sociologist, health is whatever is regarded as the normal biological condition of an individual in a society that has institutionalized a medical gaze and conception of reality. Illness is any perceived departure from this condition that is subject to medical treatment (Freidson 1970).

People in different societies may be affected by a similar viral infection, but their conditions may be socially defined quite differently. In contemporary societies, such a person is likely to be seen as 'ill'. In many pre-modern societies, which lack a concept of 'virus' and have no institutionalized medicine, they may be seen as suffering from the effects of witchcraft or evil spirits. In the same way, it is only recently—and still only in part—that those who suffer from persistent fatigue and depression have been defined as suffering from chronic fatigue syndrome (sometimes called ME or myalgic encephalomyelitis) rather than being seen as malingerers. The social construction of health and illness makes it impossible to set out any kind of general and absolute idea of what it is to be healthy. Conceptions of health are inextricably linked to ideas of personal identity and social acceptability.

Consider the case of dental health. It might be thought that this could be defined in terms of the presence or absence of tooth decay. Much dental treatment, however, is preventive and opens up many ambiguous areas of treatment. The removal of crowded teeth, the straightening of crooked teeth, and the whitening of yellowed teeth are treatments that owe as much to cosmetic considerations as they do to preventive dentistry. It is impossible to decide with any certainty which particular dental interventions are necessary for good health.

In the same way, it might be thought that those who are overweight are unhealthy. However, it is impossible to define what is meant by being overweight independently of social considerations. Conceptions of what it is to be overweight, as we show below, are impossible to disentangle from ideas of what it is to be slim and attractive. This kind of ambiguity has drawn doctors into medical treatments aimed at slimming and into various types of cosmetic surgery.

Sociologists do not, of course, deny that there is a biological basis to illness, nor do they fail to recognize physical suffering. This would be obviously absurd. Two fundamental points are being made in theories of the social construction of illness:

- Even biological concepts of health are imprecise. The World Health Organization defines health in relation to 'well-being', for example, but the Royal College of General Practitioners sees it as 'adjustment' to circumstances. Medical definitions leave many areas of uncertainty that can shift as medical knowledge changes. This medical knowledge is itself the product of a complex social process of clinical and scientific investigation.

- Social contexts shape both the meanings that are given to biological conditions and people's reactions to them. While doctors need to employ biological conceptions of illness in order to diagnose and treat particular disorders, the sociologist is more interested in the social behaviour of those who are labelled as 'sick' and those who do this labelling. Medicine and sociology have complementary concerns. An understanding of health and illness requires both a biological knowledge of the causes of illness and a sociological understanding of how sick people behave and how others react to their sickness.

Medical control and the body

Foucault (1976) showed the way in which the medical gaze transformed the prevailing view of the human body and introduced new disciplines of anatomical control. Organized medicine has been expanding its power by extending its claims to competence to more and more areas of social life. Matters that used to be the responsibilities of priests, social workers, teachers, and others are now seen as 'medical' matters. Illich (1977) sees this **medicalization** as undermining the power of ordinary people to make their own decisions. The right to make decisions is handed over to the technical 'expert' (see also Zola 1975).

In this section we will look at the idea of the sick role, which has been widely used as a way of understanding how these disciplines of the body have been organized in contemporary societies. We will also look at some of the reproductive technologies through which the fertility and sexuality of women have been disciplined. Finally, we look at the discipline of the body in death.

The sick role

In his discussion of health and illness, Talcott Parsons (1951) described the emergence of what he called the **sick role**. This role is defined by normative expectations that people who are ill should behave in ways that minimize the disruptive effects that their illness can have on ordinary social life. Those who are ill may not be able to continue with their usual activities, or they may behave in unacceptable ways. In either case, there may be much disruption of normal, everyday life. Minor forms of illness and disability are often disregarded, but those disorders that are long-lasting or debilitating are likely to cause particularly pressing problems for others as well as for the sufferer. The deviance that might result from such illnesses can be minimized and normalized if the ill person conforms to the expectations of the sick role. Through their knowledge of the sick role—a knowledge that is acquired during their socialization—people learn how to be ill in socially acceptable ways.

There are three principal elements in the normative expectations that define the sick role in that a sick person:

- is exempted from any personal responsibility for her or his illness;

- has permission to withdraw from many normal family and work commitments;

- is obliged to seek medical help and to become a 'patient'.

In our society, illness is not seen as something that sufferers bring upon themselves. It is something that is beyond their control. The physical or organic character of an illness is seen as having no direct connection with the previous behaviour of the sick person. This general principle is not, of course, completely clear-cut, and there are many areas of ambiguity. The health risks that result from heavy smoking are now well known, and there has recently been some discussion about whether heavy smokers should be entitled to medical treatment for lung cancer. Even more controversially, public opinion on AIDS/HIV-infection has sometimes tended to see it as a 'self-inflicted' illness. It is seen as a consequence of deviant sexual behaviour and, therefore, as less deserving of treatment than are other illnesses. These are, however, highly problematic and contentious areas. In most cases, exemption from responsibility is given to the sick person, who is then permitted to act in ways that would not normally be tolerated.

Briefing: self-inflicted illness and non-diseases

Should smokers receive NHS treatment for illness caused by their smoking? Some have argued that such illnesses are self-inflicted and, in a situation of limited resources, should not receive treatment at the public expense. This issue first hit the headlines in the early 1990s, when Harry Elphick, a heavy smoker aged 47, was refused hospital treatment at Wythenshawe Hospital in Manchester for his heart condition. Mr Elphick stopped smoking, but died a week before his next hospital appointment.

In early 2002 a woman aged 35 wrote to the *Guardian* to complain that her GP had refused her a repeat prescription for the contraceptive pill unless she stopped smoking. In this case, the refusal of the prescription was justified by doctors on the grounds that the combination of heavy smoking and oestrogen (the active ingredient in the pill) would increase the woman's risk of heart attack or stroke.

Alcohol, like tobacco, has been seen as a possible cause of self-inflicted harm and disease: through liver and heart damage, cancer, and the effects of drunken violence, alcohol is estimated to cost the NHS £3 billion a year. A report by Alcohol Concern suggested that heavy drinkers needed to be identified in order to reduce the burden on the health service.

A recent survey on medicalization asked doctors to name the main things for which they were consulted that they thought should be regarded as 'non-diseases' that required no treatment. The top ten non-diseases named were:

1 Ageing
2 Work
3 Boredom
4 Bags under the eyes
5 Ignorance
6 Baldness
7 Freckles
8 Big ears
9 Grey or white hair
10 Ugliness

Sources: *Independent*, 28 January 1997; *Guardian*, 21 February 2002; *Guardian*, 1 March 2002; *Guardian*, 10 April 2002.

 Under what circumstances do you think that such patients should be refused medical treatment? What considerations are relevant to this decision? What does this debate tell us about the relative powers of doctors and patients in constructing the sick role?

The recognition of 'sickness', then, is one way of normalizing deviant behaviour. When people are recognized as suffering from a sickness for which they have no responsibility, they are seen as having a legitimate right to abandon many of their normal day-to-day responsibilities. They may be entitled to take time off work without loss of pay, they can take to their bed and leave domestic chores to other household members, and they may even be able to disregard some of the normal niceties of polite behaviour. None of these dispensations would usually be allowed to people experiencing problems that were seen as their responsibility. The person who becomes incapable of work because of a drinking spree, for example, is not normally seen as having a legitimate right to take a day off. Those who find themselves in such a situation may often invent a 'bug' or a bout of 'flu' to legitimate their time off work. In doing so, they trade on the social acceptability of the sick role.

This permission to withdraw from normal commitments is not absolute, but is conditional on the person seeking medical help. The sick role is a temporary role, and the sick person must see her or his state of sickness as undesirable, as something to be escaped from as soon as possible. Those who 'wallow' in their illness and who show no sign of trying to recover will rapidly find that the permission to withdraw from normal interaction and the exemption from responsibility are taken away from them. They will be seen as 'malingerers'. The normal assumption is that real sufferers will visit a doctor's surgery or arrange a visit from a doctor to their home. It is normally doctors who confirm that a person is ill and so legitimate occupancy of the sick role. The sick person is permitted to continue in this role by those family members, friends, and work colleagues who accept the medical definition of the illness. Doctors authorize the sick person's withdrawal from normal life and make available their medical expertise to treat her or him as a patient.

Central to an understanding of the sick role, then, is the doctor–patient relationship. The relationship between the role of the doctor and the role of the patient is one of authority. There is a fundamental difference in power between the two, rooted in the claim that the doctor makes to scientific expertise (T. Johnson 1972). The patient must submit to the doctor's power, because continued occupancy of the sick role rests upon an acceptance of medical authority. People who deny the authority of a doctor must give up any claim to have a legitimate sickness. They may, indeed, be ill, but they cannot expect any allowance to be made for this by others because they have rejected the institutionalized requirement to seek and to accept medical help.

This difference in power between doctor and patient is brought out in the use of the very word 'patient', a word that originally described someone who exercises 'patience' and is, therefore, 'passive'. This power difference is magnified when there are also differences of class, gender, or ethnicity between doctors and their patients.

Reproductive bodies

The difference in power between doctors and their patients is especially marked in the medical care of pregnancy and childbirth. In these medical encounters, the doctors are overwhelmingly male and the patients are exclusively female. Their power relations are shaped by the wider context of gender differences and gender inequalities. Medical intervention in child-bearing is, in fact, an intervention in the central defining characteristic of sex–gender roles in contemporary societies.

There has been a major shift in the way in which child-bearing has been controlled over the last century and a half. Until well into the nineteenth century, childbirth was an event that took place within the private sphere of the home, perhaps with the help and support of female relatives and neighbours. The rise of modern medicine that we have traced brought childbirth and the whole surrounding area of sexuality, pregnancy, and child health into the medical arena, under the control of doctors. Obstetricians, gynaecologists, and paediatricians, supported by midwives and other nurses, achieved a high level of control over these aspects of women's lives (Oakley 1984). By 1927, 15 per cent of all births took place in hospital; by 1980 this figure had reached 98 per cent.

Pregnancy and childbirth are not, of course, illnesses. Their incorporation under the medical gaze, however, has eliminated or reduced many of the dangers to health that women and their babies previously faced. Death during childbirth, for example, was once far more common than it is today, and we have also shown how much neonatal and infant mortality have been reduced. A consequence of this involvement of medical experts has been that pregnant and would-be pregnant women have been required to adopt a variant of the sick role that legitimates the further medicalization of their lives. As a patient, they must accept the authority of the doctor (H. Roberts 1985). They must subordinate their own knowledge of their body and their control over it to the expertise of the doctor. The obstetrician, for example, expects to have the same degree of control over a woman's reproduction as a neurosurgeon has over patients during brain surgery.

The medicalization of reproduction has involved the expansion of a whole complex of reproductive technologies, under the control of doctors. Many of these technologies have, of course, made childbirth safer, but they have also introduced new risks to health. Indeed, the expansion of medical technology has resulted in a significant increase in the health risks that women face when undergoing treatment.

There are four principal technologies of reproduction (Stanworth 1987a: 10–11):

- contraception technologies;
- childbirth technologies;
- foetal technologies;
- conception technologies.

Contraception technologies are among the oldest available and include a whole array of techniques for preventing and terminating pregnancies. The legalization of abortion in Britain in 1968 reduced the very large number of deaths and injuries that resulted from illegal 'back-street' and self-induced abortions. The technology of termination, however, means that abortion of a foetus is now possible at a much later age. There have been renewed debates about the ethics of abortion and who has the right to decide whether an abortion should take place. Condoms and barrier methods of contraception have been used for a very long time, and about one-third of sexually active people use them—the rates are higher among those with more than one sexual partner (see Figure 8.7). One of the greatest revolutions in contraceptive technology, however, has been the introduction of the contraceptive pill. As a technology, working through the regulation of hormones in the woman's body, it is highly effective. It has, however, been linked with thrombosis and some forms of cancer.

Childbirth technologies include such procedures as the long-established caesarean section and the somewhat

---

Figure 8.7 Use of condoms in the previous four weeks, by number of new partners of the opposite sex (1999–2001)

Great Britain	Percentages	
	Existing partner only	One or more new partners
Males		
Used on every occasion	20	46
Used on some occasions	9	17
Not used at all	70	38
Females		
Used on every occasion	17	37
Used on some occasions	8	16
Not used at all	76	48

Note: Numbers rounded up in original source.

Source: *Social Trends* (2004: table 7.23).

newer induction of deliveries. Drug technologies for inducing births have allowed hospitals to schedule childbirth to correspond with staff shifts and rotas, reducing the number of overnight births, but induction is not without its dangers to women and their babies. Particularly important forms of childbirth technology have been those concerned with monitoring and treating the pain and distress of the mother and baby. Painkilling injections and foetal-monitoring equipment, for example, were introduced as ways of making childbirth more comfortable and of increasing the chances of the baby being born healthy.

Foetal technologies have been introduced and extended in order to monitor foetal development and eliminate birth defects. These technologies include the use of ultrasound and X-ray to examine the foetus, amniocentesis to identify genetic problems, and, most controversially, the expanding area of genetic engineering. The results of monitoring programmes have been used to identify potential 'problems'—such as a foetus that is likely to develop into a baby with Down's syndrome—and to recommend terminations. The aspiration of many medical scientists involved in the area, however, is that it may be possible, instead, to intervene directly and alter the genetic material of the foetus. The idea of 'cloning' human beings is the latest development in this area.

Finally, *conception technologies* are concerned with the promotion of pregnancy and the treatment of infertility. Informal arrangements for the 'donation' of ova and sperms and for 'surrogate motherhood' have long existed, but the medical profession has increasingly become involved in formalizing and medicalizing these arrangements. The development of drug treatments for infertility and the use of *in vitro* fertilization (so-called test-tube reproduction) have expanded the power that the medical profession has to decide who may have children and when they may have them. The most recent technology to be explored in this area is the genetic cloning of embryos. Experiments on animals led to the first successful cloning of a sheep, and doctors in Korea and Britain have announced the successful cloning of a human embryo.

The development and expansion of new reproductive technologies must be seen in the context of the occupational strategies of medical experts. While they may indeed remove some dangers, they create new risks, and their introduction and use have not been led by their health effects alone. Doctors involved in such high-profile work at the leading edge of research are able to enhance the status of their professional specialism and strengthen their arguments for higher levels of funding. The expansion of reproductive technologies is also driven by the interests of the big drug and medical supply companies, for whom reproduction has become big business.

In this context, women can become quite powerless. For this reason, feminists have seen it as critical to the whole debate over women's health and their control over their own bodies (Dworkin 1983). Reproductive technologies allow the medical profession to weaken—and perhaps to break—the link between sex and motherhood. A predominantly male medical profession usurps activities that were formerly a primary concern of women, making women's bodies into objects of the new technologies. Reproductive technologies are integral parts of the socially structured medical practices that centralize control over the regulation of populations and human reproduction.

Learning to die

It may be accepted that physical illness is socially constructed in various ways, but surely death is an undeniable biological fact? In one sense, of course, this is true, though there are numerous differences of medical opinion as to exactly when someone can be regarded as 'dead'. There are very real medical difficulties involved in determining the moment of death and in deciding whether those in a persistent vegetative state on a life-support machine are, in fact, 'dead'. This has generated much debate over the rights of relatives to switch off the life-support systems of patients who are in long-term comas. In a wider sense, however, death must also be seen as a socially constructed event around which there are all sorts of values and norms. While people do, of course, die—an undeniable physical event, however difficult it might be to identify in some cases— there are numerous and very different subjective meanings that can be given to this event. For some, death is the end of their existence, for others it is merely a point

New technology **Online diagnosis**

To deal with a shortage of doctors, nurses, and health provision, the British government has introduced online and telephone diagnosis systems. By logging on to **www.nhsdirect.nhs.uk/ index.asp**, people can consult a database of symptoms to try to identify their medical problems and recommended action.

Linked to the online service is a 24-hour telephone service on which patients can speak to a nurse, who will advise on symptoms and treatments. It is intended to integrate these services with the existing 'out-of-hours' call-out service provided by GPs.

of transition to some higher, 'spiritual' life, and for yet others it may mark the point at which the 'soul' is released for rebirth in another body. Physical death is the end stage of a social process of 'dying', and this can be understood in the same way as other forms of social behaviour.

Dying, then, must be understood as a social process. This view was one of the central insights of Durkheim's (1897) great study of suicide. Durkheim showed that suicide could be understood only if it was recognized that rates of suicide varied quite considerably from one social group to another. Douglas (1967) extended this argument, showing the varying social meanings that are given to unexpected deaths by the perpetrator (for example, in a suicide note), by friends and relatives, doctors, the police, coroners, and others.

In their powerful study of death, Glaser and Strauss (1965) have shown that, except in cases of sudden accidents that result in instantaneous death, a person's death is a process that takes time. Sometimes this is days, sometimes weeks, sometimes years. In many cases, dying is the final phase of a long occupancy of the sick role, and it involves the continued 'management' of the patient, which today generally takes place in a hospital. Relatives and medical staff will have certain expectations about when and how a patient will die, and they construct a **death trajectory** that they expect the patient to follow. The trajectory becomes, in effect, a role that is expected of the dying person.

It is difficult for these role expectations to be imposed on a dying patient if the patient is unaware that he or she is dying, and Glaser and Strauss have shown the considerable variations in role behaviour that occur with varying degrees of awareness. Doctors and nurses make medical assessments of a patient's condition, which they record in case notes and that influence their behaviour towards the patient. The medical professionals must decide how much of this information is to be passed on to the patient and to his or her relatives. In some cases, patients and relatives may be made fully aware of the situation, while in others they may be kept in the dark.

The various participants in a death, therefore, act on the basis of varying states of awareness. Where all the participants share a common state of awareness, there may be a high degree of consensus over the death trajectory that will be followed. When awareness varies, however, there will be much scope for conflict and misunderstanding and for deviance on the part of the dying patient. The person may, for example, be perceived as dying in unexpected or 'inappropriate' ways. Glaser and Strauss identify four different **awareness contexts** that surround dying in hospitals. These are:

- *closed awareness*: the patient is kept in ignorance of the condition and does not know that he or she is dying;
- *suspected awareness*: the patient suspects that he or she is dying;
- *mutual-pretence awareness*: both staff and patient know, but maintain the fiction that the patient does not know;
- *open awareness*: patient and staff are all fully aware.

In a closed-awareness context, the patient does not know his or her true condition, and the medical staff will strive to ensure that this remains the case. To this end, they employ various tactics to prevent the patient from even suspecting the truth. Doctors will not tell patients that they are dying, unless asked a direct question, and all staff may talk 'around the houses' in order to avoid making any direct statements that would give the game away. There is a structure of collusion and secrecy among the staff and the relatives, all of whom try to construct plausible accounts of events and experiences that might otherwise lead the patient to question his or her chances of recovery. In these circumstances, it is difficult to make patients conform to expectations about how to die properly, as they do not know that they are dying.

Because of the collusion and the potential for misunderstanding, closed awareness is difficult to sustain, and it often slips into a situation of suspected awareness or open awareness. Where a patient discovers the truth, he or she may, nevertheless, pretend not to have done so, and the staff—if they are aware of this pretence—are also likely to try to maintain the fiction. This context of mutual pretence is also particularly difficult to sustain.

An open-awareness context is far easier for staff to manage. In this situation, expectations of proper behaviour can be explicitly imposed on patients. Their awareness means that they can be seen to have responsibility for their own actions as dying persons: not for the fact that they *are* dying, but for *how* they die. When people know that they are dying, they are expected to present a *dying self* to the world, and this self-presentation is expected to conform to particular standards that define a 'proper' death:

> The patient should maintain relative composure and cheerfulness. At the very least, he [*sic*] should face death with dignity. He should not cut himself off from the world, turning his back upon the living; instead he should continue to be a good family member, and be 'nice' to other patients. If he can, he should participate in the ward social life. He should co-operate with the staff members who care for him, and if possible he should avoid distressing or embarrassing them. A patient who does most of these things will be respected. He evinces what we shall term 'an acceptable style of dying'. (Glaser and Strauss 1965: 86; see also Glaser and Strauss 1968)

Patients who do not die 'properly' are sanctioned in attempts to make them conform to the role expectations. They will be reprimanded, scolded, and ordered; they will be coaxed and coached in how to behave; and they may even be offered rewards for cooperation. Staff may be more likely to be friendly and helpful if the patient cooperates with ward routines, and the relatives of the patient are drawn into this process of social control.

Medicalization and the mind

We have looked at the sick role in relation to physical illnesses, but there exists a whole array of other illnesses that are seen as having mental rather than physical effects. Schizophrenia, depression, and other mental illnesses are often seen as having an organic basis and as being treatable through drug therapies. They are, however, generally seen as a different type of illness from the purely physical.

Mental disorders are seen in a rather more ambiguous light than are physical and physiological disorders. There is a lack of public understanding about the nature of mental disorders, and there is often an unwillingness on the part of sufferers to recognize their own symptoms. There is, in a very real sense, public disagreement over whether mental illness is really an illness at all. Many people feel that those who are depressed should 'pull themselves together', that psychological states are less 'real' than physical states, and that, in many respects, people are responsible for their own mental states.

If people are seen as having at least a degree of responsibility for their own illness, then the sick role cannot be played in the usual way. From this point of view, mental illness—unlike physical illness—comes to be seen as a type of deviant behaviour itself. Mentally ill people not only deviate from expectations about normal, everyday behaviour, they also deviate from the expectations surrounding the sick role. Many of the ambiguities and contradictions that are inherent in the treatment of the mentally ill and in the low prestige of psychiatric doctors can be explained by this ambivalence over the character of mental *illness* itself.

Becoming schizophrenic

Scheff (1966) has set out a model of those forms of mental illness that are diagnosed by psychiatrists as forms of 'schizophrenia' or 'psychosis' (see also Coulter 1973). These diagnoses are usually employed where people experience serious delusions or hallucinations and are seen as a threat to themselves and to others. Scheff aimed to show that these forms of mental illness, which often involve long periods of hospitalization, can be understood as forms of deviant behaviour.

Schizophrenia is rooted in what Scheff calls **residual rule-breaking**. 'Residual rules' relate not to specific kinds of interaction and relationship, but to the very nature of social interaction itself. These rules involve deeply embedded assumptions about the nature of ordinary, day-to-day encounters. They specify such things as the expectation that people who are engaged in a conversation should face one another, maintain a certain distance, take proper turns in the conversation, remain attentive to what is going on, and so on. Those who violate these expectations on a regular basis or in especially visible ways tend to be seen as particularly strange, bizarre, or frightening. They violate the very expectations without which 'normal' interaction is impossible. Their behaviour is seen as unreasonable (Busfield 1996).

Behaviour that may be seen as violating residual rules includes withdrawal, hallucination, muttering, unusual gesturing or posturing, and distraction. Many of these behaviours are acceptable in some contexts, but objectionable in others. Kneeling down, muttering, and hallucinating, for example, are regarded as perfectly acceptable behaviour in a Christian Church—they define a devout act of prayer—but they are not regarded as appropriate in a job interview. It is when such types of behaviour occur in inappropriate situations and in ways that threaten normal interaction that they are likely to be seen as deviant behaviour.

Nevertheless, residual rule-breaking is quite frequent in everyday encounters. We all, quite regularly, encounter those who seem to be distracted while we talk to them, or who continually interrupt and refuse to allow others to speak. In most cases, this behaviour goes unnoticed, is ignored, or is explained away—it is normalized in one way or another. People are seen as 'tired', 'busy', 'under the weather', or as in some other way experiencing difficulties that account for their behaviour in terms of 'normal' motivations. When residual rule-breaking is normalized, it has little continuing significance for any of those concerned.

In some cases, however, the behaviour goes beyond the bounds of what is regarded as normal, exceeding the normal tolerance levels of friends, family, or work colleagues. It may, for example, be particularly visible, extreme, or long-lasting. In these circumstances, the behaviour is seen as being unreasonable, abnormal, and incomprehensible. It is seen, therefore, as needing to be acted upon. In contemporary societies, such behaviour is likely to be labelled as a symptom of 'mental disorder'. In other societies, argues Scheff, the same behaviour might be seen as symptomatic of 'spirit possession' or of 'witchcraft' (see Szasz 1970). The term 'mental disorder' is likely to be used today because our culture has become permeated by medical and psychiatric concepts—often only partially understood—that make the imagery of mental 'abnormality', 'madness', and 'insanity' familiar.

Stereotyped images of mental disorder are learned from early childhood, and they are reinforced in the mass media. These images are conjured up through the use of such terms as 'crazy', 'loony', 'mad', 'insane', or 'deranged'. In appropriate circumstances, these labels may be applied to others or even to ourselves. People grow up with a particular image of mental disorder and, therefore, of the ways in which they expect those who suffer from it to act. As a result, there is a specific version of the sick role, the **insanity role**.

Many forms of depression and anxiety may be normalized by families, or treated within the conventional framework of the sick role; those who seem to experience seriously disruptive mental problems are more likely to be treated in terms of the insanity role. As with the sick role proper, the medical profession is called in to accredit the insanity. The person's friends and family may, for example, call in the general practitioner, who may refer the case to a psychiatric specialist. In these ways, residual rule-breaking is medicalized, and the medical professionals initiate a process of treatment.

When people act in terms of the insanity role, incorporating it into their sense of identity, residual rule-breaking is transformed into the form of secondary deviation that is called 'mental illness':

> When the deviance of an individual becomes a public issue, the traditional stereotype of insanity becomes the guiding imagery for action, both for those reacting to the deviant and, at times, for the deviant himself [sic]. When societal agents and persons around the deviant react to him uniformly in terms of the traditional stereotypes of insanity, his amorphous and unstructured rule-breaking tends to crystallize in conformity to these expectations, thus becoming similar to the behaviour of other deviants classified as mentally ill, and stable over time. The process . . . is completed when the traditional imagery becomes a part of the deviant's orientation for guiding his own behavior. (Scheff 1966: 64)

But why should anyone conform to such a role? Scheff argues that this occurs because residual rule-breakers are encouraged by others to accept the image of insanity as an 'explanation' for the problems that they have been experiencing. At the same time, they are refused the opportunity to act in more conventional ways: if mentally ill people deny their illness and do not accept the treatment, then this simply shows how ill they really are. They may, for example, find it difficult to enter or to retain employment or to continue with normal domestic responsibilities. The people labelled are, furthermore, likely to be highly suggestible to the opinions of others. The hostility that they may feel and the strength of the opinions held by professionals all leave them feeling highly vulnerable.

To see schizophrenia as a form of deviance is not to deny that many people do face serious mental problems and that they may need help in dealing with them. Nor is it to deny that there may be a biological basis to some forms of residual rule-breaking. The point that Scheff is making is that mental illness is always to be seen as a social fact as well as a physical fact. Psychiatric diagnoses—such as 'schizophrenia', 'phobia', and 'neurosis'—are made in social contexts and are applied to people who have already been labelled as a problem by others. It is only those who have come to be seen as problematic by non-psychiatrists —by friends, relatives, or colleagues—who come to the attention of psychiatrists. For this reason, psychiatrists have most of their professional contact with those who have entered the stage of secondary deviation and are already playing the insanity role. In this context, psychiatric diagnoses cannot be seen as neutral acts that are independent of processes of social control.

The moral career of the mental patient

Goffman (1961b) has also explored the life of seriously ill schizophrenics and psychotics, paying particular attention to their 'moral career'. This term refers to the changing sense of self that develops as they experience the particular contingencies and constraints that occur with their hospitalization.

Goffman sees the transition from primary deviation to secondary deviation for the mentally ill as involving a movement from the status of a *civil person* to that of a *patient*. Whereas the civil person is an individual with full civil rights as a member of society, the patient loses certain rights and powers. Hospitalized mental patients in Britain, for example, cannot vote in general elections, and hospital staff have the power to act on their behalf in many areas of life. As we show in Chapter 14, the admissions procedures adopted by mental hospitals emphasize the new status that the person has acquired. With the status of patient, the person fully enters the insanity role, and a career of mental illness becomes possible.

The patient stage of the insanity role is seen by Goffman as involving three phases. First, there is the *home-patient phase* (Goffman calls this the pre-patient phase). This is when the person remains at home, but is under the supervision of a general practitioner. Second is the crucial *in-patient phase*, when the person has been hospitalized, voluntarily or forcibly, and begins a period under the close control of hospital staff. Third is the *ex-patient phase* that follows the patient's release. Ex-patients experience a continuing public reaction, and may face many constraints on their opportunities. They are seen in terms of their status as a former mental patient and this may, for example, make it difficult for them to get a job. Many ex-patients relapse into illness, re-entering the hospital for further in-patient treatment. Goffman's argument is summarized in Figure 8.8.

Goffman's own work was concerned mainly with the in-patient phase. He saw the mental hospital as an arena in which staff and patients struggle with each other to define

Figure 8.8 The career of the mentally ill

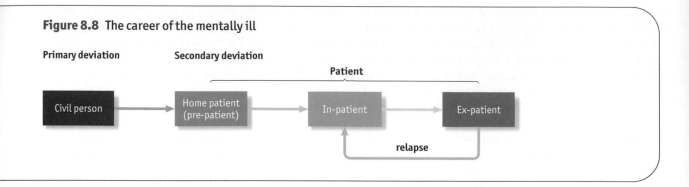

the reality of the patient experience. Patients will initially respond to hospitalization by denying that they are sick. They selectively draw on pre-hospital experiences that allow the presentation of a convincing and self-respecting account of the reasons for their new status: 'It's all a mistake', 'I was under a lot of pressure', 'I'm not like all the other patients', and so on. These kinds of accounts are difficult to sustain in the long term, as they are incompatible with the medical definition of the situation that staff are constructing.

This medical definition is embodied in the case notes and underpins the treatment that is carried out. It is structured into the very power relations of the hospital. The staff construct the image of the patient as a sick person. He or she is seen as someone who has suffered some kind of collapse or breakdown on the outside and is currently unable to act in his or her own best interests. As the patient attempts to put a positive interpretation on his or her situation, so staff will make comments or highlight evidence that contradicts this. When patients attempt to show staff how 'normal' they are, this is simply taken as a sign of how ill they are: they are so ill that they cannot even recognize their own illness.

Striking evidence in support of Goffman's argument comes from a remarkable study carried out by Rosenham (1973). In this study, Rosenham and seven colleagues feigned psychiatric symptoms—they claimed that they heard voices—and they got themselves admitted to psychiatric hospitals in various parts of the United States. Following admission, they gave up the pretence of hearing voices and began to act in 'normal' ways once more. In all cases, it was some considerable time before staff accepted that they were 'well enough' to be discharged. One of the researchers remained in hospital for a month and a half before being released. On their release, being ex-patients, none of the researchers was defined as having been 'cured' or as having returned to mental health. All were diagnosed as being 'in remission', a diagnosis that meant that the doctors felt that their 'illness' could recur at any time.

Goffman's study focused on the activities that were undertaken by staff to manage the lives of their patients. The staff included not only the doctors and the nurses, but also cleaners, porters, administrators, athletics instructors, therapists, and many others. When in hospital, Goffman argued, patients must conform not only to the medical definition of their 'case', but also to the demands of the organizational routines on which staff work activities depend. Patients must, for example, fit into ward routines and staff shift patterns, they must receive their meals and post at times convenient for the catering, delivery, and cleaning staff, they must have their visits properly regulated, and so on. The hospital—like any organization—is a *negotiated order*, a stable system of recurrent relationships and interactions that results from conflict, bargaining, and compromise among the various participants. Each participant has different kinds and amounts of power resources that they can bring to the situation (Strauss *et al.* 1963). The patient, of course, is the least powerful participant. He or she is enticed into accepting the staff definition of the situation by the rewards that can be offered for conformity.

A key to this system of rewards in the hospitals that were studied by Goffman was the ward system. The various wards were arranged in an informal hierarchy of conditions, facilities, and privileges, and patients could be moved from one ward to another in accordance with their perceived 'progress'. This progress, of course, was measured by the extent to which the patient had come to accept the staff definition of their situation as that of a person in need of treatment. Protestations of sanity and rejection of the hospital routines were regarded as signs of illness or of a lack of insight. Patients with such signs could be punished through being 'demoted' from a privileged ward to a less privileged one. A patient who accepted the medical staff's definition of the situation and cooperated with attendants and orderlies was seen as developing an insight into his or her illness. Such patients could be rewarded through 'promotion' up the ward system.

Deprived of the social supports that sustained their self-image in the outside world, patients are particularly vulnerable to these processes of control. They are, therefore, likely to show a gradual submission to staff views. In order to achieve a speedy release from hospital, 'The patient must "insightfully" come to take, or affect to take, the hospital's view of himself' (Goffman 1961*b*: 143). By accepting the staff definition of the situation, patients reconstruct their biographies as those of people who are 'ill', but are 'getting better'.

'Community' care

Both Scheff and Goffman looked mainly at the situation of schizophrenics and psychotics, and especially at those who receive hospital treatment. With the expansion of psychiatry, however, there has been a shift away from the nineteenth-century model of the asylum as the principal focus of psychiatric treatment. The total number of patients in mental hospitals in England and Wales increased continually over the twentieth century until its peak year of 1954. After this year, however, the number declined constantly, despite an increase in the total population over the same period. Thus, the rate per 10,000 people had declined to a level in 1980 that was close to its level of 100 years before. Today, approximately three-quarters of all psychiatric patients are treated on an out-patient basis. Data for the United States show a similar pattern, the peak year for hospitalization being 1955.

What was happening over this period was that more and more patients were being treated 'in the community', rather than as hospital in-patients. This is the process of

decarceration that we discuss in Chapter 14, pp. 566–7. This change in treatment was associated with a shift in the psychiatric gaze. The expansion of psychiatry led its practitioners to give relatively less attention to the severe psychotics and schizophrenics and relatively more attention to the less severe 'depressive' disorders. Depressive states had long been recognized as illnesses by the psychiatric profession, but it was only during the twentieth century that more precise diagnostic criteria were established. At first, such patients were treated in hospital, but they rapidly became candidates for out-patient treatment.

> **⊃ Connections**
>
> Read our discussion of Goffman's concept of the total institution in Chapter 14, pp. 543–4, and consider how useful you think it is in understanding mental hospitals. Look also, in the same chapter, at our discussion of decarceration on pp. 566–7.

It has been suggested that new drug therapies using tranquillizing drugs such as Largactil (chlorpromazine) were responsible for this change in treatment, but this has been overstated. These drugs undoubtedly had some effect in controlling symptoms and so allowing patients to be treated at home, but the shift away from treatment in a mental hospital began before tranquillizer treatment was at all widely available. Scull (1984) has convincingly argued that decarceration became a possibility only because of changes in the system of welfare provision. With the establishment of improved welfare systems from the 1930s,

Care in the community?
© Alice Chadwick

and especially since the Second World War, the cost of hospital treatment has been far greater than the cost of out-patient treatment for a person receiving welfare benefits. Given the choice, then, medical authorities have preferred to treat patients in the community rather than in the asylum.

By the 1960s a formal policy of 'community care' had been adopted. Long-term patients, thought not in need of active medical treatment, were processed through hostels, 'half-way houses', and training centres, while others remained at home. Instead of becoming or remaining in-patients, they have the status of home patient and the task of care is placed upon their families and their neighbours. Many mental problems are now treated by general practitioners and a growing number of counsellors. This process was especially rapid in the 1980s, as Thatcherism promoted the commercialization of care by encouraging private hostels and residential care homes. It has been estimated that the total cost of community care for elderly people suffering from dementia, depression, or anxiety is over £2 billion. These costs include not only medical treatment but also the cost of such things as home helps and meals on wheels. The Labour government reviewed this policy and introduced new legislation in 2000.

The lack of proper funding for community-care programmes has meant that many schizophrenics and psychotics who are released from the mental hospitals have had to live in rundown hostels or have become homeless. These are the very conditions that perpetuate their difficulties and that may allow them to drift into other forms of primary deviation. There have been a number of well-publicized cases of schizophrenics in community care who have become involved in dangerous actions or crimes of violence that would not have been possible if they had been hospitalized. It has been shown, however, that the number of murders committed by the mentally ill has fallen since 1957. In 1979, 121 murders were committed by those classified as mentally ill, but by 1995 this had fallen to sixty. Critics of government policy suggest that the decrease in hospitalization cannot, therefore, be seen as having brought about a greater risk of such murders and violent attacks. Whether mental illness should be treated in hospital or in the community is not a matter that can be resolved by the murder statistics.

Depression, stress, and gender

The largest number of people suffering mental disorders and being treated 'in the community' are those suffering from depression. Like many psychiatric diagnoses, 'depression' is only loosely defined. It is seen as involving feelings of general helplessness, and is closely associated with 'anxiety' and 'stress', as well as with extreme lethargy, loss of appetite, and with both suicide and attempted

 Briefing: schizophrenia and community care

There have been a number of notorious cases of schizophrenic patients released into the community and subsequently carrying out violent acts. Christopher Clunis, for example, stabbed a complete stranger in the street, killing him. Clunis's career as a mental patient had included treatment at ten different hospitals before the events of 1992. He had also stayed in a probation hostel, two prisons, a sheltered housing scheme, and five bed and breakfast hotels. He had been seen by five different Social Services departments. The family of the victim, Jonathan Zito, pressed for an official inquiry, which found that Clunis's records had not been properly kept, that there had been no proper plan for his care after his last release into the community, and that no one had overall responsibility for supervising his case.

⊃ *When you have read our discussion of the meaning of community in Chapter 13, you might like to return to this case and think about the implications for the idea of care in the community.*

suicide. The disorder is highly gendered, and women form the core of those receiving treatment for depression.

Studies of depression (Busfield 1996: chapter 10) have come to focus on various distressing experiences that put people under 'stress' and so predispose them to feelings of depression and anxiety. Events associated with stress have been said to include job change, moving home, divorce, bereavement, loss of work, being the victim of crime, illness, heavy demands at work, and so on. Stress levels have been found to vary with subordination and oppression, as people in these situations are more likely to experience unemployment, ill health, family breakdown, violence, poor housing, and crime. Women and the poor, for example, have higher rates of diagnosed and self-reported depression than have men and the more affluent. It has been estimated that between 12 per cent and 17 per cent of women have suffered from clinical depression at some stage in their life, compared with only 6 per cent of men. Women are also far more likely to be taking or to have taken tranquillizers: 23 per cent of the population in 1984 had been prescribed tranquillizers at some stage in their life, and women were twice as likely as men to have used them (Blackburn 1991: 103).

In practice, the idea of 'stress' is difficult to define with any precision. The question of what is and what is not stressful is very much a subjective matter, and it may be as much a *consequence* of depression and anxiety as it is a *cause*. The fact that women are far more likely to experience depression than men, for example, has been related to the way in which emotions are structured into gender identities. Conventional gender identities involve an expectation that women will express their emotions and take on the 'emotional work' of dealing with others, and this has become a central part of their responsibilities within families (Duncombe and Marsden 1993; see also Hochschild 1983). Men, on the other hand, are expected to 'hold things in'. When men do express their emotions, this is more likely to be outwardly, in the form of violence or in the use of alcohol. The inward direction of emotions by women has been seen as responsible for the self-blame and lower self-esteem that predisposes them to depressive responses to stress. It has been suggested, for example, that because women tend to have more emotionally charged relationships with others to whom they are close, they are, themselves, more likely to be emotionally affected by the problems faced by others in their family and the circle of close friends.

These issues were explored by Brown and Harris (1978) in their investigation into the links between potentially stressful life events and depression in a large sample of women in south London. They show that women who become depressed are far more likely to have experienced serious and severe stressful events (life-threatening illness in the family, loss of job, and so on) over a long period than were those who did not become depressed. They argue, however, that the susceptibility of women to stressful events depends upon what they call 'vulnerability'. By this they mean the social supports that are available through social ties and social networks and that help, or hinder, people's ability to cope with stress. They identify four

particular 'vulnerability factors' that predispose certain women to depression:

- the absence of an intimate relationship;
- employment outside the home;
- having three or more children under 14 at home;
- loss of their own mother before the age of 11.

Those women who have these experiences—especially the first one—are far more likely to experience depression if they are faced with stressful events. Women with an intimate partner, with few or no small children, without paid employment, and who have not lost their mothers appeared to find it easier to cope with stressful events and were less likely to fall into depression. The important point made by Brown and Harris is that these factors do not, in themselves, induce depression: they make people more or less vulnerable to the stressful events that actually trigger depression (see Figure 8.9). Further stress after the onset of depression reinitiates the process and deepens depression.

The vulnerability factors are clearly linked to conventional gender roles and to ideas about the domesticity of women. Having small children at home and being responsible for them is a central feature of the *captive wife* described by Gavron (1968). It is the combination of this with involvement in paid work that has placed conflicting pressures on many employed women in contemporary Britain. Their two principal roles—employee and mother—involve contradictory expectations and may make it more difficult to cope with stress. Those factors that help women to combine the two roles may, thereby, reduce the impact of stressful events on them. The availability of effective childcare facilities, for example, helps those who have many small children.

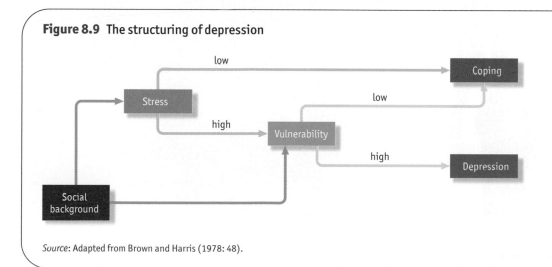

Figure 8.9 The structuring of depression

Source: Adapted from Brown and Harris (1978: 48).

Femininity, medicine, and beauty

As the boundaries of medicalization have expanded, there has also been a counter-movement in which patients are, at least in formal terms, seen by governments as 'consumers' of health with the right to choose in medical matters in the same way that they choose the education of their children, the type of car that they drive, and the kind of food that they eat. The power of patients to choose is limited in a whole variety of ways, just as their powers to choose in other areas of life are limited. However, the growing popularity of alternative medicines is a sign, perhaps, of the weakened authority of doctors. Indeed, patients are able to exercise a degree of consumer power in areas such as 'beauty', where medicine has stretched beyond the more clear-cut boundaries defined by notions of 'disease' and 'illness'.

In this section, we will look at two very different ways in which people 'choose' their own state of health. We will look at cosmetic surgery and eating disorders as responses to contemporary images of femininity.

Images of femininity

There is, in contemporary Western culture, a strong positive value attached to the idea of the slim, attractive woman, who is seen as both independent and self-assured. This cultural ideal contrasts sharply with the traditional image of female domesticity. The conventional image was vociferously challenged by the women's movement of the 1960s and 1970s in the wake of Friedan's (1962) critique of the 'feminine mystique'. This critique encouraged the view that caring for a family is a mundane and undemanding task and that women needed to develop their potentialities outside the home.

The new image of femininity closely combines conceptions of 'beauty' and 'attractiveness' with conceptions of 'health' and 'fitness' (Wolf 1991; Kathleen Davis 1995). A whole complex of industries and processes surround this image. The cosmetics industry, the fashion industry, pharmaceuticals companies, and other organizations concerned with dieting and 'healthy eating', as well as the medical profession itself, are all involved in perpetuating the new cultural ideal. These are, in turn, reinforced by advertising images of all kinds, and not only by advertising

Thinness as glamour: image and reality.

© Getty Images/Gustavo Caballero

© Getty Images: Zubin Shroff

for 'beauty' products themselves. Consumer pressure groups and television programmes that publicize the health implications of food also tend to reinforce the image of the healthy and fit woman.

Cultural ideals can change rapidly, and the ideal female body of the 1950s and 1960s became the 'full figure' of the 1980s and after. It has been shown that, over the period from 1959 to 1979, the average size of women depicted in fashion and other magazines decreased substantially. At the same time, changes in diet have meant that average weight in the population as a whole has increased. While women are getting larger, models and media ideals have been getting thinner. Pressures to be slim have grown and the size of the ideal body image has diminished (Mennell *et al.* 1992). The British Medical Association has estimated that a healthy woman has 22–26 per cent body fat, while models and actresses have an average of 10–15 per cent body fat. In mid-2000, the British government organized a seminar at which fashion editors and others discussed the idea that the mass media were promoting unrealistic body images, but the editors felt that they were reflecting, not creating, the views of their readers.

> **⮑ Connections**
> You might find it useful to turn to Chapter 10 and look at our discussion of images of women in the media in 'Representation', pp. 377–9.

Through their socialization, women have come to internalize this conception of femininity and to accept it as an ideal. The strength of the image is such that the great majority of women learn to scrutinize and monitor their size, shape, and food intake. They compare themselves with the cultural ideal, and feel themselves to have some kind of spoiled identity (Goffman 1963*b*). They may feel that they are overweight or fat, or they may feel that they have some particular blemish that marks them out as different from other women: their nose is the wrong shape, their breasts are too small or too big, or they have too many wrinkles.

The tyranny of the cultural ideal means that it is almost impossible not to develop a negative self-image. In pursuit of the cultural ideal, women seek to control and to shape their bodies in the desired direction. Dieting—restricting the amount of food that is eaten—becomes, for many, a normal part of their life. Large numbers of women are drawn not only into diet, exercise, and jogging, but also into body-building, the use of slimming pills, and increasingly into cosmetic surgery. Young girls are also exposed to these pressures and grow up feeling that it is unusual not to diet for weight loss. Their attitudes are affected by the views about health and fitness held by their own families and friends and by the classes on 'healthy eating' that now figure in the school curriculum.

Diet and eating habits have changed considerably over time. As a result of poor diets and overeating among the relatively affluent, many British people are now medically overweight. Few people engage in any strenuous activity during an ordinary day. They drive to work, are mainly involved in sedentary, non-manual work, and take little or no exercise. Less than half of the population is at a weight that is medically recognized as appropriate for their height and body shape. In 1980, 39 per cent of men and 32 per cent of women were medically overweight, and by 1999 these figures had risen to almost two-thirds of men and over a half of women. Significant numbers of men and women are classified as 'obese' or dangerously overweight. As shown in Figure 8.10, the problem of overweight is marked by a sharp social-class gradient. This increase in the problem of overweight was also apparent in the United States, where 60 per cent of adults are estimated to be overweight. The incidence of these conditions was lowest among young people and increased with age. It has been linked with the incidence of heart disease and other serious medical disorders.

Among many young people—and especially among young women—there is also a serious problem of being medically 'underweight'. This problem affected between 5 and 7 per cent of those surveyed in 1993. In the 16–24 age group, 14 per cent of males and 18 per cent of females were underweight. This is caused principally by a deliberate restriction of food intake as part of a slimming diet. Lack of body weight is linked to menstrual and fertility problems in women, as well as to such conditions as osteoporosis (brittle bones).

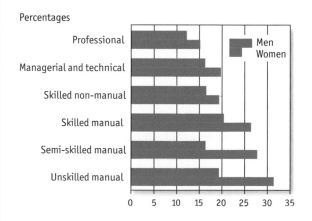

Figure 8.10 The overweight problem

Source: Social Trends (2002: chart 7.20).

We will look at two different responses to the desire to lose weight, both of which aim at empowerment and control. In the case of those women who choose to undergo cosmetic surgery, we will show that control is sought through a faith in medical experts and the quick surgical fix. In the case of those women who experience eating disorders, we will show that control is sought through the adoption of a strict and disciplined way of life.

The surgical fix

Various forms of plastic surgery have been performed for many centuries in the past, but it was not until the Crimean War that these techniques became at all reliable. These surgical techniques were driven by the need to repair the war-ravaged bodies of male soldiers, and great advances were made in the two world wars. Only in the second half of the twentieth century has plastic surgery for the aesthetic improvement of healthy bodies become a major area of medical specialization.

Indeed, plastic surgery is now the fastest growing medical specialism. Cosmetic surgery now accounts for about 40 per cent of all plastic surgery. About two million Americans received cosmetic surgery in 1988. Ninety per cent of them were women who were given face lifts, breast augmentations, liposuction (fat removal), and so on. This is, perhaps, the clearest expression of a consumerist 'choice'

 Briefing: having a face lift

Cosmetic surgery can involve major surgical intervention, as this account shows:

> I saw a face lift performed—the surgeon's hand inside the woman's face, punching and tearing, her separated skin only anchored at the nose and mouth. . . . The laser has added a further dimension to face lifting. The woman's face is now cut, separated, trimmed and reattached, the skin then burnt with a laser to get rid of the fine lines around the mouth.

A survey in the United States found that in 2003 there were 8.3 million surgical and non-surgical procedures for plastic surgery, 87 per cent of these were performed on women. The number of surgical procedures had increased by 87 per cent since 1997. The five most popular surgical cosmetic procedures in 2003 were: liposuction (384,626 cases), breast augmentation (280,401), eyelid surgery (267,627), rhinoplasty (172,420), and breast reduction (147,173).

Sources: Joanna Briscoe, *Guardian*, 18 February 1997; **www.cosmeticplasticsurgerystatistics.com/statistics.html**

orientation in contemporary medicine. Having a new nose or new breasts is seen almost in the same way as having a new hairstyle: it is something chosen by a woman in order to achieve a particular, desirable presentation of self.

Kathleen Davis (1995) has shown that cosmetic surgery is seen as an option by those women who, comparing themselves with others, develop a fear and loathing of a particular feature of their own body. This feature comes to be seen as a blemish that in some way discredits them as women. Their nose, their breasts, or their buttocks, for example, do not fit with the image of what they feel they 'really' look like. It does not match the rest of their body.

Davis argues, then, that these women are not in search of absolute perfection or an exceptional beauty. They are, rather, responding to a perceived stigma. She notes, however, that the perceived stigma is rarely disfiguring, or even apparent, in any objective sense. The cultural pressures on women, however, have led many to be hypersensitive towards their appearance. They are constantly concerned about anything that is 'not quite right'. They hope to rectify a specific blemish that, they feel, prevents them from appearing 'ordinary' and is responsible for their (actual or imagined) exclusion and derogation by others. They feel different and they feel that they are constantly noticed by others because of their assumed peculiarity. These women use the word 'ordinary' when they mean having an appearance that is within the normal aesthetic range for contemporary women. An ordinary women is not noticed in her everyday encounters. Their perception of normality, however, is heavily influenced by the cultural ideal of femininity.

The first step towards cosmetic surgery, then, is a feeling of being blemished. The second step, however, is coming to a decision that cosmetic surgery is an appropriate solution to this. In a society where more and more areas of life have become medicalized, the surgical fix becomes a more realistic possibility for ever-increasing numbers of people.

Those that take this decision, Davis argues, are involved in a renegotiation of their identity and sense of self. It is seen as a last-ditch attempt to rectify a situation that is perceived to be unbearable:

> Cosmetic surgery is not about beauty, but about identity. For a woman who feels trapped in a body which does not fit her sense of who she is, cosmetic surgery is about exercising power under conditions which are not of one's own making. In a context of limited possibilities for action, cosmetic surgery can be a way for an individual woman to give shape to her life by reshaping her body. (Kathleen Davis 1995: 163)

Women come to believe that by controlling their bodies they are controlling their lives. Cosmetic surgery comes to be seen as a way of enhancing their power. Their identity is renegotiated, however, in relation to a prevailing image of femininity and a medicalized definition of reality. Their freely chosen option of the surgical fix is as much a sign of subordination as it is of empowerment. The dilemma of cosmetic surgery is that the desire for power and control is pursued by subordination not merely to a cultural ideal of femininity but also to the power of the medical profession.

Femininity, weight, and eating

There has been growing public concern in recent years over anorexia nervosa. Indeed, there has been something of a moral panic. Anorexia comprises a number of physical symptoms that revolve around an abnormally low body weight for the age, height, and sex of the sufferer. This is brought about by a sustained and deliberate restriction of food intake. Although the condition first appeared as a medical diagnosis in the middle of the nineteenth century, it is only since the 1970s that it has become of epidemic proportions. The condition is found mainly, but not exclusively, among young, white, and relatively affluent women, and it is the causes and consequences of anorexia in this group that have been so keenly discussed. Its incidence is difficult to gauge, but it is thought to be a serious problem for one in every 200 or 250 women between the ages of 13 and 22. About double this number are thought to be significantly affected in some way by problems of anorexia. The number of deaths is small, but they may amount to over 10 per cent of those who receive long-term medical treatment as hospital in-patients.

The loss of body weight in anorexia may vary from a condition of being mildly underweight to a state of extreme emaciation. Medical discussions have tended to suggest a physiological model in which the former leads inexorably to the latter. The medical view does, however, correctly identify a number of physiological changes that result from extreme weight loss and that characterize established sufferers. These physical effects include secondary amenorrhoea (cessation of menstruation as a result of hormonal changes), feelings of extreme coldness as a result of a lowered rate of metabolism and blood circulation, disturbed sleep, the growth of fine body hair, and a thickening of head hair. There are also likely to be stomach and intestinal upsets, such as constipation and abdominal pain. These are, however, much worse in the related problem of bulimia, where 'binge' eating is followed by induced vomiting or diarrhoea. Abstinence from food over a long period of time reduces body weight below the level at which normal physiological mechanisms can operate to regulate the state of the body, and total physical breakdown is, indeed, inevitable unless treatment is accepted (Palmer 1980).

In relatively affluent and comfortable families, there is often great pressure on children to succeed in their lives.

In the case of young women, this is likely to involve an encouragement—experienced as pressure—to take up opportunities that were not available to earlier generations of women. This encouragement involves a rejection of, or at least an ambivalence towards, the traditional feminine role and an implicit endorsement of the new cultural ideal. This new ideal of independent and assertive femininity, however, is something that many young women find difficult to accept. They are anxious about their ability to meet these expectations, concerned about how they could ever compare with the ideal.

It is these anxious individuals, it seems, who are especially likely to be drawn into anorexic behaviour (Bruch 1973, 1979; Chernin 1985). Their anxiety leads them to be uncertain about their own goals, unable to decide what to do. They become confused about who they are and what they might be in the future. This uncertainty over their identity, and the associated feeling that they have no control over their own lives, leads them to focus their attention on more immediate goals that are set by parents and teachers. Educational success, for example, becomes an end in itself, and, striving to please, they tend to adopt a perfectionist attitude towards their school work. In doing so, they set unrealistic goals and so are constantly unable to meet their own rigorous standards. If they do meet these standards, they feel that they must, after all, have been too low. This is the classic example of the inferiority complex described by Adler (1928).

In their search for a solution to their problems of identity, these young women have not completely abandoned the cultural ideal of femininity. It is something that is still important to them, but about which they feel ambivalent and inadequate. Like others of their age, and like many of their mothers' generation, they are drawn to the ideal and to the practices of bodily control that are associated with it. Slimming and fitness training, for example, may be adopted as exploratory experiments in their ability to meet this ideal. Such experiments often begin around the time of puberty and are associated with the natural weight gain and changes in body shape that occur at this time. For those who misinterpret the nature of these changes, they can be seen as signs that they are getting 'fat'. It is in these circumstances that the drift into anorexia becomes a possibility.

Many young women begin to diet, perhaps by avoiding what they see as unhealthy or fatty foods. Many—perhaps most—are unsuccessful in losing weight and may drift in and out of dieting for the rest of their lives. Some of those who are successful, especially the anxious perfectionists, are likely to feel a degree of pleasure in having achieved their goal. They enjoy the feeling of accomplishment and control that it gives them. Achieving a weight loss provides a sense of purpose that seems to resolve some of the confusions that they feel about the direction that their lives should take. Dieting becomes one area of life where it seems possible to exercise total control (Bordo 1993: 148–50).

The anorexic solution

The person who drifts from experimental dieting into incipient anorexia is one who gets great satisfaction from finding, at last, something that she has chosen and that she is good at. Dieting seems to resolve her sense of identity even more than immersion in school work. It becomes something that is very difficult to give up. If it is the one area where she feels that she can 'succeed', then what does she have left if she gives it up? She becomes committed to the activity into which she has drifted, gaining satisfaction and even enjoyment from it. Continued weight loss, rather than a fixed target weight, becomes her goal. The original aspiration to achieve attractiveness and independence is partially displaced into a mastery of the body for its own sake. She begins to enter what we describe in Chapter 7, as secondary deviation. She begins a *career* of anorexia, which becomes a way of life that, paradoxically, becomes increasingly detached from the cultural ideal of femininity.

The anorexic way of life revolves around a commitment to *ascetic* practices and values that are deeply rooted in our culture and were first explored by Max Weber (1904–5; see also B. Turner 1996). Asceticism is the pursuit of a disciplined life of self-denial and abstention from material comforts and pleasures. The asceticism of the early Puritans, he argued, was the basis of their business success. In the favourable circumstances of seventeenth- and eighteenth-century England, it helped the expansion of the capitalist system. These values subsequently became much weakened, but they became the basis of a so-called work ethic that limited consumption and leisure by subordinating them to the expansion of production. As we suggest in the discussion of drug use in Chapter 7, the work ethic involves the idea that consumption and leisure can be enjoyed only *after* work commitments have been met in full. The right to enjoy one's leisure must be earned through hard work (J. Young 1971).

The work ethic is linked to a specific structuring of sex–gender roles. Participation in the 'public' world of paid work and politics has been mainly an activity of men. Women have largely been confined to the 'private' domestic world of unpaid work. In the conventional family household, women have been responsible for intimate and emotional matters and the man has been the 'breadwinner'. It is precisely this feminine role that many young women today reject, reflecting a fundamental cultural shift that has involved a weakening of the work ethic and a possibility for the more open pursuit of pleasure.

For those who are ambivalent towards the contemporary images of femininity and who drift into anorexic practices, the adoption of a purer form of asceticism, closer to the Puritan original, is highly conducive. In this sense, the anorexic way of life is an ascetic way of life. Asceticism for the anorexic is a response to anxiety and inner loneliness, as much as it was for the Calvinist. In her case, however, the anxiety does not concern religious salvation but personal autonomy and independence.

Bordo (1993) sees these women as in a state of implicit 'protest' against the culturally institutionalized images of femininity that, in crucial respects, they fear and seek to avoid. This is not, however, an absolute rejection, and their feelings are highly ambivalent. As young girls, they are socialized into an acceptance of these images, which become deeply embedded parts of their sense of self. Nevertheless, they find it impossible to embrace them wholeheartedly as examples to follow in their own lives. The anorexic, then, is in protest against these prevailing images of women—attracted by both, but fearing and rejecting aspects of them as well. This protest, however, is not a conscious and planned political protest, but a *bodily* protest. The anorexic engages in what Orbach (1986) calls a 'hunger strike' against contemporary femininities.

In the stage of secondary deviation that is marked by the adoption of an ascetic way of life, the central element in the young woman's identity is no longer an aspiration to a cultural ideal of femininity. Instead, it is the maintenance of an image of a person who is in control of her own life through her control over her own body. The anorexic way of life establishes a regime in which size must be constantly reduced. The search for a slender, controlled body involves a constant watch for any increase in weight and for any unwanted bumps that must be eliminated. With continued weight loss to well below 'normal' levels, the sufferer becomes committed to being thin rather than to meeting the cultural ideal of femininity itself. Being thin—and so being 'straight' rather than 'curvy'—is *safe*, as it allows her to withdraw from the competitive pressure to be an attractive and independent woman. A return to normal weight is feared for the problems of identity that would return with it.

As the goal becomes that of attaining ever greater slenderness, any soft flesh comes to be seen as unsightly, as fat. Sensations of emptiness become a sign of health and

 Briefing: asceticism

We discuss Weber's argument in Chapter 11, pp. 411–12, and you might find it useful to review what we say there. You might also find it useful to look at our discussion of hedonism and the work ethic in Chapter 7, pp. 257–60. These issues are well covered in Lupton (1996).

achievement, while eating above the very restricted level that has been adopted leads to feelings of being 'bloated' and, therefore, 'fat'. Paradoxically, the slimmer a woman gets, the more obtrusive becomes any normal roundness in body shape, and the greater becomes the internal pressure towards continued size reduction. As the sufferer gets drawn further into these patterns of behaviour, so the inevitable physical hunger pains and other physical symptoms of starvation also come to be seen as things that must be suppressed or ignored and, therefore, controlled. This victory over pain may even be secretly enjoyed as yet another sign of control.

It has been suggested that a sufferer from anorexia experiences perceptual distortions as a direct result of her physical condition—she misdescribes her own body as fat rather than thin. This view, however, has been challenged. It may simply be that words are used to obscure her new, secret identity as someone who has escaped from contemporary femininity through the hunger strike. By describing herself as fat, the anorexic legitimates a continuation of the ascetic practices that she believes have helped her to escape from the tyranny of the cultural ideal.

As her physical condition worsens, however, a sufferer may begin to feel that there is something wrong with her. This is tempered by a continuing commitment to her lifestyle and new identity as someone who is in control. Wearing many layers of clothing will keep her warm, partly offsetting the physical coldness that she feels, but it may also help to hide the extent of her weight loss from friends and family. She continues to tell herself that she fears putting on weight because she would no longer be attractive or healthy, and she may put these arguments to others if challenged about her appearance or behaviour. These explanations, however, become less convincing.

From reading magazines, watching television, and talking to others, the anorexic adopts the idea of an 'eating disorder' to account for her behaviour. As she struggles to understand her own feelings, she may come to accept, in private, the idea that she is suffering from anorexia. Because anorexia has been socially defined as abnormal or unacceptable—by family, by friends, and in the media—this self-definition is likely to remain a private matter. Outwardly, the anorexic wishes to appear as normal, but privately she feels that only she may know the practices and routines through which this appearance is produced. The idea of anorexia is incorporated into her identity and given a positive interpretation, but it must remain secret, something that can be admitted only in private. By maintaining an outward front-region appearance of normality and conformity, she can feel that she is able to remain in control.

In the back region—in the privacy of her bedroom—the sufferer voraciously consumes books about anorexia and eating disorders, and she comes to redefine and to reconstruct her biography in the same terms that they use. There is, however, a curious ambivalence about the medical diagnosis. This is likely to be rejected at the same time as many of its features are accepted. There can be no easy acceptance of the idea of being ill when the sufferer feels that she is in control.

Successful reversal of the anorexic condition has been shown to depend upon a self-recognition of it and an acceptance of the need to struggle against the illness. Such a decision is by no means easy, as a positive view of anorexia has become a central feature of the sufferer's identity. Any departure from the ascetic regime that she has been following for so long is likely to result in feelings of guilt, and guilt is likely to lead to re-adoption of the regime in an even more rigorous form. The ascetic shaping of the body and its physical consequences reinforce one another. Eventually the deteriorating physical condition of the sufferer may destroy the possibility of any proper control and autonomy. Lack of energy, depression, and sheer starvation make almost all physical and mental activity impossible. The search for control *over* the body can all too easily end in the control of the searcher *by* her own body.

Stop and reflect

In this section we have looked at the medicalization of ever more areas of life. We looked not only at physical health and mental health, but also at the medicalization of reproduction and beauty.

- There is no necessary conflict between medical and sociological views of health and illness. Both are important, but they have differing purposes and concerns.

- Illness in contemporary society is organized in terms of a sick role that establishes norms of behaviour for the sufferer and for others. Death is also disciplined through definite role expectations.

- Depression has its origins in particular life conditions that are experienced most particularly by women.

- Why did Goffman say that hospital treatment of mental illness involves a definite 'moral career' for patients?

We argued that the medicalization of life raises important questions about the meaning of 'health'.

- Reproductive behaviour has increasingly come to be defined in medical terms. Sex and motherhood have both come under the medical gaze.
- Contemporary concerns about feminine beauty have had a major impact on women's lifestyles. They have been a major causal factor in the growth of cosmetic surgery and eating disorders.
- To what extent are the mass media responsible for the growth in eating disorders?

◁▷ *Chapter summary*

In the first section of this chapter we looked at a number of theoretical issues in the study of body, health, and population.

- We traced Foucault's ideas on the growth of regulation and discipline in the control of human populations and the bodies of their members. We saw this in relation to the practices of surveillance that developed within nation states.
- As part of this growth in surveillance, we identified the medical gaze through which new techniques were employed to shape the body and the mind.
- Techniques of measurement through censuses, surveys, and civil registration were established and became institutionalized as means for collecting data about populations. There was a huge growth in the collection and compilation of criminal statistics, unemployment statistics, demographic statistics, and many other statistics.

The following section discussed a range of statistics on population and health, covering issues of fertility, mortality, and migration. We argued that:

- Population in modern societies is the result of a demographic transition in which birth and death rates have altered.
- There is a corresponding demographic transition in which causes of illness and death have altered with modernization.
- We also looked at debates on impairment and disability, considering the social model of disability and its idea of disability as stigmatization and social exclusion.

In the final section we focused on the medicalization of social life, examining both physical health and mental health as well as the medicalization of reproduction and beauty.

- The sick role is an important feature of the organization of health and illness, defining norms of behaviour for those involved.
- Mental illness has its origins in the social reaction to behaviour that is seen as 'abnormal' or unusual. Hospital treatment reinforces this definition by defining a moral career and confining the patient to the role of the mental patient.
- Both reproductive behaviour and ideas of beauty have come to be defined in medical terms. We traced this through the growth of cosmetic surgery and eating disorders.

⌗ *Key concepts*

- anatomo-politics
- awareness contexts
- biopolitics
- client control
- death trajectory
- demographic transition
- disability
- disciplinary society
- emigration
- fertility
- health transition
- illness
- immigration
- impairment
- insanity role
- medical gaze
- medicalization
- mortality
- professional control
- residual rule-breaking
- sick role
- surveillance

Workshop 8

Study 8 Enforcing normality

L. J. Davis (1995) has explored the cultural assumptions underpinning conceptions of deafness in Europe and the United States. Taking a historical approach, Davis shows that the idea of disability was something that became organized during the eighteenth and nineteenth centuries as part of a more general project to control the body. It emerged at a time when categories of crime, sexuality, gender, disease, and so on were all emerging in relation to transformations in the state and the economy. Those with problems of hearing came to be regarded as 'deaf' and, therefore, as subject to particular forms of regulation and control.

Western culture, Davis argues, is based around an assumption that it is normal for humans to speak and hear—just as it assumes that the norm of gender is seen as masculine, the norm of race is seen as white, and the norm of sexuality is seen as heterosexuality. Such an assumption, he claims, rests upon a particular view of the body and power. It is possible to imagine, he argues, that a developed sign or gesture language preceded oral language and so has an equal right to be considered as the norm. He makes what he admits is an extreme point in order to highlight the arbitrariness of the cultural assumption and the fact that its relevance for the future can be questioned.

'Normalcy' is socially constructed, and we cannot avoid living in a world of norms, constructed from averages and typical occurrences. The idea of the disabled body emerged in relation to a conception of the normal body. The focus of discussion, therefore, should be on the constructions or representations of disability rather than the disabled person as an object. It is the way in which normalcy is constructed that makes disability into a 'problem'. It was in the eighteenth century that deafness came to be a matter of central cultural concern. It became the visible subject of discourse among those professionals who felt that an inability to participate in the spoken culture of the Enlightenment reduced the level of a person's humanity. The deaf as a social category were brought into being by this form of discourse. Prior to that time the deaf were isolated within their own families and there was no public, enlightened discourse from which they were excluded. Writings about deafness began to appear at the same time as writings about language and communication: the Enlightenment view that language was central to humanity defined the 'problem' of deafness as a condition that was not truly human. It developed alongside the discourse of nationalism, as the shared language of a national population was seen as central to civilized human existence.

Davis raises the question of how the deaf can challenge their categorization. The disabled generally have received less political attention than many other minorities. Discussions of sexism, racism, and heterosexism, for example, are now commonplace, but the social model of disability has only slowly led to corresponding ideas of 'disablism'. Those with hearing problems are less visible as a minority even than many other disabled groups, and there has been little criticism of 'audism'. Concerns over the categorization of hearing problems as disabilities, Davis argues, has led many deaf people to define themselves as members of a 'linguistic minority'—and he suggests that a similar challenge to the general idea of disability might be posed by a term such as 'physical minority'.

❷ How useful is it to think of deafness as having been invented in the eighteenth century?

❷ Collect some advertisements for hearing aids from your local newspaper. What image of the deaf is conveyed in the advert?

❷ Consider the debate over the cochlea implant (discussed on p. 294 above). What are the main issues that deaf parents should consider when deciding whether to allow their deaf children to be surgically treated and given a form of hearing?

Media watch 8 Care in the community

The process of decarceration, with its shift to care in the community for the mentally ill, has resulted in the closure of large numbers of hospitals. For years, mental patients were treated in the large 'asylums', many of which had been built in Victorian times. One hundred Victorian hospitals have been closed, with just twenty now surviving. Many of the patients now released had spent the bulk of their lives within the hospitals, and they have found it difficult to come to terms with the outside world.

Annemarie Randall, now aged 60, was an adopted child who was treated violently by her adoptive parents. She married at 16 and suffered violence from her husband. Two children died as newborn infants before a healthy son was born. When her son was 6 years old, Annemarie's husband insisted that his pregnant mistress move into the house, and Annemarie and her son moved out. Six years later her son, Robert, was killed in a road accident. Annemarie blamed herself for having bought his bicycle, and she began a period of self-abuse. She left her flat and wandered the streets; she stabbed herself with a bread knife eleven times, and she attacked herself with razor blades and broken glass. It was not long before she was picked up by the police and she was sent to a mental hospital.

In Oakwood Hospital, Maidstone, she spent four years and was given insulin therapy and ECT (electro-convulsive therapy); she spent a great deal of time in a padded cell. She escaped from the hospital a number of times, but was always brought back. When she was released she spent her time in hostels and bed sits and, for a while, lived with an older woman whom she nursed through

the final stages of cancer. When her friend died, Annemarie once more fell into depression and was taken into Banstead Hospital, in Surrey. She spent ten years in Banstead until it closed, when she was transferred to a small hospital and then to a hostel. Although life had been comfortable in Banstead, Annemarie felt that she had not been given the opportunity to talk to therapists and had, instead, been given unhelpful drug treatments. She now lives alone, apart from her cat, suffering from chronic heart and blood problems that she believes will eventually result in a fatal stroke.

Source: *Observer*, 7 April 2002

➲ Consider our account of Goffman's model of the moral career of the mental patient and the argument of Brown and Harris about the social origins of depression.

❷ What elements in Annemarie's life story support the Brown and Harris argument?

❷ Which aspects of her story demonstrate the impact of organizational processes on her sense of self?

❷ Consult the article that we have cited: you can find it at www.guardianunlimited.co.uk. In the article you will find other accounts of patients' lives. Note down further evidence that helps you to explore the above questions. Do any of the accounts provide evidence on the effectiveness—or otherwise—of the policy of care in the community?

Discussion points

Review the various 'Stop and reflect' points in this chapter. You may find it useful to consider these in relation to our discussion of socialization, identity, and deviance in Chapters 4 and 7. We considered a number of substantive areas, as well as the methodological problems of using official statistics.

Medicine, health, and illness

In our discussion of medicine, we looked at both physical illness and mental illness. We showed that each must be seen as socially constructed:

● Make sure that you understand how the following terms can be used: medical gaze, medicalization, sick role, and moral career.

● Consider the implications of the increasing use of technology in relation to contraception and childbirth.

● Try to grasp the key ideas associated with: Foucault, Parsons, Scheff, and Goffman.

The social body

Foucault figures again in our review of the social body. You should spend a little time thinking about the links between his views on medicine and his arguments about population:

● How does Foucault distinguish between regulation and discipline?

● How would you define the terms anatamo-politics and biopolitics? How do these relate to his idea of surveillance?

Understanding fertility and mortality requires a little bit of statistical knowledge, and you should try to practise some of your skills and consolidate your knowledge of the statistical concepts used to study populations:

- What do you understand by the following demographic measures: crude birth rate, crude death rate, age-specific fertility, standardized mortality rate, life expectancy, neonatal mortality, ageing population? Do not worry about giving precise definitions, but just ensure that you understand the general idea.

- Using the figures in Figure 8.1, draw a pie chart to show the distribution of world population across the various regions. Using the data in Figure 8.2, calculate the periods in which the UK population increase has been most rapid. What conclusions would you draw from the figures in these graphs?

- How would you word a question on ethnic identity for use in a government social survey? How would you expect the conclusions reported on pp. 285–6 to be affected by a change in question wording?

Food, beauty, and lifestyle

Issues of beauty and eating have increasingly come to be seen in medical terms, and we discussed a number of matters that have arisen. Issues of health and lifestyle are now closely associated with each other.

- What is the significance of the idea of the family meal? What factors have contributed to its decline?

- Why do you think there has been a growth in smoking among young people?

- Why do you think that the cultural ideal of femininity is so important to most women?

- What do you understand by the following terms: cosmetic surgery, asceticism, hunger strike?

Explore further

Good general discussions of the issues covered in this chapter can be found in:

Foucault, M. (1963), *The Birth of the Clinic* (New York: Vintage Books, 1975). *Hard going, but it repays the effort.*

Coleman, D., and Salt, J. (1992), *The British Population: Patterns, Trends and Processes* (Oxford: Oxford University Press). *A large and comprehensive summary of population trends since the nineteenth century.*

Pilcher, J. L. (1995), *Age and Generation in Modern Britain* (Oxford: Oxford University Press). *A very useful and well-written overview of population issues related to age and ageing.*

Freidson, E. (1970), *The Profession of Medicine* (New York: Dodd Mead). *An important study of the medical profession and its power.*

Goffman, E. (1961), *Asylums: Essays on the Social Situation of Mental Patients and Other Inmates* (New York: Doubleday). *Once again, we recommend a book by Goffman. This one was said to have inspired the feature film* One Flew Over the Cuckoo's Nest.

Lupton, D. (1996), *Food, the Body and the Self* (London: Sage). *A useful overview of the sociology of food that considers many of the issues discussed in this chapter.*

Busfield, N. J. (1996), *Men, Women and Madness: Understanding Gender and Mental Disorder* (London: Macmillan). *A good, recent account of the gendered character of mental illness.*

Stanworth, M. (1987) (ed.), *Gender, Motherhood and Medicine* (Cambridge: Polity Press). *Important for Stanworth's Introduction and for other contributions on the new reproductive technologies.*

Bordo, S. (1993), *Unbearable Weight: Feminism, Western Culture, and the Body* (Berkeley and Los Angeles: University of California Press). *A collection of Bordo's papers that examine anorexia from a feminist standpoint.*

Wolf, N. (1991), *The Beauty Myth: How Images of Beauty are Used against Women* (New York: Wm. Morrow). *A good critique of the cultural ideal of beauty and how it constrains and coerces women.*

Busfield, J. (2000), *Health and Health Care in Modern Britain* (Oxford: Oxford University Press). *An excellent overview of the whole area that is comprehensive and authoritative.*

Online resources

Visit the Online Resource Centre that accompanies this book to access more learning resources and other interesting material on the body, health, and medicine at:

www.oxfordtextbooks.co.uk/orc/fulcher3e/

Much useful information can be found through the World Health Organization at:

www.who.int/home-page

World Health Organization statistical information can be found at:

www.who.int/whosis

The United Nations Population Fund can be found at:

www.unfpa.org

The British government's Department of Health website is useful for official information and policies:

www.doh.gov.uk

Interesting video resources on topics covered in this chapter include:

One Flew Over The Cuckoo's Nest, a film that explores issues of mental illness and illustrates many aspects of Goffman's argument.

My Left Foot, a film that raises issues of disability in relation to those of class and ethnicity.

The Hand Maiden's Tale, a novel by Margaret Atwood and a film, that explores a futuristic society in which women are enslaved for enforced reproduction.

The website of the British Sociological Association's Medical Sociology Study Group contains information on seminars and conferences and links to a variety of sources on the sociology of health:

www.britsoc.org.uk/about/medsoc.htm

The website of the Eating Disorder Association is at:

www.edauk.com

We have discussed Foucault a great deal in this chapter. Casey Alt has set up an animated introduction to *The Birth of the Clinic* at:

www.stanford.edu/dept/hps/BirthoftheClinic

culture, knowledge, and belief

PART THREE

education

Contents

09

More choice or less?

Choice of school is now an accepted parental right but what happens if too many parents choose the best school in the area? If a popular state school has three applications for every place, only a third of the children who have applied will get the school their parents have chosen. The school can select the child, rather than the family choosing the school.

In theory popular schools should expand and make more places available but there is inevitably a considerable time-lag if schools do this. Most popular schools would not anyway want to do it, since their size is an important aspect of the character of the school and they would risk losing their distinctive ethos and their popularity if they became too big.

Parents can face very difficult choices, since they have to take into account not only the quality of the available schools but also the likelihood of getting into them. They can drop down the popularity scale in order to be surer, if by no means certain, of getting a place at a reasonably good school, but then have to settle for 'second best'. They may look further afield but then face expensive and time-consuming journeys. They may decide to opt for private education, with all its costs, though their children will still have to pass through the private school's selection process.

There are always some schools somewhere with places available and a school will always be found for a child by the local authority. If schools have spare places because they are unpopular, this probably means, however, that they are remote or perform badly or have more than their fair share of problems. As the *Guardian* has put it, 'the end result is a combination of unacceptable and unobtainable schools'.

Sources: *Guardian Education*, 29 January 2002; *Independent*, 28 April 2005.

Parental choice has become one of the accepted principles of British education but many parents are unable to exercise that right effectively. As our opening piece shows, if too many parents choose the 'best' school in the area, some will not get the school of their choice. Furthermore, information in league tables about the relative examination success of schools, and the recent setting up of elite 'academies', increases the demand for the 'best' school. The right to choose and league tables are established features of the British educational scene but they are, in fact, very recent innovations and in this chapter we examine how and why they came into existence, and the problems they raise.

High demand for some schools means that these schools can select whom they admit. The issue of selection has dominated the educational debate in Britain since the 1960s. This is not just because it clashes with the right to choose but because it also conflicts with another fundamental principle, equality of opportunity. It has been argued that this can only be provided if there is no selection process and comprehensives take all the children in their area, irrespective of the child's background or ability. We examine this issue in the context of a more general discussion of equality of opportunity and its relationship to class, gender, and ethnicity.

But we begin this chapter by considering the broader question of the relationship between education and society, and the main sociological theories of this. What is education for? Is it a means by which children are turned into useful members of society? Is it a means of providing equality of opportunity? Does it merely serve the interests of employers?

Understanding education

The central issues of the sociology of education focus on the relationship between education and society. Our starting-point here is the significance of education in the socialization process, before moving on to the issue of inequality, and finally the relationship between capitalism and education.

Education and socialization

Education is central to the process of socialization. As we show in Chapter 4, p. 118, *primary* socialization is carried out within the family, but this takes the process only so far. Both Émile Durkheim (1925) and Talcott Parsons (1959) argued in their different ways that education plays a key role in *secondary* socialization by performing functions that the family cannot perform.

One way in which education does this is by providing the skills needed to perform the specialized occupations characteristic of industrial societies. As the division of labour became more specialized, it was no longer possible for skills to be handed down within the family. Children could acquire these skills only through formal education. How well schools perform this function has become a matter of growing concern in Britain, as occupational and technological change have altered the skills required.

More fundamentally, education turns children into members of society by socializing them into the common values and norms of their society. Through education, children learn religious and moral beliefs. They also develop a sense of national identity through education, learning national languages and customs, the symbols of nationality, and the history of the nation.

Durkheim was particularly concerned with the moral aspects of making children members of their society. It was through school discipline that children learned to behave in a moral way. Punishment and the authority of the teacher played an important part in this but he argued that it was not just a matter of forcing children to obey but also of getting them to appreciate the moral basis of society. They needed to understand the reasons for moral behaviour, so that they behaved morally because they wanted to do so. Social rules had to become internalized as part of the individual's personality, so that discipline became self-discipline.

Durkheim emphasized the moral aspect of education because he was concerned with the increasing individualism of nineteenth-century French society. For Durkheim, the key function of education was that it subordinated the individual to society and made people aware of their responsibilities to each other and to the wider collectivity. This view of education has more recently been expressed by Hargreaves (1982), who drew extensively on the work of Durkheim. He argued that British schools and teachers had become dominated by a culture of individualism. They were far too concerned with meeting the needs of the individual child and too little concerned with the school's functions for society. He called for schools to promote social solidarity by generating a sense of community among their pupils and linking this to the wider community and society as a whole.

Parsons too recognized the moral significance of education, but in the rather different social context of mid-twentieth-century America he placed more emphasis on the value of individual achievement. It was through education that children acquired the value of achievement and learned how to achieve. This value was central to the functioning of an industrial society but families could not instil it, for they treated children in a *particular* way according to who they were not according to how they achieved. In school, however, success depended upon achievement and this was measured by the *universal* standards of examinations, which took no account of who you were and simply measured how well you performed.

Although they differed in their emphasis, both Durkheim and Parsons viewed education in terms of the *functions* that it performed for society. Education does do the kinds of things that Durkheim and Parsons saw it doing but, as we show in Chapter 2, pp. 48–50, there are problems with **functionalism** and these have led to criticism of their views.

First, functionalists argue in terms of the needs of society as a whole. It may be questioned, however, whether we can speak of the needs of the society as a whole in this way. Who defines these needs? Does education perform functions for society or does it rather serve the interests of those who rule the society and control education?

Secondly, functionalists tend to assume that the members of a society share common values. Many different cultures exist within most societies, however, and there can be conflicts between them, often grounded in religious differences, over moral and cultural issues. The values, beliefs, and identities transmitted by schools are also open to challenge by those who do not hold them, who may well set up alternative educational institutions. Education may, therefore, not so much create a sense of membership of a common society as perpetuate particular cultures within it and reinforce social divisions.

Controversy and debate Faith schools

According to the British government's September 2001 White Paper on education, 'we wish to welcome faith schools, with their distinctive ethos and character, into the maintained sector, where there is clear local agreement'.

There is, however, nothing new about state-funded faith schools (the state pays the teachers and 85 per cent of the capital costs). In January 2001, 35 per cent of the 18,069 state primary schools in England were already faith schools, mainly Church of England or Roman Catholic. There were 4,509 Church of England schools (25 per cent of all primary schools) and 1,747 Roman Catholic schools (9.7 per cent). There were also 28 Methodist schools, 47 of other Christian faiths, 26 Jewish schools, two Muslim and one Sikh school.

At secondary level, there were fewer faith schools—17 per cent of the 3,481 state schools. There were 357 Roman Catholic schools (10.3 per cent of all secondary schools) and 191 Church of England schools (5.5 per cent). There were also 77 schools of other Christian faiths, five Jewish schools and one Sikh school.

There are also independent faith schools and these have recently been growing rapidly in number, rising from 170 in September 2003 to 276 in January 2005. Muslim independent schools have been growing faster than those of other religions. In 2005 more than 14,000 pupils were being taught in Muslim independent schools, as compared with 9,500 in Jewish schools and about 5,000 in evangelical Christian schools. The government is reportedly planning to encourage the movement of independent faith schools into the state-funded sector, in order to increase choice and gain some control over the faith school curriculum.

There is much debate over the merits of faith schools. Those in favour claim that they are popular, meet local needs, strengthen moral beliefs, and achieve high educational standards. Those against argue that they reinforce social divisions, generate conflict between communities, and prevent the social integration of minorities. Some have suggested that there should be *multi-faith* schools which would both meet the needs of the various local religious communities *and* make children aware of other faiths than their own.

Sources: *Guardian Education*, 14 November 2001, 8 January 2002, and 21 January 2005; see also Gardner *et al.* (2004).

❷ What did Durkheim consider to be the key functions of education? Do religious schools perform these functions?

❷ As faith schools have long existed, why has this recently become such an issue?

❷ Do faith schools integrate or divide society?

Do faith schools 'light the way' in education?
© Hymers College, Hull

Education and inequality

The relationship between education and inequality has been one of the main issues in the sociology of education and a main concern of educational policy in Britain, which has gone through two major processes of reform intended to produce greater equality. The 1944 Education Act and the later movement to introduce comprehensive schools both claimed to provide equality of opportunity.

Equality of opportunity?

As we have just shown, Parsons argued that education instilled the value of achievement. This was closely linked to another shared value, a belief in equality of opportunity, which was also central to the functioning of industrial societies. It was crucial to the allocation of human resources, for it enabled people with ability to find their way into the jobs that required those abilities. In industrial societies status was not determined by birth but by achievement, and, according to Parsons, equality of opportunity enabled those with ability to achieve success.

It also performed another key function in getting those who did not succeed to accept their failure. Industrial societies motivated people to achieve by providing them with superior rewards. This inevitably resulted in inequality, but those who did not succeed accepted this because they believed that everyone had had an equal opportunity to succeed. Thus, the belief that equality of opportunity existed legitimated the stratification of society.

Parsons considered that education was the main mechanism of equality of opportunity. In schools there was competition on equal terms, for examinations applied universal standards and performance in examinations determined educational success. Those who succeeded educationally did so on the basis of superior performance. Furthermore, it was clear to all that success was the reward for achievement. The key values of achievement and equality of opportunity were transmitted through education. The problem with this approach is that it assumes that there is competition on equal terms in schools. Others have argued that this is not the case and we now need to consider their views.

> **➔ Connections**
> We discuss equality of opportunity and the related concept of meritocracy in Chapter 18, pp. 723–4.

Class, culture, and language

It has long been argued that class background shapes educational success through material advantages and disadvantages. The better off can buy educational success, either by buying entry to better schools or by buying assistance with education, such as private coaching or extra books. It is not just money that counts, however, for it has been shown that such factors as health and quality of housing, which are related to class background, influence educational success (see Lee 1989).

Others have argued that it is not so much a matter of *material* as *cultural* advantages and disadvantages. One approach of this kind has been labelled **cultural-deprivation theory**. This held that working-class children have been disadvantaged in the educational system by working-class values and beliefs. These placed a low value on education and focused on the immediate rewards of earning money rather than *deferring gratification* until educational qualifications had been obtained. This could, for example, result in a lack of parental interest in education, which Douglas (1964) found to be the single most important factor in explaining children's educational attainments. It could also result in children leaving school early in order to earn money. Similar arguments have been put forward to explain some ethnic minorities' lack of achievement in education.

Such approaches have been criticized for the negative views they present of particular class or ethnic-minority cultures. These views often seem to reflect prejudices rather than real knowledge of the culture concerned. It is also difficult to separate out cultural from situational factors. Leaving school early, for example, may not mean that education is undervalued but rather that a family desperately needs more earners. A lack of interest in education may reflect *material* rather than *cultural* deprivation.

These criticisms indicate that one must be careful in relating educational achievement to culture, but they should not lead us to rule out cultural explanations, for people's values and beliefs do shape their behaviour. Culture must, however, be placed in its social context, for culture and social situation are closely interrelated. This can be seen in Basil Bernstein's theory of the relationship between speech patterns and educational success.

Bernstein developed an approach to class differences centred on differences in the use of language. In his early work (1961), he distinguished between two speech patterns:

- **Restricted codes.** This refers to speech patterns where meanings are implicit. They are typical of situations where people have so much in common that they do not have to spell out what they mean. Few words are needed. Sentences tend to be short and have a simple grammatical structure. Much may be communicated by gesture or tone of voice rather than the words themselves. While this form of language works well in situations where people know each other, its capacity to communicate is limited because it is *context bound* to a particular situation.

Figure 9.1 Language and class

Language and context	Restricted code	Elaborated code
Speech forms	Small vocabulary and short, simple sentences	Large vocabulary and longer, more complex sentences
Meaning	Implicit	Explicit
Communication context	Particularistic and context bound	Universalistic and independent
Family structure	Positional	Person-centred
Class	Working	Middle

❷ Imagine that a parent is telling a child to switch off the television and go to bed. How would this be expressed in speech using restricted and elaborated codes?

- **Elaborated codes**. This refers to speech patterns where meanings are made explicit. People spell out fully what they mean in longer and more complex sentences. While restricted codes are *particularistic*, elaborated codes are *universalistic*. They are *context independent* and enable people who do not share a particular social situation, or who do not know each other, to communicate.

Educational success requires an ability to use elaborated codes. These are the language of instruction. Restricted codes are no use for essay-writing! Bernstein argued that while middle-class children can typically communicate in both restricted and elaborated codes, working-class children are generally accustomed to restricted codes only and are therefore likely to be less successful in education. He did, however, recognize that schools can teach elaborated codes to those who have not acquired them beforehand.

These cultural differences were linked by Bernstein to differences in class situation. Middle-class people speak in elaborated codes because their non-manual occupations require more complex verbal skills. There are also differences in family structure. Working-class families tend to be *positional* in character—that is, their members treat each other according to their position in the family. Relationships are unambiguous and can be expressed through restricted codes. Middle-class families tend to be *person-centred*. They are more individualized and relationships are worked out through discussion which involves the use of elaborated codes (Bernstein 1977).

This is an influential theory which links educational success to class culture and class situation through language rather than values and beliefs. It has been criticized for the rather crude distinctions that it makes between the middle and working classes, and for having insufficient evidence to back up its statements (Rosen 1974). Bernstein (1997) has rejected such criticisms, however, and claims that the

THEORY AND METHODS

Pierre Bourdieu

Pierre Bourdieu (1930–2002) was born in south-eastern France. He trained initially as a philosopher in Paris in the early 1950s. His two years as a conscript in the French army in Algeria had a major impact upon him. He was shocked by the gap between the views of Parisian intellectuals and his experiences from the Algerian war. At this time he began to move towards sociology via anthropology. In the 1960s he established himself as a leading sociologist in Paris, where he became a Professor of Sociology at the College of France in 1981. His best-known work on education is *Reproduction in Education, Society, and Culture*, published in 1977. Other influential works are *Distinction* (1984) and *Homo Academicus* (1988). Richard Jenkins (1992) provides a helpful account and discussion of his life and work.

theory is supported by a large body of research carried out under his leadership.

Cultural capital

The French sociologist Pierre Bourdieu argued that success depends not just on having appropriate language abilities but on having a broader cultural capital. **Cultural capital** consists of various cultural advantages that can be turned into economic gains. Bourdieu (1997) identifies three forms that it can take:

- *The embodied state*. This consists of what Bourdieu calls 'long-lasting dispositions of the mind and body'. Put crudely, this is the culture that we carry around 'in our heads'.

- *The objectified state*. This is the culture that is found in 'things', the culture that exists in possessions, such as books, or paintings, or clothing.
- *The institutionalized state*. This is typically culture as represented in qualifications.

The term 'cultural capital' is a means of highlighting the importance of culture in occupational success, for this does not just depend on material resources. Money alone cannot enable a person to become, say, a successful and high-earning architect or barrister, because examinations have to be passed and professional qualifications acquired.

Bourdieu argued that success in examinations depended on possessing the right culture. Educational standards might appear to be objectively established and unrelated to the class structure but in reality they reflected this structure. Standards of excellence in schools were established by the dominant culture of those who ruled the society. Those whose family backgrounds enabled them to acquire the dominant culture before they came to school had a hidden advantage, for they already possessed a cultural capital that enabled them to do well in examinations. In this way education simply maintained the existing class structure by assisting those from the top and excluding those from the bottom. Education led to the **reproduction of class**.

Education also maintained the class structure in another way. It legitimated inequality by making the success of upper-class children and the failure of lower-class children appear to be the result of objective procedures. Those who succeeded did so because examination procedures were stacked in their favour but it appeared as though they had superior ability. Similarly, those of lower-class origin who failed had stood little chance of succeeding, but failure appeared to be the result of their own inadequacies. Furthermore, some did succeed, which made the system appear fair and reinforced the idea that those who failed did so because of their own failings.

Acquiring cultural capital was not just a matter of passing exams and gaining qualifications. Bourdieu argued that correct manners, the right 'taste' in, say, dress, and an appreciation of 'high culture' were all part of cultural capital. They could be crucial in determining whether someone got a high-status job or gained admission to elite circles.

A number of criticisms have been made of Bourdieu's analysis of education (Jenkins 1992: 15–19). It has been criticized for taking insufficient account of the opportunities provided by education for those of lower-class origin. It assumes that it is the legitimation of inequality by education that maintains the social order. This may not actually be the case at all and those at the bottom of society may accept inequality not because they see it as justified but because there is little that they can do about it. Bourdieu also presents a rather circular picture of class structures endlessly reproducing themselves through static cultural mechanisms. This makes social and cultural change appear almost impossible but both do happen.

Bourdieu has, none the less, provided important insights into the interrelationships between class, culture, and education. His concept of cultural capital has been widely used. There has been broad acceptance of the idea that apparently objective exam procedures actually embody the values of a dominant culture and load the dice in favour of the bearers of that culture. A similar point has been made

Acquiring 'cultural capital'? What do sociologists mean by this term?
© Alice Chadwick

Frontiers Subcultural capital?

Sarah Thornton has taken up the concept of cultural capital and applied it to social success in the world of clubbing.

'Subcultural capital confers status on its owner in the eyes of the relevant beholder. It affects the standing of the young in many ways like its adult equivalent. Subcultural capital can be *objectified* or *embodied*. Just as books and paintings display cultural capital in the family home, so subcultural capital is objectified in the form of fashionable haircuts and carefully assembled record collections (full of well-chosen, limited edition "white label" twelve-inches and the like). Just as cultural capital is personified in "good manners" and urbane conversation, so subcultural capital is embodied in the form of being "in the know", using (but not over-using) current slang and looking as if you were born to perform the latest dance styles. Both cultural and subcultural capital put a premium on the "second nature" of their knowledges. Nothing depletes capital more than the sight of someone trying too hard. For example, fledgling clubbers of 15 and 16 years old wishing to get into what they perceive as a sophisticated dance club will often reveal their inexperience by over-dressing or confusing "coolness" with an exaggerated cold blank stare.'

Source: Thornton (1997: 202–3).

❷ How do you think that subcultural capital is acquired?

❷ What kind of advantages do you think that subcultural capital confers on those who have it?

❷ Can it be converted into economic capital?

by those who argue that apparently objective tests for grammar-school entry in Britain actually favour children from superior class backgrounds.

Social capital

It is not only cultural capital that matters but also social capital. **Social capital** is a broader notion that goes beyond the cultural advantages that aid educational and career success to those conferred by the membership of networks and the knowledge of how to use them. Although there are a number of different versions of this notion, Bourdieu's approach is again seminal and has been developed by Stephen Ball (2003*a*, 2003*b*) in his recent study of middle-class families' strategies and practices in education.

Ball takes from Bourdieu two key dimensions of social capital. The first of these is social networks, 'that is, group membership, contacts and shared identities, accumulated exchanges and obligations, and actual or potential support and access to other valued resources'. The second is what Bourdieu called 'the unceasing effort of sociability' (Ball 2003*a*: 82). The network provides resources but it is the interpersonal skills of sociability that actually enable the building of networks, access to them, and use of them. The knowledge and manners provided by cultural capital (see above) are here crucial to network membership and sociability.

Ball's argument is that middle-class families have far more social capital than working-class families. This is demonstrated through the competition for places in higher education and the planning of careers. The families of students from working-class backgrounds have little knowledge of higher education and the best routes into it. The families of middle-class students have that knowledge and contacts that can help with choice of course and university, and make the right connections between higher education and professional careers.

Social capital could be especially important at times of crisis, if, for example, an exam has been failed or a student is on the edge of dropping out, and an appropriate intervention can help to restore the situation. This shows that social capital is not just something possessed but involves work, requiring the expenditure of time and effort, the investment of 'emotional capital' (Ball 2003*a*: 95).

Private education played an important role in the accumulation of social capital. As Ball puts it:

> In effect when parents invest in private education for their children they are buying into a broad and complex body of social capital that is made available to the children and in relation to which the young people develop their own investment skills. (Ball 2003*a*: 86)

This brings out the links between economic capital and social capital, for it is the financial situation of the family that determines whether it can buy this social capital through private education.

The use of social capital within state education is closely linked to the development of educational policy. As we shall show in the section on 'A regulated market-place' (see pp. 348–51), the post-1980s emphasis on providing choice of school and the growth of parental involvement in the management of schools has played into the hands of those with social capital.

Education and capitalism

As we argued earlier, the functionalist approach to education assumed that education met the needs of society. Marxist writers on education have argued that we should not refer to the needs of society as a whole, for within societies there is a fundamental conflict of interest between capital and labour, which have different needs. Education does not meet the needs of society but serves the interests of the owners of capital.

The supply of labour

Samuel Bowles and Herbert Gintis (1976) carried out the classic study of the relationship between capitalism and education through an examination of education in the United States.

To Bowles and Gintis, education was the main means by which capital subordinated labour. Capitalism required obedient and disciplined workers prepared to carry out boringly repetitive work in a highly unequal society. Labour could not be subordinated by the use of force alone, either within the factory or in the society at large, because force on its own was self-defeating and generated resistance. Effective subordination depended on getting workers to accept the capitalist system and it was education that produced this acceptance. Thus, education not only led to the reproduction of class, it was also crucial to the **reproduction of labour**.

In explaining how education does this, Bowles and Gintis referred not to the *content* of education but to the *structure of social relationships* within it. Their key concept is the **correspondence principle** (Bowles and Gintis 1976: 131). Thus, relationships of authority at school corresponded with those at work. Competition between students in school corresponded to the competition between workers which employers seek to encourage. Students were *externally* motivated by the award of grades not the satisfactions of learning, just as workers were motivated by pay not the satisfactions of work. Children were prepared for work because schools taught them how to behave like workers.

In focusing on these aspects of education, Bowles and Gintis drew attention to what Ivan Illich (1973) had called the **hidden curriculum** (see box on Illich). While the formal curriculum provided children with skills, knowledge, and qualifications, the hidden curriculum more importantly taught them how to work and obey.

The correspondence principle also operated in another way by relating levels in education to occupational levels. The lower levels of education emphasized obedience to rules, as required in low-level occupations. Intermediate levels required students to work independently without continuous supervision, as did middle-ranking positions in

Illich and the 'hidden curriculum'

Ivan Illich (1926–) was born in Vienna, studied theology and philosophy in Rome, obtained a Ph.D. in history at the University of Salzburg, and became for a time a Catholic priest. His career led him to Latin America, where he became a severe critic of economic development. He saw this as destroying the skills, knowledge, and self-sufficiency of pre-industrial societies and forcing people into a passive dependence on experts and organizations.

One of his most well-known books is *Deschooling Society* (1973), where he called for the abolition of schools. He argued that education has been confused with schooling and that most learning occurred outside schools, which do nothing for the poor and turn people into passive consumers.

Illich originated the widely used concept of the hidden curriculum. This strikingly expressed the idea that schools do not just teach the subjects of the formal curriculum, they also teach values, attitudes, and patterns of behaviour through the organization and social relationships of the school. This hidden curriculum maintains the existing social order and has a far greater influence on social life than the formal curriculum of subjects taught. While this is an important insight, the concept has been used in widely varying ways to refer to almost any aspect of education outside the formal curriculum. It is also in some ways a misleading term, because it does not refer to an identifiable curriculum as such but to the whole context of education in the school.

organizations. In higher education students were expected to internalize the institution's norms, so that they were self-motivated and self-disciplined, just as those in senior posts in organizations were expected to be. If students were unable to make it to the next stage of education, they moved into the occupational level corresponding to the stage they had reached. Thus, while reproducing labour, education also reproduced the occupational divisions of the class structure.

While this approach started from a different theoretical perspective, it overlapped in many ways with the functionalist approach. The points made by Bowles and Gintis about the importance of school discipline and competitiveness to life in the wider society were quite similar to those made by Durkheim and Parsons. Although Bowles and Gintis saw education as serving the interests of capital rather than the needs of society, they too were examining the importance of education to the socialization process, the economy, and the maintenance of social order.

But does education actually function in this way to produce subservient students? Does it actually provide employers with the workers they need?

An oppositional culture

Bowles and Gintis treat the working class as culturally passive, absorbing and accepting the values of the school and the employer. In doing this, they argued in a similar way to those who have claimed that there is a *dominant culture* imposed by the ruling class on the rest of the population. Another stream of research has, however, examined the way that *resistant subcultures* grow out of the experience of the working class.

> ⮞ *Connections*
>
> We discuss the concepts of dominant culture and subculture in Chapter 10, pp. 366–7, and you may find it helpful to refer to this discussion.

In *Learning to Labour* Paul Willis (1977) carried out a well-known study of the emergence of an **oppositional subculture** in a secondary-modern school. He argued that this subculture was hostile to authority, rejected the value of mental work, and celebrated physicality and violence. The authority of teachers was constantly challenged but in subtle ways that undermined it while stopping short of open confrontation. Willis argued that this oppositional culture was generated by the school itself, though its content was provided by the wider culture of the working class.

His study was based mainly on the observation of twelve working-class 'lads', who were selected because they were members of a minority opposition group. They were not therefore representative of the boys in the school or of working-class boys in general. Indeed, Phillip Brown (1989) has argued that most working-class children adopt a strategy of limited compliance rather than opposition. They recognize the importance of qualifications for jobs and go along sufficiently with the school to 'achieve modest levels of attainment' that will improve their job prospects.

Willis's focus on working-class boys now seems a little dated. Oppositional cultures are not just found among boys, and class is not the only basis of opposition. Carolyn Jackson (2006) explores the emergence of 'ladette' behaviour among schoolgirls and its consequences for achievement and order in the class-room (see Media watch 5 on p. 191 for a discussion of ladettes). She found that 'girls, just as much as boys, suggested that it is not seen to be cool for them to work hard in school' (2006: 79). Arguably, with the decline of class organization and with greater ethnic diversity, oppositional class subcultures have anyway declined and those based on ethnicity have become more salient (O'Donnell and Sharpe 2004).

Whatever the extent and the basis of an oppositional subculture, the main point here is, however, that it cannot be assumed that educational institutions socialize children into the work habits and obedience that capitalist production requires. Education does not automatically reproduce labour.

The workers the employer needs?

If education does not always produce subservient workers, perhaps in other respects it does not always produce the labour that the capitalist economy needs. It has been argued that one of the reasons for Britain's poor economic performance during the twentieth century was the failure of educational institutions to produce the skills required by modern industry. This was to become a key issue in the 1970s, when the declining competitiveness of the British economy and rising levels of unemployment led to much discussion of the reasons for British economic decline. Politicians, employers, and trade unionists called for the reform of education to make it more relevant to economic needs.

This was partly to do with changing economic requirements. The decline of traditional industries and occupational changes meant that there was less need for unskilled manual labour. As we show in Chapter 17, pp. 694–6, the changes associated with post-Fordism led to employers seeking adaptable, committed, and cooperative workers rather than simply obedient ones. They wanted workers who could cope with the demands of technical change, turn their hands to whatever job needed doing, and produce the high-quality goods and services demanded by customers. The kinds of workers that Bowles and Gintis saw the education system producing no longer corresponded to the needs of the employer.

The approach taken by Bowles and Gintis rightly draws our attention to the importance of the relationship between education and the capitalist economy. As we show in the section on 'Education and economy', pp. 345–8, an understanding of this relationship is crucial to an understanding of recent changes in British education. It is also clear, however, that there is nothing automatic about the relationship, that education may not meet the needs of the employer.

 *Stop and reflect*

In this section we first considered the part played by education in the process of socialization.

- Durkheim saw education as turning children into moral members of their society.

- Parsons paid more attention to the way in which it instilled values of individual achievement.

- Do faith schools exemplify their notions of the functions performed by education?

We then considered the relationship between education and inequality.

- Parsons considered that education was the main mechanism providing equality of opportunity.

- Others have argued that education reproduces the material and cultural advantages and disadvantages of social background.

- How do the concepts of 'cultural capital' and 'social capital' help us to understand the relationship between education and inequality?

Lastly, we examined the relationship between education and capitalism.

- In their different ways both functionalist and Marxist perspectives argue that education meets economic requirements.

- Does education provide the workers that employers need?

The development of education in Britain

As we showed in the 'Understanding education' section, key issues in the sociology of education have been whether educational institutions provide equality of opportunity and meet the needs of the economy. Before examining these questions further, we need to set them in context by outlining the development of educational institutions in Britain. Bear in mind that there are important institutional differences between England (and Wales), on the one hand, and Scotland, on the other.

The nineteenth-century growth of education

At the beginning of the nineteenth century there was no national system of education. In England elementary education for the poor was provided by charity and church schools, and various local private schools that charged parents for widely varying standards of usually very basic education. Secondary education was not widely available and was provided mainly by the so-called public schools, which catered not for the public in general but for fee-paying pupils, and a scattering of grammar schools in the towns. The only universities were Cambridge and Oxford, which were very exclusive institutions admitting only about 300 fee-paying students a year in the mid-eighteenth century (Royle 1987: 368). They were primarily concerned with educating the sons of the upper class to become Church of England clergy.

In eighteenth-century Scotland education was rather more developed at both ends of the spectrum. There was a system of publicly funded parochial schools provided by the Church, though this failed to keep up with the growth of urban populations. The local schoolmaster was expected to be a graduate who was able to teach up to university-entrance level. Five universities existed and during the later eighteenth century they established a high academic reputation through such leading thinkers of the Scottish Enlightenment as David Hume and Adam Smith. Student numbers were higher and university education was far more accessible than it was in England and Wales. About a quarter of the students at Glasgow University at the end of the eighteenth century were of working-class origin (Royle 1987: 373).

Education of all kinds expanded in the nineteenth century. Elementary schooling for the poor grew initially through church provision, but after the 1870 Education Act in England and the 1872 Act in Scotland through state education administered through school boards. In England the new schools plugged the gaps in existing educational provision and 'large Board Schools were erected like mission stations in working-class urban areas'. In Scotland existing local schools were taken over and incorporated in a 'nation-wide network of nearly a thousand School Boards' (Royle 1987: 354). The public schools too grew, with the creation between 1837 and 1869 of thirty-one new boarding schools in England, which provided an elite classical education for effectively the whole of Britain

Briefing: maintaining order through education

'The great object to be kept in view in regulating any school for the instruction of the children of the labouring class, is the rearing of hardy and intelligent men, whose character and habits shall afford the largest amount of security to the property and order of the community.'

Source: Sir James Kay Shuttleworth, 1838, quoted by Digby and Searby (1981: 118).

(Royle 1987: 360–1). The founding of the University of London in 1828 was a key step in the growth of higher education, and towards the end of the century colleges were set up in the provinces and the industrial cities, many of them shortly becoming universities.

The expansion of elementary education had more to do with religious, moral, and political than economic concerns. At this stage of economic development, practical workshop skills rather than technical knowledge or even literacy were required. Religious organizations competed, however, to set up schools in the cities. Schools for the poor were seen as a means of establishing order and countering radicalism in the new industrial cities. There was also a popular demand for education, and radicals called for it to be taken out of religious hands and made available to all on a free and equal basis. Education became a battleground between conservatives and radicals, though both agreed that more education was needed.

The expansion of 'public school' education for the middle and upper classes was linked to state and empire rather than commerce and industry. The bureaucratization of the nineteenth-century state (see Chapter 14, p. 545) meant that there was a growing emphasis on qualifications. The route to office in the growing apparatus of the imperial state was through success in school, university, and civil-service examinations. As Royle has put it:

> Ambitious middle-class parents knew they would have to make the necessary sacrifices to buy a public-school education for their sons if they were to make their marks in the world. Purchase of office had been the eighteenth-century method; purchase of education replaced it in the nineteenth. (Royle 1987: 390)

The public schools, together with Cambridge and Oxford universities, produced a cohesive ruling class with bureaucratic skills, the shared culture of a classical education, and a gentlemanly set of norms and values centred on public service and sportsmanship.

Nineteenth-century education clearly reproduced the class structure. In England elementary education was considered the most that the working class required and too much education was seen as threatening the social order. The public schools provided education for the upper class and those members of the middle class who could afford them. Grammar schools were the main providers of education for the middle class. Some became increasingly exclusive, keeping the children of the local poor out because fee-paying parents did not want their children rubbing shoulders with those from a lower class. In Scottish education there was more of an ideal of classlessness, though in practice the town schools were dominated by the middle class and the poor were 'left to attend charity mission schools created especially for them in working-class districts' (Royle 1987: 358).

State schools for all

A national system of schooling was slowly constructed between 1870 and 1944. Free and compulsory elementary education was gradually built up during the twenty years or so after the 1870 Education Act. Education Acts at the beginning of the twentieth century began to create a national system of secondary education, though it was not until the 1944 Act in England (in Scotland the 1945 Act) that free secondary education was made available to all.

The 1944 Act has been seen as a major social advance that transformed education. It created a *tripartite* structure of three different types of school for children of different abilities. There were grammar schools for the academic, technical schools for those with technical abilities, and secondary-modern schools for the rest. In Scotland there were academic 'senior' schools and non-academic 'junior secondaries'. This was a selective system that distributed children into a type of school on the basis of their performance in examinations at age 11. It was described as meritocratic, because it supposedly allocated children to schools entirely on the basis of their ability or merit (for a discussion of meritocracy, see Chapter 18, pp. 723–4). It certainly exemplified the *correspondence principle* of Bowles and Gintis, for types of school corresponded clearly to types of occupation.

If private education is included, there were, however, not three but five different levels in secondary education:

- public schools;
- direct-grant grammar schools (charging fees);
- grammar schools;
- technical schools;
- secondary-modern schools.

In many ways the post-1944 system perpetuated the existing structure of British education. The top two categories continued to provide a superior education for the

Briefing: development of a national school system in England

Elementary education

1833   The state began to provide some funding for religious schools.

1844   Factory Act required children in employment aged 8–13 to spend half the week in school.

1870   Education Act to provide cheap, publicly funded local schools.

1880   Attendance made compulsory up to the age of 10.

1891   Right to free elementary education established.

1893   School-leaving age raised to 11.

1899   Leaving age raised to 12.

Secondary education

1902   Education Act to create national secondary education: state grants for grammar schools in exchange for some 'free places' for children from elementary schools; new state-funded secondary schools created on grammar-school model.

1918   School-leaving age raised to 14.

1944   Education Act introduced tripartite system of grammar, technical, and secondary-modern schools. Free secondary education for all.

1947   School-leaving age raised to 15 (1972 to 16).

small minority of families who could afford to pay for it. For most of the population, education meant either a grammar school or a secondary modern, the fourth category of technical schools never becoming widely available. The grammar schools became the elite institutions of the state sector, while the secondary moderns were essentially a continuation of elementary education for the working class. As Simon (1991: 74) has put it: 'after all the discussion and legislation, the country emerged with an hierarchical educational structure almost precisely as planned and developed in the mid-late nineteenth century . . .'.

The 1944 structure soon attracted criticism. It was criticized for maintaining class inequality and wasting talent. Most working-class children ended up in secondary moderns and the *Early Leaving Report* of 1954 showed that over half of those who did get into grammar schools dropped out or failed to get three GCE O level passes (GCE O level

was the examination that preceded GCSE). It was rejected by the Labour Party but there was also some middle-class dissatisfaction, for middle-class children who failed the 11+ examination also ended up in secondary moderns. From a national point of view, it was argued that an elitist system wasted talent and created social divisions. Comparisons were made with other economically more successful countries, like the United States, that did not have selective state education.

Comprehensive schools were put forward as the answer to these problems. The principle of comprehensive education was that all the children within a particular area would go to the same secondary school, irrespective of ability or background. Education was gradually reorganized along comprehensive lines through local-authority action and the 1964 Labour government's education policy. Although comprehensive schools came to dominate British education, the fact that selective schools (and private education) still existed and 'creamed off' many of the more able students meant that a genuinely national system had still not, however, been established. Furthermore, the selective principle still operated *within* most comprehensive schools through the streaming of children into different ability groups.

Higher education for some

The founding of the University of London in 1828 broke the Oxbridge monopoly of English higher education and established a major new institution that soon became the biggest in the country. It also helped to spread higher education, for the colleges emerging in the industrial cities taught external London degrees until they had acquired the expertise and status to award their own and become 'red-brick' universities. By the 1930s there were twenty-one universities in Britain but higher education was still relatively undeveloped, especially in England, as comparison with other industrial countries shows (see Figure 9.2).

It has, indeed, been argued, notably by Wiener (1980), that the character of British education largely accounts for Britain's failure to keep pace with other industrial countries and eventual economic decline in the 1960s and 1970s. This was because an anti-industrial culture had developed in elite educational institutions during the nineteenth century.

British industrialists concerned with increasing international competition had played an important part in establishing the new colleges in industrial cities during the 1870s and 1880s. Civic leaders insisted, however, that these colleges taught the liberal arts as well as applied studies, and they eventually became universities teaching a broad range of subjects. Any aspirational educational institution modelled itself on the public schools or on Cambridge and Oxford universities, where the arts were dominant. Where

Figure 9.2 Higher education in industrial countries, 1934

Country	Number of inhabitants per university student
Great Britain	885
England	1,013
Scotland	473
Wales	741
Italy	808
Germany	604
Holland	579
Sweden	543
France	480
Switzerland	387
United States	125

Source: Simon (1991: 30).

science was taught, it was pure rather than applied science. Comparisons with Germany showed that technology was much more highly valued there and the provision of education in technology and applied science much greater.

Mass higher education began with the expansion of higher education between the 1950s and the 1970s. This was driven by the increasing numbers of 18 year-olds with the necessary qualifications for entry and a government commitment to provide high education for all those who could benefit from it. During the years 1957–72 the number of full-time students in higher and further education rose from 148,000 to 470,000 (Simon 1991: 597). In the 1970s the expansion of higher education slowed down and barely kept pace with the growing number of 18 year-olds until the current burst of expansion began in the late 1980s.

The 1960s growth of higher education had taken a binary form. The 1964 Labour government decided to halt the creation of new universities and build up a distinct public sector from existing colleges and new polytechnics. The rationale for this binary system was that a separate public sector would boost the development of new, vocationally relevant institutions of higher education that would not be dominated by the elite universities. It inevitably created, however, a two-class system of higher education with the polytechnics being seen by many as second-class rather than different institutions. The polytechnics themselves tried to become more like universities by awarding degrees and developing university-type courses. They were eventually allowed to take the title of university with the abolition of the binary system in 1991.

Comparative issues

We have been examining the development of British education up to the 1970s. We will now briefly consider the distinctiveness of the British system by comparing it with other societies.

The 1944 Education Act had established a national system of education that was less centralized than the French system but much more centralized than the American. There was no centrally controlled national curriculum as in France. There was, none the less, more of a national system in Britain than in the United States, where funding was decentralized and local communities had more control. In Britain state education was centrally funded and school organization was at least shaped by national education policies. The British system was, however, a mixed one that allowed the competing principles of the 'tripartite' structure and comprehensive schooling to coexist according to local decisions. In most European countries there was a uniform national structure.

Under the tripartite system established by the 1944 Act in Britain, selection and specialization took place at age 11. Internationally speaking this brought about a very early separation of the academic and non-academic routes. Even after comprehensive education was introduced, the continued existence of many grammar schools and a large private secondary sector, both with their main entry at age 11, have perpetuated early selection and specialization. In many other countries there has long been a fully comprehensive system of education up to the age of 15 or 16, with a separation into academic and vocational routes only after this age.

We showed above that the expansion of higher education was slow in Britain. Into the 1980s a far lower proportion of 18 year-olds entered higher education than in comparable countries (Halsey 1997: 642). Those who did had their fees paid by the state and, at that time, a generous system of maintenance grants. Graduates were a small and highly subsidized elite. British higher education was also elitist in another way, for the more vocational polytechnics were widely considered to be lower in status than universities. Although the polytechnic institutions of France, Germany, and Sweden were not strictly comparable, they were high-status institutions, often having higher status than universities.

It is, however, difficult to compare national educational systems, because there are so many sources of variation within them. This is particularly the case in Britain. It is, indeed, difficult to speak of a British system. There are, first, important historical differences between the institutions of England and Scotland, as we noted earlier (see p. 329). In England itself, many different traditions of education coexist. Furthermore, what applies to school

Global focus   Education in Japan

Education in Japan developed rapidly towards the end of the nineteenth century. Indeed, by 1910 Japan, although much less developed economically, had overtaken Britain in participation rates. Enrolment ratios are the proportion of the relevant age group participating in formal education.

This rapid development of education was driven partly by economic needs as Japan embarked on industrialization and sought to replace imported foreign experts with home-grown ones. The political functions of education were also of immense importance, since education was a means of indoctrinating the population with nationalism, loyalty to the emperor, and obedience to the government. The content of the curriculum, textbooks, and the recruitment of teachers were closely controlled by the state.

The Japanese system of education undoubtedly contributed to Japan's post-war economic miracle. It produced highly educated engineers and an obedient labour force. Japanese education apparently provided exactly the employees that Japanese companies needed. It was also highly meritocratic, because of the competitiveness of Japanese education, its unstreamed and comprehensive character, and the links between educational achievement and career success. Indeed, Dore (1987) considered Japan to be the most meritocratic society in the world.

This seemed to many to be a model system but more recently there has been much criticism of it. Such a highly competitive system has resulted in an 'examination hell' and lots of after-hours work in private crammers that have subjected Japanese children to terrible pressure. This, combined with the over-controlled and oppressive atmosphere of schools, has produced many pathologies—bullying, suicides, violence, and refusal to go to school. There has, indeed, been a growing awareness that Japan's conformist schools have not been producing the creative and innovatory people increasingly needed in a post-Fordist world. Attempts have been made to reform the system but it remains highly controlled and highly competitive.

Sources: Dore (1976, 1987); Yoneyama (1999).

Figure 9.3 Occupational structure and educational participation in Britain and Japan, 1870 and 1910 (%)

| | Percentage of labour force in non-agricultural occupations | | Enrolment ratios (%) | | | | | |
| | | | Primary | | Secondary | | Tertiary | |
	Japan	Britain	Japan	Britain	Japan	Britain	Japan	Britain
1870	17	85	28	40	1	2	–	–
1910	41	92	98	100	12	4	2	2

Source: Dore (1976: 40).

education may not apply to higher education. Thus, private schooling is highly developed in Britain but higher education is dominated by public-sector institutions, while the opposite is the case in Japan.

Although institutional differences are undoubtedly important and certainly shape the way that education is delivered, they may, anyway, tell one little about how it is actually experienced. As the box on 'Education in Japan' shows, an apparently model system of education looks very different when the daily realities of school life are brought to light. What is clear, however, is that British education has developed in a quite distinctive way and has emerged from a very particular history.

Stop and reflect

In this section we have outlined the development of educational institutions in Britain.

- The nineteenth-century growth of elementary education was driven by religious, moral, and political, rather than economic, concerns.
- A national system of primary and secondary schooling was constructed between 1870 and 1944.

- Make sure that you know the main features of the 1944 Education Act.
- Why were comprehensive schools introduced and to what extent did they replace the tripartite structure set up in 1944?
- Can one meaningfully speak of a British system of education?

Inequality in British education

In 'Education and inequality' we discussed different approaches towards the relationship between education and class inequality. In 'The development of education in Britain' we showed that attempts have been made to reform education in order to increase equality of opportunity. Whether these reforms did so or not has been the subject of considerable sociological research, which we now draw on in order to examine their impact on patterns of inequality. We start by considering class inequalities and then move on to those of gender and ethnicity.

Class

Nineteenth-century education clearly reproduced the class structure but twentieth-century reforms, first the 1944 Education Act and then the introduction of comprehensive schools, were intended to provide equality of opportunity, irrespective of class background.

The tripartite system

The 1944 Act made free secondary education available to all, with access to grammar schools determined by performance at the 11+ examination alone. Did this create equality of opportunity?

In a classic study, Halsey *et al.* (1980) examined the impact of organizational changes in education on patterns of class inequality. They studied the educational careers of 8,529 men by examining four age 'cohorts' (an age cohort consists of all those born between two dates). Since two of their cohorts were educated before the 1944 Education Act came into operation and two afterwards, the researchers could make a 'before and after' comparison.

Under the tripartite system, entry to selective schools was crucial in determining educational success. Only those going into these schools could obtain academic qualifications and go on to university. Halsey *et al.* found that class continued to determine boys' chances of getting into these schools. Making grammar-school education free and selecting children for it on the basis of the 11+ examination made no appreciable difference to class differentials. About one-fifth of the working-class children in their earliest (1913–22) cohort and their last (1943–52) cohort entered selective schools (Halsey *et al.* 1980: 63).

The 11+ examination was basically an intelligence test, which assumed that there was some general underlying ability called intelligence, which could be measured objectively. Any such ability is not, however, independent of class (or ethnicity). Tests of this sort have been shown to embody cultural and linguistic assumptions that are themselves linked to class and ethnic background (see Chapter 18, pp. 731–2). Performance at intelligence tests can, anyway, be improved through training, which families with superior resources can buy. As we showed earlier, Bourdieu argued that examinations are not objective because they are framed by the dominant culture. The greater success of those from higher classes in intelligence tests and examinations reflected both their material and cultural advantages.

Class differences then carried through to university entrance. The increasing availability of university places meant that the proportion of working-class children getting into university certainly increased but so did the proportion of those from higher classes. Indeed, while the proportion of working-class children at university tripled, the proportion of children from the higher classes nearly quadrupled (see Figure 9.4). Those in classes I and II clearly benefited far more than the other classes. Their entry to university increased by 19 per cent, as compared with a

Education in Japan—meritocratic but conformist.
© Getty Images/Paul Chesley

Figure 9.4 Attendance at university by birth cohort, 1913–52 (%)

Father's social class	Birth cohort	
	1913–32	1943–52
I and II (service)	7.2	26.4
III, IV, and V (intermediate)	1.9	8.0
VI, VII, and VIII (working class)	0.9	3.1

Note: This study used the Goldthorpe class categories (see Chapter 19, p. 783).

Source: Adapted from Halsey *et al*. (1980: 188).

6 per cent increase for the intermediate classes, and a mere 2 per cent for those at the bottom.

Comprehensive schools

Did comprehensive schools make any difference? It is difficult to explore this still-debated question because a fully comprehensive system was not created. As selective schools still existed and could 'cream off' the more academically successful children, comparisons between the tripartite system and comprehensive schools could not easily be made.

Anthony Heath (1989) argued that comprehensive reorganization made no real difference, but his conclusion was challenged by McPherson and Willms (1989), who examined later data from Scotland, where comprehensive reorganization had been more extensive. Their evidence showed that since comprehensive reorganization the gap between the examination performance of working-class and middle-class children had narrowed slightly, as working-class children started to catch up. Differences remained great, however, and it is clear that the performance of children in comprehensive schools was still substantially related to their class background.

Stephen Ball's (1981) case study of 'Beachside' comprehensive school showed some of the reasons why. Like many comprehensives, Beachside was internally streamed into three ability bands. He found that banding reproduced the traditional academic/non-academic split in British education. Band one, the academic band, consisted mainly of middle-class children, bands two and three of working-class children. On entry children were allocated to bands on the basis of primary-school reports. There was some movement between bands in the first term but little after this point, certainly little movement into band one. Band differences in curriculum, syllabus, teaching methods, and relationships with teachers created two different kinds of education within the school.

The significance of primary-school reports for banding showed that selection originated largely at the previous stage of education. Success in primary education was, therefore, critical to future success in education. Douglas *et al*. (1968) had demonstrated that the social-class composition of the primary school had a persistent influence on secondary-school performance. Children from predominantly working-class primary schools did less well in whichever type of school they went on to at age 11.

Beachside comprehensive did make a limited shift to mixed-ability classes, largely it seems because of persisting discipline problems in band-two classes, where an oppositional culture had established itself (see our discussion of oppositional culture on p. 328). The mixing of children with different abilities was, however, limited. 'Sets' for children of different abilities emerged in some subjects, notably maths and languages, while mixed-ability classes came to an end after the third year.

Ball argued that mixed-ability classes did not, anyway, change teacher attitudes. Teachers still classified children in terms of their ability and treated them accordingly. He made the important point that the classroom mixing of children of different abilities did not mean that there was mixed-ability *teaching*. His research showed that the shift to mixed-ability classes enabled the more effective socialization of children into the school and better control of their behaviour. The social divisions found within banding were, none the less, broadly reproduced in mixed-ability classes.

Class background or school?

It would be easy to conclude from all this that class background is decisive in shaping educational success and that schools do not matter. Do the material, cultural, and linguistic advantages of children from higher social classes mean that they will inevitably be more successful in education? Was Bernstein (1970) right in declaring that 'education cannot compensate for society'?

Halsey *et al*. (1980) certainly believed that the school mattered. Whether children went to public schools or grammar schools made little difference to their examination performance but whether they went to selective schools (public and grammar) or secondary moderns was critical. Boys with similar social backgrounds and similar abilities fared very differently according to this decision. Class had a major influence on the kind of school a boy ended up in, but its influence then diminished as the school took over. It has, indeed, been argued that grammar schools, with their strong academic culture, provide a better route upwards for those working-class children who do manage to get into them than comprehensive schools do.

Rutter *et al*. (1979) carried out a rather different study of twelve non-selective secondary schools in the London

Does education enable upward mobility or reproduce inequality?

© Alice Chadwick

area. Although the composition of a school's intake influenced both academic success and delinquency rates, neither were wholly explained by this. Differences in the schools as 'social institutions' were systematically related to their results. They listed such factors as teaching practices, school values, and the amount of responsibility given to children. These all to some degree depended on a school's staff and training and were not determined by its social environment. Furthermore, these factors interacted to give a school an *overall character*, which itself influenced results.

Mortimore reviewed the literature on school differences and concluded that they do account for about 10 per cent of variations in examination performance (1997: 479). This may seem a very low proportion but he pointed out that this 10 per cent variation can have a critical effect on the qualifications achieved and future educational and occupational career. A 10 per cent difference in performance at GCSE could amount to the difference between obtaining seven C and seven E grades.

This shows that we should be wary of overdeterministic explanations of educational success that relate it solely to class background and do not take account of the character of the school. Parental interest in school choice certainly suggests that parents are in little doubt about the school's significance.

Phillip Brown (1995) argued that middle-class interest in school choice has increased as middle-class jobs have become more insecure. On the one hand, organizational changes, intensifying international competition, and declining security of employment mean that the middle class can no longer rely on an easy passage for its children into stable bureaucratic and professional careers. On the other hand, mass higher education has produced larger numbers of graduates seeking entry to such careers. Middle-class parents have responded by seeking to use their material and cultural capital to maximize their children's educational advantages.

This has been translated into a pressure for greater choice in education. The more choice there is, the greater the opportunity for middle-class parents to use their advantages to get their children into higher-quality, higher-status institutions. We will return to this issue on pp. 348–9, where we examine the provision of greater choice in education during the 1980s.

Higher education for more

Higher education expanded rapidly after the late 1980s, with the proportion of 18 year-olds entering it doubling from 15 per cent in 1988 to 30 per cent in 1994. How did this impact on class inequality?

This expansion certainly increased greatly the access of those at the bottom of the class structure to higher education. Thus, between the years 1991–2 and 1998–9 the participation in higher education of those with an unskilled manual background more or less doubled, rising from 7 to 13 per cent. Expansion had clearly substantially increased the numbers of those using it as a means of escaping from the bottom of the social heap. No other class category came close to doubling its participation rate and this might suggest that expansion has disproportionately benefited those at the bottom (see Figure 9.5).

On closer examination, however, it becomes clear that class differentials in access have been maintained and it is actually those from the highest social class who have gained most from this expansion. With the limited exception of the partly skilled, the higher up the social hierarchy one goes, the greater the increase in the percentage going into higher education. The most striking feature of Figure 9.5 is in fact the disproportionate increase in the participation of those coming from a professional background.

A recent study of intergenerational social mobility rates in different countries concluded that mobility rates in

Figure 9.5 Social class and participation in higher education during the 1990s (%)

Social class	1991–2	1998–9	Change
Professional	55	72	+17
Intermediate	36	45	+11
Skilled non-manual	22	12	+7
Skilled manual	11	18	+7
Partly skilled	12	17	+5
Unskilled	13	7	+6
All	23	31	+8

Source: Glennerster (2001: table 11).

❓ Who has benefited most from the expansion of higher education?

> ⊃ *Connections*
> As the education of women has reflected persisting nineteenth-century ideas of their place in the world, you may find it helpful to refer to our discussion of this in Chapter 5, pp. 168–70.

Britain were comparable to those in the United States and lower than in Canada and Scandinavia. Social mobility had in fact been falling in Britain and this was at least partly explained by the close and increasing relationship between family income and educational achievement, particularly access to higher education. The expansion of higher education in the 1990s had reduced not increased the social mobility between generations, by enabling much greater access to higher education for the children of the better off (Blanden *et al.* 2005).

As with the greater emphasis on school choice (see the previous section), middle-class families have been using the opportunities provided by the expansion of higher education to make sure that they pass their advantages on to their children.

Gender

The literature on education and class has been mainly concerned with the persistence of inequalities in educational achievement. In examining gender inequalities we find not so much persistence as transformation. Historically, girls were excluded and sidelined but in recent years they have overtaken boys in educational achievement.

The separation of girls

According to the nineteenth-century domestic division of labour, women were destined for housework and child-rearing and, therefore, had little need for formal education beyond elementary level.

By 1880 elementary education was compulsory for all children up to the age of 10. The limited skills taught were differentiated by gender, girls learning domestic skills and boys craft skills and elementary arithmetic. Education was considered less necessary for girls and their truancy was treated more permissively than that of boys, because it was considered acceptable for girls to stay at home helping their mothers and acquiring domestic skills (Abbott and Wallace 1990).

Secondary schools for upper- and middle-class girls were gradually established during the second half of the century. One model for their education was provided by Cheltenham Ladies College, founded in 1854, which saw its function as providing an improved training for women's traditional roles. North London Collegiate, which opened as a day school for girls in 1850, had the very different mission of providing an academic education for girls. It provided a model for the Girls' Public Day School Company, which was funding thirty-eight schools by 1901 (Royle 1987: 363). Secondary schools for girls were well established by the beginning of the twentieth century but far less numerous than those for boys.

Women were excluded from universities for most of the nineteenth century. It was in 1878 at the University of London that they were for the first time allowed to take degrees. Cambridge and Oxford were particularly slow to open their doors to women. Some separate colleges for girls were established around 1880 but women were not allowed to receive full degrees until 1920 in Oxford and 1948 in Cambridge. The numbers of women in higher education remained low for a long time. In 1961 only 13 per cent of students at Cambridge and Oxford were women (Royle 1987: 381).

Integration and discrimination

The 1944 Education Act made free secondary education available to all but secondary education for girls did not mean that they pursued the same curriculum as boys. It was still believed that girls should take different subjects in order to prepare them for a domestic and reproductive role. This was not just a matter of the formal curriculum, for, even when girls and boys were integrated in the same classes in co-educational comprehensive schools, a *hidden curriculum* differentiated between them (see our discussion of this on p. 327).

The role expectations of both staff and students steered girls and boys towards specialization in different subjects as they moved higher up the school and into higher education.

Even when all subjects were available, girls moved towards those that were extensions of the domestic role and boys towards technical and scientific ones. This was clearly not just a function of the school, for it involved gender-role expectations in the wider society and different patterns of employment. The introduction of a national curriculum in the 1980s counteracted this to some extent by establishing the same curriculum for boys and girls up to age 16.

Requiring girls and boys to take the same subjects did not remove gender issues from the curriculum, as the debate over the gendering of science shows (Heaton and Lawson 1996). Feminists argued that science was taught in a 'masculine' way. Three responses to this problem emerged:

- *girl-friendly science*: making science more attractive to girls by introducing topics that interest them;
- *feminine science*: replacing competitive masculine behaviour in the laboratory with a more cooperative feminine approach;
- *feminist science*: challenging masculine ways of thinking by arguing that scientific method should give more weight to feminine intuition.

Is science a masculine activity?
© Hymers College, Hull

This debate exemplifies the conflict between the liberal and radical tendencies in feminism (see Chapter 5, p. 161, for a discussion of this). Liberal feminism seeks equal opportunities for women within the existing system, but radical feminism argues that this results in women thinking and acting like men. According to radical feminism, masculine ways of behaving and thinking should be challenged and replaced by feminine ones. If the 'feminist science' approach is adopted, this can, however, lead to the response that scientific method, as it stands, is essential to science and, if it is treated as masculine in character, this means that girls cannot be as good at science as boys.

Research by Spender (1982) and Stanworth (1983) showed the importance of different gender-role expectations in the classroom. This applied not only to subject choice but also to other aspects of student–teacher interaction. Boys got more attention and interest than girls. Boys tended to receive higher marks than girls for comparable work and were expected to perform better in examinations. This was not just due to teacher expectations but to the expectations of the children and the way that boys and girls behaved. Boys, for example, demanded more attention. This led some to conclude that girls would be better off in schools for girls only or girls' classes in mixed schools.

The educational superiority of girls

In spite of their well-documented disadvantages, girls have increasingly performed better than boys in some public examinations (see Figure 9.6). The growing success of girls in school examinations has been reflected in their access to higher education, where women now considerably outnumber men, even on full-time postgraduate courses—if part-timers are included they heavily outnumber men here too (see Figure 9.7).

How is girls' increasing and now greater success at examinations to be explained?

There is, first, the claim that attempts to counteract educational discrimination against girls have worked. These include such initiatives as GIST (Girls into Science and Technology) and the introduction of single-sex classes. More generally, there has been a greater awareness of, and sensitivity to, gender issues in schools.

There is, secondly, the argument that it is changes in the relationship between education and work that account for the superior performance of girls. The growing employment of women has arguably raised girls' expectations and confidence (see Chapter 5, p. 180). The decline of traditional male jobs has led to the disillusionment and disaffection of many boys, who no longer bother with education and take refuge in an oppositional culture, of the kind described by Willis (see p. 328). Weiner *et al.* (1997) have suggested that the impact of organizational changes and a growing

Figure 9.6 Achievement of two or more GCE A levels or equivalent by gender, 1990/1—2003/4

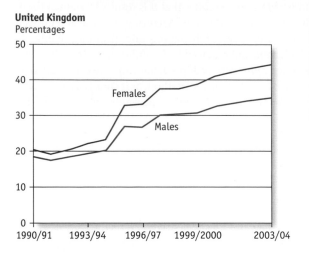

United Kingdom
Percentages

Source: Social Trends (2006: 42).

❷ Why do you think that girls have become increasingly successful in A level examinations?

insecurity of employment in middle-class male careers may have had similar effects on middle-class boys. These theories are linked to wider notions of a male identity crisis, which we discuss in Chapter 5, pp. 183–4.

Although plausible, these explanations tend to make general statements about boys and girls that take insufficient account of class location or of different responses to change. Thus, the greater employment of women in paid work does not just mean that educationally qualified girls are moving into professional or managerial careers. As Mac an Ghaill (1996) has pointed out, many are moving into low-paid, part-time, and insecure jobs, which they have to combine with traditional domestic duties. He also emphasized that a wide range of male peer groups and masculinities, not just oppositional cultures of the kind described by Willis, can be found in schools. For some working-class boys, new vocational routes are opening up into areas such as business studies, technology, and computing.

The educational success of girls should not, anyway, be taken to mean that older patterns of male domination have disappeared. Thus, gender still plays a part in subject choice, which steers men and women towards different careers. The introduction of a national curriculum reduced

Figure 9.7 Students in higher education* by type of course and gender, United Kingdom, 1970/1–2003/4 (000s)

	Undergraduate		Postgraduate		All higher education
	Full-time	Part-time	Full-time	Part-time	
Males					
1970/71	241	127	33	15	416
1980/81	277	176	41	32	526
1990/91	345	193	50	50	638
2000/01	511	228	82	118	940
2003/04	543	261	110	138	1,054
Females					
1970/71	173	19	10	3	205
1980/81	196	71	21	13	301
1990/91	319	148	34	36	537
2000/01	602	320	81	124	1,128
2003/04	664	445	111	170	1,392

*Includes both home and overseas students, and students at the Open University.

Source: Social Trends (2006: 38).

❷ Why do you think that there are more women than men in higher education?

gender differences in subject choice before age 16, but by A level traditional gender differences have re-emerged and these continue in higher education. Thus, 93 per cent of the students sitting the vocational A level in Health and Social Care in 2001 were female, while in Computing 79 per cent of entrants were male (*Independent*, 16 September 2001).

Male domination of education has also persisted in other ways. This can be seen in higher education and in managerial positions in education. Men become more numerous as one moves up the career ladder in higher education, which also means that university procedures and decision-making bodies tend to be dominated by men (Hodges 2000). Senior positions in schools, governing bodies, local education authorities (LEAs), and the Department for Education and Skills have also been male-dominated (Weiner *et al.* 1997).

In response to girls' greater examination success, there have been calls for something to be done to help boys catch up. In 2000 the government launched pilot schemes that would provide separate classes for boys, in order to restore discipline and improve results. While this may well improve the performance of boys, it may also benefit girls, and had indeed long been advocated as a means of improving their performance—so it may not reduce the current gender gap! Research on this issue has been carried out by the Rising Boys Achievement Project and can be accessed at www.rba.educ.cam.ac.uk/index.html.

The worry about boys' examination performance has been accompanied by a concern with their much higher rate of exclusion from school for misbehaviour. In English schools the rate of exclusion for boys has in recent years been four times higher than the rate for girls (DFES 2006). It has been argued, however, that too much attention has been paid to boys' problems and that girls' less visible problems have been neglected. According to Osler *et al.* (2002) girls are more involved than boys in some of the less formal and less visible forms of exclusion, such as isolation within the school and self-exclusion through disengagement from work or withdrawal from school.

Ethnicity

Variations in educational achievement have been linked to ethnicity, though the relationship between ethnicity and achievement is particularly complex.

Ethnicity and achievement

A growing concern with ethnic variations in educational achievement led to the Rampton (1981) and Swann (1985) reports, which showed that there were important ethnic differences in attainment. A considerable literature then developed to explain the relationship between ethnicity and educational achievement. Some claimed that ethnic

variations could be explained by differences in inherited intelligence (Herrnstein and Murray 1994). Alternatively, it was argued that cultural differences explained these variations. Thus, African-Caribbean culture placed a low value on education, though some Asian cultures highly valued it. Others have suggested that growing up in a white-dominated society with few positive 'black' role models leads to low self-esteem, low aspirations, and educational underachievement among African-Caribbean children.

> ⊃ *Connections*
> We examine biological explanations of ethnic differences in Chapter 6, pp. 197–200, and biological explanations of differences in intelligence in Chapter 18, pp. 731–2.

There are many problems with the literature on the educational performance of ethnic minorities. First, there is the problem of categories. The collective term 'ethnic minorities' conceals great differences in ethnicity and educational achievement (see Figure 9.8). Some are performing at higher levels than the white majority, some at lower levels. The notion that ethnic minorities underachieve is simply wrong.

There are major gender variations within ethnic groups. Thus, in Figure 9.8 the 35 per cent figure for blacks conceals the fact that 44 per cent of black Caribbean girls achieved these grades but only 27 per cent of boys. This led Trevor Phillips, the chairman of the Commission for Racial Equality, to call for separate classes for black boys in order to improve their particular performance (*Independent*, 7 March 2005).

There is also the difficulty of distinguishing between *ethnicity* and *class*. Particular ethnic groups, such as African Caribbeans or Bangladeshis, may perform badly because of their class rather than their ethnicity.

The need to take account of class was demonstrated by an important study of nineteen 'multi-racial' comprehensives in the early 1980s. Smith and Tomlinson (1989) explored the significance of ethnicity for educational achievement. They found ethnic differences at age 16 in GCE/CSE grades (the examinations that preceded GCSE), but class was far more strongly related to attainment than ethnicity. They stated that it was also quite possible that the ethnic differences that they found reflected class differences. The relatively low score achieved by those from families of West Indian and South Asian origin could well have resulted from their mainly working-class backgrounds.

Smith and Tomlinson concluded that the performance of children depended, above all, on the school they attended. As we showed earlier (see p. 337), Rutter *et al.*

Figure 9.8 Attainment of five or more GCSE grades A*–C in year 11, 1992–2004, England and Wales (%)

Ethnic origin	1992	2004	Change
White	37	54	+17
Black	23	35	+12
Indian	38	72	+34
Pakistani	26	37	+11
Bangladeshi	14	46	+32
Other Asian	46	66	+20
Other ethnic group	46 (1996)	59	+13
All	37	54	+17

Source: Social Trends (2006: 41)

❓ Do these figures show that educational achievement varies according to ethnicity?

Figure 9.9 Permanent exclusion rates in primary, secondary, and special schools, 2002–3

England	Rates per 10,000 pupils
White	12
Black Caribbean	37
Black African	12
Other black	32
Indian	3
Pakistani	8
Bangladeshi	6
Chinese	2
Other ethnic group	12
Mixed	22

Source: Social Trends (2005: 35).

❓ What is the significance of differences in these rates for patterns of educational achievement?

(1979) had demonstrated that school character made a difference. Smith and Tomlinson went further than this. They argued that school character far outweighed ethnic background in determining educational success. What really mattered was the quality of the school attended. This led them to the policy conclusion that 'the measures that will most help the racial minorities are the same as those that will raise the standards of secondary education generally' (Smith and Tomlinson 1989: 307).

There is also the need to take account of change and not see a particular level of performance as a fixed feature of a particular group (see Figure 9.8). While all groups have been improving their performance, some previously disadvantaged groups have been catching up, and some have overtaken others who previously performed better.

Performance in a school examination is, anyway, a limited way of measuring educational success. It does not take account of those who have already dropped out of education or have been excluded from it. There are very pronounced ethnic variations in rates of exclusion (see Figure 9.9).

Racism in schools?

Ethnographic studies, such as that by Cecile Wright (1988), have demonstrated the existence of racially discriminatory behaviour in schools. Observational and interview techniques have been used to investigate the interaction between different ethnic groups and teachers. They have shown teachers interpreting the behaviour of

African-Caribbean children as disruptive and then reacting in a punitive way that was inappropriate to the situation. This fits with the much higher rate of exclusion of black children from school because of 'bad' behaviour.

Rattansi (1988) referred to the *institutional racism* embedded in taken-for-granted features of school organization and curriculum (see Chapter 6, p. 202, for a discussion of this term). By this he meant the way that such matters as dress requirements or school meals arrangements or aspects of the curriculum failed to take account of non-white cultures.

Mason (2000) recognized the existence of these practices but was concerned that the term 'racist' had become overused. He argued that many such practices should be viewed as *ethnocentric* rather than *racist*. They show an ignorance and disregard of other cultures that is typical of a widely found ethnocentrism but they are in principle no different from practices that discriminate against the customs and cultures of, say, people from Ireland or Poland who live in Britain. Mason preferred to keep the term 'racism' for beliefs that involved the idea of biologically distinct races.

Ethnocentrism and racism do not themselves determine children's behaviour, for much depends on how children respond. Brah and Minhas (1988) described

How significant is ethnicity in educational achievement?
© Alice Chadwick

the emergence of an oppositional response by Asian schoolgirls. They were well aware of the operation of ethnocentric stereotypes in their schools and responded to the notion that Asians had language difficulties by pretending not to understand their teachers' instructions and speaking Urdu in class. Their resistance to the ethnocentric culture of the school took a collective form as they created mutual support groups. Fuller (1983) reported a rather different response by African-Caribbean girls, who reacted to low teacher expectations by combining defiance with educational success. They were well aware of the importance of educational qualifications and demonstrated that they could achieve results as good as anyone else's.

Nor is it simply a matter of the interaction between teachers and pupils, for interactions between the pupils themselves have an important bearing on all this. In a study of excluded black students, Wright *et al.* (1998) showed how the stereotypes of male black youth held by white students, stereotypes that combined fear and awe, interacted with those of teachers to generate an oppositional black masculinity that in turn reinforced the stereotype.

Policy responses to ethnocentrism and racism in schools may have gone some way to counter racism and ethnocentrism.

Multicultural education recognized cultural diversity and tried to treat cultures as different but equal. It involved changes to the curriculum that would better reflect cultural diversity by, for example, bringing black writers into the study of literature and recognizing religious diversity, but it has come under much criticism. It provoked a hostile reaction from those who believed that it threatened British national identity or justified unacceptable cultural practices, such as the wearing of the *burqa* by Muslims. It was also criticized by black activists for colluding with *cultural racism* (see Chapter 6, p. 224) and trying to assimilate minorities into a racist society that it did not openly challenge.

The second more radical response was *anti-racist* education. This more directly challenged racism by insisting that it must be recognized and confronted. It sought to raise awareness of all aspects of racism and train teachers in anti-racist policies. Its broad definition of racism treated all forms of disadvantage or discrimination affecting ethnic minorities as racist, labelling as racist practices which Mason would consider ethnocentric. It certainly brought racism out into the open but has been criticized for intensifying and racializing conflicts between ethnic groups.

Class, gender, and ethnicity

Class, gender, and ethnicity have all been sources of inequality of opportunity in education. Similar mechanisms are involved in each case. There are patterns of class, gender, and ethnic disadvantage. The expectations of parents, children, and teachers may be shaped by stereotypes of class, gender, or ethnicity. These are sometimes expressed in open hostility or discrimination but are often hidden in ways of thinking and behaving that are taken for granted. They may be buried in a *hidden curriculum* or embedded in organizational structures.

Factors both outside and inside educational institutions produce patterns of disadvantage. Employment, occupation, housing, health, and wealth all affect educational success from outside education. Stereotyped expectations originate and operate outside education but can be reinforced within it. Selective processes within schools through streaming, option choice, and career guidance can reproduce external structures of disadvantage.

It is important to stress that educational institutions can also counteract out-of-school sources of inequality. Studies of the 'school effect' show that school character can outweigh social background. Patterns of discrimination may also be openly countered through equal opportunities policies and programmes to make teachers sensitive to the effects of disadvantages and expectations.

Inequalities both persist and change. Class inequalities seem to be the most persistent, as changes in the organization of education appear to have had only marginal effects upon them. Gender inequalities in educational achievement do, however, seem to have diminished, indeed to have been reversed. There is clear evidence too that ethnic patterns of achievement have changed. Where inequalities are linked primarily to beliefs and expectations, social movements and policy changes can have an impact. Where they are linked to the more material factors associated with class position—employment, occupation, income, and housing—or the possession of cultural capital, they seem to persist more strongly.

While we have considered class, gender, and ethnicity separately, they intersect in complex ways. Ethnic differences are difficult to separate from class differences and it may well be that much of the difference in educational achievement between ethnic groups is explained by differences in their class composition. On the other hand, average figures for classes or ethnic groups may mean little if there are major gender differences within these categories. This means that we should not deal with class, gender, or ethnicity in isolation from each other and should always take account of location along all three dimensions.

 *Stop and reflect*

In this section we examined patterns of class, gender, and ethnic inequality.

Class inequalities:

- In spite of their intentions, neither the 1944 Education Act nor comprehensive schools made much impact on class differences in educational achievement.
- Why do you think that class inequalities have been so persistent?

Gender inequalities:

- The gendering of occupational and educational expectations disadvantaged girls until recent times.
- In recent years, however, girls have outperformed boys in many public examinations.
- How would you account for this change?
- Does it signal the end of the male domination of education?

Ethnicity:

- Variations in educational achievement have been linked to ethnicity.
- Would it be true to say that ethnic minorities underachieve?
- Consider whether class, gender, and ethnicity should be treated as separate dimensions of inequality.

Education in transformation

Since the 1980s, British education has been transformed. There has been a new emphasis on gearing education to the needs of the economy and developing its training function. Parental choice and greater competition between educational institutions have exposed education to market forces. Local education authorities (LEAs) have lost much of their control over education, but central state regulation has increased. The proportion of students staying on in education after the age of 16 rose sharply and higher education entered a new phase of rapid expansion.

Education and economy

As we showed on p. 331, education has been held responsible by some for Britain's declining international competitiveness. Britain's economic problems in the 1970s, increasing international competition, and the consequences of globalization resulted in a growing concern with education's contribution to the economy.

Education and economic success

Bowles and Gintis (1976) (see p. 327) had argued that the key function of education was the supply of labour to the capitalist economy. Economic changes have made this function even more important. In Britain, unskilled manual labour has declined and work requiring skills and qualifications has become more important. The spread of information technology into all areas of life means that new skills in processing and communicating information are needed. Knowledge and the capacity to use and communicate it has become vital to the economic success of

countries and the earnings of individuals. Furthermore, in a world of growing economic integration, investment in education has become one of the main ways of increasing international competitiveness (see box on 'Education and globalization' on p. 346).

It is now widely agreed that education is important to economic success, but which aspects of education matter most to the economy? Four different answers to this question can be identified:

- *Technical skills.* Education needs to train workers in the particular skills required by industry. Industry needs, for example, workers trained in information technology.

- *Transferable and interpersonal skills.* In a more competitive, more uncertain, and rapidly changing environment, employers are looking less for training in specific skills, which may soon go out of date, and more for adaptable and flexible workers with transferable skills. Employers need workers with skills of communication and teamwork, who can work well with others.

- *Level of education.* Economies require workers educated and trained to higher levels. Competitive economies need well-developed systems of post-16 and higher education.

- *Standards.* It is not so much the content or the level of education that are problematic but the standards reached. Standards of literacy and numeracy especially need to be improved.

Global focus Education and globalization

Growing state intervention in education has been, in part at least, a response to globalization. Increasing global integration has demolished many of the walls around national economies and made it more difficult for governments to protect industries against foreign competition. The ease with which capital can move from one country to another has weakened the capacity of governments to direct the development of national economies. One of the few ways in which they can increase the international competitiveness of an economy is through investment in human capital by putting resources into education and training.

This argument particularly relates to the old industrial societies. Their traditional manufacturing industries cannot compete with those of developing countries where labour costs are far lower. This also applies to clerical work and data processing, which can now be done by teleworkers in lower-cost countries because of advances in communications technology. The industrial societies can compete only by upgrading their skills and capitalizing on their knowledge and expertise.

All this means that it is the more highly educated members of these societies who will flourish. According to Reich (1997), those who can only do routine production and service work will lose out, while it is the highly educated 'symbolic analysts'— scientists, consultants, engineers, financial experts, and all those who can manipulate oral and visible symbols—whose skills and knowledge are in global demand. The implication is that inequality will be more related to level of education than ever before.

Brown and Lauder (1997) have argued that recent changes in education have made this problem particularly acute in Britain, for the increased emphasis on market forces and competition has inevitably resulted in greater inequality between schools and therefore in children's educational opportunities (see the section on 'Choice, selection, and inequality' below). They argue that this is not just a matter of social justice, for only when there is equality of educational opportunity will the full educational potential of the population be realized, and international competitiveness maximized.

Data from the OECD suggest that the UK has not been doing well here. Figures for the percentage of 15–19 year-olds staying on in education in 2002 ranked the UK twenty-fourth out of the twenty-seven countries surveyed. The earning power of university graduates was, however, relatively high, with the UK coming fifth in the international league table for the boost in earnings provided by higher education. This suggests that British education remains comparatively elitist, with much of the educational potential of the population untapped and international competitiveness correspondingly diminished.

Sources: Brown and Lauder (1997); Reich (1997); *Independent*, 15 September 2004.

While it is clearly possible for governments to try to improve all these aspects of education, given limited resources they imply conflicting priorities. Thus, the improvement of general numeracy requires higher investment in schools, while the raising of the overall level of education suggests that more money should be put into further and higher education.

The new vocationalism

The concern to improve education's supply of labour to employers led in the 1980s to what has been called the **new vocationalism**. This sought to change education to make it more closely related both to the occupational requirements of the economy and to students' need for jobs. The established liberal and academic traditions of British education were challenged. The liberal approach to education aimed to develop an individual's full potential in all aspects of life and did not particularly concern itself with education for work. The academic tradition valued knowledge for its own sake and was not concerned with how it was used.

Knowledge was now considered less important than the capacity to learn, communicate, and work cooperatively with others. A more vocational, more motivating, more student-involving education was needed that would raise the numbers of 16–19 year-olds staying on in education. Widespread changes followed in both secondary and tertiary education:

- *Course construction*. The modularization of courses into shorter, more flexible units with specified objectives.

- *Skills*. A shift of focus from knowledge to work-related skills, such as skills in numeracy and information technology, in communication, problem-solving, and personal management.

- *Learning*. More emphasis on student-centred learning through project work rather than the teaching of factual information, and group cooperation rather than individualist competition.

- *Enterprise*. Development of entrepreneurial skills by encouraging students to take part in profit-making business activities.

- *Assessment*. Profiles, records of achievement, and transcripts to recognize what has been achieved and replace traditional grading systems, together with certification that a defined level of competence has been reached.

It was no good, however, developing work-relevant skills if they were not valued by the educational system or employers or indeed the students themselves. This was a deep-rooted problem in Britain, where academic qualifications had always been more highly valued than vocational ones. The response to this problem was to build a new system of National Vocational Qualifications (NVQs), which tested not just knowledge but competence in specific work situations. General NVQs (GNVQs) were developed to meet the requirements of groups of related occupations, such as health care, and provide a vocational route into further and higher education. Advanced GNVQs or 'vocational A levels' were created to give equality of status with A level and provide a route into higher education through vocational qualifications. Smithers (1994) described this creation of new qualifications as 'a quiet educational revolution'.

Figure 9.10 Academic education versus the new vocationalism

Academic education	New vocationalism
• Teaching	• Learning
• Knowledge	• Competence
• Subject specific skills	• Transferable skills
• Individual achievement	• Team work

➲ Think about the course that you are taking.

❓ Does it reflect the new vocationalism?

The new vocationalism may have brought about a quiet revolution but it upset some on both the right and the left of politics. It was resisted by supporters of the academic tradition, who thought that traditional knowledge-based and subject-based A levels were a 'gold standard' to be defended at all costs. Left-wing critics argued that it subordinated education to the requirements of work in a

Can entrepreneurial skills be learned in schools and colleges?

© Hymers College, Hull

capitalist economy. Indeed, it seemed to vindicate the Bowles and Gintis (1976) analysis of the relationship between education and the capitalist economy. Was education only for work?

A regulated market-place

The drive to make education more responsive to the needs of British society led also to an introduction of market principles that should have reduced state control of education but paradoxically involved extensive state intervention and greater state regulation. Similar processes of change went on in all sectors of education but we will first consider changes in schools and colleges and then higher education.

Market forces

The introduction of market principles in the 1980s reflected the Conservative government's belief that the British economy could be revitalized by allowing market forces to operate more freely. This involved two key interacting processes, greater competition between institutions and greater parental choice.

Before the 1980s reforms, entry to state schools was based on catchment areas. Children were allocated to schools by the LEA according to the area they lived in. If parents did not like the local school, they either had to educate their children privately or move house into the catchment area of a 'good' school. Schools did not have to compete for children and parents had very little choice within the state system.

The 1980 and 1988 Education Acts gave parents the right to choose which school their children attended. The removal of restrictions on entry meant that in theory popular schools could expand, while unpopular schools might be forced eventually to close. Schools were also allowed to specialize in areas like technology and modern languages. Schools now had to compete for pupils and glossy school brochures multiplied.

Competition was encouraged in other ways by reducing LEA control over schools. The delegation of management and budget control to the schools themselves gave them greater freedom to compete, for they could decide how to use their resources most effectively. Schools could increase their resources by attracting more pupils, but in this new competitive climate they also began to raise more money from parents, sponsors, and commercial operations.

Similar changes occurred in further education, where colleges were removed from local-authority control and had their funding transferred to a national funding council appointed by the government. They were now controlled by new governing bodies on which local industry was heavily represented. Funding linked to student numbers forced the colleges into competition

Figure 9.11 Schools enter the market-place

Before the 1980s	After the 1980s
• Catchment areas	• Open entry
• LEA allocation of places	• Parents' right to choose
• LEA coordination of provision	• Competition between schools
• LEA control	• Governor authority, delegation of management, opting out
• LEA services	• Private services

with each other and also with those schools providing post-16 education.

Another kind of competition was also introduced. Educational services had previously been provided by the LEAs, which had built up large staffs to provide services as various as in-service training and grounds maintenance. Schools could now choose whether to buy LEA services or go to private suppliers. The LEAs had to compete on the same basis as private companies to win contracts from schools. Education services, just like many other local-authority services, had been privatized.

Choice, selection, and inequality

It was claimed that these changes in education increased parental choice but they also increased the capacity of schools to select, and inevitably resulted in greater inequality.

Choice results in a growing inequality between schools and therefore in the resources and facilities available to their pupils. As money follows pupils, resources flow to popular schools. If there is a high demand for places, popular schools can be more selective in deciding which child to accept. By selecting children with greater ability they improve their results and become still more popular. At the other extreme, 'sink' schools emerge that face a downward spiral of pupils, resources, and results.

As both our opening piece and Media watch 9 (see p. 357) suggest, the opportunity to choose schools has turned out to be illusory for many people. Popular schools simply cannot expand sufficiently to accommodate the demand for places in them. As these schools become more selective, the choice for many parents is reduced and most of those who cannot get their children into their school of choice have to settle for less desirable schools.

The capacity to exercise choice effectively is inevitably related to social class. There are straightforward material factors, such as the availability of transport and the pressures of work, which limit the choices of those who are poor. Cultural and social capital (see pp. 324–6) also play their part, as knowledge of education and networks helps some parents to get their children into better schools. The better the school is (in reputation at least), and the more competition there is for places, the more strongly these mechanisms operate.

In a study of school choice in Greater London during 1991–2, Ball *et al.* (1995) found two patterns of choice that corresponded to social class:

- *Working-class locals.* Their choice was governed by practical considerations and immediate concerns, such as transport arrangements.
- *Middle-class cosmopolitans.* They gave higher priority to school reputation and longer-term career concerns, and had more money for travel or private education.

A growing competition for jobs, together with the inflation of qualifications by mass higher education, led middle-class parents to use their full weight in the education market in order to give their children a competitive edge. To do this, they needed greater choice. Phillip Brown (1995) has claimed that there has been a shift in the ideology of the middle class from **meritocracy** to *parentocracy*. He contrasted these two ideologies through two equations:

- **meritocracy**: ability + effort = merit
- **parentocracy**: resources + preference = choice.

There is also an ethnic dimension to this whole issue of choice. Research has shown that parents from ethnic minorities are concerned to find a school 'with a critical mass of children from their own ethnic background'. There are also patterns of 'ethnic aversion', when schools are avoided because of their ethnic composition. This applies particularly to schools with a high proportion of refugee children. Those at the bottom of the ethnic hierarchy were, needless to say, least able to exercise choice effectively and ended up at locally labelled 'bad' schools. Patterns of ethnic disadvantage were reinforced by the machinery of (non) choice (J. Williams 2005).

Thus, in these various ways, greater choice can mean more inequality. It increased inequality between schools. It created a new line of division between those who got the school of their choice and those who did not. It reinforced existing inequalities, as those with superior material and cultural resources were better placed to pursue their preferences and obtain the kind of education that they wanted for their children.

More state regulation

The government did not, however, simply leave education to the operation of market forces and the exercise of parental choice.

The 1988 Education Act introduced a national curriculum for children aged 5–16. This was a fundamental change in British education, which had never before experienced such a regulation and standardization of its content. As Chris Pole has pointed out, this considerably changed the role of the teacher:

> By the end of the 1980s, central government was firmly inside the classroom, reducing the role of the teacher from that of professional who had previously made decisions about the curriculum to that of technician who merely delivered it. (Pole 2001: 4)

With the national curriculum went national testing. GCSE already provided a national test at age 16 but new tests were introduced at younger ages. The requirements of the national curriculum and the testing of all subjects overloaded teachers and led to heavy protests from the teaching unions and teacher boycotts of testing. This resulted in a slimming-down of the curriculum and some restriction of testing, though critics did not see these changes as dealing with the problem and protests have continued to the present day.

National testing enabled the construction of league tables that allowed the comparison of schools' performances. A major problem with these tables was, however, that performance was largely determined by a school's intake. This created a powerful incentive for schools to both be more selective in their intake and exclude children likely to perform badly.

It was not only pupils who were tested, for a new system of school inspection run by the Office for Standards in Education (OFSTED) was introduced. This involved not only the inspection of the workings of the school but also meetings with parents at which teachers were not present. OFSTED reports were then made available to parents. This fitted well with the government's belief in parent power and parent choice.

The heavier state regulation of education was in constant tension with the emphasis on free competition elsewhere in government education policy. In their day-to-day running, schools had been given greater freedom from local-authority control but they were now instead tightly controlled by the central state.

Higher education

Similar changes took place in higher education. This was expanded rapidly from the late 1880s but expansion was not matched by increased funding. The proportion of 18 year-olds in higher education rose rapidly from 15 per cent in 1988 to 30 per cent in 1994, rising slowly thereafter to 43 per cent in 2006. Funding per student declined during the 1980s and the 1990s, dropping by almost a half in real terms. Universities have responded by allowing the number of students per lecturer to rise from a student–staff

Controversy and debate   Education and disability: integration or segregation?

Should those with a disability be educated in special schools that provide for their particular needs or should they be integrated into mainstream schooling?

Following the 1978 report by Baroness Warnock, the 1981 Education Act established a framework for educating children with 'special needs' in mainstream schools. The needs of such children would be assessed and their schools would be given additional support by local education authorities. This was a reaction against both the traditional 'dumping' of many such children in special schools and the absence of any special provision in mainstream schools for those with learning difficulties.

According to the Audit Commission, between 1981 and 1991 the number of special school places in England fell from around 130,000 to around 100,000, but, contrary to public perceptions, has only slowly declined since. In 2001, 61 per cent of children with 'special needs' in England were educated in mainstream schools and 34 per cent in special schools (most of the remainder were educated in independent schools).

This integration policy reflected broader changes in the way that the disabled were viewed. Traditionally, disability had been considered an individual medical problem that required treatment in a specialist institution. Increasingly, the problem was seen as lying with society, which discriminated against and excluded those with 'special needs', depriving them of their rights. Integration was part of a broader process of decarcerating people from institutions (see Chapter 14, pp. 566–7 for a discussion of this). Education of the disabled in mainstream schools was also paralleled by the policy of 'care in the community' (see Chapter 8, pp. 303–4).

Those critical of the integration policy argue that the specialized staff and facilities of special schools make them much better at meeting 'special needs', while support in mainstream schools is erratic, inadequate, and difficult to obtain from local education authorities. They claim that the disabled suffer neglect and bullying in mainstream schools, which are anyway sometimes reluctant to admit them and often exclude them.

Those in support of integration argue that segregation is wrong and that the problems faced by mainstream schools would be solved if they were properly resourced. Those with 'special needs' can benefit greatly from contact with other children. It is also argued that some specialist schools are themselves inadequately staffed and resourced, and have changed little since the time when Baroness Warnock made her report.

Sources: Audit Commission (2002); *Sunday Times*, 12 June 2005; *Guardian*, 10 June 2005.

---

ratio of 10 to 1 in 1986 ('old' universities), to 18 to 1 by 2002/3.

Universities have tried to find new sources of income. They have tried to recruit more overseas students (who pay much higher fees), expanded their postgraduate courses (seeking overseas students), and developed distance learning programmes. The academic market-place has become global. They have also tried to raise more money from renting out accommodation, conferences, and appeals to their alumni.

Pressures on students increased in various ways. The most obvious were the shift from grants to loans, and the introduction of student fees. Students have increasingly earned their way through university by taking paid work in term-time as well as vacations. They have also come under other forms of pressure through library, equipment, and accommodation shortages, larger classes, and cramped conditions in university buildings.

Research too has been affected by a financial squeeze. This is not only the result of reduced state funding but also greater competition for research money from the Higher Education Funding Council. This became more intense when the polytechnics became universities and began to seek a share of the limited funds available. Researchers have been forced to seek funds increasingly from private industry or government departments. This means that research has become more directed by outside organizations seeking the information that they want, which they may not wish to be disclosed to competitors or to the public.

Under these pressures, universities, like other organizations, have had to become more competitive and more flexible in their internal workings. More flexible courses have been created through modularization and credit accumulation structures. Universities have also, like schools and many other employers, moved towards greater flexibility of employment (see Chapter 9, pp. 350–1). They have a *core* of full-time, permanent staff members, and a *periphery* of part-timers and short-term contract staff. This provides them with a 'numerical flexibility' that enables them to respond to changes in their financial situation.

Greater organizational flexibility has been created by decentralizing management and the control of budgets to

New technology E-Universities?

It is claimed that information and communication technology (ICT) is transforming education. What matters, however, is how it is used. E-moderators (teachers and trainers who work with learners online) can adopt different roles. Gilly Salmon (2004: chapter 6) has sketched out four scenarios, which are not predictions but a way of helping us to think about the range of possibilities and the choices that we face. She takes us on a voyage to a new planetary system.

Planet Contenteous

On this planet 'content is king'. The latest technologies are used to make as much content as possible available to everyone. The traditional transmission model of teaching is dominant. Experts pass on their knowledge to students. Students are assessed frequently through automated testing of their ability to reproduce, comprehend, and critique the material they receive. Communication skills are at a premium but communication is increasingly at a distance and there is little interpersonal contact between staff and students. The e-moderator combines the roles of e-librarian, e-lecturer, and e-mentor. The most successful can become media stars.

Planet Instantia

Here the key things are instantaneity and flexibility. E-learning takes place through integrated information technology devices that are available everywhere in the institution and are online all the time. Learners are concerned with whether their particular and immediate needs are met. They ask: 'Is this learning just for me, just in time, just for now, and just enough?' The content of learning is employment and organization-oriented. Assessment is concentrated on performance in meeting work or professional needs and is integrated with learning activities. E-moderators facilitate 'autonomous learning' and focus on the development of the skills that this requires. They are considered professionals, loyal to their professions or organizations, and tend to have a 'human resources' background.

Planet Nomadic

This planet provides 'portable learning for mobile lifestyles'. Here wireless technology is the norm. 'Learning devices were once carried, then worn and are now often embedded subcutaneously.' Learning is independent of time and place. Assessment is largely through projects and outcomes, which students can choose or at least negotiate. E-moderators are as mobile as their students. They may work for different organizations and move around the globe. They are also mobile intellectually and freely cross subject boundaries. They are enthusiasts who enjoy helping people to learn, get on well with students, and have themselves moved from e-learning to e-moderation, working when the spirit moves them.

Planet Cafelattia

On this planet ICT is used for the exchange of knowledge, for collaborative activities, and for community purposes. Technology does not replace social interaction but provides a means of achieving it. Academics do not have a monopoly of knowledge and there is an egalitarian spirit of sharing experiences of all kinds. There is a 'strong social context to learning' and learners 'express themselves freely'. Assessment is not performance-oriented but a means of enhancing the process of learning and takes a group or peer form. E-moderators can think globally *and* act locally. They have highly developed social skills and typically come from a background in community work or social movements.

Source: Salmon (2004: chapter 6). (Note that this is not in the first edition.)

➔ For further information and examples, visit www.e-moderating.com and click on 'scenarios'.

❓ Which of these planets is your institution on (or heading for)? Which would you like to inhabit?

departments. As with schools, this kind of decentralization has, in principle, allowed greater freedom to operate in a more competitive environment but resources have been ever more tightly controlled by university administrations and greater departmental autonomy has largely been illusory.

Universities, like schools, have also come under closer state scrutiny, as their teaching and research have been audited and graded. Results have been published and league tables constructed. Research performance is linked to funding, though teaching performance has not yet been.

Thus, although greater competition and flexibility have been introduced into higher education, there has also been a tighter and more bureaucratic control by the state. Both teaching and research have come under closer surveillance. The institutions of higher education have lost much of their earlier autonomy and now have to operate within a framework imposed by the state.

From Thatcherism to New Labour

In recent years education has been more thoroughly transformed by government than ever before. In this section we will review the state's role in Britain and consider what difference the Labour government has made to education policy.

The Conservative transformation

It was the Thatcher governments of the 1980s that initiated the transformation of British education. **Neo-liberalism** was central to this. Neo-liberals believed that British education could most effectively be reformed by introducing market principles. This led to policies that increased competition between schools, reduced local-authority control over them, and provided more choice for parents.

> ⊃ *Connections*
>
> For an account of the broader neo-liberal changes in government policy see Chapter 15, pp. 601–2.

There was also another strand in Conservative policy, an appeal to the beliefs and values of ordinary people, which has been labelled **authoritarian populism** (Dale 1989). Populism rejected the views of experts and called for a return to the common sense and 'natural instincts' of the people. It was associated with 'parent power' and parental choice; a return to Christian education; stricter school discipline; the teaching of patriotic versions of British history. It also sought to maintain traditional subjects, 'chalk-and-board' teaching methods, traditional examinations, and A levels. This strand of Conservatism came into conflict with many of the reforms sought by the new vocationalists.

While politicians generally agreed on the importance of education, they were also under pressure to control state expenditure. The Conservatives were committed to the reduction of taxation and very concerned to keep public spending under control. Schools were squeezed financially through the government's tighter control of local-authority spending. There were frequent calls on higher education to make 'efficiency gains' as the government reduced the value of the student fee paid at this time by the state. The Conservatives also gradually shifted the funding of students' maintenance from a grant to a loan basis.

New Labour in government

Most of the changes introduced by the Conservatives were strongly opposed by the Labour Party, but have the post-1997 Labour governments reversed the Conservatives' transformation of education?

Comprehensive schools have long been one of the main battlefields of education policy. Historically, Labour has promoted non-selective comprehensive schools, while the Conservatives supported diversity and selection. Things have, however, changed and in a famous outburst in February 2001 Alistair Campbell, the prime minister's press adviser, declared that 'the day of the bog-standard comprehensive is over', while New Labour has enthusiastically pursued diversity and, in practice at least, accepted selection.

The acceptance of selection was a big reversal of Labour's traditional posture on this issue. Labour had been hostile to selection when in opposition and the Labour Party remains in principle opposed to selection at age 11, but the post-1997 Labour governments have pursued policies that increase it. Increased selection within schools takes place through the required 'setting' by ability. Increased selection by schools results from the multiplication of specialist schools and the creation of city academies (see box on 'City academies'), both allowed to select up to 10 per cent of their pupils.

British education has become more hierarchical than ever with the addition of new layers below the elite public schools and grammar schools (164 grammar schools still existed in 2004). Specialist schools constitute one new layer, which has been further differentiated with the creation of 'advanced specialist schools', charged with raising standards and training teachers. There are also some elite city technology colleges and, increasingly, the city academies. Faith schools too are being encouraged (see box on p. 322). The comprehensive school is being replaced by a new diversified hierarchy of schools.

The government also appears to be going much further along the path of 'parent power'. Parents have been promised more choice through the further diversification of schools. Proposals to increase the power of parents include the power to call on ministers to replace the management of failing schools, in effect to 'sack heads'. Parents would also have a greater role in the management of the independent trust schools proposed by the government in early 2006.

The process of privatizing education has continued. Labour has allowed private companies to take over the management of some state schools and some local education authorities. New specialist schools and city academies have been privately sponsored by business and religious interests. Labour's 2006 plans to turn schools into independent trusts appeared to be handing them over to private bodies, which could well be controlled by business or religious organizations (*Guardian*, 20 February 2006). School building has been financed by private finance initiatives,

Controversy and debate City academies

Academies are state-maintained but independent schools, which are partly financed and largely managed by sponsoring organizations. The sponsor is expected to contribute £2 million to the cost of establishing the school (total cost of the early academies was £25 million), the state paying the rest and all future costs. The academies have to follow the national curriculum and are subject to OFSTED inspections but in return for their 10 per cent initial investment the sponsors have considerable control over the content of teaching, the employment and payment of teachers, and the selection of pupils. The academies were launched in 2000 as a scheme to replace failing schools in disadvantaged areas with innovative schools that would bring in business skills and enterprise, and raise standards. Government plans to have 200 running by 2010 (in 2005 some 17 were open) suggest that they will become much more widespread.

Much concern has been expressed about the character of the sponsoring organizations. As the *Independent* has put it: 'By the end of the decade, the bankers, the churches, the millionaire philanthropists and leaders of the country's private schools will be in charge, in the name of more choice for parents.'

It was claimed in 2004 that Sir Peter Vardy, the head of a large car dealing company, was building a network of 'creationist' academies, where creationist accounts of human origins would be presented as an alternative to Darwinism, but a local revolt by parents and teachers blocked the foundation of one such school in Doncaster. Another plan by Global Education Management Systems, the second largest provider of private education in Britain, to set up two academies in Milton Keynes was blocked by a parents' revolt in 2005. There has also been considerable debate over whether the academies actually do improve educational standards.

Sources: Independent, 8 July 2004 and 15 October 2004; *Times,* 15 June 2005.

❓ Which features of Labour education policy do city academies exemplify?

❓ What are the advantages and disadvantages of city academies?

---

while services once provided by local education authorities are increasingly provided by private agencies.

There has certainly been no let-up in the central state regulation of education. The state regulation of the curriculum has continued, while OFSTED school inspections subject schools to an intense and highly public scrutiny. Performance targets have been laid down at every level. Schools that are judged to be failing and schools that miss targets are subject to a range of interventions to bring them into line. There is not only a continuing preoccupation with educational standards but also a growing concern with behavioural problems, linked to wider public order and criminality issues.

In higher education, too, New Labour has largely continued Conservative policies. Expansion has continued and Labour's target is to raise the participation rate of 18 year-olds to 50 per cent. It has also continued to shift the funding of higher education from the taxpayer to students and their parents. It was under Labour that the student grant was abolished and the student payment of fees was introduced, with reductions and exemptions for low-earning families. The rationale for this shift was the higher earnings that graduates could command, though estimates of the additional career income earned by graduates were revised down sharply in 2005, from the previous government claim of £400,000 to £150,000 (*Guardian Education,*

31 May 2005). Whether the greater burden placed on students and their families is compatible with the continued expansion of higher education remains to be seen.

From 2006 universities (in England) will be able to increase their fees up to £3,000 per year. Payment will be made easier, since the fees can be financed by loans that are not repayable until a graduate is earning at least £15,000 per year. In principle, variable fees will allow a market to develop, but in practice most universities are planning to charge the full £3,000, since even those with recruitment difficulties fear they will appear second-rate if they do not charge the full amount. Competition between universities will take place through the bursaries that they offer students, the facilities they provide, and the effectiveness of their branding and marketing. Universities charging increased fees are required to conclude an Access Agreement with the Director of the Office for Fair Access, known appropriately as OFFA, to show that they have safeguarded access for underrepresented groups. All this illustrates well the problems involved in trying to contrive an education market-place while pursuing directive policies.

Labour has increased the state funding of education and declares that it will continue to do so. Extra funding has gone particularly into the education of under-fives, for this is seen as critical to greater equality of opportunity. Particular efforts have also been made to increase the number of teachers and recruit classroom support staff to assist them. Higher education has not done well, with funding per student continuing to fall until 2004–5, and a shifting of the financial burden from the state to students and their families. As a proportion of GNP, state expenditure on education in the UK was still no higher in 2005 than in 1995 (*Guardian Education*, 26 April 2005). Thus, although education has been declared a high national priority, a higher proportion of national resources has not been directed towards it.

Greater opportunities

While there are differences of emphasis and detail between Conservative and Labour education policies, the continuities are very striking. Diversity, competition, league tables, choice, selection, and standards have been as characteristic of Labour policy as that of the Conservatives. Labour governments, like the previous Conservative governments, have combined increasing state regulation with the development of market mechanisms and privatization. The pressure on children, students, teachers, schools, colleges, universities, and local education authorities to improve standards has steadily increased.

But what about the old Labour agenda of increasing equality of opportunity? Here New Labour has employed the rhetoric of 'levelling up' and inclusion. Equality is to be achieved by forcing up the standards of institutions, bringing state schools up to the standards of the private sector, and raising the standards of poorly performing state schools to those of the best. Pockets of illiteracy and innumeracy are to be eliminated by special policies that target them. Greater access to higher education will mean that more young people will be able to go to university.

The raising of standards and the widening of access may be highly desirable goals but it is difficult to see that they will actually increase equality of opportunity, because so many mechanisms are operating against this:

- the increasing diversity and hierarchy of educational institutions;
- greater competition for resources and growing inequality *between* educational institutions;
- more selection placing hurdles in front of those with disadvantages;
- parental choice giving advantages to those with more knowledge and resources.

Opportunities have increased but this does not mean that there is an increasing equality of opportunity. Some of those from disadvantaged backgrounds will benefit, since they will obtain educational qualifications that they would not otherwise have achieved. Those with knowledge and resources are, however, much better placed to exploit these opportunities. Recent changes in British education have been driven by the pressures of international competition in an ever more globalized world rather than the earlier drive to reduce inequality.

◆ *Stop and reflect*

In this section we have examined the transformation of education in the 1980s and 1990s. We first considered the changing relationship between state and economy in Britain.

- Governments have placed increasing emphasis on the economic functions of education.
- Consider the relationship between globalization and education policy.
- Do recent changes in education provide support for the approach taken by Bowles and Gintis?

We went on to examine the introduction of 'a regulated market-place' in first schools and then higher education.

- Market principles were introduced by diminishing local education authority control, increasing competition, and providing more parental choice.

- Do these changes result in more rather than less state control?
- Consider the implications of these changes for patterns of inequality.

Lastly, we discussed the character of government education policy.

- The reforms of the 1980s were driven by 'neo-liberalism' and 'authoritarian populism'. Make sure that you understand the meaning of these terms.
- Have the post-1997 Labour governments simply continued the policies introduced by the previous Conservative governments?

◆ *Chapter summary*

In the 'Understanding education' section of this chapter we examined different approaches to the relationship between education and society.

We first considered the part played by education in the process of socialization:

- According to Durkheim, education provided a sense of common membership in society and taught moral behaviour and self-discipline.
- According to Parsons, education transmitted values of achievement and taught children to achieve.

We went on to the relationship between education and inequality, which has been one of the main issues in the sociology of education:

- According to Parsons, education provided equality of opportunity and also legitimated inequality.
- Other sociologists, notably Bernstein, Bourdieu, and Ball, have shown how class background confers important advantages on those who are better off.

Lastly, we considered the relationship between education and capitalism:

- Functionalists saw education as meeting the needs of society.
- Marxist writers argued that it served the interests of the owners of capital.
- Willis showed, however, that education could generate an oppositional culture as well.

The next section outlined 'the Development of education in Britain':

- The expansion of elementary education in the nineteenth century was driven by religious, moral, and political concerns rather than economic needs.
- Free state secondary education for all was not provided until the Education Act of 1944, which created a tripartite structure with selection at age 11.
- Concerns with the unreliability, unfairness, and waste that resulted from selection at age 11 led to a movement to introduce comprehensive schools.
- Higher education was slow to develop and Britain's economic problems have been blamed on an anti-industrial culture in elite educational institutions.
- Mass higher education began with the expansion of universities in the 1960s and the Robbins Report's principle that all those who could benefit from higher education should have access to it.

- British education was internally divided, selective, and elitist in comparison with other industrial societies.

The next section examined 'Inequalities in British education'.

We first considered the impact of educational reforms on class inequality:

- It has been demonstrated that selection at age 11 on the basis of ability had no significant effect on class differences in boys' entry to selective schools.
- There is evidence that comprehensive schools marginally reduced class differences in educational achievement but streaming has reproduced them.

We then considered the significance of gender:

- During the nineteenth century girls were educated separately and largely excluded from higher education.
- Although the schooling of boys and girls became increasingly integrated, gender differences persisted through both formal and hidden curricula.
- Recently girls have overtaken boys in educational performance, though gender differences persist in subject choice.

Variations in educational achievement have also been linked to ethnicity:

- Ethnic groups vary in their educational achievement, though their success rates also change.
- Much of this variation may be explained by class differences and there are also important gender differences within ethnic groups.

In 'Education in transformation' we examined the transformation of education in the 1980s and 1990s.

Increasing international competition and occupational changes led governments to place more emphasis on the economic functions of education.

- There was a new emphasis on skills, standards, and vocational education.
- Higher education was expanded to meet the supposed needs of a 'knowledge-based economy'.

Schools were subjected to market forces but also greater state regulation:

- The introduction of market principles involved less local education authority control, greater competition, and increased parental choice.
- Greater diversity and increased selection strengthened the hierarchical tendencies in British education.

Continued

- Selection and choice led to greater inequality.
- There was increased state regulation through the national curriculum, national testing, and intensified inspection.
- Similar processes occurred in higher education:

  The transformation of education was driven by government policy:

- Conservative policies in the 1980s were motivated by increasing international competition, neo-liberal beliefs, and authoritarian populism.
- The post-1997 Labour governments have largely continued, indeed, strengthened, the main features of the Conservative education revolution.

Key concepts

- authoritarian populism
- correspondence principle
- cultural capital
- cultural-deprivation theory
- education
- elaborated codes

- functionalism
- hidden curriculum
- meritocracy
- neo-liberalism
- new vocationalism
- oppositional subculture

- parentocracy
- reproduction of class
- reproduction of labour
- restricted codes
- social capital

Workshop 9

Study 9 The employability of graduates

The economy's need for more highly educated employees has become one of the truisms of education policy. Not only is it argued that a knowledge-based economy requires more and better graduates, it is also claimed that higher education is a passport to a good job and higher earnings. In *The Mismanagement of Talent*, Brown and Hesketh (2004) have subjected these notions to a searching critique, supported by research into company selection practices and the experience of graduates.

They reject the idea that we now live in a knowledge-based economy. In the most advanced economy in the world, the US economy, only one-fifth of the current labour force could reasonably be described as 'knowledge workers'. In the United Kingdom the proportion of knowledge workers is probably higher and may be around one-third of the labour force. Most workers are still engaged in service or routine production work. This leads them to conclude that 'there is no prospect of the graduate labour market expanding in line with the increased supply of graduates' (2004: 63).

The result is inevitably an intense graduate competition for jobs. The employability of graduates is supposedly a matter of whether they have acquired the right skills and knowledge for the job but so many applicants for any given job have these skills and knowledge that their possession does not make someone employable. Brown and Hesketh argue that employability should be redefined to include what they call the realities of 'positional conflict' (2004: 7). Whether one secures employment depends on one's competitive position and this is a matter of the 'personal capital' that has been accumulated.

Personal capital includes the 'hard currency' of qualifications, work experience, and other objective achievements but also the 'soft currency' of interpersonal skills, leadership qualities, appearance, and accent (2004: 35). Cultural and social capital (see pp. 324–6 of this chapter) are clearly of great importance here, as is the status of the educational institutions attended. In spite of their demands for the supply of better qualified labour and their recruitment rhetoric, many companies still select on the basis of elitist criteria. The assumption is that 'the best students go to the best universities because they are the most difficult to get into' (2004: 219).

From their interviews with graduates, Brown and Hesketh construct two ideal types: *players* and *purists*. Players saw the search for employment as a competitive game with rules that had to be learned and followed if one was to be successful. Purists saw this search as a technical and meritocratic process of matching abilities with job requirements in which those who were best for the job would win out. Players would present themselves in ways that enabled them to win the game, while purists would act as they really were. Players saw their work as a means of developing their career, while purists saw it as expressing their true selves. The players' approach to their career was to maximize their advancement by moving around between employers, while purists were more concerned with progression within an organization (2004: 125).

Interviewees did not fit these types exactly but roughly one-third could be placed in each with a third falling between them. Graduates falling into one type might anyway change their strategy as a result of their experience. One might expect that the players would tend to win out but Brown and Hesketh warn that their success depends on properly understanding the rules of the game, learning to play it effectively, and convincing employers that they are genuine and not 'faking it'.

The intensification of graduate competition for jobs has broader implications for education. It creates great anxiety among the middle classes, which increases the competition for access to elite institutions at every level. One aspect of this is the ongoing debate over entry criteria to universities and the complaint that some universities, pushed by government policy, are now privileging those from state schools. Another is the greater importance attached to choice and the frantic parental manoeuvring to get children into the 'best' schools.

Note: The arguments around the growth of a knowledge-based economy are quite similar to the debate over 'post-industrial' society and you may find it helpful to read our discussion of this in Chapter 17, pp. 691–3.

❓ What aspects of the academic market-place (see pp. 348–51) does this examination of employability highlight?

❓ Do you see yourself as a player or a purist?

Media watch 9 How do you choose a school?

Providing opportunities for parents to choose their children's schools has been a central plank of both Conservative and Labour education policies (see sections on 'A regulated market-place' and 'From Thatcherism to New Labour'). Exercising the right to choose has, however, proved a complex business.

A new system of coordinated admissions was introduced on an experimental basis for London schools in 2004. Coordination was a way of preventing parents making multiple applications to a large number of schools in different areas and then sitting on the offers until they discovered whether their favourite school had offered a place. It was a perfectly rational thing for parents to do but it greatly delayed offers to other children as the schools waited for responses to their earlier offers. This was clearly unfair to those waiting, in some cases till the beginning of the school year, to know where their child would go. The new coordinated scheme allowed parents to state a preference to their education authority for at least three schools, in rank order. A computer program would then offer a place at the highest-ranked school possible, taking account of the school's vacancies and admissions criteria. Problem solved?

Not exactly . . . Schools want to give preference to those who have made them their first choice. Some local education authorities therefore operate a first preference system, which gives priority to those who have made a school their first choice. Surrey is one such authority. This led to a difficult situation for one family, whose predicament was described in the *Guardian* article below. The family in question wanted to apply for a place at a prestigious grammar school but this would mean facing the hurdle of an 11+ exam. Their second choice was a local comprehensive with a good reputation but this was in high demand and their child might not get in if it was not their first choice. Their third choice was a much less desirable school. If they went for their first choice and their child failed the 11+, they could well end up with their third. So they felt forced to go for their second choice school.

The first preference system clearly made this situation particularly difficult but there is a fundamental problem here which no system can avoid. If parents go for a first-choice school that is in high demand or is highly selective, they risk not getting a place and then having to settle for a much less desirable school than they could otherwise have got. Choosing a school requires careful study not only of schools' qualities and achievements but also of their admissions criteria and a careful calculation of your child's chances. As Stephen Ball (2003*a*) has argued, the middle-class activation of social capital involves uncertainty and anxiety.

Source: *Guardian Education*, 26 October 2004.

❓ Parents are told they have choice but who does the choosing?

❓ How does greater school diversity affect the process of choice?

❓ Which parents benefit most from parental choice?

❓ What are the advantages and disadvantages of choice?

Discussion points

Educational capital

- How useful are the concepts of 'cultural capital' and 'social capital' in enabling us to understand patterns of educational advantage and disadvantage?

Read the sections on these concepts in 'Education and inequality' and make sure that you understand the meaning of these concepts.

- Why is the term 'capital' used in these concepts?
- What is the relationship between 'cultural' and 'social' capital?
- Are these concepts helpful in understanding patterns of ethnic and gender inequality?
- Consider whether the notion of subcultural capital is a useful extension of these ideas.

Diversity and choice

- What is the significance of increased school choice?

Read the sections on 'Choice, selection, and inequality', 'New Labour in government', and Media watch 9.

- Why did greater choice of school become a priority of education policy?
- What are the implications of greater choice for patterns of inequality? Does everyone get greater choice?
- What are the disadvantages of being given choice?
- Do you think that there should be greater diversity of schools?
- Should parents be offered greater choice?

Graduate employability

- Has higher education been over-expanded?

Read the sections on 'Education and economic success' and 'Higher education', the Global focus box on p. 346, and Study 9.

- What is meant by a 'knowledge-based-economy'?
- Why do you think that higher education has expanded?
- What have been the consequences for the employability of graduates?
- What is meant by 'personal capital'? Consider its relationship to the concepts of 'cultural' and 'social' capital.
- Think about your personal capital and try applying this concept to your employability.

Explore further

The following cover most of the issues dealt with in this chapter:

Ball, S. (2004) (ed.), *The Routledge Falmer Reader in the Sociology of Education* (London: Routledge Falmer). *A personal collection of classic and contemporary texts.*

Coffey, A. (2001), *Education and Social Change* (Buckingham: Open University Press). *A careful, reflective and theoretically informed examination of current issues in the sociology of education and education policy.*

Halsey, A., Lauder, H., Brown, P., and Stuart Wells, A. (1997) (eds.), *Education: Culture, Economy, and Society* (Oxford: Oxford University Press). *A comprehensive reader, which has become a standard work.*

Mckenzie, J. (2001), *Changing Education: A Sociology of Education* (London: Prentice Hall). *A useful introduction which examines the development of British education from 1944 to the present day.*

Particular topics can be followed up through:

Archer, L. (2003), *Race, Masculinity, and Schooling: Muslim Boys and Education* (Maidenhead: Open University Press). *A discussion of the complex interaction of gender and ethnicity through an analysis of the views of Muslim boys.*

Ball, S. (2003), *Class Strategies and the Education Market: The Middle Classes and Social Advantage* (London: Routledge Falmer). *A theoretically informed discussion of class strategies that draws on interviews with parents and children.*

Brown, P., and Hesketh, A. (with Williams, S.) (2004), *The Mismanagement of Talent: Employability and Jobs in the Knowledge Economy* (Oxford: Oxford University Press). *A powerful critique of the notion that mass higher education enhances employability.*

Chitty, C. (2004), *Education Policy in Britain* (Basingstoke: Palgrave Macmillan). *Very clear and up-to-date coverage of policy-making from 1944 to New Labour.*

Gardner, R., Cairns, J., and Lawton, D. (2004) (eds.), *Faith Schools: Consensus or Conflict* (London: Routledge Falmer). *Provides different perspectives and lots of material from Britain and other countries on a hot topic.*

Illich, I. (1973), *Deschooling Society* (Harmondsworth: Penguin). *A classic critique of schooling which argues that education should not be confused with what goes on in schools.*

Jackson, C. (2006), *Lads and Ladettes in School* (Buckingham: Open University Press). *Explores how girls as well as boys adopt laddish ways of behaving in schools, linking up theories of masculinity and femininity to the sociology of education.*

Tomlinson, S. (2001), *Education in a Post-Welfare Society* (Buckingham: Open University Press). *A very useful account of recent educational policies and the way that they have combined centralization and competition.*

 ## Online resources

Visit the Online Resource Centre that accompanies this book to access more learning resources and other interesting material on education at:

www.oxfordtextbooks.co.uk/orc/fulcher3e/

The *Guardian Education* website is a useful source of articles, special reports, and data on all aspects of education:

www.education.guardian.co.uk/

The British Educational Research Association publishes the *British Educational Research Journal* (an online version is available to subscribing libraries) and organizes conferences:

www.bera.ac.uk/

The website of the Department for Education and Skills provides information about government policy and funded research on education and training:

www.dfes.gov.uk

The National Literacy Trust has a wide-ranging website that covers all aspects of education with extensive and clearly organized links to other materials:

www.literacytrust.org.uk/

communication and the media

Contents

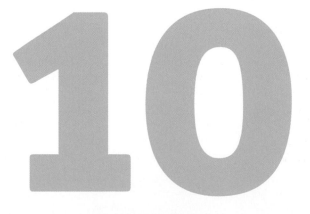

Globalizing Coronation Street

Joy Luck Street is the Chinese *Coronation Street*. In 2000 Granada signed a £15 million contract with a Beijing company to produce 500 episodes of a Chinese version of 'the street'. Script-writers and producers went out to help the Chinese produce their first soap opera. Granada hoped that this would lead to the marketing of other versions elsewhere in the world.

Granada believed that *Coronation Street* had a universal appeal. A Granada spokesman declared that 'people have affairs, they have heartbreaks, they lose their jobs, they have aspirations—all those things are absolutely universal'. *Joy Luck Street* would have characters modelled on those of *Coronation Street*, Chinese equivalents of Mike Baldwin or Audrey Roberts, though it would be less nostalgic and 'more aspirational'. There would be a local bar corresponding to the Rovers Return and the corner shop would be a store selling noodles, but *Joy Luck Street* would be located in a 'modern high-rise development'.

Some storylines and characters were, none the less, dropped. Some storylines would bewilder Chinese viewers. In a country where pregnancy terminations were common, because of its one-child policy, people would not find anguish over an abortion decision interesting or comprehensible. There were also political issues. Three Chinese censors were attached to the production team and some scripts were mysteriously changed to eliminate radically minded characters.

Even with these changes, the *Coronation Street* model proved less popular than expected and *Joy Luck Street* attracted only half the anticipated audience. The Chinese audiences considered the programme too depressing and too focused on the miseries of its characters. It was relaunched as *New Joy Luck Street* in November 2001. This time round it would be less British, have more comedy sketches, and contain characters that were attractive to Chinese viewers. According to Granada, more 'joy' would be put into *Joy Luck Street*. It continued to struggle to reach its target audience.

Sources: *Independent*, 20 June 2000; *Daily Telegraph*, 2 September 2001.

We live in a media-saturated world and the media consume a lot of our time but what influence do they have on the way we feel, think, and act? Do newspapers influence the way that we vote? Does screen violence make us behave more violently? A lot of research has gone into trying to answer these questions and we discuss in this chapter the issues that they raise.

There are another set of questions about media content. Who determines what we read in the newspapers or see on the television news? Is it the journalists, the editors, or the corporations? Or are they all simply trying to give us what we want in order to maximize audiences and sales? We examine what journalists do, and patterns of ownership and influence.

There is now a bewildering amount of choice, as terrestrial, satellite, and cable delivery systems provide us with hundreds of channels, while the Internet makes vast amounts of material available. But is this sense of choice illusory? Do we choose or are choices made for us? We consider whether governments manipulate the flow of information, and whether commercialization distorts media content.

Communications have become global. Does this mean that national cultures disappear as culture becomes global?

Or does the culture of the United States, the main exporter of films and television programmes, become *the* global culture? As our opening piece shows, those exporting programmes to other countries have to at least sometimes take account of the existing culture of the audience. Later in the chapter we examine the globalization of the media and its impact on cultural diversity.

Understanding the media

Communication and language

Animals communicate but only humans communicate through language. The distinctive feature of language is that words carry meanings, which we learn initially through socialization and education. Communication through language depends upon these meanings being shared.

We also communicate in many non-verbal ways, through, for example, body language, but the same processes of attaching and learning meaning apply. Thus, we learn that the 'thumbs up' sign means that 'things are OK'. We communicate through images too. A holiday snap can communicate our well-being on holiday and inform people that we have been somewhere fashionable. The term 'image' has, indeed, been extended to mean not just a representation of something but also the impression of ourselves that we communicate to other people. We create an image through the style we adopt, and the clothes that we wear communicate a great deal about us (see box on 'Communication through dress'). These non-verbal ways of communication carry learned and shared meanings and may also be considered languages.

Languages are much more than a means of communication, for they also express and shape the way that we see the world and the way that we see ourselves. If you say that you are British, you are not just stating which country you live in. This presupposes a way of seeing the world that divides it up between nation states. It indicates that you see yourself as British, rather than, say, English or Scottish, and carries with it ideas of national character. The importance of language is not only that it allows us to communicate, but also that it gives us an identity. Without it we would not know who we are.

Communication occurs not only through face-to-face interaction but also through various forms of recorded and transmitted images and sounds. These means of communication are generally termed the **media** (note that this is the plural of medium), because they mediate between those who give information and those who receive it. We usually use the term to refer to television, newspapers, and radio, sometimes films, and this chapter will be mainly concerned with these media, but we should bear in mind that there are many others, such as paintings, books, graffiti, and the

---

Frontiers Communication through dress

One way in which we communicate our identity is through dress and the structuring of this communication tells us a lot about a society. In some communities there are rigid dress codes which allow no individuality and require complete conformity. Religious communities have operated codes of this kind, and examples such as the *burqa* or the 'habit' readily spring to mind.

Religious dress codes may appear totally resistant to change but some religious communities have allowed greater choice of religious dress as they adapt to social change. Free choice of dress to express personal identity is indeed seen as a characteristic feature of the more complex world we now live in, though codes still operate. William Keenan suggests that the result is a 'dual dress economy':

'To survive within and pass successfully through the differentiated and multiple cultural environments we inhabit today we need to be able to adapt our dress code responses. The idea that we have at least two wardrobes, that we inhabit a dual dress economy, where a formal and a casual option is available to us, where classical and modern items mix and mingle as a matter of course within our dressways, could be said to be the characteristic message given out by the postmodern dress code system.' (Keenan 2004: 55)

❷ What does what you are wearing today communicate about your identity and your community?

❷ What processes and influences shaped your choice of clothing?

❷ What does your choice of dress say about the kind of community/society you live in?

What does the wearing of the *burqa* communicate?
© Getty Images/Yoray Liberman

Web, which all enable communication over distance and time.

The media and society

The media are central to the way our society functions. Television, newspapers, and radio have been the principal means through which people obtain information. Indeed, if the media do not cover an event or an issue, it is unlikely that anyone other than those immediately involved will know anything about it. The media not only inform us selectively about events; they actually shape them. Politicians or public relations agencies or advertisers construct 'media events' in ways that will maximize their coverage by the media and create images of a favourable kind.

The media play a key role in cultural, economic, and political activities. They largely create popular culture.

They are crucial to the functioning of the economy because of their role in the marketing of goods and services. Politicians use them to manipulate voters and elections may well be won or lost through them. Indeed, one of the first things that the leaders of any revolution or military *coup* will do is to seize control of the radio and television studios.

The relationship between the media and society has been discussed from a number of perspectives and in this section we will examine the main approaches that have emerged.

Manipulation and domination

The development of the media opened up new opportunities for the manipulation and domination of people by both governments and business. Technology enabled the media to reach ever larger numbers of people, particularly with the invention of radio and television, which could

Figure 10.1 Mass-society theory

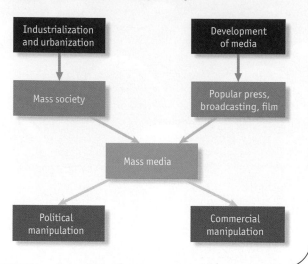

broadcast messages to huge audiences simultaneously. The media became **mass media** in the sense that they could reach the broad masses of the population.

Mass-society theory (see Figure 10.1) has explored the manipulative possibilities provided by mass media. This theory was based not only on the capacity of the media to reach large numbers of people but also on their new vulnerability to manipulation. According to this theory, industrialization and urbanization had atomized society, which had become a mass of isolated individuals after traditional community and family structures disintegrated. Social isolation meant that people were particularly open to influence by the media.

> **⟳ Connections**
> Louis Wirth's notion of an 'urban way of life', which we discuss in 'Urban society', Chapter 13, pp. 493–4, embodied ideas very similar to those of mass-society theory. He argued that the decline of community led to social disintegration and instability in the city.

Mass-society theorists, such as Kornhauser (1960), were much concerned with the dangers of both political and commercial manipulation. The fascist leaders of the 1930s, such as Hitler and Mussolini, had been very skilful at using the media to mobilize and control people. As Strinati (1995: 5) has put it, mass-society theorists believed that 'mass media equalled mass propaganda equalled mass repression'. They also believed that the rise of a 'culture industry' would result in the creation of a standardized and commercialized mass culture, a view of culture which we discuss further on pp. 366–7.

The **dominant-ideology** approach too saw the media as highly influential, though it held a very different view of the nature of society (see also our discussion of this in Chapter 20, p. 821). It rejected the idea that industrialization and urbanization produced a mass of isolated and disorganized individuals and drew from Marxist theory the notion of a society divided into classes. It argued that *subordinate* classes are dominated by the ideas and beliefs of a *ruling* class. In Marx's famous words:

> The ideas of the ruling class are, in every age, the ruling ideas: i.e. the class, which is the dominant *material* force in society, is at the same time its dominant *intellectual* force. (Marx 1845–6: 93)

This approach to the media has been much influenced by the ideas of Antonio Gramsci, who was critical of the economic determinism of some Marxists and argued that they failed to recognize the role of ideas in class domination and class conflict. According to Gramsci, the ruling class maintained its authority not just by coercion but by establishing hegemony. By **hegemony** he meant the ideological domination of society by the ruling class, which persuaded other classes to accept its values and beliefs so that a general consensus emerged around them. According to Gramsci, the reason why socialist and communist movements had failed was that the ruling class had won the battle of ideas. A revolutionary movement could not succeed unless it first challenged the hegemony of the ruling class and wrested the control of ideas from it.

Miliband (1969) spelled out the ways in which the ruling class was able to control people's ideas through the media. These were largely in private ownership, which was

---

THEORY AND METHODS

Antonio Gramsci

Antonio Gramsci (1891–1937) was born in Sardinia. He studied at the University of Turin but left to become a socialist journalist. He was closely associated with the factory-councils movement of the Turin workers, which sought to establish a system of direct industrial democracy. He was one of the founders of the Italian Communist Party in 1924 and was arrested because of his political activities in 1926. He died in prison in 1937. It was during his years in prison that he wrote his major work *Prison Notebooks*. Unlike most Marxist theorists, he developed his ideas not in a university context but out of his practical experience of political work. His most well-known contribution to Marxist theory is the concept of hegemony. An introduction to his work can be found in Ransome (1992).

concentrated in a few hands. The owners of the media were not only major capitalists in their own right but also closely connected with ruling circles. They used their control of the media to support right-wing parties by presenting ruling-class interpretations of events and preventing the discussion of alternative interpretations.

More generally, it has been argued that the media play a key part in getting people to accept inequality, for they gain most of their knowledge of the world from the media, which treat inequality as a normal, natural, and inevitable fact of life. The media also divert people's attention from the exploitation and inequality characteristic of capitalist society by glorifying and encouraging consumption (Murdock and Golding 1977).

But how dominant is the dominant ideology? There is a tension in this approach between the notion of a dominant ideology and the idea that subordinate classes have their own beliefs based on their class situation (J. Clarke *et al.* 1976). Arguably, these beliefs can provide a basis for challenging the dominant ideology. Furthermore, such challenges can be assisted by analyses of the media that reveal the ways in which people are manipulated.

The significance of ideology has also been queried. Abercrombie *et al.* (1979) recognized that a dominant ideology exists but argued that its importance in maintaining capitalism had been exaggerated. They held the view that capitalism is maintained primarily by what Marx called the 'dull compulsion of economic relations'. Workers accept capitalism because they have no real choice. They have to work in order to live and it is the capitalist economy that provides them with employment. Their beliefs have little to do with it.

Consumption and production

Both mass-society and Marxist theory assumed that the content of the media is shaped by those who own and control them. An alternative approach argues that the content of the media is determined by market forces. Thus the content of, say, newspapers is shaped not by their owners but by the readers who buy them. Newspapers and broadcasters are ultimately concerned with circulation and audience figures. The market rules and the media will serve up whatever the consumer wants.

The problem faced by this approach is that it cannot explain why the readers hold the views they do. It takes these views as given. It also treats those who own and control the media as passive, when there is plenty of evidence that many of them hold strong opinions and see the media as vehicles for their political beliefs. It is, none the less, true that most media operations have to make profits and cannot afford to alienate readers or audiences.

Yet another approach argues that it is the producers who determine the content of the media. Journalists and programme producers have an important degree of autonomy. They are professionals with their own values and their own occupational associations. There is certainly some truth in this view, for the media do depend on creative people with specialized occupational skills. An understanding of media content requires the study of those who produce it, as in Tunstall's (1971) classic study of journalists at work.

Tunstall certainly recognized, however, that the professionals work under constraints of various kinds. They have to operate within the organizations that employ them. They are controlled by editors, who are ultimately controlled by owners. Their careers depend on the approval of others and they are in competition with colleagues. They are also dependent on those who provide them with information (Tunstall 1995). At most, they have a very limited autonomy.

We will take up this issue again in the section on 'Constructing the news'.

A public sphere?

The autonomy not only of media professionals but also of a public sphere has been an important issue in the study of the media. The concept of a **public sphere** refers to a space where people can freely discuss matters of general importance to them as citizens. The eighteenth-century idea of human rights, especially the right to vote, and the rights to free speech and free assembly, was crucial in establishing this notion.

Jürgen Habermas developed an influential theory of the development and decline of the public sphere. He saw this as first emerging in eighteenth-century coffee houses, where people of all kinds could meet and freely discuss any matter in a non-commercial atmosphere, uncontrolled by church or state. He considered that the rise of commercialized and manipulative mass media led to the decline of the public sphere. This contrast was, however, overdrawn. The coffee houses were hardly accessible to the public as a whole, while the mass media do in various ways allow for the discussion of matters of public interest. In Britain, the BBC was established within a public-service framework and public-service ideals remain influential in British broadcasting. Habermas's ideas have, none the less, struck a chord among those concerned with the decline of the public functions of the media (Boyd-Barrett 1995).

The relationship between the state and public sphere has been a complex one. The public sphere needs protection from commercial pressures if it is to flourish and such protection depends on state regulation of commercial interests. The state is in other ways, however, an enemy of the public sphere, for governments seek to control or manipulate the political content of the media and turn them into an instrument of government. The public sphere needs protection from the state as well. The BBC has had an uneasy relationship with governments and, as we shall show later, its ideal of public service has at times appeared to mean service to the state. In 'Decline of the public sphere?', we examine the increasing pressures on this sphere from both governments and commercial interests.

The idea of a public sphere also implies some distinction between public and private matters. Media space and time have become increasingly taken up with material from private life, which pushes out the discussion of public affairs. While commercial pressures have largely driven this, politicians and other public figures have played their part by using the media to project their personalities and families. Media revelations can, however, do considerable damage to public figures, and this has led to calls for privacy legislation to regulate unwelcome media intrusions. Significantly, the concern is with the protection of privacy rather than the maintenance of a public sphere where matters of general interest to citizens are discussed.

The media and culture

Culture has been central to the issues that we have been discussing. If the media shape the way that people think and live, then it is largely through popular culture that they must do this. There has been a growing interest in the sociology of 'popular culture' and in this section we will examine what we mean by this term and the main approaches to it, but we first need to set popular culture in the context of the development of different kinds of culture.

Folk, high, and popular culture

The distinction between **folk culture** and **high culture** originated with pre-industrial society, where there was a *high* culture of the aristocratic elite that was separate from the *folk* or *low* culture of the ordinary people. Folk culture consisted of local customs and beliefs that were handed down by word of mouth from one generation to the next. While high culture was associated with the arts, folk culture was associated with crafts.

With industrialization and urbanization, a new, increasingly commercialized culture emerged among the people. It was a mixture of elements of the old folk culture and the new way of life in the industrial cities. It affected the content of the media, as they sought larger circulations and audiences, but it was in turn shaped by media influences. This new form of culture came to be called **popular culture**.

While the term 'popular culture' is widely used, it is not easy to specify what it means. Three different meanings are commonly found:

- *That which is not high culture.* This elitist way of defining popular culture assumes that we know what high culture is and implies that popular culture is inferior. Even within its own terms it is difficult to apply, for the boundaries between the two are hard to establish and particular items of culture move across them. Thus, Shakespeare and Dickens originally provided popular entertainment but are now treated by many as high culture.

- *What most people like and do.* This raises the issue of how popular a cultural trait has to be in order to be classified as popular. Pop songs are commonly regarded as part of popular culture but the latest fashion in rock music may not actually be at all popular in this sense. The notion of a culture of the majority does not, anyway, fit easily with the diversity of culture, which varies, for example, by class and ethnicity.

- *Culture created by the people.* This gets round the problem of how popular something needs to be in order to be part of popular culture. Folk music, pigeon-fancying, train-spotting, and rugby league—the list is endless—can all be regarded as popular in this sense, even if they are all minority interests. But does pop music originate from the people or from recording studios funded by transnational corporations? The notion of 'the people' is, anyway, more than a little vague. Does it include the middle class?

The distinction between popular and high culture is rejected by post-modernists. They do not distinguish between different kinds of culture, but treat all its manifestations as equal, and combine them freely. Plentiful evidence of the mixing and interpenetration of cultural styles can certainly be found in contemporary culture, whether in architecture, cinema, or advertising. As Strinati (1995) points out, this does not mean, however, that these distinctions no longer have any meaning. Indeed, post-modernists' jokey references to high culture actually presume its existence, since they would otherwise be pointless. 'Rather than dismantling the hierarchy of aesthetic and cultural taste, post-modernism erects a new one, placing itself on top' (Strinati 1995: 242).

> **Connections**
>
> We are referring to post-modern culture here but there is a broader post-modern perspective in contemporary thought and sociological theory, which is discussed in Chapter 2, pp. 64–6.

Mass culture, dominant culture, and subcultures

According to mass-society theory, which we examined above, popular culture was **mass culture**. The 'genuine' folk culture of the people was destroyed by a highly commercialized and standardized mass culture, which also undermined the standards of high culture.

Theodor Adorno and Max Horkheimer, prominent members of the Frankfurt school, used the term 'culture industry' to describe this transformation of culture (Adorno and Horkheimer 1986). Culture had become something that was made and sold, just like any other industrial product, in order to make a profit. It was, according to this view, forced on the masses by the culture industry and turned people into passive consumers of material that did not meet their 'real needs'. Mass culture was also crucial to the maintenance of a capitalist society. Workers were willing to accept boredom and exploitation at work because they could escape during their leisure hours into the pleasures of popular culture, by watching films or listening to popular music.

A debate between elitist and populist interpretations of popular culture has run through the literature on it. The elitist view valued the high culture of the arts and treated popular culture as commercial and trivial. Populist views, on the other hand, recognized the vitality and creativity of popular culture and argued that it expressed the experience of ordinary people. They saw popular culture as rooted in subcultures related to ethnicity or class.

Subcultures are the cultures of particular groups within society. The term is generally used to refer to youth cultures or the cultures of subordinate classes. The concept of sub-

culture, which literally means an 'under-culture', implies the existence of a dominant culture, a notion similar to that of dominant ideology, which we discussed above.

Some Marxist writers have seen subcultures based in subordinate classes as resisting the **dominant culture** and, potentially at least, challenging the social order. Thus, the subcultures that emerged among the young in the working class and middle class in the 1960s were described as 'counter-cultures' (Clarke *et al.* 1976). The 1960s styles of the 'mods', 'teds', and 'skinheads' were interpreted as challenges to the dominant culture (Hebdige 1979). As we noted in our discussion of the dominant-ideology approach, there is a tension in this literature between the idea that a dominant culture is imposed by the ruling class and the possibility of subcultural resistance to this culture.

This discussion situates the analysis of culture within the framework of class relationships in a capitalist society and enables us to make important links between the structure of a society and its culture. It helps us to understand not only the content of culture but also how the existing structure of a society can be both maintained and periodically challenged through culture. One problem with this literature is, however, that it tends to neglect those aspects of culture linked to gender, ethnicity, and nationality, and the conflicts taking place between dominant and subordinate groups along these other dimensions of inequality.

Cyberculture

The Internet and the World Wide Web have provided a new medium for culture, generally labelled **cyberculture**, because it exists in cyberspace, 'the conceptual space where computer networking hardware, network software and users converge' (Gauntlett 2000: 220).

The Internet and the Web made possible a culture apparently free of many of the constraints that operated in other media. The Web was decentralized and outside the control of governments, elites, and business corporations. Information could be freely exchanged without anyone censoring or editing it. When on the Net, people were anonymous and could assume, and play with, any identity they chose. With others they could construct their own virtual communities, their own society, their own world. They were free of their relationships, their communities, their bodies.

Indeed, Sherry Turkle (1997) argues that they can become free of themselves. They are no longer constrained by a 'unified self' and can be many different selves, exploring instead of suppressing those parts of their personality that do not fit their dominant identity. In a world of screens, this virtual world can become more real to people than the 'real world' and can shape their behaviour in the 'real world'. Aspects of identity developed in the virtual world can form the basis for relationships in the 'real world'.

THEORY AND METHODS
....

The Frankfurt school

The Frankfurt school is the name given to a group of left-wing thinkers associated with the Frankfurt Institute of Social Research. Founded in 1922, the institute moved to New York during the Nazi period, returned to Frankfurt in 1949, and was disbanded in 1969. Theodor Adorno (1903–69), Erich Fromm (1900–80), Max Horkheimer (1895–1973), and Herbert Marcuse (1898–1979) were prominent members of the school. Jürgen Habermas (1929–) has continued to develop their ideas.

The Frankfurt school found much of its inspiration in the work of the young Karl Marx on alienation (see Chapter 2, p. 28, for a discussion of this concept). It emphasized the way that the culture industry integrated workers into a capitalist society. The growth of mass consumption gave capitalist societies more stability, though there were still crisis tendencies in capitalism. Habermas (1973) has produced an influential theory of a sequence of crises that spread from the economic through the political to the cultural sphere.

➔ **Connections**
We discuss virtual communities in Chapter 13, pp. 518–19
and you might like to follow up these issues there.

Marginalized groups that have difficulty in asserting or even maintaining their particular cultures can communicate and rebuild their worlds through cyberculture. Dispersed minorities can, for example, create a newsgroup through Usenet. Similarly, deviant groups that find it hard to make their voices heard can establish a presence in cyberculture, develop their specific culture, and create a virtual community.

With the growth of what Silver (2000) has labelled 'critical cyberculture studies', the celebration of cyberculture has, however, been moderated by a growing awareness of its limitations. Many familiar constraints are at work behind the scenes.

The inequalities found in society at large are present in the world of the Internet too. The rapid rise in numbers of those using the Internet led people to view cyberculture as a new popular culture but there is plentiful evidence of a growing 'digital divide' between 'haves' and 'have-nots'. The digital divide in the United States has been described as a 'racial ravine'. Cyberspace has also been considered a predominantly male space, with a typically male 'frontier culture' (Silver 2000: 26–7).

Arguably, a 'technopower spiral' has brought about control by a technical elite. This spiral is the result of the vast, and ever increasing, amount of information available on the Web, which has led to the invention of advanced tools to enable users to find what they are seeking and manage the flow of information. It has become increasingly difficult for ordinary users to operate according to their own values, as they are dependent on the tools created and controlled by this technical elite. These tools are constructed according to the beliefs and values of the elite and in the language that it has developed (Jordan 1999: 101).

Nor is cyberculture free of commercial and political pressures. Commercial pressures are blatantly present in the pop-up advertising which finances so much 'free' activity. Commercial interests also steer and manipulate users in covert ways (see p. 394. of this chapter and the discussion of Web surveillance in Chapter 14, p. 572). Governments can find ways of censoring Web content, as in the pressure exerted by the government of China on Microsoft and Google (see box on 'Internet dissent in China' on p. 395).

This raises the broad question of quite how different cyberculture is from other cultural media. That it is different to some degree is undeniable. It does provide opportunities for individuals and groups to engage in cultural exploration in a *relatively* unconstrained way. Cyberculture is by no means immune, however, from the social processes of manipulation, domination, and commercialization that operate in society at large and shape culture in general.

Media influence and the audience

The mass-society and dominant-ideology approaches both assume that the media do actually have some influence on what people think and do. Whether they have such an influence has, however, been extensively debated and researched. In this section we examine theories of the influence of the media and then go on to consider the main methods used in the study of the media and their impact on people.

Models of media influence

Three main approaches to the influence of the media can be found in the literature:

- the media-effects model;
- the active-audience model;
- the media-themes model.

Also known as the 'hypodermic model', the *media-effects* approach assumes that audiences are passive and simply absorb injections of material from the media. It is characteristic of mass-society theory, some Marxist theories, and those who blame the media for the ills of society. Its view of the audience as passive has been challenged by the second model.

According to the *active-audience* model, audiences do not simply receive messages from the media. They select what they want to hear and interpret media messages according to their existing ideas and beliefs. To put it in a nutshell, they hear what they want to hear and see what they want to see, in which case the media tend to reinforce rather than change people's views.

While this model's emphasis on selection and interpretation provided a healthy correction to the previous notion of influential and all-powerful media, it went in some ways to the opposite extreme by exaggerating the freedom and choice of the audience. The *media-themes* model pursues more of a middle path. This is the kind of approach advocated by the Glasgow University Media Group (GUMG) and developed through their studies of television news. It recognizes that audiences are active but argues that the media do, none the less, influence them. In many ways it combines the insights of the other two approaches.

The GUMG found that the themes of media reporting corresponded closely with the ideas of audience groups. This was not just a matter of the main arguments in a programme but also of subtler themes in the language used and the images created. Indeed, members of the audience might reject opinions that did not fit their pre-existing beliefs but still pick up ideas and images that affected their view of the topic.

Media influence was then reinforced by social interaction. Thus, striking events or stories acquired 'social currency' and were passed around in conversation, which reinforced them in people's minds. The GUMG studies have shown how perceptions of key social issues, such as those surrounding AIDS, child abuse, food panics, mental illness, sexual violence, strikes, and the conflict in Northern Ireland, were influenced in this way by media coverage (Eldridge 1993a).

The GUMG has brought the idea of media influence back in, but its model of it is much more complex than the media-effects one. It recognizes that audiences are selective and interpretative but argues that audience activity actually increases media influence by involving the audience's interest and emotions. An active response is far more likely to result in something being carried away from a programme, discussed with others, and incorporated into ways of thinking and acting.

THEORY AND METHODS

Audience understandings of AIDS

The GUMG study of media influence on the knowledge and understanding of AIDS showed the importance of both the words and the pictures used by the media, and the associations created by media coverage.

- **Words.** Content analysis showed that the media made frequent reference to 'mixing bodily fluids' and the 'exchange of bodily fluids'. Audience research found that these words had stuck in people's minds and led them to fear that kissing could cause AIDS through contact with saliva, even though scientists had rejected this idea.

- **Pictures.** Media coverage often showed AIDS sufferers looking thin, haggard, and depressed. This image too stuck in some people's minds and led them to think that this appearance would enable them to recognize people with the AIDS virus. This undermined the health-education message that people with this virus can look quite normal for many years before they develop AIDS symptoms.

- **Associations.** Much of the early media coverage associated AIDS with homosexuality. There was little reference to lesbians but this association led people to think wrongly that lesbians were a high-risk group.

Source: Adapted from Kitzinger (1997: 6–11).

➲ Consider the news coverage of Africa or terrorism or Islam and see whether you can identify similar patterns of influence.

Methods of media research

Methods issues have been quite central to the debate over media influence, for different approaches have tended to use different methods. Here we will examine the advantages and disadvantages of the three main methods used:

- content analysis;
- textual analysis;
- audience research.

Early approaches focused on *content analysis*. Typically this involved quantitative studies of how often a particular item was covered by the media. These could establish the extent of the coverage of a topic, and certain basic aspects of it—whether it was covered, for example, in news reports, editorials, or commentaries. It could provide useful information on, say, how often strikes were reported in newspapers or on television.

There are two main problems with this approach. There is, first, the problem of meaning, for researchers are interested not just in how a topic is covered but in the slant of the coverage. It is not just a matter of how often a newspaper covers strikes but also of how it reports and interprets them. Does it adopt a managerial or a union perspective? A purely quantitative analysis of content cannot tell us this. There is, secondly, the problem of effect. Content analysis cannot tell us anything about how a given article or programme actually affects the audience.

The problem of meaning has been addressed by the more qualitative techniques of *textual analysis*. This approach drew on the techniques developed to analyse literary texts. It was also influenced by semiotics, the study of the meaning of signs, and is sometimes called the semiotic approach. It sought to penetrate behind words and images to uncover their meaning. The words or pictures used in reporting a strike could, for example, present a managerial account by emphasizing the stoppage of work and the loss of production. Alternatively, they could present a union perspective by focusing on workers' grievances. Through careful analysis of the text, its meaning could be revealed and its bias identified.

This approach also faced problems, however. It lacked objectivity. The researcher had to make assumptions about the meaning of the text and other researchers might interpret this differently. Would ordinary readers or viewers interpret it in the same way? There was also yet again the problem of effect. This approach too could not, on its own, tell us anything about the impact of the text on the audience.

To find out about this, it was necessary to carry out *audience research*. A commonly used method for doing this was to show a programme to an audience and assess its effect by making before and after comparisons. While this approach could provide evidence of effect, it ran into other problems of its own:

- *The research situation.* The audience was put into a contrived situation. Would they react to the programme in the same way outside this laboratory situation?
- *Long-term effects.* Studies of this kind could not get at the long-term and cumulative effects of exposure to the media. Do people gradually build up a way of looking at things through repeated exposure to a particular perspective?
- *The social context of influence.* Such studies could not take account of the way that audience ideas changed after they had discussed a programme with others.

All research methods have advantages and disadvantages. In spite of their disadvantages, *content analysis* and *textual analysis* have an important contribution to make. Thus, while *content analysis* can only take one so far, it is an important starting point, which can identify issues for audience research by mapping media coverage of a topic. It can also deal with some important questions, such as whether the media report on events in a balanced way, giving equal time, for example, to the views of different political parties. *Textual analysis* may be subjective but it can uncover hidden meanings by probing behind surface content.

Audience research, whatever its problems, is, however, the only way of addressing the question of media effects. It has also become more sophisticated in order to deal with the problems raised above. The GUMG, for example, has developed discussion-group techniques and script-writing exercises in order to probe into longer-term effects and examine the social context of media influence (Kitzinger 1997).

Particular pieces of research should not be rejected because of these problems but rather interpreted in the light of them. You should certainly bear them in mind when considering any research on the media.

Stop and reflect

In this section we first examined different approaches to the study of the relationship between media and society.

- We discussed the concepts of 'mass media' and 'mass society', and the alternative 'dominant ideology' approach.
- Consider whether these approaches exaggerate the extent to which people are manipulated by the media.
- Make sure that you are familiar with Habermas's concept of the public sphere.
- What are the main threats to the functioning of such a sphere?

We then examined different types of culture.

- Make sure that you know the meaning of the following terms: high and folk culture; popular culture and mass culture; post-modern culture; dominant culture and subculture; cyberculture.
- Does cyberculture enable freedom of communication?

Finally, we identified models of media influence and examined methods of media research.

- We identified the 'media-effects', 'active-audience', and 'media-themes' models of media influence.
- We examined the 'content analysis', textual analysis', and 'audience research' methods of media study.
- Which method would you use to investigate the media coverage of terrorism?

The rise of the mass media

Industrial societies not only produce and distribute goods and services, they also produce and distribute information and entertainment. Industrialization not only led to mass production, it also created mass media. In this part of the chapter we will examine the growth of these media and situate this within the development of a capitalist industrial society.

The print revolution

The earliest known book was printed in China in the year 868 and metal type was in use in Korea at the beginning of the fifteenth century, but it was in Germany around the year 1450 that a printing press using movable metal type was invented.

Capitalism turned printing from an invention into an industry. Right from the start, book printing and publishing were organized on capitalist lines. The biggest sixteenth-century printer, Plantin of Antwerp, had twenty-four printing presses and employed more than a hundred workers. Only a small fraction of the population was literate, but the production of books grew at an extraordinary speed. By 1500 some 20 million volumes had already been printed (Febvre and Martin 1976).

The immediate effect of printing was to increase the circulation of works that were already popular in a hand-written form, while less popular works went out of circulation. Publishers were interested only in books that would sell fairly quickly in sufficient numbers to cover the costs of production and make a profit. Thus, while printing enormously increased access to books by making cheap, high-volume production possible, it also reduced choice.

The great cultural impact of printing was that it facilitated the growth of national languages. Most early books were printed in Latin, the language of educated people, but the market for Latin was limited, and in its pursuit of larger markets the book trade soon produced translations into the national languages emerging at this time. Printing indeed played a key role in standardizing and stabilizing these languages by fixing them in print, and producing dictionaries and grammar books. Latin became obsolete as national literatures were established in the sixteenth century.

Newspapers

In Britain, newspapers first established themselves in the eighteenth century. They were initially concerned mainly with providing the middle class with business information, but a radical press grew up at the end of the century (E. P. Thompson 1963). The popular press first emerged in the 1820s with Sunday papers containing stories of murders and executions. In the second half of the nineteenth century, the *Daily Telegraph* pioneered the growth of a cheaper, more popular middle-class press. Finally, in the 1890s, the *Daily Mail*, followed by the *Daily Express* and the *Daily Mirror*, created a mass market for daily newspapers.

Newspapers had become a mass production industry by the end of the nineteenth century, and their financial basis changed as advertising became a greater source of earnings. Papers could now become cheaper than ever, though a large circulation to attract advertisers was also now more important than ever.

As the popular press sought to maximize readership, newspapers changed in character. Headlines became bigger and there was more illustration. Coverage of political

Briefing: press barons: newspapers owned by the Harmsworth brothers in 1921

- Lord Northcliffe (Alfred Harmsworth): *The Times, Daily Mail, Weekly Dispatch, London Evening News*
- Lord Rothermere (Vere Harmsworth): *Daily Mirror, Sunday Pictorial, Daily Record, Glasgow Evening News, Sunday Mail*
- Sir Lester Harmsworth: A chain of local papers in the south-west of England

Source: Curran and Seaton (1991: 50).

and economic matters declined, while sport, crime, sex, and human-interest stories increased. Between 1927 and 1937 the *Daily Mirror* halved the proportion of its news covering political, social, economic, and industrial issues (Curran and Seaton 1991: 67).

We discussed earlier the idea of a public sphere (see p. 365). Arguably, the rise of mass-circulation newspapers extended this by making news and views available to larger numbers of people. These newspapers had, however, driven out of business the radical press, which had generated political debate by challenging the dominant ideology. Furthermore, the decline of serious content in the mass-circulation newspapers, as the popular press became more concerned with entertainment than information, hardly promoted public discussion.

The transformation of the press into a mass-production, mass-circulation industry led to the concentration of ownership. Production had become capital intensive and large amounts of money were needed to set up a newspaper, while costs were reduced if the machinery was used to produce more than one. Small-circulation papers could not compete with the new mass dailies and were driven out of business. Already in 1910, 67 per cent of national daily circulation was in the hands of three owners and 69 per cent of national Sunday circulation in the hands of another three. By 1921 the Harmsworth brothers owned papers with a circulation of over six million (Curran and Seaton 1991: 51–2).

The era of the press barons raised acutely the question of press influence and the power of its owners. They made no secret of their intentions to use their papers for political purposes. They certainly exercised a detailed control over editorial content. But did their views actually influence their readers? Curran and Seaton have argued that it was not so much their direct as their indirect influence that mattered: 'Their main significance lay in the way in which their papers provided cumulative support for conservative values and reinforced opposition, particularly among the middle class, to progressive change' (1991: 61).

The barons' era has gone but ownership is still concentrated and the issues it raises have not gone away. We will return to these questions in 'Ownership and control'.

Cinema

The history of the press is long and readership built up steadily over a long period, but 'movies' burst upon the world at the end of the nineteenth century. They arrived in England in 1896 and by 1914 there were already 500 cinemas in London. As Corrigan (1983: 27) has put it, 'by 1914 going to the picture palace had become a normal activity'. The reproducibility of film meant that multiple copies could be made and films could be shown simultaneously to audiences across the world.

Going to the cinema could become a mass activity, however, only if ordinary people had the time and money for it. The reduction of working hours provided more leisure time, and in the 1920s and 1930s cinemas benefited from

the enforced leisure resulting from higher unemployment. The introduction of unemployment benefit meant that the unemployed could afford cheap seats. Films appealed particularly, however, to the young and to women. John Eldridge *et al.* (1997) have suggested that film-going was the first permissible leisure activity outside the home for women.

Films are often seen as an art form, with inspirational directors drawing on the creative talents of writers, actors, and camera crew to craft unique products. Such films have been made, but most have been produced on an industrial basis. Picture houses in Britain were eventually showing two new programmes each week, each typically containing two feature films. To meet this demand, studios had to churn them out on a routine basis and to a tight schedule. Like any other form of mass production, they were large-scale operations with a high division of labour and a bureaucratic structure.

Production and distribution were integrated and concentrated in the hands of Hollywood companies. Control of distribution was crucial, for this guaranteed outlets for production and shut out the competition. Distribution networks were able to dominate the market because film copies were cheap to produce and could be rented to a large number of cinemas at the same time. The distributors built up cinema chains to give them direct control of outlets and kept their grip on audiences through the star system (see box on 'The Hollywood star system'), for stars were the best guarantee of a large audience.

By 1914 Hollywood already had 60 per cent of the British market. In the 1920s it became completely dominant, producing 95 per cent of the films shown in Britain in 1925 (Corrigan 1983: 26). In the 1930s and 1940s Hollywood accounted for 60 per cent of world film production (Maltby and Craven 1995: 66).

As with the popular press, there has been a concentration of ownership and control in a small number of large corporations. With films, however, there is the additional twist that ownership and control have been internationally concentrated in the hands of American corporations. This raises the issue of the Americanization of popular culture, which we return to on pp. 382–3.

Radio and television

Radio and television are broadcasting media, which have quite different characteristics from cinema:

- *Domesticity*. They penetrate into the ordinary life of family and household.

- *Continuity*. They provide an endless daily programme rather than a one-off entertainment.

 Briefing: the Hollywood star system

'Far more than the type of movie, stars were the commodities that most consistently drew audiences to the movies. A "star vehicle", a movie constructed around the appeal of one or more particular stars and sold on that basis, was bound to have a set of conventional ingredients. . . . An Elvis Presley movie, for instance, offered its star several opportunities to sing, a number of girls for him to choose his romantic partner from, and a plot in which he would be misunderstood by older characters. The repetition of these standard ingredients created an audience expectation of these elements. . . . The studio system was committed to the deliberate manufacture of stars as a mechanism for selling movie tickets, and as a result generated publicity around the stars' off-screen lives designed to complement and play upon their screen images.' (Maltby and Craven 1995: 89)

❓ *Is the Hollywood star system still operating? Can you think of any contemporary examples of it?*

- *Immediacy*. They can go 'live' and communicate events to an unlimited audience as they happen.

- *Variable usage*. In the cinema people simply watch the screen, but television and radio can be combined with many other activities.

In Britain, radio provided the model for the early organization of television. In the 1920s radio was put under the control of a publicly owned monopoly, the British Broadcasting Corporation (BBC). Television then developed under the BBC's control during the 1930s. Broadcasting took this form in Britain as part of a general tendency towards the public ownership of important national services at this time.

BBC radio was established as a public service by Reith, the first Director-General of the BBC, on two basic principles:

- Universality through a national service, though with some regional programmes.

- Mixed programming to provide a mix of education, information, and entertainment, and cater for different tastes and interests.

As we argued above, the changing character of the press was making it less appropriate as a vehicle of the 'public sphere'. The control of British broadcasting by an independent public corporation meant that first radio and then television were able to take over this function to some degree, though the BBC had an uneasy relationship with the state. The government expected the BBC to be a cooperative instrument of the state and refused to allow the BBC to cover matters of political controversy or to make parliamentary broadcasts. Indeed, during the General Strike of 1926 the BBC eventually found itself assisting the government to bring the strike to an end (Curran and Seaton 1991: 143).

British broadcasting was transformed in the 1950s by the breakthrough of television and the ending of the BBC's monopoly. The number of TV licence-holders rose from 344,000 in 1949/50 to 1,165,000 in 1959/60 (Curran and Seaton 1991: 196). In 1954 a law was passed to introduce commercial television or 'Independent Television' (ITV), as it was misleadingly but cleverly called, since it may have been *independent* of the BBC but it was also *dependent* on a range of commercial interests. Pressure from the advertising and entertainment industries had combined with the Conservative Party's belief in market forces to end the BBC's monopoly.

The ending of the BBC's monopoly did not, however, destroy the public-service tradition. Indeed, it led in some ways to television becoming a more effective medium for

 Briefing: the concentration of media ownership

Concentration of ownership became a feature of all areas of the media, with a higher level of concentration in these industries than in industry generally. In Britain:

- two companies dominated the production of gramophone records by the 1930s;

- two companies dominated cinema by the 1940s;

- five companies accounted for about 70 per cent of newspaper circulation in the 1950s;

- commercial television in the 1960s was dominated by five network companies with monopoly positions in particular regions.

Source: J. Scott (1990: 142).

the public sphere. Commercial television loosened up the relationship between politics and television, and allowed increasing discussion of controversial matters. Both radio and television were able to develop their political function of informing the public about political debates and presenting opposition as well as government views. The key issue now became 'balance', the fair provision of airtime to different political views.

There was some danger that commercialization and the competition for audiences would undermine public-service principles, but their effects were limited by state regulation. The Independent Broadcasting Authority (IBA) restricted the amount of advertising, required that non-fiction programmes occupy a specified proportion of airtime, and limited repeats and imports. The public-service tradition survived.

The effects of commercial competition were also limited by monopolistic tendencies within the industry. There was little competition between ITV companies once they had won their franchises, for they operated as a national network based on regional monopolies. Competition was also limited by programming conventions. Thus, the BBC and ITV learned to schedule unpopular programmes at the same time, maximizing the audiences for, say, documentaries in the interests of both organizations. After an initial period of frantic rivalry, BBC and ITV settled down to live quite comfortably with each other during the 1960s and the 1970s, though a period of more drastic change awaited them, as we show later in the 'The limits of choice'.

◈ *Stop and reflect*

In this section we moved on to outline the rise of the mass media.

- We first examined the print revolution, the growth of the print industry, and its cultural impact.
- We then explored the interrelationships between the growth of the mass media, the development of capitalism, and the process of industrialization.
- We outlined the development of mass-circulation newspapers, cinema, and broadcasting.
- We argued that a growing concentration of ownership took place as the mass media developed.

We discussed the impact of the mass media on the public sphere.

- Return to the earlier discussion of the public sphere and make sure that you are clear about its meaning (see p. 365).
- Consider how the development of mass circulation newspapers affected the public sphere.
- We suggested that first radio and then television took over the function of providing a public sphere.
- Has commercialization weakened television's contribution to the public sphere?

The influence of the mass media

The development of the mass media had created organizations with an enormous potential for influencing people. Industrial techniques gave newspapers and films a huge production capacity, while their distribution networks could reach large numbers of people at the same time. The broadcast media could reach people instantly and give them the illusion of being present as events happened. The concentration of ownership gave great power to the small number of organizations that controlled each of the media, in some cases putting this power in the hands of individual owners prepared to use it to further their political ends.

But how much influence could those who control the media actually have on their audiences? This has been the central issue in the study of the media. As we showed in the first part of the chapter, there is no consensus on this and different models of media influence have led people to very different conclusions. In this section, we examine the research and debate on media influence in a number of key areas—information, representation, culture, and morality. In reading this part of the chapter, you should bear in mind the models of media influence that we discussed in 'Media influence and the audience', and the issues of method raised there.

Information

Although the Web is growing in importance, the mass media are still the most important sources of information in our society. We rely on 'the news' to tell us about important events and report them in a truthful and accurate way. Journalists and editors assure us that their professional values require them to provide accurate and objective information, and a balanced and representative range of opinions. But do they provide this? Is it even possible for them to do so?

Constructing the news

The starting point of the sociological study of the news is its social construction. The facts never speak for themselves.

This is partly because of the news production process. Space and time are limited and editorial **gatekeepers** select what goes into newspapers and news programmes. The news also has to be trimmed and packaged to fit newspaper layout or the structure of a broadcast news programme. The shift towards rolling news on news channels, and instant 'breaking news', have impacted on the process of news production and affected the content of the news (see box on 'Rolling and breaking news').

News does not just arrive on the editor's desk. Information is gathered by journalists, who do not collect it randomly. They are organized into a reporting network by their newspaper or broadcaster, which directs and distributes them, steering them towards information of one kind rather than another. International reporting shows this particularly well. It is inevitably patchy and decisions to send journalists to one country rather than another can have an enormous bearing on international coverage. A searchlight can be trained on a country with a particular problem, say the destruction of rainforest in Brazil, by sending a camera team to cover it for television. Problems that are not highlighted in this way hardly exist on the world stage.

New technology Rolling and breaking news

Technology has made it possible to provide direct and continuous news transmissions. Rolling news channels with 24-hour news coverage have multiplied and regular programmes are interrupted by breaking news. The viewer gets a sense of being present, of being a participant as events unfold, of having a direct access to what is going on. Martin Bell (2003) points out that there is, however, 'a lack of authenticity' in much of the coverage provided by news channels:

> It consists of correspondents perched on the roofs of hotels and television stations, exchanging guesswork with other correspondents on other roofs, about the crisis of the moment.

Instant reporting often means the transmission of unchecked rumours rather than properly investigated news stories. This lack of checking then provides an opportunity for 'spin-doctors' to present their versions of events without effective scrutiny:

> In times of crisis, of war and terrorism, the rolling-news channels have special responsibilities as the primary source of news for millions of people. They are defined by F-words. They aim to be first and fastest with the news. Their nature, too often, is to be feverish, frenzied, frantic, frail, false, and fallible.

Source: Bell, M. 'Say no to news on tap', *The Independent Review*, 16 December 2003.

➔ Next time you watch a rolling-news channel, bear in mind Martin Bell's scepticism!

The journalists themselves are guided by 'news values', which shape what they find newsworthy. They often claim that these are objective and self-evident, and Galtung and Ruge (1999) did find some evidence for this. Certain underlying principles seemed to govern the selection of events as worth reporting. The more recent, the closer, and the bigger an event, the more likely it was to be covered. Other aspects of news-gathering are, however, not objective at all and are shaped by the organization's requirements. As Tunstall (1996) has put it, each newspaper looks for the 'good story for us', the story that fits the style of a paper and its political slant.

Journalists are well aware of the need to find stories of this kind and present them in the way required by their organization. They do have occupational values of objectivity and impartiality that may well lead them to seek out information that is unpalatable to their employer but they are also socialized into the values of the organization they work for. When *occupational* and *organizational* values come into conflict, journalists can be forced to conform to editorial policies and the views of owners, if they want to keep their jobs. Editors can bring strong pressures to bear on them, and owners ultimately control editors.

This was shown well by what happened to the *Sunday Times* after it was bought in 1981 by Rupert Murdoch, who shifted its political stance to the right. A new editor was appointed and journalists were pressed to conform through the editorial hierarchy. Their articles were amended through editing. If they resisted, they could find that their pieces appeared less often, facing them with 'professional death'. It was also easier to conform than struggle every day to maintain their views. Isobel Hilton has suggested that many ended up internalizing these controls and becoming their own censors (see box on 'A journalist under pressure'). In the end, the choice was to give in or resign. Curran and Seaton (1991: 104) report that at least a hundred journalists left the *Sunday Times* between 1981 and 1986.

Briefing: a journalist under pressure

Isobel Hilton, the Latin American correspondent of the *Sunday Times* in the early 1980s, describes the pressures she experienced after its take-over by Murdoch:

> What would happen is that you would write a story and it would disappear. The copy would vanish around the building and people would write little things into it and take out other things. It would eventually appear in a very truncated form with the emphases changed. It had all been done at stages along the way. To try and make a fuss about this on a Saturday when everything was very busy was very difficult. . . . The sense of intimidation was so strong that people actually started censoring themselves because it is very unpleasant to get into this kind of argument all the time. It is not just a collection of incidents, it's a collection of incidents *and* the atmosphere, which is in the end so depressing. You stop functioning as a journalist. There are things that you just don't bother to pursue because you know you just won't get them into the paper.

Source: Curran and Seaton (1991: 104).

Much of the news is not, anyway, gathered by journalists so much as presented to them. News agencies are an important source of material, particularly from other countries. International news agencies do try hard for purely commercial reasons to present information in as neutral a way as they can. They have to sell it into countries with widely varying cultures and political regimes. Gurevitch (1996) points out that this does, however, make it easier for national editors to then manipulate the material for their own purposes. Furthermore, sources are not generally given for agency material, which frequently originates from state news agencies. An apparently neutral agency source does not make the news objective.

It is also considerably easier for journalists to write stories on the basis of information they have been given than to seek out the information themselves. It is this that keeps the public-relations industry in business, providing material that presents its clients in a favourable light, and the capacity to employ public-relations companies clearly depends on resources. In practice, this means that business corporations and the political parties they support are able to dominate the flow of information to the media.

Government information

The construction of the news provides many opportunities for governments to influence it. According to the account given by Bob Franklin (1994), some of the main ways in which British governments can influence the media are as follows:

- *Censorship*. The media are not allowed by the Official Secrets Act to publish information on 'sensitive' military or security matters, or information obtained in confidence from foreign governments or international organizations. The broad wording of these restrictions leads editors to play safe, which considerably widens the effect of censorship.
- *Control of the BBC*. The BBC depends on the government for increases in the licence fee to cover rising costs. Governments have at times threatened to withhold increases. The government also appoints the BBC's Board of Governors.
- *Provision of information*. Briefings by the prime minister's press secretary through the lobby system are an important source of information for journalists. This system feeds government information from unattributed sources into the media. Information from state agencies is released (or suppressed) to suit their purposes.
- *Pressure on investigative journalists*. There are well-known examples of governmental attacks on specific programmes, such as the 1988 Thames Television documentary *Death on the Rock*, which investigated

Briefing: 'shutter control'

The US Defense Department has the legal power to prevent civilian satellites providing images that could be used by enemies during wartime. It failed, however, to activate this 'shutter control' before the bombing of Afghanistan in October 2001. Instead, the Pentagon later bought exclusive rights to Ikonos satellite pictures of Afghanistan. It did this after reports that the bombing of training camps had led to heavy civilian casualties and backdated its rights to the beginning of the bombing. The Ikonos satellite had such high resolution cameras that it could show individual bodies lying on the ground. The Pentagon did not do this because the military needed pictures, for there were six military satellites in operation.

Source: Guardian, 17 October 2001.

the shooting of three unarmed members of the IRA in Gibraltar. Thames Television's failure to obtain renewal of its franchise in 1991 has been attributed to its conflict with the government over this programme.
- *Relationships with newspaper owners*. The newspapers take up political positions and those favourable to the government can become a mouthpiece for its views.

While all governments seek to use every means in their power to influence the media, it is important to take account of differences between societies in the relationship between the state and the media. Thus, in the United States, the law on Freedom of Information makes material available to the media which the British Official Secrets Act keeps from them, though the US government can find other ways of restricting information (see box on 'Shutter control'). In China the media are closely controlled by the state.

A contested space

The Glasgow University Media Group has demonstrated how the news favours explanations that reflect the views of dominant groups in British society. Their content analysis of strike coverage makes this point particularly well, for it is characteristic of strikes that management and union provide opposite accounts of them. The television reporting of strikes did recognize that there were two views of them but generally privileged the managerial account. Managerial explanations came up more often, were highlighted in headlines and summaries, and were adopted by the journalists themselves (Philo 1990: 169–70).

It may be said that two views were at least given, while in other societies, where television is more closely controlled by the state, that would not be the case. The creation of an illusion of balance can, however, be very manipulative. It can lead people to think that they are receiving a fair account, and therefore make them more likely to accept it as objective.

In later work on the television news reporting during 2000–2 of the Palestinian–Israeli conflict, the GUMG examined conflicting accounts of the events and found that the Israeli perspective dominated news coverage. Their analysis of news content and its impact on the audience can be found in Media Watch 10 in the Workshop section of this chapter.

The study of the process of news construction and the analysis of news content have demonstrated that the news is neither objective nor impartial. Broadly speaking, those with power and wealth are able to manage the flow of information and interpretation through the media. But it is important to recognize that they do not always succeed. Investigative reporting exists. Governments and business corporations are at times seriously embarrassed by the activities of journalists.

As Eldridge (1993a: 20) has put it, 'the media occupy space which is constantly being contested'. Subordinate groups organize and challenge the dominant ideology. Conflicts within the elite itself often provide journalists with leverage through the leak of information that governments would like to keep quiet. This is where the journalists' occupational values of independence, objectivity, impartiality, and balance come into play. Even if these values do not and cannot produce objective news, they can enable the voice of dissent to be heard.

Representation

The media can influence their audience not only through the information they provide but also through the way they represent people. In this section we consider the representation of class, gender, ethnicity and disability.

Class

Representations of class have a long history. Dodd and Dodd (1992) argued that, in the late nineteenth century, middle-class commentators created an image of the British working class which shaped later representations of it. The working class was invariably situated in industrial communities of the north. It was contrasted with the middle class by making a set of oppositions which represented workers as physical and practical in character rather than intellectual; decent and simple rather than sophisticated; local rather than national.

This image of the working class persisted through the twentieth century and can be found in the writings of Orwell, Hoggart, and Sillitoe, and in 1960s films such as *Saturday Night and Sunday Morning* or the much later *Letter to Brezhnev* of the 1980s. It can also be found in soap operas, as in *Coronation Street's* close-knit community located in a northern city.

Continuities can be found with the 1980s soaps, *EastEnders* and *Brookside*, but these also broke new ground. Although they too focused on local communities, they were concerned 'not so much with what holds a community together but with what threatens to splinter or disrupt it' (Geraghty 1992: 137). These soaps were aimed at a wider audience that included male and young viewers and tried therefore to break away from the *Coronation Street* model. There was more emphasis on social diversity, conflict, deviance, and crime. *EastEnders*, for example, recognized the multi-ethnic character of the British working class and included black, Asian, and Turkish-Cypriot families. As the Dodds have pointed out, the values of community were still there, however, for the community is defended against the criminal and racist forces threatening it from the outside.

Although the image of the working class was created by the middle class, it was adopted by intellectuals of working-class as well as middle-class origin. It was then adapted to the audience needs of television and became part of popular culture through the soap opera. The extent to which it has shaped conceptions of the working class is an open question, but the soap operas have certainly reached a mass audience. At a time when class communities were in decline, as we show in Chapter 13, pp. 515–16, the only working-class community in the lives of most people was the community in the soap opera.

Gender

Feminists have often criticized the media for reinforcing traditional gender stereotypes. Tuchman (1981) reviewed evidence on the representation of women by the American media during the period from the 1950s to the 1970s. She claimed that women were portrayed mainly in terms of their sexual attractiveness and their performance of domestic roles. When they were shown in occupational roles, these were extensions of the domestic role. Women appeared as nurses rather than doctors, secretaries rather than lawyers. The exclusion, marginalization, and trivialization of women's activities resulted in what Tuchman called the 'symbolic annihilation of women' (1981: 183).

But have media representations of women changed? Television content in the United Kingdom and the United States has increasingly featured 'strong women' performing male occupational roles in, for example, the police, or the armed forces, or the professions more generally. Arguably, television has over-compensated for its past deficiencies and misleadingly gives women more power than they actually have in society at large. Against this, there is in some programmes the continued representation of women as being primarily concerned with romance, marriage, and domesticity (Bernstein 2002).

This somewhat contradictory picture is found also in soap operas, which as a 'feminine genre' have been the focus of much feminist interest. Research here has emphasized that the significance of soap operas is not just a matter of how they represent women but also of the pleasure that they give them. As Pilcher has summarized it:

> soap operas are potentially both a ghetto, where femininity is valued but firmly based within the domestic and the personal, and a beneficial cultural space, where women audiences can actively enjoy the struggles of strong, independent, women characters. (1999: 114)

It is also necessary to take account of social interaction within the audience, as argued by the GUMG (see p. 369). A study of the soap opera audience has claimed that much of the pleasure that women take in them results from the opportunities they provide for discussion of the characters and events. This can build solidarity among women and resistance to patriarchy (M. Brown 1994).

The content of girls' and women's magazines has been another major focus of interest. McRobbie's well-known study of the teenage magazine *Jackie* started off a debate that raised important issues of method. McRobbie argued that the stories, images, problem pages, and articles on fashion, beauty, and pop music combined to focus girls on personal and emotional matters, as though these were the only things that mattered. Relationships between boys and girls were treated solely in 'romantic' terms. As McRobbie put it, 'the girl is encouraged to load all her eggs in the basket of romance and hope it pays off' (McRobbie and McCabe 1981: 118).

This approach went well beyond content analysis by using techniques of textual analysis to discover hidden

Do girls' magazines shape the way they think?
© Getty Images/M Nader

meanings, but inevitably had to make assumptions about the text's meaning. Martin Barker (1989) examined McRobbie's analysis and came up with a different reading. He argued that these magazines at times undermined rather than reinforced the romantic love model, and that McRobbie's approach treated the reader as a passive receiver of messages. Frazer (1987) studied reader responses to *Jackie* through discussions among girls. She found that they distanced themselves from the fictional characters, criticized the magazine, and were well aware of the process through which it had been produced.

> ⊃ *Connections*
>
> We discuss femininities and masculinities in Chapter 5, pp. 163–4, and recent changes in gender on pp. 181–4. Read these pages with this discussion of media representations.

In her later work, McRobbie (1996) acknowledged these criticisms and adopted more of an 'active audience' approach. This time she examined magazines such as *Just Seventeen, More!,* and *19.* She found that the content of these magazines was focused on sexuality rather than romance. They treated the reader as more 'knowing', and adopted an ironic, mocking attitude towards traditional femininities. The young women professionals who produced and edited them were highly educated and familiar with gender politics. These magazines promoted a bolder, more confident, more challenging identity for women, though in some respects they still reinforced established femininities through their predominantly heterosexual assumptions.

While the literature on gender has been dominated by feminist concerns, there has been a growing interest in media representations of men. Media representations of sportsmen have embodied **hegemonic masculinity** (see Chapter 5, p. 164) in their emphasis on competitiveness, strength, and aggression. Alternative gay masculinities have been generally mocked and marginalized. Some soap operas have introduced 'gay' characters and taken them seriously, but they still approach them from a heterosexual viewpoint, concerning themselves with the issue of tolerance and the reaction of heterosexuals to gays (Bernstein 2002).

Men's magazines, as Edwards (1997) has argued, have been permeated by traditional images of masculinity. This applies particularly to those celebrating laddism, which have gloried in such images, though even here a certain irony has crept in. As Pilcher has put it, they are 'sexist but in an ironic, self-conscious "should know better" way' (1999: 128).

There is an interplay here between representations of men and women. As representations of women have

changed, they have challenged the established model of femininity and, therefore, the hegemonic masculinity that depends upon this. This challenge, together with the assertion of gay subcultures, has resulted in some questioning of the hegemonic model but has also provoked a masculinist response. The challenge should not, anyway, be exaggerated, for the heterosexuality that lies at the heart of established models of femininity and masculinity seems as pervasive as ever, if not quite so compulsory.

Ethnicity

The media have reinforced racial as well as class and gender stereotypes. Solomos and Back argue that media racism has two core features. The culture of black people is presented as alien to the British way of life and their presence is seen as a threat to British culture (Solomos and Back 1996: 184).

> ⊃ *Connections*
>
> It is important to bear in mind the cultural form taken by racism in Britain. As we show in Chapter 6, pp. 224–5, the discrediting of an openly biological racism led to its replacement by a 'new racism' emphasizing national cultural differences.

The press in particular has presented a negative image of black people, though the content of this image has shifted over time. Solomos and Back have suggested that there have been three successive stereotypes (1996: 183):

- the 1960s 'welfare scrounger';
- the 1970s 'mugger';
- the 1980s 'rioter'.

The emphasis was always on the problems presented by black people rather than their contribution to British society, or the problems that British society created for them. Thus, welfare scrounging was emphasized rather than the contribution of black immigrants to the staffing of the National Health Service. The black mugger was highlighted rather than rising numbers of racist attacks on blacks by whites. Headlines such as 'Black War on the Police' presented the disorders in 1980s British cities as 'race riots', in which blacks attacked the police, rather than as the outcome of urban deprivation, exclusion, or changes in methods of policing (we discuss these disorders in Chapter 13, pp. 522–5).

Similar negative images can be found in television. Alvarado *et al.* (1987) identified four historical stereotypes of black people:

- the 'exotic', as in British media coverage of international tours by the Royal Family;

- the 'dangerous', as in the portrayal of Indians in westerns;
- the 'humorous', as in sit-coms like *Till Death Do Us Part*;
- the 'pitied', as in coverage of famines.

Such representations place blacks, and other minorities treated in a similar way, in a special 'different' category, whether to be feared, patronized, or ridiculed. Deliberately presenting positive images might seem one way of counteracting negative ones but can also reinforce stereotypes. Thus, black success stories, such as very occasional Oscars for black film stars, not only show that some blacks can succeed but may also suggest that success is exceptional and that most fail. Furthermore, success or failure are seen in individualist terms and do not take account of the disadvantages and deprivations that make such stories exceptional. Arguably, negative images are best countered by the representation of blacks as ordinary people, which it is claimed that *EastEnders* has done (Abercrombie 1996).

This is not only a matter of how blacks are presented but also of their absence. Soap operas may have recognized their existence, but there has been, at least until recently, little recognition of them in advertising. The ordinary family in the television advert has historically been a white family. Tuchman's term 'symbolic annihilation' would seem appropriate here too.

Multi-ethnic adverts did become fashionable in the late 1980s (Solomos and Back 1996). These presented people from different ethnic backgrounds and emphasized their harmony and unity. Thus, a 1995 British Airways campaign featured a Danish woman next to an Indian woman, with the caption 'there are more things that bring us together than keep us apart'. The rationale for adverts of this kind is easy to see. They fit nicely into the marketing strategy and image of transnational corporations selling products across the globe.

Solomos and Back point out that these apparent celebrations of ethnic difference can, none the less, reinforce racist stereotypes. They might seem anti-racist in their positive representation of ethnic diversity and their emphasis on harmony between different peoples. They can, however, reinforce racial stereotypes by emphasizing the physical characteristics that these are based on. Thus, for example, in one Benetton advert a blue-eyed blonde white child is flanked by a 'negroid' black child and an 'oriental' Asian child.

As with much of the discussion of representations, what we do not know much about is the impact they make on the audience. The analysis of content is an essential starting point, but it does leave open the whole issue of the *effect* of representations on the audience? How important are negative images of blacks in shaping their sense of identity?

Do adverts reinforce ethnic stereotypes?
© Alice Chadwick

It has been claimed that in British television things are now really changing, that there is an across-the-board increase in the representation of non-white people in both adverts and programmes, and also in media employment. The BBC's 2004 documentary, *The Trouble with Black Men*, was, however, criticized for perpetuating negative stereotypes through its title and its presentation of black men as 'promiscuous, lazy, and obsessed with rap'. The BBC defended itself by arguing that the title was intentionally provocative, that statistics showed that Afro-Caribbean boys were three times as likely as white boys to be excluded from school, and that other programmes presented black men in a positive light (*Independent*, 19 August 2004).

Disability

Media representations of disability reflect the broader cultural identification of the disabled as 'different' from ordinary people. This way of treating the disabled has a long history, stretching back through medieval times to ancient Greece and Rome. Because they were different, those with some perceived disability, such as 'dwarfs', were a source of entertainment in households and royal courts. They could be the target of abuse and humiliation as their difference removed them from the constraints that normally regulated behaviour. 'Freak shows', where visitors would pay money just to see people with some disability, real or fake, were at one time a common feature of travelling fairs and circuses.

The mass media continued this treatment of the disabled as different. This is reflected in both their absence and their presence. Research on television programmes has shown that the disabled rarely appear in normal roles. When they do appear, they are typically presented as 'dependent, unproductive and in need of care'. Storylines, and this applies to newspaper coverage as well, have taken a 'personal tragedy approach' that focuses on the suffering of the disabled, their medical treatment, or their achievements in spite of their disability (Barnes and Mercer 2003: 94).

In the *Cinema of Isolation*, Martin Norden (1994) identified three stages in the portrayal of the disabled in films. The first stage, between the 1890s and the 1930s, was an exploitative continuation of the 'freak show' tradition. In the second stage, 1930s to 1970s, a more exploratory 'personal tragedy' approach was taken. Disabled individuals struggled to overcome their difficulties. This was followed by a third and more positive stage in which disability was treated in varying contexts in a more 'incidental' way. While some normalization was taking place, examples of negative stereotyping in films none the less continued to appear.

As pointed out above, one of the problems with research in this area is the lack of research into audiences. *Disabling Prejudice*, a report by Jane Sancho (2003), commissioned by UK broadcasting organizations, has, however, carried out important research on audience attitudes and responses. A postal survey of a representative panel, which therefore included disabled people, was carried out, with a response rate of 75 per cent. This research identified five different types of respondents, demonstrating the importance in media research of differentiating the audience (Sancho 2003: 7–8):

- *Issue-driven* respondents (14 per cent of sample), who were disabled or associated with disabled people, and were 'vocal and active on behalf of disabled groups';
- *Transformers*, who were younger people (9 per cent), some of whom were disabled, and were less critical but looked for role models and wanted more opportunities for the disabled and 'a normalization of portrayals';
- *Progressives* (36 per cent), who were mainly non-disabled, educated, and middle-class, and considered that television had 'a role to educate and normalize';

- *Followers* (26 per cent), who are described as 'mainstream', mainly non-disabled, with no interest in the disability issue, who saw television as entertainment, and were 'surprised by more hard-hitting portrayals';
- *Traditionalists* (15 per cent), who were older viewers, some of whom were disabled, who had a stereotyped and prejudiced view of minority groups, saw television as entertainment, and were 'shocked by hard-hitting portrayals'.

One of the interesting findings of this research was that the audience seemed to have advanced further than the professionals who were also interviewed. Some 69 per cent of survey respondents said that 'it would not bother them if a disabled person read the main evening news' and 63 per cent 'thought it would be good to see more disabled presenters on different programmes'. However, the professionals interviewed 'are inclined to believe that audiences are not ready to accept an increase in disability portrayals yet …' (Sancho 2003: 16).

Media organizations are under pressure to normalize the representation of the disabled. As with gender and ethnicity, greater organization, 'voice', and anti-discrimination legislation have been making an impact. As Barnes and Mercer have put it, 'disability politics has been caught up in the wider flow of identity politics and the celebration of difference' (2003: 132). Media research has been crucial in all of this, for it is research that has brought to light the way that people are represented in the media and has informed the campaigns of minority groups.

Culture

Now we turn to examine the broader impact of the mass media on the development of culture. We argued on p. 367 that two broad views of popular culture have emerged, the *elitist* and *populist*. Here we will discuss these views in relation to audience involvement and Americanization.

Audiences: passive or active?

Media corporations are successful enterprises because people enjoy their products but those who hold a manipulative view of the media regard audience pleasure as dangerous. When people enjoy a story, film, or programme, their guard is down and they are most likely to absorb media ideologies and stereotypes. Thus, feminists have argued that women who enjoy romantic films or stories receive a powerful reinforcement of traditional conceptions of womanhood by identifying with the heroine. The implication is that alternative films and stories with more appropriate messages should be produced.

Briefing: identifying with a vampire

'I knew I was supposed to feel relieved when the vampire got staked. I didn't. . . . I knew I was supposed to find vampires frightening, and my home, family, and their expectations of me comforting, safe. I didn't. I identified with the vampires. *They* were the rebels I wanted to be. They didn't have elders bugging them. I dreamed of independence and revelled in the vampires' anarchic force: they spurned families, marriage and other social conventions. . . . Although loners themselves, they found others like them and were united by a shared difference against the mass of humanity.' (Quoted in Eldridge *et al.* 1997: 153)

Apart from the practical difficulties of producing an alternative and persuading audiences to buy it, the problem with this approach is that it disparages the daily pleasures of millions of people. One researcher into the content of women's magazines has expressed this nicely:

> I felt that to simply dismiss women's magazines was also to dismiss the lives of millions of women who read and enjoyed them each week. More than that *I* still enjoyed them, found them useful, and escaped with them. And I knew I couldn't be the only feminist who was a closet reader. (Winship 1987: xiii)

As we showed in our discussion of the representation of women in teenage magazines, readers are anyway not passive and can retain their critical faculties while they enjoy reading.

Research on audience response has shown that people do not just absorb representations. They frequently identify with film and television characters in unexpected ways. Eldridge *et al.* (1997) have listed many examples of this. A study of responses to westerns showed that some Native Americans rejected them and were critical of the way that 'Indians' were portrayed, but others actually identified with the Indian-hating John Wayne because they appreciated the freedom of the cowboy way of life. Audience members can also identify with minor or deviant characters, even with vampires (see box on 'Identifying with a vampire'). The term 'identification' is itself misleading, for it suggests that people accept the whole character presented. In reality, they select aspects of a given character, say beauty, or cleverness, or strength, to identify with. They can inter-pret and reconstruct characters to suit their particular needs and fantasies.

Television is usually treated as the medium which induces most passivity. Viewers are regarded as 'couch potatoes' who soak up whatever 'the box' throws at them. This is, however, a quite misleading notion of what viewers actually do. Researchers have mounted video cameras inside television sets and watched the watchers. They have found that viewers engage in all sorts of other activities while watching and frequently do not watch at all, and, when they do watch, do so with widely varying degrees of attention (Abercrombie 1996).

This may seem an obvious finding but it has consider-able implications for assessments of the impact of tele-vision. Viewing figures based on reports of hours spent watching or programmes watched are likely to exaggerate greatly actual watching time. The term 'watching' is itself misleading, as it implies that people are either watching or non-watching, when in reality they may well be 'half-watching'. While television is in some ways the most powerful of the media, since it penetrates into the private life of a household, this very feature also lessens its influ-ence. It is part of everyday life, which goes on around it. The combination of watching with a lot of non-watching dilutes the impact of television.

The notion of an active audience corrects the mislead-ingly passive view of audiences embodied in many theories of the impact of the mass media on popular culture. As Eldrige *et al.* (1997) have pointed out, it does, however, carry with it the danger of uncritically celebrating the way that people enjoy and use the media. It can all too easily suggest that content no longer matters, that there are no representation issues, that it does not really matter who owns and controls the media. The fact that people select and interpret does not mean they are uninfluenced, as the GUMG's research has shown (see p. 369).

Americanization

The conflict between *elitism* and *populism* has taken another form in the debate over the Americanization of popular culture (see Strinati 1992*b*). It was the domin-ation of film production by Hollywood which raised this issue, but almost any item of popular culture may be American in origin. If we eat a 'Big Mac' or wear jeans, we are consuming items of American culture.

American culture was certainly exported on a massive scale. As we showed on p. 372, Hollywood dominated world film production in the 1920s and 1930s but American interests also continued to control film production and distribution into the television age. Given this dominant position, even films produced, financed, and distributed by non-American interests were likely to be influenced to some degree by the Hollywood model.

Those holding *elitist* views of culture have been hostile to Americanization. They have viewed it as popular, com-mercial, and generally responsible for the mass culture which threatened to swamp British cultural traditions. This view of Americanization treated audiences as passive recipients of American influence.

Americanization has been interpreted very differently from a *populist* perspective, which has seen audiences as active rather than passive. This view claimed that America was popular not because American dominance of the media shaped what people liked but because American culture gave them what they actually wanted. America was a source of democratic and popular forms of culture that had been suppressed in a class-dominated Britain. Young members of the working class could draw on American culture to create subcultures that enabled them to resist and challenge the dominance of middle-class culture. According to this view, America was a diversifying rather than a standardizing influence on British culture.

The populist view may seem a healthy corrective to the rather patronizing treatment of American culture by elitists, but the import of American culture does present problems, such as the preservation of other national cultures and the maintenance of production and employment in other countries. We will return to these issues again when we consider whether globalization has led to Americanization (see p. 395).

Morality

We focus here more specifically on the way that the media handle behaviour judged to be criminal or immoral. On the one hand, they have been held responsible for criminal or immoral behaviour. On the other hand, they have been accused of generating moral panics through the exaggerated and distorted reporting of events.

Sex and violence

The powerful visual impact of film meant that almost as soon as films were introduced into Britain, concerns were raised about their dangers. They were seen as generating crime, promiscuous sexual behaviour, and violence. There was particular concern because of the large numbers of women and children who went to the cinema. Some claimed that children learned how to commit crime by seeing crimes on the screen. Others worried that screen stories of romantic love affairs would undermine marriage and threaten the family. The film industry decided to stave off state regulation by setting up its own British Board of Film Censors in 1912 and this still operates, though its standards and rules have inevitably changed (Eldridge *et al.* 1997).

Later developments in the media have intensified worries about their corrupting effects. Broadcasting media, especially television, penetrate into the home and are easily accessible to children. The content of videotapes, videogames, and the Internet has been not only easily accessible but also more difficult to regulate because of the way their material is distributed and disseminated.

Videotapes have attracted much blame. A well-known example of this was the James Bulger case in 1993, when the murder of a 2-year-old child by two 11-year-old children was blamed on horror videos. One particular video, *Child's Play 3*, was blamed for this murder, though there was no evidence that either of the children had seen it (Newburn and Hagell 1995).

There is a long history of research into whether the media are responsible for rising violence but it is an exceptionally difficult issue to investigate. This is partly because of definitional and measurement problems:

- *The definition of violence.* It is hard to define this objectively. What some would consider a violent act, others would not. Is smacking a child a violent act?
- *The acceptability of violence.* Boxing is considered by some but not others to be a legitimate form of violence, as is the use of military force.
- *The measurement of violence.* It is difficult to assess the amount of violence involved in different kinds of violent act. This applies to both attempts to measure violent behaviour and attempts to assess the amount of violence in the media.

Controversy and debate What is violence?

- A cruise missile attack;
- A fatal shooting;
- A 'beating up';
- A boxing match;
- Verbal abuse;
- An execution by lethal injection;

- An execution by beheading;
- Corporal punishment.

❷ Which of these would you consider 'violent'?

❷ Can you rank them in terms of degree of violence?

❷ What do you think makes one act more violent than another?

Studies of television and violence have commonly found evidence of a relationship but have had difficulty in isolating the effect of media violence from the wide range of other factors which may be said to cause violent behaviour. If violent children are found to be big watchers of violence, this may be because they are attracted to violent programmes. Experiments can be designed to investigate causality by exposing groups in laboratory situations to different amounts of violence and then measuring their aggressiveness. Such experiments have demonstrated a relationship between exposure and aggressiveness but are open to the criticism that the experimental situation is artificial and bears no relation to the social situations in which people actually watch the screen. In Study 10 at the end of the chapter, we report an important attempt to get beyond these methodological problems.

Although many studies may be flawed and a causal link between television watching and violence may not be proven, this does not mean that there is no relationship between the two. Crude notions that one causes the other may not stand up to examination, but the research by the GUMG (see p. 368) has shown that on a number of issues the media do influence the audience in subtle and long-term ways. The discussion of moral panics shows how complex this influence may be.

Moral panics

The literature on 'moral panics' provides another approach to these questions. The argument here is not that the media cause people to behave badly but rather that they report bad behaviour in an exaggerated and distorted way. This results in a societal reaction out of proportion to the initial problem, a reaction that can itself generate deviance.

The concept of the **moral panic** was first developed in Stan Cohen's (1972) study of the 'mods and rockers' of the 1960s. These were rival youth groups which engaged in some minor violence in Clacton during the Easter weekend of 1964. The newspapers reported widespread violence and large numbers of arrests with such headlines as 'Day of Terror by Scooter Groups' (*Daily Telegraph*) and 'Youngsters Beat Up Town—97 Leather Jacket Arrests' (*Daily Express*). These exaggerated reports awoke public fears and a hostile reaction to the youth groups, which were seen as a major threat to public order. Mod and rocker subcultures received publicity, which led more teenagers to adopt these styles, further increasing public fears. Mods and rockers became what Cohen called the *folk devils* of their time.

Cohen's analysis of this moral panic made an important contribution to the theory of deviance, which we outline in Chapter 7, pp. 238–41. Its two key notions were:

- *The labelling of behaviour.* What were little more than subcultural styles, the riding of scooters and the wearing of leather jackets, became defined as deviant behaviour.

Do the media generate moral panics?

© Alice Chadwick

THEORY AND METHODS

Moral panics

- Can you think of a recent moral panic?
- What form did the primary deviance take?
- What role did the media and the politicians play in its amplification?
- Were any folk devils created?
- Can you identify any secondary deviance that resulted from this process?
- Why do you think this moral panic occurred?

➲ You may find it helpful here to return to the discussion of deviance in Chapter 7, pp. 238–41.

- *Deviance amplification.* The social reaction to the *primary* deviance, the minor violence in Clacton, generated *secondary* deviance, the spread of deviant subcultures. This developed the distinction between *primary* and *secondary* deviation made by Becker (1963) and Lemert (1967), though Cohen used the term 'deviance' rather than 'deviation'.

The concept of a moral panic was an important addition to the vocabulary of sociology. It identified important mechanisms in the media representation of deviance and showed how the media could amplify it. The main problem that it faces is whether a moral panic actually affects people's attitudes and behaviour. A readership accustomed to exaggerated media stories may well view them with some scepticism. Newspapers may also pander to *existing* popular taste in constructing folk devils. The effects of media labelling and amplification may therefore be more limited than this concept suggests.

‹› *Stop and reflect*

In this section we considered the various ways in which the mass media have been said to influence people.

We first examined the media presentation of information.

- We showed how the social construction of news shapes the way that information is presented by the media.
- Do those with wealth and power control the news?

We then considered the media representation of class, gender, ethnicity, and disability.

- Do the media perpetuate stereotypes?

We moved on to explore the influence of the media on culture.

- Make sure that you understand the difference between the elitist and populist perspectives, and the passive and active conceptions of audience.

- These different approaches affect attitudes towards the Americanization of popular culture.
- Is Americanization a myth?

Lastly, we considered the influence of the media on moral issues.

- We examined the difficulty of establishing the influence of the media on violent behaviour.
- We also explored the notion that the media generate 'moral panics' by reporting 'bad behaviour' in an exaggerated and distorted way.
- Should the media be held in any way responsible for 'immoral' behaviour?

The limits of choice

We have examined the growth of the mass media and their influence on culture and society but times have changed. The media have now lost much of their previous mass character with the shift to multiple outlets providing specialized programmes to particular, not mass, audiences.

The multiplication of the media has apparently greatly increased consumer choice. Until quite recently there were only four television channels in Britain—BBC1, BBC2, ITV, and Channel 4. Hundreds of channels now compete for audiences. Similar changes have happened in other media, as cinemas have gone multiplex and a huge range of special-interest magazines has appeared. The Internet has hugely expanded the availability of information. Choice has arguably been enhanced by globalization, which has increased the international availability of information and television programmes.

But how much diversity is there, how much information, and how much real choice? What are the limits to choice? These are the questions that we examine in this part of the chapter. We first examine diversity, before considering ownership and control, the fortunes of the public sphere, and the implications of globalization.

Diversity and choice

Greater choice has come about through a combination of technical, economic, political, and cultural changes, which we examine first. We then consider how real the greater diversity and choice have actually turned out to be.

Technology or politics?

Technological change has opened up new ways of delivering information to the household. Satellite and cable

➜ Connections

In this section we situate changes in the media within the context of broader changes in the economy, in politics, and culture. It will help you to understand the changes in the media if you follow up the cross-references in the text.

delivery systems, together with digital transmission, have made hundreds of television channels possible. Satellites make programmes available across national boundaries. The Internet is an alternative delivery system that can provide almost limitless digital material. Telly-surfing and web-surfing have become part of everyday life and

THEORY AND METHODS

Measuring audiences

It is crucial for all the channels to find out how big an audience particular programmes attract. The commercial channels set their rates to advertisers on the basis of audience size, while the BBC needs to show that audiences for its programmes are big enough to justify the licence fee.

Audiences are measured by the Broadcasters Audience Research Board (BARB), which is jointly owned by the BBC, ITV, Channels 4 and 5, BSkyB, and the Institute of Practitioners of Advertising. It was set up in the 1970s to replace the separate monitoring of audiences by the BBC and ITV, which inevitably produced figures that did not agree. Audience data are sold to television companies and other commercial interests.

BARB audience data are provided by a panel of 5,100 volunteers, selected after interviews to represent the main demographic characteristics of the British population. The volunteers regularly receive £10 Argos vouchers as a reward for their participation. Viewers, and any guests they have, are required to press a button on a set-top box every time they start watching and press it again when they stop or leave the room, even briefly. The box transmits data to processing companies. Telephone calls are made every eighteen months to ask whether the volunteers are viewing and check with the data from the box.

Source: *Guardian*, 20 November 2001, 21 January 2002.

❓ What problems do you think there are in collecting and interpreting the data? Think about the selection process, problems posed by the existence of multiple channels, viewing habits, and use of the set-top box. You may find it helpful to refer to the section on 'Selection and sampling' in Chapter 3 (see pp. 93–6), and the discussion of audiences on p. 382 of this chapter.

interchangeable as the boundaries blur between TV, computer, and phone.

Choice of viewing has been enhanced by a shift of power from the programme scheduler to the viewer, from a 'push' to a 'pull' system. The breakthrough here was the video cassette recorder (VCR), which liberated the viewer from what was immediately available, either on TV or at the local cinema. Further technical advances have provided huge personal storage facilities and made searching much easier. Ads can be bypassed, which means that commercial television advertisers can no longer be sure they are reaching consumers. The spread of pay-per-view TV has enabled consumers to buy precisely what they want.

Politics was also involved, however. In Britain, the post-1979 Conservative governments held a neo-liberal ideology that advocated deregulation and competition (see the discussion of Thatcherism in Chapter 15, pp. 601–3). It was argued that greater competition would result in more choice for the consumer, though this was not the only motivation for it. Greater competition would also cut costs by forcing programme producers to be more efficient and could be used to break the power of the unions, which were seen as having a stranglehold over BBC and ITV production.

Competition certainly increased as cable and satellite delivery systems were allowed to develop but changes in the state regulation of ITV also played an important part in this. The ITV companies were forced into greater competition by the 1990 Broadcasting Act, which put ITV franchises out to competitive tendering. The highest bid would get the franchise, though certain quality requirements still had to be met. The Independent Broadcasting Authority, which regulated the content of commercial television, was replaced by a 'lighter-touch' Independent Television Commission that allowed the commercial companies to operate more freely. As in other areas of life, the promotion of market forces required a combination of regulation and deregulation.

Post-Fordism and post-modernism

Product diversity in the economy as a whole has been increased by broader changes in production and consumption that have been labelled '**post-Fordist**' (see Chapter 17, pp. 693–7). The saturation of markets with mass-produced goods has resulted in the production of a more diverse range of products aimed at *niche* rather than *mass* markets. Advertising has similarly become more sophisticated and increasingly targets particular markets.

Post-Fordist changes have occurred in the media too. The creation of Channel 4 in 1982 has been seen in terms of a public-service concern to provide programmes for minorities, but it also made commercial sense, as these minorities were niche markets for advertisers. Entirely

Greater diversity or more of the same?
© Alice Chadwick

specialized television channels, providing sport or films, and specialized radio stations, such as Classic FM, have taken this process one stage further. There is also the proliferation of special-interest magazine titles. If you are selling pesticides to gardeners, the best way to reach them is to put adverts in a gardening magazine or attach them to a gardening programme on commercial radio or television.

Another important post-Fordist change has been the emergence of more flexible forms of organization that contract out functions to a network of smaller specialist firms (we discuss network organizations in Chapter 14, pp. 553–5). This has occurred in television with the introduction of the *publisher* model to replace the *producer* model. Both the BBC and the ITV companies were traditionally *producer-broadcasters*—that is, they largely made the programmes that they transmitted. Channel 4 was set up as a *publisher-broadcaster* to commission programmes made elsewhere and the other channels too now do this extensively.

Figure 10.2 The sources of diversity

Technology	New delivery and storage systems
Politics	Deregulation and competition
Consumption	Niche marketing
Production	Post-Fordist product diversification
Organization	Publisher broadcasting
Culture	Post-modern pluralism

The state played a part in this through the 1990 Broadcasting Act, which forced both BBC and ITV companies towards the publisher model by requiring them to take at least 25 per cent of their output from independent producers. Small and often short-lived independents have multiplied. This has diversified production and enlarged the range of products available. It has also greatly reduced security of employment and weakened the union organization of workers in the television industry.

The cultural changes associated with **post-modernism** (see p. 366) have contributed to diversity in other ways by creating a non-hierarchical plurality of cultures. The distinction between *high* and *popular* culture has become ever more blurred, as the domination of an elite *high* culture has been increasingly challenged by *popular* forms of culture disseminated by the media. Culture has also become less hierarchical as diverse class, ethnic, and national subcultures have become increasingly valued in their own right.

It is, however, not only the coexistence of a plurality of cultures that is characteristic of post-modernism. It is also the way that they are mixed and combined. People move more freely across cultural boundaries, as they consume culture just like any other product. They adopt styles and follow fashions in dress or food, picking and mixing from the various cultural resources available to them. Styles from different places and times are combined, whether in architecture or popular music or television adverts. This can be done for effect, to surprise and attract attention by deliberately breaking cultural rules. As Strinati (1992a) points out, there is often a subversive jokiness in the combination of apparently incompatible styles.

So, there are multiple sources of greater diversity, and choice has apparently greatly increased. Before celebrating this, however, we must also consider processes diminishing and limiting it.

Increasing or declining diversity?

As is so often the case, increased competition was followed by consolidation. Many of the new and highly specialized channels launched on a wave of entrepreneurial enthusiasm could not attract the audiences they needed to stay afloat.

Competitive pressures have also put ITV and the BBC under greater pressure to maximize their audiences. The multiplication of channels inevitably reduced the audiences for the main BBC and ITV channels. This was particularly serious for ITV, which had to compete with Channels 4 and 5 for advertising revenue and a host of other channels for audiences. If audiences fall, advertisers will not pay for advertising or will, at least, force down the rates they pay. The BBC also has to compete, as it can only justify the licence fee by having a large audience.

The growing competition for audiences has arguably reduced diversity. BBC1 and ITV have shown more frequent episodes of popular programmes, especially soap operas, and this has driven other programmes from peak viewing times. The main BBC and ITV channels are wary of taking risks, as they once did, with minority programmes at peak times. Nor can they force 'educational' programmes on a mass audience, as they also once could, by scheduling, say, documentaries at the same time, for there are plenty of other channels for watchers to migrate to. Educational, documentary, and minority programmes have been relegated to non-peak times or left to the niche channels, which have fewer resources for making such programmes.

There is a greater diversity of channels and more consumer choice but greater competition has also led to the pursuit of popularity by the main terrestrial channels and this has probably lessened diversity in the *mass* media.

Access

Diversity may make choice possible, but, as always, the exercise of choice depends on income, knowledge, time, and control.

Almost everyone in Britain has access to a television, but access to satellite, cable, and digital transmissions requires extra expenditure and some events, particularly major sports, are becoming accessible only by this means. The capacity to exercise choice is related to income, and those living in poverty will be increasingly excluded from full media participation. A section of the population may be deprived of what is increasingly regarded as a normal part of social life (see 'Poverty and deprivation', Chapter 18, pp. 751–8).

Knowledge, time, and control are closely related to the division of labour and distribution of power in the household. Gray (1992) studied household use of VCRs. She found that men had more knowledge of the technology and exercised more control over the choice of programmes. Housework, anyway, reduced the time, especially uninterrupted time, available to women for television-watching. Indeed, some of the women she interviewed saw television

Briefing: how much choice do YOU have?

- Look at one of the weekly magazines listing television programmes.
- How many channels are listed?
- How many do you have access to?
- List the things that limit your choice of viewing.

and VCR as a last-resort leisure activity, for household obligations meant that it was difficult to escape work at home and they preferred to go out. Women benefited less than men from the opportunities for increased choice.

Choice is not simply a matter of the availability of options and depends on the capacity to choose.

Ownership and control

Greater competition has also led to greater concentration, as control of the media fell into fewer hands. In this section we first consider changes in the pattern of ownership and then its significance for political choice.

Ownership

As we showed on pp. 371–2, ownership became more concentrated as the media developed. This process has continued and become more complex with the multiplication of media:

- concentration within media;
- multi-media ownership;
- transnational ownership.

Ownership has become concentrated within particular media. Murdoch's News Corporation's papers have accounted for one-third of the weekly sales of British national papers. ITV is moving towards ownership by a single corporation. As in any other areas of the economy, concentration is a way of increasing profits by eliminating competitors and creating economies of scale.

Even more striking has been the growth of *multi-media* empires. Conglomerates have emerged with wide-ranging interests spanning newspapers, book and magazine publishing, television companies, film studios, and radio stations. Ownership across the media facilitates the promotion of related products, such as books based on television series, transfers of content between, say, film production and television, and the pooling of communications expertise. Rupert Murdoch's News Corporation,

Global focus 'Planet Murdoch': Rupert Murdoch's News Corporation in 2004

Area	Newspapers	Book and magazine publishing	Television, radio and film
Global		Harper Collins UK, US, and Australia Inc. (Operations in 30 countries)	20th Century Fox
Asia and Middle East		Harper Collins (India)	Star TV (satellite covering China, India, Saudi Arabia, and 50 other countries)
			Phoenix satellite TV
			China Network Systems
Australia	*The Australian* and over 100 other titles	Various magazine titles	Fox Studios
			Foxtel
Europe (outside UK)			Sky Radio
			Sky Italia
			Balkan News Corporation
Latin America			Sky Latin America
			Direct TV Latin America
United Kingdom	*The Times, Sunday Times, News of the World, Sun*	*TES, TLS*	BSKYB (satellite)
United States	*New York Post, Weekly Standard*	*Gemstar TV Guide*	Fox Entertainment, 35 Fox TV stations
			Cable Network Programming
			Direct TV
Other	Interests in Fiji and Papua New Guinea		

Note that in 2005 News Corporation began to acquire Internet companies.

Source: S. Shah 'Planet Murdoch', *Independent*, 18 October 2004.

? See if you can find out which companies providing Internet services have become part of Planet Murdoch. Why do you think News Corporation has moved in here?

with its major interests in film and television, as well as newspapers, again provides a good example, and in 2005 began buying Internet companies. Note that News Corporation's television interests include terrestrial stations, and cable and satellite channels. Time Warner's merger with America Online (AOL) in 2000 showed another multi-media empire extending its interests into the Internet. The BBC has created online services, closely interconnected with its programmes and with the extensive commercial operations it has recently developed.

The big media corporations are all *transnational* corporations with a global reach. Murdoch's News Corporation has major interests in Australia, Britain, Hong Kong, and the United States, and minor interests in many other countries. A small number of global corporations, notably Walt Disney, Time Warner, News Corporation, Viacom, Bertelsman, and Sony dominate the world's media.

Newspaper politics

But does ownership matter? In this section we focus on the consequences of the concentration of newspaper ownership for the political process. Do owners politically manipulate their readers or merely follow their views?

There is little doubt that newspapers were moving to the political right during the period from the 1960s to the 1980s. The *Sun* in particular moved from supporting Labour to supporting the Conservatives in 1979. The Labour Party faced a largely hostile press in the 1980s and by 1987 papers supporting the Conservative Party accounted for 72 per cent of national daily circulation (Curran and Seaton 1991: 124).

Their shift to the right can be explained in two different ways. First, there is the argument that it resulted from the interests of capital. As owners of capital, the owners of newspapers have a general interest in maintaining

Controversy and debate Labour government and media concentration

Traditionally the British labour movement has been hostile to the increasing concentration of media ownership but in 2003 a Labour government passed legislation that makes this easier. The 2003 Communications Act removed various rules designed to prevent media corporations building a dominant position both within particular sectors and across them. The rationale for this Act was the 'neo-liberal' belief that deregulation would improve the efficiency and competitiveness of media

companies (see p. 386). Economic arguments took priority over the need to maintain media 'plurality'. Some critics have suggested that the government's relationship with Rupert Murdoch's News Corporation may have had something to do with this Act, which allowed newspaper companies greater freedom to buy into radio and television.

Source: Doyle (2004).

capitalism. More specifically, their profits are heavily influenced by their labour costs, and they therefore have a direct interest in 'bashing the unions'. Tunstall (1996) suggests that their support for Thatcherism was linked to its attack on union power. The anti-union legislation passed by the Thatcher government certainly helped Rupert Murdoch to take on and defeat the print unions in the crucial battle over the movement of newspaper production to Wapping in 1986. This defeat destroyed their previously considerable control of newspaper production.

The alternative explanation is in terms of market pressures. In the end profits depend on selling newspapers and no owner can run a paper at a loss for long. People are unlikely to buy papers on a regular basis if they express unpopular views. The electorate as a whole shifted to the right in the later 1970s and it can be argued that the newspapers simply followed it in order to maintain their sales. There were good commercial reasons for the rightward shift of the press.

The significance of this shift to the right is also difficult to assess. The *Sun*'s support for the Conservatives has been considered a major factor in their election victories, but, as we showed earlier (see p. 369), it is very difficult to demonstrate media effects on behaviour. It is claimed, none the less, that in the 1987 election the *Sun* and the *Star* markedly influenced politically uncommitted readers towards voting Conservative (B. Franklin 1994). Through its support for Thatcherism, the press probably played some role in the Conservative victories of the 1980s and 1990s, but it is difficult to assess how important this was. The Labour Party and the labour movement were weak during this period for other reasons and their weakness cannot be attributed to a hostile press alone.

This was not, however, the end of the story, for in March 1997 the *Sun* changed sides (as did some other right-wing newspapers) and it supported Labour in the 1997, 2001, and 2005 general elections. It may be that the *Sun* simply

recognized that Labour was going to win and wanted to be on the winning side so that it could exert some influence on the government. It has been more specifically suggested that Rupert Murdoch's alliance with Labour was motivated by a concern to head off any legislation on media ownership that might obstruct his plans.

Murdoch's strong opposition to Britain joining the Euro might have been expected to prevent him supporting a pro-Euro Labour government. However, Murdoch is reported to have told Tony Blair that the *Sun* would support Labour if it changed its policy and called a referendum on the Euro (given the unpopularity of the Euro, a referendum would probably block entry). Labour did, indeed, change its policy in April 2004 and newspapers owned by Murdoch just happened to be the first to break this news (*Independent*, 20 April 2004).

It is difficult to assess the actual significance of newspaper support for the outcome of elections but it is clear that politicians take it very seriously. In deciding who to support, newspaper owners are influenced by their established ideological positions, which are related to their target readership. They also have clear interests as owners in securing governments with policies that favour their corporate interests. They have to bear in mind, however, the danger of losing influence if they back the wrong horse. In the 1980s there was no problem, as all these considerations pointed the same way—support for the Conservatives. Since the middle of the 1990s Murdoch in particular has faced more difficult choices but so far his interests have kept him supporting Labour.

Decline of the public sphere?

As we showed on p. 365, the concept of a 'public sphere', where people can freely discuss matters of importance to them, has been much discussed in social and political theory. It has been argued that a strong public sphere must be maintained if the electorate's political choice is to be free and informed. Growing commercial and political pressures have, however, encroached on the public sphere, though the Internet has recently provided it with an alternative medium.

The commercialization of the media

Here we consider first the continued commercialization of the press and then the commercialization of broadcasting. Commercialization threatens the public sphere because of both the commercial manipulation of media content and the displacement of information and debate by entertainment.

The commercialization of the press (see p. 371) continued after the Second World War. A widening gap emerged, however, between the popular and the 'quality' press, where the coverage of public affairs was maintained. Curran and Seaton (1991) claimed that this gap had important political consequences, for working-class

Which aspects of this front page reflect commercialization?

© Alice Chadwick

readers were denied serious coverage of public affairs. This was not because there was no demand for this material. Market research showed that people wanted it but their lack of purchasing power meant that advertisers were not interested in supporting newspapers that might meet this demand. 'An elite press thus came to dominate by default the field of serious journalism, thereby reinforcing elite domination of political life' (Curran and Seaton 1991: 118).

Both the ITV network and the BBC have come under increasing commercial pressure since the 1980s. ITV companies found that the arrival of Channel 5, followed by the multiplication of satellite and cable channels, intensified the competition for audiences and advertisers. The BBC's licence fee did not increase sufficiently to cover its rising costs and it sought alternative sources of money, by, for example, creating magazines linked to programmes.

One of the effects of commercialization has been the steady breakdown of the barrier between programme content and advertising. Advertising agencies seek to break through this barrier because advertising that is *integrated* with content is more effective than advertising *segregated* in slots. Integration enables the use of what Vance Packard (1963) famously called 'hidden persuaders'. It also reaches a larger audience through repeats and international sales, and cannot be bypassed by the 'zapper' or by recording technologies.

Graham Murdock (1992) has traced this process. In the early 1980s both BBC and ITV came to accept sponsorship. The televising of sport was a key battleground, for advertisers wanted to associate their products with healthy activities and reach large, often international, sport audiences. The BBC gave way on this and by 1986 was showing some 350 hours of sport per year sponsored by tobacco companies, which were not allowed for health reasons to advertise their products in ITV slots. ITV sponsorship rules were relaxed by the 1990 Broadcasting Act, which allowed sponsorship of an increasing range of programmes, including weather forecasts but excluding news programmes.

Sponsorship is now an accepted and ever more widespread part of television. The Independent Television Commission bans the influence of programme content by sponsors, but there is clearly a risk that those who fund programmes will find ways of influencing them. It has certainly happened in other countries, particularly through 'product placement', which inserts products into programmes. Although this is not allowed in British television, advertisers try to 'beat the system' and, since the 1980s, placement has occurred increasingly in films, which, sooner or later, get shown on television (see box on 'Product placement' on p. 392). Murdock has pointed out that sponsorship anyway gives commercial interests the power to determine which programmes are made, thereby threatening broadcasting as a public sphere (Murdock 1992).

Briefing: product placement

'The present intensification of placement activity dates from 1982, when the alien in *ET* was enticed from his hiding place by a trail of Reese's Pieces sweets, producing a 300 per cent increase in the brand's sales. Since then, placement has become an integral part of Hollywood film-making, with Associated Film Promotions and similar agencies continually scanning new scripts for placement opportunities for their clients. Sums for onset promotions regularly range from the $100,000 Kimberly-Clark paid to have Huggies nappies used in *Baby Boom* and to use its infant star in publicity, to Philip Morris's $350,000 outlay on *Licence to Kill* to have James Bond use their Lark cigarette brand.' (Murdock 1992: 227)

Commercialization operates in other ways, by, for example, mixing information with entertainment to produce 'infotainment'. Hallin (1996) examined this process in American television. In the 1960s professional journalism became well-established in the networks' news divisions, which were insulated from commercial pressures. Increasing competition in the 1980s led, however, to the spread of 'reality-based programming'. This mixed news and entertainment in magazine-style programmes that became the main output of the news divisions.

One consequence of this was a greater interest in the private lives of public figures. Presidential elections in the United States came to revolve largely around personalities rather than policies. Politicians were, of course, happy to exploit and manipulate this interest in private lives but commercial pressures lay behind the shift of news content that brought this about.

Hallin saw some virtues in a more popular and less elitist presentation of news, but he was concerned about the consequences of commercialization for the political process:

> The nation's political agenda, its stock of social knowledge, its style of political discussion, all are shaped by the news media, and there is no reason to suppose that they will be 'optimized' by profit-seeking programmers and advertisers. (Hallin 1996: 259)

The state and the public sphere

The relationship between the state and the media is crucial to the maintenance of the public sphere. The state is in many ways the guardian of this sphere but also the main threat to it.

In Britain, the media regulator, the Office of Communications (OFCOM), has been charged by the Communications Act of 2003 with a duty to 'further the interests of citizens in relation to communications matters'. The state sets the framework for public-service broadcasting by regulating the programming of the public-service providers, which include not only the BBC channels but also ITV, Channel 4, and Channel 5. ITV is, for example, required to provide arts, religious, children's and regional programmes.

The continuing shift to digital broadcasting is expected to undermine existing public-service provision as unregulated channels multiply and take more viewers. OFCOM has proposed a relaxation of the public-service requirements on ITV, which is expected to have difficulty competing with commercial channels unburdened with these requirements. It has also proposed the creation of a new public-service broadcaster that would be in competition with the BBC. OFCOM is trying to maintain a public-service provision threatened by growing commercial pressures, a high rate of technical change, and the rise of global media corporations.

The state also provides important information to the public. In 1980s Britain, the flow of information to the media about politics and policies grew enormously. Television gained access to parliament, with the admission of cameras to the House of Lords in 1985 and the House of Commons in 1990. New 'league table' information, of great interest to the public, on the performance of hospitals, schools, and universities became available for the first time.

While the state in these ways promotes the public interest, it is also one of the main threats to the public sphere. Governments have, since the 1980s, engaged in increasing manipulation of the media. The 'packaging' of politicians and policies for the media rapidly developed at this time. The political parties increasingly employed media consultants, public-relations experts, and advertising agencies to promote their policies and personalities (B. Franklin 1994).

While all political parties did this, the governing party had control of the apparatus and resources of the state and the Conservative governments of the 1980s made much greater use of the media. The prime minister's press secretary more actively managed and coordinated the flow of information to journalists. By 1989 the government had become Britain's biggest advertiser as huge amounts of money were spent on campaigns to promote the government's privatization policies.

There were also growing government attempts to censor and regulate media information. The government attacked media coverage of the Falklands War and the conflict in Northern Ireland. New bodies were established to regulate broadcasting, the Broadcasting Complaints

Commission of 1981 and the Broadcasting Council of 1988. The 1990 Broadcasting Act required the practice of 'due impartiality' in matters of 'political or industrial controversy or relating to current public policy'. This enabled governments to attack media they judged were giving too much publicity to opponents.

The post-1997 Labour governments have further developed the techniques brought in by the Conservatives in the 1980s. The prime minister's press secretary has tried to control the government's relationship with the press. Special political advisers, nick-named 'spin-doctors', were appointed to ministries to handle the presentation of policies, and, some have said, to shape those policies in ways that would gain good publicity for the government.

One aspect of government news management that has attracted much comment has been not the promotion of good news but the concealment of bad news. When the twin towers of the New York World Trade Center came down on 11 September 2001, Jo Moore, a special adviser at the Department of Transport, notoriously e-mailed colleagues to tell them that it was 'a good day to bury bad news'.

The state's relationship to the public sphere is ambivalent. The control of the commercialization of broadcasting and the maintenance of public-service provision depend on state regulation. The state is also, however, an instrument of governments seeking to manipulate and restrict the information available to the public. The state is both the main protector of the public sphere and the greatest potential threat to it.

The Internet and the public sphere

Arguably, as commercialization and government manipulation increasingly threaten the public sphere, the Internet and the World Wide Web have created new opportunities for developing it.

Figure 10.3 The state and the public sphere

The state's positive contribution	The state's negative contribution
● Public service framework of TV	● Censorship
● Regulation of commercial interests	● Promotion of government policy
● Provision of information	● News management

Although the Internet was created for military purposes (see box on 'Net and Web'), it was then developed as a means of exchanging knowledge for education and research. It was decentralized, committed to 'free speech', and open to all who had the skills to access it, qualities that made it a highly suitable vehicle for the public sphere, though until the growth of the Web its use was restricted to a highly educated elite. It was the invention and expansion of the Web that opened up the Internet to a wider public.

The Web itself was designed to perform public-sphere functions. Tim Berners-Lee, who was more responsible than anyone else for developing its organization and protocols, was an idealist dedicated to the principles of communication, cooperation, and participation.

> When I proposed the Web in 1989, the driving force I had in mind was communication through shared knowledge, and the driving 'market' for it was collaboration among people at work and at home. By building a hypertext Web, a group of people of whatever size could easily express themselves, quickly acquire and convey knowledge, overcome misunderstandings and reduce duplication of effort. This would give people in a group a new power to build something together. (Berners-Lee 2000: 174)

New technology Net and Web

The 'Net'

● The Internet is a network of interconnected computers.

● Its origins lay in a military network developed in the United States in the 1960s.

● After technical developments in the 1970s, the Internet was established in the 1980s to transmit information between American universities and laboratories.

The 'Web'

● The World Wide Web is a network of interlinked files accessed via the Net. The Hyper Text Transfer Protocol (http), provides

the common rules that enable the transmission of these files between computers.

● The World Wide Web was created by Tim Berners-Lee in 1990, while working at the Cern European Particle Physics laboratory in Geneva.

● The invention at the University of Illinois of an easy-to-use web browser called Mosaic, later to become Netscape Navigator, resulted in the rapid expansion of the Web after 1993.

Sources: Berners-Lee (2000); Gauntlett (2000).

The creation of the Web was, however, followed by the commercialization of the Internet. Rapidly growing Internet usage provided an opportunity to access an expanding and relatively affluent market. Companies discovered that they could have an 'electronic shopfront', combining 'signage, catalogues, product information and pictures, advertising, a virtual tour, contacting a business, meeting staff' (Goggin 2000: 105). Advertisers found a new medium for reaching consumers. Pornographers found that they could transmit powerful erotic images directly to individuals. Financial service companies realized that they could transact their business cheaply online. By the end of the 1990s e-commerce had really taken off and has continued to grow.

Arguably, this commercialization has eaten into the public-service functions of the Web. It is not only that commercial activity has occupied growing amounts of Internet space. Technological advances have made it possible for commercial interests to accumulate information about individuals' interests and target them with advertising tailored to their interests. Portals can steer the browser towards the products that sponsor them or advertise through them. Consumers' profiles can, indeed, be bought and sold. Net-users are therefore exposed to various kinds of covert commercial manipulation.

Goggin cautions us, however, against jumping to the conclusion that commerce has taken over the Web. Although commercial activity has rapidly increased, there is still plenty of cultural, educational, political, and individual activity:

Some of the traditional public spaces have been reinvented and reconceived online, often deliberately so—whether libraries, community or selfhelp groups, public broadcasters, news, public service announcements or information services. An individual or group's ability to make a space for themselves on the Internet—public or private—is still arguably far greater than in other media. (Goggin 2000: 111)

The public functions of the Internet can, in other words, coexist with its commercial functions but it is not just a matter of their survival. Arguably, the vast expansion of the Internet would not have occurred unless people could make money out of it. Use of the Web has been made easy because it was only through making it user-friendly that the market for Web services and products could be maximized. Like commercial television, much 'free' Internet provision, such as the search engines, is financed by advertising. Without commercialization, the Internet would have remained a high-minded but exclusive club for a highly educated elite. Access remains an issue, for this costs money and requires expertise, but there can be little doubt that commercialization has widened it.

The public functions of the Internet/Web have been relatively free of state regulation. It is more difficult for the state to control its content than that of the press or radio and television, though that has not stopped the Chinese government trying (see box on 'Internet dissent in China'). Furthermore, the Internet/Web enables the cross-border organization of dispersed or fragmented opposition movements. With the growth of wireless technologies, the Web can be accessed from anywhere within a communication

Frontiers News on the Net

One area in which it is claimed the Internet contributes to the public sphere is through the diffusion and democratization of news. Established news providers, such as the newspapers or the BBC, can reach out faster and further by going online. Arguably, news has also been democratized, for it is no longer controlled by established commercial or political organizations but can be provided by any individual able to create a website. 'News receivers' can become 'news producers'. The news provided by Web sources can escape the state regulation and manipulation that distort the news provided by newspapers and broadcasters.

There are also problems, however, with online news. One, which we discussed in the box on 'Rolling and breaking news' on p. 375, is that the instant transmission of news may be the transmission of unchecked rumour. Untrained news producers on the Web may lack the standards of detachment and impartiality that, in principle at any rate, govern the provision of news by estab-

lished providers. The source of news and the credentials of the news producer may be obscure. News from Web sources may also be distorted and manipulated, and subject to commercial pressures. If people turn increasingly to the Web for news, they may use established providers less, and these may lose commercial viability. Newspapers may shut down and the established public sphere may be diminished.

Sources: Gunter (2003); 'Doors', *Sunday Times*, 5 June 2005.

❷ When you want to find out 'the news' about something, where do you look?

❷ Do you think that Web sources are 'better' than established providers?

❥ As an exercise, compare news coverage of an event by an established provider and by Web sources.

Global focus Internet dissent in China

The media have long been tightly controlled by the Communist Party in China. Journalists have recently been challenging censorship by reporting on mining and environmental disasters, official corruption, and the social problems caused by economic growth. The government has responded by closing down publications and jailing journalists.

Increasing Internet use, particularly by the young, is an alternative means of criticizing the government and voicing dissent. Print journalists have taken to the Net to publish what the censors have blocked. The government has responded by blocking websites, introducing filtering software, and monitoring Internet cafes and registering their users. According to Jonathan Watts of the *Guardian*: 'An Internet police force—reportedly numbering 30,000—trawls websites and chatrooms, erasing anti-Communist comments and posting pro-government messages.'

The government has also enlisted the help of Yahoo, Microsoft, Cisco, and Google. Yahoo helped the government identify a dissident, who was subsequently jailed for ten years, through his e-mail account. Microsoft has blocked Chinese searches on key words, such as 'democracy'. Cisco has provided surveillance software. Google, supposedly the guardian of Internet freedom, has agreed that its Chinese branch will obey Chinese censorship laws. The Chinese market is so big that these companies dare not risk exclusion from it.

Source: *Media Guardian*, 20 February 2006.

❷ Can the Internet undermine authoritarian regimes?

---

satellite's footprint. So far, people's concerns have focused more on the absence of regulation, which has allowed racist and other hate groups, and paedophile networks, to flourish on the Net, than on the dangers of state regulation.

The Web is not, however, free of state surveillance. Messages can be traced, because there is always an electronic record, in transmission and storage machinery, that cannot easily be destroyed, and China provides an example of this too (see box on 'Internet dissent in China'). Encryption may make it difficult to break codes but historically ways have always been found of breaking the apparently unbreakable. If commercial agencies can construct consumer profiles, governments can certainly construct political ones. Although state control of content may be difficult, surveillance may inhibit communication by making it too dangerous to communicate subversively or illegally.

The ingenuity of Internet users has so far run ahead of most attempts to police the Net, but there are some reasons for doubting whether it can replace the media as the main vehicle of the public sphere:

- *Access.* This requires technical skills as well as equipment. Although computers are becoming ever more available and knowledge of how to use them is spreading fast, the Internet is still a long way from being as accessible as radio, television, or newspapers (see box on 'The digital divide' in Chapter 16, on p. 646).

- *The interface with politics.* There is much exchange of information and opinion on the Web, but currently the connection between its world and mainstream political discussion and communication is limited.

There are, then, good grounds for the view that the Net can contribute importantly to the public sphere. Although commercialization has diverted the Net's development away from the goals and values of those who created it, commercialization has arguably made it more accessible without destroying its public functions. Governments are making greater attempts to monitor and regulate it but have much lee-way to make up, and it is not clear how successful they will be in this. The Internet cannot, however, replace the established media, which still have a crucial function to perform in the public sphere.

Media globalization

Global communication has made television a 'window on the world', bringing world events into one's room as they happen. Potentially, it has provided greater choice both through access to a greater diversity of programmes and new opportunities to break free from national cultures. This is, however, contested by those who believe that globalization has destroyed diversity by imposing on the world one national culture, that of the United States. They claim that globalization means Americanization. The global diffusion of American culture has also been seen as a **media imperialism** that promotes continued domination by American corporations, values, and policies.

American global domination?

American media corporations have become increasingly dominant globally. In 1993 the top American multi-media company was only the fourth largest in the world but by

Controversy and debate Al-Jazeera

CNN has been a powerful vehicle for the global diffusion of the American view of the world. The domination of 24-hour news broadcasting by CNN was, however, challenged by the rise of Al-Jazeera, an Arabic satellite channel launched in Qatar in 1996 and modelled on CNN. Al-Jazeera has been financially dependent on funding by the emir of Qatar, though there are plans to privatize it.

Al-Jazeera's news coverage has been heavily criticized by United States leaders and officials. It has been accused of giving voice to Al-Qaeda by broadcasting Osama bin-Laden's videotapes. It has been criticized for showing 'raw' the bloody consequences of warfare and insurgency in Iraq. It has been seen as a mouthpiece of the insurgents because of its 'slanted' reporting of the civilian deaths and destruction caused by military operations. Its offices in Kabul and Baghdad were bombed by American planes and its operations in occupied Iraq have been shut down.

Al-Jazeera is seen as providing the Arabic alternative to Western news channels but its position is not as simple as that. It has undoubtedly provided an independently minded and very different coverage of events, and in its debate programmes has allowed the expression of strong and controversial opinions (quite different in this respect from the region's state-controlled broadcasters). It has, however, drawn Arabic criticism because it has given voice through interviews to Israeli and American politicians. It has also been seen as siding with Sunni muslims against Shias. The rival Al-Arabiya news channel, set up by Saudi interests in Dubai in 2003, is popular in Iraq and Saudi Arabia.

What does the future hold for Al-Jazeera? It certainly has global ambitions. It launched an English-language channel, presented by David Frost, in March 2006. A new competitor for its audience in the Middle East is, however, coming over the horizon. The BBC is launching its own Arabic news channel, funded by the British Foreign Office, in 2007.

Sources: 'Arab satellite television', *Economist*, 26 February 2005; Miles (2005); 'BBC goes head-to-head with Al-Jazeera', *Guardian*, 26 October 2006.

❷ What does this account tell us about media globalization, American global domination, and cultural pluralism?

1998 American corporations occupied three out of the top four places. Walt Disney was the largest, followed by Time Warner, but Time Warner then merged with AOL in 2000 to become number one (Van Gompel *et al.* 2002: 190). These corporations provide one of the main vehicles for the export of American culture.

Hollywood has increased its domination of world film production. Although it established this domination long ago (see p. 372), film industries elsewhere did, none the less, develop but these have declined in recent years. Between 1987 and 1996 Hollywood's share of the European film market rose from 56 per cent to 70 per cent. By 1996 Hollywood had 83 per cent of the Latin American market. Mexico had at one time produced a hundred films a year but by 1995 was only making forty and by 1998 less than ten (United Nations Development Programme 1999: 33).

This American cultural domination of film production is paralleled by a domination of television schedules. In the 1990s some 62 per cent of television programming in Latin America came from the United States, 8 per cent from Asia and Europe, and only 30 per cent from within the region (United Nations Development Programme 1999: 34). American exports accounted for three-quarters of world programme exports in the mid-1990s (C. Barker 1997: 50).

Cultural pluralism

The claim of Americanization is opposed by those who argue that the emergence of local production has led to a growing cultural pluralism. Sreberny-Mohammadi (1996) lists a number of ways in which national cultures can resist media imperialism:

- *The domestication of output.* Home-produced programmes can oust imports because they are more attractive for linguistic and cultural reasons.
- *Reverse flows.* Ex-colonial countries can start to export their own programmes to the old imperial societies. Increasing international migration has paved the way for this. Bollywood films provide a good example.
- *Going global.* Local producers can themselves create transnational corporations. For example, ZEE TV, a Hindi-language Indian commercial station, took over TV Asia in Britain.
- *Controls on distribution.* Television imports to terrestrial channels in Britain have been limited to a quota of some 14 per cent of programmes. It is more difficult to control satellite television, but some countries, such as Singapore, Malaysia, Saudi Arabia, and Iran, have banned the sale of satellite dishes.

Bollywood—a reverse flow?
© Getty Images/Arko Datta

American penetration of markets does vary considerably. It is high, as we saw above, in Latin America, though Brazil is an important independent centre of production there. It has been much lower in some Asian markets, especially India. A 1994 study reported that in India 92 per cent of television programming was of domestic origin. This was much higher than in Europe, though there were considerable variations between European countries, with Sweden producing 81 per cent, but Italy producing only 58 per cent, of its output. The figures for Australia were lower still at 46 per cent (Sreberny-Mohammadi 1996: 188).

The notion of Americanization is also open to the criticism that it is based on the *media-effects* model of media influence, which we discussed on p. 368. It assumes that American programmes automatically inject American values. Studies of the impact of the American *Dallas* series, which was exported to more than ninety countries, have shown that it is not as simple as that. *Dallas* apparently celebrated the values of American capitalism, but Ang (1985) demonstrated that Dutch viewers were perfectly

capable of enjoying the story and its emotions while disapproving of its values and rejecting them.

As we showed earlier, audience identification with film characters is a complex process. The audience may simply reverse the apparent values of a Hollywood film by siding with the 'bad guys' rather than the 'good guys'. People respond to cultural imports within the context of their own situation and values.

Global corporations anyway recognize that they can market their products more effectively by adapting them to local needs. Indeed, the term 'glocalization' was invented to describe the Japanese marketing strategy of adapting global products to meet local requirements. In the media case, this can mean adapting to the requirements of the national state. The behaviour of Google in China (see box on 'Internet dissent in China' on p. 395) provides a good example of this.

This means that there are dangers in uncritically celebrating pluralism. As Sreberny-Mohammadi (1996) points out, local producers will generally be under the

Global focus 'Reality TV' goes global

The *Big Brother* format was created in 2000 and by early 2004 there were already twenty-four different versions across the world. The twenty-fifth was *Big Brother Middle East*, which was the first in a muslim area. There was much local concern that unmarried men and women would be sharing the same house and might fall in love. None the less, the programme went ahead but with separate living rooms and prayer rooms for men and women. Cameras in the bathroom, dance marathons, and the practice of chaining people together for long periods were all dropped!

In 2005 *The Apprentice* arrived in China. There it is called *Wise Man Takes All*. In the American and British versions contestants competed to secure employment with such well-known entrepreneurs as Donald Trump and Alan Sugar, who set them complex tasks, judge their performance ruthlessly, and fire those who do not perform. In the Chinese version the show has more of an educational character. Contestants have to submit business plans, to be judged by a panel of business school professors, and the winner receives one million *yuan* to invest in their business. There is no humiliation of contestants and no one gets fired!

Source: *Independent*, 28 February 2004, 18 August 2005.

❷ Does the international spread of 'reality TV' weaken or strengthen local cultures?

control of their nation state, which may well be trying to stamp out local resistance to its authority. Similarly, the banning of satellite dishes may be little to do with preserving local culture and a lot to do with maintaining the existing social order. In highly patriarchal societies, male domination may be threatened by the import of programmes embodying a more liberated conception of the role of women.

Thus, the debate over the control of media imports must be placed in the context of conflicts of interest and authority relationships *within* society as well as the context of conflicts *between* cultures and international relationships.

‹› *Stop and reflect*

In this section we examined the movement from a small number of mass media outlets towards a world of more specialized multiple media.

- Technical change, neo-liberal politics, post-Fordist organization, post-modern culture, and globalization have broadly resulted in greater media diversity.

  Greater media diversity has in principle provided more choice, but in practice this has been limited by other processes of change.

- The exercise of choice depends on access, which requires resources, knowledge, time, and control.

- The concentration of ownership has increased not only within particular media but also across the media and internationally.

- What implications has this concentration had for political choice?

We also considered the impact of media changes on the public sphere.

- Revisit the discussion of the consequences of the growth of the mass media for this sphere on pp. 371–3.

- The commercialization of newspapers and broadcasting have weakened the autonomy of the public sphere.

- We have argued that the state is to some extent a guardian of this sphere but also a threat to it.

- Do you think that the Internet has revived the public sphere?

  Technical change has facilitated media globalization.

- This has potentially provided access to a far greater range of cultures and experiences.

- Has it led to Americanization?

Chapter summary

In the 'Understanding the media' section we outlined the main approaches to the study of the media. We first considered concepts and theories:

- The concept of 'mass media' is linked to the mass-society theory of the atomizing of society by industrialization and urbanization.

- Dominant-ideology theory saw the media as maintaining ruling-class hegemony.

- Other approaches argued that consumers and producers, as well as owners and controllers, shape the content of the media.

- We discussed the concept of a public sphere, and the mass media's contribution to it.

We went on to discuss different conceptions of culture:

- Popular culture emerged out of a folk culture distinct from high culture.

- Elitist and populist views provide competing interpretations of popular culture.

- Cyberculture is apparently new and free but older constraints of social inequality and commercial pressures still operate.

We concluded by examining models of media influence and methods of research:

- We distinguished media-effects, active-audience, and media-themes models.

- Media research used methods of content analysis, textual analysis, and audience research.

We then outlined the growth of the mass media. This reflected the general features of the development of capitalist industrialism:

- Large, capital-intensive enterprises mass produced newspapers and films.

- Markets were controlled by integrating production and distribution, and driving out competitors.

- Ownership became highly concentrated.

We also considered the impact of the growth of the media on the public sphere:

- Newspaper readership grew but commercial pressures diminished 'serious' content.

- The BBC was established on public-service principles but was also an agent of the state.

- Although commercial television was introduced in the 1950s, public-service regulation and limited competition restricted the effects of commercialization.

In the next section we considered the influence of the mass media. We first examined media presentation of information:

- The social construction of the news shapes the way that information is presented by the media.

- The superior resources of those with wealth and power enable them to influence but not wholly determine the content of the news.

We moved on to consider media representations of class, gender, ethnicity, and disability:

- The media reproduce stereotypes, but representations none the less change as society changes.

In the section on the 'Limits of choice' we explored the degree to which greater media diversity has provided more choice. Technical change, neo-liberal politics, post-Fordist organization, and post-modern culture have resulted in greater media diversity:

- The exercise of choice depends on access, which requires resources, knowledge, time, and control.

- Choice has been diminished by the concentration of ownership.

We considered the political significance of ownership:

- Newspaper owners arguably played a significant part in the Thatcherite transformation of British politics.

- While newspapers have ideological positions, they also take account of market considerations and the likely character of the next government when deciding which political party to support.

We then discussed changes in the media's contribution to the public sphere:

- Commercial pressures reduced coverage of public affairs in the popular press and broke down the barriers between programming and advertising.

- The flow of information about politics and policies has increased but so have political manipulation and attempts at censorship.

- The Internet has enlarged choice and provided an important new medium for the public sphere, but it too is subject to political and commercial influence.

Globalization has potentially provided access to a greater range of cultures and experiences:

- Cultural diversity may, however, be lost through Americanization.

- Various mechanisms do, none the less, perpetuate cultural pluralism.

🔑 *Key concepts*

- cyberculture
- dominant culture
- dominant ideology
- folk culture
- gatekeepers
- hegemony
- hegemonic masculinity

- high culture
- mass culture
- mass media
- mass society
- media
- media imperialism
- moral panic

- popular culture
- post-Fordism
- post-modernism
- public sphere
- subcultures

Workshop 10

Study 10 Television and violence

The impact of television watching on violence has been a much debated issue. As we argued on p. 384, it is one thing to show that there is some association between watching violence on television and violent behaviour, but it is more difficult to show that it was the watching that led to the violence, rather than the other way round. People with a violent disposition or in a situation that made them violent might simply be attracted to violent programmes.

The results of a sophisticated longitudinal study that tried to tackle this problem have been published by Johnson *et al.* (2002). This was a study of 707 families in the state of New York. It was carried out over seventeen years, beginning in 1975 with randomly selected families with a child under the age of 10. Data on television viewing and aggressive or criminal behaviour were collected by interviews with the children and their mothers in the 1980s and the 1990s. Information was also collected on other aspects of these families, such as intelligence, education, income, psychiatric disorders, and child neglect, and on neighbourhood characteristics, including levels of aggression and school violence.

The study found a significant association between the amount of television watched in the early teenage years (at an average

age of 14) and aggressive acts reported in the later teenage years or early adulthood (at average ages of 16 and 22). Thus, it was reported that 25 per cent of those who had watched more than three hours of television per day in their early teenage years were involved later on in assaults or fights that resulted in injury. This compared with 18 per cent of those who watched between one and three hours, and 6 per cent of those who watched less than one hour.

There was also an association between amount of television watched in early adulthood (at an average age of 22) and aggressive acts reported later (at an average age of 30), though this was not so strong.

There were important differences between boys and girls. The early teenage boys who watched a lot of television were far more likely to be involved in assaults or fights later on—some 42 per cent of those who had watched more than three hours a day, compared with 27.5 per cent of those watching one to three hours, and only 9 per cent of those watching less than an hour. The association was much less strong with girls at this age and not statistically significant.

The picture changed dramatically later on. There was a much stronger association between television watching and later aggression among young adult women than young adult men. While 17 per cent of the women who watched more than three hours of television engaged in aggressive acts later, only 4 per cent of those who watched between one and three hours did so (none of them watched less than an hour).

These associations suggest that large amounts of television-watching may lead to violence later but what about other possible explanations? There was still a significant association between amount of watching and amount of later aggression after controlling other variables, such as poverty or bad parenting, that might account for both. What about the argument that those with aggressive tendencies were more likely to watch a lot of television in the first place? An association was found between amount of watching and later violence, whether or not there was a history of previous violence.

What conclusions can be drawn from this study? The authors state that their study could not, by its very nature, demonstrate a *causal* connection between amount of television-watching and later violence. Some environmental factor that they had not taken into account could possibly explain the association. Only a controlled experiment could demonstrate causation and a study of that kind would be unethical. The leader of the research team was, however, confident enough to state that: 'Our findings suggest that, at least during early adolescence, responsible parents should avoid permitting their children to watch more than one hour of television a day' (*Independent*, 29 March 2002).

Note that this study did not show an association between the *amount of violence* seen on television and later violence. The association was between *amount of watching* as such and later

violence. The authors refer to other studies that show there are on average between three and five violent acts per hour of prime time television and 20–25 in an average hour of children's television.

Sources: Johnson *et al.* (2002); *Independent*, 29 March 2002.

❷ Can you think of any possible explanation of the association between amount of television watching and later violence other than the violent content of television programmes?

❷ What model of media influence (see pp. 368–9) was used in this study? How would other models suggest that this issue should be investigated?

❷ Given the results of this study, should children's television viewing be restricted to one hour a day?

❷ Try making a content analysis of the violence portrayed in a drama or some other similar programme on television (record it first). List incidents of violence, their duration, their consequences, different types of violence, the relationship in which the violence occurs and its context. Before doing this you must think carefully about the meaning and types of violence, and construct lists and grids to help you record what you see (see p. 383 of this chapter and the discussion of domestic violence in Chapter 12, pp. 478–82). How far can a content analysis take one in investigating the significance of violence on television?

Media watch 10 News from Israel

In *Bad News from Israel* (2004), Greg Philo and Mike Berry from the Glasgow University Media Group examined the process of news production, the content of news broadcasts, and their impact on audiences. They interviewed journalists and other broadcasting professionals. They analysed TV news coverage of Israel from September 2000 to April 2002. They investigated audience responses through a questionnaire distributed to students in Britain, the United States, and Germany, and through the extensive use of focus groups, in which journalists and other broadcasting professionals participated.

This study is set in the context of the historical conflict between Israel and the Palestinians. Two key events are identified:

● the displacement of Palestinians from their homes and land when the state of Israel was set up in 1948;

● the establishment of Israeli military control of the occupied territories after the war of 1967.

Recent events can only be understood and explained when placed in the context of these historic events. Very different accounts of these historic events have, however, been provided by the two sides, which makes the job of the journalist extremely difficult.

Content analysis showed that TV news reporting was dominated by Israeli perspectives. The Palestinians were seen as the source of trouble and Israel as only responding or retaliating. There was more coverage of Israeli than Palestinian casualties, even though more Palestinians died, and a different language was used to describe Israeli and Palestinian casualties. Israeli deaths but not Palestinian ones were, for example, described as 'mass murder' (2004: 259). Israeli perspectives tended to dominate the headlines.

Philo and Berry comment on the lack of historical explanation in news reports. This could partly be due to the production process. News bulletins had to fit a time frame. A concern for audience ratings favoured images of violence, fighting, and destruction, rather than dry explanation. A focus on bombings rather than the situation that gave rise to them suited, however, the Israeli view of the conflict, while the 'war on terror' language of news reports demonstrated the dominance of an Israeli/American perspective. There are, of course, lobbies for both sides but the dominance of this perspective reflected the greater power of the pro-Israel lobby in Britain and the United States, and the superior effectiveness of the Israeli public-relations machinery.

The content of the news is clearly important but what *effect* does it have on the audience? This was partly assessed through questionnaire responses but the focus groups were crucial, since they made it possible to explore the reasons given for answers and to discuss the issues raised. Focus-group members also participated in a news writing exercise to see whether they reproduced the language and explanations found in news broadcasts.

Most participants in the audience study had little idea of the history, which 'made it very difficult for people to understand key elements of the conflict' (2004: 216). But there was plentiful evidence that the audience had absorbed many features of the news treatment of the conflict. It was, for example, often seen as initiated by the Palestinians with the Israelis then responding, while the news writing exercise showed the audience reproducing the themes of TV news. Those who obtained

information from other sources could, however, be critical of TV news coverage and present alternative views.

Discussion in the focus groups brought out a 'strong feeling . . . that the news should explain origins and causes and that journalists should speak more directly to viewers about what was happening and why' (2004: 240). When people learned more about the history of the conflict through the focus group discussions, their interest in the news increased, while 'incomprehension led to detachment and increased the sense of powerlessness some people felt when watching terrible events with which they could not engage or relate to' (2004: 257). This led Philo and Berry to argue that the existing structure and content of TV news programmes should be changed in order to provide better information for people.

❷ What do we learn from this study about the uses and limitations of content analysis?

❷ Why do Philo and Berry think that there should be more explanation of origins and causes in TV news?

❷ How do you think that journalists should deal with conflicting accounts of the events that they report?

❷ Should the structure and content of the main television news programmes be changed, and if so, how?

Discussion points

Television violence

Before discussing this issue, read the section on 'Morality' and Study 10.

● Why do some people think that violence on TV makes people more violent?

● Why do others think that TV violence has no such effect?

Consider what 'violence' means, and how violence should be defined.

● Can we really speak of violence in general?

● How can violence be differentiated? What kinds of violence are there?

Carry out a content analysis of the kind suggested by Study 10.

● Is there good evidence that TV violence makes people more violent?

● Or is the concern with TV violence just a 'moral panic'?

Cultures

Before discussing this, read 'The media and culture', and the later sections on 'Media globalization'.

● Consider the terms high culture, folk culture, and popular culture. How are they to be distinguished? Find examples of each.

● How would a post-modern approach view such distinctions?

● Do *you* think these distinctions are meaningful?

● What is cyberculture?

● How free is it from the constraints operating in other media?

● Why is it thought that globalization is leading to Americanization?

● Does globalization mean that local cultures are disappearing?

● What were the last three television programmes that you watched?

● Where was each produced?

● Did any of them show signs of American influence? Consider the type of programme, its format, and style.

● Did these programmes reflect your own national culture in any way?

The public sphere

Before discussing this, read 'A public sphere?', 'The rise of the mass media', and 'Decline of the public sphere?'. Make sure that you are clear about the meaning of the 'public sphere'.

- Where do you think the public sphere is?

- Which institutions and organizations of your society contribute to its public sphere?

- Why is it important that a society has a functioning public sphere?

- What reasons are there for thinking that the public sphere is in decline?

- Is there still a functioning public sphere in your society?

- Do you think that your society needs a larger or stronger public sphere?

- Does the Internet/Web provide a means of reviving the public sphere?

- Is the Internet/Web free of the pressures on the other media?

- Will the Internet/Web become the main medium of the public sphere?

Explore further

The following references cover most of the issues dealt with in this chapter:

Eldridge, J., Kitzinger, J., and Williams, K. (1997), *The Mass Media and Power in Modern Britain* (Oxford: Oxford University Press). *A discussion of the power of the media, examining their history, and reviewing different approaches to their influence.*

Fleming, D. (2000) (ed.), *Formations: A 21st Century Media Studies Textbook* (Manchester: Manchester University Press). *An advanced reader that goes well beyond introductory material and consists of specially written pieces.*

Newbold, C., Boyd-Barrett, O., and Van den Bulck, H. (2002) (eds.), *The Media Book* (London: Arnold). *A clear and comprehensive introductory reader that works through all the key issues in media studies.*

Particular topics can be followed up through:

Abercrombie, N. (1996), *Television and Society* (Cambridge: Polity Press). *Although this is focused on television, it is a very clear and full analysis of all aspects of the sociology of the media.*

Barker, C. (1999), *Television, Globalization, and Cultural Identities* (Buckingham: Open University Press). *A perceptive and theoretically* aware discussion of the issues of identity and representation raised by the globalization of television.

Bell, D., and Kennedy, B. (2000), *The Cybercultures Reader* (London: Routledge). *A very extensive collection of pieces out on the frontiers of the study of culture.*

Curran, J., and Seaton, J. (2002), *Power without Responsibility: The Press and Broadcasting in Britain* (6th edn., London: Routledge). *A theoretically informed account of the development of the press and broadcasting from the nineteenth century onwards.*

Gauntlett, D. (2000) (ed.), *Web.Studies: Rewiring Media Studies for the Digital Age* (London: Arnold). *An informative and lively collection that usefully extends the various areas of media studies into the age of the Internet.*

Seabrook, J. (2004), *Consuming Cultures: Globalization and Local Lives* (Oxford: New Internationalist). *A highly readable discussion of the impact of globalization and Americanization on cultural diversity, with lots of examples.*

Strinati, D. (2000), *An Introduction to Studying Popular Culture* (London: Routledge). *A clear and comprehensive guide to the study of popular culture.*

Online resources

Visit the Online Resource Centre that accompanies this book to access more learning resources and other interesting material on communication and the media at:

www.oxfordtextbooks.co.uk/orc/fulcher3e/

The Resource Center for Cyberculture Studies is 'an online, not-for-profit organization whose purpose is to research, study, teach, support, and create diverse and dynamic elements of cyberculture':

www.com.washington.edu/rccs/

Transparency, a site created by American writer and media critic Ken Sanes, provides very clear and theoretically informed accounts and reviews of contemporary material on the media and popular culture. Lecturers and students have apparently found his work very helpful:

www.transparencynow.com/

Based in the United States, the Center for Media and Public Affairs is a 'nonpartisan research and educational organization', and conducts research into many different aspects of media content and influence:

www.cmpa.com/index.htm

The Campaign for Press Broadcasting Freedom campaigns for the reform of the media and is linked to the unions and the labour movement:

http://keywords.dsvr.co.uk/freepress/

religion, belief, and meaning

Contents

11

Pagan beliefs

Cassandra Latham is a qualified nurse and counsellor. She is also a witch. She makes charms and spells for the residents of her village in Cornwall, and she makes them available to a larger audience through her website (www.villagewisewoman.co.uk). Maureen Brown is a psychotherapist, and she, too, is a witch. Maureen has been a member of a coven in Croydon for twenty-six years.

Witches are followers of the Wiccan religion. There are about 10,000 in Britain today, and most are affiliated to the Pagan Federation, which has 100,000 members. Its practitioners adopt magical means to cast spells, mix love potions, and engage in other rituals aimed at enhancing a person's powers and abilities. These aspects of Wicca are familiar from such story-book images as those of the Harry Potter books. Wiccans, however, base their magic and rituals on their belief in a so-called Mother Goddess, who is closely associated with the Horned God. They celebrate the winter and summer solstices, the autumn and spring equinoxes, and they hold festivals at Lammas (harvest time in August) and Halloween (October).

Cassandra Latham: Village Wisewoman.

© Simon Burt of Apex Agency

Paganism is little understood. It is often confused with Satanism or with the demons depicted in *Buffy The Vampire Slayer*. In fact, it is a very respectable religion. The Pagan Federation comprises druids, witches, shamans, wizards, and others who are united by their adherence to ancient Celtic, Germanic, and Norse beliefs. For a long time, those beliefs have been ignored and were actively suppressed in the witchcraft persecutions of the sixteenth and seventeenth centuries. The Witchcraft Act was not repealed until 1951, and Wicca, like other Pagan religions, has grown rapidly since then—and especially since the 1970s. Contemporary Wicca and Paganism have few direct links with past generations of believers and are, in many respects, recent creations: Wicca was effectively founded as an organized religion by Gerald Gardner in the early 1950s.

Sources: *Guardian*, 28 October 2000; *Sunday Times Magazine*, 23 December 2001.

For every person in Britain today who subscribes to Pagan beliefs, there are many more whose religious beliefs appear more conventional. For these people, religion is something for Sundays and for holy days, and is practised largely in and through a Church. Yet others adopt highly emotional belief systems and may talk in tongues, engage in faith healing, or actively convert others on their own doorsteps. In many societies in the past, levels of religious activity were much greater than they are for most people in Britain. Even today, many societies have very high levels of religious activity. In fact, the strength of religious commitment is quite variable from one type of society to another. What, then, is religion, and what part does it play in social life?

In this chapter we will look at religions of all kinds and, in particular, at the historical trend of religion and belief in modern societies. In the section on 'Understanding religion' we consider the nature of religion and the major sociological theories of religion. The second section on 'Religion in modern society' examines the idea that modern societies have undergone a process of secularization in which religious beliefs and practices have declined. The final section, on 'The rise of new religions', looks at the significance of the many new religions that are today experiencing a growth in membership.

Understanding religion

A religion is a system of beliefs through which people organize and order their lives. This is often thought to involve a belief in a god or gods, but this is not the case for all religious beliefs. The central meaning of the word 'religion' is, in fact, simply the way in which shared beliefs establish regulations, rules, or bonds of obligation among the members of a community. In its broadest sense, then, religion can be seen as involving devotion or attachment to a system of beliefs that defines the moral obligations and responsibilities that people have towards one another. These beliefs define a code of behaviour that regulates personal and social life. It is notoriously difficult to produce any generally acceptable definition of religion. Wallis and Bruce, however, have come up with a useful, if rather complex, definition. According to these writers, a religion comprises the

actions, beliefs and institutions predicated upon the assumption of the existence of either supernatural entities with powers of agency, or impersonal powers or processes possessed of moral purpose, which have the capacity to set the conditions of, or to intervene in, human affairs. (Wallis and Bruce 1992: 10–11)

While this definition contains a number of quite complex ideas, it is a good starting point for our discussion, and you will find it useful to return to it from time to time.

The sacred and the secular

Religious beliefs and rites have generally been organized around objects and activities that are held to be sacred because they are seen as having superior power or dignity to the objects and activities of everyday life. Sacred things have 'a quality of mysterious and awesome power' (Berger

1969: 34; see also Durkheim 1912; Pickering 1984). They have a spiritual quality that leads them to be venerated as holy and to be set apart from everyday things. By contrast with natural objects, they are *supernatural*. These sacred objects are the basis of the moral standards by which the non-sacred, or *secular* world is judged. Religious activity involves special forms of communication and action—such as prayer and ritual—through which those in the secular world can come into contact with the sacred world.

Religion forms what Berger (1969) calls a *sacred canopy*. By this he means an overarching framework of meanings that gives a larger, cosmological significance to the ordinary world of practical action and that legitimate particular social institutions. Everyday matters can be seen as significant if they have a place in a wider context of meanings. When covered by a sacred canopy, routine, day-to-day social reality comes to acquire a significance that goes beyond the immediate, practical interests and concerns of everyday life. Instead of appearing as arbitrary and precarious, it appears as part of some larger purpose. People conform to the expectations defined by this social reality because they feel a sense of duty or obligation to something beyond themselves. Sacred social institutions may compete for control over people's lives with those institutions that are purely secular.

Religions differ from one another in terms of those particular things that they regard as sacred or holy. Typically, the ultimate sacred object is some kind of higher power, such as a god, though this may often be seen in highly abstract terms. What are called theistic religions are those that involve devotion to a superhuman or controlling power that is seen as being the source of all moral values and that requires an attitude of reverence or awe. Such a sacred power becomes the object of worship. The major monotheistic religions—Judaism, Christianity, and Islam—have all accorded this kind of devotion to a single, personified God. In Christian theology, for example, representations of God are at the heart of the spiritual significance given to sacred texts (especially the Bible), to sacred buildings (churches and chapels), and to sacred music and works of art.

Polytheistic religions, on the other hand, are organized around a large number of separate gods. The religions of ancient Greece and Rome, for example, were polytheistic. In fact, they invoked a similar set of gods. For the Greeks, Zeus ruled the spiritual world from Mount Olympus, along with such other gods as Athena, Poseidon, Hermes, and Artemis. For the Romans, the counterpart gods were the spiritual ruler Jupiter, together with Minerva, Neptune, Mercury, and Diana. In both religions, the events of the natural and social worlds reflected the relations of cooperation and competition that existed among the various gods.

In practice, however, the distinction between monotheistic and polytheistic religions is difficult to draw with any precision. Early and medieval Christianity, for example, saw God—personified always in male terms—as standing at the head of a celestial hierarchy of other spiritual beings: seraphim, cherubim, thrones, dominations, virtues, powers, principalities, archangels, and angels. The various prophets and saints inspired by God also became objects of religious devotion, as did—above all—Mary, the mother of God. In this system of religious belief, then, monotheism was combined with the recognition of a vast number of lesser spiritual beings.

Not all religions are theistic. Buddhism, for example, has no conception of a personal god, although it does require that people regulate their lives by specific values and standards. It sees people as going through a series of reincarnations until they achieve an enlightened, sacred state that releases them from their earthly existence. They achieve 'nirvana'. The moral standards that Buddhists must follow, therefore, have an ultimate, supernatural significance, but they are not derived from the demands of any supernatural being. Though recognizing no personified gods, Buddhists do revere those people who have achieved perfect enlightenment. They are termed Buddhas and Bodhisattvas and are held up as exemplars for others to follow. The founder of the religion—often referred to simply as Buddha—was Sidartha Gautama, the most important of the Buddhist saints. Buddhism merges easily with other religions, and many of the gods of the traditional Brahman religion of India, from which Buddhism originated, were simply transformed into Buddhas. The number of holy entities recognized in some forms of Buddhism can, in fact, be very high.

Buddhism is a religion in which the ultimate state of existence (nirvana) is *transcendent*. That is to say, it goes beyond the everyday world and exists only on a purely spiritual plane. Similarly, the Christian heaven is an ultimate state that transcends the everyday world. In some non-theistic religions, however, the ultimate state of existence is *immanent* rather than transcendent. This means that it is rooted in the natural, practical world itself and is seen as an actual state of affairs that can or will result from practical actions. The secular world—as it is or as it might become—is itself given a sacred status.

Soviet Communism, for example, justified commitment to the existing political order in relation to the ideal Communist society that was being built. The state's role in building this ideal legitimated conformity to its demands. Despite the absence of gods and transcendent states of existence, Soviet Communism was a religion as we have defined it. Marxist–Leninist ideas were drawn upon to construct images of such sacred entities as the proletariat and the party, and these became the objects of reverential attachment. Exemplary thinkers and practitioners of Marxism were accorded a holy status, and some became the objects of cult attachments. Marx, Engels, Lenin, and Stalin were all treated in this way. Lenin's body, for example, was preserved in a special mausoleum in Moscow and was the focus of many ceremonies of state. Party Congresses and other party meetings provided the ritualized contexts in which these ideas and values could be reaffirmed. Even after the collapse of the Communist regime, cult attachments persisted, and the new authorities did not rush to remove Lenin's body from public display.

Theories of religion

The pioneer sociologists of the nineteenth century recognized the central part that religion has played in human history. They were particularly concerned, however, with the implications that modern science had for traditional forms of religion. Both Comte and Marx saw the specifically supernatural aspects of religious belief as being incompatible with an acceptance of modern scientific knowledge. Both of them held that traditional forms of religion would disappear as modern societies matured. Their claim concerned the secularization of modern society, or the declining significance of religion in the day-to-day lives of people in the modern social world.

The founders of classical sociology—most particularly Durkheim and Weber—drew on these ideas and developed them into more sophisticated understandings of the social significance of religion and scientific knowledge. Durkheim, like Comte, saw modern society as evolving new forms of religion that were more compatible with scientific knowledge and with the structures of complex, advanced societies. Weber was more pessimistic. He anticipated the complete disappearance of all religion and held that individuals would, therefore, be unable to make any sense of their lives. Weber undertook a range of comparative and historical studies of religion, looking particularly at the link between religion and the rise of capitalism. A useful overview of theories of religion can be found in Beckford (1989) and Aldridge (2000).

Comte and Marx: religion and science

Comte saw traditional religions as having either a theistic or a metaphysical character. They constructed sacred canopies around ideas of supernatural beings or of abstract forces and powers. The Catholic Church in medieval Europe was typical of such a traditional religion. These kinds of religious ideas, Comte held, have been undermined by the growth of modern science. In the modern world, he argued, no theistic or metaphysical religion can stand up to the advance of scientific knowledge. He held,

 ## Briefing: Catholicism

Christians believe that Jesus was the Son of God, the Messiah prophesied in the Jewish religious texts. Christianity was adopted as the official religion of the Roman Empire in the fourth century AD. The Roman Church termed itself Catholic because it claimed to be a universally valid religion for all who lived within the Empire. The Roman Catholic Church has always had a centralized structure and is headed by the Pope, who has ultimate, infallible authority over its members. The authority of the Church is exercised through a hierarchy of cardinals, archbishops, bishops, and priests.

With the fall of the Roman Empire, the Roman Catholic Church was separated from the Eastern Orthodox Church, a federation of independent churches that rejected the authority of the Pope but retained the core beliefs and rituals of the Roman Church. The Orthodox Church remains strong in Greece, the Balkans, and Russia, while the Roman Catholic Church is strongest in Italy, Spain, and Latin America.

however, that modern societies did still require a system of beliefs that would function as religion had in the past to regulate social activities and produce social order. This new form of religion he found in science itself.

Positive, scientific thought, Comte held, would become the basis of a new kind of religion that could provide the cohesion and consensus that is necessary for social integration. It could do this without resorting to theistic or metaphysical ideas. Only a scientifically based religion could provide sacred ideas and a moral code that is compatible with the modern scientific outlook. Central to all religious beliefs are ideas about the nature of social life itself, and Comte therefore held that the science of society —sociology—would be at the heart of this new religion. Comte set out to help build a positivist religion of humanity that could provide the necessary cement to hold modern societies together (B. Turner 1991: chapter 2).

> **➲ Connections**
> You might like to look back at our review of the development of sociological theory in Chapter 2. There you will find accounts of Comte and the various other theorists that we look at in this section. Comte's religion of humanity followed from his law of the three stages, which we discuss on p. 26.

A more radical view of religion was taken by Marx, though he too recognized the role that it played in furthering social cohesion. Like Comte, Marx believed that theistic forms of religion would disappear as modern societies matured. He believed, however, that this would occur only when the capitalist features of these societies had been abolished and they had become socialist societies.

Marx saw theistic and metaphysical religions as expressions of the deepening alienation that people experienced in a modern capitalist society. Traditional religious thought was simply a distorted reflection of the real class relations that connected and divided people from one another. In a capitalist society, Marx held, class divisions took a particularly sharp form, but they were obscured by religious ideas of unity and common brotherhood. The cohesion and integration that this produced simply served the interests of the dominant class and not the whole of society.

According to Marx, then, traditional religion had an *ideological* function and could not be understood apart from the underlying social divisions and conflicts of a society. Although it appeared to provide a sense of meaning for those who were subject to economic exploitation, this was an illusion. It merely obscured their subordination and oppression and made it less likely that they would challenge the existing social order. Religion deflected social conflict by encouraging people to accept their social position. It was, in Marx's words, both 'the sigh of the oppressed' and 'the opium of the people'. By providing illusions to live by, it effectively drugged people into the acceptance of social relations that exploited and alienated them. Religion would be swept completely away when capitalism was overthrown and when, in consequence, alienation and class divisions finally disappeared from human history.

Durkheim: religion and individualism

Durkheim followed Comte in recognizing the part played by religious belief and ritual in social cohesion and social integration (Beckford 1989: 25–31). He also agreed with Comte that the theistic aspects of religion would disappear in modern society. Though he rejected Comte's religion of humanity, he did say that modern societies would come to be organized around a 'cult of man' or cult of individualism.

Durkheim approached religion from an analysis of its most primitive or elementary forms. These he found in the **totemism** of tribal societies. All forms of religion, he argued, had their origins in totemistic beliefs, though he believed that these survived only among native Australians and some North American tribes. These tribes, he argued, were divided into clans, which were the real bases of social solidarity. People felt strong sentiments of attachment to their clan, because it defined their relations to all other members of their tribe. Each clan identified itself with a particular animal or plant. This was its emblem or totem, and it symbolized the clan. Members of a clan might say, for example, that they were the fox clan, and that they were quite distinct from the beaver clan. These totems were, then, marks of social identity.

Because clan membership was fundamental to the whole way in which people lived their lives, the totem had a sacred quality. It was in this imputation of sacredness to particular objects that Durkheim found the basis of all religion. In more advanced forms of totemism, sacredness was not so likely to be seen in natural objects such as animals, plants, winds, stars, rocks, rivers, and so on. Instead, social identity became focused around spiritual entities such as souls, demons, spirits, saints, or gods. A people might, for example, regard themselves as the 'chosen people' of a particular god. The further development of religion, as societies advanced beyond the tribal stage, led to the complete disappearance of its totemistic elements. The sacred objects of a society became more abstract.

Durkheim had only a rather limited knowledge of the Australian tribes, and his views on totemism have been seriously questioned by later writers (Lévi-Strauss 1962). What has not been challenged, however, is his general view of the relationship between the sacred sphere and the religious attitude, on the one hand, and the structure of society, on the other.

Durkheim, like Marx, saw religion as having a social basis. The origin of the idea of the sacred was to be found in society itself. Religious forces and entities are, he held, mere representations of the moral forces and constraints that people experience in their social relations. In their social interaction, people build what Durkheim called **collective representations**. These include shared images and ideas about the moral obligations that they feel to bind them together as members of their society. These representations are so fundamental to their social relations that they come to have a sacred character. They are, under some circumstances, personified as gods or other spiritual beings. The idea of god is an expression of society itself.

Ideas of divinity, then, are reflections of the ways in which people attempt to understand their social relations with one another. Religion is also central to the production of a sense of moral community. It is through religion that the symbols and ideas that sustain social life and that underpin the social order are sustained. Durkheim called these symbols and ideas, in French, the *conscience collective*. This is a difficult term to translate, and so is generally left in the French. It refers to both the consciousness that is shared among the members of a society and the moral ideas that form their consciences. Because the *conscience collective* is so central to social life, Durkheim held, the disappearance of religion would mean the disappearance of

Religion and society

> Religious force is only the sentiment inspired by the group in its members, but projected outside of the consciousnesses that experience them, and objectified. To be objectified, they are fixed upon some object which thus becomes sacred. (Durkheim 1912: 229)

Durkheim's statement is quite complex, and you will not fully understand it the first time that you read it. Read it through once or twice, picking out the key words and try to get the gist of what he is saying. The key words are 'sentiment', 'projected', and 'objectified'. Can you see how he applied these ideas to totemism?

 Briefing: Protestantism

This is a Christian religion that originated in Martin Luther's 'protestation' against the authority of the Roman Catholic Church in the sixteenth century. Luther emphasized the authority of the Bible, as the direct word of God. He rejected the Catholic view that priests were able to interpret God's wishes. Luther held that each individual must open his or her mind to God and must rely on conscience as the sole guide to conduct.

social order itself. For this reason, he concluded that any society that is to persist must have some form of religion. This is why Durkheim is often said to have focused his attention on the functions of religion in creating social solidarity.

Although traditional forms of supernatural religion disappear as societies become more modern, other forms of religion will take their place. This new form of religion, Durkheim argued, centres around the idea of the individual. Individualism is the system of ideas most compatible with the social division of labour and the market relations that are central to modern society. This is manifested in moral systems that emphasize human rights, freedom, and equality, and in the encouragement of individual autonomy and choice in all things. Moral individualism, centring around a cult of the individual, is, according to Durkheim, the normal form taken by religion in modern society. This idea has been taken up in the discussions of Soviet Communism and 'civil religion' that we refer to on pp. 33–9 below.

> ⮕ *Connections*
>
> Read our discussion of Durkheim's wider theoretical ideas in Chapter 2, pp. 33–9. We show there how he saw anomie and egoism as pathological expressions of the normal condition of moral individualism in modern societies. Can you see why religion was so important in Durkheim's theory of suicide?

Weber: religion and capitalism

Weber's particular concern in his sociology of religion was to look at the relationship between religious values and economic action. He carried out comparative studies of the religions of China, India, and ancient Israel, but his

most important study was set out in a book on *The Protestant Ethic and the Spirit of Capitalism* (Max Weber 1904–5). The problem that he set himself to examine was why modern capitalism developed first in western Europe, and he found the answer in its particular religious pattern.

Weber saw the central characteristic of modern capitalism as its spirit, its particular cultural attitude towards commercial activity. The **spirit of capitalism** is a system of beliefs that encourages the accumulation of income and assets through productive activity. This spirit encourages people to see excessive consumption as wasteful and, therefore, as something to be avoided. The profits of business have to be reinvested rather than consumed in luxurious and extravagant expenditure. This spirit emerged first among those who became active capitalist entrepreneurs in the seventeenth and eighteenth centuries, and Weber wanted to uncover its origins. He concluded that these origins were to be found in certain characteristics of the Protestant religion.

Weber looked, in particular, at the Calvinist forms of Protestantism that developed from the ideas of John Calvin. Calvinists believed that only a small minority—the elect—were destined by God for salvation and would join Him in heaven. The remainder were destined for eternal damnation. Nothing that people did during their lives could make any difference to their destiny, which reflected God's choice, and there was no way in which any individual believer could know whether he or she was destined for salvation or damnation. As a result, Calvinists experienced what Weber called 'inner loneliness'. They were completely on their own, having no one to whom they could turn for authoritative guidance on their eternal destiny.

This extreme anxiety about their fate caused great uncertainty about how they should behave. Protestant ministers and teachers responded to this by stressing those other aspects of Calvinism that might help to resolve the anxieties of their parishioners. Calvin had said that success in a person's calling might be seen as a sign that he or she was destined for salvation. A calling or vocation was the particular way of life to which one had been called by God. Calvin's followers concluded that God would hardly allow worldly success to those whom he had damned. The Puritan sects of the seventeenth century—especially the Quakers and the Baptists—developed an ethic that saw success in an occupation, business, or profession as giving people some indication of whether they were saved or damned. They began to encourage their members to be diligent and hard-working in their work and disciplined in all aspects of their lives. Those who worked hard found that they were, indeed, likely to be successful, and this helped to lessen their sense of anxiety about their destiny (G. Marshall 1982).

Weber described this lifestyle as one of *asceticism*. The ascetic lifestyle involved hard work, discipline, the avoidance of waste, and the rigorous and systematic use of time. This rational and calculative attitude was applied in all aspects of life. In the Puritan world-view, eating and sexuality were seen as stimulating the bodily appetites and, therefore, as things to be controlled. Fasting, the avoidance of non-reproductive sex, and, outside marriage, a life of chastity and celibacy were all seen as means of self-control through which a mastery of the body could be attained (B. Turner 1996).

The pursuit of these values by seventeenth-century merchants in the Puritan sects led them to greater business success than their counterparts in other religions. Their ascetic way of life stressed the avoidance of excessive income and wasteful or luxurious consumption, and this led them to plough back their profits into their businesses

and so to expand their scale of operations. Asceticism gave a new meaning to practical economic life. A distinctively modern view of commercial activity and an ethic of hard work were encouraged, and it was this new outlook and orientation that allowed capitalist business enterprises to expand on an unprecedented scale in the eighteenth and nineteenth centuries. The Protestant ethic, Weber argued, had given birth to the spirit of modern capitalism.

In the favourable conditions provided by the nation states of western Europe in the seventeenth and eighteenth centuries, this spirit helped to produce the modern capitalist system of production. This system rapidly spread across Europe and into the wider world. In the longer term, however, the success of the capitalist system undermined sacred, religious meanings. In expanding capitalist societies, Weber argued, individuals are forced to work by economic necessity, and not by any spiritual commitment to it as a calling. For most people there is simply no alternative to capitalist economic activity: if employers do not make a profit, then the pressures of competition will force them out of business; and if employees do not work hard, they will be sacked and replaced by those who will. The spirit of modern capitalism disappears, and modern life becomes increasingly empty and meaningless.

Weber's ideas on religious ethics and their influence on economic activity have been taken up in some contemporary discussions of the economic development of overseas Chinese communities in the Far East, where forms of religion now operate in much the way that the Protestant ethic operated in seventeenth-century Europe (Redding 1990).

‹› *Stop and reflect*

In this section we have looked at the nature of religion and the principal sociological theories about the development of religion in modern societies.

- A religion is an overarching system of beliefs and practices that helps the members of a society or community to organize and order their lives.

- Central to religious thought is a distinction between the sacred and the secular.

We sketched the views of the main sociological theorists of religion. Their ideas are relevant to the many issues that we discuss in the rest of this chapter.

- Comte saw a conflict between religion and science, though he held that science could itself become the basis of a new religion and a new form of social cohesion.

- Marx related religion to class divisions and alienation. It is an important factor in the legitimation of social divisions.

- Durkheim saw modern societies as organized around a religion of moral individualism that corresponded to its social differentiation and division of labour.

- Weber gave an account of the rise of modern capitalism that saw the social ethic of the Protestant churches as a crucial factor in generating the attitudes and outlook of the capitalist entrepreneur.

- Is it necessary to choose between these differing views of religion?

Religion in modern society

It is often claimed that belief in God is less common in Europe and America today than was the case in the past. This loss of traditional religious belief is seen as showing that modern societies must be seen as increasingly secular societies. This follows Comte's argument that positive, rational knowledge would free people from traditional forms of religious belief. Atheists have seen this in a favourable light, seeing it as liberating people from superstitious and irrational beliefs. Those who remain committed to traditional forms of religious faith, on the other hand, have seen it in more negative terms. For them, it undermines morality and destroys the possibility of a disciplined communal life. Most sociologists prefer not to take sides on these theological issues, seeing religious faith as a purely personal matter. They concern themselves only with the actual question of whether modern societies have, in fact, undergone a process of secularization.

Secularization and modernity

The sociological concept of **secularization** involves two closely related ideas. First, it implies that there has been a *disengagement* of religion from public institutions. This means that religious beliefs and practices are detached from major social institutions and become purely private matters of individual belief and choice. Indeed, the word 'secularization' was originally used to denote the removal of a territory from the legal control of a church. It was generalized from this to mean the declining public significance of religion. The idea of secularization, secondly, implies that there has been a *disenchantment* of social life. The *disenchantment* of the world is the process through which the ultimate spiritual meaning of practical life recedes as individuals lose their traditional religious beliefs. A society is disenchanted when sacred ideas are no longer of any relevance to people and practical matters are, in consequence, emptied of any ultimate spiritual significance. Disengagement involves a *privatization* of religious belief; disenchantment involves a *loss* of spiritual concerns.

The disengagement of religion

Disengagement is 'the process by which sectors of society and culture are removed from the domination of religious institutions and symbols' (Berger 1969: 113). This is apparent in the separation of church and state, the removal of education and welfare from control by religious bodies, and the withdrawal of churches from their attempts to regulate economic behaviour and control matters of morality. In Europe, this disengagement was apparent in the transformation and weakening of the Roman Catholic Church.

Medieval Europe was built around the cultural dominance of the Catholic Church, which was allied with all its major states and was the main focus of unity across the continent. The Catholic Church established a virtually compulsory framework for religious observance. People were born into membership of the Church, just as they were born into membership of a particular state. There was no choice about either. Place of birth fixed a person's subjection to church and state. The Church hierarchy was closely allied with the political hierarchies of the states of the Christian world, and the Pope was at least the equal of the European kings and princes.

Sociologists introduced the term **ecclesia** to describe the specific form taken by religion in this period. This type of religious organization is sometimes referred to simply as a 'church', but this word is now used so widely and in such a general sense that it has lost its original and more specific meaning. A church, in its broadest sense, is any form of

Redundant churches have been turned into trendy bars, restaurants, and retail outlets.

© Freud

association that is organized around the relations of its members to a sacred sphere of meaning and action. The word 'church' is even used to refer to the buildings in which religious activities take place.

An ecclesia is a specific kind of church, most clearly illustrated by medieval Roman Catholicism. It is a universal and inclusive religious organization that claims total spiritual authority over all of those who live within a particular territory. It generally claims a degree of political authority too. The medieval Catholic Church claimed spiritual authority over virtually the whole of Europe. An ecclesia is organized around an orthodox doctrine. This is a systematically codified body of beliefs that is protected as the one true faith and is given authoritative interpretation by the church's leaders. People are born into membership of an ecclesia and they are socialized into its beliefs and practices. An orthodox doctrine may be the basis of a rigid social conformity: heretics (deviants from the religious orthodoxy) are not tolerated and may be relentlessly persecuted.

The ecclesia can be distinguished from the **denomination**. A denomination is a church that is organized around *voluntary* rather than compulsory membership. It occurs where there is a separation between church and state. A denomination is a church that is disengaged from the many political and public functions undertaken by an ecclesia. A denomination does not claim a monopoly of religious truth and it accommodates itself to the legitimacy of secular states and to the beliefs of other denominations. This contrast between ecclesia and denomination is important when comparing different forms of religion (Martin 1962; see also Niebuhr 1929).

By the nineteenth century, neither Roman Catholicism nor Anglicanism could be regarded as ecclesia. They had come closer to being mere denominations. Anglicanism had, and still has, certain privileges and powers in relation to the state. It forms the established 'Church of England'. However, it is far weaker than it was in the past (B. R. Wilson 1966: 252). In virtually all the societies of Europe, religion became denominational, and states have gradually come to tolerate the existence of numerous separate denominations. At the same time, the various denominations tend to be more tolerant of one another than any ecclesia would be towards unorthodox beliefs and practices. In Britain, for example, such churches as the Methodists and the Baptists emphasize voluntary commitment to the church and accommodation to other religions.

Denominations often have a social base in a particular social class or ethnic group, and religious struggles in a denominational society can often be closely associated with the social struggles of these groups for power. For example, nonconformist (i.e. non-Anglican) Protestantism was strongest in nineteenth-century England in the working-

---

THEORY AND METHODS

Ecclesia and denomination

The contrast between the ecclesia and the denomination—often discussed as a contrast between 'church' and denomination—is of great importance. According to Weber, an ecclesia is a form of administration that organizes religion into a structure of what he called 'hierocratic coercion'. It is characterized by:

- a claim to universal authority: control that is not restricted by kinship, ethnicity, or other particularistic claims;
- a systematic dogma and set of rites, generally recorded in texts that are objects of disciplined training;
- a professional priesthood, having specific duties and being controlled through salaries and promotions;
- compulsory membership for all who live within the territory over which it claims authority.

A denomination, on the other hand, exercises fewer and more restricted controls over its members. Although it may have a professional priesthood, these do not have the powers held by priests in an ecclesia. Specifically, the denomination is characterized by:

- a tolerance towards other religions, which are recognized—in principle—as having an equally legitimate right to attract members and spread their views;
- a voluntary membership based on an act of choice made by a believer.

Examples of ecclesia are medieval Catholicism and Islam. Examples of denominations are the Methodist and Baptist churches in nineteenth- and twentieth-century Britain, and the many branches of Buddhism in Japan. Anglicanism is intermediate between the ecclesia and the denomination.

---

class communities of the industrial north. Methodist, Baptist, and Congregationalist chapels provided a focus for communal cohesion and bases for opposition to the Established Church. The conflict between 'chapel' and 'church' became an important thread in British politics, persisting well into the twentieth century. In big cities, where there were substantial numbers of Irish migrants, Catholicism played a similar part in building the solidarity of the Irish working-class communities.

The disenchantment of the world

The second aspect of secularization is what Max Weber called the *disenchantment* or 'desacralization' of the world.

By this he meant that modern societies experience a loss of the spiritual meaning that had been provided by traditional religious belief. While it is important not to overstate the depth and the consistency of religious belief in the past, Weber correctly identified a major difference between the medieval and the modern world-view.

Most ordinary people in the medieval world did hold to a broadly Christian world-view. The details of Christian theology and its specific doctrines were often unfamiliar or poorly understood, but Christianity provided a taken-for-granted sacred canopy that helped them to organize their everyday lives. The spiritual content of this religion was reinforced by equally strong beliefs in a whole array of supernatural and magical powers. For most people, witches, spirits, and fairies were every bit as real as the angels and saints of orthodox Christianity. These heretical views were tolerated by the Catholic Church, so long as its own position was not threatened. More systematic and intellectually consistent Christian beliefs were held by the literate, though even here there was a willingness to believe in magical forces (K. Thomas 1971). Medieval people, then, lived in an enchanted world, a world in which the secular activities of everyday life were permeated by supernatural forces.

The Reformation of sixteenth-century Europe challenged the Catholic orthodoxy and popular beliefs. The new Protestant beliefs recognized far fewer spiritual beings and emphasized a much greater degree of doctrinal purity. In a wider context, this helped to produce the fundamental shift in intellectual outlook that has been described as the Enlightenment. In one sphere of intellectual enquiry after another, knowledge was freed from religious constraints and opened up to rational criticism (Merton 1938a). As Comte had recognized, an increasingly scientific world-view gave greater priority to rational considerations over matters of faith. Protestantism and Enlightenment thought together destroyed the medieval world-view, encouraging a separation of religious from practical matters. Protestantism eliminated much of the spiritual content from religion, and scientific knowledge soon began to challenge any kind of theistic religion. Traditional religious beliefs could no longer be taken for granted, and they became progressively more difficult to sustain.

Many people, then, experienced a loss of faith in traditional religious ideas. Miracles, mysticism, saints, and sacraments all played a much smaller part in everyday life when religion took a specifically rational form and placed less emphasis on the supernatural. As Berger (1969: 117) has written: 'The Protestant believer no longer lives in a world on-goingly penetrated by sacred beings and forces.' In the modern world, it is science and technology that are looked to for solutions to practical problems. While most people do not have the knowledge that would allow them to assess scientific ideas critically, their faith is now placed in the powers of the scientific expert rather than the world of the spirits. They are also less likely to believe in the power and effectiveness of witches, demons, and fairies. Such ideas are confined to the world of fiction, fairy tales, and horror films. People find it more difficult to believe in things that run counter to scientific principles of explanation.

> **⌕ Connections**
>
> Does Weber's argument about disenchantment explain why the witchcraft beliefs of Cassandra and Maureen, whom we introduced at the beginning of this chapter, appear so strange to so many people? Later in this chapter (on pp. 433–438) we look at the growth of 'New Age' beliefs. You might like to come back to this discussion when you have read those pages and see whether you think that this new spirituality marks a move away from the disenchantment that Weber described.

With the growing rationalization of modern culture, the sense of spiritual meaning that had formerly been provided by religion was lost. Weber took a particularly pessimistic view of this. He saw people living in a cold, soulless, and calculating world. They no longer had any sense of mystery about supernatural forces that could be understood only through magic or religion. They had lost sight of any values or goals except those that were tied to their immediate economic and political concerns. Modern society was becoming a vast and relentless machine, and individuals became mere 'cogs' in this machine. They played their parts out of necessity and not for any ultimate spiritual purpose.

In these circumstances, Weber held, it becomes more and more difficult to justify a commitment to any values and ideals (B. R. Wilson 1976; Wallis 1984). Individuals no longer feel that they have any basis for choosing the values by which to live their lives. They must make arbitrary choices among the competing values that face them, and they cannot rely on the guidance formerly provided by traditional religions. Such arbitrary choices provide them with no foundation for moral commitment to the rational and impersonal world in which they live. Practical matters lack any moral legitimacy.

Durkheim was less pessimistic than Weber. Like Comte, he accepted that there had been a decline in people's willingness to believe in spiritual beings and forces. He recognized, however, that a new form of religion—moral individualism—was developing and that this could give a moral significance to social life. Moral individualism, as it developed, would help to offset the calculative and soulless aspects of modernity that Weber had identified. Only where moral individualism had not fully developed did

THEORY AND METHOD

Anomie

Anomie is a term that was introduced by Durkheim to describe a failure of moral regulation. The word literally means 'without norms', and Durkheim used it to mean the absence of a normative framework or sacred canopy. Individual desires and interests for wealth and power are left uncontrolled.

Anomie is seen as a pathological condition that exists when the moral basis of modern society (moral individualism) has not properly developed. The full development of moral individualism produces the organic solidarity that Durkheim saw as the key to social cohesion in modern societies.

- In Chapter 2, p. 38 and pp. 47–8, we look at how Durkheim and Merton defined anomie. We will use Merton's ideas later in this chapter.

modern life break down into anomie. For Durkheim, then, disenchantment could be seen as involving a decline in traditional religious beliefs, but not a decline in religion as such. Religion had been transformed, but not displaced. Religion in the modern world may be less spiritual and less theistic, but it could still sustain a sacred canopy.

Differentiation and religious pluralism

In medieval society, the Catholic Church was able to claim a monopoly of moral authority. In a secular society, there are numerous denominations and they must compete for believers. In this situation, religion becomes much more a matter of individual choice and preference (Berger 1961a, 1961b). The roots of this religious pluralism and the need for choice can be traced to certain central features of Protestant Christianity itself.

The Protestantism of Luther and Calvin, as we have shown, rejected the authority of priests and of the church hierarchy. It emphasized, instead, the need for each individual to read the Bible and to listen directly to the voice of God. Individuals had to use their powers of reason to arrive at their own decisions about what is right and what is wrong. The Protestant obligation to consider all matters rationally and critically encouraged, albeit unintentionally, the very existence of God to be questioned. By the nineteenth century, all the major elements of traditional Christian belief—the Trinity, miracles, and the Virgin birth—were legitimate subjects for rational debate. They were no longer simply matters of faith (B. R. Wilson 1966). In this cultural context, religious denominations felt an increasing need to ensure that their doctrines and

teachings would appear plausible to rational believers. They could not rely on an uncritical acceptance of traditional authority.

These features of Protestantism have meant that none of its denominations has found it easy to maintain a plausible claim to a monopoly of truth. It has been said that 'Protestantism is essentially fissile': it tends always to split into competing schools of thought (Bruce 1985, 1986). Unlike Roman Catholicism, there is no unified and coherent system of Protestant doctrine and practice. Existing interpretations of the word of God are always open to challenge in the light of rational argument or personal inspiration, and so there is a strong tendency to schism and sectarianism. Protestant churches must compete to maintain the loyalty of those who have the obligation to make their own religious choices.

When religion is a matter of personal choice and private belief, societies face a problem of moral legitimacy. Traditional religion can no longer provide an authoritative guide for moral decision-making. There can be no intellectually convincing statement of what is right and what is wrong. Modern societies must live with the possibility of moral relativism. The moral individualism of modern society provides only a very weak basis for a shared commitment to any other ideals.

Contemporary societies are not, however, in a chronic state of anomie. In addition to the bonds of moral individualism, there do remain certain areas of *shared* belief. It is those who are most concerned with intellectual matters who are the most likely to pursue the rational criticism of accepted values. Most people, for most of the time, do not question the values into which they have been socialized. While these values are, in principle, subject to rational criticism, they are generally taken for granted in everyday situations. People are born into specific cultural and religious traditions, and these shape the way that they approach religious and moral questions. Religious commitment becomes weaker, but religious and moral beliefs tend to be relatively standardized throughout a society. As a result, competition between religions tends to be limited in scope. They can compete through the marginal differentiation of their ideas within a broadly shared religious framework.

Individual attachment to this framework is, however, weak and precarious. It is constantly subject to intellectual criticism, and there is always the danger that individual adherents will take these intellectual problems seriously. The inherited religious framework is in constant danger of erosion in the face of the secularizing tendencies built into modern society. Religious attachment must also compete with other calls upon people's time. When religion becomes a matter of individual preference, people see it as a leisure-time activity to be engaged in on a purely voluntary basis. It must, therefore, compete with the many other leisure-time activities that have become such important aspects of modern life. As B. R. Wilson has argued, choice in religion becomes equivalent to the consumer choice between 'pushpin, poetry, or popcorn' (1976: 96).

Religion in Britain

Early Protestantism in Britain was divided into numerous churches organized as 'sects'. A **sect** is a schismatic group, a body of people whose views diverge from those of others within the *same* religion. Following the Reformation, the number of sects multiplied as they diverged from one another within the broadly Protestant framework. The sociological concept of the sect was used by Troeltsch (1912) in his study of how the early Baptists, Quakers, and Methodists split from the Anglican and other Protestant faiths in the seventeenth and eighteenth centuries. These sects were quite diverse. The followers of Devon-born Joanna Southcott believed that she had received messages from the Spirit of God warning of impending dangers and disasters. These prophecies were placed in a 'Great Box' to be opened only when humankind was ready to receive the true message. George Fox's Society of friends—known as the 'Quakers'—believed in the power of quiet contemplation as a means to spiritual enlightenment. They believed in the importance of telling the truth at all times and refused to swear oaths, even in court.

Like the ecclesia, the sect claims to possess a monopoly of religious truth, but it is organized on a voluntary basis rather than through compulsory membership. Members are recruited through the conversion of non-members or through their personal decisions to join. People are born into an ecclesia, but they *choose* to join a sect. Sects establish sharp boundaries between members and non-members, and they expect a high level of involvement and commitment from their members. They stress the earnestness of individual faith and there is a heightened sense of commitment and morality. They tend, therefore, to be highly emotional in character and to adopt an evangelistic stance towards non-members. A denomination is tolerant towards other religions, but a sect stresses its sole and exclusive claim to religious truth.

Sects also place a great emphasis on individual decision and choice. This has meant that there is a greater lay involvement in religion. There is far less differentiation between lay people and clergy than there is in either the ecclesia or the denomination, and so they have more fluid and democratic structures of leadership. Niebuhr (1929) showed that sects tended to evolve into denominations as they grew and matured. The early Protestant sects in Britain, for example, had gradually been transformed into denominations by the nineteenth century. The Protestant sects had rejected Episcopalianism—rule by bishops—and relied, instead, on quite informal and democratic structures of leadership. In their denominational forms, church government was formalized into congregational or presbyterian structures.

It was this transition from sect to denomination that allowed the secularizing potential of Protestantism to make itself felt in Britain. The emerging denominations relaxed their earlier claims to possess a monopoly of religious truth, and they accommodated one another and Anglicanism. This pattern of denominational pluralism—the competition of rival but mutually tolerant denominations—became the characteristic religious pattern in Britain and the United States. Sects such as the Jehovah's Witnesses and the Seventh Day Adventists have survived only through very active proselytization and conversion.

Church and nation

The high point of religious participation, for all denominations, was the second half of the nineteenth century, after which it declined quite considerably. Rates of church attendance and of membership fell rapidly, and only a quarter of adults in England were even nominal members of a religious group by the 1950s (B. R. Wilson 1966; Martin 1967). Between 10 per cent and 15 per cent of the population were regular Sunday churchgoers, compared with about 40 per cent a century earlier. This decline in membership and attendance was especially marked during the last decades of the nineteenth century. Decline began first among Anglicans, and it then set in among the nonconformist denominations.

The decline in membership was greater in towns and cities than in rural districts, though the extent of the decline varied quite considerably from district to district within the major cities. Inner-city and working-class housing estates, for example, had very low rates of churchgoing, while middle-class suburbs showed significantly higher rates. The Catholic Church in Britain was more successful in retaining relatively high levels of church attendance, partly because of the large numbers of those who migrated to England from Ireland. For this reason, Catholics came to form a large proportion of the total churchgoing population.

While Protestantism in Britain took this highly pluralistic form, the Church of England remained the religion of the majority until well into the twentieth century (B. R. Wilson 1966: 119). The Church is the Established Church, having a constitutionally defined role in relation to the monarchy and the political system. The monarch is both Head of State and Head of the Church, appointing all bishops and archbishops and acting as 'Defender of the Faith'. The Church retained a strong association with the major social institutions of British society. As the

Briefing: surviving sects

- **Jehovah's Witnesses** believe in the literal truth of the Bible. They hold that the world was actually created in seven days and that there will soon be an apocalyptic battle between God and Satan. The sect actively recruits new members through a door-to-door ministry.

- **Seventh Day Adventists** believe that Jesus Christ will soon return to earth and will rule for 1,000 years. Founded in the 1840s when William Miller prophesied the end of the world, the sect is active in missionary work and has Saturday as its holy day.

Established Church, it was very much the church of the aristocracy, the old professions, and the middle classes.

Despite its official status, however, the Church of England is a denomination, not an ecclesia. It is a state church whose religious monopoly is limited by the existence of a substantial bloc of dissenting religion (Davie 1994). It has consistently sought to accommodate its practices to those of the leading Protestant denominations that have split from it over the years. Methodism, for example, has been particularly successful in attracting large numbers of working-class adherents, but the two churches have cooperated in a number of religious and secular activities.

A majority of people in England in mid-century (just under two-thirds) continued to describe themselves as 'Church of England' when asked. A nominal affiliation to the Church was seen as a part of what it was to be 'English'. It was an expression of English national identity and allegiance to English social institutions (B. R. Wilson 1966: 24). Other religions in Britain had much smaller numbers of adherents. About one in ten people were Catholics, and there were similar numbers in the Church of Scotland. There were as many Jews as there were Catholics, and one in ten of the population were members of smaller nonconformist denominations. In 1966 these smaller denominations included about 700,000 Methodists, 280,000 Baptists, 200,000 Congregationalists, and about 250,000 people in total spread among the Unitarians, Presbyterians, Quakers, and the Salvation Army. Between 1 and 2 per cent of the population were affiliated to small sects, such as the Christian Scientists and the Jehovah's Witnesses. Religious pluralism was especially high in Wales, where there were many dissenting sects and denominations. As in England, however, religion was linked with national identity. The chapels were the carriers of a distinctively Welsh identity, nurturing generations of Liberal and Labour supporters and politicians.

Only a very few people were willing to describe themselves—at least in public—as non-religious. An opinion poll in the middle of the 1960s found just 6 per cent of the English population stating 'none' as their religion. Only 9 per cent claimed that they had no belief in a 'spirit, god or life-force'. Almost a half of the people (43 per cent) claimed that they said regular prayers, and the majority wished to retain religious instruction in schools (Forster 1972).

Britain was a nominally Christian nation, and for the majority it was an Anglican nation. Although the level of emotional commitment to religion was low, involvement in the major rituals of the Christian calendar persisted. Church services were important markers of various critical stages in the life course. Two-thirds of all children were baptized into the Church of England between 1885 and 1950, and a quarter of the population in the early 1960s had been confirmed into the Church. One-fifth of children attended Sunday school over the period from 1895 to 1940. In this period the marriage rate was high and marriage in church was very common. The proportion of church marriages declined from the high level of 70–80 per cent that it achieved between 1850 and 1880. Nevertheless, over a half of all marriages were still being solemnized in the Church of England until after the Second World War.

Religion in the United States

While England had a national church, and there were similar institutions in Scotland and Wales, this was not the case in the United States. While the US Constitution guaranteed religious freedom for all its citizens, it gave no privileged position to any denomination. Political differences in the United States did not, therefore, take a religious form—there were no nonconformist or dissenting churches that could link religious opposition to an established religion with political opposition to an established state (Tocqueville 1835–40). The numerous religions that migrant settlers brought from their home countries to the United States all found their place within a strong pluralistic structure. Some of the older Protestant sects did retain a sectarian form, though they have often found it difficult to survive. The Shakers, for example, have died out, while the Amish have been much reduced in numbers.

Despite their different histories, Britain and the United States have moved towards similar forms of denominational pluralism (B. R. Wilson 1966: chapter 6). Levels of church membership in the United States have been higher than in Britain, however, and church involvement has substantially increased since the turn of the century. Twenty per cent of the US population were church members in 1880, and by 1962 the figure had increased to 63 per cent. Membership of Protestant denominations, for example, increased from 27 per cent of the population in 1926 to

Briefing: declining sects

- **Shakers** originated in the United States in the eighteenth century. They were celibate communities that lived apart from the rest of society and followed a simple life. They originally practised religious activities that involved shaking, trembling, or convulsions. There are no longer any Shaker communities, and they are now famous for their highly valued antique furniture, produced in their communities to simple, clean designs.

- **Amish** originated in a Swiss sect of Anabaptists in the seventeenth century. They maintain a strict Puritan lifestyle, living apart from the world in isolated communities. They are now found in Pennsylvania and the Midwest. Contemporary 'Old Order' Amish still dress in the same way as their founders and they make no use of modern technology such as cars and televisions (Sim 1994).

Being religious and being American.
© Alice Chadwick

35 per cent in 1950. The number of Catholics increased from 16 per cent to 23 per cent over the same period. Until well into the post-war period, almost a half of all Americans attended church every week.

The religious melting pot

These high levels of church attendance and membership do not mean, however, that the United States is not a secular society. An important study by Herberg (1955) showed that mainstream religions in the United States were losing their specifically theological character and were coming to be more closely identified with a sense of national identity. Herberg traces this to the particular experience of migration in the United States.

The United States is a nation of migrants. Successive waves of migrants arrived with their specific ethnic identity and religious affiliation. There was never a single, dominant denomination, and nor was there a single, dominant ethnic group. While the great bulk of all nineteenth- and twentieth-century migrants were white, they were ethnically diverse: there were Germans, Poles, Irish, Dutch, Norwegians, Russians, and many others. This produced what has been called an ethnic 'melting pot' (Glazer and Moynihan 1963). While first-generation migrants retained strong emotional ties to their home countries, second- and third-generation migrants tried to forge stronger identities for themselves as Americans and identified themselves closely with the social institutions of American public life.

> **⊃ Connections**
> The idea of the melting pot has been central to many discussions of race and ethnic relations. We discuss this and the associated idea of assimilation in Chapter 6, pp. 203 and 213–15. You will find it useful to consider those discussions alongside our discussion of Herberg's argument.

Central to the American way of life—or so it seemed to the newcomers—was regular churchgoing, and members of the ethnic minorities sought acceptance by mainstream American society through their own churchgoing. At church, they met those who had already successfully completed the process of migration and settlement, and they could get much needed practical help, including help with the language. Most importantly, they could acquire a sense of belonging in their new society. In their dealings with others, religious differences were minimized, as they built a shared sense of being religious and, therefore, of being 'American'.

Commitment to a church was a matter of practical commitment to the American way of life and American national identity. It was not a sign of high levels of religious faith or devotion. High levels of church membership and attendance, then, went hand in hand with secularization. Religions in the United States were disengaged and American society was disenchanted. It was the particular situation of the United States as a nation of migrants that led to such high levels of church involvement in a secular society. Churchgoing was an expression of one's citizenship, of being a 'good American'. To be a good American did not, however, require adherence to any particular religion. Someone could be a good American by being a good Protestant, a good Catholic, or a good Jew.

The various denominations identified themselves with the American state and society and the American way of life. As a result, the moral teachings of the principal religions became more and more similar, and their theologies became looser and more liberal in character. Once religiosity is identified with national identity in this way, a withdrawal from or denial of religion comes to be seen as a withdrawal from or denial of the American way of life. People are locked in to high levels of church attendance and to the public statement of religious values. To do anything else would be 'un-American'. Churchgoing strengthens a sense of national community. It reinforces the symbolically bounded imagined community that unites all together in a common activity and with a common identity.

Civil religion

In both Britain and the United States there has been a close association between religion and national identity. In Britain, this took the form of the nominal affiliation of a majority of the population to the Church of England. In the United States, it took the form of high levels of church attendance. This identification of religion and national community has led many sociologists to suggest that secular societies can be seen as organized around a characteristic pattern of **civil religion**.

In a civil religion, the secular world itself has a sacred character (Bellah 1967, 1970; Bocock 1974; see also Warner 1953). Secularized religions of this kind are a result of the partial, but not complete disenchantment of the modern world. Despite growing disenchantment, modern societies have been able to rely on a residue of traditional attachment to established social institutions. The traditional symbolism of national identity provides a common cultural framework for all members of society, cutting across differences between particular denominations. The nation itself can become an object of religious veneration, and distinctive civic rituals are focused on it. Presidential inaugurations, Thanksgiving, Independence Day, Veteran's Day, and other public occasions in the United States, for example, provide opportunities for the expression and reaffirmation of a sense of shared national identity and commitment.

Bellah, like Herberg, sees the United States as having been united by a religious belief in the sacred character of America and a consequent loyalty to the American nation. God is almost seen as an American. Where children's prayers end with 'God bless Mummy and Daddy', political speeches end with 'God bless America'. Saintly figures from American history have been central to the maintenance of American values. The story of Abraham Lincoln's rise 'from the log cabin to the White House', for example, is central to the mythology of America as an open, classless society and to the maintenance of the 'American Dream'.

Involvement in civic rituals is a way in which existing religious organizations can maintain a role for themselves in a secular society. In Britain, for example, the Church of England remains the nationally Established Church. It is closely involved in major parliamentary occasions and in the celebration and commemoration of national values and events. The Royal Family has for long been associated with the civic rituals of the major national occasions. Many specific rituals surround the Royal Family itself: the Coronation, the Queen's Birthday, the Christmas speech, the Trooping of the Colour, the State Opening of Parliament, Remembrance Day, and so on. The link between the nation, the monarch, and the church has been central to the legitimation of the state.

This view of religion and ritual in British society was first explored in an influential article on the Coronation of Queen Elizabeth II in 1953 (Shils and Young 1953). The Coronation was seen as one of a number of occasions—others might be royal weddings—in which a sense of national community could be affirmed and the basic moral values of the society reinforced. The Coronation of 1953 was the first major televised spectacular in which a large mass audience could simultaneously participate in the same civic ritual. Twenty million viewers watched seven hours of live coverage of the Coronation. Even in 1981,

---

➔ Connections

You will find it useful to look at what we say about national identity in Chapter 16, pp. 619–21. Pay particular attention to the idea of nationalism as allegiance to an imagined community.

The situation that we are describing is that which existed in its strongest form until the 1960s. How far do you think it still applies to Britain? How have the personal problems of the Royal Family affected the Church of England and its role in civil religion? What does public reaction to the deaths of Diana, Princess of Wales, and the Queen Mother tell us about religious beliefs and attitudes towards the monarchy? Were these reflected in celebrations of the marriage of Prince Charles to Camilla Parker-Bowles?

Presidential inaugurations: a ceremony of the civil religion?
© Getty Images/Alex Wong

39 million people watched the televised wedding of the Prince of Wales, and there was a doubling in sales of video recorders.

The idea of civil religion offers, perhaps, the best framework for understanding the religious character of Soviet Communism that we mentioned earlier. The Marxist–Leninist creed identified the revolutionary role of the proletariat with the Soviet state and its leaders, and many public ceremonials and rituals reinforced its moral values and legitimated its power (C. Lane 1981). Public occasions were marked by the parading of portraits of Communist leaders as national symbols from the Communist past. On the anniversary of the Communist Revolution, the major national event of the year, lengthy military and industrial parades marched past the political leaders in their enclosure above Lenin's mausoleum. The Red Flag, the Red Army, and Red Square were the symbols of Soviet identity.

It is important not to overemphasize the consensual character of civil religions (K. Thompson 1992). For many people, involvement in public ceremonies and rituals reflects a pragmatic acceptance of them rather than any kind of normative commitment. In a disenchanted society, people may not be individually and genuinely committed, in terms of their personal and private beliefs, to the moral authority of political leaders and national symbols. They may, nevertheless, conform to the rituals and observances as public acts, and as part of the routine of their daily lives. This conformity may reflect the power of taken-for-granted attitudes, or the wish not to deviate from what is taken to be public opinion. It may result from calculations of personal advantage, or it may be enforced by coercive political authorities (Abercrombie *et al.* 1979).

> **⊃ Connections**
>
> We look at the political structure of the Soviet Union in greater detail in 'Totalitarianism and command societies', in Chapter 20, pp. 834–6. You may like to return to our discussion of civil religion when you read that chapter. What evidence is there from television and newspapers of a civil religion in the new post-Communist Russia?

◆ *Stop and reflect*

In this section we have looked at patterns of secularization in modern society. We began by looking at the concept of secularization itself.

- Secularization can be seen in terms of the two processes of disengagement and disenchantment.

- In Europe, secularization involved a transition from the Catholic ecclesia to a situation of denominational pluralism. Many denominations evolved from earlier sects.

- In modern societies, religious belief has become more of a private matter and religious activities have to compete with the other activities among which individuals must choose to allocate their time.

- If beliefs have become simply a matter of choice and lifestyle, can they still be regarded as 'religious'?

We then turned to reviewing religious practices and beliefs in Britain and the United States from the middle of the nineteenth century to the 1960s.

- There was a decline in religious participation in Britain, but a majority of the population continued to see themselves as nominal members of the Church of England.

- There was an increase in religious participation in the United States, where a nation of migrants saw church membership as a symbol of American national identity.

- Civil religion is a secularized form of religion that identifies religion with national identity and state ceremonial. Is it compatible with the existence of privatized religions of choice?

The rise of new religions

In the previous section we traced patterns of religious belief and practice up to the 1960s. As in so many other areas, the 1960s were a turning point for religion. Since then old and established forms of religion have declined, and those that have prospered have done so by adapting their beliefs and practices to the new times. Moreover, civil religion has weakened, and now exists in only a very feeble form. The residue of traditional social attachment on which it could trade in the past has continued to decline in the face of growing disenchantment. Traditional authority in the state and other social institutions is increasingly difficult to sustain, and, with the decay of tradition, so civil religion is weakened. At the same time, however, new religious sects and cults have multiplied. While the scale of religious involvement remains quite low, new forms of religion have become an important element in the lives of many people.

Belonging and believing

The post-war period in Britain has seen a continued decline in church membership and attendance. Although church involvement in the United States remains higher than in Britain, membership is no longer growing and attendance seems to be falling. There has been a considerable weakening of religious belonging. People are now less likely to belong to organized religions or to be actively involved in their rituals and practices. There has not, however, been a comparable decline in religious belief. The majority of

people continue to subscribe to broadly religious beliefs, though their adherence is very loose. Their beliefs are not tied to particular doctrines or practices and they are a matter of only very low-key adherence.

For many people, then, religious belief is a real, but rather unimportant part of their lives that has no particular significance for their moral or political attitudes. For a minority, however, the common religion does not suffice. These are the people who are attracted into active and reinvigorated Protestant sects or into new, non-Christian forms of cult religion. In this section we will look at trends in religious behaviour and the nature of the common religion, and we will then turn to a discussion of the variety of new religions.

From civil religion to common religion

The proportion of the British population who actually belong to a Christian church fell from 19 per cent in 1970 to 12 per cent in 1990. This was less than half the level that it had been at the turn of the century. About two-thirds of church members were Protestants and one-third were Catholics. Just under 4 per cent of the adult population were active members of the Church of England in 1990 (Bruce 1995: 37). Only one-fifth of the population now attend church at least once each month. Some estimates have put this figure even lower, though a survey in 1978 found just over one-third of English Catholics to be regular church attenders.

Figure 11.1 Active membership in Christian churches, United Kingdom, 1975–2000

Church	1975	1985	1995	2000
Anglican	2,297,571	2,016,593	1,785,033	1,653,980
Roman Catholic	2,518,955	2,204,165	1,914,396	1,768,036
Presbyterian	1,641,520	1,384,997	1,088,098	988,812
Other Protestants	1,345,273	1,318,644	1,299,916	1,277,927
Orthodox	196,850	223,686	196,995	234,690
Total	8,000,169	7,148,085	6,284,438	5,923,445

Sources: Davie (1994: 46, table 4.1); *Religious Trends* (2001: table 2.22).

Church membership and attendance are highest among older women and among non-manual workers than they are, in general, among men and manual workers. Among those who see themselves as 'frequent' or 'regular' church attenders, two-thirds are women. Among Protestants, members of the Anglican denominations (the Church of England, the Church in Wales, the Episcopal Church in Scotland, and the Church of Ireland) were in a minority. The great majority of active Protestants are members of Presbyterian, Methodist, or Baptist denominations (Davie 1990). Church membership remains particularly high in Northern Ireland, among both Catholics and Protestants. About a quarter of Catholics in England are first-generation migrants from Northern Ireland or the Republic.

Britain has one of the lowest levels of church membership in Europe. Although comparative figures are notoriously difficult to compile, it seems that about 15 per cent of the adult British population are members of one church or another, compared with just over 20 per cent in France and Denmark, and about 30 per cent in Finland and Norway. Overt religious activity is still very high in the United States. Over two-thirds of the population of the United States claim to be church members, and just over a half of the population still attends a church at least once each month.

Figures 11.1 and 11.2 show some recent trends in church membership and church allegiance in Britain. A comparison of the two tables brings out clearly the discrepancy between the numbers claiming a nominal adherence to a religion and the numbers who are actively involved as members of one or another church. About 40 million people in 1995 claimed to have some kind of religious allegiance, over a half of them claiming to be Anglican. Very few of these nominal Anglicans were active members or attended church regularly. It would seem that only about one in twenty of those who claim to be Anglicans are actually members of the Church. This discrepancy was less marked for other denominations. In most cases, about a half or more of their adherents were active members.

The Anglican and Catholic churches both lost large numbers of members between 1975 and 2000. The Protestant sects and denominations have held up slightly better than the Anglicans. Nevertheless, the Baptists, the Methodists, and the Presbyterians each lost about a

Figure 11.2 Expressed church allegiance, United Kingdom, 1975–2000

Church	Allegiance (millions)			
	1975	1985	1995	2000
Anglican	28.2	27.1	26.1	25.6
Roman Catholic	5.6	5.6	5.7	5.8
Presbyterian	2.9	2.7	2.6	2.6
Other Protestants	3.1	3.3	3.2	3.2
Orthodox	0.4	0.4	0.5	0.5
Total	40.2	39.1	38.1	37.7
Hindus	0.3	0.4	0.4	0.5
Jews	0.4	0.3	0.3	0.3
Muslims	0.4	0.9	1.2	1.4
Sikhs	0.2	0.3	0.6	0.6
Others	0.8	1.3	1.6	1.7
Total	2.1	3.2	4.1	4.5
Totals	42.3	42.3	42.2	42.2

Source: *Religious Trends* (2001: tables 2.3.1 and 10.7.2).

❷ How do you think a question on religious allegiance might have been worded for these surveys?

❷ Is it useful to study religious beliefs using survey methods?

Figure 11.3 shows the growth in various religions across the world since 1900. Which religions have shown the greatest rate of growth over this period? Which have been the slowest to grow?

You can calculate growth rates by subtracting the 1900 figure from the 2000 figure and dividing this amount by the 1900 figure. Christianity, for example, has grown by (1999.6–508.1)/588.1, or by 2.58 times. Note that you cannot calculate this accurately for Baha'is, who were so small in numbers in 1900 that there were not enough of them to be recorded in this table. (The technical reason for this calculation problem is that it would involve you dividing by zero—and anything divided by zero is infinity.)

Now calculate similar growth rates for the increase between 1970 and 2000.

Can you come up with any explanation for the rates of change that you have found? Total world population increased from 1,620 million in 1900 to 3,696 million in 1970 and 6,055 million in 2000—what does this tell you about the overall trend in religious attachment? Can you find any evidence for secularization in this table?

The comparative data shown in Figure 11.4 is taken from the World Values Survey, which asked people whether they attended church at least once per week. Such measures are very unreliable, but some broad patterns are clear. Rates of church attendance are especially low across northern Europe, Russia, China, and Central and East Asia. Moderately high rates are found through the Americas, and the highest rates of all occur in Nigeria, the Philippines, Ireland, and South Africa. Data were not collected for many Muslim countries in Africa and the Middle East, where attendance at religious services might be expected to be very high.

Figure 11.3   World religions 1900–2000

	1900	1970	1980	1990	2000
	no. in millions				
Christian	558.1	1,236.4	1,482.6	1,747.5	1,999.6
Muslim	199.9	553.5	759.0	962.4	1,188.2
Hindu	203.0	462.6	578.7	686.0	811.3
Chinese folk religion	380.0	231.9	288.4	347.7	384.8
Buddhists	127.1	233.4	275.7	323.1	360.0
Animists	117.7	160.3	180.9	200.0	228.4
Sikhs	3.0	10.6	14.2	19.3	23.3
Jains	1.3	2.6	3.2	3.9	4.2
Jews	12.3	14.8	14.0	13.2	14.4
Baha'is	0	2.7	3.8	5.7	7.1
Other religions	14.0	93.8	105.4	116.7	130.0
Non-religious	3.2	697.5	774.2	853.8	918.2

Source: Religious Trends (2001: table 1.2.2).

Figure 11.4   Church attendance (1997)

Percentage of adults surveyed who claimed that they attend church services one or more times per week

1.	Nigeria	89%
2.	Ireland	84%
3.	Philippines	68%
4.	South Africa	56%
5.	Poland	55%
6.	Puerto Rico	52%
7.	Slovakia	47%
8.	Portugal	47%
9.	Mexico	46%
10.	Italy	45%
11.	Belgium	44%
12.	United States	44%
13.	Turkey	43%
14.	Peru	43%
15.	India	42%
16.	Canada	38%
17.	Brazil	36%
18.	Netherlands	35%
19.	Uruguay	31%
20.	Venezuela	31%
21.	Austria	30%
22.	United Kingdom	27%
23.	Spain	25%
24.	Chile	25%
25.	Argentina	25%
26.	Croatia	22%
27.	France	21%
28.	Hungary	21%
29.	Romania	20%
30.	Lithuania	16%
31.	Switzerland	16%
32.	Australia	16%
33.	Korea, South	14%
34.	Czech Republic	14%
35.	Taiwan	11%
36.	Georgia	10%
37.	Bulgaria	10%
38.	Moldova	10%
39.	Ukraine	10%
40.	China	9%
41.	Armenia	8%
42.	Serbia and Montenegro	7%
43.	Azerbaijan	6%
44.	Belarus	6%
45.	Denmark	5%
46.	Norway	5%
47.	Latvia	5%
48.	Sweden	4%
49.	Iceland	4%
50.	Estonia	4%
51.	Finland	4%
52.	Japan	3%
53.	Russia	1%

Source: www.nationmaster.com/graph-T/rel_chu_att

quarter of their members between 1970 and 2000. Among Christian churches, only the Orthodox Church has shown an increase in numbers, largely as a result of migration over the period.

About two-thirds of children born between 1885 and 1950 were baptized into the Church of England, but the figure had fallen to a half by 1960. By 2000 the figure had dropped to only just over a quarter. There were 122,000 infant baptisms and 36,300 confirmations in 2000. Less than one in ten children were then attending Sunday school, compared with one in five during the period from 1895 to 1940. There was also a decline in church marriages, as couples became more likely to have a civil ceremony. One-third of English marriages were civil marriages in the period from 1952 to 1962, compared with one-quarter in 1929 and just one in eight in 1879 (B. R. Wilson 1966: chapter 1). By 2000, however, well over a half of all marriages took place in a register office or in 'approved premises', such as hotels and public halls. Marriage itself had become less popular (see Chapter 12, pp. 465–9).

These falls in membership and attendance have been associated with organizational changes in the churches. The number of Church of England ministers declined from over 20,000 in 1900 to 10,750 in 2000, and the number of Methodist ministers declined from 3,800 to 2,456 over the same period. The number of Catholic priests in England and Wales, by contrast, increased for a while as the number of migrants from Eire and Northern Ireland also increased. It has now fallen back in line with declining membership. In Scotland, the number of ministers in Presbyterian denominations has fallen from 3,600 to less than 1,500 (Bruce 1995: 32–3). An important trend, however, has been an increase in the number of women clergy. About 12 per cent of Anglican ministers and 18 per cent of Methodist ministers are now female.

These trends show, then, a decline in religious *belonging*, as measured by conventional churchgoing and church involvement. They do not, however, give any direct evidence of a decline in religious *believing* (Davie 1994). In fact, religious belief appears to remain quite strong. A survey carried out in the 1980s found that 76 per cent of people in Great Britain believed in God, 50 per cent engaged in regular prayer, and only 4 per cent described themselves as atheists. In 1990, 71 per cent claimed to believe in God, 53 per cent prayed or meditated, and 44 per cent said that they drew personal strength from their religious beliefs. Fifty-three per cent of people believed in 'Heaven', and 25 per cent believed in 'the Devil' and in 'Hell' (Davie 1994: 79, see also Jowell *et al.* 1991). In a survey in 1995, only 11 per cent said that they definitely did not believe in God, while 21 per cent had no doubts at all about the existence of God (see Figure 11.5). During 1996, the then leaders of all three major political parties claimed that they prayed regularly to God. By 1999, only 32.5 per cent

of the population claimed to believe in God (Voas and Bruce 2004).

In the United States, religious belief seems to be somewhat higher. A massive 95 per cent of the population claim to believe in God. In many cases, Americans subscribe to creationist ideas that run counter to the conclusions of contemporary science. In the early 1980s, a survey reported that 44 per cent of Americans believed that God had created human beings within the last 10,000 years.

Though most people in Britain and the United States describe their religious beliefs as 'Christian', they are not those of conventional Christianity. For many people, Christian and non-Christian ideas have been fused into loose and amorphous systems of personal belief. They claim no specific biblical or priestly authority for these beliefs, regarding them as things that they simply accept or have worked out for themselves. Forty-two per cent of those who believed in God saw this god as 'some sort of spiritual or vital force' rather than as the personal God of traditional Christianity (Bruce 1995: 50).

Beliefs in a god are directly and closely linked with 'superstitious' beliefs and practices and with beliefs in astrology, psychic phenomena, ghosts, and paranormal experiences. Just under a quarter of the British population in 1991 believed that good-luck charms were effective, just over a quarter believed in the accuracy of horoscopes, and 40 per cent believed in the powers of fortune tellers (Jowell *et al.* 1991). For many people, these beliefs were held alongside beliefs in alternative medicine, the power of crystals, and reflexology.

This was true also of those who identified themselves as Catholics, a significant number of whom held unorthodox beliefs or rejected certain aspects of traditional Catholicism. These 'heterodox Catholics' formed a majority among Catholic non-attenders at church. They were younger than

Figure 11.5 Belief in God, Great Britain, 1995

	(%)
Do not believe in God	11
Do not know if God exists and cannot find evidence for God's existence	15
Believe in a higher power of some kind	12
Believe sometimes	12
Doubt, but believe	23
God exists, with no doubts	21
Can't choose/not answered	7
	100

Source: *Social Trends* (1997: table 13.23).

the average English Catholic—two-thirds of them were under age 35—and they were more likely to be second or later generation than recent migrants. A survey of their attitudes concluded that they might never have been anything more than nominal Catholics (Hornsby-Smith *et al.* 1982; see also Hornsby-Smith 1987, 1991).

Organized religion, both conventional denominational religion and state-oriented civil religion, is no longer a major factor in the lives of most people. Those religious beliefs that they do retain are loose and free-floating and are not organized into any formal participation in churches or rituals. Mainstream religious belief in Britain is no longer tied to conventional Christianity or to regular church attendance. What Davie (1994) has termed the common religion is a non-sectarian and eclectic form of religious belief. People 'continue to believe in God, but . . . are reluctant to express this belief in either churchgoing or church membership' (Davie 1990). Their conception of God, furthermore, bears little relationship to the scriptural God of the Christian tradition. The common religion is a private system of belief that draws on a pool of shared ideas that derive from both Christian and non-Christian sources.

What is striking, however, is that the common religion has no significant moral implications for how people should live in society. There is some sign of a growing sense of the environmental implications of these religious beliefs—of the need to protect the earth and its natural resources—but there is no equivalent sense of any need to build or to defend particular kinds of social order. The common religion does not provide the moral bonds and regulations that were central to traditional religion. In a secular society, the uncommitted mainstream religion of the vast majority of the population is a sprawling and amorphous array of beliefs that form a framework of taken-for-granted ideas that, for most people, are an integral, if rather marginal, aspect of their day-to-day lives. This raises the question of whether such collective beliefs can still be said to constitute 'religious' beliefs in the fullest sense of the term.

> **⮞ Connections**
>
> The idea of the common religion raises questions about the definition of religion. What do you think about this? Look back at the definition given on p. 407 at the beginning of this chapter. You might like to talk to friends and family about their beliefs to see if they are similar to those described here.

Varieties of new religion

The common religion is a widely shared framework of ideas, but for many people it is not enough. Nor does the more general framework of moral individualism meet their need for truly spiritual values. Some of these seekers after the sacred have turned to more fundamental forms of traditional Christianity, but others have found a greater appeal in new religions. The number of these new religions, both Christian and non-Christian, has increased since the Second World War, in both Britain and the United States. This growth has been especially rapid since the 1960s. These new religions are often described as cults, though this term has been given a wide variety of meanings.

In the original definition given by Troeltsch (1912), the **cult** was contrasted with the sect. Troeltsch defined the cult as a loosely organized grouping without sharp boundaries and with no exclusive system of beliefs. Cult beliefs are not rigid and exclusive; they are open and flexible. They comprise a set of common themes and ideas, and individual members are able to contribute their personal views to the pool of ideas. A cult is very open to new recruits, it is tolerant towards other beliefs, and it makes no demand that its members should completely abandon their other beliefs. Many people today, for example, adhere to cult beliefs in UFOs and alien abductions. These beliefs are remarkably diverse, and those who adhere to such beliefs are united by little more than their common concern and interest. There is no central organization or rigidly codified and enforced set of beliefs.

Cults are often short-lived. They depend upon the personal leadership of a founder or key member, and they dissolve when this leader dies. An example of a long-lasting cult is spiritualism, which has drawn its adherents from the membership of many churches, as well as from those who are members of none (Nelson 1969). Troeltsch argued that, if a cult can establish a more secure base of recruitment, it can establish a more permanent organization. Such a cult may even develop into an ecclesia, as happened when early cult Christianity was taken up by the Roman emperor and became the Roman Catholic Church. On the other hand, however, cults may remain apart from political and economic power and evolve into sects.

The word 'cult' has also been used in popular discussions, but here it tends to be a derogatory term. For many people, then, a cult is a contemporary religious organization, often a tight and exclusive sect, whose aims and methods they reject. Cults are accused of brainwashing or kidnapping those who join them, and they are often accused of financial, sexual, or political deviance. Because the original sociological meaning of cult has been obscured by its contemporary popular use as a label for religious deviance, many sociologists now prefer to use the more neutral term 'new religious movement'. This term, too, can be a little misleading, as all religions were, at some stage, new, and many of the growing religions of the 1960s have long-established roots.

The established Christian and non-Christian denominations and sects—Methodists, Baptists, the Reformed Church (Presbyterian and Congregationalist), Anglicans, Catholics, Jews, Spiritualists, Mormons, Jehovah's Witnesses, and the Salvation Army—have, in general, continued to decline in numbers or have, at best, maintained their membership through active proselytizing. The big growth in numbers of members and believers has largely occurred among those sects that have returned to or have emphasized the fundamental beliefs of their faith and those religions that have based themselves on radically new sets of ideas that are often non-theistic in character.

In the rest of this chapter, we will look at the four main forms of religion in which there has been a growth of activity. They are:

- inspirational Protestantism;
- world-rejecting religions;
- world-affirming religions;
- religions of ethnic protest.

Inspirational Protestantism comprises a number of fundamentalist, reformed, and evangelical sects and denominations that have split from the established denominations or that have been set up in direct opposition to them. Examples are the Pentecostalist churches and the Southern Baptist Convention. World-rejecting religions are a variety of generally non-Christian sects and cults that reject established religion and many aspects of modern society. They adopt a 'utopian' or millennial point of view. Examples are the Unification Church and Krishna Consciousness. World-affirming religions, on the other hand, include a variety of sects and cults that embrace the values of modern society. They aim to provide their members with better means to achieve them. Examples are Scientology and Transcendental Meditation. Finally, religions of ethnic protest are religions of migrants and ethnic minorities who have been excluded from full participation in the mainstream of modern society. The religion becomes a means of protest and opposition to their exclusion and oppression. Examples are Rastafarianism and some contemporary forms of Islam.

Inspirational Protestantism

Those who are attracted to inspirational Protestantism do so in reaction to the increasingly liberal religious attitudes of the mainstream Protestant denominations. As we have shown, Protestant beliefs have encouraged and reinforced the tendency to secularization, and this has meant that the beliefs of the Protestant denominations themselves have been marked by a disenchantment. To those who look for traditional religious beliefs, the Protestant denominations have little to offer. In moving in an increasingly liberal direction, the Protestant denominations have estranged many of their own adherents.

These people decry the loss of any distinctively religious content in the teachings of the churches. They resent the abandonment of what they still regard as religious certainties, especially when it is bishops and other senior leaders of the churches who seem to be denying the central tenets of their belief. When, in the early 1990s, the Bishop of Durham gave a rational, liberal interpretation of the Virgin birth, many of the most active members of the Church felt that he was no longer speaking as a truly Christian clergyman.

Those who retain traditional Christian beliefs lose confidence in a church that they see as moving rapidly away from them in an increasingly secular direction. They reject attempts to be relevant to contemporary concerns and to update the liturgy and rituals. They disapprove of the translation of the Bible into contemporary English. The involvement of the churches in social work and political controversies is seen as a departure from their primary purpose of preaching the gospels. The Protestant denominations have lost members, at least in part, because their liberal beliefs are out of line with the more conservative religious beliefs and attitudes of many of their members. These disaffected Protestants are attracted to the more fundamentalist Protestant sects that have managed to increase their memberships in recent years. These sects have prospered by retaining traditional beliefs in an

THEORY AND METHODS

Sect and cult

We have identified four concepts that form a typology of religious organizations. These are ecclesia, denomination, sect, and cult. You should review the definitions of ecclesia and denomination on p. 414.

A sect is characterized by:

- a claim to a monopoly of religious truth;
- voluntary, not compulsory membership;
- a high level of emotional commitment;
- non-hierarchical forms of leadership.

In so far as the concept of a cult can still be used in its original sociological sense, it refers to religious groups that are characterized by:

- great openness to all who wish to join;
- loosely defined beliefs and concerns;
- non-institutionalized forms of leadership.

Presbyterianism in Northern Ireland is a basis of ethnic loyalism.

© Neil Jarman

increasingly secular age. As Bruce (1983: 466) has argued, 'The group of Protestants who do most to preserve their faith from the ravages of the secular world have survived the last quarter century in better shape than have those who argued for compromise with the modern world.'

Most of the Presbyterian denominations in both Scotland and Northern Ireland, for example, have experienced declining membership over the course of the century. The more conservative Free Presbyterian Churches, however, have experienced huge increases in membership since the middle of the 1950s. Ian Paisley's Free Presbyterians have built up a massive 10,000 membership in Northern Ireland since its formation in 1951, its role as the defender of the 'loyalist' ethnicity of Ulster Protestants having helped to strengthen its appeal (Bruce 1983).

The Protestant sects that have attracted this growth in membership have been the inspirational sects and we now need to look a little closer at the nature of inspirational Protestantism and those who support it.

Fundamentalism and Pentecostalism

Two principal forms of inspirational Protestantism can be identified in Britain and the United States. These are fundamentalism and Pentecostalism. Fundamentalists adopt a particularly conservative attitude towards their religion. They subscribe to the Protestant reliance on the Bible as the direct word of God and, therefore, as the fundamental source of all knowledge, and they hold that its meaning is self-evident to all who read it. The Bible requires no interpretation by priests or others: it is not allegorical or mythical, it is literally true. God's will and the truth of human creation are claimed to be discoverable by a simple and direct reading of the Bible.

Things are not, of course, this simple, as no text can be understood in a strictly literal sense, without interpretation. The meaning of the Bible, or, indeed, of any other text, is far from straightforward. This is clear from the fact that there are divergent forms of biblical fundamentalism. There are, for example, differences between reformed and evangelical Protestantism. Calvinist or Reformed Protestants believe in a doctrine of predestination according to which only a small group of the elect are destined for salvation. Evangelical forms of fundamentalism, on the other hand, encourage people to choose God and, through being 'born again', to *achieve* salvation.

In reality, then, fundamentalism must rely on the authoritative interpretations given to the Bible by the preachers and teachers who have played a leading role in the social organization and development of the particular sects. Fundamentalists are inspired by the direct word of God, as recorded in the Bible, but they must rely on charismatic, inspiring preachers to guide their reading. Fundamentalist readings of the Bible are attractive to those who, by prior belief or social background, are predisposed towards conservative responses to its message.

Pentecostal Christians also subscribe to the literal truth of the Bible, but they combine this with an overriding emphasis on personal religious experiences, such as spiritual possession, speaking with tongues, healing, and the working of miracles (Bruce 1985). In this kind of religion, the word of God in the Bible is supplemented by the direct voice of God. Pentecostalists believe that they can learn God's wishes for them through opening their hearts and minds to His spirit. They believe that they can learn from direct spiritual inspiration and from observing the religious experiences and inspiration of others in their church.

Large numbers of Pentecostalists in Britain are African Caribbean. First-generation migrants arrived in Britain in the 1950s with more conservative religious attitudes than most of the white population. They were particularly attracted by Pentecostalism. It has been estimated that just under one in five African Caribbeans attend church

Briefing: Pentecostalism

According to the Bible, the Holy Spirit descended on the disciples on the fiftieth day (Greek *pente koste*) after the Passover festival. The Holy Spirit gave the disciples gifts of prophecy, healing, and speaking in foreign tongues. In the contemporary Christian calendar, this is celebrated at Whitsun.

Pentecostal churches believe that these gifts are still available to true believers, and their services are designed to create the conditions for this. Services involve loud and joyful singing and prayer, and members of the congregation may exhibit signs of the Spirit's 'gifts'. The Pentecostal movement began in the United States around 1900 and soon spread to Britain. The principal Pentecostal church in the United States is the Assemblies of God. In Britain, most Pentecostalists are members of the Elim Pentecostal Church or the Apostolic Church. There are also many independent black Pentecostalist churches.

regularly, about four-fifths of these attending Pentecostal churches. Pryce (1986) has shown the high level of support for Pentecostalism in a particular area of Bristol. African Caribbeans in Bristol reported that they were oppressed as both black and working class. Their religion helped them to minimize the significance of this oppression while they awaited salvation in the next world. Black Pentecostalism, then, is a form of *cultural defence* (Bruce 1995: 78) for African-Caribbean ethnicity.

The new Christian right

The social and political influence of fundamentalism grew particularly rapidly in the United States during the 1960s and 1970s. Underlying this growth was a feeling that a weakening of the civil religion and an associated spiritual decline in American society into permissiveness and moral relativism was something that needed to be reversed through a reassertion of traditional Christian values. Moral individualism, also, was felt to be unsatisfying in itself because it lacked the enchantment and spirituality of traditional religion. Specific targets were the liberal intellectuals who were seen as responsible for this spiritual decline.

This demand for moral revival emerged in what Bruce has called conservative social milieux or subcultures. These are loose networks of individuals and organizations that are united by shared beliefs and values but are not formed into any single organization or political movement (Bruce 1984: chapters 3 and 7). These milieux are particularly strong in the southern states, but they extend nation-wide.

Those who live in the conservative milieu build supporting institutions that strengthen it and allow it to extend its influence. Separate and distinct schools and colleges, for example, have allowed conservative Protestants to socialize their children away from the permissiveness and liberalism that they see in the mainstream schools. Similarly, the publication of fundamentalist books, films, and music helps to enlarge the subculture of fundamentalism. Most recently, these cultural efforts have been solidified through radio and television evangelism. There are now a number of satellite and cable television channels dedicated to evangelistic Protestantism and its charismatic leaders.

Evangelical crusades have been of major significance in attracting new recruits to particular churches, and in preventing the sons and daughters of subcultural adherents from falling away from their faith. Conservative Protestant movements have, however, recruited mainly from those who were already predisposed towards traditional, conservative forms of religion. The principal recruits have been the children of people who were already associated with one or another of the conservative Protestant churches. The crusades have been occasions for reviving and revivifying the religious beliefs of those who are already predisposed towards conversion.

When existing religious world-views lose their plausibility, many young people in the conservative milieux find the message of the fundamentalist churches attractive. This cultural affinity builds on the close personal links that they and their families have to the churches and other institutions of the subculture of fundamentalism. Personal social relations are also able to reinforce their commitment once their religious choice has been made. More than a half of all converts to the conservative Protestant churches are recruited between the ages of 12 and 20, and they have generally been introduced to the church through a parental Christian influence (Bruce 1984: 56–7). For these reasons, fundamentalist churches have made few converts from outside the milieux, and the evangelical crusades have not resulted in the mass conversion of the uncommitted:

> The people who go forward are almost all the sons and daughters of believers. What they signify with such a move is not that they have found a new and previously alien belief-system convincing but rather that they have come to make a positive commitment to a set of beliefs with which they are already familiar. (Bruce 1984: 102)

It was from these conservative cultural milieux that the so-called new right emerged in the 1970s. Media evangelists were key figures in mobilizing cultural support for the Moral Majority, which was formed in 1979 as an organizational focus for the new Christian right. Conservative Protestants formed the leading members of the new right in the political sphere, though it also built its support through alliances with right-wing thinkers in the Catholic, Jewish, Mormon, and other churches. This movement built a large bloc of support that helped to secure the election of Ronald Reagan in his first term as president.

> **⟳ Connections**
>
> If you want to know more about the growth and influence of the new right in the United States and Britain, turn to Chapter 15, pp. 601–3.

The processes that helped the formation of the new Christian right in the United States were much weaker in Britain. The conservative Protestant churches have, however, been the least likely to embrace the move to toleration and secularism in politics. Bruce has shown that smaller religious organizations in Scotland and Northern Ireland, especially those with a predominantly working-class membership and a strong regional identity, have maintained a sectarian stance towards other churches and have opposed moves that would undermine their own particular identity (Bruce 1986). In Northern Ireland, conservative Protestantism has developed into a strong social force with an anti-Catholic character, and these fundamentalist churches have been particularly important social bases of support for the Orange Order, a Masonic body that pursues charitable and, above all, political goals. Orangeism in Northern Ireland, drawing widely in its recruitment from among the Protestant population, has been especially strongly shaped by the views of those associated with the conservative Protestant sects.

World-rejecting and world-affirming religions

The religious needs that many people feel can no longer be met through any of the conventional forms of Christianity. They seek forms of religion that seem to be more in accord with contemporary life. To understand this, we can draw on the work of Merton, whose ideas on anomie we looked at in Chapter 2, pp. 47–8. Merton looked at the strains and tensions that can occur in cultural systems and at the varying responses that individuals may make to these. The growth of affluence and consumerism in the 1950s and 1960s generated two characteristic responses to the mainstream religious culture on the part of those who felt unable to achieve their goals through the conventional means available to them:

- *Retreatism*: this involves a rejection of the goals and means of the conventional society and a withdrawal from it;

- *Innovation*: this involves seeking out alternative ways of achieving the conventional goals.

Wallis (1984: 4–6, 9) argued that each of these responses was associated with the growth of a particular kind of religion. Corresponding to the retreatist response are the **world-rejecting religions** that denigrate the central values and assumptions of the modern world. Examples of such religions are The International Society for Krishna Consciousness (ISKCON) and the Unification Church. ISKCON—popularly known as Hare Krishna—is based around a form of Hinduism that requires a particular ascetic and communal way of life from its followers. Corresponding to the innovative response are the **world-affirming religions** such as Transcendental Meditation (TM) and Scientology. These religions embrace many of the central cultural goals and values of contemporary societies but claim to offer new means to achieve them. TM, founded by the Maharishi Mahesh Yogi, stresses the personal and practical benefits of regular meditation, while Scientology uses methods closer to psychotherapy.

Many of these religions take a cult form. They engage in worldly activities and allow people to drift in and out of participation as they sample the beliefs on offer. TM, for example, is associated with a political party (the Natural Law Party) that fights general elections on policies that advocate the benefits of TM and 'yogic flying' for solutions to individual and social problems. Even such groups as the Unification Church and Scientology, which are relatively closed to outsiders, do not typically hold on to their members for long periods.

Utopian religion and world rejection

World-rejecting, utopian religions grew rapidly in the 1960s, when many young people were attracted by retreatist responses. In the early 1960s this had been expressed in the hippie, drug-user subculture of American and European youth, which, as Jock Young (1971) showed, rejected the work ethic and the impersonality and bureaucracy of modern society. In place of these values, hippies emphasized spontaneity and hedonism. The subculture proved especially attractive to white, middle-class, college drop-outs. It was the perceived failure of hippie utopianism to achieve its aims that produced many recruits for new religions that offered more radical solutions. Those who identified with the values of the hippie culture, even if they had not directly experienced it, sought new ways of meeting its values of community and fellowship.

These religions see present-day problems as symptoms of a departure from an authentic and more natural way of life, and their appeal derives not so much from the specific content of their beliefs as from the communal lifestyles with which the groups have been identified. Familiarity

→ *Connections*
You might like to read the discussion of Jock Young's work in Chapter 7, pp. 257–8. This will give you an overview of the hippie subculture.

with the beliefs generally came *after* young people had joined the groups. Potential members have been attracted by the communal group solidarity that the religions espouse, and it is this—rather than brainwashing—that has tied people to them. These religious communities appeared to offer an escape from the impersonality of modern society and a solution to the perceived loss of community in the wider society.

These religions tend to have a clear and specific conception of a god or gods, regarded as the source of moral norms and obligations. They have a sense of their religious mission that is sometimes allied with a search for political influence and social change. Some, however, are millenarian. That is to say, they anticipate the destruction or collapse of the world, followed by their own salvation. The Children of God, for example, await the return of Jesus to save the world. Yet other groups anticipate the arrival of extra-terrestrial life forms (Festinger *et al.* 1956). What such groups tend to hold in common is a view that

> the prevailing social order . . . [has] departed substantially from God's prescriptions and plan. Mankind [*sic.*] has lost touch with God and spiritual things, and, in the pursuit of purely material interests, has succeeded in creating a polluted environment; a vice-ridden society in which individuals treat each other purely as means rather than ends; a world filled with conflict, greed, insincerity and despair. The world-rejecting

movement condemns urban industrial society and its values, particularly that of individual success as measured by wealth or consumption patterns. It rejects the materialism of the advanced industrial world, calling for a return to a more rural way of life, and a reorientation of secular life. (Wallis 1984: 10)

The religions tend to organize themselves as total institutions, and there is a great emphasis on their separate, enclosed, and disciplined communal life. This often involves engaging in economic and fund-raising activities that help to provide for the group's own subsistence. Those religions that have been particularly successful in this and have become very wealthy have often attracted external criticism, especially when their wealth seems to provide extravagant lifestyles for the leadership.

Social control within the group operates mainly through a *persuasion* that draws on people's commitment to the group and their love for its leaders, its ideals, and their fellow members. In these circumstances, individual identity is subordinated to collective identity. Although the exercise of coercion over members is not usual, it does occur, and a degree of coercive control may be accepted by members as necessary to maintain the group in a hostile environment. In some extreme cases, suicide may be accepted as a necessary way to affirm the group's identity and beliefs when they are under threat from the outside. This is known to have been the case with the mass suicides of members of the Heaven's Gate group in San Diego in 1997, and it is thought to have played a major part in the destruction of the Branch Davidian group in Waco, Texas, in 1993. Durkheim (1897) called this fatalistic suicide.

The end of the long period of sustained affluence in the mid-1970s was marked by static or declining membership for the world-rejecting religions. In response, some of them became more world-accommodating in character and have since recruited older people. The term **world-accommodating religions** describes those religions that adopt an attitude of mild disapproval or of acceptance of the world as it is, rather than an attitude of complete rejection. In such groups, religious beliefs often come to be seen as separate from the principal activities of everyday life (Wallis 1984). As religions become world-accommodating, they tend to attack established religious organizations rather more than they do the secular world, and they recruit those who are searching for a more direct experience of the sacred than established religions can provide. The religions provide a feeling of certainty in a relativistic culture, and Wallis suggested that world accommodation is the end-stage for all world-rejecting sects and cults.

Therapeutic religions and world affirmation

The second response that we identified to the mainstream religious culture is the innovative response of the

 Briefing: Moonies

A characteristic world-rejecting religion is the Unification Church, popularly known as the 'Moonies' after its founder the Reverend Moon. Drawing on both Christian and Buddhist sources, the religion rejects the materialism of the contemporary world and advocates a disciplined, ascetic lifestyle. It requires that its members should give their income and assets over to the use of the church. Moonies see their task as bringing about a physical kingdom of God on earth that actualizes the spiritual kingdom that had been established by Jesus. The Reverend Moon is believed to be the new Messiah who leads adherents towards this goal. A good study is E. Barker (1984).

world-affirming religions. These religions have a worldly character. That is to say, they embrace the goals and values of modern society. They combine their religious orientation with an acceptance of magical and manipulative techniques that allow their members to achieve conventional goals through unconventional means.

Many of these religions adopt a psychotherapeutic stance towards the solution of their members' problems, and they 'straddle a vague boundary between religion and psychology' (Wallis 1984: 35). They generally lack any developed theology or ritual, and their conception of God, if any, is that of a diffuse, universal force that manifests itself in individuals. They are oriented towards the perfectibility of the individual through specific therapeutic practices, and they work towards promoting individual achievement within the existing society. They might claim, for example, that they can unlock a person's potential by providing him or her with the appropriate discipline or training. These advantages are held to be open to anybody who joins the group and learns its techniques.

These religions have deeper roots and a more long-lasting base of recruitment than do the world-rejecting religions. They expanded considerably during the 1950s and 1960s, and they recruited from among relatively

Briefing: Scientology

A characteristic world-affirming religion is Scientology. Founded by the science-fiction writer L. Ron Hubbard, Scientology draws on psychotherapy to provide practices and techniques that alter the consciousness of its members and enable them to act in more positive and effective ways to achieve their worldly goals: a better job, a higher income, or greater happiness in what they are doing. It claims to give its members spiritual powers, such as the ability to see, hear, and manipulate people and objects at great distances, purely by mental forces. The religion works through training and therapy sessions in closed communities, but it has many similarities to a conventional business operation: recruits pay fees for their training and counselling, and many full-time workers are employed to manage the church. An inquiry in the 1990s alleged widespread financial fraud on the part of the church. Prominent adherents today include the Hollywood actor Tom Cruise. A good description of Scientology can be found in Wallis (1976).

THEORY AND METHODS

World-rejecting and world-affirming religions

	World-rejecting	World-affirming
Conception of good	Personal entity distinct from humanity	Element of every human life
Present world	Debased: its values all contrary to the ideal; in need of total transformation	Much to offer if one has the means to secure the good things available
Commitment required	Complete, including separation from family and career. Movement is a 'total institution'	Partial, a largely leisure-time pursuit while one continues one's activity in the world
Economic base	Wealth and labour of converts, supplemented by street solicitation of donations	Fees for goods and services marketed by the movement
Sexual morality	Ascetic (i.e., tightly regulating sexual activity) or antinomian (permitting promiscuous sexual relationships)	Largely indifferent to sexual conduct
Conversion	Rapid, abrupt after contact, attitude of 'surrender' required from outset	Typically a sequence of stages of progressive personal transformation
Leader	God's emissary or representative	Technical innovator
Social organization	Communal	Corporate
Examples	Unification Church, ISKCON, Children of God, People's Temple, Manson's Family	Transcendental Meditation, Human Potential Movement, Est (Erhard Seminars Training), Silva Mind Control, Scientology

Source: Wallis (1984).

affluent people in their twenties and thirties who were seeking ways of helping themselves towards greater individual achievement, happiness, and success in a consumer society (B. R. Wilson 1966: 216).

While Scientology has tended to adopt a sectarian form of organization, the so-called New Age movement is a much looser world-affirming cult. It combines elements of Eastern religions with mythology and Jung's psychoanalysis to form a complex and diverse system of beliefs that embraces crystal healing, the use of essential oils, astrology, acupuncture, herbalism, dowsing, UFOs, Paganism, certain aspects of witchcraft, and various other strands. New Age ideas became especially popular in the 1980s, and they have had an impact on mainstream culture beyond its own adherents. Those who see themselves as part of the New Age movement promote their preferred therapies and ideas through advertising, setting up shops, and publishing books. These promotional activities bring non-believers into contact with the movement, and they have been behind the massive popularity of such techniques as aromatherapy. This technique, which involves the use of essential oils, appeals to those, for example, who are also attracted to the forms of alternative medicine and personal strategies of well-being that challenge the authority of medical experts.

Despite the growth in their numbers, the world-rejecting and world-accepting religions together comprise only a very small proportion of the population. The membership of any one group is tiny. There have, for example, never been more than 1,000 'Moonies' in Britain. There are less than 500 members of ISKCON, and only a few hundred members of TM (E. Barker 1989).

Religions of ethnic protest

Religious beliefs have long played a central part in defining and developing ethnic identities. In many religions, a particular ethnic community is seen as being in some way special to the gods. Jewish holy texts, for example, define the Jews as the chosen people of God, and the indigenous religious beliefs of Japan trace the origins of the Japanese to *Ama-terasu*, the sun goddess. As A. Smith (1991: 7) has shown, for most of human history, religion and ethnic identity have been very closely entwined, each people having its own gods and sacred texts, and its distinctive religious practices, priests, and places.

Migration into Britain and the births of second- and later-generation members of migrant families have altered the religious mix. Migrants from the Caribbean, as we have shown, brought conservative Protestant religions with them, but migrants from elsewhere have brought about an expansion of non-Christian religions. Those from India, Pakistan, Bangladesh, and East Africa have swelled the

numbers of Hindus, Muslims, Sikhs, Jews, and others. This religious diversity is increased by the divisions that exist within each religion. About one in ten British Muslims are Shi'as, while most of the rest are Sunnis. The Sunnis, however, are divided into Barelwi, Deoband, and Tablghi Jamaat branches. Similarly, Hindus are divided into loose traditions, as well as being divided by caste (Bruce 1995: 79 ff.).

There are now more than one million Muslims in Britain, there are just under a half a million Hindus, and there are the same number of Sikhs. Membership of these religions has tripled since 1970. The state has long financed denominational schools—through the system of voluntary aid—for Anglicans, Catholics, Methodists, and Jews, and there is a growing demand for similar support for Muslims.

Growth in the numbers of those affiliated to ethnic-minority religions is not, however, what is meant by the term 'religions of ethnic protest'. A multi-ethnic, multi-religion society is an essential condition for the emergence of religions of ethnic protests, but it is not the same thing. Religions of ethnic protest are those that have grown within particular ethnic-minority communities and are used by their members to voice their protest at their exclusion, on the grounds of their ethnicity, from full participation in their society.

> ⊃ **Connections**
> You will probably find it useful to remind yourself about what we say on ethnicity and ethnic identity and on migration in Chapter 6, pp. 200–2 and 223–4. You will also find useful our discussion of ethnicity and national identity in Chapter 16, pp. 619–21.

Rastafarianism and the Nation of Islam

The two most characteristic religions of ethnic protest in contemporary Britain are Rastafarianism and the Nation of Islam.

The deeply felt experience of deprivation and exclusion that is found in the poor, inner-city districts of Britain where many African-Caribbean people are forced to live contrasts sharply with the optimistic expectations of the migrants who arrived in Britain during the 1950s and 1960s. Many of the first generation, as we have shown, have given voice to their situation through inspirational Protestantism. Those of the second and third generations —like their young white counterparts—have sought answers in newer and more radical forms of religion. Among these people, Rastafarianism has had a particularly strong appeal, as its social ethic seems to talk directly to their experiences.

Membership grew particularly during the 1970s with the success of the singer Bob Marley and the popularization of reggae. Its musical style, along with its style of dress and the use of cannabis (ganja), have sprung from and contributed to the wider growth of a consciousness of black identity (Alexander 1996). Its lifestyle and ethic of social non-conformity were attractive to many inner-city African Caribbeans. Many of these adherents were attracted by its musical and fashion styles, and they did not necessarily make any serious commitment to its religious beliefs and practices. The committed Rastafarian refuses to become involved in crime and deviance for its own sake, stressing the need to build a sense of black dignity (Pryce 1986).

Drawing on a shared memory of the African diaspora, this black consciousness forms part of what Gilroy (1993) has called the 'Black Atlantic', a cultural framework that links Africa, Britain, the Caribbean, and the Americas. This consciousness, however, is not without its divisions. In 1996, Rastafarians attended a service for the dead Crown Prince of Ethiopia at an Ethiopian Orthodox church in London. The Rastafarians saw the Prince as the son of a God (Haile Selassie), a direct descendant of King Solomon and the Queen of Sheba. He was also heir to the throne of their spiritual homeland. The Ethiopian Orthodox Church, part of the Eastern Orthodox Church, refused to be publicly linked with these claims, and many Ethiopians resented the presence of the Rastafarians in their church.

The Nation of Islam was central to the civil-rights movement in the United States. One of its principal aims is the promotion of black consciousness, and it was a major force behind campaigns stressing 'Black Power' and 'Black is Beautiful'. Those who were excluded from the ethnic melting pot also felt excluded from any sense of American identity and participation in the civil religion. Total membership in the United States is estimated at about 100,000. Membership in Britain, where they began recruiting in 1986, is relatively small, and is thought to be about 2,500. In the United States, it takes a high-profile stance in African-American politics. Its leader, Louis Farrakhan, has been at the centre of attempts to build cross-faith solidarity among African-Americans (Lincoln 1973).

The British Nation of Islam, which is more closed and secretive in its organization than the American one, is in some rivalry with the Rastafarians for recruits. It has been suggested that those African Caribbeans who identify with Africa are attracted to the Rastafarians, while those who identify with black Americans are attracted to the Nation of Islam. In many respects, the Nation of Islam adopts conservative attitudes, stressing traditional morality and the value of the family. To this moral conservatism, however, it adds a radical political programme of black consciousness-raising and black segregation.

Briefing: Nation of Islam

The Nation of Islam, also known as the Black Muslims, was founded in the United States by Fard Mohammad and his deputy Elijah Muhammad in the 1930s. They promoted the adoption of Islam by African-Americans as a return to the pre-slavery religion of their ancestors. Those who join the Nation of Islam adopt new Muslim names, and many of the men wear smart suits and a bow tie as a mark of their membership. For many years the chief spokesman for the group was Malcolm X, but he was expelled in the 1960s. The beliefs of the group are far from pure Islam, and there is much reliance on the Christian New Testament. Some activists hold that the founders of the Nation of Islam are orbiting the earth in a spaceship.

The current leader of the Nation of Islam, Louis Farrakhan, was excluded from Britain between 1986 and 2001 because of claims that his views would encourage racial hatred. These claims were based on Farrakhan's views on Jews and white people. He has said that Judaism is a 'gutter religion' and that Jews are 'selfish, self-centred, vindictive, and unforgiving'. White people have been described as 'our mortal enemy', and Farrakhan has denounced sexual relations between blacks and whites. Slavery, he argues, was a Jewish conspiracy against Africans, and African-Americans should be given eight or ten states to form a black USA.

You might like to look at our summary of black nationalism in Chapter 6, p. 222.

Briefing: Rastafarianism

Rastafarianism originated in Jamaica. Marcus Garvey had claimed that Africans were the 'lost tribe' of biblical Israel, and that this tribe had been further dispersed across the world by the enslavement of Africans and their transportation to the West Indies and the Americas. Africans, African-Americans, and African Caribbeans were, therefore, seen as a chosen people of God. Their oppression and exploitation could be ended only by a return to Africa and the establishment there of societies free of colonial and post-colonial domination. Seeing the former Emperor of Ethiopia Haile Selassie (otherwise known as Ras Tafari) as a Messiah, Garvey advocated and encouraged such a return. There are estimated to be about 70,000 believers world-wide, but the religion is not united under a single leadership.

Islam in a global context

Islam is the second largest religion in the world today and is a major force in many societies of the world. Its growth over the centuries has been linked with huge advances in knowledge and scholarship—indeed, one of the earliest sociological writers, Ibn Khaldun, wrote from an explicitly Muslim standpoint in the fourteenth century. Today it has become an important element in the everyday lives of millions of people across the world. In many places, however, particularly radical forms of Islam have grown in recent years.

The globalization of economic, political, and cultural relations has posed a threat to many local, indigenous communities that had not previously been drawn directly into the modern world. As we show in Chapter 16, pp. 635–9, these communities have not been isolated from the expanding world-system—far from it—but they have not until now been so directly penetrated by forces that come from outside their own immediate world. In many parts of Africa, the Middle East, and the Far East, for example, strongly anti-modern and, therefore, anti-Western sentiments have been aroused. Similarly, migrants from these areas to western and central Europe have generally experienced an exclusion from mainstream society that reinforces their sense of difference from white Westerners. The post-colonial experience—in the metropolitan centres and in the local communities—provides fertile ground for an emphasis on 'traditionalism' and traditional religion.

Fundamentalism occurs in areas that have been relatively secure from outside influence and have suddenly experienced major disruptions to their way of life. In those parts of the world that have a Christian tradition, as we have shown, Christian fundamentalism has attracted large numbers of adherents, while Muslim areas—which make up a significant proportion of all areas that are greatly affected by the forces of globalization—have shown a growth in radical forms of Islam often misleadingly called Islamic fundamentalism.

This radical Islam stresses that traditional religious truths, far from being undermined by modern society, have an ever-greater relevance to its problems. Essential religious truths are reaffirmed in a context where the globalizing forces of modernity have disrupted highly valued traditional ways of life. The reassertion of traditional ideas and values, however, is not a simple restatement of an unchanging tradition. It is, rather, a creative reinterpretation of that tradition through a selective drawing on inherited social meanings in the light of their present circumstances. It is a reworking of the shared values and beliefs of a Muslim community aimed at uncovering their central principles in the face of modernizing forces seen as

Briefing: Islam

Islam is a monotheistic religion that shares much of the Old Testament tradition with Jews and Christians. Its main beliefs, however, are contained in the Qu'ran, which contains the teachings of the sixth- to seventh-century prophet Muhammad. The Qu'ran is seen as the revealed will of God (Allah). It has no priestly hierarchy or authoritative interpretation of its orthodoxy, and no distinction is made between the spheres of religion and politics. Sunni Muslims are the more orthodox, while Shi'as have added to the original teachings of Muhammad. About one-fifth of the world's population is nominally Muslim. The largest areas of settlement are in the Middle East, the Indian subcontinent, South East Asia, Turkey, and West Africa. The largest single community is found in Indonesia. In Western Europe, the largest numbers of Muslims are in France, mainly migrants from north and west Africa, with smaller groups in Britain and Germany.

Friday prayers in a Muslim Mosque
© Getty Images/Paul Chesley

imposing a 'Western' or 'American' way of life. It takes the form of 'Islamism', a radical reading of holy texts that allies their principal tenets with social exclusion and nationalism. This need to rework and re-create tradition is made all the more necessary by the fact that migration and the globalization of cultures make each local group more aware of the diversity that exists within Islam. No set of beliefs can any more be simply taken for granted. They have to be taken back to their basic principles.

A key characteristic in radical Islam, then, has been its development in reaction to a specifically *Western* form of modernization. This form of Islam achieved its earliest success in Iran in 1979, where it produced a revolutionary overthrow of the pro-Western regime of the Shah and established a Shi'ite Islamic Republic. Powerful and important radical Islamist movements played a major role in Lebanon, in Egypt, in Syria, and in Afghanistan, and Islamist regimes have been established in Algeria and Sudan. Moderate—generally Sunni—forms of Islam are the official creeds of many Arab states. The growth of Islamist regimes has been greatest wherever globalization results in the oppression or exclusion of those from a particular ethnic group—in many cases, therefore, radical Islam strengthens a sense of national identity.

The image of 'Islamic fundamentalism' in the West focuses on its links with the political violence, kidnapping, and hijacks undertaken by terrorist groups such as Hezbollah and Al-Qaeda, though these are minority activities. More typically, Islamists argue their position in peaceful, though forcible, discussion. Nevertheless, political regimes based on Islamist principles have tended to take a very restricted view of personal and political rights, such as those of women.

There is some evidence of a growth of radical Islamist views among some young second-generation Muslim migrants in Britain. While many have abandoned their religion altogether, the experience of unemployment, poor housing, and racial discrimination leads others to be receptive to radical solutions. Just as disadvantaged African-Caribbean youths have embraced Rastafarianism rather than the Pentecostalism of their parents, so many young Muslims find Islamist ideas appealing.

◈ *Stop and reflect*

In this section we have looked at the emergence of a number of new forms of religious belief and practice and at how there has also been a growth of traditional beliefs.

- There has been a continuing decline in both church attendance and church membership. At the same time, the civil religion has weakened, in both Britain and the United States.

- There is strong evidence for the existence of a loose and unorthodox common religion that has little similarity with traditional Christianity.

- Where do the various beliefs that comprise the common religion come from?

We looked at how the growth of liberal Protestantism has encouraged many believers to seek out more inspirational forms of Christianity.

- Conservative Protestantism takes two main forms: fundamentalism and Pentecostalism. These forms of conservative Protestantism have been closely associated with the new right and the moral majority.

The new religions that have grown in numbers have tended to be non-Christian sects and cults.

- World-rejecting religions are utopian or millennial and reject many aspects of contemporary social life. World-affirming religions are therapeutic and tend to embrace the values of modern society.

- Why are so many people worried about the rise of religious cults?

We finally looked at the relationship between religion and ethnicity. We showed how Britain had become a multi-ethnic, multi-religious society, and we examined global changes in religion.

- There has been growing support for religions of ethnic protest.

- Islam is one of the fastest-growing religions in the world.

- Why is there such a strong link between religion and ethnicity?

‹› *Chapter summary*

In 'Understanding religion' we looked at the varying ways in which sociologists have tried to explore religion and its characteristics in modern societies.

- We defined religion as comprising the overarching systems of beliefs and practices that help people to organize and order their lives.

- We identified a distinction between the sacred and the secular, which has led to discussions of the varying relationships between the two spheres.

- For Marx, religion could legitimate class divisions and had to be seen as a form of alienation.

- Durkheim saw social differentiation and the growing division of labour in modern societies as producing higher levels of individualism. He saw religion as taking the form of a moral individualism, which would be the basis of an organic solidarity.

- Weber was particularly interested in the influence that religious beliefs had on economic activities, tracing this through his account of the impact of Protestantism on modern capitalism.

In the following section we explored religion and modernization through the debate over secularization, understood as involving processes of disengagement and disenchantment.

- European belief systems were secularized through the transformation of a unified Catholic world into a pluralistic pattern of largely Protestant denominations and a growth of secular and scientific concerns.

- Nominal Church membership remains strong, despite a decline in the numbers of active participants in organized religion. It is particularly strong in the United States.

- In both Britain and the United States, forms of civil religion remain strong and link religious participation with national identity.

- Religious belief has, however, become largely a private matter rather than a public obligation. Participation in religious activities is limited by the fact that individuals feel they must choose how to allocate their time among the various private interests and concerns that they value.

In the final section we looked at a number of new religious beliefs and groupings that challenge traditional forms of belief.

- A loose and unorthodox 'common religion', with little similarity to traditional Christianity, has grown in importance.

- The growth of Liberal Protestantism has encouraged many who value a traditional religious outlook to take up inspirational and charismatic forms of Christianity such as fundamentalism and Pentecostalism. These have been closely associated with the conservative views of the new right and the moral majority.

- Non-Christian sects and cults have attracted larger numbers of adherents. Some are 'world-rejecting' or utopian, while others are 'world-affirming' and are therapeutic in orientation.

We finally looked at the relationship between religion and ethnicity. We showed how Britain had become a multi-ethnic, multi-religious society, and we examined global changes in religion.

- Multiculturalism and ethnic diversity have been associated with growing support for religions of ethnic protest among those who feel excluded from their society.

⊶ *Key concepts*

- civil religion
- collective representations
- *conscience collective*
- cult
- denomination

- ecclesia
- sect
- secularization
- spirit of capitalism
- totemism

- world-accommodating religion
- world-affirming religion
- world-rejecting religion

Workshop 11

Study 11 The New Age

We have pointed to New Age beliefs as a contemporary form of world-affirming religion, and we have noted that certain New Age beliefs even form a part of the 'common religion' espoused by many people in Britain. Paul Heelas (1996) has traced the growth and development of New Age ideas, showing how they originated in the late nineteenth century but flowered in the 1960s and 1970s during the so-called 'Age of Aquarius'. The phrase 'New Age' was introduced in the last third of the nineteenth century when the ideas of Swedenborg and others were taken up in such belief systems as Theosophy and Jungian psychotherapy.

Behind the borrowings from Buddhism, Hinduism, Christianity, Paganism, and spiritual therapies, the core element in New Age belief systems is what Heelas calls 'self-spirituality'. The individual self is seen as a sacred object. The task of the believer is to make contact with the spirituality that lies within the individual person. People must distance themselves from the contamination and pollution of the profane world in order to discover the sacred inner world. This is expressed in practices of healing and therapy in all areas of human life, the aim of which is 'enlightenment'.

Heelas argues that the New Age reintroduces pre-modern ideas of mysticism, shamanism, and magic as a response to the cultural uncertainties of contemporary life. New Age beliefs help to resolve the anxieties and uncertainties that face the contemporary self. Paradoxically, however, New Age beliefs appeal because many of them are in tune with modernist ideas: they promise the rational promotion of people's interests and desires.

- Review our discussion of the reflexive project of the self in Chapter 4, p. 149. Return to this discussion of the New Age when you have familiarized yourself with the key arguments of Giddens on this.

- Visit your local bookshop and examine the books in the 'Mind, body, and spirit' section. (Most shops have a section with this title or something similar.) What specific issues and topics are covered in these books, and which of them would you characterize as New Age? Are these books sold alongside other New Age materials (such as music cassettes or tarot cards)? Are there any other shops in your local high street that sell New Age materials (jewellery, ornaments, incense, aromatic oils, etc.)? Try to compile a list of the particular techniques and themes stressed in the New Age.

- How many people in your class or lecture group subscribe to any New Age beliefs, and how many engage in, or have some interest in, New Age practices such as aromatherapy? Do they typically regard their beliefs as 'religious', and do they see any incompatibility with other religious ideas? What does this tell you about a common religion?

- What differences—apart from the obvious differences of intellectual content—do you find between the New Age and a religion such as Islam? What are their respective views of the self and their views of morality? Does the New Age specify a particular moral way of life to which individuals should conform? Find out about the beliefs of Baha'i: to what extent can this be seen as a New Age Islam?

In addition to Heelas (1996), you will find useful background information in Roszak (1971), Reich (1971), Ferguson (1982), and Merchant (1992). These cover the background and influence of New Age ideas in a number of contexts.

Media watch 11 Moral panic over Islam

A growing moral panic over the role of religious teaching in mosques was brought to a head in the public and press reaction to the London bombings in the summer of 2005 and the bombing conspiracies uncovered in the summer of 2006. Great concern was expressed about the role of 'radical clerics' in encourag-

ing and supporting violent political opposition and acts of terrorism.

Abu Hamza Al-Masri came to Britain from Egypt in 1979 and was regularly portrayed in the press as a leading spokesperson and supporter of Al-Qaeda from his base in the Finsbury Park

Mosque in London. He came to particular prominence in 2002, when he addressed a meeting of Al-Muhajiroun, whose members openly support Al-Qaeda and when he spoke in support of Osama bin-Laden. He was banned from preaching at his mosque and the government launched plans to deport him. Subsequent to this he was arrested, pending extradition hearings for terrorist charges made in the United States and a trial for offences allegedly committed in Britain.

Omar Bakhri Mohammed lived in Britain for twenty years but was banned from returning after a visit he made to Lebanon. It was allegations that he supported the London bombers that led to his exclusion.

Columnist Melanie Phillips had earlier commented that 'Muslim clerics in Britain were appalled at militant figures from "Mujahidin-type organisations" who run what are advertised as prayer groups from private homes but which are in reality recruiting missions' (**www.melaniephillips.com/diary/archives/ 000091.html**). The blame, she argued, lay with the failure of Muslim communities to regulate their own affairs.

This is part of a wider concern about the conservatism of many Islamic clerics. Much press comment has centred on the recruitment of clerics from Middle Eastern countries and from poor, rural backgrounds, rather than training imams in Britain. It is claimed that such clerics are out of touch with the views of most British Muslims and that more 'modern' attitudes should be promoted in the mosques. Such issues have sparked a wider debate over education in separate faith schools and the extent to which religious attitudes and practices should be expressed in public life. In many schools, wearing of the *hijab* by girls has been banned as incompatible with a standard school uniform. This is not unique to Britain. In France, a new law prohibited the wearing of any religious symbols or emblems at school, and this was widely seen as a law aimed specifically at Muslims.

Collect copies of daily newspapers for a week and mark all the stories that refer to religion, distinguishing those that relate to Islam and those that relate to other religions. Then consider the following questions:

- What differences can you see in the type of language used to describe followers of each religion and their activities?

- Is religion linked to other social phenomena in the articles (for example, to health or crime)? Can you see any differences in the claims made about Muslims and non-Muslims?

- If you have examples of different kinds of newspapers, can you identify any differences in their treatment of Muslims?

Sources: *The Times*, 20 October 2004; *Guardian*, 19 October 2004; www.bbc.co.uk/bbcfour/documentaries/profile/abu-hamza.shtml; http://thescotsman.scotsman.com/index.cfm?id=1773172005; http://news.bbc.co.uk/1/hi/world/europe/3619988.stm

Discussion points

Theories of religion

Make sure that you are familiar with the main ideas on religion of Marx, Durkheim, and Weber. Try to make sure that you understand the idea of the sacred and the secular and the importance of the distinction.

- Can Weber's ideas on the influence of the Protestant ethic on the spirit of capitalism help us to understand the contemporary relations between religion and economic activity?

Secularization and mainstream religion

The idea of secularization has dominated discussions of religion in the modern world. We drew on the work of Weber to explore some of its implications. We started off by seeing secularization as involving the two processes of disengagement and disenchantment:

- Try to draw up a classification of forms of religious organization in which you distinguish between ecclesia, denomination, sect, and cult. Give examples of each type.

Which description is most appropriate for each of the following contemporary religions: Krishna Consciousness, Jehovah's Witnesses, Children of God, Pagans, Hinduism, Shinto, Unification Church, Scientology, Rastafarianism, Nation of Islam. If you are not familiar with the beliefs and organizations of these religions, use your library resources to find out more about them.

- We have presented some evidence to show that women are more likely to be active churchgoers than are men. In view of this, why do you think that there was such opposition to the ordination of women in the Church of England.

- Why does Steve Bruce claim that 'Protestantism is essentially fissile'? What are the implications of this?

- Figures 11.1 and 11.2 give some evidence on church membership and church attendance in Britain. How do you think that these data might have been collected? What other kinds of data would be useful to assess the extent of secularization?

New religions and growing religions

We examined a number of new and growing forms of religion, some of which are renewed and more strident expressions of traditional religious beliefs:

- How useful is the distinction between world-rejecting religion and world-affirming religion?

- Is conservative, inspirational Protestantism characteristic of particular regions or classes?

- How would you go about collecting evidence on the extent and significance of New Age beliefs in Britain today?

- How useful is it to see the spread of Islam as a religion of ethnic protest and a response to globalization?

- What are the implications of the banning of religious dress in French schools? Is this government action directed specifically at Muslim pupils?

The study of religious belief raises some of the most fundamental questions about the nature of knowledge and the role of science. You might like to consider some of these issues. (We do not expect you to come up with the answers!):

- What is religion? Do you think that the definition given by Bruce and Wallis (p. 407) is useful?

- Are the claims of religion and science compatible with one another? Is it possible to be both a rational scientist (for example, a sociologist) and a religious believer?

Explore further

Extremely good general accounts of religion can be found in:

Turner, B. (1991), *Religion and Social Theory* (2nd edn., London: Routledge). *A useful overview of theories that discusses many of the key issues.*

Bruce, S. (1995), *Religion in Modern Britain* (Oxford: Oxford University Press). *A brief and very readable account of contemporary trends in British religion.*

Ling, T. (1968), *A History of Religion, East and West* (Houndmills: Macmillan). *A very useful comparative study of the origins and development of the major religions.*

Hamilton, M. (1998), Sociology and the World's Religions (Houndmills: Macmillan). *A well-argued overview of key debates.*

Wilson, B. R. (1976), *Contemporary Transformations of Religion* (Oxford: Oxford University Press). *One of the key sources by the principal writer on contemporary forms of secularization.*

Wallis, R. (1984), *Elementary Forms of the New Religious Life* (London: Routledge and Kegan Paul). *A classic account of the variety of new religions. You should follow this with a reading of Wallis (1976) and Barker (1984).*

More detail can be found in the following. You should *try* reading the books by Durkheim and Weber, but be warned that they are rather difficult.

Festinger, L., Riecken, H. W., and Schachter, S. (1956), *When Prophecy Fails* (New York: Harper & Row). *A wonderful case study* of a millenarian, flying-saucer cult. The methodological appendix is particularly good for highlighting the practical and ethical problems of participant observation. The research was fictionalized in Alison Lurie's novel Imaginary Friends *(New York: Coward, McCann, 1967).*

Herberg, W. (1955), *Protestant, Catholic, Jew* (New York: Doubleday). *A classic study of mainstream American religions in relation to ethnicity.*

Lane, C. (1981), *The Rites of Rulers: Ritual in Industrial Society— The Soviet Case* (Cambridge: Cambridge University Press). *A useful investigation of ritual in Soviet society, which brings out the religious aspects of Communist systems.*

Wallis, R. (1976), *The Road to Total Freedom* (London: Heinemann). *A study of Scientology.*

Barker, E. (1984), *The Making of a Moonie* (Oxford: Basil Blackwell). *A study of the Unification Church.*

Durkheim, E. (1912), *The Elementary Forms of the Religious Life* (London: George Allen & Unwin, 1915, but also in various other editions). *Sets out Durkheim's argument about totemism and the origins of religion.*

Weber, Max (1904–5), *The Protestant Ethic and the Spirit of Capitalism* (London: George Allen & Unwin, 1930, but also in various other editions). *Sets out Weber's account of the part played by religion in the rise of modern capitalism.*

Online resources

Visit the Online Resource Centre that accompanies this book to access more learning resources and other interesting material on religion, belief, and meaning at:

www.oxfordtextbooks.co.uk/orc/fulcher3e/

A useful general source is the Virtual Religion Index at Rutgers University:

http://religion.rutgers.edu/vri/index.html

Trends in organized Christian religions are covered by the Church of England at:

www.cofe.anglican.org

and by the World Council of Churches at:

www.wcc-coe.org

A more independent source of factual information on a variety of religions can be found at:

www.adherents.com/

For new religious movements you should consult the Inform website:

http://virtualreligion.net/vri/

Links to information about many different religious organizations can be found at:

www.academicinfo.net/religindex.html

For conferences and seminars on the sociology of religion, consult the website of the British Sociological Association's Sociology of Religion Study Group at:

www.britsoc.co.uk/new_site/index.php?area=specialisms&id=56

social organization and control

PART FOUR

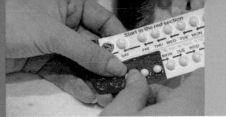

family and life course

Contents

12

'How many households are normal?'

Most people's idea of a normal household is a married couple with children. Does this any longer correspond with the reality of people's lives? In 2005 only 22 per cent of British households consisted of a couple with dependent children, compared with 35 per cent in 1971. In 2005 considerably more households, 29 per cent, actually consisted of people living entirely on their own (*Social Trends* 2006: 22). Marriage used to be considered the cornerstone of family life but by 2000 over two-thirds of respondents from the *British Social Attitudes* survey thought that 'it is all right for a couple to live together without intending to get married' (Park *et al.* 2001: 32).

One might conclude from this that family life is in decline, and some have indeed reached this conclusion and argued that this decline is responsible for many of the ills of today's society. There is, however, an alternative view that family life in particular and households in general have simply become more varied. Family life should not be measured against some impossible ideal that is no longer appropriate. Indeed, some have argued that the traditional family was constrictive and damaging to all concerned.

What we mean by 'the family' has been the subject of much debate and in this chapter we begin with this question. Family life involves relationships between people at different stages of their lives and we go on to examine ways of thinking about the 'life course'. In the next section, we discuss the historical development of the family and the division of the life course into distinct stages. In the last section, we examine a range of contemporary family issues, from divorce and parenting to ethnic diversity, from the domestic division of labour to domestic violence and sexual abuse.

Understanding family lives

Before examining the development of the family and changes in the life course, it is necessary to be clear about the meaning of the various concepts used in this area and the different approaches to the study of the family. We first examine the main concepts used by sociologists.

What is the family?

This might seem a question that does not have to be asked. Surely everyone knows what a family is. When we refer to 'our family', or indeed someone else's, there is usually little doubt about what we mean by this.

A little reflection shows, however, that it is actually far from clear what 'our family' means. It may refer to those with whom we share a household. It may mean a wider group that includes our parents and/or our children, whether or not they live with us. Divorce(s) and remarriage(s) may make this an extensive and complex group with uncertain boundaries. It may mean a much wider group of relatives with whom we have occasional contact

by phone or at family meetings. It may mean a group of blood relatives, extending perhaps to cousins, grandparents, uncles, and aunts, which includes people with whom we have no contact at all.

Families and family practices

Different views of the form the family *ought* to take have coloured notions of what the family *is*. Conceptions of the family are indeed highly politicized and it is difficult to arrive at a neutral or objective description of the family.

Traditionalists see the family as centred on marriage and a domestic division of labour between a breadwinning husband and a housewife responsible for childcare and housework. A definition of the family in these terms excludes single-parent families, and unmarried couples, heterosexual or homosexual, even though they may consider themselves to be families and act together in family ways. This definition also builds the domestic division of labour into the family, instead of treating it as just one way in which families can organize their work lives.

Controversy and debate What is the family?

'The family is a social group characterized by common residence, economic co-operation and reproduction. It includes adults of both sexes, at least two of whom maintain a socially approved sexual relationship, and one or more children, own or adopted, of the sexually cohabiting adults.'
(Murdock 1949: 1)

❓ This is a well-known and much-quoted definition of the family. What problems do you think that it faces in the light of the discussion in the text?

❓ Have a look at other definitions in dictionaries and sociological works (use indexes to locate definitions). How well do they cope with these problems?

❓ Do you think that the definition that we offer in the text is a satisfactory one?

To avoid these problems, Diana Gittins (1993) argued that instead of referring to 'the family' we should refer to 'families'. By doing this we could recognize the various forms taken by the family and avoid privileging any one of them. This practice has now been widely adopted in sociology but it does not really solve the problem, for families must logically have something in common that leads us to call them families. There would still seem to be the problem of what we mean by the term 'family'.

There is also the issue of how a family should be distinguished from other similar social units. Sue Heath has carried out research into relationships between young adults in shared households. The sharing of housing has become increasingly common as young adults delay forming couples until they are well into their twenties or thirties. These shared households can be seen as 'families of choice'. As Sue Heath has put it:

> In the broader context of risk-laden transitions to adulthood, many of the sharers we met appeared to be looking to their peers to provide the sense of communality, support and intimacy that they might hitherto have drawn from 'settled' family commitments, commitments which they were deferring, whether by choice or constraint. (Heath 2004: 10)

A friendship unit of this kind would not in the past have been considered a family but, if it performs the functions of a family, is there any reason why we should not consider it to be one?

A more radical approach is to reject the whole idea of defining the family as a social unit. David Morgan (1996, 1999) has argued that instead of concerning ourselves with what the family is, we should focus on 'family practices', on what families do and what they consider to be family activities (see box on 'Family practices' on p. 448). This is in many ways a refreshing and liberating approach. It suggests that instead of engaging in rather sterile discussions about the boundaries and membership of family units, we should concentrate on exploring what goes on in family life and how people view it.

The problem of what we mean by the family does not really go away, however. The notion of 'family practices' begs the question of how we distinguish these practices from non-family ones. Furthermore, the notion of a family unit is still important to people and the question of whether particular units should be viewed as families or not does matter to them. It matters, for example, whether gay couples or single parents with children see themselves as families and are treated as families. So, while recognizing the difficult issues raised by the question 'What is the family?', it is necessary to arrive at a working definition.

In moving towards a sociological definition, we should consider that families have two main things in common:

- *The closeness of family relationships.* Relationships are closer within a family than with people outside it. There is a boundary around a family, a sense of family identity, that separates it off from other people.

- *A sense of obligation and responsibility.* Family responsibilities are not fixed and are continually negotiated by family members, but there is, none the less, something distinctive about them which makes family commitments different from, say, those to friends.

The **family** may then be defined as a small group of closely related people who share a distinct sense of identity and a responsibility for each other that outweighs their commitments to others. This group is commonly, but not necessarily, based on marriage, biological descent, or adoption. Indeed, there is much to suggest that these criteria are becoming less important in the way that people think about the family unit. We have therefore put forward a deliberately broad definition that includes established notions of the family but takes account of social change

Frontiers Family practices

According to David Morgan: ' "Family" represents a constructed quality of human interaction or an active process rather than a thing-like object of detached social investigation' (1999: 16). He prefers to use the term 'family practices'. Instead of worrying about the composition of the family, we should study what families do and what people themselves consider to be family activities. He claims that much of the literature is too concerned with the family as an institution of society and a focus on family practices makes it possible to give more attention to the everyday activities of family life, the ordinary ways in which families eat together, enjoy leisure activities, and care for each other, which are not trivial but things that really matter to families. Family activities should also not be sealed off from other areas of life in a kind of 'family box', for family practices interpenetrate with, say, work practices or leisure practices. Family practices are not something fixed but constantly change as people construct and reconstruct family life.

So how does Morgan define family practices? In his words:

. . . 'family practices' are those practices described as being in some measure about 'family' by one or more of the following: individual actors; social and cultural institutions; the observer. . . . They are also practices which matter to the persons concerned and which are seen in some way as being 'special' or 'different'. To 'mean' something to somebody is not simply to be able to identify, but also to invest that object of identification with a degree of emotional significance. It should be stressed that this emotional/evaluative aspect need not be positive; in family matters, as many have noted, we are dealing with love and hate, attraction and repulsion, approval and disapproval. (1999: 19)

➲ List up to five activities that you have engaged in during the past week that you consider to be family practices.

❓ Compare your list with those compiled by others. Is there any agreement between you?

❓ What are the differences and what do they suggest about views of the family?

❓ Do you agree that we should stop worrying about what the family is and get on with studying family practices?

by avoiding the exclusion of people who live together in a family way but do not fit the traditional conception of the family.

Families, households, and kinship

Sociologists distinguish between families and households. A **household** consists of a person or group of people living in a particular residential unit. But is a common residence enough to make them a household? The Labour Force Survey defines a household as 'a single person, or a group of people who have the same address as their only or main residence and who either share one meal a day or share the living accommodation'. This definition goes further than common residence, since it assumes that the members of a household must in some meaningful way share its facilities. A household is, in other words, more than a collection of people who happen to live in the same place.

The members of a family may well live in different households. On the one hand, when children leave home and set up their own households, this does not mean that they leave their family. On the other hand, while the members of a household *may* consist of members of one family, they may well not be bound together by family ties. Indeed, some groups opposed to the idea that people should live in families have created households based on the idea of community rather than family.

Sociologists also distinguish between family and kinship. **Kinship** refers to a network of relatives (kin) who are connected by common descent or by marriage. Common descent means that all can trace their ancestry back to the same person, real or, as is often the case, mythical. Kinship therefore extends well beyond the smallish group that we usually take the term 'family' to mean, though there is also an intermediate term, the 'extended family', which we discuss below.

Kinship structures have been central features of small-scale societies, such as hunting and gathering bands or tribes, and social anthropologists have discovered many different principles of kinship in them. They have, for example, distinguished between *matrilineal* structures that trace descent from a female ancestor, and *patrilineal* structures that trace descent from a male. These differences have been very important in societies which have not developed state structures of coordination, because such societies have been largely organized around kinship patterns. While most contemporary societies are not primarily structured in this way, kinship networks are certainly found within them and perform important functions for their members.

Nuclear and extended families

The most common forms of the family distinguished in the literature are nuclear and extended families. The **nuclear**

A nuclear family.
© Alice Chadwick

The nuclear family

'The nuclear family is a state of mind rather than a particular kind of structure or set of household arrangements. It has little to do with whether the generations live together or whether Aunt Mary stays in the spare bedroom. Nor can it be understood with kinship diagrams and figures on family size. What really distinguishes the nuclear family—mother, father, and children—from other patterns of family life in Western society is a special sense of solidarity that separates the domestic unit from the surrounding community. Its members feel that they have much more in common with one another than they do with anyone else on the outside— that they enjoy a privileged emotional climate they must protect from outside intrusion, through privacy and isolation.' (Shorter 1976: 205)

family is usually defined as a two-generation unit consisting of parents and unmarried children. A distinction is generally made here between the 'family of origin' and the 'family of destination'. People will commonly be members of at least two nuclear families, the family of *origin* into which they were born and the family of *destination*, which they created themselves. Divorce and remarriage may mean that they create a series of such families.

The **extended family** includes other family members. It extends *vertically* to include at least three generations— that is, at least grandparents and grandchildren. It extends *horizontally* to include 'in-laws', cousins, aunts, and uncles, though how far it extends will vary and depends upon perceptions of the composition and boundaries of the family. It is important to recognize that terms such as 'aunt' are not universal. The language of kinship and the kinds of relationship that exist between family members vary greatly between societies. In some societies, for example, aunts on the mother's side are distinguished from aunts on the father's side and there is no common word for aunt.

There has been much debate over the relationship between these two forms of the family. Talcott Parsons (1949) argued that industrialization resulted in a shift from the extended family characteristic of traditional societies to the nuclear family typical of industrial societies (see our discussion of his theory on p. 450). Against this view, Peter Laslett and Richard Wall (1972) claimed that in Britain the nuclear family has always been the dominant form. Also against this view but in a different way, the well-known studies by Michael Young and Peter Willmott (1957) and by Michael Anderson (1971) found that the extended family still performed important functions in industrial societies. We examine this question in the next section (see pp. 458–9).

The nuclear family is usually defined in residential terms, as parents and children living together on their own, but in many ways its key feature is less a matter of 'who lives with who' than of the family's relationship to other people. The nuclear family is a relatively isolated and inward-looking unit that is centred on domestic life and held together by close emotional relationships. It is this rather than whether or not a grandparent lives in the household that really marks out the nuclear family. Edward Shorter has nicely expressed this view of the nuclear family (see box on 'The nuclear family').

Perspectives on the family

Here we work through the main perspectives on the development of the modern family and link them to contemporary debates.

Functionalist

Parsons (in Parsons and Bales 1956) took a functionalist approach to the development of the family, starting from the assumption that social institutions developed to meet the basic needs of society. There were two such needs that the family, and only the family, met: the needs for primary socialization and personality stabilization. Primary socialization was the process through which children acquired the basic values of society from their family during their early years. Family life also stabilized the adult personality by providing emotional support through marriage and enabling adults to satisfy childish impulses that could not be indulged in public, by, for example, playing games with their children.

This theory of the development of the family was set in a more general theory of social change. Parsons argued that the pre-industrial extended family was a multifunctional unit that met most of people's daily needs. Modernization involved institutional differentiation, with distinct and specialized institutions emerging to meet particular needs. The family lost many of its functions to other institutions, as production moved from the household to the workplace, and education and health care were provided by specialist occupations and organizations. The family itself became more specialized around its core functions of socialization and personality stabilization.

> ⊙ *Connections*
>
> We deal with primary and secondary socialization in Chapter 4, pp. 117–18, and you will find it helpful to refer to this chapter for a more detailed discussion of these concepts. We discuss the functionalist approach in Chapter 2, pp. 48–50, and the theory of social change put forward by Parsons, also in Chapter 2, on p. 50.

Parsons claimed that the nuclear form of the family was particularly well suited to an industrial economy. Within the nuclear family roles were specialized, with one adult earning money through paid work and the other bringing up the children. The small nuclear family without obligations to an extended family and with only one 'breadwinner' could be geographically mobile, which was important in an industrial society with a high rate of change. Such a society required a mobile workforce prepared to move to where the work was. This close fit between the nuclear family and the requirements of the economy integrated the institutions of industrial society.

The nuclear family also fitted an industrial society because it kept separate the worlds of work and family. Industrial societies were based on values of *achievement* and *universalism*, which meant that people were rewarded according to their achievements and judged according to universal standards of qualification and competence. The family, however, operated on the basis of the opposite values of *ascription* and *particularism*. Thus, status was ascribed and depended on who one was—husband, wife, child, or grandparent, etc.—rather than what one did. Parents would do their best to advance their children, whatever their children's abilities might be. If family units and work units overlapped, there would be endless tension and conflict between the incompatible value-systems of work and family relationships. With the nuclear family the two worlds were kept separate and linked only by the male breadwinner.

This approach has been much criticized. It appeared to justify a gendered division of labour between male breadwinner and female housewife by arguing that this alone met the requirements of an industrial economy. It emphasized the fit between the nuclear family and industrial society, and did not take account of the tensions between the two. It said nothing about observable variations in the structure and composition of families in industrial societies. It also treated the family as a harmonious institution and did not deal with its internal conflicts and their consequences.

Marxist

A different theory of the development of the modern family was put forward by a 1970s group of Marxist writers, who explained its development in terms of the needs of a capitalist economy.

Their central argument was that the capitalist system exploits the free domestic labour of the housewife through the **domestic division of labour**. A key point here is that housework and child-rearing should not be considered family activities *outside* the operation of the capitalist economy but rather an *essential* part of it. The male breadwinner can work long hours for the employer only because the domestic work of looking after the household and bringing up children is done by the housewife. The family also reproduces labour by beginning the process of producing submissive workers, which is then continued by education (see Chapter 9, pp. 327–8). Although domestic labour is therefore essential to the capitalist economy, employers pay only for the work of the male breadwinner and get the housewife's contribution free. If the housewife was paid for her labour, the wage costs of the capitalist employer would increase considerably.

It has also been argued that the family provides an outlet for the tensions and frustrations generated by the alienating work of a capitalist economy. Workers are under constant pressure from the employer to work harder and faster, often carrying out boring and repetitive work in very poor conditions, over which they have little control. Family life provides a temporary escape and a means of relieving the tensions generated by work, which may well be at the expense of wife and children, particularly if these tensions are expressed in a violent way. The bullied worker may restore his self-esteem by bullying his family. The build-up of an explosive discontent at work is avoided through the safety valve provided by the family and the 'emotional labour' of the wife.

Many housewives do, however, work in paid employment and have always done so. As the main role of the woman in the nuclear family was to be a housewife and the male breadwinner earned a 'family wage' to support the whole household, employers could pay women low wages. They could also treat women as a 'reserve army' that could be drawn into work when there was a labour shortage and returned to the home when demand was slack. Thus, the nuclear family also provided employers with a useful additional supply of cheap labour.

In spite of its evident differences from the functionalist approach, this analysis shared with it the assumption that a particular form of the family fits the requirements of the economy. It treated the nuclear family with a gendered division of labour as the standard form of the family, much as Parsons did, and similarly said little about variations in the structure and character of the family. It was an approach that was taken up by some Marxist feminists, such as Veronica Beechey (1987), who saw the dynamics of capitalism as central to the subordination of women.

> ↪ *Connections*
> We discuss the employment of women in paid work, and the concept of a 'reserve army', in Chapter 17, p. 688.

Feminist

An alternative feminist approach focused in a similar way on the domestic division of labour but rejected the idea that it can be explained by capitalism. This approach argued that the domestic division of labour preceded the rise of capitalism and resulted from an age-old domination of women by men. For these 'radical feminists', as they were called, it was not capitalism that was the problem, but patriarchy. By **patriarchy** they meant a universal structure of male authority that is found in all societies but expressed in many different institutional ways. It is the power that men have over women, not the dynamics of capitalism, that explains the domestic division of labour.

> ↪ *Connections*
> We discuss feminism, the concept of patriarchy, and the problems it raises in Chapter 5, pp. 160–3.

Thus, Delphy (1977) saw the exploitation of women's labour as rooted in 'the domestic mode of production' in the household, not in the capitalist mode of production. Men held a superior position within the domestic mode of production and exploited through marriage the labour of women. The subordination of women in the household and the domestic division of labour resulted from male exploitation. The family was an institution for the exploitation of women by men.

Walby (1986) too rejected the idea that the development of capitalism accounted for the emergence of a domestic division of labour, though she argued that there are other patriarchal structures besides the family. It was not so much that men kept women subordinated in the home as that men excluded them from the paid employment that would enable them to be independent. The capitalist employer actually wanted to employ women as a cheaper source of labour and it was the patriarchal structures of the state and the trade unions that excluded women from work. Thus, Walby argued that women's domestic labour was a *result* of the exclusion of women from paid work rather than a *cause* of it.

Those that have used the concept of patriarchy to explain the domestic division of labour have advanced the debate on this issue. They have moved away from the functionalist notion of the family as a harmonious institution adapted to the needs of industrial society. They have also avoided the economic determinism of the Marxist approach. There are, however, problems with explanations that rely on patriarchy alone. If patriarchy is a universal feature of human societies, it cannot explain changes in the relationships between men and women. We will return to this question in our section on 'The development of family life'.

Contemporary debate

These perspectives have been associated with very different evaluations of the contemporary family. Those who believe in 'family values' have a view of the family close to the functionalist perspective. They see the correct performance of the socialization function as critical to the maintenance of the social order and believe that only the traditional family can perform this function. They are much concerned with what they consider to be the decline of this family.

Their idea of the family is based on marriage, a gendered division of labour within the household, and sex only within marriage. They call for divorce to be made more difficult and do not consider that cohabitation is an acceptable alternative to marriage. Wives should focus their lives on the upbringing of children and the maintenance of the household. There is a general hostility towards sex education, homosexuality, and abortion.

Single-parent families headed by lone mothers have come under attack from this perspective. These are not considered to be 'proper' families. The absence of a father figure is said to weaken the control of children and deprive boys of a male role model. Fatherless families have been blamed for rising crime, educational failure, lack of interest in work, and dependence on state welfare. According to Charles Murray (1990), fatherless families are responsible for the emergence of an underclass (see our later discussion of 'Parenting').

Against this view, it is argued that the single-parent family should not be held responsible for these problems. Mothers are forced by low income, absent fathers, and government policy to take employment. The difficulties of one-parent families are, anyway, not so much the result of their one-parent character but of their poverty and their children's consequent lack of opportunity. The focus on the decline of the family as the source of social problems diverts attention from their broader economic and political origins. This approach is critical not of the family but of the existing social order and is typical of a Marxist perspective.

> **⊃** *Connections*
> The theoretical assumptions behind these positions on the single-parent family are further discussed in Media watch 2 on p. 69.

In *The Antisocial Family*, Michele Barrett and Mary McIntosh (1991) combined a Marxist with a feminist approach. They argued that the family is the central mechanism through which inequality is passed from one generation to the next through the inheritance of wealth. They also emphasized what is often called the 'dark side' of family life. The family is not, as it is often seen, a refuge from the pressures of the world but a prison, which isolates women, leaves them vulnerable to domestic violence, and generates mental illness. The family oppresses women sexually and financially, through marriage and the domestic division of labour.

The problem is not only what the family does to people but also that it is a 'privileged institution', which devalues life outside it. As they put it, 'the family ideal makes everything else seem pale and unsatisfactory' (1991: 77). Nonfamilial institutions, such as old people's homes, nurseries, or children's homes, may well provide better care or a more stimulating environment than the family, but they are always viewed in negative terms because of the dominance of the family ideal. Furthermore, people become so wrapped up in family life that they do not have time and energy for other relationships and activities. The family is presented here as an exclusive and suffocating institution,

which 'sucks the juice out of everything around it, leaving other institutions stunted and distorted' (Barrett and McIntosh 1991: 78). To Barrett and McIntosh, the problem is not that the family is in decline but that it is too strong.

These consequences of family life are certainly recognizable, and, as we shall see in the section on 'Domestic violence and abuse', there is plentiful evidence for the 'dark side' of family life. This critique of the family also usefully counteracts the dominant and idealizing view of family life presented by those who believe in 'family values'. It does, however, attribute rather too much to the family itself. This is not the only patriarchal structure in society, and cannot be held solely responsible for inequalities between men and women, or for the failure of other institutions.

The life course

Families involve relationships between people of different ages who are at different stages of life. People are also themselves moving through these stages as they pass through the 'life course'. These generational relationships and stages are important aspects of family life, which have been receiving increasing attention from sociologists in recent years (Pilcher 1995; Hunt 2005).

Age and generation

People of different ages are often described as belonging to different generations. Two different usages of the term **generation** should, however, be distinguished.

- *Those born during a particular period.* Examples of this usage are the 'sixties generation' or the 'pre-war generation' or 'my generation'.
- *Kinship groups defined by parent–child relationships.* Children and their cousins; their parents, aunts, and uncles; their grandparents, great-aunts, and great-uncles; (and so on) each constitute a generation.

Pilcher (1995) has argued that this double usage of the term creates confusion. She suggests that it is best to use the term **cohort** for all those born in a particular year or group of years and reserve generation for kinship groups. The term 'intergenerational relationships' would then refer to, say, relationships between parents and children or grandparents and grandchildren, rather than to the relationship between 'pre-war' and 'post-war' generations.

Such intergenerational relationships are certainly central to the functioning of a family. The process of socialization operates through intergenerational relationships, as adults pass on their knowledge and experience to the young. This process can also operate in the other direction, however, as when the young pass on their knowledge of, say, information technology or the Web to the old.

Intergenerational processes are also crucial to caring and this demonstrates the importance of taking account of changes in the relationships between generations as families adapt to the social changes occurring around them. One consequence of the rise of the two-earner family in which both parents take paid employment is that a greater burden of childcare falls on grandparents.

While intergenerational relationships enable the family to function, they are also a source of tension and conflict. Growing longevity, the smaller size of families, and changes in social policy have made the old a greater financial and care burden on the young. This can lead to 'elder abuse'. It can also result in a broader conflict between those at work and those in old age, between those paying taxes and those receiving state benefits and care.

These relationships must be put in the context of the changing generational composition of families and households. Increasing longevity means that there are growing numbers of multi-generation families that include not only grandparents but great-grandparents. As the family has become generationally stretched, intergenerational relationships have become more complex and more salient.

Stages in life?

As we grow older we pass through various stages in life. Childhood, youth, adulthood, middle age, and old age are terms commonly used to describe the stages we pass through.

The term 'life cycle' has often been used to describe this process. This term has biological origins and implies that a process of biological ageing shapes the stages of life. It contains the idea that there is a fixed sequence of stages that everyone passes through as they age. The traditional British notion that there are clearly bounded stages, such as adulthood beginning at the age of 21 or retirement starting at the age of 65, reflects a life-cycle way of thinking.

The idea of a life cycle cannot, however, easily accommodate two features of the stages:

- differences in stages between societies;
- changes in stages.

In many pre-industrial societies there has not been a youth stage but rather a direct transition from childhood to adulthood (Hunt 2005). If stages vary in this way between societies, it is difficult to see them in life-cycle terms. There has also been considerable change in both the number and the timing of stages in Britain. For example, the notion of a 'new middle age' of active but non-work life between adulthood and 'old age' has recently emerged and 'old age' has been shifted to a later time of life (Pilcher 1995).

In sociology, the more flexible term **life course** has now superseded life cycle. This accommodates better the *social construction* of life's stages and gets away from the idea that these are biologically determined or fixed. Furthermore, as Pilcher (1995) has pointed out, life course also carries with it a sense of the cumulative character of a person's movement through life. The way that a person starts the course and moves through it will shape the way that he or she finishes it.

If stages are so variable and changeable, do they have any real basis in social reality? Post-modern theorists have argued that it no longer makes much sense to see the life course in terms of stages. The boundaries between stages have become blurred and are no longer fixed at particular ages. Instead of living in a way appropriate to their stage in life, people choose lifestyles regardless of their age. Indeed,

Frontiers Disability and the life course

Mark Priestley has developed a life-course approach to the study of disability. He claims that:

> This perspective is important, because it highlights how disabling societies and practices affect people of different generations in different ways (e.g. children, young people, adults or older people). It also allows us to consider some important disability issues at the very beginning and end of the life course (i.e. at birth and death). This in turn enables us to see more clearly how societies organize generational boundaries and life course transitions in a collective way, and how this shapes our understanding of disability in the social world. (Priestley 2003: 1)

An example of this approach is his examination of the distinctive way in which the young disabled are regarded. The treatment of disabled adults as impaired, incompetent, and passive has been challenged effectively by disability activists but this has not happened with disabled children, who are still treated in this way. They are still viewed as a distinct category, as a social problem, rather than as individuals with their own personalities, needs, and wishes. As they become older, they are denied the transition of youth. This is generally seen as a transitional stage of preparation for adulthood but for the disabled 'true adult status is neither envisaged nor attained' (2003: 113). The disabled young are therefore locked into a kind of 'enduring adolescence' and also find themselves excluded from a youth culture centred on images of bodily perfection.

Does the notion of the stages of life still have any meaning?
© Getty Images/Philip Lee Harvey

they go to great lengths to counteract or conceal their biological age through exercise regimes or cosmetic surgery. In an age of individualization, consumerism, and choice, life is no longer divided into stages (Hunt 2005).

The idea of stages in life is still, however, embedded in ordinary discourse, in the language which people use to describe themselves and each other. They still commonly call themselves 'young' or 'middle-aged' or 'old'. They mark transitions from one stage to another with twenty-first birthday or retirement parties. It therefore still makes sociological sense to conceive of stages in the life course, so long as this notion is used flexibly and takes account of changing conceptions of these stages. Indeed, charting changes in the way that people divide up the course of their lives is one means by which sociologists can monitor processes of social change.

Stop and reflect

We began this part of the chapter by considering what is meant by the family.

- In everyday usage the family is given many different meanings and notions of the family have been highly politicized.

- Some sociologists therefore prefer to refer to 'families' and 'family practices'.

- We have provided a broad definition of the family in terms of a distinct sense of identity and mutual responsibility.

  We went on to outline different perspectives on the family.

- Make sure that you are clear about the functionalist, Marxist, and feminist approaches.

- How would these differ in their interpretation of the rise of single-parent families?

  Lastly, we examined the concepts used to explore the life course.

- Make sure that you are clear about the meaning of the terms 'generation' and 'cohort'.

- Intergenerational relationships are central to family life and have changed with the changing generational composition of the family.

- Why is the term 'life course' preferable to 'life cycle'?

- Is the notion of 'stages' in life still useful?

The development of family life

Many aspects of contemporary family life are treated as 'taken for granted' or 'natural' characteristics of the family. The existence of strong emotional bonds between family members is, for example, considered a natural feature of family relationships. The life course is seen as passing through certain natural stages. There is, however, nothing natural about family life and in this section we examine the processes of social change that have produced the contemporary family and life course.

The rise of the nuclear family

As we argued earlier (see p. 449), the nuclear family is usually defined as a residential unit consisting of parents and unmarried children, but in many ways what really matters is not so much its composition as its relationship to the wider society. The nuclear family is a relatively isolated and inward-looking unit centred on domestic life and characterized by intense emotional relationships.

Emergence of the nuclear family

According to the classic model of the development of the family, as presented by Talcott Parsons (1949), the extended family unit of pre-industrial society gave way to the nuclear family of industrial societies. In pre-industrial societies production depended on the amount of family labour available to work the land. Large families were therefore economically advantageous, and the extended family was the most appropriate unit. In industrial societies, the household became increasingly separated from production and the nuclear family with one breadwinner became the dominant form. This view needs considerable qualification in the light of later historical research.

The nuclear family was, in fact, emerging long before industrialization. According to Lawrence Stone (1977), in the upper and middle classes the isolation of the nuclear family from the extended family began as early as the sixteenth century. Before this time there was no boundary between the two. Relationships between husbands and wives, parents and children, were no closer than their relationships with other relatives or neighbours. From this time on, the family became increasingly focused on the upbringing of children and the emotional needs of their parents. By the eighteenth century the nuclear family had become 'walled off' both from the community and the wider network of relatives.

In line with this view, Leonora Davidoff (1990) has argued that family life in the upper class became more private and more domestic during the eighteenth century. There was less involvement in public activities and a greater interest in the pleasures of home and family. In the country house, the life of the household became less centred on the semi-public great hall and more on the small private rooms of the family. One important architectural change was the building of corridors, which allowed people to go from one room to another without disturbing each other's privacy. Servants were increasingly segregated in their own quarters.

Catherine Hall (1982a) has shown how a similar domesticity was emerging in the middle class. During the eighteenth century the better-off shopkeepers became dissatisfied with living over the shop and wanted their home to be separate from their workplace. Their wives 'were furnishing their living apartments elegantly, putting their servants into livery, and refusing to be seen in the shop themselves, as it was not considered to be ladylike' (C. Hall 1982a: 4).

In the family life of the lower classes, the great change in the eighteenth century was the break-up of the household as the unit of production. Previously, all members of the family had been expected to engage in productive activities —working on the land, keeping animals, producing craft goods, collecting wood, or foraging for food. Young people often became servants or apprentices in the larger households, where they were treated as members of the family. Indeed, the family at this time was taken to mean all members of the household. Servants and apprentices had the same status and were treated in much the same way as members of the biological family (Davidoff 1990).

The pre-industrial development of wage labour broke up the household as a unit of production. With the growth of capitalism in eighteenth-century Britain, production was carried out increasingly not by members of the family but by workers paid a wage for their labour. The family was becoming a unit of *consumption* rather than *production*. Its members no longer worked together but rather used the wages they had earned elsewhere to buy the goods they consumed as a family.

The family also became a more exclusive unit held together by kinship alone. Its members were linked now only by marriage and birth (or possibly adoption). Apprentices and servants were no longer treated as members of the family. Apprentices now learned their trade in the workplace, while domestic servants increasingly became wage workers. The family had become both biologically and emotionally a tighter 'nuclear' unit that was focused on the home.

Husbands and wives

According to the sentiments school of sociologists and historians (see box on 'Emotions and documents'), family members have not always been bound together by strong emotional relationships. There was no affection in the relationships of the early family. It was only with the emergence of the nuclear family that family life developed an emotional quality.

Stone (1977) called this process the 'growth of affective individualism' (affective simply means emotional). People began to treat each other as unique individuals with personal and emotional needs. Family relationships took on a new quality as its members became concerned with their feelings for each other. The main function of the nuclear family increasingly became the satisfaction of emotional needs.

THEORY AND METHODS

Emotions and documents

The classic studies of the development of the family were carried out during the 1960s and 1970s by Philippe Ariès (1962), Edward Shorter (1976), and Lawrence Stone (1977). They have been labelled the 'sentiments approach' by Michael Anderson (1980), because of their focus on the emotional aspects of the development of the family.

The work of the 'sentiments school' of family studies was inevitably dependent on documentary sources. It is, however, difficult to draw conclusions about the emotional quality of relationships or the way that people actually behave from sources of this kind. These sources also become scarcer as one moves down the social order and the discussion of historical changes in the family tends to be dominated by evidence from upper- or middle-class families.

➲ We discuss the problems of using documentary sources in Chapter 3, pp. 89–93. Read these pages and consider how our account here of the development of the nuclear family ought to be qualified.

❓ Imagine that in a hundred years time a sociologist was writing about family life at the beginning of the twenty-first century. What sources would be available to the sociologist? What evidence would the sociologist be able to find on the emotional quality of family life?

He argued that these changes could be seen in marriage. In the sixteenth century, marriage in the upper ranks of society was a means of joining together two kinship groups, for economic or political purposes. Mate selection was controlled by parents and the wider family. By the end of the eighteenth century emotional concerns had become much more important to marriage. Economic considerations and parental influence still mattered, especially when large fortunes or estates were at stake, but love and companionship were also seen as essential. Rejection of a chosen partner on the grounds of incompatibility was allowed, and choice based on mutual attraction was becoming more common. It was also recognized that loveless marriages would inevitably lead to extramarital affairs.

One sign of these changes was the proliferation of match-making occasions for upper-class families. Balls, card parties, and other social events in the 'assembly rooms' that were being built in eighteenth-century towns enabled young members of the elite to meet potential marriage partners and exercise some choice over who they

Briefing: eighteenth-century wife sales

'As described in 1727, the husband "puts a halter about her neck and thereby leads her to the next market-place, and there puts her up to auction to be sold to the best bidder, as if she were a brood mare or a milch-cow. A purchaser is generally provided beforehand on these occasions". This procedure was based closely on the sale of cattle. It often took place in a cattle market and was accompanied by the use of a symbolic halter, by which the wife was led to market by the seller, and led away again by the buyer. . . . In the popular mind, this elaborate ritual freed the husband of all future responsibility for his wife, and allowed both parties to marry again. Very often, perhaps normally, the bargain was pre-arranged with the full consent of the wife, both purchaser and price being agreed upon beforehand.' (Stone 1977: 40)

What does the symbolism of this ritual tell us about the relationship between husband and wife?

married. London and Bath became the centres of the national marriage market established at this time.

Lower down the social order, in the middle class and among skilled workers, economic considerations remained more central to mate selection, because capital was scarce and the financial aspects of marriage were that much more crucial. Among the propertyless poor there was less at stake. Premarital sex was common and partners were freely chosen, and discarded, or abandoned. Desertion and bigamy were, according to Stone (1977), common, while 'wife sales' by 'mutual consent' provided an unofficial means of divorce (see box on 'Eighteenth-century wife sales').

As marriage became more emotional, it also became less stable. The nuclear family was held together less by wider kin relationships and depended more on internal bonds. Women found themselves torn between the competing demands of children and husbands as family relationships became emotionally more intense. The eighteenth-century changes in marriage created 'very severe stresses' for the institution and these have arguably been with it ever since (Stone 1977: 404).

Parents and children

The sentiments historians argued that the relationship between parents and children also became more emotional. It was the pioneering work of Ariès (1962) on the history of childhood that started the discussion of this aspect of the family.

Aries claimed that childhood did not exist in medieval times. Once children no longer required constant care, they were treated like adults. This was shown by the way that they were dressed. Until the seventeenth century there were no special clothes for children, who were dressed like small adults. Children did not lead separate lives and generally mixed with adults. They were expected to earn their keep, and to fight in war, as soon as they were physically able to do so.

Relationships between parents and children were at this stage unemotional. Adults took no pleasure in their relationships with children and were indifferent to their emotional needs. They left children alone for long periods, put them out to wet-nurses, and showed little concern when they died, which they often did, for infant mortality was very high. Indeed, this meant that it was best not to invest too much emotion in them. The lack of parental feeling for children was shown by the harsh punishments that were used to discipline them.

According to Aries, it was in the seventeenth century that attitudes began to change, at first in the aristocracy and among educated people. Parents began to take pleasure from watching and playing with children, and began to treat them as different from adults. Clothes, games, toys, and stories specifically created for children made their first appearance. Also, a sense of special parental responsibility for the welfare and success of children began to emerge. Child-rearing now became a central function of the family in a way that it had not been before.

The idea that parents had previously lacked emotional feelings for their children has, however, been challenged by Linda Pollock (1983). She used diary and autobiographical material to show that sixteenth-century parents grieved for their children when they died and did not treat them as harshly as the sentiments historians had suggested. Hugh Cunningham (1995) has reviewed the literature on this issue and concluded that there were, none the less, significant changes in attitudes towards children, particularly in the eighteenth century. A greater concern for the welfare of children and a greater sense of parental responsibility emerged in the middle class and spread downwards to the working class after industrialization.

Patriarchy and the domestic division of labour

The development of the nuclear family involved not only changes in the emotional quality of relationships but also in power relationships. The nuclear family was a patriarchal family in which men dominated.

> **➔ Connections**
> We discuss the concept of patriarchy in Chapter 5, pp. 160–3.

The domestic division of labour was central to the patriarchal nuclear family of the nineteenth century. Men went out to work and controlled the family income, while women were confined within the home doing the housework and bringing up children. As we showed earlier (p. 450), Marxist writers have argued that it was industrial capitalism that brought about this domestic division of labour. There is also, however, evidence of a pre-industrial division of labour between men and women. Harriet Bradley (1989) has reviewed the literature on this question.

Women were engaged in a wider range of productive tasks in pre-industrial Europe but tended to carry out those that were of lower status and linked to the home. Segalen's (1983) study of French peasant households showed that women worked in the house, the barn, the farmyard, and the garden more often than out in the fields. Middleton (1979) held that women in medieval Britain carried out many different agricultural tasks, but it was the men who did the high-status work of ploughing. In the towns, women were engaged in a variety of occupations but the main crafts were male-dominated and women took part in craftwork in a less specialized and more intermittent way, generally through family connections.

Although a gendered division of labour existed, there was much variation and flexibility. In some places women were very active in trade and shopkeeping, which could give them independence and lead to their playing important public roles. Widows and unmarried women could indeed be heads of households in the same way as men. Bradley (1989) has stressed that the gendering of the pre-industrial division of labour was quite flexible. She suggested that the greater uncertainties of life in pre-industrial societies made it necessary for the various members of a household to cooperate in a flexible way.

With industrialization there was a much sharper separation of production from consumption, of paid work from the household. This resulted in a more systematic separation of the male and female spheres (see Chapter 5, pp. 168–70). In the middle class there was a clear separation of the male sphere of work and, more generally, public life from the female domestic sphere. Women were excluded from public activities and more than ever confined within the home. This separation was less marked in the working class, where many women went out to work, but this paid work was seen as secondary to their domestic role and subordinate to it.

It was also in the nineteenth century that an ideology of the domestic division of labour became established. The belief that women's primary responsibilities and duties lay in the home acquired a new moral force. Men and women were seen as having different identities, which were grounded in what were presumed to be their very different natures.

It is, then, clear that the gendered division of labour characteristic of the 'classic' nuclear family did not originate with industrialization. It existed in pre-industrial times but with a lot of local variation and flexibility according to household circumstances. With industrialization came a greater standardization of male and female roles and an ideological rationale for them that became deeply embedded in people's beliefs about the differences between the work of men and women.

The persistence of the extended family

Domesticity did not, however, mean that the nuclear family cut itself off from contact with relatives. According to Davidoff (1990), the nineteenth-century middle-class family was typically large, with families interlinked by marriage into an extensive network. People kept in touch with their relatives through letter-writing, visiting, and the exchange of gifts. The domestic focus of the middle-class household clearly did not prevent important relationships with a wide circle of relatives. Technological change later made this easier, with the telephone providing a new means of keeping in contact.

In the working class, the modern pattern of the nuclear family, focused on home life and separated from the workplace, had become generally established in the nineteenth-century industrial city, but this did not mean that the working-class family was completely isolated. Michael Anderson (1971) argued that in 'critical life situations' there was a continued dependence on the extended family. These situations occurred through illness, death, unemployment, difficulties in finding work or accommodation, and the problems of old age. In such circumstances it was only the family that people could fall back on and the extended family remained a crucial means of support.

In their well-known study of Bethnal Green, Michael Young and Peter Willmott (1957) found that the extended family was still alive and well in a stable working-class community in the 1950s. They particularly emphasized the importance of the mother–daughter relationship. Even when daughters had married and set up their own households, mothers and daughters relied upon each other for help and advice, and had frequent contact. In their sample, a fifth of those married couples who had parents that were still alive had them living in the same street. This was not just a feature of family life in Bethnal Green, for similar family relationships could be found in other places, such as Liverpool, Wolverhampton, and Swansea (Willmott 1988).

Communities of this kind did, then, change as the extensive rehousing of inner-city communities dispersed their members to other locations during the 1960s. Willmott and Young (1960) showed that the rehousing of Bethnal Green families to an estate in Greenleigh broke up extended family relationships and led people to lead a more isolated life focused on the nuclear family household. Women now depended much less on their mothers and more on their husbands. It was not only a matter of community upheavals, for changing leisure patterns, the rise of home ownership, and increasing domestic consumption resulted in a growing focus on the private life of the family. Furthermore, Geoff Dench, Kate Gavron, and Michael Young (2006) argue that the role of older women changed as the welfare state and professional social workers took increasing responsibility for welfare:

> What seems to have happened is that the welfare state has appropriated the role which older women used to play. The growth of a national family—the nanny state in some accounts —has created an additional system of public care and support which now goes beyond helping ordinary families and is instead taking power and meaning away from them. (Dench *et al.* 2006: 118)

Some studies have, none the less, shown that contacts with the extended family still survive, to a perhaps surprising degree. In a study of part of North London, Willmott (1986) found that two-thirds of couples with young married children saw relatives at least weekly. Working-class couples saw their relatives more often than middle-class couples did, though the differences were not great. O'Brien and Jones (1996) found similarly that 72 per cent of households in an area of East London had been visited by a relative during the previous week. Indeed, they concluded that contact with relatives had not changed significantly since a study of the area carried out by Wilmott in the 1950s.

Arguably the extended family is once again becoming more central to people's lives. As life expectancy has increased, the number of old people has risen and they have required more care, but state care for the old has declined with the closing of local-authority homes and geriatric wards. Similarly, with the closure of mental hospitals, care of the mentally ill was shifted back into the community via community care, but inadequate resources meant that in practice a growing burden fell on to families (see Chapter 8, pp. 303–4 for a discussion of community care). This is not only a matter of the greater dependence of the old on the family but also of the greater dependence of the family on the old. Increasing numbers of working women, especially the working mothers of small children, have made extended family assistance with childcare, particularly through grandparents, more important.

There is then plentiful evidence that the extended family has remained important to people in industrial societies. Extended kin are still a source of help and support, and this function may well have recently increased in importance. This does not contradict the idea that the nuclear family has become increasingly isolated. The

separation of production from the household, the rise of domesticity, the spread of home ownership, the decline of local communities, and a growing focus on private life have gradually isolated the nuclear family. It does, however, show that the notion of a transition from the extended to the nuclear family is oversimple.

Changes in life's stages

As the family developed, the life course changed. Stages in the life course that are now commonly taken for granted actually emerged historically at different times. In this section we examine the social construction of the stages of life.

Childhood and youth

As we showed earlier, attitudes towards children were changing, in the upper levels of society at least, by the seventeenth century, but childhood, as people think of it today, did not become clearly established until the nineteenth century. Two key changes during this century were the restriction of child labour by the Factory Acts and the development of compulsory education. This was gradually lengthened until the school-leaving age reached 16 in 1972. These changes created a space for childhood between infancy and adulthood and kept children in the parental home for a longer period.

Recent changes have to some extent undermined the distinctiveness of childhood. Television's penetration into the household has given children virtually unrestricted access to the adult world. They early become fully-fledged consumers of adult products, rather than special products designed for children. Children have also been increasingly treated as individuals in their own right. Thus, the Children's Act of 1989 made changes in their legal status,

---

Figure 12.1 Main stages in the development of the nuclear family

1 Pre-industrial emergence of domesticity.

2 Pre-industrial break-up of the household as a unit of production.

3 Increasing focus of the family on emotional life.

4 Separation of home from work by capitalist production and industrialization.

5 Separation of male from female sphere, standardizing of a domestic division of labour, and growth of a domestic ideology during the nineteenth century.

6 Further isolation of the nuclear family through the break-up of communities and the privatizing of leisure and consumption during the later twentieth century.

Frontiers Children in their own right

James, Jenks, and Prout (1998) have argued that the study of children has been dominated too long by the notion that childhood is a stage of socialization through which people pass on their way to be adults. They call for a new sociology of childhood that would focus on the child 'as being' rather than 'as becoming'. They identify four discourses of childhood, which could provide the basis for a new approach to the study of children:

1 *The social structural child*. Children should not be treated as marginal but 'as a constant and recognizable component of all social structures' (1998: 210). As a category of people, children should have the same conceptual status as a social class.

2 *The minority group child*. Children are 'structurally differentiated within societies' (1998: 211). Within all

societies children are a minority within society, which, like other minorities, is exploited and discriminated against.

3 *The socially constructed child*. 'There is no essential child' (1998: 212). Childhood is constructed through social practices and perceptions, and is culturally and historically variable.

4 *The tribal child*. Children inhabit their own cultural world with a 'self-maintaining system of signs, symbols and rituals that prescribes the whole way of life of children within a particular sociohistorical setting' (1998: 215).

❓ In the light of this approach, should we give up the idea of childhood as a stage of life?

---

treating them less as minors without rights and more as individuals, with the right to have their wishes and feelings taken into account by, for example, the courts or those running children's homes (Lavalette 1996; Winter and Connolly 1996).

There has, however, been a reaction against these changes that has re-emphasized the distinctive status of children. On the one hand, there has been a growing concern to protect them from drugs, violence, sexual abuse, exploitative child labour, and 'adult' television. On the other hand, politicians have sought to reassert parental authority over children and establish parental responsibility for their behaviour. Boyden (1997) has argued that these twin concerns with the protection and control of children have informed the globalization of a concept of childhood that is not in the interests of children (see box on 'The globalization of childhood').

Between childhood and adulthood comes youth, though it is a less clearly defined stage in the life course. Pilcher (1995) suggests that it is best treated as a stage of transition between the two, which involves two particular transitions:

- from compulsory, full-time education to employment;
- from family of *origin* to family of *destination*.

Modern conceptions of youth as a distinct stage date in Britain from early in the twentieth century, when special prisons, courts, employment, and welfare agencies for young people were established. Special organizations and institutions were required to deal with teenagers who were no longer really children but not yet recognized as adults.

It was not until the 1950s and 1960s, however, that distinctive youth cultures emerged. During these years of growing affluence, teenagers found jobs quickly and could earn large amounts of money. Their spending power and minimal financial obligations to the household made them important consumers and industry responded by creating products that marked youth out as having a distinctive style of clothing and leisure. Their earnings, their greater independence, and their lifestyle brought them into a conflict with 'the older generation' that sharpened awareness of age differences.

The affluence of the young was not to last and with the changes of the 1980s the *celebration* of youth arguably gave way to its *marginalization* (Coffield 1987). The spending power of youth declined because of unemployment, insecure employment, and the lengthening of education. A much higher proportion of young people now stay in some form of education or training to the age of 21. The ending of maintenance grants and the introduction of student contributions to higher education fees have led to more dependence on the family during higher education.

Adulthood, post-adolescence, and middle age

Adulthood became a more distinct stage as its boundaries with childhood and old age grew sharper. It came to be seen as the time between education and old age, during which people made a productive contribution to society. Its boundary with old age became more distinct with the notion of retirement from work and the creation of the

Global focus   The globalization of childhood

There has been much media concern with the global plight of children. As Boyden has put it: 'international media coverage of the young paints an especially stark picture, of innocent and vulnerable child victims of adult violence and maltreatment; of "stolen" childhoods in refugee camps and war zones' (1997: 191).

In response, international agencies have been created with a mission to protect children from the adult world and provide them with a safe and happy childhood. The work of these agencies has led to the globalization of a particular notion of childhood based on a concern for the rights of children. Behind this concern for children's rights, however, lies the export of a particular conception of childhood. This is 'culturally and historically bound to the social preoccupations and priorities of the capitalist countries of Europe and the United States' (1997: 192). These involved not only welfare concerns but also adult fears of children becoming indisciplined and getting out of control. Such a conception of childhood is two-edged, treating street children as 'both the most deprived and the most depraved members of society' (1997: 196).

Boyden is concerned that this conception can 'have the effect of penalizing, or even criminalizing the childhoods of the poor' (1997: 207). Governments treat street children as vagrants or delinquents but, if their families are to survive, children must earn money by selling goods and providing services on the streets. These customary family practices become the target of inappropriate state intervention by governments that are anyway primarily concerned with maintaining order and protecting the interests of the rich rather than promoting the welfare of the poor.

Forcing children into school may actually be of little benefit to them, as the kind of work available when they leave does not require formal skills, and education may merely subject them to indoctrination by the state. They can more appropriately prepare for adult life by acquiring work experience and survival skills on the streets.

Boyden, then, is sceptical of the benefits to children and their families of the globalization of a concept of childhood that may appear grounded in a concern for universal rights but is in fact culturally specific and not appropriate to the cultures, customs, and circumstances of most poor countries.

➜ Look up newspaper reports of the treatment of children in poor countries.

❓ Are there situations where governments should intervene to protect or educate children?

❓ Should governments in poor countries leave children alone?

---

old-age pension in 1908. Recently, however, both the early and the late boundaries of adulthood have come into question.

The early boundary has been challenged by those who have argued for the existence of a new stage in the life course, variously labelled 'late adolescence', 'young adulthood', or 'post-adolescence'. We will call it **post-adolescence**. This is a period in the life of those in their twenties and thirties when they are relatively independent of their families of origin but have not acquired the responsibilities associated with adulthood, in particular those connected with marriage and parenthood. Some have evaluated this negatively as a period of inability, or selfish refusal, to take on the responsibilities of adulthood. Heath and Cleaver (2003) suggest that it should be seen more positively as a time when people are working out for themselves how to 'do' adulthood. They are experimenting with relationships and choosing how to live but not freely, because they have to operate within the constraints of the housing and labour markets. Indeed, class position plays a key part in enabling or preventing this. As Heath and Cleaver (2003: 184) have put it: '. . . this new phase is by no means universal, but is particularly associated with well educated graduates and young professionals, who are increasingly choosing to sideline some of the more traditional markers of adulthood, in some cases indefinitely'.

Gender has become less significant, as young women have gained increasing access to higher education and professional careers. The post-adolescence of young women has, however, resulted in much popular disquiet because of its questioning of traditional, gendered notions of adulthood. For women especially, marriage and child-bearing have been the markers of adult status. Post-adolescence marks not just a new stage on the way to adulthood but also a rethinking of the criteria of adulthood, a social reconstruction of what adulthood means.

At the later end of adulthood, 'new middle age', covering the later years of working life and extending into what used to be considered 'old age', has, however, recently emerged. This time of life has been reconstructed as an active phase with its own distinctive features, as changes in employment and welfare have enabled a period of active

Controversy and debate   Ages and stages?

There are four ages of life:

- The *first age* is the period of childhood, characterized by socialization and dependent status.
- The *second age* is the period of full-time employment, family-building, and adult responsibility.
- The *third age* covers the years 50–74 and is the 'new middle age' of active independent life, post-work and post-parenting.

- The *fourth age* is old age proper, characterized by increasing dependence on others.

Source: Pilcher (1995: 89).

❓ How well does the notion of four stages describe the life course?

❓ How would post-modern theorists view this notion of stages (see p. 453).

non-work. Earlier retirement has released people from the constraints of paid work, while state-subsidized occupational pension schemes have provided them with the means to maintain a reasonable standard of living. The growing purchasing power of the over fifties has led to the creation of magazines, holidays, insurance schemes, retirement homes, and residential communities designed specifically for them. The University of the Third Age was set up to provide an educational forum for the exchange of accumulated knowledge and expertise.

Pilcher (1995) has pointed out that the capacity to enjoy a leisurely and affluent 'third age' is not, however, equally available to all. Lower-paid jobs and intermittent work histories, because of child-rearing, mean that women may have to resume or continue paid work into 'old age', while there is no retirement from housework. Redundancy may bring employment to an end before sufficient pension contributions have been accumulated to provide for a comfortable retirement (and the closing of many final salary schemes will anyway make this retirement less comfortable). Those in lower-paid work without occupational pensions have to rely on state pensions, whose value relative to earnings has been declining since 1982, when they were linked to changes in prices rather than earnings. Some ethnic minorities are disproportionately represented in this group. The world of the third age may largely be inhabited by white, middle-class, males.

Old age

In contrast with the active, up-beat presentation of the *third age*, images of the *fourth age* tend to be negative, treating old age as a period of dependence, disability, and decline. It is important to understand that these images are not simply descriptions of the characteristics of old people. Like the other stages of life, old age is socially constructed, not biologically fixed.

There are two main ways in which people become classified as old. The *first* is based on chronological divisions. Old age is often taken to mean the age at which people become entitled to the state pension, which in the past meant that men became old at 65 and women at 60, though in future both will receive the pension at 65. Problems in funding pensions for a longer period, as people live longer, may well lead to this age rising towards 70. The *second* is the way that they look. Grey hair and wrinkles are, for example, commonly taken to indicate that people are old.

Once people are classified as old, they tend to be treated as dependent, and as physically and mentally incapacitated, irrespective of their characteristics as individuals. This stereotyping of old age has led to those who would conventionally be considered old rejecting the term as inappropriate for them. People who *look* old frequently state that they do not *feel* old. There is, as Pilcher (1995) points out, a tension between interpretations of external appearance and sense of identity.

The stereotyping of old age has been associated with patterns of prejudice and discrimination labelled ageism, in the same way as patterns of racial and sexual prejudice and discrimination are called racism and sexism. In the case of older women, ageism tends to be combined with sexism, for women are judged more in terms of personal appearance than men are. Old women have also been particularly caricatured in folk tales and children's stories.

The stages of life are, therefore, anything but fixed. The boundaries between one stage and another have often shifted, and new stages have been created as views of the life course have altered. Arguably, the social constraints of a person's stage of life have been loosened as stereotypes have been challenged and people have exercised a more individual choice of lifestyle. A post-modern rejection of the idea of stages (see p. 453) probably goes too far, however, for the notion of stages of life still provides a framework within which people can locate and identify themselves and a means of ordering and managing their lives.

Generations and families

The age composition and generational shape of families has been changing. There are growing numbers of multi-generation family units that include grandparents and great-grandparents. Two long-term demographic changes operating since the nineteenth century were the main causes of this:

- Greater longevity resulting in the older generations living longer;
- The earlier age of child-bearing reducing the age gap between generations (though in recent years the age of child-bearing has increased).

Four- and five-generation families have become more common. Thus, about half of all people over the age of 65 are now great-grandparents.

Multi-generation families have combined with a lower birth rate to restructure the family. While the number of generations in a family increases, a lower birth rate means that people have fewer siblings within their generation. The structuring of kinship networks is increasingly by relationships *between* generations rather than relationships *within* them. Families have been extended *vertically* rather than *horizontally* (see Figure 12.2).

These changes have also brought about a shift in the age distribution of the population. Greater longevity and a falling birth rate mean that the care of the old has become a greater burden on the young. The contrast in the age distributions of the population in 1821 and 2004 demonstrates this very clearly (see Figure 12.3). Furthermore, the smaller size of the lower age groups in 2004 indicates that there will in future be even fewer people of working age to support the growing numbers of old people.

The growth of this burden is not just, however, the result of demographic changes in age distribution, since recent social policy changes have shifted more of the care of the old on to the family. The state funding of the residential care of the old has declined and this has increased the financial and social burden on the family. Furthermore, as Janet Finch (1989) has pointed out, the care burden on the family has increased as the capacity of the young to look after the old has diminished. As families have become smaller, there are fewer children to share the responsibility for care of the old. Care of the old also tends to fall on daughters rather than sons and the increasing employment of women means that daughters have less time available.

There is some danger, as we noted above, of treating the old merely as a burden. They can clearly make a very positive contribution to family life. Grandparents can, in particular, assist with childcare as mothers increasingly go out to work. The old do, none the less, require more care as they get older and more of this care seems to be descending on the family at a time when it is less able to provide it. There is the potential here for a growing conflict between generations. In this context, the problem of 'elder abuse',

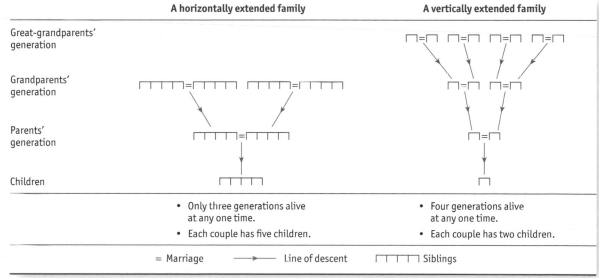

Figure 12.2 Horizontal and vertical families

	A horizontally extended family	A vertically extended family
Great-grandparents' generation		⊓=⊓ ⊓=⊓ ⊓=⊓ ⊓=⊓
Grandparents' generation	⊓⊓⊓⊓=⊓⊓⊓⊓ ⊓⊓⊓⊓=⊓⊓⊓⊓	⊓=⊓ ⊓=⊓
Parents' generation	⊓⊓⊓⊓=⊓⊓⊓⊓	⊓=⊓
Children	⊓⊓⊓⊓⊓	⊓

- Only three generations alive at any one time.
- Each couple has five children.

- Four generations alive at any one time.
- Each couple has two children.

= Marriage　　⟶ Line of descent　　⊓⊓⊓⊓ Siblings

Figure 12.3 Population by sex and age, 1821 and 2004, Great Britain (millions)

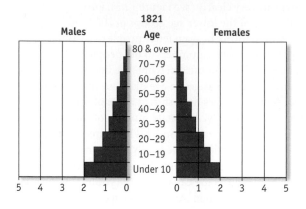

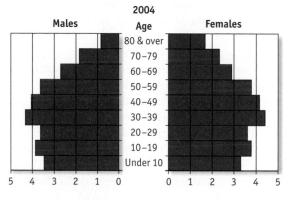

Source: Social Trends (2006: 11).

Grandparents can assist with childcare.

© Alice Chadwick

which was 'discovered' in the United States during the 1980s (Gelles and Cornell 1987), may become a more serious issue in the future.

Thus, changes in the life course have had important consequences for family structure, family relationships, and family life. As we have shown, the family gradually became more focused on the nuclear, domestic unit, but extended family relationships remained important. These extended family relationships have, however, themselves changed as families have become vertically rather than horizontally extended. Changes in social policy have then led to these vertical relationships placing a greater burden of care on the nuclear family at a time when it is strained by other processes of social change.

 Stop and reflect

In this part of the chapter we first examined the historical development of the family as a distinct domestic unit.

- Make sure that you know the meaning of the terms 'nuclear family' and 'extended family'.
- According to the sentiments approach, relationships within the family became increasingly emotional as it developed.

- With industrialization the family became a more domestic unit of consumption rather than production.
- Did this result in a transition from the extended to the nuclear family?
- Is the extended family becoming more important in people's lives today?

We went on to consider changes in the life course, the stages of life, and the relationships between generations.

- Childhood became a more distinct stage of life in the nineteenth century and youth emerged as a distinct stage during the twentieth.

- Is childhood still a distinct stage?

- Adulthood too became more distinct, though it has been claimed that new stages of 'post-adolescence' and 'new middle age' have recently emerged within it.

- Intergenerational relationships have changed with the shift from a horizontally to a vertically extended family.

- What have been the consequences of this shift for family life?

Family life in transformation

By the middle of the twentieth century the nuclear family had become established as the main form of the family in Western industrial societies. This did not mean, as we have shown, that extended family relationships ceased to be important. The nuclear family was, none the less, a distinct unit centred on marriage and children, focused on domestic life, and based on a gendered division of labour. This form of the nuclear family had also become ideologically dominant and was enthroned as 'the family'.

Since the 1960s this model has been undermined by changes in sexual life, marriage, and employment, also by a growing awareness of the dark side of family life, and by greater ethnic diversity. These changes have led to the debate over the decline of the family. Those who believe in 'family values' have defended the model against the changes undermining it. Those critical of this model have called for a greater acceptance of new forms of the family. This debate has coloured the discussion of all the issues that we cover in this section.

Sex, marriage, and divorce

We start by considering the so-called 'sexual revolution' of the 1960s and its consequences. Marriage was a cornerstone of the established form of the family. Has the sexual revolution changed this? Rates of marriage have declined and the divorce rate has increased. Does this mean that marriage is in decline?

A sexual revolution?

The 1960s has been generally considered a period of sexual liberation. This was particularly the case for women, who could free themselves from the risk of unwanted pregnancies through the contraceptive pill. A redefinition of female sexuality took place as sex became a source of pleasure, rather than a means of producing children. The sexual behaviour of women has arguably become more like that of men (see Chapter 5, pp. 184–6).

Jeffrey Weeks (1991) has set this sexual revolution in the context of post-war changes in capitalism and their impact on the working class in particular. Drawing on the ideas of the Frankfurt school, which we examine in Chapter 10, p. 367, he argued that post-war mass consumption commercialized all aspects of life and ended the social isolation of the working class. There was a shift from the traditional virtues of self-denial and careful saving to compulsive spending. Weeks associated this with a new

Did 'the pill' lead to a sexual revolution?
© Alice Chadwick

pleasure-seeking attitude towards life, which spilled over into sexual behaviour and was manipulated through the more explicit use of sexual imagery in advertising.

The relationship between sex and marriage has certainly been changing. According to the British Social Attitudes Survey, the proportion of respondents thinking that there was nothing wrong with premarital sex rose from 42 per cent in 1984 to 62 per cent in 2000 (Park *et al.* 2001: 32).

Marriage has itself changed. A growing importance was attached to the sexual aspects of the marital relationship and a satisfying sex life became one of the expectations of marriage (Richards and Elliott 1991). This continued the process of changing marriage from a primarily economic to a primarily emotional relationship, which, as we showed earlier, started long ago.

> ➲ *Connections*
>
> You may find it helpful to place this account of changes in the relationship between sex and marriage in the context of our discussion of changes in sexual behaviour in Chapter 5, pp. 184–6.

Marriage and cohabitation

The permissiveness of the 1960s was seen as a threat to the institution of marriage. Would people bother in future to get married? Would they instead simply live with whomever they chose for however long they chose?

Statistically, marriage appears to be in decline. The number of first marriages per year has gone down steadily since the 1960s (see Figure 12.4). The number of marriages is, however, not a good guide to the popularity of marriage, as it in part reflects the size of the population and its age distribution. Rate of marriage figures provide a better guide. The proportion of adult men who are married dropped from 71 per cent in 1971 to 53 per cent in 2000, the proportion of adult women from 65 per cent to 52 per cent (*Social Trends* 2002: 42). More people are living on their own or cohabiting.

One of the most striking changes is the increasing number of people who live on their own. The number of households containing only one person rose from 11 per cent in 1961 to 29 per cent in 2001 and 2005 (see Figure 12.5). This partly reflected an increase, up until the 1980s, in the number of women outliving their partners. More recently, it results particularly from the rising proportion of working-age men living on their own. Between 1986–7 and 2004–5, the proportion of men aged 25–44 living on their own rose from 7 to 16 per cent, while the proportion of men aged 45–64 on their own rose from 8 to 17 per cent. The proportion of women in these age groups living on their own also increased but to a lesser extent (*Social Trends* 2006: 23).

Figure 12.4 Marriages, divorces, and remarriages, United Kingdom, 1950–2003 (000s)

1 For both partners.
2 Includes annulments. Data for 1950 to 1970 for Great Britain only.
3 For one or both partners.

Source: *Social Trends* (2006: 26).

❷ Is marriage in decline?

Cohabitation, that is an unmarried couple living together, has also sharply increased. In 1986 11 per cent of non-married men under the age of 60 were in cohabiting relationships, but by 2004 this figure had risen to 24 per cent. The comparable figures for women were 13 per cent in 1986 and 25 per cent in 2004 (*Social Trends* 2006: 27). Cohabitation relationships need to be differentiated, however, and fall into three different categories:

- long-term relationships similar to marriage, which are often called consensual unions;
- short-term relationships with little commitment;
- pre-marriage relationships, a group that to some degree overlaps with the other two, for relationships can clearly change.

Cohabitation as an alternative to marriage became particularly established in Scandinavia, especially in Sweden. It is much more common there than in other European countries and has become institutionalized as a stable relationship very similar to marriage. The proportion of Swedish women who marry has consequently long been much lower than in other countries. In 1988 the proportion of women married by the age of 50 was only 55 per

Figure 12.5 Households by type of household and family, Great Britain, 1961–2005 (%)

Type of household/family	1961	1971	1981	1991	2001	2005
One person	11	18	22	27	29	29
Two or more unrelated adults	5	4	5	3	3	3
One family households						
Couple						
No children	26	27	26	28	29	29
1–2 dependent children	30	26	25	20	19	18
3 or more dependent children	8	9	6	5	4	4
Non-dependent children only	10	8	8	8	6	6
Lone parent						
Dependent children	2	3	5	6	6	7
Non-dependent children only	4	4	4	4	3	3
Multi-family households	3	1	1	1	1	1
All households (= 100%) (millions)	16.3	18.6	20.2	22.4	23.8	24.1

Source: *Social Trends* (2006: 22).

❓ What have been the main changes in households and families since 1961, as shown by this table?

cent, as compared with 78 per cent in England and Wales (F. R. Elliot 1996: 15).

Cohabitation in Britain has commonly taken the form of a pre-marriage relationship. Thus, data from 1998 show that 76 per cent of cohabiting men and 71 per cent of cohabiting women expected to marry, which suggests a slightly greater attachment of men to the idea of marriage. Looking at this the other way, about three-fifths of those who had got married in their thirties had cohabited before marriage (*Social Trends* 2002: 42). The rising rate of cohabitation clearly does not then mean that cohabitation is replacing marriage, for cohabitation more often than not leads to marriage.

It is important when considering these figures to set marriage within the life course of the individual. The declining proportion of the population in marriages in part reflects a later date of marriage. The average age of first marriage considerably increased between 1971 and 2003, for men from 25 to 31, for women from 23 to 29 (*Social Trends* 2006: 25). Marriage may be delayed for various reasons, such as the lengthening of education or the pursuit of a career, but this does not mean that people are less likely to become married during their life.

Cohabitation is, none the less, seen increasingly as an alternative to marriage, particularly among the young. Thus, according to *Social Trends* (2004: 33), 88 per cent of those aged 18–24 consider that 'it is all right for a couple to live together without intending to get married'. There

are also signs that the government is moving towards greater rights for cohabitees, who do not have the same legal protection as divorcees if they split up, though these moves have been opposed by defenders of the institution of marriage.

The greater acceptability of premarital sex, a higher rate of cohabitation, and more people living on their own, all indicate that marriage is considered less necessary than it once was. It remains, however, a generally accepted ideal and a valued institution. Thus, although attitudes to premarital sex have become more permissive, this does not appear to be happening with attitudes towards extramarital sex. According to the British Social Attitudes Survey, in 2000 about 60 per cent considered that extramarital sex is 'always wrong', the same figure as in 1984.

Divorce and remarriage

While people are still keen to get married, the divorce rate has risen. Does a rising divorce rate mean that marriage is in decline?

The number of divorces in the UK rose steadily after the 1960s (see Figure 12.4). This might suggest that marriage as an institution has declined, that it has become less stable and more likely to break down. There are, however, two reasons for qualifying such a conclusion. First, the divorce rate reflects not only the state of marital relationships but also the ease of separation. Secondly, there is also the high rate of remarriage.

Controversy and debate   Gay marriage?

Gay couples have long sought the right to marry. Although gay couples had acquired registration rights in Scandinavia in 1996, it was in the Netherlands that same-sex marriages were first allowed, and two took place in Amsterdam City Hall on 1 April 2001.

Same-sex marriages are not allowed in Britain but in 2004 the government passed a Civil Partnership Act to give legal rights to same-sex partners equivalent to those of married couples in such matters as property, inheritance, pensions, and benefits. Partners can now register at a Registry Office and sign an official document on its steps. The first civil partnership ceremonies in Britain took place in December 2005. The only way of ending a civil partnership is through a divorce.

❷ What does this tell us about the institution of marriage?

Celebrating a gay marriage.
© Getty Images/Martin Sanmiguel

Figure 12.6 Divorce and the law

Main laws	Main provisions
1857 Divorce Act	Made divorce available through the courts rather than special Act of Parliament. Husbands could divorce wives on the basis of adultery but wives had to prove other offences, such as cruelty and desertion as well. The expense of the procedure made it unavailable to the mass of the population.
1923 Divorce Reform Act	Wives now allowed to divorce husbands on adultery grounds alone.
1937 Divorce Reform Act	Allowed divorce on the basis of desertion, cruelty, and insanity as well as adultery.
1949 Legal Aid and Advice Act	Legal aid for divorce proceedings made divorce available to the poor.
1969 Divorce Reform Act	Irretrievable breakdown made the only basis of divorce. Evidence of breakdown is adultery, unreasonable behaviour, desertion, or separation (two years with consent or five years without).
1984 Matrimonial and Family Proceedings Act	Divorce now allowed after one rather than three years of marriage.
1996 Family Law Act	A wait of nine months (fifteen if there are children) required after a statement of marital breakdown and conciliation meetings. No evidence of breakdown required.
2001 Suspension of 1996 Act	Government declares that implementation of the 1996 Act's divorce provisions would cease and these would be repealed.

❷ What have been the main changes in the process of divorce since 1961?

❷ What effect do you think that legislation has had on divorce?

❷ Why do you think that the divorce rate has increased?

An unhappy marriage leads to divorce only if the couple are able to end it. Permissive changes in the law have here been crucial and invariably followed by a rise in the divorce rate. The 1969 Divorce Reform Act made divorce far easier and was followed by the big rise in divorce (see Figure 12.4). Ease of separation depends not only on the law but also on the practicalities of life after divorce. The growing employment of women in paid work, and the greater availability of state benefits, have made it easier for wives to leave marriages.

In the 1990s a further move to make divorce easier ran into fears that this would undermine the institution of marriage. The rather contradictory 1996 Family Law Act faced both ways on this. Its 'no-fault' divorces apparently continued the process of making divorce easier. This Act also, however, slowed down the divorce process by forcing people to wait for nine months (fifteen if there were children) and undergo a process of conciliation. It was argued that divorce had become too easy and people resorted too quickly to it when problems arose in relationships. Then in 2001 the Labour government decided to abandon the idea of 'no-fault' divorce, ceased implementation of the 1996 Act's divorce provisions, and announced that they would be repealed.

As the divorce rate went up at the end of the 1960s, so did the number of remarriages (see Figure 12.4). People have increasingly passed through more than one marriage. The term **serial monogamy**—that is, a sequence of marriages—is used to describe this process. The fact that so many divorced people remarry means that divorce indicates a dissatisfaction with a particular partner rather than a rejection of the institution of marriage.

In assessing whether marriage has declined, much depends on the view taken of it. If marriage is taken to mean a life-long relationship, which provides the only proper framework for a sexual relationship, then sexual permissiveness, increasing cohabitation, and a rising divorce rate undoubtedly mean that it has declined. This is the view of marriage put forward by those who believe in 'family values' and they are in no doubt about its decline.

If the essence of marriage is taken to be a mutually satisfying relationship, it has arguably been strengthened rather than weakened by cohabitation and divorce. Neither has stopped people marrying, while both can be seen as improving the quality of marital relationships. Cohabitation enables a more informed selection of partners and a preparation for marriage, while the greater ease of divorce makes 'empty-shell' marriages less likely.

Parenting

The model of family relationships held by those who believe in 'family values' sees marriage as essential to parenting. According to this view, the only right way to bring up children is within the marriage that has produced them.

Marriage has, however, become increasingly dissociated from parenthood. This has occurred in three main ways:

- a rising number of childless couples;
- the increasing birth of children outside marriage;
- a rising rate of separation and divorce.

We will not concern ourselves here with childless couples but concentrate on the consequences of this dissociation for the parenting aspects of family life. One result is increasing numbers of single-parent families. Another is more complex stepfamilies when parents remarry after divorce.

Single-parent families

The proportion of families with dependent children headed by single parents has tripled since the beginning of the 1970s (see Figure 12.7). There are two main routes to single-parenthood: the birth of children outside marriage, and divorce, which are roughly equal causes of it (*Social Trends* 2002: 48).

The proportion of children born outside marriage in the United Kingdom has risen sharply, from about 10 per cent in the 1970s to 42 per cent in 2004. This is an inter-

nationally high figure, exceeded only by Scandinavian countries, where cohabitation is institutionalized, and France (see Figure 12.8). When it comes to teenage pregnancies, Britain is in a league of its own. In other European countries teenage birth rates have been falling but in Britain they have remained at the same level as in the early 1980s.

There is evidence that many of the children born outside marriage in Britain are born into a household with two parents. Cohabitation relationships may be less stable than marriages, but they do mean that two parents are present, and they may well lead to marriage. The joint, as opposed to sole, registration of births can be taken as an indicator of a stable cohabitation relationship. In England and Wales in 1975 less than half the children born out of marriage were jointly registered but by 2000 about four-fifths were (*Social Trends* 2002: 47). Furthermore, data from the British Social Attitudes Survey have shown that people are becoming markedly more willing to accept cohabitation as a basis for parenthood. When respondents were asked in 2000 whether 'people who want children ought to get married', only 54 per cent thought so, as compared with 70 per cent in 1989, a considerable change in eleven years (Park *et al.* 2001: 37).

Figure 12.7 Percentage of children living in different family types, Great Britain, 1972–2005 (%)

Family type	1972	1981	1992	2005
Couple families				
1 child	16	18	17	18
2 children	35	41	38	36
3 or more	41	29	28	23
Lone mother families				
1 child	2	3	5	7
2 children	2	4	6	8
3 or more	2	3	5	6
Lone father families	1	2	2	2
All dependent children	100	100	100	100

Source: *Social Trends* (2006: 24).

❷ What changes in children's experience of family life does this table suggest have taken place since the 1970s?

❷ What issues are raised by the category 'couple families'?

❷ Does this table provide evidence for change or stability in family life?

Figure 12.8 Births outside marriage, European Union, 2004 (%)

Austria	36
Belgium	31 (2003)
Denmark	45
Finland	41
France	45 (2003)
Germany	28
Greece	05
Ireland	31
Italy	15 (2003)
Luxembourg	26
Netherlands	33
Portugal	29
Spain	23 (2003)
Sweden	55
United Kingdom	42
EU–15 average	33

Source: *Social Trends* (2006: 30).

❷ Why do you think there are such wide variations in the rate of births outside marriage?

❷ Why is the United Kingdom rate so high?

Single-parent families have been the focus of much debate. To right-wing commentators they are a defective form of the family that cannot function properly and causes social problems. They are seen as resulting from a lack of moral responsibility that is often blamed on the permissiveness of the sexual revolution. Those on the political left attribute the problems of these families to poverty and see them as needing support rather than criticism.

This debate has particularly centred on whether single-parent families are a source of social problems. They are mainly headed by women (see Figure 12.7), and it has been argued that the absence of a father results in inadequate socialization, particularly for boys who, without an appropriate male role model, fail to learn correct patterns of male behaviour.

> **⊃ Connections**
>
> Charles Murray (1990) has argued that single-parent families are largely responsible for the creation of an underclass. We discuss his theory of the underclass in Chapter 18, pp. 730–1. You may also find it interesting to compare this theory of paternal deprivation with the theory of maternal deprivation discussed in Chapter 4, pp. 134–5.

But is it the absence of a father that leads to problem behaviour? Rodger (1996) reviewed many alternative explanations. The key factor may be not whether fathers are *present* but whether they are actively *involved* in upbringing, and this applies to two-parent families as well. Children in single-parent families may turn out to be disturbed not because of the absence of a father but because of the conflict and disruption caused by separation and divorce. Single-parent families experience greater deprivation than two-parent families and it may be the poverty of the household rather than the absence of a male role model that is crucial. Rodger reported that research on delinquency in children has, anyway, related it not to 'broken' but to 'bad' homes, to the way children are treated, supervised, and disciplined rather than the composition of the household.

The British government has introduced the Sure Start programme to help overcome the parenting problems faced by children in deprived areas. This programme has aimed to connect up high-quality childcare, parenting classes, work training for mothers, and health advice. By 2005, 524 such schemes had been set up at a cost of £3.1 billion and the programme was to be extended to 3,500 by 2010. Although early results from the scheme did not provide much evidence that children had benefited, it is popular with parents, has wide support, and is 'expected' to provide important benefits in the longer term (*Guardian*, 13 September 2005).

One major concern of governments has been the cost to the state of supporting one-parent families. This led to the establishment of the Child Support Agency (CSA) in 1993

What proportion of single-parent families are headed by lone fathers?

© Lucy Dawkins

to make absent parents support their children financially. The administration of the CSA ran into huge and persistent problems, which eventually led to the February 2006 decision to abolish it and create a new system of child support. The problem of the costs of one-parent families has also been addressed in another way, by getting single parents back to work and off income support through Labour's Welfare to Work programme, which has provided more state-funded childcare and put pressure on the mothers of school-age children to seek work.

Parenting after divorce

Divorce ends a marriage but it does not end a couple's relationship, at least where children are involved, for the divorced partners have to continue working out their relationship as parents. Remarriage may then lead to complex parenting relationships. Here, we first consider parenting after divorce, before going on to the 'reconstitution' of families by remarriage.

Bren Neale and Carol Smart (1997) have explored the issue of parenting after divorce in the context of the shift, brought about by the 1989 Children's Act, from **custodial parenthood** to **joint parenting**. Under the earlier system of *custodial parenthood*, one parent, usually the mother, ended up with responsibility for care of the child. Under the new system of *joint parenting*, parents are required to share responsibility and are expected to cooperate in the continued care of their children. Disputes between parents are settled by a process of mediation rather than by decisions in the courts.

A growing concern, which we examined above, with the problem of absent fathers motivated this change. According to Burghes (1994), 40 per cent of absent fathers had lost all contact with their children within two years, which was a problem not only for the children but also for the father. In recent years there has been a strong movement to reassert fathers' rights after divorce.

This issue has been linked to broader changes in family relationships by Beck and Beck-Gernsheim (1995). They held that the growth in the employment of women combined with their continued responsibility for childcare to generate growing marital conflict. Both parents then sought greater emotional satisfaction in their relationship with their children. The emotional intensity of the family increased and, when divorce led to children staying with the mother, fathers felt all the more deprived.

They argued that the idea that wives now 'have everything', both a career and the children, has caused resentment in some fathers. Previously, fathers had been willing to allow 'non-working' mothers to have the children, as they would otherwise 'have nothing'. The growing insecurity of male employment added to this sense of injustice, as men found themselves ending up with neither jobs nor

After divorce who should get the child?
© Alice Chadwick

children. This led to the claim that 'true equality' should mean that, just as women are entitled to a career, men are entitled to the emotional satisfactions of parenthood. It was therefore an assertion of fathers' rights, in combination with a social-policy concern with absent fathers, which promoted a model of joint parenting after divorce.

Joint parenting may have been an advance but it was not sufficient to meet fathers' concerns and pacify the fathers' movement. It was claimed that men were still often excluded from contact with their children and that the courts were biased against men when arriving at access and residence decisions. It was also claimed that mothers benefited far more than fathers from state benefits after divorce. The Fathers 4 Justice organization called for children to be shared 'fifty-fifty' between parents, who should be given equal contact with children, and should share parental state benefits.

In response to a highly publicized campaign, the government promised in 2005 to improve child contact arrangements. The Courts would be given more power to deal with parents who flouted access orders—in other words to force mothers withholding access to fathers to obey the law. There would also be new funding for child contact centres. The call for equally shared contact, for 'shared parenting', was, however, rejected as not being in the interests of children.

Others have argued that too much attention has been paid to the demands of the fathers' lobby. It is said that only a very small proportion of fathers are refused access through courts or are then denied access by their ex-partners. It is also suggested that the real problem for families is not the exclusion of fathers but their failure to keep contact with their children and involve themselves in their childrens' lives. The strength and activism of the fathers' movement none the less indicates that there is a strong sense of grievance among some fathers.

Reconstituted families

Post-divorce parenting has been made more complex by the reconstitution of families after remarriage. These new families have been traditionally called stepfamilies, but are described as **reconstituted** (or hybrid) **families** today. This situation is by no means new, for the death of one parent led frequently to the reconstitution of families in earlier times. The contemporary reconstituted family is, however, new in two key respects.

First, the commonness of a divorce background means that reconstituted families are different in composition. Traditional stepfamilies generally took the form of the replacement of a dead or disappeared parent but the contemporary reconstituted family often involves the bringing together into one unit of children from different families after divorce or separation. In 2004–5, 10 per cent of families in Great Britain with dependent children contained one or more stepchildren, 81 per cent of whom were from the woman's previous family (*Social Trends* 2006: 28).

Secondly, the traditional stepfamily was an attempt to recreate a nuclear family which had lost a key member through death or separation. Stepfamilies sought to present themselves as no different from any other ordinary family. Increasingly, when marriages split up today, ex-partners are still around, maintaining some contact with their children, and taking part in their parenting. The reconstituted family cannot so easily present itself as a traditional nuclear family unit (Crow 2002).

Reconstituted families are generally regarded as experiencing additional tensions and problems. The marital relationship itself is likely to be less stable, as the divorce rate for second marriages is higher than that for first marriages. Children have to establish new relationships with step-parents and possibly step-siblings. They experience conflicts of loyalty between their parents and between parents and step-parents. Parents have to juggle feelings

and responsibilities between biological children and stepchildren. Ex-partners generally have access rights and the conflicts of the previous family may well re-emerge and cast a shadow over the new one. The process of working out all these relationships is a long and complex one (Robinson and Smith 1993).

This somewhat gloomy view of the reconstituted family has, however, been challenged. It has been argued that it compares stepfamilies with an idealized and unrealistic image of the nuclear family. It also neglects the advantages of the new kind of extended family created through remarriage(s) (see Figure 12.9 on p. 474). In such a family a child can draw on the support and resources of a greater array of relatives. Family life can be flexible and adaptable, with few fixed boundaries and an opportunity for considerable choice of relationships within the family network.

One policy response to these changes in parenting has been to defend, and try to revive, the traditional family, on the grounds that this is the only context in which proper parenting can take place. The alternative response is to accept the growing diversity of family life, recognize that there are positive aspects to other forms of the family, and provide appropriate support for the new kinds of family that are emerging.

Ethnicity and family diversity

Ethnic diversity due to increasing international migration is another source of family diversity. It is, however, important to bear in mind the diversity *within* as well as *between* ethnic groups, and to take account of change. Static stereotypes that exaggerate the differences between groups and ignore the diversity and change within them must be avoided.

We consider here both Caribbean and Asian family structures. In each case, we begin by outlining family structures in the area of origin and then consider how these have changed in the context of British society.

African-Caribbean families

The literature on family patterns in the Caribbean suggests that the lower-class Caribbean family is particularly centred on the role of the woman. Marriage is weakly institutionalized, men 'wander', and women commonly head households. Relationships between mothers and children are much stronger than those between fathers and children. Family life is held together by a network of women. Children are cared for through this network and women other than the biological mother often take on a mothering role (Elliot 1996; Berthoud 2000).

This pattern is certainly evident among those of African-Caribbean descent in Britain today. The rate of marriage

Frontiers A new form of the extended family

Figure 12.9 Jennie's extended family

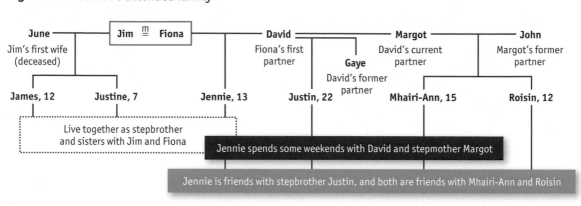

'Alongside the nuclear family of parents and their children, a new social organism is developing: the extended network of stepparents, stepchildren, cousins, aunts, uncles and grandparents. It is a grouping that is simply reflecting demographics, expanding and adapting to increased rates of divorce and remarriage. . . .

Take Jennie, 13, whose mother Fiona, 38 . . . separated from her partner David six years ago to marry Jim, 45. She now enjoys strong relationships with both sets of parents and their respective partners as well as various step- and half-relations across the country. For Jennie there have been many positive aspects to this complex merger of relatives and strangers.

"I like having this sort of family," says Jennie. "My mum seems much happier and so does my dad. I also feel I've got more people to support and care for me—I've always got lots of different relatives to visit and things to do".'

Source: Emma Cook, 'The Nuclear Family is Dead: Long Live the Extended Family', *Independent on Sunday*, 11 November 1996.

is low and lone-parent families are common (see Figure 12.10). It should not be thought that this is simply a matter of the persistence of an African-Caribbean culture, for this pattern is stronger among those born in Britain than it was among the first generation of migrants. Some have explained it in terms of increased black male unemployment and the assertion of black cultural identity, in response to patterns of racist exclusion.

Faith Robertson Elliot (1996) has linked the African-Caribbean family form to the high involvement of women in economic activity, their distinctive attitudes to work, and independence from men. African-Caribbean women have been more economically active than women from any other ethnic group. They see paid work as a basis for financial independence and are more likely to control the use of their earnings than Asian or white women. This high involvement in economic activity is, however, only made possible by the sharing of the mothering role with other women.

Asian families

Although there are considerable cultural differences between the various South Asian nationalities that have come to Britain, there are certain underlying similarities. Families from rural areas in South Asia typically take a more extended form. They include three generations in the household, and are organized through a network of males. They are also strongly bound together by beliefs in brotherhood and family loyalty. Marriages are arranged and seen as a contract between two families. This type of family structure contrasts strongly with both the contemporary nuclear family in Britain and the mother-centred African-Caribbean family.

Migration to Britain severely disrupted extended families of this kind and many women especially found themselves socially isolated at home and unsupported by kin. A period of dislocation was followed by the rebuilding of extended family structures. The family network was an important resource for the individual, as well as a source of identity, a means of maintaining cultural distinctiveness, and a defence against local hostility.

F. R. Elliot argued that South Asian communities have adapted to the British environment but according to 'their own cultural logic' (1996: 52). Sikh households have become more focused on couples and women have renegotiated traditional authority patterns through the greater independence paid work has given them. They were able to do this because Sikh religious traditions emphasized equality and allowed Sikh women a degree of independence (Bhachu 1988). In contrast, women from Pakistani and Bangladeshi cultures have been limited to homework or work in family businesses by the Islamic prohibition of contact with unrelated men. This can lead to the exploitation of women as cheap labour and their confinement within the home. They have, none the less, been becoming more assertive and influential within the family, and have also developed some independence through their own neighbourhood networks (Werbner 1988).

Marriage rates are very high (see Figure 12.10) and divorce rates are very low within the minorities of South Asian origin. Divorce is permitted under certain circumstances but strongly discouraged. This lower rate of divorce can be linked to the greater strength of communal and kinship bonds, to the patriarchal control of women by men, and the lower involvement of women in paid employment outside the family. There is evidence that the family life of young Asian couples has become more focused on the marital relationship and less involved with wider kin networks but that they still have a strong sense of obligation to the extended family (Elliot 1996).

Some commentators have pictured young Asians as caught between cultures and in conflict with their parents, particularly over arranged marriages. Ethnographic studies have, however, suggested that they have often been able to make compromises between cultures or find ways of combining them. Thus, they have accepted the institution of the arranged marriage but have become more involved in the arrangement process and have been allowed to defer the marriage until they have completed higher education. Conflict does clearly occur, however, particularly when arranged marriages are forced marriages and some young Asians have rejected their parents' plans, chosen their own partners, or engaged in secret relationships (Elliot 1996; Berthoud 2000).

The issues raised by forced marriages have recently attracted increasing attention. There has been a particular problem with British girls of Pakistani or Bangladeshi background being sent by their families to marry men in these countries, though it is not confined to girls. Foreign and Commonwealth officials have reported that in at least 15 per cent of the cases they investigate the injured party is male. These officials reported in 2004 that since 2000 nearly a thousand cases of this practice had been investigated by British government officials but these are, of course, only the ones that came to their attention. The police and social services have tried to mediate between girls and their families but it has been claimed that this can lead to girls finding themselves defenceless back in the families that have been pressurizing them (*Independent*, 25 March 2005).

Both the African-Caribbean and the various Asian patterns of family life originated in agrarian societies but first persisted and then developed in their own ways within British industrial society. As both are quite different from the standard nuclear family, their adaptation to life in an industrial society leads one to question Parsons' notion that the nuclear family is the form appropriate to an industrial society (see p. 450). They similarly show that family forms are culturally diverse and that the standard nuclear family is not really standard at all but just one cultural form that the family has taken.

Figure 12.10 Families with dependent children, by ethnicity and family type, UK, 2001 (%)

	Bangladeshi	Black (African)	Black (Caribbean)	Chinese	Indian	Pakistani	White
Married couple	79	44	32	79	85	78	63
Cohabiting couple	3	8	12	3	2	3	12
Lone parent	18	47	57	18	13	19	25
	100	100	100	100	100	100	100

Source: Social Trends (2006: 25).

❷ What evidence can you find in this table to support the points made in the text about ethnic differences in family life?

Work and money

The traditional family has also been challenged by changes in work patterns and we now move on to consider their impact on gender-roles within the family. We begin by discussing whether the growing employment of women has led to changes in the domestic division of labour, and then consider whether it has affected the management of money in the household.

> ⮕ *Connections*
>
> The discussion of the domestic division of labour should be placed in the context of changing employment patterns, which we examine in Chapter 5, pp. 179–81, and Chapter 17, pp. 705–7.

A changing domestic division of labour?

Changes in employment have challenged the rationale for a domestic division of labour, not only because of the growing employment of women in paid work, but also because of the declining employment of men. Does this mean that the domestic division of labour is coming to an end?

The domestic division of labour established in nineteenth-century Britain was gendered. It was a division of labour between the male *breadwinner* and the *housewife*, though this was not an absolute division. First, men did some household tasks. These too were gendered, for some tasks, such as gardening and house repairs, were defined as men's work, while others, such as routine cleaning and childcare, were defined as women's work. Secondly, many women did paid work, but this was regarded as secondary to their domestic work. It has often been said that women in this situation had to carry a **double burden** or work a 'double shift', because they were still expected to carry out their domestic work.

A 1990 study by Warde and Hetherington (1993) of households in the Manchester area showed that the domestic division of labour still operated. Housework was overwhelmingly done by women rather than men. There was also a clear division of household tasks between men and women. Women did the more routine cleaning, cooking, and childcare tasks. Men mainly did jobs such as home repairs, home improvement, car maintenance, and also various intermittent tasks such as brewing alcohol, cooking barbecues, and collecting takeaways. Weeding the garden appeared to be the only ungendered task.

This suggested that little had changed but, according to Jonathan Gershuny (1992), important changes have taken place. Gershuny used detailed diaries to measure the time spent by men and women on all their various daily activities, including housework and paid work. He argued that,

even though the distribution of housework was still far from equal, the proportion of housework done by men had been increasing and the *total* work done by men and women had become almost equal. If their total work was almost equal, it could not be argued that women carried an extra, 'double' burden.

Gershuny suggested that a process of lagged adaptation was taking place. There was inevitably a lag between women taking on paid work and households adapting to change but they did eventually adapt. His data showed that the longer that a woman had been in paid employment, the more equal had become the sharing of the total household workload. He argued that there was also a generational dimension to change, for children socialized in a changing household may be expected to acquire different conceptions of gender-roles, which they then practise later on in their own households.

Sullivan (2000) has used national time-budget data from different years to compare couples in 1975, 1987, and

Does a continued domestic division of labour mean that patriarchy continues?

© Alice Chadwick

Figure 12.11 Women's share of domestic work by employment status of partners, Great Britain, 1975, 1987, 1997

Employment status	1975	1987	1997
Both partners full-time	68	62	60
Husband full-time, wife part-time	80	70	69
Husband full-time, wife not employed	82	73	73
Other[a]	61	55	59
All	77	67	63

[a] This category consisted largely of couples with husbands either not employed or working part-time.

Source: Adapted from Sullivan (2000: 443, table 1).

1997. She found that women's share of domestic work had dropped overall by nearly a fifth between 1975 and 1997 (see Figure 12.11). A decline in their shares had occurred across all her employment categories, and in both working-class and middle-class households, suggesting that this was a very general social change. In all categories women, none the less, still did more domestic work than men in 1997. Her data also showed that the *more* that women were employed, the *lower* was their share of the domestic work, but also that the *less* that men were employed, the *more* they did at home.

Sullivan analysed this data to discover how many 'egalitarian' households there were in her various employment categories. She found that when both were working full time, the woman was doing *less than half* the domestic work in only 15 per cent of the couples in 1975, in 20 per cent of them in 1987, but in 32 per cent of them in 1997. Thus, by 1997, in a third of these couples the husband was doing more than the wife, though in two-thirds the wife was still doing more than the husband. Sullivan argued that her data indicated 'a general trend towards a more egalitarian domestic division of labour' (2000: 450).

Sullivan also put together the time spent in paid work and in domestic work to arrive at the total work contribution. She found that women's share of the total work-time was about 50 per cent in each of her three years, which broadly supports Gershuny's argument against the double burden, as it suggests that the total workload was equitably distributed. However, she also found that those women doing more than five hours of paid work a week, particularly those in full-time work, did do slightly more than 50 per cent of the total work. This provides some support for the notion of the 'double burden' carried by women in paid work, though Sullivan notes that these women were only working between 3 and 5 per cent longer than men, rather less than the amount suggested by other studies.

From this we may conclude that:

- the proportion of domestic work done by women has generally declined;
- women still do more housework than men;
- the amount of housework done by women is related to their employment status, and that of their husbands;
- the proportion of 'egalitarian' households has increased;
- there is, none the less, still some evidence to support the existence of a double burden.

Crompton, Brockmann, and Lyonette (2005) have carried out a comparative study of the domestic division of labour and attitudes towards it. They demonstrate significant and persisting international differences in the domestic division of labour between Britain, the Czech Republic, and Norway. Norway, with its Social Democratic welfare state, is the least traditional. The Czech Republic, which has been moving away from state socialism, is the most traditional. Britain lies somewhere in between.

By comparing data from national surveys in 1994 and 2002, this study develops an interesting argument on the relationship between attitudes and social change. Crompton *et al.* found that in all three countries *attitudes*, especially those of women, towards the domestic division of labour had become less traditional. The *actual* domestic division of labour had, however, changed much less in all three countries, indeed reverting towards a more traditional division in Britain (see Figure 12.12).

They argue that Gershuny's process of lagged adaptation has 'stalled', a result, they suggest, of an intensification of work pressures. As international competition increases and companies demand greater commitment from their employees, men in demanding careers are forced to devote more time and energy to their paid work. This stalling, at a time when women's attitudes were changing, is linked to

Figure 12.12 Households with traditional and non-traditional division of domestic labour (%)

	Britain		Czech Republic		Norway	
	1994	2002	1994	2002	1994	2002
Traditional	46	49	63	58	40	39
Non-traditional	54	51	37	42	60	61
	100	100	100	100	100	100

Source: Crompton *et al.* (2005: 217).

greater 'home life stress' among British and Norwegian women in households with a traditional division of labour.

There are a number of hidden issues in this whole discussion that need to be brought out. First, there is the problem of how housework is defined. Does this, for example, include gardening or car maintenance? Different conclusions will be reached according to the range of tasks included in a study.

Secondly, a focus on the amount of work done does not take account of its meaning. When men carry out an increasing share of housework, do they take on the boring routine jobs that are particularly soul-destroying? Or do they focus on intrinsically more interesting tasks, such as gardening, which could reasonably be considered leisure rather than work (see our discussion of these issues in Chapter 17, pp. 675–6)?

Thirdly, the listing of tasks takes no account of the hidden 'emotion work' that women do. Duncombe and Marsden (1995) carried out a study of forty couples who had been married for at least fifteen years. They found what they called a general 'gender asymmetry' in emotional behaviour. Men were reluctant to express emotions and the emotional labour of the household had to be done disproportionately by the women. It has been argued (see p. 450) that it is through the emotion work of the wife that the male breadwinner copes with the tensions generated by work in a capitalist economy. It has also been suggested that this additional emotion work means that women carry not a *double* but a *triple* burden.

Fourthly, married couples are not the only couples. As about a third of couples are in cohabitation relationships, and these will inevitably be, on average, younger couples, it would be interesting to know how the domestic division of labour operates here. There are also same-sex couples. Gillian Dunne carried out a study of lesbian couples and found that: 'the allocation of household tasks bore no relationship to the gender-segregated patterns that characterize dominant trends for heterosexual couples' (1999: 68).

Money management

The management of money is a key issue in most households. Studies of the distribution of tasks commonly find that this is one that is either shared or mainly done by women. Does this mean that women control household finances and that patriarchy is a myth?

Routine *management* of money matters does not necessarily mean *control* of money. It may, for example, mean sorting out how the 'housekeeping' money is spent, but not deciding how much is allocated to it. Furthermore, as Crompton points out, when income is low, sorting out the household budget may be 'more a chore than a source of power' (1997: 92). The statement that both partners are involved may also be quite misleading, for Pahl (1989)

found that when both were said to control finances, in practice it was the husband who made the major decisions.

Pahl (1993) identified four main ways of organizing household money in a randomly selected sample of 102 couples, who all had at least one child under the age of 16. The couples were sorted into the following groups according to whether they pooled their income in a joint bank account and according to the wife's response to the question 'Who really controls the money that comes into the house?'

- *Husband-controlled pooling* (39 couples). A joint account but the husband paid bills and checked the bank statement. This was typical of higher income groups where the wife was not in paid employment. If the wife had a job, it was one of lower status than her husband's or part-time.

- *Wife-controlled pooling* (27 couples). This was particularly common among middle-income groups, where both partners were in full-time paid work. The higher the wife's earnings and educational level, as compared with the husband's, the greater the wife's financial control.

- *Husband control* (22 couples). This occurred typically on the traditional model of a housekeeping allowance. The husband had his own bank account and gave his wife an allowance. The man was the sole or main earner.

- *Wife control* (14 couples). This was most commonly found in low-income families, where both partners were unemployed and household income came mainly from social-security payments.

Thus, women had most control when there was least to control. There was otherwise a clear relationship between the paid employment of women and the influence they had over household finances. A later study by Vogler and Pahl (1993) showed that the traditional practice of husbands giving wives a housekeeping allowance was in decline. This was probably related to increasing male unemployment. The relationship between employment and control over money shows how important employment is to power in the household.

Domestic violence and abuse

The established form of the nuclear family has also come into question because of an increasing awareness of what is often called the 'dark side' of the family. The family home is not only a place of comfort and affection but also a place where violence and sexual abuse occur.

Both family violence and sexual abuse have become major issues. There are three possible explanations and each may partly account for this.

- *Changes in behaviour.* The behaviour concerned has been increasing. This is the explanation that first springs to mind but it is by no means the only one.

- *The redefinition of behaviour.* Behaviour once considered acceptable or only a minor form of deviance has been redefined as unacceptable or serious. The beating of children or 'date rape' are examples of this.

- *Increasing awareness.* Unacceptable behaviour that was previously concealed has come to light. There has been a process of rediscovering and investigating the 'dark side' of the family since the 1960s.

Child abuse and child protection

The problem of separating out changes in behaviour from changes in attitudes and reporting applies to both the physical and sexual abuse of children. It must be emphasized that there is little agreement about what constitutes 'abuse', that conceptions of this vary and change (see Corby 2000 for a discussion of the definitional issues).

Violence against children is certainly nothing new, but it is only since the 1960s that it has been treated as physical abuse. Corporal punishment and firm discipline within the family had long been considered essential to the maintenance of social order. In the 1960s, however, the 'battered-baby syndrome' was discovered, and in 1973 the death of Maria Colwell at the hands of her stepfather led to a public inquiry that established child abuse as a problem. The work of professionals in medicine and childcare was clearly important in bringing child abuse to light, but Hendrick (1994) has argued that it became a major issue because ideological conflict was increasing at that time.

The Colwell case was used by the New Right to highlight the dangers of permissiveness and moral decline.

The *reported* abuse of children increased rapidly in Britain during the 1980s. The number of children on child protection registers in England and Wales increased from a rate of one per thousand children in 1984 to four per thousand in 1991, then dropping back to three per thousand in 1999, largely it seems because of changes in registration procedure and the faster removal of cases from the register. New registrations continued to rise during the 1990s (Corby 2000: 88–9). Clearly, with rates of this kind small changes in reporting and definition can have a big impact. The publicity given by the media not only to the Maria Colwell case but to a number of other tragic cases at this time could well have impacted on this.

The discovery of the physical abuse of children was followed shortly by the discovery of sexual abuse. Historical data on rates of sexual abuse are more available for the United States than for Britain. In the United States there was an increase of 71 per cent in reported cases during the three years 1976–9, an increase so great over such a short period that it could only be due to changes in reporting or definition (Russell 1986: 75). There is, however, some American evidence of a long-term increase in the sexual abuse of children (see box on 'Child sexual abuse in the United States).

Varying definitions of sexual abuse certainly have an enormous effect on reported rates. F. R. Elliot (1996: 156) points out that different definitions have resulted in estimates of its prevalence in Britain ranging from 3 to 46 per cent of children. A key issue here is whether non-contact offences, such as exposure or obscene telephone calls, are included.

Controversy and debate Child sexual abuse in the United States

Diana Russell (1986) carried out a study of sexual assaults through a survey of 930 women in San Francisco in 1978. Women of all ages (aged 18 or above) were interviewed and rates of abuse could therefore be established for women born from the early years of the century up to the early 1960s. Russell concluded that rates of both incestuous and non-familial child sexual abuse had increased fourfold between 1909 and 1973. Instances of incestuous abuse amounted to 16 per cent of the total reported child abuse. There were, however, problems with the representativeness of these findings, as 36 per cent of those approached refused to participate.

Why had child sexual abuse increased in this way? The main explanations suggested by Russell related to changes in sexual behaviour and gender relationships. She pointed to the increasing availability of child pornography and the permissiveness generated by the sexual revolution of the 1960s. She also suggested that a reaction against women's demands for sexual equality might be involved. Women's challenge to male power deflected men towards children as sexual objects, for children were dependent on adults and less able to resist their demands. This is consistent with the generally accepted explanation of child sexual abuse as due to the availability and vulnerability of children rather than their sexual attractiveness.

In Britain there was an upsurge of concern with the sexual abuse of children within the family during the 1980s. This was clearly connected with the high publicity given to a series of cases in Cleveland. In 1987, 545 complaints of child sexual abuse were referred to Cleveland Council and action was taken in 265 cases to protect the children involved. Social workers advised by doctors using new techniques of diagnosis removed a large number of children from families suspected of child abuse. According to Rodger (1996), the main reason why these cases caused so much shock was that they involved apparently normal middle-class families that were conventionally regarded as immune to such problems. Studies have shown that abuse is equally likely to be found in all social classes (F. R. Elliot 1996: 160).

There was a very public conflict in Cleveland between the police, on the one hand, and social workers and doctors, on the other. The police rejected the medical evidence of sexual abuse and refused to act on it. Gittins (1993) has interpreted this as a conflict between a patriarchal police force denying the existence of child sexual abuse, which is mainly carried out by men, and social services seeking to protect children. Media coverage largely took the side of the police, and social workers found themselves heavily criticized by the media and politicians. They were, in fact, under attack from two different quarters, for failing to protect children and for overzealously removing them from their families. There was simply no agreement between the various professions involved about how much abuse had actually been occurring.

There has subsequently been a shift towards a more legalistic and formal system of child protection. Rodger has claimed that social work became more bureaucratic and defensively concerned with rules and procedures in order to avoid criticism. It has also focused increasingly on the investigation and surveillance of families rather than family support. He argued that a concept of the 'dangerous' family has replaced notions of the 'vulnerable' or 'troubled' family (Rodger 1996: 188). There has, indeed, been a tendency for the state to intervene increasingly in family matters, to concern itself with the health and behaviour of children, and the adequacy of parenting.

There is no real way of knowing whether child abuse has increased or whether there is simply greater awareness of it. It is clear from all this that the greater publicity given to child abuse and policy towards it have little to do with child abuse itself and much to do with changes in professional interest, ideology, and politics. We do, however, now have much better information on the amount of violence and abuse of British children, from a recent NSPCC (National Society for the Prevention of Cruelty to Children) survey, which is reported in Study 12 at the end of this chapter.

Marital violence and coercion

Attitudes towards violence between husband and wife have also changed markedly in Britain since the 1960s. Feminism has here played a crucial part in exposing the hidden violence within marriage and rejecting the idea that it is simply part of normal married life. The creation of women's refuges was an important practical consequence of the new attitude towards domestic violence.

Changes were made in British law during the later 1970s to provide greater protection for women. Housing rules were changed so that women leaving home because of male

---

 ## Briefing: marital rape

Marital rape is a key issue in the study of changing attitudes to domestic violence. This is because marital rape was until recently not treated in most countries as a crime. Indeed, it was regarded as a legal impossibility. The law assumed that men were entitled to sexual intercourse whenever they wished it, while married women were required by their marriage vows to obey men. In the United States the law on this point was changed in most states by 1990. In Britain, it was not until 1991 that a House of Lords ruling established that rape could occur within marriage.

Diana Russell carried out a pioneering study of marital rape, using material from the same 1978 survey that she used for her study of child sexual abuse (see box on 'Child sexual abuse in the United States'). Definitions of rape vary from the narrow legal definition of forced intercourse to the much broader notion of forced sexual activity of any kind. Russell adopted an intermediate definition that included forced oral and anal sex and forced digital penetration as well as intercourse. She found that 14 per cent of the married women in her sample reported that they had experienced rape or attempted rape by a husband or ex-husband (Russell 1990: 57, 67).

Marital rape, as defined in this way, has been regarded as but one form of sexual coercion. Some feminists have argued that there is a continuum from entirely mutual sexual acts to rape, which then becomes a somewhat arbitrary line drawn across the continuum at a certain point. Indeed, Russell argued that 'much conventional sexual behaviour is close to rape' (1990: 74). Twenty-six per cent of Russell's sample reported some kind of 'unwanted sexual experience' with their husbands, and interviewers then had to probe further to establish whether this experience fell into the study's definition of rape.

violence were no longer regarded as making themselves homeless and therefore losing the right to council housing. New laws gave women greater legal protection against violent husbands through injunctions that could be issued quickly by magistrates and followed by imprisonment if breached.

Action through the courts has, however, proved difficult, because of women's dependence on their men, fear of the consequences of taking them to court, and an unwillingness to testify against them. Courts have also had a reputation for treating men leniently and not imprisoning them for acts of domestic violence. To address this situation, the Home Office awarded funding in 2000 for twenty-seven projects designed to reduce domestic violence. Special Domestic Violence Courts have been established and domestic violence awareness training has been introduced for magistrates, prosecutors, and defence lawyers (*Independent*, 8 June 2005).

The focus on husbands' violence against wives has been challenged. A national survey carried out in the United States in 1985 by Straus and Gelles (1986) showed that women were, in the domestic situation, at least as violent as men. The most common situation involved violence by both parties but, after this, violence by women against men was more common than violence by men against women. Even in the severe-violence category, wives were violent more often than husbands (see Figure 12.13). Straus and Gelles argued that these findings were supported by a number of other studies.

A recent survey in Britain apparently demonstrated, however, that domestic violence is overwhelmingly the violence of men against women. A survey of all police forces in the United Kingdom found that on one day in September 2000 there were 1,300 reports of domestic violence. Of these, 81 per cent involved a male attacking a female. Only 8 per cent were attacks by females on males.

Attacks by females on females accounted for 4 per cent and males on males 7 per cent (*Independent*, 26 October 2000).

There are also data from the 2001 British Crime Survey. Here, 6 per cent of women and 4.5 per cent of men reported that they had been subject to non-sexual domestic violence (abuse, threat or force), during the past year. The figures for severe domestic force alone were 1.6 per cent of women and 1.2 per cent of men (Walby and Allen 2004: 14). These figures do indicate that men are more violent than women in the domestic situation but nothing like the extent suggested by the 2000 survey of British police forces.

How are these very different conclusions to be reconciled? One explanation lies in the method of investigation used. Archer has reviewed eighty-two different studies of 'inter-partner aggression' in Western societies. He found that studies based on *reports* showed that women were more often the victims but *social surveys* showed that men were more often the victims. Surveys also showed that this was not because women were in some way acting in 'self-defence', as has often been argued, since women were at least as likely as men to initiate the violence. The discrepancy is explained by women being much more likely than men to report violence to the police.

The kind of information collected about the violence is also crucial. James Nazroo (1999) studied ninety-six couples in Britain. He too found that there were significantly more attacks by women on men than by men on women, and this was the case even with severe acts of violence, but when he looked at how dangerous the acts were, he found a very different situation. Men were far more likely to engage in dangerous violence with an intention to harm, while women were more likely to be seriously injured. Violence by men was also more likely to be continuous and repeated and there were higher levels of anxiety about violence among women.

Nazroo's study was not nationally representative but the advantage of his in-depth approach was that he was able to probe into the character, meaning, and consequences of violence. His findings also point towards an explanation of the higher rate of reporting by women, and are consistent with the well-known fact that far more women than men are murdered.

Research has, then, revealed not only that there is much hidden violence towards women in Britain but that there is also a hidden violence towards men that has attracted far less attention. This does not, however, detract from the view that it is the violence towards women that is the more serious problem, as its consequences are more serious.

This area is a difficult one to investigate but there is no doubt that research has revealed a 'dark side' of family life. The inward focus of the nuclear family and its characteristic isolation of family life from wider kin and community networks have hidden violence and abuse from public

Figure 12.13 Marital violence in the United States, 1985 (per 1,000 couples)

	Husband and wife	Wife-to-husband	Husband-to-wife
Overall violence	158	121	113
Severe violence	58	44	30

Notes: Acts of severe violence were: kicked, bit, hit with fist; hit, tried to hit with something; beat up; threatened with gun or knife; used gun or knife. Overall violence included minor acts as well: threw something; pushed/grabbed/shoved; slapped or spanked.

Source: Straus and Gelles (1986: 470).

Global focus Domestic violence across the globe

According to a United Nations Population Fund report, 'violence against women is a pervasive yet under-recognized human rights violation' that takes many forms: the infanticide of unwanted female children; suicides following domestic violence; rapes, sexual violence, and prostitution; genital mutilation; so-called 'honour' killings.

In many countries domestic violence towards women has been considered legitimate, and often by the women themselves. Thus, a survey in Ghana found that 43 per cent of men and nearly half of women considered that wife-beating was justified if a woman used a family planning method without her husband's consent. In Egypt many women in rural areas thought that beatings were justified if women refused to have sex with their partners.

The report claimed that 'honour' killings, when girls and women were murdered, usually by family members after supposed infidelity or immoral behaviour, often after being raped, were on the increase. They had been reported in Bangladesh, Brazil, Ecuador, Egypt, India, Israel, Italy, Jordan, Morocco, Pakistan, Sweden, Turkey, Uganda, and the United Kingdom. They most commonly occurred in Muslim communities and countries.

Source: United Nations Population Fund (2000).

❷ Should domestic violence against women be considered a universal feature of human society?

view. Furthermore, the growing emotionality of family relationships as the nuclear family developed may well have created an emotional intensity that finds expression in greater violence and abuse. Those who believe in 'family values' face the problem that the very form of the family that they defend may also be the one most likely to generate behaviour that violates other widely held norms and values.

Stop and reflect

This part of the chapter has been concerned with the recent transformation of family life. We began by considering the sexual revolution and changes in marriage.

- Since the sexual revolution of the 1960s the relationship between sexual behaviour and marriage has been changing.

- The rate of marriage has been falling as people increasingly live on their own or cohabit, and the divorce rate has risen.

- Does this mean that marriage is in decline?

We then considered changes in parenting.

- Parenting has become increasingly separated from marriage.

- What have been the consequences of this for family life?

A growing ethnic diversity has been another source of family change in Britain.

- Consider the implications of ethnic diversity for the different perspectives on the family examined earlier (see pp. 473–5).

We then moved on to the domestic division of labour, and the management of the household.

- There have been some changes in the domestic division of labour but it nonetheless persists.

- Do women have more say in money matters nowadays?

- Do women in paid employment still carry a 'double burden'?

Lastly, we examined the 'dark side' of family life.

- In this area it is very important to distinguish between changes in behaviour, the redefinition of behaviour, and the increasing awareness of behaviour.

- There has been a growing concern with child abuse and domestic violence.

- Do studies of domestic violence show that women are as violent as men?

Chapter summary

In the 'Understanding family lives' section we considered different approaches to the study of family life.

We first discussed the definitional and theoretical issues raised by 'the family':

- The politicization of the family makes it difficult to arrive at an agreed definition.
- Some consider it preferable to refer to 'families' and 'family practices'.
- We distinguished between family, household, and wider kinship network, and discussed the nuclear and extended forms of the family.

We also discussed different approaches to the study of the life course:

- Families involve relationships between people at different stages of life, who are also moving through these stages.
- The concept of a 'life course' is preferable to 'life cycle', because the latter implies a biological sequence of stages.
- The notion of stages has itself been challenged but still has a reality in people's lives.

In the 'Development of family life' we examined the development of the nuclear family and changes in the life course.

We began by considering the nuclear family:

- Family relationships became increasingly emotional as the nuclear family developed.
- The nuclear family emerged before industrialization, though industrialization further separated home from work and male from female spheres.
- Extended family relationships remained an important means of support and became stronger as stable working-class communities became established.
- Housing relocation during the 1950s and 1960s, along with other social changes, further isolated the nuclear family.

We then considered changes in the life course and their impact on intergenerational relationships:

- Childhood, youth, adulthood, and old age became established as distinct stages during the nineteenth and early twentieth centuries.
- As multi-generational families became more common, families became vertically rather than horizontally extended.

- The family became increasingly burdened with the care of older generations, though the old also helped to care for the young.

In 'Family life in transformation' we discussed recent challenges to the standard nuclear family.

We began by considering the sexual revolution and changes in marriage:

- The sexual revolution of the 1960s changed attitudes to both unmarried sex and sex in marriage.
- The rate of marriage has declined and cohabitation has increased, though cohabitation often leads to marriage.
- Divorce rates have risen but so has the rate of remarriage.

We then moved on to consider changes in parenting:

- Parenting has become increasingly separated from marriage.
- This has led to rising numbers of single-parent families, post-divorce conflicts over children, and the reconstitution of families after remarriage.

A growing ethnic diversity has been another source of family diversity:

- African-Caribbean backgrounds are associated with households headed by women.
- Asian backgrounds are associated with strong extended family networks.
- Divorce rates in Asian families are lower but there has been a growing concern with the practice of forced marriages.

We then considered the effect of the growing employment of women in paid work on home life:

- The domestic division of labour and the double burden have persisted, though there is evidence of changes in attitude and some adaptation of households to the employment of women.
- Men more commonly control household finances than women, but control of money is related to employment and employed wives have more financial control.

The standard nuclear family has also been challenged by a growing awareness of the 'dark side' of family life:

- There has been a growing concern with child abuse and the legal protection of children.
- There has also been a growing awareness of domestic violence by men against women, though there is also much evidence of violence initiated by women.

🔑 *Key concepts*

- cohabitation
- cohort
- custodial parenthood
- domestic division of labour
- double burden
- extended family

- family
- generation
- household
- joint parenting
- kinship
- life course

- nuclear family
- patriarchy
- post-adolescence
- reconstituted families
- serial monogamy

Workshop 12

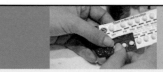

Study 12 The extent of child abuse

Reliable information about the amount of violence and abuse experienced by children is very hard to come by. Most information is from official sources and is based on cases reported to the authorities. As families are secretive about such sensitive matters—child abuse can lead to criminal prosecutions, social worker interventions, and the removal of children—data from such reports are bound to underestimate the size of the problem. There are also well-known problems with official statistics (see Chapter 3, pp. 102–3, where we discuss these issues).

We now have much better information about the situation in Britain from a national study carried out by the NSPCC and reported in *Child Maltreatment in the United Kingdom* (Cawson *et al.* 2000). This was based on a national probability sample of households and achieved a response rate of 69 per cent. The sample consisted of 1,235 men and 1,634 women aged between 18 and 24. This age group was interviewed because of the difficulties involved in interviewing children themselves but it did mean that there would be problems of recall, particularly with incidents in early childhood. The restriction of the study to people living in households, the response rate, and recall problems meant that the amount of abuse would be under- rather than overestimated.

It was found that a total of 24 per cent had experienced physical abuse of some kind from parents or carers. This figure was broken down into the following categories:

Serious physical abuse	7%
Intermediate physical abuse	14%
Cause for concern	3%
Total	24%

In making sense of these figures, definitions are clearly crucial. *Serious physical abuse* was defined as the use of violence that either caused injury, or carried a high risk of doing so if it continued, and regular violent treatment. Such actions as choking, scalding, hitting with fists or objects, and violent shaking came into this category. *Intermediate physical abuse* either involved occasional violence that did not cause injury or regular physical treatment resulting in 'pain, soreness or marks lasting at least a day'. Regular smacking or slapping, if it left marks or caused pain, would be intermediate abuse. The '*cause for concern*' category referred to less serious physical maltreatment that occurred regularly and indicated 'problems in parenting or the quality of care which could escalate or lead to continued distress' (2000: 34–5). The category a respondent fell into was determined not by self-assessment but by the researchers' evaluation of the information provided by the respondent.

There are clearly many problems with these categories. They combine both the severity of the action and its frequency. The movement of the boundaries between them through small changes in definition would produce a different picture. It was considered important, however, to carry out some form of grading, since a global figure, covering everything from really serious injury to regular smacking, would not be very meaningful on its own. The global 24 per cent figure did, none the less, indicate that almost a quarter of the child population at least sometimes experienced treatment in their families that 'breached the standards shown by previous research to be accepted by over 90 per cent of the population' (2000: 37).

There were many other interesting findings on physical abuse. The person responsible was most often the mother (49 per cent of cases) rather than the father (41 per cent), though this is no doubt largely explained by mothers' greater responsibility for childcare. Physical abuse appeared to be related to class, with 12 per cent of social grade DE respondents coming into the serious abuse category, as compared with 7 per cent of C1s, 5 per cent of C2s, and 4 per cent of ABs. Girls (8 per cent) were more likely than boys (6 per cent) to have suffered serious abuse.

This study not only dealt with physical abuse but also covered emotional and psychological maltreatment and was, indeed, the first UK study of the incidence of this in the general population. The problems of studying this are clearly even greater than those of studying physical abuse, where more objective indicators, such as physical damage, can be used. The approach taken was to identify from the literature the following seven dimensions:

- Psychological control and domination, including attempts to control the child's thinking and isolation of the child;
- Psycho/physical control and domination, that is, physical acts that control by causing distress rather than pain or injury;
- Humiliation/degradation, including verbal and non-verbal attacks on sense of worth or self-esteem;
- Withdrawal of affection and care, including exclusion from the family or from benefits received by other children;
- Antipathy by showing marked dislike by word or deed;
- Terrorizing by threatening the child, or someone or something loved by the child, or making the child do something frightening;
- Proxy attacks on someone or something loved by the child or valued by the child.

A score was produced for each respondent. The maximum possible score was 14 but 7 was taken as a cut-off point indicating

serious emotional maltreatment. Six per cent of respondents had scores of 7 or above. The most common maltreatment was terrorizing, which was experienced by a third of children, while a quarter had experienced extreme psychological domination, and almost a fifth had suffered from psycho/physical domination and humiliation.

Data were also collected on sexual abuse. This was defined as any of the following:

- Acts involving a parent or carer;
- Behaviour against the respondent's wishes;
- Consensual sex with someone other than a parent who was five or more years older when the child was aged 12 or under.

Some 16 per cent of respondents reported acts of sexual abuse, though only 1 per cent reported abuse by a parent or carer, and 3 per cent abuse by another relative. Girls were more likely than boys to have suffered sexual abuse by a *parent* or *carer* but there certainly were reports from boys, though numbers were too small for any generalizations to be made. It was, however, nearly always a male parent who was responsible. Class differences in abuse rates were minimal. Definitions are crucial and if 16, the legal age of consent, rather than the age of 12 had been put into the definition, much more sexual abuse would no doubt have been reported.

This is just a brief summary of a major study and does not do justice to the amount of data it provides, the complexity of the issues, and the methodological discussion. This study also reports on other aspects of maltreatment, such as neglect, and contains very useful reviews of the literature and a bibliography. Further reports based on this survey are available from the NSPCC.

Source: Cawson, P., Wattam, C., Brooker, S., and Kelly, G. (2000), *Child Maltreatment in the United Kingdom: A Study of the Prevalence of Child Abuse and Neglect* (London: NSPCC).

❷ What problems are involved in seeking to establish the extent of child abuse?

❷ How can each of the problems that you have identified be expected to affect the results?

❷ Should child abuse be considered a normal feature of family life?

Media watch 12 The family in 2020

The recent transformation of the family has attracted much media attention. In 'Family fortunes', Madeleine Bunting has reflected on these changes for *The Guardian* and projected them forward to the year 2020.

She argues that four of the tendencies that we have examined in this chapter—increasing cohabitation, divorce, births outside marriage, and single parenthood—will continue. This will mean that 'the brittle nature of the core relationship between the parents' will be accepted as a 'general rule of family life' in 2020. It is not the trends that will change but attitudes towards them, as the new ways of life resulting from them become socially acceptable.

Parental relationships are, however, becoming stronger and more important. Bunting claims that 'the major characteristic' of the twenty-first century family is the charging of the parental relationship 'with a much greater intensity, commitment and pleasure'. Parenting is not just a matter of bringing up children but a process to be enjoyed in its own right for its own sake, and by fathers as well as mothers. Furthermore, the longer financial dependency of children, as more go through an increasingly expensive higher education and property prices rise, means that 'parenthood is well on its way to becoming a minimum 25-year deal'.

Families will be far more diverse in 2020, with more single-parent families and complex reconstituted families after separation/divorce and remarriage. This diversity does not, however, mean that the family is breaking down or in decline but rather that it is undergoing a process of 'reinvention'. People value family life as much as ever but the traditional family unit has been taken apart and the bits reassembled as people have 'adapted family structures in line with their aspirations to autonomy, self-definition and emotional integrity'.

The number of single-person households is, however, steadily increasing. More people live on their own. There are more childless women. Couples often no longer live together in the same households. Bunting suggests that this means that for a substantial minority of people family relationships will not be as important in their lives as friendship. There will be a greater reliance on friends than on family for help with the crises of life. This will leave some, particularly the old, in a vulnerable position, with loneliness and depression becoming more common.

This links to what may be the most difficult problem for the family in 2020—a 'care deficit'. Increasing longevity, old people living on their own, and the rising costs of medical and nursing care are making care a huge burden. Women used to be responsible for care in the family but 'the transfer of their labour from the family to the paid economy has opened up a care deficit'. This is made worse by the lengthening of hours of work.

Does new technology offer a solution? The new communications technologies of the internet, e-mail and mobile telephones can help family members stay in contact but cannot solve the problem of care. Care requires carers and it is not clear where they will come from in 2020. The declining birth-rate in European countries will make this problem worse. Either carers will have to be paid more or the gap will have to be filled by migrant labour.

Source: Bunting, M. (2004), 'Family Fortunes', *Guardian*, 25 September.

❓ What is meant by the 'brittle nature of the core relationship', the 'greater intensity' of parenting, and the 'reinvention' of the family?

❓ Are families becoming a matter of choice rather than biology?

❓ Is friendship replacing family?

❓ Do you think that the family will be a weaker institution in 2020?

➲ Revisit our discussion of what the term 'family' means on pp. 446–8. and consider the usefulness of our definition.

Discussion points

Domestic violence

Before discussing this, read the section on 'Domestic violence and abuse' and Study 12.

- Should domestic violence include acts of physical violence only or also verbal and emotional violence?
- Does it make sense to refer to domestic violence in general?
- Can domestic violence be defined objectively or is it a matter of how actions are viewed by those involved?

- How does one know when an act of domestic violence is taking place?
- Why has domestic violence and abuse become considered a problem?
- Is it because violence has increased, norms and values have changed, or awareness has increased?
- Are males as much a victim of domestic violence as females?
- Does the gendering of violence vary between societies?
- Has the gendering of violence changed over time?

Is the family in decline?

Before discussing this read 'Families and family practices', 'Contemporary debate', 'Family life in transformation', and Media watch 12.

- It is important to be clear about what you mean by 'the family'. What problems are there in defining it?

- Should we not worry about definitions and simply study 'family practices'?

- How important is marriage to the family?

- Does increasing cohabitation mean that the family is in decline?

- Does a higher divorce rate mean that the family has declined?

- What is the significance of the registration of civil partnerships for the institution of marriage?

- Consider the increasing diversity of family life. What forms has this growing diversity taken?

- Does this diversity indicate the decline of the family or its vitality?

- Are the bonds of friendship replacing those of the family among young adults?

- Are people born into families or can they choose them?

Explore further

The following provide general discussions of the nature of the family and family life:

Allan, G. (1999) (ed.), *The Sociology of the Family* (Oxford: Blackwell). *A standard and comprehensive reader on the family, with important and interesting contributions on key contemporary issues.*

Allan, G., and Crow, G. (2001), *Families, Households, and Society* (Basingstoke: Palgrave). *Provides useful and up-to-date coverage of the issues of diversity and change in the family, focusing particularly on the family and the life course.*

Elliot, F. R. (1996), *Gender, Family, and Society* (Basingstoke: Macmillan). *A detailed and comprehensive review of the literature on recent changes in the family, focusing on ethnic differences, unemployment, ageing, violence and sexual abuse, and AIDS.*

Gittins, D. (1993), *The Family in Question: Changing Households and Familiar Ideologies* (2nd edn., London: Macmillan). *A critical examination of the gulf between the ideology of 'family values' and the realities of family life, which challenges the whole idea of 'the family' and argues that only 'families' exist.*

Morgan, D. H. J. (1996), *Family Connections: An Introduction to Family Studies* (Cambridge: Polity Press). *Not so much an introduction as a thoughtful discussion of current issues in the sociology of the family, arguing that it should be studied through the notion of 'family practices'.*

For further reading on specific topics, see the following:

Barrett, M., and McIntosh, M. (1991), *The Anti-Social Family* (2nd edn., London: Verso). *A classic critique of the family.*

Berthoud, R. and Gershuny, J. (2000), *Seven Years in the Lives of British Families* (Bristol: Policy Press). *This is an invaluable source of information on social change in the family, based on annual interviews with 10,000 adults.*

Carling, A., Duncan, S., and Edwards, R. (2002) (eds.), *Analysing Families: Morality and Rationality in Policy and Practice* (London: Routledge). *A collection of pieces on different aspects of family life, dealing with a range of policy issues, and focusing on the interplay of rationality and morality.*

Chapman, T. (2004), *Gender and Domestic Life: Changing Practices in Families and Households* (Basingstoke: Palgrave Macmillan). *Moves beyond 'the family' to consider domestic practices in a range of households, including single-person, gay and lesbian, and communal households.*

Dench, G., Gavron, K., and Young, M. (2006), *The New East End: Kinship, Race, and Conflict* (London: Profile Books). *Updates the classic Bethnal Green study of the family and raises fundamental issues concerning the interrelationships between change in the family, the welfare state, ethnicity, and politics.*

Ferguson, H. (2004), *Protecting Children in Time: Child Abuse, Child Protection, and the Consequences of Modernism* (Basingstoke: Palgrave Macmillan). *A sophisticated examination of the development of child protection policy and practice that draws on the 'risk society' ideas of Giddens and Beck.*

Heath, S., and Cleaver, E. (2003), *Young, Free and Single?: Twenty-somethings and Household Change* (Basingstoke: Palgrave Macmillan). *Brings the life-course literature up to date and relates it to contemporary debates by very clearly reviewing the literature on 'post-adolescence' and presenting the results of a survey of young adults.*

Hockey, J., and James, A. (2003), *Social Identities across the Life Course* (Basingstoke: Palgrave Macmillan). *A re-conceptualization of the life course, which examines the interaction between structure and agency, assesses the post-modern perspective, and emphasizes the embodiment of identity.*

James, A., Jenks, C., and Prout, A. (1998), *Theorizing Childhood* (Cambridge: Polity Press). *This book brings together the new ideas on the sociology of childhood that were developed in a number of important projects and publications during the 1990s.*

Pilcher, J. L. (1995), *Age and Generation in Modern Britain* (Oxford: Oxford University Press). *A clear and thorough account of changes in the life course, examining all its stages and discussing the relationships between generations.*

Silva, E. and Smart, C. (1999) (eds.), *The New Family?* (London: Sage). *This collection pushed out the frontiers on the family with contributions that challenge established views of it both within society and within sociology.*

Online resources

Visit the Online Resource Centre that accompanies this book to access more learning resources and other interesting material on family and the life course at:

www.oxfordtextbooks.co.uk/orc/fulcher3e/

The Institute of Economic Research at the University of Essex carries out research into families and households and is particularly well known for its longitudinal and life-course studies. Electronic versions of publications and papers are available at:

www.iser.essex.ac.uk/

Information about the University of Leeds Centre for Research on Family, Kinship and Childhood and its research activities can be found at:

www.leeds.ac.uk/family/

The Centre for Research on Families and Relationships (CRFR) is a collaborative venture between Glasgow Caledonian University, and the Universities of Aberdeen, Edinburgh, and Glasgow. Information about its research and publications is available from:

www.crfr.ac.uk/

cities and communities

Contents

13

Dubai: a global consumer city

In Dubai, a global city of consumption is emerging from the desert. Since Dubai lacks the oil and gas reserves of neighbouring states, investment is going instead into hotels, shopping malls, apartment blocks, theme parks, artificial islands, and tourist attractions, and into the transport facilities required to bring in goods and people.

Dubai, located midway between Europe and the Far East, is at the heart of a rapidly growing and global communications network. The Dubai-based Emirates airline has ordered forty-two Boeing 777s, the biggest order that Boeing has ever received. Dubai Ports has acquired port facilities all over the world and in 2006 bought P & O, the British shipping and ports company, awakening fears in the United States that this would give an Arab corporation control of American ports.

Huge construction projects have drawn in migrant labour. There is a labour force of some 250,000 workers, mainly from India and Pakistan. They are closely controlled and crammed into shared accommodation in camps. There were reports in 2005 and 2006 of strikes, demonstrations, and riots by construction workers complaining about low pay and exploitation. According to Adam Nicolson (2006), it would cost one of these workers the equivalent of six months' wages to buy one night's stay in one of the luxury hotels. As Nicolson has put it:

> This is the Dubai sandwich: at the bottom, cheap and exploited Asian labour; in the middle, white northern professional services, plus tourist hunger for glamour in the sun and, increasingly, a de-monopolized western market system; at the top, enormous quantities of invested oil money, combined with fearsome social and political control and a drive to establish another model of what modern Arabia might mean in the post-9/11 world.

Source: A. Nicolson, 'Boom Town', *Guardian*, 13 February 2006.

As the example of Dubai shows, cities are dynamic places, changing the world and constantly changing themselves. Capitalism drives this urban dynamism as the ceaseless search for profit transforms the urban landscape and urban society by revolutionizing production and consumption. Cities are also the control centres of the global capitalist economy, the location of transnational corporation headquarters and the financial markets that move capital around the world. We begin this chapter by examining the changing relationship between cities and capitalism.

What, however, is it that makes the city distinctive? How is urban society different from rural society? Can one speak, as the sociologist Louis Wirth argued, of an 'urban way of life' or are there many different ways of life that coexist within the city? Have the differences between life in the city and life in rural areas largely disappeared as both are shaped by the dynamics of consumer capitalism? We

move on to examine different approaches to the distinctiveness of urban society.

According to some urban sociologists, social isolation and the absence of community were the distinctive features of urban society. Others have, however, claimed that strong communities *can* form in the city, indeed that city life actually creates the conditions in which people are able to form certain kinds of community. The strength of community has been one of the main issues of urban sociology and we take this up at various places in this chapter. We also consider whether globalization is leading to the decline of local communities and the rise of virtual ones.

Social change in the city has taken new directions in recent years. As cities grew they developed a centralized structure and acquired a local state that provided urban management and public services for their residents. More recently, major economic activities have been decentralized to the city's periphery and city centres have changed their character, while the local state and public services have been subjected to processes of privatization. The structure of this chapter is shaped by a contrast between the processes of centralization and decentralization, of the growth and decline of urban management.

Changes in the city are most obvious in its buildings, in the new clubs and bars of the inner city, or the new retail and leisure complexes along the motorways that ring it. These changes in buildings are, however, closely connected with changing relationships between people. In this chapter we examine the changing relationships in the city between classes, sexes, and ethnic groups. We discuss increasing inequality and rising violence. In the changes of the city we see in concentrated form the changes that have been taking place in society as a whole.

Understanding cities and communities

In this section of the chapter we examine and discuss sociological approaches to the study of the city. We begin by outlining the ideas of those who set the development of the city in the context of the rise of capitalism. We go on to consider the debate on the differences between urban and rural life, which leads us to the study of community, and the debates around this.

Capitalism and the city

The development of capitalism has been the driving force behind the growth of the city, while the city has played a key part in the rise of capitalism. If we are to understand the dynamism of the city and the character of urban society, we must first examine the relationship between capitalism and the city.

This relationship was central to Max Weber's work on the city. To Weber (1923), the *medieval city* was 'a fusion of fortress and market'. It was there that the markets central to the rise of capitalist economies were first established, in the context of emerging legal and political institutions that protected property, established the rights of citizens, and gave merchants and craftsmen the stability and security they needed to engage in their economic activities. The independence of the city was crucial too, for this allowed capitalism and citizenship to emerge within a feudal society hostile to both. This is where the fortress came in, for political independence depended on military security.

A network of independent cities provided a framework for the early development of international capitalist trading in Europe but these early cities did not maintain their leading economic and political role. Although the medieval European city created favourable economic and political conditions for the growth of capitalist *trading*, these later inhibited the capitalist transformation of *production*. This occurred outside the city, for detailed guild regulations in the cities protected traditional crafts and new forms of production could be more easily established elsewhere. Cities also lost their independence as they fell under the control of the developing political and administrative structures of the nation state. These changes were symbolized by the dismantling of medieval city walls, which marked the city's subordination to the modern state and its incorporation within a national economy.

> **⊃ Connections**
> You may find it helpful here to refer to Chapter 16, p. 628, where we examine the rise of the nation state, and Chapter 17, pp. 671–2, where we discuss capitalism and industrialism.

Capitalist production led to industrialization and the emergence of a new kind of city, the *industrial city*, in the nineteenth century. It was this growth of the industrial city that resulted in the urbanization of society, that is in the emergence of the first societies that were predominantly urban in character. Industries employed large numbers of people and became the centres of new concentrations of population that were far greater in size than the older cities dating from medieval times.

The industrial city was quite different from the medieval city. The medieval city was shaped by the contours of the land, for its streets and walls followed the land's shape. In a capitalist society urban land was not just ground that was suitable to be built on but had a market value. Land was bought and sold. As Lewis Mumford (1961) emphasized, the spatial patterns of the capitalist city were not *dictated* by the shape of the land but were *created* by a market in land. And re-created, for cities have been involved in a constant process of restructuring as developments in production, communication, and consumption have changed property values and altered land use.

Industrial capitalism shaped the city not only through these economic transformations of its physical structure but also through the changing relationship between capital and labour. This aspect of the city was explored by Manuel Castells, who argued that capitalism could function only if the employer was provided with an educated, healthy,

Figure 13.1 Capitalism and the city

Type of city	Relationship between capitalism and the city
The medieval city	• Cities as early centres of capitalist trading • Citizenship and self-government • Military and political independence • European economy controlled by a network of trading cities
The industrial city	• New centres of industrial production outside the medieval city • Growth of industrial cities shaped by capitalism • City incorporated by nation state • Growth of collective consumption
The consumer city	• Cities reshaped by investment in means of consumption • Cultural restructuring • Marketing of city image • Increasing employment in production of services and images
The global city	• Cities as control centres of emerging global economy • Empires administered by imperial cities • In the post-colonial world, global cities are headquarters of TNCs and manage the global flow of money • New network of cities outside national control

and housed labour force that was able to work (Castells 1977). Employers, if they were to make profits, could not bear the costs of providing these services themselves. The costs were, therefore, increasingly borne by the state through what Castells called **collective consumption**. By this he meant that the education, health, and housing consumed by labour were not obtained from the market on an individual basis but collectively provided by the state, largely through local authorities in cities. Labour movements played an important part in forcing the state to provide these services.

As services were expensive to provide, the rising costs of collective consumption led eventually to urban crisis and political conflict. In the 1970s, cities cut back on services and came into conflict with political movements struggling to maintain them. Castells believed that collective consumption was essential to the maintenance of capitalism, and saw no way out of this crisis but in the 1980s public services were privatized and consumption was individualized, a process that we examine in 'City management in decline'.

Out of this process emerged the *consumer city*. Central areas of the city had always been devoted to consumption but towards the end of the twentieth century cities were reshaped as capital flowed into the construction of shopping malls, peripheral stores and leisure facilities, new pubs and clubs in city centres. Cities began to market themselves as centres of consumption that attracted consumers and tourists from whole regions, indeed from other countries, as travel became easier and cheaper. The image of the city became all-important, and cities engaged in 'cultural restructuring' (see pp. 525–6) to maximize their attractiveness. Consumer capitalism had produced the consumer city (Miles and Miles 2004).

This does not mean that urban production had become a thing of the past. The production of goods was in decline but the production of services was growing and providing increased employment. Furthermore, as the cultural aspects of city life became more important, the production of culture increased. A decline in the production of goods should not be confused with a decline of production in general, for the services and images consumed in the city all have to be produced. Consumer cities are still full of employees engaged in production, in producing services and images (and goods too). These expanding areas of production are, however, more directly and immediately related to consumption, and the shape of the city is determined more by the requirements of consumption than the requirements of production.

One group of cities, *global* or *world cities*, have come to play an increasingly important part in directing the development of the world economy. In their first guise, the global cities were imperial cities that administered colonial empires. Now they are financial centres that manage the flow of money and investment around the world. The headquarters of transnational corporations (TNCs) are located in them. They form a new urban network that directs economic forces that have an enormous impact on national economies but are largely outside the control of the nation state. Indeed, Saskia Sassen (2001) has argued that global cities have become in many ways detached from national economies. We examine the rise of global cities on p. 511.

The independence of the medieval city enabled the emergence of an early form of capitalism within it but cities lost their independence with the rise of the nation state, while capitalist production initially developed outside them. New industrial cities eventually grew up that were shaped by industrial capitalism, class conflict, and state intervention. The growth of individualized consumption then reshaped cities into centres of consumerism. With the rise of a network of global cities, the city has, however, regained some of the directive autonomy that it had in much earlier times.

Consumer city—why
have stores moved
to the periphery?
See p. 511.
© Lucy Dawkins

Urban society

The new cities of the nineteenth and twentieth centuries presented a sharp contrast to the predominantly rural societies in which they emerged. How different was the social life of the city from the social life of rural areas? And is it still different?

The urban way of life

Louis Wirth (1938) has made the most well-known attempt to identify the differences between urban and rural life. He saw the defining characteristics of the **city** as:

- the large size of its population;
- its high population density;
- its social diversity.

These features of the city resulted in a quite distinctive **urban way of life**, though Wirth was careful to emphasize that the city's influence on surrounding areas meant that this way of life was found to some degree outside the city. The large and dense population of cities resulted in a high division of labour. People performed specialized roles and this meant that social relationships were segmental and secondary.

Relationships were **segmental** because people did not know each other as rounded individuals and saw only the segment or section of personality related to a person's role as, say, shop assistant or employer. This contrasted with rural society, where people knew about many different aspects of each others' lives and had all-round relationships that were not limited to particular roles.

The term 'secondary' referred to a distinction made by Charles Cooley (1909), another member of the Chicago school of sociology, between *primary* and *secondary* groups. **Primary groups** involved face-to-face interaction, of the kind found in the family or among friends. **Secondary groups** were much larger associations in which relationships were distant and impersonal, as in organizations, such as factories, unions, or political parties, where the

---

members of the organization did not all know each other as individuals.

According to Wirth, urban society was weakly integrated. City-dwellers had frequent but brief and superficial encounters with many different people rather than enduring relationships. Their involvement in the organizations that dominated city life was limited to the task or activity concerned. Thus, although people were crammed together, they felt isolated and 'on their own', a feature of city life also emphasized by Simmel (see box on 'The mental life of the city'). This weak integration meant that city life was unstable and social order was liable to break down. People living in cities were more likely than those living in rural areas to suffer mental breakdowns, commit suicide, or become victims of crime. Weak integration and instability also meant that city-dwellers were easily manipulated by politicians and the media.

Urban diversity

Wirth's notion of a distinctive urban way of life was criticized by Gans (1968). He argued that Wirth focused too much on the inner city and ignored the majority of the urban population who lived in quite stable communities which protected them from the worst consequences of urban living. He also argued that there was not just one way of life in the city. Five different ones could be distinguished.

- *Cosmopolites.* Students, artists, writers, musicians, entertainers, and other intellectuals and professionals,

---

THEORY AND METHODS

The mental life of the city

In a famous essay with this title, Simmel explored the individualism of city life and its consequences.

Simmel argued that in cities endless variety and constant change result in a continuous stimulation of the senses that leads to an 'intensification of emotional life'. People protect themselves against an intolerable level of excitement by becoming detached, reserved, indifferent, and *blasé*. This means that, although they are physically very close in 'the metropolitan crush of persons', they are also distanced from each other emotionally. They can experience a more intense loneliness in the city than anywhere else.

In the city individualism becomes extreme. The only way to stand out from the mass of people and establish a distinct identity is to be different, and a person's distinctiveness has to be highly visible if it is to register with people in a world of brief and fleeting contacts. As Simmel put it:

> This leads ultimately to the strangest eccentricities, to specifically metropolitan extravagances of self-distanciation, of caprice, of fastidiousness, the meaning of which is no longer to be found in the content of such activity itself but rather in its form of 'being different'—of making oneself noticeable. (Simmel 1903, in Levine 1971: 336)

➲ Next time that you are in the centre of a city, look around and see whether you can identify in people's appearance and behaviour 'the mental life of the metropolis'.

'Making oneself noticeable' in the city?
© iStockphoto.com/TerjeBorud

who chose to live in the city for cultural and educational reasons. Insulated from city life by their subcultures, they had no wish to be integrated and were detached from the neighbourhood they lived in.

- *The unmarried and childless.* The geographically mobile, who lived in areas of high population turnover and were not interested in local services because of their stage in life. They too had little interest in the neighbourhood in which they lived, did not seek local ties, and did not suffer from social isolation.

- *Ethnic villagers.* Groups with a common ethnic background. Heavily reliant on kinship and the primary group, they were little involved with secondary associations and lived outside the formal controls of society in highly integrated communities that identified strongly with their neighbourhood.

- *The deprived.* The poor, the emotionally disturbed and handicapped, single-parent families, and people experiencing racial discrimination. Forced to live in deprived areas with the cheapest housing, they did suffer from social isolation.

- *The trapped.* Old people on small pensions, or the downwardly mobile, who had been left behind when others moved out to the suburbs and had to continue to live in an area after its character had changed. They had lost their social ties and they too suffered from social isolation.

Of these five ways of life, only two, the *deprived* and the *trapped*, experienced the social isolation that Wirth saw as typical of urban life. Gans argued that ways of life depended not so much on people's urban or rural location as on their class situation and stage in life. He concluded that there was no such thing as 'an urban way of life' and also nothing distinctive about suburban life either (Gans 1995). The age of an area and the cost of its housing had a greater bearing on the characteristics of the people who lived in it than its location.

Giddens (1981) too has rejected Wirth's idea that there is a distinctive urban way of life. He argued that there were sharp differences between urban and rural society at the time of the pre-capitalist city but modern capitalism has eliminated them. Whether people live in the city or the countryside makes little difference, for capitalism has transformed both. What really matters is that they sell their labour to an employer in return for a wage. They then buy similar goods with these wages and live a similar lifestyle. It is wage labour, not where they live, that shapes most people's lives.

In a short essay Wirth had provided a coherent, wide-ranging, and forceful analysis of urban life that has been highly influential but also much criticized. Although he mentioned some of the positive sides of city life, notably the greater choice, freedom, and tolerance it provides, the image he presented of it was, on the whole, negative and emphasized its loneliness, insecurity, and superficiality. There was an anti-city bias in Wirth's approach that reflected a widely found nostalgia in industrial societies for the life of the rural village.

Community

Louis Wirth believed that city life was incompatible with community. A contrast has, indeed, been commonly drawn between the integrated communities of rural society and the isolation of the individual in the city. It has also been argued, however, that this contrast is misleading, that city life is perfectly compatible with community, while plenty of conflict can be found in supposedly integrated rural communities.

Urbanism and community

Wirth followed in the steps of the nineteenth-century theorists who contrasted traditional communities with the urban industrial society they saw emerging around them. The best-known exponent of this view is Ferdinand Tonnies, who distinguished between community (*Gemeinschaft*) and association (*Gesellschaft*).

According to Tonnies (1887), in *communities* there were strong and emotional bonds of unity based on kinship and sustained by close, personal relationships within a small population. In contrast, *associations* were characterized by rational and impersonal relationships between isolated individuals. These relationships were typical of business enterprises and large populations, such as those of the industrial city or the nation state. While custom ruled in communities, relationships were regulated by contract and law in these larger groups and organizations. In communities there was a strong emotional attachment to the place where people lived but this was absent in the city. The distinction made by Tonnies between community and association corresponded closely to Wirth's distinction between primary groups and secondary associations.

But is urban society so hostile to community life? Gans demonstrated that communities of what he called 'ethnic villagers' could be found in American cities. Young and Willmott (1957) showed that a strong working-class community still existed in Bethnal Green in 1950s London (we discuss the working-class community on p. 505).

Indeed, it can be argued that urban life actually enables the formation of communities through a process of

Figure 13.2 Rural integration and urban isolation

	Rural integration	Urban isolation
Ferdinand Tonnies	Community	Association
	• Emotion	• Reason
	• Unity	• Individuality
	• Custom	• Contract and law
	• Loyalty to place	• Non-attachment to place
Louis Wirth	Ruralism	Urbanism
	• Primary group	• Secondary association
	• 'All-round' personality	• Segmental roles
	• Personal relationships	• Impersonal relationships
	• Integration	• Isolation and disorder

Figure 13.3 Changing views of the relationship between cities and communities

Communities and cities incompatible	Wirth, Tonnies
Communities do exist in cities	Gans, Young and Willmott
Cities facilitate formation of communities	Fischer
Social isolation is none the less a feature of city life	Savage and Warde

gravitation. Fischer has claimed that cities allow thinly spread minorities, such as artists or students, to gravitate together and produce a 'critical mass' that enables them to establish 'thriving social worlds' (1975: 1326). This kind of argument can also be applied to ethnic or religious minorities, who in cities can form communities that would be impossible to create in rural areas or small towns, where such minorities would be individually isolated and excluded.

Mike Savage and Alan Warde (2002) have, none the less, argued that the presence of communities in cities has been overstated. They suggest that those studying communities have found evidence of social integration partly because they were looking for it. They neglected isolated people, who are inevitably less visible and more difficult to contact. Furthermore, people move through many different situations in their daily lives and can sometimes behave as members of a community but at other times experience social isolation. In other words, people's involvement in a city community does not mean that they live their whole lives within it.

What is community?

The debate over the impact of the city on community raises the issue of what we mean by community. This term has been given many different meanings and used in countless different ways, often loosely to refer to any group assumed to share a common way of life, as in references to the diplomatic community or the black community, or simply to those who live in the same place, the local community. These everyday usages should be distinguished from the use of the term in sociology, where it indicates that a group has certain sociological characteristics.

While sociological definitions themselves vary in their emphasis, they do share certain common features. A **community** may be said to have the following characteristics:

- *Common situation.* Those living in a community will share some common feature that binds them together. This may be their place of residence, but may also be their class, their ethnicity, their religion, or some other feature. A distinction is commonly made between *residential* and *non-residential* communities.

- *Common activities.* Communities involve all-round relationships between people. They are all-round in the sense that they are not limited to work, or politics, or sport, or any other single activity but extend into most areas of life.

- *Collective action.* People have some sense of a common interest, and may well organize collective action in pursuit of this common interest. Thus, those living in a particular place may organize action to prevent a road being built through it or to raise money for a community centre.

- *Shared identity.* There is a sense of belonging to a distinct group that has an identity. With this identity goes a certain emotional charge, a feeling of belonging to a larger unit and some loyalty to it.

Definitions are important not only for what they contain but also for what they leave out. In the above definition, we deliberately make no reference to *integration* or *place*, which are commonly seen as characteristics of community. This is because there has been much argument over their links with community and we will now examine the issues they raise.

The classic discussions of community assumed that communities were unified or integrated. This was particularly considered to be the case with rural communities. Those who have studied rural society have often found high levels of conflict, however. Frankenberg (1966) found plenty of conflict in the Welsh village that he studied in the 1950s. One example of this was the conflict within the village football committee over whether outside players, who would increase the team's strength but diminish its local character, should be selected. The conflict in the committee was apparently settled by resignations but then spread into the wider community, as those who had left sabotaged the committee's actions. Eventually the conflict became so intense and widespread that village football collapsed and village interest switched to other activities. These went through the same cycle of intensifying conflict followed by collapse. There was no apparent end to these sequences, though some of the people involved were driven out of the village or left.

Thus, features of the community that are commonly thought to produce integration actually generated a conflict that weakened it. The emotionality of community life, its frequent face-to-face contacts, and the multiple connections between those involved made conflict more intense and harder to resolve through avoidance or compromise. In the end village unity could only be maintained by 'adopting an enemy, real or imagined, outside' (Frankenberg 1966: 273).

It is also commonly assumed that communities are identified with places. The classic community studies certainly demonstrated the importance to many communities of a sense of place. This is a feature of most residential communities, but there are also non-residential communities whose members do not live in the same place.

The significance of spatial location has been particularly questioned by those who have studied social networks. One of the features of the city is that ease of travel enables the creation of network communities spanning large areas. Communities can be constructed that are not tied to a particular locality. In the city, community relationships can be liberated from the constraints of place. They do not even require face-to-face contact. The invention of the telephone enabled the creation of voice-to-voice networks well beyond the confines of the city. The ultimate liberated community is provided by the spatially unlimited *virtual communities* of the Web, which we discuss on pp. 518–19.

William Flanagan (1993) has emphasized that people who live in an area where there is a residential community may not be a part of that particular community. Their particular social network may connect them more strongly with people in other parts of the city, or nation, or world. The cosmopolites identified by Gans provide a good example of this. Global communications and extensive international migration, which mean that local people may hardly figure in some social networks, have made this more true than ever before.

There are strong arguments for moving away from the old *container* idea of community to a *network* conception of it. The container idea saw communities as consisting of all those who lived within certain geographical boundaries. They were seen as members of that community, who belonged to it. People's social relationships are not, however, actually contained in this way and extend across such boundaries. Some living in a particular place may have minimal connections with locals and may well be in networks that span the globe (Crow and Allan 1994).

If we adopt a network conception of community, these problems can be overcome. A network conception allows for greater openness, for individuals' varying connectedness with a particular community, and for a person to be a member of multiple communities. It also makes room for the approach to community developed by Gerard Delanty (2003), who advances the view that individuals actively construct communities through communication with others as they search for meaning and a sense of belonging in a meaningless and fragmented world.

A network conception of community is still perfectly compatible with the idea of a local community. A local community can be said to exist when many local networks overlap to produce a high local density of social relationships. Thus, the concept of community is liberated by a network conception from the restrictions of place, for communities can exist that are not bound together by their location, but the important idea of the 'local community' can be retained. The existence of locally networked communities in particular places can be recognized, though there is no assumption that all those living in the place are involved in the community network.

Socioscapes

The rather different concepts of 'socioscape' and 'sociosphere' have been put forward by Albrow *et al.* (1997) as a way of describing local relationships in the contemporary city. A study of the London area of Tooting showed that many of those living there were members of networks created by global migration. They were part of an 'imagined community' based on a global network that was non-spatial in character. Furthermore, different networks coexisted within the same area without coming into much real contact with each other. There was no local community as such.

Albrow uses the term **sociosphere** to refer to the separate worlds of those living in such an area, worlds which may be based on very different structures, from the relics of traditional communities to global networks. Some people may have an almost entirely local life, while others may be, what Gans called, cosmopolites (see p. 495). But however global their networks are, all do, none the less, have a local existence, where 'their sociosphere touches the earth', for everyone lives somewhere. The lack of local contact between those who live in a place means, however, that there is no local culture of the kind described by the classic studies of local communities. People use the locality in many different ways, according to their needs, but pay little attention to each other.

> They live stratified existences, just as airliners operate in different air spaces according to the length of their journeys and cross each other's path at different heights in co-ordinated but unconcerned ways. (Albrow 1997: 53)

The sociospheres intersect in a **socioscape**, a concept derived from Appadurai's (1990) term 'ethnoscape'. An ethnoscape is a space that people *pass through* rather than *live in*, much as tourists pass through a landscape rather than settling in it, experiencing it from the perspective of their own worlds. People similarly pass through a socioscape, carrying with them their own very different worlds. Since they live in the area, they do also, however, interact on a regular basis, for they have established routines and ways of getting on with each other that enable them to coexist, though their interactions do not produce anything as substantial or as stable as a local culture or community. The term 'socioscape' refers to these regular but superficial interactions.

These are interesting concepts, which try to get to grips in an innovative way with the interaction between the

> **Connections**
> The relationship between the global and the local is a central issue in the discussion of socioscapes and we discuss this in Chapter 16, pp. 624–5.

global and the local in particular places. The researchers clearly felt that established notions of the 'local community' could not grasp the social realities of the areas they were investigating. The absence of a local community of this kind does not, however, mean that the people living there were not part of a community at all. People may interact locally in a socioscape but still be members of, say, a religious or ethnic community network, which could well stretch across countries and continents.

For and against community

Why, you might ask, has there been so much concern with community? Built into much of the literature is the idea that communities meet deep human needs for integration, identity, and mutual support. Tonnies and Wirth, for example, clearly believed that community life was desirable and held negative views of the city because they thought that city life was incompatible with it.

A belief in community is still very much alive today. It is found, for example, among architects and planners who want to reconstruct our cities in ways that would revive local communities. The ideal of the community has also recently experienced a revival in the *communitarian* movement associated with the American sociologist Amitai Etzioni. Such ideas have struck a chord with the British government, eager to promote social inclusion and local participation (see box on 'Community spirit' on p. 500).

Communitarianism advocates the strengthening of community structures so that people will take a shared local responsibility for what happens to them (Etzioni 1995). Those who take this view are opposed to fashionable neo-liberal beliefs in individual freedom and responsibility but equally opposed to the left-wing idea that the state should bear responsibility for people's welfare. They argue that people should take a collective, mutually supportive responsibility for each other's well-being through the institutions of the local community. It is these institutions that should mediate between the individual and the wider society.

It might seem that, like apple pie and motherhood, no one could be against community, but Richard Sennett has

A socioscape—what social interactions are taking place here?
© Lucy Dawkins

Controversy and debate Community spirit

Until recently the government's enthusiasm for community was unabating. After the election, David Miliband was appointed the first cabinet minister with communities in his job title. After the London bombings on July 7 . . . the picture has darkened. Communities may be seedbeds of extremism, places where malign values are nurtured. 'Community leaders' may endorse beliefs and behaviour that threaten the wider community.

So wrote David Walker in *The Guardian* in 2005. As he also pointed out, ministers might insist that 'there is a rich seam of untapped activism out there, people panting to get more involved' and might 'give them decisions to make about bins, bollards, and the siting of bus stops. . . . But what if the people wanted to decide more exciting things such as if a hospital should stay open or a school [be] put into special measures?'

Community spirit is generally regarded as desirable and constructive but actual communities also have another side to them. They can generate social conflict, encourage unacceptable behaviour, or indeed obstruct government policy, though this may not necessarily be a bad thing. . . .

Source: D. Walker, 'View from the Top', *Guardian*, 27 July 2005.

❓ Should community spirit be encouraged or discouraged?

> **➔** *Connections*
>
> Communitarianism needs to be placed in the context of neo-liberalism and different approaches to social policy, which we discuss in Chapter 15, pp. 587–9. There are many similarities between this movement and the pluralist approach to politics, which we examine in Chapter 20, pp. 838–9.

written a powerful critique of the community ideal. He argued that communities are based on a belief in sameness, that 'people feel they belong to each other, and share together, because they are the *same*' (Sennett 1973: 40). This belief leads to conformism, an intolerance of difference and deviance, and the risk of violent confrontations with other communities. It can result in the dangerous myth of what Sennett calls the 'purified community'. These dangers have been particularly great where a community has defined itself in terms of a shared religion or shared racial characteristics.

To Sennett, communities were an immature adolescent response to the uncertainties and insecurities of life. He believed that people had to come to terms with their differences and conflicts, and learn to deal with each other in an adult way. This could happen only if they had frequent contact with many different kinds of people. He condemned any attempt by planners either to construct communities or zone activities in ways that would reduce contact between those who were different. To him, the great thing about cities was that they made such contacts possible through their high population density and their diversity. Thus, Sennett celebrated exactly those aspects of city life that Wirth criticized.

In some people's minds the word 'community' may conjure up images of harmonious village life, but in the minds of others it may be associated with racism and ethnic cleansing.

Stop and reflect

We began this section by considering the relationship between the development of the city, capitalism, and industrialism.

- Cities played a key role in the development of capitalism, which then became the driving force in the later development of the city.
- Are cities now shaped by consumption rather than production?

We went on to consider the distinctiveness of urban society.

- Make sure that you understand the following terms: urban way of life; segmental relationships; primary and secondary groups; cosmopolites and ethnic villagers.
- Also make sure that you are familiar with the main arguments of Simmel, Wirth, Gans, and Giddens on this issue.
- Consider whether urban life has distinctive characteristics.

We then discussed the issues raised by community.

- We argued that the features of community were a common situation, common activities, collective action, and a shared identity.

- Can you identify any communities in the area where you live? What makes you think that they are communities?

- Are communities desirable?

Urbanization and centralization

Cities are constantly changing but the structures of the past are still evident in the contemporary city. A knowledge of the development of the city is therefore essential for an understanding of the present day city. In this section we outline the process of urbanization in Britain, the growth of large, centralized cities, and their characteristic structures. We also discuss the ecological approach to the analysis of these cities and examine the impact of urbanization on class, ethnicity, and gender. We go on to consider the creation of the 'managed city' through the development of local state structures.

Urbanization

The term **urbanization** is used in two ways. In the broadest sense of the term, it means the growth of cities and this began with the earliest known civilizations. It was not until the eighteenth and nineteenth centuries, however, that urbanization, in its second sense of a shift of population from rural to urban areas, really got under way. It is with urbanization in this second sense that we are concerned here.

Industrialization and urbanization

Industrial capitalism turned Britain into a predominantly urban society by the second half of the nineteenth century (see Figures 13.4 and 13.5). It was not only that Britain had become a predominantly urban society, it was also that the new industrial cities were so much larger than their predecessors. Leaving aside London, which we discuss below, the five largest cities in early eighteenth-century Britain—Bristol, Exeter, Newcastle, Norwich, and York—had populations of under 20,000 but by 1851 Liverpool had 376,000 inhabitants, Manchester 303,000, and Birmingham 233,000. There had been an urban as much as an industrial transformation of Britain.

Industrialization led to urbanization not only because of the building of factories but also because it resulted in new patterns of travel and leisure, which contributed significantly to urbanization. In the second half of the nineteenth century the spread of the railways led to the growth of Swindon, Crewe, York, and Derby as railway centres. There was also another kind of urban growth

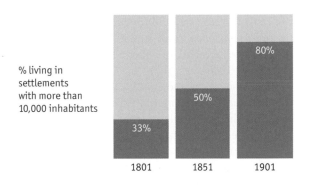

Figure 13.4 The urbanization of British society 1801–1901

% living in settlements with more than 10,000 inhabitants

Source: Lawless and Brown (1986: 18).

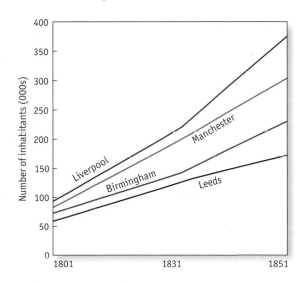

Figure 13.5 The growth of the British industrial city, 1801–1851

Source: Lawless and Brown (1986: 14).

Figure 13.6 The rise of the seaside resort, 1851–1911

Resort	1851	1911
Bournemouth	700	78,000
Blackpool	4,000	60,000

Source: Lawless and Brown (1986: 14).

associated with the railways—the rise of seaside resorts (see Figure 13.6). Railways made it possible for workers to reach the coast for days out and longer holidays, which both became a regular feature of people's lives as distinct periods of leisure were created (see Chapter 17, pp. 688–90) (Lawless and Brown 1986).

It is also important to emphasize that in many parts of the world an urbanizing industrialization still goes on. In China the industrialization of the area around Hong Kong has led to the construction of a new industrial city, Shenzen. This is part of a growing conurbation of some 30 million people, which Byrne has described as 'the world's largest industrial metropolis' (2001: 24).

Imperialism and urbanization

Urbanization was not just, however, the result of industrialization and any account of the urban transformation of Britain must deal also with the growth of London (see Figure 13.7).

In 1500 London already had a population of some 60,000 and by the mid-eighteenth century this had risen to 750,000—well before industrialization had made much progress. Trade was at the heart of London's growth, and something like a quarter of London's population depended on port employment in the eighteenth century. During the nineteenth century employment in financial and administrative, as well as trading, activities grew rapidly. By the mid-1930s London and its suburbs contained eight million people, about a fifth of the British population. London had by then become a major industrial city but its growth had been driven mainly by its role as a global centre of trade and finance.

Hong Kong—in China an urbanizing industrialization continues.
© Getty Images/Paul Chesley

A hierarchy of cities provided a network of control for the overseas empires that divided up the world during the nineteenth century. It also established the framework within which a global process of urbanization took place during the nineteenth and twentieth centuries. The colonial cities became the 'mega-cities' of the ex-colonial states during the later twentieth century.

> **⊃** *Connections*
>
> The process of globalization, the dividing-up of the world between empires, and the urbanization of ex-colonial territories are examined in Chapter 16.

Thus, while industrialization has certainly resulted in urbanization, it is important to see this as a broader and global process that was generated by the growth of both a world economy and colonial empires.

The centralized city

We now turn to examine the structure of the large cities produced by urbanization. After considering the specialized structure of the city, we discuss the ecological approach to its study, and then examine the processes of ethnic, class, and gender segregation that took place within it.

Differentiation and centralization

As cities grew, areas within them became functionally specialized in different activities. The term *differentiation* is often used to describe this process of specialization. Thus, particular areas became devoted to factories, shopping, leisure, finance, and housing. Commercial and industrial activities were concentrated in the centre and residential areas spread outwards to the edge of the city and beyond. Residential areas themselves became differentiated by their class or ethnic composition.

The growing size and area specialization of cities generated problems of coordination that led to centralization, as centrally organized services and local government developed with important planning and regulatory functions. A local state apparatus emerged in nineteenth-century Britain to manage and control the life of the city (an aspect of the city that we take up in 'Managed cities', pp. 506–9).

As cities spread, residential suburbs were built at some distance from the city centre. The growth of suburbs might suggest that a process of decentralization was also taking place. There is some truth in this, as suburbanization involved a decentralization of population from overcrowded central areas. Suburbs were, however, by their very nature part of a centralized structure. They were tied

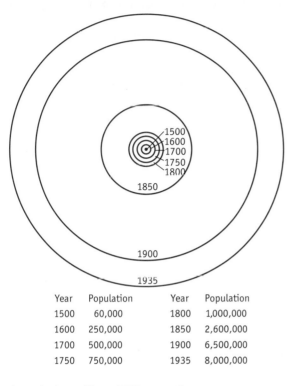

Figure 13.7 The growth of London, 1500–1935

Year	Population	Year	Population
1500	60,000	1800	1,000,000
1600	250,000	1850	2,600,000
1700	500,000	1900	6,500,000
1750	750,000	1935	8,000,000

Source: Lawless and Brown (1986: 6, 14, 18).

London's global role was closely linked to its position at the heart of the world's largest overseas empire, and this was reflected in its still highly visible imperial buildings. During the early twentieth century the area around Trafalgar Square and the Strand was rebuilt to accommodate the administration of the Empire with the opening of Australia House (1914), India House (1924), Canada House (1925), Africa House (1928), and South Africa House (1933). In the inter-war period companies based on imperial trade, such as ICI, Shell, and Unilever, built impressive corporate headquarters on sites along the Thames. The growth of other British cities too, such as Bristol and Liverpool, Glasgow and Dundee, was based on the import and processing of raw materials from the Empire.

Imperialism was linked not only to urbanization in Britain but also to urbanization in its colonial territories. Anthony King (1990: 33) distinguished three types of colonial city:

- the *metropolitan capital*, such as London or Paris;
- the *colonial capital*, such as Delhi or Canberra;
- the *colonial port or regional capital*, such as Calcutta or Hong Kong.

to the city centre by transport networks, for this was where employment, services, leisure facilities, and shops were mainly concentrated.

The process of area differentiation was first systematically studied by sociologists working in Chicago during the period from the 1910s to the 1930s. They mapped out the specialization of the various areas of the city by activity and residential group (see Figure 13.8). Prominent members of this group were Ernest Burgess, Robert Park, and Louis Wirth.

Their approach is commonly described as **urban ecology**, because of their use of an ecological model of the city derived from biology. Note that this approach is labelled ecological not because of its members' concern with preserving the natural environment but because they treated the city as though it was such an environment. They argued that specific social groups colonized areas, just as specialized plant forms occupied particular habitats in the natural environment. These groups then competed for dominance, in the same way that natural species competed for habitats, and areas periodically changed hands.

One example of this process was the competition between ethnic groups or classes for possession of an area. Another was the conflict between business and home-owners over the use that should be made of an area. The Chicago sociologists focused particularly on the invasion by business interests of the innermost residential areas around the central business districts of cities. This created what they called a zone of transition. As this invasion made the inner city less attractive to residents, those who could move out did so, leaving an area of decline occupied by the poor, and marginal and deviant groups. This area was seen

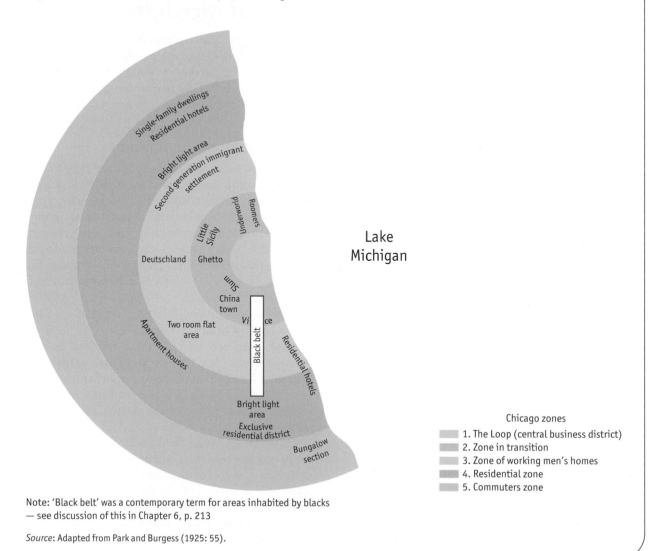

Figure 13.8 The zones of the metropolis: Chicago in the 1920s

Lake Michigan

Chicago zones
- 1. The Loop (central business district)
- 2. Zone in transition
- 3. Zone of working men's homes
- 4. Residential zone
- 5. Commuters zone

Note: 'Black belt' was a contemporary term for areas inhabited by blacks — see discussion of this in Chapter 6, p. 213

Source: Adapted from Park and Burgess (1925: 55).

as particularly exemplifying the disintegrated character of urban life, as described by Louis Wirth (see p. 493).

Processes of area specialization, and changes in the use and social composition of areas, have undoubtedly been important aspects of the development of urban society. The biological assumptions of urban ecology have, however, been strongly criticized as inappropriate to the analysis of social behaviour. In nature, if one species is better adapted to a particular environment, it will force out other, less well-adapted, species. Thus, grey squirrels have gradually pushed out red ones in most of Britain. But in a city there may be successful local resistance to invasion, for people can organize to keep out the invaders. Furthermore, local politicians and planners may well intervene and control changes in the occupation and use of areas, as we will now show.

Ethnic competition

John Rex and Robert Moore (1967), in their well-known study of race relations in Birmingham, found the ideas of the Chicago school useful, especially the notion of competition for areas and the concept of a zone of transition. Their analysis also demonstrated, however, the importance of external intervention, for the control of areas was not simply a matter of competition between groups and depended on the allocation of housing.

They examined the role of urban **gatekeepers**, such as landlords, building-society managers, and Housing Department officials, in the distribution of accommodation. These were quite literally gatekeepers, as they controlled access to housing, though the term has also been used more generally to refer to those who control access to any resource. The local authority's procedures for allocating council housing were particularly critical in determining which groups occupied which housing in which areas.

Eligibility for council housing depended first on being a resident for five years and then on the number of points accumulated, which took account of such matters as existing housing conditions, health, and war service. Rex and Moore pointed out that these criteria inevitably disadvantaged the ethnic minorities, who were forced into lodging houses by the five years' residence rule. Furthermore, when they had met this requirement and accumulated enough points to make them eligible for council housing, they generally found that they were allocated poor-quality housing in slum areas. Rex and Moore noted that the criteria used by the Housing Visitor, who allocated council housing, were not made public, and there was plenty of scope here for discrimination on racial grounds.

This study demonstrates well the limitations of an ecological model in understanding ethnic competition for areas. Such competition has certainly occurred but within a framework of local-authority regulation and a structure of ethnic relationships. The criteria used by local authorities have, however, changed since then and allocation on the basis of need has generated much resentment in some areas when locals on waiting-lists have found themselves overtaken by immigrants judged to be in greater need (Gavron 2006).

Class segregation

The growth of the city led to class as well as ethnic segregation. Distinct working-class communities became established in the inner areas of cities, while the middle class lived in the suburbs.

As we showed in our earlier discussion of community, nineteenth-century theorists and their twentieth-century followers thought that urbanization led to the decline of community because city life was incompatible with it. This was far from the case. When urban society had settled down after the turbulence of industrialization and the population movements of urbanization, relatively stable communities could emerge.

There were many features of working-class life that encouraged the growth of strong communities. The workers in one area would often be employed largely in one particular trade, such as mining or dock-work, and sometimes largely by a single local employer. Conflict with this employer and the growth of trade unions could generate local solidarity, while the deprivations and insecurities of life in early industrial cities made people reliant on local structures of support. Opportunities for social or geographical mobility were limited and most people lived most of their lives within a restricted area. Common situation, collective organization, mutual dependence, and social segregation produced the conditions in which strong communities could become established.

Once they were established, the strength of their networks, organizations, and identities enabled them to perpetuate themselves and resist external changes. In the most famous study of a working-class community in Britain, that of Bethnal Green in 1950s London by Young and Willmott (1957), the authors expected to find that post-war social changes were leading to the breakdown of community, but instead they discovered that it was alive and well.

The middle class became concentrated in the suburbs. The building of most suburbs was financed by the sale of houses to owner-occupiers, and middle-class people were more able to afford homeownership and the cost of travelling in and out. Suburban living also enabled the middle class to separate itself off socially by spatially distancing itself from the working class.

As Savage and Warde (2002) have argued, suburbanization reinforced social inequality. By excluding those with lower incomes from new residential areas, it consolidated a distinctive middle-class culture and strengthened middle-class solidarity. The process of suburbanization itself contributed to class formation.

Gendered urban space

The growth of the city was also associated with gender segregation, which was linked to the separation of home life from work life in the nineteenth-century city (see Chapter 5, pp. 168–70).

The public life of the city became dominated by men, who could travel freely through it, and there has been much discussion in the feminist literature of the 'male gaze' of the wandering man or *flâneur* (the French term generally used), which expressed male domination and treated women as sexual objects. The presence of women in public places was associated with prostitution, as in the term 'street-walker'. The male domination of public space was particularly apparent in the predominantly male character of sporting events and sports places. As Doreen Massey has observed, this started early in life (see box on 'The male domination of public space').

Elizabeth Wilson (1995) has cautioned us, however, against taking this view of the male domination of the city too far, for the city is also a place of opportunity for women. Employment in the city gave women some possibility of escaping from unpaid labour in the household, while shopping became one of the few legitimate public activities for women. One consequence of the growth of female white-collar work in the city and the rise of the department store was the appearance in late nineteenth-century cities of a range of eating places specifically designed for women. So, women too could wander in the city, albeit within certain limits, and men could not in the end keep them out of public life.

Suburbanization hardened the separation of gender roles in the household. The male breadwinner commuted into the city, while the housewife remained at home with little else to do but engage in housework and child-rearing. As compared with the inner city, there was unlikely to be much local employment for women. Furthermore, transport was designed to meet the needs of the male commuter, and the poor provision of local public transport within the suburb confined the housewife even more to the home. Distance from other members of the family intensified the housewife's social isolation and substituted telephone for face-to-face contact.

Thus, suburbanization not only segregated classes, it also segregated men and women, reinforcing gender, as well as class, inequalities.

Briefing: the male domination of public space

'I can remember very clearly a sight which often used to strike me when I was nine or ten years old. I lived then on the outskirts of Manchester, and "Going into Town" was a relatively big occasion; it took over half an hour and we went on the top deck of a bus. On the way into town we would cross the wide shallow valley of the River Mersey, and my memory is of dank, muddy fields spreading away into a cold, misty distance. And all of it—all of these acres of Manchester—was divided up into football pitches and rugby pitches. And on Saturdays, which was when we went into Town, the whole vast area would be covered with hundreds of little people, all running around after balls, as far as the eye could see. . . . I remember all this very sharply. And I remember, too, it striking me very clearly—even then as a puzzled, slightly thoughtful little girl—that all this huge stretch of the Mersey flood plain had been entirely given over to boys.' (Massey 1994: 185)

 Does this male domination of open space still occur? Observe your local park at the weekend and see who makes most use of its space and sporting facilities.

Managed cities

During the nineteenth century, institutions were established to manage the sprawling concentrations of population brought about by urbanization. To understand the rise of the 'managed city', we must place it in the context of the growth of capitalism, class relationships, state intervention, and collective consumption, which we outlined and discussed earlier in this chapter (see pp. 491–2).

In Britain a local state was constructed by the national state in the nineteenth century. Parliament passed laws that enabled the development of local democratic institutions and empowered local government to create a wide range of authorities and services. This provided an opportunity for the labour movement to gain a foothold by first establishing its political presence on local councils and local school boards. What has been called 'municipal socialism' led to councils taking water and gas supply into public ownership, and developing modern transport systems. The management of the city later extended to planning of the use of land.

We examine elsewhere the issues of order (Chapter 14, pp. 546–8), health (Chapter 8, pp. 289–90), and education (Chapter 9, pp. 329–30). We concentrate here on the public provision of housing and the development of planning.

Housing classes

Perhaps the best example of collective consumption in the city is the public provision of housing. In this section we outline the growth of public housing through the building of council houses before examining the concept of *housing classes*.

THEORY AND METHODS

Housing classes

1 Owner-occupiers;

2 Council-house tenants;

3 Tenants of whole private houses;

4 Owners of lodging houses;

5 Tenants of rooms in lodging houses.

Rex and Moore (1967) developed the concept of 'housing classes'. Their ideas can be linked to the debate between Marxists and Weberians on stratification. Rex and Moore followed the Weberian tradition in arguing that class situation is not simply a matter of the ownership or non-ownership of capital. These issues are discussed in 'Class and status', Chapter 19, pp. 773–4.

❓ How useful is the notion of 'housing classes'?

The rapid growth of the industrial city in the nineteenth century soon produced severe problems of overcrowding in poor-quality housing. There were calls for slum clearance and house-building programmes. The 1890 Housing Act enabled both processes to start, but for a long time progress was slow and it was not until the 1960s that they came to a climax. In London, one in ten houses was demolished between 1967 and 1971. At its high point in 1979 the public sector accounted for what must now seem a quite astonishing one-third of British households.

Up to this time, the social significance of the ownership and control of housing had been rather neglected in sociology, but Rex and Moore (1967) tried to remedy this through their concept of **housing classes**. This started a debate over whether the housing situation should be treated as a separate dimension of stratification.

In their study of Birmingham (see also p. 505), Rex and Moore argued that lack of housing was a more serious problem in people's lives than lack of employment. They claimed that ownership of domestic property was as important in determining class situation as the ownership of industrial property, though there were also important differences within the categories of owners and non-owners. They concluded that 'there is a class struggle over houses and this class struggle is the central process of the city as a social unit' (Rex and Moore 1967: 273). As we showed on p. 505, they also argued that 'urban gatekeepers' played a key role in determining the distribution of housing.

The whole idea of separate housing classes has, however, been found wanting, as position on the housing market is so closely related to other aspects of stratification. If housing situation is largely determined by income, there is little to be gained by creating a separate housing dimension of stratification, though it must be said in defence of Rex and Moore that they did demonstrate that access to housing was not *only* a matter of income. They also showed how the local state played an important part in distributing 'life chances' and reinforcing patterns of inequality.

Planning

Nineteenth-century British cities grew but twentieth-century cities were increasingly planned, and the planning process has shaped the environment in which we now live.

Planning was strongly influenced by conceptions of the ideal city. Two influential conceptions were Howard's *garden city* (see Figure 13.9) and Le Corbusier's *radiant city*

Figure 13.9 Ebenezer Howard's garden city

Published at the end of the nineteenth century, this vision of the city envisaged a group of six garden cities, each the size of a small town, surrounded by green belts, and linked to a larger central city, the whole complex comprising a 'Social City'. Each garden city would be self-sufficient, with its own industries, residential areas, and cultural, recreational, and service facilities. The residential areas would be divided into neighbourhoods, to facilitate the growth of communities. There would be an emphasis on public transport, and cycling would be encouraged. Housing would be small-scale and traditional. Howard believed in the collective ownership of land and the development of public welfare services at local level.

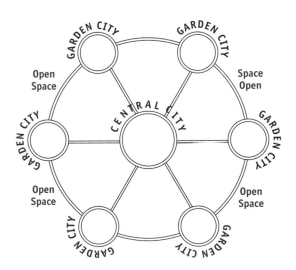

Source: Adapted from Howard (1898).

Figure 13.10 Le Corbusier's radiant city

This 1920s vision of the city saw it as 'towers in a park'. Population density would be far higher than in the garden city or, indeed, existing cities, but the construction of tower blocks sixty storeys high would leave most of the land free of building and available as green spaces for sport and leisure. There would be a great central open space for restaurants, cafés, and various public buildings. The techniques of mass production would be used to standardize building and cut its costs. This city was designed for the car, with arterial roads, one-way systems, and underground routes for heavy vehicles and deliveries. Although Le Corbusier too believed in the public ownership of land, there was less concern for community in his vision of the city, which sought to maximize the freedom of the individual by, for example, facilitating travel by car.

'*Note*: The centre of the city seen from one of the terraced cafés surrounding the Great Central Station square. The station can be seen between the two sky-scrapers on the left, only slightly raised above ground level. Leaving the station, the 'speedway' continues to the right in the direction of the Park. We are in the very centre of the city, the point of greatest density of population and traffic; there is any amount of room for both. The terraces containing the cafés are much frequented and serve as boulevards. Theatres, public halls, etc., are scattered in the open spaces between the sky-scrapers and are surrounded by trees.'

Source: Le Corbusier (1947: 258–9).

Figure 13.11 Garden city versus radiant city

Garden city	Radiant city
● Small population	● High population density
● Decentralized	● Centralized
● Green belts	● Green spaces
● Neighbourhood housing	● Tower blocks
● Public transport and cycling	● Cars and trucks
● Collectivist	● Individualist

Figure 13.12 New towns, Great Britain

Source: Lawless and Brown (1986: 134).

(see Figure 13.10). Howard's garden city sought to combine the advantages of urban and rural life. Le Corbusier presented the radiant city as a 'vertical garden city' that would preserve open space for grass and trees and prevent urban sprawl but in a more realistic way compatible with large concentrations of population. The radiant city was, none the less, radically different from the garden city in its size, architecture, and transport arrangements.

Jane Jacobs has argued that both these conceptions were, in spite of their differences, fundamentally anti-urban in spirit, as they devalued street life, imposed conformity, forced activities into zones, and left no space for the spontaneity, diversity, innovation, and dynamism, which she saw as the essence of urban life (1961: 16–23). Their elitist blueprints catered for the interests of planners, architects, and engineers but did not allow for popular involvement and did not give people any say in the construction of the environment in which they would have to live, travel, and work.

More down-to-earth concerns with the growing size of cities, overcrowded housing, and uncontrolled building motivated politicians' interventions. Legislation, especially the 1947 Town and Country Planning Act, established a framework for planning. Implementation involved the locally elected bodies of councils, their planning committees, and the officials who influenced and implemented local planning decisions.

What has been the impact of planning on the development of towns and cities? The construction of self-sufficient 'new towns' (see Figure 13.12) and the preservation of green belts around cities showed the influence of Howard's ideas. These fitted well with the anti-urban sentiments of the British elite, which has always valued country rather than city life. The protection of the countryside and agricultural land was one of the main themes of British planning. In spite of these views, population growth after the Second World War and a rising demand for homes in suburban and rural areas created pressures that could not be resisted and led to development in rural areas (Murdoch and Marsden 1994).

Le Corbusier's conception of the city became influential in the 1950s. The high density and industrial building techniques that he advocated provided cheap solutions to the problems of overcrowded cities and badly built slums. His ideas were seized upon by city councils, architects, engineers, and builders. His legacy is visible in the tower blocks, system building, and urban motorways of British cities.

In the 1960s there was some shift of emphasis from transformation to conservation. The 1967 Civic Amenities Act gave local authorities greater power to protect listed buildings and trees. Particular areas of historic or architectural interest could be designated Conservation Areas, though development in them was allowed, if it could be presented as consistent with the area's character. In general, employment, transport, and housing were higher priorities than conservation and the reshaping of the urban environment continued apace.

Planning is a bureaucratic process carried out by experts, but group interests are heavily involved and exert pressure on the planners. Incoming middle-class residents seek to conserve rural areas, but farmers often want to sell their land to developers, and local workers are primarily interested in new economic activities that will give employment. Conservation Areas in cities have been used by the urban middle class to protect the quality of its environment and increase the value of its property, bringing them into conflict with developers who are alive to every opportunity to build more houses in sought after locations. So-called 'slums' in working-class areas have, however, been cleared without much concern for conservation and little reference to the people whose homes were demolished.

Those who are most organized and have most resources are most able to represent themselves effectively, pay for professional assistance, and influence planning procedures. This not only means that the middle class is likely to be more effective than the working class in protecting its interests, it also means that the interests of capital tend to prevail over those of conservation groups seeking to halt development. Planning is not a neutral bureaucratic process, for decisions are shaped by class interests and class power.

‹› *Stop and reflect*

In this section we have outlined the process of urbanization and linked it to other processes of change.

- In Britain, industrialization led to urbanization but this was also the result of the development of a global trading economy and the growth of empire.

We then considered the structure of the centralized city that resulted from nineteenth-century urbanization.

- Cities developed zones that were differentiated by function, class, and ethnicity.
- Key functions were located in the centre and communications radiated from it.

- What contribution did the ecological perspective make to the study of the city and what were its limitations?

We went on to examine the emergence of managed cities.

- In the nineteenth century a local state was constructed and collective consumption began to develop.
- Key features of the managed city were the public provision of services and housing, and the growth of planning.
- How useful is the concept of 'housing classes'?
- What ideas and interests shape the planning process?

The contemporary city

Here we explore recent changes in the city that have reversed many of the tendencies examined above. Decentralization has spread the city out and blurred its boundaries with the countryside. Depopulation and industrial decline have turned many inner cities into problem areas. Long-established communities have been broken up. Local government has lost power and resources, while social order has been threatened by a return of the urban riot.

Cities have not just experienced decline, however. There have also been processes of gentrification and regeneration. Cities have acquired a new lease of life through cultural restructuring and investment in new economic activities. New kinds of community have emerged. Although global economic changes inflicted considerable damage on industrial cities, global cities have benefited greatly from them. Out of all these changes has emerged a new kind of city—the post-modern city—and we conclude the chapter with a discussion of this.

Deurbanization or deruralization?

After a long period of urbanization, the halting of city growth and the actual decline of some city populations suggested that some degree of deurbanization was happening. It can also be argued, however, that the influence of the city has actually penetrated further into rural areas. Has deurbanization or deruralization been taking place?

Urbanization had been going on for so long that it seemed an unstoppable process, but in the 1950s it began to slow down and eventually reverse in both Britain and the United States. Large cities lost population to towns and rural areas—a process called deurbanization (sometimes counter-urbanization). This resulted from two important processes:

- the decline of urban employment;
- the decline of urban residence.

Between 1951 and 1981 some two million manufacturing jobs were lost in the larger cities of Britain. Between 1961 and 1978 Greater London lost 47 per cent of its manufacturing jobs, though increasing service employment partly compensated and the decline in total employment was only 17 per cent. The decline of urban employment was due in part to a general collapse of manufacturing, as competition from low-cost countries increased. It was also due to a shift of employment towards the outskirts of cities, smaller towns, and rural areas, where land was cheaper and

communications were easier (Lawless and Brown 1986; D. King 1987).

Those who worked in cities have increasingly lived outside them. Road- and house-building, together with the spread of car and home ownership, made it easier for people to live in preferred or cheaper rural or semi-rural locations and commute. Motorways and rail electrification brought a huge area of the country, including the Midlands, East Anglia, and even parts of Wales and Yorkshire, into commuting range of London. Information technology enabled some to telework and made it possible for them to pursue city careers a long way from cities.

> ⊃ **Connections**
> It is important to emphasize that the decline of city populations occurred only in a limited number of rich countries. In most countries of the world urbanization has continued and the world as a whole is becoming more urban (see Chapter 16, pp. 643–5).

London has, none the less, recently entered a period of renewed growth. In the 1990s its population began to rise rapidly again, from 6.8 million in the 1980s to 7.5 million in 2001, with predictions that it will be over eight million by 2016. London is exceptional, however, because of its global functions as a centre of financial services and its attractiveness to immigrants at a time of increasing global migration (see Media watch 13 on p. 533). The fortunes of global cities have been different from those of cities in general (see box on 'Global cities').

Does the movement of jobs and homes out of the city anyway indicate a process of *deurbanization* or *deruralization*? If people with an urban culture and urban living patterns are dispersed into rural areas, closely linked by commuting and shopping patterns to cities, do not these areas become urbanized? Furthermore, declining employment in an ever more capital-intensive agriculture has led rural inhabitants to seek urban employment, while the new stores and services around the edge of cities are accessible from rural as well as urban areas. Rural areas are also increasingly devoted to the provision of leisure pursuits for city-dwellers. Are the golf courses, theme parks, and garden centres that take up areas of the countryside in any sense rural?

The term 'deurbanization' certainly draws our attention to important changes in the distribution and location of population and employment, but it must be placed in the context of a broader urbanization of rural areas that makes

Global focus Global cities

Globalization has led to the emergence of a new kind of **global city** that is centrally involved in the growing economic integration of the world. The rise of the global city and the shifting of capital out of the old industrial cities were part of the same process.

In her study of *The Global City* Sassen (2001) argued that the *dispersal* of production from the old industrial societies to other parts of the world made greater coordination necessary and resulted in the *concentration* of control in a small number of global cities. These are the 'command' cities, where transnational corporations (TNCs) and financial institutions have their headquarters.

Sassen concentrated her attention on London, New York, and Tokyo and argued that, although they have very different histories, cultures, and national traditions, these three cities have become increasingly alike because of their similar global functions. These three cities are linked together in a global financial network that has produced 'one transterritorial marketplace' (2001: 327). Their geographical positioning means that as one closes down at the end of the day, another opens for trading.

Sassen also argued that the global role of these cities has partially *unhooked* them from their societies. They have followed patterns of economic growth different from those of the national economy. At a time when the industrial cities in Britain, America, and Japan were in decline, their global cities were booming.

These cities produce the services and financial innovations required by TNCs and the international financial industry. They are, therefore, centres of managerial, legal, insurance, marketing, communications, public relations, design, and accountancy occupations. They are also centres of innovation where the latest technologies are applied to the development of these services. Sassen rejected the distinction between goods and services and emphasized that 'the "things" a global city makes are services and financial goods' (2001: 5).

While these global functions have revived the fortunes of the cities concerned and provided them with new sources of employment, not all of those who live in them have benefited. As we show on p. 513, London contains areas that have experienced severe deprivation as growing global economic integration has led to the decline of their traditional industries.

A growing inequality has resulted from the occupational changes generated by London's global financial functions. While higher-paid managerial and professional occupations have expanded, so have the low-paid occupations of the clerical workers, cleaners, and security staff employed in the office blocks. Other low-paid occupations, such as restaurant workers, bar staff, and shop assistants, have expanded to meet the consumption needs of the higher-paid professionals. Sassen suggested that this gap between the higher and lower paid has been widened by the global city's orientation to world markets and diminished sensitivity to local poverty, local problems, and local politics.

The notion that global cities are new is in some ways misleading. As we showed earlier (pp. 502–3), London and other comparable cities have long performed global functions. But they did so within the framework of the imperial state, and there is certainly something new in the emergence of a network of global cities that are partially unhooked from national economies. This network has opened a new chapter in the evolving relationship between capitalism and the city (see p. 492).

---

it ever more difficult to argue that social life in rural areas is still distinctive. As we saw earlier, some sociologists have been sceptical of the notion that urban and rural societies are any longer different from each other (see p. 495). They were different during the period of city growth, when cities were becoming centralized and city populations looked inwards to the city centre, but the processes we have just been examining suggest that this difference may be disappearing.

The decentralized city

We now turn to examine the emergence of a new type of city, the decentralized city, with multiple centres and activities dispersed to the city's periphery.

Decentralization and dedifferentiation

Decentralization is associated with a process of dedifferentiation, reversing the differentiation that we discussed earlier (see p. 503). The various parts of a city have become less specialized in their activities and land use. Retail stores, for example, are spread through the city and are no longer concentrated in a shopping district. While at one time there were distinct inner-industrial areas, numerous small industrial estates are now dotted around the city.

New urban development is particularly focused on the periphery of the city as new stores, warehouses, leisure facilities, hotels, schools, and hospitals are built around its edge. The term 'edge city' has come into use to describe the new shape of cities. People increasingly travel out of

Figure 13.13
The centralized city

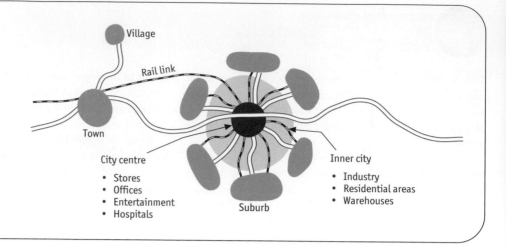

Village

Rail link

Town

City centre
- Stores
- Offices
- Entertainment
- Hospitals

Inner city
- Industry
- Residential areas
- Warehouses

Suburb

Figure 13.14
The decentralized city

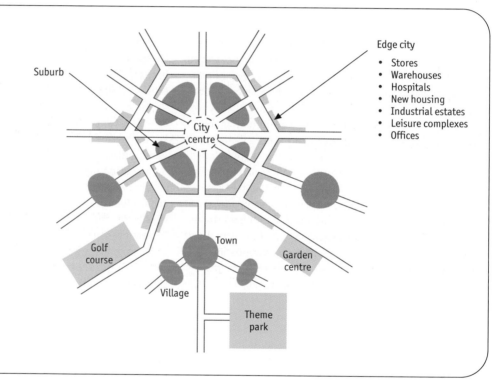

Suburb

City centre

Edge city
- Stores
- Warehouses
- Hospitals
- New housing
- Industrial estates
- Leisure complexes
- Offices

Golf course

Town

Garden centre

Village

Theme park

the city for shopping or leisure, and many now work on the city's edge. With this growth of the periphery, cities have spread out and incorporated outlying towns and villages into an urban network.

These changes are linked to changes in communications. The centralized city typically had radiating railway lines, which brought people in and out of the centre and connected one city with another. The decentralized city has a network of motorways that link its multiple centres and give access to the periphery. The prime location for many commercial organizations is now the motorway junction. Graham and Marvin (2001) argue that the growth of networks connecting together the most valued parts of cities but bypassing places and people of low value is leading to the fragmentation of cities and 'splintering urbanism'.

The best and probably only example of a totally decentralized city is Los Angeles, which has no discernible centre. Most cities still have a clear centre and a communications system focused on it. One of the great problems of the contemporary city is how to reconcile the centralized structure inherited from the past with the decentralizing tendencies of the present, and produce a working city out of them.

Inner-city deprivation

Decentralization 'hollowed out' the city, as the loss of economic activity, employment, and population from inner areas drained their resources and concentrated deprivation in them. Changes in the character of the local state, such as privatization and a tighter central control of local government funds, which we examine later, made the problems of the inner city worse.

The growing problems of the inner city have been described in Paul Harrison's (1985) study of Hackney, one of London's inner-city boroughs. Jobs in manufacturing dropped by 40 per cent between 1973 and 1981. Furthermore, the industries that were left—for example, in clothing and footwear—were labour intensive and highly vulnerable to competition from poor countries with cheaper labour. Then, in the early 1980s, employment by Hackney Council, the largest employer in the borough, was hit by various government policies aimed at reducing local-authority expenditure (P. Harrison 1985: 49–51).

Since the 1980s, the decline of housing provision for the poor, as council houses were sold and council-house building plummeted, resulted in a growing problem of homelessness. The number of households in England recognized as homeless by local authorities increased from 57,000 in 1979 to 137,000 in 2003–4 (*Social Trends* 2005: 140). Latterly, rapidly rising house prices have made it more difficult for those in low-paid jobs, let alone those without jobs at all, to find somewhere to live.

Poverty and ill health are linked and concentrated in the inner city. The concentration of deprivation in the inner city was demonstrated by the 1985–6 study of London by Peter Townsend and his colleagues (Townsend 1991). Of the ten most deprived areas that they studied, only two were in outer London. Townsend and his colleagues also showed a clear relationship between deprivation and death rates. The death rate for those under the age of 65 was almost twice as high in the most deprived areas as in the least deprived. Townsend reported that other studies of Manchester, Birmingham, and Liverpool showed similar links between inner-city deprivation, ill health, and premature death.

It is not only, however, in the inner city that such deprivation is found. Meegan (1989) described the intense deprivation experienced by those living on estates in Kirby and Speke on the edge of Liverpool. The fortunes of this area changed drastically when the transnational corporations that had invested there during the 1950s and 1960s either closed their plants or reduced their labour forces.

Studies of these problems also emphasize that some inner-city areas are not deprived and that in the least deprived areas some people experience great deprivation.

Gentrification

Inner-city decline has resulted in deprivation for some but opened up opportunities for others. In some parts of inner cities, property developers and middle-class owner-occupiers have moved in to 'upgrade' areas, a process known as gentrification. Instead of moving out to the suburb, some middle-class people, typically young singles and childless couples, settle in the inner city (Butler 1996). Changes in class composition have led to the appearance of boutiques, galleries, delicatessens, restaurants, and similar enterprises that have also helped to revitalize inner-city areas.

Following Warde (1991), gentrification can be defined as involving four processes:

- the displacement of one group of residents by another of higher social status;
- the transformation of the built environment as housing is renovated and new shops and services arrive;
- the emergence of a new urban lifestyle with a distinctive pattern of consumption;
- rising property values.

Why does gentrification occur? The decline of the inner city itself provides an opportunity, as lower property prices

Figure 13.15 The experience of deprivation, London, 1985–6 (%)

Form of deprivation	Percentage experiencing deprivation as a major problem in	
	Most deprived areas	Least deprived areas
Health of someone in the family	33.8	29.1
Vandalism and theft	30.3	14.5
Poor public transport	20.4	11.2
Unemployment	20.1	6.7
Street/estate violence	17.7	4.6
Poor housing	16.4	1.3
Being alone and isolated	12.1	6.9
Poor local schools	8.2	3.0
Conflict at home	7.1	4.5
Racial harassment	7.0	1.4

Source: Adapted from Townsend (1991: table 5.6).

Gentrification.

© Lucy Dawkins

attract both developers and owner-occupiers. The disappearance of factories, warehouses, and docks have made cheap ex-industrial buildings and sites available for 'loft-living' conversions and developments.

Savage and Warde (2002) linked gentrification to changes in household formation, composition, and employment. Rising population after the post-war baby boom led in the 1960s to a greater demand for housing, which could not be satisfied by suburban house-building. Gentrified areas provided housing particularly suitable for the smaller households that have become steadily more common. The growing employment of women in salaried occupations was also a factor, for living in the city suited dual-career couples by giving easier access to work and to cheap domestic labour from those living in the deprived areas.

Cultural reasons for preferring to live in the inner city have played a significant part in the process. These may involve access to the cultural facilities of big cities or a rejection of suburban values and lifestyles. Some people are attracted into the city by the opportunity to pursue deviant lifestyles in a more anonymous, more tolerant urban society.

Suburbanization, as we showed earlier, segregated classes residentially, while gentrification is a movement of middle-class groups back into predominantly working-class areas. Has it reversed class segregation? Tim Butler (1996: 104) has argued that in gentrified areas of Hackney 'there is little evidence that spatial togetherness leads to any lessening of social distance'. Furthermore, while gentrification upgrades areas, it pushes house prices out of working-class reach, reduces the rented accommodation available to those who cannot afford to buy houses, and generally displaces the lower paid. There is little to suggest that gentrification has diminished class differences or class segregation.

Degendering urban space?

We argued earlier that the spatial differentiation of the centralized city further separated the spheres of home and work, and therefore intensified the segregation of gender-roles. Suburban life distanced housewives from the public life of the city centre and left women isolated in the home, often without transport. Have recent decentralizing and dedifferentiating tendencies reversed this process?

Decentralization means that the local availability of services has increased in most suburban areas, as have employment opportunities, and suburban isolation has therefore diminished. The new superstores and leisure services on the edge of cities offer part-time work consistent with the domestic role. Public transport to the city edge may be poor, however, so access to many of these decentralized activities may still be dependent on car ownership and availability, which is itself gendered, as men tend to control car use.

Gentrification too has arguably contributed to the degendering of the domestic division of labour. One of the attractions of inner-city living is that it provides easier movement between workplace and home for dual-career households trying to juggle with the competing demands of work and family.

The situation in declining areas of the inner city is quite different. Single parents with small children, who, after the collapse of many city communities, may well lack local support networks, can be confined to the home by the demands of childcare. Their incomes are not high enough to buy it and state nursery provision in Britain has been minimal, though it is now improving. The decline of employment with the collapse of inner-city manufacturing has forced many women to take up low-paid homework and work for long hours within the home.

New housing estates with leisure facilities often limited to male-dominated clubs and pubs may leave women with little alternative, apart from bingo, to private leisure in front of the television. Bingo is a predominantly female activity, which, Dixey has argued, 'plays a vital role in providing a semi-public space which is local and handy, and, as an extension of the community, brings feelings of rootedness and "at-homeness"' (1988: 126).

According to a study of Manchester and Sheffield by Ian Taylor, Karen Evans, and Penny Fraser (1996), men still dominate urban space. Their street survey found that men consistently outnumbered women in public spaces at all times of day and night, particularly at night. They came across only 31 women for every 100 men in the streets during the early evening hours (Evans 1997).

 Briefing: a landscape of fear?

A study of Manchester and Sheffield showed that women's use of the city was shaped by safety concerns and a 'landscape of fear', which identified areas to be avoided. These varied according to the time of day, and shopping areas that attracted women in day-time became a 'dead space' that was avoided or passed through hastily at night. For an analysis of night-time life in the city, see Study 13 at the end of this chapter.

Source: Taylor *et al.* (1996).

➲ *Try comparing male and female responses to these questions.*

❓ *Have you ever felt frightened in a public place? If so, when did this last happen? At what time of day did it happen? Where did it happen?*

❓ *What frightened you about the situation that you were in? Is there any part of the city you live in (or a city that you visit) which you would avoid visiting? During the day-time? At night?*

❓ *In what ways do you think that the city could be made safer?*

Valentine (1992) has suggested that a vicious circle comes into operation. The male dominance of public space in cities leads to women avoiding some areas by day and all areas by night, which increases male dominance, which intensifies women's fears. The responses of both the police and the media to incidents of violence against women reinforce their fears by suggesting that by putting themselves at risk in dangerous places they are partially to blame for the violence against them.

Even though some of the social changes that gendered urban space have been reversed, there is in the end little to suggest that recent changes in the city have done much to degender the use of space within it.

Changing communities

In this section we examine the implications of recent changes for community life in both urban and rural areas. We also consider the emergence of a new kind of community, the 'virtual community'.

Declining working-class communities

Working-class communities may have been still flourishing in the 1950s (see p. 505) but this situation was about to change. Slum clearance and relocation shattered the residential base of many of these communities during the 1950s and 1960s.

In a classic study, Peter Willmott and Michael Young (1960) followed what happened to forty-seven young married couples who moved from Bethnal Green in London to Greenleigh, a council housing estate twenty miles away. The move to Greenleigh immediately broke up the extended kinship network that was a prominent feature of Bethnal Green, while fewer public meeting places, such as pubs and shops, meant less opportunity for social interaction. Greenleigh also brought together people from many different places who were strangers to each other. People lived a much more private existence focused on the household and the nuclear family.

Where communities survived these changes, they were weakened by the more general growth of privatism that we examine in Chapter 19, p. 805. These focused people's energies increasingly on home and household. When Bethnal Green was restudied in the early 1980s, it had become much more home-centred (see box on 'Bethnal Green revisited' on p. 516).

The changes in the inner city that we have been examining above further weakened those working-class communities that were still there. The decline of urban manufacturing destroyed their economic base. Those left in inner-city areas were disproportionately the old, the unemployed, one-parent families, the homeless, and the chronically ill. Socially isolated, they looked to support

Briefing: Bethnal Green revisited

'One striking difference was how home-centred most Bethnal Green families had now become. In the 1950s, this had been a feature of the Woodford families. Mothers with a three-month old child are, of course, likely to spend more time in the home than outside it. But it was noticeable how many husbands in Bethnal Green today were almost as much around, when they could be, as Woodford husbands. DIY, even in rented property, and television—not to mention the baby—were clearly strong competitors of the pub and the football ground. . . .

But whatever the draw towards the home, or occupation within it, the corollary in Bethnal Green to this new home-centredness was the emptiness of the streets and corridors and staircases in the housing estates. Markets still flourished. Children sometimes played outside. Small groups of adults occasionally congregated. But no longer could it be said that people in Bethnal Green were (in Young and Willmott's words) "vigorously at home in the streets . . .".' (Holme 1985: 45)

Who looks after people when communities collapse?
© Alice Chadwick

from the welfare state rather than from relatives or community. Furthermore, Geoff Dench *et al.* argue that the welfare state, with its 'army of social workers', has taken away the authority of the older women who used to hold the community together through family networks (2006: 118).

Rural communities

Decentralization and deurbanization also impacted on rural communities. The spread of urban commuters into rural areas meant that the dividing line between urban and rural came to run *through* villages rather than *between* them and the city. As commuters leading essentially urban lives became an increasing proportion of village inhabitants, the village community could be weakened and divided. Ray Pahl commented on this long ago: 'The middle-class people come into rural areas in search of a meaningful community and by their presence help to destroy whatever community was there' (1965: 18).

In his study of class relations in East Anglia, Newby (1977) interpreted this situation rather differently. He argued that a common opposition to newcomers had strengthened the sense of community between agricultural workers and farmers. In the nineteenth century the landowners had tried with little success to create a spirit of community between themselves and labourers. They failed

because the class structure and the conflicting interests of landowners and labourers generated an oppositional culture among the latter. This culture was, however, weakened by the decline in the number of agricultural workers. The invasion of outsiders from the city then strengthened the bonds between farmers and their workers by generating a shared hostility to the newcomers.

Thus, according to Pahl, the incomers destroyed the community, while, according to Newby, they stimulated the emergence of a community. These apparently conflicting interpretations are, however, perfectly compatible, for Pahl and Newby were referring to different kinds of community. Pahl was concerned with the decline of the residential community, as village unity and identity became weaker, while Newby drew attention to the strengthening of a countryside community, in the face of an invasion from the outside. As one kind of community declined, another was formed.

Ethnicity and community

Ethnicity as well as class has provided a basis for city communities. As we showed in the first part of the chapter, Gans argued that *ethnic villages* had a distinctive way of life based on strongly integrated communities. Immigrant communities are nothing new in Britain but increased immigration in the 1950s and 1960s led to their proliferation in British cities.

> **⊃** *Connections*
>
> In considering ethnic communities, it is important to be clear about the meaning of *ethnicity* and its relationship to *race*, which we discuss in Chapter 6, pp. 200–2.

Various aspects of the situation of ethnic minorities facilitate community formation. They tend to be spatially concentrated, while ethnicity itself provides a strong basis for community because of the distinctive linguistic, cultural, and religious traditions that can bind members of an ethnic minority together (see Media watch 13 for a discussion of ethnic concentration). This is reinforced by the ethnic conflicts and racism that commonly accompany ethnic diversity. Indeed, racism is, as Jewson has put it, 'a particularly intrusive, explicit, involuntary, and powerful determinant of collective identity' (1990: 171). Ethnic communities are not just the product of shared customs and beliefs. They are also the result of common experiences of exclusion and discrimination, and the creation of organizations for mutual support and protection.

While attention has been focused on the ethnic communities of black and Asian minorities, whites too have ethnic identities. Ethnicity has provided a basis for white communities as well. Jeffers *et al.* (1996) examined the emergence of what they call 'defended communities' among whites in the East End of London and on the Beaumont Leys estate in Leicester. These communities saw themselves as threatened by blacks and Asians, though this did not mean that any actual threat existed. The scarcity of housing and jobs in these areas easily generated fears and conflicts. As we showed on p. 505, ethnic competition for housing has been a long-standing feature of city life.

Ethnicity as a basis for community can come into conflict, however, with efforts to develop multi-ethnic organizations that bring together those living in a particular area. Community Relations Councils and Community Associations provide examples of efforts to 'improve race relations' by creating local organizations that include different ethnic groups. The launch of an Institute of Community Cohesion in Leicester in 2006 provides another example.

Jeffers *et al.* (1996) have examined the relationships between these conflicting principles of community. They studied the success of seven community initiatives to overcome ethnic and racial divisions in Bristol, Leicester, and Tower Hamlets in London. They concluded that one important factor in their success was whether the various ethnic groups were interdependent. When they were interdependent because they shared a common interest, maybe in a sporting activity or in improving a housing estate, an appropriately organized initiative could reduce ethnic and racial conflict.

The form taken by state initiatives could have a considerable bearing on these relationships. Government funding strategies that encouraged competition for public resources often generated ethnic conflict, as ethnically based groups competed for funds and claimed they had 'special needs'. On the Bancroft estate in Tower Hamlets, both blacks and whites were, however, dependent on a multi-ethnic Tenant Management Committee for access to modernization funds, and racial conflicts on the estate declined. Ethnic interdependence can be promoted if government interventions are designed appropriately.

Jeffers *et al.* (1996) point out that much also depended on how such initiatives were carried out. They needed to strike a difficult balance between working against racism in public and allowing people to maintain their private attitudes and feelings, even if these were racist in character. It was important that cultural differences were not ignored or suppressed but instead recognized and accommodated. The Leicester Institute of Community Cohesion has explicitly recognized the importance and value of difference.

Ethnicity has then provided a basis for community in contemporary Britain, but ethnic communities were not only generated by the distinctive customs and cultures of groups. They also arose because of patterns of exclusion, racial discrimination, and the competition of groups for resources. Attempts have been made to reduce ethnic conflicts by constructing multi-ethnic community organizations that seek to establish a broader community cohesion. We shall return to these issues in the section on 'riots' (see pp. 522–5).

Gay villages

The hollowing-out of the city (see p. 513) has provided the space for another kind of community to emerge, one based on sexual orientation. Taylor *et al.* (1996) have examined the growth of a gay village in the centre of Manchester.

They advance an argument similar to Fischer's 'gravitation' theory by suggesting that the sheer size of the city's population meant that it contained a sufficient number of gay people to sustain an openly identifiable gay area (Taylor *et al.* 1996: 182). Also, the existence of various ethnic communities in Manchester, including a Chinatown

Controversy and debate Gay communities and city interests: the Gay Games in New York

'The games are more than an athletic competition for a special group. They are supposed to exemplify the solidarity and pride of homosexuals, burnished by political organizations and ravaged by AIDS. In the publicity surrounding the games, as well as in the athletic and cultural program, homosexuality is represented as if it were an ethnicity with its own traditions and roots. It is also represented as a lifestyle, with its own entertainment forms and consumption choices. Lifestyle is inescapably linked to marketing, as it is often pointed out that most individual homosexuals in the United States have higher incomes than most households. Thus the Gay Games have drawn the support of large corporate sponsors (manufacturers of consumer goods), feature T-shirts and other commercial memorabilia, and are praised for bringing tourist dollars to the city.' (Zukin 1995: 264)

and distinct Indian and Jewish areas, facilitated the tolerance of a gay village as just one more minority culture. As Zukin (1995) has pointed out, even though it is not based on ethnicity, a gay community has many features in common with an ethnic minority and may present itself as ethnically distinct.

The emergence of gay communities must be set in the context of changing attitudes towards sexual orientation. The partial decriminalizing of gay sexuality by the Sexual Offences Act of 1967, the rapid spread of openly gay pubs and clubs in the 1970s, and the emergence of a distinctive gay lifestyle prepared the way for the establishment of gay villages. But these were not simply the result of a growing tolerance that enabled gays to associate openly in public.

Indeed, Taylor *et al.* (1996) suggested that it was the 1980s resurgence of political and media hostility to gays, partly occasioned by the association of AIDS with gay sexual activity, that precipitated the withdrawal of gays into their own space. Gay communities are then the result of 'gay-bashing' as well as gay association. Thus, while gay villages clearly require a degree of tolerance, they also stem from a more general intolerance, which leads gays to travel considerable distances to find an area where they can be open, relaxed, and at home with others of the same persuasion.

The creation of a gay village in Manchester was also linked to gentrification, as it upgraded a derelict area of inner-city warehouses. There was investment in shops and places of entertainment, and the renovation of buildings and streets, which involved both commercial interests and local-authority regeneration programmes. The so-called 'pink pound', the exceptional spending power of gay consumers, with their lower family and household commitments, attracted the interest of entrepreneurs, both gay and straight. To a local authority, a gay village could be a means of reviving a flagging local economy, revitalizing a derelict area of the city, and attracting tourists.

Virtual communities

In our earlier discussion of community (see pp. 497–8), we discussed the network conception of community and argued that this was superior to the older container notion. **Virtual communities** provide the purest example of a network community.

Older communications technologies allowed the *extension* of communities but it is the Net that has enabled the creation of the virtual community. National postal systems and telephone networks made it possible to develop and maintain communities without everyday face-to-face contact. Mobile phones even allow people to, in a sense, carry their community around with them, but do not provide an independent basis for community in the way that the Net does. The bulletin boards, chat rooms, and multi-user domains of the Net escape the one-to-one limitations of the phone and make it possible for whole groups of people to interact electronically.

The idea of virtual communities has been promoted by enthusiasts such as Howard Rheingold (www.rheingold. com), who have engaged actively in building such communities. A by now classic example of them is 'The Well', which describes itself as 'a cluster of electronic villages on the Internet, inhabited by people from all over the world' (www.well.com/aboutwell.html). Such communities can be constructed by any group of like-minded people. As Rheingold has put it:

> The great value of virtual community remains in its self-organizational aspects. Any group of Alzheimer's care-givers, breast cancer patients, parents of learning disabled children, scholars, horse-breeders—any affinity group—can start an e-mail discussion group, a chat-room, or a Web-forum. (Rheingold 2000: 173)

But are these really communities? Sceptics argue that so-called virtual communities are little more than a means

New technology LunarStorm: a Swedish web-community?

Advances in mobile phone technology have made possible the creation of extensive 'mobile virtual communities'. One such web-community, called 'LunarStorm', has been created in Sweden. It claims a membership of over a million, with nearly half of all Swedish teenagers between the ages of 12 and 17 visiting it each month. More than 300,000 visit it each day. LunarStorm provides its members with a wide range of contact and information services.

It is a commercial operation, run by the LunarWorks company, which provides a LunarMarket and operates LunarMobil phones with a special direct text link to LunarStorm. When someone joins LunarStorm, they accept the right of LunarWorks to send them product information and commercial offers. LunarWorks collects useful intelligence about which products or services are likely to appeal to particular members through the information provided about their usage of its services through 'cookies'. Members also have to accept the company's right to sell any data it collects on its membership, though not the personal details of particular members.

Source: www.lunarstorm.se

❷ Do you think that such an organization can be meaningfully considered a 'community'?

---

of exchanging information. If relationships are formed, they are brief and not sustained. They are also partial, concerned only with some shared interest, and do not involve the whole person. Some consider that electronic contact cannot be sufficient for the creation of a community, for a 'real' community must have face-to-face interaction (Wellman and Gulia 1999).

Furthermore, some of these communities are, more or less, disguised commercial operations. They provide yet another means of targeting people with advertisements and selling them goods and services. Some are, indeed, sponsored by mobile phone companies, for the growing linkages between the Net and mobile phones mean that these companies have an evident interest in stimulating electronic interactions that provide them with revenue.

There is also the argument that virtual communities operate at the expense of real communities. Participation in a virtual community and long hours on the Net isolate people from their local community, arguably providing a pale substitute for real community relationships.

In defence of virtual communities, it is claimed that they are far more than a means of communication. Many of them do provide emotional support for their members. Some become highly organized, with rules to regulate interactions, sanctions against those who break them, and governing institutions. Some generate face-to-face interaction, when community members arrange real meetings and conferences. Some result in common action, when they bring people together in a common cause that leads to fund-raising or political action.

The dangers of commercialization can be exaggerated. Rheingold thinks that opportunities for commercial exploitation are limited and that commercial operations will only succeed if they allow genuine communities to emerge, a process that requires considerable time and skill: 'If you squeeze your community to make a profit at the same time as you are trying to coax it into taking its first breath, you will simply kill your enterprise' (Rheingold 2000: 173).

Wellman and Gulia have reviewed the literature and concluded that there *are* meaningful virtual communities that maintain 'strong, supportive community ties' and 'may be increasing the number and diversity of weak ties' (1999: 185). Weak ties should not be neglected because they may be a bridge to stronger relationships and anyway have considerable social significance in their own right.

They make the important point that virtual communities should not be contrasted with some mythical rural community that no longer exists in an individualized and privatized world. Social relationships 'online' are much like 'offline' ones, which too are 'intermittent, specialized, and varying in strength'. Weak electronic ties are, anyway, better than no ties at all and can perform important functions by extending networks into new areas.

In deciding whether virtual communities are real communities, conception of community is clearly crucial. If face-to-face interaction or location in the same place is made a defining characteristic of a community, they are not communities. They do not fit the traditional 'container' model of a community but they are perfectly compatible with the network conception of community, which we argued for above (see p. 497).

This certainly should not, however, be taken to mean that *all* electronic networks are communities, for most will not meet the minimum requirements of a community (see p. 496), either because they are primarily concerned with information or are too single-stranded, too narrowly focused on one particular interest or activity.

Community diversity

So many different kinds of community exist that one cannot sensibly speak of a general decline of community. Communities based on class have been generally in decline but not communities based on ethnicity. Residential communities have been weakened by privatism, as people's lives become increasingly focused on the home, but virtual communities are anchored in the home computer.

The changes that weaken one kind of community may well enable another to establish itself. Thus, the movement of commuters into villages weakened local residential communities but stimulated the emergence of a defensive countryside community. The emptying out of inner-city working-class communities may lead to the creation of new communities, such as gay villages or middle-class communities generated by gentrification.

One kind of community may, indeed, be in conflict with another. Thus virtual communities may arise at the expense of residential communities, and ethnic communities may become stronger at the expense of multi-racial communities. Communities can, however, coexist and it should not be assumed that a person can be part of only one community at any one time.

What does seem clear is that people do experience a need for the practical and emotional benefits of community, and commonly seek to identify themselves with a community of some kind. It is important to understand that communities do not just emerge in the right conditions but are actively constructed by people. If the social basis for one kind of community breaks down, they are likely to seek actively to create a community of another kind. This is where the Net comes in, for it provides new opportunities for them to do this.

City management in decline

We showed in 'Managed cities' how urbanization led to the growth of a local state to establish order, manage the city, and provide collective consumption. In recent years this process has in some respects been reversed and in this section we examine the decline of city management with the privatization of local services, and the re-emergence of urban disorder.

Privatization

In Britain the local state came under attack from a Conservative government seeking to reduce local-government powers and spending after its victory in the 1979 election. Local government lost much of its autonomy as a result and its finances fell under the control of the central state. The Conservatives also initiated an extensive programme of **privatization** based on the principle of individuals

choosing services from providers competing in a marketplace.

As we showed earlier (p. 492.), Castells (1977) believed that collective consumption was necessary to the maintenance of capitalism, since it provided the capitalist employer with a supply of healthy, educated, and housed workers. Saunders took a different view. Collective consumption was not a requirement of capitalism but rather a 'holding operation' that covered people's basic consumption needs until they were able to take responsibility for meeting these needs themselves (Saunders 1986: 316). In future most people would satisfy their consumption requirements through private purchases, leaving a minority that was unable to do so dependent on what was left of the welfare state. Privatization was not something forced on people by the government, for it met a real desire by consumers for greater control over their lives. It was not something that Saunders (rightly) expected some future Labour government to reverse.

> **⊃ Connections**
>
> These changes in the local state need to be placed in the context of changes in the state as a whole and the general crisis of capitalism that lay behind these changes in the state. We discuss all this in Chapter 15, pp. 601–3, and also consider there New Labour's approach to privatization.

Some of the main forms taken by privatization in the city were:

- compulsory competitive tendering;
- delegation of education budgets;
- deregulation of bus services;
- sale of council houses;
- privatizing of public space.

Compulsory competitive tendering required local authorities to allow private companies to compete for contracts to provide local services and give contracts to the cheapest provider. Local-authority services were, in effect, privatized, since they had to behave like private companies in order to compete with them. Refuse collection, road maintenance, street cleaning, and school-meals provision were privatized in this way.

This was linked to the *delegation of education budgets* to schools. The funds for local education authority services were largely transferred to schools, which could then buy in the services they chose to have from a provider of choice.

The *deregulation of bus services* took away their monopoly of routes from municipal bus companies, which now had to compete with (sometimes transnational) private

A transnational company operates a local bus service—find out how many countries this bus company operates in.

© Lucy Dawkins

companies. As we show elsewhere, privatization is closely linked to globalization (see Chapter 14, pp. 563–4).

The *sale of council houses* too was driven by government policy, which forced local authorities to allow their tenants to buy their houses. Between 1981 and 1989 1.5 million council houses were sold. New council-house building fell and rent subsidies to council-house tenants were reduced.

Although the sharp decline of council housing in the 1980s was the result of government policy, there had been a steady increase in owner-occupation during the twentieth century (see Figure 13.16). Saunders (1990) has pointed out that house ownership is particularly high in Britain and societies originally settled by the British— Australia, Canada, New Zealand, and the United States— in contrast with the countries of continental Europe. He argued that it is related to a strong culture of individualism going back to medieval British society.

Saunders saw private ownership as meeting real needs, giving people greater control over their lives, security and identity. In enabling greater homeownership the Conservatives generated considerable popular support, particularly in the working class, which helped them to stay in government until 1997. It did have its disadvantages too. For some people, it turned into a personal disaster, when they lost their jobs, found themselves unable to service their loans, and lost their homes. It also led to a shortage of social housing, exacerbating tensions between local whites and incoming migrants in areas like East London and providing an opportunity for the British National Party to exploit local white discontent (Gavron 2006).

Figure 13.16 Housing tenure changes, Great Britain, 1914–2001 (%)

Year	Types of tenure		
	Owner-occupiers	Council tenants/ social sector	Other rented
1914	10	0	90
1945	26	12	62
1961	43	27	31
1971	53	31	16
1981	54	34	12
1991	67	24	10
2001	70	21	9

Sources: Jewson (1989: 130); *Living in Britain* (1996: 229); *Social Trends* (2002: 167).

Another less obvious form taken by privatization was the *privatizing of public space*, which had been one of the central features of urban life (Bianchini and Schwengel 1991). Examples of it are:

- *Shopping malls*. The essentially public shopping street has been replaced by privately owned or privately managed shopping malls. Access to these is controlled by private security companies, who can exclude buskers and expel 'undesirables'.

Is it important to keep public spaces in cities?
© Alice Chadwick

- *Privately controlled streets*. Homeowners' Associations and Business Improvement Districts in the United States have acquired the authority to carry out surveillance and control the streets.
- *Fortified estates*. Walled estates with controlled entry, surveillance by camera, and patrol by private security companies have been built, not only in American but also in British cities.
- *Privately managed parks*. The transfer of park management to private companies is commonly found in American cities (Zukin 1995).

The privatizing of public space reflects not only the spread of private ownership but also a growing concern with public order. The exclusion of 'undesirables' is in part a response to rising crime, the growth of begging and busking, squatting in shop doorways, and 'sleeping rough' in the parks. These are in turn at least partly a consequence of unemployment, homelessness, and the closing of mental hospitals.

It is also linked to the privatizing of law enforcement. The financial crises of the state, local and central, have led to the transfer of security and policing to the private sector, which pays lower wages, provides a cheaper service, and transfers some of the costs to private individuals. This process has gone furthest in the United States, but it has been happening in Britain too (see Chapter 15, p. 610).

Riots

Riots were a common feature of the pre-industrial and early industrial city, but during the nineteenth century conflict became increasingly organized, managed, and contained. The main form it took was class conflict and this was organized in the industrial sphere by unions or in the political sphere by political parties. Violent riots still occurred from time to time but were exceptional events. In the 1980s, rioting re-emerged. Beatrix Campbell (1993: xi) went so far as to claim that 'riot became routine' in the 1980s and 1990s.

The one thing that most riots have had in common is their occurrence in working-class areas with high levels of unemployment and deprivation, whether areas of the inner city, such as Brixton, or outer estates, such as Meadowell, or deindustrialized mill towns, such as Oldham. While high local unemployment is one of the most important conditions that has led to rioting, it can, however, only provide a partial explanation. Riots have not occurred in all areas of high unemployment and were not a feature of the 1930s, when unemployment and deprivation were very much higher.

Ethnicity has been a major factor in many riots. Jewson (1990) suggested that a common feature of the 1980s riots was the involvement of ethnic minorities experiencing racial discrimination and exclusion from full participation in British society. He argued that in Britain political organization has been on class lines and there is no tradition of organized ethnic politics. Ethnic minorities had not, therefore, been politically incorporated as they had in the United States, where there was a much greater representation of ethnic minorities in city governments.

The ethnicity dimension is linked to another feature of some riots in British cities—conflicts with the police. In

In the 2001 riots, ethnicity was again a central feature. In Oldham, where the most serious disorder took place, rioting occurred against a background of deteriorating relationships between whites and Asians, mainly with a Bangladeshi or Pakistani background, in a town with high unemployment and poor housing. There were white suspicions that scarce local resources were being channelled towards the Asian community, who in turn considered that they were being discriminated against. There were Asian fears of racist attacks and claims that the police were racist and not providing protection, though Asian self-defence actions and counter-violence led to white accusations of attacks by Asians. Both Asians and whites claimed that they were being excluded from 'no-go' areas. Both the British National Party (BNP) and Islamic militants were said to have exploited local fears and discontents (*Independent*, 17 and 28 May 2001).

The background to the 2001 riots was investigated by a Community Cohesion Review Team, set up by the government and chaired by Ted Cantle. This not only investigated the riots but also considered ethnic relations in other cities, such as Leicester and Nottingham, where there had not been riots. It argued that an ethnic polarization, which generated mutual fear and suspicion, lay behind the riots (see box on 'Ethnic polarization' on p. 524). Some of its main recommendations were:

- The need for a clearer concept of the rights and responsibilities of citizenship, which should be embodied in a statement of allegiance.

- The development of 'a new compact or understanding between all sections of the community', which should include an expectation of competence in the English language, a recognition of women's rights, a commitment to the 'full representation of all minority groups', and 'respect for both religious differences and secular views'.

- A 'community cohesion strategy' for each area, which should include 'a new and vigorous approach to recruitment and career progression, in all key agencies, such as the police, local authorities, health authorities and regeneration agencies'.

- A 'programme of cross-cultural contact' in schools and moves to desegregate education by getting all schools to offer 25 per cent of places to 'other cultures or ethnicities within their local area', and establishing ethnically mixed catchment areas for new estates.

- A change in regeneration strategies to avoid funding area projects linked to the interests of distinct ethnic communities but also action to 'bust myths' about the way that resources were distributed.

Figure 13.17 Major riots since the 1980s

1980	April	Bristol (St Paul's)
1981	April	London (Brixton)
	July	London (Brixton)
	July	London (Southall)
	July	Liverpool (Toxteth)
	July	London (Brixton)
1985	Sept.	Birmingham (Handsworth)
	Sept.	London (Brixton)
	Oct.	London (Broadwater Farm)
1991	Aug.	Cardiff (Ely)
	Sept.	Oxford (Blackbird Leys)
	Sept.	Tyneside (Meadowell)
1992	May	Coventry (Wood End)
	July	Bristol (Hartcliffe)
1995	June	Bradford (Manningham)
	July	Leeds (Hyde Park)
	July	Luton (Marsh Farm)
	Dec.	London (Brixton)
2001	April	Bradford (Lidget Green)
	May	Oldham
	June	Burnley
2005	Sept.	Belfast
	October	Birmingham (Lozells)

---

some ethnic minorities a counter-culture associated with drug-dealing and petty crime emerged and this brought people into conflict with the police. Police stop-and-search tactics that seemed to discriminate against blacks resulted in a deterioration of relationships between the police and black communities during the 1980s and early 1990s. In response, the police have scaled down this practice and made serious efforts to deal with accusations of 'institutional racism' (for a discussion of this concept see Chapter 6, p. 202).

Ethnicity was not a major factor in generating the outer estate riots of the early 1990s, though other forms of exclusion were involved. According to Campbell, 'these estates had been living with permanent high unemployment and decline, while they were encircled by evidence of prosperity and renewal' (1993: 303). Campbell gave as an extreme example of this the proximity of the Scotswood Estate to the Gateshead Metro centre (see box on 'A themed shopping centre' on p. 529). Conflicts with the police were again also a feature, for the estates had become centres of burglary, car theft, ram-raiding, and joy-riding.

Briefing: ethnic polarization

'Whilst the physical segregation of housing estates and inner city areas came as no surprise, the team was particularly struck by the depth of polarization of our towns and cities. The extent to which these physical divisions were compounded by so many other aspects of our daily lives, was very evident. Separate educational arrangements, community and voluntary bodies, employment, places of worship, language, social and cultural networks, means that many communities operate on the basis of a series of parallel lives. These lives often do not seem to touch at any point, let alone overlap and promote any meaningful interchanges.

A Muslim of Pakistani origin summed this up: "When I leave this meeting with you I will go home and not see another white face until I come back here next week".

Similarly, a young man from a white council estate said: "I never met anyone on this estate who wasn't like us from around here".

There is little wonder that the ignorance about each others' communities can easily grow into fear; especially where this is exploited by extremist groups determined to undermine community harmony and foster divisions.'

Source: Home Office (2001).

For a discussion of ethnic concentration, see Media Watch 13.

❓ *Under what conditions does the formation of communities lead to a polarization of this kind?*

❓ *In what ways can polarization be broken down?*

• More action by the police to ban 'inflammatory marches' but also a recognition by minorities that they have tolerated 'certain types of criminality'.

Polarization is not just a consequence of ethnicity. Indeed, perhaps the most extreme example of urban polarization in the United Kingdom has resulted from the religious divisions of Northern Ireland in general and Belfast in particular. The residential segregation of Catholics and Protestants has increased during recent decades. In Belfast it has become almost total in public housing and working-class areas. Where Catholic and Protestant areas are not kept apart by roads or commercial properties, they are separated by the high walls of the 'peace lines' (*Independent*, 6 April 2004).

In this context it is not surprising that riots returned to the Northern Ireland scene in September 2005. There were violent disorders in seven locations within Belfast and five locations outside. The riots were apparently initiated by Protestants and the event that triggered them was the re-routing of a traditional Protestant march away from a Catholic area. The rioting was fuelled by Protestant discontent with government housing policy, which, it was claimed, favoured Catholics, and also conflicts between the police and Protestant paramilitaries.

There were deeper, long-term causes of Protestant anger. There was said to be a Protestant sense of abandonment by the British government as it searched for an accommodation with Sinn Fein and the republican movement. Further in the background lay the decline of traditional Protestant working-class communities. These had suffered from the consequences of deindustrialization and were losing out demographically to Catholics. They were also experiencing a crisis of identity in the face of a new confidence among Irish Catholics (*Guardian*, 12 and 13 September 2005; Howe 2005).

Riots are very complex social events and in understanding and explaining them it is important to separate out:

• the underlying social conditions;
• the dynamics of conflict generation;
• the triggering incident;
• later responses to the situation;
• the explanations of those involved.

The *underlying social conditions* can be linked to the changes in the city that we have examined earlier—the decline of the inner city, concentrated deprivation in the inner city and on outer estates, and ethnic segregation.

The *dynamics of conflict generation* involve the vicious circles that easily develop around policing, criminality, and resources. Conflicts over these issues intensify discontent and create a combustible situation. Politicization through the involvement of external political agents, such as the British National Party, can play an important part in this.

Some *incident*, very often of a quite minor kind, can ignite a riot, but the way the riot unfolds depends on *responses* to the situation and it might take on a quite new character in its later stages.

After the riot those involved provide their own *explanations*, which derive from their own particular experiences, their beliefs about social conditions, and their concern to justify their actions. Rioters focus attention on the injustice or unfairness of the incident that precipitated the riot and accuse the police of worsening the situation by overreacting to legitimate protests. The 'authorities' deny that legitimate grievances have played any part in generating a riot and accuse extremists or looters of engineering it for their own purposes. Alternatively, the media are blamed for publicizing previous riots and triggering off 'copycat' incidents.

It is important to emphasize that there is no single or simple reason why such a complex event as a riot occurs. It passes through many stages in its development and at each one new factors can influence its course. It involves complex interactions between many different groups of people with differing perceptions of what is going on. The explanation of a riot must take account of the whole process and not fasten on one particular stage of it or one particular group's view of it.

Urban regeneration

We have given much attention to changes that are symptoms of urban decline—deurbanization, the problems of the inner city, the decline of the local state, and the return of the riot. Cities have also, however, become centres of regeneration and we move on to the role of culture and sport, and the part played by the state, in urban revival.

> ➲ *Connections*
> We have already touched on urban regeneration in our discussion of gentrification (see pp. 513–14), which can revive particular areas. In Study 13, at the end of this chapter, we examine the part played by the night-time economy of clubs and pubs in reviving the urban economy (and generating urban disorder).

Cultural restructuring

Culture is making a growing contribution to the city economy. Zukin has argued that 'cultural consumption' has become a central activity of the contemporary city:

> With the disappearance of local manufacturing industries and periodic crises in government and finance, culture is more and more the business of cities—the basis of their tourist attractions and their unique competitive edge. The growth of cultural consumption (of art, food, fashion, music, tourism) and the industries that cater to it fuels the city's symbolic economy. (Zukin 1995: 2)

By the 'symbolic economy', Zukin means the production and distribution of images rather than goods. Tourism, for example, sells sights, captured as images by the camera, rather than objects. Employment has steadily increased in a range of occupations concerned with the symbolic economy. Advertising, public relations, the media, designers, and software companies in various ways all make and sell images. Goods are, of course, still produced, but their design has become an ever larger component of their value.

The image of the city itself has become an important means of attracting investment through 'place marketing'. Culture, tourism, and investment are here closely tied together. Cultural attractions enable image-makers to sell cities to tourists, who bring money into the city, make it more widely known, and attract corporate investment. The focus on urban culture is therefore linked to the growth of global tourism (see Chapter 16, pp. 649–51) and is yet another aspect of the increasing integration of cities in the global economy.

Higher education is tied into this cultural complex, for universities are major employers and an ever-increasing source of local consumer demand as the government pursues its goal of having 50 per cent of 18 year olds in higher education. The image of the city is important in attracting student consumers as well as tourists.

The growing economic importance of culture, tourism, and education have made *cultural restructuring* one of the chief ways of regenerating cities in economic decline. The revival of Glasgow as 'European City of Culture' in 1990 has provided the best-known example in Britain, but the process has been going on in towns and cities up and down the country, and across Europe. In Spain, the Guggenheim made Bilbao a tourist destination and demonstrated that architecturally exciting art galleries could lead a city renaissance.

As employment in manufacturing has collapsed, the heritage industry has turned industrial landscapes into tourist attractions. The conversion of ex-industrial buildings into museums, galleries, and restaurants combines nostalgia for the past with the attraction of the new, as in the conversion of Southbank power station into Tate Modern. Cultural restructuring not only provides local employment and brings in tourists but also makes places more attractive to live and work in, and therefore brings in other businesses in the symbolic economy which can locate themselves where their employees want to be.

Sport cities

The attraction of major sporting events can perform a similar function to cultural activity in promoting an image, bringing in visitors and investment, and improving city facilities. As Urry (2002) has pointed out, such events can enable a city to reinvent itself by creating a new identity unrelated to the city's past or geographical location. The intense and global competition to host major sporting events shows the importance that cities attach to them. Huge sums are spent in the competition to host, especially, the Olympic Games and the football World Cup.

Taylor *et al.* (1996) have discussed the part played by sport in the regeneration of Manchester and Sheffield. Manchester's (unsuccessful) bids for the Olympic Games were an important part of that city's regeneration strategy,

Briefing: the cultural restructuring of Lancaster

'As industry has departed from the city centre Lancaster has been reconstructed as a modern consumption centre preserving the shells of past rounds of economic growth to house new functions—the old customs house as a maritime museum, the warehouses of the riverfront as gentrified homes, canal-side mill buildings as new pubs. One of the main thrusts of all of this is to construct "Lancaster" as an object of the tourist gaze. It has many of the ingredients of a modern tourist mecca: a castle (which in 1991 will become entirely usable for tourist purposes); a river and a gentrified river front; the folly on the hill (Ashton Memorial) just restored at a cost of some £1.5 million; four museums, three of which have been recently completed; well-conserved old, interesting streets with 270 listed buildings; cultural events including the Lancaster Literature festival, and so on.'
(Bagguley *et al.* 1990: 161)

Can you think of any examples of cultural restructuring in the area where you live?

and the bidding process alone attracted funds and improved facilities. Sheffield's success in attracting the World Student Games in 1992 was more of a mixed blessing, generating jobs and sports facilites but also imposing a financial burden on the city that led to cuts in local-authority services and jobs.

Manchester's (successful) bid for the 2002 Commonwealth Games was similarly double-edged. It was claimed that this would regenerate the eastern side of Manchester, attract tourists and capital, generate jobs, and enhance Manchester's image world-wide. Expenditure on the Games did, however, lead to the shutting down of fourteen Housing Department offices, redundancies among council employees, and the closing of two swimming pools and a boxing club (*Guardian*, 25 July 2001).

Will the London Olympics in 2012 regenerate East London and improve London transport or divert expenditure away from public services and other sports facilities?

Sport stadia play a crucial part in the competition to host major sporting events. The Commonwealth stadium and national velodrome were built in East Manchester to provide the main venue for the Commonwealth Games. The Millennium Stadium has brought major events to Cardiff. The building of new stadia can, however, lead to the closing of old ones and this can have a devastating effect on the local businesses that have grown up around them and the community that depends upon them.

The attraction of major sporting events, and indeed cultural restructuring, depend on a positive local response to change. They require not only investment by local entrepreneurs but also the active involvement of local authorities in promotion, coordination, reconstruction of the urban landscape, and the provision of facilities. The economic fortunes of cities do then depend not only on the impact upon them of movements of capital but also the local response, for this can be critical in shaping where the capital flows.

The state's role

Having contributed more than a little to the creation of an urban crisis through their cuts in local-authority spending, the Conservative governments of the 1980s became involved in urban regeneration. This was, however, to be brought about by private capital and the state's role was initially merely to encourage 'enterprise', to provide a context in which capital would invest.

Thus, the Conservatives' first regeneration initiative was the creation of Enterprise Zones, where planning regulations would be relaxed and companies would be exempt from certain taxes. As with the Free Trade Zones established in such countries as Mexico (see Chapter 16, pp. 648–9), capital would be attracted by creating a favourable environment for it.

A more interventionist approach followed with the creation of twelve Urban Development Corporations, the most well-known of which was the London Docklands Development Corporation (LDDC), which bypassed local authorities. These corporations could compulsorily purchase large areas, invest in infrastructure, and ignore normal planning restrictions. As the LDDC has shown, they could have a big impact on the environment, but whether this benefited the people who lived there was another matter. The LDDC certainly attracted international capital to build the office blocks, most famously at Canary Wharf, that now dominate the east London skyline, but did not provide much employment for local people accustomed to dock-work and other kinds of manual labour. While there was a huge expansion of private housing in the area, the prices were out of the reach of most locals, while funding cuts halted council-house building (Coupland 1992).

The City Challenge programme of 1993 initiated a period of greater local involvement. It brought in local authorities as major partners, and took more account of local needs and local people (Pratt and Fearnley 1996). This programme also went beyond the built environment to target particular areas' housing, education, and crime problems.

The Labour government's 2000 Urban White Paper basically continued this programme. It put forward a coordinated approach to regeneration that would deal with the multiple problems of particular areas. It also focused increasingly on 'community' and neighbourhood level, through New Deals for Communities and Neighbourhood Renewal Units. The government appears to be moving towards the provision of new powers to bodies at this level, such as a power to buy waste land in order to create parks, playgrounds, or community centres (*Guardian*, 13 October 2005).

The modernist idea of constructing a whole city, whether in the total vision of the 'ideal city', which we examined earlier (see pp. 507–9), or the comprehensive plan typical of the 'new town' is long gone. The focus is not now on the city as a whole but the local community and the neighbourhood. This has been described as a process of 'post-modern' regeneration that creates 'islands of renewal' in a piecemeal and fragmentary way (Wilkinson 1992).

The post-modern city

The idea that cities have recently entered a new stage in their development has led to the notion of the **post-modern city**, which is similar to the concepts of post-Fordism and post-modern organization and related to the changes that they describe. In this section, we use the concept of the post-modern city to draw together the various changes that we have been examining and link them to changes in city culture and city life.

Like the post-modern organization, the post-modern city is decentralized. The shifting of production and services to the periphery has hollowed out the city and decentralized its activities to the city's edge, where large units readily accessible by car and truck have been constructed on green-field sites. City centres have more recently experienced a revival through regeneration projects and the growth of the night-time economy of clubs and pubs but, while in the past people typically used public transport to head into the centre for shopping and services, they now drive in their cars to facilities on the periphery.

> **⊃ Connections**
> See Chapter 17, pp. 693–6 for our examination of post-Fordism and Chapter 14, p. 556 for the post-modern organization. Post-modernism is discussed in Chapter 2, pp. 64–6, and post-modern culture in Chapter 10, p. 366.

The post-modern world is particularly focused on consumption and culture, and this is reflected in urban life. The economy of the post-modern city is based less on the production of goods and more on the consumption of goods and services. Cities that were once known as centres of production, as cotton or hosiery or pottery or steel 'towns', now tend to be known for their shopping centres. There is also a much greater emphasis on the symbolic economy, on the production and consumption of images of all kinds. City politicians have recognized these changes and tried to revive their economies through cultural restructuring and the improvement of the city's image to draw in tourists, investors, and consumers in general.

The manufacturing of goods still, of course, goes on, but style and image have become a more important aspect of the product. Product diversity has become increasingly important and variations in style are one means of creating this. Furthermore, a style can extend across a range of products, so that furnishing, clothing, and personal appearance can be combined to create a certain image. The projection of an image lies at the heart of the attractiveness of a style.

Similarly, style and appearance rule in the *post-modern* city, as compared with the *modern* city, where function shaped appearance, and where products and buildings were mass-produced in standard forms. Modernism produced efficiently functioning structures that were universally applicable and almost indistinguishable. One tower block looked like another. Post-modern architecture has reacted by playfully creating façades that have nothing to do with the function of the building, often borrowing and combining styles from the past.

This emphasis on style and surface appearance took on an all-embracing form through the simulation of complete worlds. In the *modern* city people went to the cinema to transport themselves into another world, for this was the only way that most people could 'escape reality'. The film industry went on, however, to create in the various versions of Disneyland complete cities, where we can visit, and for

Figure 13.18 Modern and post-modern cities

The modern city	The post-modern city
● Centralized	● Decentralized
● Production	● Consumption
● Manufacturing	● Symbolic economy
● Function	● Style
● Faceless architecture	● Façades
● Reality	● Simulation
● Collective consumption	● Private consumption
● Public life	● Private life
● Integration	● Fragmentation

Las Vegas—the ultimate post-modern city?
© Getty Images/Robert Glusic

a time stay in, another world and accompany its characters. The experience of other places is simulated in a safe and sanitized environment. In the *post-modern* city people can escape reality by actually entering simulated worlds.

A process of what Bryman (1999) has called Disneyization has spread Disney principles into many areas of consumption. Theming, the contriving of an experience of another world, is not only found in Disneyland and theme parks but in themed hotels, themed restaurants, and themed shopping centres (see box on 'A themed shopping centre'). Theming has found perhaps its most famous expression in Las Vegas, where visitors to its hotel-casinos can sample simulations of Venice, Rome, ancient Egypt, and so on. The Disney company has constructed a whole new town in Florida, called Celebration, on theme park principles, to recreate the feeling of a traditional American small town.

Theming makes cities placeless. Placelessness is one of the most remarked upon features of the contemporary city. The location of the city and its history become irrelevant as theming creates a fictitious place that isolates the themed area from its geographical and historical context. The standardized superstores, shopping malls, hotel chains, and burger bars that are such a feature of the contemporary city have no sense of place about them. The domination of the high street by brand name chains selling identical products in every town or city has resulted in the 'cloning' of urban centres as they lose their distinctiveness of place. Perhaps the ultimate example of the placeless urban experience is the cruise ship (see box on 'The cruising city'), a floating city which is not only wholly contrived but always moving between places and insulated from them.

The isolation of the individual from place is reinforced by the increasingly private character of life in the

Briefing: the cruising city

Steven Miles and Malcolm Miles argue that in the cruise ship 'consumer capitalism' has created a 'placeless city':

> . . . in its determination to find new markets through the commodification of city life, consumer capitalism has reached the stage where it can now actively transcend place in the form of a mobile city, a city without place, but *with* consumption. (2004: 134)

The cruise ship provides round-the-clock consumption for its passengers. Services are available throughout the day. Food and entertainment are continuously provided. A wide variety of shops, personal services, and leisure activities make available anything a person might wish to buy 'under one roof'. Furthermore, this is a captive market, since opportunities to purchase goods and services elsewhere are extremely limited.

Indeed, although cruises are sold on the basis of visits to romantic tourist destinations, it is the cruise ship itself which is for many people the main attraction. Contact with local destination cultures is extremely limited and carefully controlled. The local culture that is made available is inevitably commercialized, sanitized, and non-authentic. The consumption of local products is also minimal, since cruise ships are fully stocked with consumables before they leave their home port. Thus, cruising is placeless in the sense that passengers hardly experience the places they visit.

The society of the cruise ship, like urban society, is stratified and segregated. There is the division between passengers and crew but the passengers themselves are divided into classes, while the crew are stratified into occupational hierarchies. The crew are ethnically diverse but also ethnically stratified as different ethnicities occupy different occupational positions. Segregation excludes from specific areas of the ship members of different passenger classes and categories of crew.

The placeless city has, however, gone beyond cruising with the construction of mobile residential ships. The first such ship, *The World*, has 110 private apartments and claims that it enables people to travel the world without leaving home. The projected *Freedom Ship* describes itself as a 'floating city' with 18,000 living units, 3,000 commercial units, 2,400 time-shares and 10,000 hotel rooms. It claims that it will have a 'world-class' medical facility, a school system, and an international trade centre.

Sources: Miles and Miles (2004); *The World* and *Freedom Ship* websites.

❓ *What do you think is meant by 'the commodification of city life'? (Visiting the glossary and the index will help you with this.)*

➲ *Assess the claim that 'cruise ships are the cities of the future' (Miles and Miles 2004: 140).*

---

post-modern city. The privatizing changes that we have examined in this chapter, the privatizing of consumption and entertainment, the spread of homeownership, the privatizing of public space, focus people more on their domestic and private lives. As public and communal life has declined, people are less inclined to go out into their city and experience what is left of its particular qualities as a place. The particularity of the place where they live loses importance in their lives.

All these various changes have resulted in the urban society of the post-modern city becoming more fragmented. The city has been fragmented by decentralization and the dispersal of population. The public life that once brought people at least superficially together has declined and public space is increasingly seen as dangerous and best avoided. Cities have also become more divided by inequality and ethnic diversity. The well-off have withdrawn behind their fortifications, while the poor have been isolated in inner-city areas of deprivation and outer-city estates without employment. Ethnic fragmentation has produced some strong communities but also juxtaposed and polarized cultures that do not communicate much with each other.

It would be misleading, however, to suggest that the city has completely changed. Decentralization does not mean that city centres no longer exist, and central shopping areas have fought back against the peripheral stores, often by creating a kind of 'inner periphery' of enclosed shopping malls or retail parks. There are still rush hours, as those living in the suburbs travel into work in the centre, while city centres have acquired new life from the clubs and pubs that pull in people from suburban areas at night (see Study 13 below).

The post-modern city is superimposed on the modern city, which still surrounds us and still structures our lives. While being aware of continuities, we do, none the less, need to find ways of grasping change, and the notion of the post-modern city helps us to do this. It highlights the reversal of many previous tendencies and connects together into a coherent pattern many of the features of the contemporary city.

Briefing: a themed shopping centre

'Looking across the river from Scotswood, the residents see another miracle of the Enterprise Zone, the £200 million Gateshead Metro Centre, Europe's biggest retail park, which was built on 115 acres of derelict land, and was fuelled by tax allowances and an exemption from rates until 1991. It provided a creche for customers, but not for its projected four thousand workers. Looking like an eyeless fortress, topped with stiff plastic flags around its periphery, the Metro Centre is a cornucopia of pastiche—customers walk around two million square feet of retail space down colour-coded routes, along 42nd Avenue, or around the Grecian Terrace, or through the Victorian Arcade lit darkly with a night sky all day long. People go for the day to the Metro Centre; they have been seen with flasks and sandwiches as if they were on holiday. The Metro Centre is a shopping resort.'
(B. Campbell 1993: 305)

 In what ways can such a shopping centre be considered post-modern?

 Stop and reflect

In 'Deurbanization and deruralization' we discussed the relationship between recent changes in capitalism and changes in the city.

- There is some evidence of deurbanization in rich countries but arguably a broad process of deruralization has also occurred.
- Global cities have grown in size and become to some degree detached from their surrounding areas.
- What is it that makes the global city distinctive and how have its global functions affected urban society?

We then examined the emergence of a new kind of decentralized city.

- Decentralization was associated with dedifferentiation.
- Cities were 'hollowed out' and deprivation grew in central areas as they lost employment and resources.
- More recently a reverse process of gentrification has occurred.
- Has urban space been degendered?

In 'Changing communities' we examined the effects of various social changes on a range of communities.

- Make sure that you are clear about the meaning of 'community' and revisit pp. 496–7 if you are not.

- Although some communities have been weakened, others have become stronger, and some new forms of community have emerged.
- How would you explain the emergence of gay villages?
- Are virtual communities real communities? Visit a virtual community on the Net and see what features of 'community' you can identify.

We moved on to consider 'City management in decline' and 'Urban regeneration'.

- Privatization has resulted in the decline of 'collective consumption'.
- Urban riots 'returned' in the 1980s.
- Cities have also, however, been regenerated through 'cultural restructuring', investment in sport stadia, and government initiatives.

Lastly, we examined the broad notion of the 'post-modern' consumer city.

- Make sure that you understand the meaning of 'theming' and 'placelessness'.
- How have they affected the city's appearance and the experience of city life?
- Can a cruise ship be described as a 'floating city'?
- Has the 'post-modern' city replaced the 'modern city'?

Chapter summary

In the 'Understanding cities and communities' section we examined the distinctiveness of urban society and the relationship between city and community.

We first considered the relationship between the development of the city, capitalism, and industrialism:

- A network of medieval cities was at the heart of the early development of capitalism.
- Industrial cities were shaped by the requirements of production but more recently cities have been reorganized around consumption.
- Global cities have emerged as centres of a new network directing economic development.

We went on to consider the distinctiveness of urban society:

- Wirth defined cities in terms of their size, population density, and diversity, which he thought produced a distinctive urban way of life.
- Gans and Giddens argued that way of life is shaped by class, life cycle, and capitalism rather than location.

We then discussed the issues raised by community:

- Wirth and Tonnies saw the city as incompatible with community, but others argued that communities can thrive in cities.
- The concept of a socioscape has been put forward as a more appropriate term for areas where people from different social worlds coexist.
- Although people still hanker after community life, community has negative as well as positive connotations for social integration.

In 'Urbanization and centralization' we outlined the modern city's development and its social divisions.

We first examined the process of urbanization:

- Industrialization led to the urbanization of British society through changes in production, travel, and leisure patterns.
- Urbanization also resulted from the growth of global trading and financial activities, and the creation of overseas empires.

We went on to analyse the centralized city's character and structure:

- City space was differentiated by function and segregated by ethnicity, class, and gender.
- Although urbanization disrupted communities, they re-established themselves in working-class areas of the city.

- As the centralized city developed, the local state and collective consumption grew.
- Land use was increasingly planned by public officials, though organized interest groups influenced the planning process.

In 'The contemporary city' we explored the consequences of decentralization, its impact on communities, and the emergence of the 'post-modern' city.

We first examined the decentralization of the city and its consequences:

- This led to both deurbanization and deruralization.
- Decentralization 'hollowed out' the city but there has also been a reverse process of gentrification.
- There has been some reversal of gender-role segregation, but city space has remained highly gendered.

We went on to consider the effects of urban change on communities:

- Some existing urban and rural communities were weakened but others formed.
- Ethnic communities established themselves, and attempts have been made to construct multi-ethnic communities.
- Although local communities have often declined, the Internet has provided opportunities for the creation of virtual communities.

Changes initiated by government have weakened the local state and diminished its capacity to manage urban society, but it has been involved in urban regeneration:

- Collective consumption has declined, as services, housing, and space were privatized.
- Urban rioting became a regular feature of city life during the 1980s.
- Cultural restructuring and investment in sport have attracted capital and tourists.
- Government initiatives have brought private capital in to regenerate the city.

Recent changes in the city can be conceptualized as a shift from the modern to the post-modern city:

- The post-modern city has been superimposed on the modern city.
- In the post-modern city function gives way to style and surface appearance.
- Post-modern cities are also decentralized, divided, and fragmented.

🔑 *Key concepts*

- city
- collective consumption
- communitarianism
- community
- gatekeepers
- global city

- housing classes
- post-modern city
- primary groups
- privatization
- secondary groups
- segmental relationships

- socioscapes
- sociospheres
- urban ecology
- urbanization
- urban way of life
- virtual communities

Workshop 13

Study 13 Cities in the night

At night British city centres are taken over by young drinkers frequenting a mass of late-night bars and clubs. In a lively and intriguing article, 'Receiving shadows . . .', Dick Hobbs *et al.* (2000) explore the causes and consequences of the rise of a night-time economy that has become a central feature of the 'post-industrial' British city.

This new economy has emerged against the background of industrial cities in decline. As we showed on pp. 512–13, the movement of production to lower-cost locations elsewhere has emptied industrial cities of much of the manufacturing that was once at the heart of the urban economy. The vacuum left by local deindustrialization has been filled by services, as cities have reinvented themselves as centres of leisure and consumption. The night-time economy of bars and clubs has also provided flexible employment for the young, who can combine night-time work with day-time jobs or studies.

The growth of this economy has not, however, simply been an economic process. Hobbs *et al.* (2000) argue that it is also closely connected with a 'new urban governance'. Local government went into partnership with private capital in a 'municipal capitalism' that contrasts with the 'municipal socialism' of old (see p. 506 of this chapter). City councils engaged in an intense competition to regenerate their cities by attracting scarce capital to them. Instead of limiting and regulating city-centre bars, they encouraged them, by relaxing licensing and planning rules in order to attract breweries, pub chains, and leisure companies to invest.

The rapid growth of licensed premises has brought about an intense and homogenizing competition between the various bars and clubs for the young drinkers' market. Old-style pubs, with a diverse, local clientele, give way to 'fun pubs'. Stone floors are replaced by wooden dance floors, entertainment is introduced, and 'a cross-section of quality bitters is replaced by a narrow selection of strong lagers' (Hobbs *et al.* 2000: 709). In the city centre investigated by Hobbs *et al.*, only four of the fifteen traditional pubs that were there ten years ago had survived. Few city centres can maintain their own distinctive leisure culture in the face of such pressures.

According to Hobbs *et al.*, areas that are shopping and business districts in the day-time take on a different character during night-time. The line between day and night is a division between work and leisure, safety and danger. Night-time gives 'a release from the rigours and restraints of the daylight hours' but also 'inspires fear and apprehension'. It is a time of 'liminality', by which they mean enjoyment of a separate area of life outside its normal boundaries. People can escape the routines of ordinary existence and abandon normal restraints in the experimental pursuit of excitement and illicit pleasures (Hobbs *et al.* 2000: 710–11).

Pubs and clubs exploit this desire for liminality and seek to give people the feeling that they are in a distinctive community of free and equal people, in order to attach their customers to a particular venue. Hobbs *et al.* consider that this is, however, illusory. There is no real community or freedom or equality, but rather commercial manipulation and control by business interests, maintained by a subculture of criminality and violence.

They examine this subculture in another article, based in part on a covert ethnographic study carried out by a member of the research team working as a bouncer (Winlow *et al.* 2001). A 'door culture' had emerged among the bouncers 'as a strategy of economic and personal survival, control and domination within a hostile and chaotic working milieu' (Hobbs *et al.* 2002: 355). Verbal skills, local knowledge, and physical presence were important attributes of the bouncer but it was their fighting skills that were crucial. Bouncers often had a criminal record and there was plenty of scope for criminal abuse of their power.

> As informed by our interviewees, this scope for abuse ranges from the potential for an 'over-the-top' heavy handed response to problem punters, to the opportunist theft from a marooned handbag, to the planned conspiracy to supply, wholesale, a venue's drug of choice. (Hobbs *et al.* 2002: 360)

The maintenance of order in the city at night-time had largely fallen into the hands of bouncers. Manchester city centre attracted about 75,000 people on Friday and Saturday evenings and they were controlled by almost 1,000 bouncers, as compared with some thirty police officers normally charged with public order duty. The maintenance of order in the night-time world of the city had effectively been privatized and placed in the hands of people with criminal connections and often a criminal record. The state had apparently abandoned its historic monopoly of

the right to use physical force (see our discussion of this in Chapter 15, p. 581).

Registration schemes for bouncers operated by local authorities are supposed to provide a degree of official control and exclude those with a criminal record, but Hobbs *et al.* (2002) do not consider that they are effective or could ever be, even if their role were strengthened by legislation and the proposed creation of a Security Industry Authority. They conclude that 'local police divisions with their wealth of local knowledge and experience are likely to remain better situated to manage and enforce regulation at both a formal and informal level' (Hobbs *et al.* 2002: 363).

Sources: Hobbs, D., Lister, S., Hadfield, P., Winlow, S., and Hall, S. (2000), 'Receiving Shadows: Governance and Liminality in the Night-time Economy', *British Journal of Sociology*, 51; Hobbs, D., Hadfield, P., Lister, S., and Winlow, S. (2002), 'Door Lore: The Art and Economics of Intimidation', *British Journal of Criminology*, 42; Winlow, S., Hobbs, D., Lister, S., and Hadfield, P. (2001), 'Get Ready to Duck: Bouncers and the Realities of Ethnographic Research on Violent Groups', *British Journal of Criminology*, 42.

? What does this study tell us about the relationship between capitalism and the city? Go into your local city and try systematically comparing a traditional pub and a cheap alcohol bar under the following headings: the environment; the venue; processes of commercial operation; mechanisms of social control; staff appearance and behaviour; staff interactions with customers; customer appearance and behaviour.

 Media watch 13 Cosmopolitan London

In September 2005 a speech by Trevor Phillips, Chairman of the Commission for Racial Equality, was given much media attention. Phillips argued that a process of ghettoization was taking place in British cities. Multiculturalism has, in Phillips's view, failed and the populations of British cities are becoming segregated into ethnic communities which do not intermix.

He claimed that research showed that the residential concentration of people of Pakistani origin in Leicester and Bradford is increasing: 'The number of people of Pakistani heritage in what are technically called "ghetto" communities trebled during 1991–2001; 13% in Leicester live in such communities (the figure 10.8% in 1991); 13.3% in Bradford (it was 4.3% in 1991)'. He concluded that 'the fragmentation of our society by race and ethnicity is a catastrophe for all of us' (Phillips 2005).

Leo Benedictus (2005) carried out for the *Guardian* an analysis of the residential distribution of different ethnic groups in London, using data from the 2001 Census. He found that around a third of the population of London had been born outside Britain and many more of its residents were descendants of immigrants who

identified with minority ethnic groups. Ethnic minorities only rarely, however, amounted to more than 50 per cent of the population of a ward. He claimed that 'there are no true ghettoes in the city'.

The Bangladeshis have become the most concentrated ethnic group. In 1991 there were about 37,000 of them in Tower Hamlets but there were 67,000 by 2001. Over a third of Tower Hamlets residents considered themselves to be Bangladeshis and in one ward they amounted to nearly 60 per cent of the population. Pakistanis were much less concentrated and were less than 20 per cent of the population in all wards in their areas.

Indians were mainly concentrated in a large area of West London, where in some wards they were over 50 per cent of the population. What appeared to be a solid Indian area was, however, divided by religion, with a Hindu part to the north and a Sikh part to the west, though in some wards they overlapped. The notion of a solidly Indian area here was misleading because it concealed two different communities.

Afro-Caribbeans were concentrated in three distinct blocks, in the east, south, and west, where there were large and overlapping black African and black Caribbean populations. The notion of three 'black' areas may again, however, be at least partly misleading, as may be the term 'Afro-Caribbean: 'The two halves of the black community often live close together, sharing shops, schools and history, and yet they have acquired a reputation for not getting along—nowhere more famously than in Peckham . . .' (Benedictus 2005).

The Chinese population was much more dispersed than any of these groups and was nowhere more than 6 per cent of the population of a ward. This was said to be because they prefer to set up their restaurants at a distance from each other!

The white British were concentrated in a ring of outer boroughs, where in a large number of wards they amounted to over 75 per cent of the population, and in one East London ward over 90 per cent.

This is just a brief outline of the distribution of some of the larger ethnic groups and it is important to bear in mind the sheer ethnic diversity of London. Benedictus claimed that London is probably the most ethnically diverse city in the world.

'Altogether, more than three hundred languages are spoken by the people of London, and the city has at least fifty non-indigenous communities with populations of ten thousand or more' (Benedictus 2005).

Sources: Benedictus, L. (2005), 'London: The World in One City', *Guardian*, 1 January (a *Guardian* special report, with maps, is obtainable from its website); Phillips, T. (2005), 'After 7/7: Sleepwalking to Segregation', speech given to the Manchester Council for Community Relations, 22 September.

➔ See what you can find out about the original meaning of the term 'ghetto' and the history of its use.

❓ Do you think that 'ghetto' is an appropriate term for the ethnic minority residential patterns found in Britain?

❓ Where do you think that the most residentially segregated places in the United Kingdom are?

❓ Under what conditions do ethnic groups become residentially segregated?

Discussion points

Community

Before discussing this, read the sections on 'Urban society', 'Community', 'Changing communities', and Media watch 13.

- What are the key features of a community?
- How important is identification with a place?
- What are the differences between the 'container' and 'network' conceptions of community?
- Is city life compatible with community life?
- Should 'gay villages' be considered communities?
- Do communities integrate people?
- Do communities increase social conflict?
- Are communities a desirable feature of urban life?
- Are virtual communities 'real' communities?
- Visit a virtual community on the Web and see what features of 'community' it has.
- Do virtual communities increase or decrease a person's participation in community life?
- Do you think that you are a member of a community?
- Why do you think it is a community?
- What effect does it have on your social relationships?

The post-modern city

Before discussing this read 'Capitalism and the city', 'Cultural restructuring', and 'The post-modern city'.

- What is distinctive about the city that you know best?
- Has it undergone a process of cultural restructuring?
- What image do you think that the city has?
- What is the main basis of employment in the city?
- Has there been a shift from manufacturing to services?
- Has there been a shift from production to consumption?
- Is this city losing its distinctiveness?
- List any ways in which it is becoming 'placeless'.
- Do you think that the identity of the city matters any longer to the people who live there?
- What aspects of contemporary urban life does the notion of a post-modern city draw attention to? See if you can find those aspects in a city that you know.
- Can you also find the main features of the modern city?
- How post-modern do you think this city is?

Explore further

Clear and comprehensive coverage of the main issues and the literature on cities and communities can be found in the following texts:

Byrne, D. (2001), *Understanding the Urban* (Houndmills: Palgrave).

Crow, G. and Allan, G. (1994), *Community Life: An Introduction to Local Social Relations* (Hemel Hempstead: Harvester Wheatsheaf). *This is an extremely useful introduction to community, which brings the concept up to date by developing a network perspective.*

Savage, M., and Warde, A. (2002), *Urban Sociology, Capitalism and Modernity* (2nd edn., London: Palgrave Macmillan).

Wide-ranging collections of articles and extracts can be found in these readers:

Kasinitz, P. (1995) (ed.), *Metropolis: Centre and Symbol of Our Times* (London: Macmillan).

Legates, R. T., and Stout, F. (1996) (eds.), *The City Reader* (London: Routledge).

Westwood, S., and Williams, J. (1997) (eds.), *Imagining Cities: Scripts, Signs, and Meanings* (London: Routledge).

For further reading on particular topics:

Delanty, G. (2003), *Community* (London: Routledge). *Ranges across multiculturalism, globalization, post-modernism, and the virtual world in order to reconceptualize this concept in a way appropriate to the contemporary world.*

Dench, G., Gavron, K., and Young, M. (2006), *The New East End: Kinship, Race, and Conflict* (London: Profile). *Following up on the work of Young and Willmott, this examines the impact of immigration and the welfare state on East London communities and ethnicities.*

Eade, J. (1997) (ed.), *Living the Global City: Globalization as Local Process* (London: Routledge). *An innovatory and influential collection of pieces on the relationship between global and local changes in London.*

Low, S. (2003), *Behind the Gates: Life, Security and the Pursuit of Happiness in Fortress America* (London: Routledge). *Life in the gated communities that are becoming increasingly common in the United States but also spreading into the United Kingdom.*

Miles, S., and Miles, M. (2004), *Consuming Cities* (Basingstoke: Palgrave Macmillan). *A lively, wide-ranging, and sophisticated examination of the relationship between consumption and urban life, illustrated with detailed examples from around the world.*

Sassen, S. (2001), *The Global City: New York, London, Tokyo* (2nd edn., Princeton, NJ: Princeton University Press). *Second edition of a classic study that argues that these three cities form a transterritorial market-place, detached from their national economies.*

Smith, M., and Kollock, P. (1999) (eds.), *Communities in Cyberspace* (London: Routledge). *This interesting collection goes beyond the hype to examine the realities of communities formed on the Internet.*

Taylor, I., Evans, K., and Fraser, P. (1996), *A Tale of Two Cities: Global Change, Local Feeling, and Everyday Life in the North of England. A Study in Manchester and Sheffield* (London: Routledge). *A plentiful and fascinating source of material on recent changes in these two cities and how they have affected many different aspects of the lives of those who live in them.*

Thorns, D. (2002), *The Transformation of Cities: Urban Theory and Urban Life* (Basingstoke: Palgrave Macmillan). *This thoughtful and wide-ranging book moves from the industrial city to the 'sustainable' city via topics such as the global city, consumption in the city, and urban social inequality.*

Zukin, S. (1995), *The Culture of Cities* (Oxford: Blackwell). *Highly readable analysis of cities as centres of cultural consumption and production, which examines the Disneyfication of the city.*

Online resources

Visit the Online Resource Centre that accompanies this book to access more learning resources and other interesting material on cities and communities at:

www.oxfordtextbooks.co.uk/orc/fulcher3e/

For information about virtual communities on the Internet, visit the website of Howard Rheingold, one of the pioneers of their development, but bear in mind that he is promoting the idea:

www.rheingold.com

The *Guardian* special report on the ethnic diversity of London (see Media watch 13) can be found through the *Guardian* website:

www.guardian.co.uk

The ambitiously (and acronymically) named Global Urban Research Unit at the University of Newcastle carries out a wide range of projects, including some on the theme of 'neighbourhood diversity and social inclusion':

www.ncl.ac.uk/guru/home.htm

organization, management, and control

Contents

Organizing the McDonald's way: the McDonald's operations manual

'It told operators exactly how to draw milk shakes, grill hamburgers, and fry potatoes. It specified precise cooking times for all products and temperature settings for all equipment. It fixed standard portions on every food item, down to the quarter ounce of onions placed on each hamburger patty and the thirty-two slices per pound of cheese. It specified that french fries be cut at nine thirty-seconds of an inch thick. And it defined quality controls that were unique to food service, including the disposal of meat and potato products that were held more than ten minutes in a serving bin.

Grill men were instructed to put hamburgers down on the grill moving from left to right, creating six rows of six patties each. And because the first two rows were farthest from the heating element, they were instructed (and still are) to flip the third row first, then the fourth, fifth, and sixth before flipping the first two.'

Source: Love (1986: 141–2, quoted in Ritzer 1996: 32).

We spend much of our daily lives working for organizations or trying to obtain goods or services from them. Schools, hospitals, companies, trade unions, churches, government departments, armies, prisons, and theatres are all organizations. We tend to think of them as very different in character because they carry out such different tasks, but they do all have certain basic features in common. Indeed, as you will find in this chapter, the insights obtained from the study of one organization have often been applied to apparently very different ones.

Most of the organizations that we come across are bureaucracies and we have mixed feelings about them. Bureaucratic organizations do meet important needs by providing us, for example, with employment, health care, and education. They also often seem impersonal, obstructive, and unconcerned with our particular requirements. In this chapter we discuss the functions of bureaucratic rules and how they are used and interpreted. We also consider whether there are alternative, less bureaucratic and more effective ways of organizing activities.

An orderly society depends on discipline. Hospital patients are required to accept treatment, soldiers to obey orders, employees to do their work, and students to write essays. But why do people act in the way required by organizations? How do organizations know that they are behaving in the correct way. We examine the basis of discipline, the development of methods of control, and the surveillance techniques used to monitor people's behaviour.

Organizations require management. Those who run them have to ensure that they achieve their goals. What is the best way to do this? One way is to divide work up into simple tasks, give workers detailed instructions, and see that they carry them out, as in the McDonald's restaurant. Is it, however, better for managers to leave it to the workers to decide how best to carry out tasks and concentrate themselves on motivating workers to do their best? How then can people best be motivated? We examine these issues too in this chapter.

We also consider who actually controls an organization. In most organizations there are experts with a specialized knowledge of the activity concerned, but do they control what goes on? In a business organization, is it the managers who are in control or those who own it? In many industries and services there have recently been major changes in ownership with their transfer from the public to the private sector through privatization. What difference does private or public ownership make? We consider too the global corporation and the amount of control it exercises over its operations in different countries.

You will find that we discuss many different organizations, from departments of government and business corporations to mental hospitals and prisons. As you read the chapter, try and apply what you learn about organizations to any that you have personal experience or knowledge of.

Understanding organizations

We begin by considering briefly what we mean by organizations, before discussing Max Weber's analysis of bureaucracy, which has been central to the sociological study of organizations. One of the defining features of bureaucracy is discipline and we go on to examine Foucault's influential analysis of this. We also consider his concept of carceral organization and Goffman's similar notion of the total institution.

Organizations

The term **organization** is used in a very general way in sociology. You should not worry too much about the definition of this term, but it is worth sketching out briefly what sociologists have in mind when they refer to organizations. An organization is basically a structure for carrying out a particular social activity on a regular basis and will generally have the following features:

- a specific goal;
- a defined membership;
- rules of behaviour;
- authority relationships.

Continuity is a key characteristic of an organization. It has an existence independent of the particular individuals who make it up at any one time. There may be frequent changes of personnel, as people enter and leave it or move between its different positions, but the organization continues to exist.

The range of social units that come into the category of organizations is not particularly well defined. It is clear that, for example, business corporations, trade unions, hospitals, schools, churches, and armies are all organizations, for they all have the features listed above. It is equally clear that some social groups, such as a community or a class, are not, for they do not have specific goals or rules of behaviour, though they may provide the social basis for organizations that do.

The term 'organization' is also used to refer to the *process* through which a group becomes organized. Social-class organization provides a good example of this. A social class consists of those who share a common economic situation (see our discussion of class in Chapter 19, pp. 774–5) and is not itself an organization, but it can become organized through the creation of class organizations, such as trade unions or political parties.

There is some ambiguity in the use of the terms 'organization' and 'institution'. Strictly speaking, organizations are not institutions. **Institutions** are established practices that regulate the various activities that make up social life. A wedding or a funeral are, for example, institutions but not organizations. These practices became, however, increasingly organized as society developed and the term 'institution' is often used to refer to the organizations which now carry out these practices. Thus, churches, schools, hospitals, and prisons are often described as institutions, though they should really be called organizations. Goffman, whose work we shall discuss shortly, uses the term 'total institution' to refer to mental hospitals and other organizations of this kind.

Bureaucracy

Bureaucracy is only one type of organization but one that became increasingly widespread as society developed. Most of the organizations that we come into contact with in our daily lives are bureaucratic in character, though not all. Small businesses, for example, are not usually run on bureaucratic lines. In this section we consider the meaning of bureaucracy and the issues raised by bureaucratic organization.

Weber's ideal type

Weber's *ideal type* of **bureaucracy** has been the starting point of the sociological study of organizations. The term 'ideal type' can be a little confusing and it is important to be clear about its meaning, which we discuss in Chapter 2, p. 40. Weber's ideal type was a statement not of what bureaucracies *ought* to be like but rather of the *key features* of bureaucratic organization.

According to Weber (1914), bureaucracies have the following characteristics:

- *Specialist expertise*. Bureaucracies contrast with earlier forms of organization where there was no systematic specialization of tasks. Expertise depends on education and training, and bureaucracies require qualifications for entry. As Weber put it: 'bureaucratic administration means fundamentally the exercise of control on the basis of knowledge' (1920: 225).
- *Hierarchy*. There is a hierarchy of officials, with those in higher positions having authority over those lower down. The duties of the different positions are laid down in writing and behaviour is closely supervised.
- *Impersonal rules*. Particular cases are dealt with by reference to general rules. Bureaucrats are expected

to apply rules impersonally and take no account of the particular character of the person with whom they are dealing. This applies whether they are dealing with each other or with the outside world.

- *Discipline.* Bureaucrats are required to obey the rules and carry out their duties in a disciplined way. The bureaucrat is expected to be self-disciplined but, if the rules are broken, the official concerned is punished.

- *Salaries.* Bureaucrats are paid salaries. This means that they do not have to earn their living as they perform their duties. Their private interests and their public duties are clearly separated.

- *Careers.* Bureaucrats have full-time and permanent posts. Their security of employment enables them to act impartially without fear or favour. They are promoted on the basis of merit and seniority.

The interrelationships between these elements are central to the ideal type. Thus, career officials can operate impersonally because of the independence and security provided by their salaries and their permanent posts. Similarly, disciplined behaviour is bound up with hierarchy and the application of impersonal rules in a non-emotional way.

Since Weber's time there have been numerous studies of bureaucracy that have criticized or revised the ideal type. Martin Albrow (1970) argued that much of the criticism of Weber was ill-founded, because it misunderstood or over-simplified what he wrote. The critics of Weber have been concerned with the *efficiency* of bureaucracy, while Weber was primarily interested in its *rationality*. Weber's writings on bureaucracy should certainly be placed in the context of his general interest in broader processes of rationalization (see Chapter 2, p. 42). He did, none the less, make many statements that indicated his belief in the technical efficiency of bureaucracy:

> The decisive reason for the advance of bureaucratic organization has always been its purely *technical* superiority over any other form of organization. The fully developed bureaucratic mechanism compares with other organizations exactly as does the machine with the non-mechanical modes of production. Precision, speed, unambiguity, knowledge of the files, continuity, discretion, unity, strict subordination, reduction of friction and of material and personal costs—these are raised to the optimum point in the strictly bureaucratic administration . . .
> (Max Weber 1914: 973)

The functions of rules

Much of the literature on bureaucracy has focused on the operation of rules. One question it raises is whether obedience to the rules results in effective organization. It also raises more fundamental issues to do with their use and interpretation by different groups.

THEORY AND METHODS

Alvin Gouldner

Gouldner (1920–80) was born in New York and spent most of his career as a Professor of Sociology at Washington University. His *Patterns of Industrial Bureaucracy* (1954a) and the follow-up *Wildcat Strike* (1954b) were path-breaking studies that explored empirically and theoretically a number of issues raised by Weber's work on bureaucracy. He is probably best known, however, for *The Coming Crisis of Western Sociology* (1970), in which he examined the historical development of sociological thinking and tried to develop a middle path between the functionalist and Marxist approaches that dominated sociology at that time. He also founded the journal *Theory and Society*. The major influences on Gouldner's thinking were Weber, the Frankfurt school (see Chapter 10, p. 367), and C. Wright Mills.

Robert Merton (1940) examined the *dysfunctions* of rules. He argued that obedience to the rules could prevent an organization achieving its goals, instead of enabling it to function efficiently. Obedience to the rules is considered so crucial that officials are trained to obey them to the letter and this can lead to decisions that are inappropriate to a particular situation. The application of rules can become 'an end in itself' rather than a means of achieving the organization's goals. Merton called this a **displacement of goals**, for the bureaucrat's goal became the correct application of the rules rather than the achievement of the organization's goals. Bureaucrats therefore acquired what Merton called a *trained incapacity* to work effectively.

In a well-known study of an American factory, Alvin Gouldner (1954a) argued that the operation of bureaucratic rules should be understood not in terms of the needs of the organization as a *whole* but rather in terms of the interests of *various groups* within it and the relationships between them. Thus, while some rules might be imposed on workers by managers, others were forced on management by workers, while still others emerged in a more 'democratic' way through consultation and discussion. Gouldner identified three patterns of bureaucracy within the factory:

- *Mock bureaucracy.* This referred to rules, such as no-smoking rules, that were not enforced by management, except when the insurance inspector visited. This non-enforcement helped to create solidarity between managers and workers against the interfering outside world.

- *Representative bureaucracy.* This referred to rules that were implemented with the consent of workers. Thus, workers accepted the need for safety rules. He labelled this kind of bureaucracy as representative, because the workers themselves were involved, in part through union safety committees, in the process of developing and implementing these rules.

- *Punishment-centred bureaucracy*. This referred to rules that one side tried to impose on the other against resistance. Management tried to enforce a non-absenteeism rule on the workers. The workers tried to force management to fill vacancies according to the procedure laid down by a collective agreement, which required any new job to be offered to existing workers and restricted the managers' freedom of action.

Gouldner emphasized that in other situations a particular rule might fall into another pattern. On an oil rig, the evident dangers of smoking might mean that a non-smoking rule would become an example of representative rather than mock bureaucracy. Arguably, the diminishing cultural acceptance of smoking has anyway tended to shift non-smoking rules into this pattern. The fundamental point is that rules do not exist in some vacuum but have to be interpreted and enforced before they become a social reality. The interests of groups and the relationships between them are crucial in shaping the way that this happens.

This important study also documented a process of bureaucratization and observed its consequences. Gouldner showed how the *succession problem* created by the arrival of a new boss led to a greater reliance on rules. The new boss lacked the informal contacts that his predecessor had developed. He was also under instructions to increase production by tightening up on worker behaviour, thereby violating what Gouldner called the *indulgency pattern* established by his predecessor. As he tried to enforce the rules, he met worker resistance, lost the workers' cooperation, and fell back even more on the formal structure of supervision and control. The workers then retaliated by 'working to rule' and insisting that management obeyed the rules laid down in the collective agreement. A vicious circle of conflict developed and led to the unofficial strike that Gouldner (1954b) analysed in a follow-up study.

In another well-known study, Anselm Strauss *et al.* (1963) examined the way that rules were used and interpreted in a mental hospital. They pointed out that hardly anyone knew all the rules, which were frequently ignored or forgotten, and then reinvented when a particular crisis showed that they were needed. The rules were only actually used in conflicts between groups, as when nurses invoked 'the rules of the hospital' to fend off the demands that some doctors made on them. Rules also always required interpretation before they could be implemented. Did they apply to *this* person, in *this* situation and, if so, to *what* degree and for *how* long?

The various occupational groups in the hospital—psychiatrists, psychologists, nurses, students, occupational therapists, social workers—not only had different interests but had been trained in different ways and held varying and strongly held professional ideologies. Whether a rule should be implemented and how this should be done were always matters for negotiation. This went on all the time and Strauss *et al.* saw the hospital as based on what they called a **negotiated order**.

In a similar way to Gouldner, Strauss *et al.* drew attention to the realities of rule use. Rules should not be seen as fixed and objective structures that somehow exist in their own right and regulate people's behaviour. They are always subject to interpretation and implementation. It is important, however, to be aware of differences between organizations in the way that rules are applied. Hospitals are different from factories. The negotiated order of the hospital reflected a distinctive occupational structure, where staff had a degree of autonomy because of their professional or semi-professional status. This autonomy gave them a greater capacity to negotiate than ordinary employees usually have.

For and against bureaucracy

It is wrong to think that Weber was an uncritical advocate of bureaucracy. He was certainly impressed by its efficiency

Figure 14.1 Gouldner's patterns of industrial bureaucracy

Pattern of bureaucracy	Example of rule	Who enforces the rule?	Management–worker relationship
Mock	No smoking	Outsiders	Solidarity
Representative	Safety	Management *and* workers	Agreement
Punishment-centred	Non-absenteeism	Management	Conflict
	Vacancy-filling	Workers	Conflict

but also very concerned about its implications for both creativity and democracy.

He was particularly interested in the character of the bureaucratic state and the relationship between bureaucrats and politicians. Bureaucrats should in principle be the servants of government but they tended to become a force in their own right. Although they were supposed to be detached and objective, like any other group they had their own interests, while their expertise and authority made it difficult for politicians to resist them. As Weber (1914: 991) put it, 'the political "master" always finds himself, namely the trained official, in the position of a dilettante facing the expert'.

Weber was very aware of the dangers of bureaucratic domination under socialist regimes. He was sceptical of the socialist belief that the abolition of the private ownership of industry and the introduction of a planned economy would lead to a more equal and more productive society. He thought that the bureaucrats in charge of planning would become a secretive, selfish, and all-powerful elite. The result would be repression and inefficiency. A capitalist society based on market principles was more flexible and more responsive to people's needs.

While the development of state socialist societies bore out Weber's fears, capitalist societies too became increasingly managed and controlled by bureaucratic organizations. This occurred particularly through the nationalization of major industries and services, the growth of state welfare, and the state management and state planning of the economy. Then, in the 1970s and the 1980s, the economic crisis of the old industrial societies led to a revival of the belief in market forces and an attempt to shift from bureaucratic control to market regulation, in part through privatization (see p. 563).

Debureaucratizing tendencies have occurred within the management of business corporations as well. Debureaucratization can be seen both in the search for new organizational forms (see pp. 553–9) and in changing management techniques (see pp. 559–63). These changes too became particularly evident in recent years, as technological change, increasing international competition, and globalization increased the pressure on business organizations to be more responsive and flexible.

There has also been a re-evaluation of the importance of emotion in organizations. Weber had stressed the rational and non-emotional character of bureaucracy:

> The more perfectly bureaucracy develops, the more it is 'dehumanized', the more completely it succeeds in eliminating from official business love, hatred, and all purely personal, irrational and emotional elements which escape calculation. (Weber 1914: 975)

The rediscovery of the emotional aspects of organizations began with the emphasis placed by the human-relations school of management on the emotional needs of the worker and the significance for productivity of relationships with supervisors and other workers (see pp. 559–61). From a different perspective, the Weberian model of bureaucracy has been criticized by feminists for its typically male concerns with hierarchy, formality, and impersonality rather than the female qualities of caring and sharing (see pp. 556–8).

In spite of its negative image, bureaucracy continues to perform key functions in today's society. It is all too often used merely as a term of abuse. When people are asked to fill in forms, or find themselves regulated by apparently unnecessary rules, or wait endlessly for their case to be dealt with, or feel that they are being treated in too impersonal a way, they accuse organizations of 'bureaucracy'. This fails to take account of the vital role it plays in many areas of life. Health and safety rules protect us against accident and disease. The protection of the environment requires the bureaucratic implementation of legislation. Impersonal treatment guards against favouritism and corruption.

Bureaucracies, at least in principle, treat people impartially and equally. They may work slowly but they usually also work thoroughly. When bureaucracy protects us, treats us fairly, and operates efficiently, we never sing its praises. It is important to take a balanced view of its positive and negative aspects.

Discipline, carceral organizations, and total institutions

Discipline is not only a key feature of bureaucratic organization. According to Michel Foucault (1975), it is a central feature of society as a whole, for we live in a 'disciplinary society'. In this section we discuss Foucault's analysis of discipline and examine the organizations that most embody it.

Discipline

Foucault's disciplinary society is based on techniques of control that were first developed in the seventeenth and eighteenth centuries to produce what he called 'docile bodies'. These techniques attained their most developed form in the nineteenth-century prison, which became a model not only for other organizations but also for techniques of surveillance and control that have spread throughout society.

According to Foucault, discipline involved:

- control of the body;
- surveillance;
- punishment.

Discipline required a detailed *control of physical activities* through the systematic subdivision of space, time, and bodily activity. Thus, criminals were spatially confined in prisons, which were divided into blocks or wings, which were in turn subdivided into cells. Time was divided up by the timetable, which broke it down into short periods, and provided a means of organizing activity, and eliminating idleness. Bodily activity was split up through drills and exercises. The loading and firing of a gun, for example, was carried out through a specified sequence of movements. Once activity had been divided up, it could be reassembled in a coordinated and directed manner.

Discipline was dependent on *surveillance*, the continuous observation of those subject to discipline by those enforcing it. Foucault stressed the importance of visibility. People were under the gaze of those who controlled them, though the controllers remained invisible. The military camp, for example, was laid out in lines of tents with prescribed spaces between them, specified routes, and carefully positioned entrances and exits, so that all movement could be observed. This principle was eventually extended to many other areas of life. 'For a long time this model of the camp or at least its underlying principle was found in urban development, in the construction of working-class housing estates, hospitals, asylums, prisons, schools . . .' (Foucault 1975: 171–2).

Discipline involved new methods of *punishment* centred on the prison. In pre-industrial times offences, even relatively minor ones, were punished by public execution of the offender. This might involve torture and bodily mutilation, particularly when the offence challenged the authority of the ruler. Rulers were concerned primarily with the public demonstration of their authority, by displaying their power over the bodies of their subjects. Laws were implemented and offenders punished in an erratic and arbitrary way. In the late eighteenth century a much more systematic approach to law enforcement and the punishment of criminals emerged. Punishment was increasingly by imprisonment, with its duration related to the seriousness of the crime. Punishment was now concerned not with demonstrating royal power but with maintaining order.

According to Foucault, these disciplinary techniques were most developed in the nineteenth-century prison. The growth of systematic punishment through imprisonment initiated a process of **incarceration**, which basically means shutting people away from society. The regime of the nineteenth-century prison was different from that of earlier prisons because it cut off prisoners' contact with the outside world. The new prison also controlled prisoners by isolating them from each other, and keeping them under constant surveillance. Foucault used the term **carceral organization** to refer to organizations that controlled

Guy Fawkes and his co-conspirators in the Gunpowder Plot of 1605 are publicly hanged, drawn and quartered. Why were they punished in this way? Why are people not punished in this way nowadays?

© Getty Images/Hulton archive

Frontiers Aesthetic organizations

The classic studies of the ways in which organizations control their members have focused on the use of incentives and punishments to secure obedience to the rules. Control operates through the conscious minds and rational actions of the organization's members. They might not always obey but disobedience too was treated as a conscious and rational process, as in Gouldner's 'patterns of bureaucracy' (see pp. 539–40).

There has recently been a growing interest in the control of people through their bodies rather than their minds. This can be seen in Foucault's emphasis on the discipline of bodies. It can also be found in the recent interest in the aesthetic character of organizations. By this is meant aspects of their physical environment, such as office décor, furniture, and building design, which impact on the senses. The physical environment is used to

make employees feel in certain ways about each other and about the organization. It is not the symbolism of the physical environment that counts here, for this operates through the mind, but the feelings created through the senses.

The concept of aesthetic labour, which we discuss in Chapter 17, p. 683, conveys the similar idea that the bodily characteristics of the worker, the way that the worker's physical appearance impacts on the senses of customers, have in many occupations become an essential part of work and a condition of employment.

An exploration of these issues can be found in Gagliardi (1996). An analysis of the aesthetic character of organizations and a case study of a hotel chain can be found in Witz *et al.* (2002). Felstead, Jewson, and Walters (2005) discuss the aesthetic aspects of the 'collective office'.

---

people in these ways. We examine nineteenth-century incarceration and the new prison in 'Disciplined organizations'.

The process of incarceration extended beyond the prison, however. This was partly because the prison became the model for other carceral organizations, such as hospitals and factories, which similarly isolated and watched people. It was also because the techniques of control developed within prisons have been generalized *throughout* society. Thus, according to Foucault, people at large have been increasingly controlled by dividing them up into isolated compartments and keeping them under surveillance. The same principles governed the construction of the housing estate as the prison. The working class was controlled by isolating workers on estates, where they were under the surveillance of the police. This generalization of techniques of control led him to use the terms 'carceral city' and 'carceral society'.

Giddens has criticized Foucault for over-extending the idea of carceral organization. Giddens holds that factories are not carceral organizations. Some factories may well have adopted disciplinary and surveillance techniques similar to those used in prisons, but workers remain 'free wage labour', able to leave if they wish. Workers have not been isolated from the rest of society and, unlike prison inmates, can organize themselves in unions to resist the power of the employer (Giddens 1981: 172). While Foucault's notion of the generalizing of control techniques is interesting and insightful, Giddens clearly has a point.

It has also been argued by Scull (1984) that the process of incarceration was reversed by decarceration in the 1960s.

In both Britain and the United States there was a shift from locking up 'the mad and the bad' to dealing with them through community programmes. We discuss Scull's work on decarceration on pp. 566–7.

Total institutions

Although some organizations, particularly those that employ people, may make heavy demands on our time and energy, most leave us with a separate private life. This is not the case, however, with one class of organizations, those that were labelled **total institutions** by Erving Goffman in his book *Asylums* (1961b). His study of these institutions was based on his observations of life in a mental hospital, but he was struck by the similarities between mental hospitals and other organizations, such as prisons, boarding schools, monasteries, merchant ships, and military barracks, that apparently performed very different functions.

> ### ➲ *Connections*
> Goffman was particularly interested in people's daily rituals and face-to-face interactions, with the construction, maintenance, and change of their sense of identity, and with the way that they present themselves to others and are seen by others. We outline his views on these issues in Chapter 4, pp. 128–9, and you may find it helpful to place the discussion of total institutions in the context of his broader approach.

Total institutions had in common the following features, though not all would be found in every institution:

- *The disappearance of private life.* All daily activities were carried out within the same organization. Any sense of a separate work or private life disappeared.

- *Life in common.* Each daily activity was carried out at the same time by all the inmates together. Eating, for example, became a communal activity. People were moved around in batches that were treated alike.

- *Planned and supervised activities.* Activities were timetabled and controlled in accordance with an overall plan for the organization.

- *Inmate/staff division.* There was a sharp division between staff with access to the outside world and inmates separated from it. There was little contact or communication between the two groups, which held stereotyped images of each other.

- *The mortification of the self.* Inmates experienced the 'death' of their previous identity. They lost their roles in the wider world, at work or in the family, which were central to their sense of identity and self-esteem.

Goffman particularly emphasized the way that people were systematically stripped of their previous identity. When they entered a total institution, they were required to change their clothing, while personal objects important to their sense of self were removed. Routine humiliations forced them to act in ways that contradicted their previous identity. This stripping of identity involved the penetration of the private space that protected their identity from the surrounding world. Goffman called this process a 'contamination' of the self:

> The model for interpersonal contamination in our society is presumably rape; although sexual molestation certainly occurs in total institutions, there are many other less dramatic examples. Upon admission, one's on-person possessions are pawed and fingered by an official as he itemizes and prepares them for storage. The inmate himself may be frisked and searched to the extent—often reported in the literature—of a rectal examination. Later in his stay he may be required to undergo searchings of his person and of his sleeping quarters, either routinely or when trouble arises. In all these cases it is the searcher as well as the search that penetrates the private reserve of the individual and violates the territories of his self. (Goffman 1961b: 35–6)

Goffman was particularly interested in the changes brought about by total institutions in the inmates' sense of self, and their responses and adaptations to the situation they found themselves in. He described these organizations as 'forcing houses for changing persons' (Goffman 1961b: 22).

Goffman's concept of the total institution is similar to Foucault's notion of the carceral organization, though Foucault was more interested in the techniques of control developed in these organizations than in changes of the self. Although Goffman recognized that some of the features of the total institution could be found in other organizations, he treated total institutions as a distinct class of organizations, while Foucault argued that the control techniques of the carceral organization were extended throughout society.

◆ *Stop and reflect*

We began this section by discussing the concept of organization before examining Weber's ideal type of bureaucracy and the issues that it raises.

- Make sure that you understand the distinctive character of bureaucratic organizations.

- Later studies of bureaucracy argued that many of its features could be dysfunctional for the achievement of an organization's goals.

- Make sure that you understand the following terms: the dysfunctions of bureaucratic rules; the displacement of goals; and trained incapacity.

- Other studies have argued that there are different types of bureaucratic organization, as in Gouldner's typology of mock, representative, and punishment-centred bureaucracy.

- Consider what is meant by a 'negotiated order'. Do all organizations have this?

- Why do you think that bureaucracy has acquired a negative image? Has this view of it been taken too far?

We then considered discipline, carceral organizations, and total institutions.

- Make sure that you understand the following terms: carceral organization and total institution.

- According to Foucault, discipline involved control of the body, surveillance, and punishment.

- Are there good reasons for thinking that we live in a 'carceral society'?

- Goffman claimed that many organizations are 'total institutions'.

- A key feature of these organizations was the 'mortification of the self'. What is meant by this?

- Can you identify the characteristics of a total institution in any organization that you have been in?

The administrative and managerial revolutions

We tend to see the nineteenth-century transformation of society as driven by industrialization but it was also transformed by the development of a technology of social control. There was an administrative as well as an industrial revolution. This was followed by the development of management and, arguably, a managerial revolution.

In this section we first examine the emergence of the disciplined organizations that were at the heart of the administrative revolution. We then consider the growth of management, the changing relationship between managers and owners, and the rise of public ownership.

Disciplined organizations

Discipline was the key feature of the new organizations, which developed ways of much more closely controlling people, whether in the army, or the factory, or the prison. These organizations emerged through a process of bureaucratization.

Bureaucratization

Although bureaucratization was central to the administrative revolution, bureaucracies of a kind had long existed. We will briefly consider these earlier forms of bureaucracy in order to highlight the distinctiveness of the new bureaucracies of the nineteenth century.

Weber (1914) recognized that earlier forms of bureaucracy had been created by the empires of ancient Egypt, Rome, and China to administer the huge territories they conquered. The officials in these early bureaucracies were, however, usually paid in kind, taking a share of the produce from the land they governed. They were often simply given control of this land to extract as much from it as they could. They became preoccupied with the exploitation of the people they governed, failed to carry out their official duties, and were largely outside the ruler's control. This was not a disciplined bureaucracy in the modern sense of the term.

The creation of salaried bureaucrats was crucial to the rise of modern bureaucracies. Payment by salary, as Weber recognized, meant that bureaucrats could be full-time officials devoted wholly to their duties and under the control of their superiors. Salaries could only be paid, however, if rulers had funds at their disposal, which they could acquire only if there was a money economy for the state to tax. The growth in Europe of a highly commercialized capitalist economy was therefore an essential condition for the emergence of the modern career bureaucrat.

Bureaucratization resulted from rulers' attempts to gain greater control over their territories. The appointment of salaried officials enabled rulers to escape an administrative dependence on the loyalty of uncontrollable feudal lords, a dependence which had been the central problem faced by the medieval monarch. There was also a parallel process of military bureaucratization, as rulers developed disciplined and professional military forces that were loyal to the state (Dandeker 1990).

> ⊃ *Connections*
> Later on bureaucratization was linked to other aspects of the development of the state, which we examine in Chapter 15. See especially, pp. 581–2, and the discussion of the relationship between state welfare and bureaucratization on pp. 590–1.

While the foundations of modern bureaucracy had been laid by these earlier changes, it was during the nineteenth century that there was a general bureaucratization of society. According to Weber (1914), modern societies developed bureaucratic organization partly because of the problems of administering large, heavily populated territories, but the pre-industrial empires too had faced difficulties of this sort. What distinguished modern societies was the multiplicity of administrative tasks found within them and the importance of expertise in carrying these out. All this resulted from what Weber called 'the increasing complexity of civilization', which was due to the greater wealth, increasing social problems, and growing size of organizations in industrial societies.

The bureaucracies that emerged in the nineteenth century were highly rational organizations. They operated on the basis of the expertise of their officials and the knowledge stored in their files, rather than on traditional customs and beliefs. They functioned in a disciplined and unemotional manner, and their activities were calculated, systematic, and predictable. As we showed in our earlier discussion of his work, Weber considered that the sheer technical superiority of bureaucracy over other forms of organization meant that it would triumph in all fields of human activity, in the business corporation, the church, and the university, as well as the state.

Incarceration

The prison was as typical an organization of the nineteenth century as the factory. Incarceration in a prison eventually became the normal method of punishment for almost all offences, and the prison a characteristic organization of modern society.

The prison embodied all the new techniques for instilling discipline which Foucault has identified. Local jails had certainly existed earlier but prisoners had not been incarcerated. They had not been shut off from contact with the outside world, or confined in cells, or subjected to silence rules, as they were in the new prison or penitentiary, as it was called to emphasize its punitive and disciplined character. Techniques of surveillance and control were steadily tightened and culminated in the 1842 opening of Pentonville, a new model prison, in London. Prisons had become carceral organizations.

The ultimate example of discipline and surveillance was the *panopticon*, the name given to Jeremy Bentham's nineteenth-century design for a prison. This was a circular building with the cells on the periphery and the guards in a central tower. The cells extended the full width of the building and had a window on each side, so that prisoners could be observed from the tower and were silhouetted by the light coming from the outer window. Venetian blinds in the tower windows would make the guards invisible to the prisoners, who would not know whether they were under observation at any particular moment.

Cellular subdivision, the total visibility of those under control, and the invisibility of those in control, were all exemplified by this design. It also minimized costs by enabling the supervision of a large number of prisoners by a small number of guards. No prison was ever built exactly according to Bentham's design but its basic principles of surveillance and control have been commonly applied in prison construction.

The growth of imprisonment was linked to the development of industrial capitalism. A more systematic means of punishment was needed because of the rise in crime that accompanied industrialization. This was not just because more crimes were committed, but also because there were new laws to protect the private property crucial to the functioning of a capitalist society. Industrial capitalism also involved the widespread trading and movement of goods, which created new opportunities for crime and meant that property required greater protection (Ignatieff 1978).

Industrialization generated disorder as craftsmen reacted against changes that threatened their livelihoods, through, for example, the Luddite machine-breaking movement. Workers challenged the authority of the employer by organizing themselves in unions and taking strike action. Economic fluctuations produced unemployment and some of those without any means of subsistence resorted to crime. There was a general problem of disorder in the new industrial cities, where large masses of people were concentrated outside the traditional rural structures for maintaining order.

Prisons were a means of isolating and managing those who threatened social order, as was the asylum for the mentally ill, which was also established at this time. In pre-industrial society, deviants could be absorbed and

Why are so many prisons in nineteenth-century buildings?
© Alice Chadwick

Briefing: from jail to penitentiary

The eighteenth-century jail

'It was common for wives to appear daily at the gates bearing meals for their jailed husbands. They were given the run of prison yards from dawn until locking up, and a judiciously placed bribe would make it possible to remain inside at night. The sexual commerce between the inside and the outside was vigorous. As far back as the seventeenth century, one prisoner had observed that whores flocked to prison like "crowes to carrion". . . . Walls often no more than eight feet high, could not stop passers by from tossing food, notes, and letters over the other side, or stop prisoners from conversing with people in the street, or on occasion splashing them with dirty water.' (Ignatieff 1978: 34–5)

The nineteenth-century penitentiary

'At Gloucester an eighteen-foot wall was constructed around the institution. Outsiders required written permission from the magistrates to get inside. For next of kin, visits were allowed only once every six months. No food, bedding, books, or furniture were allowed in from the outside. The penitentiary enforced a new conception of the social distance between the "criminal" and the "law-abiding". Walled away inside Gloucester, "deviants" lost that precarious membership in the community implied by the free access once allowed between the old jail and the street.' (Ignatieff 1978: 101–2)

 In what ways did the new penitentiary embody the techniques of discipline identified by Foucault?

managed locally within the community. This was not possible in the new industrial cities, so they were separated and controlled in carceral organizations.

The state was closely involved in the process of incarceration. Governments passed the laws which defined behaviour as criminal, increased the powers of local magistrates, and created new police forces to catch the new criminals (Ignatieff 1978). The state also funded, directed, and inspected both prisons and asylums.

Conceptions of deviance, of both criminality and madness, were changing. Criminals had previously been considered innately wicked and the mad were treated as uncontrollable animals. In the nineteenth century it was increasingly believed that both the bad and the mad could be reformed through the application of scientific expertise. Prisons and asylums were places where deviants could

be cured as well as disciplined and isolated. It was indeed at this time that the medical model of madness emerged. Asylums became seen as mental hospitals where the mentally ill could be treated by psychiatry, which was establishing itself as a branch of medicine.

Factory discipline

The maintenance of discipline was also of great importance to the new industrialists. Discipline was crucial to profitable production. Punctuality and uninterrupted work during fixed working hours were essential, for the division of labour made one worker's labour dependent on that of others, while expensive machinery had to operate continuously if owners were to maximize the return on their capital.

Sidney Pollard (1965) argued that the widespread employment of children presented the early British industrialists with a particular problem of discipline. In the early nineteenth-century cotton industry, some 40 per cent of those employed were under the age of 18. Child labour was not new but when production had been on a small workshop or household basis children were controlled by their parents or guardians. According to Pollard, 'the new mass employment removed the incentive of learning a craft, alienated the children by its monotony, and did this just at the moment when it undermined the authority of the family, and of the father in particular' (1965: 217).

In early nineteenth-century Britain employers relied overwhelmingly on dismissal or the threat of dismissal to maintain discipline. This was a method that could work only when alternative sources of labour were freely available, which at this time was generally the case, for there was considerable labour migration and unemployment was often high. The use of fines or deductions from pay to maintain discipline was also widespread. Corporal punishment too was widely used, particularly where children were employed.

Techniques of labour management developed slowly, for the early entrepreneurs were preoccupied with such matters as machinery, transport, and finance. Specialized managers to take over responsibility for these various matters, and indeed for the management of labour, did not yet exist. Some of the more advanced employers, such as Robert Owen, did invent more subtle methods of control, but these were quite exceptional (see box on 'Silent monitors' on p. 548). In the harsh conditions of the Industrial Revolution, the means used to maintain discipline were overwhelmingly negative and relied, as Pollard has put it, on 'compulsion, force and fear' (Pollard 1965: 243).

The factory was not a prison, but it was certainly a place of punishment, and the prison was there in the background to back up the authority of the factory-owner. Behind the employer stood the magistrate and laws that made worker

Figure 14.2 Controlling child labour

Different means used by firms to discipline children in British industry, 1833

Negative means	No.	Positive means	No.
● Dismissal	353	● Kindness	2
● Threat of dismissal	48	● Promotion or higher wages	9
● Fines, deductions	101	● Reward or bonus	23
● Corporal punishment	55		
● Complaints to parents	13		
● Confined to mill	2		
● Degrading dress, badge	3		
Total	575	*Total*	34

Source: Factory Commission Survey of 1833 (Pollard 1965: 222).

Briefing: silent monitors

New techniques were invented to monitor work performance in the early industrial factory. Best known of all were the 'silent monitors' of Robert Owen. He awarded four types of mark for the past day's work to each superintendent, and each of them, in turn, judged all his workers; the mark was then translated into the colours black–blue–yellow–white, in ascending order of merit, painted on the four sides of a piece of wood mounted over the machine, and turned outward according to the worker's performance. These daily marks were entered in a book as a permanent record, to be periodically inspected by Robert Owen himself.

Source: Pollard (1965: 225).

organization illegal and breach of the contract of employment a crime. Employers (and farmers) could use the courts to discipline their workers. Thus, the prison and the courts played an important part in maintaining discipline in the factory.

Management and ownership

It was the growth of larger and more complex businesses that led to the emergence of specialized and professional management. In this section we examine first the development of 'scientific' labour management. We go on to consider the increasing power of managers and changes in the relationship between them and owners. Lastly, we consider the growth of public ownership and its implications for management.

Scientific management

As we showed above, the techniques used to manage labour in the early factories depended largely on punishment. Later in the nineteenth century, there was a movement towards the greater use of incentive schemes intended to increase productivity by paying workers according to the amount they produced. This approach was most systematically developed by the school of thought known as **scientific management**, which emerged in the United States in the 1880s.

The most famous exponent of scientific management was the engineer Frederick Taylor, who published his *Principles of Scientific Management* in 1911 (scientific management is sometimes referred to as Taylorism). Its key ideas were as follows:

- *The subdivision of labour*. Work is broken down into the smallest possible tasks requiring a minimum of skill. Workers can then be trained easily to carry out a particular task in the shortest possible time.

- *Measurement and specification of work tasks*. 'Time-and-motion' study shows scientifically the best way of performing a task, the exact movements required, and the time that they should take (see Figure 14.3).

- *Selection and training*. Workers are selected according to their ability to carry out a particular task and then trained in the best way to carry it out.

- *Motivation and reward*. Workers are solely motivated by the wages they earn. They should be paid not by the hour but according to the amount they produce. The price per item produced should be determined by the time taken to carry out the movements involved.

- *Individualism*. Workers are motivated by individual self-interest. Social contact distracts them and should be kept to a minimum. Unions are unnecessary, as rates of pay can be determined scientifically and there is therefore no basis for a conflict of interest between workers and managers.

- *Management*. Management is completely separated from labour. Production is planned by management, which gives workers detailed instructions, which they follow obediently and exactly.

This method of management appeared to be scientific because it was based on experiments, and involved the careful measurement of behaviour by work study engineers trained in its techniques. It was certainly an engineering approach to the management of labour, for it treated workers as machines without feelings or culture, and there was no recognition that work was a meaningful activity. This meant, however, that it was not really scientific at all, for it was not based on a genuinely scientific knowledge of people. Its claim to be scientific was, none the less, an important means of legitimating it in an age when science was identified with progress. Weber (1914) considered it to be the ultimate example of rational factory organization but also of the dehumanizing consequences of rationalization.

Figure 14.3 Scientific management in action. How long does it take to open a drawer?

An American corporation's unit time values for clerical tasks?

Actions	Minutes
Opening and closing	
File drawer, open and close, no selection	0.04
Folder, open or close flaps	0.04
Desk drawer, open side drawer of standard desk	0.014
Open centre drawer	0.026
Close side drawer	0.015
Close centre drawer	0.027
Chair activity	
Get up from chair	0.033
Sit down in chair	0.033
Turn in swivel chair	0.009
Move in chair to adjoining desk or file (4ft. max.)	0.050

Source: Braverman (1974: 321), quoting a 1960 guide to office clerical time standards.

Scientific management was essentially a means for exploiting labour more effectively. Its emergence in the United States towards the end of the nineteenth century is usually explained in terms of declining industrial profits at this time and the rise of labour movements (Clegg and Dunkerley 1980). Declining profits stimulated employers to develop positive ways of increasing productivity through incentives, rather than simply relying on punishment or the threat of dismissal. Scientific management was also a means of responding to the growing power of unions by taking a tight managerial control over labour. It particularly attacked the power of the craft unions of skilled workers, since it deskilled labour by subdividing it into the simplest possible tasks, which could be carried out by unskilled workers.

While it developed new techniques of management, it also embodied the features of industrial capitalism identified by Marx and the technology of organizational control analysed by Foucault. The division of labour, its individualization, and the reliance on monetary incentives were considered by Marx to be typical of capitalist production. The subdivision of tasks, the training of the body in specified movements, and the individualist isolation of the worker exemplify Foucault's analysis of new disciplinary techniques. Scientific management also involved the close surveillance of labour by management, for it required the constant monitoring of a worker's movements and performance.

> ⟴ *Connections*
> See 'Capitalism', in Chapter 17, p. 671, for an outline of Marx's analysis of the capitalist mode of production. In Chapter 17, pp. 679–80, we also discuss the implications of scientific management and deskilling for the meaning of work.

Managerial capitalism

The growing size and complexity of organizations made management more important and this led to the rise of managers as a distinct and powerful group. Some have argued that they took control of industry away from the owners of capital, though others have rejected this view and claim that control actually passed at this time into the hands of finance capitalists.

Ownership and control were originally fused in the person of the industrial entrepreneur, who combined the work of financier, works manager, engineer, and accountant. The problems of coordinating an increasingly specialized division of labour, rapid technical development, and the growing size of companies made it impossible, however, to carry on in this way. Owners retained overall control, but the detailed control of a company's activities was delegated to a managerial bureaucracy. Increasingly, specialist managers developed a degree of professional autonomy. Thus, personnel management and marketing, for example, eventually became distinct fields in their own right, with their own career structures, qualifications, and professional institutes.

Ownership too changed. In the first half of the nineteenth century ownership was *personal*. Factories were owned by an individual, a family, or a small number of partners. Mid-century legislation then made possible *impersonal* ownership through joint-stock companies. These were owned by shareholders, who could be any members of the general public who had invested in the company through the Stock Exchange. The new companies were controlled by directors, who were elected by and responsible to the shareholders. These companies allowed businesses to draw on a much wider pool of capital to finance investment. Apparently rather technical changes in company law were immensely important, for they made possible the growth of the giant corporations that dominate the world economy today.

There have been widely differing interpretations of these changes. On the one hand, there were those, such as Berle and Means (1932) and Alfred Chandler (1962), who argued that ownership and control had actually become separated. They claimed that share ownership had become so fragmented among a mass of small shareholders that owners no longer had any control over corporations. Control had passed into the hands of managers and a **managerial revolution** had taken place. Some indeed argued that the exploitative capitalist had been replaced by the 'socially responsible' manager, who was concerned not so much with profitability as keeping the company going by balancing the competing claims of all those who had a stake in it, from shareholders to trade unions. A post-capitalist social order had emerged.

On the other hand, Marxists, such as Hilferding (1910) and Aaronovitch (1961), claimed that ownership was more important than ever. The spread of share ownership reduced the power of *individual* owners, but enabled financial organizations with large shareholdings to become the *effective* owners. Effective owners were those who were able to use their ownership of shares to exert influence over the company, even though they might not own a majority of a company's shares. Economic power became increasingly

---

Figure 14.4 Ownership and control

The network of control

In contemporary Britain, just under a half of the top 250 enterprises are controlled through constellations of interests. Their controlling constellations overlap a good deal and form a large intercorporate network of controllers, linked through cross-shareholdings and interlocking directorships. Less than a hundred enterprises are at the heart of this network (Scott 1997).

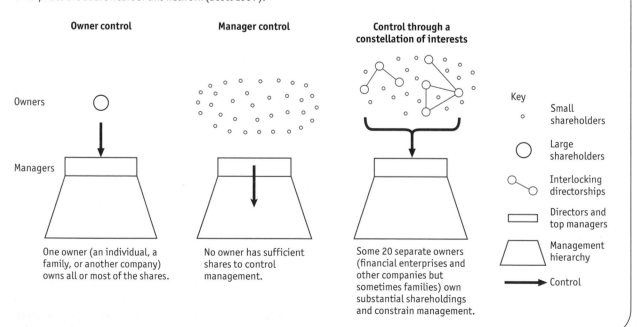

concentrated as a small number of large banks became the effective owners and gained control of the large corporations that monopolized production. The age of industrial capital had been followed by the age of **finance capital**.

These writers too argued that ownership was separated from production, since finance capital was interested only in profit and not concerned with the management of production, so long as this was profitable. It was not, however, the managers but the finance capitalists, those who controlled the big banks and other financial organizations, who had ultimate power. They could hire and fire managers at will. Indeed, their concern with profit alone made them more ruthless than traditional industrial entrepreneurs, who had been deeply involved in the day-to-day running of their businesses.

John Scott (1997) has examined this debate in the light of the accumulated research and concluded that owners still exercise control. By owners he means, however, not small individual shareholders, for he agrees that they are powerless, but those in effective possession, who are typically a loose grouping of major shareholders. Scott has called these groupings 'constellations of interests'. These constellations are dominated by financial institutions, such as insurance companies, banks, and pension funds, but often include other non-financial companies as well and also some executives and wealthy families with large shareholdings. They are linked together by interlocking directorates. These involve the directors of one company having seats on the boards of others (see Figure 14.4).

The opposed theories of managerial revolution and finance capital have each recognized important aspects of social change, but neither can be accepted in its entirety. Managers do, indeed, have day-to-day power and much autonomy in their decision-making, but they are constrained by the interests and pressures of the leading shareholders. These shareholders are in most cases not a tightly integrated group but a looser constellation of interests. The insights of the two theories need to be combined if we are properly to understand how business is controlled.

Figure 14.5 Interpreting changes in ownership

Issues	Managerial theorists	Marxists
Ownership	Dispersed	Concentrated
Controllers	Managers	Banks/financial corporations
Social order	Post-capitalist	Finance capitalism

Public ownership

Changes in ownership were not just a matter of changes in the private ownership of capital, for in some societies the state began to take over the ownership of certain industries and services. This led to another aspect of the managerial transformation of capitalism, the growing state management of production.

Public ownership was seen by socialists as an essential step in the transition from a capitalist to a socialist or communist society. Marx and his followers considered that the private ownership of the means of production was the central feature of capitalism. Some Marxist writers believed that the growing concentration of ownership under finance capitalism had made it easier for the state to take control of industry, for it would only have to take over the small number of companies that were already in effective control of the economy.

Public ownership did develop in Britain but for rather different reasons. It began during the later nineteenth century with moves by city councils to control the supply of water, gas, and electricity, and improve methods of urban transport. The first major expansion of state control was driven by the imperatives of war. During the First World War the government took control of coal mining, the railways, shipping, and the munitions industry. All this was dismantled at the war's end, but there was some movement towards greater state control and public ownership during the inter-war years. This was motivated by nationalist rather than class concerns, by the problem of reorganizing Britain's more archaic industries, particularly coal mining, and the belief that new services, such as broadcasting and civil aviation, should be kept under state control.

The main extension of public ownership was carried out by the Labour governments of 1945–52. This was certainly in part motivated by the labour movement's belief that key areas of the economy should be brought under public control, but it mainly resulted from continued nationalist concerns with the backward, inefficient, and fragmented character of key industries and services. Public ownership was a means of overcoming backwardness and reorganizing these industries and services into more effective and modern units. Significantly, this extension of public ownership was described as the nationalization, not the socialization, of ownership.

What difference did nationalization make? Those who had hoped for a socialist transformation of the economy were soon disappointed. Since each industry was run by its own relatively independent board, nationalization did not result in the increased planning of economic development. Although some token worker–director schemes were introduced, workers and their unions found that they had no greater influence over management than before

Figure 14.6 The growth of public ownership in the United Kingdom 1850–1950

Years	Main extensions of public ownership
1850s–70s	Municipal ownership of water, gas, and trams
1892–1912	Nationalization of telephone companies
1914–18	State takes temporary control of transport, coal mining, and munitions
1920	Law passed to combine 120 railway companies into four regional groups
1926	British Broadcasting Corporation created
1926	Central Electricity Board created to buy and distribute electricity
1933	London Passenger Transport Board created to control buses, trams, and underground lines
1938	Coal Act takes coal reserves into state ownership
1940	British Overseas Airways Corporation created
1946	Bank of England nationalized
1946	Coal, cable and wireless, and civil aviation nationalized
1947	Road and rail transport nationalized
1947	Electricity generation nationalized
1948	British Gas created
1948	National Health Service created
1949	Steel industry nationalized

nationalization. The nationalized industries anyway had to operate within the framework of a capitalist economy and were soon themselves required to make a normal commercial profit on their operations.

This is not to say that nationalization achieved nothing. It was, however, more a vehicle for the state reorganization and coordination of particular industries and services than a means of controlling the economy or changing the capitalist relations of production. It led to greater state control but not to workers' control.

In state socialist societies, public ownership and state planning did become the norm. The ruling party directed economic development, planned production, and controlled the factories. Although factories were supposedly controlled by workers' councils, these actually became a means through which the ruling party controlled and disciplined labour, except in Yugoslavia. There, after a degree of independence from the Soviet bloc had been achieved in the later 1940s, workers' councils did acquire some real autonomy. There were no independent trade unions in state socialist countries, including Yugoslavia.

Broadly speaking, in state socialist countries the state was in control and Weber's bureaucratic nightmare had been realized. As we pointed out in our discussion of Weber's view of bureaucracy, he was deeply concerned that bureaucratization would weaken democracy and result in a loss of freedom and creativity. He considered that this was particularly likely to happen under socialism, for the power of the bureaucrat would no longer be balanced and limited by the power of the owner of private capital.

◀▶ *Stop and reflect*

This section has been concerned with the administrative and managerial revolutions that began in the nineteenth century. We began by examining the emergence of disciplined organizations.

- We argued that the prison should be considered as typical an organization of the nineteenth century as the factory.
- What was new about the nineteenth-century penitentiary?
- Discipline also had to be maintained in the factory.
- Why was discipline so important in the factory?
- How was the factory related to the prison?

We went on to consider the development of management and the changing relationships between managers and owners.

- Make sure that you understand the following terms: scientific management; managerial revolution; and finance capital.
- What was scientific about scientific management?
- Ownership and management became increasingly distinct.
- Did this mean that owners lost control?
- From the 1850s to the 1950s public ownership increased in Britain.
- Did the extension of public ownership introduce socialism?

Towards new structures of control

The techniques of control developed during the nineteenth and early twentieth centuries enabled a massive expansion in both the productive capacity of industrial capitalism and the apparatus of the modern state. More recently, these techniques have been challenged, and new methods of control began to emerge that reacted against earlier tendencies. We examine these new methods of control in this last section of the chapter and consider whether they have transformed organizations or merely further developed the framework established by the administrative revolution.

Debureaucratization?

Although Weber was highly critical of bureaucracy, he thought that its technical superiority would make it the dominant form of organization in modern societies. As we showed on p. 539, the efficiency of the bureaucratic model has, however, been questioned, and we consider here the alternative forms of organization that have emerged. We also discuss the feminist argument that bureaucracy is patriarchal in character and organizations should be feminized.

Organic organization

Rigidity was one of the main features of bureaucracy revealed by case studies of organizations. More flexible organizations, which are claimed to be more appropriate to situations of rapid technical change or market uncertainty, have been developed.

In their classic study of the Scottish electronics industry, Burns and Stalker (1961) examined the emergence of a more flexible form of organization, which they called *organic* and contrasted with *mechanistic* organization, which they also found within this industry.

The *mechanistic* type had a clearly specified division of labour, coordinated by a hierarchy of managers. Everyone knew exactly what their job required and what their responsibilities were. Decisions were taken at the top of the organization, where knowledge of business matters was concentrated. Orders came from the top down and subordinates were expected to obey instructions. This structure led to conflicts between *line* and *staff* managers, an example of the conflict between hierarchy (line) and expertise (staff), which is commonly found in bureaucratic organizations. As Gouldner (1954) pointed out, there is a tension in the Weberian model of bureaucracy between authority based on expertise and authority based on hierarchical position.

The *organic* type was much more flexible. Jobs changed as the company's projects changed and relationships

Figure 14.7 Mechanistic and organic organizations

Mechanistic	Organic
● Rigid division of labour	● Flexible tasks
● Hierarchy	● Network
● Authority based on position	● Authority based on expertise
● Obedience to authority	● Collective problem-solving
● Instructions	● Advice and consultation
● Defined duties/ responsibilities	● General commitment to goals
● Vertical communications	● Lateral
Stability	*Change*

Source: Adapted from Burns and Stalker (1961: 119–22).

evolved within the organization. Roles were not clearly defined and there was little sense of particular responsibilities. Positions were still stratified by seniority but authority was exercised by those with most expertise, wherever they were located, and through a network rather than a hierarchy. Communication tended to be lateral rather than vertical. The ethos of the organization was not obedience to authority but collective problem-solving. Commitment was not to the duties of the job but to the goals of the company and wider values of technical progress.

The *mechanistic* organization was clearly the more bureaucratic of the two. Its machine-like character made it inflexible and it responded poorly to the demands of change in an industry with a high rate of technical innovation. Burns and Stalker concluded that the more flexible *organic* form was much more appropriate to such an environment. They did not, however, argue that it was superior to the mechanistic form or that bureaucratic organization was outmoded, for they recognized that the *mechanistic* form was more appropriate to situations of stable production.

Network organization

A more radical and more recent departure from the classic bureaucratic organization is the network organization, which is a much more open structure based on *information technology*. Computer networks can link not only those inside a company but those outside, so that a factory, its

Are network organizations non-bureaucratic?
© Alice Chadwick

component suppliers, and retailers are all interlinked. Instead of operating on the basis of the detailed regulation of its members' behaviour, the network organization plugs them into production on a contractual basis when it requires their work. It operates on the basis of market rather than bureaucratic coordination.

Thus, the organization can subcontract work through the network to self-employed teleworkers or specialist outside organizations who provide services when required. Instead of directly employing designers or marketing specialists, it can simply call them in through the network when it needs them. At the other end of its activities, instead of selling its products, it can produce according to the orders coming through the network from retailers or franchised outlets. Rapid communication and a highly flexible structure make a network organization appropriate to post-Fordist production, which we discuss in Chapter 17, pp. 693–6.

It is hard to establish the boundaries of a network organization or distinguish between its internal and external activites. Benetton is one of the best-known examples of such an organization (Clegg 1990). If it is defined by its employees, Benetton consists of certain design and production facilities in north Italy. But are not Benetton's thousands of retail outlets, franchised operations that are not staffed by Benetton employees but sell only Benetton products, part of its organization? What about the hundreds of small firms and the homeworkers who make Benetton products or carry out certain stages in production, such as finishing off clothing?

The subcontracting of components production or the use of homeworkers to finish goods is nothing new, but what distinguished Benetton was that the bulk of its production was carried out in this way. Stewart Clegg has suggested that Benetton should be thought of 'less as an organization *per se* and rather more as an organized network of market relations premised on complex forms of contracting made possible by advances in microelectronics technology' (1990: 121).

Virtual organization

The ultimate network organization is the virtual organization that exists only in an electronic form and this is promoted by some as the future form that organizations will take. It is important, however, to distinguish between organizations that make an extensive use of electronic communications and virtual organizations that only exist in an electronic world. Most organizations of any size will use electronic means of communication, and this may well enable them to develop more of a network structure, but it does not make them virtual organizations. There are few existing organizations that can take a purely electronic form.

Virtual organization is particularly appropriate for organizations whose activity mainly involves information and communication, and this would include some financial organizations. Not all such organizations can, however, take such a form. Call centres, which carry out such functions, are far from virtual in character and have many of the characteristics of much older workplaces (see Chapter 17, p. 693). Apparently electronic organizations, such as *Amazon*, have offices, warehouses, and distribution systems that are far from virtual.

Virtual organization may also be appropriate for short-lived operations, which assemble people electronically for a particular purpose and are disbanded once a project is completed. Social movements, such as the anti-globalization movement (see Chapter 16, p. 654), may be largely virtual organizations that bring people together for particular demonstrations, though these are anything but virtual.

The advocates of virtual organization have argued that it has a special character that distinguishes it from all previous forms of organization. It is claimed that virtual organizations are by their very nature decentralized and unhierarchical. This claim may well, however, reflect ideal conceptions of what the world of the Internet should be like rather than descriptions of how such organizations actually operate. Even virtual communities have rules and some form of government by those who formulate the rules and enforce them.

> **⊃ Connections**
> We have a section on virtual communities in Chapter 13, pp. 518–19, and you may find it interesting to compare them with virtual organizations.

It is important to stress that information networks of all kinds actually facilitate central control. They do certainly enable the flow of information across the organization, so that communications can be lateral and less *dependent* on central coordination or a managerial hierarchy. They also enable the decentralization of management. They do, however, provide those who control an organization with access to very detailed information about the behaviour and performance of its members. Electronic communication, particularly when combined with the huge potential for surveillance that this provides (see our discussion of this on pp. 571–3), can be a highly effective vehicle of central control.

Cultural alternatives

Much of the early literature on organizations assumed that the principles of organization were universal, but later studies have argued that there were important international variations in the character of organizations.

The economic success of East Asian countries has led to a growing interest in their organizational patterns and the possibility of learning from their experience. We will consider here Stewart Clegg's (1990) account of the Japanese and Chinese patterns of organization.

Japanese industrial organization typically involves less specialized and more flexible occupations than a Western industrial organization. Workers are not seen as having particular skills but are expected to carry out any task required by management. They are moved through the various operations in a factory and acquire a knowledge of the connections between its various parts, which improves communication and develops lateral networks. Research and development are less separated from production, for their personnel will have had experience of each other's work. Management is similarly unspecialized and there is a regular rotation of managers through different functions.

> **Connections**
> To understand the wider context in which this kind of organization has developed, refer to the discussion of the integrative character of Japanese industrial relations in Chapter 17, pp. 699–700.

Chinese business organization in Taiwan is radically different from both the modern Western and Japanese models. Chinese businesses are organized on a family basis. The head of the family that owns the business controls it, and the key tasks of managerial surveillance and control are kept, so far as possible, inside the family. Authority is related to age. Relationships are personal, familial, and based on trust—quite opposite in character to the impersonal and formalized relationships of bureaucratic organizations.

As Clegg points out, the key point is that while small family businesses everywhere will tend to have these features, in Taiwan they are found in large organizations as well. Indeed, the need to provide an inheritance for sons, who will receive equal shares of the father's estate, has driven the expansion of Taiwan family businesses. When profits lead to the accumulation of capital, new businesses are founded, which are run by members of the family, usually by sons, who inherit them on their father's death.

These examples show that unbureaucratic forms of organization can work well in the contemporary world. They also show that there is no such thing as a single East

---

THEORY AND METHODS
....

Modern and post-modern organizations

Modern (Fordist)	Post-modern (post-Fordist)
● Differentiated	● Dedifferentiated
● Specialized roles	● Unspecialized
● Centralized	● Decentralized
● Hierarchy	● Network
Mass production	**Flexible production**

Stewart Clegg (1990) argued that the changes that we have been discussing in this section have created **post-modern organizations**. He identified *modern* organization with the Weberian model of bureaucracy and *post-modern* organization with various alternative organizational structures. Organic organizations, the East Asian models, and network organizations are all examples of post-modern organization and Clegg is at pains to emphasize that there is no single post-modern form. Modern and post-modern organizations broadly correspond with the distinction between Fordist and post-Fordist production (see Chapter 17, pp. 693–6).

Asian model. Japanese and Taiwanese businesses are organized on very different principles but both have been highly successful. The success of these models suggests that the structures promoting organizational effectiveness are culturally specific. What works in one society with one set of beliefs and practices will not necessarily work in another.

Clegg warns, however, against jumping from a universalism that ignores culture to a cultural determinism that explains everything in terms of it. Both Japan and Taiwan are predominantly Confucianist in culture, but they have developed very different organizational patterns. Clegg proposes instead an *embedded* view of organization. This accepts that organizations are based in a particular societal context but includes in this not only the culture but also the institutions, laws, and policies of the society. It also recognizes that the character of organizations is not *determined* by their context, for they are actively *constructed* out of the 'materials available' (Clegg 1990: 7).

Feminizing the organization

Another line of criticism has come from those who argue that Weber's emphasis on the formality and impersonality of bureaucracy conceals its gendered character.

Bureaucracy and patriarchy have arguably been historically interrelated and mutually reinforcing. Nineteenth-century bureaucratization took place in a highly patriarchal

Can organizations be feminized?
© Alice Chadwick

depended on the housewife, whose servicing and emotional labour enabled the husband to give time and energy to his organization. The bureaucrat's self-disciplined devotion to duty, which was central to Weber's ideal type, depended on the domestic division of labour.

If gender is important to office relationships, what about sexuality? The classic literature on organizations has focused on their rational and non-emotional character, leaving sexuality out. Rosemary Pringle has argued, however, that sexuality pervades the life of the office 'in dress and self-presentation, in jokes and gossip, looks and flirtations, secret affairs and dalliances, in fantasy, and in the range of coercive behaviours that we now call sexual harassment' (Pringle 1989: 90).

Some have treated this as inappropriate behaviour that spills into the work setting but is nothing to do with work. Thus, Rosabeth Moss Kanter (1977) recognized the existence of sexual behaviour in the office but treated it as a hang-over from pre-bureaucratic relationships that should be eliminated. This approach maintained the Weberian view of bureaucracy as an impersonal structure in which emotional and sexual relationships should play no part.

Others have argued that it is an integral part of authority relationships. According to this view, sexual harassment at work is not just an overflow of non-work behaviour into the work situation; it is one of the means by which male superiors establish their power over female inferiors. It is also used to justify the exclusion of women from occupations that involve 'serious' work by treating them as irrational reservoirs of sexuality and emotionality.

Treating sexual behaviour at work as sexual harassment presents other problems, however. Pringle accepted that sexual behaviour is a means by which women are subordinated but also pointed out that it can make women 'the pathetic victims of sexual harassment'. Account must also be taken of 'the power and the pleasure' that women can get from sexual interaction at work (Pringle 1989: 101–2).

Feminist responses to the patriarchal character of traditional bureaucracies have varied. Some have argued that they should be forced to open their senior positions to women but, although the opening-up of careers to women may reduce discrimination, it does not necessarily make organizations less patriarchal in character. Women may have to act like men in order to reach and hold senior positions. Crompton and Le Feuvre reported that many of the women managers they studied 'had felt constrained to behave as "surrogate men"—even to the extent of remaining childless' (1992: 116).

Women in senior posts can, none the less, make a difference. Watson (1992) claimed that 'femocrats' in the relatively open Australian state bureaucracy have been able to make some important, though limited, changes in

society and produced male-dominated organizations. During the twentieth century these organizations increasingly employed women but in junior clerical positions, where they were excluded from promotion.

Banking provides a good example of this. Up until the 1960s sex discrimination in banking was quite explicit, with separate salary scales for men and women, and the requirement that on marriage women had to resign from their jobs, though they were usually then reappointed to non-career grades. It was not until the 1980s that this situation really changed, after the recruitment practices of Barclays Bank had been referred to the Equal Opportunities Commission (Crompton 1997).

Patriarchy operated not only through the exclusion of women from bureaucratic careers, but also through the dependence of the male career on gendered domestic roles. This applied both inside and outside the office. Inside the office, secretaries became 'office wives', who carried out personal caring functions and provided emotional support for the boss. Outside the office, the successful male career

Briefing: solicitors and secretaries

'The most claustrophobic example of control through sexuality (no-one had yet labelled it "harassment") concerns a legal practice which was, for a country town, quite large. The atmosphere was one of compulsory jocularity: solicitors and secretaries gaily exchanged insults and sexual banter with each other all day, and there was a great deal of friendly fondling and patting of bottoms. They also intermarried and had a shared social life of parties and barbeques. Ex-secretaries with their babies were regular visitors, and often came back to work on a part-time or temporary basis. Beneath the enforced egalitarianism and informality there was a rigidly enforced sexual division of labour. The partners could not imagine taking on a woman lawyer or the possibility that any of the "girls" might have the capacity to do "law".... The women were clear that their role was to service men and were willing to put up with what was constant sexual innuendo. The overall feel of the place was not dissimilar to a brothel. While the secretaries made continuous use of mockery and parody, it seemed only to reaffirm them in "traditional" boss–secretary relationships.' (Pringle 1989: 93–4).

? *Have you come across examples of sexual behaviour or the use of sexual language in organizations that you have worked for?*

? *What effect has this had on work relationships?*

policies, laws, services, and the bureaucracy itself that are favourable to women.

A more radical approach has argued that organizations cannot be feminized by women in senior positions because bureaucracies are inherently masculine in character. Their emphasis on hierarchy, formality, and impersonality is typically male. Women should instead seek to create a different kind of organization that embodies the female qualities of 'caring and sharing'.

There are two strands to this argument:

- a belief that activities can and should be organized in a more democratic, more participatory, and cooperative way;
- the notion that women are more able than men to create this kind of organization, as the organizations created by the women's movement are said to have shown.

Figure 14.8 Three ways of feminizing organizations

- **Femocracy:** increasing women's access to senior positions.
- **Feminine organizations:** creating alternative feminine organizations.
- **Degendering activities:** redistributing activities equally between men and women.

As Witz and Savage have pointed out, the problem with this approach is that it assumes 'gender differentiated modes of social action' (1992: 20). It presupposes that women are socialized into more participatory, cooperative, caring, and sharing patterns of behaviour. This kind of socialization is itself, however, a consequence of patriarchy, since it is male domination that pushes women into caring roles in the household. The notion of the feminine organization is, in other words, itself bound up with patriarchal assumptions.

Witz and Savage suggest that, instead of attaching different principles of organization to gender, we should recognize that organizations require both 'male' and 'female' activities and that both men and women can carry out both sets of activities. What matters is the relationship between these activities, and the way they are divided and distributed between men and women. Witz and Savage argue that work activities should be degendered. As they nicely put it, 'men can no longer go on simply organizing the world; they have to take responsibility for tidying it up too' (Witz and Savage 1992: 26).

Continued bureaucracy

Bureaucracy has been challenged and to some degree reversed. Has a process of **debureaucratization** taken place?

A growing awareness of the disadvantages of bureaucracy and of the existence of alternatives that seem to work better has led to the construction of less bureaucratic forms of organization. The growth of organizational studies has contributed to this process by stimulating reflection on organizational character and structure, drawing attention to structures embodying different principles and values, and designing more appropriate organizations for specific purposes. Organizations have also had to adapt to changes in their environment, to advances in information technology, changing markets, and feminist challenges.

These changes have occurred only in some organizations, however. George Ritzer has argued that the broad tendency of organizational development is towards greater rationalization and bureaucratization, which he calls the

Frontiers Customer-oriented bureaucracy in call centres

Marek Korczynski (2001) argues that Ritzer's concept of McDonaldization fails to grasp the full character of service bureaucratization. The Weberian rationalization of production certainly operates in service organizations but these are distinctive in the *simultaneity* of production and consumption, which operate according to different principles. The discipline of production conflicts with the customer's pleasure of consumption. At least some service organizations have to satisfy customers in an immediate way. The requirements of a customer-orientation contradict those of rational organization and set up tensions within the organization.

Korczynski discusses this issue on the basis of a study of five call centres in different countries (we also discuss call centres in Chapter 17, pp. 682–4). Call-centre employees were expected to empathize with customers and seek to meet their needs. Indeed, employees were selected partly on their capacity to do this and were trained to do so. Managers sought also, however, to minimize costs and control employee behaviour by standardizing responses and limiting the length of calls. A rationalized emotional labour was required from employees and this set up tensions within them, particularly when they had taken on this

work out of a desire 'to help people'. Call-centre workers found their work both satisfying and highly stressing. They were torn between the 'pleasures and pains' of call-centre work.

Korczynski points out that this may not apply to all call centres, as some may operate on a more professional basis, while others may be concerned solely with sales. He also argues, however, that:

> there are many other forms of front-line work that can be illuminated through the lens of the customer-oriented bureaucracy. The work of the nurse, the care assistant, the retail worker, the bank teller, the restaurant worker, the hotel worker, the bar-worker can all be analysed usefully against the ideal type of the customer-oriented bureaucracy. (Korczynski 2001: 98).

❓ Have you ever worked in a customer-oriented bureaucracy? Did you experience such tensions and contradictions? If so, what form did they take and how did you deal with them? If not, why do you think that there were no contradictions or tensions between customer service and rational organization?

McDonaldization of society. He claims that the principles of the fast-food restaurant exemplify the rationalizing tendencies identified by Max Weber as characteristic of modern society. McDonald's offers efficiency, calculability, and predictability. It also tightly regulates its employees (see the opening extract of this chapter), and even controls the behaviour of its customers, by, for example, providing uncomfortable seats that 'lead diners to do what management wishes them to do—eat quickly and leave' (Ritzer 1996: 11).

There has, furthermore, been no debureaucratization of society as a whole. Bureaucratic organization remains the principle way of organizing large-scale activities and information technology has simply improved their coordination and increased central control of them. Although the bureaucratic model has been challenged in some businesses, where greater flexibility and higher commitment have become crucial to competitiveness, in others bureaucratic organization is still considered the best way of coordinating the routine production of standard goods and services. Bureaucratic organization also remains central to activities concerned with health, safety, equal opportunities, and protection of the environment, where objectivity, consistency, and impersonality are essential.

As we show in Chapter 15, pp. 607–8, although deregulatory government policies may have diminished state regulation in some important areas of activity, the overall level of regulation has increased—and regulation almost always means bureaucratic organization. The term 'debureaucratization' is a useful means of drawing attention to important changes in some organizations, but these must be placed in the context of continued bureaucratization elsewhere.

The transformation of management

The organizational changes examined above were paralleled by changes in management techniques. Management thinking shifted from an emphasis on formal to informal structures, from authoritarian to integrative styles of control, from specialization to general commitment. In this section we examine the development of the human-relations approach and then go on to consider human resource management.

Human relations

The development of these new techniques began with the **human-relations school** of management. This grew out of, but also reacted against, the scientific-management approach that we examined on pp. 548–9. The human-relations approach emerged from interpretations of the experiments conducted during 1924–32 at the Hawthorne factory of the Western Electric Company in the United States. These experiments are important not only because of their significance for the development of management thought but also because of their methodological implications.

The first experiments were in the scientific-management tradition. They examined the effects of changes in lighting on worker productivity. The experimenters found, to their surprise, that almost any changes they made, whether, for example, they increased or decreased the amount of light, resulted in higher productivity. They also found that productivity rose in the control group as well as the experimental group. From this, they concluded that the conduct of the experiment had itself raised productivity. The interest shown by the investigators in the workers had changed their attitudes to their work and this had more effect on their behaviour than the experimental changes. They had discovered what has been labelled the 'Hawthorne effect'—that is, the effect of a study on the behaviour of those being studied.

This discovery led to many further experiments that showed that productivity was not a matter of individual responses to monetary incentives, as assumed by scientific management. Production was regulated by the group, which established output norms and put pressure on those who over- or under-produced to conform to them.

The behaviour of work groups was in turn seen as largely the result of supervisory style. The restriction of output was interpreted as a defensive response by workers fearing managerial interference in their work lives. Supervisors who allayed workers' anxieties, and encouraged their participation in decision-making, obtained higher levels of production.

The human-relations approach is generally considered an advance on scientific management. It recognized the importance of group influences on the individual, and took account of the informal as well as the formal structure of the workplace. It established the significance of workers' emotional needs and argued for an essentially integrative style of management based on meeting these needs. It led to schemes that sought to make work more meaningful by rotating tasks between workers, and by enlarging and enriching jobs to include more varied work. It also promoted the rise of personnel managers as human relations specialists. In general, it treated workers as human beings rather than machines—hence the term *human relations*.

It was claimed that the Hawthorne experiments provided a scientific basis for the human-relations approach,

 Briefing: the work-group rules!

The rules established by one group observed during the Hawthorne experiments.

- 'You should not turn out too much work. If you do, you are a "rate-buster".
- You should not turn out too little work. If you do, you are a "chiseler".
- You should not tell a supervisor anything . . . to the detriment of an associate. If you do, you are a "squealer".
- You should not attempt to maintain social distance or act officious. If you are an inspector, for example, you should not act like one.' (Roethlisberger and Dickson 1939: 522)

but the results of the experiments have been interpreted in other ways (Carey 1967). Rose (1975) argued that the restriction of output was not necessarily a response to supervisory practices, for, at a time of high unemployment, it was quite rational to restrict output in order to make a job last as long as possible. Thus, the conclusions drawn by the human-relations approach reflected a particular interpretation of the experiments' results.

The human-relations approach derived not only from the results of the experiment but also from a particular social theory. One of the leading exponents of the approach, Elton Mayo, who directed some of the experiments, believed that the integration of workers in a work community could counteract societal tendencies towards an individualism that he considered excessive. Influenced by Emile Durkheim's ideas, he believed that the problem of *anomie* could best be solved by developing integrated industrial communities (for Durkheim's theory of anomie, see Chapter 2, pp. 37–8).

The human-relations approach has been criticized for its managerial assumptions, for its focus on the work situation alone, and for its neglect of technology (see Chapter 17, pp. 679–83 for a discussion of the significance of technology). Its understanding of worker behaviour was, however, an advance on scientific management, while in its later stages it became considerably more sophisticated in its analysis of the experience of work and work relationships, and took more account of organizational structure, technology, and conflict. It was also based on a substantial body of research, which greatly increased our knowledge of social behaviour at work.

Figure 14.9 Human relations versus scientific management

Aspects of management	Scientific management	Human relations
Motivation of worker	Money	Social needs
Unit of analysis	Individual	Work-group
Organizational structure	Formal	Informal
Work tasks	Subdivided	Rotated, enlarged, enriched
Management style	Coercive	Integrative
Interpretation of worker behaviour	Rational, calculative	Irrational, emotional

Human resource management

Human resource management (HRM) is the name given to a new emphasis in management thought since the 1980s on the central importance of a company's labour force in creating competitiveness. Like the human-relations approach, HRM seeks to integrate workers into the company but it has gone considerably further in its aims and techniques. According to HRM, personnel issues are too important to be left to personnel managers as human-relations specialists. They must become a central concern of *all* managers, especially top management, for a company's human resources are its most important resources. It is also more ambitious than the human-relations approach in its mission to change the whole culture and organization of the workplace.

Exponents of HRM argue that *cultural* change is crucial to competitiveness, because it is employee attitudes and beliefs that really matter. Management should not seek a bureaucratic obedience to company rules but rather the total commitment of employees to the company. Mission statements, cultural change programmes, staff development, and appraisal are typical techniques for developing this commitment. The selection of employees is also crucial, to make sure that company recruits are capable of this kind of commitment.

Cultural change requires *organizational* change. Organizations should be decentralized to shift responsibility

---

THEORY AND METHODS

Critical management studies

Critical management studies (CMS) emerged in business schools in the 1980s and has now established itself as a distinctive perspective in the study of management. It brings together many different critiques, from Marxist, Foucauldian, and feminist approaches, of the managerial ideologies dominant in the 1980s. Grey and Wilmott (2005) have identified three common threads in CMS:

- de-naturalization;
- anti-performativity;
- reflexivity.

De-naturalization rejects any notion that management structures and practices are natural. Hierarchy or competition, for example, are often treated as self-evident features of management. CMS rejects the idea that any aspect of management should be taken for granted in this way.

Anti-performativity opposes the idea that management should be evaluated solely in terms of its success in attaining the goals of the organization. Ethical and political criteria matter.

Reflexivity refers to the importance of reflecting upon the assumptions that inform business school teaching and research. These must always be subject to questioning and challenge.

Critical management studies has attracted a following among academics in business schools but faces the problem that business schools earn their money from training managers who come from, or will seek careers in, organizations that operate on the basis of the assumptions that it is criticizing. The ultimate test of CMS is whether it can move beyond academic critique to impact upon the practices of management in business organizations.

downwards in order to empower the workforce. Instead of allocating workers to specified tasks, managers should create flexible teams that can take responsibility for carrying out whatever work is required to meet the objectives of the company. Workers should be involved in the process of quality improvement.

This highly integrative approach to the management of labour leaves little room for an independent trade unionism. Unions are, after all, based on the assumption that there is a conflict of interest between employers and employees, while HRM emphasizes the cultural unity of a company as it engages in an intensely competitive struggle with its rivals. HRM is, therefore, wary of collective bargaining and seeks to individualize the relationship between employee and company, through individual contracts, appraisal, and performance-related pay.

HRM requires cultural and organizational changes in management as well as labour. Managers must alter their own customary ways of thinking, if they are to bring about cultural change and introduce the new programmes to achieve it. Intermediate layers of management should be stripped out, partly because they are no longer necessary if responsibility is devolved, and partly because HRM calls for a closer and more direct relationship between management and labour.

> **Connections**
>
> HRM and the Japanese-style integration of employees into the company are closely linked to 'the "new" industrial relations', which we discuss in Chapter 17, pp. 699–700.

These ideas have been linked to Japanese-style management practices. Japanese companies out-competed many Western companies and one reason for their success appeared to be their much higher levels of employee commitment. Japanese workers have been expected to stay with their company throughout their careers and subordinate themselves totally to it. They have had to take part in quality-circle meetings and suggest ways of improving production. They have had to work long hours and sacrifice weekends and holidays to the requirements of their company. They have been expected to spend much of what leisure time is left attending company social events or engaging in bonding activities with colleagues after work. It is no accident that the Japanese have a word—*karoshi*—for death through overwork.

Some have taken a sceptical view of HRM and treated it as little more than managerial rhetoric. Karen Legge (1995) found little to distinguish HRM from the standard prescriptions of personnel management, and argued that practice anyway fell far short of the claims made by its exponents. She saw HRM as a management fad generated

Briefing: work in a Japanese car factory

'In recent years demand for the company's product has been brisk and two hours of overtime are routinely required. . . . With overtime the working day from start to finish is typically 11 hours long. . . . Even though their day is long, workers can expect little free time for rest and relaxation in the course of the working day. The scheduled meal breaks are often taken up with company business, such as Quality Circle meetings. When the norm is 32 suggestions per worker per year, membership of an 8 or 10 person Quality Circle imposes real obligations. Workers are formally entitled to 2 days off each week but, in recent years, they have been obliged to work 6 days so that the company can extract more output from existing capacity. Their one day off may not be completely free because loyal workers are expected to join in company sports and social events. Finally, the day off may be taken mid-week at the convenience of the company and the inconvenience of the worker's family. In the summer of 1987 Nippon Car chose to work Saturdays and Sundays because the local electricity utility charged a lower tariff at weekends.' (K. Williams *et al*. 1994: 61)

by those, such as business gurus, management consultants, business schools, and publishers, who made money by riding new bandwagons. Managers used HRM qualifications to advance their careers, while personnel managers became HRM missionaries at a time when the decline of labour organization had diminished their role as managers of industrial relations.

Storey (1995*a*) argued, however, that HRM is distinctive and that management has really been changing. He presented survey evidence that showed the growing use of HRM techniques, though he found that few companies had adopted the full HRM package. HRM is interrelated with other changes, such as post-Fordist methods of production, which we examine in Chapter 17, pp. 693–6. Similar pressures for more competitive, more flexible, more customer-oriented organizations lie behind all these innovations, and they have been influenced by a growing interest in the merits of non-Western alternatives.

New management styles and new methods of control have certainly developed in some companies, but this does not mean that older techniques of management have been superseded. HRM techniques may not be appropriate in businesses where production is labour intensive, work tasks are routine, and profits depend on producing large quantities of goods at the lowest possible cost. In such circumstances, the most effective management of human resources may be simply to use financial incentives or coercion to get employees to work as hard as possible. In some companies the most effective management of human resources may not require HRM techniques at all!

Privatization

The literature on organizational and management change makes little reference to ownership, but in a capitalist society the control of an organization lies ultimately in the hands of its owners. We showed earlier that there had been a considerable extension of public ownership in Britain since the mid-nineteenth century. Since the 1980s this has been substantially reversed by privatization. Private capital has been drawn into public services in many different ways but here we will focus on public utilities sold to the private sector.

> **⇨ Connections**
>
> We examine the economic and political context of privatization in 'The crisis of the 1970s', Chapter 15, pp. 599–601 and its continuation by New Labour on p. 606. Its consequences for industrial relations are considered in Chapter 17, p. 703.

We argued earlier that nationalization made little difference to the capitalist character of British society. The nationalized industries had to operate within a capitalist society and therefore operated on capitalist principles. This implies that it mattered little whether businesses were privately or publicly owned, but the privatizing Conservative governments of the 1980s and 1990s clearly did believe that ownership was important. They associated public ownership with sluggish, bureaucratic, inefficient, and unresponsive organizations and claimed that privatization would make them dynamic, efficient, and responsive to consumers. We cannot here make a general assessment of the effects of privatization, but what consequences did it have for organization and management?

Julia O'Connell Davidson (1993) studied the consequences of privatization for the organization of water companies. Changes in their organization were designed to replace *centralized* and *bureaucratic* structures with *decentralized* and *contractual* ones. Supposedly decentralized profit centres were, however, tightly controlled by company boards, which did not allow them to buy in services freely from the outside. The threat of contracting out functions to lower-cost providers was in practice used to force more work out of employees afraid of losing their jobs.

Privatization has had an impact on managerial careers. Kate Mulholland (1998) found that it led to changes in career paths and in the relationship between the employing organization and the manager. Previously this relationship had been one of trust and commitment, with the manager giving loyal service in return for a salary and a secure career. After privatization, employment depended on performance. The bureaucratic career was replaced by a 'portfolio career', where individuals took responsibility for their own futures, moving between organizations, and capitalizing on their employability. A division opened up between 'public-sector survivors', who tried to hang on to their jobs, and 'movers and shakers', who were constantly on the lookout for better opportunities elsewhere.

The privatization of the utilities had enabled the most senior managers to operate more freely, for they became relatively independent of both owner and market control. Ownership was now dispersed among many small and passive shareholders, while the monopolistic position of the utilities left them relatively free from market regulation. This freedom enabled them to diversify company operations into other activities both at home and abroad. They sharply increased their salaries, while also benefiting from share ownership and share options. They abandoned the industrial-relations and career conventions of the public sector.

The senior managers were not wholly free of external constraints, however, for they were subject to new bureaucratic controls. The privatized utilities were supervised by new regulatory authorities, such as the Office of Water Regulation (OFWAT), which were charged with preventing them from abusing their monopolistic position. Their prices, standards of service, investment programmes, and impact on the environment were all subject to regulation. These authorities were controlled by bureaucrats with a high degree of autonomy but the effectiveness of regulation has been a matter of considerable debate. The regulators have certainly at times intervened strongly, though they have had no control over many aspects of company operation and policy.

Thus, privatization involved both debureaucratization and bureaucratization. A limited debureaucratization took place internally and through some shift from state control to market control. New external bureaucratic controls were, however, created to regulate some aspects of the behaviour of the privatized utilities.

Globalization

While privatization reversed earlier nationalizing tendencies, one process that has not gone into reverse has been the rise of transnational corporations (TNCs). Their rapid growth since the end of the Second World War has created some corporations whose operations are so extensive that they are considered to be global in character (see Chapter 16, p. 647, for a discussion of this). Here we will

Controversy and debate Global Tesco

Tesco's increasing dominance of the UK retail sector has attracted growing comment. In 2005 four companies between them controlled 74 per cent of the national grocery market. Morrisons had 11.4 per cent, Sainsbury's had 15.6 per cent, Asda had 16.7 per cent, but Tesco had 30.3 per cent. It was estimated that Tesco actually controlled more than 40 per cent of the grocery market in fourteen towns. This was not only because of the number of large Tesco stores but also because Tesco had recently been buying up local convenience stores, which it plans to increase up to 1,200 in number. There are calls for intervention by the Office of Fair Trading to halt this process, which is plausibly said to be driving independent retailers out of business. Tesco could be forced to sell off some stores if it is found to have broken competition laws.

Expansion abroad has not come up against such barriers. Tesco declared in 2000 that 'food retailers will have to go global to succeed'. By 2005 a quarter of its stores were outside the United Kingdom. In Europe it had a further 25 stores in the Czech Republic, 69 in Hungary, 87 in Ireland, 78 in Poland, and 30 in Slovakia. In Asia it had 31 stores in China, 104 in Japan, six in Malaysia, 38 in South Korea, and five in Taiwan. While this was hardly a global coverage, Tesco had clearly expanded strongly in Eastern Europe and Asia. This expansion occurred partly through the opening of new stores, partly through the purchase of existing chains, as in Japan, where Tesco bought a chain of 78 convenience stores in 2003.

Tesco also has a global reach through its sourcing of products. It has been criticized by ActionAid for using its huge purchasing power to force down the prices it pays for South African fruit and therefore the wages of South African farmworkers.

> Tesco is the UK's biggest buyer of South African fruit. Despite the company's commitment to corporate social responsibility and the Ethical Trading Initiative (on minimum labour standards)—and the existence of good national laws to protect farm labourers—ActionAid found unacceptable conditions among the temporary labourers interviewed on Tesco accredited farms. (ActionAid 2005)

The mainly women farmworkers were paid below the minimum wage, exposed to pesticide spraying, and excluded from benefits provided by labour legislation.

Sources: ActionAid UK, press release, 11 April 2005, www.actionaid.org.uk/1580/press_release.html; *Guardian*, 10 November 2005; Tesco annual review 2005.

---

consider the organizational and management issues raised by globalization, but it is first worth pointing out the relationship between globalization and privatization.

Globalization has interacted with privatization in various ways. State ownership tended to keep the operations of companies within national boundaries, while privatization released them from this restriction. Equally, privatization allowed foreign companies to buy into previously nationalized activities. Globalization has in turn promoted privatization, because the increased global mobility of capital has put pressure on governments to attract and retain capital, in part through privatization. Furthermore, bodies like the World Bank have put pressure on governments to privatize, as a condition of receiving loans.

Concentration and globalization have led to decentralizing changes in organizational structure. According to the traditional *functional* model, a corporation was divided into specialized departments, such as personnel, research and development, and marketing, that were coordinated by a centralized management structure. As corporations became transnational and grew larger, they shifted to *divisional* structures with *product* or *area* divisions, each having a complete range of specialized departments within

it. Sometimes product and area structures were combined in *matrix* structures that tried to get the best of both worlds (Child 1984). Coordination was carried out at the divisional level and management was largely decentralized to this level, though financial control and strategic direction remained centralized in the corporate headquarters, which was always firmly located in a particular country.

Since the 1980s, American and British companies have become increasingly decentralized along *project* lines (Scase 2002). Cumbersome bureaucratic structures engaged in coordinating many different operations were broken down into more flexible units to carry out particular business projects and focus specifically on their success. These were leaner operations, where occupational boundaries were broken down, high levels of commitment and cooperation were required from employees, and performance was closely monitored.

This model could deliver impressive results but Richard Scase has commented that it was geared to short-term performance and liable to burn out those involved. This essentially American model has been widely diffused but adoption has been far from universal and companies in continental Europe have continued to operate on more bureaucratic lines. Further converts to the American corporate model are now perhaps less likely, at least for the time being, after the spectacular failure of Enron and WorldCom, where fraudulent accountancy ended in corporate disaster (see Fulcher 2003).

Some aspects of this leaner model originated in Japan. As we showed in 'Cultural alternatives' (on p. 556), there has been much interest in the less bureaucratic organizational structures found in East Asia, while HRM has tried to apply Japanese-style techniques for generating greater employee commitment and loyalty. A debate has developed between those who believe that Japanization has been taking place and those who argue that Japanese organizational forms are dependent on the Japanese context and cannot travel.

> ⮩ *Connections*
>
> We discuss globalization and the rise of transnational corporations in Chapter 16, pp. 646–8. In Chapter 17, pp. 699–700, we discuss whether Japanese industrial-relations practices have been transplanted into Britain.

Japanese companies themselves provide an interesting test case, given the number of foreign plants that these companies have set up since the 1970s. There is much anecdotal evidence of the diffusion to the 'transplants' of typical Japanese practices, such as quality circles, exhaustive selection procedures, and various kinds of management–worker mixing. Case studies suggest, however, that there are barriers to the full implementation of Japanese management techniques outside Japan. One such study has concluded that overseas Japanese companies find it 'difficult or impossible to Japanize because they cannot recreate Japanese levels of workforce consent and commitment' (K. Williams *et al.* 1994: 87).

But do Japanese companies even try to Japanize their foreign operations? A study of HRM practices in Japanese companies in Australia has suggested that a distinction be made between the *core* and *periphery* of Japanese companies (Dedoussis and Littler 1994). In Japan itself, the distinctive features of Japanese management, such as lifetime employment, do not operate within the periphery, which consists of small subcontractors that supply the core company (see Chapter 17, p. 700). Dedoussis and Littler

Japanization? Workers at the Japanese-owned Auto Parts Alliance factory in Guangdong, China.
© Getty Images/Peter Parks

argue that overseas plants are treated as part of this periphery, particularly when they are 'screwdriver' operations assembling Japanese components abroad in order to penetrate local markets. There is no need to introduce there the expensive personnel practices used to create and maintain worker loyalty in core plants at home.

Global corporations do put pressure on countries to standardize the economic and financial environment within which they operate. Governments deregulate and privatize in order to attract investment and this results in the partial dismantling of distinctive national structures, often within special zones (see Chapter 16, pp. 648–9). Globalization has not, however, standardized corporate structures and cultures, and, in spite of their advocates, neither the American nor the Japanese model have become universal, for both have had limited applicability outside their country of origin.

Decarceration and recarceration

We showed on pp. 546–7 that incarceration in prisons and hospitals was a characteristic feature of the new industrial society emerging during the nineteenth century. In the 1950s and 1960s a process of **decarceration** got under way as community alternatives to imprisonment and hospitalization were developed. There was then, however, a reaction against this and a process of recarceration began. In this section we examine these processes but also consider the privatizing of prisons, for the rising prison population has been increasingly accommodated in privately managed prisons. Lastly, we consider surveillance, for arguably recarceration has extended to the whole of society as surveillance has spread and intensified.

Decarceration

In the 1960s there was a growing criticism of the incarceration of people in prisons and mental hospitals. Goffman's (1961*b*) analysis of the dehumanizing effects of *total institutions* on their inmates became one of the fashionable texts of the time (see pp. 543–4). It was argued that such institutions did not help either to cure or to rehabilitate those shut up inside them and, indeed, often made them worse by 'institutionalizing' them. The symptoms displayed by patients in mental hospitals were attributed to the institution itself or the adoption of an inmate role, with patients losing their ability to cope with the outside world. It was claimed that prisons actually increased criminality, because inmates were brutalized by their prison experiences and learned new criminal skills while they were inside.

The alternatives put forward involved various forms of *community care* for the mentally ill and *community correc-*tions for criminals. Community care was made easier by the availability of new drugs that made it possible to treat mental patients without taking them into hospitals. There were 130 large mental hospitals in England Wales in 1975 but by 2005 only fourteen of these were left and with much smaller populations. Crimes were punished increasingly by fines rather than imprisonment and new forms of punishment were created, such as community service, suspended sentences, attendance by day at specified centres, or residence in supervised hostels (see Figure 14.12 on p. 570).

According to Andrew Scull (1984), the emergence of superior comunity-based alternatives to the prison and the mental hospital did not, however, explain decarceration. He claimed that there was no evidence to support the idea that treatment in the community was more effective than hospital care. Furthermore, those who believed in community care had no idea what it really meant.

> What has the new approach meant in practice? For thousands of the old, already suffering in varying degrees from mental confusion and deterioration, it has meant premature death. For others, it has meant that they have been left to rot and decay, physically and otherwise, in broken down welfare hostels or what are termed . . . 'personal-care' nursing homes. For thousands of younger psychotics discharged into the streets, it has meant a nightmare existence in the blighted centres of our cities, amidst neighbourhoods crowded with prostitutes, ex-felons, addicts, alcoholics, and the other human rejects now repressively tolerated by our society. (Scull 1984: 2)

Scull also argued that 'community corrections' were an inadequate way of controlling and rehabilitating criminals and delinquents. Those charged with supervising them were overloaded with cases and supervision became a token process involving no more than short weekly interviews. Criminals drifted into decaying inner-city areas, where they were largely left alone by the police. As both the mentally ill and the criminals congregated in these areas, there was the danger of a violent backlash against them from the local inhabitants.

Scull explained decarceration as a response to the crisis of welfare capitalism. The expense of the welfare state had generated a financial crisis. It was cheaper to deal with deviants through community programmes and welfare payments than to lock them up in heavily staffed and expensive institutions. This was not just a matter of the running costs of these institutions, but also the need for greater capital expenditure. Most of them had been built in the nineteenth century and urgently needed replacement.

> **➲ Connections**
>
> You may find it helpful to look up our discussion of changes in welfare in other chapters. See Chapter 8, pp. 303–4, and Chapter 15, pp. 602–5.

Controversy and debate Electronic tagging

Electronic tagging, otherwise known as the 'home detention scheme' (HDS), was introduced in the 1990s and has now become an established part of the British courts' repertoire of punishments. It involves the wearing of a device that enables the private security companies operating the scheme, under contract from the Home Office, to know whether the wearer is within a particular area, normally their home, during a specified time period.

Electronic tagging was seen initially as a means of preventing re-offending. It would permit the early release of offenders from prison, so that they could maintain or re-establish their family and community lives, and possibly return to work, while continuing their punishment. It has been claimed that it helps an offender to resist peer pressure to re-engage in criminal activity after release.

Increasingly, however, it has been seen as a means of relieving the problems caused by the overcrowding of prisons. In 2005 the continued rise in the prison population led to a government proposal to allow early release on HDS during the last six months of a sentence rather than the last four and a

half months. Ministers have regularly called for the greater use of electronic tagging.

Mike Nellis has claimed that instead of being an extra means of supervising offenders, it is becoming the dominant means, displacing the traditional functions of the probation service. This marks 'an emerging shift in the community field from a humanistic to a surveillant paradigm' (Nellis 2003: 63). Powerful commercial interests are involved, for tagging is carried out by private companies using the products of companies selling ever more advanced surveillance machinery.

Sources: *Independent*, 22 March 2002; *Guardian*, 14 October 2005; Nellis (2003).

❷ Why do you think that electronic tagging was introduced?

❷ Do you think its use should be extended?

❷ Is the growth of electronic tagging evidence of decarceration?

Scull's theory of the decarceration of the mentally ill has been criticized for its economic determinism. The critique of the total institution together with a movement in psychiatry away from a *medical* towards a *behavioural* model of psychological problems was at least partly responsible for the shift from hospital to community-based treatments (Nettleton 1995: 246). Scull was, none the less, right to emphasize the importance of financial pressures, and Baggott has concluded that in Britain it was the 'economic argument which has been the driving force behind the development of community care policies' (Baggott 1994: 220).

There has been a more fundamental critique of the whole notion of decarceration. Stanley Cohen (1985) argued that community punishments do not decarcerate but extend surveillance and control into the society at large. Instead of surveillance and control being concentrated in specific institutions, they now operate in the outside society through probation, community service, and electronic tagging (we discuss surveillance in a separate section below). This leads us back to Foucault's argument that the disciplinary and surveillance techniques of the carceral *organizations* of the nineteenth century were but the first step towards a disciplinary or carceral *society* (see p. 543).

Recarceration

Mental illness in the United Kingdom is, in principle, now handled by community care, with only the most serious cases leading to some form of hospitalization. Highly publicized cases of murder by the mentally ill, growing concerns with public safety, and attempts to get the homeless off the streets have, however, contributed to what two community psychiatrists have called a process of 'reinstitutionalization'. Turner and Liebe contend that: 'Whether you call something a continuing care unit, a 24-hour nursing staffed hospital or a medium secure rehabilitation unit does not really matter, since essentially you are reproducing the asylum' (2002: 253).

So far as punishment is concerned, there has been a rise in imprisonment going back to the 1970s, resulting from both a greater recourse to imprisonment as a punishment and longer sentences. This was most evident in the United States, where incarceration returned to favour as a way of solving the problem of rising crime by taking criminals off the streets. Prison terms became longer, most notoriously with the 'three-strikes' law introduced in 1992, which meant that in some states conviction for three crimes of any kind resulted in mandatory life imprisonment. The prison population in the United States increased at a

Figure 14.10 Rates of imprisonment in selected countries

Country	Prison population per 100,000 inhabitants	Date
United States	701	2002
Russian Federation	606	2003
South Africa	402	2003
Iran	226	2002
Chile	212	2002
Brazil	160	2003
England and Wales	141	2003
Scotland	129	2003
China	117	2002
Kenya	111	2002
Saudi Arabia	110	2000
Germany	98	2003
France	93	2003
Sweden	73	2002
Japan	53	2002
India	29	2002

Source: *World Prison Population List*, Home Office (2003) (can be found at www.homeoffice.gov.uk).

➔ Note that definitional and recording practices do vary between countries.

❓ What factors do you think affect the rate of imprisonment in a country?

staggering speed, doubling every decade, rising from 316,000 in 1980 to 740,000 in 1990 and 1,428,000 in 1999/2000 (*Guardian*, 15 February 2000). Currently, the United States has much the highest rate of imprisonment in the world (see Figure 14.10).

In Britain, the rate of increase was much slower, though rising sharply in the 1990s (see Figure 14.11). British penal policy has been driven by the conflicting imperatives of a concern with costs *and* a law-and-order ideology emphasizing punishment rather than rehabilitation. There has been a 'twin-track' strategy that made greater use of both non-custodial punishments and imprisonment (Cavadino and Dignan 2002). In the case of lesser offences, attempts have been made to keep the prison population down by the use of cautions, non-custodial punishments, and shorter sentences. More serious crimes have been punished by a greater use of imprisonment (see Figure 14.12).

A rising prison population has led to the building of new prisons but prison-building has not been able to keep pace. This has led to recurrent overcrowding crises, with rising numbers of prisoners per cell and a growing pressure on educational and exercise facilities. With cuts in expenditure leading to lower staffing levels and reducing prisoners' out-of-cell time, rehabilitation work with offenders has suffered. One expedient adopted to deal with the crisis was the purchase of a prison ship from the United States. Another has been the greater use of imprisonment at home through electronic tagging.

While there is evidence to support the idea of decarceration, since there has been a considerable decarceration of

Figure 14.11 Prison population, England and Wales, 1980–2004

Source: *Social Trends* (2006: 142).

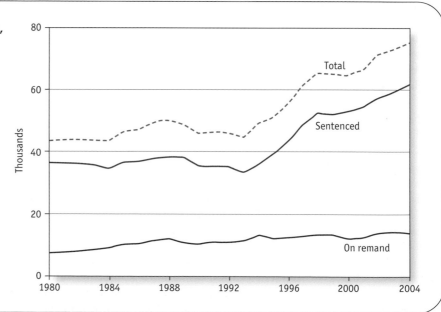

The prison ship in Portland harbour. Is this the solution to the overcrowding of British prisons?
© Getty Images/David Goddard

the mentally ill and a greater use of non-custodial punishments for criminals, there is also evidence of increasing incarceration in rising prison populations. A parallel can here be drawn with the notion of debureaucratization and decarceration. Both these concepts usefully draw our attention to important changes in techniques of control, which have partially reversed previous tendencies. But just as debureaucratization has occurred in some organizations within an increasingly bureaucratic society, decarceration has taken place in some institutions within an increasingly carceral society.

Private prisons

As prison populations rose, prisons were privatized. In this section we consider the consequences of this process, drawing on a study by Adrian James *et al.* (1997).

In the 1980s the prison population began to grow sharply in the United States and it was there that the private prison was first revived. The American example was then followed by Australia, various European countries, including Britain, and more recently New Zealand. The international scope of privatization has, indeed, resulted in leading American companies, such as the Corrections Corporation of America, becoming transnational corporations involved in prison management in Australia and Europe, another example of the interaction between privatization and globalization.

In Britain, privatization began in 1992 with the handing over of the management of the Wolds Prison in Yorkshire to Group 4. Two other prisons have had their management privatized, while eight have been constructed and managed by private companies. There were many reasons for privatization:

Figure 14.12 Changing patterns of punishment, England and Wales, 1938–2003 (%)

Sentencing of adult offenders	Percentage of offenders			
	1938	1975	1994	2003
Imprisonment	33.3	13.4	18.2	24
Probation	15.1	7.0	12.0	–
Community service	–	0.5	10.7	–
Combination order[a]	n.a.	n.a.	2.4	–
Community sentence[b]	–	–	–	33
Fines	27.2	55.3	34.9	23
Suspended sentence	–	11.2	1.1	1
Discharge	23.4	12.0	18.2	15
Other	1.0	0.6	2.4	4
	100.0	100.0	100.0	100.0
Total no. of offenders	38,896	209,709	215,500	334,000

[a] After the 1991 Criminal Justice Act probation could be combined with other penalties.
[b] Community sentence now includes probation, community service, and other community punishments.

Sources: Cavadino and Dignan (1997: 207, table 8.1); *Social Trends* (2005: figure 9.17).

❓ What are the main changes that have taken place in methods of punishment since the 1930s and since the 1970s?

❓ Do these figures suggest that there has been a process of decarceration?

- It was believed that the private sector would be able to manage prisons more efficiently and more economically than the state.

- It was hoped that private prisons would be innovative, would improve the conditions for prisoners, and reduce disorder.

- Privatization was also a means of weakening union power, for the powerful Prison Officers' Association was seen as an obstacle to reform in state-managed prisons.

At Wolds, Group 4's contract required it to achieve higher standards—for example, in prisoner education—than were required elsewhere in the prison service, but gave Group 4 a relatively free hand in how it achieved them. In order to make a fresh start, Wolds employed staff without previous experience of working in prisons. Unlike other British prisons, it was to have remand prisoners only, which meant that it was dealing with non-convicted prisoners who were legally 'innocent until proved guilty'.

The regime established at Wolds set out to minimize the carceral aspects of imprisonment. Its management declared that, since the prisoners were on remand only, they should have as much freedom as possible within an environment that was as normal as possible, and should make productive use of their time. Thus, they were allowed out of their cells for fifteen hours a day and were to receive six hours of education and gym each week. Maintenance of contact with their lives outside the prison was a high priority and they were encouraged to have substantial daily visits and given access to card-phones.

The American practice of *direct supervision* was introduced. This involved prison officers having closer contact with prisoners and treating them more positively. The idea was that greater officer involvement would make destructive prisoner behaviour less likely and enable the construction of cheaper prisons that did not have to withstand violent assault. In Wolds, direct supervision occurred through Unit Supervisors, who took charge of living units of fifty prisoners and had a general responsibility for meeting prisoners' needs. It was believed that the isolation of the supervisor from other staff would lead to closer relationships between staff and prisoners.

The realities of prison life turned out to be somewhat different. Problems in controlling prisoners led to restrictions on their movements, while 'trouble-makers' had to be segregated under a tougher regime. Supervisors complained of isolation and more staff had to be appointed to the units. While some prisoners valued out-of-cell time, others, who were used to greater restriction, found the lack of constraint hard to manage and complained of boredom. Many services, such as education and library services, were contracted out to external providers, which had difficulty supplying them to the required level, because competition for contracts had forced them to cut costs.

In assessing the Wolds experiment, James *et al.* (1997) concluded that it was, none the less, innovatory and successful. The majority of the prisoners they interviewed thought that their relationships with staff were better than those they had experienced elsewhere, while the staff too thought relationships were good. They noted that there was also some evidence that the relative freedom of movement in Wolds had led to more bullying and drug use. It was the staffing problems of the Wolds that gave James *et al.* most cause for concern and they argued that in private prisons inexperienced staff face greater stress and insecurity.

The Director of the Prison Service stated in 2001 that he had initially been opposed to the idea of private prisons, since it seemed immoral to make profits from imprisonment, but they had, none the less, been 'a massive step forward'. They had been innovatory and had established benchmarks for the public sector, though the public sector had in some respects caught up since. Two prisons had, indeed, been transferred back to the public sector after the prison service had outcompeted private management. Privatization had, he thought, stimulated a healthy competition between the public and the private sector (*Financial Times*, 2 October 2001). This notion of healthy competition between the private and public sectors has been one of the central features of Labour's policy towards public services.

Organizational surveillance

As we showed earlier (see p. 542), surveillance was one of the key features of Foucault's disciplinary society. Those who control organizations have always wanted to keep those they control in view. Technology has now made it far easier to watch workers at a distance through web-cams and CCTV, with the added bonus that they do not know when they are being observed (see Study 14 for an investigation into the consequences of CCTV surveillance).

Technology has also, however, made it less necessary to have people actually in view, for their location and activity can be tracked electronically. Thus electronic tagging means that convicts can be imprisoned in their own homes outside the view of guards or warders. In call centres it is not necessary to watch operators to see whether they are answering calls correctly and efficiently, as call durations are monitored electronically and conversations are recorded. In retail operations, sales volume tracking enables managers to check not only what is being sold but who is doing the selling. Surveillance of this kind is much tighter than it ever was in the traditional workplace, where workers could devise ways of avoiding the supervisor's eye or pretend to be working when they were not.

As communication becomes increasingly electronic, surveillance becomes easier and tighter. Cheap surveillance software allows managers to monitor communications, while some systems even enable them to detect and track union activities (Lyon 2001). Written communications can be destroyed but electronic messages leave traces that cannot be removed by those who have sent them. It was never easy, if not impossible, to monitor private face-to-face conversations but such conversations, and movement around the workplace to conduct them, are disappearing as electronic communication becomes the norm.

David Lyon (2001) has pointed out that an individualizing of surveillance parallels the individualizing of work. Workers are expected to be individually mobile and work variable hours (see our discussion of flexible work in Chapter 17, pp. 696–7). Payment is increasingly linked to the individual's performance. Workers' locations, performances, and other activities can now all be monitored electronically on an individual basis.

Frontiers From panopticon to polyopticon

Felstead, Jewson, and Walters (2005) argue that in some workplaces there is a shift from panopticon to polyopticon surveillance. The panopticon (see p. 546 of this chapter) enables those in authority to view subordinates from a central location. The polyopticon provides 'all-round, 360–degree, observation by both senior and junior co-workers at all times' (Felstead *et al.* 2005: 84). In the polyopticon everyone is watching everyone else.

Felstead *et al.* observed this kind of surveillance in a 'collective office', where employees had no fixed work stations and were frequently moving around a workplace with glass walls and uninterrupted lines of sight. Furthermore, senior staff as well as junior staff were highly visible and their behaviour too was open to view and subject to gossip and comment. In the polyopticon control was not just vested in those with authority, for all employees were potentially agents of control.

For an account of the social dynamics of the 'collective office', see Chapter 17, pp. 697–9.

A surveillance society?

Surveillance does not just occur *within* organizations. Through electronic linkages one organization's data can easily become another's. As Lyon has put it, the surveillance containers that once 'were pretty well sealed' are now 'leaky' (2001: 37). This applies particularly to information collected by state agencies, which can be passed from one to another.

Private information hardly exists any longer. More and more financial, consumption, and health data about individuals are stored by organizations, and can be transferred between them. They commonly sell data to each other. In 1998 the Web portal *Geocities* sold people's registration information to commercial interests, in spite of online promises that it would not do this (Gauntlett 2000). According to Lyon, 'the fiction that the inside of a home is a haven from outside demands and pressures is subverted by the ways in which electronic devices take data into and out of the house, sometimes without our knowledge' (Lyon 2001: 17). Increasing use of the Internet is one of the main ways in which such personal data are collected (see Media Watch 14).

Body surveillance techniques that record and store physical and biological data about individuals are being rapidly developed. People can be identified by palm prints, iris or retina patterns, and DNA, which can now be analysed from the traces left by breathing on, say, buildings, cars, or furniture. CCTV can be programmed to identify and track individuals from stored profiles of their facial features or

to home in on those engaging in specified movements defined as suspicious. Information about health or drug-taking habits can also be obtained in unexpected ways. Workers at a British Toyota plant were surprised to find that their urine was being routinely and automatically analysed when they went to the washroom (Lyon 2001: 9).

Surveillance not only penetrates into people's private lives and bodies, it also extends globally. Airlines, for example, routinely collect and exchange data about their passengers' travelling habits and medical conditions. Police surveillance has been globalized, not only to trace individual criminals and pass data on them from one country to another but also to identify and track the international movement of targeted groups, such as minorities. The computerized Echelon system intercepts virtually all electronic communications across the world, to pick out and store messages that include names or other words listed in 'dictionaries' compiled by intelligence agencies. There is, however, an ongoing battle between surveillance agencies and commercially available cryptographic techniques designed to protect privacy (Lyon 2001).

It is the increasingly routine character of surveillance that makes the notion of a 'surveillance society' particularly appropriate (Ball and Webster 2003). There is, of course, a deliberate targeting of those considered to be a particular threat but huge amounts of data are routinely collected about ordinary people as they go about their daily activities. Using the telephone, surfing the Web, going through a supermarket checkout, just walking or driving along a road covered by CCTV, can all result in the accumulation of

Watch where you go in London!

© Lucy Dawkins

information somewhere about one's behaviour, movement, and lifestyle (see Media Watch 14). This routine information can inform marketing. It can become a commodity to be bought and sold. It can be trawled by state agencies searching for criminals, or terrorists, or simply opponents.

Lyon (2001) insists that an information society is inevitably a surveillance society. It is the development of information and communication technology that makes greater surveillance possible but, as he also emphasizes, it is wrong to adopt a position of technological determinism. These technologies are invented and applied because those with power seek to maintain and extend their control through surveillance. They are also driven forward by a capitalist society, where the relentless competition between business organizations gives them strong incentives to increase surveillance, in order to find ways of extracting more work from their employees and obtaining more information about the consumers who buy their products.

◀▶ *Stop and reflect*

In this section we explored the emergence of new techniques and structures of control that partially reversed the processes of bureaucratization and incarceration. We began by considering debureaucratization.

- Make sure that you understand the following terms: mechanistic and organic organization; network organization and virtual organization; McDonaldization and customer-oriented bureaucracy.

- There are important international differences in the character of organizations and in some East Asian societies less bureaucratic forms of organization have been effective.

- The increasing employment of women has arguably led to a debureaucratizing feminization of organization.

- Do you think that society *is* becoming less bureaucratic? Do you think that it *should* become less bureaucratic?

We went on to examine the changes that had occurred in management.

- Make sure that you understand the terms: scientific management; the Hawthorne effect; the human-relations approach; human resource management.

- Is HRM anything more than the latest version of the human-relations approach?

- The privatization of the British utilities resulted in important, and partially debureaucratizing, changes in organizational character and managerial careers.

- Globalization has exerted debureaucratizing pressures on company organization but distinctive national organizational structures have persisted.

- Has the rise of Japanese transnational corporations resulted in the Japanization of management in other societies?

Lastly, we explored processes of decarceration, recarceration, and increasing surveillance.

- Make sure that you are familiar with Scull's theory of decarceration.

- Some degree of decarceration has taken place but there have also been processes of recarceration.

- As prison populations have risen, prisons have been privatized.

- Organizations have increased their surveillance of employees but surveillance techniques have changed and it has been argued that the 'panopticon' has been replaced by the 'polyopticon'.

- It has been claimed that an 'information society' is necessarily a 'surveillance society'. Why should this be the case?

- Do you think that you live in a 'carceral society'?

◀▶ *Chapter summary*

In the 'Understanding organizations' section, we focused mainly on the issues raised by bureaucracy and discipline.

We first outlined and discussed Weber's ideal type of bureaucracy:

- According to Weber, bureaucracies are hierarchical, disciplined, and impersonal organizations of salaried, career officials.

- Later studies of bureaucracy showed that obedience to the rules could be dysfunctional, while rule use and interpretation varied between groups and organizations.

- We argued that criticism of the rigidity and formality of bureaucracy should be balanced by an awareness of its efficiency and impartiality.

We then examined disciplinary techniques of control and the organizations that practise these techniques:

- Foucault argued that discipline involved control of the body, surveillance, and punishment.
- Disciplinary techniques were most fully developed in the prison, which became the model for other carceral organizations.
- Goffman's concept of the total institution was similar to Foucault's concept of carceral organization, though Goffman was primarily concerned with the impact of the total institution on the self.

In the next section we sketched out the main features of the administrative and managerial revolutions.

We began by outlining the processes leading to the emergence of disciplined organizations:

- Bureaucratization involved the development of hierarchical organizations staffed by salaried and disciplined officials, and regulated by impersonal rules.
- The rise of industrial capitalism resulted in the systematic punishment of offenders through imprisonment and the establishment of carceral organizations to isolate and control deviants in a cost-effective way.
- The early industrialists maintained discipline largely through the threat of dismissal, though they also used fines, corporal punishment, and punishment through the courts.

We went on to consider the growth of management and the changing relationships between managers and owners:

- Scientific management developed new techniques for the management of labour, based on individual incentives, the subdivision of work tasks, and the detailed control of the worker's movements.
- The growing power of managers, the spread of ownership, and the increasing ownership of companies by financial organizations separated management from ownership, though the owners of capital were still in ultimate control.
- Increasing public ownership resulted in greater state control, particularly in state socialist societies, but not greater workers' control.

In 'Towards new structures of control' we explored the emergence of new techniques and structures that partially reversed the processes of bureaucratization and incarceration.

We began by considering processes of debureaucratization:

- More flexible forms of organization have emerged, together with a growing awareness of less bureaucratic Asian models.
- The patriarchal character of traditional bureaucracies has been challenged by the feminizing of organizations.
- Debureaucratizing changes have, however, taken place within a broader context of continued bureaucratization.

We then examined related changes in the character and techniques of management:

- The human-relations school developed an integrative approach to the management of labour.
- HRM emphasized the importance of cultural and organizational change to generate greater worker loyalty and commitment to the company.
- The privatization of utilities led to internal debureaucratization but also a new bureaucratic control by regulatory authorities.
- Global corporations have developed decentralized organizations within a framework of central control.
- Japanese transnational corporations have exported Japanese management techniques to their overseas operations only to a limited extent.

Finally we discussed decarceration and recarceration processes, and the growth of surveillance:

- Community-based treatments and punishments developed as an alternative to incarceration in mental hospitals and prisons.
- Decarceration was linked to a growing crisis in welfare capitalism, though this crisis also generated disorder and recarceration.
- Recarceration increased the state's financial burdens and governments responded by privatizing prisons.
- Technological advances have placed increasingly powerful surveillance techniques in the hands of those who run organizations.
- In a 'surveillance society' there is a network of surveillance that penetrates into people's private lives and even into their bodies, but also extends globally.

Key concepts

- bureaucracy
- carceral organization
- debureaucratization
- decarceration
- displacement of goals
- finance capital

- human-relations school
- human resource management (HRM)
- incarceration
- institutions
- managerial revolution

- negotiated order
- organization
- post-modern organization
- scientific management
- total institutions

Workshop 14

Study 14 CCTV surveillance at work

There is much awareness of the growing use of CCTV to watch the streets, but rather less of the growing surveillance of the workplace, though that is where 80 per cent of the money invested in CCTV is spent. McCahill and Norris (1999) carried out a study of twenty-four retail and manufacturing businesses in a northern town in England.

CCTV was partly used to protect businesses against external threats to their profitability. On the manufacturing sites, it was used to maintain perimeter security; in the stores, to deter shoplifting and card frauds. The visibility of cameras was an important means of deterrence and some were placed to record till transactions in order to deter card fraudsters. The cameras were used not only to observe theft in progress but also to identify potential shoplifters from a 'rogue's gallery' and alert security staff. CCTV recordings could be used to train staff to identify known shoplifters and spot suspicious activities.

There were also internal threats from the employees themselves. CCTV was used to monitor staff handling of cash, where camera visibility was again an important deterrent, but also to observe cleaning staff and loading bays. If particular employees were suspected, they were often targeted by a covert camera. Monitoring of cash handling was also carried out via EPOS (Electronic Point of Sale) systems, which enabled managers to obtain a printout for each till of expected and actual takings. At the manufacturing sites CCTV was used to prevent staff pilfering.

Managers found that CCTV could help them to monitor and improve staff performance. Store managers could observe customer service and procedures at fitting rooms, which were also crucial to the prevention of shoplifting. Staff were subject to a quite penetrating surveillance of their body language when dealing with customers. Staff movement and activity were also checked, to make sure they were actively engaged in serving customers and not just standing around or chatting among themselves. At manufacturing sites, CCTV enabled managers to check that workers complied with health and safety regulations, and handled goods and machinery correctly. Carelessness that caused damage could be recorded and the recordings used to discipline those involved. The amount of time spent on work breaks could be checked.

Surveillance could be subverted, however. One CCTV operator turned a 'blind eye' and did not report workers engaged in pilfering, because he identified with them rather than management and, indeed, took part in the pilfering himself. Operators subverted the system in other ways, by neglecting their screens or watching what people got up to 'for fun'. Some security managers responded by installing their own covert systems to make themselves independent of CCTV operators.

McCahill and Norris argue that in evaluating CCTV surveillance, account must be taken of its unintended consequences. Fiddling and pilfering are accepted practices, particularly in poorly paid work, and their suppression may lead to higher wage demands, industrial conflict, or loss of staff. Managements may, in fact, prefer workers to take part of their earnings in this way, since this reduces wage costs and losses may be covered by insurance.

Surveillance may also destroy trust, since it implies a managerial distrust of employees. Workers may take the attitude that, as they are not trusted, they may as well behave in an untrustworthy way, if they can get away with it. Surveillance can lead to a situation where workers only comply, and only work properly, when they know they are in view. To understand surveillance and its consequences, we must, then, place it in the context of the overall relationship between employers and employees, between managers and workers.

This study showed that surveillance for one purpose, say reducing theft, may become surveillance for another, monitoring worker performance. It showed that surveillance itself does not result in discipline and control, for these depend on human actions. Indeed, the commonly found notion that surveillance is purely a matter of installing the appropriate technology is quite wrong, for its effectiveness depends on operators, who have

their own interests and inclinations. Surveillance technology has potentially increased managerial control over workers but whether this does actually increase depends both on managerial actions and worker responses. Lastly, tighter surveillance may appear to be obviously in the managerial interest but its costs and the damage it does to relationships may outweigh its benefits.

❷ Look up the discussion of bureaucratic rules on pp. 539–40. What are the implications of greater surveillance for 'mock bureaucracy' and 'indulgency patterns'?

❷ Look up the discussion of Foucault's concept of a 'disciplinary society' on pp. 541–3. What does the above study tell us about the relationship between discipline and surveillance?

❷ Think of somewhere where you have done paid work. What managerial surveillance practices were you aware of? Think of electronic ones but also of other ways in which your work was observed and checked. Were you able to escape surveillance? Did an 'indulgency pattern' operate?

Media watch 14 Electronic surveillance

Managerial control of workers is becoming ever tighter as electronic surveillance techniques become widespread at work. Call-centre workers are particularly exposed to this kind of surveillance. Their calls and conversations are routinely monitored by supervisory staff. It is reported that 3,000 AA call-centre staff are going to have their online time electronically monitored to make sure that they do not exceed a total of 82 minutes of free time per day. This has to include lunch, tea breaks, and visits to the lavatory.

It is not just early release prisoners who are electronically tagged. Tagging is being introduced as a means of tracking the movements of employees. Electronically tagged jackets are being brought in for security workers, and warehouse workers are being required to wear tracking devices. Some companies are tracking delivery workers by satellite. Two London companies are reportedly thinking of introducing the satellite tracking of sandwich board holders! It is always claimed that these devices are designed to enable workers to be directed more efficiently to the places where they are needed but they also mean that workers are under constant surveillance.

Information about consumers is being collected not only through card use but by trawling for information from electoral rolls, the Land Registry, where all property transactions are registered, the Office for National Statistics, and surveys of various kinds. Tesco is reportedly constructing a profile not only of its own customers but of every consumer in the country, with informa-

tion not only on what they buy, and where and when they buy it, but on their lifestyle, their travel habits, and even such matters as how charitable they are and how eco-friendly. This commercially valuable information is sold by Dunnhumby, the Tesco subsidiary that collects the data, to other retail organizations.

There are plans to collect information about people's movements from road-side cameras installed every 400 metres along motorways. Automatic number-plate recognition will enable the identification of owners/drivers and automatic cross-checking with other databases listing people that state agencies have an interest in. Thus, those without insurance, fine defaulters, criminals, terrorists, and members of radical movements, to list some obvious examples, could be traced and intercepted. A system of this kind already operates through cameras installed around the Meadowhall shopping centre in Sheffield.

Surveillance of computer use is widespread. 'Cookies' are routinely inserted by a website on a user's browser to save information about the user and the user's browsing activities and transmit it back to the website. Cookies can be an innocent means of speeding up access to a given website and tailoring it to the user's interests but they can also be used to monitor web-browsing habits and target advertising on a user. Furthermore, employers or other interested parties can track a user's web-browsing by examining the cookies they have acquired. Spyware is more sinister software that is covertly inserted on your computer to collect personal information, possibly login information and passwords, which can be put to commercial and criminal use. AOL research has found that 80 per cent of home computers are infected with spyware and Earthlink has found on average three pieces of spyware per machine tested.

Sources: Hencke, D. (2005), 'AA to Log Call Centre Staff's Trips to Loo in Pay Deal', *Guardian*, 31 October; Mitchell, S. (2005), 'Keeping Spies Off Your Computer', *Sunday Times*, 10 April; Pandya, N. (2005), 'Ocado gets Big Brother Tag', *Guardian*, 11 June; Smith, E., and Gadher, D. (2005), 'Spy Cameras to Spot Drivers' Every Move', *Sunday Times*, 13 November; Tomlinson, H., and Evans, R. (2005), 'Tesco Stocks Up on Inside Knowledge of Shoppers' Lives', *Guardian*, 20 September.

❷ Should greater surveillance be seen as resulting from the development of information technology?

❷ How useful is the notion of an 'electronic panopticon' for analysing surveillance in contemporary societies? For a brief description of the panopticon, see p. 546. The relevance of this notion has been discussed in Chapter 4 of David Lyon's *The Electronic Eye* (1994), which is available at **http://home.fnal.gov/~annis/ digirati/otherVoices/Lyon.html**

 # Discussion points

For and against bureaucracy

Before discussing this, read the sections on 'Bureaucracy' and 'Debureaucratization'.

- Why did Weber think that bureaucracies were highly rational organizations?
- What did he think were the negative consequences of bureaucracy?
- What dysfunctions of bureaucratic organization were demonstrated by later studies of bureaucracies?
- Why have bureaucracies been considered patriarchal organizations?
- Should organizations be feminized?
- What alternatives are there to the bureaucratic organization of work?
- Can these be developed in any work situation?
- Is debureaucratization possible?
- Is debureaucratization desirable?

Decarceration

Before discussing this, read the sections on 'Discipline, carceral organizations, and total institutions' and 'Decarceration and recarceration'.

- What did Foucault mean by 'carceral organization'?
- What did Goffman mean by the 'contamination of the self' in total institutions?
- Why was incarceration such a feature of nineteenth-century British society?
- Why did a process of decarceration get underway during the second half of the twentieth century?
- Is it better to care for the mentally ill in the community?
- Are there any disadvantages with community care?
- Is it better to punish offenders with community sentences?
- Should electronic tagging be used more often?
- Does greater surveillance mean that we live in a 'carceral society'?
- Is intensified surveillance of any benefit to ordinary people?

Explore further

Further reading on bureaucracy, organization, and management can be found in the following:

Clegg, S. R. (1990), *Modern Organizations: Organization Studies in the Postmodern World* (London: Sage). *Travels from the Weberian model to East Asian and post-modern organizations.*

Clegg, S. R., and Hardy, C. (1999), *Studying Organization: Theory and Method* (London: Sage). *A wide-ranging reader that seeks to convey the diversity of the field of organization studies.*

Grey, C., and Wilmott, H. (2005), *Critical Management Studies: A Reader* (Oxford: Oxford University Press). *A wide range of readings critical of management orthodoxy, and includes both classic and contemporary critiques.*

Ritzer, G. (1996), *The McDonaldization of Society: An Investigation into the Changing Character of Social Life* (rev. edn., Thousand Oaks, CA: Pine Forge Press). *A wide-ranging and highly readable application of the Weberian approach to contemporary life, which argues that it is becoming ever more rationalized and bureaucratic.*

Scase, R. (2002), *Living in the Corporate Zoo* (Oxford: Capstone). *A lively and perceptive analysis of current corporate practices that discusses their implications for organization, management, careers, education, and life in general.*

Storey, J. (1995) (ed.), *Human Resource Management* (London: Routledge). *A collection of readings on HRM, which includes supporters and critics.*

Further reading on punishment, imprisonment, incarceration, and decarceration can be found in the following:

Cavadino, M., and Dignan, J. (2002), *The Penal System: An Introduction* (3rd edn., London: Sage). *A systematic analysis of punishment and imprisonment, which deals with privatization and discusses Scull's approach.*

Goffman, E. (1961b), *Asylums: Essays on the Social Situation of Mental Patients and Other Inmates* (New York: Doubleday). *A classic set of essays on life in a mental hospital.*

Scull, A. (1984), *Decarceration: Community Treatment and the Deviant—A Radical View* (2nd edn., Cambridge: Polity Press). *Forcefully advances a theory of decarceration and includes an appendix which updates the original study and responds to critics.*

For further reading on particular topics, see the following:

Ball, K., and Webster, F. (2003) (eds.), *The Intensification of Surveillance: Crime, Terrorism and Warfare in the Information Age* (London: Pluto Press). *An up-to-date and wide-ranging collection.*

Elger, T., and Smith, C. (1994) (eds.), *Global Japanization: The Transnational Transformation of the Labour Process* (London: Routledge). *Examines the degree of Japanization in many different countries.*

Lyon, D. (2001), *Surveillance Society: Monitoring Everyday Life* (Buckingham: Open University Press). *A powerful statement of the proposition that we live in a surveillance society.*

Scott, J. (1997), *Corporate Business and Capitalist Classes* (Oxford: Oxford University Press). *An examination of the growth, power, and influence of big business.*

Online resources

Visit the Online Resource Centre that accompanies this book to access more learning resources and other interesting material on organization, management, and control at:

www.oxfordtextbooks.co.uk/orc/fulcher3e/

The HRM Guide Network provides a series of linked websites with articles, features, and links on Human Resource Management:

www.hrmguide.co.uk/

In its own words: 'Critical Resistance works to build an international movement to end the Prison Industrial Complex by challenging the belief that caging and controlling people makes us safe':

www.criticalresistance.org/index.php

the state, social policy, and welfare

Contents

15

Choosing health care

'For the first time patients in the NHS will have a choice over when they are treated and where they are treated. The reforms we are making will mark an irreversible shift from the 1940s "take it or leave it" top down service. Hospitals will no longer choose patients. Patients will choose hospitals.

By 2005 all patients and their GPs will be able to book appointments at both a time and a place that is convenient to the patient. This might include NHS hospitals locally or elsewhere, diagnostic and treatment centres, private hospitals or even hospitals overseas. They will be able to compare different waiting times in different hospitals. By then the latest IT systems will allow GPs and patients to see which hospitals have capacity available to treat more patients quickly and book on line.'

Source: Department of Health (2002), *Delivering the NHS Plan* (London: HMSO).

In this document the government has committed itself to an 'irreversible shift' in the way that health care is provided. This is but one example of the fundamental changes that have recently taken place in state policy and one aim of this chapter is to examine and discuss these changes. A key question here is whether the founding principles of the welfare state have now been left behind. Is welfare becoming a matter of consumer choice rather than public need? Are the Labour governments that have ruled Britain since 1997 abandoning the welfare state that the Labour Party did so much to create and defend after the Second World War?

Before considering recent changes, we shall first outline the earlier development of the state. We take for granted a framework of services provided by the state but if we go back to the early nineteenth century, none of these services existed. There were no state schools, there was no state medical care, and there were no state pensions. If you fell on hard times, there was precious little help from the state. Why did the state become so involved in our welfare. How was the welfare state created in the first place and what were its key principles?

We have already made many references to 'the state'. This may seem a remote and vague abstraction but the state's influence is actually present in everything that we do. The state regulates the contents and packaging of the food we eat, the television programmes we watch, the construction of the house we live in, the content of lessons in school, the way that we drive down the road, and the environment in which we work, study, or play. Indeed, the state is involved in so many activities that it is difficult to pin down what we mean by it and that is the first problem we shall address in this chapter.

Understanding the state and state welfare

What do we mean by 'the state'? In this section we begin by discussing this vexed question and different perspectives on its development, before moving on to the issues raised by state welfare.

What is the state?

People commonly think of the government as being 'in charge of the country'. The government is, however, but a small part of what we call 'the state' and is wholly dependent upon it. The government would be powerless without civil servants, tax collectors, diplomats, and the police, to name only the more obvious employees of the state. When sociologists refer to 'the state', they mean both the government and the complex of organizations that enable governments to govern.

It is fairly easy to say what the government is. Even if we cannot remember all their names, we know that in Britain a group of about twenty Cabinet ministers is collectively responsible for taking key decisions on our behalf. It is much more difficult to define what we mean by the state because it is such a complex and extensive structure.

The best way to approach this question is to identify the key functions that states perform. The **state** can then be said to consist of the institutions and organizations involved in performing these functions. Most sociologists would agree that the state is engaged in all the following activities:

- the maintenance of order;
- policy-making and implementation;
- taxation;
- political representation;
- the management of external relationships.

The *maintenance of order* involves most obviously a legal system and a police force, with the military to back it up when necessary, but it is not only the police and the military who maintain order. This also depends on a horde of inspectors, regulators, and other officials, such as air-traffic controllers, traffic wardens, auditors, health-and-safety officials, and school inspectors.

Policy-making and implementation extend into all areas of society. Most of the work of government departments is concerned with policy but this is also a key function of local government, for local authorities are charged with carrying out many important policies, such as those concerned with housing, education, and planning.

Taxation provides the resources that enable the state to exist. Without some form of taxation the 'unproductive' officials of the state cannot be supported. Taxation also, however, performs other functions, because it is one of the main ways through which governments implement their policies. Thus, it is partly through its taxation policies that a government controls the economy, and regulates the distribution of income and wealth.

Political representation occurs through parliamentary bodies and political parties, which we examine in Chapter 20, pp. 825–32, though the amount of power these bodies have varies greatly. Governments may largely ignore the views of elected representatives and treat parliaments as a rubber stamp for government decisions. All contemporary state structures have such bodies, however, if only because they enable governments to legitimate their actions by presenting them as 'the will of the people'.

The management of external relationships has always been a key function of the state. It was initially mainly concerned with territorial boundaries, which were the subject of diplomacy and war, but it has increasingly become concerned with economic and environmental issues, which are regulated by international institutions, such as those of the European Union and the United Nations, which we discuss in Chapter 16 pp. 659–61. This regulation has extended into what were previously internal matters. Indeed, internal matters and external relationships can hardly now be separated in many areas of policy.

While sociologists broadly agree that the state does these things, they hold differing views on the question of who the state does these things for. Thus a *functionalist* approach to the maintenance of order would treat this as an activity performed by the state to meet one of the basic needs of society. A *Weberian* approach would see the maintenance of order in terms of the control of society by its rulers. A *Marxist* approach would argue that the maintenance of order is a means by which one class uses the state apparatus to dominate and exploit another. In societies split by ethnic or religious divisions, the maintenance of order can similarly be seen as one way in which other dominant groups control subordinate ones.

The development of the state

Different approaches to the state provide different accounts of its development. In this section we examine three different accounts of the development of the state. We first draw on the work of Max Weber to consider the authority of the state. We go on to discuss the notion of democracy and democratization. We then draw on the Marxist approach to set the development of the state in the context of class relationships.

Authority and control

In his discussion of the development of the state, Weber was primarily interested in the process through which rulers acquired control of their territories. Control of physical force was crucial to this, though Weber emphasized that the state did not rule through force alone but also by establishing its authority. In 'Politics as a Vocation', he declared that the state's defining feature was that it 'successfully claims the monopoly of the legitimate use of physical force within a territory' (Weber 1919: 78). There are three key notions here that are central to the understanding of the state's development:

- monopoly of the use of force;
- legitimacy;
- territory.

States seek to gain a *monopoly of the use of force* because otherwise they cannot command the allegiance and obedience of their citizens. The efforts made by rulers to establish such a monopoly led to the early development of the state in Europe. In the feudal societies of medieval Europe the use of military force was decentralized in the hands of local lords. Rulers had no direct control over their subjects and rather little control over the local lords themselves. These were obliged by their feudal oaths to provide military service to the ruler, but rulers frequently had great difficulty in getting them to do this and often faced military revolts by them. The beginnings of the development of the modern state can be seen in the ruler's subordination of the feudal lords. The destruction of their castles and the creation of military forces paid to serve the ruler were crucial steps in this process.

A monopoly of the use of force was not, however, sufficient on its own, for control of the population depended on the *authority* of the ruler, which itself required **legitimacy**. People obey rulers not simply because they are forced to do so but because they recognize the authority of those they obey. They accept this authority when they consider it legitimate. This notion of legitimacy becomes clearer when one considers the three types of authority identified by Weber:

- traditional authority, when particular individuals or groups have held a customary authority since ancient times;
- charismatic authority, which is held by particular individuals through personal qualities of leadership that, in the eyes of their followers, legitimate their decisions;
- rational–legal authority, which is held by politicians and officials whose actions are legitimate because they occupy certain positions in the state and exercise powers laid down by law.

Weber had created what he called 'ideal types' (on these see Chapter 2, p. 40), in order to explore the logic of these different types of authority. The types certainly correspond to distinct and identifiable patterns of political leadership, but it should be emphasized that they are often found in combination. For example, political leaders whose authority is rational–legal, because it is based on their position as prime minister or president, may well also develop a charismatic relationship with their followers.

Weber argued that there was a tendency for traditional and charismatic authority to give way to rational–legal authority as societies developed, though charismatic leaders could still emerge at any time. This movement towards rational–legal authority took place through bureaucratization, which provided rulers with a corps of professional administrators, who had specified official duties and were under the ruler's direct control. Whether these administrators have remained under the ruler's control is another matter, for they have often taken over, or tried to take over, the running of the state. In democratic states, there is always a tension between the top civil servants and the elected political leaders, a tension that Weber explored at length in his work.

> **⟳ Connections**
>
> We have examined important aspects of the development of states in other chapters. The bureaucratization of the state is covered in Chapter 14, p. 545, the development of the nation state in Chapter 16, pp. 619–20. Authority is discussed in Chapter 19, p. 777.

The state's authority is exercised within a *territory*. The emergence of a consolidated national territory under a unified national administration was a central feature of the construction of nation states. This territorial aspect of the state leads us to the issue of how the state has managed its external relationships, which have greatly influenced its internal development.

The development of the state apparatus has indeed been largely driven by international conflict. It was war, above all, that led to the centralization of the state in order to mobilize and control the population. The demands of war lay behind the development of taxation, which was the main function of the administrative apparatus of the early state. Through an analysis of state finances Michael Mann showed that state spending has been overwhelmingly on military matters. He calculated that in Britain from the twelfth to the nineteenth century between 70 and 90 per cent of state expenditure was on the military (Mann 1986: 485).

Democratization

As states developed, a process of democratization also took place. Indeed, most rulers nowadays seek to legitimate their authority by claiming that they have been democratically elected. Before discussing this process, we need to consider what democracy means and the issues that it raises.

Democracy means rule by the people. It comes from the ancient Greek words *demos*, the people, and *cratia*, rule. It contrasts with *aristocracy*, rule by an elite defined by birth, and *monocracy* (more commonly called monarchy), rule by a single individual.

But how is 'the people' defined? In the so-called democracies of ancient Greece women and slaves had no political rights, for they were not considered citizens. The definition of citizenship is crucial to democracy. Simply living in a country does not make one a citizen, for citizenship is conferred only on those considered full members of a society (see Chapter 18, p. 722, for a discussion of citizenship). A large part of the population may in this way be excluded from political participation.

There is then the issue of how 'the people' can rule. A distinction is made here between *direct* and *representative* democracy. *Direct* democracy means that citizens collectively take political decisions. While this may be possible in very small societies, in social units of any size it is clearly impossible. One possible substitute is the referendum, in which all citizens vote on a particular issue, but this can only be used to decide a limited range of matters where there is a fairly clear and simple choice. Generally, democracy has taken a *representative* form, where government is carried out by representatives of the people, who are chosen through elections.

For elections to be meaningful, there must be a free choice for the electorate. If only one party is allowed to put up candidates or there are restrictions on political activity, there is only the semblance of democracy. Single-party states are not usually considered to be democracies, though they may well claim that the existence of elections and parliamentary bodies makes them democratic. Representative democracy requires a multi-party system, free competition between parties, and free political activity. This kind of political system is often labelled 'liberal democracy', because it is based on liberal ideas of the freedom (liberty) of the individual.

There must also be voter participation in elections. Concerns with turnout are not, however, simply a matter of democratic principle, for the main political parties tend to lose out when turnout falls and fear that single-issue or politically 'extreme' parties, with highly committed supporters, will benefit from this. Recent declines in the turnout at British elections have led to a discussion of ways

to increase it by greater use of the postal vote or e-mail voting. Some have proposed making the vote compulsory, as in Australia, with fines for non-voters.

By **democratization** is usually meant two main processes, the emergence of representative assemblies with political power and the extension of the right to vote to all adults. Parliamentary assemblies existed in medieval times, but it was only after a series of revolutions, in seventeenth-century Britain and eighteenth-century America and France, that such bodies began to acquire real power. The extension of the vote took much longer. In most countries only men with a certain amount of wealth or income were initially allowed to vote, while colonial peoples were largely excluded from the political process until after the Second World War.

As we argued above, the existence of parliaments and elections is not enough to make a society democratic, for democracy also requires party competition and free political activity. These were not found in the totalitarian regimes of Germany, Italy, and Spain, or the state socialist countries of the Soviet bloc, which we discuss in Chapter 20, pp. 834–6. With the defeat of fascism in the 1940s and the collapse of state socialism at the end of the 1980s, the 'liberal democracies' were apparently victorious, and this led Francis Fukuyama (1989) to proclaim 'the end of history' in a much-publicized essay. What he meant by this

Frontiers Internet democracy

Can the Internet solve the problems faced by democracy? It has been claimed that the Internet provides a 'technology of democracy' by making information freely available, facilitating communication, and enabling organization by opposition or campaign groups. It has also been argued that it can counteract declining popular participation and involvement in the political process, as shown by low turnout figures at elections.

The Internet does provide a way of accessing information, and one that is independent of selection and manipulation by newspapers and television channels, which in many societies are state controlled. Much of this information does, however, consist of official or commercial material that is not exposed to the critical examination which the established media do at least sometimes provide. Minority and dissenting views are more readily available on the Internet but they still have to be found and search engines are increasingly steered by commercial interests (see Chapter 10, pp. 393–4). The greater availability of information can, none the less, reasonably be seen as enhancing the democratic process.

The Internet particularly provides a vehicle for campaigning groups. It is a useful additional tool for established organizations, such as the environmental movement, and has become an absolutely crucial means of contact and document delivery for loosely organized campaigning organizations, such as the anti-capitalist, anti-globalization movement and also for local campaigns, such as anti-road protests. It also plays a key part in the organization and functioning of dispersed groups, such as exiled opposition or diasporic movements. It must be added, however, that the Internet does also facilitate the organization of 'hate' groups that are far from democratic in spirit.

Access remains a key problem. It is unlikely that the Internet will do much to increase popular participation, as 'the Internet remains in the hands of the relatively privileged minority who are already more inclined to participate' (Lax 2000: 168).

⊃ Note that we discuss the significance of the Internet in Chinese politics in Chapter 10, p. 395.

❓ Has access to the Internet increased your knowledge of political matters or increased your political activity?

rather misleading phrase was that the historical struggle between different political systems had come to an end. Liberal democracy had won.

However, this notion of the victory of 'liberal democracy' hardly conveys the reality of contemporary world politics. The collapse of the Soviet Union was not the same as the triumph of democracy, which still had to be fought for in the successor states, as the 'orange revolution' in the Ukraine showed. Many countries are ruled by nominally democratic but repressive regimes with little regard for the liberties essential to a functioning democracy. China, with a fifth of the world's population, remains a one-party state.

Class and state

A very different perspective on democracy has emerged from the Marxist analysis of the relationship between capitalism and the state. This places the state in the context of class relationships and treats it as an instrument of class domination. The institutions of representative democracy are seen here as a means through which the capitalist bourgeoisie could pursue its interests. According to this approach, the modern state was essentially a capitalist state.

We shall see later in our discussion of 'liberal capitalism' how the early steps of democratization in Britain produced a parliament that acted in the interests of capital.

The domination of the state by capital was challenged by the growth of labour movements. Marx believed that class conflict would lead to the emergence of a revolutionary labour movement (see Chapter 20, pp. 819–21) but most European labour movements pursued an alternative, non-revolutionary strategy of gaining control of the state by parliamentary means. Before they could do this, they had to force through a democratization that would enable workers to use their weight of numbers to vote in pro-labour governments. The power of the state could then be used to reform society and create a fairer and more equal distribution of resources. Indeed, some argued that in this way a non-revolutionary transition could be made from a capitalist to a socialist society (see box on 'From capitalism to socialism in Sweden').

Labour governments were certainly elected, notably in Britain and Scandinavia, but did this mean that the state became an instrument of the working class? A transition to socialism was never really on the agenda. Labour

History has not ended—the 'orange revolution' in Ukraine 2005.
© Getty Images/Sergei Supinsky

Global focus   From capitalism to socialism in Sweden?

The Swedish labour movement has been the most powerful in the world and the Social Democratic Party has dominated Swedish politics since the early 1930s. Radical Social Democrat thinkers believed that a non-revolutionary transition could be made from capitalism to socialism by using the numerical strength of the labour movement. Once political democracy had been achieved, the labour movement could secure control of the state and establish first social democracy, through the construction of a welfare state, and then economic democracy, by giving workers control over the organizations that employed them. This would finally enable the transition from capitalism to socialism to take place.

The Swedish labour movement produced in the 1970s an ingenious scheme to make this transition. The Meidner Plan, as it was called, proposed to end the power of capital by legislating a shift in the ownership of industry from private capital to union-controlled funds, which would be created by taxing excess profits. The higher the profits made by a company, the faster it would be taken over by the workers! After intense debate a law was passed in 1983 to set up such funds, but by this time the plan had been thoroughly deradicalized and turned into a means of increasing investment in industry and supporting pension funds. The Social Democratic state remained a capitalist state.

Source: Fulcher (1991*a*).

governments accepted that the economy had to be run on capitalist lines. They did introduce welfare reforms, but, as we shall see in 'Welfare capitalism', it was the middle class that benefited most from these.

Why did Labour governments not introduce more radical reforms? In a study of Labour government in Britain, Ralph Miliband (1969) argued that the economic power of capital inevitably limited any government's freedom of political action. The resources of private capital, which were so much greater than those of labour movements, enabled it to bring pressure to bear on governments, parliaments, and the civil service. Miliband also emphasized the ideological **hegemony** of the ruling class (see Chapter 20, pp. 821–2, for a discussion of this concept). Radical alternatives were developed only weakly, because the mass media and education were dominated by conservative views.

Labour governments are now arguably more than ever constrained by the economic power of capital. As we show in Chapter 16 p. 647, increasing global economic integration means that capital can be shifted more easily than ever from one country to another. If governments pursue policies that threaten the interests of capital, it is liable to move elsewhere, with serious consequences for the national economy, and this enables large companies to blackmail governments into pursuing the policies that favour them. We discuss this issue in the 'Globalization and international convergence?' box on p. 606.

If we are to understand the development of the state, we must certainly place this in the context of class relationships and the relationship between the state and the economy but there is a danger of then treating the state

as no more than the instrument of a class. There is also the problem of economic determinism, of explaining the development of the state solely in terms of changes in the economy.

These problems have been recognized by Marxists themselves, and Nicos Poulantzas criticized Miliband for his 'instrumentalist' view of the state. Poulantzas (1975) argued that the state could act in the interest of capital *as a whole* only if it had a degree of independence from it, what he called a **relative autonomy**. This enabled the state to arbitrate between the conflicting interests of different sections of capital and take a long-term rather than a short-term view of the interests of capital as a whole. There was still, however, an underlying economic determinism in his approach, as he still saw the state's actions in terms of the interests of capital.

Theda Skocpol (1985) held that the state had much more autonomy than this. She returned to the Weberian tradition to emphasize the territorial character of the state, which involved it in interstate relationships. States face outwards as well as inwards, and their international involvements have given rulers some independence from the economic power of capital. Thus, as we shall show in 'The state takes responsibility', the imperatives of the First World War allowed the British state to take control of the economy and, at least to some extent, override the interests of private capital.

Governments do have some freedom of action, though the term 'autonomy' is rather misleading, since it suggests that the state can somehow be an independent force. It is better to see governments as having a limited freedom of action that has to be exercised within the various constraints acting upon the state. They are constrained by both internal interests and interstate relationships. They are also constrained by the consequences of democratization, for, in the liberal democracies at least, rulers can rule only if they succeed in persuading the electorate to give them the power and authority to do so.

State welfare

States have since earliest times been involved in the maintenance of order, the raising of taxes, and conflicts over territory. It is only since the nineteenth century that they have become drawn into the provision of welfare. Since then the questions of how much welfare they should provide and what means they should use in providing it have become ever more important issues.

While most countries have developed some form of *state welfare*, not all of these have developed a *welfare state*. Although the term **welfare state** is used by some to refer broadly to all states that provide welfare, others use it to refer only to states that have at least attempted to provide welfare on a 'universal' basis for the whole population. We use it in the latter sense.

In this section we first consider rival explanations of the extension of the state's activities into welfare provision. We will then examine the central issue of social policy—the relationship between the state and the market.

Theories of state welfare

The functionalist approach to the development of state welfare, as taken by Wilensky (1975), explains it in terms of the 'new needs' generated by industrialization, which destroyed self-sufficiency. People moved from the land to the city, where they became dependent on employment in paid work. Industrial economies were prone to sudden slumps, when people were thrown out of work and lost the capacity to support themselves. Furthermore, traditional means of community support were largely absent in the new industrial cities. Urbanization also created new concentrations of population, where there were severe problems of health and housing. The state stepped in to deal with the problems created by industrialization.

There can be little doubt that the development of state welfare was in some sense a response to the problems generated by industrialization but the difficulty with this approach is that it assumes that the 'new needs' would be met. It does not deal with the contested political process through which the welfare state was established. Nor can it explain international differences in social policy.

These issues have been addressed by those who link the development of the welfare state to class conflict. According to this approach, the welfare state developed because of the growth of a labour movement. The starting point here is not so much the needs of an industrial society as the class conflict generated by capitalism. Thus, Esping-Andersen and Korpi (1984) have argued that state welfare was most developed in countries such as Sweden, where the working class was well organized and gained political power through a strong labour movement.

According to Esping-Andersen (1990), decommodification is central to the development of the welfare state by labour movements. In order to understand this term, we must first consider **commodification**, which refers to the process through which capitalism turned all aspects of life, including health care and education, into 'things' (or commodities) that were bought and sold. Access to them then depended on people's capacity to buy them, which was in turn related to their 'market situation', that is, their earning power or wealth. **Decommodification** was the opposite process, through which people became independent of the market by means of the state provision of welfare as a matter of right.

Decommodification led to what Habermas (1981a) has called **juridification**. By this he meant that welfare was provided through legal (or juridical) and administrative procedures. Rights to welfare were specified by laws, which were administered by state agencies. Although welfare had become a matter of legal entitlement, the application of laws to particular cases always, however, required interpretation by administrators. This frequently led to disputes between agencies and clients, and reference to the courts for the resolution of conflicts. State provision generated its own problems.

According to Esping-Andersen, decommodification was crucial to the collective solidarity and therefore the strength of labour movements. If welfare was provided by the state on a universal basis, this would prevent divisive conflicts between the higher paid, who had to pay for state welfare through taxes, and the lower paid, who received it. Greater worker unity would then strengthen the collective power of workers. This was one reason why labour movements have tried to use their political power to create welfare states.

This general emphasis on the role of labour movements in the development of state welfare has in turn been criticized on the grounds that it was often initially created not by Labour or Social Democratic governments but by Liberal or even Conservative ones, which was the case in Britain (Pierson 1998). It can, none the less, be argued that the pressure of a labour movement generally lay in the background, leading other parties to introduce state welfare to prevent the growth of a revolutionary movement or stop a labour party gaining power.

The development of state welfare must also be set in the context of bureaucratization and interstate relationships. State welfare was in part a product of the administrative

revolution, which we examine in Chapter 14, pp. 545–7. International considerations also played a part, for the military and economic effectiveness of the nation state depended on its having educated and healthy soldiers and workers. The provision of state welfare on a national basis was also a means of unifying society at a time of war. As we shall see on pp. 592–3, war and the development of state welfare have at times been closely associated with each other.

Market versus state

A central issue in the contemporary discussion of welfare is the relationship between the market and state provision of welfare. Two main types of social policy have emerged:

- the market model;
- the welfare-state model.

The *market model* is based on the principle of selective state benefits for the poor. Benefits are means-tested—that is, they are given only to those whose means (income and wealth) fall below a certain level. Everyone else is expected to buy welfare from the market by, for example, subscribing to private health insurance. Apart from the state provision of a safety net for the poor, welfare is the responsibility of the individual not the state. This approach is often called 'liberal', because its supporters believe in the freedom (liberty) and responsibility of the individual.

The *welfare-state* model is based on the idea that state welfare should be not selective but universal, in two senses. It should provide benefits for all, irrespective of income. It should also provide a comprehensive range of benefits, including pensions, health care, education, and employment. By providing equal and comprehensive access to welfare, the welfare state seeks to reduce the inequality generated by market forces. It also does this by funding state welfare through 'progressive' taxation, which requires those with higher incomes to pay more tax (as opposed to 'regressive' taxation, such as sales taxes, which bear most heavily on the poor). One of its central principles is that employment should not be left to market forces. The state should manage the economy in order to maintain full employment.

> **➲ Connections**
>
> These two concepts of welfare are linked to corresponding notions of democracy and citizenship. The market model is linked to *liberal* ideologies that emphasize the importance of political democracy and see citizenship in terms of civil and political rights. The *welfare-state* model is based on a social-democratic concept of citizenship that sees it as also involving social rights to employment, education, health, and welfare. See our discussion of citizenship in Chapter 18, pp. 722–4.

The relationship between these welfare principles has been the main issue in the development of state welfare. Those who support a 'market model' argue that limited state resources should be targeted on those with most need. Dependence on the state should be discouraged and people should take responsibility for their own welfare. In a society dependent on a market economy, state intervention and taxation should be kept to a minimum. This approach is usually linked to a belief in the virtues of capitalism and the importance of maintaining the free market central to the workings of a capitalist economy.

Those who advocate the welfare state argue that benefits should be universal because this commits the whole society to the welfare state and prevents a backlash against high taxation from those who rely on private schemes. Universal welfare also establishes high standards of state welfare, as it has to meet the needs of the middle as well as the working class. Universal benefits avoid the problem of the 'poverty trap', which occurs in means-tested systems when claimants' incomes increase and they lose benefits, leaving them no better off and with no incentive to seek work and support themselves. In its hostility to the market principle, this approach has been particularly supported by socialists seeking to restrict the scope of the market, if not transform capitalist society.

Until the 1970s it seemed as though there was a general tendency for the social policies of industrial societies to move towards welfare-state principles. In the 1970s, however, the market model was revived by **neo-liberalism**, which simply means 'new liberalism'. Neo-liberals sought to restore the individual's freedom and choice, which they thought had been taken away by the growth of state welfare. They called for the targeting of state welfare on those who were most in need. The rest of the population should be encouraged to enter private insurance schemes. This would not only keep state expenditure down, it would also prevent people becoming dependent on the state, and enable market forces to work. We discuss neo-liberalism further in the section on 'Thatcherism'.

Neo-liberalism is often associated with the idea that the state should be 'rolled back', to allow market forces to operate and provide individuals with greater choice. Neo-liberal policies have indeed rolled back the *welfare* state, but this has not meant that the state as a whole has taken a back seat. Andrew Gamble (1994) has argued that neo-liberalism, like liberalism itself, actually required a strong state to protect the rights and freedom of the individual and create the conditions in which markets could flourish. As we shall see in 'A weaker or stronger state?', pp. 607–10, the neo-liberal policies of the Thatcher governments in 1980s Britain led to a strengthening of the authority of the state.

From welfare to workfare

The notion of workfare has been another departure from the classic welfare-state model. Indeed, Jessop (2002) has argued that there has been a shift from a welfare to a workfare state. The idea of 'workfare' first emerged in the United States, and influenced Conservative policy in Britain, but was then taken up enthusiastically by the 1997 Labour government in its 'welfare to work' programme.

Exponents of **workfare** argue that social policy should be designed to get those who have become dependent on state welfare back into work. This is not only arguably good for them, it is also good for state finances. It is claimed that unemployment can be better reduced by improving the work skills and general readiness for work of the unemployed than by the state creation of jobs (Finn 2003). Social policy becomes a means not of insulating people from the market by decommodifying welfare (see our discussion of decommodification on p. 586) but of increasing their market effectiveness.

Improving work skills through better education and training also improves the quality of the labour force and increases national competitiveness. The development of workfare is part of the process of constructing what Evans and Cerny (2003) have called the 'competition state'. 'The competition state is the successor to the welfare state, incorporating many of its features but reshaping them, sometimes quite drastically, to fit a globalizing world' (Evans and Cerny 2003: 24).

> **◆ Connections**
> Social policy links closely here to education policy, which has come to be seen as one of the main means by which governments can increase national competitiveness in a globalizing world. See Chapter 9, pp. 345–8.

Workfare is related to a movement away from the idea that people are simply entitled to welfare. This has been expressed in two ways:

- A process of, what Peter Dwyer (2004) has called, 'creeping conditionality' has weakened welfare rights by making the provision of welfare increasingly dependent on the fulfilment of certain conditions. State benefits for the unemployed, lone parents, and the disabled have, for example, become conditional on attendance at interviews designed to get them back into work. In this vein, 'unemployment benefit' has been replaced by the 'job-seeker's allowance'.

- There has been a growing emphasis on the responsibilities of the citizen. People should take responsibility for their own welfare instead of simply depending on the state to provide it (Lewis 2003). Thus, instead of relying on the state to provide them with pensions, people should save for the future, and the state should provide them with incentives to do this.

Another New Labour theme has been the ending of exclusion and the promotion of an 'inclusive society'. One of the main means of doing this is getting those out of work back into it. Ruth Levitas (2005) has examined New Labour's rhetoric on this issue and distinguished between three discourses of exclusion:

- a *redistributionist* discourse that sees exclusion as a consequence of poverty and inequality;
- a *moral underclass* discourse that treats the excluded as culturally distinct and responsible for their own exclusion (see Chapter 19, p. 807, for our discussion of the underclass concept);
- a *social integrationist* discourse that sees exclusion and inclusion in terms of participation in the labour market.

Levitas argues that New Labour has gradually shifted away from the redistributionist discourse towards the other two. Exclusion has been detached from inequality. Those at the bottom of society have themselves been made responsible for their position. Indeed, as Levitas points out, the very use of the term 'exclusion' diverts attention from inequality by drawing the main line of division in society between the included and the excluded rather than, say, the rich and the poor.

> **◆ Connections**
> Different concepts of welfare provision are linked to corresponding notions of citizenship. The market model is linked to *liberal* ideologies that emphasize the importance of political democracy and see citizenship in terms of civil and political rights. The *welfare-state* model is based on a social-democratic concept of citizenship that sees it as also involving social rights to employment, education, health, and welfare. This principle of citizenship has been undermined by the 'creeping conditionality' that makes welfare payments dependent on the meeting of certain conditions by claimants. See our discussion of citizenship in Chapter 18, pp. 722–4.

These conceptions of welfare have been brought together under the 'third way' label. In *Beyond Left and Right*, Anthony Giddens (1994) argued that both the market and the welfare-state approaches to the provision of welfare were out of date. He called for a 'third way' programme of 'positive welfare' that would address what he saw as the real welfare problems of the contemporary world. The notion of a 'third way' became one of the slogans of the 1997 Labour government and Giddens further developed his ideas on welfare in *The Third Way* (1998). We discuss the 'third way', and whether Labour policy may be described in these terms, later in this chapter.

Stop and reflect

In this section we began by considering what is meant by 'the state' and then examined different approaches to the explanation of its development.

- We argued that the uncertain boundary of the state made it best to define it in terms of its functions.
- Make sure that you are familiar with the main features of the Weberian and Marxist perspectives on the state.
- Weber claimed that there was a tendency for traditional and charismatic authority to give way to rational–legal authority.
- The Marxist perspective saw the development of the state as an instrument of class domination but others have argued that it must be set in the context of both class conflict and interstate relationships.
- We examined the process of democratization but treated with scepticism Fukuyama's notion that the triumph of liberal democracy had resulted in the end of history.
- Has a democracy now been established in Iraq?

We went on to examine different approaches to state welfare.

- Make sure that you understand the meaning of the following terms: commodification and decommodification; the market and welfare-state models; means-testing; progressive and regressive taxation; workfare.
- Esping-Andersen saw the development of the welfare state as a process of decommodification.
- The welfare-state model of the provision of welfare developed to replace the market provision of welfare but has been challenged by a revived market model.
- New Labour (and Anthony Giddens) have claimed that there is a 'third way' between these two models.
- Jessop has argued that the welfare state has been replaced by a workfare state.
- Do you think that the welfare state belongs to the past?

The development of the state in Britain

In this section we examine the development of the state in Britain from the early nineteenth century through to the 1970s, setting it in the context of the theoretical issues that we have just discussed.

Liberal capitalism

Our starting point is the period of liberal capitalism during the first half of the nineteenth century. Industrial capitalism was making its breakthrough at this time. There was minimal state interference with the activities of the early industrialists—hence the term liberal capitalism— and state regulation initially declined, though in the 1830s new forms of bureaucratic regulation began to appear.

Deregulation

The politically dominant ideas were those of the eighteenth-century economist and philosopher Adam Smith, who believed in a society of freely competing individuals. Smith argued that competition in a free market would be to the benefit of all. It would not only reduce prices but also increase wages, for employers seeking to expand production would compete for labour and wages would rise. The capitalist employer's search for profits would also make sure that industry only produced goods for which there was a demand. If this was insufficient, prices and profits would fall and industrialists would switch their investment into producing the things that people really did want to buy.

Although Smith believed that the state should allow market forces to operate freely, he did recognize that it had some important duties to perform. These involved not only defence and the administration of justice, but also other tasks important to the community that could not be carried out by profit-seeking entrepreneurs. This aspect of his ideas is often forgotten by his modern-day followers.

Briefing: free trade

The apparently obscure repeal of the Corn Laws in 1846 was one of the most important events of nineteenth-century history and typical of the era of liberal capitalism. The Corn Law of 1815 had been introduced to protect the interests of British farmers and landowners by keeping out cheap foreign corn. Its repeal in 1846 marked the victory of the industrial over the agricultural interest. Cheap food imports meant that industrialists could pay lower wages to their workers and it was argued that this would make British industry more competitive and enable it to expand production. British agriculture would be forced to become more efficient and diversify its products. There was more to it than this, however. If other countries were able to export food to Britain, they would be able to buy industrial goods from Britain. This repeal was a key step in the development of an international division of labour, which we discuss in Chapter 16, pp. 629–30.

During the first half of the nineteenth century, key aspects of economic activity were deregulated. In 1815 the regulation of wage rates and food prices was ended, though the freeing of international trade took longer. The key step in this was the ending of import duties on corn in 1846 (see box on 'Free trade'), which was followed by a general removal of import duties in the 1850s and 1860s.

The liberal state was clearly a capitalist state, since deregulation was in the interests of industrialists, who wanted to be free to develop their activities without state interference. They wanted wage rates to be set by the labour market not by the state. They also wanted free trade, in part to assist exports but also because imports of cheap food would allow them to pay lower wages. Whether liberal capitalism was in the interests of workers, as Adam Smith believed, was another matter. Skilled workers in high demand could certainly use their market power to push up their wages, but workers with weak bargaining power could be freely exploited. Agricultural labourers found that their bargaining position was greatly weakened by the import of food produced by cheap agricultural labour abroad.

Allowing market forces to operate freely did not, however, mean that the state was weak. Indeed, the very reverse was the case, for market forces could operate freely only within an orderly society. The maintenance of order required a strengthening of the state at a time when capitalist industrialism was generating disorder. Strikes, rioting, machine-breaking, and crimes against property were threatening both production and social order, while trade unions and radical political movements emerged to challenge the capitalist employer and the state. In response, there was a general tightening-up of law and order, which we outline in Chapter 14, pp. 546–8. The military were used to quell riots and demonstrations, and the law was used to suppress trade-union activity.

Limited state intervention

There was a growing awareness of social problems as Britain became an industrial society, population increased, and new industrial cities rapidly grew. Unemployment became a recognized problem, for industrial workers were entirely dependent on paid work, though the economists of the time saw unemployment as the inevitable result of the operation of market forces and believed that there was nothing that could be done about it. Indeed, they believed that the labour market central to a capitalist economy would work only if there was a steady supply of labour seeking employment.

An industrial society anyway needed workers to labour for long hours in the unpleasant work conditions of the early factories. The poor had to be forced to work and in 1834 the Poor Law Amendment Act introduced a new system of relief to do just that. Only those who entered a 'workhouse' would be given support. Conditions there would be made worse than those experienced by the poorest paid worker, so that only the absolutely desperate would enter. Families were broken up, men and women segregated. This law unsurprisingly generated enormous hostility among the poor. It illustrates well the attitude of the state to poverty during the period of liberal capitalism.

People who fell on hard times were otherwise dependent on the local community, charity, pawn shops, and self-help schemes. Insecure employment and irregular wages encouraged the emergence of the pawn shop, where a loan could be obtained on the security of some item of personal property. In 1830 in London alone there were an estimated 500–600 unlicensed pawnbrokers, in addition to some 342 licensed ones (Royle 1987: 186). Those with higher earnings could insure themselves against future disasters by making weekly payments to 'friendly societies', which would support them in ill health or unemployment or pay for their funeral.

In some areas of welfare the state did begin to intervene, for there was a growing concern with work conditions in the factories. Reformers were concerned not just with the length of work hours but also with issues of morality, health, education, and family relationships, which were all affected by unregulated labour in mines and factories. From 1833 a series of Factory Acts began to restrict the hours of work, though many employers resisted or circumvented them, and progress was very slow. The 1833 Act also required employers to provide two hours of

Women having their dinner at a workhouse in London, around 1900.

© Getty Images/General Photographic Agency

education per day for child workers. In 1844 another Act prohibited women and children working in the mines.

> **⊃ Connections**
>
> We refer in this section to aspects of welfare discussed in other chapters. In Chapter 17, pp. 697–8, we examine the problem of unemployment. In Chapter 18, pp. 729–31, we discuss the distinction between the 'deserving' and 'undeserving' poor.

The other main area of state intervention was in public health. The 1848 Public Health Act required the establishment of local boards of health and the appointment of medical officers in places with higher than average death rates. The state did not become involved in health care as such, though in the 1840s workhouses began to provide some very basic medical care for the poor, which was otherwise provided by charities and public dispensaries.

Although the state's actual involvement in welfare was limited by the liberal principles dominant at the time, a new bureaucratic approach to social problems was establishing itself. This involved state investigation, the collection of information, legislation, regulation, and inspection. Inspectors' reports then fed back into the process. For example, the reports of the Factory Act inspectors shaped the development of factory legislation. There were still many barriers to effective legislation and regulation, but a bureaucratic state-welfare machinery was coming into being.

Origins of state welfare

New attitudes towards poverty and new policies towards welfare gradually emerged during the later years of the nineteenth century. The work of Booth and Rowntree created more awareness of poverty and understanding of its causes (see Chapter 18, pp. 737–41). In Britain it was during the years before the First World War that the breakthrough to the state provision of welfare was made, though in Germany the development of state welfare had started much earlier.

The state takes responsibility

It was during the ten years or so before the First World War of 1914–18 that the British state began to take responsibility for the unemployed, the sick, the old, and the young. The initial focus was on improving the welfare of children through state-funded school meals, a school medical service, and the 1908 Children's Act, which made the parental neglect of children's health an offence and made the community responsible for the care of neglected children. In 1908 state pensions were brought in for the over seventies. In 1911 the National Insurance Act established unemployment benefit, sick pay, maternity and disability benefits, and free medical treatment from general practitioners.

The state welfare introduced by these measures was, however, limited in important ways. It was limited by the insurance principle, for both unemployment benefit and health benefits were introduced on this basis, which meant

Global focus   State welfare in Germany

State welfare developed much earlier in Germany than in Britain, even though industrialization occurred there much later. In Germany legislation providing social-insurance schemes for accidents, sickness and disability, and old age was passed in the 1880s, a good twenty years earlier than in Britain. This legislation was initiated by Bismarck in an attempt to detach the German working class from the Social Democratic Party, which it failed to do. The background to this early welfare legislation was the earlier extension of the vote, which was given to all adult males in 1871, and the earlier growth of a socialist political movement. This shows the significance of democratization and class organization in the development of state welfare.

that they depended on weekly national-insurance contributions paid by those in employment. As Derek Fraser has put it, 'the state was compelling its citizens to provide insurance for themselves rather than providing simple state medicine and sickness benefits' (1984: 166). Only those who had paid contributions were entitled to benefits and non-working wives, who had not contributed, were excluded from the benefits of the 1911 Act. The health care provided by this Act was limited to general-practice medicine and a national hospital system had to await the creation of the National Health Service in 1947.

Some have argued that this burst of legislation marked the beginning of the welfare state but the dominance of the insurance principle meant that it was a long way from the welfare-state idea that all citizens are entitled to welfare by right. None the less, its importance can hardly be exaggerated, for the state had taken a substantial responsibility for people's welfare in a quite new way.

Democratization and the labour movement

To understand these reforms we must take into account the changing character of class relations, going back to the mid-nineteenth century. At this time, the strategy of the British ruling class shifted from *repressing* discontent to *containing* it by incorporating the growing labour movement. By **incorporation** is meant the process of including working-class organizations in institutions of bargaining and political representation.

Incorporation involved democratization. The vote was gradually extended to all adult males by the Reform Acts of 1867, 1884, and 1918, which led to a growing competition for the working-class vote between the two main political parties of the time, the Conservative and Liberal parties. It also led gradually to the independent political organization of the working class, and in 1906 the unions finally created the Labour Party to represent them in parliament.

It was not, however, the Labour Party that was responsible for the welfare legislation of the years before the First World War. This was introduced by the Liberal government of 1906–14. Why would a Liberal government do this, given the non-interventionist principles of the liberal state?

The growth of the labour movement and the development of socialist ideas had put pressure on the political elite to head off the threat of more radical changes. The Liberal Party, which had close links with many of the trade unions and relied on the support of organized labour, felt particularly threatened by the emergence of the Labour Party. Thus, the growth of a labour movement did lie behind the Liberal welfare legislation. It was ultimately the class conflict and class organization generated by a capitalist industrial society that resulted in the development of state welfare.

The First World War

The development of state welfare must also be placed in the context of interstate conflict. The growing international rivalry that led towards the First World War made its own contribution to the development of state welfare. Many British politicians were keenly aware of the superior development of state welfare in Germany. The significance for national military strength of a healthy population and an integrated society was well recognized. Indeed, it was the revelation of the poor physical state of British soldiers by the Boer War of 1899–1902 that gave rise to the measures to improve children's health.

The First World War itself then gave an additional momentum to the development of the state. Often described as the first 'total war', it made huge demands on the populations and resources of all the participating countries. In Britain, the state intervened massively to organize production and control society. Some of its main interventions were:

- conscription to the armed forces in 1916;
- the creation of the Ministries of Food, Health (1919), Labour, Munitions, and Shipping;
- state control of wages and prices, food and raw materials, housing and rents;

- state control of industrial production and transport;
- state arbitration of industrial conflict;
- a sixfold increase in state expenditure.

The war had a lasting effect on the development of the state and its relationship with British society (see Runciman 1993). Higher state expenditure and taxation never fell back to their pre-war levels. The wartime experience of state control of the economy provided a model for its later extension and prepared the way for a more state-managed form of capitalism. The state's wartime involvement in industrial relations stimulated both unions and employers to strengthen their organization at a national level and establish relationships with the state. The 1918 extension of the vote to women over the age of 30 followed the heavy involvement of women in the war effort.

Welfare capitalism

It was during the Second World War and the years immediately after it that the *welfare state* was established. In this section we examine the creation of the welfare state and set it in the context of corporatism, for welfare depended upon the state management of the economy by corporatist means. We also consider the implications of the welfare state for social inequalities by discussing its patriarchal character and its redistributive consequences.

The Second World War and the post-war settlement

The Second World War had a far greater impact on the development of state welfare than the First World War had done. It was during the Second World War that Keynesian economic policies to manage the economy gained official acceptance. The Beveridge proposals for a new system of social insurance emerged during the war years. The 1944 Education Act, which we discuss in Chapter 9, pp. 330–1, at last established free secondary education for all. Thus, the foundations of the welfare state were laid during the war.

Why did the Second World War have such an impact? The political situation had changed considerably since the First World War. Welfare ideas and policies had developed further, while the Keynesian idea of the state management of the economy had emerged in the inter-war period. The labour movement had grown in strength and the Labour Party participated in the wartime coalition government. The war itself had a more general and more immediate impact on the British people through the extensive bombing of British cities, which destroyed or damaged about a quarter of the British housing stock. The government recognized that the construction of a welfare state was the price that had to be paid for the wartime mobilization and sacrifices of the British people.

Briefing: Beveridge and the welfare state

William Beveridge (1879–1963) has been seen as the architect of the welfare state. He had an early career in the civil service before becoming Director of the London School of Economics during the years 1919–37. In 1941 he was appointed chairman of a committee of civil servants charged with inquiring into the whole field of social insurance. The Beveridge Report of 1942 emerged from the work of this committee. In 1944 he became a Liberal MP for a year and then a Liberal peer.

The Beveridge Report made wide-ranging proposals for welfare reform. It called for a war on the 'five giant evils' of 'Want, Disease, Ignorance, Squalor, and Idleness'. Beveridge was torn, however, between his universalist desire to 'cover everything and everyone' and his belief in contributory insurance through employment, which meant that benefits would be related to years of employment. The report immediately became a bestseller and generated a popular impetus for welfare reform (Glennerster 2000).

The outcome was what is generally called the 'post-war settlement'. This was a settlement in two rather different senses. First, it settled the broad framework of social policy until the 1980s. Secondly, it was a compromise between capital and labour. The labour movement accepted capitalism, while business accepted the welfare state and greater state intervention in the economy. The settlement was broadly accepted by all the main political parties.

The welfare state and corporatism

A Labour government was elected in 1945 and by 1948 the Keynesian welfare state had been established. It was based on three key principles:

- full employment;
- universal welfare;
- free health care and education for all.

Full employment was considered essential to welfare and would be maintained by the Keynesian management of the economy. *Universal welfare* was provided by the National Insurance Act of 1946, which introduced a basic minimum level of welfare for all. *Free health care* was provided by the National Health Service (NHS) in 1948 and *free secondary education* had already been provided by the 1944 Education Act.

What was the connection between the Second World War and the welfare state?
© Getty Images/John Turner

While these measures transformed state welfare, they did not provide equal welfare for all. There was, certainly, an extensive *decommodification* of welfare, as education and health care were now freely available to all, but the persistence of private medicine and private education set clear limits to this, as superior education and superior health care could still be bought. There was a complete range of benefits for the whole population 'from the cradle to the grave', but in some respects this was less than universal. While there was a basic minimum for all, the actual level of benefits received depended on the contributions made during employment. The insurance principle, which related benefits to contributions, still remained (Glennerster 2000).

Welfare depended not only on specific social policies but also on the effective management of the economy to provide jobs, give people a good standard of living, and fund state expenditure on welfare. It was at this time believed that effective management of the economy depended on the participation of both the unions and the employers in making and implementing policy. From the 1950s to the 1970s, Conservative and Labour governments tried to involve both unions and employers in economic management through various corporatist arrangements.

Corporatism involved the state developing a cooperative relationship with the organizations (or corporations) of major interest groups, such as unions and employers' organizations. It recognized the power of these organizations and tried to bring them into the state apparatus by appointing their representatives to policy-making bodies. In exchange for being given some influence over policy, they were expected to become agents of the state and implement government policies on, for example, prices and incomes (Fulcher 1991*a*).

As we showed earlier, the British ruling class had shifted from a strategy of repressing the unions to one of incorporating them during the second half of the nineteenth century. The corporatism of the 1960s and 1970s was the final stage of this process.

The patriarchal welfare state

It was widely believed that the welfare state would lead to greater equality but it was in practice less egalitarian than it appeared to be. We consider here the issues raised by its patriarchal character, and then in the next section its redistributive consequences.

The British welfare state was based on patriarchal assumptions. It assumed a gendered division of labour between men in paid employment and women at home carrying out unpaid domestic and childcaring tasks. Thus, the welfare state assumed that men in paid work would support women doing domestic work and married women, therefore, received a lower rate of benefit until the 1975 National Insurance Act. The insurance principle also meant that they received lower benefits because they had made fewer contributions, due to years off work rearing children. As Pateman (1989) argued, men were treated by the British welfare state as full citizens but women as wives and mothers.

Rodney Lowe (2004) recognized the force of these arguments but pointed out that the 1940s changes did, none the less, greatly improve the position of women. They provided free medical care, which non-working women had not previously been entitled to. The payment of pensions at age 60 to women, five years earlier than to men, together with their greater longevity meant that women obtained greater benefit from state pensions. The issue is not simply a matter of the amount of benefit received, however, for patriarchal welfare assumptions reinforced patriarchal beliefs about women's role and therefore strengthened patriarchy generally.

The welfare state also depended on women carrying out much of the work of caring for children, the sick, and the old on an unpaid basis. In other words, the welfare state was based on the provision of welfare by the state *and* by women. This was not just a matter of unpaid work but also of the absence of state childcare facilities, which led to British state childcare provision being the lowest in Europe (Phillips and Moss 1988). The assumption was that mothers looked after pre-school children. If they chose to work, they had to make their own childcare arrangements without assistance from the state.

This assumption has not been made in all industrial societies. In Sweden there has been extensive state provision of pre-school childcare. Furthermore, in Sweden either parent has long been entitled by law to take paid leave to look after sick children (A. Gould 1993: 189).

A redistributive welfare state?

The welfare state was widely expected to create greater equality in two main ways. First, it was to provide universal benefits and equality of access to education and health. Secondly, state welfare expenditure would be redistributive, because taxation would be progressive and the poor would benefit most from state expenditure. Progressive taxation meant that tax rates increased as income rose. The poor would benefit most from spending on social security, education, health, and other social services. Increased spending on social security and social services should therefore redistribute resources from those with higher to those with lower incomes.

In a number of important ways, however, the welfare state soon departed from the principles of universalism and free and equal access through:

- means-testing;
- charges;
- income-related benefits.

The *means-testing* of state benefits had become quite widespread by the 1970s. While this was an apparently reasonable way of containing costs, it created a complex poverty trap and moved away from welfare-state universalism.

Health care soon became less free as *charges* were introduced for prescriptions and for some services, such as dentistry. These charges inevitably took a higher proportion of income from those with lower pay.

The principle of *relating benefits*, such as unemployment benefit and pensions, *to income* was introduced in the 1960s. This meant that a lower income resulted in lower benefits. These were all processes of recommodification, for they made welfare more dependent on market situation (Glennerster 2000).

More fundamentally, redistribution through taxation and state spending has not occurred. So far as taxation is concerned, the growth of indirect taxation has placed a greater burden on those with lower incomes. An increasing proportion of the money raised by tax has come from indirect taxes on widely used products, such as beer,

➲ *Connections*

We discussed the meaning of commodification and decommodification on pp. 586–7, and the opposed principles of means-testing and universalism. If you are unclear about any of this, return to this discussion. The issue of equality of access to education is taken up in Chapter 9, pp. 335–43.

cigarettes, and petrol. There is also a general sales tax—VAT. As these taxes are paid on consumption not on income, they cannot take account of income level. If you are too poor to pay income tax, you still pay tax on most things that you buy and at the same rate as the rich.

So far as spending was concerned, Julian Le Grand (1982) showed that public expenditure has mainly benefited the better off and this has been confirmed by later studies reviewed by Colin Hay (1996). The better off have made more use of the NHS, because of their greater knowledge of what they could get from it, and their social and cultural connections with those who provide care. The children of the better off stayed in education longer and gained higher qualifications, which, of course, improved their career prospects and earnings potential. There were similar patterns in housing expenditure and transport subsidies. Le Grand concluded that 'almost all public expenditure on the social services in Britain benefits the better off to a greater extent than the poor' (1982: 3). Note that this conclusion was reached on the basis of 1970s data, before changes in social policy increased inequality during the period of Conservative government after 1979.

Arthur Gould (1993) developed this argument further. He pointed out that the middle class benefited not only because of its capacity to exploit state welfare but also because of the jobs it provided for the middle class. The welfare state has generated large numbers of salaried white-collar, professional, and semi-professional occupations in health, welfare services, and education.

Three worlds of welfare

So far we have been focusing on the development of state welfare in Britain. In this section we set the British experience in an international context by considering different systems of state welfare and their consequences. Esping-Andersen (1990) has provided a framework for doing this and we will first outline his 'three worlds of welfare' before examining their consequences for employment and social stratification.

As we showed earlier, Esping-Andersen's central concept was the decommodification of welfare, which essentially means making people's welfare independent of the market. He carried out an international comparative study of the extent of decommodification in 1980. This study measured the degree of decommodification in the provision of pensions, and sickness and unemployment benefits. These measures were then combined into an index to capture the extent to which the 'average worker' had become independent of the market.

When countries were ranked according to their position on this index, he found that they clustered in three groups. He also examined the history of their social policies and found that these corresponded with his three clusters. This led him to identify three types of state welfare (see Figure 15.1). Not all countries fitted his clusters neatly. Britain, for example, showed a relatively low level of decommodification but its social policy combined liberal and social democratic principles. Esping-Andersen pointed out that particular societies always combined different

Figure 15.1 Esping-Andersen's three types of welfare

Type of welfare	Degree of decommodification	Principles of social policy	Countries
Liberal	Low	Individualistic self-reliance	Australia
			Canada
			United States
Conservative	Medium	Loyalty to state and preservation of existing social order	France
			Germany
			Italy
Social democratic	High	Equality and social solidarity	Denmark
			Netherlands
			Norway
			Sweden

principles of social policy to some degree and therefore never fitted his types of state welfare exactly.

Two of his types correspond broadly with the two models of social policy we examined in 'Market versus state', p. 587. The *liberal* type corresponded to the *market* model, providing state welfare for the poor only and expecting everyone else to take responsibility for their own welfare and buy it on the market. The *social democratic* type was essentially based on the *welfare-state* model of providing universal state welfare.

The third *conservative* type sought to protect traditional structures against both the individualism of the market and the egalitarian tendencies of socialism. The state provided more welfare than in the liberal model but channelled it largely through workers' entitlements to benefits and pensions. The assumption was that the male worker would provide for his family through a 'family wage' and through the benefits and pensions paid to him. Traditional gender roles were maintained and the family was expected to play a central part in welfare. State benefits could be quite generous but were related to occupation. The links between occupation and welfare meant that welfare depended on the labour-market situation and was only partially decommodified.

Esping-Andersen was interested not just in the development of state welfare as such but also in its important, and often overlooked, consequences for employment and social stratification. Welfare work was a crucial source of 'post-industrial' employment, particularly for women, at a time when jobs in manufacturing industry were shrinking. Depending on the type of social policy, employment in welfare services could lead to what he called 'good' or 'bad' jobs. The outcome was very different patterns of social stratification. He explored these issues by examining Sweden, the United States, and Germany as examples of each of his 'worlds of welfare'.

In Sweden the development of a universalist welfare state led to the creation of many public-sector jobs in health, education, and social services. These enabled Sweden to maintain full employment even though manufacturing industry was contracting, while a strong labour movement kept up the wages of service workers and prevented the emergence of bad jobs. A non-patriarchal welfare state enabled women to pursue full-time and relatively uninterrupted careers in service jobs. The principle of providing welfare for all also resulted in a high degree of social solidarity stretching across the working class and the middle class.

The expansion of the public sector generated a conflict within Sweden's centralized union federations between private- and public-sector unions. This corresponded closely to a gender division, between male workers concentrated in the private sector and predominantly female workers in the public sector. The gender segregation of occupations was high in Sweden, where managerial, professional, and technical occupations were dominated by men and caring occupations by women.

In the United States too health, education, and social services provided increasing employment, but the reliance on market provision led to much more expansion of private sector services, subsidized in various ways by the state. Private-sector expansion and a weak labour movement resulted in a dual labour market with a widening gap between good and bad jobs. The good jobs were in well-paid managerial and professional occupations with plentiful 'fringe benefits' providing welfare for those employed in them. The bad jobs involved routine and menial work in low-paid services, where pay was low and workers received hardly any additional benefits.

The result was increasing inequality and social division. Initially the good jobs were monopolized by white males and the bad ones were carried out largely by women, and by black and Hispanic workers. Esping-Andersen argued that Affirmative Action and Equal Opportunities programmes have, however, opened up routes for these groups into better jobs. He suggested that this may mean that in future social divisions will be based on class rather than ethnicity or gender.

In Germany there had been less service expansion and employment was still largely dependent on a highly productive manufacturing industry, which provided diminishing employment. The decline of employment was managed through early retirement but unemployment too was high. Lack of service jobs and the preservation of the traditional family resulted in fewer women entering the labour market than in Sweden and the United States.

The result was a large number of economically inactive people, consisting of housewives, the unemployed, and pensioners, who were supported by a relatively small and highly taxed labour force in manufacturing industry. The main line of social tension was between insiders jealously guarding their jobs and unemployed outsiders. The insiders resented the high taxes they had to pay to provide welfare for the outsiders. One form taken by this conflict was hostility to foreign workers, who were regarded as 'job thieves' or 'welfare-scroungers'.

Where does Britain come in? In 1980 Britain was probably closest to the Swedish case but then moved away from it towards the American. The British welfare state had some universal features but low-paid and insecure private-sector jobs in areas such as cleaning and care were expanding on American lines. Britain was moving from a social democratic welfare state towards the liberal/market model.

This is one of the problems with Esping-Andersen's typology, for there has been a general tendency, eventually

Figure 15.2 Welfare worlds, employment, and social divisions

Country	World of welfare	Development of post-industrial employment	Social divisions
United States	Liberal	'Dual' expansion of 'good' and 'bad' private-sector jobs and low unemployment	Concentration of women, blacks, and Hispanics in 'bad' jobs but 'equal opportunities' programmes
Germany	Conservative	Low expansion of service jobs and high unemployment	Tax-paying 'insiders' with jobs/unemployed 'outsiders'
Sweden	Social democratic	Expansion of 'good' public-sector jobs and low unemployment	Private-sector male workers/public-sector female workers

even in Sweden, for all countries to move towards the liberal/market model. Some criticism has been made of the way he identified his three clusters and other groupings have been proposed. More generally, it is argued that he made the character of paid employment too central to his typology at a time when, in developed countries, it was occupying a diminishing part of people's lives (Pierson 1998). Feminists have argued that he dealt only with women's paid work and ignored their unpaid and uncommodified domestic labour (Crompton 1997).

None the less, in evaluating Esping-Andersen's work it is important to recognize its originality and the comprehensiveness of its framework. It brought statistical and historical analysis together in a fruitful and broadly convincing way. It provided a framework for studying the development of state welfare within a comparative framework. It also broadened the study of social policy by examining its consequences for employment, occupational structure, stratification, and social conflict. We will return to his typology when we place the changes of the 1980s and 1990s in comparative perspective.

⟨⟩ *Stop and reflect*

In this section we first considered the state's role during the period of liberal capitalism.

- Important areas of economic activity were deregulated.
- What was the significance of the 1934 Poor Law Amendment Act?
- Did state intervention decline during this period?

We went on to examine the growth of state welfare.

- The origins of the modern British welfare state can be found in the years before the First World War.
- The principles of the welfare state were established during and after the Second World War.
- The welfare state was linked to the management of the economy through corporatist structures that involved both unions and employers.

- The egalitarian goals of the welfare state were compromised by the continued importance of market power in access to welfare, the patriarchal character of the state, and the lack of redistribution.
- Was the growth of state welfare driven by class conflict or international conflict?

We set the development of the British welfare state in a comparative perspective.

- Make sure that you are familiar with Esping-Andersen's typology of state welfare and the consequences of the different types for employment and social divisions.
- How does Britain fit into his typology?

Crisis and transformation

We now move on to the transformation of the British state during the 1980s. This transformation was central to the development of all aspects of government policy since, and that includes the policies of the post-1997 Labour governments.

We begin by considering the economic crisis of the 1970s, for it was largely in response to this crisis that the state was transformed. We then examine the changes in the state brought about by the Conservative governments of the 1980s and 1990s, and the changes in social policy that broke decisively away from the principles of the welfare state. We move on to law and order, for the policy changes of the 1980s had at least contributed to increased conflict and crime, which the government tried to contain by strengthening the forces of law and order.

Finally, we discuss state welfare at the beginning of the twenty-first century. Has the Labour government made any difference? Is Labour pursuing a new 'third way'? Are changes to social policy the result of an international convergence towards the market model of welfare? Will Esping-Andersen's three worlds of welfare continue on their separate paths?

The crisis of the 1970s

The transformation of the state was rooted in the crisis of British society in the 1970s. In order to understand contemporary policies and issues we must go back to this crisis and examine why it occurred.

The decline of profitability was at the heart of the 1970s crisis. The profitability of British industry declined during the 1960s and 1970s to the point at which much of it was hardly making a profit at all. This is shown by the net profit rate, which measures the return on capital after allowing for the cost of replacing worn-out or out-of-date equipment. The net profit rate of British manufacturing as a whole fell from 17.5 per cent in 1960 to a low of 1.7 per cent in 1981. The crisis was particularly severe in Britain but it occurred in other countries too (see Figure 15.3).

Profit is the driving force in a capitalist economy. If profitability falls, then industry collapses, companies go bankrupt, and workers lose their jobs. Without the expectation of profit there will be no investment and no creation of new jobs. Governments face growing financial problems, as higher unemployment leads to higher welfare expenditure at a time when their income from taxation falls. They are likely to face a growing discontent and increasing disorder. So the crisis spreads rapidly from the economy to the state.

Figure 15.3 Net profit rate of manufacturing industry, selected countries, 1960 and 1981 (%)

Country	1960	1981
Canada	17	14
France	18	1
Germany	29	8
Japan	44	13
United Kingdom	18	2
United States	22	10

Note: Figures to nearest 1 per cent.
Source: Armstrong et al. (1984: 464).

Contradictions and competition

The internal causes of crisis lay in the problems created by the system of welfare capitalism established by the post-war settlement. These problems became particularly severe, however, because of increasing international economic competition, which particularly threatened the economies of the old industrial societies.

As we showed on p. 593, the establishment of a welfare state in 1940s Britain has been interpreted as a settlement between capital and labour. Although this settlement apparently solved the problem of class conflict, welfare capitalism then generated 'vicious circles', which led to greater conflict in the 1960s and the crisis of the 1970s. These vicious circles have been seen by Marxist writers as resulting from the contradictions of welfare capitalism (Gough 1979). By this they mean that essential elements of welfare capitalism were in fundamental conflict with each other.

One of these vicious circles centred on state spending. The welfare state led to growing expenditure on health, education, pensions, and social services generally (see Figure 15.4). Increased state spending in capitalist societies resulted in what has been called the **fiscal crisis** of capitalism (Gough 1979: 125). The higher taxation of both workers and companies in various ways diminished the profitability of industry. Workers, for example, found that their take-home pay declined as taxes rose, and they therefore demanded higher wages in compensation. Higher wages then diminished the profits of the companies who employed them. As the economy got into a worse state, it became more and more difficult for the government to raise the taxes it needed.

Figure 15.4 Welfare spending, Great Britain, 1900–2001

Source: Glennerster (2001: 228).

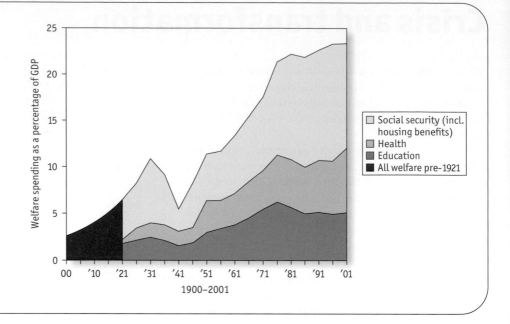

This vicious circle interacted with another one, centred on the maintenance of full employment. This was one of the key principles of the welfare state, but it increased the bargaining power of workers, who could take strike action in pursuit of higher wages with little fear of losing their jobs (see Chapter 17, p. 679), and resist attempts by employers to change work practices in order to increase productivity. Thus, the full employment of the 1960s and 1970s had consequences that weakened the competitiveness of British industry.

These economic problems were particularly serious because increasing international competition led to a general crisis of profitability, as Figure 15.3 shows. Even Japan suffered, though not as severely as the old industrial countries. Britain's crisis was one of the worst, because of economic weaknesses dating back to the nineteenth century. Three main problems are commonly identified:

- an archaic industrial structure, resulting from early industrialization;

- the domination of financial and trading interests, established in the nineteenth century;

- the absence of an effective state industrial policy.

Thus, the problems generated by the contradictions of welfare capitalism were worsened by an increasing international competition, which Britain was poorly equipped to meet because of the legacy of its nineteenth-century industrialization.

From economic to political crisis

Crises can, however, be managed and they lead to breakdown and transformation only if crisis management fails.

As we showed on pp. 594–5, the governments of the 1960s and 1970s responded to Britain's growing economic problems by seeking to construct a system of corporatist cooperation between the state, the unions, and the employers. Although numerous attempts were made to achieve this, they all failed and corporatism eventually collapsed in the later 1970s.

Why did corporatism fail? It failed largely because it required the unions to control their members, but this conflicted with their basic goals, for they had been created to represent their members' interests. It failed also because of the organizational structure of both unions and employers' associations. In Britain these bodies were weakly centralized and had little control over their members. They were reluctant to act as agencies of the state and could not deliver on the agreements that governments forced them into. In other countries, such as Sweden, where more centralized organizations had emerged, corporatism was more successful (Fulcher 1991a).

While the corporatist experiments of the 1960s and 1970s may now seem rather remote, their failure and the way they failed shaped the transformation of the British state in the 1980s.

By the late 1970s the post-war settlement was becoming strained. First, the institutions of the welfare state were coming under growing criticism, because it was becoming more apparent that the welfare state was falling short of its egalitarian goals, and because they were seen as unresponsive to consumers and providing insufficient choice. Secondly, British governments had been unable to handle the growing economic crisis and the state's role in managing the economy was increasingly questioned. Thirdly, the political consensus on the welfare state was breaking down.

British politics polarized as alternatives emerged on the left and the right. Both agreed that there was a crisis and their diagnoses were remarkably similar. It was a crisis of profitability and the welfare capitalism established in the 1940s had failed. Their ways out of the crisis were, however, very different.

According to the left, capitalism was collapsing and a transition should be made to a socialist society. The left-wing alternative was not, however, viable in a capitalist society. Sweden was the capitalist society that came closest to a socialist transition but this was never a realistic prospect even there (see the box on 'From capitalism to socialism in Sweden?' on p. 585).

To the right, capitalism was collapsing and needed reinvigoration. The right was politically resurgent in many countries in the 1970s. In Britain, the right-wing alternative won at the polls and after the 1979 election eighteen years of Conservative government began.

Thatcherism and the transformation of the state

Thatcherism emerged victorious out of the polarizing of British politics in the 1970s. It was more than a new set of policies, for it sought to bring about long-term changes in the basic assumptions of British politics. It rejected the values of compromise, consensus, welfare, and equality, putting in their place enterprise, market discipline, consumer choice, and freedom. In this section we will first examine the beliefs and principles of Thatcherism before considering the changes made to the structure of the British state.

Thatcherism

The roots of Thatcherism can be found in the thinking of the New Right, which became dominant in the Conservative Party during the 1970s. This combined two rather different strands of thought, *neo-liberalism* and *neo-conservatism* (Hay 1996). The prefix 'neo' indicates that both were new versions of old ideas. There was at the time much talk of a return to Victorian values by those who believed that Britain could be rescued from its crisis by reviving the values and beliefs associated with its period of greatness in Victorian times.

Neo-liberalism was a restatement of the beliefs in individual freedom and market forces, beliefs which had been dominant during the period of liberal capitalism in the early nineteenth century (see p. 587). Britain's economic problems were seen as the result of the growing power of the unions, increasing state intervention, and the growth of the welfare state. These all interfered with the operation of market forces and took freedom, choice, and responsibility away from the individual. Neo-liberals advocated the curbing of union power, an ending of dependence on the welfare state, and the restoration of the rights and responsibilities of the individual.

Neo-conservatism was a reassertion of the traditional values of the Conservative Party. It involved strengthening morality, reviving the traditional family, and restoring 'law and order'. The problems of Britain were seen as moral rather than economic. This strand was also strongly nationalist and concerned both to defend British sovereignty against federal tendencies in Europe and to protect British identity by controlling immigration. Stuart Hall and Martin Jacques (1983) used the concept of **authoritarian populism** to describe this aspect of Thatcherism. They argued that Thatcherism generated support for extending the authority of the state by appealing to popular anxieties about union militancy, permissiveness, crime, and immigration.

These two strands of Thatcherism were in some conflict with each other. The neo-liberal belief in freedom, choice, and market forces conflicted with the neo-conservative emphasis on order, morality, and tradition. Market forces are no respecters of tradition and ignore moral concerns. Neo-liberalism and neo-conservatism could unite, however, in their joint hostility to welfare dependence on the 'nanny state' and to the power of trade unions. They could also unite in the defence of property, for the protection of property rights was central to both.

Hay (1996) argued that the populist authoritarianism of the *neo-conservative* strand was crucial in generating political support for Thatcherism. It was, however, the *neo-liberal* strand that mainly informed the policies that transformed the state.

Marketization

The central objective of the Conservative transformation of the state was **marketization**. This basically meant expanding the role of market forces in British society. It is very important to grasp that, although this involved a withdrawal of the state from some of its activities, it also led to the extension of state control as well. We examine this issue in the section 'A weaker or stronger state?', p. 607.

There was a shift from the corporatist management of the economy to a greater reliance on market mechanisms. Thus, the Conservatives abandoned corporatism and dismantled corporatist structures that involved unions and employers in policy-making. The government neither consulted with union and employer organizations nor used them to implement its policies. Although it continued to control the wages and salaries of public-sector employees, it did not try to control wage levels in the economy as a whole through incomes policies but left the market to set them.

The market sphere was more generally expanded through **privatization**, which transferred production, services, and property from the public to the private sector. Some of the main ways in which this occurred were as follows:

- Publicly owned companies were sold to the private sector. British Airways and British Telecom were examples of this kind of privatization.

- Local and central state services previously carried out by state employees were increasingly carried out by private companies under contract. Examples of this were the school-meals service or refuse collection or privately operated prisons.

- Public property was sold, as when councils were forced to sell council housing to tenants wishing to buy their houses.

- Privatization occurred in a rather different way by encouraging or forcing people to pay for services they had previously relied on the state to provide. Thus, people began increasingly to pay privately for health, education, and the care of the old.

When services could not be privatized, 'internal markets' were introduced. This meant that services remained in public ownership but those who provided the service were forced into competition with each other, *as though* they were operating in the private sector. Thus, hospitals were forced to compete with each other, as were schools and colleges.

The reduction of state expenditure and taxation was one of the most important goals of neo-liberalism. This was certainly attempted but the Conservatives were unable to bring about an overall reduction, largely because higher unemployment resulted in higher social-security spending. The overall level of taxation was not brought down, but income-tax rates were reduced by shifting the burden of taxes from income tax to indirect taxes on goods and services.

The 1980s changes in the state were quite fundamental and reversed many long-term processes of change. They reversed the corporatist tendency, dating back to the First World War, to involve the unions and the employers in the management of the economy. They reversed the nationalization of important industries and services, which also went back to the First World War. They reversed the growth of local-authority services, which dated back well into the nineteenth-century. Furthermore, the clear distinction that had been established between the public and the private spheres began to break down as public activities were privatized.

Away from the welfare state

The Conservative governments of the 1980s were hostile to the universalism of the welfare state. They argued that people should not be dependent on the state and should take individual responsibility for their own welfare through insurance and savings schemes provided by the private sector. State welfare should be targeted on those unable to provide for themselves. Conservative policy was also driven by the need to save money on public spending.

Some of the main changes in welfare policies during the Thatcher years were as follows:

- *Priority to control of inflation*. Employment was central to most people's welfare and the maintenance of full employment was one of the principles of the welfare state. This principle had already been abandoned in 1976 by a Labour government but the first Thatcher government made it clear that the main aim of government economic policy was to control inflation.

- *Delinking of pensions to earnings*. After 1982 pensions were increased in line with price increases not increases in average earnings. This cut the cost of the basic pension by a third during the next ten years (Glennerster 1995: 182). Retirement would now result in an ever greater drop in living standards for those dependent on the state pension alone.

- *Reductions in unemployment benefit*. As we show in Chapter 3, p. 105, entitlement to unemployment benefit was restricted in various ways and benefits were cut. This was the beginning of the move from welfare to workfare.

- *Increased means-testing*. The shift from universal benefits to means-tested ones did not start with Thatcherism but it certainly continued. Child benefit remained universal but its level was frozen, so inflation reduced its value and cost.

- *From grants to loans*. The freezing of maintenance grants for students forced them to rely increasingly on loans, preparing the way for abolishing the student grant.

- *Less state support for the old*. State support for the residential care of the old was sharply cut by making local authorities responsible for it through community care and by means-testing.

- *Parental responsibility for children*. The Child Support Act of 1991 created the Child Support Agency, designed to transfer the financial support of single-parent families from the state to the absent parent (see Chapter 12, pp. 471–2).

There were also important changes in health policy. An 'internal market' was introduced by requiring self-governing hospital trusts to compete for contracts from health authorities and 'fund-holding' general practitioners. A creeping privatization took place as the boundary between public and private health was blurred by the provision of private care by hospital trusts and the use of public funds to buy care from private hospitals. People were encouraged to take out private health insurance.

There was, broadly speaking, a shift towards **welfare pluralism**, the provision of welfare by a number of agencies rather than just the state—yet another example of reversal, for the state had gradually displaced other welfare agencies to become the dominant provider of care by the 1940s. Welfare pluralism was not just the result of privatization, important as this was, but also of a greater reliance on voluntary organizations, charities, the family, commercial sponsors, and the funding of projects through the new state lottery.

State welfare in decline?

State welfare had moved away from the central principles of the welfare state. We identified these earlier as full employment, universal welfare, and free and equal health and education. Full-employment policies had been abandoned. Welfare had become increasingly selective and benefits had been cut in various ways. Free health and education were still available, but people found themselves under a growing pressure to buy them.

In Esping-Andersen's terms, a process of *recommodification* had taken place. Welfare was once again becoming a commodity provided by the market, with access dependent on market situation. The level of employment depended less on government policy and more on the competitiveness of British businesses in international markets and the attraction of foreign investment. State benefits had been restricted, reduced, and means-tested. The quality of health care and education depended increasingly on purchasing power and the operation of market mechanisms.

This does not, however, mean that state spending on welfare declined. Indeed, the proportion of national income spent on state welfare continued to rise (see Figure 15.4 on p. 600). The major components in this rise were spending on health and social-security benefits. More and more people became dependent on state benefits, largely because of higher unemployment, the rise in non-working single parents, and higher rents, which led to the increased payment of housing benefit.

Nor did a movement away from *welfare-state* principles necessarily mean that *state welfare* was in decline. It is important to keep in mind the distinction between the welfare state and state welfare, and the existence of different models of state welfare, which we discussed above on pp. 586–9. Whether a movement from the welfare state to the market model means that there has been a decline in state welfare depends on one's views on the merits of these two models. It is also important to recall that there had been a sense in the 1970s that the welfare state was not providing good enough services. As Glennerster has put it:

What Mrs. Thatcher saw, with her populist insight, was that there was a growing dissatisfaction with state services that gave little choice to their users, in which the professional view was dominant and the parent or patient in the waiting-room seemed to count for little. In a growingly sophisticated consumer society this compared poorly with the market sector. (Glennerster 1995: 192)

The 1980s *can* be seen not as a period of decline in state welfare but rather as one of reform, which addressed long-standing problems in the welfare state and injected a healthy dose of market discipline.

New Labour

The transformation of the state in the 1980s was carried out by Conservative governments but since 1997 Labour has again been in power. The election of 1997 appeared to be a political watershed, as Labour had won its largest ever majority and then went on to win two more general elections in 2001 and 2005.

In this section we consider how much impact the return of Labour government has made on the British state and social policy, focusing on the key areas of state welfare and the relationship between the public and private sectors. Before considering these areas, we examine the notion of a 'third way' in British politics. 'New Labour' has claimed that it is pursuing a distinctive 'third way' between the 'old left' and the 'new right', while Anthony Giddens has provided an academic rationale for this idea.

A 'third way'?

The notion of a **third way** must be set in the context of Labour's political situation in the 1990s. After a series of general election defeats, the Labour Party needed to distance itself from 'old labour' in order to regain its popularity. It also needed to distinguish itself from the Conservative Party and the policies that it had been pursuing.

This notion should also be put in the context of broader social changes, notably the growth of individualism and globalization. The policies of 'old labour' were based on collectivism and the state direction of the economy. With the decline of trade-union membership, the growth of consumerism, and the greater emphasis on individual freedom and choice, basing a party on old-style collectivism was no longer a viable political strategy. Governments could not realistically pursue economic policies that ignored the increased global mobility of capital. A 'third way' was needed that would recognize the existence of individualism and globalization but also take account of their costs and limits.

As a political position, the 'third way' was most clearly advanced by Tony Blair in a Fabian Society pamphlet (Blair 1998). A longer and more academic reflection on 'third-way' politics was produced by Anthony Giddens (1998) in *The Third Way*, though many of the ideas that informed this book had already been developed in *Beyond Left and Right* (1994). Here we outline some of the main points made in *The Third Way*.

- Central to the politics of the 'third way' is a strengthening of civil society. Social problems cannot be solved by either leaving things to the market (the 'new right') or to the state ('old labour'). Politics should be based on an 'active' civil society, where community organizations and voluntary agencies play a key part. Citizenship is about the obligations as well as the rights of citizenship.

- The basic institution of civil society is the family but the family must be democratized. Changes in family life make it impossible to return to the traditional family but that does not mean that 'anything goes', as the children of single-parent families *do* suffer. A democratized family would recognize the equality of the sexes, and encourage a more equal sharing of childcare and joint responsibility for children.

- The democratic state requires further democratization to counteract distrust in politicians and the formal political process. A decentralizing devolution of power will strengthen not weaken the state by giving it greater legitimacy. There should be experimentation with new ways of reconnecting government and citizens, through, for example, electronic referenda.

- A new mixed economy should be created. The public sector should draw on the dynamism of the private sector thorough joint projects, while keeping the public interest paramount. Business should be involved in partnerships with government and community. There must, however, be a balance between the economic and the non-economic in a 'social investment state', which is concerned with equality and welfare.

- Equality remains a key issue but 'the cultivation of human potential should as far as possible replace "after the event" redistribution' (Giddens 1998: 101). 'The new politics defines equality as *inclusion* and inequality as *exclusion* . . .' (Giddens 1998: 102, original italics). Inclusion means having the rights and obligations of citizenship, full involvement in public life, and access to education and work.

- An outmoded welfare state should be replaced by 'positive welfare'. Instead of reliance on the bureaucratic state, there should be greater self-reliance. The role of the state should be to provide the conditions in which people can themselves take welfare initiatives. The welfare state sought to eliminate risk but risk has a positive, entrepreneurial

side to it, and people should seek to manage, not avoid, it. The aim should be to develop 'a society of "responsible risk-takers in the spheres of government, business enterprise and labour markets"' (Giddens 1998: 100).

- A new role is required for the nation state in a globalized world. It is wrong to think that globalization is destroying the nation state, which is, indeed, the main defence against political fragmentation, but to be effective the nation state must change and become more *cosmopolitan*. It must move away from monolithic and exclusive ideas of the nation to accommodate ethnic and cultural diversity. It should also become part of a global system of governance that can alone manage economic and environmental problems that are global in character.

Much of the policy and rhetoric of recent Labour governments are informed by ideas of this kind. There are important departures from 'old labour' thinking, notably the emphasis on the responsibilities rather than the rights of citizens, and the redefinition of equality in terms of inclusion rather than redistribution. As we argued earlier, the third way sought to replace the welfare with the work-fare state (see pp. 588–9).

Welfare and workfare

What actually happened to state welfare when Labour returned to power in 1997? Did it reverse Conservative policies, continue them, or pursue a 'third way'?

Labour did not in fact abandon redistribution. An 'old labour'-style minimum wage was introduced, though the main thrust of policy has been on reducing poverty, especially child and pensioner poverty. Labour set itself the goal of abolishing child poverty and it was claimed in 2006 that a quarter of children in poverty had already been lifted out of it through tax credits and benefits. Pensioner poverty too was reduced through tax credits. According to Polly Toynbee (2006), 'Labour has redistributed more to the poor than any government since the war'. The focus has, however, been on poverty rather than inequality, and the gap between rich and poor has increased since Labour came to power. Furthermore, Labour's policies became increasingly means tested rather than universal, with all the problems that this entails (see p. 587).

Welfare policy was also a matter of helping people to help themselves. The phrase 'a hand up, not a hand out' became one of the government's slogans. We can see here a continuation of the Thatcherite hostility to the 'nanny state' and emphasis on the responsibility of the individual.

This can also be seen in Labour's policy towards the unemployed. While in opposition, Labour politicians had criticized the Conservatives' abolition of an unconditional

Have Labour governments significantly reduced
pensioner poverty?

© Alice Chadwick

unemployment benefit but when in government Labour
continued down the same track. Its 'Welfare to Work'
programme required unemployed people receiving state
benefits to accept a subsidized job, carry out voluntary
work, or take up full-time education or training. As the
Chancellor of the Exchequer put it when delivering his first
budget in 1997: 'when the long-term unemployed sign on
for benefit they will now sign up for work or training'.

Indeed, 'routes into work' became absolutely central to
Labour's social policy, not just towards the unemployed,
but to anyone on benefit. A tougher stance towards those
living 'on welfare' was signalled by moves to get lone parents off benefits and back to work. They would be helped
back to work through state-funded childcare and assistance
with finding jobs. They were expected to earn their living
rather than depend upon state welfare. Work was made
more attractive by reducing the taxation of those on lower
earnings (Glennerster 2000). In 2005 the government
announced a drive to reduce the number of people on

disability benefit by getting them too back to work. There
is much evidence here to support the idea that there has
been a shift from a welfare to a workfare state.

> ➲ *Connections*
>
> We are not dealing with education policy here because
> this was covered in 'From Thatcherism to New Labour',
> Chapter 9, pp. 352–4. Education policy is an important part
> of social policy, however, and in considering the issues we
> discuss here you will find it helpful to refer to Chapter 9.

As we have shown, the rhetoric of the 'third way' equated
social inequality with social exclusion. Labour placed great
emphasis here on the coordination of policy across government departments and set up a cross-departmental
Social Exclusion Unit, with eighteen Policy Action Teams,
immediately after the 1997 election. 'Welfare to Work' and
the ending of child poverty were presented as policies to
end exclusion. Another means of ending it was by improving access to education, through programmes like Sure
Start. This was not just about helping the poor out of
poverty, however, for there was also a punitive element
aimed at disciplining the poor in Labour's approach to
social exclusion.

In her evaluation of Labour's policies on social exclusion, Susanne MacGregor (2003) found that all three of
the discourses identified by Levitas (see p. 588) were present. As Macgregor has put it:

> The attention given to social exclusion in Britain at the turn
> of the 21st century has been primarily about redrawing the
> boundaries between acceptable and unacceptable behaviour.
> But this effort has focused almost entirely on distinguishing the
> genuinely unemployed from those who are not, the genuine
> asylum-seeker from the economic migrant, the disreputable
> from the respectable poor. This concentrates on bad behaviours
> among the poor, ignoring the drug taking, infidelities, frauds
> and deceptions and other human frailties found among the rich,
> the better off and the not-quite-poor. (Macgregor 2003: 72)

Broad continuities with Conservative policy are evident,
though that does not mean that Labour government has
made no difference. A Conservative government would
not have introduced a minimum wage, or targeted child
poverty in the way that Labour has done. Many of the ideas
expressed in the 'third way' can, as we have shown, be
traced in Labour's policies. Whether Labour's policies are
sufficiently distinctive to justify the 'third way' label is more
debatable. From a longer-term perspective, the division
between different eras in social policy would seem to lie in
1979 rather than 1997.

Continued marketization

In proposing that the private sector be given a greater
role in public services and emphasizing the importance

Global focus Globalization and international convergence?

We have been considering recent changes in state welfare in Britain in the context of British politics but we also need to set them in a global perspective. Has Britain been merely conforming to global tendencies that are moving all countries away from the welfare-state model of state welfare?

It has been argued that countries can no longer afford the cost of a welfare state in a world of increasing international competition and global economic integration. There are three main steps in the argument:

- First, international competition has put pressure on the old industrial societies, which had higher costs and found themselves out-competed by the new industrializers, to reduce the costs of state welfare.

- Secondly, a growing global economic integration has made it easier for capital to move around the world. Any country whose government adopts welfare policies judged to diminish its competitiveness or likely to increase inflation will find money leaving its shores for lower-cost and safer places.

- Thirdly, the economically more successful countries, such as Japan and the other Asian tigers, have not developed

welfare states on the European model. Lower rates of taxation have made them more competitive. Furthermore, in Japan the development of company welfare schemes has enabled companies to integrate and control their core workers. Their competitive success can be partly explained by the high commitment and high productivity of workers integrated in this way (see Chapter 17, p. 700).

Will Esping-Andersen's three worlds of welfare (see pp. 596–8 of this chapter) therefore become one? Nick Ellison and Chris Pierson argue that countries in his 'conservative' and 'social democratic' categories have moved in a neo-liberal direction but there is not a general convergence towards one model. National governments have a 'bounded autonomy'. They adapt national welfare systems but view the pressures of globalization through the 'lens of the domestic policy agenda' and preserve national distinctiveness. Governments' political concerns to maintain their electoral popularity and pressures from organized interest groups set limits to change (Ellison and Pierson 2003: 2–5). There still are many different worlds of welfare.

of choice, the 'third way' advocated marketization and privatization.

There are many different ways in which privatization has occurred and it is important to distinguish between them. There is first the transfer of ownership from the public sector to the private sector, effectively selling public-sector enterprises to private capital. This was the kind of privatization carried out by the Conservatives but Labour has not, on the whole, privatized in this way. Labour has not, however, reversed the Conservative privatizations, with the exception of Railtrack, and this was only a very limited reversal of rail privatization, as the train operating and leasing companies, and other components of rail transport, are still owned by private companies.

Another form taken by privatization is to draw private capital into the financing of public services and public enterprises, without transferring their ownership. The Conservatives began using private capital to finance un-privatized parts of the public sector through the Private Finance Initiative and Labour has continued this through its Public Private Partnerships. Private capital has, for example, been used to finance hospital and school-building. Complex privatization schemes drew private capital into the modernizing of air-traffic control and the London

Underground. Private capital has also been drawn into the delivery of public services. Failing schools and failing education authorities have been turned over to private management (see Chapter 9, p. 352).

In opposition, Labour had opposed attempts by the Conservatives to revitalize health care through market mechanisms. Once in government, it abolished the internal market established by the Conservatives but has, none the less, made extensive and increasing use of market mechanisms. Great emphasis is being placed on the provision of choice to patients and the principle that funding should follow patients. Private clinics and hospitals are being used to supplement NHS provision. If all this indicates considerable continuity with the Conservatives' changes to the NHS, it should be recognized that the government has hugely increased spending on the NHS and has rejected insurance-based schemes of the kind favoured at times by the Conservative Party. See Study 15 and Media watch 15 at the end of this chapter for further discussion of Labour's health policies.

Labour's privatizations have focused less on the transfer of ownership to the private sector and more on complex partnerships between the public and private sectors. Labour has also made piecemeal use of the private sector

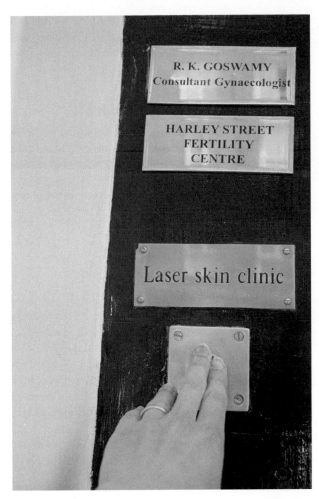

Is greater use of private clinics the best way to increase NHS capacity?

© Alice Chadwick

to deal with specific public-sector problems, while the Conservatives adopted a more thoroughgoing and doctrinaire approach to whole industries. None the less, there is also much continuity here. Privatization has been partly driven by the problem of how to increase investment in the public sector without raising taxes, as it was under the Conservatives. There is also the same conviction that private management can succeed where the public sector has failed, that private management possesses superior skills. As with the Conservatives, the provision of greater choice to the consumer has been an important consideration, most notably in Labour's 2002 plan for the NHS.

Has Labour pursued a 'third way'? The involvement of the private sector in the provision of public-sector services was certainly one element in the 'third way' prescription provided by Giddens. New Labour has, however, hardly steered a middle path between the 'new right' and the 'old left', and may be judged much closer to the former here. Labour has, indeed, gone much further in bringing private capital into public-service provision than the Conservatives ever did. New Labour has here accepted and further developed the transformation of the state initiated by the Conservatives in the 1980s.

A weaker or stronger state?

The transformation of the state that began in the 1980s sought to revive market forces and increase choice. It was often claimed that this would lead to the 'rolling back' of the state. Privatization certainly transferred companies and functions from the public sector to the private sector. Choice was increased by bringing in private producers of goods and services or requiring public providers to act as though they were private companies. But did this lead to a weakening of the state?

Increased regulation

Deregulation was one of the watchwords of the 1980s but attempts to revive market forces actually led in various ways to greater regulation.

This is not to say that there were no processes of deregulation. There were certainly clear examples of this. The deregulation of local bus services allowed private companies to enter the field of public transport and led, at least initially, to intense competition to provide it. The deregulation of financial services permitted building societies to become banks and freed up the movement of capital between countries. The deregulation of opening hours allowed the 24/7 opening of stores and pubs.

Deregulation did not automatically mean, however, that competition would increase, at least not in the long term. One of the consequences of allowing competition to take place is that the strongest companies rapidly come to dominate the market. Although capitalism is generally characterized as a system of free enterprise, it also manifests strong monopolistic tendencies. When the British water, gas, and electricity industries were privatized, there was the evident danger that new private monopolies would emerge to replace the publicly owned monopolies that had previously provided these services. These monopolies would have customers at their mercy. A whole range of new bureaucratic bodies, such as Ofwat, Oftel, and Ofgas, were created to maintain competition and protect the consumer through the regulation of these and other privatized industries. The maintenance of competition actually requires strong regulation by the state, not its withdrawal.

The abandonment of state incomes policies, which we described on p. 601, did not mean that the state simply withdrew from the labour market. It combined deregulation with regulation in its policies towards labour. The unions, by their very nature, obstructed the free operation of the labour market. The whole point of union organization is, indeed, to mobilize the collective power of labour, in order to protect individual workers against exploitation by the employer, who has far greater market power. The Conservative governments' drive to free up the labour market resulted in a whole series of laws being passed during the 1980s and the early 1990s to restrict the activities of the unions, laws which were left largely intact by New Labour. The unions became more regulated than they had ever been before and their opposition to regulation was ruthlessly suppressed.

> **⊃** *Connections*
>
> We examine many of these changes in other chapters: the regulation of trade-union activity in Chapter 17, pp. 700–1; the introduction of market forces and greater state regulation are discussed in relation to education in Chapter 9, pp. 352–4.

Another example of the combination of deregulation and regulation can be found in the changes to the licensing laws. The laws that regulate the sale and consumption of alcohol have been gradually relaxed since the later 1990s, in part as a means of regenerating city centres hollowed out by the shift of economic activity to the city periphery (see Chapter 13, pp. 532–3). In 2005 changes in the law finally allowed 24-hour drinking in those premises licensed to provide this. This reform has, however, been coupled with increased regulation. The police and local councils have been given new powers to 'crack down' on disorderly behaviour and disorderly premises, while tougher penalties were introduced for shops that are caught selling alcohol to minors.

The maintenance of law and order

There has also been a greater emphasis since the 1980s on law and order. This too was closely connected with the policy changes of Thatcherism, which generated greater disorder.

The policies of the 1980s contributed to growing disorder in three main ways:

- unemployment and crime;
- urban deprivation and riots;
- industrial relations policy and strikes.

Crime-rates rose (continuing their 1970s rise). Recorded offences increased by 56 per cent between 1979 and 1990. While this rise may be partly due to changes in recording and reporting, an increase of this magnitude suggests that crime itself had increased. Loveday (1996: 84–8) has summarized plentiful evidence of an association between high rates of local unemployment and crime. While government policy was certainly not the sole cause of higher unemployment, the Conservatives' adoption of a tough anti-inflationary policy in the 1980s had clearly contributed to it, and government policy can therefore be held partly responsible for increases in crime.

Why has there been a greater emphasis on law and order since the 1980s?

© Alice Chadwick

Riots resulted partly from increased urban deprivation. Higher levels of unemployment and associated deprivation were linked to the rioting that became a regular feature of city life (see Chapter 13, pp. 522–5). Feelings of deprivation became particularly acute as the individualist consumerism promoted by the neo-liberal ideology of Thatcherism took hold.

Strikes became more violent. Government industrial-relation policies led to new confrontations in the 1980s and industrial disorder reached a new height in the violent battles of the 1984–5 miners' strike. The use of the police against strikers was crucial to the government's defeat of the unions in this and other 1980s strikes (see Chapter 17, pp. 700–1).

There was also a discernible shift in social policy from the principle of removing the causes of disorder through state welfare to the containment and suppression of disorder through the police and the courts. The Conservatives rejected the idea that disorder resulted from social conditions and saw it in terms of the moral responsibility of individuals for their actions. If they failed to act responsibly, they had to be punished and forced to obey the law.

The state was strengthened through various changes in policing. Control of the police was centralized and largely taken out of the hands of locally controlled police authorities. The police were given new equipment and trained in new tactics for dealing with public-order situations, a process that has been described as *para-militarization*. As P. A. J. Waddington (1996: 124) has put it: 'No longer are officers deployed as a collection of individuals acting more or less at their own discretion; police now act as squads under superior command and control.'

The powers of the police were extended in various ways. In 1984 the police acquired the power to hold for questioning for seven days those suspected of terrorism. In 1986 the police were given greater powers to ban and control demonstrations and marches. The 1994 Criminal Justice Act changed the 'right to silence' by allowing the silence of defendants when questioned by the police to be used against them in court. It also increased police powers in dealing with such groups as football hooligans, travellers, squatters, hunt saboteurs, and road protesters. Changes in policing were backed up by changes in the penal and judicial process, with punishments for serious offences being made more severe (see Chapter 14, pp. 568–9).

These tendencies continued under New Labour, notably with the introduction of anti-social behaviour orders (ASBOs) in 1999. The police, local authorities, and social landlords can all initiate proceedings against individuals considered to have been behaving in an anti-social way. ASBOs typically restrict the movement of offenders, banning them from particular areas, and restrict their association with other people. While an ASBO is a civil order that does not result in a criminal record, breaches of an ASBO are a criminal offence and can lead to a prison sentence of up to five years. Particular local authorities, notably Manchester, have made extensive use of these orders.

New Labour's general style of government may be described as authoritarian. One of the slogans of education

What is anti-social behaviour?
© Alice Chadwick

policy has, for example, been 'zero tolerance for failure'. This policy has been implemented through a tough school inspection regime and severe penalties, such as the closure of failing schools and the suspension of failing education authorities (see Chapter 9, pp. 352–3). In 2005 the government announced plans under its 'respect agenda' to make greater use of parenting orders that would make parents responsible for ensuring the good behaviour of their children (*Guardian*, 2 September 2005).

There are here too evident continuities with Conservative policies. The *authoritarian populism* considered a feature of 1980s Conservatism (see p. 601) has turned out to be a feature of New Labour as well. We live in 'new times' with greater disorder and governments have been strengthening the state in order to deal with it.

Privatizing law and order

While the state's apparatus for maintaining law and order was being strengthened, it was also being privatized, though this resulted from long-term privatizing tendencies as well as new government policies. Privatization has taken three main forms:

- the growth of private security;
- the privatizing of law and order functions;
- active citizenship.

Private security companies probably employed more people by the 1990s than the public police force. This was a long-term process going back to the 1920s, which was linked to changes in industry and retailing, such as the growth of large commercial sites (Johnston 1992). The widespread introduction of bouncers to police entry to clubs and, in effect, control the surrounding area has led to the claim that the maintenance of order in cities at night has been privatized (see Study 13 on p. 532). Gated communities staffed by guards provide another example and there has also been the appearance in some local areas of street patrols by private security companies, funded by local residents.

There has been an extensive *privatizing of law-and-order functions*. Prisoner escort duties, to and from courts and prisons, have been privatized. Prison-building has been privately financed and the management of some prisons has been privatized (see Chapter 14, pp. 569–71). Electronic tagging is operated by private companies (see Chapter 14, p. 567). There has been a programme to identify 'non-essential' police functions for transfer to private companies.

Active citizenship involves private citizens in police functions. There are various state-sanctioned schemes, such as Neighbourhood Watch. Television programmes such as *Crimewatch* and hotlines providing information to the police are other examples. Active citizenship may also take non-legitimate forms, such as vigilante activity.

These privatizing processes raise the possibility of police functions becoming fragmented between various competing organizations. In this vein, Les Johnston (1996: 63) listed seven alternative providers of policing in British cities:

- private security patrols of streets and residential properties;
- private security companies contracted by municipal authorities to patrol streets and protect council property;
- municipal security organizations;
- municipal constabularies—bodies of sworn constables who police parks and other public places;
- 'activated' neighbourhood watch patrols authorized by the Home Office;
- vigilantes;
- security companies set up by police organizations in order to compete locally with the private sector (proposed by several chief constables).

These various processes of privatization may be seen as reversing the nineteenth-century development of a public police force. They raise the issue of whether the modern state is losing the 'monopoly of the legitimate use of force', which, as we showed earlier (see p. 581), was considered by Max Weber to be its key feature. At the very least, the privatization of the maintenance of order blurs the distinction between public and private services in the performance of a key function of the state.

◆ *Stop and reflect*

In this section we began by considering the links between the crisis of the 1970s and the transformation of the British state in the 1980s.

- There was an international crisis of profitability, which was particularly severe in Britain, in the 1970s.

- Corporatist attempts to manage this crisis failed, and the corporatist welfare state was seen by some as responsible for the crisis.
- Politics became polarized between Right and Left alternatives.

- The Conservative Party led by Margaret Thatcher won the 1979 election and then initiated the 1980s transformation of the state.

  We went on to analyse the Thatcherite transformation of the state.

- Make sure that you understand the meaning of neo-liberalism, neo-conservatism, authoritarian populism, and marketization.

- What were the main features of the transformation of the state?

- How did state welfare change and do you think that it went into decline?

  We then considered the period of Labour government after 1997.

- New Labour's welfare policies were informed by notions of a 'third way'.

- Labour governments introduced a minimum wage and pursued some redistributive measures but also sought to tackle inequality by ending social exclusion.

- Labour social policy has been interpreted as a shift from the welfare state to the workfare state.

- The marketizing and privatizing of public services continued.

- Was Labour reversing or continuing Conservative policies, or pursuing a 'third way'?

  Finally, we discussed whether the state had been weakened or strengthened by the changes that had occurred since the 1980s.

- Governments had privatized public companies and public services.

- There had been some deregulation of economic activities but also increased regulation of education and industrial relations.

- Government policies also arguably created social disorder and responded to this disorder in an authoritarian way.

- Neo-liberals had called for the state to be 'rolled back'. Do you think that it was?

‹› *Chapter summary*

In the 'Understanding the state and the welfare state' section we examined the nature of the state and its development, and the main approaches to state welfare.

  We began by considering what is meant by 'the state':

- We defined the state in terms of its functions of maintaining order, policy-making and implementation, taxation, political representation, and the management of external relationships.

  We went on to examine different aspects of the development of states:

- Weber saw the state as establishing a monopoly of the legitimate use of physical force within a territory.

- As states developed they underwent a process of democratization through the emergence of representative bodies and the extension of citizenship.

- A functioning democracy also required free political activity and competition between parties.

- The development of the state must be set in the context of both class conflict and interstate relationships.

  Lastly, we considered the main approaches to state welfare:

- The growth of state welfare was a response to the problems generated by industrialization but was shaped by changing relationships between capital and labour, and interstate relationships.

- The development of the welfare state involved a process of decommodification that made welfare independent of market situation.

- State welfare has been provided according to two main models, the 'market model', which gives state benefits to the poor only, and the 'welfare state', which provides universal state benefits.

- The welfare state approach has given way to a revival of the market model through neo-liberalism and workfare.

In 'The development of the state in Britain', we outlined the growth of state welfare and its relationship with the development of capitalism.

  We first considered the stage of 'liberal capitalism':

- During the first half of the nineteenth century the state deregulated important areas of economic activity but strengthened law and order.

- The 'workhouse' was introduced to keep the costs of supporting the poor down and force them to work.

- The state introduced protective factory legislation and public health measures.

We then considered the establishment of state welfare during the years before the First World War:

- Child welfare measures, old-age pensions, unemployment benefit, and sick pay were introduced.
- Democratization, the growth of a labour movement, and the imperatives of international conflict lay behind these reforms.

We went on to consider the 1940s establishment of the welfare state:

- This involved universal benefits, free and equal access to health and education, and the maintenance of full employment through the Keynesian and corporatist management of the economy.
- The egalitarian character of the welfare state was, however, limited by its movement away from universal principles, its patriarchal assumptions, and its redistributive failure.
- In 'Three worlds of welfare' we linked the British welfare state to Esping-Andersen's three types of state welfare.

In 'Crisis and transformation', we examined the crisis of the 1970s and subsequent changes in the state and state welfare:

We first analysed the crisis and its origins:

- There was a growing economic crisis centred on the decline of profitability.
- This crisis had its roots in the contradictions of welfare capitalism and increasing international competition.

Thatcherism responded to this crisis by transforming the British state:

- There were both neo-liberal and neo-conservative strands in Thatcherism.
- The transformation of the state involved marketizing and privatizing processes.
- Social policy shifted from the welfare-state model towards the market model and the recommodification of welfare.

The return of Labour government in 1997 raised the issue of whether the changes of the 1980s would be reversed:

- New Labour's social policy was informed by notions of a 'third way'.
- Although Labour carried out some redistribution, it placed more emphasis on ending exclusion and moved from welfare state to workfare state policies.
- Labour continued the process of marketizing and privatizing public services.
- Although there is an international tendency to move towards market models, many different 'worlds of welfare' still exist.

We then considered whether marketization had rolled back the state:

- Although some deregulatory policies had been pursued, marketization actually led to greater state regulation.
- Greater disorder led to an authoritarian concern with strengthening law and order.
- Privatizing processes also occurred in this area of the state's activities.

Key concepts

- authoritarian populism
- commodification
- corporatism
- decommodification
- democracy
- democratization
- fiscal crisis

- hegemony
- incorporation
- juridification
- legitimacy
- marketization
- neo-conservatism
- neo-liberalism

- privatization
- relative autonomy
- state
- third way
- welfare pluralism
- welfare state
- workfare

Workshop 15

Study 15 A new NHS?

In April 2002 the Labour government unveiled its plan for transforming the NHS through a massive increase in NHS resources but also major reforms in the way that the NHS operated.

Patient choice was at the heart of the plan. Instead of patients waiting for their local hospital to provide the treatment or surgery they required, they and their doctors would choose when and where they would be treated. Information about waiting times and success rates would be freely available, so that patients could make appropriate choices, and their doctors could book them in electronically. The principle of free care was maintained but the notion that this would be provided entirely by the NHS had been abandoned.

Market mechanisms would play an important part in raising performance. Hospitals would compete for patients. Those hospitals that attracted more patients would get extra funding. As an extra incentive, successful hospitals could acquire 'foundation status', which would allow them to raise capital for expansion, pay their staff at higher rates, and operate more independently. Improved performance would, therefore, be achieved not by commands from the top but by decentralization, incentives, and 'payment by results'.

Improved performance would not, however, be left solely to the operation of market forces, for there would also be much more regulation of hospitals and doctors. The National Institute for Clinical Excellence (NICE) would ensure that the most cost-effective treatments were used. National Service Frameworks (NSFs) would lay down standards of treatment. A 'health super-regulator', called the Commission for Healthcare Audit and Inspection, would be created to monitor performance and scrutinize complaints by patients. Another body, the Commission for Social Care Inspection, would regulate nursing and the care of old people. Thus, the government's plan involved not just incentives and decentralization but also bureaucratization and central control.

Furthermore, the NHS has to meet literally hundreds of targets spelled out in the government's *National Plan for Health*. There are targets for the reduction of death rates from major diseases, the reduction of waiting times, the recruitment of staff, the improvement of hospital cleanliness and hospital food, and the computerizing of doctors' surgeries. Success in achieving these targets will be monitored by an extensive auditing

apparatus. Critics have pointed out that there was a danger that 'micro-management' of the detailed activities of the NHS would obstruct the workings of the market mechanisms on which the government set so much store.

There would be a big increase in NHS capacity in order to reduce waiting times and meet the government's various health targets. This expansion would be funded by a £40 billion increase in expenditure, which would take spending on health from 7.7 per cent of Gross Domestic Product in 2002 to 9.4 per cent by 2008, with long-term plans to raise it to 12.5 per cent by 2023. Some commentators consider this a return to 'old labour' tax and spend. There has also been much concern that increased funding would be swallowed up by higher salaries and other costs, so that there would, in the end, be little to show for increased spending and higher taxation.

The government's own summary of its changes is as follows:

	1948 Model	New model
Values	Free at point of need	Free at point of need
Spending	Annual lottery	Planned for 3/5 years
National standards	None	NICE, NSFs and single health-care inspectorate/ regulator
Providers	Monopoly	Plurality—state/private/ voluntary
Staff	Rigid professional demarcations	Modernized flexible professions benefiting patients
Patients	Handed down treatment	Choice of where and when to get treatment
System	Top down	Led by front line—devolved to primary care
Appointments	Long waits	Short waits, booked appointments

There was no doubt that the UK had lagged way behind comparable societies in expenditure on health. OECD figures for the late 1990s show it actually coming bottom (out of 21 countries) in the number of acute-care beds, bottom (out of 25) in physicians per 1,000 population, and twentieth (out of 23) in nurses per 1,000 population (*The Independent*, 16 April 2002). Expenditure has increased sharply, rising from 6.8 per cent of GDP in 2000 to 9 per cent in 2005. Nursing staff increased from 320,000 in 1998 to 390,000 in 2003; GPs from 3,749 in 1997 to 6,030 in 2003; consultants from 17,500 in 1999 to 24,300 in 2004; cardiologists from 467 in 1999 to 692 in 2004 (*Guardian*, 2 February 2005).

The debate has been not so much over whether funding should be increased but over the best way of channelling money into health. Tax-funded systems are considered to be fairer and more efficient, while insurance-based systems, where employers and employees share the costs of health insurance, with the state covering those who are uninsured, are considered to provide more choice and to be more responsive to patients. The British government has opted for a tax-funded system but is trying also to introduce more choice and stimulate greater responsiveness through incentives and market mechanisms.

Source: Department of Health (2002), *Delivering the NHS Plan* (London: HMSO), available at www.nhsia.nhs.uk/nhsplan/

- ⊖ List the ways in which the government is seeking to improve the performance of the NHS.
- ❓ Are there any significant differences between its policy and that of previous Conservative governments (see p. 602 of this chapter)?
- ❓ Which of Esping-Andersen's three worlds of welfare does the government's policy on health come closest to?
- ❓ Do you think that its health policy indicates a commitment to the principles of the welfare state or an abandonment of them?

Media watch 15 For and against NHS marketization

Since publishing its NHS plan the government has been pressing ahead with schemes to increase the efficiency of the NHS by using market mechanisms. Greater choice is being provided, and waiting lists are being reduced, by bringing in private clinics. Markets are being created by separating the purchase and the provision of health care. Providers are being driven towards greater competition.

According to an article by Polly Toynbee of the *Guardian*, 'Manic marketization is driving the NHS into cut-throat chaos'. She accepts that there are good reasons for using the private sector to cut waiting lists and she is not against patient choice, but she fears that the government's increasing emphasis on competition will 'cause nuclear melt-down in the NHS'.

Toynbee raises many questions. What will be the effect of competition on cooperation? How can organizations that are supposed to cooperate also compete? What will happen to units that are driven into financial failure by competition? Will they be closed down if they are essential to the delivery of health care in a particular area? 'Just watch how many services will need rapid rescue when wards or clinics prove indispensable (or local protest threatens marginal seats)'.

Marketization increasingly turns the NHS into a purchaser of services rather than a provider of services. Toynbee thinks that turning primary care trusts into purchasers rather than providers will destroy the local relationships that have built up between doctors and health visitors, school nurses, community nurses, and midwives, as these become 'self-employed entrepreneurs' or are bought up by organizations that sell their services to the trusts.

She worries about the consequences of 'payment by results', particularly if this spreads to emergency and chronic care. Paying for 'cold surgery' is one thing but how can the medical care of the old, who often have long-term and complex medical problems, be paid for in this way? She fears that payment by results could lead to 'expensive overtreatment', as hospitals earn extra money by carrying out procedures or prescribing medication that are unnecessary. Payment by results 'will create a tidal pull for extra patients to fill hospital beds—and coffers'.

Julian Le Grand, one of the architects of government health policy, responded a few days later. He argues that the NHS has failed to live up to its principles. There have been long waiting lists, unhappy patients with no choice of care, unless they paid for it privately, and no incentives to reward providers of good care or force bad providers to improve. Increased funding alone will not remedy its deficiencies.

Targets have helped but they were 'too blunt an instrument' and required a constant monitoring of performance. Incentives to improve were needed. Giving patients choice was a step forward but could not on its own provide sufficient incentives. That is why it is necessary to introduce payment by results as well, 'where money follows choice'. Le Grand claims that the 'overtreatment' danger should be avoided by making general practitioners the purchasers, for 'experience has shown GPs to be good gatekeepers, effectively managing referrals to hospitals and drug costs'.

He argues that alternative providers are also needed to make choice work. The government is therefore introducing new providers—foundation trusts, social enterprises, and independent centres for diagnosis and treatment.

Toynbee describes the outcome of successive NHS reforms as 'a cat's cradle of contradictory policies' leading to chaos, but Le Grand sees health policy as having 'an underlying logic and consistency' that will produce 'a service that is responsive, fair, efficient, free, and robust enough to last'.

Sources: Toynbee, P., 'Manic Marketization is Driving the NHS into Cut-throat Chaos', *Guardian*, 7 October 2005; Le Grand, J., 'Payment by Results Will Save Our Health Service', *Guardian*, 12 October 2005.

When considering these questions, use material from Study 15 as well:

❷ Do you think that the government's health policy leads to a 'cut-throat chaos' or has 'logic and consistency'?

❷ What do you think are the advantages and disadvantages of: greater choice; payment by results; increased competition?

Discussion points

Thatcherism and New Labour

Before discussing this, read the section on 'Crisis and transformation'.

- What were the 'two strands' of Thatcherism?
- Were they compatible with each other?
- What forms did marketization take?
- What is meant by the 'third way'?
- What continuities can you find between the policies of Thatcherism and New Labour?
- What differences can you find?
- Do you think that the post-1997 Labour governments continued Thatcherism, reversed it, or pursued a 'third way'?
- What are the grounds for thinking that the British state entered a new era in the 1980s?
- How would you explain the transformation of the British state?

State welfare

Before discussing this, read the sections on 'State welfare' and 'Three worlds of welfare', the 'welfare' sections of 'Crisis and transformation', the Global focus box on p. 606, Study 15 and Media watch 15.

- What is the difference between state welfare and welfare state?
- What policies towards state welfare are advocated by neo-liberalism?
- What did Esping-Andersen mean by the 'three worlds of welfare'?
- Which world does Britain fit in?
- Are the three worlds becoming one world?
- What are the main features of Labour's NHS plan?
- Has New Labour pursued the same health policy as the Conservatives?
- What are the main features of NHS marketization?
- Do you think that the NHS should be marketized?

Explore further

The following references explore the development of the state and its transformation in recent years:

Gamble, A. (1994), *The Free Economy and the Strong State: The Politics of Thatcherism* (2nd edn., London: Macmillan). *An influential examination of the crisis of the 1970s, the rise of Thatcherism, and the transformation of the state during the 1980s.*

Hay, C. (1996), *Re-Stating Social and Political Change* (Buckingham: Open University Press). *A sophisticated review of the literature on the state and an account of its development from the 1940s to the present, with a lot of helpful tables and diagrams.*

Held, D. (1992), 'The Development of the Modern State', in S. Hall and B. Gieben (eds.), *Formations of Modernity* (Cambridge: Polity Press). *Provides a clear outline of the historical development of European states and different approaches to their study.*

Miliband, R. (1969), *The State in Capitalist Society* (London: Weidenfeld & Nicolson). *A classic study of the relationship between capitalism and the state, which deals not only with government but also with the civil service, the military, the judiciary, the mass media, and education.*

Wainwright, H. (2003), *Reclaim the State: Experiments in Popular Democracy* (London: Verso). *A discussion of alternatives to the neo-liberal state, drawing on examples of experimentation at the level of the local state in various countries.*

Clear and full accounts of the development of state welfare in Britain are provided in:

Glennerster, H. (2000), *British Social Policy since 1945* (2nd edn., Oxford: Blackwell).

Hill, M. (2003), *Understanding Social Policy* (7th edn., Oxford: Blackwell).

Lowe, R. (2004), *The Welfare State in Britain since 1945* (3rd edn., London: Macmillan).

Contemporary state welfare issues are also examined in:

Cochrane, A., Clarke, J., and Gewirtz, S. (2001) (eds.), *Comparing Welfare States* (2nd edn., London: Sage). *Compares social policy in Britain with other European states and the United States.*

Ellison, N. and Pierson, C. (2003) (eds.), *Developments in British Social Policy 2* (Basingstoke: Palgrave Macmillan). *All aspects of Labour's social policy are covered here.*

Levitas, R. (2005), *The Inclusive Society: Social Exclusion and New Labour* (2nd edn., Basingstoke: Palgrave Macmillan). *This is a penetrating analysis of Labour's policies on social exclusion and their relationship to inequality.*

Online resources

Visit the Online Resource Centre that accompanies this book to access more learning resources and other interesting material on the state, social policy, and welfare at:

www.oxfordtextbooks.co.uk/orc/fulcher3e/

A debate on the 'third way' hosted by the Nexus think tank, with contributions from sociologists and social policy experts, can be found at:

www.netnexus.org/library/papers/3way.html

A site maintained by the *Guardian* newspaper, providing access to news about British politics, political commentary, opinion polls, editorials and links to special reports on key issues, can be found at:

http://politics.guardian.co.uk/

The full text of the British government's plans for the transformation of the NHS, and various additional documents, are available at:

www.nhsia.nhs.uk/nhsplan/

The Centre for the Analysis of Social Exclusion at the London School of Economics can be found at:

http://sticerd.lse.ac.uk/case/

globalization

Contents

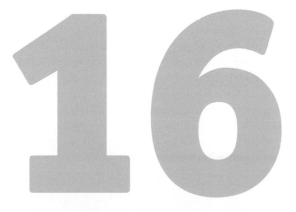

16

Global cigarettes

'Hollywood' cigarettes are very popular in Brazil and are manufactured there by British American Tobacco (BAT). Many of the 'Hollywood' cigarettes smoked in Brazil have, however, gone on a strange journey to Europe and back before they reach Brazilian smokers.

By late 1999 some 20 million 'Hollywood' cigarettes a month were being shipped from Brazil to Helsinki in Finland, supposedly so that they could be sold in Europe. These cigarettes, highly taxed in Brazil, were going 'duty free' for export. When, as BAT put it, 'sales did not materialize', the cigarettes were shipped to the Romar Freezone Trading Company on the small island of Aruba, a Dutch colony in the Caribbean. The cigarettes were then smuggled into Colombia and from there went across the border into Brazil, to be sold cheaply in Manaus. Cigarettes also came in this way from BAT factories in the United States and Venezuela. BAT reportedly made twice-weekly checks of stock levels and prices at the place in Colombia where the cigarettes came ashore. Extensive documentation of BAT's involvement in this trade was provided by Alex Solagnier, a former Romar director turned whistle-blower.

Romar's claims were denied by Kenneth Clarke, the prominent Conservative MP and ex-minister, who had become Deputy Chairman of BAT, but in 2004 fresh allegations were made. Researchers found BAT documents suggesting that it had been involved in extensive cigarette smuggling operations in Asia during the 1990s. China had restricted cigarette imports into its huge market, the biggest in the world, which had been targeted by cigarette manufacturers as Western consumption declined. These restrictions were circumvented by the smuggling of cigarettes through Hong Kong. These allegations embarrassed BAT at a time when it was seeking permission to set up a factory in China that would produce one billion cigarettes a year.

Sources: Duncan Campbell, 'The Multi-million Dollar Trade Route', *Guardian*, 22 August 2001; Rachel Stevenson, 'BAT Hit by Fresh Claims It Used Smuggling to Expand into Asia', *Independent*, 24 November 2004.

Globalization means that we live in a world where goods are increasingly made in one country and sold in another. Transnational corporations (TNCs) increase their profits by producing in countries where the costs are lowest and selling their products in the high-consumption markets of the developed world. Sales in countries, such as Brazil and China, have, however, become ever more important to cigarette companies, as they face increasing regulation, and negative publicity about the health consequences of smoking, in their traditional markets. As the example of BAT shows, they also increase their profits by keeping the taxes they pay to a minimum, in this case evading duty by pretending to export cigarettes and then importing them through the back door.

The growth of TNCs and increased movement across national borders have made it ever more difficult for national governments to regulate and tax companies. In this chapter we examine the way that globalization has challenged the integrity and authority of the nation state. This problem of national control applies not only to business corporations but also to many other activities, such as migration, terrorism, the spread of ideas and images that threaten particular regimes, and the laundering of illegally acquired money.

We also examine the growing interdependence of countries, which have become dependent on each other economically, politically, and environmentally. It is often claimed that the world is in crisis, that 'planet earth' is threatened by exploding populations, sprawling cities, ever-increasing pollution, and diminishing resources. We consider the growth of new global movements that seek to address these problems and the United Nations' attempts to protect the environment through 'earth summits' and international treaties. This leads us on to the UN's role as a 'world government' and the rise of other supranational bodies, such as the European Union.

Countries' dependence on each other does not, however, mean that they have become more equal. Indeed, there is plentiful evidence of increasing international inequality. We examine the origins and growth of the inequalities between rich and poor countries. We also consider the efforts made by poor countries to develop, the strategies they have adopted, and the problems they continue to face.

Understanding globalization

The key issue in understanding globalization is its relationship with the nation state. Globalization has, indeed, been defined as the stretching of social relationships beyond the nation state and many have argued that with globalization the age of the nation state is coming to an end. We therefore begin this section by considering what is meant by the 'nation state', and the related concepts of nation and nationalism. Most of the world's nation states were created after the collapse of the European overseas empires, and we move on to consider the emergence of these new states and theories of the relationship between developed and developing societies. This leads us to the issue of globalization itself, different approaches to globalization, and the debate around the consequences of globalization for the nation state.

Nation states, nations, and nationalism

We first need to consider the relationships between nations, nation states, and nationalism. Although these relationships might seem self-evident, there are many problems here that require careful exploration.

Nation states

A **nation state** is a political unit that has:

- national citizens;
- a national territory;
- a national administration.

Nation states are based on the idea that their citizens are members of a nation that lives within a defined territory. This territory comes under a unified administration, which, at least formally speaking, treats all citizens in the same way, though we must remember that some of those, such as migratory workers who live within the territory, are not treated as citizens. All citizens are subject to the

nation state's laws, are entitled to its protection, and have the same rights and responsibilities. The national character of a state, the claim that it is the political embodiment of a nation, is an essential element in the legitimacy of most states. Thus, government actions towards both its citizens and other governments are often justified by the claim that it represents the nation.

The distinctiveness of the nation state becomes clearer when we compare it with the 'dynastic states' that preceded it in Europe. These states were the family possessions of their ruling dynasties and their territories would change after marriage, which could instantly enlarge greatly a country's size. There was no sense that all those who lived within the state were members of the same nation. There was no unified administration and each territory would have its own institutions of government and its own laws. The state's inhabitants were the ruler's *subjects*, not *citizens* with rights, and the ruler's actions required no legitimation, for monarchs ruled by 'divine right'.

Nations

Nation states are based on the idea that political units correspond to nations. But what is a nation? A **nation** may be defined as a people with a sense of identity. While a nation state is defined objectively by its territorial boundaries and administrative structure, a nation is subjectively defined by the sense that its members have something in common that distinguishes them from others. Max Weber expressed this idea by defining a nation as a 'community of sentiment' with 'a specific sentiment of solidarity in the face of other groups' (1920: 922).

According to Benedict Anderson (1991), this is an 'imagined community'. Nations are a community because they possess a strong sense of fraternity or comradeship, powerful enough to motivate people to die for their country. The community is 'imagined' because 'the members of even the smallest nation will never know most of their fellow-members, meet them, or even hear of them, yet in the minds of each lives the image of their communion'

(B. Anderson 1991: 6). People identify with such a community through the emergence and communication of national languages, though state formation also plays a key role by constructing the units within which imagined communities emerge.

What then is the relationship between the nation and the nation state? Here we need to distinguish between two sources of nationality that often come into conflict with each other:

- the emergence of distinct peoples;
- the construction of nations by the state.

According to Anthony Smith (1994), the 'ethnic elements' of nationality existed long before the nation state. He claimed that the origins of nations lay in the much earlier emergence of distinct peoples with their own languages and cultures. Their distinctiveness was expressed in myths of their historic origin, which commonly referred to an ancestor or a deity, from which the nation was said to be descended.

Although these ethnic elements provided the 'raw material' of nationality, it was the state that forged the modern nation out of this material. Thus, Giddens (1985) argued that a nation did not exist until the state had constructed a national administration that stretched over its territory. It was the state's unification of its citizens into a single entity that created the nation. Indeed, when nation states were later created from the colonies of the European empires there was often no previous sense of national identity and one of their governments' first tasks was to 'build the nation'. The term *nation-building* expresses well the idea that nations did not just emerge and had to be constructed.

The ethnic elements of nationality and its construction by the state may well, however, be in conflict. Nationalities created by the state may be strongly resisted by peoples within its territory that either already have a sense of national identity or stretch across state boundaries. Such peoples may feel strongly that they have the right to form their own nation states. The Kurds, for example, form sizeable minorities in a number of states and have been in almost constant revolt against them as they seek to build their own state (see box on 'Kurds and Kurdistan'). Nation states and nations often do not coincide and this has been and still is a most potent source of conflict in our world.

This tension between concepts of nationality shows that nationality is not something fixed and objective that exists in the outside world. People construct their own sense of nationality for their own purposes. 'Post-classical' approaches to nationalism see nationality not just as the outcome of historical development but as a means through which people make sense of the world around them, of their experiences and their relationships with others (Day and Thompson 2004). This approach brings people back in as agents, treating them not as members of some pre-existing sociopolitical grouping but as active creators of the nation, who make it and remake it. Their nationality is, furthermore, but one strand of their identity, which they interweave with, say, their ethnicity, their gender, their religion, their class, their sense perhaps of being a citizen of the world, to give them a sense of who they are.

Nationalism

Nationalist movements typically seek to create new states on the basis of a presumed national identity. They claim that a nation has the right to self-government through its own independent state. This claim made nationalism a powerful force in the break-up of empires, whether the nineteenth-century Austrian Empire in Europe, the colonial empires of European states, or, indeed, Soviet Russia, which was an empire of sorts. Nationalism also challenges many contemporary nation states, which commonly include people who believe that they have a distinct national identity. Welsh and Scottish nationalists in Britain provide a case in point.

Nationalism is more than this, however, for it asserts that national unity and national identity should take priority over membership of any other group. It claims that one is first and foremost a member of a nation rather than a member of, say, a family, or a class, or a religion. One's obligations as a member of a nation must take priority over any other duties or responsibilities. Nationalism does not, therefore, come to an end once an appropriate nation state has been constructed. Indeed, one of the consequences of the formation of nation states is an international conflict that fuels nationalism.

Nationalism is not just some natural outgrowth of feeling from the nation. It is an ideology that can be used by many different groups in pursuit of their own purposes and interests. Politicians excluded from government may

Figure 16.1 Dynastic states and nation states

Features of the state	Dynastic state	Nation state
Territory	Possessions of ruling family	Land occupied by nation
Administration	Local institutions	Unified structure
Inhabitants	Subjects of ruler	National citizens and dependants
Legitimation	Ruler's divine right	Embodiment of nation

Briefing: Kurds and Kurdistan

Kurds are often in the news as they struggle to establish their own state against the opposition of other countries in a volatile and conflict-ridden part of the world.

They trace their history back to the Hurrian people, who occupied the area now called Kurdistan between 4,000 and 600 BC. Kurdish nationalism dates back to the sixteenth century, when it emerged in response to the division of the area between the Ottoman and Persian Empires. The Kurds hoped to establish their own state of Kurdistan after the First World War but, in the 1923 Treaty of Lausanne, Britain and France, the main imperial powers in the area, divided them up between Turkey, Syria, Iraq, and Iran.

They are a people with a distinct sense of identity, a history, a language, and literature but they remain divided between several nation states. An estimated ten million of them live in Turkey, five million in Iran, four million in Iraq, one million in Syria, and a few hundred thousand in the post-Soviet republics. In all of these states they are a smallish minority, with their main population amounting to some 20 per cent of the population of Turkey.

In 1991 the notion of a Kurdistan achieved some political reality when the Iraqi Kurds became a self-governing entity under United Nations protection. After the invasion of Iraq in 2003, a Kurdistan Regional Government was established. The Kurdish leaders now have to tread a political tight-rope. There are popular demands for a truly independent Kurdistan but this would be unacceptable to neighbouring countries, especially Turkey, with large numbers of Kurdish inhabitants, and military intervention could well follow. If the Regional Government continues to operate within a nominally unified Iraq, it has to make contributions to this state, accept a degree of Iraqi government, and make concessions to Iraqi Arab interests, all of which diminish its autonomy and anger its supporters.

Sources: The Kurdistan Regional Government at **www.krg.org/**; Charles Glass, 'Welcome to Kurdistan (While It Lasts)', *Independent*, 23 November 2004.

❷ *Does Kurdistan have a future inside or outside Iraq?*

❷ *The Kurds see themselves as a nation but will they ever be permitted to form their own nation state?*

---

launch a nationalist movement to set up a breakaway state as a vehicle for their ambitions. Governments seeking to mobilize a population for war will commonly use the rhetoric of nationalism to justify it and motivate people to fight for their country. Employers faced with troublesome unions may accuse them of dividing the nation. Racists may seek to justify their actions by wrapping themselves in the national flag and claiming that they are defending national identity.

Development, modernization, and underdevelopment

The post-colonial emergence of a large number of new nation states raised the whole question of their future development. Many different meanings have, however, been given to this term. To some **development** means becoming like the West, to others it simply means economic growth of any kind. Broader concepts of development take account of a range of social and economic indicators. Thus, the United Nation's Human Development Index combines three dimensions: health and longevity; knowledge and education; standard of living.

A growing concern with the environmental consequences of development has led more recently to the important and widely used concept of 'sustainable development', which we discuss on pp. 657–8. The term 'development' does not, therefore, have a fixed or agreed meaning and, as policy aims and circumstances have changed, so has the meaning of development.

Theories of development

There have been two main approaches to the study of development:

- modernization theory;
- dependency theory.

Modernization theory was an approach widely adopted in the 1950s and 1960s by both academics and policy-makers but similar assumptions still underly much contemporary thinking. Modernization theorists emphasized the differences in values and attitudes between traditional, pre-industrial and modern, industrial societies, arguing, as Talcott Parsons did, that modern societies held values of achievement and universalism that were not found in traditional societies (see Chapter 9, p. 321). Becoming modern meant adopting the values of the already developed countries of the West.

This approach put forward a 'diffusion' model of development. Modernity would spread from the developed to the developing world, as the latter acquired from the former modern technology, organization, ideas and attitudes. The main obstacles to development were traditional institutions and attitudes. Once these were overcome, development would occur. When economic growth proved slower than expected, failure was blamed on the selfishness or incompetence of governments and elites.

This approach has much in common with the widely held contemporary view that development will result from the economic integration of poor countries into the global economy. These countries should adopt the market-based institutions of the developed world, privatize state-owned industries and services, remove tariff barriers, and allow in foreign capital. Failure to develop results from inappropriate policies or corruption.

According to **dependency theory**, this failure was, however, inevitable because of the exploitative relationship between developed and developing societies, which kept the latter economically dependent on the former. This approach emerged during the 1930s among radical Latin American economists, who argued that, although Latin American countries were *politically independent*, they were still *economically dependent* on the industrial societies. The developed countries did not diffuse modernity but actually prevented other countries from developing.

The most well-known exponent of this view was Andre Gunder Frank (1967), who rejected the idea that countries were undeveloped because they were traditional societies that had not yet been incorporated in the modern world. The real situation was the exact opposite of this. Their lack of development was due to their involvement in the international capitalist economy and their exploitation by the developed societies. In using the phrase 'the development of **underdevelopment**' he went further than the dependency theorists by arguing that the industrial societies had actually *reduced* the level of development in the rest of the world. Cheap industrial goods had driven manufacturing crafts in other parts of the world out of business. As the industrial societies became more developed, the rest of the world became less developed.

This was not simply a matter of exploitation by the developed countries, for the *ruling classes* of undeveloped countries were also involved in this exploitation. It was not only the coffee importers in London who exploited coffee producers in Brazil but also the merchants exporting the coffee and the landowners, who both enjoyed a good lifestyle at the expense of the landless agricultural workers who actually produced the coffee. The merchants and landowners were quite content for Brazil to remain a dependent coffee producer, even if this left Brazil at the mercy of international coffee prices controlled by foreign

markets. A chain of exploitation relationships ran between what Frank rather awkwardly called *metropoles* and *satellites* (see box on 'Frank's metropolis–satellite relationships: the example of Chile').

Those holding this perspective generally argue that development requires the active intervention of the state to protect people from exploitation, keep out foreign capital and foreign goods, and develop publicly owned industries and services to meet the needs of the people. According to Frank, underdeveloped societies would develop only if the relationships of exploitation were broken by a socialist revolution. This may now seem a rather dated approach but it lives on in Latin America, not only in Fidel Castro's Cuba but also in the Venezuela of Hugo Chavez and the Bolivia of Evo Morales.

The conflict between the modernization and underdevelopment approaches dominated and rather paralysed the sociology of development for many years. Each drew attention to an important aspect of the relationship between the developed and undeveloped societies but each was one-sided. While the modernization approach could not really explain the failure of many poor countries to develop, the underdevelopment approach could not account for the success of countries such as Singapore. Neither of them left much scope for local variations and initiatives.

An action approach

The more recently developed **action approach** emphasizes the ability of local people to take initiatives rather than seeing their behaviour as determined by the constraints of wider structures. Norman Long argues that here modernization theory and dependency theory actually have much in common:

> . . . the two models are similar in that both see development and social change emanating primarily from external sources of power via interventions by the state or international bodies, and following some broadly determined developmental path, signposted by 'stages of development' or the succession of different regimes of capitalism. (Long 2001: 11)

What Long calls the 'actor-oriented approach' returns agency to the people, takes account of local activities, and

Controversy and debate An obituary for the Third World

'The Third World is disappearing. Not the countries themselves, nor the inhabitants, much less the poor who so powerfully coloured the original definition of the concept, but the argument. Third Worldism began as a critique of an unequal world, a programme for economic development and justice, a type of national reformism dedicated to the creation of new societies and a new world. It ends with its leading protagonists either dead, defeated or satisfied to settle simply for national power rather than international equality; the rhetoric remains, now toothless, the decoration for squabbles over the pricing of commodities or flows of capital.' (Harris 1986: 200)

recognizes that the same external forces may stimulate very different responses from people. This more social anthropological perspective takes account of the widely varying cultures and customs found in different societies and does not dismiss them as either traditional obstructions (modernization theory) or irrelevancies (dependency theory).

David Booth (1993) has reviewed this approach and points out that there is a danger that it may open a gap between the study of local situations and wider structures. Apparently flourishing local initiatives can be suddenly destroyed by economic changes or wars originating elsewhere. Furthermore, globalization, as we shall show shortly, means that different areas of the world have become ever more closely connected with each other, so that distant changes are more likely to impact on a particular locality.

As in other areas of sociology, the problem is to find a balance between structure and agency. The sociology of development must take account of local initiative and local diversity but set the local within the context of national and international relationships. The value of the modernization and dependency approaches is that they draw attention to crucial, if contrasting, aspects of these relationships. Their weakness is that they leave out local responses to them.

A Third World?

Developing societies have been commonly regarded as the **Third World**, a term that came into use in the very different economic and political context of the 1950s and 1960s but is still very widely used today.

They were called the Third World to distinguish them from the First World of the industrial-revolution countries and the Second World of the Soviet bloc, which had pursued a socialist rather than a capitalist route to modernity. It was believed that the ex-colonial societies could somehow develop together in their own way and avoid the evils of both capitalism and socialism. There was a third route to modernity.

These distinctions now appear more than a little dated. Any idea of the ex-colonial countries pursuing a common path disappeared quickly, as the Cold War between the United States and the Soviet Union forced them to align themselves politically with one side or the other. The Second World then collapsed with the break-up of the Soviet bloc and the general abandonment of the socialist route. It is, anyway, difficult to see the countries of the Third World as any longer sharing common features. While the Asian 'tigers' rival the old industrial societies, some African countries seem stuck in an almost permanent condition of deprivation and poverty.

Globalization makes the notion of distinct worlds ever more out of date, though this idea was always somewhat misleading, for there have from the start been close relationships between the First, Second, and Third World countries. Indeed, as we will show on pp. 629–30, a capitalist world economy has long existed. It has never made much sense to conceive of three different worlds within it.

Globalization

Our sense that the world is increasingly becoming one place is most commonly expressed by use of the term 'globalization'. We first need to consider carefully the meaning of this widely used term. We will then return to the issue of the nation state and the impact of globalization upon it.

What is globalization?

This word is often used as a short-hand term for growing economic integration. There is an important economic dimension to globalization but it embraces all aspects of our lives, all institutional areas of society. Processes of cultural and political as well as economic globalization are at work. Religion and the media, crime and sport, work and leisure have all been globalized. To make sense of globalization we have to provide a definition which can apply to all these different areas and activities.

Globalization refers to a complex of interrelated processes, which have in common the idea that relationships and organizations have increasingly spread across the world, bringing about a growing awareness of the world as a whole. Its key components are:

- the destruction of distance;
- the stretching of relationships beyond national boundaries;
- a growing awareness of the world as a whole;
- an increasing interdependence between different parts of the world.

Globalization *destroys distance* through communications technologies that bring places closer together, as in such terms as the 'shrinking' or 'compression' of the globe (see Figure 16.2). Faster travel does this but it is most strikingly exemplified by the telecommunications technologies that allow the instant communication of information between distant places. As Anthony Giddens has put it, this is 'action at a distance'. Globalization was 'the intensification of world-wide social relations which link distant localities in such a way that local happenings are shaped by events occurring many miles away' (1990: 64).

Others have defined globalization as the development of relationships and organizations that *cross national borders and extend beyond the nation state*. Held *et al.* consider that 'globalization implies first and foremost a stretching of social and economic activities across frontiers . . .' (1999: 15). Transnational organizations provide the clearest example of this stretching process and Sklair has argued for a 'conception of the global system based on transnational practices' (1991: 6).

The distinction between the transnational and the international is conceptually very important, since they have very different implications for the nation state:

- International organizations, such as the United Nations (UN), are controlled by the representatives of nation states and operate through national structures.

- Transnational organizations, such as transnational corporations (TNCs), operate across national boundaries and have some autonomy from the nation state.

There are, however, problems in equating the transnational with the global and excluding the growth of international organizations from the globalization process. Many TNCs operate in only a small number of countries and are hardly global in character (see pp. 646–7). On the other hand, an international body, such as the UN, is the most globally extensive organization one can think of. It makes little sense to treat all TNCs as global organizations but then exclude the UN from this category. Globalization should, therefore, be taken to refer to the development of both international and transnational relationships and organizations.

As Held *et al.* (1999) have emphasized, a distinction also needs to be made between regional and global organizations. By 'regional' organization is meant here the organization of distinct regions of the world, such as Europe or Africa. Both regional and global organizations extend beyond the nation state but they are very different in character. As groupings of nation states that have a common interest, regional organizations such as the European Union (see pp. 659–61) act in some ways like self-interested superstates. A global organization, such as the UN, which represents all nation states and tries to reach compromises and agreements between them, is quite different in character.

Global organizations not only extend across the world, they also penetrate into local society, both shaping what happens locally and adapting to it. The term **glocalization** has been employed to refer to the interpenetration of

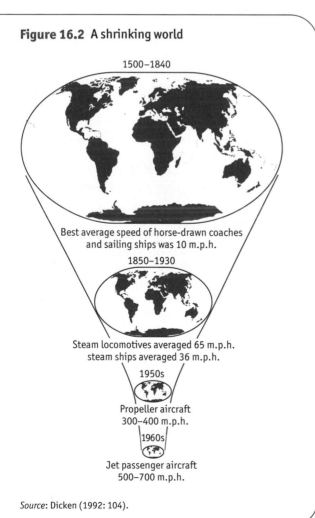

Figure 16.2 A shrinking world

1500–1840

Best average speed of horse-drawn coaches and sailing ships was 10 m.p.h.

1850–1930

Steam locomotives averaged 65 m.p.h. steam ships averaged 36 m.p.h.

1950s

Propeller aircraft 300–400 m.p.h.

1960s

Jet passenger aircraft 500–700 m.p.h.

Source: Dicken (1992: 104).

the global and the local. It was first used by Japanese business corporations to describe the adaptation of their managerial practices to local cultures and conditions. It was then taken up by Roland Robertson (1992) and has now become widely used by, for example, Ulrich Beck (2000*a*). Beck has gone further and emphasized the ways in which the global penetrates into people's lives, so that the conflicts between different worlds are reproduced within them (see box on 'Place polygamy and the globalization of biography'). We should not then treat global relationships and processes as though they exist solely at some high level above the national society, for the global impacts on the local and, indeed, the personal, while local responses affect global structures.

Globalization is not just to do with communication and organization. It also involves the growth of an *awareness or consciousness* of the 'world as a whole' or the 'world as a single place'. Thus, Robertson has argued that globalization means 'the intensification of consciousness of the world as a whole' (1992: 8). Notions such as 'one earth', the 'new world order', or the 'global economy' are examples of this consciousness. Indeed, Giddens considers that the growing use of the word 'globalization' is itself an indicator of it (1999: i). Another term that has been used by Martin Albrow (1996) and Robertson (1992) to convey the notion of a new global awareness is 'globality'.

This growing awareness is partly due to the increasing *interdependence* of widely separated areas of the world. This interdependence is another key feature of globalization. It is particularly evident in economic matters. Vegetables from Kenya, or wine from New Zealand, or cameras from Japan are produced for global markets. Producers in one country are dependent on retailers and consumers in another, and vice versa. An economic crisis in one part of

---

THEORY AND METHODS

Place polygamy and the globalization of biography

In *What is Globalization?* (2000*a*) Ulrich Beck argues that globalization not only reaches down into local society, it penetrates into our personal lives. Globalization means that we live simultaneously in many different social worlds. He gives the example of a German lady who travels between homes and social networks in Bavaria and Kenya, belonging to neither place and to both. He calls this 'place polygamy':

> Transnational place polygamy, marriage to several places at once, belonging in different worlds: this is the gateway to globality in one's own life; it leads to the globalization of biography. (Beck 2000*a*: 73)

By this he means not only that we may have homes, friends, and families in different countries but that this brings many different worlds into our lives. Furthermore, the simultaneous presence of different worlds means that the conflicts between them are reproduced inside each one of us.

Globalization of biography means that the world's oppositions occur not only out there but in the centre of people's lives, in multicultural marriages and families, at work, in circles of friends, at school, in the cinema, at the supermarket cheese counter, in listening to music, eating the evening meal, making love, and so on.

→ Note that we outline some of Beck's other ideas on the consequences of globalization (for work, employment, and leisure) in Chapter 17, p. 698.

? Think of what you have done in the past week—at work, at leisure, at home. Can you find examples of the world's oppositions in your daily life?

Global food—Who is more dependent, those who produce the food or those who sell it?
© Alice Chadwick

the world can be swiftly transmitted to another. Environmental concerns too have intensified this awareness of the world as a whole, for global warming ignores boundaries.

According to Robertson (1992), people now see themselves less as members of this community or that country and more as members of humanity, of a single threatened species. This focus on awareness makes culture and identity central to the process of globalization. While Robertson agreed with Giddens that the 'compression of the world' was one of the defining characteristics of globalization, he criticized Giddens for not taking this cultural aspect of globalization sufficiently seriously.

Globalization and the nation state

The relationship between globalization and the nation state has been the subject of a long and ongoing debate. This is not just a matter of the prospects of the nation state, for it is crucial to such questions as the protection of human rights, the future of the environment, and the treatment of refugees. We will examine here the positions that have been taken up on the future of the nation state but later in the chapter we will consider their implications for these various policy areas.

In one of the classic discussions of globalization, Giddens (1990) treated the development of the nation state as interconnected with the process of globalization. The nation state existed from its very beginnings in a system of nation states, which was initially European but then expanded to become a global system. Some have seen this system as weakening the sovereignty of the state but Giddens insisted that sovereignty has always been dependent upon the system itself. It has been through the international system that states have recognized each other's sovereignty and sorted out their boundary disputes. He argued that loss of sovereignty to a supranational UN has been exaggerated, for the UN has actually presided over the establishment of many new nation states during the post-colonial era. The existence of the nation state was bound up with the development of a global system of nation states.

A chorus of recent writers has, none the less, declared that globalization is now resulting in the decline of the nation state. Some refer to its 'demise' (Castells 1996: ii, 275), others to its 'withering away' (Bauman 1998: 57). The nation state is seen as losing its control of society and its autonomy in the world. According to Albrow (1996: 64), 'the nation state loses control of the forces it previously contained' (we outline his theory in Chapter 2, p. 65). According to Manuel Castells, 'globalization, in its different dimensions, undermines the autonomy and decision-making power of the nation state' (1996: ii, 261).

The specific arguments made by these various authors are as follows:

- the growth of international law and organization leads to a loss of national sovereignty;
- global economic integration undermines national control of the economy, constrains the actions of national governments, and weakens the state;
- national governments are challenged 'from below' by transnational social and religious movements;
- the growth of global communication makes it more difficult for states to police their borders;
- national unity is fragmented by a growing ethnic and religious diversity that stimulates communal demands for autonomy from the state.

Does all this mean that the nation state is on the way out? Are national societies being superseded by a global society? Albrow seems to think so but others have suggested that weaker versions of the old nation state will survive. Thus, Zygmunt Bauman (1998) has argued that global capitalism promotes the proliferation of weak states that can maintain order but are not strong enough to interfere with the movement of capital between countries and its activities within them.

It is often claimed that nation states can no longer control their borders. Ohmae argued in *The Borderless World* (1990) that the global flow of information is 'eating away' the boundaries between states. The broader term 'deterritorialization' is used to describe the decline of distinct territories and of social organizations based on *bounded* units, from the nation state to the local community. It is argued that instead of being members of distinct units, people are linked by networks that spread across all boundaries.

> ⮕ *Connections*
> You may find it interesting to follow up this issue in our discussion of container and network conceptions of community in Chapter 13, pp. 497–8.

Bauman has, however, made the important point that the significance of borders depends on social position. He has sharply contrasted the situation of the rich and poor:

> For the inhabitants of the first world—the increasingly cosmopolitan, extraterrestrial world of global businessmen, global culture managers or global academics, state borders are levelled down, as they are dismantled for the world's commodities, capital and finances. For the inhabitants of the second world, the walls built of immigration controls, of residence laws and of 'clean streets' and 'zero tolerance' policies, grow taller; the moats separating them from the sites of their desire . . . grow deeper, while all bridges, at the first attempt to cross them, prove to be drawbridges. (Bauman 1998: 89)

Paul Hirst and Grahame Thompson (1996) have firmly rejected the idea that the nation state is in decline. They criticized the belief that transnational corporations are, somehow, free-floating organizations detached from nation states. They argued that TNCs still have national headquarters and national cultures. TNCs still depend on the nation state's institutions and support for their activities. They also argued, like Giddens, that international political organizations do not take authority away from nation states for these are represented in such bodies and participate in their decision-making, while these bodies inevitably depend on nation states to implement their policies. Hirst and Thompson concluded that government has certainly become a multi-layered matter, but that the nation state remains essential to it.

The impact of globalization on the nation state raises a range of important questions, which are in many ways the most pressing issues of the world today. We will come across them at many points in this chapter.

The timing of globalization

Globalization is commonly treated as a recent process. The world does seem to have 'shrunk' since the 1960s, with the much greater speed of travel and communication resulting from key developments at that time, such as the introduction of wide-bodied passenger jets and geostationary satellites. People, goods, information, images, and money began to move around the world much more freely. Globalization might then appear to be a recent phenom-enon and some sociologists have treated it in this way. Albrow (1996) argued that globalization occurred during the transition from the modern to the global age, a transition which he dated very precisely to the years 1945–89.

Robertson (1992) considered, on the contrary, that globalization began in the fifteenth century with the European voyages of discovery and the beginnings of the European colonization of the world. Similarly, Immanuel Wallerstein (1974), whose ideas we will examine in the next section, argued that a capitalist world economy was already coming into existence at that time. Certainly, by the time of the nineteenth century there were major communications advances—steam travel, the telegraph, and the telephone —which 'shrank' the world. We take the view that globalization is a long-term process that stretches back to the fifteenth century.

Hirst and Thompson (1996) have challenged what one might call the 'onwards and upwards' notion of globalization. They claimed that the world economy was more integrated by trade and finance during the period before the First World War than it is today, though they did recognize that some globalizing processes, such as the growth of TNCs, have recently accelerated. The global movement of people through international migration, which we examine on pp. 630–2 and pp. 651–2, certainly slowed down after the First World War, before accelerating again after the Second World War. It should not be assumed that globalization is a continuous and ever-increasing process of world integration.

◈ *Stop and reflect*

We began this chapter by considering the nation state, and its relationship to the nation and to nationalism. Reflect on your own nationality.

- What nation state are you a citizen of?
- List the main rights and obligations that citizenship of your nation state involves.
- What do you consider your nation to be?
- What are the distinguishing features of your nation?
- Does your nation correspond with your nation state?
- How important is nationality to your sense of identity?

We then considered issues raised by the development of post-colonial nation states.

- Modernization theory and dependency theory provided contrasting approaches to development.

- While evidence from different countries can be found to support each of these approaches, both gave insufficient attention to local diversity and local initiative.
- Consider whether the action approach provides a better way of addressing development issues.

We went on to consider globalization.

- Although globalization is often taken to refer to the growing economic integration of the world, it embraces all aspects of people's lives.
- Make sure that you are clear about the key components of globalization, which we list on p. 624.
- What is meant by the notion of a 'shrinking' world?
- Consider Beck's concept of 'place polygamy' and its consequences. Think about what you have done in the past week—at work, at leisure, and at home. Can you find examples of the 'world's oppositions' in your daily life?

Empires in a global economy

In this part of the chapter we examine the development of nation states and the early stages of globalization. We deal with the rise of empires and the growth of a world economy. We go on to consider the huge movements of population that resulted from empire-building and global economic integration. Lastly, we consider global divisions and the globalization of warfare.

From nation state to empire

The origins of European nation states can be traced far back in history. Anthony Smith (1994) argued that the ethnic elements of nationality already existed in medieval times. The various peoples of Europe had a sense of their distinctiveness because of differences of language and culture, and the historical myths that traced their origins back to distant ancestors.

Linguistic diversity had always existed in Europe but distinct national languages had to be created. In medieval Europe educated people communicated with each other through the international language of Latin. The creation of national languages involved the displacement of Latin, the consolidation of local dialects into a standard and stable language, and the elimination of rival languages. The fifteenth-century invention of the printing press and the growth of the print trade played a crucial part in this process (see Chapter 10, p. 370).

At this time Europe was divided between dynastic states, of the kind that we describe on p. 619. In the sixteenth and seventeenth centuries the monarchs that ruled these states began to build new administrative structures that gave them more control over their populations and resources. They constructed royal administrations to collect taxes and maintain order within distinct territories with defined borders. They encouraged the growth of national languages as part of the process of unifying their territories. Nation states were now emerging.

⮞ Connections

Other closely related aspects of the development of states are discussed elsewhere. The bureaucratization of the state is discussed in Chapter 14, p. 545, and the development of the ruler's authority in Chapter 15, pp. 581–2.

Interstate conflict played an important part in the process by driving rulers to find new ways of raising armies and financing wars. The nation state, international warfare, and international relations emerged together. As we pointed out above, Giddens (1985) argued that the growth of nation states can be understood only if they are seen as parts of an international system. The importance of relationships between nations in the growth of the nation state can be seen clearly in the British case.

According to Colley (1992), it was the long eighteenth-century conflict between Britain and France, lasting until the defeat of Napoleon in 1815, which forged the British nation. This conflict made three crucial contributions:

- *National administration.* The construction of an effective system of national taxation and the building of a 'massive military machine'.

- *National identity.* The creation of a British identity, with religion playing an important part in this, for war with Catholic France unified the Protestant peoples of Great Britain and Northern Ireland.

- *Empire.* The unifying of the various British nationalities through their combined involvement in building, administering, and exploiting the Empire.

Then, in the nineteenth century a unified national administrative structure was constructed through the administrative revolution, which we examine in Chapter 14, p. 545. The railways, improved postal services, and the telegraph created national communication networks.

Within this framework other changes integrated and strengthened the nation. The nineteenth-century democratization of government involved the British people, and the peoples of other European states, in national politics. State education, state employment, and national military service generated loyalty to the state. Governments standardized national languages, built national monuments, revived ancient myths of national origin, and generally glorified the nation (Hobsbawm 1977). Industrialization and urbanization broke down local ties and brought people into larger groupings where they could identify with the 'imagined community' of the nation.

The rise of the nation state and the construction of overseas empires were closely interconnected. Conflicts over territory in Europe extended to conflicts over territory elsewhere in the world, while overseas rivalries contributed to nation-building in Europe. The construction of national empires must, however, be set in the context of economic change as well and we now go on to the rise of a global economy.

The emergence of a global economy

The beginnings of a global economy can be found in the late fifteenth-century expansion of Europe through voyages of exploration that led to trading relationships with other continents. In this section, we first discuss the emergence of a 'capitalist world economy' and then go on to examine its integration by industrialization and the establishment of an international division of labour.

A capitalist world economy

The concept of a 'capitalist world economy' comes from Immanuel Wallerstein's work on world systems (1974). A **world system** is, in his terms, a unit within which there is a complete division of labour that extends across various ethnic and cultural groups. World systems can take the form of world empires or world economies. **World empires**, such as ancient Rome or imperial China, had a single political centre and were integrated by a bureaucratic administration. **World economies** had multiple political centres and were integrated economically rather than politically.

Wallerstein argued that a capitalist world economy first established itself in Europe and then gradually extended to include the whole world. After the collapse of the Roman world empire, no other imperial power had been able to take control of Europe, which fragmented into competing national states. Although Europe was politically divided, it became economically integrated by the capitalist merchants in the trading cities of north-west Europe, who created a network of economic relationships that eventually extended across the whole world. A capitalist world economy had come into existence.

The central feature of this world economy was the relationship between its *core* and *periphery*. It was initially dominated by a group of *core* countries in north-west Europe—Britain, France, and the Netherlands—but this later included Germany and the United States. These were the economically most advanced areas, where the manufacturing of goods was already well established, and were later to be at the centre of the Industrial Revolution.

The *periphery* supplied raw materials to the core and imported manufactured goods from it. It initially consisted of eastern European countries, but in the late fifteenth century began to expand to include Africa, Asia, and Latin America. Military domination by the strong states of the core countries kept state structures weak in the periphery. The construction of overseas empires played an important part in this, though the core also dominated the periphery by financial means.

The importance of Wallerstein's approach is that he established that:

- we should not examine national economies in isolation but always consider their place in the whole system of economic relationships;
- from its very beginnings the development of capitalism brought about a growing economic integration of the world;
- the end of empire did not end the core's domination of the periphery. Thus, when Latin American countries became independent from Spain and Portugal, their domination by core countries continued, for Britain and the United States still controlled their economies.

Industrialization and the international division of labour

While a world economy was *created* in the sixteenth century, it was industrialization that really *integrated* it by generating a much closer interdependence between the

Controversy and debate Re-orienting world thinking

In the 1970s Andre Gundar Frank (see p. 622) found Wallerstein's ideas congenial and began working with him. Frank saw the lack of development in Latin American countries as resulting from their position in the capitalist world economy and their exploitation by economically developed countries. By the end of the 1980s, Frank and Wallerstein were, however, moving apart and in his 1998 book *ReORIENT: Global Economy in the Asian Age*, Frank accused Wallerstein, and indeed Marx, Durkheim, Weber, and many others, of providing a Eurocentric version of world history.

Wallerstein had argued that a capitalist world economy emerged in Europe in the sixteenth century. In *ReORIENT*, Frank claimed that Asia was actually ahead of Europe in its level of economic development until the nineteenth century. Europe's early economic development was in fact a consequence of the earlier development of Asian economies. It was only in the nineteenth century that the West overtook Asia. The later rise of Asian economies in the second half of the twentieth century, and their future dominance of the world economy, should not be seen as something new but rather as a return to their world dominance of earlier times.

core and the periphery. This interdependence resulted from the international division of labour established in the nineteenth century. The industrial societies specialized in producing manufactured goods and the rest of the world in raw materials and food (usually called primary products, to contrast them with the secondary, processed goods made in the industrial countries). This global division of labour was said to be in the common interest, as each country could concentrate on what it was best at doing.

Interdependence meant, however, that some were more dependent than others and the result was increasing international inequality. The primary producers found that most of the benefits of the international division of labour seemed to go to the industrial countries. It was the growing awareness of this that led to the *dependency* theory of the relationship between the industrial and primary producer countries (see p. 622).

There were many reasons for the growth of international inequality between the industrial societies and the primary producers:

- *Profits on capital.* The industrial countries were the source of the capital that financed tea estates in India or rubber plantations in Malaya, and took the profits from primary production.

- *Control of prices.* These were controlled by trading corporations and markets located in the industrial countries. The prices of industrial goods were kept high, while raw material prices tended to fall.

- *Product dependence.* The economies of the industrial countries were highly diversified, but the economies of the primary producers were often dependent on one product, such as coffee in Brazil or bananas in the Caribbean. A fall in the price of these products had a catastrophic effect on these countries.

- *Imperialism.* Through their empires the industrial countries were in political, administrative, and military control of many primary producers, and could make sure that colonial economies were subordinated to imperial interests.

Nineteenth-century empire-building was linked to industrialization. The spread of industrial methods of production from Britain to Europe and the United States led to an increasing international competition for markets and raw materials. The best way to protect markets and raw-material supplies was to construct an imperial fence around them. Economic concerns were not, however, the only motivation behind imperial expansion. Having an empire was regarded as one of the defining characteristics of a 'great power' and late-comers to the competition, such as Germany and Italy, scrambled for areas with little obvious economic value.

A divided world

Different parts of the world had become increasingly integrated through both the administrative structures of empires and the capitalist world economy. Globalization was well under way. The world also, however, became more divided by racial divisions and by imperial rivalries that led eventually to world wars.

Ethnic and racial divisions

The growth of a world capitalist economy generated a series of migrations that created ethnically diverse societies. At a time when people were learning to identify themselves as nations, they also began to think of themselves as belonging to distinct races.

It is estimated that between 1500 and 1800 some six million Africans were transported by the slave trade to the colonies of America and the Caribbean (Emmer 1993: 67). This was not the only trade in slaves, for they were also traded from parts of Africa to the Islamic countries of North Africa and the Middle East.

Briefing: the slave-ship *Zong* jettisons its cargo

The *Zong* was a Liverpool slave-ship that sailed in 1781 from West Africa to Jamaica with a cargo of slaves. On the initiative of its captain, and with the compliance of the crew, 131 sick slaves were thrown overboard as it approached its destination, in order to save drinking water and make a claim on the ship's insurers. When this became known, Granville Sharp, a leading campaigner against the slave trade, tried to bring a prosecution against the crew for murder.

Two cases came to court in 1783, though these were concerned not with the murder of the slaves but with the shipowner's insurance claim, which was contested by the underwriters. The Solicitor-General represented the slave-owners and declared in court that a prosecution for murder 'would be madness: the blacks were property'. The judge agreed and stated that 'the case of the slaves was the same as if horses had been thrown overboard'.

The only response of the British state to this and similar cases seems to have been the Act of 1790 that ruled out insurance claims 'on account of the mortality of slaves by natural death or ill treatment, or against loss by throwing overboard of slaves on any account whatsoever'.

Source: Walvin (1993: 18–21).

Figure 16.3 The transatlantic slave-trade triangle

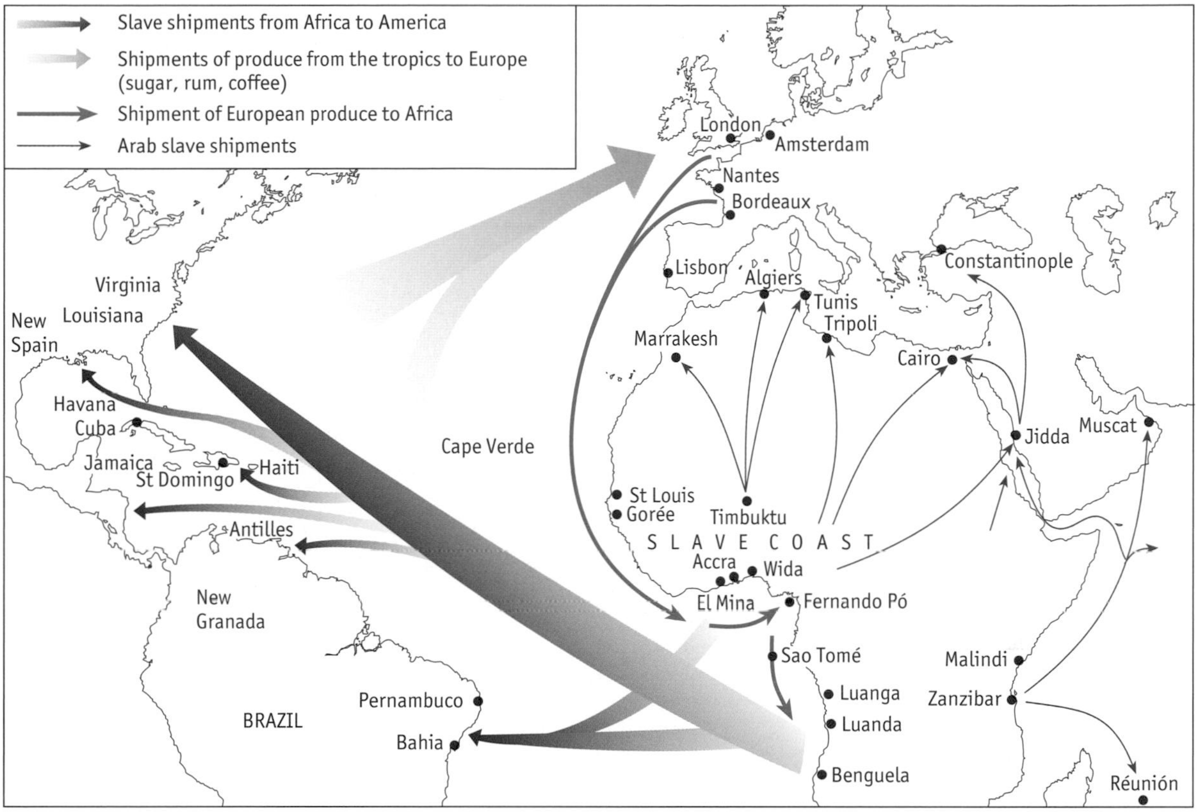

→	Slave shipments from Africa to America
→	Shipments of produce from the tropics to Europe (sugar, rum, coffee)
→	Shipment of European produce to Africa
→	Arab slave shipments

Source: Potts (1990: 42).

The defining characteristic of **slavery** is that it treats people as property. Slaves are the possessions of slave-owners, who can buy and sell them at will (see the box on 'The slave-ship *Zong* jettisons its cargo').

The labour provided by slaves was crucial to the emerging capitalist world economy. They were used to work the gold and silver mines of South America, to produce sugar in Brazil and the Caribbean, to grow tobacco and cotton in North America. Native populations had often been exterminated by a combination of colonial conquest and colonist-spread disease, or else were hard to subdue into a reliable labour force. Slaves transplanted from their societies of origin and forced into submission were a cheap and controllable source of labour.

This trade in people was also central to the capitalist world economy in another way, for it formed one side of the Atlantic trade triangle of the eighteenth century. Goods shipped from Britain and France were used to buy slaves on the West African coast, who were transported across the Atlantic and sold to plantation-owners. The ships could

then return to Europe with a cargo of colonial products, typically sugar or tobacco or cotton. From Europe they shipped industrial products back to Africa for sale there (see Figure 16.3).

While most people have at least heard of the slave trade, the far greater transportation of the indentured labour that succeeded it, after its nineteenth century abolition, is often forgotten. Unlike slavery, indentured labour involved the payment of wages, but in other respects it was little different, since workers were subject to enslaving contracts. Some 30 million indentured workers were transported from India to other British colonies, to work, for example, on sugar plantations in the Caribbean or to build railways in East Africa (Massey and Jess 1995: 12).

There was also an extensive migration of settlers from Europe to the 'new world', particularly during the nineteenth century (see Figure 16.4). Between 1815 and 1914 an estimated 60 million people left Europe for America, Africa, and Australasia combined (Hirst and Thompson 1996: 23). Between 1860 and 1920 an estimated 30 million

Figure 16.4 International migrations, 1820–1910

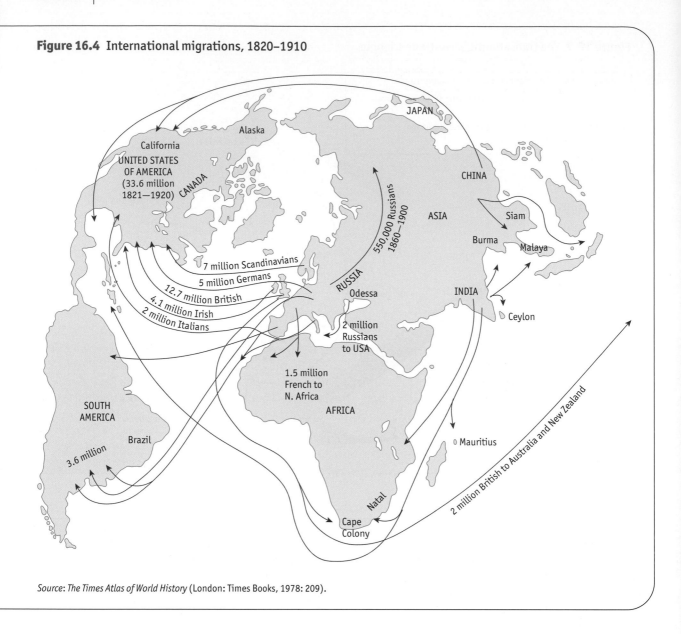

Source: *The Times Atlas of World History* (London: Times Books, 1978: 209).

emigrated from Europe to the United States alone (Castles and Miller 2003: 51).

This migration is often described as voluntary, to distinguish it from the forced migrations of African slaves and the coercive recruitment of indentured labour. There clearly was a difference, but the term 'voluntary' is more than a little misleading. The migration of nearly two million Irish people to the United States during the potato famine in the 1840s was hardly voluntary. How voluntary was the migration of the Jews persecuted in Eastern Europe? Some migrants were motivated by dreams of making their fortunes in the colonies or on the American frontier, but, for many, emigration was the only means of escaping from hunger, poverty, or death.

These international migrations created ethnically diverse societies stratified by ethnicity. In the United States, white Anglo-Saxon Protestants (WASPS) were dominant, other groups of European origin, such as Italians, Irish, and Poles, came below them, and the black descendants of African slaves were at the bottom. In many British colonial territories, Asians occupied an intermediate position between the British settlers and native populations. These hierarchies resulted from differences in power and wealth, but notions of superiority and inferiority were quickly attached to ethnicity. Stereotyping resulted in crude characterizations used to justify inequality. The ethnic stratification of these colonial societies was seen as reflecting in-born racial characteristics rather than resulting from power and wealth.

➔ *Connections*
We discuss race and ethnicity in Chapter 6, pp. 197–207, and stratification in Chapter 19, pp. 772–3. You may find it helpful to refer to these discussions while reading this section.

It was imperialism that led to the identification of race with skin colour. Europeans justified their rule over Africa and Asia by claiming the superiority of the white race over the black, brown, and yellow peoples of the world. As Malik (1996: 118) has put it, ' "the colour line" now became the chief way of understanding and dividing the world'.

With imperialism, race also became a matter of popular belief that helped to unify the class-divided societies of Europe. The British workers who had been treated as inferior by the upper class could now see themselves as members of a superior white race that ruled the world.

Imperial divisions

By the end of the nineteenth century, almost the whole world was divided up between the rival empires of the European states, the United States, and latterly Japan. Where they did not formally incorporate territories, they established competing spheres of influence, as in China.

Expansion overseas not only gave these countries new territory; it also consolidated them as nation states. The economic benefits of imperialism produced employment and higher wages, while those who were discontented or adventurous could emigrate to the colonies. Empire also provided a sense of national superiority that counteracted class divisions and strengthened popular identification with the nation. Hobsbawm (1987) has noted that the politicians of the time were well aware of the 'social benefits' of imperialism.

Unlike Wallerstein's world empires (see p. 629), these overseas empires were not complete world systems but parts of a *system* of nation states. The empires of Rome and China had been for a time contemporary civilizations, but they were isolated from each other and each had arguably established a 'world of its own'. The overseas empires of the nineteenth century had not established such worlds and were in constant competition, which drove them into wars with each other.

Industrial production, national railway systems, and bureaucratic administrations provided nation states with a new capacity for war. It was now possible to organize and mobilize whole populations and whole economies for 'total war'. A popular nationalism motivated and legitimated this mobilization, with an effectiveness that exceeded the expectations of governments. At the beginning of the First World War governments were surprised by the enthusiasm with which people plunged into a conflict that was to kill at least 20 million of them (Hobsbawm 1987).

Conflict between nation states had gone global. Periodic warfare between rival overseas empires had begun as soon as they acquired colonies, but the nineteenth-century division of the world brought about a more intense economic, political, and military competition between them. It also led to the construction of complex alliances stretching across the world, as in Britain's 1902–21 alliance with Japan to contain the expansion of Russia.

The First World War was still essentially a European war that drew in allies and colonies, but the Second World War between 1939 and 1945 was truly global in its scope. In Europe, German expansion resulted in something of a rerun of the First World War, while in Asia the expansion of the Japanese Empire collided with the imperial interests of Britain, France, the Netherlands, and the United States. The European and Pacific 'theatres' were linked by global alliances, which joined the United States to the Soviet Union, Britain, and France, and joined Japan to Germany and Italy.

Ideological divisions

The Cold War was a world war of a different kind. It was a war between rival socio-economic systems led by the Soviet Union and the United States. It started as the Second World War ended and lasted until the Soviet Union began to collapse at the end of the 1980s. The world was more divided into two blocs than ever before and countries that tried to remain neutral found themselves under heavy pressure to join one side or the other. Many were split by political struggles or civil wars between forces sponsored by the two sides.

The Cold War in some ways marked the end of the imperial stage of globalization. The European colonial empires collapsed, partly because the United States and the Soviet Union supported independence movements. There was also an ideological dimension to the Cold War conflict between 'capitalism' and 'socialism' that was absent from the earlier conflicts between the colonial empires.

There were, none the less, continuities with the imperial past, for the United States and the Soviet Union can be considered the last two empires. The United States continued to regard Latin America, the Caribbean, and the Pacific as its sphere of influence and took military action against Soviet attempts to penetrate them. Much of the Soviet Union was not ethnically Russian and consisted of countries conquered by the pre-revolutionary Russian Empire, while its 'allies' were controlled by military occupation.

The conflicts between nation states had led to the construction of empires that both integrated and divided the world. They integrated the world by bringing almost all peoples into a small number of political and military structures that stretched across the continents. They divided the world through the racial divisions they generated and the rivalries that led to world wars. The world was both more integrated *and* more divided than ever before.

Figure 16.5 Africa under European rule in 1913

Note: With the exception of Ethiopia and Liberia, the whole of Africa was divided up between the European empires by 1913.

Source: *The Times Atlas of World History* (London: Times Books, 1978).

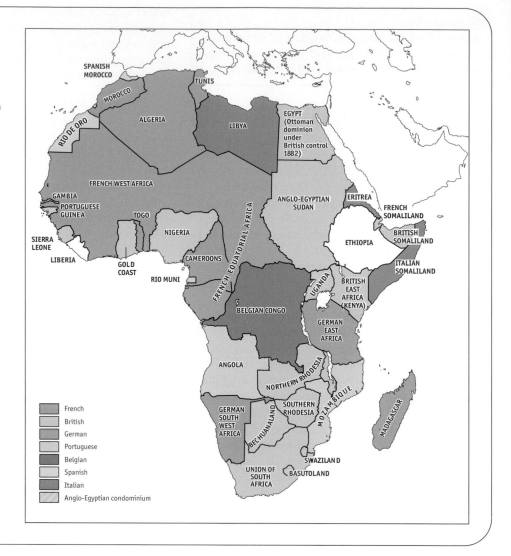

◆ *Stop and reflect*

In this section we first considered the development of nation states, the growth of a capitalist world economy, and the construction of overseas empires.

- Make sure that you are clear about the meaning of 'nation state', 'world empire', and 'capitalist world economy'.

- The ethnic components of nationality have long existed but it was in the nineteenth century that the modern nation state was constructed.

- A capitalist world economy originated in the fifteenth century and after industrialization an international division of labour was established.

- Most of the world was divided up between overseas empires. Should they be considered 'world empires'?

We have also been examining the early stages of globalization.

- Return to our definition of globalization on p. 624 and consider in what ways globalization occurred during the centuries covered by this section.

- It is often said that globalization integrates the world. In what ways did the world become more integrated and in what ways more divided during these centuries?

Development and globalization in post-colonial times

The European overseas empires collapsed after the Second World War, the Soviet Empire some forty years later. In this section we consider the problems of development faced by post-colonial nation states, going on to discuss the issues raised by population growth and urbanization. We then consider globalization in the post-colonial era and examine global movements of capital and people, and global challenges to the nation state. Lastly, we discuss whether we can be said to live in one world, taking up in this context environmental issues and world government.

New nation states

We begin by outlining the foundation of most of the world's nation states during the post-colonial era and considering the problems of development they have faced.

From empires to state nations

The overseas empires, which had appeared so permanent at the end of the nineteenth century, were self-destructive. The European states could not administer their huge colonial territories without involving and educating local people to do most of the work for them. Education brought local people into contact with the political movements and democratic institutions of the home countries. Nationalist movements calling for the same institutions to be established in the colonial territories inevitably emerged. The Second World War then weakened their control over their colonial territories.

After this war, world politics were dominated by the United States and the Soviet Union. The United States opposed colonialism and wanted the European empires opened up to its exports. The Soviet Union supported independence movements in the hope of establishing politically favourable regimes in the ex-colonial countries, which led the United States to sponsor rival movements. As for the Soviet Union, its economy was eventually unable to sustain the military expenditure required by the Cold War and its collapse brought the last of the European empires to an end.

As the empires collapsed new nation states were created. Between its foundation in 1945 and the end of the century the membership of the United Nations tripled from fifty to over 150. The ex-colonial nation states faced difficult political problems. They rarely corresponded to a people with a clear national identity. Their boundaries were determined by the way the empires had divided territory between them. They often included ethnically diverse peoples, with different languages, religions, and cultures. They had, therefore, to construct new nations within their state boundaries and for this reason have been called *state nations* rather than *nation states*.

The new state apparatus would often be dominated by one ethnic group at the expense of others, and subordinate ethnicities frequently found this situation intolerable. Military *coups*, civil wars, leading at times to genocide, became a feature of the newly independent states.

Aid or trade?

The new states faced the question of how they could catch up with the developed industrial societies. Would the rich countries of the West, which had exploited them for so long, assist them? According to modernization theory, which we examined earlier (see p. 621), economic growth would spread from rich to poor countries. Economic aid would help this process along.

More economic aid has often been seen as the solution to the continuing problems faced by the new states. The United Nations has called on rich countries to give 0.7 per cent of their gross national product annually as aid, though few have given as much as this (in 2005 the European Union's fifteen rich member states agreed that they would meet this target—by 2016). The G8 summit in 2005 and the Live-8 Concert focused on the provision of more aid to solve the problems of Africa. Arguably, the problem with economic aid is not, however, whether there is enough of it as whether it can actually do much to help poor countries.

The economic significance of aid is problematic. When it takes the form of a loan, debt repayments can become a huge burden. Debt cancellation has indeed become one of the main objectives of those seeking to help poor countries. Economic aid has often been misdirected into large and highly visible prestige projects, typically dams (see box on 'The biggest dam ever' on p. 636), or siphoned off into conspicuous consumption by the elite. Even if it is directed into projects likely to benefit the mass of the population, the country's infrastructure and institutions may not enable effective implementation.

Aid-giving countries also generally attach 'strings' to aid. It may be given on condition that it is spent on projects that benefit exporting companies in the donor country. Aid has often been steered politically to countries adopting

Briefing: the biggest dam ever

The Three Gorges dam in China, due to be completed in 2009, will create a reservoir stretching some 400 miles up the Yangtse. It is estimated to cost £15 billion and roughly a third of its costs are to be paid by the World Bank.

The dam will enable better control of the Yangtse, which periodically floods huge areas, drowning large numbers of people. It will also provide cheap hydroelectric power to meet rising industrial and consumer demand in a huge and rapidly developing country. It will displace an estimated 1.9 million people, who will be moved into 114 resettlement townships.

Environmental groups in China and abroad are very concerned about its multiple impacts on the environment. Large quantities of silt are expected to accumulate above the dam and there is the danger that, as happened with the Aswan dam in Egypt, this will be prevented from reaching the agricultural lands beyond in both China and other South-East Asian countries, which have historically been refertilized by periodic floods. It is also feared that the reservoir will accumulate pollution from the cities up-river, which contain a population of 31 million, and the areas flooded, which will include '1,300 local mines, 300,000 square metres of latrines, and 2.8 million tons of rubbish, as well as graveyards, abattoirs, medical centres and other potential hazards'.

Source: John Gittings, 'Industrial Waste Will Pour into China Dam', *Guardian*, 21 January 2002.

the 'right' political and ideological stance. Loans have been made conditional on governments pursuing 'correct' economic policies that may not be appropriate to their circumstances. The International Monetary Fund has notoriously made loans conditional on structural adjustment programmes that require governments to cut state expenditure, open themselves up to trade, and privatize state enterprises, actions which may not be in their national interests.

Trade is, anyway, more important than aid. Many poor countries are, for example, heavily dependent on the export of one product and the price of, say, bananas, or tea, or coffee is far more important to them than the amount of aid they receive. They also find that, although they have been forced to open their borders, the European Union, the United States, and Japan maintain their barriers, particularly to the import of agricultural goods, and subsidize their own exports. Aid and debt relief are generally easier

options for rich countries' politicians than the lifting of trade barriers, since this damages powerful economic interests. Indeed, dramatic declarations of increased aid can be used to divert attention from a failure to address the trade issue.

Aid can undoubtedly benefit countries stricken by disasters and specific projects may well be beneficial but it is doubtful whether aid leads to much economic development. Other aspects of the economic relationships between rich and poor countries are of much greater significance.

Development strategies

If development was to occur, it would depend largely on the efforts of the poor countries themselves. What strategy should they pursue? Industrialization seemed the best way to achieve economic growth. As we showed earlier, the international division of labour made non-industrial societies dependent on industrial ones, which suggested that the new states needed to industrialize if they were to achieve economic independence and raise standards of living.

But how was industrialization to be achieved? The strategy advocated in the 1950s and 1960s was *import substitution*, which involved the state setting up industries and protecting them against cheap imports from the industrial countries by erecting tariff barriers. This policy could rapidly establish new industries but these could then devour state resources and become out of date and inefficient in the absence of competition.

The emphasis shifted in the 1970s to the state promotion of *export* industry, for Japan had taken this approach and very successfully penetrated the markets of the West. A group of other countries, notably South Korea, Taiwan, Singapore, Brazil, and Mexico, which were labelled the newly industrializing countries (NICs), followed Japan along this path.

Ashton and Sung (1997) have, however, argued that education, rather than state direction, was the key to the rise of the East Asian tiger economies. In the case of Singapore, economic development resulted not from centrally directing investment but from providing conditions that attracted to Singapore companies that would produce high-value goods and services. These companies were given the skilled labour they needed by state policies designed to upgrade the skills of those entering the labour force.

Since the 1980s, increased global economic integration has shifted policy from the state direction of development

The 'Make Poverty History' demo at the 2005 G8 summit—can more aid do this?

© Getty Images/Nicolas Asfouri

to the provision of conditions that will attract foreign capital. This is partly a matter of the easier movement of capital but also to do with the greater speed and volume of the movement of goods, information, and people. The goods and services that result from investment can be more easily exported to rich countries.

The availability of cheap labour in poor countries is important in attracting capital but it is clearly not as simple as this. Following Ashton and Sung above, it is the availability of suitably educated labour that is crucial. In the Indian case, the availability of English-speaking labour has facilitated the outsourcing of call-centre jobs from Britain, while Bangalore became a major centre of software production because a labour force that was both English-speaking and highly educated was available.

The degree of state regulation, the extent of trade unionism, and the level of taxation are also important considerations. The growth of TNCs has led many countries to create Export Processing Zones, where foreign companies can operate freely with minimal constraints of regulation and taxation, and where unions may well be banned (see p. 648).

Since the 1980s the free movement of capital has been promoted by the American-dominated World Bank and International Monetary Fund (IMF). These important institutions have advocated free market policies as the route to development, making these policies a condition for the provision of aid. They called for fiscal austerity to reduce wasteful government spending and loose monetary policies that would cause inflation. They called for privatization to get rid of inefficient public enterprises, introduce market discipline and reduce government expenditure. Trade barriers should be lifted in order to increase trade. These policies reflected the 1980s dominance of neo-liberalism in the United States.

> ⟶ **Connections**
>
> Neo-liberalism comprises a crucial set of ideas about economic policy that have had a great impact on all areas of government policy. For an outline of these ideas see Chapter 15, pp. 601–2.

These policies have, however, attracted much criticism. Water privatization was advocated as a means of solving water shortages by bringing in investment but it has been heavily criticized for giving Western companies highly profitable monopolies at the expense of the poor, who find they have to pay high prices for their water. Stiglitz (2002), a senior figure at the World Bank between 1997 and 2000, has argued that although free market policies could bring benefits in some circumstances their indiscriminate and over-hasty imposition could be disastrous. Valuable state

projects could be destroyed. Mass unemployment could result. Assets could be plundered.

The contrast between the Russian and Chinese experiences is instructive here. After the collapse of state socialism, Russia followed IMF advice and the resultant 'shock therapy' led to mass poverty, while China's gradual and controlled transition 'entailed the largest reduction in poverty in history in such a short time span' (Stiglitz 2002: 181–2). China did not engage in mass privatization but allowed foreign capital to enter and private enterprises to emerge within the existing social order. The conditions were created that would encourage foreign capital to enter, in order to exploit China's huge market and reserves of cheap labour, but within a framework controlled by the state.

The focus in this section has been on industrial development but other areas of the economy should not be neglected. The growth of tourism has become very important to the economic development of some societies (see pp. 649–51). The economies of most of the new states are agricultural and it makes little sense to ignore agricultural development.

In agriculture, two different strategies can be found. One is to invest capital in large, modern units with economies of scale and the latest technology, which could produce for export markets. The technological advances of the 'green revolution', which invented new, more productive crop varieties, required this kind of unit. Countries such as Colombia, Mexico, and the Philippines went down this route. It could work well but only within fertile areas, leaving most of rural society with its productive potential untapped. Success tended to be short term, for these crops needed an ever greater use of expensive and environmentally damaging fertilizers and pesticides.

Some countries have tried to increase agricultural production within small-scale traditional units, sometimes combining this with land reform to break up large estates and return the land to those who worked it. Taiwan is commonly cited as an example of the success of this strategy. Cooperatives and community development projects have been set up in many countries to help traditional farmers raise production by pooling resources, acquiring modern technology, and improving organization. Results have, however, often been disappointing, largely it seems because inappropriate structures imposed by bureaucrats have alienated local people (Hulme and Turner 1990). A more flexible approach, of the kind advocated by the 'action perspective' (see p. 622), would give locals more involvement and more choice.

The search for an appropriate strategy is a difficult one. Particular strategies and specific models have been strongly advocated by their supporters but these generally fail to take account of the varying circumstances, institutions,

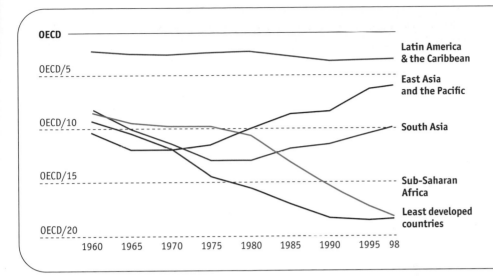

Figure 16.6
A comparison of the incomes of developing regions and high-income OECD countries, 1960–98

Regional average GDP per capita as a ratio of that of high-income OECD countries

Source: Human Development Report (2001: 16).

and cultures of poor countries. What works in South Korea will probably not work in Somalia. Top-down strategic thinking anyway often fails to take account of local diversity, or involve local people. Lastly, strategies are constrained by external forces, as the imposition of policy conditions by the World Bank and the IMF shows. If governments have no freedom of manoeuvre, no choice of strategy is possible.

International inequality

How successful have developing states been in closing the gap with developed countries? Figure 16.6 shows a strikingly divergent picture. In 1960 most developing regions had an average per capita income about one-tenth that of the rich countries (the OECD). The East Asian and Pacific region have reduced this gap and in 1998 had almost one-fifth the income of the rich countries. The relative gap between the rich countries and the sub-Saharan African and least developed countries has, however, widened considerably as their income has sunk to about one-eighteenth that of the OECD. Given this divergence it makes little sense to refer to all these countries as the Third World.

Figure 16.7 shows a similar picture emerging from changes in the broader Human Development Index, which combines data on life expectancy, education, and income. The rich countries have, on the whole, maintained their relative advantages, though East Asia and the Pacific have closed the gap to some degree, while sub-Saharan Africa has fallen further behind.

This divergence suggests that there is some truth in both the modernization and dependency perspectives discussed earlier on pp. 621–2. Development has diffused to some societies, though this has not been the automatic process envisaged by modernization theorists and has largely

resulted from the strategies pursued successfully by some states. In others development has been weak and they have remained highly dependent on the rich countries, reliant on primary product exports and, indeed, on aid. An adequate theory of development would have to incorporate something from both perspectives and, above all, take account of the diverse experiences of poor countries.

An over-populated world?

As they struggled to develop, poor countries found themselves faced with a rapid growth of population, much of which collected in large urban concentrations. In this section we examine population growth and then consider whether over-urbanization is taking place.

Over-population?

Population increase is basically a matter of there being more births than deaths, though migration may have some impact on population size when the population is small. The post-1945 population increase in poor countries was quite simply the result of rapidly falling death rates as the technology of disease control spread from the industrial countries. Malaria, for example, could be wiped out by spraying wet-lands with DDT.

Death rates had fallen in the industrial countries too but this had happened gradually over the previous century and was cancelled out by falling birth rates. Industrial countries had passed through a **demographic transition**, moving from one relatively stable state to another as they shifted from high birth and death rates to low birth and death rates (see Figure 16.8). In poor countries death rates fell very rapidly after the Second World War but birth rates remained very high. Thus in the mid-1950s birth rates in

Controversy and debate Poverty in Africa

Is Africa responsible for its poverty or are the developed countries to blame? In 2004 Tony Blair set up the Commission for Africa to investigate the reasons for African poverty and to recommend measures to reduce it. The seventeen-strong Commission consisted of political leaders, public servants, and private sector representatives. A majority were from African countries.

Sub-Saharan Africa as a whole has not only failed to develop, it has gone backwards since the 1970s, with GNP per capita actually lower in 2002 than in 1975. While average income in Sub-Saharan Africa was twice that of East Asia in 1975, by 2002 it had fallen below half that of East Asia. Average life expectancy has been falling since 1990 and in 2003 was only 46 years, as compared with 63 years in South Asia and 69 in East Asia (*Our Common Interest* (*OCI*): 102–5).

What are the causes of this situation? The Commission highlighted 'poor governance' as the main obstacle to development in Africa. Governments were often undemocratic, corrupt, and incompetent. Wars and other civil conflicts created and perpetuated poverty. These political problems, together with transport difficulties, deterred investment. Manufacturing had developed late and Africa was still heavily dependent on the export of primary products. Agriculture had been held back by lack of investment, transport problems, and trade barriers. Poor health and weaknesses in education contributed to stagnation. Debt was a huge burden, with Sub-Saharan Africa governments on average spending more on debt servicing than health.

The Commission concluded that 'internal factors have been the primary culprit for Africa's economic stagnation or decline' (*OCI*: 113) but recognized that Africa's relationship with the developed world was also important. Poor governance was partly a legacy of the colonial period and external business interests were complicit in corruption but 'governance is in large measure made at home' (*OCI*: 106).

What should be done? The most important task was to improve governance, since 'without progress in governance, all other reforms will have limited impact'. Developed countries could help with this but it is 'first and foremost the responsibility of African governments and people' (*OCI*: 14). Conflict should be tackled by building up the capacity of African states to prevent and manage conflict. More resources should be provided for health and education. Africa needed to produce more marketable goods, though rich countries' barriers to trade had to be removed.

How should these changes be resourced? Donor countries should immediately provide an extra $25 billion in aid per year, and a further $25 billion a year by 2015, and there should be 100 per cent debt cancellation.

How did developed countries respond? The leaders of the eight most developed promised an extra $50 billion in aid at the G8 meeting in Edinburgh in July 2005, though critics have claimed that much of this would not actually be 'new money'. The debts of eighteen countries, which had met certain conditions, such as trade liberalization and privatization, would be cancelled. Critics argued that these conditions would harm the countries concerned and far more countries needed to have their debts cancelled. On trade barriers there were fine words but no specific measures. The European Union has, however, promised reforms that would reduce barriers to the import of sugar.

Source: *Our Common Interest: Report of the Commission for Africa* (2005), available at: www.commissionforafrica.org/

❷ Do you think it is right to place the main responsibility for African poverty on African countries?

❷ Will increased aid solve the problem of African poverty?

❷ Can one generalize about Africa?

the industrial societies ranged between fifteen and twenty-five births per 1,000 people per year but in most poor countries they were between forty and fifty births per 1,000 (Hurd 1973: 70).

> ⮑ **Connections**
> We discuss the demographic transition in more detail in Chapter 8, pp. 286–9.

It is easy to see why death rates declined so rapidly in poor countries, but why did birth rates stay so high?

In the industrial societies birth rates had declined because people needed large families less and wanted smaller ones. With education becoming a longer and more compulsory process, children became less a source of additional income and more a cost. Family income would be maximized by women going out to work rather than having children. Also, pensions, state health care, and residential homes for the elderly meant that there was less need for children to provide support in old age.

In poor countries most of this did not apply. Much of the population was still engaged in agriculture and more children meant more farmhands. Child labour was and still

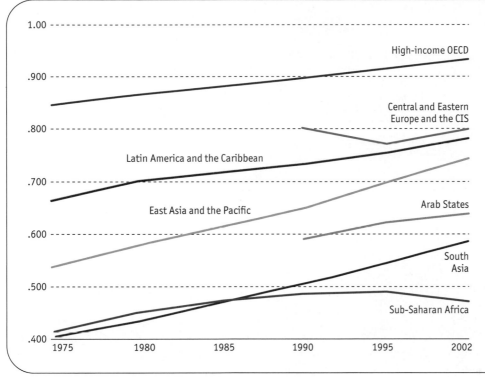

Figure 16.7 Global inequalities in human development, 1975–2002

Source: *Human Development Report* (2004: 134), available at www.undp.org.in/hdr2004/HDR2004_complt.pdf

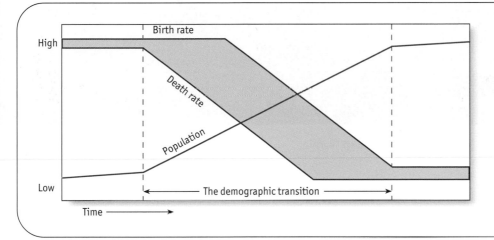

Figure 16.8 The demographic transition

➲ You might like to read our other discussion of the demographic transition in Chapter 8, pp. 286–9.

is common not only in agriculture but also in workshops and factories, while in the cities children make good beggars, thieves, and scavengers. A larger family means a larger income and, in societies where there is little state provision for the sick or old, more support in illness or old age.

By the 1960s there was a growing concern with a *population explosion*. Although having more children might be a rational strategy for the individual household, an increasing population had serious consequences for countries trying to develop. It led to higher unemployment and increased welfare expenditure, pressure on the land and over-urbanization. It resulted in growing poverty, which might lead to disorder. There was also much concern with the impact of rising populations on the environment.

If population increase was a serious problem, what was to be done about it? The first approach was to spread birth-control techniques through family-planning clinics and free contraception. Another has been to bribe or coerce people to limit their families. A coercive policy was particularly followed in China, where a one-child-per-family

A Cambodian girl goes through garbage looking for things to sell.
© Getty Images/Paula Bronstein

policy was adopted. In terms of results, this policy was highly successful and a birth rate of thirty-seven births per 1,000 people in 1952 was reduced to eighteen per 1,000 by 1979 (Hulme and Turner 1990: 125). This policy had, however, unacceptable consequences. The preference for boys led to the abandonment of girls in orphanages, where some were left unfed to die. The policy has been officially relaxed to allow those born since it was introduced to have two children, and to allow those in rural areas whose first child is a daughter to have another child.

Fears of an uncontrolled population explosion have, however, diminished somewhat. The United Nations has recently revised downwards its estimates of future population growth. According to its medium scenario, it expects world population to rise from 6.1 billion in 2000 to around nine billion in 2050 but to then stabilize at or below this level (United Nations 2004a: 2).

This reduction reflects remarkable evidence of falling fertility, which in many countries has fallen below the level at which the population is replaced. The replacement fertility rate is said to be 2.1 children per woman in countries where mortality is low. In the 1970s fertility in only twelve developed countries was below replacement level, but by the 1990s forty-one countries had dropped below this level. More surprisingly, while in the 1970s only one 'developing country' was below replacement level, by the 1990s nineteen were. In developing countries, average fertility levels had dropped from over 5.9 children per woman in the

1970s to about 3.9 children per woman in the 1990s (United Nations 2003*b*: xviii). Many poor countries are now going through the demographic transition, with later marriage, the spread of contraceptive techniques, smaller numbers of children, and increasing divorce rates.

There is also the impact on population of increased mortality, due to the return of apparently conquered but now resurgent diseases, such as malaria and tuberculosis, and the spread of AIDS. It is estimated that in 2025 the population of the thirty-eight most AIDS-affected countries in Africa will be at least 156 million lower than it would otherwise have been, due not only to AIDS deaths but also to the early deaths of women of reproductive age (United Nations 2003*a*: 28). Although AIDS will have a great impact on the population of some countries, such as Botswana, it is changes in fertility rather than mortality which are expected to be the main determinant of population growth.

Population growth may then be less of a problem than it was thought to be. There are, however, many variables operating here and the UN's various scenarios predict a range of outcomes for total world population in 2050, from 10.6 to 7.4 billion (United Nations 2004*a*: 4) and a far wider spread for dates further into the future. Even if the medium scenario is correct, its prediction of nine billion in 2050 would still mean that the world's population had increased more than threefold in one century.

Over-urbanization?

As with population growth, urbanization in poor countries is often considered out of control. League tables do certainly show that the cities of Asia, Africa, and Latin America are overtaking in size those of Europe and North America (see Figure 16.10). Terms such as 'mushrooming cities' or 'the urban explosion' are used.

The notion of over-urbanization is based partly on the idea that urbanization in the poor countries of Africa, Asia, and Latin America has been much faster than in the developed countries at a comparable stage in their development. The rate of urbanization in nineteenth-century Britain did not get much above 1 per cent a year, while annual rates in poor countries reached between 3 and 6 per cent during the period 1950–90.

It has been argued that cities in poor countries are *parasitic* rather than *generative*. They are said to drain resources from rural areas and contribute nothing to them, instead of creating economic growth, as cities are supposed to do. Urban elites have been criticized for leading unproductive lives, focused on the consumption of imported goods, and assisting foreign capital in the exploitation of their societies.

It is also argued that cities cannot cope with their increasing populations. Employment opportunities have

Figure 16.9 Fertility rates in selected countries

Country	Fertility rate
Argentina (2000)	2.5
Australia (2000)	1.7
Bangladesh (1997)	3.4
Botswana (2001)	5
China (2001)	1.4
Egypt (1999)	3.6
France (1999)	1.8
Ghana (1998)	5.6
India (1997)	3.3
Iran (2000)	2.2
Italy (2000)	1.2
Japan (2000)	1.3
Mexico (1996)	2.7
Nigeria (1997)	5.1
Peru (1998)	3
Saudi Arabia (1994)	6.1
Sweden (2001)	1.6
United Kingdom (2000)	1.6
United States (2000)	2.1
Venezuela (2000)	2.7

Source: United Nations (2003*b*).

➲ List countries above and below the replacement rate (see text for this).

❷ What patterns do you see emerging from this list and how would you explain it?

➲ Consider the implications of fertility rates for age distribution, labour force, and welfare.

❷ What do you think are the implications of this list for patterns of migration?

not kept pace and large numbers of people have been forced into the informal economy, which shades into such activities as begging, scavenging, and prostitution, in order to survive. Many of them have to live in shanty towns without decent housing or sanitation. Unmanageable concentrations of population have built up that cannot be provided with proper services and are a source of crime and disorder.

However, comparisons between the cities of rich and poor countries may well exaggerate the differences between them. Many cities in poor countries have grown larger by extending their boundaries, while some cities in the old industrial countries have retained old boundaries that no

Figure 16.10 The world's largest five cities, 1950–2015

1950		1990		2015 (projected)	
City	Population (m.)	City	Population (m.)	City	Population (m.)
1 New York	12.3	1 Tokyo	25	1 Tokyo	36.2
2 London	8.7	2 New York	16.1	2 Bombay	22.6
3 Tokyo	6.9	3 Mexico City	15.1	3 Delhi	20.9
4 Paris	5.4	4 São Paulo	14.8	4 Mexico City	20.6
5 Moscow	5.4	5 Shanghai	13.5	5 São Paulo	20.0

Sources: United Nations Population Fund (1996: 32–3); United Nations (2004*b*: 9).

Figure 16.11 Have poor countries become over-urbanized?

Aspects of urbanization	Yes	No
Rate of urbanization	Higher than in rich countries	Comparable rates at a similar stage
Size of cities	Larger than in rich countries	Differences in boundary definitions
Contribution to economy	Parasitic	Generative
Living conditions	Cities unable to provide decent living conditions	Living conditions better than rural areas

longer reflect their true size. Thus, London has kept administrative boundaries that give no real idea of its spread. Greater London in 1991 had a population of 6.4 million, which made it the twenty-third largest city in the world, but a definition in terms of its metropolitan region would have given it a population of 12.5 million, which would have made it the world's sixth largest (United Nations Centre for Human Settlements 1996: 17).

While the world as a whole is certainly becoming increasingly urban, poor countries are not predicted to

Briefing: the 'street-finders' and 'collectors' of nineteenth-century London

'These men, for by far the great majority are men, may be divided, according to the nature of their occupations, into three classes:

1 The bone-grubbers and rag-gatherers . . . the pure-finders, and the cigar-end and old wood collectors.

2 The dredgermen, the mud-larks, and the sewer-hunters.

3 The dustmen and nightmen, the sweeps and the scavengers.

The first class go abroad daily to *find* in the streets, and carry away with them such things as bones, rags, 'pure' (or dogs' dung), which no one appropriates. These they sell, and on that sale support a wretched life. The second class of people are also as strictly *finders*; but their industry, or rather their labour, is confined to the river, or to that subterranean city of sewerage unto which the Thames supplies the great outlets. . . . The third class is distinct from either of these, as the labourers comprised in it are not finders, but *collectors* or *removers* of the dirt and filth of our streets and houses, and of the soot of our chimneys.' (Mayhew 1861*a*: ii. 136)

❓ *Were conditions in nineteenth-century British cities much different from those in poor countries today?*

Overurbanization?—a shanty town in Ho Chi Minh City, Vietnam.
© Getty Images/Paul Chesley

have significantly higher urban populations than rich ones. In 2030 the population of Africa is predicted to be 53 per cent urban, of Asia 54 per cent, and of Latin America 85 per cent. These are certainly high figures but the population of Europe is predicted to be 80 per cent urban and North America 87 per cent (United Nations 2004*b*: 6).

The concept of 'over-urbanization' may also present too negative an image of city life in poor countries. There may be insufficient employment in the formal economy to absorb the population but migrants are drawn to cities because they offer better prospects than the areas the migrants come from. Conditions may be bad in the cities but they are worse elsewhere. The condemnation of apparently squalid shanty towns also neglects the success of community-based self-help initiatives in improving them and obtaining transport, water supplies, and electricity.

Flanagan (1993) has suggested that the differences between the cities of rich and poor countries have been exaggerated. Many cities in rich countries are afflicted by serious poverty and unemployment. Furthermore, in an increasingly globalized world all cities face problems generated by the dynamics of the international economy. He concluded that the study of the Third World city has been a separate field for too long and now needs to be integrated with the study of the cities of the developed world.

Global movements of capital

We showed in 'The emergence of a global economy', pp. 629–30, that global economic integration is nothing new but in recent years the transformation of communications has speeded up the process. In this section we examine the global movement of capital and in the next we consider movements of people. First, we must briefly outline the changes in communication that have made all this possible.

A shrinking world

In the nineteenth century, a revolution in communications 'shrank' the world as steam power transformed travel with railways and steamships. Air travel has now made it possible to reach most of the world within a day or so. Speed is certainly important, and the growing speed of travel is shown in Figure 16.2 on p. 624, but too much emphasis can be placed on this alone. The regularity and cheapness of transport are fundamental to global integration. It was the wide-bodied passenger jets introduced in the 1960s that made cheap mass travel possible. The container revolution of the 1970s enormously cheapened the transport of goods by sea and enabled a huge growth in the volume of trade.

It is not only travel that matters but also the communication of information. The invention of the telegraph in 1837 and the telephone in 1876 'destroyed distance' by separating communication from travel. As Giddens (1990: 141) has pointed out, the telephone made it possible to be in more intimate and private contact with someone on the other side of the globe than someone on the other side of the room.

The launching of geostationary satellites in the 1960s and 1970s further transformed communication. Satellites made global communication cheap and enabled the transmission of huge quantities of information and money, which now circulates mainly in an electronic form. Digital transmission has subsequently increased greatly the amount of information that can be sent.

Since the 1990s, the spread of the World Wide Web on the Internet has brought about another communications revolution, though different parts of the world are plugged very unequally into the global information network. The figures in the box on 'A digital divide?' show that Internet use is increasing fast in the less developed regions of the world but is still at a relatively low level there. There is also a 'digital divide' within countries, with Internet use concentrated among those who are educated, young, male, and live in cities.

Transnational corporations

Faster communication facilitated transnational economic organization through the **transnational corporation** (TNC). The key feature of the TNC is that it does not just *trade* across borders. International trading is as old as national frontiers. TNCs actually *produce* goods and services in more than one country. They first emerged in the nineteenth century, but it was the new economic conditions stemming from the collapse of empire and increasing international competition in the 1960s and 1970s that made them a dominant force in the world economy.

Increasing international competition and declining profits drove companies in the old industrial countries to set up operations in countries where labour costs were lower. Another strategy, typical of the vehicle industry, was to buy up or merge with competing companies in other countries. Transnational organization was also stimulated

New technology A digital divide?

The World Bank has questioned the need for the United Nations' campaign to increase access to technology. According to the World Bank, 'the digital divide is rapidly closing'. According to the World Summit for the Information Society, the 'divide is very much real and needs to be addressed' (BBC News, 25 February 2005). Have a look at the figures below and see what you think.

Figure 16.12 World Internet usage

World Regions	Usage growth 2000–5 (%)	Users as % of population
Africa	258	2
Asia	183	9
Europe	161	37
Middle East	312	8
North America	107	68
Latin America/Caribbean	277	12
Oceania/Australia	116	49
World as a whole	*160*	*15*

Source: Internet World Statistics (2005) at: **www.internetworldstats.com/**

by the erection of tariff barriers to protect domestic producers, as one way of forestalling this was to produce goods and services inside other countries. That is one of the main reasons why Japanese companies built factories in Europe.

Global corporations have also come to dominate agriculture. According to an ActionAid report, two companies, Chiquita and Dole, control half the world's trade in bananas. Dupont and Monsanto dominate two-thirds of the world seed market for maize. Three companies control 85 per cent of world tea production (ActionAid, *Power Hungry* 2004, www.actionaid.org). Vandana Shiva (2000) has argued that agriculture is increasingly dominated by 'life science' corporations, which cut across agribusiness, biotechnology, the chemical and pharmaceutical industries.

TNCs provide services as well as goods, and there are global hotel chains, global advertising agencies, global car rental companies. These global service corporations are sometimes seen as the camp followers of global manufacturers. Up to a point they are, but this is not the whole story. Hilton hotels do not just provide standard rooms for travelling American executives. They provide standard rooms for tourists too (see 'Global tourism', pp. 649–51).

There are also global superstores like the United States-based Wal-Mart, which in 2002 employed 300,000 workers outside the United States. Wal-Mart controls 40 per cent of Mexico's retail sector and has acquired the ASDA chain in Britain. Tesco has forty-eight stores in Thailand, where 36 per cent of all food sales are through TNCs (ActionAid, *Power Hungry* 2004: 13). In 2004 the B&Q do-it-yourself chain had eighteen stores in China and planned to have seventy-five by 2008 (*Sunday Times*, 30 May 2004).

While access to cheap labour and control of markets largely motivate the growth of TNCs, changes in culture and way of life are also very important. The global expansion of McDonald's was not just to provide burgers for American travellers, whether business executives or tourists. It more importantly provided a standard and fashionable fast food for local people. The popularity of McDonald's was largely a result of the globalization of the media, which has spread American culture and the consumption of American products world-wide. The growth of TNCs is linked to global changes in culture and living patterns as well as the economic advantages of production in other countries.

> **⊃ Connections**
> The globalization of the media is an important aspect of globalization. We discuss this, and the issue of Americanization, in Chapter 10, pp. 395–8.

TNCs pose a particular threat to the authority of the nation state, as they threaten its control over the economy. By shifting investment from one country to another they can move capital and employment between countries, and, as the opening piece of this chapter shows, TNCs can find ingenious ways of avoiding taxation. If they do not like a government, they can move their operations elsewhere or, at least, threaten to do so, putting pressure on states to act in ways that will maximize their profits. Arguably, we now live in a world where governments have to dance to the tune of the TNC and power has shifted from the nation state to the global corporation.

But are TNCs really independent of the nation state? Hirst and Thompson (1996) have claimed that very few TNCs are really transnational, as their main operations are always located in a particular country. Even if they do produce in many countries, they must have a national base where their headquarters and other central functions are located. They rely on national educational and financial institutions, and benefit from mutually supportive relationships with central and local government. TNCs are not at all averse to using the diplomatic and military power of their home country to advance their operations elsewhere. If they are still dependent on nation states, this means that national governments can exert some influence over them.

Dicken (2003) similarly argues that *transnational* corporations are at the same time *national* corporations. He is also sceptical of the commonly used term 'global corporation'. Some TNCs, such as Coca-Cola, or Hilton, or McDonalds, do have operations in most countries of the world, but most TNCs do not really have a global character and operate in a relatively small number of countries.

Furthermore, economic nationalism is far from dead, though the willingness of countries to open themselves up to foreign companies varies internationally. There is quite a contrast here between Britain and France. Rising energy prices led to much debate about the behaviour of European energy corporations. Tony Blair was happy to declare in March 2006 that 'the electricity in Number 10 Downing Street is supplied by a French company, the water by a German company. On gas, you've got a choice of four companies, three of which are non-British.' The French government was, however, concerned to keep energy supply in national hands and refused to allow an Italian company to take over Suez, the Franco-Belgian utility group (*Independent*, 27 March 2006).

The freedom and independence of the TNC should not then be exaggerated but equally it must be recognized that they have a considerable capacity to move production, employment, and profits across borders. They may depend on their nation state of origin, but they are much less dependent on the other states in which they operate. Governments certainly compete to attract investment by offering TNCs special grants and subsidies, and by adopting policies that provide a favourable context for TNC operations. While TNCs are rooted in particular countries, their transnational organization does give them some autonomy and considerable leverage on national governments.

A new international division of labour?

One of the main consequences of the growth of TNCs was the emergence of what Frobel *et al.* (1980) called a new international division of labour. According to the old international division of labour established in the nineteenth century, the industrial societies specialized in exporting manufactured goods, while Africa, Asia, and Latin America provided primary products. According to the new international division of labour, the industrial societies now export capital and expertise, while poor countries provide cheap labour for manufacturing.

One feature of this new international division of labour has been the creation of Export Processing Zones or Free Trade Zones. To attract capital, governments have cut taxes and allowed unregulated production in these zones, as the example of the Mexican *maquiladoras*, the local name

Briefing: export processing zones in Mexico

There are nearly 5,000 production units, known as *maquiladoras*, along Mexico's border with the United States. The number doubled after the North American Free Trade Agreement (NAFTA) treaty removed trade barriers between the two countries in 1994. A huge range of goods and services are produced in this area for export to the United States. Ciudad Juarez is called 'Little Detroit' because so many car components are produced there rather than in the United States.

The *maquiladoras* are owned by European and Asian, as well as American, companies. Production is cheap not only because of low wages but also because labour is weakly organized and work is unregulated. Attempts to form independent trade unions have been obstructed and crushed by the employers and the state. Mexican health and safety regulations are more or less the same as those of the United States but are not enforced. The availability of cheaper labour in China is, however, threatening to lure away companies that have invested in Mexico.

Source: 'Double Standards', *Multinational Monitor*, November 2000, 21: 11; International Trade Data System (2004) at www.itds.treas.gov/index.html

Figure 16.13 Changes in the international division of labour (IDOL)

Groups of societies	Old IDOL	New IDOL
Industrial societies	Manufactured goods	Capital and expertise
Rest of the world	Primary products	Cheap labour

for these zones, shows (see box on 'Export processing zones in Mexico').

The exploitation of cheap labour in poor countries has resulted in the increasing employment of women and children. TNCs prefer young women workers, for they can be paid less and are considered easier to control than male workers, and easier to dispose of by returning to the household if the employer needs to shed labour. Child labour has similar advantages and is widely exploited in many poor countries.

There is no doubt that capital has moved into poor countries to exploit cheap labour but the concept of a new international division of labour is in some respects misleading.

First, this new division of labour has not replaced the old one. Although the old industrial societies lost some manufacturing to the newly industrializing countries (NICs), they still have important exporting industries, such as, for example, the arms industry. Furthermore, poor countries are still heavily involved in producing food and raw materials for the rich countries. The old international division of labour lives on.

Secondly, much of the cheap labour carried out in poor countries involves little investment, if it is done in small workshops or at home. This applies particularly to international telework, which is spreading as companies based in rich countries seek to have their calls answered, their software written, or their data processed by cheap labour in poor countries. There may be little transfer of capital to the poor country where the goods or services are produced.

Thirdly, most transnational investment is between rich countries. Europe, Japan, and the United States, the main sources of international capital, have been directing most of their investment to each other. The share of global investment going to Africa and Latin America has actually fallen since the 1960s.

Fourthly, rich countries attract capital from poor countries. Thus, in the mid-1990s South Korean capital was drawn into Britain, particularly to Wales, where the closure of steelworks and coal mines had depressed wage levels. In 2005 a Chinese company bought up parts of MG Rover after this had gone bankrupt. Rich countries have courted this kind of investment with grants and loans.

Fifthly, most of the money moving between countries is not productively invested. There is a huge circulation of speculative money that moves between currencies, commodities, and shares, to exploit market changes.

The concept of a new international division of labour gives an oversimple picture of the movement of capital and the complex international relationships between capital and labour. It is, however, quite correct in drawing attention to the way in which cheap labour in poor countries has been drawn increasingly into the production of manufactured goods and services for rich countries.

Global movements of people

The literature on global economic integration has focused on the movement of capital, rather than the movement of people. One of the main features of globalization is, however, the greater movement of people across national borders. Here we examine two very different examples of this, global tourism and migratory labour.

Global tourism

International tourism has become one of the main activities in the global economy. In 2003 it represented 6 per cent of world-wide exports of goods and services. Its growth has been phenomenal, from 25 million international tourist arrivals in 1950 to an estimated 763 million in 2004 (World Tourism Organization, 'Tourism Highlights' 2005, www. world-tourism.org/facts/menu.html).

Global tourism is clearly a consequence of faster and cheaper international travel but it has also generated this itself, by increasing the demand for travel and opening up routes to new destinations, which have often acquired airports in order to receive tourists. Similarly, greater global awareness through media coverage has stimulated tourist interest in new holiday destinations, but tourist travel has also generated a demand for travel programmes on television, travel books, and information about far-off places. Global tourism results from globalization but also promotes it.

As with the circulation of money, the circulation of tourists is mainly between the rich countries of the world, between the United States, Europe, and Japan. The United States and European countries are the main earners from tourism and dominate the top ten positions in the earnings league table, though China comes seventh and Turkey eighth (World Tourism Organization 'Tourism Highlights' 2005). Tourism has, none the less, become very important to the economies of poor countries and is the main 'export' in many of them.

 Briefing: sex tourism

Sex tourism is one form of global tourism that has grown rapidly. It is another example of the exploitation of the cheap, unregulated labour in poor countries by people from rich ones. Tourists can engage in immoral or illegal activities more cheaply, more easily, and more safely than they can in their own countries. Prostitution in sex tourist destinations is largely organized by local entrepreneurs, though expatriates from the countries that supply the tourists can become involved. Major corporations based in the West also make profits from sex tourism, however. O'Connell Davidson has argued that 'the airlines which transport prostitute users half way around the globe and the hotels (many of which are owned by international conglomerates) in which they stay, as well as the travel agents which arrange their flights and accommodation, are probably the prime beneficiaries of sex tourism' (O'Connell Davidson 1998: 86).

Tourism can be seen as the spearhead of global capitalism. It can penetrate rapidly into areas of the world that have little capacity to produce goods or other services for the world market. Indeed, the most traditional societies attract tourists because of their traditionality. Their religious festivals, cultural objects, and way of life can suddenly acquire a monetary value. Tourism also creates paid labour in bar and hotel work, and prostitution. It generates a greater demand for food production and transport, and may well provide the basis for the local manufacturing of souvenirs. The earnings from tourism will increase the circulation of money and the import of manufactured goods, and establish new consumption patterns.

The question of who gains from tourism has been much discussed. Poor countries apparently gain a new economic activity that generates employment, encourages local businesses, and earns foreign currency. But how much of the benefit stays in the country concerned? Global tourism is organized by TNCs, which return most of the profits on tourism to the rich countries. Price competition between companies drives down the wages paid to locals, who may be expected to risk life and limb in dangerous but unregulated work. Agriculture may well suffer from a shortage of labour as people take up new jobs, while tourism may be seasonal and not support people through the year. Land and property prices may be pushed out of the reach of local people.

This leads to the wider issues of the cultural and environmental impact of tourism. Customs may lose their

Thai bar girls—global tourism can increase local employment but at what cost?

© AFP/Getty

authenticity when commercialized, though commercialization may at least keep them alive in some form. Hotel-building and the sheer weight of tourist numbers may damage the natural environment, though tourists may also provide an incentive to preserve vanishing species and maintain natural environments. Much depends on the kind of tourism involved. The rise of 'alternative tourism' and 'eco-tourism' may mean that a tourism more compatible with the preservation of the environment has become commercially viable.

Whether tourism benefits poor countries is a complex matter, which ultimately depends on value judgements, on the relative value attached to employment, the environment, culture, and so on. What can be said is that surveys

 ## Briefing: trekkers and porters

'Nepal's spectacular beauty draws 40,000 Britons a year, most of whom are unaware of the ugly underbelly of the trekking business.

A hundred thousand men are estimated to be carrying the industry on their backs. It is a measure of how little importance is attached to their welfare that there is no register of how many are working in areas known to be dangerous. They come, they go. Some never return. There was talk last year of a dozen bodies or more appearing after a sudden thaw at the Gokyo Pass in the Everest region: twenty porters are said to have died in the Makalu-Barun National Park in the past few years.

They die perhaps partly because of the convenient myth that they are supermen. Physically small, the prowess they display in lifting and carrying seemingly impossible loads never fails to impress the pampered Western tourist. . . .

Most porters risk life and limb for the equivalent of the price of a pint of a beer. When they pocket as little as £2 or £3 a day, buying their own weatherproof gear is simply not an option. . . .

Proper shelter, decent medical care in the event of an illness and, above all, adequate protective gear to face the extreme conditions—these are the sort of expenses trekking agencies could work into their overheads—but Deepak Thapa (a Nepalese journalist) is pessimistic about the chances of agencies putting their own house in order. He sees no political will to improve. Any change, he says, will be in response to foreign consumer pressure, when trekkers themselves insist on ethical treatment of porters before making a booking.'

Source: Sankha Guha, 'All the Risks, None of the Rewards', *Telegraph Travel*, 2 September 2000.

have indicated that ordinary people in poor societies take a positive view of tourism and say they want more of it (D. Harrison 1994).

Migration

Globalization has brought not only an international flow of tourists but also increasing numbers of migrants.

As we showed earlier (see pp. 631–2), there was an extensive international migration during the nineteenth century. This died down after 1914 but there was a new wave of international migration after 1945, as the growing economies of North America, north-west Europe, and Australia sucked in labour from both the peripheral countries of Europe and the colonial and ex-colonial territories of Africa and Asia. Since then migration has been less dominated by colonial relationships and has become increasingly global in character.

Stephen Castles and Mark Miller (2003: 7–9) have identified five main tendencies in recent patterns of migration:

- The 'globalization of migration' as more and more countries have been affected by it at the same time;
- The 'acceleration of migration' as international movements of people increase;
- The 'differentiation of migration' as different types of migration, such as labour migration and refugee movements, develop;
- The 'feminization of migration' as the labour migration of women workers increases;
- The 'politicization of migration' as politics at all levels was increasingly affected by migration.

The increasing migration of women has been the focus of much interest (see Study 16 on p. 663). In rich countries the demand for female labour has been rising. Service occupations that typically employ women have expanded, as has paid domestic work. In the Gulf States, the growing employment of women in professional and managerial occupations led to the recruitment of Asian maids to do the housework, and this has happened in Hong Kong and London too. Female migrants have been drawn into prostitution and sex tourism, while there has also been a growing trade in 'mail-order' brides. Asia was their main source initially but more recently they have come from eastern Europe, after the collapse of the state socialist economies led to unemployment and poverty there.

Entry barriers rose in Europe during the 1970s, as unemployment increased, but in the 1980s worsening conditions in many poor countries increased the pressure to migrate. Rising populations, the failure of economic growth, famine, and war increasingly drove people in poor countries to seek entry to rich ones. Illegal immigration increased and this led to a general tightening of border and entry controls in the 1990s. Airlines, employers, educational institutions, and social security offices all became agents of entry control. Highly organized people trafficking developed as migrants tried to find ways around these controls.

Some employers have had an interest in employing illegal entrants and economies can become highly dependent upon them. In the United States, the 1986 Immigration Act introduced fines and imprisonment for employers hiring illegal migrants, but huge protests from agricultural and industrial interests followed, particularly in California and New Mexico, where there was also a widespread employment of illegal migrants in housework and gardening. Concessions were made and enforcement was ineffective. It was its very illegality that made Mexican and Central American labour so cheap, for illegals were extremely vulnerable and willing to work for very low wages, while their employers avoided having to make social-security payments (N. Harris 1995).

While it is mainly the poor who want to migrate, in the hope of a better life elsewhere, it is easy to buy your way into countries if you have wealth or, increasingly, skills. Thus, the United States Immigration Act of 1991 allowed the entry of up to 10,000 migrants willing to invest $1 million and create ten jobs within six months. Australia and Canada have operated similar schemes with lower requirements. Indeed, Harris argued that there is an international competition to attract wealthy immigrants, with one country trying to outbid another. This supports Bauman's contention that the significance of borders depends on whether you are rich or poor (see p. 626).

As host countries put up the barriers to migrants, the number of refugees and asylum seekers increased. This was partly because, by claiming asylum, migrants could circumvent immigration controls, but also because famine, wars, and oppression have forced so many more to leave their countries. The United Nations High Commission for Refugees (UNHCR) reports that the global number of 'persons of concern', which includes internally displaced people as well as refugees, rose from 15 million in 1990 to 19 million at the end of 2004 (UNHCR 2005).

It is often thought in Britain that these refugees overwhelmingly arrive on its particular shores. Applications for asylum did increase from 25,000 in 1990 to 103,000 in 2002. They were then, however, reduced to 30,500 in 2005, in part because of a halving in the total number of asylum seekers since 2001. The United Kingdom was the largest receiver of asylum seekers in Europe during 2001–5, but when the size of the domestic population is taken into account, it drops below Austria, Belgium, Ireland, Norway, Sweden, and Switzerland (UNHCR 2005).

Why did asylum seekers become such a big issue in Britain?

© Alice Chadwick

Immigration policy

Immigration policy is torn between contrasting views of immigrants as a threat and a resource. They are viewed as a threat by those concerned with the maintenance of a traditional national identity. In particular areas they are often considered a threat by those with whom they compete for jobs, housing, and local resources. At a time of growing labour shortage in Britain, immigrants have, however, provided cheap labour without which some sections of the economy would grind to a halt. Agriculture, construction, care and cleaning services, education, hotels and restaurants, medicine, and transport have all become dependent on immigrant labour. Furthermore, the failure of the domestic populations of Europe to reproduce themselves (see Figure 16.9 on p. 643), and the ageing of these populations, is worrying economists.

The identity issue has become particularly emotive. Defenders of traditional national identities have called for the restriction of an immigration which they see as threatening them. 'Traditional' identities are themselves, however, the product of past waves of immigration, while the composition of national populations has already become more diverse with the increased migration of recent times. Castles and Miller (2003) suggest that ideas of national identity have to come to terms with greater diversity. As they put it:

> all countries . . . are going to have to reexamine their understanding of what it means to belong to their societies. Monocultural and assimilationist models of national identity may no longer be adequate for the new situation. Immigrants may be able to make a special contribution to the development of new forms of identity. It is part of the migrant condition to develop multiple identities, which are linked to the cultures both of the homeland and of the country of origin. Such personal identities possess complex new transcultural elements. (Castles and Miller 2003: 289)

Faced with political turmoil on the immigration issue before the 2005 general election, the government proposed a five-year immigration and asylum strategy (Home Office 2005). This sought to limit permanent immigration further, while maintaining the flow of immigrant labour into areas of shortage. Its main proposals were:

- A four-tier points system for those applying to work or study in Britain;

- Only the highly skilled in tier one, such as doctors, engineers, finance and IT experts, allowed in without a job offer and a sponsor;

- Only those in tiers one and two (skilled workers in shortage areas, such as nurses and teachers) allowed to apply to stay in Britain;

- Small quotas for tier three low-skilled non-EU nationals in specific shortage areas and for fixed periods with a guarantee of departure;

- Tier one and two applications to stay allowed only after five rather than the current four years, and applicants required to pass language and UK knowledge tests, and to demonstrate that they can support themselves and their dependants;

- Ending of 'chain migration' which allowed dependents of those permitted to stay to bring in further dependants;

- Successful asylum seekers only to be given temporary leave to stay and expected to return home when it is safe;

- Tighter border controls and health checks, with finger printing of visa applicants;

- Crack-downs on people trafficking and the employment of illegal labour.

Controversy and debate Should Britain import nurses?

UK health care has become heavily dependent on nurses (and doctors) from overseas but every nurse who comes to Britain is one less in their country of origin. In order to stop the drain of nurses from countries that cannot afford to lose them, an NHS code of practice bans the recruitment of nurses and doctors from poor countries. Over 3,000 nurses from countries on this list were, however, registered in Britain during 2004–5. Of the 200 nurses trained in Swaziland during 2004–5, 150 came to Britain, at a time when the nurse shortage there was becoming acute because of the AIDS epidemic, which was also killing many nurses (300 during 2003–4). These nurses were recruited in Britain by private agencies and private-sector nursing homes, often working there for a short time but then entering the NHS.

Source: *Guardian*, 20 December 2005.

Challenges to the state

We argued in 'Globalization and the nation state' (see pp. 626–7) that a key issue raised by globalization is its consequences for the nation state. The global movements of capital and people that we have examined in the two sections above weaken the nation state's control over its economy and population. In this section we explore more direct challenges to the state's authority.

Global communication

The speed and volume of communication in today's world has challenged the nation state's capacity to control information. Any person with access to a mobile or a satellite dish can communicate information and images to anywhere in the world. Dissidents can easily transmit anti-government material across frontiers and terrorists can operate through global communication networks.

In some countries the state has responded by making the possession of a satellite dish illegal or regulating satellite channels, but such relatively crude attempts to prevent communication do not exhaust the state's counter-measures, for there has been a massive increase in the state's surveillance capacity. Indeed, in their attempts to control terrorism and drug trafficking, states rely now not on random searches at borders but on electronic intelligence-gathering operations. Satellite communications are routinely intercepted and checked by massive computers for the use of key words and names in e-mails and phone calls (see our discussion of surveillance in Chapter 14, pp. 572–3).

Furthermore, communications technology is at the service of the nation state as well as those who wish to undermine it. A modem or a satellite dish in every house can give people uncontrolled access to the Internet, but a television in every house can enable a government to flood the nation with its own account of events by manipulating the news. The idea put about by Internet enthusiasts that technology has taken the world into a new age of individual freedom should be treated with some caution.

Although communications technologies may have made it more difficult for national states to prevent people communicating information across borders, they have also greatly increased the state's opportunities for surveillance and manipulation.

Global social movements

Global communication has assisted the growth of trans-national movements. The 'new social movements' of feminism, the peace movement, and, above all, environ-mentalism, have become globally organized.

> ➔ *Connections*
> Our main discussion of social movements is in Chapter 20, pp. 847–51, and you may find it helpful to look this up as you read this section.

The new social movements challenge the authority of the nation state by appealing to universal values and human rights. They have used information and communication technology to create networks that extend across national boundaries and enable them to spread their messages and mobilize international opinion against the regimes, policies, and actions of particular states. They have attached themselves through non-governmental organizations (NGOs) to the United Nations and promoted their causes through its programmes and conferences. They have used the global media to generate publicity by staging spectacular dramas.

These movements both reflect and create a new aware-ness of the responsibility of individuals for the fate of the world. They show the sense of insecurity and risk, and the distrust of experts, which Ulrich Beck (1992) and Anthony

Giddens (1990) have examined in their analysis of 'risk society' (see Chapter 4, pp. 147–9). This changed way of viewing the problems of the world has resulted in political actions of a more individualized and more direct kind, such as:

- direct action against the destruction of the environment or harm to animals;
- consumer boycotts of environmentally harmful products or goods manufactured by child labour or exported by politically unacceptable regimes;
- personal conservation activities such as recycling or the purchase of forest to prevent its destruction.

'Green consumerism' has stimulated some travel companies to switch to eco-tourism (see pp. 649–50) and some stores to stock environmentally friendly 'green products'. Moves of this sort have, however, been viewed with some scepticism, for they can just mean relabelling existing products in order to cash in on the 'green market'. Yearley (1991) has suggested that companies make such changes to their products where they can do this easily and cheaply, to create a 'green' image and distract attention from other practices. Campaigners can, none the less, then draw attention to those practices that do not fit the image and press a company to justify itself. He concluded that 'on balance, green consumerism is likely to benefit the environment' (Yearley 1991: 100).

The growth and impact of the environmental movement has been quite dramatic. As environmental problems were almost by definition global in their scope, the environmental movement became globally organized. Through effective organization and lobbying, environmental NGOs acquired official recognition as legitimate participants in international policy-making, outnumbering national representatives by around seven to one at the 1992 Earth Summit (Yearley 1996). The movement has also achieved some spectacular successes in forcing governments to change their course of action, perhaps most notably in the French government's decision to call off its nuclear testing programme, after the publicity generated by environmentalist attempts to halt the Pacific tests of 1995.

The strength of global movements can also, however, be their weakness. Their global network does put them beyond the reach of any individual nation state and enables them to mobilize international opinion against a particular government. They can therefore be very effective in stopping particular government actions but to have a long-term impact on policy they need to penetrate the structures of the decision-making and resource-controlling state and their network character here makes them less effective actors. What makes Greenpeace successful makes green political parties weak, and this applies also to their

Briefing: transnational Greenpeace

'It can hardly be denied that, in order to pursue its environmental concerns around the world, Greenpeace has developed into a form of transnational organization comparable in principle and in the global extent of its activities to some of the companies which it opposes. It draws expertise from different nation states and deploys technology according to its strategic plans. It has learned to lobby governments and to mobilize public support, taking advantage of the global media and the raised consciousness of a global movement.' (Spybey 1996: 146)

Figure 16.14 An anti-globalization chronology

- January 1994. Formation in Mexico of 'People's Global Action' (PGA), also known as 'Ya Basta', Spanish for 'enough is enough', in opposition to the North American Free Trade Agreement.
- May 1996. Occupation of a section of the M41 in West London by 'Reclaim the Streets', which goes on to organize protests, street parties, and other actions in cities across the world.
- June 1998. First J18 'Carnival Against Capitalism' in cities around the world.
- November 1999. 'Battle of Seattle' demonstration by 1,200 different NGOs at the meeting of the World Trade Organization.
- April 2000. Demonstration at a meeting of the International Monetary Fund and World Bank in Washington.
- May 2000. Mayday demonstration in London, leading to the biggest police containment operation for thirty years.
- April 2001. Disruption of the Summit of the Americas in Quebec.
- May 2001. Mayday demonstrations in London and other capitals.
- June 2001. World Bank's cancellation of a planned conference in Barcelona and substitution of an online conference in order to avoid demonstrations.
- June 2001. Demonstrations at the European Union Summit in Gothenburg, Sweden.
- July 2001. 'Battle of Genoa' where some 700 anti-globalization groups were contained by Italian police at a G8 summit meeting.
- September 11, 2001. Reaction to attack on World Trade Center in New York takes the steam out of anti-globalization demonstrations, at least for a while.
- June 2005. Demonstrations at the Edinburgh G8 meeting.

❷ Can you add further events to this list?

❷ Have these demonstrations had any effect on policies?

Drama at a demo at the G8 Summit in Edinburgh 2005—what impact have such demonstrations had?
© Getty Images/Carl de Souza

international activities. The environmental movement may be highly vocal but at international meetings it can be shut out of the negotiation of policy documents or treaties by the representatives of nation states.

During the 1990s sections of the environmentalist movement joined up with the descendants of older movements in anti-globalization and anti-capitalist demonstrations. These demonstrations brought together environmentalists, socialists, anarchists, and other campaigning groups in a common opposition to the activities of the World Trade Organization (WTO), the World Bank, the International Monetary Fund, and other such organizations. There is not really an anti-globalization movement as such but rather a network of disparate single-interest groups united only by their hostility to global capitalism. At the 'Battle for Seattle' in November 1999, the key event in their emergence on the global scene, and in subsequent demonstrations, the use of the Internet played a crucial role in mobilizing so many different groups in the same place at the same time.

These demonstrations have brought different groups together, generated an international solidarity of radical groups, and created publicity for their campaigns but such demonstrations have had little real impact on governments. After being ambushed at Seattle, state authorities have responded by sealing off demonstrations with their security forces, while the targeted organizations have explored alternative, more secure and more remote, venues for meetings. Arguably, one consequence of such demonstrations is a diversion of energy from campaigns on more specific issues where movements can more easily mobilize popular support and exert leverage on politicians.

Global terror

Nation states have found global terror much more difficult to deal with.

On 11 September 2001 two airliners under the control of Al-Qaeda hijackers slammed into the World Trade Center in New York, and demolished its twin towers. Another airliner crashed into the Pentagon and a fourth failed to reach its target and was brought down after passengers attacked the hijackers. Over 3,000 people were killed. This was neither the beginning nor the end of Al-Qaeda terrorism (see Figure 16.15) but its most dramatic manifestation so far.

Before '9/11' a number of analysts had already been arguing that a 'new terrorism' had come into existence (Martin 2004). Its main features were:

- organizational decentralization;
- operational asymmetry;
- religious centrality;
- weapons of mass destruction.

Through *organizational decentralization* terrorist organizations took the form of a network of relatively independent cells. There could still be an important degree of central coordination—at the time of 9/11, Al-Qaeda had a clear base with training camps in Afghanistan. This form of organization did, however, mean that cells could operate in different countries independently of each other with minimal central direction and sometimes only a loose connection with Al-Qaeda.

In a world where one country, the United States, was unassailably dominant, there was an *operational asymmetry* between the United States (and its allies) and its opponents. Since the military defeat of the United States is currently inconceivable, its opponents have recourse to unconventional and unexpected attacks that bypass national defences. This was a big change from the Cold War situation, where the relationship between the orthodox military machines of the United States and the USSR dominated international conflict.

There is a *religious centrality* to contemporary terrorism, as compared to the centrality of either left-wing ideologies or ethno-nationalism to the terrorism of the recent past.

Figure 16.15 A chronology of global 'Islamist' terror

Year	Country	Target	Method
1993	United States	World Trade Center, New York	Car bomb
1995	Saudi Arabia	US base at Riyadh	Bomb
1996	Saudi Arabia	US base on Gulf coast	Lorry bomb
1998	Kenya/Tanzania	US embassies	Lorry bombs
2000	Aden	US warship	Exploding dinghy
2001	United States	World Trade Center and Pentagon	Aircraft hijack
2002	Tunisia	Djerba synagogue	Lorry bomb
2002	Pakistan	Karachi bus carrying naval personnel	Suicide bomber
2002	Indonesia	Bali bars	Car bombs
2002	Kenya	Mombasa hotel used by Israeli tourists	Suicide bombers
2003	Saudi Arabia	Western compounds in Riyadh	Suicide bombers
2003	Morocco	US and Jewish targets in Casablanca	Suicide bombers
2003	Turkey	Istanbul synagogues	Suicide bombers
2003	Turkey	British embassy and HSBC bank, Istanbul	Suicide bombers
2004	Spain	Commuter trains in Madrid	Bombs
2005	United Kingdom	London underground trains and bus	Suicide bombers
2005	Egypt	Sharm al-Sheikh hotels	Suicide bombers

Note that this is a list of major 'successful' attacks only. Whether they should be described as 'Islamic' is a contentious matter. The terrorists see themselves as engaged in an Islamic *jihad* but other muslims have rejected the idea that such actions are in any way Islamic. We, for this reason, use the term 'Islamist' (see Chapter 11, p. 436). The degree of Al-Qaeda involvement is uncertain, since attacks are often carried out by relatively autonomous groups only loosely associated with it.

❷ Should the July 2005 bombings in London be described as Islamic terror?

❷ What is meant by the term 'terrorism'?

This does not mean that religion is the source of terrorism but rather that terrorists draw on religion to justify their actions. They see terrorism as a weapon in the absolute struggle between good and evil. This can lead to the commission of violent acts regardless of the consequences to the actor and the victims.

There is also a willingness to use *weapons of mass destruction*. Fuel-laden airliners, as in 9/11, can become such weapons. There are fears that biological, chemical, or radiological weapons may be used.

This new terrorism can reasonably be described as global. Terrorists have used global communications to construct a global network. At the time of 9/11, Al-Qaeda's main base and training camps were in Afghanistan but the attacks were planned by a cell in Germany and financed from Dubai. Immediately afterwards, suspected members of Al-Qaeda were arrested in Belgium, Britain, France, Germany, and Spain. The Al-Qaeda network has extended through the Middle East into Europe and Africa, central, eastern, and southern Asia. As the chronology of attacks (see Figure 16.15) shows, the targets of Al-Qaeda have been worldwide.

Terrorists also use the global communications network to publicize their attacks. The crashing of the planes into the World Trade Center (and the Pentagon), was a global terrorist drama. It was an attack on the well-known symbols of American capitalism and military domination in a media-saturated world, where there was instant transmission to all points of the globe. The audience was global and people everywhere could through live television feel that they were participating in the event. Osama bin-Laden's tapes and videos of terrorist acts have similarly been diffused rapidly across the world.

The events of 9/11 have stimulated state counter-measures. These have used the apparatus of the nation state to engage in what some consider to be 'state terror'. The 'war on terror' took a conventional form with the invasion and occupation of Afghanistan to destroy Al-Qaeda bases. The global character of the terror network has been combated through the tighter regulation and closer surveillance of the movement of people, money, and messages. Nation states across the world have flexed their muscles by introducing anti-terrorist laws that increased their powers, often at the cost of established civil rights.

In some respects these counter-measures may have been effective but continued attacks show that they have not stopped terrorism. Indeed, some counter-measures may have been counter-productive by increasing support for or providing greater opportunities for terrorism. Thus, the invasion of Iraq was claimed to be part of the war on terror but has arguably generated more terrorism. The problem for the nation state is, anyway, that the 'new terrorism' does not play according to the traditional rules of international conflict.

Al-Qaeda has also changed its *modus operandi* in response to the state's counter-measures. Awareness of electronic surveillance resulted in greater use of messengers. Instruction in the techniques of terrorism was carried out via the Web rather than training camps. The destruction of Al-Qaeda bases in Afghanistan resulted in its organizational dispersal into autonomous cells, which may have only very loose connections with it. As Jason Burke (2005) has put it, with reference to the July 2005 bombings on the London underground:

> . . . we need to face up to the simple truth that bin-Laden, al-Zawahiri *et al.* do not need to organize attacks directly. They merely need to wait for the message they have spread around the world to inspire others. Al-Qaida is now an idea, not an organization.

One world?

The global social movements discussed above have helped to bring about a growing awareness of the world as a whole but has this awareness been matched by the emergence of global political organization? In this section we examine Earth Summits and world government.

Saving the earth

Environmental issues are generally considered a key area for global political organization. Nuclear radiation and pollution do not recognize national boundaries. Deforestation in one country affects the climate of another. Rivers cross borders. The consequences of climate change due to global warming impact on all countries. Ulrich Beck (2000*a*) has argued that the environmental issue can be the basis of a new and vigorous global politics.

As we have seen, there has been an active and global environmentalist movement but has political organization developed far enough to regulate the environmental relationships between nation states? The United Nations has taken on the function of coordinating national responses to ecological issues. Its 1972 Stockholm Conference on the Human Environment was followed by the founding of its Environment Programme. 'Earth Summits' took place at Rio de Janeiro in 1992 and at Johannesburg in 2002.

Environmental politics have demonstrated not so much a common interest in 'saving the earth' as conflicts of interest between countries. One line of conflict is between rich countries' concerns with resource conservation and pollution control and poor countries' development goals. The poor have accused the rich, which are the world's main polluters and consumers of raw materials, of trying to solve the problems they have created by restricting the growth of other countries. The poor referred pointedly to what they call the 'pollution of poverty' and continued to build heavily polluting coal-fired power stations to meet their growing energy needs.

This conflict led to the compromise notion of **sustainable development**, which has come into widespread use as a way of reconciling environmental and developmental concerns, in principle at least (see box on 'Sustainable development'). While the goal of sustainable development has been adopted by particular environmentally concerned organizations, often for public relations purposes, there has been little implementation at national or international level.

Although the Earth Summits have achieved little, a broad agreement on the need for a binding treaty to contain global warming by limiting carbon dioxide emissions was reached in Kyoto in 1997. A further conference was held in Bonn in 2001, to try to resolve the problems left over from Kyoto. At Bonn 186 countries signed up to implement the Kyoto protocols and accepted mandatory targets for the reduction of carbon emissions.

Conflicts between heavy polluters and light polluters were partly resolved through 'carbon sinks' and 'carbon trading'. Polluters could offset pollution by claiming carbon credits from carbon sinks created by planting forests and from agricultural practices that absorb carbon. Carbon credits could also be traded, so heavy polluters could buy credits from elsewhere and those countries reducing emissions could benefit financially. Whether all this would

sufficiently reduce carbon emissions to have much effect on global warming is questionable, but clever and typically capitalist financial solutions had been found to overcome some of the international conflicts on this issue.

But not all, for while ratification by a sufficient number of countries eventually activated the treaty, important countries remained outside. The United States, the world's largest polluter, and Australia refused to ratify it, while rising polluters, the rapidly industrializing countries of China and India, were left outside. Those opposed to the treaty have argued that, on the one hand, it would have an unacceptable impact on their economies and, on the other, that it was anyway an ineffective way of reducing carbon emissions and would not work.

In 2005 these countries declared that they were forming a partnership to pursue an alternative and technological path that would reduce carbon emissions by developing and diffusing cleaner ways of producing energy. Targets and timetables for the reduction of emissions were, however, absent from the agreement between these countries. They have been accused of seeking to undermine Kyoto and of pursuing their economic interests at the expense of the environment. In spite of the Kyoto treaty, the world remains divided by national interests in its response to global warming.

Both the opposition to Kyoto and the reluctant implementation of it have been ascribed to the influence of business on government. This has been particularly the case in the United States, where politically powerful oil industry interests see their profits threatened by any moves to reduce oil consumption. Business is generally regarded as hostile to the increased state regulation and higher costs resulting from Kyoto-type policies. The Confederation of British Industry (CBI), the main organization of British business, has taken this line, while the Department of Trade and Industry has reportedly blocked environmental policies that might make British industry uncompetitive. Global capitalism would appear to make global environmental action very difficult.

In June 2006, however, the Aldersgate Group of prominent British business leaders called on the government to take action on climate change. A failure to engage with carbon reduction technology might result in companies losing out. There are many business interests that can benefit from investment in carbon-reduction technologies —carbon reduction may indeed be the growth industry of the future. Furthermore, international competitiveness may be lost if companies fail to keep pace with a growing consumer demand for environmentally sustainable products and services. Government action was necessary because it would be so much easier for companies to justify higher investment and increased costs if a regulatory pressure was coming from above. This suggests that the Kyoto

---

THEORY AND METHODS

Sustainable development

The most common and influential definition of sustainable development is the Brundtland Commission's 'development which meets the needs of the present without compromising the ability of future generations to meet their own needs' (Adams 1995: 355). More specifically, sustainable development recognizes the need for economic growth, but this must be growth that conserves natural resources, maintains the productivity of the land, and protects genetic diversity. This concept should not be confused with President Bush's notion of 'sustainable economic growth', which takes the opposite position of arguing that unless economic growth is maintained, there will be no resources available for conservation.

❷ Is development generated by global tourism an example of sustainable development (see our discussion of this on p. 650)?

❷ Do you know of any examples of sustainable development taking place in your part of the world?

route and the technological route should not be seen as alternatives.

World government?

The United Nations was founded in 1945 as a forum for the discussion of international issues and the settlement of international disputes. The UN Charter also recognized universal human rights which transcended the sovereignty of the nation state. International law was no longer confined to agreements between nation states but was seen as expressing the 'will of the international community' (Held 1992: 84–6). The United Nations was, indeed, seen by some as an embryonic 'world government' that would eventually supersede the nation state.

The UN's activities were constrained during the Cold War by superpower polarization, for the conflict between the United States and the Soviet Union dominated world politics. After the collapse of the Soviet Union at the end of the 1980s it was declared that there would be a 'New World Order', in which the UN would assume a much more important role. The UN intervened in Iraq, Bosnia, and Somalia and there was increasing reference to 'human rights' as a justification for intervention. Interventionism was also stimulated by the huge increase in the number of NGOs attached to the UN, for these could act more flexibly and independently, with less regard for international protocol (Kegley and Wittkopf 1999: 146–7).

It may be more accurate, however, to refer to a 'new world disorder'. The collapse of the Soviet Union created many new nation states, some of which were weak and divided, out of its territory. It has also been argued that the end of the Cold War has resulted in the re-emergence of old conflicts between civilizations, though this notion has been strongly criticized (see box on 'Civilizations in conflict').

In reality, the post-Soviet world has been dominated by the United States rather than the United Nations. UN interventions have generally been dependent on the agreement and resources of the United States. American domination has been more evident than ever since 9/11 and the declaration of a 'war on terror'. The UN has condemned terrorism, passed resolutions against it, and adopted anti-terrorist conventions and treaties, but it was the United States and its allies that took action. International action means in practice action determined and carried out by the most powerful nation states. The invasion of Iraq in 2003 was a case in point.

It is important to remember that the UN is an *international* rather than a *transnational* organization. As we argued earlier (see p. 624), international organizations are importantly different in character from transnational ones. Transnational organizations cut across nation states and threaten their authority but international ones are controlled by nation states and have to act through them.

When the UN sends a military force into a country, this force is composed of units from national armies, which remain largely under the control of their respective nation states. The UN is entirely dependent for its resources on contributions from these states, which they are often slow to provide and may withhold.

Thus, the nation state does not seem to have lost much of its authority or sovereignty to global political organization. Furthermore, the UN charter affirmed not only universal human rights but also the principle of the sovereignty of the nation state (Held 1992). New nation states have eagerly sought membership for this very reason. Acceptance into this body strengthens them, by giving them recognition, legitimacy, a voice in international affairs, and some protection against attack by other states.

European Union

Between the global and national levels of organization lies the regional level, where, in the case of the European Union, political integration has gone much further than it has at a global level.

States have certainly lost some of their law-making and judicial powers to European bodies. European Union legislation is initiated by the European Commission, while in some matters European law and European courts take precedence over national law and national courts. Closer economic union through the adoption of the Euro constrains the economic policies of national governments by, for example, removing their power to set interest rates. Some policies, as in agriculture and fishing, have long been determined within European institutions.

European unification has also diminished national control of frontiers. Control over borders has always been a key issue in nation states, for their territorial integrity and policy implementation depend on the existence of frontiers. One of the features of European integration has been the weakening of border controls within the European Union, and, over much of its area, their virtual disappearance. A key issue at the moment is whether the control of immigration will remain at a national level or become the responsibility of the European Union.

European integration has threatened the integrity of nation states in another way, as subnationalisms can bypass national capitals by making their own links with Brussels. Loss of sovereignty downwards through devolution combines with loss of sovereignty upwards to European institutions to diminish the nation state.

Nation states have not, however, been superseded by the European Union, because they are centrally involved in the making of European law. National leaders negotiate and decide policy through the Council of Ministers, the most powerful body in the European Union. Furthermore, the Presidency and other positions in the European

Frontiers Civilizations in conflict

In a much-quoted article, Samuel Huntington (1993) argued that after the end of the Cold War world politics would be dominated by conflicts between civilizations. His main arguments are:

1 The ideological divisions of the Cold War have given way to an older and more fundamental division of the world between civilizations.

2 Civilizations are basic cultural entities defined by differences of language, history, religion, customs, and identity. Huntington lists seven or eight main civilizations—Western, Confucian, Japanese, Islamic, Hindu, Slavic-Orthodox, Latin American, and possibly African.

3 Globalization intensifies conflicts between civilizations because it increases the interaction between peoples from different civilizations, making them more aware of these differences and of what they have in common with other members of their own civilization.

4 Economic and social change results in the decline of local and national identities, leading people to identify increasingly with their religions, which are central to differences between civilizations.

5 Conflicts of culture are less easily resolved than political and economic conflicts through compromise, polarizing people into 'us and them' distinctions.

6 Conflicts of civilization can occur both between communities and between states, taking the form of both ethnic cleansing and war between states.

7 One particular 'fault line' of conflict, that between the Western and Islamic worlds, has existed for 1,300 years, has recently intensified, and is seen by both sides as a conflict of civilizations.

This approach seems to resonate with recent world events but it is open to considerable criticism:

1 Huntington's civilizations are units that are very different in character, including a nation state (Japan), religions (Islam), regions (Latin America), and a vague grouping of countries (the West).

2 Civilizations are not distinct units and borrow extensively from each other, as when medieval Christian Europe acquired scientific knowledge from the Islamic world.

3 Identities are complex and there are many bases of identity other than civilization, such as class, gender, nationality, community, and ethnicity, which become salient in different situations.

4 Increased interaction between people of different cultures may lead to conflict but may also lead to multicultural tolerance and hybridization, when people combine elements and construct new cultures and identities (we discuss hybridization in Chapter 6, pp. 223–50).

5 There are great variations and divisions within the civilizational units identified by Huntington, such as the division within Islam between its Sunni and Shi'a branches or the conflicts between Catholics and Protestants in Northern Ireland.

6 The expansion of the European Union may well bring countries from the Western, Islamic, and Slavic-Orthodox 'civilizations' within one political organization.

7 Civilizations are not entities but ideological constructs used by political and religious leaders to manipulate people and to justify their policies and actions.

→ Taking account of these criticisms, consider whether the events of 9/11 and its aftermath (see section on 'Global terror') can be explained in terms of a conflict of civilizations.

Commission rotate between countries. Although each state has lost some autonomy, it has also gained some new influence over other countries.

Nation states also implement European laws and policies. While the European Commission supervises and monitors the application of European laws and treaties, they are implemented by national administrations. There is not as yet a European police force or a European army, though both are on the agenda. Thus the institutions of the European Union can act only through the apparatuses of the nation states that make it up, which leads to a highly variable implementation of laws and treaties.

> ### → Connections
> This section raises a number of issues related to the definition and development of the state, which we discuss in Chapter 15, pp. 580–1.

The European Union has experienced a massive enlargement that increased its size from fifteen countries to twenty-five, and other countries are waiting in the wings. This raises in acute form the issue of the relationship between individual nation states and the Union. Federalists argue that the European Union will only be able to function

Figure 16.16 Is the nation state in decline?

Areas of change	Arguments for decline	Arguments against
Advances in communications	Loss of control over borders	Increased surveillance and manipulation of people
Transnational organization	Rise of the TNC	TNC dependence on state
Global social movements	State policies challenged	Movements ignored and resisted by state
Terrorism	Vulnerability of state to the 'new terrorism'	Development of counter-terrorist state
International government	Authority lost to international bodies	State involvement in international regulation
Identity	Revival of subnationalisms and ethnic diversity	Creation of new nations

if there is further centralization to combat national fragmentation. Given the problem of arriving at a consensus among such a large number of members, majority decisions have been proposed. Nationalists argue that greater national diversity within the European Union must be recognized and more must be left to the nation state to decide. In 2005, the rejections by some states of the proposed European constitution suggest that any further centralization and further erosion of the remaining autonomy of European nation states are unlikely.

A global society?

Some have argued that globalization is leading to a global society. Anthony Giddens (1999) has suggested that we already live in such a society. While there is no denying that a process of globalization has been taking place and that this has generated a global level of organization and a new global consciousness, this section has shown that the nation state has not been superseded. We can no longer say simply that we live in national societies but it makes no sense to conclude that we now live *instead* in a global society. We must make room too for the existence of distinct regional groupings, such as the European Union, which lie between the national and the global. The persistence of the subnational communities that we examine in Chapter 13 (see pp. 515–20) should also be put into the picture.

As the range of social relationships expands and new larger-scale units emerge, lower-level ones do not disappear but persist in a changed form and interact with higher level ones. Society is neither national nor global but multi-level in character, with communal, national, regional, and global levels of organization.

 *Stop and reflect*

We began this part of the chapter by examining the collapse of global empires and the creation of most of the world's current nation states. We then examined the problems of development faced by these states and the strategies they adopted.

- Many have called for more economic aid to be given by rich countries to poor ones. Will more aid enable them to catch up?
- Increasing population has been seen as one of the main problems faced by poor countries. Has this problem been exaggerated?
- Cities in poor countries have grown rapidly. Should they be described as over-urbanized?
- What do you think is the main problem faced by poor countries in achieving improved standards of living?

We moved on to consider global movements of capital and labour.

- Communications technology has enabled the greater and faster movement of both capital and labour.
- The growth of transnational corporations has facilitated the movement of capital between countries.
- Are such corporations truly transnational?
- Globalization has resulted in greater movements of people, through both tourism and labour migration.
- In what sense is global tourism the 'spearhead of global capitalism'?
- Is labour migration a threat to the nation state?

We have in various places examined topics that involve the impact of globalization on the nation state.

- Go back to the earlier section on 'Globalization and the nation state' and make sure that you understand the positions outlined there.

- The nation state has been challenged by the global movement of information, money, and people, and the growth of global organizations.

- Consider the implications of Jason Burke's characterization of Al-Qaeda as 'now an idea rather than an organization'.

- Should the United Nations be considered potentially a 'world government'?

- How meaningful is the notion that we live on 'one earth'?

- Do you think that we now live in a global society?

 # *Chapter summary*

In the 'Understanding globalization' part of this chapter we examined the concepts of the nation state, development, and globalization, and discussed the issues they raised.

- Nation states are based on the principle that those who live within a defined territory are national citizens but states do not always overlap with people's sense of nationality.

- Modernization and dependency theory provide contrasting approaches to development but do not take sufficient account of local initiative and local diversity.

- Globalization involves a number of interrelated processes:
  - the destruction of distance;
  - the stretching of organizations and relationships beyond national frontiers;
  - a growing awareness of the world as a single place;
  - the increasing interdependence of different parts of the world.

- Although some claim that globalization is weakening the nation state, others argue that it will remain the basic unit of international life.

In 'Empires in a global economy', we outlined the development of nation states, the growth of a world economy, and the early stages of globalization.

- Although the ethnic components of nationality had long existed, it was not until the nineteenth century that the modern nation state was constructed.

- A capitalist world economy emerged in a politically divided Europe and then expanded to include the world as a whole.

- Nineteenth-century industrialization brought about an international division of labour that created a global interdependence between countries but led to a growing international inequality.

- While the world became more integrated through globalization, it also became more divided by racial and imperial divisions.

- The Cold War between the American and Soviet empires brought the imperial stage of globalization to an end.

In 'Development and globalization in post-colonial times', we discussed the problems faced by new nation states, the impact of globalization on them, and a range of linked issues.

The new nation states that emerged from the collapse of overseas empires faced considerable problems of development.

- Aid from developed countries has been a mixed blessing and outweighed by their trading problems.

- Various development strategies have been tried, though choice of strategy has been constrained by international financial bodies.

- The economic gap between the richest and poorest countries has continued to increase.

- Although declining death rates and continued high birth rates led to rising populations, many poor countries are now going through the 'demographic transition'.

- One consequence of rising population has been the rapid growth of cities and arguably, though disputably, to over-urbanization.

New forms of global economic integration and global organization have emerged:

- The development of communications increased not only the flow of information around the world but also the flow of money.

- Increasing international competition stimulated the growth of transnational corporations.

- According to the new international division of labour, industrial societies provide capital and expertise, while the rest of the world supplies cheap labour.

- As well as a greater movement of capital around the world, there is also a greater movement of people through global tourism and international migration.

- Since the 1970s, host countries have been torn between a concern to restrict immigration and a need to import labour.

- The nation state's authority has been challenged by the global communication of information, globally organized social movements, and globally organized terror.

- There is little sign of effective global political organization to protect the environment from global warming.

- New levels of organization have emerged with the founding of the United Nations and the growth of the European Union, but these are international, not transnational, organizations.

- The continued importance of national, and the growth of regional, organization undermine the notion of a 'global society'.

 ## *Key concepts*

- action approach
- demographic transition
- dependency theory
- development
- globalization
- glocalization

- modernization theory
- nation
- nationalism
- nation state
- slavery
- sustainable development

- Third World
- transnational corporation
- underdevelopment
- world economy
- world empire
- world system

Workshop 16

 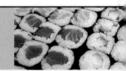

Study 16 Global women

Care, housework, and sex work for people in rich countries are increasingly done by women from poor countries. *Global Woman* (2003), edited by Barbara Ehrenreich and Arlie Russell Hochschild, explores the issues that this raises in a wide-ranging collection of pieces.

In rich countries, women's employment in paid work has grown enormously and this has diminished their capacity to carry out unpaid domestic and caring work in the household. This gap has been filled through the employment of other women, whether as au pairs, maids, or nannies. A globalization of women's work has occurred in two ways, for women in professional and managerial work have found themselves increasingly required to travel around the world, while the cheapest source of domestic labour has been migratory labour from poor countries. Poverty is not the sole reason, however, for women seeking employment in rich countries, since many migrants come from better off backgrounds and are seeking to escape the confinements of home life in their own countries.

Ehrenreich and Hochschild point out that all this is not simply a result of women's employment. In many rich countries, it is the state's failure to provide adequate child care to support women drawn into the labour force that has forced households to buy the services of other women. Furthermore, in rich countries men, many of whom have lost employment, have not been willing to fill the gap. As Ehrenreich and Hochschild (2003: 9) have put it: 'So, strictly speaking, the presence of immigrant nannies does not enable affluent women to enter the workforce; it enables affluent *men* to continue avoiding the second shift.'

Men are also responsible for the importation of women to do sex work and as sexual partners. This can reflect Western male conceptions of oriental women as exotic or as still having those traditional feminine virtues that are disappearing in the West. Many sex workers do not migrate voluntarily but are coerced by men and trafficked by them into prostitution.

Ehrenreich and Hochschild claim that the migration of women throws new light on the globalization process. Although poor countries have generally been treated as dependent on rich countries, these have now become dependent on poor country services. In their words:

The First World takes on a role like that of the old-fashioned male in the family—pampered, entitled, unable to cook, clean, or find his socks. Poor countries take on a role like that of the traditional woman within the family—patient, nurturing and self-denying. A division of labour critiqued when it was 'local' has now, metaphorically speaking, gone global. (Ehrenreich and Hochschild 2003: 11–12)

This is not only a transfer of labour from poor countries to rich countries but, as Hochschild suggests, a transfer of 'emotional resources' (2003: 26). Migrant nannies substitute the children of their employers for their own children, providing love for the former at the cost of depriving the latter.

In 'maid to order', Ehrenreich examines the increasingly commercialized 'cleaning-service chains' that employ migrant women and have turned the household into a capitalist workplace. She calls for this hidden work, and the relationships of exploitation involved in it, to be made visible.

'The feminists of my generation tried to bring some of it into the light of day, but, like busy professional women fleeing the house in the morning, they left the project unfinished, the debate broken off in mid-sentence, the noble intentions unfulfilled. Sooner or later, someone else will have to finish the job' (Ehrenreich and Hochschild 2003: 103).

See Chapter 12, pp. 476–8 for a discussion of the domestic division of labour, and Chapter 17, pp. 705–7 for the growing employment of women.

⮕ Look at the Frontiers box on p. 625 and see if you can link Study 16 to Beck's ideas.

⮕ Consider the implications of Study 16 for dependency theory (see p. 622) and the international division of labour (see p. 630).

❷ Does the globalization of women's work weaken or strengthen patriarchy?

Media watch 16 Galapagos tourism

We showed in this chapter that one aspect of globalization is the growth of global tourism. This has made an important contribution to the economic development of poor countries but at the same time can distort their economies and damage the environment. 'Eco-tourism' and 'sustainable tourism' seek to reconcile the conflicting imperatives of economic growth and conservation.

The Galapagos islands are off the Pacific coast of Ecuador and contain many intriguing plant, animal, and bird species found nowhere else in the world. Charles Darwin visited the islands in 1835 and his observations of the different finch species found there played an important role in developing his theory of evolution. These special features of the Galapagos have made them a major tourist destination.

Ecuador has tried to reap the economic benefits of tourism while controlling its impact on a fragile environment, which is, after all, the only reason for the tourist trade. The government encouraged the growth of tourism but in 1987 limited the annual entry of tourists to 25,000 in order to protect the environment. In 2004 some 110,000 tourists were, however, allowed to enter, each paying an entry fee of $100 and in other ways boosting the national economy. Increased numbers of tourists have put pressure on the environment through incursions into protected areas, the consumption of local products, the generation of waste and pollution, the stimulation of local souvenir industries, and the rising population that provides services and goods for tourists.

Human habitation is restricted to 3 per cent of the land area and 90 per cent of it has National Park status. There is also a marine reserve where fishing is restricted. The population of the Galapagos has, none the less, risen from around 6,000 in 1990 to 22,000 in 2004 and may be much higher due to illegal immigration. People are employed not only in the tourist trade but also in the fishing industry, supplying, for example, shark fins to East Asia, and conflicts have emerged between tourism's interest in conservation and the fishing industry's demands for greater access to marine stocks. Attempts have been made to create alternative employment in conservation work.

The Ecuador government has come under pressure from international bodies to protect the Galapagos from further damage to the environment but Ecuadorean politics make this difficult. A reportedly weak president has undermined the management of the National Park by distributing jobs there to political allies and is said to be dependent on support from a local politician linked to fishing interests. Recent reports suggest that conflicts between local interests are running out of control.

Source: A. Gumbel, 'Paradise lost', *Independent*, 18 April 2005.

⮕ A case study of the Galapagos and other similar situations can be found in the Trade and Environment Database's online journal at: www.american.edu/TED/class/all.htm

⮕ In the light of this case, and any others you can find, consider whether tourism preserves or destroys the environment.

❷ Is eco-tourism a contradiction in terms?

❷ Is the economic development of poor countries compatible with protection of the environment (see pp. 657–9 of this chapter)?

Discussion points

Globalization and integration

- Has globalization integrated the world?
- Read 'What is globalization?' and make sure that you know what this term means.
- Read 'Empires in a global economy' and list the ways in which the world became more integrated and more divided during the centuries covered by this section.
- Read 'One world?' and 'A global society?', and consider whether we now live in one world-wide society.

Making poverty history

'Make poverty history' became the slogan of the 2005 movement to put pressure on the rich countries to do more for poor countries. You can easily find out more about this movement by browsing the Net.

Read 'Theories of development' and 'International inequality'. How do the theories account for international inequality? Has development reduced it?

- Look at the box on 'Poverty in Africa' on p. 640. How did the Africa Commission explain poverty in Africa? Do you think this explanation is right?
- Can the Make Poverty History campaign do anything to make poverty history?

- What would be the best way to end poverty in poor countries?

Migration and the nation

- Read 'Migration'. What is distinctive about recent patterns of migration?
- Why has illegal migration increased?
- Read Study 16. Why do women migrate from poor countries to rich ones?
- Migrants have been considered both a threat and a resource. List ways in which they might be considered either.
- Look at Figure 16.9 on p. 643 and consider its significance for the migration debate.
- How does the British government's five-year immigration and asylum strategy differentiate immigrants? Should they be differentiated in this way?
- What are the implications of migration for countries of origin?
- Should migration into Britain be reduced, increased, or held stable?

Explore further

This book provides a stimulating and thought-provoking challenge to classic accounts of global economic development:

Frank, A. G. (1998), *ReORIENT: Global Economy in the Asian Age* (Berkeley and Los Angeles: University of California Press). *A critique of orthodox accounts of the growth of the capitalist world economy, arguing that Asia's significance in this has been ignored.*

The following provide general accounts of globalization:

Bauman, Z. (1998), *Globalization: The Human Consequences* (Cambridge: Polity Press). *A compact, strongly written and perceptive discussion of the relationship between the globalization of the elite and the localization of the poor.*

Cohen, R., and Kennedy, P. (2000), *Global Sociology* (London: Macmillan). *A clear, interesting, comprehensive, and user-friendly survey of all aspects of globalization, containing lots of examples and dealing with a wide range of issues.*

Held, D., McGrew, A., Goldblatt, D., and Perraton, J. (1999), *Global Transformations: Politics, Economics, and Culture* (Cambridge: Polity Press). *An extremely detailed, comprehensive, and authoritative account of all aspects of globalization.*

Held, D., and McGrew, A. (2003) (eds.), *The Global Transformations Reader* (Cambridge: Polity Press). *Accompanies the above.*

Steger, M. (2003), *Globalization: A Very Short Introduction* (Oxford: Oxford University Press). *The best introduction to this concept.*

Waters, M. (1995), *Globalization* (London: Routledge). *The most useful summary of the various theories of globalization.*

For particular aspects of globalization see:

Castles, S., and Miller, M. J. (2003), *The Age of Migration: International Population Movements in the Modern World* (3rd edn., Basingstoke: Palgrave Macmillan). *The standard work on migration, but also relevant to most of the issues discussed in this chapter.*

Dicken, P. (2003), *Global Shift: The Internationalization of Economic Activity* (4th edn., London: Sage). *A mine of information on TNCs and the economic aspects of globalization.*

Elliott, L. (2004), *The Global Politics of the Environment* (2nd edn., Basingstoke: Palgrave Macmillan). *Clear, full, and up-to-date coverage of the development of international politics on this issue.*

Meetham, K. (2001), *Tourism and Global Society* (Basingstoke: Palgrave). *A useful examination of an often taken-for-granted aspect of a globally integrated world.*

On development issues see:

Long, N. (2001), *Development Sociology: Actor Perspectives* (London: Routledge). *Breaks away from the established approaches to development by presenting an alternative action approach.*

Townsend, P., and Gordon, D. (2002), *World Poverty: New Policies to Defeat an Old Enemy* (Bristol: Policy Press). *Contains contributions that analyse inequality and poverty in both rich and poor countries.*

United Nations Development Programme (2005), *Human Development Report* (Oxford: Oxford University Press). *An up-to-date source of information on international inequality and development programmes.*

Online resources

Visit the Online Resource Centre that accompanies this book to access more learning resources and other interesting material on globalization at:

www.oxfordtextbooks.co.uk/orc/fulcher3e/

The 1999 BBC Reith lectures given by Anthony Giddens on globalization can be found at:

http://news.bbc.co.uk/hi/english/static/events/reith_99/default.htm

Belinda Weaver's site at the University of Queensland library provides links to a huge range of materials on all aspects of globalization and the debates around it:

www.journoz.com/global/

For documents, reports, statistics and discussion of world poverty visit:

http://topics.developmentgateway.org/poverty

For information on the global environmentalist movement and the latest Earth Summit, visit Greenpeace International at:

www.greenpeace.org/homepage/

The United Nations homepage is at:

www.un.org/english/

production, inequalities, and social divisions

PART FIVE

work, employment, and leisure

Contents

The new 'satanic' mills?

Call centres have been described as today's version of the nineteenth century's 'satanic' textile mills. Rows of workers, tied to their machines and tightly watched by management, endure 'sweatshop' conditions, and work continuously with minimal breaks, for low pay.

Call centres have certainly become a rapidly expanding section of the economy. In the United Kingdom in 1995 there were 2,515 call centres employing 144,000 workers. By 2003 there were 5,320, employing 494,000. Many call-centre jobs have recently been exported to India but call-centre employment in Britain is, none the less, expected to increase steadily.

Call centres are intense and low-paid workplaces. Calls are closely monitored by management and there is a constant pressure to keep their length to a minimum. The BT requirement that calls at its centres last no longer than 285 seconds triggered a strike in 1999 (*Independent*, 23 November 1999). The Automobile Asociation uses dataveillance to log all absences of its staff from their desks and allows them a total of 82 minutes' free time, which includes lunch, tea breaks, and visits to the lavatory (*Guardian*, 31 October, 2005).

Source: TUC report, 'Calls for Change', February 2001 (www.tuc.org.uk/work_life/tuc-2997-fo.cfm).

The experience of work and employment has been changed by the steady shift of employment from manufacturing into services. Some have seen this as a process of deindustrialization, though, as our opening piece suggests, it can also be argued that services themselves are becoming increasingly organized on industrial lines. In this chapter we examine the impact of such changes on the meaning and experience of work, on the relationships between workers and employers, and on the organization of labour.

Call centres largely employ women. As employment has shifted into services, more women have entered employment, and they have also broken into previously male professions. We consider the reasons for the growing employment of women, in the context of changes in patterns of employment, changes in home and family life, and in the broader relationships between men and women.

In exploring the world of work, we deal not only with the factory and the office but also the home, for the home too is a workplace. We discuss unpaid domestic labour, the mechanization of housework, and the implications of the rise of DIY. We also examine homework, which in this context means paid work in the home for an outside employer, and summarize an important recent study of this in Study 17. Homework has been growing in importance and at least partly changing in character with the spread of telework.

The home has also become the main focus of leisure. Work and leisure might seem totally different activities but they are in fact bound together. One could not exist without the other. Indeed, industrialization not only created regular employment for the first time but also leisure, for it sharply divided daily activities into work-time and leisure-time. Recent changes in both work and leisure have, however, altered the relationship between work and leisure activities, and we discuss whether it is any longer a meaningful distinction to make.

Understanding work, employment, and leisure

Our experience of work, employment, and leisure has been shaped by two powerful forces that have transformed the world—capitalism and industrialism. We begin by discussing their meaning and the relationship between them. We then move on to consider the emergence of a distinct world of work and the relationship between home and workplace, work and non-work.

Industrial capitalism

Capitalism and industrialism have been closely linked, for it was their combination in the form of industrial capitalism that led to the transformation of the world. They must, however, be carefully distinguished, for they refer to different aspects of economic organization.

Capitalism

The basic feature of **capitalism** is the financing of economic activity by the investment of capital in the expectation of making a profit. Capital simply means accumulated money that is available for investment. Money can be invested in this way in any economic activity, in trade, production, services, or agriculture. Capitalism did indeed first develop in trading activities during medieval times and it was not until much later that capitalist production became established. It was, however, capitalist production that transformed society and it is on capitalist production that we shall focus.

It was Karl Marx (1848) who first systematically analysed capitalist production. He argued that its central feature was the private ownership of the means of production. The **means of production** were the workplace, tools, and raw materials that made the production of goods possible. It was the capitalist who provided the money to set up a workplace, equip it with machinery, and buy the necessary raw materials. These means of production were therefore the private property of the capitalist and were not owned by the producers, the workers who actually made the goods.

Production was carried out by wage labour. Capitalists employed workers to produce goods in exchange for a wage. Instead of being able to consume or sell what they had made, workers received a wage in return for their labour. The producers had therefore lost control of the product of their labour, which was owned by the employer. They worked not in order to produce something that they could use or sell but in order to earn wages. They had become, as Marx put it, 'wage slaves'.

Market relationships came to dominate capitalist societies. In order to make a profit, the capitalist had to sell products in the market. Equally, producers could not consume what they had produced or produce what they needed to consume. Instead, they had to use their wages to buy in the market everything that they needed or wanted. The link between production and consumption had been broken and was now mediated by market relationships.

Marx emphasized that under capitalism those who produced lost control not only of the *product* of their labour but also the *process* of production. The capitalist employer determined what machinery should be used, how the work should be divided between employees, the hours of work, and the speed of work. This loss of control over the product of work and the process of work resulted in the *alienation* of the worker, a concept which we discuss on p. 673.

The interests of the owners of capital and labour were, according to Marx, in conflict. The employer's concern to maximize profits by squeezing as much work as possible out of labour, while paying it as little as possible, meant that the interests of the owners of capital and their employees were inevitably opposed. Marx argued that this conflict of interest would lead to the division of society into two classes, the capitalist bourgeoisie and the working class (see

---

THEORY AND METHODS

Marx and Engels on capitalism

Although Marx's name is associated with attempts to overthrow capitalism and replace it with communism, he was greatly impressed by the enormous productive potential of capitalism. In the *Communist Manifesto* of 1848, Marx and Engels wrote that:

'the bourgeoisie, during its rule of scarce one hundred years, has created more massive and more colossal productive forces than have all preceding generations together. Subjection of nature's forces to man, machinery, application of chemistry to industry and agriculture, steam-navigation, railways, electric telegraphs, clearing of whole continents for cultivation, canalization of rivers, whole populations conjured out of the ground—what earlier century had even a presentiment that such productive forces slumbered in the lap of social labour.' (Marx and Engels 1848: 85)

Chapter 19, pp. 774–5 for a discussion of Marx's theory of class conflict). Increasing conflict between these two classes would lead eventually to a revolutionary transformation of society that would bring capitalism to an end.

Industrialism

Capitalist production existed before the Industrial Revolution. In sixteenth- and seventeenth-century Europe production in households and workshops was increasingly financed and controlled by the owners of capital. These then began to bring their workers together in larger units called factories and in the eighteenth century developed the techniques of industrial production in order to make higher profits on their capital.

Industrialism refers to the new method of organizing production that became fully established in the nineteenth century. While the development of *power-driven machinery* was central to industrialization, the defining feature of industrialism was the way that production was organized. It was *concentrated* in large workplaces (factories), where work was *divided into specialized tasks* and *coordinated by managers*.

Production was transformed through the introduction of *power-driven machinery*, initially driven by water but then by the steam engine. It was the nineteenth-century introduction of steam power that led to the rapid spread of industrialism, for steam engines could be set up anywhere, while travel was transformed by the steam-driven locomotive and the steamship. Hand tools had been controlled by the worker, but in a real sense the worker was now controlled by the power-driven machine, for this determined the speed of work and shaped the work environment.

Industrialization involved the *concentration* of production in large workplaces. Workers could be controlled more easily and more closely if they were brought together under one roof, while the harnessing of water and steam power made it necessary to concentrate production in factories with power-driven machinery. The factory changed the social character of work, bringing large numbers of workers together and enabling them to organize themselves in unions.

The development of technology and the concentration of production led to the *division of labour* into specialized tasks. The division of labour did not begin with industrialization, but factory production resulted in a much more systematic division of work into specialized tasks than had existed before. This made workers highly interdependent, for the work of each depended on the work of others.

A whole new range of functions and occupations emerged to enable the *management and control* of the workplace. The concentration of labour, the introduction of new technology, and the specialization of tasks in the industrial factory generated new problems of coordination, expertise,

Figure 17.1 Capitalism and industrialism

Capitalism	Industrialism
● Profit drives economic activity	● Power-driven machinery
● Private ownership of means of production	● Concentration of production
● Employment of wage labour	● Systematic division of labour
● Control of process of production by employer	● Coordination of production by specialized management
● Conflict of interest between capital and labour	● Organization of workers in unions

and control. Employers could neither ignore these problems nor handle them on their own and began to employ increasingly professional and specialized managers.

Capitalism and industrialism have been closely related because it was the capitalist's pursuit of more profitable ways of organizing production that drove industrialization forwards. We do, therefore, frequently refer to *industrial capitalism*, but it is important to distinguish between capitalism and industrialism. As we have shown, capitalist production existed before production was organized on industrial lines. Furthermore, capitalist industrialism has not been its only form and a non-capitalist system of industrial production was created in some state socialist countries, notably in the Soviet Union, its satellite countries in eastern Europe, in China, and in Cuba. State socialism was, however, in the end unable to establish itself as a viable alternative and collapsed at the end of the 1980s (see Chapter 20, pp. 835–6).

The world of work

The development of capitalist production and industrialization separated production from the household. Previously, most production had been carried out in the household, in a workshop attached to it, or on a family farm. Under industrial capitalism the workplace became a world of its own—the world of the factory, the office, the laboratory, and the factory farm. Indeed, people now spoke of the world of work as though it were a quite separate part of life.

Employment relations

A distinct set of social relationships emerged between employers and workers. These consisted of the organization and management of work, which we examine in Chapter 14, and industrial relations, which we consider here.

The term *industrial relations* refers to the bargaining relationships that developed between employers and workers, not only in factories but also in offices and all other kinds of workplace—in stores, or schools, or hospitals, or restaurants. These relationships became a distinct area of organizational and institutional development.

The process of organization began when workers began to form unions because they were individually weak. They were dependent on employment for a living, but, unless they had skills in short supply, the employer could easily dismiss and replace them. Worker organization then stimulated counter-organization by employers, who created employers' associations.

Organization led to the gradual **institutionalization of industrial conflict**. By this is meant the increasing organization and regulation of conflict. Unions and employers made collective agreements to regulate the relationship between them. These specified wage rates and conditions of employment, and procedures for dealing with disputes and negotiating agreements. Governments often became involved in the process by creating institutions of mediation or arbitration, to avoid as much as possible the disruption and disorder resulting from open conflict.

Conflict did not, however, come to an end with institutionalization. Conflict took place within the framework of the negotiation procedures set up to regulate it. Open conflict anyway still occurred when negotiations broke down. Institutionalization also itself generated conflicts between the leaders of organizations and their members. One consequence of institutionalization was the rise of unofficial strikes, when workers took action locally in defiance of the agreements reached by their leaders.

We examine the relationship between institutionalized and open conflict in 'Industrial conflict', below.

The meaning of work

With the creation of separate workplaces, the experience of work became a distinct part of daily life. This experience was shaped by the work situation, the technology, management practices, and the work environment.

According to Karl Marx (1844), work had been and should be a creative means of self-expression, but the emergence of capitalism turned it into a non-creative activity. Traditional craftsmen had worked at their own pace in their own workshops with their own tools, creating whole and unique products, which also belonged to them. The pace of factory work was, however, set by a machine in an environment controlled by the employer. Work was fragmented by the division of labour and workers had no sense of making a complete object. They produced standard and characterless goods owned by the employer. Instead of work being a means of self-expression, it had become merely a means of earning a living.

This loss of the creative aspects of work was characterized by Marx as a process of **alienation**:

A union meeting—why do workers need unions?
© Alice Chadwick

- As the worker had lost control of the product, it had become an alien object. The worker had no feelings for it, no attachment to it, or pride in it.

- With loss of control over the product went loss of control over the production process, which dominated the worker as an alien and oppressive force.

- Workers also became alienated from each other, as they competed for employment in a labour market.

- Since it was creativity through work that was the distinctive feature of human beings, the loss of creativity was dehumanizing and alienated 'man' from his true self.

Emile Durkheim (1893) challenged this view and argued that the growing division of labour should not have such degrading consequences, because it created a new interdependence between workers. This would give them a sense of participation in a common enterprise that would make work more, rather than less, meaningful. Instead of producing alienation and conflict, the division of labour would lead to cooperation and harmony. Durkheim used the analogy of the human body, where organs were specialized but worked together in a harmonious fashion to produce what he called an **organic solidarity**.

Durkheim's views were not, however, as different from Marx's as they appear to be, for Durkheim did recognize that the division of labour would have these integrative consequences *only if* people were able to carry out freely chosen tasks appropriate to their abilities. The difference between them was that Marx believed that this was impossible in a capitalist society, while Durkheim thought that it would normally be the case. When it was not, perhaps because social change had been too rapid, society was, according to Durkheim, in an abnormal state of anomie (see Chapter 2, p. 37).

Marx and Durkheim were concerned with the general impact of industrial capitalism on work, but many *different* kinds of work situation have emerged within industrial societies, and we examine these on pp. 679–84.

Outside the world of work

Industrialization not only created a new world of work, it also changed people's ways of thinking about their work and non-work activities.

Work at home

We discussed the experience of work as though work always means paid work outside the home. Commonly used phrases such as 'going to work' or 'hours of work' define work in this way, as does the term 'workplace'. Where, however, does this definition of work leave housework or homework?

One of the problems here is that the definitions of the various kinds of work that go on in the household are far from clear. It is important first of all to distinguish two key terms:

- **Domestic labour**. This refers to all work concerned with maintaining the household. It includes both housework and domestic production, as well as other tasks that we discuss below.
- **Homework**. This is paid work carried out at home for an outside employer.

Domestic labour in the household takes up a large part of people's daily lives. Although not traditionally counted as economic activity, it undoubtedly makes an enormous contribution to the economy. People can only carry out paid work if they are fed, clothed, housed, and kept both mentally and physically well, but most of the work that goes into maintaining them in this state is provided by unpaid domestic labour. Its importance has been recognized in a recent attempt to measure its contribution, which concluded that in the United Kingdom it was equivalent to 77 per cent of Gross Domestic Product (see **www.statistics.gov.uk/hhsa**).

Domestic labour consists of many different kinds of work. The routine cleaning and maintenance tasks of *housework* are different from *domestic production*, such as baking cakes, making clothes, or growing vegetables. Other tasks, such as roof repair or decoration, are concerned with *domestic capital*, for they maintain or increase the value of property. There are also *management tasks* that deal with family finances, the distribution of work between its members, and the supervision of their work. *Emotional labour* is yet another kind of domestic work, concerned with the household's emotional needs, which are in part generated by the stress of paid work (see Chapter 12, pp. 450–1).

Is this domestic labour?
© Alice Chadwick

Domestic labour can also be carried out in various ways:

- the unpaid labour of the household members;
- waged domestic labour, when maids, gardeners, or au pairs are paid to carry it out;
- informal cooperation, an important and often omitted source of labour, ranging from mutual baby-sitting arrangements to local systems for exchanging tokens that represent amounts of labour.

Domestic labour is not the only kind of work carried out at home. There is also homework. Since industrialization, most people have earned their living in a separate work-place but some have continued to carry out paid work for an employer at home. Recent developments in communications and information technology have given homework, particularly in the form of telework, a new boost.

The home is then a workplace, within which many different kinds of work go on. The 'sociology of work' should concern itself not just with paid work outside the home but with all work going on in the society. Glucksmann (1995) has developed the concept of the *total social organization of labour* (TSOL) to convey this idea. The TSOL refers to 'the manner by which all the labour in a society is divided up between and allocated to different structures, institutions, and activities' (Glucksmann 1995: 67). This concept makes central to the study of work the relationships between the different forms that it takes.

Employment and unemployment

With industrialization, work became identified with employment. Those who made their living by providing goods and services without working for an employer were now the exception rather than the rule, and were called *self-employed*. If people lost their jobs or were unable to find paid work, they fell into the new category of those who were *unemployed*. If they were unemployed, they were considered 'out of work', even though they might be working hard to grow their own food or make their own clothes.

The definition of unemployment presents many problems. They are not simply all those not in employment, for those who are ill, retired, or in full-time education are not considered unemployed. To be unemployed, people must at least be *available* for paid work and availability is not easy to define. Some people may be available for work but not actually seeking it, because, for example, they have developed an alternative lifestyle. Should they be considered unemployed?

Definitions are important, for the official definition of unemployment determines the size of the figure for the unemployed, which is a politically sensitive issue. As we show in Chapter 3, p. 105, there have been many recent changes in the official definition of unemployment, which have mostly had the effect of reducing it.

Figure 17.2 Who are the unemployed?

Which of the following would you consider to be unemployed?

- All those not in employment?
- People who are 'out of work' and available for it?
- Those who are out of work who are seeking it?
- Part-time workers unable to find full-time work?
- Retired people who still want to work?
- Students unable to find vacation work?
- People who are between jobs?
- Those receiving unemployment benefit?
- House husbands and housewives?

Work and leisure

In daily life we usually distinguish between work and leisure. This distinction makes a sharp division between work and non-work activities, and commonly treats them as opposite in character. Work is generally seen as routine and unsatisfying, while leisure provides freedom, choice, self-expression, and creativity.

Should, however, such a sharp distinction be made? Stanley Parker (1976) showed how in some situations work is not sharply distinguished from leisure. He identified three different work–leisure patterns and linked them to differences between occupations:

- *The segmentalist pattern*. This broadly matched the conventional work–leisure distinction. It was found among routine clerical or unskilled manual workers, particularly those, such as fishermen or miners, working in harsh or dangerous conditions. Their work was a means to earn a living that provided few opportunities for work satisfaction and gave them little control over what they did. Leisure was an escape from alienating work. (See 'The working-class world', Chapter 19, pp. 790–3).

- *The extension pattern*. This did not fit the conventional distinction, for work interests spilled over into non-work time. It was characteristic of business people, professionals, and skilled workers, whose work was involving and satisfying. Work was not a negative experience and leisure was not an escape from it.

- *The neutrality pattern*. An intermediate pattern, with no sharp opposition between work and leisure but also no extension of work into leisure time. It was typical of semi-skilled manual and clerical workers.

The extension pattern suggests that too sharp and general a contrast should not be drawn between work as a negative experience and leisure as a positive one. Work can be a positive experience, while the emergence of leisure industries, and the manipulation of the consumer by the mass media and advertising, imply that leisure is not simply a time of choice, freedom, and creativity. There are pressures to consume as well as to work. Furthermore, the pressure to consume may lead to passive forms of leisure, such as television-watching. Indeed, some work activities may well be more creative and self-expressive than many leisure activities.

It has also been argued that the work–leisure distinction reflects a particularly male way of looking at the world. It does not take account of the housework that has been the main daily activity of many women, for housework is neither paid work nor leisure. Furthermore, when women are employed in paid work, they generally have to carry out housework at other times. Thus, non-work time can only become leisure if the housework is done by someone else, such as a paid servant. The work–leisure distinction has applied, therefore, most clearly to the lives of married men in full-time employment with full-time housewives.

There are then problems with the distinction between work and leisure but, as we shall show in 'The growth of leisure', industrial capitalism did, none the less, lead to a significant separation of work and leisure activities in many workers' lives. Whether it is still a meaningful distinction is another matter, which we discuss in 'A leisure society?' (see pp. 710–12).

 ## *Stop and reflect*

We first explored the significance of capitalism and industrialism.

- Make sure that you understand the meaning of these two key terms.
- What is the relationship between them?

We went on to discuss the emergence of a separate world of work in the workplace.

- Make sure that you understand the approaches of Marx and Durkheim to the experience of work.
- How do they differ and do they have anything in common?

We then moved outside the 'world of work' to examine the relationship between workplace and home, work and non-work.

- We distinguished between 'domestic labour', which is work concerned with the maintenance of the household, and 'homework', which is work carried out at home for an outside employer.
- We argued that people can be 'out-of work' for many reasons but it is only when they are available for work that they should be considered unemployed. Do you agree?
- Daily activities are commonly seen as divided between work and leisure. What problems are there with this distinction?

The impact of industrial capitalism

In this section we examine the main features of the new world of work created by industrial capitalism. This concentrated labour in the workplace and generated industrial conflict. It made the experience of paid work a central feature of people's lives and separated work from non-work in people's minds—the workplace from the home, the employed from the unemployed, and work from leisure.

Industrial conflict

Industrial capitalism generated industrial conflict. There was a conflict of interest between the owners of capital and their employees, since profits depended on keeping labour costs to a minimum by paying as few workers as possible as little as possible for as much work as possible. Industrialization concentrated workers together in large units and made it easier for them to organize themselves in unions and stand up to the capitalist employer.

Workers organized themselves in different ways, however, and pursued different strategies, while employers too became organized and developed counter-strategies. Before considering industrial conflict, we need first to consider the process of organization on both sides of industry.

Organization and strategy

The first strong unions in Britain were the *craft* unions that established themselves in the middle of the nineteenth

Figure 17.3 Labour organization, strategy, and employer response

Labour organization	Membership	Strategy	Employer response
Craft union	Skilled workers	Control of entry	Deskilling
Industrial union	All workers in an industry	Collective bargaining	Employer associations
Labour party	All workers	Use of political power	Influence on parties and state

century. They organized workers within a particular craft or occupation, such as printing, and their main strategy was to keep wages high by controlling the supply of labour. They did this by both controlling entry to the craft and restricting jobs to their members. They were in conflict as much with other crafts and with less skilled workers as with employers. Employers tried to counter their strategy by using less skilled labour, a process known as **deskilling**, by either breaking work down into simpler tasks or introducing machinery that could be operated by workers with less skill (we discuss deskilling on p. 678).

A similarly exclusive strategy has been operated by professions, whose associations have acted much like craft unions. They too established their bargaining power by restricting entry, and controlling the training and certification of members. Thus, during the nineteenth century the British medical profession established control of entry through the registration of medical practitioners and the control of medical education. As with the craft unions, this involved the exclusion of women from membership (Witz 1992).

The second form of organization was the *industrial* or *general* union created by less skilled workers unable to control entry. These unions relied more on collective bargaining and the strike weapon. They were inclusive, seeking to organize as many workers as possible, regardless of their skill. Their open and inclusive character led them to adopt socialist ideologies based on the principle of class organization. They have also been associated with the development of national union federations that could mobilize the strength of the working class as a whole.

Employers responded to trade unionism by constructing counter-organizations. Faced by unions that stretched across a whole industry, they organized themselves into matching employers' associations. They could respond to strikes by locking out all union members, seeking to exhaust the unions' funds by forcing them to support large numbers of out-of-work members.

The third main form of worker organization was the *labour* or *social democratic* party, which sought to advance the collective interests of labour through political rather than industrial action. In a democratic political system such a party could bring to bear the numerical advantages of the working class, for workers' votes far outweighed those of the employers. In this situation, the employers' response was to support and fund political parties themselves, and use their economic power to exert pressure on any labour government.

> **⊃** *Connections*
> We discuss labour movements and the development of the British Labour Party in Chapter 20, pp. 826–7. In Chapter 15, pp. 584–5, we discuss the relationship between labour movements and the state.

Strikes

The term 'industrial conflict' is often taken to mean strike action, but this is quite wrong. When considering industrial conflict it is important to make a number of basic distinctions:

- between *institutionalized* and *open* conflict;
- between *different forms* of open conflict;
- between *collective* and *individual* expressions of conflict.

We discussed the *institutionalization* of industrial conflict on pp. 672–3. As we argued there, institutionalization did not mean that conflict ceased, even if there was no open conflict taking place.

Open conflict commonly takes the form of strike action, but in some situations it may be more effective to use other weapons. Workers can bring considerable pressure to bear on employers by refusing to work overtime or 'going slow', without breaking agreements or contracts, and while continuing to draw their pay. Open conflict may also take the form of an employer-initiated lockout.

In situations where workers are unorganized or unable to act collectively, discontent may take the form of *individual* actions, such as going sick or simply staying away from work. The term 'absenteeism' is used for this kind of individual refusal to work. The line between individual and collective action may, however, become blurred, for unions may advise their members to go sick or may coordinate absenteeism.

While industrial conflict must not be confused with strikes, they have been the most disruptive weapon used by workers and have been extensively studied. The most common method used has been to analyse trends and variations in the amount of strike action, though there have also been some important case studies of particular strikes (Gouldner 1954b; Lane and Roberts 1971; Friedman and Meredeen 1980). British strike data are available from the Office of National Statistics. The Workplace Employment Relations Survey is an important source of data on both strike and non-strike action (Kersley *et al.* 2005).

As we show in Chapter 3, pp. 105–6, there are many problems with official statistics and this is certainly the case with the official statistics on British industrial disputes. First, strike records depend on employer reports and the preparedness of employers to treat a work stoppage as a strike. Secondly, very small disputes that involve fewer than ten workers or last less than one day are excluded (unless they result in the loss of more than 100 worker days).

Strikes are mainly measured by *worker days lost* and *strike frequency*. Strike frequency figures are unreliable because most strikes are short. The shorter the strike, the less likely it is to be reported or included by the official definition. Problems with frequency data particularly affect international comparisons, for reporting and definitional practices vary considerably between countries. Strike frequency data are, none the less, important, because they indicate workers' readiness to take strike action. The worker days lost figure is more reliable, since it is mainly determined by large or long strikes that are certain to find their way into the statistics.

Figure 17.4 shows the long-term trend of strikes in Britain. The days-lost peak in the 1920s reflects the General Strike of 1926, and other large strikes around that time. In

Figure 17.4 UK strikes, 1895–2004, five-year annual averages

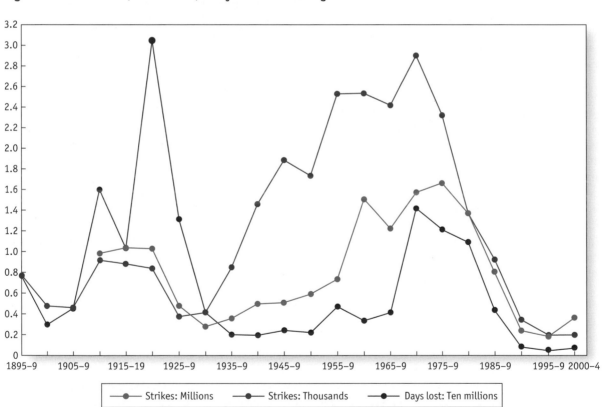

Legend: Strikes: Millions — Strikes: Thousands — Days lost: Ten millions

Sources: Grint (1999: 163); Office for National Statistics (www.statistics.gov.uk 2006: Dataset lms 21).

❓ Why did the number of strikes increase so much more than the number of strikers and worker days lost between the 1930s and the 1970s?

❓ Why have strikes declined since the 1970s?

a well-known study, Ross and Hartman (1960) argued that there had been a general decline of the strike in all the main industrial societies as industrial conflict became institutionalized but, as Figure 17.4 shows, strike measures rose to new heights in the 1950s, 1960s, and 1970s.

Relatively full employment at this time and growing union membership undoubtedly played a part in generating increased strike activity but it was argued that the archaic organizational and institutional structures inherited from the past were also responsible (Fulcher 1991*a*). Major attempts were made in the 1960s and early 1970s to reform British industrial relations. These failed, and brought the governments concerned into disastrous conflicts with the unions, but had very important consequences because they prepared the way for the legislative onslaught on the unions in the 1980s. We examine this in 'Industrial conflict and the state' on pp. 700–1.

The experience of work

We now turn to consider the impact of industrial capitalism on the experience of work. We discuss, first, the effects of different technologies and then examine the significance of factors outside the work situation. We go on to examine the experience of clerical and service work.

Technology and the meaning of work

The classic work on this is Robert Blauner's (1964) *Alienation and Freedom*. He developed and applied the concepts of Marx and Durkheim, which we discussed earlier on p. 673.

Blauner considered that technology was central to the way work was organized and experienced. It developed through four stages:

- craft production;
- machine-based factory production;
- assembly plants;
- automation.

Although these were historical stages in the development of technology, each of them still existed. He took printing as his example of craft production, textiles for the machine-based factory, the car industry for the assembly plant, chemicals for automation. These examples were appropriate at the time of his study in the 1950s, but major changes in technology have happened since. In the car industry, for example, many operations have been automated and are carried out by computer-controlled machinery. All the technologies examined by Blauner do, none the less, still exist.

In order to study the effect of different technologies on the experience of work, Blauner had to operationalize the concepts of Marx and Durkheim so that he could measure the degree of alienation experienced by workers (see Figure 17.5). His first step was to sort out the different ways in which the work situation could affect the worker. From the writings of Marx and Durkheim he extracted four dimensions of alienation:

- powerlessness;
- meaninglessness;
- isolation;
- self-estrangement.

Self-estrangement largely resulted from the effects of the other three dimensions on the experience of work. It referred to workers' inability to express themselves through their work or involve themselves in it. It is similar to Marx's idea that workers are alienated from their true selves.

Indicators had to be found for each of his dimensions. Blauner established, for example, the following indicators for the powerlessness dimension:

- non-ownership of the means of production and the product of labour;
- inability to influence general managerial policies;
- lack of control over the conditions of employment;
- lack of control over the immediate work process.

So far as non-ownership was concerned, he agreed with Marx that this characterized all workers under capitalism. But whereas this was for Marx the essential point, Blauner was primarily interested in how the degree of alienation varied within capitalism. His other indicators of powerlessness varied from industry to industry, producing different degrees of alienation.

Blauner applied all four of his dimensions to each of his four industries, using data from a survey of attitudes to work in the United States and case-study material. He found that printing retained much of the character of a pre-industrial craft and showed low levels of alienation (see Figure 17.5). Alienation increased with industrialization, reaching its maximum level with car assembly plants, but with automation returned to a level characteristic of pre-industrial work. Although Blauner accepted that under capitalism all workers inevitably experienced some alienation, he claimed that much of it could be removed by more advanced technologies that made work satisfying and meaningful again.

The idea that automation has reversed the tendency towards increasing alienation has been challenged by Harry Braverman (1974), who argued that the development of technology has deskilled workers by separating mental from manual work. Mechanization enabled management

Figure 17.5 Operationalizing the concept of alienation

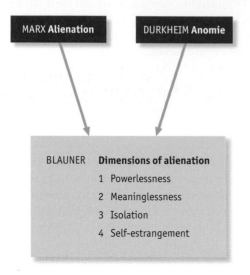

Indicators of powerlessness	Printing	Textiles	Cars	Chemicals
1 Separation from ownership	✓	✓	✓	✓
2 Inability to influence management	✕	✓	✓	✕
3 Lack of control over conditions of employment	✕	✓	✓	✕
4 Lack of control over work process	✕	✓	✓	✕

⊃ Try applying Blauner's dimensions to any work situation that you have experienced.

⊃ In Chapter 3, p. 97, we discuss whether Blauner accurately operationalizes Marx's ideas. Look at what we say there and see what you think.

to turn work into a series of simple, repetitive tasks that required little training and little mental effort. Mental work was concentrated in management, in the occupations that planned, organized, and controlled the work process. The advantages of deskilling to the employer were that it made labour cheaper and increased employer control of the work process. According to Braverman, automation was but the latest stage in this process.

He was very sceptical of Blauner's argument that workers in the chemical industry had meaningful work. The monitoring of chemical processes was a routine matter that required little skill. The only knowledge it needed was the capacity to read a dial. A case study by Theo Nichols and Huw Beynon (1977) supported this view of the chemical industry and argued that control work could be lonely and meaningless. Furthermore, however automated an industry was, it also employed many workers carrying out traditional kinds of manual work.

A more general issue is raised by both Blauner and Braverman. What is the significance of technology for the experience of work? The power of workers must in part relate to the strength of union organization and does not just vary with technology. For his part, Braverman did not take account of the way that styles of management could impact on job satisfaction through, for example, job rotation, job enlargement, and job enrichment.

> ⊃ **Connections**
>
> We discuss different approaches to management in Chapter 14, pp. 547–8 and 559–62.

From technology to orientation

The main challenge to the technological approach came, however, from the *Affluent Worker* study by John Goldthorpe *et al.* (1968a) of workers in Luton during the 1960s. This argued that the attitudes people bring to work shape their experience of it. The study covered three of the technologies examined by Blauner, the Vauxhall car assembly plant, machine-based work at the Skefko ball-bearing factory, and automated production at Laporte Chemicals.

The study did find that technology was related to the amount of *work satisfaction* experienced by these workers, but also that there was remarkably little variation in their *attitudes* to their work. These were instrumental, for they saw work as a means to earn the money they needed, rather than a means of self-expression. What mattered in their lives was not their work experience or work relationships but their private life at home, their possessions, and their families. As their work situations were so different, these attitudes could not have been generated by their work and must have been brought into the workplace.

Is this worker in control?
© Alice Chadwick

Gabriel (1988) has examined the experience of work in catering. One of the workplaces that he studied was the catering department of a community centre in a northern British city. He found that catering had been deskilled through processes of mechanization and industrialization, and the application of the techniques of scientific management, often known as Taylorism (see Chapter 14, pp. 548–9):

> The cook-freeze kitchen was a faithful adoption of Taylorist principles in mass catering, splitting up cooking from planning, breaking up work-tasks into simple and tightly controlled routines, and reducing the skill, initiative and thinking required of the cooks to a virtual minimum. . . . All freedom and creativity, the hallmarks of craft cooking, are eliminated through rules aimed at preventing the cooks from 'messing about with the recipes'. Monotony and lack of variety prevailed, each day being the same as the next. (Gabriel 1988: 87–8)

He also found, however, that the women who worked in this kitchen made their work more meaningful by taking responsibility for meeting production targets, and controlling the pace and distribution of work. Their shared interests and common home backgrounds also made work bearable by generating a feeling of togetherness that 'provided consolation for jobs devoid of interest'. They, none the less, felt trapped in their jobs and unable to seek more interesting work, because the department's work hours and holiday periods were compatible with their domestic and childcare obligations.

 Think about any paid work that you have recently done. How meaningful was it? What aspects of the work situation made it more or less meaningful? Could you make it more meaningful yourself? Did the meaning of your work matter to you?

The *Affluent Worker* study introduced the important concept of **orientation to work** to describe the attitudes that workers brought into work. Orientations were shaped by prior socialization, social background, earlier experiences of life, and the influence of the media. Orientation to work then mediated between the characteristics of the workplace, such as its size and technology, and workers' experience of it. The Luton workers typically held an *instrumental* orientation to work, but Goldthorpe *et al.* also identified *bureaucratic* and *solidaristic* orientations to produce a typology of orientations (see Figure 17.6). The solidaristic one was typical of the more traditional worker community, the bureaucratic one of white-collar workers.

This study did not claim that the Luton workers were typical of workers in general. The high wages of this area had attracted mobile workers from all over the country and selected out those who were highly instrumental. The authors of the study were well aware of the distinctive character of the Luton labour force and, indeed, studied it for this very reason.

So far we have considered classic studies of British and American workers, operating within a basically Anglo-Saxon culture. Duncan Gallie's (1978) study of oil refineries in Britain and France examined international differences in attitudes to work. His choice of highly automated plants meant that he could test Blauner's theory that automation would lead to declining alienation. Gallie concluded that Blauner's theory was culturally specific. The British refineries did broadly fit his model, for the workers were integrated and had few grievances, but in France they were in a continual state of conflict with an arrogant and

Figure 17.6 Orientations to work

Orientation	Meaning of work	Involvement in organization	Involvement in work	Relationship between work and non-work life
Instrumental	Work as source of income	Calculative only	Work not a central life interest	Sharp separation
Bureaucratic	Service to organization in exchange for career	Moral obligation to organization	Career a central life interest	Social aspirations and status related to career
Solidaristic	Work as a group activity	Identification with enterprise or work group	Work a central life interest	Strong occupational community

Source: Adapted from Goldthorpe *et al.* (1968a: 38–41).

exploitative management, whose authority they did not accept.

In accounting for these differences, Gallie first referred to differences of management. In Britain, management was willing to negotiate with the unions and conceded some control over work organization to union representatives, but in France the unions were excluded and managers were uncompromising. While this stance itself generated conflict with labour, it was also a response to the French labour movement, which was more radical, more politicized, and more threatening to management.

Gallie could not explore the origins of these differences, given the limits of his study, but they clearly went back to the different histories of industrial relations and political movements in the two societies. Gallie had, however, demonstrated the existence of international differences in orientations to work. He had also shown that attitudes to work that appeared to be the result of technology were in fact culturally specific.

White-collar work

White-collar work has often been treated as quite different from manual work. In the classic British study of white-collar workers David Lockwood (1958) argued that white-collar workers had a more personal relationship with their superiors, while their work was non-repetitive and required some skill, responsibility, and judgement. As we showed above, Goldthorpe *et al.* (1968a) considered that a distinct bureaucratic orientation to work was associated with white-collar work.

> **⊃ Connections**
> Braverman and other Marxist writers have argued that a process of proletarianization turned white-collar workers into members of the working class. We discuss changes in the class situation of white-collar workers in Chapter 19, pp. 795–6.

According to Braverman, however, the same deskilling processes operated in white-collar as in manual work and its distinctiveness has entirely disappeared. The clerk's situation was changed by bureaucratization and mechanization. Bureaucratization led to the creation of standard procedures that took much of the discretion and personal contact out of clerical work. The career opportunities for the white-collar worker declined as the number of routine jobs grew. The mechanization of clerical work and the application of the principles of scientific management led to the subdivision of tasks and deskilling, just as it had done with manual work. The creation of call centres, and their standardization of service employees' responses to customer enquiries, provides a recent example of this (Korczynski 2001).

In a study of white-collar workers between 1979 and 1981, Rosemary Crompton and Gareth Jones (1984) examined the effects of automation on a largely female workforce of clerks in three types of workplace—local-authority departments, an insurance company, and a bank. The result was a greater fragmentation of work into specialized, low-skill, routine tasks. Instead of giving the clerks more control over their work, automation actually shifted control into the hands of senior administrators. Automation had in this case increased powerlessness and alienation. Crompton and Jones did, however, find that greater contact with the public made work more satisfying and more meaningful for the bank clerks.

They also examined the significance of the career, which was central to the notion of a bureaucratic orientation to work. Here they made two main points:

• White-collar occupations have become increasingly stratified by a promotion barrier. A small number of positions involving skill and responsibility had good promotion prospects and were filled by entrants with high educational qualifications. The broad mass of routine clerical jobs involved little skill and little likelihood of significant promotion.

- It was mainly men who got promoted. The lower grades were largely filled by women, whose promotion prospects suffered because of lower educational qualifications and career breaks to have children.

White-collar work lost therefore much of its distinctiveness as it was subjected to the same processes of change as manual work. The distinction between manual and white-collar work has also diminished because all kinds of work increasingly involve the application of information technology. Computer-controlled production and electronic communication mean that manual workers have to learn the kind of technical skills associated with non-manual work.

Customer service work

Employment in industrial societies has shifted from manufacturing to service occupations. The term 'service work' includes both white-collar work in non-manual occupations that, like much clerical work, involve little or no contact with customers, and customer service work that revolves around interaction with customers. Customer service work has become steadily more important, with:

- the growth of occupations, from airline cabin crew, to hairdressers, and nurses, that involve such interactions;
- the increased emphasis in a highly competitive market-place on marketing products by providing a good service to customers.

Customer service work typically involves **emotional labour**, which we discuss in Chapter 4, pp. 146–7. Some work involves caring functions that draw upon the emotion of the employee and are a necessary part of the work, as in the case of nursing. Customer service workers are also required to manage their own emotions in order to conform to the image their employer is seeking to promote, as in Hochschild's account of the emotional labour carried out by airline cabin crews (see our discussion of this in Chapter 4). Bolton (2001) has argued that changes in health-service management mean that nurses too have experienced a growing pressure to not only be caring but also to present a 'smiley face' that may not match their real emotions when they have to deal with difficult patients. In this situation, emotional labour can involve 'multiple identities' and an 'emotional juggling' that is itself a special skill.

Emotional labour commonly requires **aesthetic labour**. Employees are expected to 'look good' and 'sound right'. The key feature of aesthetic labour is that it involves the embodiment of certain capacities and attitudes. Employers select workers in terms of their bodily appearance and train them to modify this appearance in order to conform with the image and style that the company is projecting. While this has, arguably, always been a feature of occupations that involve contact with customers, Nickson *et al.* present evidence that commercial pressures are driving more organizations to demand 'aesthetic skills and competences' (2001: 178). Increasing competition forces commercial organizations not only to improve their service to customers but also to present a more attractive image.

Customer service work involves emotional and aesthetic labour.
© Photo courtesy of ATOC

Emotional labour can give work meaning. It can make work satisfying, if the worker draws satisfaction from meeting the requirements and receiving the gratitude of a customer. As we noted above, Crompton and Jones (1984) discovered that those bank clerks who had contact with customers found their work more satisfying. Emotional labour also requires the acquisition and development of special skills and may be more meaningful for this reason too, since work that involves the exercise of a skill is usually more satisfying. If heavily scripted and controlled by the employer, and call centres are notorious for this, customer service work can, however, easily become routinized and emptied of meaning.

If, at the other extreme, it becomes too demanding, work that involves emotional and aesthetic labour can intrude into areas of workers' lives that they consider private and 'off limits' to the employer. They can feel that their emotions and their bodies are no longer their own. One way of dealing with this situation and protecting themselves is to put on a mask. The 'smiley face' may be no more than that. Customers and/or employers may then detect a lack of sincerity. If customers report that they do not feel genuinely cared for and threaten to remove their custom, the employer's business may suffer. In which case, as we note in Chapter 4, the employer may well respond by seeking to recruit more malleable employees. Another option is to retrain and remotivate workers to perform their emotional labour with a genuine emotion.

Emotional labour, like any kind of labour, can become a battlefield between employer and employees but the battle may take very different, indeed opposite, forms. Conflict may arise because the employer tries to restrict the emotional involvement of workers who want to engage emotionally with the customer, in order to speed up the process of dealing with customers and to increase the efficiency and profitability of the organization. Conflict may also occur because the employer tries to intensify the emotional involvement of workers who want to limit the emotional demands their work makes on them, in order to meet the emotional needs of the customer, increase customer satisfaction, and generate more business that way. These various tensions are further discussed in Korczynski's analysis of 'customer-oriented bureaucracy in call centres' (see box in Chapter 14, p. 559).

Job satisfaction

The classic studies of the experience of work had examined variations between the kinds of work in different industries. Michael Rose (2003) has, however, argued that differences in satisfaction are more closely related to occupational differences between *jobs* than work differences between *industries*.

Frontiers Types of emotional labour

Sharon Bolton and Carol Boyd argue that a more differentiated approach to emotional labour in work organizations is now required. They use material from their own study of aircraft cabin crew to criticize Hochschild's emphasis on the control of employees' private emotions by employing organizations. They claim that emotional labour is much less under the control of management than physical labour is.

> Cabin crew do not have to 'love' the product, the passengers or the airline. They do not have to feel estranged from the emotional labour process. Unlike the factory worker they own the means of production and, therefore, the capacity to present a 'sincere' or 'cynical' performance lies within the emotional labourer. (Bolton and Boyd 2003: 293–4)

They present a typology of four kinds of emotion management:

- *Pecuniary* management involves a purely instrumental and generally superficial display of emotion to keep the customer happy for commercial reasons, acting in accordance with company norms.
- *Prescriptive* management is governed by the need to conform to professional and organizational safety and service standards, which may supersede company concerns with customer service, as when abusive or irate passengers have to be controlled.
- *Presentational* management refers to emotional exchanges with colleagues, as when cabin crew have a laugh with each other in 'unmanaged spaces' and engage in a workplace humour that reinforces comradeship and relieves boredom.
- *Philanthropic* management refers to 'the freedom to give that little bit extra', when a genuine concern for the well-being of passengers or colleagues leads cabin crew to go beyond what is required by pecuniary or prescriptive rules.

Emotional labour is not just at the service of the employer but also meets the social and personal needs of the worker as well. Cabin crew 'juggle' with many different kinds of emotional labour and have to find a way of reconciling their conflicting requirements.

❓ Bolton and Boyd studied air crew. What is distinctive about the work situation of cabin crew? Can this typology be applied to other kinds of customer service work?

Rose analysed data from the British Household Panel Survey in 1999. He found that the material advantages of the job, which included not only pay but hours of work, security of employment, and promotion opportunities appeared more important to respondents than the work itself. *Extrinsic* factors to do with the contract of employment outweighed *intrinsic* ones linked to the quality of the work. The level of work-related stress seemed, none the less, crucial in shaping job satisfaction in some occupations, particularly among nurses, primary school teachers, solicitors, journalists, youth workers, production control clerks, and marketing managers. Degree of workplace influence was also important.

The ranking of eighty-eight occupations in terms of overall levels of satisfaction produced interesting results (see Figure 17.7). Some professional and technical occupations, such as primary school teachers, management consultants, and laboratory technicians had low scores. Some manual workers, such as caretakers, farm workers, and gardeners had high scores, though others, especially assembly-line workers, had low ones. Occupations involving personal and caring services scored high, with miscellaneous childcare heading the list, while hairdressers and barbers, care assistants and attendants, nursery nurses, secretaries and PAs, cleaners and domestics were all towards the top end. Educational assistants came fourth from the top but primary school teachers came close to the bottom! Waiters and bus drivers were right at the bottom with very low scores.

This analysis of job satisfaction both consolidates and extends earlier findings. The importance given to extrinsic, contract of employment issues is consistent with the instrumental orientation identified by the *Affluent Worker* study (Goldthorpe *et al.* 1968a). The growth of consumerism and individualism, together with the rewards and pressures of neo-liberal capitalism (see Chapter 15, pp. 601–2), have no doubt strengthened this orientation to work. Blauner's classic study of alienation is also supported, however, by the low position of assembly-line and other routine manual work, and the importance of influence in the workplace. But it is not just the alienating conditions of work that lead to low job satisfaction, for work-related stress, long hours, and insecurity at work also come out as key factors. It is also striking that so many personal service occupations, involving close contact with customers and employers, showed high levels of satisfaction, even though the extrinsic rewards of these jobs are not immediately apparent.

Work and non-work

In pre-industrial society, people worked, enjoyed themselves, and looked after their homes but did not use the concepts of employment, leisure, and housework to

Figure 17.7 A job satisfaction league table

Occupation	Number of cases	Overall job satisfaction score*
Top ten (of 88)		
Miscellaneous childcare	64	75
Caretakers	24	71
Hairdressers, barbers	27	70
Educational assistants	49	69
Farm workers	22	68
Gardeners and ground staff	23	65
Managers in building and contracting	23	65
Care assistants and attendants	138	64
Secretaries, PAs, typists	118	64
Nursery nurses	42	64
Bottom ten (of 88)		
Laboratory technicians	36	36
Metal working production and maintenance fitters	103	36
Assemblers/line workers (electrical/electronic)	56	34
Primary and nursery education teachers	98	34
Assemblers/line workers (vehicles/metal)	21	33
Plastics process operatives, moulders and extruders	28	32
Postal workers, mail sorters	56	32
Sewing machinists, menders, darners, embroiderers	32	32
Waiters and waitresses	33	24
Bus and coach drivers	31	23
All employees		50

*The score is the percentage scoring above the median for the whole sample.

Source: Rose (2003).

❷ Can you identify any common features in the top ten occupations and in the bottom ten?

❷ What are the implications of the occupational diversity at the top and bottom of the table?

describe these activities. It was the shift of production from the household by industrialization that systematically differentiated these activities and created these new ways of categorizing them. In this section we consider the impact of industrial capitalism on work and non-work outside the workplace.

Continued work at home

Although production had largely moved from a domestic setting to outside workplaces, many different kinds of work still went on in the home.

Much work in the home was still closely connected to work in the workplace, which arguably could not go on without it. Thus, paid work depended on the unpaid work of women in the home to 'reproduce labour' (see Chapter 12, pp. 450–1). Labour was reproduced not only by producing and bringing up the next generation of workers but also by attending to the domestic needs of paid workers, whose time and energy could then be devoted to their paid work. When women themselves were employed in the factories, and many were employed in the textiles industry, this paid work was considered secondary to their main role as housewives and they were expected to do the housework as well.

Routine housework was not the only unpaid labour carried out by women in the home. They continued to carry out some important productive tasks. Thus, the household's clothing was not just provided through the purchase of factory-made clothes. Some were still made at home. Indeed, production at home was facilitated by one of the new industrial products, the sewing machine.

Paid work itself was not carried out only in the workplace. Employers could economize on workplace costs and wages by giving work that did not require factory machinery to women at home, who were in a weak bargaining position, because of their isolation and their domestic responsibilities. A lot of homework was carried out in the textiles industry, where spinning, weaving, and dyeing were factory processes but 'finishing-off' was done by homeworkers. Thus, although industrialization had shifted the bulk of production out of the household, it had also resulted in the emergence of a new form of employment in the home. 'Homework' had come to have a quite new and specific meaning.

Most women who took paid work were not in fact employed in the textiles industry but in waged domestic labour in middle-class households. Women's employment in domestic service was certainly not new, but the character of this employment had changed significantly. Previously seen as members of the family, servants were now increasingly treated as wage labour. The development of industrial capitalism led not only to wage labour in factories but also wage labour in the home.

Wage labour in the home diminished in the twentieth century with the growth of clerical work and mass production. Servants became too expensive as the growing employment of women in offices and factories pushed up women's wages. The gap left by the departure of servants was filled in three different ways:

- mass-produced labour-saving machinery reduced the time taken to do some household tasks;
- domestic production declined and finished products, particularly food products such as bread, were increasingly bought;
- middle-class wives had to do more housework. Indeed, the time spent by working-class and middle-class housewives on routine domestic tasks had become virtually the same by the 1960s (Gershuny 1988).

In the 1970s, Oakley carried out a ground-breaking study of housework as work. She examined it in the same way as industrial sociologists like Blauner had studied factory work and found that housework was similarly characterized by monotony, the fragmentation of tasks, time pressure, and social isolation. When she compared her findings with work satisfaction data from the *Affluent Worker* study, she found that housework was not only more alienating than industrial work in general, it was apparently more alienating than assembly-line work, the most alienating form of industrial work (Oakley 1974) (see Figure 17.8).

Oakley found no relationship in housework between technology and work satisfaction, but, as she pointed out, the relationship between machine and worker is different in housework. In industrial work the pace of the machine controls the speed of work, but the housewife controls the pace and rhythm of housework. The alienation of housework is not, therefore, related as closely to technology as it is in industrial work. The pressures of housework are different, for they come from the standards and routines that govern its performance. Dusting could, for example, be done several times a day, once a week, or much less often. While mechanization could in principle save time, it could also lead to the more frequent repetition of tasks.

Oakley argued that in the absence of a wage the housewife had to find other rewards of a psychological kind. It was in meeting standards that housewives obtained what satisfaction they could from housework. Standards varied

Figure 17.8 Housework and industrial work

Workers	Percentage experiencing		
	Monotony	Fragmentation	Speed
Housewives	75	90	50
Factory workers	41	70	31
Assembly-line workers	67	86	36

Source: Oakley (1974: 87).

considerably but, although defined by the housewife, became powerful constraints that seemed to her to be external forces. Standards originated largely from socialization, which transmitted norms of housework from one generation to the next, though there were other influences, such as the media.

Oakley had demonstrated that housework, like industrial work, could be analysed in terms of the satisfaction or dissatisfaction that it gave, but also that it was different in character. As with industrial work, the routines of housework were imposed, but not in the same way. Because they were psychological, the pressures generated by standards were greater than the external pressures of paid work. Paid workers could also leave the workplace and, at least temporarily, escape from its pressures. The housewife could not do this so easily.

The creation of unemployment

The distinction between employment and unemployment goes back to the emergence of capitalist production. 'Work' came to mean work for an employer. If their paid work ceased, workers were now unemployed. A new category of people, the unemployed, had come into existence.

People could find themselves out of work in pre-industrial societies, but their pattern of work was irregular and included many different economic activities. With industrialization a much sharper contrast between being in work and out of work emerged. Industrialists required their employees to work continuously for long hours and work in manufacturing could no longer be combined with other kinds of work. When, however, production became unprofitable, there was no basis for continued employment and factories closed. Unemployment then had a devastating effect on workers and their families, for they had become entirely dependent on paid work for their livelihood.

Industrial capitalism by its very nature has provided insecure employment. The economic cycle has generated periods of intense work during booms, followed by recessions when demand collapses, production diminishes, and people are thrown out of work. Intense competition can also lead to the sudden closure of companies driven out of business. The high rate of technical change can result in the replacement of workers by machines and whole occupations can become obsolete.

Unemployment has had serious consequences for the individual and the society. For most of the population of working age, employment in paid work is the main source of income, but the impact of unemployment on the individual is not just financial. It reduces the variety of life, removes the satisfactions of work, makes the day structureless, diminishes social contacts, and damages identity and self-esteem (Warr 1983).

Briefing: work in pre-industrial times

'A labouring family around 1700 normally got its support, not from just one or two sources, but from a variety of activities. . . . Even in places where few commons existed, many people had small cottage gardens where they could grow potatoes, cabbages, peas and beans; cottagers very commonly kept a pig or two, which could be fattened on almost anything; some had chickens or geese, a few kept bees . . . Some of this produce they sold in the market, much of it they consumed directly. For most of them farm labour was an important source of income; and increasingly country people were taking up ancillary employments—spinning, weaving, knitting, glovemaking, metalworking, and the like—to supplement the livelihood they gained from agricultural wages, a smallholding, or common rights.' (Malcolmson 1988: 58)

The experience of unemployment has been viewed as going through a number of stages. Four have been commonly identified:

- *shock*: on learning the news;
- *optimism*: an initially optimistic search for work;
- *distress and pessimism*: a growing concern about the future and a lowering of expectations when the search fails;
- *resignation and adjustment*: acceptance of the situation.

Unemployment is not, however, experienced in the same way by all. Ashton (1986) has argued that its meaning varies. Those in middle-class occupations are more likely to be financially cushioned through savings but may suffer a more serious psychological loss, because their work allows self-expression and is important to their identity. Skilled workers may well experience unemployment in a similar way and have some cushioning through redundancy payments. Unskilled or semi-skilled workers are in a different situation. They are less likely to receive redundancy payments and are more affected by loss of income but suffer less from a loss of identity, as they express themselves less through their work and take an instrumental attitude towards it.

The effects of unemployment also depend upon its duration. The longer people have been unemployed, the more difficult it becomes to re-enter employment, partly because motivation diminishes, partly because technologies and

The reserve army of labour

The concept of the **reserve army of labour** was important to Marx's theory of capitalism. He argued that labour was increasingly replaced by machinery as capitalism developed. This process created a reserve army of the unemployed, which made workers available for the further expansion of production. The reserve army also kept wage levels down and forced workers to submit to a more intense exploitation of their labour, by increasing the competition between them for jobs.

The notion of a reserve army was taken up by Veronica Beechey (1987), who argued that married women are part of the reserve army. They can be drawn into production when there is a shortage of labour and returned to the household to resume their primary role as housewife when no longer required. This happened in Britain during the First and Second World Wars but also in the 1960s, when a labour shortage developed in British industry. The growth of part-time work enabled women to continue performing their domestic role.

Beechey emphasized that it is the 'sexual division of labour' and traditional assumptions about the role of women that make them part of the reserve army. Furthermore, women's wage rates are lower than those of men, because their domestic role is their primary role. The availability of female labour depresses wage levels.

occupations change, so that previous experience becomes out of date. Long-term unemployment leads to poverty and dependence on the state. A vicious circle can develop that makes unemployment self-perpetuating.

Unemployment has wider consequences for society as a whole. There is plentiful evidence that it leads to higher levels of physical and mental illness, divorce, crime, and violence (Ashton 1986; Gallie and Marsh 1994). State benefits paid to the unemployed may seem inadequate to those receiving them but are a major item of state expenditure, while unemployment also reduces the state's tax revenue and, therefore, its capacity to pay out benefit. So far as the economy is concerned, unemployment reduces spending power and the demand for goods and services, thereby throwing other people out of work and threatening to cause a cumulative decline of economic activity.

It must also be recognized that unemployment has some positive consequences for employers and for the state. A certain level of unemployment is arguably beneficial, because it damps down inflation, forces people to work harder in order to keep their jobs, and increases international competitiveness. Unemployment also provides a

reserve army of people available for work (see box on 'The reserve army of labour'), which helps to keep down wage levels, undermine collective bargaining, and reduce union militancy. Governments that give a higher priority to these matters may decide, as happened in early 1980s Britain, to allow unemployment to rise.

The growth of leisure

Recreational and creative activities, such as sport or play, or painting or conversation, which are commonly regarded nowadays as leisure pursuits, have existed since the earliest known human societies. The *idea* of leisure as something distinct and separate from work was, however, another result of the impact of industrial capitalism on daily life. 'Leisure' is not simply a descriptive term for these activities but a way of thinking about them.

In pre-industrial times, the days of the landed gentry were largely occupied with such activities as field sports, gambling, social events, reading, eating, and drinking, which were not seen as leisure pursuits but as normal pastimes. Work was considered inappropriate to their class and socially demeaning. Their wealth enabled them to employ others to carry out both the management of their estates and the running of their households. Their lifestyle demonstrated their wealth and signified their high social status to others.

Ordinary people necessarily spent most of their time in productive activities, as they tried to provide themselves with a living, though there were some clear non-work times in their lives. There were seasonal festivals, such as Christmas and Easter, and saints' days with fairs and sporting events. But there was no clear distinction between work and leisure time in daily life, for work hours were irregular and often seasonal. At harvest-time, for example, work would be day-long, while at slack periods of the year there might be no work available. The pre-industrial craftsman determined his own pace of work and could combine it with other non-work activities. Craftwork, anyway, had a creative quality and work was not a meaningless activity that had to be balanced by recreation outside work hours.

Industrialization was associated with a very different attitude towards work. Capitalist entrepreneurs put most of their time and energy into *generating* rather than *spending* wealth, while their employees were required to work regularly and continuously in a disciplined manner.

This focus on work might seem opposed to the whole notion of leisure but it had the effect of creating leisure as a distinct part of people's lives. As the regulated, supervised and continuous work typical of the factory did not permit the mixing of work with non-work activities, work and leisure became separated. Employers concluded that it was better to channel leisure into clearly organized holiday periods when their factories shut down than have production interrupted and disorganized by workers taking time off during traditional holiday periods. Then, as workers became organized, their unions pressed for shorter working days and a fixed number of working hours per week.

The state too played an important part in the development of leisure by creating a legal framework for it. Health and welfare concerns, the pressure from religious movements to protect Sundays, and demands from the labour movement for shorter hours and restrictions on the work of women and children, all put pressure on governments to pass laws that protected and extended leisure time. The Factory Acts of the 1840s and 1850s restricted the hours of work of women and children. Sunday Observance Laws were enforced and extended to prohibit most commercial activity on Sundays. In 1871 four bank holidays were created. Later, in 1938, the Holidays with Pay Act was passed and paid holidays gradually became a normal feature of work-life.

The creation of 'free' leisure time for workers did not mean that they could simply be left to enjoy their leisure as they pleased. As early nineteenth-century factory-owners sought ways of controlling the work behaviour of their employees, a campaign began to regulate and 'improve' their non-work lives as well. This was not just due to the employer's need for disciplined labour, important though this was, for there was also the problem of maintaining order in the cities. The urban poor, who worked and lived in appalling conditions, engaged in disorderly, sometimes violent, political and recreational activities.

Leisure activities became increasingly regulated and organized. Traditional popular pastimes, such as drinking, bull-baiting, cock-fighting, and dog-fighting, could be tolerated and contained within the established and relatively stable framework of rural communities but endangered social order in the cities. By 1835 a law had been passed to prohibit sports involving cruelty to animals. From 1830 to 1914 a series of laws increasingly restricted

Southsea beach, 1895—why did seaside holidays become so popular in the nineteenth century?
© Getty Images/F J Mortimer

the opening hours of public houses. Disorderly pre-industrial sports were brought within a framework of increasingly detailed rules of behaviour. Local sporting activities were organized within the framework of the club, with its members, officials, rules, and committees. Sports eventually came under the control of bodies, such as the 1863-founded Football Association, which regulated competition nationally.

New leisure activities were developed, particularly by the growing middle class and the 'respectable' working class, who established their social status through leisure activities that were different from both the traditional pastimes of the landed gentry and the popular entertainments of the poor. They sought 'improving' recreations compatible with their religious values, and the growth of a civic, municipal culture in the new cities led to the emergence of publicly funded colleges, libraries, museums, and art galleries to improve the mind. Local clubs for sports such as cricket, bowling, cycling, and swimming improved the body. Tennis, golf, and croquet became popular and socially exclusive sports for the middle class.

In a capitalist society the growth of leisure also provided new opportunities for profit-making and led to the rise of leisure industries. The emergence of the weekend stimulated the commercialization of sport, particularly through the Saturday afternoon football match. Football itself became a capitalist enterprise towards the end of the nineteenth century, and the popularity of football and horse-racing provided the basis for the development of a gambling industry. By the 1930s sixteen times as many people gambled through the football pools on the results of matches as actually went to watch them (Royle 1987: 269).

The spread of the railways enabled cheap and fast travel to sporting fixtures and seaside resorts. Organized tourism dates from 1841, when Thomas Cook of Leicester arranged a railway trip to a temperance meeting at the neighbouring town of Loughborough for some 400 people. Cook went on to organize international holidays, pioneer the conducted tour and the guidebook, arrange travel and hotel bookings, and ultimately create the package holiday. As Lash and Urry (1994: 262) have put it: 'Cook's was responsible for a number of innovations which transformed travel from something that was individually arranged and full of risks and uncertainty into one of the most organized and rationalized of human activities based on considerable professional expertise'.

Briefing: key steps in the nineteenth-century commercialization of football

- Charging for entry to matches
- Wages for players
- Transfer fees
- Investment of capital by local businessmen
- Formation of a union by players
- Emergence of professional management
- Clubs becoming limited companies
- Formation of Football League (1888)

❓ *Can you add steps that have happened since?*

During the twentieth century new manufacturing industries emerged to provide the *mass-consumer* products, such as cars, televisions, and washing machines, that became used during non-work time by most people. *Mass production* depended on a steady demand for products and this stimulated the rise of yet another industry, advertising. Leisure time, leisure activities, and the marketing needs of both consumer goods and leisure industries in turn provided the conditions in which the modern *mass media* could emerge (see Chapter 10, pp. 371–3).

The significance of leisure had changed since the early years of industry. The first industrialists tried to make their employees work long hours, for this enabled them to keep their costs low and maximize their profits. But by the twentieth century the economy increasingly revolved around the consumption of goods and services during leisure time. One person's leisure provided another person's employment. Production had now become dependent in a quite new way on the earnings, non-work activities, and spending patterns of the population as a whole. Mass consumption also made it possible for governments to manage the economy in Keynesian fashion by controlling purchasing power through taxation or control of credit. Consumption, production, and state economic management had become interdependent by the 1950s.

Stop and reflect

In exploring the impact of industrial capitalism, we first examined the organization of workers and employers, and the development of industrial conflict.

- Why did workers become collectively organized?

- Worker organization was countered by employer organization, worker strategies by employer counter-strategies.

- Consider the various forms taken by industrial conflict. Make a list of the ways in which conflict has been expressed in any work organization you have been in.

We went on to the experience of work and the ways in which this has varied.

- Make sure that you understand the following terms: alienation, self-estrangement, deskilling; orientation to work; emotional and aesthetic labour.

- Blauner argued that the degree of alienation was linked to the type of technology.

- The *Affluent Worker* study showed that attitudes to work were not, however, determined by technology and reflected broader orientations to work.

- Customer service work involves emotional labour, which can provide work satisfaction, though tight supervision may empty it of meaning.

- According to Rose, work satisfaction is more closely related to the job than the industry.

- What kind of paid work have you found most satisfying? Does your experience of work exemplify any of the above studies?

We then examined the changing relationship between work and non-work.

- Industrialization concentrated production outside the household.

- Did it remove work from the home?

- In what sense did it create unemployment?

- Why did leisure emerge in the nineteenth century?

The transformation of work, employment, and leisure

During the period of economic expansion from the end of the Second World War to the early 1970s industrial capitalism continued to develop along the lines established before the war. Mass production and mass consumption flourished, while the high demand for labour resulted in full employment. In Britain the labour movement continued to grow and Labour governments alternated with Conservative ones. The British unions saw off various attempts to reform them.

All this was changing by the 1980s. International competition had intensified with the rise of new industrial societies, particularly in the Far East. Profitability fell and the old industries of Europe and America struggled and contracted. Unemployment rose sharply and new forms of insecure, part-time, and temporary employment emerged. As jobs in manufacturing disappeared, service occupations grew. Men lost jobs, while the employment of women increased. The labour movement declined and unions came under increasing state control. Innovations in communications and information technology had a huge impact on both production and consumption. Economic, political, and technological changes combined to transform work, employment, industrial relations, and leisure.

Post-industrialism, post-Fordism, and flexibility

How should this transformation be conceptualized? Some have argued that society is now post-industrial and we begin with a discussion of this approach. We then go on to the more limited notion of post-Fordism, which enables us to contrast new forms of both production and consumption with the Fordist mass production and mass consumption of the past. We examine the 'flexible firm' and the growing emphasis on the need for flexible employment to accommodate a high rate of economic and technological change. Lastly, we consider the emergence of the 'flexible office'.

Post-industrialism

It was Daniel Bell (1973) who popularized the notion of a **post-industrial society**. His starting point was the shift of economic activity from the production of *goods* to the provision of *services*. Manual work was in decline and machine operators were being replaced by robots, while non-manual service occupations were expanding.

These service occupations were engaged in the processing of knowledge and information. For example, financial occupations, teachers, advertisers, market researchers, scientists, and social workers all worked with different kinds of information. According to Bell, economies were now driven not by the search for more efficient ways of producing goods but by the generation of knowledge and the processing of information. Indeed, he used the term **information society** to describe a society in which knowledge was the prime resource.

Employment has certainly been shifting from manufacturing into services, as Figure 17.9 shows. Some traditional industries, such as shipbuilding, have been virtually wiped out. Since the miners' strike of 1984–5 the number of coal miners has fallen from 170,000 in 170 mines to a mere 4,000 in eight mines in 2005 (*Guardian*, 4 March 2005). Employment in services has soared, especially in financial and business services, but also in other areas: distribution; travel and tourism; communications and the media; leisure activities; personal services such as hairdressing, catering, and cleaning; education and health; care and welfare.

Does this mean that Britain is deindustrializing? The term 'deindustrialization' has been much used, particularly when shipyards, or mines, or steel mills, or factories close, and many have closed since the 1970s. Those who lose their jobs directly or indirectly no doubt have a strong sense that deindustrialization is taking place. New industries, such as those concerned with electronics, or biotechnology, or software, have, however, grown up in the old industrial societies, often in new science parks near universities.

Nonetheless, there is no disputing the declining weight of manufacturing in the economy. Does this mean that we are at least moving towards a post-industrial society? Although there is now less production of goods in Britain and the other old industrial societies, it must be kept in mind that they still distribute and consume manufactured goods. The production of goods has not ceased but moved elsewhere as other societies, notably at present China and India, industrialize. Arguably, we now live in a global society which is far from post-industrial in character.

It should not anyway be assumed that service work is non-industrial. Industry should not be confused with manufacturing. As we showed on p. 672, the term 'industry' refers to the way in which production is organized but industrial principles of organization can apply to the production of *services* as well as *goods*. The characteristic features of industrialism listed earlier are found in service organizations too. Catering, for example, provides a service, but, according to Gabriel (1988) has increasingly become industrialized (see box on 'Catering work' on p. 681). It can similarly be claimed that health care has undergone a process of industrialization (see box on 'The industrialization of health care').

Figure 17.9 From manufacturing to services: employee jobs by sex and industry, 1984–2004

United Kingdom	Percentages					
	Males			Females		
	1984	1994	2004	1984	1994	2004
Distribution, hotels, catering and repairs	18	20	23	26	26	26
Financial and business services	12	17	21	14	17	19
Manufacturing	28	24	18	16	11	7
Public administration, education and health	14	14	14	34	36	38
Transport and communication	10	10	8	2	2	3
Construction	8	7	8	2	2	1
Agriculture	2	2	1	1	1	1
Energy and water supply	4	2	1	1	–	–
Other community, social and personal services	3	4	5	5	5	6
All employee jobs (=100%) (millions)	12.3	11.3	13.3	10.2	11.7	12.9

Source: *Social Trends* (2005: 52).

Briefing: the industrialization of health care?

- Mechanization: the use of ever more sophisticated machinery to investigate and treat illness and injury.
- Concentration: the emergence of large regional hospitals and the closure of small local ones; the concentration of particular health-care functions, such as accident and emergency work or childbirth, in the hospital.
- Specialization: the specialization of hospitals, as particular ones become transplant centres or centres for the treatment of particular conditions, such as spinal injury; the specialization of medical, surgical, and nursing occupations, with, for example, physicians, surgeons, and nurses specializing in cancer care.
- Management: the creation of a distinct stratum of professional managers who distribute resources and develop policy.

❓ *Do you think that health care is an industry?*

❓ *Can you identify similar changes taking place in your school, college, or university? Do you think that education has been industrialized?*

The growth of call centres provides another interesting case. This is undoubtedly service work but it shows many of the features of industrial organization. Machinery, in the form of the phone or the monitor screen, determines the pace of work. A function that used to be dispersed through many local offices is concentrated in large workplaces. Call answering has become a specialized work activity that reflects an increased division of labour. The workplace is closely supervised by managers. Indeed, work conditions have been reportedly so poor that call centres have been described as the modern equivalent of the 'dark satanic mills' of the nineteenth-century textile industry (*Management Issues*, 8 January 2004).

The idea of post-industrial society draws attention to important and undeniable changes in economy and occupational structure. The term 'post-industrial' is, however, misleading for industrial organization remains the dominant form of work organization and industrialization is an ongoing process. The world is becoming more industrial not less.

Post-Fordism

Post-Fordism is a similar but more specific term that is used to describe changes in production and consumption

but, before discussing it, we need to consider briefly what Fordism means.

Fordism refers to the system of mass production created by Henry Ford in the car factories he set up in the United States during the early twentieth century. This became the model for the low-cost production of standardized goods for a mass market. Mass production and mass consumption were interdependent and linked by the advertising provided by the mass media.

> **⊃ Connections**
> Changes in production and consumption were closely linked with changes in the media, which are discussed in Chapter 10, pp. 371–2.

Fordist production exemplified the deskilling of work that Braverman considered characteristic of capitalist production, while in Blauner's terms, its assembly-line

Is mass production a thing of the past?
© Alice Chadwick

technology maximized alienation. Work was fragmented into small tasks which could be carried out repeatedly by low-skilled labour with very little training. There was a clear division between a mass of semi-skilled workers and a small number of skilled workers carrying out key tasks. Production was controlled by a centralized management, sharply separated from labour. Trade unionism was strong and there was a lot of open industrial conflict.

The very success of Fordism meant, however, that markets quickly became saturated. One refrigerator was enough for most households! Market saturation, together with increasing competition, resulted in a growing emphasis on quality, product diversity, and innovation. Long production runs were replaced by frequent changes of product and small batch production, to meet particular market opportunities and respond to changes of style. The Ford company had been famous for the production of the standard model T Ford, which could be obtained in any colour, 'so long as it was black'! Car factories now provide a wide range of models, each with many variations in style and engine power, and many optional extras.

The decline of mass production was interwoven with the decline of mass consumption, where major changes were also taking place. The decline of class and community as sources of identity and the growth of individualism meant that consumer goods were seen increasingly as an expression of personal identity. This was no longer a matter of the work a person did or the place they came from but of what they wore, what they drove, where they took their holidays. Function became a less important product feature and the image projected more important. The shift from an emphasis on use or function to image can be seen particularly in advertising, which has both reflected and promoted this change.

The growing significance of image resulted in the **stylization** and **aestheticization** of consumption. Images were given meaning by styles and the concept of 'lifestyle' emerged as an organizing principle. The purchase of a group of products and experiences sharing the same style enabled a consumer to establish a certain identity. The creation of styles by, for example, magazines has become crucial to marketing and a business in its own right. The importance of image has also resulted in the aestheticization of products, as culture has become more influential in their design, packaging, and advertising. Once the meaning rather than the function of a product has become crucial, culture comes into its own, for meanings are essentially a cultural matter (Lury 1996).

The diversification of products, frequent changes of style, and a more aesthetic approach to design made the techniques of mass production less appropriate. Production was reorganized to meet the requirements of quality, diversity, innovation, and change. This involved the interrelated changes in the organization of work, personnel policies, and industrial relations, which have been described as **post-Fordism**.

The post-Fordist organization of work required greater skill, flexibility, and commitment from labour. Workers were expected to be adaptable and multi-skilled, which made trade unions organized on occupational lines less

Why have image and style become more important?

© Lucy Dawkins

Figure 17.10 From Fordism to post-Fordism at Ford

DAGENHAM 1975

DAGENHAM 1995

Clock—nearly 5 and time to knock off

Clock—the time is irrelevant

PRODUCTIVITY TARGETS: APRIL

Team effort boosts morale and output

Union card—the workers united will never be defeated

Multi-tasking—the last of today's jobs completed ahead of schedule—as usual

STRIKE FOR 10% NOW!

Wonkey bumper—'not perfect but it'll pass—and it's not my job anyway'

Quality's the name of the game— no detail is too small to check

Work area so clean you could eat your lunch off it

Source: Independent, 20 April 1995.

appropriate. Flexible production and quality products implied a highly motivated and highly trained labour force, a more decentralized management, and a more cooperative, less conflictual style of industrial relations. The techniques of human resource management (see Chapter 14, pp. 561–3) were designed to mobilize these higher levels of commitment and employee integration.

The concept of post-Fordism has generated considerable debate. Its advocates challenged the notion that capitalism continually deskilled and degraded labour and claimed that work would become multi-skilled and more varied. Paul Thompson (1993) has, however, been sceptical of this view and has argued that requiring workers to do a wider range of tasks does not upgrade their work or increase its skill content. He suggests that it would be more accurate to describe this as multi-tasking than multi-skilling. Wood (1989) has similarly argued that many of the post-Fordist changes in work organization and management are merely minor modifications to basically Fordist methods. He prefers the term neo-Fordism—that is, a new form of Fordism—to post-Fordism.

It must also be said that post-Fordist changes in some industries do not mean the end of Fordism everywhere. There is still a market for many cheap, simple, functional goods that can best be produced by mass production techniques. In some industries Fordism is arguably on the increase. The changes taking place in catering, as described by Gabriel (1988), fit a Fordist rather than a post-Fordist model (see box on 'Catering work' on p. 681).

Figure 17.11 Fordism and post-Fordism

Aspects of production	Fordism	Post-Fordism
Product	Standard	Diverse
Priority	Cheapness	Quality
Market	Mass	Segmented/niche
Work tasks	Fragmented and repetitive	Multiple and varied
Skills	Mainly semi-skilled work	Multi-skilled worker
Labour force	Occupationally divided	Integrated and flexible
Management	Centralized	Decentralized
Industrial relations	Conflictual	Cooperative
Trade unionism	Multiple and independent	Single and integrated

It is also important to emphasize that post-Fordist production remains capitalist in character. Employers still seek to maximize their profits and minimize their labour costs. Managers still control the production process. If anything, more is demanded from labour than before, for workers are required to produce higher-quality work, carry out a greater range of tasks, adapt to frequent changes of product, and continue working as long as it takes to

Figure 17.12
The flexible firm
Source: J. Atkinson (1984: 29).

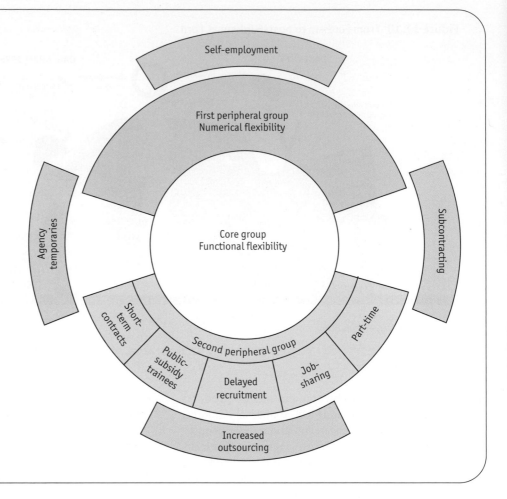

complete the job. The weakening of labour movements (see pp. 700–3) was probably a condition of these changes, for it enabled management to take greater control of the workplace.

The flexible firm

The flexible use of labour was central to the post-Fordist organization of production. John Atkinson (1984) constructed an influential and widely discussed model of the **flexible firm**, which particularly focuses on this issue (see Figure 17.12).

> **Connections**
> The flexible use of labour is closely linked to new organizational forms, which we discuss in Chapter 14, pp. 553–5.

Atkinson identified three different kinds of flexibility—functional, numerical, and financial:

- *Functional* flexibility. This required workers to carry out any task assigned by management.
- *Numerical* flexibility. This enabled management to vary the size of the labour force according to the demand for labour.
- *Financial* flexibility. This referred to financial changes, such as performance-related pay, that enabled companies to control their operations more flexibly.

This model particularly drew attention to numerical flexibility. The uncertainties generated by greater competition and faster change, together with the need to minimize costs, have led employers to seek ways of adjusting the size of the labour force to their actual need for staff. One way of doing this is to employ more workers on a part-time basis, as when stores employ extra staff at checkouts during peak shopping times. Another way is to offer short-term contracts, perhaps for a particular production run or, in education, the duration of a course. An extreme example is the zero-hours contract, which requires employees to be available for work but does not specify their hours of employment and only pays them when the employer calls them in.

The flexible firm created a new division within labour, between *core* and *periphery* (see Figure 17.12). The *core* consisted of permanent, full-time employees with security of employment, promotion prospects, and company benefits of various kinds. In exchange for these privileges, they were expected to be loyal and flexible employees. The *periphery* was composed of those with a looser and less secure relationship to the organization. Atkinson divides it into two groups. The first consists of full-time workers with jobs rather than careers, who have less security of employment than the core groups. The second group consists of various kinds of temporary or part-time workers. Further flexibility is provided by an outer ring of workers brought in under contract but not employed by the organization.

This division between core and periphery has had important consequences for the organization of labour and the stratification of society, for it has weakened the class solidarity of workers (Coates 1989). Ulrich Beck (2000*b*) sees the greater flexibility and insecurity of employment as combining with globalization to divide societies into four different groups (see the box on 'Globalization and Brazilianization' on p. 698).

Like post-Fordism, the model of the flexible firm has been much criticized. It has been argued that its work organization and employment are nothing really new. The practice of contracting out work rather than directly employing workers is long established. Capitalist employers have always tried to cut their employment costs at the expense of the security of labour and are simply finding new, or rediscovering old, ways of doing this (Pollert 1991).

The term 'flexibility' arguably gives too positive an image of change. Greater numerical flexibility can also be described as the *casualization* of labour. The labour movement has long struggled to improve the security of employment by getting rid of casual work, only to find it re-emerging under the banner of flexibility. Pollert (1988) has, indeed, claimed that the flexible firm is essentially a political notion put about by government and employers to spread and justify changes in employment relationships resulting in greater insecurity for workers.

Greater flexibility can also have negative as well as positive consequences for the employer, costing more than it saves. Temporary employees may be poorly motivated and unreliable. Subcontracted work may not be carried out to the correct standards. Product quality may suffer and safety may be compromised. Indeed, the fatal rail crash at Potters Bar in 2002 has been attributed to poor maintenance of the track by subcontractors using inexperienced flexible labour to do the work.

Like post-Fordism, the concept of the flexible firm usefully highlights changes in employer practices. It is important to see both concepts not as *descriptions* of work organization or employment relations but as simplified *models* of reality that help us to grasp processes of change by drawing contrasts and suggesting interrelationships between processes. The critics of these concepts do, however, rightly point out the dangers of exaggerating change and emphasizing its positive rather than negative consequences.

The flexible office

Another instance of greater flexibility is the more flexible use of space in what Felstead, Jewson, and Walters (2005) have called the *collective*, as opposed to the *personal*, office. In the collective office there are no longer fixed and personal places of work. People 'hot-desk' and 'touch down', moving around through relatively open spaces to use the available work stations. Felstead *et al.* emphasize that this new working environment should not be confused with the open plan office, which retained individual and personal workplaces.

This spatial flexibility enables a company to cut considerably its office costs, for it no longer has to pay for the construction and upkeep of offices unoccupied by employees working elsewhere, travelling, or away ill. There is, however, much more to the flexibility of the collective office than this.

In the *personal office*, the bureaucratic principles of hierarchy and specialization resulted in highly specified positions in the organization. As Felstead *et al.* put it, 'workstations and workplaces were demarcated as rigidly as occupational roles' (2005: 65). The spatial flexibility of the *collective office* matches the organizational flexibility of the post-bureaucratic company, where the emphasis is on teamwork, flexible job descriptions, and, indeed, the collective achievement of the company's goals rather than the individual performance of specified tasks.

> **Connections**
>
> The collective office reflects the new styles of management associated with post-bureaucratic organization and you may find it helpful to look up our discussion of this in Chapter 14, pp. 561–3.

The collective office has a very different culture of interaction. Informality, chance encounters, and social gatherings are characteristic features of the work experience. Information is collected not through communication channels but through the 'osmosis' of 'unobtrusive overhearing, eavesdropping and observing co-workers' as people move about and temporarily occupy work stations

Global focus Globalization and Brazilianization

In *The Brave New World of Work* (2000*b*), Ulrich Beck lays out what he sees as the likely consequences of globalization for the work, employment, and leisure of different groups of people. He describes this as Brazilianization rather than Americanization, for the future of Western societies can be glimpsed in Brazil rather than the United States. He sees Brazilianization as producing 'a political economy of insecurity', which has two key features:

- the growth of informal and temporary jobs, with 'inferior' productivity, working conditions, contractual terms, social security, and legal protection;

- deregulated labour relations that bypass and weaken collective bargaining and the power of unions.

He argues that Europe has been stable since the Second World War partly because of opportunities for people to be upwardly mobile and partly because of their willingness to accept factory work and discipline in exchange for 'greater income, social security and leisure time', which he calls a 'Fordist consensus' (2000*b*: 104–6). This stability is being undermined by a Brazilianization, which will fragment society into four groups:

'1 *The 'Columbus' class of the global age.* These are the winners from globalization, the owners of globally active capital and their top managerial executors. The income of this minority has been rising exponentially as a result of downsizing, wage compression and lower social contributions. Like Columbus, they set out to conquer global space and subject it to their economic goals. . . . They have the technological and material resources of globalization at their command— but they pay a high price for this in the form of time poverty. For the global elites lack what the most impoverished local rejects have in abundance: time. . . .

2 *Precarious employees at the top of the skills ladder.* These earn a lot, but have to be constantly on the ball to avoid being pushed aside by rivals. They are temporary workers, the spurious self-employed, people with their own business, and so on, in high-paid positions that assume similarly high educational qualifications. . . . Leisure time is a foreign word, social life—'vacations'—an endemic problem. Anyone who cannot be reached anytime and anywhere is running a risk. . . .

3 *The working poor.* The jobs of 'low-skilled' and 'unskilled' workers are directly threatened by globalization. For they can be replaced either by automation or by the supply of labour from other countries. In the end, this group can keep its head above water only by entering into several employment situations at once. . . .

4 *Localized poverty.* Zygmunt Bauman has pointed out one essential difference from the poverty of earlier epochs: namely, the localized poor of the global age are no longer needed. . . . Their position may be thought of as complementary to that of the globalized rich. The localized poor have time in abundance, but they are chained to space.' (2000*b*: 106–7)

Beck claims that these adverse consequences of globalization could be counteracted by creating a society of active citizens, which is no longer fixed within the container of the national state and whose activities are organized both locally and across frontiers (2000*b*: 5).

➡ Note that the reference to Bauman is to p. 56 of his book on *Globalization* (1998), which we discuss in Chapter 16, p. 626.

❓ Can you identify such groups in British society today?

❓ Can you think of examples of a 'political economy of insecurity' in Britain?

---

near each other (Felstead *et al.* 2005: 86). The separation of work and non-work activities and concerns breaks down as people interact informally at work and take work home.

This does not mean, however, that work is uncontrolled by the employer. Although not regulated by detailed rules, it is controlled by performance measures and appraisal. As with homework (see Study 17 on p. 714), the burden of day-to-day management is placed on employees, who have to manage and regulate their own daily activities, but they are still under employer control. Furthermore, informal social interaction is a means of instilling motivation and commitment to the organization, of binding the worker emotionally to the corporate mission. In this context, engaging in casual interpersonal interaction is not a permitted indulgence but a required behaviour.

Nor should it be assumed that employees simply conform. Felstead *et al.* describe the practice of 'stalling'. In the collective office employees are not supposed to take possession of particular spaces or work stations by leaving their belongings there or otherwise colonizing them. Employees do, however, seek to do this—to mark out their own territory. They may want to have a base or to work near a particular person or make sure that they have access to a particular facility. They may therefore lay claim to a work station by leaving personal items there, perhaps placing a jacket over a chair. These practices will not seem unusual to anyone who has worked in a university library! Management can respond with 'stallbusting' sweeps to clear away anything personal left at a work station or by instructing personnel to move around.